Not For Tourists Guide to LONDON

Not For Tourists, Inc

Skyhorse Publishing

designed by:
Not For Tourists, Inc
NFT$_{TM}$—Not For Tourists$_{TM}$ Guide to London
www.notfortourists.com

Printed in China
Print ISBN: 978-1-5107-5808-7
Ebook ISBN: 978-1-5107-5809-4
ISSN# 2162-7215

13th Edition

www.skyhorsepublishing.com

10 9 8 7 6 5 4 3 2 1

Dear NFT User,

We've seen a lot these last couple of years. There was the Royal Wedding, which cheered up even the most miserable bastards among us. The glorious sight of spitfires and hurricanes flying over the capital was enough to make one feel proud to be British, and a style icon was born when Kate Middleton wore Alexander McQueen up the aisle. Then the 2013 arrival of His Royal Highness Prince George of Cambridge. And in 2015, Princess Charlotte. The year 2018 brought the birth of Prince Louis of Cambridge followed by another Royal Wedding of beautiful Meghan Markle and everyone's favorite ginger, Prince Harry.

Then there were the Olympics: otherwise known as that running-jumping-swimming-cycling-diving event thingummy, the name of which we cannot mention for trademark reasons; luckily it all went smashingly, we were ready (eat it, Mitt Romney!), and Britain's dignity, respectability, and credibility remained intact. Well, there was that moment when Boris got stuck on the zip wire…oh, and the mix up with the North and South Korean flags…Russell Brand at the lacklustre closing ceremony. But other than that, all good. Well done everyone, jolly good show.

Elsewhere—specifically, "Sarf of the river"—we have a new Renzo Piano-designed 72-storey glass shard-like pyramid-idoididooby tower. Once destined to be the tallest building in Europe…well, with all that new Russian money that we knew wouldn't last, but we'll always have the view. We could make a joke about the best thing about the view is that it's the one place you can't see The Shard, but that would be a little shabby. Anyway, so that happened.

And to think all this happened amid a backdrop of financial collapse, Mayan nihilism and Danny Boyle's supremely dreary view of the Industrial Revolution. But that's where a stiff upper lip comes in handy. All of which is to say, here it is, a guide to the most delicious, intoxicating, awe-inspiring, groovy destinations in the city. The best places for quaffing, boogying, spending, and caffeinating ourselves silly in one of the best cities in the world. Or just spots that we like—those that become part of our everyday as Londoners and which we've chosen to share with you.

Don't forget to visit us online at www.notfortourists.com for updates and added content. And while we're at it, check out the NFT app—it's a great way to take the little black book on the go. No, we'll never shake the tactile pleasure of the printed page, but that doesn't mean we won't find new ways to reach out and connect. As usual, don't hesitate to let us know how you feel—your comments (and criticism!) are always very much appreciated.

Central London

West London

North London

East London

Southeast London

Southwest London

Parks & Places

Colleges & Universities

Sports

Transport

General Information

Arts & Entertainment

Regent's Park
REGENT'S PARK
SOMERS TO
ST. JOHN'S WOOD
LISSON GREEN ESTATE
EUSTON
Euston Rd
Tavistock Sq
Gower St
Marylebone Rd
MARYLEBONE
Portland Pl
Great Portland St
FITZROVIA
Tottenham Court Rd
Montague Pl
Bloomsbury St
York St
Gloucester Pl
Baker St
Marylebone High St
Welbeck St
Goodge St
Chapel St
LISSON GROVE
Cavendish Pl
Cavendish Sq Garden
Oxford St
Soho Square Garden
St. Giles
Portman Sq
SOHO
PADDINGTON
Seymour St
James St
New Bond St
Conduit St
Regent St
WEST END
Shaftesbury Ave
Charing Cross Rd
Marble Arch
MAYFAIR
PICCADILLY
Haymarket
Waterloo Pl
Hyde Park
Park Ln
Piccadilly
St. James's St
Pall Mall
ST. JAMES'S
Green Park
St. James's Park
Kensington Gardens
Hyde Park Corner
Buckingham Palace Gardens
Grosvenor Pl
KNIGHTSBRIDGE
Broad Sanctuary
Great Smith St
Victoria St
King's Rd
Pont St
SOUTH KENSINGTON
BELGRAVIA
Rochester Row
WESTMINS
Sloane St
Eaton Gate
Buckingham Palace Rd
BROMPTON
Vauxhall Bridge Rd
Belgrave Rd
Pimlico Rd
SLOANE SQUARE
PIMLICO
CHELSEA
Grosvenor Rd
1
2
3
4
9
10
11
12
19
20
21
22
23

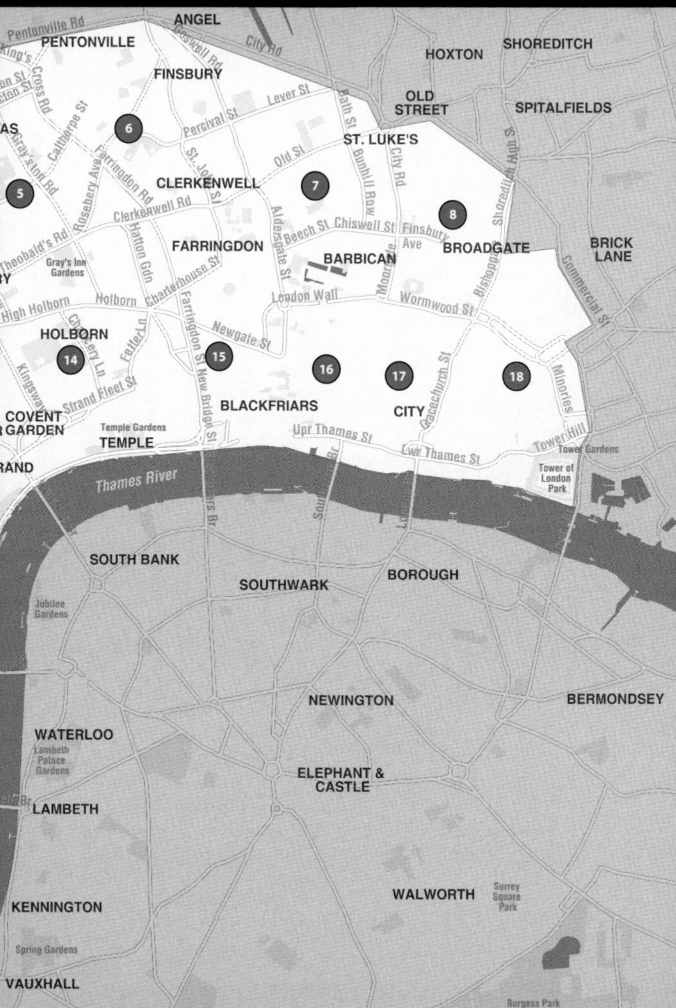
ANGEL
PENTONVILLE
Pentonville Rd
FINSBURY
HOXTON
SHOREDITCH
OLD STREET
SPITALFIELDS
ST. LUKE'S
CLERKENWELL
FARRINGDON
BARBICAN
BROADGATE
BRICK LANE
HOLBORN
COVENT GARDEN
TEMPLE
STRAND
BLACKFRIARS
CITY
Thames River
Tower of London Park
Tower Gardens
Temple Gardens
Gray's Inn Gardens
SOUTH BANK
SOUTHWARK
BOROUGH
NEWINGTON
BERMONDSEY
WATERLOO
Lambeth Palace Gardens
Jubilee Gardens
ELEPHANT & CASTLE
LAMBETH
WALWORTH
Surrey Square Park
KENNINGTON
Spring Gardens
VAUXHALL
Burgess Park
5
6
7
8
14
15
16
17
18

Map 1 • Marylebone (West)

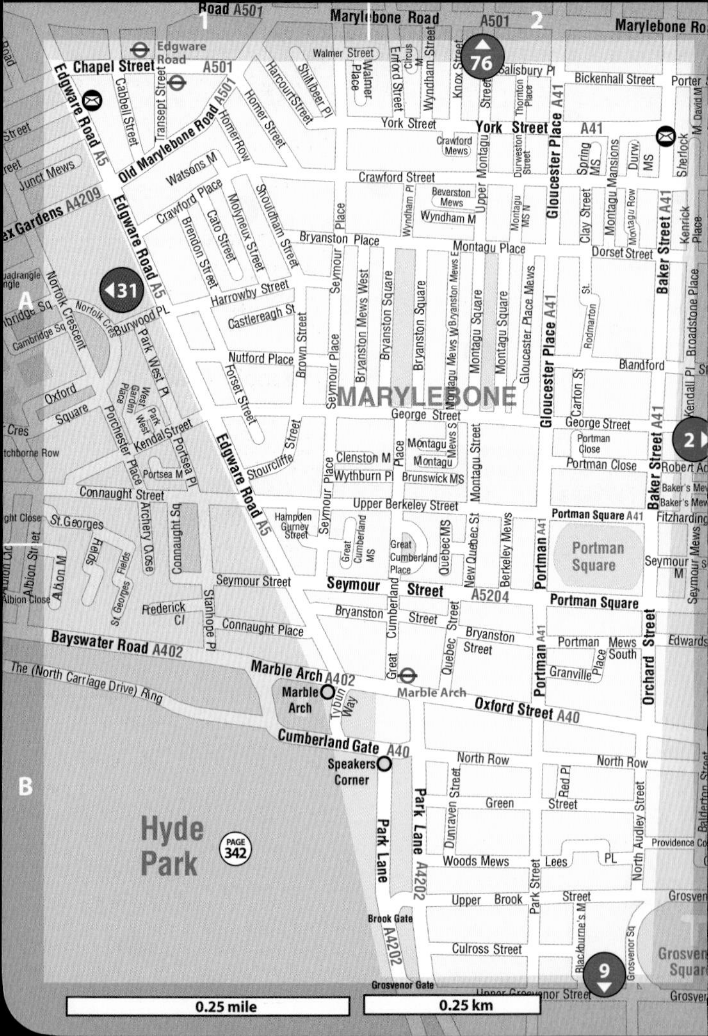

Where the mullah meets the hookah, a stroll down Edgware Road is soundtracked by gurgling shisha pipes and bangin' Arabic pop music. To the east, ostentatiously bejewelled madams patrol Montague Square. They'd turn their noses up at a shawarma at **Beirut Express**, and probably wouldn't deign to shop at **Maroush Deli**. Good, more for the rest of us.

Cinemas

- **Everyman Baker Street** • 96 Baker St

Coffee

- **Bagel Factory** • 39 Paddington St
- **Borough Barista** • 60 Seymour St
- **Caffe Nero** • 184 Edgware Rd
- **Daisy Green** • 20 Seymour St
- **Eat.** • 400 Oxford St
- **Pret A Manger** • 556 Oxford St
- **Starbucks** • 26 Edgware Rd

Landmarks

- **Marble Arch** • Oxford St & Park Ln
- **Speakers' Corner** • Cumberland Gate & Park Ln

Nightlife

- **Arizona Lounge** • 134 Marylebone Road
- **Duke of York** • 45 Harrowby St

Post Offices

- **Baker St** • 111 Baker St
- **Edgware Rd** • 354 Edgware Rd

Restaurants

- **Beirut Express** • 56 Edgware Rd
- **Daisy Green** • 20 Seymour St
- **Locanda Locatelli** • 8 Seymour St
- **Maroush VI Express** • 68 Edgware Rd
- **Twist** • 42 Crawford St

Shopping

- **Maroush Deli** • 45 Edgware Rd
- **Phil Parker** • 106 Crawford St
- **Primark** • 499 Oxford St
- **Spymaster** • 11 Howard St
- **Totally Swedish** • 32 Crawford St

Supermarkets

- **Sainsbury's** • 116 Baker St

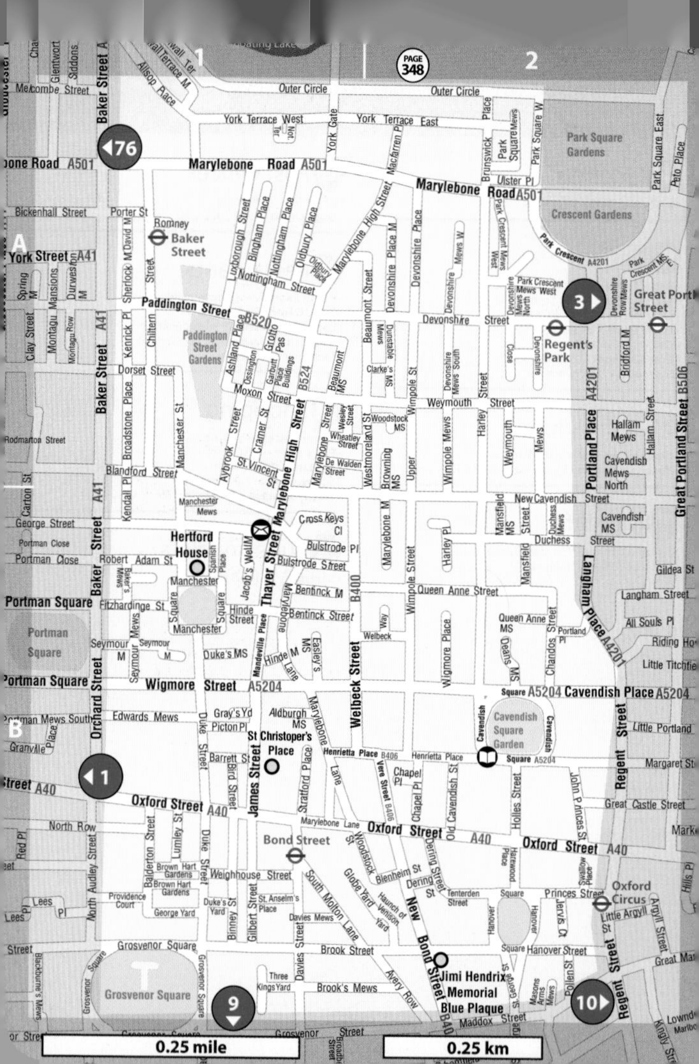

1
2
PAGE 348
A
B
Outer Circle
York Terrace West
York Terrace East
York Gate
Allsop Place
Baker Street A41
76
Marylebone Road A501
Melcombe Street
Glentworth
Siddons
Park Square Gardens
Park Square East
Park Square W
Park Square Mews
Brunswick Place
Ulster Pl
Macfarren Pl
Peto Place
Crescent Gardens
Park Crescent A4201
Park Crescent Mews West
Park Crescent Mews E
Bickenhall Street
Porter St
Romney
Baker Street
York Street A41
Luxborough Street
Bingham Place
Nottingham Place
Oldbury Place
Marylebone High Street
Devonshire Place M
Devonshire Place
Mews W
Nottingham Street
3
Great Portland Street
Sherlock M
David M
Spring M
Montagu Mansions
Durweston M
Paddington Street
B520
Paddington Street Gardens
Ashland Place
Grotto Pas
Beaumont Street
Devonshire Street
Devonshire Mews North
Devonshire Mews West
Devonshire Row Mews
Regent's Park
Bridford M
Clay Street
Montagu Row
Kenrick Pl
Chiltern Street
Ossington
Garbutt Place
Buildings
B524
Beaumont MS
Dunstable Mews
Clarke's MS
Wimpole St
Devonshire Mews South
Devonshire Close
A4201
B506
Dorset Street
Moxon Street
Weymouth Street
Harley Street
Broadstone Place
Manchester St
Rodmarton Street
Cramer St
Marylebone Street
Wesley Street
Wheatley Street
Woodstock MS
Westmoreland St
Hallam Mews
Hallam Street
Aybrook Street
St Vincent St
De Walden Street
Browning MS
Upper
Wimpole Mews
Weymouth Mews
Mews
Portland Place
Cavendish Mews North
Great Portland Street
Blandford Street
Carton St
Kendall Pl
A41
Manchester Mews
New Cavendish Street
Mansfield MS
Mansfield Street
Duchess Mews
Cavendish MS
George Street
Portman Close
Hertford House
Cross Keys Cl
Marylebone M
Harley Pl
Duchess Street
Gildea St
Robert Adam St
Spanish Place
Jacob's Well M
Thayer Street
Bulstrode Pl
Bulstrode Street
Wimpole Street
Langham Place
Baker's Mews
Manchester Square
Bentinck M
B400
Queen Anne Street
Langham Street
Portman Square
Fitzhardinge St
Hinde Street
Marylebone Lane
Bentinck Street
Welbeck Way
Queen Anne MS
Chandos Street
Portland Pl
All Souls Pl
Portman Square
Seymour M
Seymour Mews
Mandeville Place
Hinde M
Easley's MS
Welbeck Street
Wigmore Place
Deans MS
Riding House
Little Titchfield
Duke's MS
Lane
A4201
Orchard Street
Wigmore Street A5204
Cavendish Place A5204
Portman Mews South
Edwards Mews
Gray's Yd
Aldburgh MS
Cavendish Square Garden
Little Portland
Place
Granville
Picton Pl
St Christopher's Place
Henrietta Place B406
Vere Street
Regent Street
Duke Street
Barrett St
Bird Street
James Street
Stratford Place
Chapel Pl
Margaret St
Street A40
Oxford Street A40
Chapel Place
Old Cavendish St
Holles Street
John Princes St
Great Castle Street
North Row
Marylebone Lane
Oxford Street
A40
Oxford Street A40
Red Pl
Balderton Street
Lumley St
Bond Street
Woodstock St
Dering Street
Harewood Place
Swallow Place
Hills Pl
North Audley Street
Brown Hart Gardens
Weighhouse Street
South Molton Lane
Blenheim St
Dering St
Tenterden Street
Princes Street
Oxford Circus
Argyll Street
Lees Pl
Providence Court
Duke's Yard
Gilbert Street
St. Anselm's Place
Globe Yard
Haunch of Venison Yard
New Bond Street
Hanover Square
Jervis Ct
Little Argyll St
George Yard
Binney St
Davies Mews
Grosvenor Square
Davies Street
Brook Street
Hanover Street
Great Marlborough
Blackburne's Mews
Grosvenor Square
Three Kings Yard
Brook's Mews
Avery Row
Jimi Hendrix Memorial Blue Plaque
St George St
Masons Arms Mews
Pollen St
10
Kingly Street
9
Maddox Street
Grosvenor Street
B406
0.25 mile
0.25 km

Marylebone (East)

Map 2

Granted, the plush boutiques and old moneyisms of Marylebone are far removed from most Londoners' lives, but that's not to say you can't go window shopping, and with **VV Rouleaux** nearby, you could even craft your own outfit. Don't forget to stop in at **Claridge's** to tell Gordon Ramsay to f*** off, then sedate yourself in the beautiful book haven that is **Daunt**.

Coffee

- **Apostrophe** • 23 Barrett St
- **Back on Track Coffee** • 3 Wimpole St
- **Caffe Nero** • 273 Regent St
- **Costa** • 69 Wigmore St
- **Eat.** • 9 Avery Row
- **Eat.** • 319 Regent St
- **Eat.** • 92 Wimpole St
- **Eat.** • 400 Oxford St
- **Paul Rothe & Sons** • 35 Marylebone Ln
- **Pret A Manger** • 31 Cavendish
- **Pret A Manger** • 18 Hanover St
- **Starbucks** • 22 Princes St
- **Starbucks** • 14 James St

Landmarks

- **General Sikorski Statue** • Portland Place
- **Hertford House** • Manchester Sq
- **Jimi Hendrix Memorial Blue Plaque** • 23 Brook St
- **St. Christoper's Place** • 23 Barrett St

Libraries

- **Royal College of Nursing Library** • 20 Cavendish Sq

Nightlife

- **Claridge's Bar** • 55 Brook St
- **Inn 1888** • 21 Devonshire St
- **The Phoenix** • 37 Cavendish Sq
- **Purl** • 50-54 Blandford St

Post Offices

- **Marylebone** • 24 Thayer St

Restaurants

- **Casa Becci** • 32 Paddington St
- **Chiltern Firehouse** • 1 Chiltern St
- **Comptoir Libanais** • 65 Wigmore St
- **Diwan** • 31 Thayer St
- **Fischer's** • 50 Marylebone High St
- **The Golden Hind** • 73 Marylebone Ln
- **Goodman Mayfair** • 24-26 Maddox St
- **Hush Brasserie** • 8 Lancashire Ct
- **Patty & Bun** • 54 James St
- **Pollen Street Social** • 8 Pollen St
- **Royal China** • 24-26 Baker St
- **Royal China Club** • 40-42 Baker St
- **Trishna** • 15 Blandford St
- **Zoilo** • 9 Duke St

Shopping

- **Browns** • 24 S Molton St
- **Content Beauty/Wellbeing** • 32 Cavendish St
- **Daunt Books** • 83 Marylebone High St
- **Divertimenti** • 227-229 Brompton Road
- **Fenwick** • 63 New Bond St
- **French Sole** • 61 Marylebone Ln
- **Gray's Antique Market** • 58 Davies St
- **John Lewis** • 300 Oxford St
- **La Fromagerie** • 2 Moxon St
- **Monocle** • 2 George St
- **Niketown** • 236 Oxford St
- **Paul Smith** • 38 Marylebone High St
- **Postcard Teas** • 8 Dering St
- **Selfridges & Co.** • 400 Oxford St
- **VV Rouleaux** • 102 Marylebone Ln
- **Zara** • 242 Oxford St

Supermarkets

- **Marks & Spencer** • Bond St Station
- **Waitrose** • 98 Marylebone High St

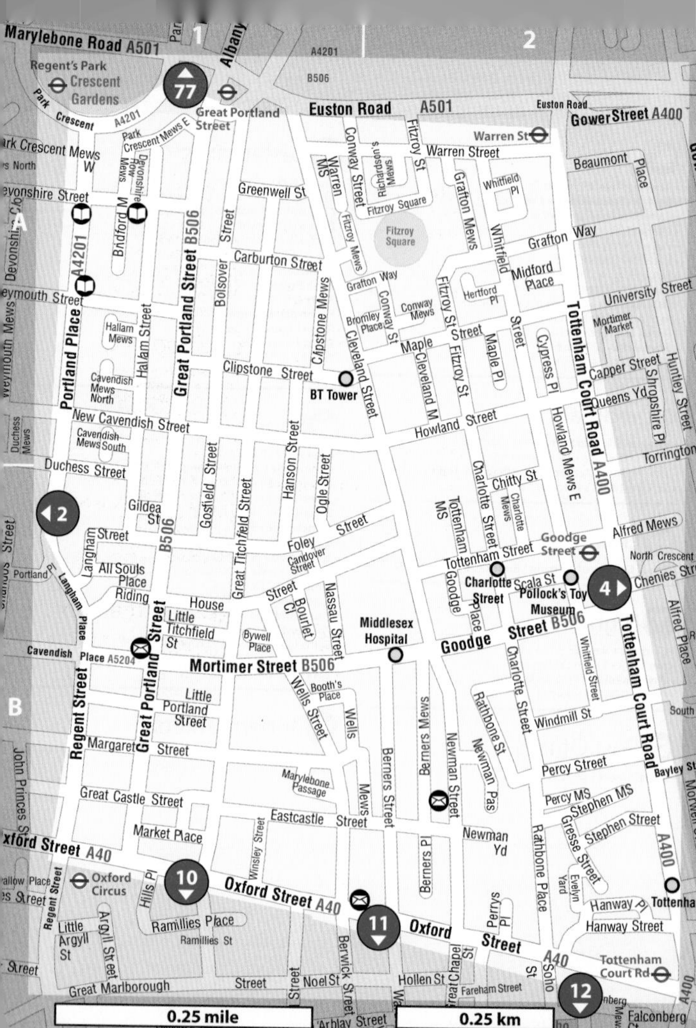

1
2
A
B
Marylebone Road A501
Regent's Park
Crescent Gardens
Park Crescent
A4201
77
Albany
A4201
B506
Great Portland Street
Euston Road
A501
Euston Road
Gower Street A400
Warren St
Warren Street
Park Crescent Mews E
Park Crescent Mews W
Devonshire Row Mews
Devonshire Street
Conway Street
Warren MS
Richardson's Mews
Fitzroy St
Fitzroy Square
Fitzroy Mews
Grafton Mews
Whitfield Pl
Whitfield
Beaumont Place
Greenwell St
Bridford M
A4201
Great Portland Street B506
Bolsover Street
Carburton Street
Grafton Way
Grafton Way
Midford Place
Hertford Pl
Conway Mews
Bromley Place
Conway St
Fitzroy St
Maple Street
Maple Pl
Street
Cypress Pl
University Street
Mortimer Market
Weymouth Street
Weymouth Mews
Portland Place
Hallam Mews
Hallam Street
Clipstone Mews
Cleveland Street
Cleveland M
Fitzroy St
Tottenham Court Road A400
Capper Street
Queens Yd
Shropshire Pl
Huntley Street
Cavendish Mews North
Clipstone Street
BT Tower
New Cavendish Street
Cavendish Mews South
Howland Street
Howland Mews E
Torrington
Duchess Mews
Duchess Street
Gosfield Street
Great Titchfield Street
Hanson Street
Ogle Street
Charlotte Street
Chitty St
Charlotte Mews
Tottenham MS
2
Gildea St
B506
Langham Street
Foley Street
Candover Street
Goodge Street
Alfred Mews
North Crescent
Portland Pl
All Souls Place
Riding House Street
Tottenham Street
Charlotte Street
Scala St
Pollock's Toy Museum
4
Chenies Street
Langham Place
Little Titchfield St
Bourlet Cl
Nassau Street
Middlesex Hospital
Goodge Place
Goodge Street B506
Whitfield Street
Alfred Place
Cavendish Place A5204
Bywell Place
Mortimer Street B506
Regent Street
Great Portland Street
Little Portland Street
Wells Street
Booth's Place
Wells Mews
Berners Mews
Newman Street
Rathbone St
Charlotte Street
Windmill St
South
Margaret Street
Marylebone Passage
Newman Pas
Percy Street
Bayley Str
John Princes St
Great Castle Street
Berners Street
Percy MS
Stephen MS
Gresse Street
Stephen Street
Eastcastle Street
Market Place
Winsley Street
Berners Pl
Newman Yd
Rathbone Place
A400
Oxford Street A40
Oxford Circus
10
Hills Pl
Oxford Street A40
Evelyn Yard
Hanway Pl
Tottenham
Regent Street
Perrys Pl
Hanway Street
Little Argyll St
Argyll Street
Ramillies Place
Ramillies St
11
Oxford Street
A40
Berwick Street
Chapel St
Soho St
Tottenham Court Rd
Great Marlborough Street
Noel St
Hollen St
Fareham Street
12
A400
0.25 mile
0.25 km
D'Arblay Street
Falconberg Ct
Falconberg Mews

There's a whole recent trend for upmarket Fiztrovians to roam east in return for trendsetting East Enders giving their neighbourhood a bit of cool cred—they're all swapping galleries and premises and god knows what else in some kind of grown-up-exchange programme. Fitzrovia has its own history of cool though; you might be lucky enough to see a star or two at the BBC on Great Portland.

Map 3

Cinemas

- **Odeon Tottenham Court** • 30 Tottenham Ct Rd

Coffee

- **The Attendant** • 27 Foley St
- **Black Sheep Coffee** • 5 Goodge St
- **Caffe Nero** • 79 Tottenham Ct Rd
- **Caffe Nero** • 187 Tottenham Ct Rd
- **Caffe Nero** • 2 Charlotte St
- **Eat.** • 94 Tottenham Ct Rd
- **Kaffeine** • 66 Great Titchfield St
- **Lantana** • 13 Charlotte Pl
- **Mother's Milk** • 12 Little Portland St
- **Pret A Manger** • 298 Regent St
- **Starbucks** • 203 Oxford St
- **Starbucks** • 51 Goodge St
- **Tapped and Packed** • 114 Tottenham Court Rd

Landmarks

- **BT Tower** • 60 Cleveland St
- **Charlotte Street** • Charlotte St
- **Middlesex Hospital** • Mortimer St & Cleveland St
- **Pollock's Toy Museum** • 1 Scala St
- **Sinner Winner Man** • 216 Oxford St
- **Tottenham Court Road** • Tottenham Ct Rd

Libraries

- **RIBA British Architectural Library** • 66 Portland Pl
- **Royal Institute of British Architects** • 66 Portland Pl

Nightlife

- **100 Club** • 100 Oxford St
- **The Albany** • 240 Great Portland St
- **Bourne & Hollingsworth** • 28 Rathbone Pl
- **Bradley's Spanish Bar** • 42 Hanway St
- **Bricklayers Arms** • 31 Gresse St
- **Charlotte Street Hotel** • 15 Charlotte St
- **The Cock** • 27 Great Portland St
- **The Fitzroy Tavern** • 16 Charlotte St
- **The Jerusalem Tavern** • 55 Britton St
- **London Cocktail Club** • 61 Goodge St
- **Market Place** • 11 Market Pl
- **The Remedy** • 124 Cleveland St
- **Rising Sun** • 46 Tottenham Ct Rd
- **The Roxy** • 3 Rathbone Pl
- **Shochu Lounge** • 37 Charlotte St
- **The Social** • 5 Little Portland St
- **Yorkshire Grey** • 46 Langham St

Post Offices

- **Great Portland St** • 55 Great Portland St

Restaurants

- **Archipelago** • 53 Cleveland St
- **Ask** • 48 Grafton Way
- **Bao** • 31 Windmill St
- **Barrica** • 62 Goodge St
- **Berners Tavern** • 10 Berners St
- **Bonnie Gull Seafood Shack** • 21 Foley St
- **Brazilian Gourmet** • 70 Cleveland St
- **Crazy Bear** • 26 Whitfield St
- **Gitane** • 60 Great Titchfield St
- **Govinda's** • 9 Soho St
- **Honey & Co** • 25 Warren St
- **Iberica** • 195 Great Portland St
- **ICCo** • 46 Goodge St
- **Kin Cafe** • 22 Foley St
- **Koba** • 11 Rathbone St
- **Market Place** • 11 Market Pl
- **Portland** • 113 Great Portland St
- **Ragam** • 57 Cleveland St
- **The Riding House Cafe** • 43 Great Titchfield St
- **Roka** • 37 Charlotte St
- **Salt Yard** • 54 Goodge St
- **Thai Metro** • 38 Charlotte St
- **Yalla Yalla** • 12 Winsley St

Shopping

- **The Aquatic Design Centre** • 26 Zennor Trade Park
- **Bravissimo** • 28 Margaret St
- **Computer Exchange** • 32 Rathbone Pl
- **Chess & Bridge** • 44 Baker St
- **Fan New Trimmings** • 14 Great Titchfield St
- **Harmony** • 103 Oxford St
- **Hobgoblin Music** • 24 Rathbone Pl
- **Mango** • 225 Oxford St
- **Paperchase** • 213 Tottenham Court Rd
- **Scandinavian Kitchen** • 61 Great Titchfield St
- **Topshop** • 216 Oxford St
- **Urban Outfitters** • 200 Oxford St

Supermarkets

- **Marks & Spencer** • 55 Tottenham Ct Rd
- **Sainsbury's** • 35 Mortimer St
- **Sainsbury's** • 17 Tottenham Ct Rd
- **Sainsbury's** • 145 Tottenham Ct Rd
- **Tesco** • 10 Goodge St

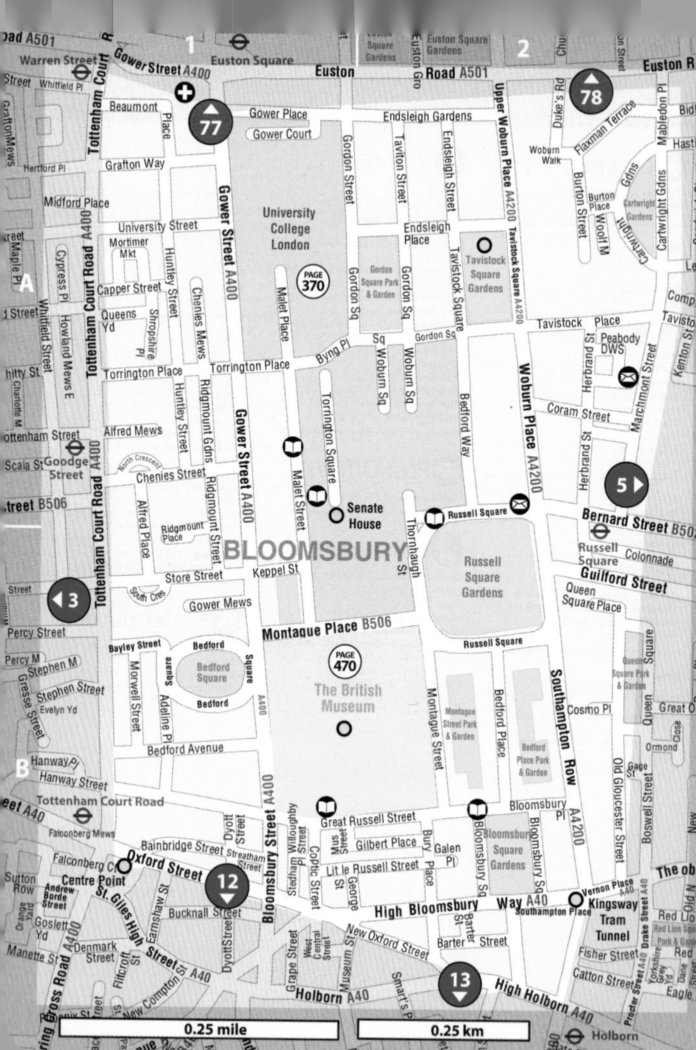
1
2
A
B
Euston Road A501
Warren Street
Gower Street A400
Euston Square
Euston Square Gardens
Euston Road A501
Whitfield Pl
Tottenham Court Road
Beaumont Place
77
78
Gower Place
Gower Court
Endsleigh Gardens
Upper Woburn Place A4200
Duke's Rd
Flaxman Terrace
Mabledon Pl
Woburn Walk
Grafton Mews
Hertford Pl
Grafton Way
Midford Place
University Street
Mortimer Mkt
Capper Street
Queens Yd
Shropshire Pl
Cypress Pl
Maple Pl
Whitfield Street
Howland Mews E
Tottenham Court Road A400
Huntley Street
Chenies Mews
Gower Street A400
University College London
PAGE 370
Malet Place
Gordon Street
Taviton Street
Endsleigh Street
Endsleigh Place
Gordon Square Park & Garden
Gordon Sq
Tavistock Square
Tavistock Square Gardens
Tavistock Square A4200
Burton Street
Burton Place
Woolf M
Cartwright Gdns
Cartwright Gardens
Tavistock Place
Peabody DWS
Herbrand St
Marchmont Street
Kenton St
Torrington Place
Byng Pl
Woburn Sq
Gordon Sq
Bedford Way
Woburn Place A4200
Coram Street
Ridgmount Gdns
Alfred Mews
Torrington Square
Goodge Street
North Crescent
Chenies Street
Scala St
Ottenham Street
Charlotte M
Malet Street
Senate House
Russell Square
Bernard Street B502
Alfred Place
Ridgmount Place
Ridgmount Street
BLOOMSBURY
Thornhaugh St
Russell Square Gardens
Russell Square
Colonnade
Guilford Street
Keppel St
Store Street
South Cres
Gower Mews
3
5
Montague Place B506
Queen Square Place
Percy Street
Bayley Street
Bedford Square
PAGE 470
The British Museum
Russell Square
Queen Square
Queen Square Park & Garden
Percy M
Stephen M
Stephen Street
Gresse Street
Evelyn Yd
Morwell Street
Adeline Pl
A400
Montague Street
Montague Street Park & Garden
Bedford Place
Bedford Place Park & Garden
Southampton Row
Cosmo Pl
Great Or
Ormond Close
Bedford Avenue
Hanway Pl
Hanway Street
Tottenham Court Road
Bloomsbury Street A400
Old Gloucester Street
Gage St
Boswell Street
Falconberg Mews
Dyott Street
Stedham Willoughby Pl Street
Great Russell Street
Bloomsbury Pl
A4200
Bainbridge Street
Streatham Street
Mus Street
Gilbert Place
Bury Place
Galen Pl
Bloomsbury Sq
Bloomsbury Square Gardens
Falconberg Ct
Oxford Street
12
Coptic Street
Little Russell Street
George St
Sutton Row
Centre Point
Andrew Borde Street
St. Giles High Street
Earnshaw St
Bucknall Street
High Bloomsbury Way A40
Southampton Place
Vernon Place A40
Kingsway Tram Tunnel
Drake Street
Red Lion Square Park & Garden
Orange Yard
Goslett Yd
Dyott Street
New Oxford Street
Barter St
Barter Street
Fisher Street
Red L
Manette St
Denmark Street
Flitcroft St
Grape Street
West Central Street
Museum St
Catton Street
Yorkshire Grey Yd
Dane St
Eagle St
Charing Cross Road A400
Holborn A40
Smart's Pl
13
High Holborn A40
Proctor Street
New Compton St
0.25 mile
0.25 km
Holborn

Bloomsbury (West)

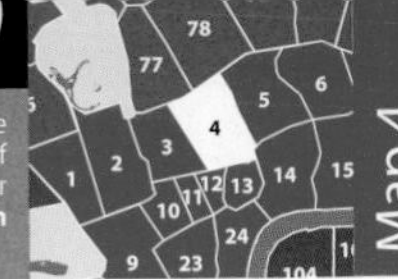

Map 4

Bloomsbury didn't incite and excite Britain's most prolific set of literature writers for no good reason. These streets ooze the kind of romanticised idea of London that had Virginia Woolf and E.M Forster zoned in as inspiration. Clever people have lived here in Bloomsbury and cleverer people still visit. **The British Museum**'s Age of Illumination collection highlights the world's learners.

Cinemas

- **Horse Hospital** • 30 Colonnade
- **Odeon Tottenham Court** • 30 Tottenham Ct Rd

Coffee

- **Black Sheep Coffee** • 5 Goodge St
- **Costa** • 104 New Oxford St
- **London Review Cake Shop** • 14 Bury Pl
- **Pret A Manger** • 40 Bernard St
- **Pret A Manger** • 44 New Oxford St
- **Ruskins Cafe** • 41 Museum St
- **Starbucks** • 112 New Oxford
- **Starbucks** • 425 Oxford St
- **Store Street Espresso** • 40 Store St

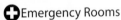

Emergency Rooms

- **University College Hospital** • 235 Euston Rd

Landmarks

- **Bloomsbury Square Garden**
- **British Museum** • Great Russell St
- **Centre Point** • 101 New Oxford St
- **Kingsway Tram Tunnel** • Theobald's Rd & Southampton Row
- **Senate House** • Malet St & Torrington Sq
- **SOAS** • Thornhaugh St
- **Student Central** • Malet St
- **Tavistock Square** • Tavistock Sq
- **University College London** • Gower St

Libraries

- **Anthropology Library** • Great Russell St
- **Birkbeck College Library** • Malet St
- **German Historical Institute Library London** • 17 Bloomsbury Sq
- **Institute of Advanced Legal Studies Library** • 17 Russell Sq
- **University of London, Senate House Library** • Malet St

Nightlife

- **All Star Lanes** • Victoria House, Bloomsbury Pl
- **Bloomsbury Bowling Lanes** • Bedford Way
- **Marquis Cornwallis** • 31 Marchmont St
- **The Old Crown Public House** • 33 New Oxford St
- **The Plough** • 27 Museum St
- **The Princess Louise** • 208 High Holborn
- **ULU** • Malet St

Post Offices

- **Marchmont St** • 33 Marchmont St

Restaurants

- **Alara** • 58 Marchmont St
- **Bi Won** • 24 Coptic St
- **Savoir Faire** • 42 New Oxford St

Shopping

- **Blade Rubber Stamps** • 12 Bury Pl
- **British Museum shop** • Great Russell St
- **Gosh!** • 1 Berwick St
- **James Smith & Sons** • 53 New Oxford St
- **London Review Bookshop** • 14 Bury Pl
- **Paperchase** • 213 Tottenham Ct Rd

Supermarkets

- **Waitrose** • Brunswick Sq

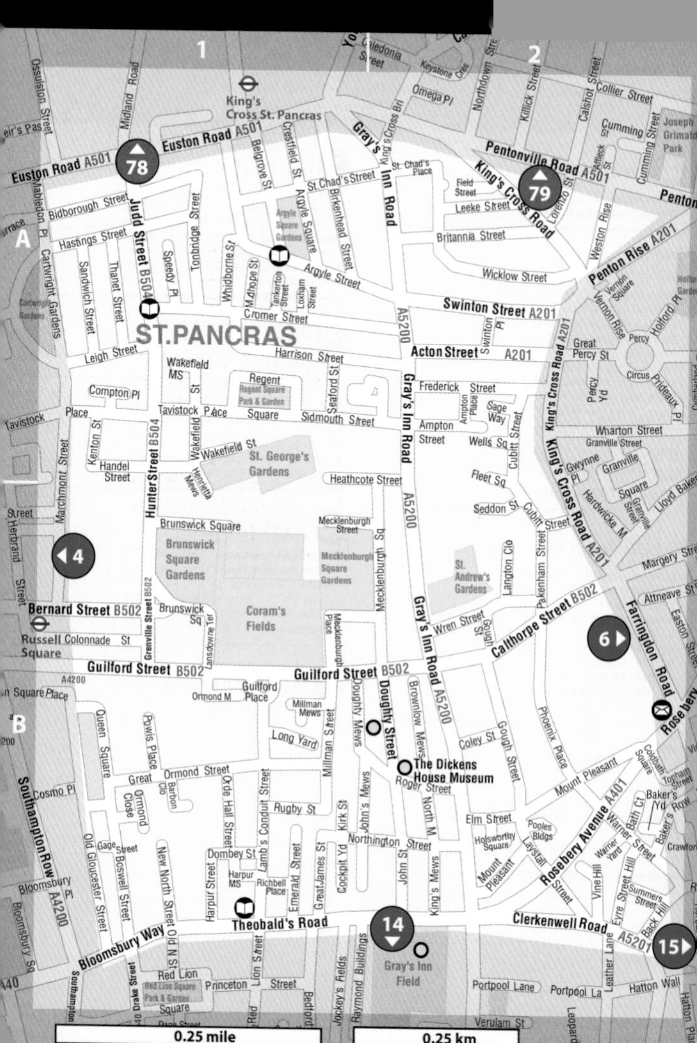

1
2
A
B
King's Cross St. Pancras
Caledonia Street
Keystone Cres
Omega Pl
Northdown Street
Killick Street
Calshot Street
Collier Street
Cumming St
Cumming Street
Joseph Grimaldi Park
Ossulston Street
Midland Road
Euston Road A501
Belgrove St
Crestfield St
Gray's Inn Road
King's Cross Bri
St. Chad's Place
St. Chad's Street
Argyle Square
Argyle Square Gardens
Birkenhead Street
Field Street
Leeke Street
Pentonville Road A501
King's Cross Road
Affleck St
Lorenzo St
Penton
78
79
Mabledon Pl
Bidborough Street
Hastings Street
Judd Street
Tonbridge Street
Britannia Street
Weston Rise
Cartwright Gardens
Sandwich Street
Thanet Street
Speedy Pl
Whidborne St
Midhope St
Tankerton Street
Loxham Street
Argyle Street
Wicklow Street
Penton Rise A201
Vernon Square
Vernon Rise
Holford Pl
Judd Street B504
Cromer Street
Swinton Street A201
ST.PANCRAS
A5200
Swinton Pl
Acton Street
A201
King's Cross Road A201
Great Percy St
Percy
Circus
Prideaux Pl
Leigh Street
Harrison Street
Wakefield MS
Regent Square
Regent Square Park & Garden
Seaford St
Frederick Street
Ampton Place
Sage Way
Percy Yd
Compton Pl
Tavistock Place
Tavistock Place
Wakefield St
Sidmouth Street
Ampton Street
Wells Sq
Cubitt Street
Wharton Street
Granville Street
Kenton St
Marchmont Street
Handel Street
Hunter Street B504
Wakefield St
Henrietta Mews
St. George's Gardens
Heathcote Street
Fleet Sq
Gwynne Pl
Granville Square
Hardwicke M
Granville Street
Lloyd Baker
Seddon St
Cubitt Street
Brunswick Square
Brunswick Square Gardens
Mecklenburgh Street
Mecklenburgh Sq
Mecklenburgh Square Gardens
St. Andrew's Gardens
Langton Clo
Pakenham Street
Margery Stre
Herbrand Street
4
Bernard Street B502
Grenville Street B502
Brunswick Sq
Lansdowne Ter
Coram's Fields
Mecklenburgh Place
Gray's Inn Road
Wren Street
Gough St
Calthorpe Street B502
Farringdon Road
Attneave St
Easton Street
6
Russell Square
Colonnade
St
Guilford Street B502
Guilford Street B502
A4200
Square Place
Ormond M
Guilford Place
Millman Mews
Doughty Mews
Doughty Street
Brownlow Mews
Gray's Inn Road A5200
Phoenix Place
Rosebery
Queen Square
Powis Place
Long Yard
Millman Street
Coley St
Gough Street
Coldbath Square
The Dickens House Museum
Roger Street
Great Ormond Street
Barbon Clo
Ormond Close
Orde Hall Street
Lamb's Conduit Street
Rugby St
Kirk St
John's Mews
North M
Mount Pleasant
Topham Street
Southampton Row
Cosmo Pl
Elm Street
Pooles Bldgs
Baker's Yd
Baker's Row
Bath Ct
Rosebery Avenue A401
Warner Street
Warner Yard
Old Gloucester Street
Gage Street
Boswell Street
New North Street
Dombey St
Northington Street
Holsworthy Square
Mount Pleasant
Laystall Street
Crawford
Bloomsbury Pl
A4200
Harpur Street
Harpur MS
Richbell Place
Emerald Street
Great James St
Cockpit Yd
John St
King's Mews
Vine Hill
Eyre Street Hill
Summers Street
Back Hill
Bloomsbury Sq
Bloomsbury Way
Old N St
Theobald's Road
14
Clerkenwell Road
A5201
15
Leather Lane
Southampton
Drake Street
Red Lion Square
Red Lion Square Park & Garden
Princeton Street
Lion Street
Jockey's Fields
Raymond Buildings
Gray's Inn Field
Portpool Lane
Portpool La
Hatton Wall
Bedford
Verulam St
Leopards
Hatton Place
Eagle Street
0.25 mile
0.25 km

Bloomsbury (East)

Map 5

Agog with students, this tract of Bloomsbury is a bustling cultural playground. The brilliant **Renoir Cinema** resides in the belly of the **Brunswick Centre**, a Brutalist masterpiece with some posh shops thrown in for good measure. For contrast, stroll over to Lamb's Conduit Street and enjoy some boutique shopping.

Cinemas

- **Renoir Cinema** • 1 Brunswick Sq

Coffee

- **Café Lumen** • 88 Tavistock Place
- **The Espresso Room** • 31-35 Great Ormond St
- **Knockbox Coffee** • 29 Lambs Conduit St
- **Pret A Manger** • 15 Theobald's Rd
- **Store Street Espresso** • 54 Tavistock Place

Landmarks

- **Charles Dickens Museum** • 48 Doughty St
- **Gray's Inn Field** • Theobald's Rd
- **Doughty Street** • Doughty St & Guilford St

Libraries

- **Holborn Library** • 32 Theobald's Rd
- **Royal National Institute of the Blind Research Library** • 105 Judd St
- **St Pancras Library** • Argyle St

Nightlife

- **The Blue Lion** • 133 Grays Inn Rd
- **Calthorpe Arms** • 252 Gray's Inn Rd
- **The Clerk & Well** • 156 Clerkenwell Rd
- **The Lamb** • 94 Lamb's Conduit St
- **The Perseverance** • 63 Lamb's Conduit St
- **Pimp Shuei** • 59 Mount Pleasant
- **The Water Rats** • 328 Grays Inn Rd

Post Offices

- **Mount Pleasant** • Farringdon Rd & Rosebery Ave

Restaurants

- **Banh Mi Bay** • 4-6 Theobalds Rd
- **Ciao Bella** • 86 Lamb's Conduit St
- **The Food Bazaar** • 59 Grays Inn Rd
- **Fryer's Delight** • 19 Theobald's Rd
- **Itadaki Zen** • 139 King's Cross Rd
- **The Lady Ottoline** • 11 Northington St
- **Mary Ward Centre** • 42 Queen Sq
- **Paolina Thai Snack Bar** • 181 King's Cross Rd
- **You Me Sushi** • 180 Grays Inn Rd

Shopping

- **Bibas Hair and Beauty** • 72 Marchmont St
- **The Brunswick** • Hunter St
- **The Flash Centre** • 68 Brunswick Centre
- **Folk** • 49 Lamb's Conduit St
- **Gay's the Word** • 66 Marchmont St
- **International Magic** • 89 Clerkenwell Rd
- **JOY** • 22 Brunswick Centre
- **Magma** • 117 Clerkenwell Rd

Map 6 • Clerkenwell

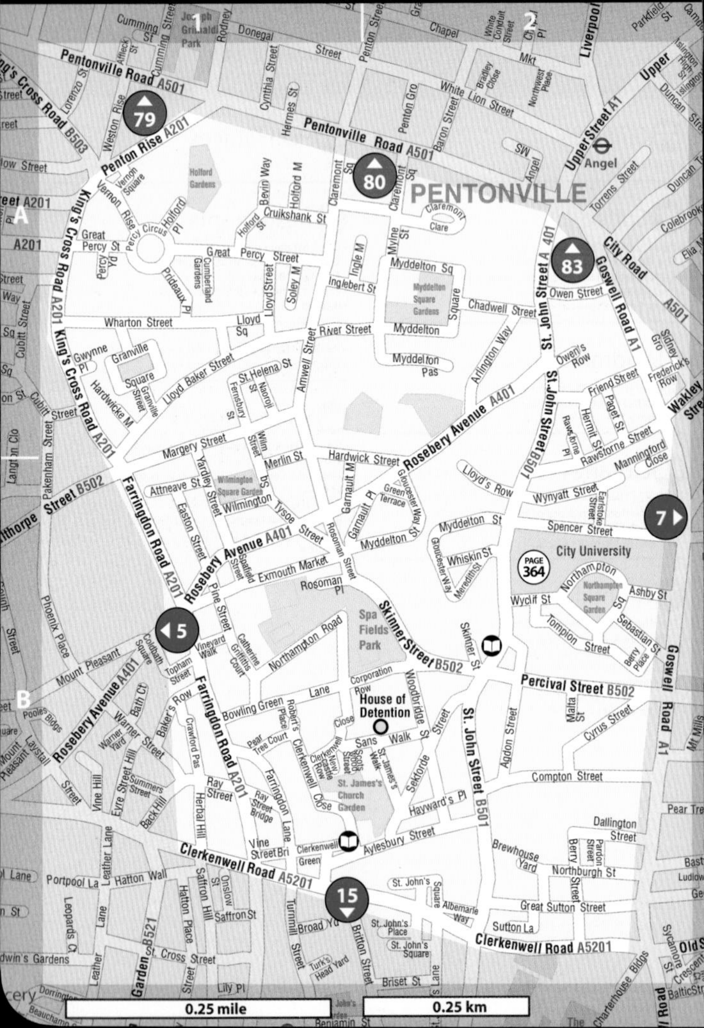

N

PENTONVILLE

Joseph Grimaldi Park
Cumming St
Cumming Street
Affleck St
Rodney
Donegal Street
Penton Street
Chapel Mkt
White Conduit Street
Liverpool
Parkfield St
Pentonville Road A501
King's Cross Road B503
Lorenzo St
Weston Rise
Cynthia Street
Hermes St
Penton Gro
Baron Street
White Lion Street
Bradley Close
Northwest Place
Upper Street A1
Islington High St
Duncan Street
Angel
Penton Rise A201
Holford Gardens
Vernon Square
Vernon Rise
Percy Circus
Holford Pl
Bevin Way
Holford M
Claremont Sq
Cruikshank St
Claremont Close
Torrens Street
Colebrooke
City Road
Goswell Road A1
King's Cross Road A201
Great Percy St
Percy Yd
Great Percy Street
Cumberland Gardens
Prideaux Pl
Lloyd Street
Soley M
Ingle M
Mylne St
Myddelton Sq
Myddelton Square Gardens
Inglebert St
Chadwell Street
St. John Street A401
Owen Street
Wharton Street
Lloyd Sq
River Street
Myddelton Pas
Arlington Way
Owen's Row
Sidney Gro
Frederick's Row
Gwynne Pl
Granville Square
Granville Street
Lloyd Baker Street
St. Helena St
Fernsbury St
Naoroji St
Amwell Street
Rosebery Avenue A401
St. John Street B501
Friend Street
Paget St
Hermit St
Rawstorne Pl
Rawstorne Street
Manningford Close
Wakley Street
Hardwicke M
Cubitt Street
Pakenham Street
Langton Clo
Margery Street
Wilmington Street
Merlin St
Hardwick Street
Garnault M
Gloucester Way
Green Terrace
Lloyd's Row
Wynyatt Street
Earlstoke Street
Calthorpe Street B502
Attneave St
Yardley Street
Wilmington Square Gardens
Wilmington Sq
Tysoe Street
Garnault Pl
Myddelton St
Spencer Street
Farringdon Road A201
Easton Street
Spafield Street
Exmouth Market
Rosoman Street
Whiskin St
Meredith St
City University
PAGE 364
Northampton Sq
Northampton Square Garden
Wyclif St
Ashby St
Rosoman Pl
Pine Street
Spa Fields Park
Skinner Street B502
Skinner St
Tompion Street
Sebastian St
Berry Place
Phoenix Place
Mount Pleasant
Coldbath Square
Topham Street
Vineyard Walk
Catherine Griffiths Court
Northampton Road
Corporation Row
Woodbridge St
Percival Street B502
Rosebery Avenue A401
Bath Ct
Pooles Bldgs
Warner Street
Warner Yard
Baker's Row
Crawford Pas
Bowling Green Lane
Robert's Place
Close
House of Detention
Malta St
Cyrus Street
Mount Pleasant
Laystall Street
Coldbath Hill
Eyre Street Hill
Summers Street
Pear Tree Court
Clerkenwell Close
Newcastle Row
Scotswood Street
Sans Walk
St. James's Walk
Sekforde Street
Agdon Street
Compton Street
Vine Hill
Back Hill
Ray Street
Ray Street Bridge
Farringdon Lane
St. James's Church Garden
Hayward's Pl
Pear Tree
Herbal Hill
Vine Street Bri
Clerkenwell Green
Aylesbury Street
Brewhouse Yard
Berry Street
Pardon Street
Dallington Street
Northburgh St
Clerkenwell Road A5201
Leather Lane
Hatton Wall
Saffron Hill
Onslow St
Portpool La
Leopards Ct
Hatton Place
Saffron St
Turnmill Street
Broad Yd
Britton Street
St. John's Square
Albemarle Way
St. John's Place
Great Sutton Street
Sutton La
Sycamore St
Old St
Baldwin's Gardens
Garden B521
St. Cross Street
Lily Pl
Turk's Head Yard
Briset St
Charterhouse Bldgs
Dorrington
Beauchamp
Benjamin St
Baltic St
79
80
83
7
5
15
A
B
1
2

0.25 mile
0.25 km

A village in the city provides a perfect contrast of a pretty green square separated by only a row of shops from the rest of the corporate world. **The Modern Pantry** is where suits gather for a business power-breakfast, while lunchtimes centre on Exmouth Market. Potter off the main square for back-alley Belgium beers at **The Dovetail**.

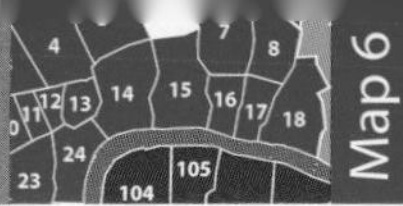

Coffee

- **Ground Control** • 61 Amwell St

Libraries

- **Finsbury Library** • 245 St John St
- **Marx Memorial Library** • 37 Clerkenwell Green

Landmarks

- **City University London** • Northampton Sq
- **The House of Detention** • St James's Walk

Nightlife

- **1920** • 19 Great Sutton St
- **Bandstand Busking** • Northampton Sq
- **The Betsey Trotwood** • 56 Farringdon Rd
- **Café Kick** • 43 Exmouth Market
- **The Dovetail** • 9 Jerusalem Passage
- **The Harlequin** • 27 Arlington Wy
- **Hat & Turn** • 3 Hatton Wall
- **Old Red Lion** • 418 St. John St
- **The Slaughtered Lamb** • 34 Great Sutton St
- **The Three Kings** • 7 Clerkenwell Close
- **Wilmington Arms** • 69 Rosebery Ave

Restaurants

- **Badabing** • 120 St. John St
- **Caravan** • 11 Exmouth Market
- **Dans Le Noir** • 30 Clerkenwell Green
- **The Eagle** • 159 Farringdon Rd
- **The Modern Pantry** • 47 St. Johns Sq
- **Morito** • 32 Exmouth Market
- **Moro** • 34 Exmouth Market
- **Pham Sushi** • 159 Whitecross St
- **SandwichMan** • 23 Easton St
- **Sushi Tetsu** • 12 Jerusalem Passage

Shopping

- **EC One Jewellery** • 41 Exmouth Market
- **The Family Business Tattoo Shop** • 58 Exmouth Market
- **London Tattoo** • 332 Goswell Rd
- **Metro Imaging** • 32 Great Sutton St
- **Timorous Beasties** • 46 Amwell St
- **The Wyvern Bindery** • 56 Clerkenwell Rd

Supermarkets

- **Tesco Express** • 1 Brewnhouse Yard
- **Waitrose** • Ayelsbury St & St. John St

ST.LUKE'S
BARBICAN
City Road A501
Goswell Road A1
Lever Street B502
Old Street A5201
Bunhill Row B144
Whitecross Street
Golden Lane
Aldersgate Street A1
London Wall A1211
Beech Street B100
Chiswell Street
Clerkenwell Road A5201
St. John Street B501
Charterhouse Street B500
Kings Square Garden
St. Luke's Garden
Radnor Street Open Space
Fortune Street Garden
Bunhill Fields Burial Grounds
Bunhill Fields
LSO St. Luke's
Barbican Centre
Church of St Bartholomew the Great
St. Giles's
Barbican
Old Street
Moorgate
The Green
PAGE 324
83
84
6
8
15
16
A
B
1
2
0.25 mile
0.25 km

Barbican / City Road (South)

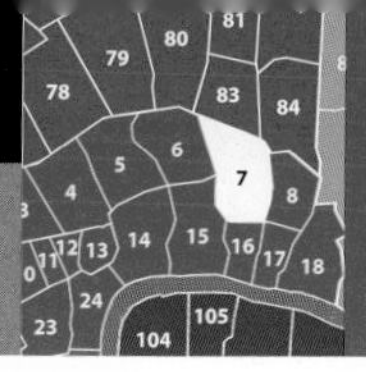

Map 7

Jgly as the brutalist Barbican might be, its surrounds have happily morphed nto one of those areas that thrives on its appalling looks and survives on a jeneration of media peeps. Where the cool crowds flow, top notch hang-outs vill follow. Old Street, or Silicon Roundabout, was designed for those who nainline coffee for survival while **Bunhill Fields** provides necessary respite.

Cinemas

- **Barbican Centre Cinema** • Silk St & Whitecross St

Coffee

- **Caffe Nero** • 40 City Rd
- **Costa** • 68 Goswell Rd
- **Costa** • Ropemaker St
- **Fix** • 161 Whitecross St
- **Look Mum No Hands!** • 49 Old St
- **Pitch 42** • Whitecross St Market
- **Popular Cafe** • 85 Lever St
- **Pret A Manger** • 9 Goswell Rd
- **Pret A Manger** • Ropemaker St
- **Shoreditch Grind** • 213 Old St

Landmarks

- **Barbican Centre** • Silk St
- **Bunhill Fields Burial Ground** • 38 City Rd
- **Church of St Bartholomew the Great** • Kinghorn St
- **LSO St Luke's** • 161 Old St
- **St. Giles** • Fore St

Libraries

- **Barbican Library** • Silk St
- **Wandsworth Town Library** • 11 Garratt Ln

Nightlife

- **The Gibson** • 44 Old St
- **Nightjar** • 129 City Rd
- **The Two Brewers** • 121 Whitecross St

Post Offices

- **Old Street** • 205 Old St

Restaurants

- **Carnevale** • 135 Whitecross St
- **Nusa Kitchen** • 9 Old St
- **Original Bagel Bakery** • 22 Goswell Rd

Shopping

- **Evans & Witt** • 58 Long Lane
- **Red Dot Cameras** • 86 Goswell Rd
- **Whitecross Market** • Whitecross St

Supermarkets

- **Waitrose** • Whitecross St

Map 8 • Liverpool Street / Broadgate

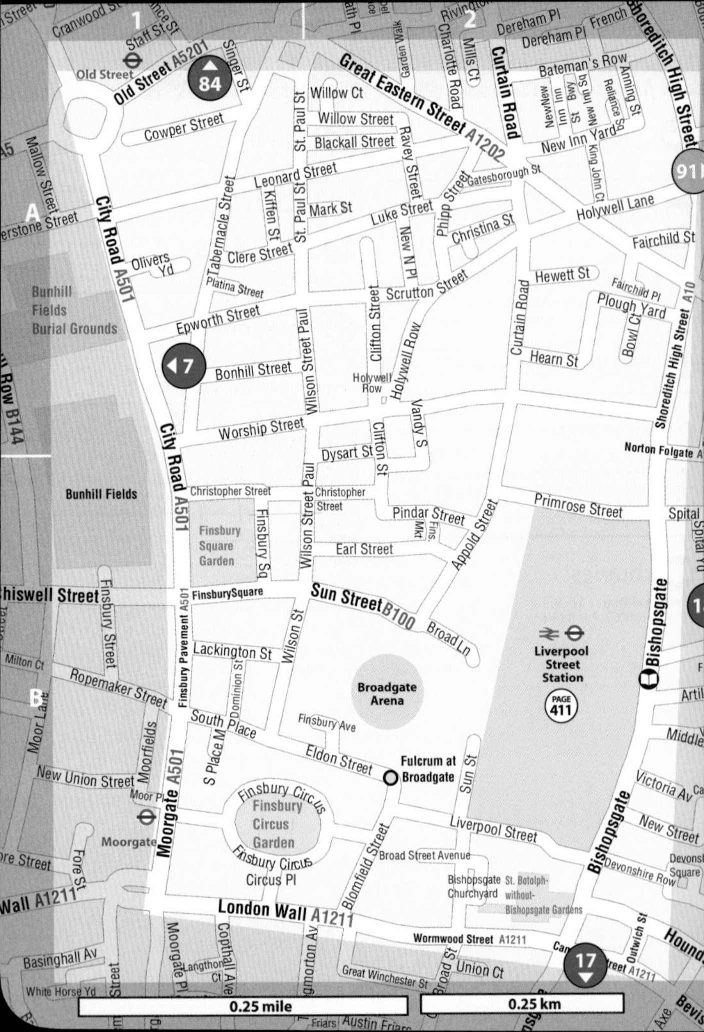

Old Street
Old Street A5201
84
Cranwood St
Staff St
Singer St
Cowper Street
City Road A501
Mallow Street
Tabernacle Street
Olivers Yd
Platina Street
Epworth Street
7
Bonhill Street
Worship Street
Bunhill Fields Burial Grounds
Bunhill Fields
Chiswell Street
Finsbury Street
Christopher Street
Finsbury Square Garden
Finsbury Sq
FinsburySquare
Finsbury Pavement A501
Lackington St
Dominion St
Milton Ct
Ropemaker Street
Moor Lane
Moorfields
South Place
S Place M
New Union Street
Moor Pl
Moorgate
Moorgate A501
Fore St
Fore Street
Wall A1211
Basinghall Av
White Horse Yd
Moorgate Pl
Langthorn Ct
Copthall Ave
Finsbury Circus
Finsbury Circus Garden
Circus Pl
London Wall A1211
Throgmorton Av
Great Winchester St
Austin Friars
Willow Ct
Willow Street
St. Paul St
Blackall Street
Leonard Street
Kiffen St
Mark St
Clere Street
Luke Street
Ravey Street
New N Pl
Garden Walk
Great Eastern Street A1202
Charlotte Road
Rivington
Mills Ct
Curtain Road
Dereham Pl
French
Bateman's Row
New Inn Bwy
New Inn Sq
Reliance Sq
Anning St
New Inn Yard
King John Ct
Shoreditch High Street
91
Gatesborough St
Phipp Street
Christina St
Holywell Lane
Fairchild St
Fairchild Pl
Scrutton Street
Clifton Street
Holywell Row
Hewett St
Plough Yard
Bowl Ct
Hearn St
Shoreditch High Street A10
Wilson Street
Paul
Vandy S
Dysart St
Clifton St
Norton Folgate
Primrose Street
Spital
Spital Yd
Pindar Street
Mkt
Fins.
Appold Street
Earl Street
Sun Street B100
Broad Ln
Wilson St
Broadgate Arena
Finsbury Ave
Eldon Street
Fulcrum at Broadgate
Sun St
Liverpool Street Station
PAGE 411
Bishopsgate
Artil
Middle
Victoria Av
New Street
Liverpool Street
Blomfield Street
Broad Street Avenue
Bishopsgate Churchyard
St. Botolph-without-Bishopsgate Gardens
Devonshire Row
Devonshire Square
Wormwood Street A1211
Outwich St
Camomile Street A1211
Hounds
17
Old Broad St
Union Ct
Bevis
Axe

0.25 mile
0.25 km

Liverpool Street / Broadgate

grimy maw that spews trendos onto Bishopsgate, Liverpool Street is the ateway to the nowness of Brick Lane and Shoreditch. Its arse-end lets out uits and money into the borders of the City.

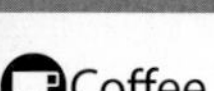

Coffee

- **AMT** • Liverpool St & Broadgate Circle
- **Caffe Nero** • 155 Bishopsgate
- **Caffe Nero** • 40 City Rd
- **Caffe Nero** • 22 Wormwood St
- **Costa** • 1 Ropemaker St
- **Costa** • 18 Liverpool St
- **Eat.** • 95 City Rd
- **Eat.** • 34 Broadgate Circle
- **Eat.** • 80 Old Broad St
- **Starbucks** • Liverpool St Station
- **Starbucks** • 28 Broadgate Circle

Landmarks

- **Fulcrum** • Broadgate

Libraries

- **Bishopsgate Library** • 230 Bishopsgate

Nightlife

- **The Book Club** • 100 Leonard St
- **Callooh Callay** • 65 Rivington St
- **Lounge Bohemia** • 1 Great Eastern St
- **McQueen** • 55 Tabernacle St
- **Red Lion** • 1 Eldon St
- **Worship Street Whistling Shop** • 63 Worship St
- **XOYO** • 32 Cowper St

Restaurants

- **Duck and Waffle** • 110 Bishopgate
- **Gaucho Broadgate** • 5 Finsbury Ave
- **Hoxton Grill** • 81 Great Eastern St
- **Lantana** • 55 City Road
- **The Princess of Shoreditch** • 76 Paul St

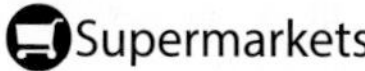

Supermarkets

- **Tesco** • 158 Bishopsgate

Map 9 • Mayfair / Green Park

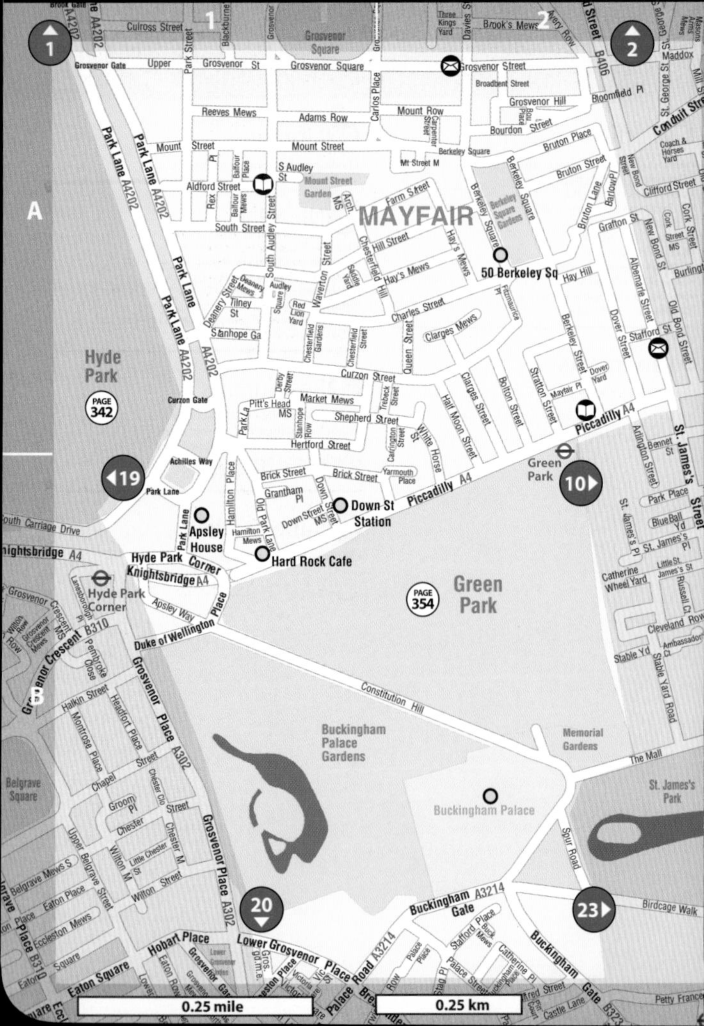

N

1
2
A
B
1
2
19
10
20
23

Culross Street
Upper Grosvenor St
Grosvenor Gate
Park Street
Blackburne's
Grosvenor Square
Grosvenor Square
Carlos Place
Three Kings Yard
Davies St
Brook's Mews
Avery Row
Grosvenor Street
Broadbent Street
Grosvenor Hill
Bourdon Place
Bourdon Street
Bloomfield Pl
Maddox
Conduit Street
St. George St
Masons Arms Mews
Mill St
Reeves Mews
Adams Row
Mount Row
Carpenter Street
Berkeley Square
Bruton Place
Bruton Street
Bruton Lane
Barlow Pl
Coach & Horses Yard
New Bond Street
Clifford Street
Cork Street
Cork Street MS
Mount Street
Mount Street
Mt Street M
S Audley St
Mount Street Garden
Aldford Street
Rex Pl
Balfour Place
Balfour Mews
South Street
Arch. MS
Farm Street
MAYFAIR
Berkeley Square
Berkeley Square Gardens
50 Berkeley Sq
Grafton St
Hay Hill
New Bond St
Albemarle Street
Burlington
Old Bond Street
Park Lane A4202
Park Lane A4202
Park Lane
Park Lane A4202
A4202
South Audley Street
Waverton Street
Hill Street
Chesterfield Hill
Saddle Yard
Hay's Mews
Hay's Mews
Deanery Street
Deanery Mews
Tilney St
Audley Square
Red Lion Yard
Stanhope Ga
Charles Street
Fitzmaurice Pl
Clarges Mews
Queen Street
Chesterfield Gardens
Chesterfield Street
Berkeley Street
Dover Street
Stafford St
Dover Yard
Hyde Park
Curzon Gate
Curzon Street
Derby Street
Market Mews
Pitt's Head MS
Park La
Stanhope Row
Shepherd Street
Trebeck Street
Carrington Street
White Horse St
Half Moon Street
Clarges Street
Bolton Street
Stratton Street
Mayfair Pl
Piccadilly A4
Arlington Street
Bennet St
St. James's Street
Hertford Street
Achilles Way
Park Lane
Hamilton Place
Brick Street
Brick Street
Yarmouth Place
Green Park
Grantham Pl
Down Street
Down Street MS
Down St Station
Piccadilly A4
Old Park Lane
Hamilton Mews
Park Lane
Apsley House
Hard Rock Cafe
Park Place
Blue Ball Yd
St. James's Pl
St. James's Pl
South Carriage Drive
Knightsbridge A4
Hyde Park Corner
Knightsbridge A4
Hyde Park Corner
Lanesborough Pl
Grosvenor Crescent
Grosvenor Crescent MS
Grosvenor Crescent Mews
Wilton Row
Apsley Way
Place
Duke of Wellington Place
Green Park
Catherine Wheel Yard
Little St. James's St
Russell Ct
Cleveland Row
Ambassador's Ct
Stable Yd
Stable Yard Road
Grosvenor Crescent B310
Pembroke Close
Halkin Street
Headfort Place
Grosvenor Place A302
Constitution Hill
Montrose Place
Chapel Street
Chester Clo
Buckingham Palace Gardens
Memorial Gardens
The Mall
St. James's Park
Belgrave Square
Groom Pl
Chester Street
Chester M
Buckingham Palace
Upper Belgrave Street
Wilton M
Little Chester St
Grosvenor Place A302
Spur Road
Belgrave Mews S
Eaton Place
Wilton Street
Eccleston Mews
Buckingham Gate A3214
Birdcage Walk
Eaton Square
Hobart Place
Lower Grosvenor Place
Palace Road A3214
Palace Place
Stafford Place
Buck Mews
Catherine Pl
Buckingham Gate B323
Buckingham Place
Palace Street
Castle Lane
Petty France
Eaton Row
Lower Grosvenor Garden
Victoria Sq
Place B310
Eaton Square

0.25 mile
0.25 km

A taste of Old Money is a decent enough reason to visit Mayfair; splashing out on High Tea at **The Ritz** is pretty much an investment in one's cultural education. The upside to might-rich neighbourhoods? Art galleries. Ones that give away wine. All the time. Pop down Cork Street on an eve to quaff all the free champagne at a private view then go off somewhere far more interesting.

Cinemas

- **Curzon Mayfair** • 38 Curzon St

Coffee

- **Apostrophe** • 10 Grosvenor St
- **Caffe Nero** • 50 Curzon St
- **Caffe Nero** • 70 Piccadilly
- **Costa** • 9 Eldon St
- **Eat.** • 8 Berkeley Sq
- **Starbucks** • 52 Berkeley St

Landmarks

- **50 Berkeley Square** • 50 Berkeley Sq
- **Apsley House** • 149 Piccadilly
- **Buckingham Palace** • The Mall
- **Down Street Station** • Down St & Piccadilly
- **Hard Rock Cafe** • Piccadilly & Old Park Ln

Libraries

- **Mayfair Library** • 25 South Audley St
- **Royal Society of Chemistry Library and Information Centre** • Piccadilly

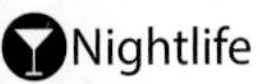

Nightlife

- **1707 Wine Bar** • 181 Piccadilly
- **bbar** • 43 Buckingham Palace Rd
- **Funky Buddha** • 15 Berkeley St
- **Mahiki** • 1 Dover St
- **Shepherd's Tavern** • 50 Hertford St

Post Offices

- **Mayfair** • 32 Grosvenor St

Restaurants

- **Alain Ducasse at The Dorchester** • Park Ln
- **Burger & Lobster** • 29 Clarges St
- **Corrigan's** • 28 Upper Grosvenor St
- **El Pirata of Mayfair** • 5 Down St
- **The English Tea Room at Brown's** • Albemarle St
- **Galvin at Windows** • Park Ln, 28th Floor
- **Gymkhana** • 42 Albemarle St
- **Kitty Fisher's** • 10 Shepherd Market
- **L'Autre** • 5 Shepherd St
- **Momo** • 25 Heddon St
- **Nobu** • 19 Old Park Ln
- **The Ritz** • 150 Piccadilly
- **Theo Randall** • 1 Hamilton Pl

Shopping

- **Diane Von Furstenberg** • 25 Bruton St
- **Dover Street Market** • 17 Dover St
- **Green Valley** • Berkeley St
- **Stella McCartney** • 23 Old Bond St

Supermarkets

- **Marks & Spencer** • 78 Piccadilly
- **Sainsbury's** • 38 Stratton St

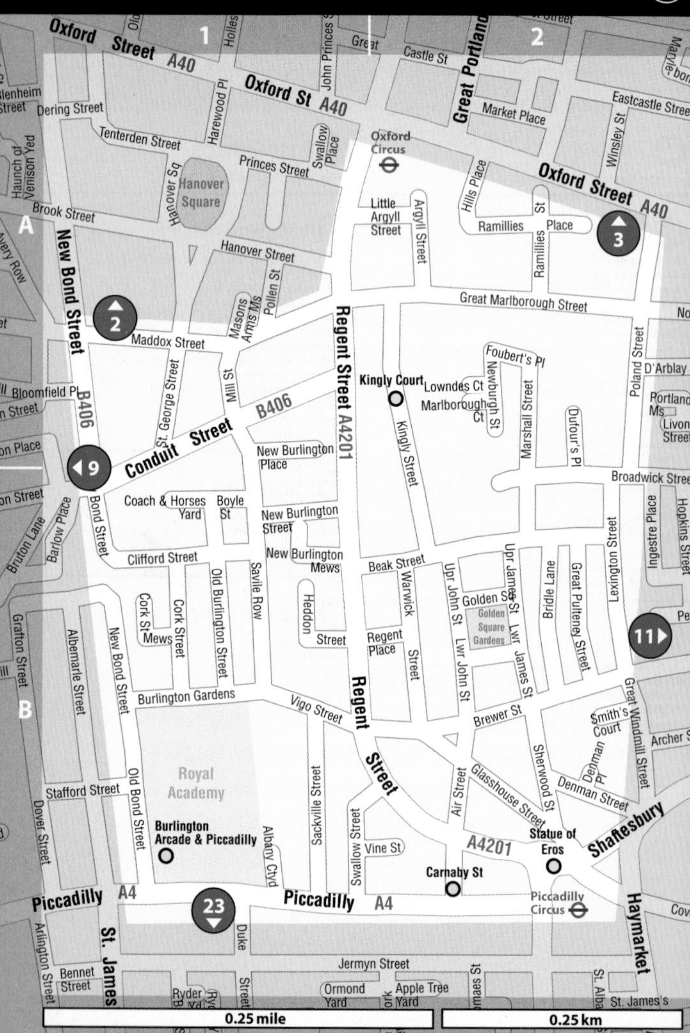

Oxford Street A40
Oxford St A40
Oxford Street A40
Oxford Circus
Regent Street A4201
Regent Street
Conduit Street
B406
New Bond Street
Great Marlborough Street
Kingly Court
Burlington Arcade & Piccadilly
Royal Academy
Statue of Eros
Carnaby St
Piccadilly A4
Piccadilly Circus
Shaftesbury
Haymarket
Jermyn Street
Golden Square Gardens
Hanover Square
0.25 mile
0.25 km

Piccadilly / Soho (West)

orget visions of Austin Powers "yeah baby" grooviness, Carnaby Street is a slick study in consumerism with all major streetwear labels present, but the grand dame of department stores, **Liberty**, retains top marks for a unique shopping experience. Have a coffee in Sacred if you can find a seat or else retreat to **Milk & Honey** for a cocktail. **Polpo** restaurant is a winner in the small plates game.

Coffee

- **Caffe Nero** • 62 Brewer St
- **Caffe Nero** • 26 Piccadilly
- **Costa** • 11 Argyll St
- **Eat.** • 19 Golden Sq
- **Eat.** • 8 Vigo St
- **Pret A Manger** • 298 Regent St
- **Pret A Manger** • 27 Great Marlborough
- **Rapha Cycle Club** • 85 Brewer St
- **Sacred Cafe** • 13 Ganton St
- **Tonic Coffee Bar** • 15 Sherwood St
- **Yunchaa** • 45 Berwick St

Landmarks

- **Burlington Arcade** • Piccadilly
- **Carnaby Street** • Carnaby St
- **Kingly Court** • Kingly St & Foubert's Pl
- **Statue of Eros** • Piccadilly Circus

Nightlife

- **5th View** • 203 Piccadilly
- **Ain't Nothing But…** • 20 Kingly St
- **Beyond Retro** • 58 Great Marlborough St
- **The Blind Pig** • 58 Poland St
- **Courthouse Bar**• 19 Great Marlborough St
- **The John Snow** • 39 Broadwick St
- **Milk & Honey** • 61 Poland St
- **The Red Lion** • 14 Kingly St
- **The Windmill** • 6 Mill St

Restaurants

- **Bao** • 53 Lexington St
- **Bob Bob Ricard** • 1 Upper James St
- **Bodean's BBQ** • 10 Poland St
- **Brasserie Zedel** • 20 Sherwood St
- **Cecconi's** • 5 Burlington Gardens
- **Dehesa** • 25 Ganton St
- **Detox Kitchen** • 10 Kingly St
- **Dishoom** • 22 Kingly St
- **Kulu Kulu** • 76 Brewer St
- **Le Pain Quotidien** • 18 Great Marlborough St
- **Mildred's** • 45 Lexington St
- **Nordic Bakery** • 14 Golden Sq
- **The Photographers' Gallery** • 16 Ramillies St
- **Ping Pong** • 45 Great Marlborough St
- **Polpo** • 41 Beak St
- **San Carlo Cicchetti** • 215 Piccadilly
- **Sartoria** • 20 Saville Row
- **Sketch** • 9 Conduit St
- **Social Eating House** • 58 Poland St
- **Taro** • 61 Brewer St
- **Tibits** • 12 Heddon St
- **Yauatcha** • 15 Broadwick St
- **Yoshino** • 3 Piccadilly Pl

Shopping

- **Abercrombie & Fitch** • 7 Burlington Gardens
- **Anthropologie** • 158 Regent St
- **Apple Store** • 235 Regent Street
- **Beyond Retro** • 58 Great Marlborough St
- **Burlington Arcade** • Burlington Arcade
- **Cos** • 222 Regent St
- **Fortnum & Mason** • 181 Piccadilly
- **Hamley's** • 188 Regent St
- **Hatchards Bookshop** • 187 Piccadilly
- **Hoss Intropia** • 211 Regent St
- **Lazy Oaf** • 19 Fouberts Pl
- **Liberty** • 214 Regent St
- **Lillywhites** • 24 Lower Regent St
- **Lucky Voice** • 52 Poland St
- **Muji** • 41 Carnaby St
- **Phonica** • 51 Poland St
- **Richard James** • 29 Savile Row
- **Rigby & Peller** • 22 Conduit St
- **Twinkled** • 1 Kingly Ct
- **Whole Foods Market** • 69 Brewer St

Supermarkets

- **Whole Foods Market** • 69 Brewer St

A40
Oxford Street
A40
1
2
3
A
B
Berwick Street
Great Chapel St
Hollen St
Fareham St
Soho St
Falconberg
Marlborough St
Noel St
Poland Street
Sheraton St
D'Arblay Street
Carlisle St
Soho Square Garden
Soho Square
Sutton
Portland Ms
Livonia St
Wardour Ms
Dean St
Chapone Place
Dufour's Pl
John Snow Water Pump
Flax. Court
Richmond Buildings
Broadwick Street
Ingestre Place
Hopkins Street
Berwick Street
Duck La
Wardour Street
Richmond Ms
Royalty Mews
Bateman Street
Frith Street
Greek Street
Lexington Street
Berwick Street Market
Meard Street
12
Beak Street
Great Pulteney St
Bridle Lane
10
Peter Street
Bourchier St
Old Compton Street
SOHO
Romilly Street
Brewer Street
Rupert Street
Winnett Street
Shaftesbury
Gerrard Pl
Lower James Street
Great Windmill St
Smith's Ct
Archer St
A401
Horse & Dolphin Yard
Brewer Street
Sherwood St
Dansey Pl
Mac. St
Avenue
CHINATOWN
Shaftesbury
Denman St
Lisle Street
Street
Rupert Street Mkt
Leicester St
A4201
Huge Tree In Pub (Waxy O'Connor's)
Piccadilly Circus
Coventry Street
23
Whitcomb
Leicester Square Garden
0.1 mile
0.1 km

By day, the turning out of London's new favourite caffeine kick—the flat white courtesy of the Aussies—is relentless at **Milk Bar**. All the better to fuel the night's activities: This is still the heart of the red light district, but it's no longer such a sordid affair. Berwick Street is still loved for its record shops and market.

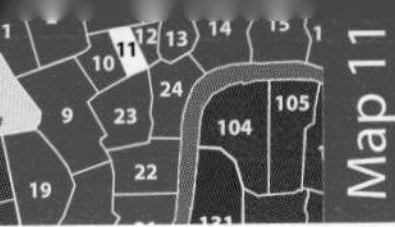

Cinemas

- **Apollo Theatre** • Shaftesbury Ave
- **Curzon Soho** • 99 Shaftesbury Ave
- **Prince Charles Cinema** • 7 Leicester Pl

Coffee

- **Flat White** • 17 Berwick St
- **Kaffeine** • 66 Great Titchfield St
- **Milk Bar** • 3 Bateman St
- **Prince Charles Cinema** • 7 Leicester Pl
- **Starbucks** • 60 Wardour St
- **TAP Coffee** • 193 Wardour St
- **Toi & Moi Cafe** • 38 Berwick St

Landmarks

- **Berwick Street Market** • Berwick St & Rupert St
- **John Snow Water Pump** • Broadwick St
- **Waxy O'Connor's** • 14 Rupert St

Nightlife

- **Blue Posts** • 22 Berwick St
- **The Blue Posts** • 28 Rupert St
- **The Comedy Store** • 1 Oxendon St
- **De Hems** • 11 Macclesfield St
- **Experimental Cocktail Club** • 13 Gerrard St
- **Freedom** • 66 Wardour St
- **The French House** • 49 Dean St
- **The Lyric** • 137 Great Windmill St
- **Village** • 81 Wardour St
- **The Yard** • 57 Rupert St

Restaurants

- **Balans** • 60 Old Compton St
- **Bar Bruno** • 101 Wardour St
- **Blanchette** • 9 D'Arblay St
- **Bocca di Lupo** • 12 Archer St
- **Bone Daddies** • 31 Peter St
- **Brewdog Soho** • 21 Poland St
- **Busaba Eathai** • 110 Wardour St
- **Copita** • 27 D'Arblay St
- **Ember Yard** • 60 Berwick St
- **Gelupo** • 7 Archer St
- **Honest Burgers** • 4 Meard St
- **Leggero** • 64 Old Comton St
- **Jazz Club** • 10 Dean St
- **Maoz** • 43 Old Compton St
- **Mildred's** • 45 Lexington St
- **The Palomar** • 34 Rupert St
- **Princi** • 135 Wardour St
- **Randall & Aubin** • 16 Brewer St
- **Snog** • 9 Brewer St
- **Soho Joe** • 22 Dean St
- **St Moritz** • 161 Wardour St
- **Tamarind Kitchen** • 167 Wardour St
- **Tokyo Diner** • 2 Newport Pl
- **Won Kei** • 41 Wardour St

Shopping

- **Algerian Coffee Store** • 52 Old Compton St
- **Cass Art Soho** • 24 Berwick St
- **Gerry's** • 74 Old Compton St
- **I. Camisa & Son** • 61 Old Compton St
- **Reckless Records** • 30 Berwick St
- **Sister Ray** • 34 Berwick St
- **Snog** • 9 Brewer St
- **Sounds of the Universe** • 7 Broadwick St

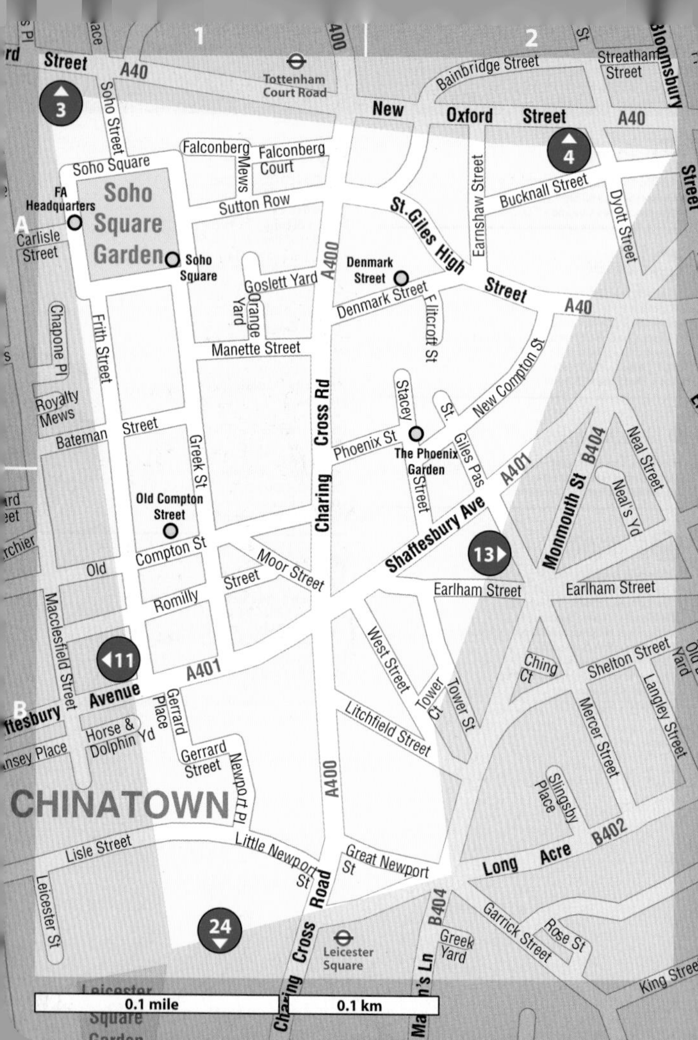

1
2
A
B
Oxford Street
A40
Tottenham Court Road
New Oxford Street
Bainbridge Street
Streatham Street
Bloomsbury Street
3
4
Soho Street
Soho Square
Soho Square Garden
FA Headquarters
Carlisle Street
Falconberg Mews
Falconberg Court
Sutton Row
Bucknall Street
Earnshaw Street
Dyott Street
St. Giles High Street
Denmark Street
Goslett Yard
Orange Yard
A400
Flitcroft St
Manette Street
Chapone Pl
Frith Street
Royalty Mews
Bateman Street
Greek St
Charing Cross Rd
Stacey St
Phoenix St
The Phoenix Garden
New Compton St
Giles Pas
A401
Shaftesbury Ave
B404
Monmouth St
Neal Street
Neal's Yd
Old Compton Street
Compton St
Moor Street
Old Street
Romilly Street
13
Earlham Street
Macclesfield Street
11
Avenue
West Street
Tower Ct
Tower St
Ching Ct
Shelton Street
Old Yard
Langley Street
Mercer Street
Shaftesbury
Gerrard Place
Horse & Dolphin Yd
Litchfield Street
Gerrard Street
Newport Pl
CHINATOWN
Slingsby Place
Lisle Street
Little Newport St
Great Newport St
Long Acre
B402
Leicester St
Charing Cross Road
24
Leicester Square
Greek Yard
Garrick Street
Rose St
King Street
0.1 mile
0.1 km
Leicester Square Garden

While **The Three Greyhounds** (opposite Soho House) might be one of the cheapest pubs in central London, **Jazz After Dark** on Greek Street certainly isn't, but it does have an undeniably attractive ambiance. Blend in with the winos at Soho Square with a shop-bought bottle while **G-A-Y** showcases the more colourful side of Soho.

Cinemas

- **Vue West End Cinema** • 3 Cranbourn St

Coffee

- **Caffe Nero** • 32 Cranbourn St
- **Caffe Nero** • 43 Frith St
- **Eat.** • 16 Soho Sq
- **Eat.** • 155 Charing Cross Rd
- **Maison Bertaux** • 28 Greek St

Landmarks

- **Denmark Street** • Denmark St
- **FA Headquarters** • 25 Soho Sq
- **Old Compton Street** • Old Compton St
- **The Phoenix Garden** • 21 Stacey St
- **Soho Square** • Soho Sq

Nightlife

- **68 and Boston** • 5 Greek St
- **Bar Termini** • 7 Old Compton St
- **Cafe Boheme** • 13 Old Compton St
- **The Borderline** • Orange Yard
- **Comptons** • 53 Old Compton St
- **The Crobar** • 17 Manette St
- **G-A-Y Bar** • 30 Old Compton St
- **G-A-Y Late** • 5 Goslett Yard
- **Garlic & Shots** • 14 Frith St
- **Jazz After Dark** • 9 Greek St
- **Karaoke Box** • 18 Frith St
- **Ku** • 30 Lisle St
- **Milroy's** • 3 Greek St
- **The Montagu Pyke** • 105 Charing Cross Rd
- **Ronnie Scott's** • 47 Frith St
- **Salsa!** • 96 Charing Cross Rd
- **The Royal George** • 133 Charing Cross Rd
- **The Three Greyhounds** • 25 Greek St
- **The Toucan** • 19 Carlisle St

Restaurants

- **10 Greek Street** • 10 Greek St
- **Baiwei** • 8 Little Newport St
- **Baozi Inn** • 26 Newport Court
- **Bar Italia** • 22 Frith St
- **Barshu** • 28 Frith St
- **Bi Bim Bap** • 11 Greek St
- **Boheme Kitchen and Bar** • 19 Old Compton St
- **Ceviche** • 17 Frith St
- **Garlic & Shots** • 14 Frith St
- **Gay Hussar** • 2 Greek St
- **Haozhan** • 8 Gerrard St
- **Imperial China** • 25 Lisle St
- **The Ivy** • 1 West St
- **Koya** • 49 Frith St
- **La Bodega Negra** • 16 Moor St
- **La Porchetta Pollo Bar** • 20 Old Compton St
- **Le Beaujolais** • 25 Litchfield St
- **Maison Bertaux** • 27 Greek St
- **Sartori** • 15 Great Newport St
- **Soho's Secret Tea Room** • 29 Greek St
- **The Three Greyhounds** • 25 Greek Street

Shopping

- **Angels Fancy Dress Shop** • 119 Shaftesbury Ave
- **Fopp** • 1 Earlham St
- **Forbidden Planet** • 179 Shaftesbury Ave
- **Foyles** • 113 Charing Cross Rd
- **Hank's Guitar Shop** • 27 Denmark St
- **Macari's** • 92 Charing Cross Rd
- **Quinto Bookshop** • 72 Charing Cross Rd
- **Rockers** • 5 Denmark St
- **Wunjo Guitars** • 20 Denmark St

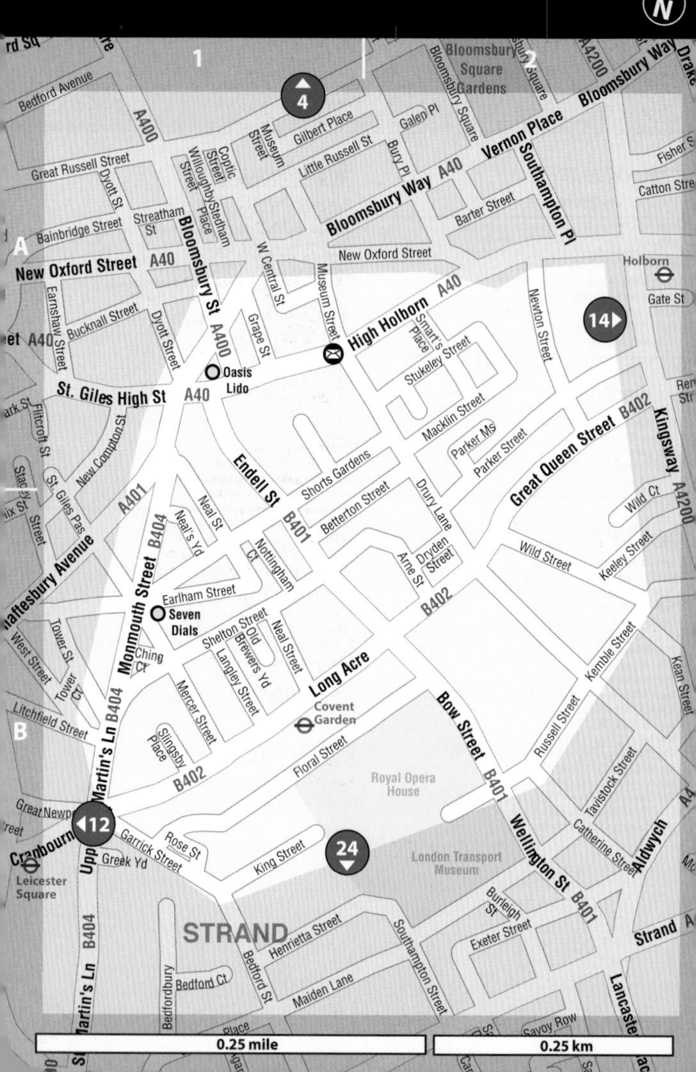

Bloomsbury Square Gardens
Bedford Avenue
A400
Gilbert Place
Museum Street
Galen Pl
Bloomsbury Square
Bloomsbury Way
Vernon Place
Great Russell Street
Coptic Street
Willoughby Street
Little Russell St
Bury Pl
Bloomsbury Way A40
Southampton Pl
Fisher St
Catton Street
Dyott St
Stedham Place
Barter Street
Bainbridge Street
Streatham St
Bloomsbury St
W Central St
New Oxford Street
New Oxford Street A40
Holborn
Museum Street
Gate St
Earnshaw Street
Bucknall Street
Dyott Street
Grape St
A400
High Holborn A40
Smart's Place
Newton Street
Stukeley Street
Oasis Lido
St. Giles High St A40
Macklin Street
Flitcroft St
New Compton St
Parker Ms
Parker Street
Great Queen Street B402
Kingsway A4200
St. Giles Pas
Endell St
Shorts Gardens
Drury Lane
Wild Ct
A401
Neal St
Neal's Yd
B404
Betterton Street
B401
Nottingham Ct
Dryden Street
Arne St
Wild Street
Keeley Street
Shaftesbury Avenue
Monmouth Street
Earlham Street
Seven Dials
B402
Tower St
West Street
Shelton Street
Old Brewers Yd
Neal Street
Kemble Street
Ching Ct
Langley Street
Long Acre
Kean Street
Tower Ct
Mercer Street
Covent Garden
Bow Street
Russell Street
Litchfield Street
St Martin's Ln B404
Slingsby Place
Floral Street
B402
Royal Opera House
B401
Tavistock Street
Great Newport
12
Cranbourn
Garrick Street
Rose St
King Street
24
Wellington St
Catherine Street
Aldwych
London Transport Museum
Upper
Greek Yd
Leicester Square
Burleigh St
B401
STRAND
Henrietta Street
Exeter Street
Strand
B404
Southampton Street
Lancaster
St Martin's Ln
Bedford St
Maiden Lane
Bedford Ct
Bedfordbury
Savoy Row
0.25 mile
0.25 km
A
B
1
2
4
14
N

Covent Garden is a shopper's delight, especially on Endell Street and Neal Street. However, such activity will not offer a respite from the Piazza and its hordes of spatially unaware folk. Stop for fish and chips at **Rock & Sole Plaice**. Come the evening, sip cocktails at **Freud** or convene with the ghost of Bernard Shaw at the **Lamb & Flag**.

Map 13

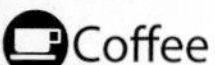

Coffee

- **Bagariat** • 24 Rose St
- **Bagel Factory** • 18 Endell St
- **The Black Penny** • 34 Great Queen St
- **Caffe Nero** • 30 Monmouth St
- **Caffe Nero** • 83 Long Acre
- **Pret A Manger** • 65 Long Acre
- **Starbucks** • 10 Russell St
- **Timberyard** • 7 Upper St Martin's Ln

Landmarks

- **Oasis Sports Centre** • 32 Endell St
- **Seven Dials** • Upper St Martin's Ln & Earlham St

Nightlife

- **Compagnie Des Vins Surnaturels** • 8-10 Neal's Yard
- **The Cross Keys** • 31 Endell St
- **Freud** • 198 Shaftesbury Ave
- **Lamb & Flag** • 33 Rose St
- **The Poetry Cafe** • 22 Betterton St

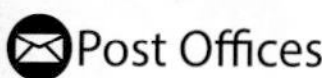

Post Offices

- **High Holborn** • 181 High Holborn

Restaurants

- **Battersea Pie** • Covent Garden Piazza
- **Belgo Centraal** • 50 Earlham St
- **Café Mode** • 57 Endell St
- **Flat Iron** • 17 Henrietta St
- **Flesh & Buns** • 41 Earlham St
- **Great Queen Street** • 32 Great Queen St
- **Lanzhou Noodle Bar** • 33 Cranbourne St
- **Lima Floral** • 14 Garrick St
- **Mon Plaisir** • 21 Monmouth St
- **The Punjab** • 80 Neal St
- **Rock & Sole Plaice** • 47 Endell St
- **Sarastro** • 126 Drury Ln
- **Souk Medina** • 1 Shorts Gardens
- **Wild Food Cafe** • 14 Neal's Yard

Shopping

- **The Astrology Shop** • 78 Neal St
- **Ben's Cookies** • 13 The Piazza
- **Blackout II** • 51 Endell St
- **Cath Kidston** • 28 Shelton St
- **Coco de Mer** • 23 Monmouth St
- **Libidex at Liberation** • 49 Shelton St
- **London Graphic Centre** • 16 Shelton St
- **Lululemon** • 19 Long Acre
- **Neal's Yard Dairy** • 17 Shorts Gardens
- **Poetry Cafe** • 22 Betterton St
- **Pop Boutique** • 6 Monmouth St
- **Rokit** • 42 Shelton St
- **Rossopomodoro** • 50 Monmouth St
- **Stanfords** • 12 Long Acre
- **Tabio** • 66 Neal St
- **Urban Outfitters** • 42 Earlham St

Supermarkets

- **Sainsbury's** • 129 Kingsway

HOLBORN
Theobald's Road A401
High Holborn A40
Holborn A40
Holborn
Chancery Lane
Kingsway A4200
Gray's Inn Road A5200
Clerkenwell Road
Hatton Garden B521
Hatton Garden
Gray's Inn Gardens
Sir John Soane's Museum
Lincoln's Inn Fields (Fickets Fields)
The Old Curiosity Shop
London School of Economics
Royal Courts of Justice
Site of Sweeney Todd's Barber Shop
BBC Bush House
Somerset House
Aldwych Tube Station
King's College
Inner Temple Gardens
Temple
Aldwych A4
Strand A4
Fleet Street
Chancery Lane B400
Fetter Lane A4
New Fetter Lane A4
Great Queen Street B402
Southampton Row A4200
Bloomsbury Way A40
Drury Lane
Wellington Street B401
Bow Street B401
Lancaster Place A301
Victoria Embankment A3211
River Thames
PAGE 368
PAGE 366
4
5
13
15
24
A
B
1
2
0.25 mile
0.25 km

Map 14

An essential cog in London's machine, this area is resplendent with curios (**Old Curiosity Shop, Sweeney Todd's**), public squares full of depressed lawyers and legions of serious-looking people being integrated into The System. The ghosts of London's past hover around Temple and the Strand, where you'll also find **Aldwych Film** for brunch and a flick.

Cinemas

- **Aldwych Film** • 1 Aldwych

Coffee

- **Caffe Nero** • 333 High Holborn
- **Department of Coffee and Social Affairs** • 14 Leather Ln
- **Eat.** • 34 High Holborn
- **Eat.** • 7 Kingsway
- **Eat.** • 77 Chancery Lane
- **Fleet Street Press** • 3 Fleet St
- **Pret A Manger** • 10 Leather Ln
- **Pret A Manger** • 240 High Holborn
- **Prufrock Coffee** • 23-25 Leather Ln
- **Starbucks** • 10 Kingsway
- **Starbucks** • 99 Kingsway

Landmarks

- **Aldwych Tube Station** • Strand & Surrey St
- **BBC Bush House** • Aldwych & Kingsway
- **Hatton Garden** • Hatton Garden
- **Inner Temple Garden** • Inner Temple
- **King's College London** • Strand
- **Lincoln's Inn Fields** • Newman's Row
- **London School of Economics and Political Science** • Houghton St
- **The Old Curiosity Shop** • 13 Portsmouth St
- **Royal Courts of Justice** • Strand
- **Sir John Soane's Museum** • 13 Lincoln's Inn Fields
- **Sweeney Todd's Barber Shop** • 186 Fleet St
- **Somerset House** • Somerset House Trust, The Strand

Libraries

- **British Library of Political and Economic Science** • 10 Portugal St

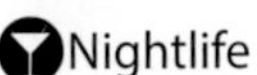

Nightlife

- **Bar Polski** • 11 Little Turnstile
- **Bounce** • 121 Holborn
- **Cittie of Yorke** • 22 High Holborn
- **The Craft Beer Co.** • 82 Leather Ln
- **The Enterprise** • 38 Red Lion St
- **The Seven Stars** • 53 Carey St

Post Offices

- **Aldwych** • 95 Aldwych
- **Grays Inn** • 19 High Holborn

Restaurants

- **Asadal** • 227 High Holborn
- **Casanova's Treats** • 13 Lamb's Conduit Passage
- **Indigo** • 1 Aldwych
- **MEATmarket** • Jubilee Market Hall, Tavistock St
- **Radio Rooftop Bar** • 336 Strand

Shopping

- **Konditor & Cook** • 46 Grays Inn Rd
- **Topshop** • 60 The Strand

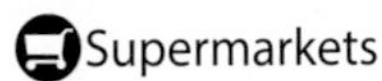

Supermarkets

- **Sainsbury's** • 129 Kingsway
- **Sainsbury's** • 60 Fetter Ln
- **Sainsbury's** • 71 High Holborn

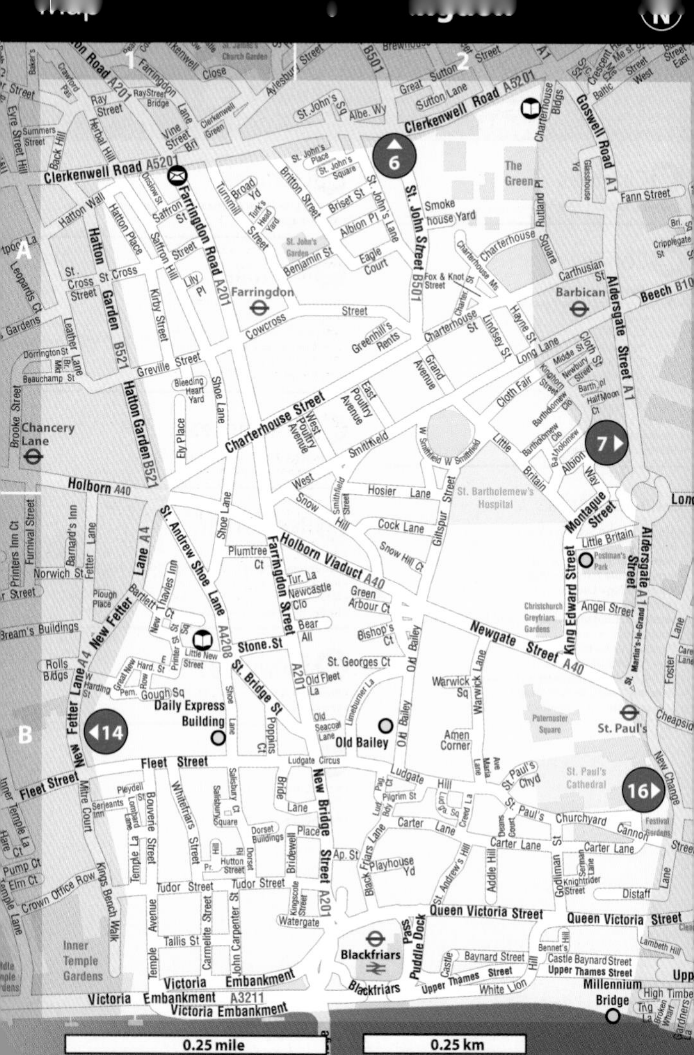

1
2
A
B
Clerkenwell Road A5201
Clerkenwell Road A5201
Farringdon Road A201
Farringdon Lane
Ray Street
Ray Street Bridge
Vine Street Bri
Clerkenwell Close
Clerkenwell Green
Aylesbury Street
St. John's Sq
Albe. Wy
Great Sutton Street
Sutton Lane
Charterhouse Bldgs
Goswell Road A1
Crawford Pas
Baker's
Eyre Street Hill
Summers Street
Back Hill
Herbal Hill
Hatton Wall
Hatton Place
Hatton Garden B521
Onslow St
Saffron St
Saffron Hill
Saffron Street
Turnmill Street
Broad Yd
Turk's Head Yard
Britton Street
St. John's Place
St. John's Square
Briset St
Albion Pl
St. John's Lane
St. John's Gardens
Benjamin St
Eagle Court
St. John Street B501
Smokehouse Yard
The Green
Rutland Pl
Glasshouse Yd
Fann Street
Charterhouse Square
Charterhouse Ms
Carthusian St
Barbican
Aldersgate Street A1
Beech B10
Cripplegate St
Fox & Knot Street
Charter St
Charterhouse St
Lindsey St
Hayne St
Long Lane
Cloth St
Middle St
Newbury Street
Kinghorn Street
Barth. pl
Half Moon Ct
Cloth Fair
Bartholomew Clo
Little Britain
Albion Way
Montague Street
Farringdon
Cowcross Street
Greenhill's Rents
Grand Avenue
East Poultry Avenue
West Poultry Avenue
Charterhouse Street
West Smithfield
W Smithfield
St. Cross Street
St. Cross
Kirby Street
Lily Pl
Leather Lane
Dorrington St
Brooke Street
Beauchamp St
Greville Street
Bleeding Heart Yard
Shoe Lane
Ely Place
Chancery Lane
Holborn A40
Leopards Ct
Gardens
Hosier Lane
Giltspur Street
St. Bartholomew's Hospital
Smithfield Street
Snow Hill
Cock Lane
Snow Hill Ct
Postman's Park
King Edward Street
Aldersgate Street A1
Little Britain
Christchurch Greyfriars Gardens
Angel Street
St. Martin's-le-Grand
Foster Lane
Newgate Street A40
Holborn Viaduct A40
Plumtree Ct
Farringdon Street
Tur. La
Newcastle Clo
Green Arbour Ct
Bear All
Bishop's Ct
St. Georges Ct
Old Bailey
Warwick Sq
Warwick Lane
Paternoster Square
St. Paul's
Cheapside
St. Andrew Street
Shoe Lane A4208
Thavies Inn
Bartlett Ct
New St Sq
Printer St
Little New Street
Stone St
St. Bride St
A201
Old Fleet La
Limeburner La
Old Seacoal Lane
Amen Corner
Ave Maria Lane
Printers Inn Ct
Furnival Street
Barnard's Inn
Fetter Lane
Norwich St
Plough Place
New Fetter Lane A4
Bream's Buildings
Rolls Bldgs
Hard. St
Great New St
Gough Sq
Pem. Row
W Harding St
Daily Express Building
Poppins Ct
New Fetter Lane A4
Fleet Street
Fleet Street
Ludgate Circus
Ludgate Hill
St. Paul's Chyd
St. Paul's Cathedral
New Change
St. Paul's Churchyard
Cannon
Festival Gardens
Pilgrim St
Ludgate Sq
Creed La
Carter Lane
Carter Lane
Carter Lane
Deans Court
Godliman St
Sermon Lane
Knightrider Street
Distaff Lane
Inner Temple La
Hare Ct
Mitre Court
Pleydell St
Serjeants Inn
Lombard Lane
Bouverie Street
Whitefriars Street
Salisbury Ct
Salisbury Square
Bride Lane
Dorset Buildings
Dorset Ri
Bridewell Place
New Bridge Street A201
Ap. St
Black Friars Lane
Playhouse Yd
St. Andrew's Hill
Addle Hill
Temple La
Pump Ct
Elm Ct
Crown Office Row
Kings Bench Walk
Tudor Street
Tudor Street
Hutton Street
Pr.
Kingscote Street
Watergate
Queen Victoria Street
Queen Victoria Street
Lambeth Hill
Temple Lane
Temple Avenue
Tallis St
Carmelite Street
John Carpenter St
Blackfriars
Pass
Puddle Dock
Castle
Baynard Street
Upper Thames Street
White Lion Hill
Bennet's Hill
Castle Baynard Street
Upper Thames Street
Millennium Bridge
High Timber
Broken Wharf
Gardners La
Inner Temple Gardens
Victoria Embankment
Victoria Embankment A3211
Victoria Embankment
Blackfriars
6
7
14
16
0.25 mile
0.25 km

The choices for eating out and drinking in this quarter are myriad, but we recommend getting your chops around a side of cow: **Smith's** and **Gaucho** are two solid options. Get a feel for sixteenth-century London with a potter around the old Livery Halls, then make like a Dickensian Oliver in the gated Charterhouse Square.

Coffee

- **Alchemy Coffee** • 8 Ludgate Broadway
- **Caffe Nero** • 30 Newgate St
- **Caffe Nero** • 118 Newgate St
- **Costa** • 13 New Bridge St
- **Costa** • 46 Cowcross St
- **Pret A Manger** • 101 Turnmill St
- **Pret A Manger** • 5 St John's Sq
- **Pret A Manger** • 19 Ludgate Hill
- **Pret A Manger** • 110 Pasternoster Sq
- **Pret A Manger** • 101 New Bridge St
- **Pret A Manger** • 143 Fleet St
- **Starbucks** • 1 Paternoster Sq
- **Starbucks** • 3 Fleet Pl
- **Starbucks** • 30 New Bridge St
- **The Wren** • 114 Queen Victoria St

Landmarks

- **Daily Express Building** • 121 Fleet St
- **Millennium Bridge** • Millennium Bridge
- **Old Bailey** • Old Bailey
- **Postman's Park** • Little Britain

Libraries

- **Shoe Lane Library** • Little New St
- **Society of Genealogists Library** • 14 Charterhouse Buildings

Nightlife

- **Fabric** • 77 Charterhouse St
- **Fox and Anchor** • 115 Charterhouse St
- **The Happenstance** • 10 Paternoster Sq
- **The Hat and Tun** • 3 Hatton Wall
- **Ye Old Mitre** • 1 Ely Pl
- **Ye Olde Cheshire Cheese** • 145 Fleet St
- **Ye Olde London** • 42 Ludgate Hill

Post Offices

- **Farringdon Road** • 89 Farringdon Rd

Restaurants

- **Bleeding Heart** • Bleeding Heart Yard
- **The Fat Bear** • 61 Carter Lane
- **Gaucho Smithfield** • 93 Charterhouse St
- **Hix Oyster And Chop House** • 36 Cowcross St
- **Le Cafe du Marche** • 22 Charterhouse Sq
- **Pho** • 86 St. John St
- **Smiths of Smithfield** • 67 Charterhouse St
- **St. John** • 26 St John St
- **Tinseltown** • 44 St John St
- **Vivat Bacchus** • 47 Farringdon St
- **Ye Olde Cheshire Cheese** • 145 Fleet Street
- **Yo! Sushi** • 5 St Paul's Church Yard

Supermarkets

- **Sainsbury's** • 23 Farringdon Rd

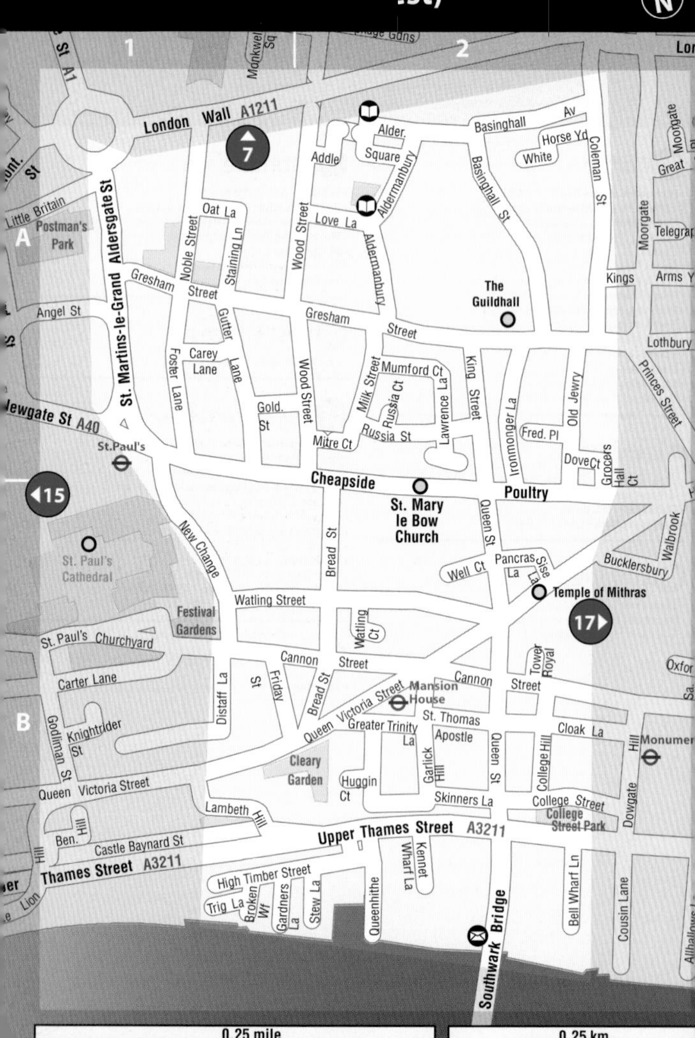

London Wall A1211
Aldersgate St
St. Martins-le-Grand
Little Britain
Postman's Park
Angel St
Newgate St A40
St.Paul's
St. Paul's Cathedral
Festival Gardens
St. Paul's Churchyard
Carter Lane
Godliman St
Knightrider St
Queen Victoria Street
Ben. Hill
Castle Baynard St
Thames Street A3211
Noble Street
Oat La
Staining Ln
Gresham Street
Foster Lane
Carey Lane
Gutter Lane
Gold. St
Wood Street
Addle
Alder.
Square
Aldermanbury
Love La
Basinghall Av
Basinghall St
Horse Yd
White
Coleman St
The Guildhall
Moorgate
Great
Telegrap
Kings
Arms Y
Lothbury
Princes Street
Milk Street
Mumford Ct
Russia Ct
Russia St
Lawrence La
King Street
Ironmonger La
Old Jewry
Fred. Pl
Dove Ct
Grocers Hall Ct
Mitre Ct
Cheapside
St. Mary le Bow Church
Poultry
New Change
Bread St
Queen St
Well Ct
Pancras La
Sise La
Bucklersbury
Walbrook
Temple of Mithras
Watling Street
Watling Ct
Cannon Street
Tower Royal
Distaff La
Friday St
Bread St
Queen Victoria Street
Mansion House
Greater Trinity La
St. Thomas Apostle
Garlick Hill
Queen St
College Hill
Cloak La
Hill
Monumer
Cleary Garden
Huggin Ct
Skinners La
College Street
College Street Park
Dowgate
Lambeth Hill
Upper Thames Street A3211
Kennet Wharf La
High Timber Street
Trig La
Broken Wf
Gardners La
Stew La
Queenhithe
Southwark Bridge
Bell Wharf Ln
Cousin Lane
Oxfor
0.25 mile
0.25 km

Aah, the City, that faceless square mile at which we direct such disgust and vehemence for the state we're in. Despite meltdowns and protests, the world continues to turn, stocks are traded, and bonuses return. This place has always been empty at the weekends so you can enjoy the caryatids and Doric columns in peace. And of course take in the duomo at San Paulo (so much more romantic sounding, don't you think?)

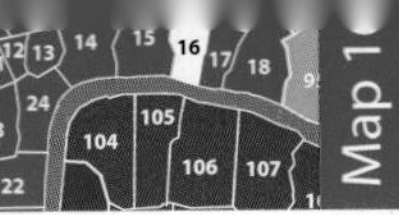

Coffee

- **Costa** • 99 Gresham St
- **Eat.** • 143 Cheapside
- **Pret A Manger** • 30 Gresham St
- **Starbucks** • 143 Cheapside

Landmarks

- **The Guildhall** • Gresham St
- **St Mary le Bow Church** • Cheapside
- **St Paul's Cathedral** • St Paul's Church Yard
- **Temple of Mithras** • Queen Victoria St

Post Offices

- **Southwark** • 136 Southwark Bridge Rd

Libraries

- **City Business Library** • Aldermanbury Sq
- **Guildhall Library** • Aldermanbury

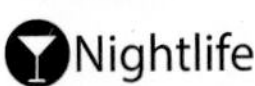

Nightlife

- **Planet of the Grapes** • 74 Queen Victoria St
- **The Samuel Pepys** • Stew Ln
- **Three Cranes** • 28 Garlick Hill
- **Ye Olde Watling** • 29 Watling St

Restaurants

- **Barbecoa** • 20 New Change Passage
- **Coq d'Argent** • 1 Poultry
- **Planet of the Grapes** • 74 Queen Victoria St
- **Sweetings** • 39 Queen Victoria St

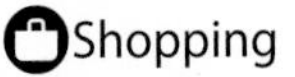

Shopping

- **Church's** • 90 Cheapside
- **Space NK Apothecary** • 145 Cheapside

Supermarkets

- **Marks & Spencer** • Cannon St Station

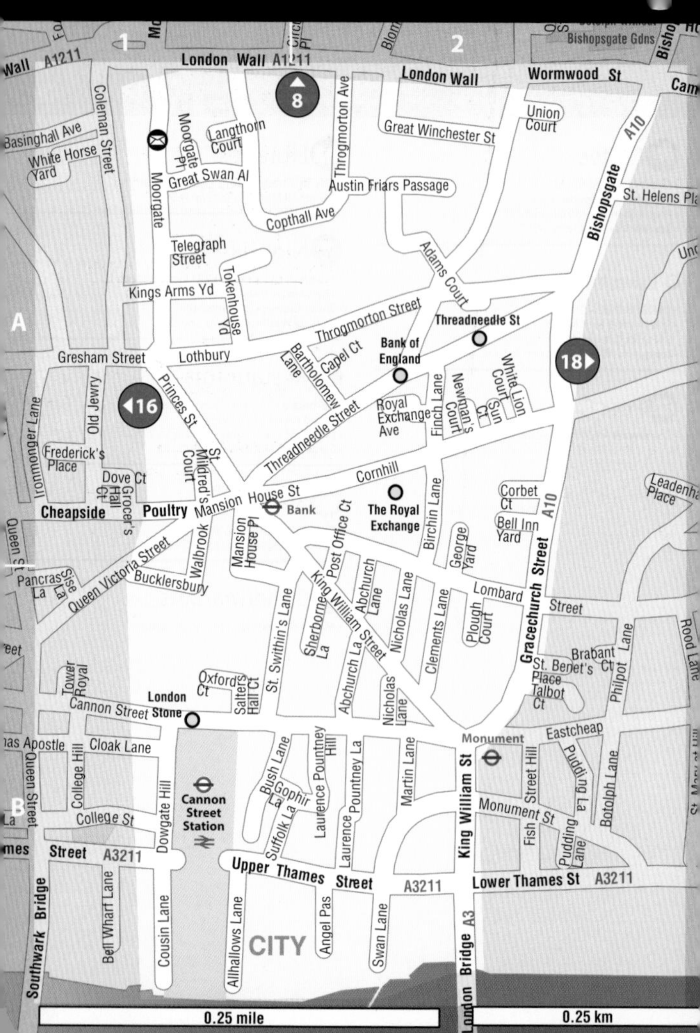

London Wall A1211
Wormwood St
Bishopsgate Gdns
Coleman Street
Moorgate
Basinghall Ave
White Horse Yard
Langthorn Court
Moorgate Pl
Great Swan Al
Throgmorton Ave
Great Winchester St
Union Court
Austin Friars Passage
Copthall Ave
Bishopsgate
A10
St. Helens Pl
Telegraph Street
Tokenhouse Yd
Kings Arms Yd
Adams Court
Throgmorton Street
Threadneedle St
Bank of England
Gresham Street
Lothbury
Capel Ct
Bartholomew Lane
Princes St
Old Jewry
Ironmonger Lane
Frederick's Place
Dove Ct
Grocer's Hall Ct
St. Mildred's Court
Threadneedle Street
Royal Exchange Ave
Finch Lane
Newman's Court
Sun Ct
White Lion Court
Cornhill
The Royal Exchange
Birchin Lane
Corbet Ct
Bell Inn Yard
Leadenhall Place
Cheapside
Poultry
Mansion House St
Bank
Mansion House Pl
Post Office Ct
George Yard
Gracechurch Street
Queen Victoria Street
Walbrook
Bucklersbury
Pancras La
Sise La
St. Swithin's Lane
Sherborne La
King William Street
Abchurch Lane
Nicholas Lane
Clements Lane
Lombard Street
Plough Court
Brabant Ct
St. Benet's Place
Talbot Ct
Philpot Lane
Rood Lane
Tower Royal
Cannon Street
London Stone
Oxford Ct
Salters Hall Ct
Abchurch La
Nicholas Lane
Monument
Eastcheap
Cloak Lane
College Hill
Queen Street
Dowgate Hill
Cannon Street Station
Bush Lane
Gophir La
Suffolk La
Laurence Pountney Hill
Laurence Pountney La
Martin Lane
King William St
Fish Street Hill
Pudding La
Botolph Lane
Monument St
Pudding Lane
College St
Street A3211
Upper Thames Street
A3211
Lower Thames St A3211
Southwark Bridge
Bell Wharf Lane
Cousin Lane
Allhallows Lane
CITY
Angel Pas
Swan Lane
London Bridge A3
0.25 mile
0.25 km

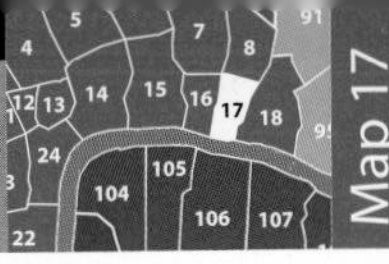

London's most Jekyll-and-Hyde-like hood. **The Counting House** is for after-work beers, while the possibility of shopping at the Royal Exchange is laughable, but who says you have to buy? By night, well, just don't go there.

Coffee

- **Caffe Nero** • 22 Wormwood St
- **Eat.** • 54 Cornhill
- **Pret A Manger** • 43 King William St
- **Starbucks** • 48 Gracechurch St

Landmarks

- **Bank of England** • Threadneedle St
- **London Stone** • 111 Cannon St
- **The Royal Exchange** • Cornhill
- **Threadneedle Street** • Threadneedle St

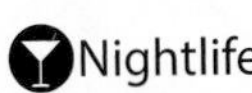

Nightlife

- **The Counting House** • 50 Cornhill
- **Royal Exchange Grand Cafe** • Royal Exchange

Post Offices

- **Moorgate** • 45 London Wall

Restaurants

- **Burger and Lobster** • 52 Threadneedle St
- **Coya Angel Court** • 31 Throgmorton St
- **Gaucho City** • 1 Bell Inn Yard
- **Hispania** • 72 Lombard St
- **The Mercer** • 34 Threadneedle St
- **Nusa Kitchen** • 2 Adams Ct
- **Simpson's Tavern** • 38 Ball Court Alley, Cornhill
- **Wasabi** • 52 Old Broad St

Shopping

- **Bremont** • 12 The Royal Exchange
- **Paul A Young Fine Chocolates** • 20 Royal Exchange
- **Pretty Ballerinas** • 30 Royal Exchange

Supermarkets

- **Marks & Spencer** • Cannon St Station
- **Sainsbury's** • 10 Lombard St

Tower Hill

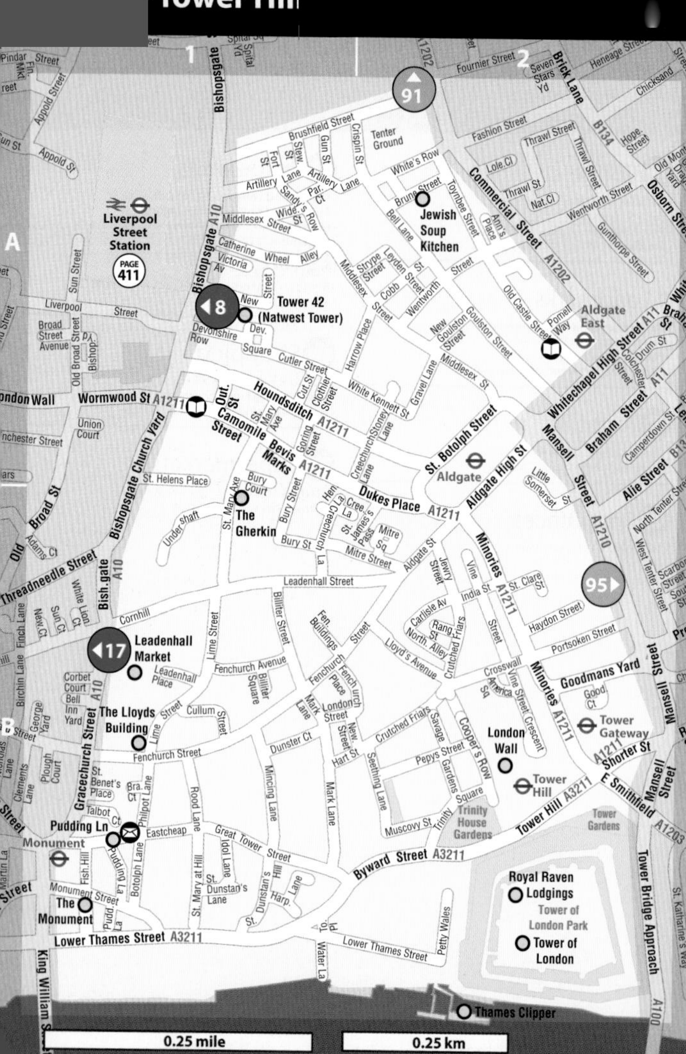

1
2
A
B
Liverpool Street Station
PAGE 411
91
8
17
95
Bishopsgate
Bishopsgate A10
Brushfield Street
Tenter Ground
Gun St
Crispin St
Fort St
Stew. St
Artillery Lane
Artillery Lane
Par. Ct
Sandy's Row
Wide. St
Middlesex Street
Catherine Wheel Alley
Victoria Av
White's Row
Brune Street
Jewish Soup Kitchen
Bell Lane
Toynbee Street
Fournier Street
Seven Stars Yd
Brick Lane
Heneage Street
Fashion Street
Thrawl Street
Thrawl St
Lolo Cl
Nat.Cl
Hope Street
Chicksand Street
Commercial Street A1202
Wentworth Street
Gunthorpe Street
Osborn Street
Ann's Place
Old Castle Street
Pomell Way
Aldgate East
Whitechapel High Street A11
Braham St
Colchester Street
Drum St
Braham Street
Camperdown St
Alie Street
Mansell Street
Little Somerset St
North Tenter Street
West Tenter Street
Tower 42 (Natwest Tower)
New Street
Dev. Sq
Devonshire Row
Cutler Street
Strype Street
Leyden Street
Cobb Street
Wentworth Street
New Goulston Street
Goulston Street
Middlesex Street
Harrow Place
White Kennett St
Gravel Lane
Middlesex St
Houndsditch A1211
Out. St
Camomile Street
St. Mary Axe
Bevis Marks A1211
Goring Street
Cut St
Clothier Street
Creechurch Lane
Stoney Lane
St. Botolph Street
Aldgate
Aldgate High St
Dukes Place A1211
Bury Court
Bury Street
The Gherkin
Hen. Ct
Cree. La
St. James's Pass
Mitre Sq
Bury St
Creechurch La
Mitre Street
Aldgate St
Jewry Street
Vine St
Minories A1211
St. Clare St
India St
Haydon Street
Portsoken Street
Liverpool Street
Broad Street Avenue
Old Broad Street
Bishop. Yd
Sun Street
Appold Street
Appold St
Pindar Street
Wormwood St A1211
London Wall
Union Court
Winchester Street
Bishopsgate Church Yard
St. Helens Place
Undershaft
Old Broad St
Adams Ct
Threadneedle Street
Bish.gate A10
White Lion Ct
Sun Ct
New Ct
Finch Lane
Birchin Lane
Cornhill
Leadenhall Street
Leadenhall Market
Leadenhall Place
Lime Street
Billiter Street
Fen. Buildings
Street
Carlisle Av
Rang. St
North. Alley
Crutched Friars
Lloyd's Avenue
Fenchurch Avenue
Billiter Square
Fenchurch Place
Fenchurch Street
Mark Lane
London Street
Corbet Court
Bell Inn Yard
George Yard
The Lloyds Building
Cullum Street
Lime Street
Gracechurch Street
Fenchurch Street
Dunster Ct
New. Street
Hart St
Crutched Friars
Savage Gardens
Cooper's Row
Crosswall
America Sq
Vine Street Crescent
Minories A1211
Goodmans Yard
Good Ct
Tower Gateway
A1211
Shorter St
E Smithfield
Mansell Street
London Wall
Tower Hill
Tower Hill A3211
Pepys Street
Seething Lane
Trinity Square
Trinity House Gardens
Muscovy St
Tower Gardens
St. Benet's Place
Bra. Ct
Philpot Lane
Plough Court
Clements Lane
Talbot Ct
Pudding Ln
Eastcheap
Rood Lane
Mincing Lane
Mark Lane
Monument
Great Tower Street
Idol Lane
St. Mary at Hill
St. Dunstan's Lane
St. Dunstan's Hill
Harp. Lane
Byward Street A3211
Fish. Hill
Pudding La
Botolph Lane
Monument Street
The Monument
Pudd. La
Lower Thames Street A3211
Lower Thames Street
Water La
Petty Wales
Royal Raven Lodgings
Tower of London Park
Tower of London
Thames Clipper
Tower Bridge Approach A100
St. Katharine's Way
A1203
King William Street
0.25 mile
0.25 km

Tower Hill / Aldgate

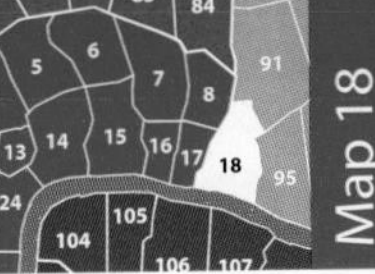

Though on the fringe of the financial cesspit, Aldgate is brilliant to walk and gawp around in. After stodge at **Jeff's**, head south, past the Erotic **Gherkin** (ahem), and go siege the **London Wall** alongside the tourists. Alternatively go become one yourself at **Pudding Lane**.

Coffee

- **Cafe from Crisis** • 64 Commercial St
- **Caffe Nero** • 1 Fenchurch Pl
- **Caffe Nero** • 88 Leadenhall St
- **Curators Coffee** • 9 Cullum St
- **Eat.** • 122 Minories
- **Market Coffee House** • 52 Brushfield St
- **Pret A Manger** • 3 Cutler St
- **Starbucks** • 48 Gracechurch St
- **Starbucks** • 48 Minories
- **Trade Coffee** • 47 Commercial St

Landmarks

- **The Gherkin** • 30 St Mary Axe
- **Jewish Soup Kitchen** • Brune St & Tenter Ground
- **The Lloyd's Building** • 1 Lime St
- **Leadenhall Market** • Gracechurch St
- **London Wall** • Cooper's Row & Trinity Sq
- **The Monument** • Monument St
- **Pudding Lane** • Pudding Ln
- **St Dunstan-in-the-East** • St Dunstan's Hill
- **The Ravens** • Tower Hill
- **Thames Clippers** • Tower Pier
- **Tower 42** • 25 Old Broad St
- **Tower of London** • Tower Hill

Libraries

- **Camomile Street** • 15 Camomile St
- **The Women's Library** • 25 Old Castle St

Nightlife

- **Kenza** • 10 Devonshire Sq
- **The Minories** • 64 Minories
- **Revolution** • 140 Leadenhall St

Post Offices

- **The City of London BO** • 12 Eastcheap

Restaurants

- **Gunpowder** • 11 White's Row
- **Jeff's Cafe** • 14 Brune St

Shopping

- **Montezuma's** • 51 Brushfield St
- **Petticoat Lane Market** • Middlesex St
- **Precious** • 16 Artillery Passage

Supermarkets

- **Sainsbury's** • 45 Fenchurch St

Map 19 • Belgravia

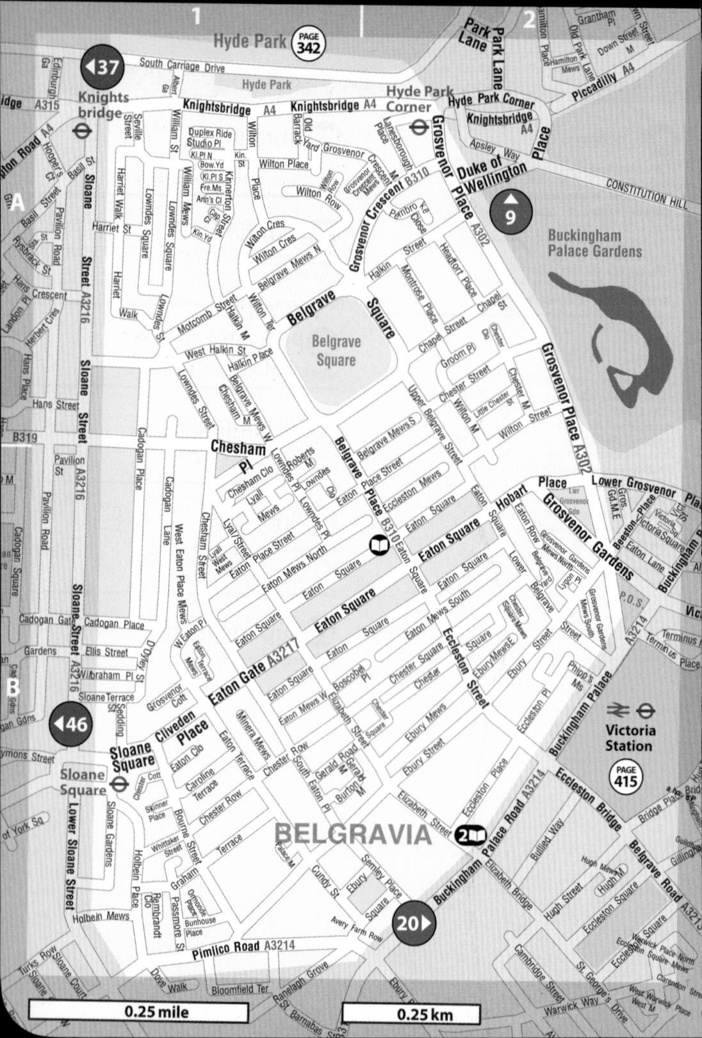

Ugg and Range Rover fetishists are in a constant state of climax around here. It sure is pretty when the sun isn't being blocked by expensively coiffured bouffants, but one suspects the plummy accents and tasteless richness would dent anyone's enthusiasm for chic dog clothes (**Mungo & Maud**) or curry (**Amaya**).

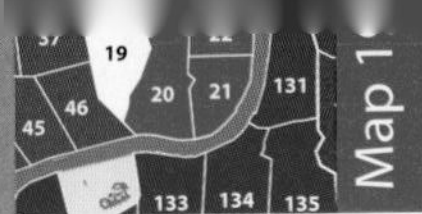

Coffee

- **Tomtom Coffee House** • 114 Ebury St

Libraries

- **Instituto Cervantes** • 15 Devereux Ct
- **Victoria Library** • 160 Buckingham Palace Rd
- **Westminster Music Library** • 160 Buckingham Palace Rd

Nightlife

- **The Blue Bar** • The Berkeley Hotel • Wilton Pl
- **Nag's Head** • 53 Kinnerton St
- **The Plumber's Arms** • 14 Lower Belgrave St

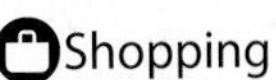

Restaurants

- **Amaya** • Motcomb St
- **Boisdale** • 15 Eccleston St
- **Colbert** • 50 Sloane Sq
- **Noura** • 12 William St
- **The Pantechnicon** • 10 Motcomb St
- **The Thomas Cubitt** • 44 Elizabeth St
- **Yo! Sushi** • 102 Knightsbridge

Shopping

- **Daylesford Organic Farmshop and Cafe** • 44 Pimlico Rd
- **Mungo & Maud** • 79 Elizabeth St
- **Peter Jones** •Sloan Sq

Supermarkets

- **Waitrose** • 27 Motcomb St

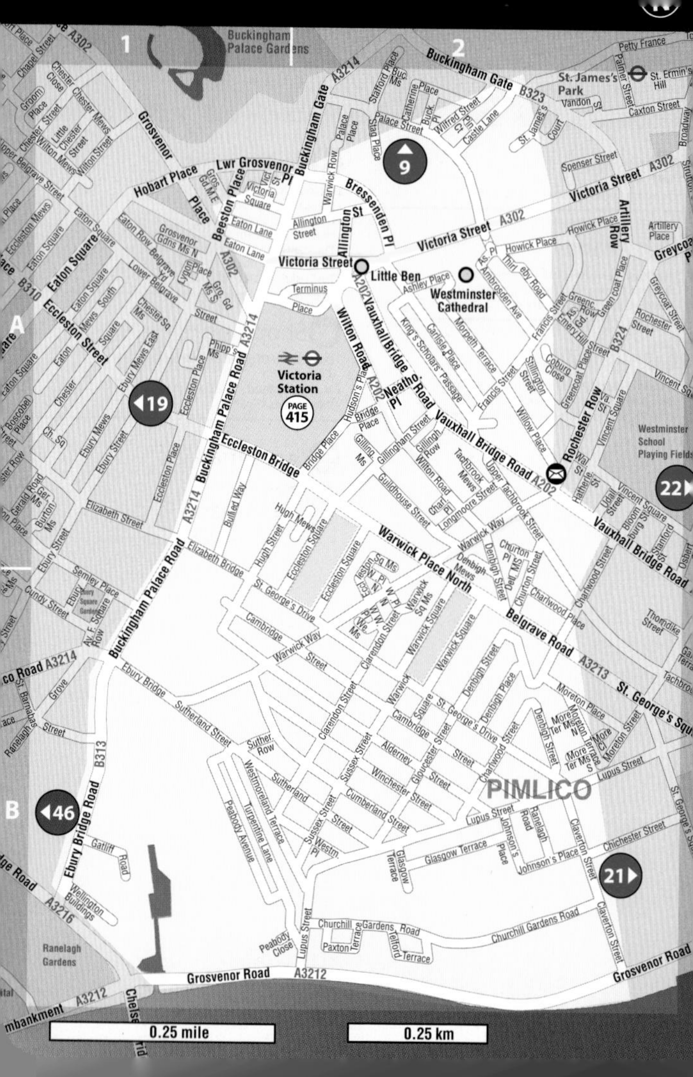
1
2
A
B
Buckingham Palace Gardens
Buckingham Gate
B323
St. James's Park
Petty France
Caxton Street
Victoria Street
A302
Grosvenor Place
Hobart Place
Lwr Grosvenor Pl
Eaton Square
B310
Eccleston Street
Buckingham Palace Road
A3214
Victoria Station
PAGE 415
Little Ben
Westminster Cathedral
Vauxhall Bridge Road
A202
Wilton Road
Eccleston Bridge
Warwick Way
Warwick Place North
Belgrave Road
A3213
St. George's Square
Rochester Row
Westminster School Playing Fields
Elizabeth Street
Ebury Bridge
Ebury Bridge Road
B313
Sutherland Street
Cambridge Street
St. George's Drive
Eccleston Square
Warwick Square
Denbigh Street
Lupus Street
PIMLICO
Claverton Street
Churchill Gardens Road
Grosvenor Road
A3212
A3216
Ranelagh Gardens
Chelsea Embankment
9
19
22
46
21
0.25 mile
0.25 km

Victoria / Pimlico (West)

Since the Tower of London closed for business, prisoners have been routinely tortured at weekends in Victoria Station. Surrounding the transit hubs is a dignified 'hood Churchill and Mozart called home. Do a late-night tramp photoshoot on the steps of the magnificent houses of Lupus Street (with a camera from **Grays**) before heading to **The Cask & Glass** for a knees-up with your new pals.

Coffee

- **Bagel Factory** • Victoria Place Shopping Centre • Buckingham Palace Rd
- **Caffe Nero** • 31 Warwick Wy
- **Costa** • 3 Cardinal Walk
- **Costa** • 115 Buckingham Palace Rd
- **Pret A Manger** • 173 Victoria St
- **Pret A Manger** • Unit 36B • Victoria Station
- **Pret A Manger** • 92 Buckingham Palace Rd
- **Starbucks** • Buckingham Palace Rd & Lower Belgrave St

Post Offices

- **Vauxhall Bridge Road** • 167 Vauxhall Bridge Rd

Landmarks

- **Little Ben** • Victoria St & Vauxhall Bridge Rd
- **Westminster Cathedral** • 42 Francis St

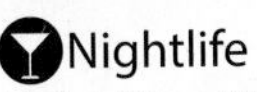

Nightlife

- **The Cask & Glass** • 39 Palace St
- **The Warwick** • 25 Warwick Wy
- **Windsor Castle** • 23 Francis St

Restaurants

- **Grumbles** • 35 Churton St
- **The Phoenix** • 14 Palace St
- **Pimlico Fresh** • 86 Wilton Rd

Shopping

- **Capital Carboot Sale** • Lupus St
- **Grays of Westminster** • 40 Churton St
- **Rippon Cheese Stores** • 26 Upper Tachbrook St
- **Runners Need** • 24 Palace St

Supermarkets

- **Marks & Spencer** • Victoria Mainline Station

Horseferry Road
Vincent Square
Westminster School Playing Fields
Vauxhall Bridge Road
Rochester Row
Greycoat Pl.
Marsham Street
Millbank
Millbank Tower
Tate Britain
PAGE 476
Chelsea College of Art & Design
St. John's Gardens
Page Street
Regency Street
John Islip Street
Atterbury Street
Bessborough Gardens
Pimlico
St. George's Square
St. George's Square Garden
Lupus Street
Grosvenor Road
Pimlico Gardens
Vauxhall Bridge
River Thames
Riverside Gardens
Victoria Tower Gardens
Tachbrook Street
Moreton Place
Claverton Street
Chichester Street
Wandsworth Road
Parry Street
Bridgefoot
22
20
0.25 mile
0.25 km

Hugging the curve of the Thames, this princely patch of Pimlico combines the stately Tate with imposing embankment architecture and ancient houses. Check out the old-money splendour of Vincent Street before grabbing lunch at the **Regency**, a true gem of a caf. Much fun can be had by pretending you actually live around here, so in this spirit head to the **Morpeth** as your local.

Landmarks

- **Millbank Tower** • 21 Millbank

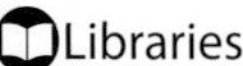

Libraries

- **Pimlico Library** • Lupus St
- **Royal Horticultural Society Library** • 80 Vincent Sq

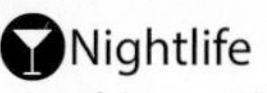

Nightlife

- **Morpeth Arms** • 58 Millibank

Restaurants

- **Goya** • 34 Lupus St
- **The Regency Cafe** • 17 Regency St
- **The Vincent Rooms** • 76 Vincent Sq

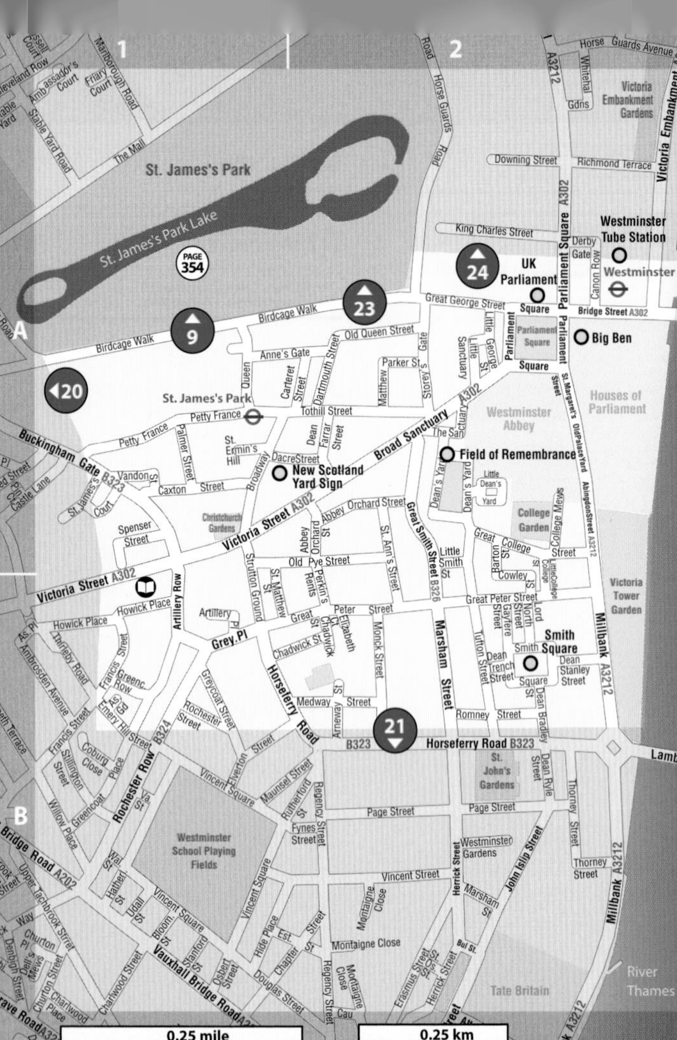
St. James's Park
St. James's Park Lake
PAGE 354
9
23
24
20
21
UK Parliament
Westminster Tube Station
Westminster
Big Ben
Houses of Parliament
Westminster Abbey
Field of Remembrance
New Scotland Yard Sign
St. James's Park
Smith Square
Victoria Embankment Gardens
Victoria Tower Garden
Parliament Square
College Garden
Christchurch Gardens
St. John's Gardens
Westminster School Playing Fields
Tate Britain
River Thames
Birdcage Walk
Great George Street
Victoria Street A302
Broad Sanctuary A302
Horseferry Road B323
Millbank A3212
Vauxhall Bridge Road
Rochester Row
Marsham Street
Great Smith Street B326
Horse Guards Road
Downing Street
Richmond Terrace
King Charles Street
Bridge Street A302
Petty France
Buckingham Gate B323
Tothill Street
Old Queen Street
Artillery Row
Horseferry Road
Page Street
Vincent Square
Vincent Street
John Islip Street
The Mall
Horse Guards Avenue
Victoria Embankment
0.25 mile
0.25 km

The long shadow of government falls over these parts, beautiful as they are. Protesters and wannabe Guy Fawkeses head to Parliament Square, where they can harangue whichever bunch of jokers are ensconced in the Houses of Parliament. Get away from tourists at the tiny **St. Stephen's Tavern**, or grab a classy cocktail at **The Cinnamon Club**. If you must shop, head to Victoria Street.

Coffee

- **Caffe Nero** • 105 Victoria St
- **Fresco Cafe Bar** • 11 Tothill St
- **Iris & June** • 1 Howick Pl
- **Pret A Manger** • 75 Victoria St
- **Pret A Manger** • 49 Tothill St
- **Starbucks** • 27 Victoria St

Landmarks

- **Big Ben** • Bridge St
- **Field of Remembrance** • Victoria St
- **New Scotland Yard Sign** • 8 Broadway
- **St. John's Smith Square** • Smith Sq
- **UK Parliament** • Victoria St & Abingdon St
- **Westminster Tube Station** • Westminster Bridge Rd

Nightlife

- **The Albert** • 52 Victoria St
- **The Cinnamon Club** • 30 Great Smith St
- **The Feathers** • 18 Broadway
- **The Speaker** • 46 Great Peter St
- **Two Chairmen** • 39 Dartmouth St
- **St. Stephen's Tavern** • 10 Bridge St

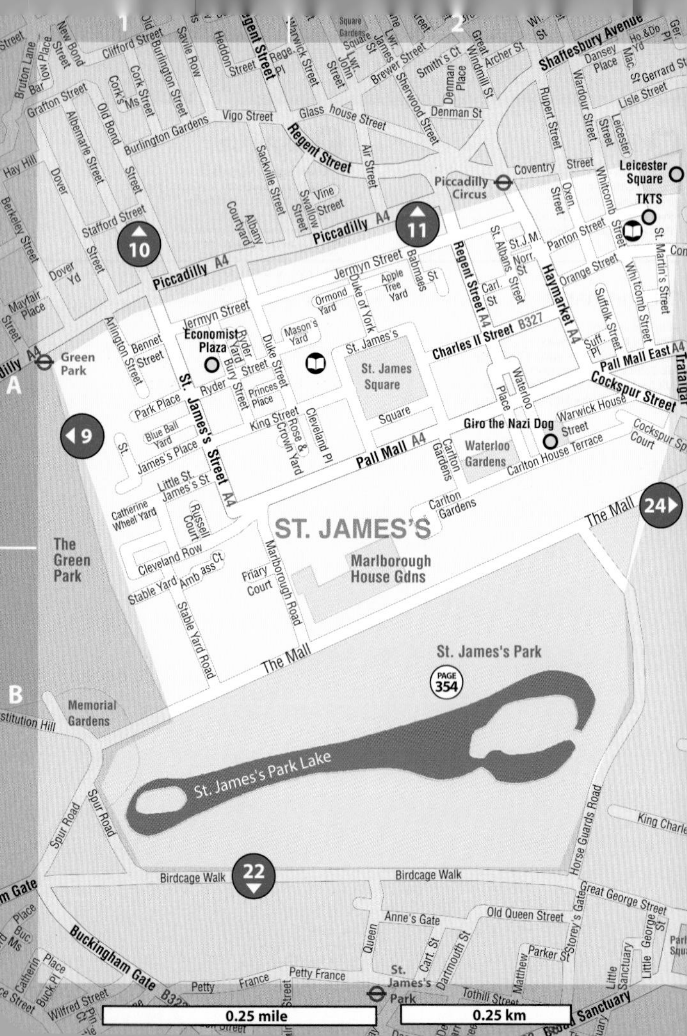

ST. JAMES'S
St. James's Park
St. James's Park Lake
The Green Park
Marlborough House Gdns
St. James Square
Waterloo Gardens
Memorial Gardens
Piccadilly Circus
Leicester Square
TKTS
Green Park
St. James's Park
Economist Plaza
Giro the Nazi Dog
Piccadilly A4
Regent Street
Jermyn Street
Pall Mall A4
The Mall
Birdcage Walk
Buckingham Gate
Haymarket A4
Charles II Street B327
St. James's Street A4
Cockspur Street
Shaftesbury Avenue
Horse Guards Road
PAGE 354
10
11
9
24
22
0.25 mile
0.25 km

)ignified, decadent, exclusive, Pall Mall and St. James's Street are where the ristobrats come out to play. With stuffy gentlemen's clubs, bespoke tailors, nd the stale scent of a cigar-fuelled colonialist past pervading, you'll want to weeten up with a macaroon at **Laduree**.

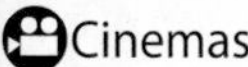

Cinemas

- **Apollo Cinema Piccadily Circus** • 19 Lower Regent St
- **Cineworld Haymarket** • 63 Haymarket
- **ICA Cinema** • The Mall & Horse Guards Rd
- **Odeon Leicester Square** • 24 Leicester Sq
- **Odeon Panton Street** • 11 Panton St
- **Odeon West End Cinema** • 40 Leicester Sq

Coffee

- **Borough Barista** • 15 Charles II St
- **Caffe Nero** • 35 Jermyn St
- **Eat.** • 319 Regent St
- **ICA Cafe** • The Mall
- **Pret A Manger** • 8 King St

Landmarks

- **Economist Plaza** • 25 St. James's St
- **Giro the Nazi Dog** • 9 Carlton House Terrace
- **King George VI & Queen Elizabeth Memorial**
- **Leicester Square** • Leicester Sq
- **TKTS** • Leicester Sq

Libraries

- **London Library** • 14 St James's Sq
- **Westminster Reference Library** • 35 St Martin's St

Nightlife

- **Dukes Hotel** • 35 St James's St
- **Institute of Contemporary Arts** • The Mall

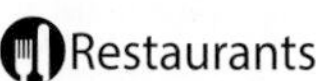

Restaurants

- **Cafe Concerto Green Park** • 61 Piccadilly
- **Laduree** • 71 Burlington Arcade

Shopping

- **Partridges Deli** • 2 Duke of York St
- **National Map Centre** • 22-24 Caxton St
- **Richard Caplan** • 60 Pall Mall

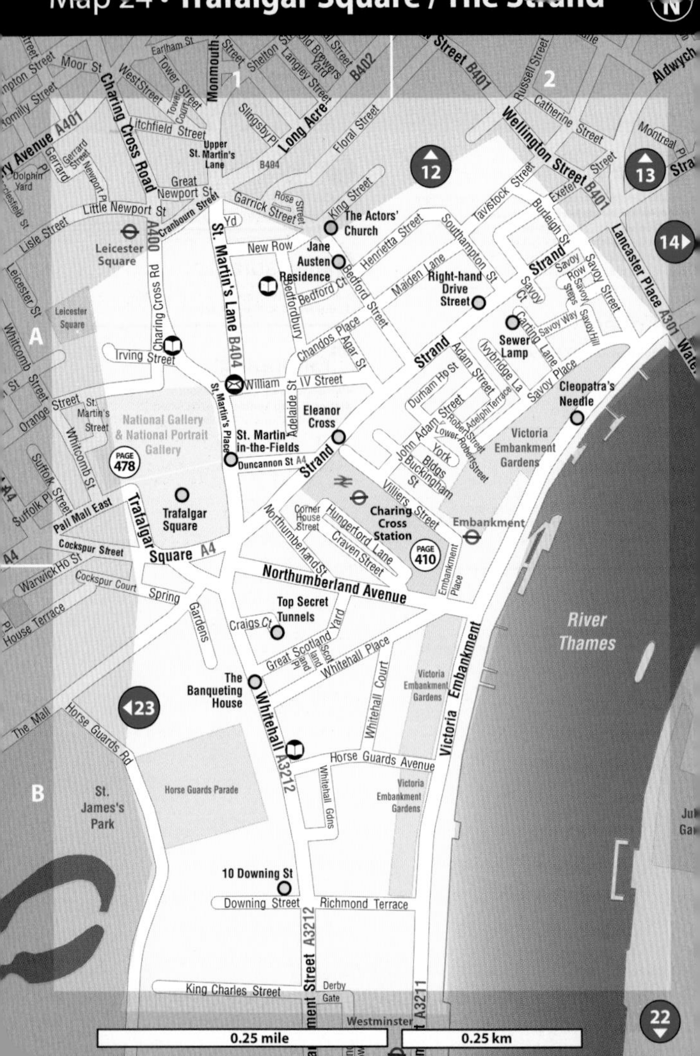
N
1
2
12
13
14
22
23
A
B
Moor St
Charing Cross Road
Earlham St
Tower Street
West Street
Monmouth Street
Shelton St
Old Brewers Yard
Langley Street
Long Acre
B402
Slingsby Pl
Floral Street
Street B401
Russell Street
Catherine Street
Wellington Street B401
Aldwych
Montreal Pl
Strand
Litchfield Street
Upper St. Martin's Lane
B404
Gerrard Pl
Gerrard Street
Newport Pl
Dolphin Yard
Great Newport St
Cranbourn Street
Little Newport St
Lisle Street
Garrick Street
Rose Street
King Street
The Actors' Church
Tavistock Street
Exeter Street
Burleigh St
Lancaster Place A301
Leicester Square
Leicester St
Yd
New Row
Jane Austen Residence
Henrietta Street
Southampton St
Bedford St
Bedford Ct
Bedfordbury
Maiden Lane
Right-hand Drive Street
Savoy Ct
Savoy Row
Savoy Steps
Savoy Street
Savoy Way
Savoy Hill
Carting Lane
Sewer Lamp
Whitcomb Street
Irving Street
St. Martin's Lane B404
Chandos Place
Agar St
Adam Street
Ivybridge La
Savoy Place
Cleopatra's Needle
William IV Street
Adelaide St
Durham Ho St
Adelphi Terrace
Robert Street
Orange Street
St. Martin's Street
National Gallery & National Portrait Gallery
St Martin's Place
Eleanor Cross
St. Martin-in-the-Fields
John Adam Street
Lower Robert Street
York Bldgs
Buckingham St
Victoria Embankment Gardens
PAGE 478
Whitcomb St
Duncannon St A4
Suffolk Street
Suffolk Pl
Pall Mall East
Trafalgar Square
Corner House Street
Northumberland St
Hungerford Lane
Craven Street
Charing Cross Station
Villiers Street
Embankment
PAGE 410
Embankment Place
Cockspur Street
Warwick Ho St
Cockspur Court
Spring Gardens
Northumberland Avenue
House Terrace
Top Secret Tunnels
Craigs Ct
Great Scotland Yard
Scotland Pl
Whitehall Place
River Thames
Victoria Embankment
The Banqueting House
Whitehall A3212
Whitehall Court
The Mall
Horse Guards Rd
Horse Guards Avenue
Horse Guards Parade
St. James's Park
Whitehall Gdns
10 Downing St
Downing Street
Richmond Terrace
King Charles Street
Derby Gate
Street A3212
A3211
Westminster
A400
A401
A4
0.25 mile
0.25 km

Trafalgar Square / The Strand

1 2 3 4 10 11 12 13 14 15 24 9 23 105 104 22 19 20 21 131 112

ıe hawkers came and removed the flying rats and lo! the Square was clean ıd visible. This ain't Mary Poppins—don't feed the birds, you dirty tourists. stead go to **Terroirs** and pretend you know a lot about wine. Eat at **Wahaca**, ıe of London's few good Mexicans, then walk it off on **Waterloo Bridge** and atch the sun set over the Thames. Aah. That's why you love London.

Coffee

- **Caffe Nero** • 10 Bedford St
- **Caffe Nero** • 36 St Martin's Ln
- **Caffe Nero** • 29 Southampton St
- **Coffee Island** • 5 Upper St Martin's Ln
- **Coffee Republic** • 79 Strand
- **Costa** • 17 Embankment Pl
- **Eat.** • 39 Villiers St
- **Notes** • 31 St Martin's Ln
- **Pret A Manger** • 135 Strand
- **Pret A Manger** • 421 Strand
- **Pret A Manger** • 7 St Martin's Ln
- **Starbucks** • 1 Villiers St

Landmarks

- **10 Downing Street** • 10 Downing St
- **The Actors' Church** • 29 Bedford St
- **Banqueting House** • Whitehall
- **Cleopatra's Needle** • Embankment
- **Eleanor Cross** • Strand
- **Jane Austen Residence** • 10 Henrietta St
- **Right-Hand Drive Street** • Savoy Ct
- **Sewer Lamp** • Carting Ln & Strand
- **St Martin-in-the-Fields** • Trafalgar Sq
- **Top Secret Tunnels** • 6 Craig's Ct
- **Trafalgar Square** • Trafalgar Sq

Libraries

- **Charing Cross Library** • 4 Charing Cross Rd
- **Royal United Services Institute Library** • Whitehall

Nightlife

- **The Chandos** • 29 St Martins Ln
- **The Coal Hole** • 91 Strand
- **Covent Garden Comedy Club** • The Arches
- **Gordon's Wine Bar** • 47 Villiers St
- **The Harp** • 47 Chandos Pl
- **Haxells Restaurant & Bar** • 372 Strand
- **Heaven** • The Arches
- **Maple Leaf** • 41 Maiden Ln
- **Punch & Judy** • The Covent Garden Piazza
- **Retro Bar** • 2 George Ct
- **Roadhouse** • 35 The Covent Garden Piazza
- **The Sherlock Holmes** • 10 Northumberland St
- **Terroirs** • 5 William IV St
- **Zoo Bar & Club** • 13 Bear St

Restaurants

- **Benito's Hat** • 19 New Row
- **Cafe in the Crypt** • 6 St Martin's Pl
- **Gourmet Burger Kitchen** • 13 Maiden Ln
- **Herman Ze German** • 19 Villiers St
- **J Sheekey** • 28 St Martin's Ct
- **Portrait Restaurant & Bar** • St Martin's Pl
- **R.S. Hispaniola** • Victoria Embankment
- **Rules** • 35 Maiden Ln
- **Thai Pot** • 1 Bedfordbury
- **Wahaca** • 66 Chandos Pl

Shopping

- **Austin Kaye** • 425 The Strand
- **London Camera Exchange** • 98 Strand
- **Rohan** • 10 Henrietta St
- **Stanley Gibbons** • 399 Strand

Supermarkets

- **Marks & Spencer** • Charing Cross Station

KENSAL RISE
WEST KILBURN
KENSAL GREEN
Kensal Green
EALING
KENSAL TOWN
25
Wormwood Scrubs
NORTH KENSINGTON
Westway
WHITE CITY
ACTON
EAST ACTON
NOTTING HILL
Wood Ln
28
SHEPHERD'S BUSH
Holland Park Ave
Acton Park
Uxbridge Rd
32
33
Shepherds Bush Green
Holland Rd
Wendell Park
Shepherds Bush Rd
TURNHAM GREEN
34
Goldhawk Rd
Dalling Rd
40
Bath Rd
Ravenscourt Park
Hammersmith Rd
Chiswick Common
39
King St
41
CHISWICK
HAMMERSMITH
Great West Rd
38
Chiswick Ln
42
Hogarth Ln
CASTELNAU
Thames River
Fulham Palace Rd
47
Fulham Cemetery
Chiswick Cemetery
FULHAM
48
University of Westminster Stadium
BARNES
Putney Park
Duke's Meadow
Fulham Palace Gardens
MORTLAKE

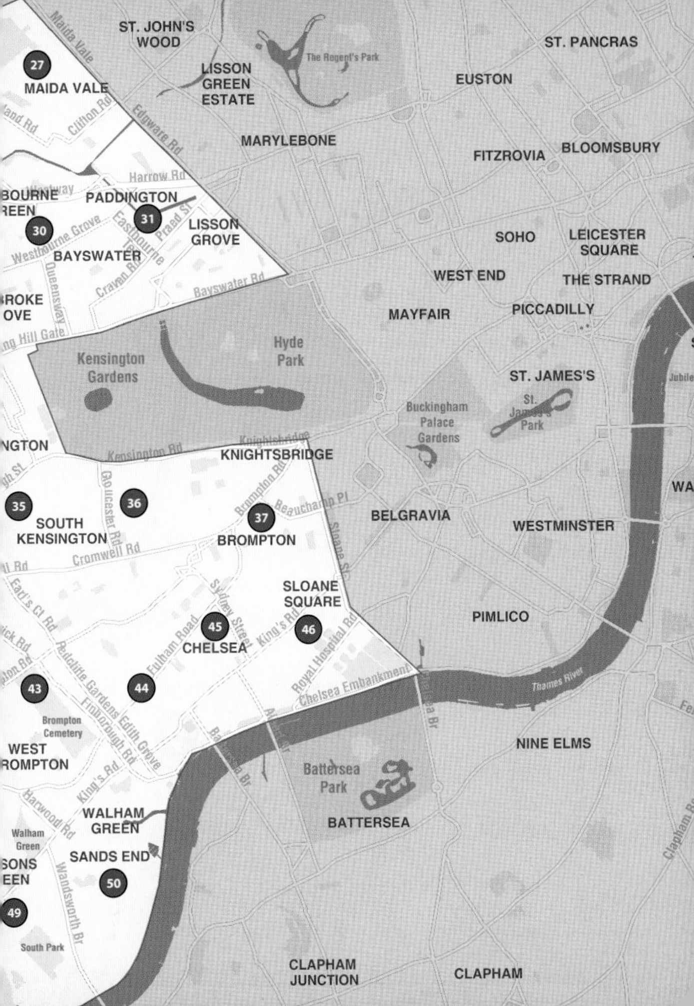

ST. JOHN'S WOOD
27
MAIDA VALE
LISSON GREEN ESTATE
The Regent's Park
EUSTON
ST. PANCRAS
MARYLEBONE
FITZROVIA
BLOOMSBURY
PADDINGTON
31
30
BAYSWATER
LISSON GROVE
SOHO
LEICESTER SQUARE
WEST END
THE STRAND
MAYFAIR
PICCADILLY
Kensington Gardens
Hyde Park
ST. JAMES'S
Buckingham Palace Gardens
KNIGHTSBRIDGE
35
36
37
SOUTH KENSINGTON
BROMPTON
BELGRAVIA
WESTMINSTER
SLOANE SQUARE
45
46
CHELSEA
PIMLICO
43
44
Brompton Cemetery
WEST ROMPTON
Thames River
NINE ELMS
Battersea Park
WALHAM GREEN
BATTERSEA
SANDS END
50
49
South Park
CLAPHAM JUNCTION
CLAPHAM

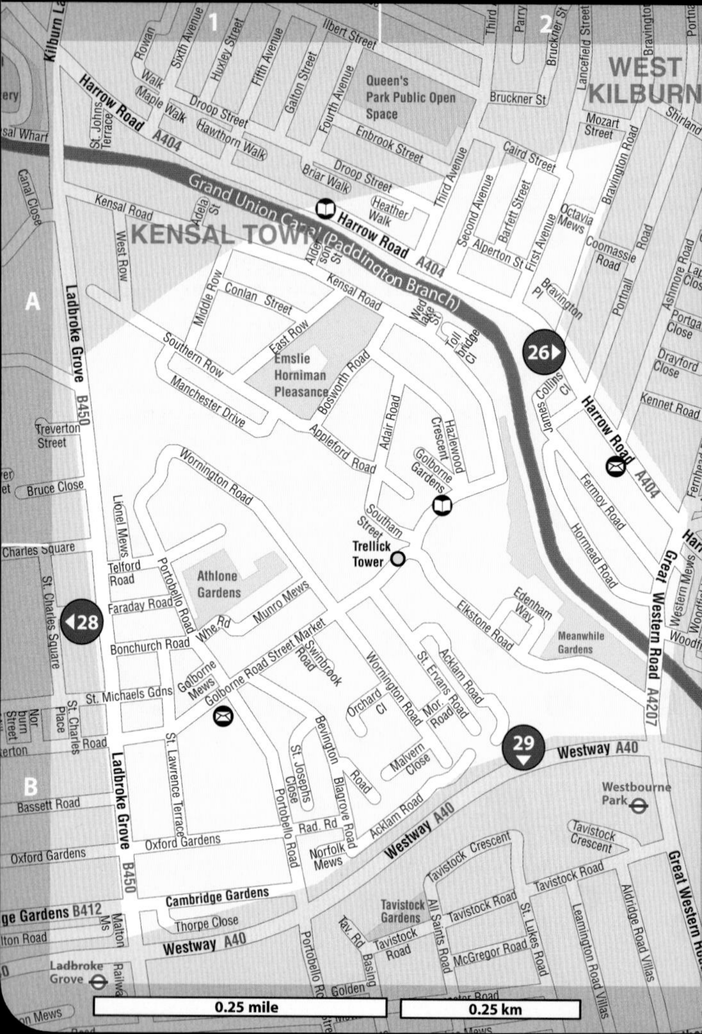

N

1
2
A
B

WEST KILBURN
KENSAL TOWN

Grand Union Canal (Paddington Branch)
Queen's Park Public Open Space
Emslie Horniman Pleasance
Athlone Gardens
Meanwhile Gardens
Tavistock Gardens
Trellick Tower
Westbourne Park
Ladbroke Grove

Kilburn La
Harrow Road A404
Ladbroke Grove B450
Great Western Road A4207
Westway A40
Rowan
Sixth Avenue
Huxley Street
Fifth Avenue
Galton Street
Fourth Avenue
Ilbert Street
Third Avenue
Parry
Bruckner St
Lancefield Street
Bravington Road
Walk
Maple Walk
Droop Street
Hawthorn Walk
Enbrook Street
Bruckner St
Mozart Street
Shirland
St. Johns Terrace
Briar Walk
Caird Street
Heather Walk
Second Avenue
Barfett Street
Octavia Mews
Kensal Road
Adela St
Alder son St
Alperton St
First Avenue
Coomassie Road
Portnall Road
Ashmore Road
Canal Close
West Row
Middle Row
Conlan Street
Bravington Pl
Wedlake St
Tollbridge Cl
Portgate Close
Drayford Close
Kennet Road
Southern Row
East Row
Bosworth Road
Manchester Drive
Adair Road
Hazlewood Crescent
James Collins Cl
Appleford Road
Golborne Gardens
Fermoy Road
Treverton Street
Bruce Close
Wornington Road
Southam Street
Hormead Road
Lionel Mews
Charles Square
St. Charles Square
Telford Road
Portobello Road
Faraday Road
Munro Mews
Edenham Way
Elkstone Road
Western Mews
Woodfi
Bonchurch Road
Whe Rd
Golborne Road Street Market
Swinbrook Road
Acklam Road
St. Ervans Road
St. Michaels Gdns
Golborne Mews
Orchard Cl
Mor. Road
Norburn Street
St. Charles Place
Road
Bevington Road
St. Lawrence Terrace
St. Josephs Close
Malvern Close
Bassett Road
Blagrove Road
Rad. Rd
Tavistock Crescent
Oxford Gardens
Norfolk Mews
Tavistock Road
Cambridge Gardens
Aldridge Road Villas
Great Western Road
Thorpe Close
Malton Ms
All Saints Road
St. Lukes Road
Leamington Road Villas
McGregor Road
Tav. Rd
Basing
Golden
Railway

26
28
29

0.25 mile
0.25 km

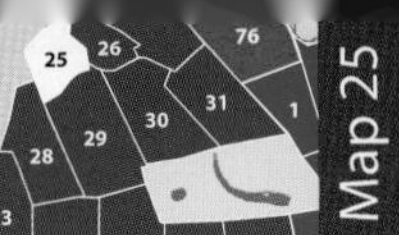

ıe "new Notting Hill" label weighs heavily on the Kensals. They look east for .spiration, ignoring the Harlesden yardies at their backs. Prepare for Carnival y visiting **What Katie Did** for exhibitionist outfits, while **Trellick Tower** is erfect for real—"I mean it, I'll jump"—attention-seekers.

Coffee

- **Camden Coffee House** • 155 Ladbroke Grove
- **Lisboa Cafe** • 57 Golborne Rd

Landmarks

- **Trellick Tower** • 5 Golborne Rd

Libraries

- **Kensal Library** • 20 Golborne Rd
- **Queen's Park Library** • 666 Harrow Rd

Post Offices

- **Maida Hill** • 377 Harrow Rd
- **Portobello Road** • 325 Portobello Rd

Restaurants

- **Lowry and Baker** • 339 Portobello Rd
- **Made in Brasil** • 12 Inverness St
- **Snaps + Rye** • 93 Golborne Rd
- **Thai Rice** • 303 Portobello Rd

Shopping

- **Honest Jon's** • 278 Portobello Rd
- **Rellik** • 8 Golborne Rd
- **What Katie Did** • 281 Portobello Rd

Supermarkets

- **Iceland** • 512 Harrow Rd
- **Miah's Oriental Foods** • 396 Harrow Rd

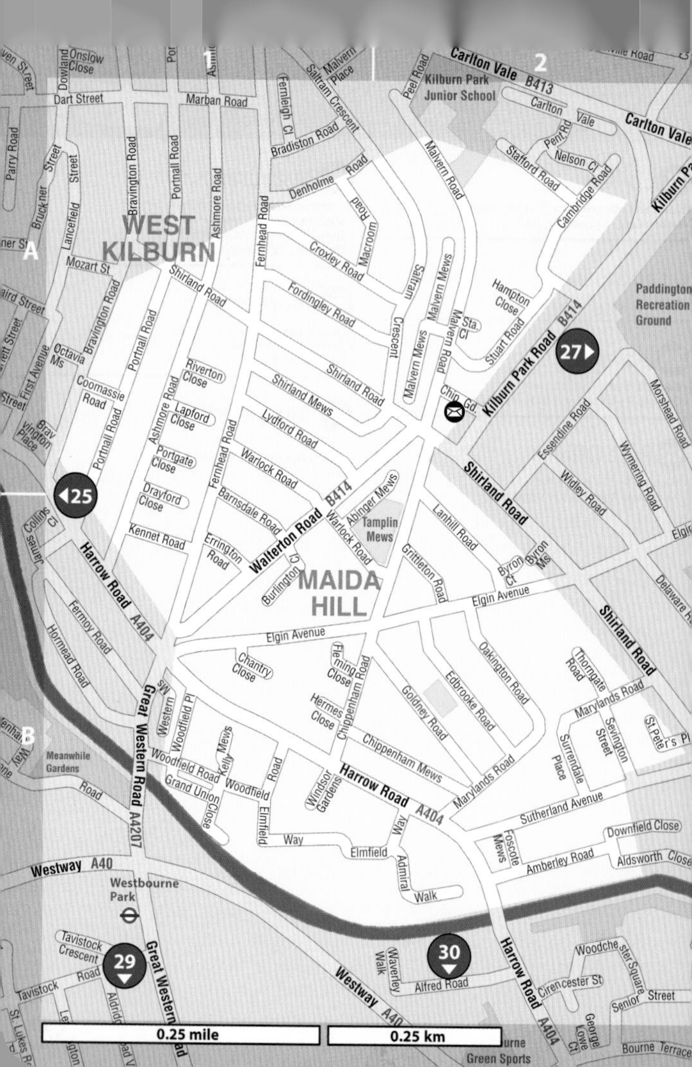

WEST KILBURN
MAIDA HILL
Carlton Vale B413
Kilburn Park Junior School
Paddington Recreation Ground
Tamplin Mews
Meanwhile Gardens
Westbourne Park
Shirland Road
Walterton Road B414
Kilburn Park Road B414
Harrow Road A404
Great Western Road A4207
Westway A40
Elgin Avenue
Sutherland Avenue
25
27
29
30
0.25 mile
0.25 km

Not as posh as Maida Vale or as cool as Ladbroke Grove, Maida Hill is slightly grubby to the south, not helped by the distinctly unlovely Harrow Road. Things get more upmarket heading north, but the beating heart of the hill can be found Saturdays around Harrow Road's new market. On one of those rare sunny London days get down to the **Union Tavern** and grab a canal side table.

Post Offices

- **Kilburn Park** • 29 Malvern Rd

Nightlife

- **Union Tavern** • 45 Woodfield Rd

Restaurants

- **Mosob** • 339 Harrow Rd
- **Tsiakkos & Charcoal** • 5 Marylands Rd

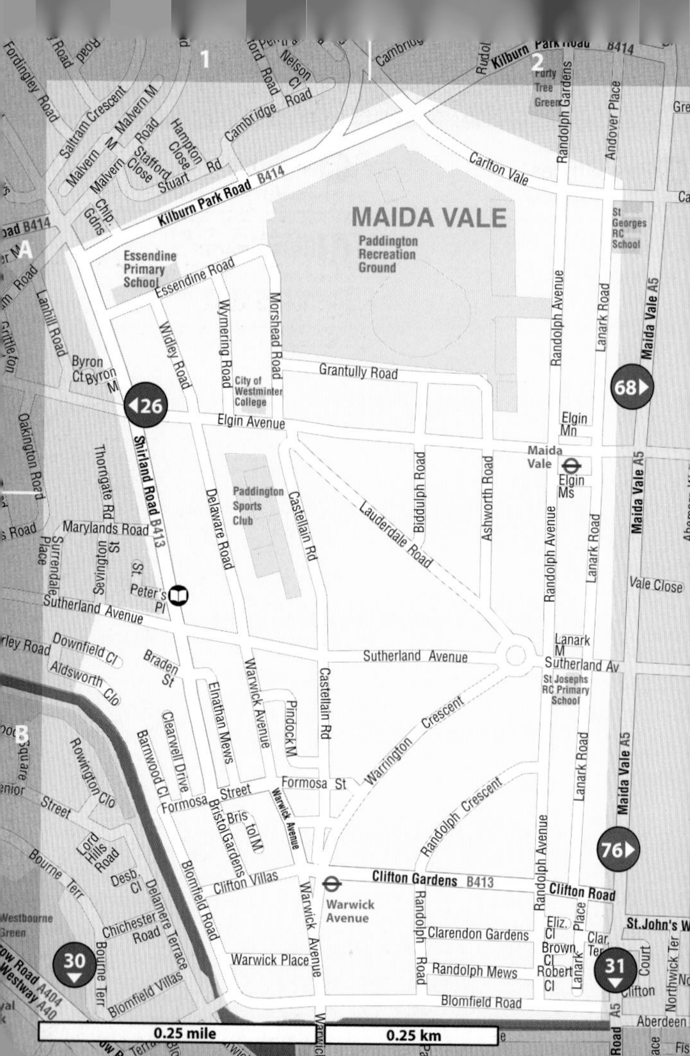

MAIDA VALE
Paddington Recreation Ground
Kilburn Park Road B414
Carlton Vale
Essendine Primary School
Essendine Road
Wymering Road
Morshead Road
Grantully Road
City of Westminster College
Elgin Avenue
Randolph Avenue
Lanark Road
Maida Vale A5
St Georges RC School
Forty Tree Green
Randolph Gardens
Andover Place
Elgin Mn
Maida Vale
Elgin Ms
Widley Road
Shirland Road B413
Delaware Road
Paddington Sports Club
Castellain Rd
Lauderdale Road
Biddulph Road
Ashworth Road
Vale Close
Sutherland Avenue
Lanark M
Sutherland Av
St Josephs RC Primary School
Warrington Crescent
Randolph Crescent
Formosa St
Formosa Street
Warwick Avenue
Pindock M
Elnathan Mews
Clearwell Drive
Barnwood Cl
Braden St
Bristol Gardens
Bristol M
Clifton Villas
Clifton Gardens B413
Clifton Road
Warwick Avenue
Clarendon Gardens
Randolph Mews
Blomfield Road
Warwick Place
Blomfield Villas
Delamere Terrace
Chichester Road
Bourne Terr
Westbourne Green
Lord Hills Road
Desb. Cl
Rowington Clo
Aldsworth Clo
Downfield Cl
Marylands Road
Sutherland Avenue
St. Peter's Pl
Sevington St
Surrendale Place
Thorngate Rd
Oakington Road
Byron Ct
Byron M
Lanhill Road
Chip. Gdns
Malvern Road
Malvern M
Saltram Crescent
Fordingley Road
Stafford Close
Hampton Close
Stuart Rd
Cambridge Road
Nelson Cl
Eliz. Cl
Brown. Cl
Robert Cl
Clar. Ter
Lanark Place
St.John's W
Aberdeen P
Clifton
Northwick Ter
26
68
76
30
31
A
B
1
2
0.25 mile
0.25 km

ou don't come to Maida Vale for the nightlife, end of story. Though pretty, canal-side alks are a different matter. Away from 'Little Venice' are endless rows of identical-oking Edwardian mansion blocks on peaceful, tree-lined avenues. It's clean, eaceful, and nice (translation: quite dull). Locals frequent the cafés and eateries round the Maida Vale tube station and on Clifton Road.

Coffee

- **Starbucks** • 168 Randolf Ave

Libraries

- **Maida Vale Library** • Sutherland Ave

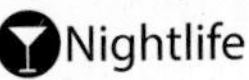

Nightlife

- **The Bridge House** • 13 Westbourne Terrace Rd
- **The Elgin** • 255 Elgin Ave
- **Prince Alfred** • 5A Formosa St
- **The Warwick Castle** • 6 Warwick Pl
- **The Waterway** • 54 Formosa St

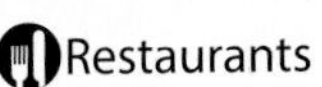

Restaurants

- **Banana Tree** • 166 Randolph Ave
- **Le Cochonnet** • 1 Lauderadale Rd

N
1
2
A
B
25
29
33
34
St. Quintin Avenue B412
Kingsbridge Road
Wallingford Avenue
Kelfield Mews
Kelfield Gardens
St. Helens Gardens
Cowper Terrace
St. Marks Road
Archway Close
St. Charles Square
Chesterton Road
Millwood Street
Norburn Street
St. Charles Place
Ladbroke Grove B450
Bonchurch Road
Golborne Road
Portobello Road
Bevington Road
St. Lawrence Terrace
St. Josephs Close
Blagrove Road
Bassett Road
Oxford Gardens
Highlever Road
Balliol Road
Finstock Road
Latimer Road
Latimer Place
Westview Close
Rad. Rd
Norfolk Mews
Acklam Rd
Cambridge Gardens B412
Malton Road
Malton Mews
Thorpe Close
Walmer Road
Westway A40
Crowthorne Road
Trinity Mews
Ladbroke Grove
Railway Mews
Ruston Mews
Lancaster Road
Golden Cross Mews
Basing Street
Alba Place
Haydens Place
Elgin Mews
Westbourne Park Road B412
Kingsdown Close
Bridge Close
Bartle Road
St. Andrews Square
Lancaster Road
Silchester Road
Ladbroke Crescent
Camborne Mews
Cornwall Crescent
St. Marks Close
St. Marks Place
Clare Gardens
Convent Gardens
Folly Mews
Dunworth Ms
Grove Mews
Talbot
Dartfield Way
Waynflete Sq
Waynflete Square
Shalfleet Drive
Blechynden Street
Lancaster Green
Latimer Road
Bramley Road
Lockton Street
Verity Cl
Dulford St
Dale Row
Blenheim Crescent
Kensington Park Mews
Kensington Park Road
Colville Mews
Elgin Crescent B415
Elgin Cr
West Cross Route A3220
Freston Road
Bard Road
Grenfell Road
Bomore Road
Runcorn Place
Whitchurch Road
Treadgold Street
Threshers Place
Avondale Park Road
Hesketh Pl
Elgood Cl
Walmer Road
Clarendon Road
Portland Road
Arundel Gardens
Vernon Yd
Westbourne
Rosmead Road
Lansdowne Road
Ladbroke Gardens
Stanley Crescent
Kensington Park
Silver Road
Evesham Street
Stoneleigh Place
Stoneleigh Street
Sirdar Road
Park Gdns
Avondale
Mary Place
Gorham Place
Heathfield Street
Portland Road
NOTTING HILL
Stanley Gdns
Olaf Street
Mortimer Square
Hunt Close
St. Anns Road
Avondale Park
Hippo. Ms
Hippo. Place
Clarendon Cross
Lansdowne Rise
Lansdowne Crescent
Kensington Park Gardens
St. Johns Gardens
Ladbroke Square Gardens
Queensdale Crescent
Wilsham Street
Pottery Lane
Princedale Road
Darnley Terrace
St. James's Gardens
Penzance Place
Penzance Street
Lansdowne Walk
Ladbroke Square
Swanscombe Road
Queensdale Place
Princes Place
Wilby Mews
Ladbroke Road
Ladbroke Walk
Queensdale Road
Norland Road
Queen Wk
Norland Square
Princes Yard
Norland Place
Ladbroke Mews
Lansdowne Mews
Boyne Terrace Mews
Kingsdale Gardens
Royal Crescent Mews
Addison Place
Addison Avenue
Taverners Close
St. Anns Villas
Royal Crescent
Royal Crescent Gardens
Holland Park
Holland Park Avenue A402
Hill Square
Campden Hill Square
Hillsleigh Road
Aubrey Road
Shepherd's Bush
Shepherd's Bush Place
Green A402
Holland Road
Lorne Gardens
Kingham Close
Holland Park Gardens
Addison Road
Holland Park Lawn Tennis Club
Holland Park Mews
Aubrey Walk
Campden Hill Tennis Club
0.25 mile
0.25 km

Ladbroke Grove/Notting Hill (West)

Look at that Westway and tell us you can't hear the opening chords of "London Calling." Maybe Rudie didn't fail but he moved up and moved out. This is the quiet, leafy Notting Hill of gated gardens away from the Hugh Grant-hungry tourists scouring Portobello Road. Head to Clarendon Cross or Portland Road for food and stuff. Grab a bite at **Julie's** or wander down to Holland Park Avenue for organic treats at **Jeroboams Deli**.

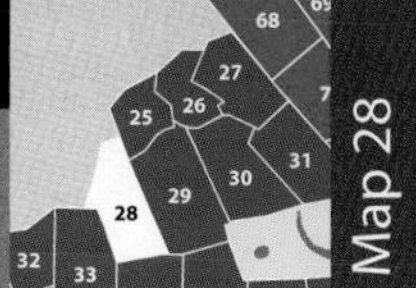

Coffee

- **Starbucks** • 76 Holland Park Ave

Nightlife

- **Julie's Restaurant & Champagne Bar** • 135 Portland Rd

Shopping

- **Cowshed** • 119 Portland Rd
- **The Cross** • 141 Portland Rd
- **Daunt Books** • 112 Holland Park Ave
- **Jeroboams** • 96 Holland Park Ave
- **Virginia** • 98 Portland Rd

1
2
A
B
WESTBOURNE GREEN
NOTTING HILL
KENSINGTON
Kensington Gardens
Westbourne Park
Ladbroke Grove
Holland Park
Notting Hill Gate
Portobello Road Market
Ladbroke Square Gardens
Campden Hill Tennis Club
25
26
28
30
34
35
PAGE 342
0.25 mile
0.25 km
Westway A40
Ladbroke Grove B450
Portobello Road
Westbourne Park Road B412
Great Western Road A4207
Chepstow Road A4207
Westbourne Grove A4206
Pembridge Villas A4206
Pembridge Road A4206
Kensington Park Road B415
Elgin Crescent B415
Holland Park Avenue A402
Notting Hill Gate A402
Kensington Church Street
Palace Gardens Terrace
Talbot Road
Lancaster Road
Colville Terrace
Ledbury Road
Artesian Road
Lonsdale Road
Westbourne Grove
Chepstow Villas
Pembridge Crescent
Pembridge Square
Dawson Place
Princes Square
Leinster Square
Moscow Road
Ladbroke Gardens
Arundel Gardens
Lansdowne Road
Lansdowne Rise
Ladbroke Square
Lansdowne Walk
Ladbroke Road
Ladbroke Walk
Ladbroke Terrace
Kensington Park Gardens
Stanley Gardens
Stanley Crescent
Blenheim Crescent
Oxford Gardens
Cambridge Gardens
Bonchurch Rd
Golborne Road
St. Michaels Gdns
Elkstone Road
Tavistock Crescent
Tavistock Road
Tavistock Gardens
All Saints Road
St. Lukes Road
Leamington Road Villas
Aldridge Road Villas
Powis Gardens
Powis Terrace
Powis Square
Colville Gardens
Colville Square
Campden Hill Road
Campden Hill Square
Aubrey Walk
Kensington Place
Peel Street
Campden Street
Bedford Gardens
Edge Street
Uxbridge Street
Hillgate Place
Linden Gardens
Clanricarde Gardens
Ossington Street
Palace Court
Chapel Side
St. Petersburgh Place
Harrow Road A404
Alfred Road
Elmfield Way
Bayswater

Notting Hill Gate

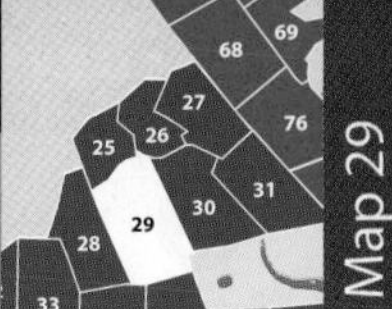

t is hard to believe that until relatively recently this now home of the mega-rich was (ensington's rough bad-boy slum. Traces of the Gate's multicultural past are in the vrinkles of the old eccentrics in the **Uxbridge Arms**, the lively **Portobello Market**, and he buzz of the summer Carnival. To feel old and bitter, go scowl at skinny jeans-clad eenagers in the **Notting Hill Arts Club**. Pig out on some of London's best gelato at)ri Dri, browse the stacks at **Rough Trade Records** and sit back in leather sofa luxury vith a Peroni for a flick at the historic **Electric Cinema**.

Cinemas

- **The Electric Cinema** • 191 Portobello Rd
- **Gate Picturehouse** • 87 Notting Hill Gate
- **Notting Hill Coronet** • 103 Notting Hill Gate

Coffee

- **Caffe Nero** • 113 Westbourne Grove
- **Caffe Nero** • 53 Notting Hill Gate
- **Caffe Nero** • 168 Portobello Rd
- **Coffee Plant** • 180 Portobello Rd
- **Coffee Republic** • 214 Portobello Rd
- **Pret A Manger** • 65 Notting Hill Gate
- **Starbucks** • 227 Portobello Rd
- **Starbucks** • 26 Pembridge Rd

Landmarks

- **Portobello Road Market** • 223 Portobello Rd

Libraries

- **North Kensington Library** • 108 Ladbroke Grove
- **Notting Hill Gate Library** • 1 Pembridge Sq

Nightlife

- **Mau Mau** • 265 Portobello Rd
- **Notting Hill Arts Club** • 21 Notting Hill Gate
- **Sun in Splendour** • 7 Portobello Rd
- **Trailer Happiness** • 177 Portobello Rd
- **Uxbridge Arms** • 13 Uxbridge St
- **Windsor Castle** • 114 Campden Hill Rd

Post Offices

- **Kensington Church St** • 190 Kensington Church St
- **Ladbroke Grove** • 116 Ladbroke Grove

Restaurants

- **Beach Blanket Babylon** • 45 Ledbury Rd
- **Cafe Diana** • 5 Wellington Terrace
- **Geales** • 2 Farmer St
- **The Ledbury** • 127 Ledbury Rd
- **Osteria Basilico** • 29 Kensington Park Rd
- **Ottolenghi** • 63 Ledbury Rd
- **The Shed** • 122 Palace Gardens Terr
- **Taqueria** • 139 Westbourne Grove

Shopping

- **& Clarke's Bread** • 124 Kensington Church St
- **Bodas** • 38 Ledbury Rd
- **The Grocer on Elgin** • 6 Elgin Crescent
- **The Hummingbird Bakery** • 133 Portobello Rd
- **Melt** • 59 Ledbury Rd
- **Mr Christian's Delicatessen** • 11 Elgin Crescent
- **Music & Video Exchange** • 38 Notting Hill Gate
- **Notting Hill Farmers' Market** • Kensington Church St
- **Portobello Road Market** • Portobello Rd
- **R Garcia and Sons** • 248 Portobello Rd
- **Retro Man** • 34 Pembridge Rd
- **Retro Woman** • 32 Pembridge Rd
- **Rough Trade** • 130 Talbot Rd

Map 30 • Bayswater

N

26
27
31
29
1
2
A
B

Sutherland Avenue
Elmfield
A404
Harrow Road A404
Foscote Mews
Downfield Close
Amberley Road
Aldsworth Close
Admiral Walk
Braden Street
Shirland Road B413
Formosa Street
Warwick Avenue
Clearwell Drive
Barnwood Close
Bristol Gardens
Bristol Mews
Clifton Villas
Clifton Gardens
Warrington Crescent
Castellain Road
Warwick Avenue
Blomfield Road
Warwick Place
Westway A40
Wav.Wk
Alfred Road
Westbourne Green Sports Complex
Cirencester Street
Senior Street
Rowington Close
Lord Hills Road
Delamere Terrace
Desborough Close
Chichester Rd
Bourne Terrace
Torquay Street
Harrow Road
Westbourne Green
Blomfield Villas
Westbourne Terrace Road
Warwick Crescent
Westbourne Park Road A4207
St. Stephens Mews
St. Stephens Gardens
Shrewsbury Road
Westbourne Park Villas
St. Stephens Cres
Westway A40
Lord Hills Bridge
Royal Oak
Harrow Road A404
PADDINGTON
Northumberland Place
Chepstow Road A4207
Bridstow Place
Hereford Road
Kildare Terrace
Kildare Gdns
Alexander Street
Alexander Mews
Durham Terrace
Westbourne Park Road
Celbridge Ms
Gloucester Terrace
West. Gardens
Sunderland Terrace
Ranelagh Bridge
Westbourne Bridge
Botts Ms
Newton Road
Burdett Ms
Porchester Square
Porchester Terrace North
Hereford Mews
Monmouth Place
Westbourne Grove Terrace
Hatherley Grove
Queensway
Pickering Mews
Porchester Road B411
Orsett Terrace
Gloucester Gdns
Bishops Bridge
Westbourne Grove A4206
Bishops Bridge Road A4206
Chepstow Place
Rede Place
Leinster Square
Garway Road
Kensington Gardens Square
Redan Place
Queensway B411
Inver Court
Eastbourne Terrace
Paddington Station
Gloucester Terrace
Westbourne Terrace Mews
Cleveland Terrace
Princes Square
Cleveland Gardens
Eastbourne Mews
Princes Mews
Porchester Gardens
Cervantes Ct
Porchester Gardens Mews
Leinster Place
Westbourne Terrace
A4205
Chilworth Street
BAYSWATER
Ilchester Gardens
Moscow Pl
Queens Mews
Salem Road
Queens Ms
Moscow Road
Inverness Terrace
Inverness Ms
Tenniel Close
Leinster Gardens
Cleveland Square
Queens Gardens
Devonshire Terrace
Upbrook Mews
Gloucester Mews
Chilworth Mews
Palace Court
Chapel Side
Ossington Street
Ossington Cl
Victoria Grove Mews
St. Petersburgh Mews
St. Petersburgh Place
Lombardy Pl
Bark Place
Caroline Place
Poplar Place
Bayswater
Inv.Pl
Queensborough Terrace
Queensborough Ms
Queens Pass
Fulton Ms
Queens Studios
Craven Hill Gardens
Craven Hill Mews
Craven Road B410
Craven Hill B410
Conduit Mews
Orme Lane
Orme Square
Orme Court
Orme Court Mews
Olympia Ms
Fosbury Ms
Queensway
Caroline Cl
Bayswater Road A402
Craven Hill
Leinster Mews
Leinster Terrace B410
Porchester Terrace
Lancaster Gate
Lancaster Mews
Craven Terrace
Brook Mews North
Smallbrook Mews
Westbourne Crescent
West. Cresc Ms
Cerney Mews
Elms Ms
Marlborough Gate House
Lancaster Terrace
Westbourne Street
A4209
Lancaster Gate
Kensington Gardens
Kensington Palace Gardens

PAGE 414
PAGE 342

0.25 mile
0.25 km

London's unofficial 'Little Beirut' seems to attract both camera-clad tourists (who have strayed too far from Hyde Park) as well as Londoners (who look for food gems on Westbourne Grove). While the place is bustling, beware of the overpriced, and frankly sh***, tourist traps on Queensway. Alternatively, do it like the Victorians did and get a rub down at **Porchester Gate Spa**.

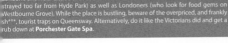

Coffee

- **Arno Coffee** • 77 Bishop's Bridge Rd
- **Pret A Manger** • 127 Queensway
- **Starbucks** • 49 Queensway

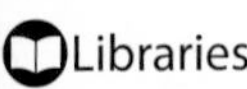

Libraries

- **Paddington Library** • Porchester Rd

Nightlife

- **All Star Lanes** • Bloomsbury Pl & Southampton Row
- **The Cow** • 89 Westbourne Park Rd
- **Redemption Bar** • 6 Chepstow Rd

Post Offices

- **Harrow Rd** • 272 Harrow Rd
- **Queensway** • 118 Queensway

Restaurants

- **Al Waha** • 75 Westbourne Grove
- **The Cow** • 89 Westbourne Park Rd
- **Royal China** • 13 Queensway

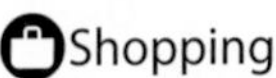

Shopping

- **Al Saqi Books** • 26 Westbourne Grove
- **Planet Organic** • 42 Westbourne Grove
- **Porchester Gate Spa** • Queensway & Porchester Rd

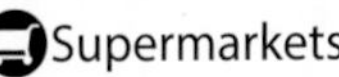

Supermarkets

- **Sainsbury's** • 88 Westbourne Grove
- **Waitrose** • 38 Porchester Sq

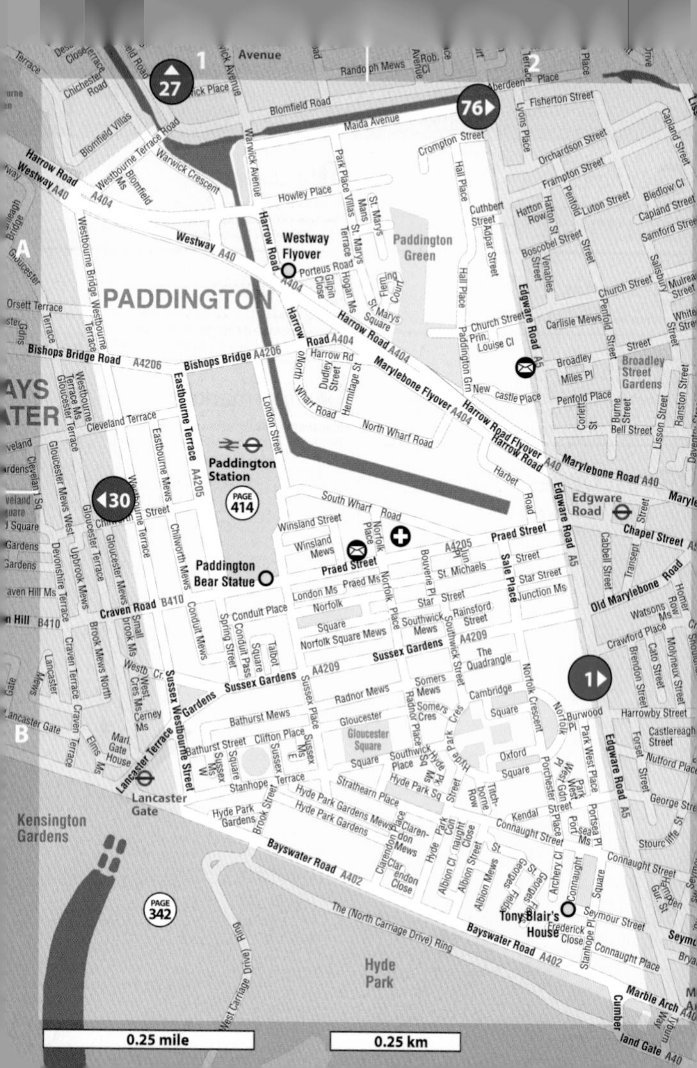
PADDINGTON
Kensington Gardens
Hyde Park
Paddington Station
Paddington Green
Westway Flyover
Paddington Bear Statue
Tony Blair's House
Edgware Road
Lancaster Gate
Broadley Street Gardens
Gloucester Square
PAGE 414
PAGE 342
27
76
30
1
A
B
1
2
Harrow Road A404
Westway A40
Marylebone Flyover A404
Harrow Road Flyover A40
Marylebone Road A40
Bishops Bridge Road A4206
Eastbourne Terrace A4205
Praed Street
Craven Road B410
Sussex Gardens A4209
Bayswater Road A402
Edgware Road A5
Marble Arch A40
Cumberland Gate A40
The (North Carriage Drive) Ring
West Carriage Drive
Westbourne Terrace
Warwick Avenue
Warwick Crescent
Blomfield Road
Maida Avenue
Randolph Mews
Aberdeen Place
Fisherton Street
Crompton Street
Orchardson Street
Frampton Street
Hall Place
Church Street
Chapel Street
Old Marylebone Road
London Street
South Wharf Road
North Wharf Road
Norfolk Square
Norfolk Crescent
Cambridge Square
Oxford Square
Connaught Street
Seymour Street
Connaught Place
Hyde Park Gardens
Hyde Park Square
Kendal Street
Sussex Place
Gloucester Terrace
Chilworth Street
Orsett Terrace
Cleveland Terrace
Lancaster Terrace
Westbourne Street
Brendon Street
Harrowby Street
0.25 mile
0.25 km

Paddington Bear may not seem so cuddly if he were one of today's commuters hanging around Paddington Station. This area can seem like zombie land, a mass of tired-looking, harassed faces grabbing food from one of the endless chain eateries. It's not all bad news though. Evening boredom can be banished by listening to famous war correspondents' exotic tales over a meal at the **Frontline Club**. For all other woes solve it with a swift half at **The Victoria**.

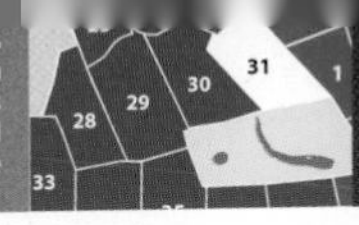

Map 3

Cinemas

- **Frontline Club** • 13 Norfolk Pl

Coffee

- **Beany Green** • 6 Sheldon Square
- **Caffe Nero** • 14 Spring St
- **Caffe Nero** • Paddington Station
- **Costa** • 254 Edgware Rd
- **Eat.** • Paddington Station
- **Markus Coffee Company** • 13 Connaught St
- **Pret A Manger** • 9 Sheldon Sq
- **Serpentine Bar & Kitchen** • Serpentine Rd

Emergency Rooms

- **St Mary's Hospital** • Praed St & Winsland St

Landmarks

- **Paddington Bear Statue** • Paddington Station
- **Tony Blair's House** • Connaught Sq & Seymour St
- **Westway Flyover** • Westway

Nightlife

- **Frontline Club** • 13 • Norfolk Pl
- **The Royal Exchange** • 26 Sale Pl
- **The Victoria** • 10 Strathearn Pl

Post Offices

- **Edgware Rd** • 354 Edgware Rd
- **Paddington** • 4 Praed St

Restaurants

- **Bonne Bouche** •129 Praed St
- **Casa Malevo** • 23 Connaught St

Supermarkets

- **Sainsbury's** • Paddington Station
- **Sainsbury's** • 12 Sheldon Sq

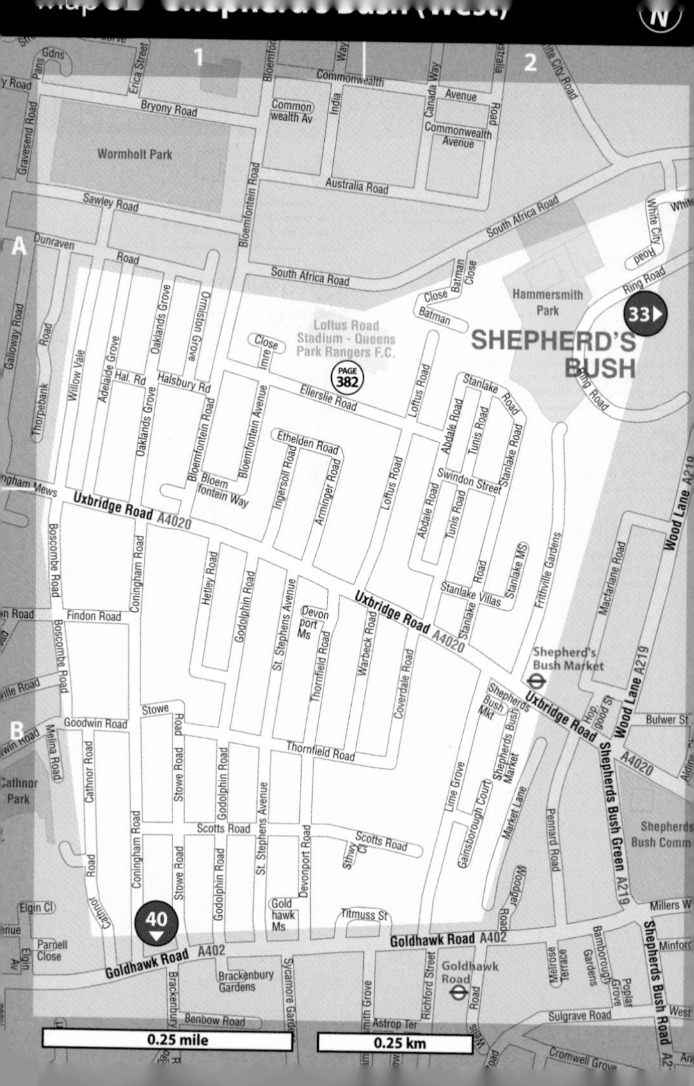

1
2
A
B
Commonwealth Avenue
Common wealth Av
India Way
Canada Way
Commonwealth Avenue
Erica Street
Bryony Road
Gravesend Road
Wormholt Park
Australia Road
Bloemfontein Road
Sawley Road
Dunraven Road
South Africa Road
White City Road
Batman Close
Close Batman
Hammersmith Park
Ring Road
33
SHEPHERD'S BUSH
Loftus Road Stadium - Queens Park Rangers F.C.
PAGE 382
Imre Close
Ellerslie Road
Galloway Road
Thorpebank Road
Willow Vale
Adelaide Grove
Oaklands Grove
Ormiston Grove
Hal. Rd
Halsbury Rd
Bloemfontein Avenue
Loftus Road
Stanlake Road
Abdale Road
Tunis Road
Ethelden Road
Ingersoll Road
Arminger Road
Swindon Street
Bloem fontein Way
Uxbridge Road A4020
Stanlake MS
Stanlake Villas
Frithville Gardens
Macfarlane Road
Wood Lane A219
Boscombe Road
Coningham Road
Hetley Road
Godolphin Road
St. Stephens Avenue
Devon port Ms
Thornfield Road
Warbeck Road
Coverdale Road
Shepherd's Bush Market
Findon Road
Stowe Road
Goodwin Road
Melina Road
Cathnor Park
Cathnor Road
Lime Grove
Shepherds Bush Mkt
Shepherds Bush Market
Gainsborough Court
Market Lane
Pennard Road
Hop. good St
Bulwer St
Shepherds Bush Green A219
Shepherds Bush Comm
Scotts Road
Devonport Road
Sthwy Cl
Woodger Road
Elgin Cl
Parnell Close
Elgin Av
Gold hawk Ms
Titmuss St
40
Goldhawk Road A402
Goldhawk Road
Millers W
Shepherds Bush Road
Brackenbury Gardens
Brackenbury Road
Sycamore Gardens
Richford Street
Melrose Terrace
Bamborough Gardens
Poplar Grove
Benbow Road
Astrop Ter
Sulgrave Road
Cromwell Grove
0.25 mile
0.25 km

Shepherd's Bush (West)

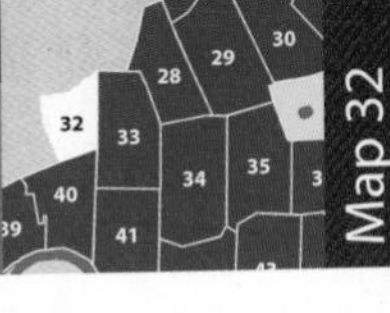

Don't be scared. This part of town won't bite ... much. Things may look a bit drab, and indeed you wouldn't want to spend your Friday nights in many of the pubs here, but on Uxbridge Road looks truly can be deceiving. While it's nothing special from the outside, **Esarn Kheaw** will blow your head off with authentic Thai green curry and leave you begging for more. Then swoon under the chandeliers to an off-the-radar act at restored dance hall **Bush Hall**.

Nightlife

- **Bush Hall** • 310 Uxbridge Rd
- **The Queen Adelaide** • 412 Uxbridge Rd
- **White Horse** • 31 Uxbridge Rd

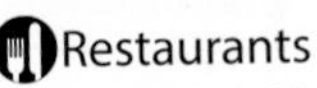

Restaurants

- **Abu Zaad** • 29 Uxbridge Rd
- **Esarn Kheaw** • 314 Uxbridge Rd
- **Vine Leaves Taverna** • 71 Uxbridge Rd

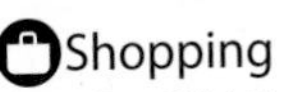

Shopping

- **Damas Gate** • 81 Uxbridge Rd
- **Nut Case** • 352 Uxbridge Rd

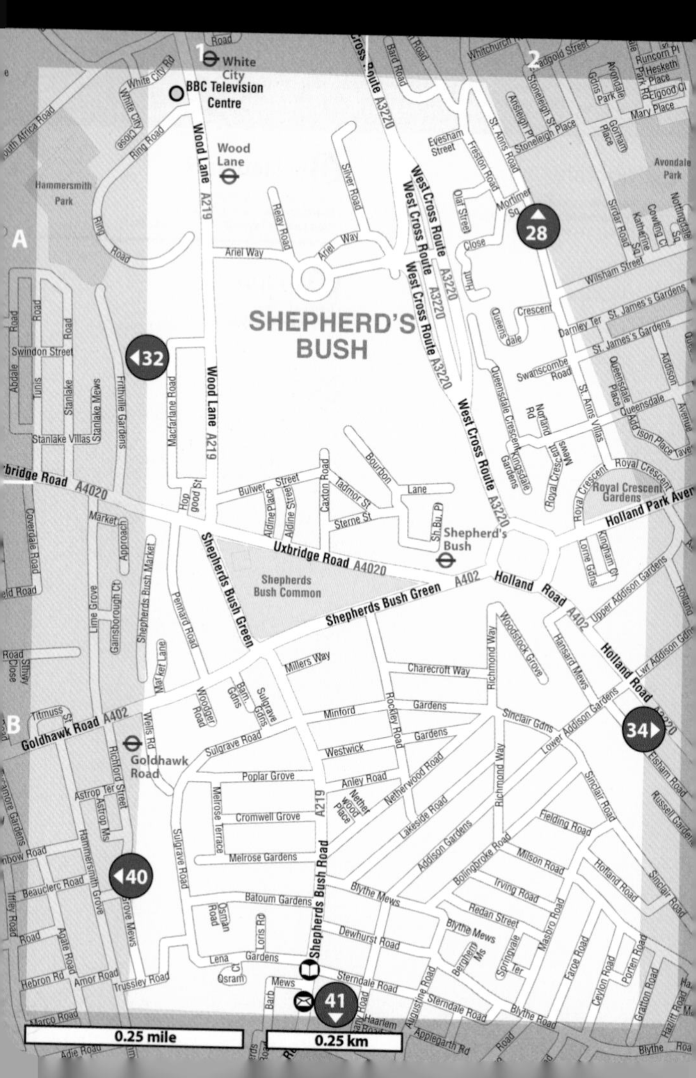

SHEPHERD'S BUSH
White City
BBC Television Centre
Wood Lane
Hammersmith Park
Shepherd's Bush
Shepherds Bush Common
Goldhawk Road
Royal Crescent Gardens
Avondale Park
Uxbridge Road A4020
West Cross Route A3220
Holland Road A402
Shepherds Bush Green
Goldhawk Road A402
Shepherds Bush Road A219
Holland Park Aver
Wood Lane A219
0.25 mile
0.25 km

'The Bush' has had a bit of a face-lift over the past few years. Once the former grime hub of West London, it now sports one of Europe's biggest shopping centres, **Westfield**, and with it comes more traffic and more chain shops. Even the Beeb is on its way out. Fear not though, for **Shepherds Bush Market** still keeps the place decidedly unpretentious, while the **Empire** continues to attract the best up-and-coming bands. Experience some in-yer-face theatre at **Bush Theatre**.

Cinemas

- **Vue Shepherds Bush** • Shepherds Bush Green & Rockley Rd

Coffee

- **Costa** • 72 Uxbridge Rd
- **Starbucks** • 62 Uxbridge Rd

Landmarks

- **BBC Television Centre** • Wood Ln & Ring Rd

Libraries

- **Shepherds Bush Library** • 6 Wood Ln

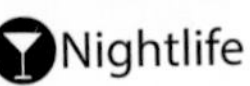

Nightlife

- **Albertine** • 1 Wood Lane
- **Bush Theatre** • 7 Uxbridge Rd
- **The Defectors Weld**• 170 Uxbridge Rd
- **O2 Shepherd's Bush Empire** • Shepherd's Bush Green

Post Offices

- **Shepherds Bush Road** • 146 Shepherd's Bush Rd

Restaurants

- **Busaba Eathai** • Westfield Shopping Centre
- **Ho-ja** • 39 Goldhawk Rd
- **Jasmine** • 16 Goldhawk Rd
- **Kerbisher & Malt** • 164 Shepherd's Bush Green
- **Mr Falafel** • Units T4-T5, New Shepherd's Bush Market
- **Popeseye** • 108 Blythe Rd

Shopping

- **Westfield Centre** • Ariel Way

Supermarkets

- **Sainsbury's** • 164 Uxbridge Rd

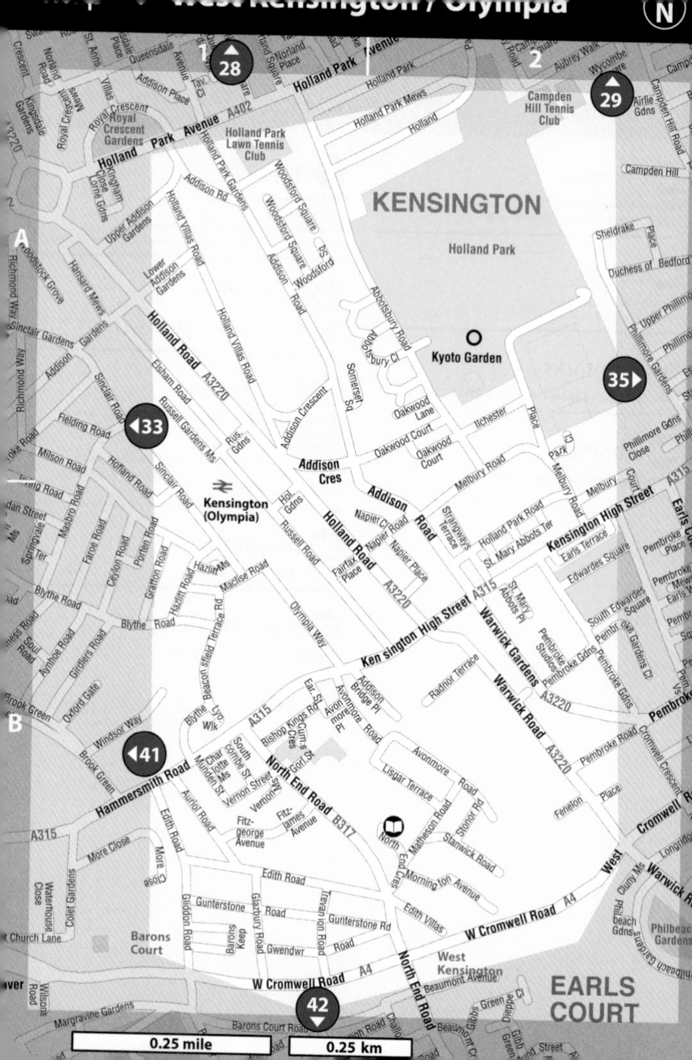
N
KENSINGTON
Holland Park
Kyoto Garden
Kensington (Olympia)
Holland Park Lawn Tennis Club
Campden Hill Tennis Club
Royal Crescent Gardens
Barons Court
West Kensington
EARLS COURT
Holland Park Avenue
A402
Holland Road
A3220
Addison Road
Addison Cres
Kensington High Street
A315
Warwick Gardens
Warwick Road
Hammersmith Road
North End Road
B317
W Cromwell Road
A4
Cromwell Road
Pembroke Road
Melbury Road
Abbotsbury Road
Holland Villas Road
Addison Crescent
Russell Road
Olympia Way
Blythe Road
Brook Green
Edith Road
Gunterstone Road
Avonmore Road
Lisgar Terrace
Stanwick Road
Matheson Road
Edith Villas
Margravine Gardens
Barons Court Road
Beaumont Avenue
Philbeach Gardens
Earls Terrace
Edwardes Square
Pembroke Gardens
Radnor Terrace
Ilchester Place
Oakwood Court
Woodsford Square
Holland Park Gardens
Addison Gardens
Sinclair Road
Fielding Road
Milson Road
Hansard Mews
Richmond Way
Windsor Way
Oxford Gate
Girdlers Road
Aynhoe Road
Masbro Road
Faroe Road
Ceylon Road
Porten Road
Gratton Road
Maclise Road
Hazlitt Road
Beaconsfield Terrace Rd
Auriol Road
Fitz-george Avenue
Fitz-james Avenue
Vernon Street
Glazbury Road
Gliddon Road
Trevanion Road
Colet Gardens
Church Lane
Longridge
Fenelon Place
Campden Hill
Phillimore Gardens
Duchess of Bedford's
Sheldrake Place
Napier Road
Napier Place
Strangways Terrace
St. Mary Abbots Ter
Holland Park Road
28
29
33
35
41
42
1
2
A
B
0.25 mile
0.25 km

West Kensington / Olympia

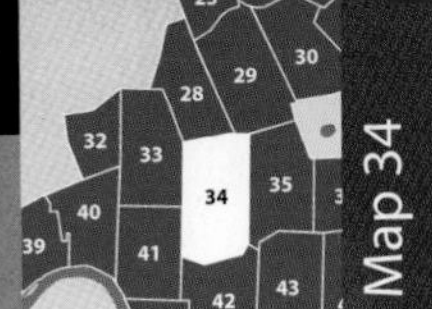

West Ken is a Jekyll-and-Hyde kind of place. The calm, village atmosphere around Holland Park soon gives way to an 'in your face' cluster of kebab shops and grime once you go south of High Street Kensington. While the hordes head to Hyde Park, locals in the know make a beeline to the more intimate Holland Park with its peaceful **Kyoto Garden**, sublime in autumn. Olympia Exhibition Centre gets that middle class blood boiling—Erotica Show anyone? Near the tube, **Café Continente** is the place to go for an irresistible stack of blueberry pancakes.

Coffee

- **Cafe Continente** • 62 N End Rd

Landmarks

- **Kyoto Garden (Holland Park)** • 100 Holland Park Ave

Libraries

- **Barons Court** • North End Crescent

Nightlife

- **The Cumberland Arms** • 29 N End Rd
- **Famous 3 Kings** • 171 North End Rd
- **Society Bar** • 380 Kensington High St

Post Offices

- **Olympia** • 8 North End Rd

Restaurants

- **Belvedere Restaurant** • Abbotsbury Rd

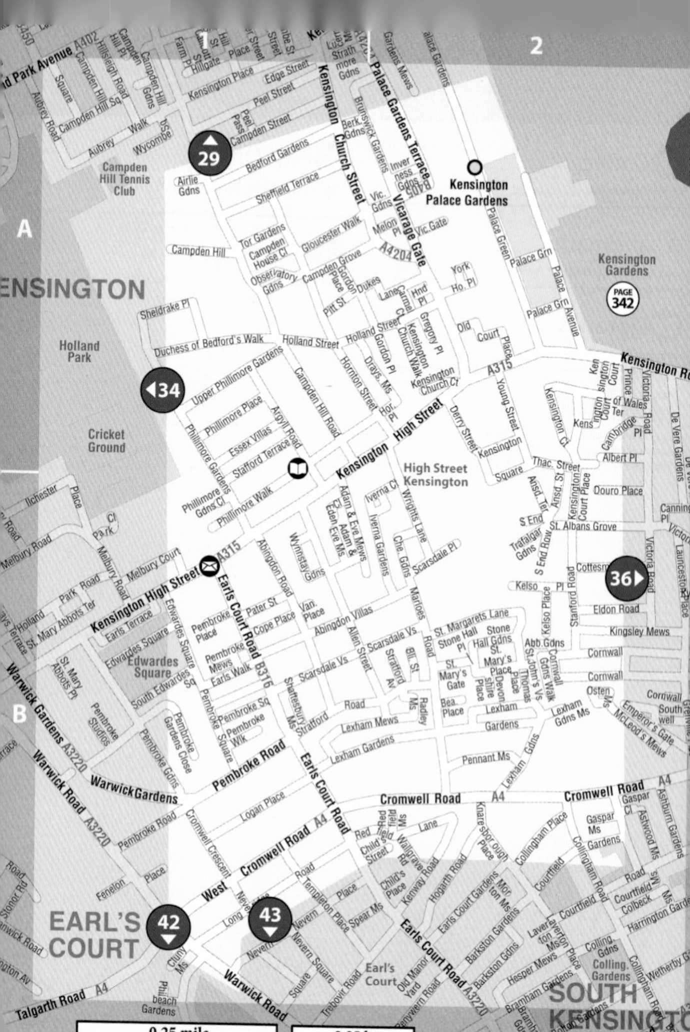

1
2
A
B
29
34
36
42
43
PAGE 342
Kensington Palace Gardens
Kensington Gardens
KENSINGTON
Holland Park
Campden Hill Tennis Club
Cricket Ground
High Street Kensington
Edwardes Square
EARL'S COURT
Earl's Court
SOUTH KENSINGTON
Kensington Church Street
Palace Gardens Terrace
Vicarage Gate
Kensington High Street
Kensington Road
Earls Court Road
Cromwell Road
West Cromwell Road
Warwick Gardens
Warwick Road
Pembroke Road
Abingdon Road
Campden Hill Road
Phillimore Gardens
Holland Street
Young Street
Derry Street
Wrights Lane
Marloes Road
Lexham Gardens
Talgarth Road
Kensington Place
Campden Hill
Campden Grove
Sheffield Terrace
Bedford Gardens
Duchess of Bedford's Walk
Palace Green
Palace Avenue
Victoria Road
Stanford Road
Kensington Court Place
St. Albans Grove
Scarsdale Villas
Allen Street
Pembroke Square
Logan Place
Knaresborough Place
Collingham Road
Courtfield Gardens
Barkston Gardens
Nevern Square
0.25 mile
0.25 km

Kensington is the London of Disney fantasy—Princesses tip-toeing around grand old homes and taking tea at 3 p.m. It's the kind of place where a gentile mews cottage will set you a back a cool mill, but if you live here you'll still have some change left over for an SUV and a box of organic veg. You're not going to score any cool points for hanging out here but there's nothing better than frisbee and a picnic (from **Whole Foods**, of course) in Hyde Park on those treasured London summer days. If you've got the cash to splash, High Street Ken has the goods but instead take a detour to **The Builders Arms** for a not-so-posh pint.

Coffee

- **Caffe Nero** • 160 Kensington High St
- **Pret A Manger** • 149 Kensington High St
- **Starbucks** • 25 Kensington High St
- **Starbucks** • 197 Kensington High St

Landmarks

- **Kensington Palace Gardens** • Kensington Palace Gardens

Libraries

- **Kensington Central Library** • Phillimore Walk

Nightlife

- **Builders Arms** • 1 Kensington Ct Pl
- **The Devonshire Arms** • 37 Marloes Rd
- **Yashin Sushi** • 1 Argyll Rd

Post Offices

- **Kensington High St** • 257 Kensington High St

Restaurants

- **Balans Soho Society** • 187 Kensington High St
- **Bone Daddies** • 63-97 Kensington High St
- **Byron** • 222 Kensington High St
- **Clarke's** • 124 Kensington Church St
- **Kitchen W8** • 11 Abingdon Rd
- **Maggie Jones's** • 6 Old Court Pl

Shopping

- **Ben's Cookies** • 12 Kensington High St
- **Trailfinders** • 194 Kensington High St
- **Urban Outfitters** • 36 Kensington High St
- **Whole Foods Market** • 63 Kensington High St

Supermarkets

- **Sainsbury's** • 162 Earl's Ct Rd
- **Tesco** • 100 W Cromwell Rd
- **Waitrose** • 243 Kensington High St

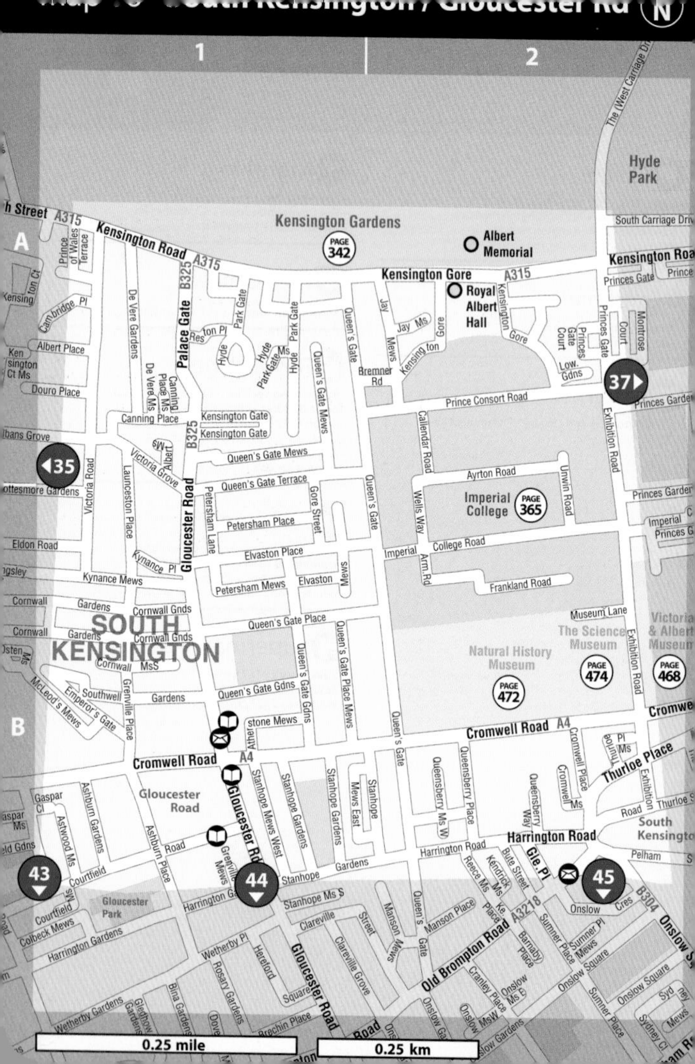

1
2
A
B
Kensington Gardens
PAGE 342
Albert Memorial
Hyde Park
The (West Carriage Drive)
South Carriage Drive
Kensington Road A315
Kensington Gore A315
Royal Albert Hall
Prince Consort Road
Princes Gate
Exhibition Road
Imperial College
PAGE 365
Ayrton Road
Wells Way
College Road
Frankland Road
Museum Lane
The Science Museum
PAGE 474
Natural History Museum
PAGE 472
Victoria & Albert Museum
PAGE 468
Cromwell Road A4
Queen's Gate
Palace Gate B325
Gloucester Road
De Vere Gardens
Victoria Road
Launceston Place
SOUTH KENSINGTON
Cornwall Gardens
Queen's Gate Terrace
Queen's Gate Place
Queen's Gate Gdns
Elvaston Place
Petersham Place
Stanhope Gardens
Queensberry Place
Harrington Road
Thurloe Place
South Kensington
Old Brompton Road A3218
Onslow Square
Gloucester Road
Gloucester Park
Courtfield
Harrington Gardens
Wetherby Pl
35
37
43
44
45
0.25 mile
0.25 km

South Kensington/Gloucester Rd

Once known as Albertopolis, this place started out as Prince Albert's playground of learning. These days the museums are the carrot that draws the tourists westwards from the buzzing centre. Free entry to museums mean more money for treats, and if it's treats you're after then fresh gelato at **Oddono's** won't fail to disappoint. If your idea of a good night out consists of more than a few quiet shandies then we suggest checking out another 'nabe.

Cinemas

- **Cine Lumiere** • 17 Queensberry Pl

Coffee

- **Café Deco** • 62 Gloucester Rd
- **Pret A Manger** • 99 Gloucester Rd
- **Pret A Manger** • 15 Old Brompton Rd
- **Raison D'etre** • 18 Bute St
- **Starbucks** • 17 Gloucester Rd
- **Starbucks** • 83 Gloucester Rd

Landmarks

- **Albert Memorial** • Kensington Gardens
- **Imperial College** • South Kensington Campus
- **Royal Albert Hall** • Kensington Gore

Libraries

- **French Institute Library** • 17 Queensberry Pl
- **National Art Library** • Cromwell Rd
- **Natural History Museum** • Cromwell Rd

Post Offices

- **Gloucester Road** • 118 Gloucester Rd
- **South Kensington Station** • 41 Old Brompton St

Restaurants

- **Da Mario** • 15 Gloucester Rd
- **Jakob's** • 20 Gloucester Rd
- **The Kensington Creperie** • 2 Exhibition Rd
- **Oddono's** • 14 Bute St
- **Tombo** • 29 Thurloe Pl

Shopping

- **Maitre Choux** • 15 Harrington Rd
- **Partridges Deli** • 17 Gloucester Rd

Supermarkets

- **Sainsbury's** • 158 Cromwell Rd
- **Waitrose** • 128 Gloucester Rd

1
2
The Serpentine
Hyde Park
PAGE 342
South Carriage Drive
Prince of Wales Gate
Kensington Road
A315
Princes Gate
Exhibition Road
Montrose Ct
Princes
Ennismore Gardens
Ennismore Gdns
Rutland Gate
Rutland Gate Ms
Rutland Gardens
Rutland Gdns Ms
Kent Yd
Knightsbridge
Holy Trinity Brompton
Knightsbridge
Trevor Place
Trevor St
Trevor Sq
Trevor Square
Raphael St
Lancelot Place
Edinburgh Gate
Seville St
Hooper's Ct
Harriet Walk
Harriet St
Princes Gardens
Ennismore Mews
Montpelier Terrace
Montpelier Pl
Montpelier St
Sterling St
Brompton Road
A4
Basil Street
Hans Road
Hans Crescent
Rysbrack St
Pavilion Road
Sloane Street
A3216
Imperial College Rd
Princes Gate Mews
Cheval Place
Fairholt Street
Relton Ms
Beaufort Gardens
Brompton Place
Brompton Square
Cottage Place
Victoria & Albert Museum
PAGE 468
Beauchamp Place
B319
Ovington Ms
Ovington Gdns
Ovington Square
Walton Place
Hans Place
Hans Street
Pont Street
Cadogan
Cromwell Rd
Egerton Gardens Mews
Egerton Place
Egerton Terrace
Egerton Gardens
Egerton Crescent
Yeoman's Row
Walton Street
Lennox Gardens
Lennox Gardens Mews
Shafto Mews
Clabon Mews
Cadogan Square
Pavilion Street
Thurloe Place
A3218
Thurloe Square
Thurloe Close
Alexander Sq
North Ter
A308
Fulham Road
South Terrace
South Kensington
Crescent Pl
Richards Pl
First Street
Hasker Street
Ovington Street
Milner Street
Moore Street
Cadogan Gate
Pelham Street
Pelham Crescent
Draycott Avenue
Donne Place
Ives St
Mossop St
Denyer Street
Rawlings Street
Halsey Street
St. Catherine's Ms
Wiltshire Cl
Cadogan Street
Draycott Ter
Cadogan Gdns
BROMPTON
Sloane Avenue
Lucan Place
Makins St
Elystan Street
Rosemoor St
Sydney Ms
Pond Place
Symons Street
Blacklands Ter
Culford Gdns
A3217
36
19
45
46
0.25 mile
0.25 km

Move on over Z-list celebrity, only the truly rich shop here! While you can't move for fur or tourists, Knightsbridge is still a great place to shop. Window shop, that is. **Harrods** and **Harvey Nics** are the big boys here, and if you're after £40 soap you are in the right place. For the rest of us there's the **Victoria & Albert Museum**—free entry, brilliant cafe to escape the crowds, and multiple naked male sculptures to ogle.

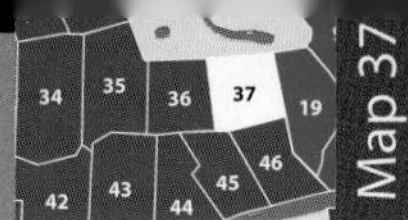

Coffee

- **Caffe Nero** • 124 Brompton Rd
- **Fernandez & Wells** • 8A Exhibition Rd
- **Pret A Manger** • 132 Brompton Rd
- **Starbucks** • 44 Brompton Rd

Landmarks

- **Holy Trinity Brompton** • Brompton Rd & Knightsbridge
- **Victoria & Albert Museum** • Cromwell Rd & Thurloe Pl

Libraries

- **Goethe-Institut Library** • 50 Princes Gate

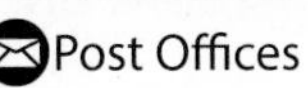

Post Offices

- **Knightsbridge** • 6 Raphael St

Restaurants

- **Bar Boulud** • 66 Knightsbridge
- **Daquise** • 20 Thurloe Square
- **L'Eto Brompton** • 234 Brompton Rd
- **Ognisko** • 55 Prince's Gate
- **Zuma** • 5 Raphael St

Shopping

- **Burberry** • 2 Brompton Rd
- **Divertimenti** • 227 Brompton Rd
- **Harrods** • 87 Brompton Rd
- **Harvey Nichols** • 109 Knightsbridge
- **Rigby & Peller** • 2 Hans Rd

Supermarkets

- **Sainsbury's** • 112 Brompton Rd

ACTON GREEN
Chiswick Common
Turnham Green
CHISWICK
39
Chiswick High Road
Turnham Green Terrace
Chiswick Lane
Hogarth Lane
Hogarth Roundabout Flyover
Great West Road
Burlington Lane
Alexandra Avenue
Dukes Avenue
Devonshire Road
Homefield Recreation Ground
Fuller's Griffin Brewery
Chiswick House Grounds
Corney Road Cemetery
River Thames
Chiswick Eyot
Leg of Mutton Nature Reserve
Harrod's Sports Ground
Chiswick Mall
Church Street
Bath Road
South Parade
0.25 mile
0.25 km

Chiswick

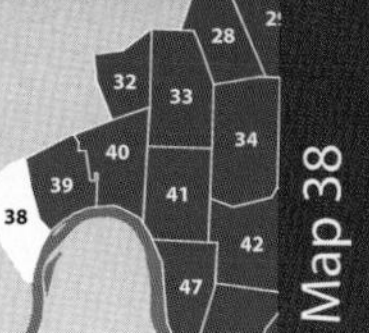

Map 38

ean, green and thankfully not so mean. Chiswick's tranquil, leafy, village feel is perhaps vhat draws families and well-heeled couples with its stacks of laid-back continental tyle pavement dining and quaint cafes on the High Road. Hit Devonshire Road for outique shopping, and on sunny days it's all about ice-cream from **Foubert's** and an fternoon chilling out on Acton Green. **The Roebuck** serves up a top-notch Sunday oast but the **High Road Brasserie** still remains the place to be seen.

Coffee

- **Tamp Coffee** • 1 Devonshire Rd

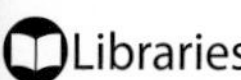

Libraries

- **Chiswick Library** • Duke's Ave

Landmarks

- **Fuller's Griffin Brewery** • Chiswick Lane South

Nightlife

- **Carvosso's** • 210 Chiswick High Rd
- **George IV** • 185 Chiswick High Rd
- **The Packhorse & Talbot** • 145 Chiswick High Rd
- **The Roebuck** • 122 Chiswick High Rd

Post Offices

- **Chiswick High Road** • 110 Chiswick High Rd

Restaurants

- **Chris' Fish and Chips** • 19 Turnham Green Terrace
- **Faanoos** • 472 Chiswick Road
- **Foubert's** • 2 Turnham Green Terrace
- **Franco Manca** • 144 Chiswick High Rd
- **High Road Brasserie** • 162 Chiswick High Rd
- **La Trompette** • 5 Devonshire Rd
- **Le Pain Quotidien** • 214 Chiswick High Road
- **Kalamari** • 4 Chiswick High Rd
- **Zizzi** • 231 Chiswick High Rd

Shopping

- **As Nature Intended** • 201 Chiswick High Rd
- **Chiswick Health & Wellness Spa** • 300 Chiswick High Rd
- **Gail's Bread** • 282 Chiswick High Rd
- **Outsider Tart** • 83 Chiswick High Rd
- **Oxfam Books** • 90 Turnham Green Terrace
- **Wheelers Garden Centre** • Turnham Green Terrace

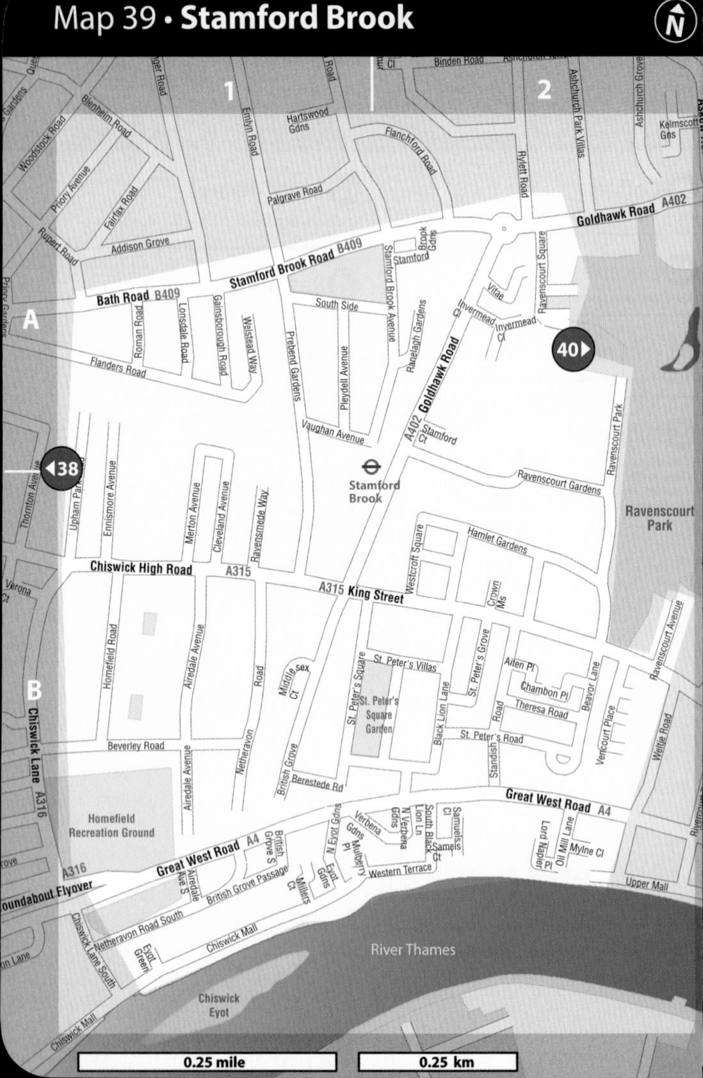
1
2
A
B
Goldhawk Road A402
Stamford Brook Road B409
Bath Road B409
Chiswick High Road A315
A315 King Street
Great West Road A4
Stamford Brook
Ravenscourt Park
Homefield Recreation Ground
St. Peter's Square Garden
River Thames
Chiswick Eyot
Chiswick Lane A316
Hogarth Roundabout Flyover
Chiswick Mall
Upper Mall
Emlyn Road
Hartswood Gdns
Flanchford Road
Palgrave Road
Rylett Road
Ashchurch Park Villas
Ashchurch Grove
Kelmscott Gns
Binden Road
Blenheim Road
Woodstock Road
Priory Avenue
Fairfax Road
Rupert Road
Addison Grove
Stamford Brook Avenue
Stamford Brook Gdns
South Side
Roman Road
Lonsdale Road
Gainsborough Road
Welstead Way
Flanders Road
Prebend Gardens
Pleydell Avenue
Ranelagh Gardens
Vaughan Avenue
Stamford Ct
Invermead Cl
Vitae
Ravenscourt Square
Ravenscourt Gardens
Ravenscourt Park
Thornton Avenue
Upham Park Road
Ennismore Avenue
Merton Avenue
Cleveland Avenue
Ravensmede Way
Westcroft Square
Hamlet Gardens
Crown Ms
Verona Ct
Homefield Road
Airedale Avenue
Netheravon Road
Middlesex Ct
St. Peter's Square
St. Peter's Villas
Black Lion Lane
St. Peter's Grove
Aiten Pl
Chambon Pl
Theresa Road
Beavor Lane
Vencourt Place
Ravenscourt Avenue
Weltje Road
St. Peter's Road
Standish Road
Beverley Road
Airedale Avenue
British Grove
Berestede Rd
Verbena Gdns
N Verbena Gdns
Lion Ln
South Black Lion Ln
Samuels Cl
Samels Ct
Lord Napier Pl
Oil Mill Lane
Mylne Cl
Western Terrace
Mulberry Pl
Eyot Gdns
N Eyot Gdns
Millers Ct
British Grove Passage
British Grove S
Airedale Ave S
Netheravon Road South
Chiswick Lane South
Eyot Green
A316
A4
38
40
0.25 mile
0.25 km

edged between Chiswick and Hammersmith, on the surface Stamford Brook may em like not much more than a tube station and some rather nice, note 'expensive', ouses. Brookites, however, know that it's all about that big blue below the A4—The ames—for a lazy Sunday stroll or long Saturday brunches at **Lola & Simon**. Farther King Street, **Tosa** serves up some authentic Japanese yakitori while thirsty Brookites ad to **The Carpenter's Arms** for oysters and a Guinness in the garden.

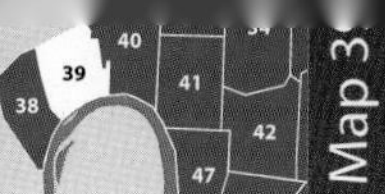

Coffee

- **Artisan Coffee** • 372 King St

Nightlife

- **The Raven** • 375 Goldhawk Rd

Restaurants

- **The Carpenter's Arms** • 89 Black Lion Ln
- **Lola & Simon** • 278 King St
- **Saigon Saigon** • 313 King St
- **Tosa** • 332 Kings St

Supermarkets

- **Sainsbury's** • 120 Chiswick High Rd
- **Tesco** • 327 King St

Shopping

- **Thai Smile** • 287 King St

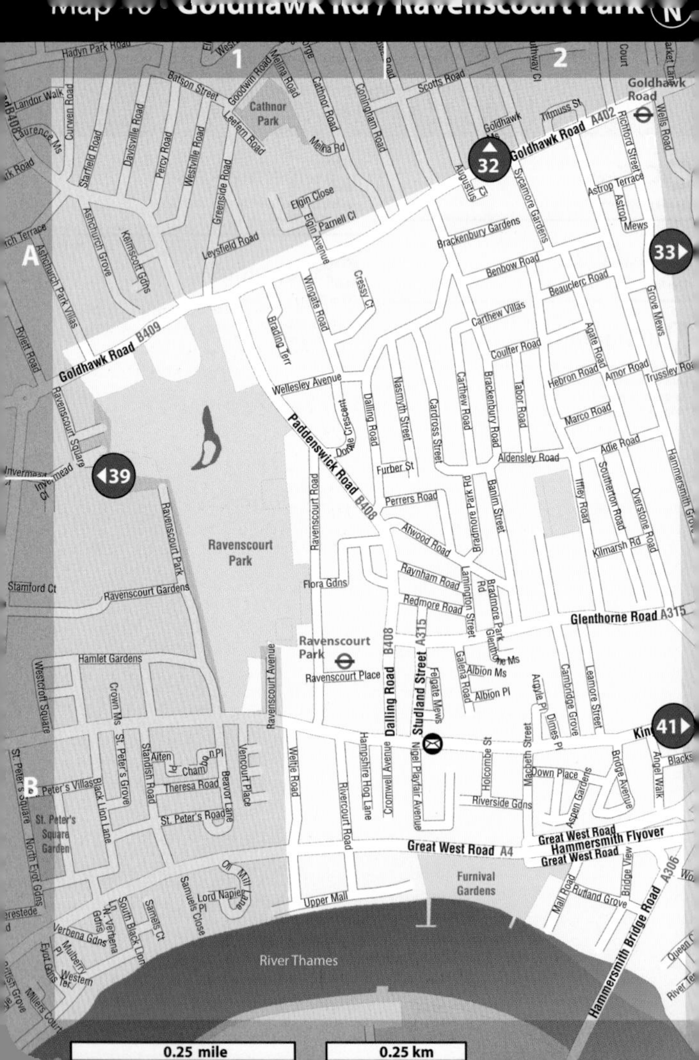

Goldhawk Rd / Ravenscourt Park
N
1
2
A
B
Goldhawk Road
Goldhawk Road A402
Goldhawk Road B409
32
33
39
41
Hadyn Park Road
Batson Street
Goodwin Road
Melina Road
Cathnor Road
Coningham Road
Scotts Road
Cathnor Park
Leefern Road
Melina Rd
Landor Walk
Curwen Road
Laurence Ms
Starfield Road
Davisville Road
Percy Road
Westville Road
Greenside Road
Elgin Close
Elgin Avenue
Parnell Cl
Leysfield Road
Ashchurch Grove
Kelmscott Gdns
Ashchurch Park Villas
Ashchurch Terrace
Rylett Road
Augustus Cl
Goldhawk Ms
Titmuss St
Richford Street
Wells Road
Sycamore Gardens
Brackenbury Gardens
Astrop Terrace
Astrop Mews
Benbow Road
Beauclerc Road
Grove Mews
Carthew Villas
Coulter Road
Agate Road
Amor Road
Trussley Road
Hebron Road
Marco Road
Adie Road
Wingate Road
Cressy Ct
Brading Terr
Wellesley Avenue
Paddenswick Road B408
Dalling Road
Nasmyth Street
Cardross Street
Carthew Road
Brackenbury Road
Tabor Road
Aldensley Road
Furber St
Perrers Road
Atwood Road
Bradmore Park Rd
Banim Street
Iffley Road
Southerton Road
Overstone Road
Kilmarsh Rd
Hammersmith Grove
Ravenscourt Square
Invermead Cl
Ravenscourt Park
Ravenscourt Road
Raynham Road
Lamington Street
Bradmore Park Rd
Redmore Road
Glenthorne Road A315
Flora Gdns
Stamford Ct
Ravenscourt Gardens
Hamlet Gardens
Ravenscourt Avenue
Ravenscourt Place
Dalling Road B408
Studland Street A315
Felgate Mews
Galena Road
Albion Ms
Albion Pl
Glenthorne Ms
Argyle Pl
Dimes Pl
Cambridge Grove
Leamore Street
King
Westcroft Square
Crown Ms
St. Peter's Grove
Standish Road
Aiten Pl
Theresa Road
St. Peter's Road
Beavor Lane
Vencourt Place
Weltje Road
Rivercourt Road
Hampshire Hog Lane
Cromwell Avenue
Nigel Playfair Avenue
Holcombe St
Macbeth Street
Down Place
Aspen Gardens
Bridge Avenue
Angel Walk
Riverside Gdns
St. Peter's Villas
Black Lion Lane
St. Peter's Square
St. Peter's Square Garden
North Eyot Gdns
Great West Road A4
Great West Road
Hammersmith Flyover
Furnival Gardens
Upper Mall
Lord Napier Pl
Samuels Close
South Black Lion
Verbena Gdns
Mulberry Pl
Western Ter
Eyot Gdns
Mall Road
Rutland Grove
Bridge View
Hammersmith Bridge Road
A306
Queen Caroline
River Thames
0.25 mile
0.25 km

Goldhawk Rd/Ravenscourt Park

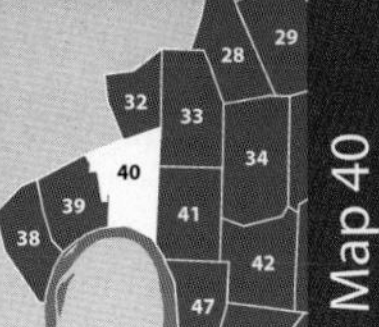

Far enough out on the tube to scare the tourists, this area is a haven for locals who want it all on their doorstep. International flavours colour the Goldhawk Road, Ravenscourt Park offers a calm little slice of green while pretty Thames walks must surely conclude with a visit to the city's most picturesque pub, **The Dove**. Furnival Gardens is the spot to watch the annual Oxbridge boat race.

Coffee

- **Caffe Nero** • 1 King St
- **Camden Coffee House** • 57 Goldhawk Rd

Nightlife

- **The Dove** • 19 Upper Mall

Post Offices

- **King St** • 168 King St

Restaurants

- **Donde Carlos** • 143 Goldhawk Rd
- **Lowiczanka Polish Cultural Centre** • 238 King St
- **Mahdi** • 215 King St
- **Sagar** • 157 King St
- **Zippy Diner** • 42 Goldhawk Rd

Shopping

- **Bushwacker Wholefoods** • 132 King St
- **Patisserie Sainte-Anne** • 204 King St

Supermarkets

- **Iceland** • 111 King St
- **Tesco** • 327 King St

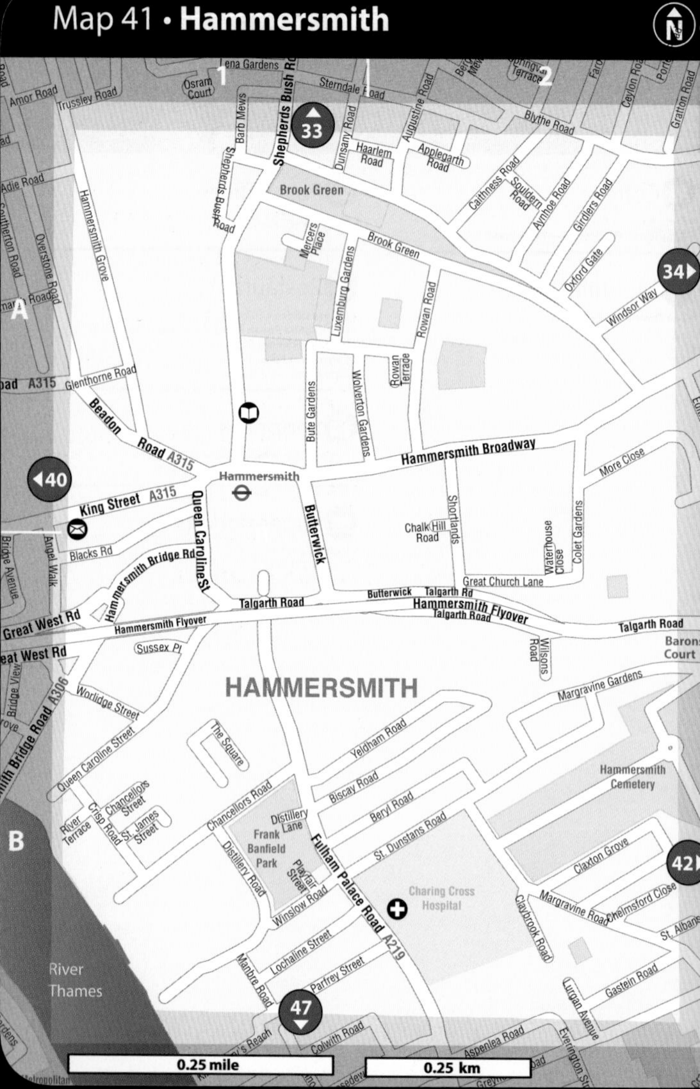

Shepherds Bush Road
Sterndale Road
Blythe Road
Brook Green
Hammersmith Grove
Glenthorne Road
Beadon Road A315
King Street A315
Queen Caroline St
Butterwick
Hammersmith Broadway
Hammersmith Bridge Rd
Talgarth Road
Hammersmith Flyover
Great West Rd
Hammersmith Bridge Road A306
HAMMERSMITH
Fulham Palace Road A219
Margravine Road
Charing Cross Hospital
Hammersmith Cemetery
Frank Banfield Park
River Thames
0.25 mile
0.25 km

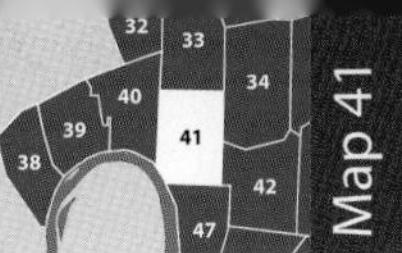

hile the shops and pubs on offer along the main drag (King Street) are all pretty ab, Hammersmith has three great venues for the more culturally inclined. **The pollo** hosts mainstream bands and big-name comedians; **The Lyric** is an fordable way to indulge in some modern theatre, and **The Riverside Studios** fer a satisfying selection of foreign and art house films. London's vegetarians ɔck to **The Gate**, with its seriously original and inventive menu.

Cinemas

- **Riverside Studios** • Crisp Rd & Queen Caroline St

Coffee

- **Starbucks** • 200 Hammersmith Rd

Emergency Rooms

- **Charing Cross Hospital** • Fulham Palace Rd & St Dunstan's Rd

Libraries

- **Hammersmith Library** • Shepherds Bush Rd

Nightlife

- **Brook Green Hotel** • 170 Shepherd's Bush Rd
- **The Distillers** • 64 Fulham Palace Rd
- **The Hampshire Hog** • 227 King St
- **Lyric Hammersmith** • King St

Post Offices

- **Hammersmith** • 168 King's Mall

Restaurants

- **The Gate** • 51 Queen Caroline St
- **Rangrez Indian Restaurant** • 32 Fulham Palace Rd

Shopping

- **Bakehaus** • 71 King St

Supermarkets

- **Tesco** • 180 Shepherd's Bush Rd

1
2
A
B
North End Road B317
Fitzjames Avenue
Mathison Road
Stonor Road
Stanwick Road
Mornington Avenue
North End Crescent
Edith Road
Gunterstone Road
Edith Villas
Gwendwr Road
Gliddon Road
Barons Keep
Glazbury Road
Trevanion Road
West Kensington
Talgarth Road A4
Beaumont Avenue
Cluny Mews
Warwick Road
Philbeach Gardens
34
Barons Court
Barons Court Road
Gibbs Green
Dieppe Close
Beaumont Crescent
Comeragh Mews
Comeragh Road
Castletown Road
Challoner Street
Challoner Crescent
Charleville Road
Palliser Road
Barton Road
41
Hammersmith Cemetery
Vereker Road
Fairholme Road
Lanfrey Place
Mund Street
Ivatt Place
Aisgill Avenue
Stamer Close
Bellamy Close
Earl's Court Exhibition Centre
Gledstanes Road
Perham Road
Cheesemans Terrace
May St
Sun Road
Franklin Square
Fane Street
Star Road
Marchbank Road
Empress State Building
Queen's Club
Norfolk Terrace
Chelmsford Close
St. Albans Terrace
Field Road
St. Andrews Road
Turneville Road
Archel Road
Thaxton Road
Lerry Close
Normand Mews
Chesson Road
Telephone Place
Lillie Road A3218
Greyhound Road
Queens Club Gardens
Queen's Gardens
Bramber Road
Spencer Mews
Tasso Road
Kinnoul Road
Musard Road
Normand Road
Mulgrave Road
Chestnut Alley
Chestnut Court
Georges Square
Sedlescombe Road
Crammond Close
Abbey Gardens
Normand Park
Jervis Road
Racton Road
Humbolt Road
Disbrowe Road
Moylan Road
Hugh Gaitskell Close
Barbara Castle Close
Coomer Mews
Coomer Road
Coomer Place
Crowther Close
Anselm Road
Lampeter Square
Laundry Road
Brecon Road
Lintaine Close
Tilton Street
Hugh Dalton Avenue
Len Freeman Place
Ancill Close
Crefeld Close
47
Bayonne Road
Margaret Ingram Close
Rylston Road
Delaford Street
Haldane Road
Armadale Road
Lillie Road A3218
Purcell Crescent
Chaldon Road
William Close
Pellant Road
Mendora Road
Prothero Road
John Smith Avenue
St. Thomas's Way
Tournay Road
Epirus Road
Epirus Mews
Hartismere Road
Fabian Road
Strode Road
Munster Road
Estcourt Road
Mirabel Road
Shorrolds Road
Palace Mews
St. John's Close
Hannell Road
Dawes Road A3219
Bronsart Road
Aintree Street
Rosaline Road
Mablethorpe Road
Sherbrooke Road
48
Rowallan Road
Orbain Road
Varna Road
Parkville Road
Gironde Road
Burnthwaite Road
Heckfield Place
Allestree Road
St. Olaf's Road
Rosaville Road
Brookville Road
Homestead Road
Wheatsheaf Terrace
Lancaster Court
Kilmaine Road
Reporton Road
Bloom Park Road
Marville Road
Darlan Road
0.25 mile
0.25 km

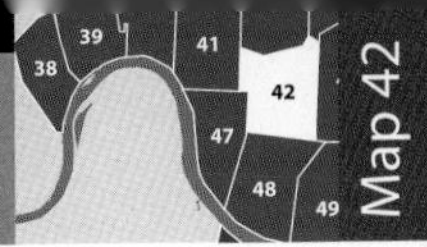

'arons Court doesn't have a scene as such, but it is elegantly lovely. Ignore North nd Road—a fried chicken blot among Edwardian mansions—and instead get ost in Lille Road's antique stores. **Curtains Up** offers intimate theatre in the pub aults. If you need a change from polished chic, seek the **Colton Arms** for a jug- int in its cottage style garden.

Landmarks

- **Empress State Buidling** • Lillie Rd & North End Rd

Nightlife

- **Colton Arms** • 187 Greyhound Rd
- **The Curtains Up** • 28 Comeragh Rd
- **The Fulham Mitre** • 81 Dawes Rd

Post Offices

- **Dawes Road** • 108 Dawes Rd
- **Olympia** • 8 North End Rd

Restaurants

- **Best Mangal** • 104 N End Rd
- **The Malt House** • 17 Vanston Pl

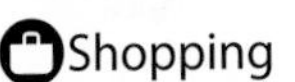

Shopping

- **Curious Science** • 319 Lillie Rd

Supermarkets

- **Co-Op** • 88 N End Rd
- **Iceland** • 290 North End Rd
- **Sainsbury's** • 342 N End Rd

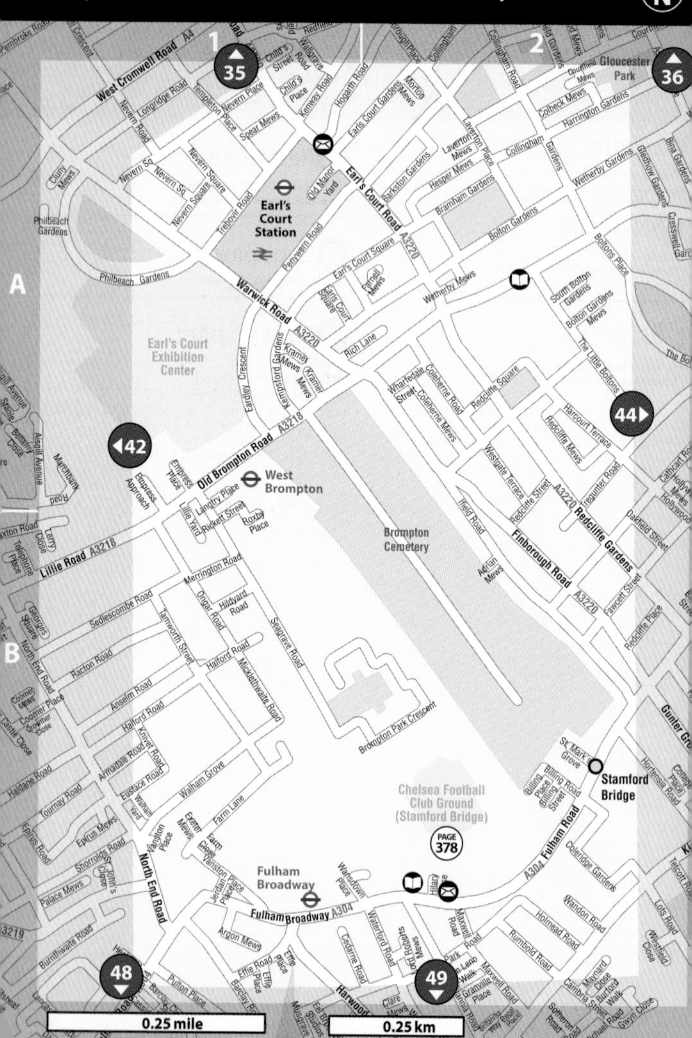

1
2
35
36
A
B
42
44
48
49
West Cromwell Road
A4
Pembroke Road
Longridge Road
Nevern Place
Nevern Road
Templeton Place
Child's Street
Child's Place
Wallgrave Road
Kenway Road
Hogarth Road
Earls Court Gardens
Morton Mews
Spear Mews
Nevern Sq
Nevern Square
Cluny Mews
Philbeach Gardens
Trebovir Road
Earl's Court Station
Old Manor Yard
Earl's Court Road
A3220
Barkston Gardens
Laverton Mews
Laverton Place
Hesper Mews
Bramham Gardens
Collingham Road
Collingham Gardens
Gloucester Park
Colbeck Mews
Harrington Gardens
Wetherby Gardens
Bolton Gardens
Gledhow Gardens
Bina Gardens
Cresswell Gardens
Boltons Place
Penywern Road
Earl's Court Square
Farnell Mews
Earls Court Square
Wetherby Mews
South Bolton Gardens
Bolton Gardens Mews
The Little Boltons
Warwick Road
A3220
Rich Lane
Earl's Court Exhibition Center
Eardley Crescent
Kempsford Gardens
Kramer Mews
Wharfedale Street
Coleherne Road
Coleherne Mews
Redcliffe Square
Harcourt Terrace
Redcliffe Mews
Old Brompton Road
A3218
West Brompton
Empress Place
Empress Approach
Langtry Place
Rickett Street
Roxby Place
Lillie Yard
Marchbank Road
Asgill Avenue
Westgate Terrace
Redcliffe Street
A3220
Redcliffe Gardens
Tregunter Road
Ifield Road
Brompton Cemetery
Adrian Mews
Finborough Road
Fawcett Street
Redcliffe Place
Lillie Road
A3218
Telephone Place
Lerry Close
Merrington Road
Sedlescombe Road
Ongar Road
Hildyard Road
Seagrave Road
Tamworth Street
Georges Square
North End Road
Racton Road
Halford Road
Mickelthwaite Road
Anselm Road
Knivet Road
Armadale Road
Coomer Mews
Coomer Place
Castle Close
Brompton Park Crescent
St Mark's Grove
Stamford Bridge
Gunter Grove
Hortensia Road
Haldane Road
Eustace Road
Walham Grove
Walham Yard
Tournay Road
Farm Lane
Billing Place
Billing Road
Billing Street
Chelsea Football Club Ground (Stamford Bridge)
Epirus Mews
Epirus Road
Exeter Mews
Farm Close
Vanston Place
North End Road
Shorrolds Road
St John's Close
PAGE 378
A304
Fulham Road
Coleridge Gardens
Palace Mews
Jerdan Place
Fulham Broadway
Wansdown Place
Hilary Close
Fulham Broadway A304
Maxwell Road
Wandon Road
Holmead Road
Lots Road
Westfield Close
Argon Mews
Waterford Road
Cedarne Road
Rumbold Road
Burnthwaite Road
Effie Road
Effie Place
Pulton Place
Harwood
Park Road
Lena Walk
Granville Place
Maynard Close
Burford Walk
Cambria Street
Michael Road
Gwyn Close
Sotheron Road
0.25 mile
0.25 km

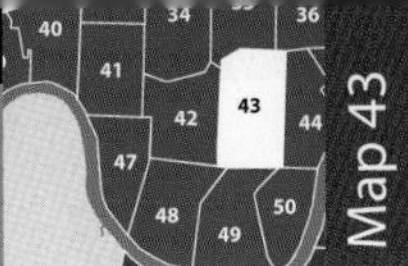

lively mix of Aussies, Saffas, rich kids, and sweaty Chelsea fans occupy these eighbourhoods. Fulham Broadway is the focus of the action offering heaving ars and clubs. Earl's Court is slightly more sedate while West Brompton s positively sleepy in comparison. On Brompton Road '60s boho café **The roubadour** is still a happening spot for live music and a coffee while **Vingt-Quatre** is a 24-hour institution serving fry-ups to clubbers in the early hours.

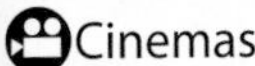

Cinemas

- **Cineworld Fulham Road** • 142 Fulham Rd
- **Vue Fulham** • Fulham Rd & Cedarne Rd

Coffee

- **Cafe du Coin** • 229 Earls Ct Rd
- **Caffe Nero** • 480 Fulham Rd
- **Caffe Nero** • 174 Fulham Rd
- **Chairs & Coffee** • 512 Fulham Rd
- **Pret A Manger** • Fulham Broadway Retail Centre
- **Starbucks** • 259 Old Brompton Rd
- **The Troubadour** • 263 Old Brompton Rd

Landmarks

- **Stamford Bridge** • Fulham Rd & Moore Park Rd

Libraries

- **Brompton Library** • 210 Old Brompton Rd
- **Institute of Cancer Research Library** • 237 Fulham Rd

Nightlife

- **Chairs & Coffee** • 512 Fulham Rd
- **The Blackbird** • 209 Earl's Court Rd
- **The King's Head** • 17 Hogarth Rd

Post Offices

- **Earls Court** • 320 Earl's Court Rd
- **Fulham Road** • 369 Fulham Rd

Restaurants

- **Bodean's** • 4 Broadway Chambers
- **Cafe Brazil** • 511 Fulham Rd
- **Couscous Darna** • 306 Earls Ct Rd
- **Flora Indica** • 242 Old Brompton Rd
- **Harwood Arms** • Walham Grove
- **Vingt Quatre** • 325 Fulham Rd
- **Yo! Sushi** • Fulham Rd

Shopping

- **Fulham Broadway Centre** • Fulham Rd

Supermarkets

- **Sainsbury's** • Fulham Rd
- **Tesco** • 459 Fulham Rd
- **Waitrose** • 380 North End Rd

1
2
A
B
36
43
45
50
Gloucester Park
Courtfield Road
Harrington Gardens
Colbeck Mews
Wetherby Gardens
Wetherby Place
Stanhope Gardens
Stanhope Mews
South Clareville Street
Clareville Grove
Manson Mews
Manson Place
Old Brompton Road
Onslow Crescent
Onslow Square
Onslow Gardens
Sumner Place
Sydney Place
Sydney Street B304
Pelham Street
Pelham Place
Rosary Gardens
Hereford Square
Bina Gardens
Dove Mews
Gledhow Gardens
Brechin Place
Cranley Gardens
Cranley Mews
Cranley Place
Roland Way
Roland Gardens
Eagle Place
Drayton Gardens
Cresswell Gardens
Cresswell Place
Ensor Mews
Foulis Terrace
Neville Street
Dudmaston Mews
South Parade
Cale Street
Chelsea Common
Chelsea Square
Dovehouse Street
Selwood Place
Elm Place
Lecky Street
Bolton Place
South Bolton Gardens
Bolton Gardens Mews
The Little Boltons
The Boltons
Redcliffe Square
Redcliffe Gardens
Harcourt Terrace
Redcliffe Mews
Tregunter Road
Finborough Road
Evelyn Gardens
Elm Park Gardens
Priory Walk
Holly Mews
Harley Gardens
Gilston Road
Milborne Grove
Fulham Road A308
Old Church Street
Manresa Road
Ramsay Mews
Carlyle Square
Elm Park Road
Elm Park Lane
Mulberry Walk
The Vale
Mallord Street
Bramerton Street
Cathcart Road
Hollywood Mews
Hollywood Road
Seymour Walk
Redcliffe Road
Holmes Place
Cavaye Place
Hemmiker Mews
Callow Street
Farrier Walk
Oakfield Street
Limerston Street
Winterton Place
Elm Park Mansions
Camera Place
Park Walk
Chelsea Park Gardens
Beaufort Street
CHELSEA
Paultons Square
Paultons Street
Waldron Mews
Danvers Street
Red Anchor Close
Justice Walk
Lavender Close
Petyt Place
Roper's Gardens
Cheyne Walk
Barker Street
Fawcett Street
Redcliffe Place
Edith Grove A3220
Netherton Grove
Nightingale Place
Gertrude Street
Hobury Street
Shalcomb Street
Lamont Road
Langton Street
Milman's Street Burial Ground
Milman's Street
Moravian Place
Ann Lane
Munro Terrace
Riley Street
World's End Passage
Apollo Place
Blantyre Street
Brompton Cemetery
Fernshaw Road
Gunter Grove A3220
Edith Terrace
Slaidburn Street
Hortensia Road
College Place
St Mark's Grove
Billing Road
Billing Place
Billing Street
Fulham Road
Edith Yard
King's Road
A308
Tetcott Road
Thorndike Close
Westfield Park
Uverdale Road
Ashburnham Road
Cremorne Road A3220
Damer Terrace
Stadium Street
Cremorne Gardens
Chelsea Wharf
Tadema Road
Coleridge Gardens
Wandon Road
Holmead Road
Rumbold Road
Westfield Close
Pooles Lane
Burnaby Street
Upcerne Road
Maynard Close
Battersea Bridge A3220
River Thames
Thorney Crescent
Whistlers Avenue
Battersea Church Road
Pavilion Drive
0.25 mile
0.25 km

his area drips old money, 4x4s, and people who own rather large things, like, ay, Devon. The only way to do Chelsea is to be seen doing it—and if you're ›aying all that money at least make it worthwhile. Engage in some (super) tar-gazing at **The Bluebird Café**. For a more sedate affair hang out with the ›cals, property investors 'n all, at local Victorian boozer **The Drayton Arms**.

Emergency Rooms

- **Chelsea and Westminster Hospital** • 369 Fulham Rd

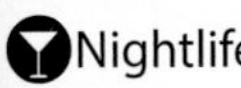

Nightlife

- **Brinkley's** • 47 Hollywood Rd
- **The Drayton Arms** • 153 Old Brompton Rd
- **The Duke of Clarence** • 148 Old Brompton Rd

Restaurants

- **The Bluebird** • 350 King's Rd
- **Eight Over Eight** • 392 King's Rd
- **Haché** • 329 Fulham Rd

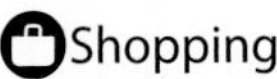

Shopping

- **Cambio de Tercio** • 163 Old Brompton Rd
- **Furniture Cave** • 533 Kings Rd
- **Richer Sounds** • 258 Fulham Rd
- **The Shop At Bluebird** • 350 King's Rd

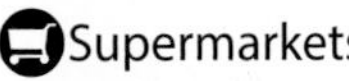

Supermarkets

- **Sainsbury's** • 295 Fulham Rd

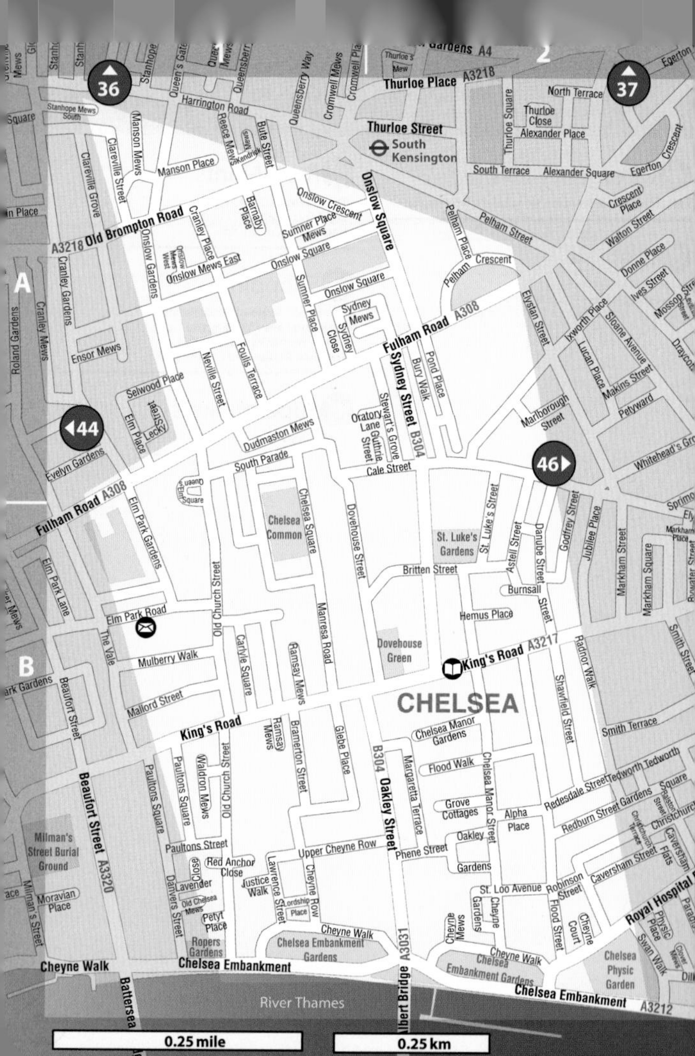

36
37
44
46
A
B
Thurloe Place A3218
Harrington Road
Thurloe Street
South Kensington
North Terrace
Thurloe Close
Alexander Place
Thurloe Square
South Terrace
Alexander Square
Egerton Crescent
Crescent Place
Pelham Street
Walton Street
Donne Place
Ives Street
Onslow Square
Onslow Crescent
Pelham Place
Pelham Crescent
Old Brompton Road
A3218
Manson Place
Manson Mews
Clareville Street
Clareville Grove
Cranley Place
Onslow Gardens
Onslow Mews East
Sumner Place Mews
Sumner Place
Sydney Mews
Sydney Close
Fulham Road A308
Sydney Street
Bury Walk
Pond Place
Elystan Street
Ixworth Place
Sloane Avenue
Lucan Place
Makins Street
Petyward
Marlborough Street
Whitehead's Grove
Cranley Gardens
Cranley Mews
Roland Gardens
Ensor Mews
Selwood Place
Neville Street
Foulis Terrace
Oratory Lane
Stewart's Grove
Guthrie Street
B304
Elm Place
Lecky Street
Dudmaston Mews
South Parade
Cale Street
Evelyn Gardens
Fulham Road A308
Elm Park Gardens
Queen's Elm Square
Chelsea Common
Chelsea Square
Dovehouse Street
St. Luke's Gardens
St. Luke's Street
Astell Street
Danube Street
Godfrey Street
Jubilee Place
Markham Street
Markham Square
Elm Park Lane
Britten Street
Burnsall Street
Elm Park Road
Old Church Street
Manresa Road
Hemus Place
The Vale
Mulberry Walk
Carlyle Square
Ramsay Mews
Dovehouse Green
King's Road A3217
Radnor Walk
Smith Street
Shawfield Street
CHELSEA
Beaufort Street
Mallord Street
King's Road
Chelsea Manor Gardens
Smith Terrace
Paultons Square
Waldron Mews
Bramerton Street
Glebe Place
Oakley Street
B304
Margaretta Terrace
Flood Walk
Chelsea Manor Street
Tedworth Square
Redesdale Street
Redburn Street
Grove Cottages
Alpha Place
Christchurch Street
Milman's Street Burial Ground
Beaufort Street A3320
Paultons Street
Upper Cheyne Row
Oakley Gardens
Phene Street
Red Anchor Close
Lavender Close
Justice Walk
Lawrence Street
Cheyne Row
Caversham Street
Moravian Place
Old Chelsea Mews
Petyt Place
Lordship Place
St. Loo Avenue
Robinson Street
Cheyne Gardens
Cheyne Mews
Flood Street
Cheyne Court
Royal Hospital Road
Physic Place
Swan Walk
Milman's Street
Danvers Street
Roper's Gardens
Cheyne Walk
Chelsea Embankment Gardens
A3031
Chelsea Physic Garden
Chelsea Embankment
Battersea
Albert Bridge
River Thames
A3212
0.25 mile
0.25 km

:helsea East is what Hollywood thinks all of London is like, full of dapper English chaps nd potential princesses. King's Road buzzes as it did when it spawned the Swinging '60s, nd foodies are spoiled around Cale Street. For a cheaper and sweeter taste of the area et to **The Hummingbird Bakery** for addictive oh-so-good cupcakes.

Cinemas

- **Cineworld Chelsea** • 279 King's Rd

Coffee

- **Caffe Nero** • 66 Old Brompton Rd
- **Starbucks** • 123 King's Rd

Libraries

- **Chelsea Library** • King's Rd

Post Offices

- **Elm Park** • 66 Elm Park Rd

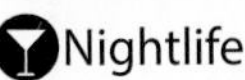

Nightlife

- **The Anglesea Arms** • 15 Selwood Terrace
- **Chelsea Potter** • 119 Kings Rd
- **The Pig's Ear** • 35 Old Church St

Restaurants

- **Chelsea Kitchen** • 451 Fulham Rd
- **Le Columbier** • 145 Dovehouse St
- **The Hummingbird Bakery** • 47 Old Brompton Rd
- **Made In Italy** • 249 King's Rd
- **My Old Dutch Pancake House** • 221 King's Rd
- **The Pig's Ear** • 35 Old Church St

Shopping

- **Anthropologie** • 131 King's Rd
- **British Red Cross Chelsea** • 69 Old Church St
- **Frock Me! Vintage Fashion Fair** • Chelsea Town Hall, Kings Rd
- **Nomad Books** • 781 Fulham Rd
- **Sweaty Betty** • 125 King's Rd

Supermarkets

- **Waitrose** • 196 King's Rd

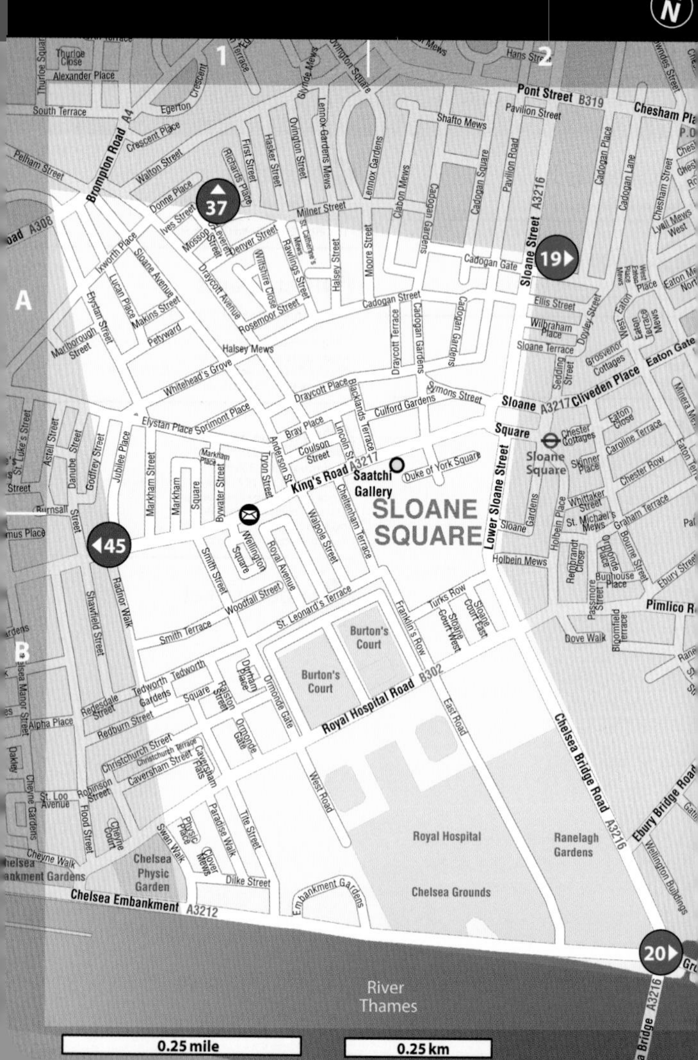

N
1
2
A
B
Thurloe Close
Alexander Place
South Terrace
Egerton Crescent
Crescent Place
Pelham Street
Brompton Road A4
Walton Street
Donne Place
Richards Place
37
First Street
Hasker Street
Ovington Street
Lennox Gardens Mews
Lennox Gardens
Ovington Square
Clabon Mews
Cadogan Gardens
Cadogan Square
Pavilion Road
Hans Street
Pont Street B319
Pavilion Street
Shafto Mews
Chesham Place
Cadogan Place
Cadogan Lane
Chesham Street
Lyall Mews West
Sloane Street A3216
19
Milner Street
Ives Street
Mossop Street
Denver Street
Rawlings Street
Halsey Street
Moore Street
Cadogan Gate
Ixworth Place
Sloane Avenue
Lucan Place
Makins Street
Draycott Avenue
Wiltshire Close
Rosemoor Street
Cadogan Street
Ellis Street
Wilbraham Place
Sloane Terrace
Elystan Street
Marlborough Street
Petyward
Halsey Mews
Whitehead's Grove
Draycott Terrace
Draycott Place
Blacklands Terrace
Culford Gardens
Symons Street
Sloane Square A3217
Cliveden Place
Eaton Gate
Elystan Place
Sprimont Place
Bray Place
Coulson Street
Lincoln St
Anderson St
Tryon Street
King's Road A3217
Saatchi Gallery
Duke of York Square
SLOANE SQUARE
Lower Sloane Street
Sloane Square
Chester Cottages
Eaton Close
Caroline Terrace
Skinner Place
Chester Row
Whittaker Street
Graham Terrace
St. Michael's Mews
Holbein Place
Sloane Gardens
Holbein Mews
Astell Street
Danube Street
Godfrey Street
Jubilee Place
Markham Street
Markham Place
Markham Square
Bywater Street
Burnsall Street
45
Wellington Square
Smith Street
Royal Avenue
Walpole Street
Cheltenham Terrace
Radnor Walk
Shawfield Street
Woodfall Street
St. Leonard's Terrace
Smith Terrace
Franklin's Row
Turks Row
Sloane Court West
Sloane Court East
Burton's Court
Royal Hospital Road B302
Tedworth Square
Tedworth Gardens
Redesdale Street
Redburn Street
Alpha Place
Durham Place
Ralston Street
Ormonde Gate
East Road
Chelsea Bridge Road A3216
Christchurch Street
Christchurch Terrace
Caversham Street
Caversham Flats
Robinson Street
St. Loo Avenue
Flood Street
Cheyne Court
Swan Walk
Physic Place
Paradise Walk
Tite Street
West Road
Royal Hospital
Ranelagh Gardens
Ebury Bridge Road
Wellington Buildings
Cheyne Walk
Chelsea Physic Garden
Clover Mews
Dilke Street
Embankment Gardens
Chelsea Grounds
Chelsea Embankment A3212
20
River Thames
Rembrandt Close
Ormonde Place
Bourne Street
Bunhouse Place
Passmore Street
Bloomfield Terrace
Dove Walk
Pimlico Road
Ebury Street
Sedding Street
Grosvenor Cottages
Dorley Street
West Eaton Place
Eaton Terrace
Eaton Mews North
0.25 mile
0.25 km

Sloane Square

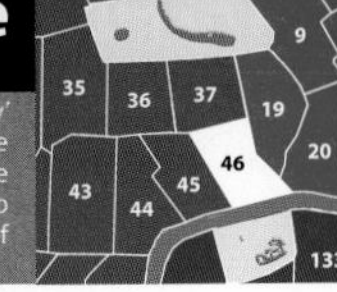

You've got to love a place that spawns an adjective. If you've never met any 'Sloaney' types and are curious as to why the whole of London gets so riled about them, take a walk along the King's Road and observe. **Peter Jones** stands tall over the square and offers everything you didn't know you wanted. This rather beautiful 'nabe also hosts some bank-breaking eateries, such as **Bibendum**, as well as its fare share of cultural fair—the **Saatchi Gallery** being the finest example.

Coffee

- **Eat.** • 82 King's Rd
- **Pret A Manger** • 80 King's Rd
- **Starbucks** • 65 Sloane Ave
- **Starbucks** • 128 King's Rd
- **Tomtom Coffee House** • 114 Ebury St

Landmarks

- **Saatchi Gallery** • Duke of York HQ, King's Rd

Post Offices

- **Kings Walk** • 122 King's Rd

Restaurants

- **The Admiral Codrington** • 17 Mossop St
- **Bibendum Restaurant & Oyster Bar** • 81 Fulham Rd
- **Foxtrot Oscar** • 79 Royal Hospital Rd
- **The Good Life Eatery** • 59 Sloane Ave
- **Restaurant Gordon Ramsay** • 68 Royal Hospital Rd

Shopping

- **Partridges** • 2 Duke of York Sq
- **Peter Jones** • Sloane Sq
- **Rigby & Peller** • 13 Kings Rd
- **Space NK Apothecary** • 307 King's Rd

Supermarkets

- **Sainsbury's** • 75 Sloane Ave

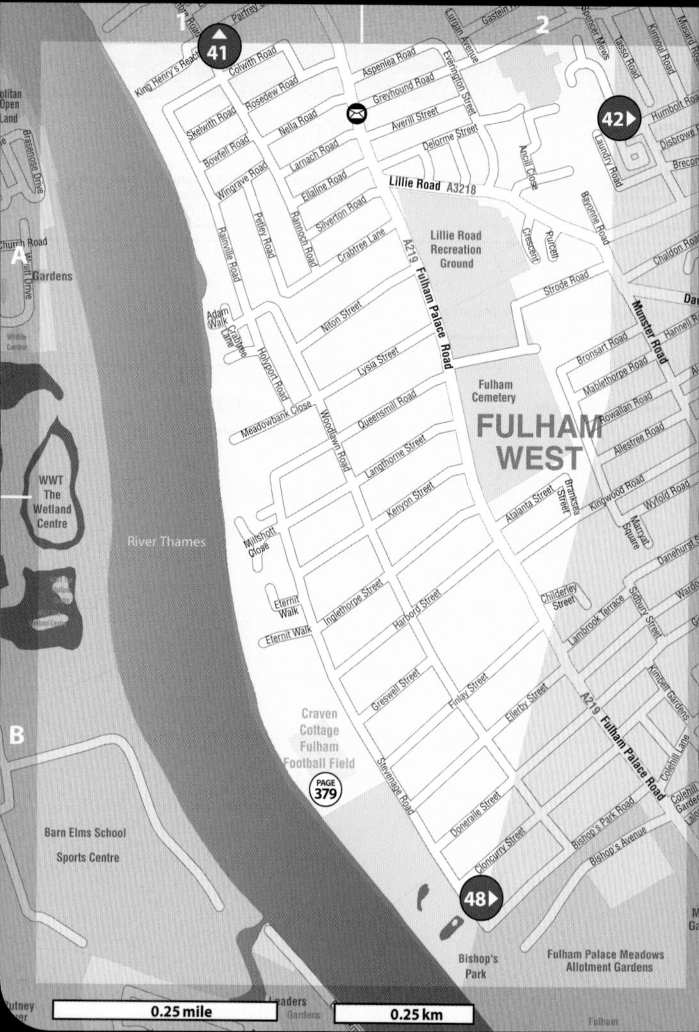

Map 47 • Fulham (West)

FULHAM WEST

Lillie Road A3218

A219 Fulham Palace Road

Lillie Road Recreation Ground

Fulham Cemetery

River Thames

WWT The Wetland Centre

Craven Cottage Fulham Football Field

PAGE 379

Barn Elms School

Sports Centre

Bishop's Park

Fulham Palace Meadows Allotment Gardens

41

42

48

0.25 mile

0.25 km

This area is an estate agent's wet dream. Leafy, well heeled, on the river, and made for families. Catch the great English game at **Craven Cottage** before making the most of the riverside and grabbing a pint at **The Crabtree Tavern**. Now that you're tipsy, head to **The River Café** where you'll feel less pained shelling out for top-notch, dead-posh grub.

Nightlife

• **The Crabtree Tavern** • Rainville Rd

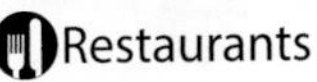

Restaurants

• **The River Café** • Thames Wharf, Rainville Rd

Post Offices

• **Fulham Palace Road** • 185 Fulham Palace Rd

Supermarkets

• **Sainsbury's** • 179 Fulham Palace Rd

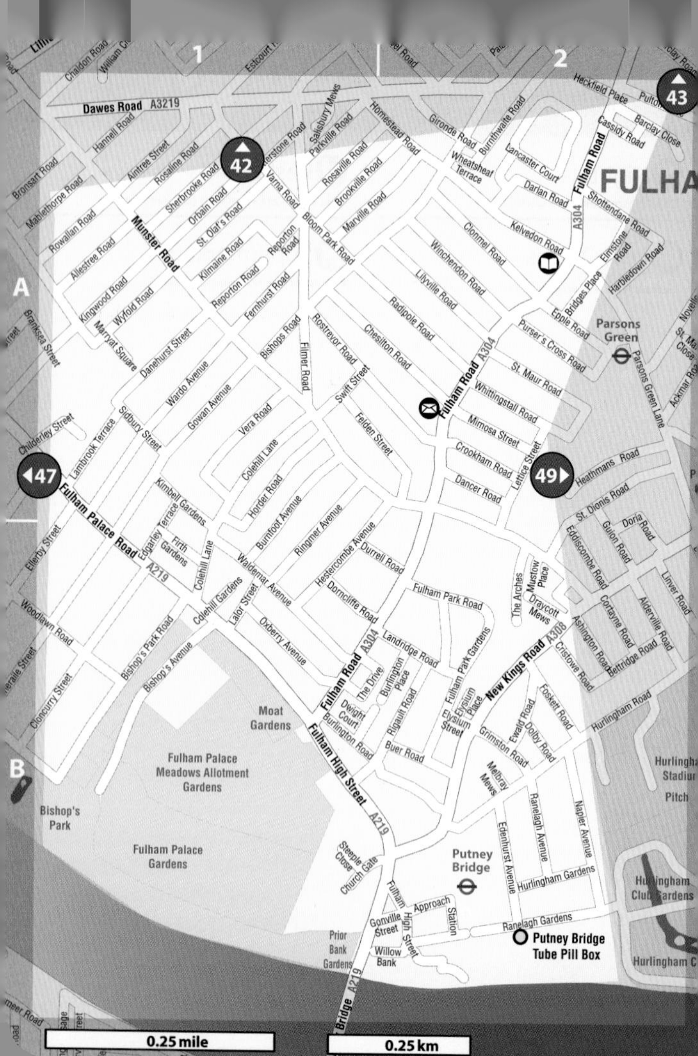

Dawes Road
A3219
Munster Road
Fulham Road
A304
FULHAM
Parsons Green
Fulham Palace Road
A219
New Kings Road
A308
Moat Gardens
Fulham Palace Meadows Allotment Gardens
Bishop's Park
Fulham Palace Gardens
Fulham High Street
Putney Bridge
Putney Bridge Tube Pill Box
Hurlingham Club Gardens
0.25 mile
0.25 km
42
43
47
49

This part of town is rather lovely and rather boring in equal measure. Expensive homes belonging to Chelsea FC players sit alongside the often overlooked romantic beauty of Fulham Palace. On the main drag of Fulham High Street is **Hurlingham Books** with its walls stacked high with texts on anything and everything. With not much else going on away from here we suggest contemplating life while staring out at the mighty Thames in Fulham Palace Gardens. When you're done then warm up in their elegant tearoom, **The Drawing Room**.

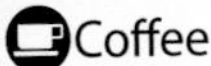

Coffee

- **Local Hero** • 640 Fulham Rd
- **Tinto Coffee** • 411 Fulham Palace Rd

Landmarks

- **Putney Bridge Tube Pill Box** • Putney Bridge Station

Libraries

- **Fulham Library** • 598 Fulham Rd

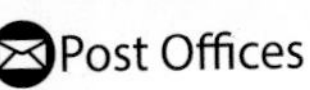

Post Offices

- **Fulham** • 815 Fulham Rd

Restaurants

- **Drawing Room Cafe** • Bishop's Ave
- **Fisher's Chips** • 19 Fulham High St
- **Royal China** • 805 Fulham Rd

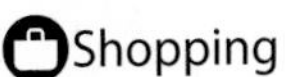

Shopping

- **Hurlingham Books** • 91 Fulham High St

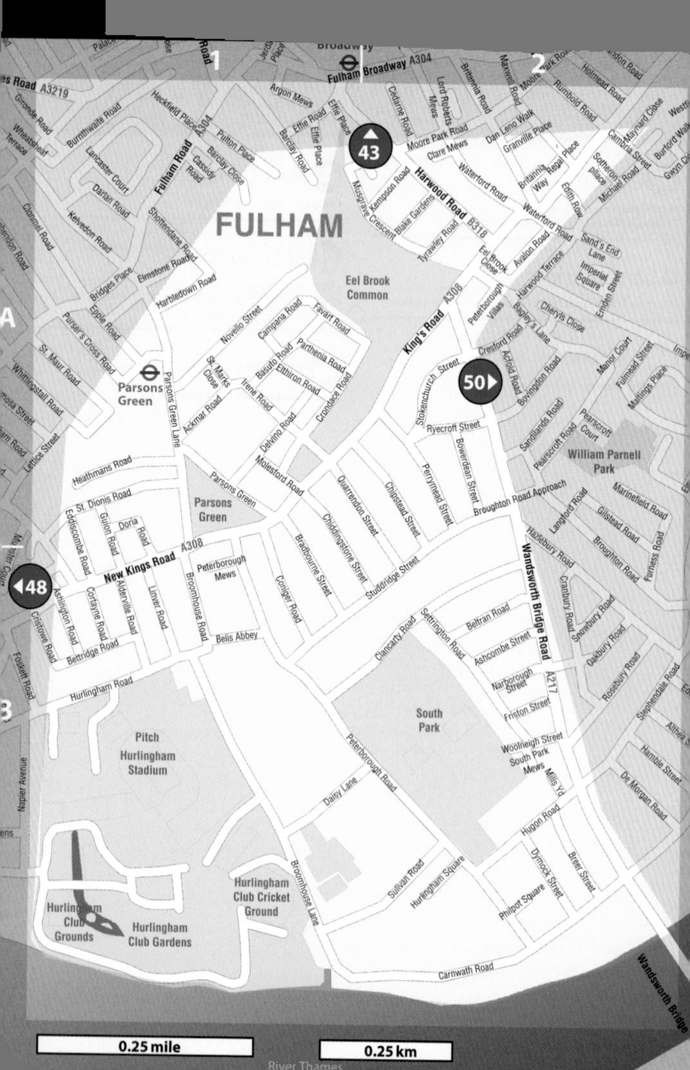
1
2
A
B
FULHAM
Fulham Broadway A304
43
50
48
Eel Brook Common
Parsons Green
Parsons Green
William Parnell Park
South Park
Pitch
Hurlingham Stadium
Hurlingham Club Cricket Ground
Hurlingham Club Grounds
Hurlingham Club Gardens
Wandsworth Bridge
River Thames
0.25 mile
0.25 km
King's Road
A308
New Kings Road
A308
Harwood Road
B318
Wandsworth Bridge Road
A217
Fulham Road
A304
Hurlingham Road
Carnwath Road
Peterborough Road
Broomhouse Lane
Broomhouse Road
Parsons Green Lane
Moore Park Road
Waterford Road
Heckfield Place
Pulton Place
Barclay Close
Cassidy Road
Shottendane Road
Elmstone Road
Harbledown Road
Bridges Place
Epple Road
Purser's Cross Road
St. Maur Road
Whittingstall Road
Lettice Street
Heathmans Road
St. Dionis Road
Eddiscombe Road
Guion Road
Doria Road
Ashington Road
Cortayne Road
Alderville Road
Linver Road
Bettridge Road
Cristowe Road
Peterborough Mews
Belis Abbey
Coniger Road
Bradbourne Street
Chiddingstone Street
Quarrendon Street
Chipstead Street
Perrymead Street
Bowerdean Street
Ryecroft Street
Stokenchurch Street
Studdridge Street
Broughton Road Approach
Molesford Road
Delvino Road
Irene Road
Ackmar Road
St Marks Close
Novello Street
Campana Road
Favart Road
Parthenia Road
Basuto Road
Elthiron Road
Crondace Road
Musgrave Crescent
Kempson Road
Blake Gardens
Tyrawley Road
Eel Brook Close
Avalon Road
Peterborough Villas
Cresford Road
Acfold Road
Bovingdon Road
Sandilands Road
Pearscroft Road
Pearscroft Court
Langford Road
Hazlebury Road
Cranbury Road
Marinefield Road
Gilstead Road
Broughton Road
Furness Road
Snowbury Road
Oakbury Road
Rosebury Road
Stephendale Road
Hamble Street
De Morgan Road
Settrington Road
Clancarty Road
Beltran Road
Ashcombe Street
Narborough Street
Friston Street
Woolneigh Street
South Park Mews
Mills Yd
Hugon Road
Dymock Street
Breer Street
Philpot Square
Hurlingham Square
Sulivan Road
Daisy Lane
Argon Mews
Effie Road
Effie Place
Barclay Road
Cedarne Road
Lord Roberts Mews
Britannia Road
Maxwell Road
Clare Mews
Dan Leno Walk
Granville Place
Britannia Way
Regal Place
Edith Row
Sand's End Lane
Imperial Square
Emden Street
Harwood Terrace
Cheryls Close
Bagley's Lane
Manor Court
Fulmead Street
Maltings Place
Rumbold Road
Holmead Road
Cambria Street
Maynard Close
Sotheron Place
Michael Road
Burnthwaite Road
Lancaster Court
Darlan Road
Kelvedon Road
Clonmel Road
Gironde Road
Wheatsheaf Terrace
Foskett Road
Napier Avenue

You know you're in a classy neighbourhood when the kebab house (**Kebab Kid**) gets people travelling across London. This part of town ain't cheap and unless you're looking for a sedate Sunday lunch you'll most likely not find yourself here. If, however, you are looking for a chow down then **The White Horse** (known locally as the 'Sloany Pony') is the place to be, hands down. Otherwise head to charming **Duke On The Green** for a pint in style—they even show the footy!

Coffee

- **Caffe Nero** • 142 Wandsworth Bridge Rd
- **Starbucks** • 95 Wandsworth Bridge Rd

Nightlife

- **Amuse Bouche** • 51 Parsons Green Ln
- **Duke on the Green** • 235 New Kings Rd
- **The White Horse** • 1 Parson's Green Ln

Restaurants

- **Kebab Kid** • 90 New Kings Rd
- **Koji** • 58 New King's Rd
- **Little H** • 267 New Kings Rd
- **Tendido Cuatro** • 108 New King's Rd

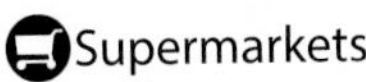

Supermarkets

- **Tesco** • 601 King's Rd

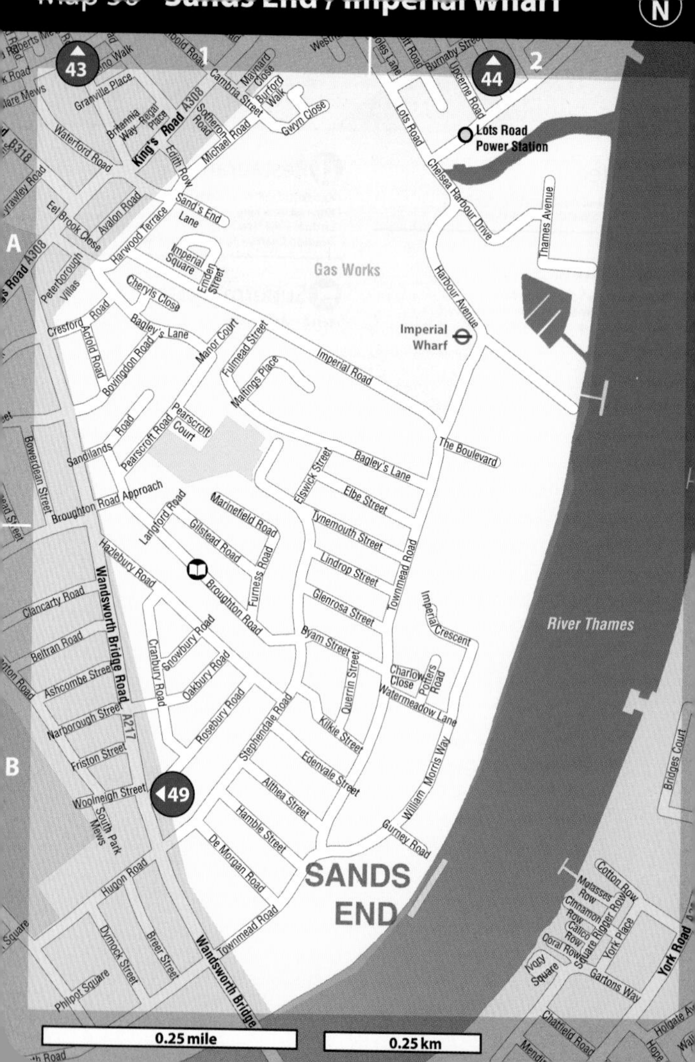

N
43
44
49
1
2
A
B
Lots Road Power Station
Imperial Wharf
Gas Works
River Thames
SANDS END
King's Road A308
Wandsworth Bridge Road A217
Wandsworth Bridge
Granville Place
Britannia Way
Regal Place
Waterford Road
Cambria Street
Maynard Close
Burford Walk
Gwyn Close
Sotheron Road
Michael Road
Edith Row
Sand's End Lane
Harwood Terrace
Avalon Road
Eel Brook Close
Imperial Square
Emden Street
Peterborough Villas
Cheryls Close
Cresford Road
Acfold Road
Bagley's Lane
Bovingdon Road
Manor Court
Fulmead Street
Maltings Place
Imperial Road
Pearscroft Court
Pearscroft Road
Sandilands Road
Broughton Road Approach
Bowerdean Street
Langford Road
Gilstead Road
Marinefield Road
Furness Road
Broughton Road
Hazlebury Road
Elswick Street
Elbe Street
Tynemouth Street
Lindrop Street
Glenrosa Street
Byam Street
Townmead Road
Imperial Crescent
The Boulevard
Harbour Avenue
Chelsea Harbour Drive
Thames Avenue
Lots Road
Upcerne Road
Burnaby Street
Clancarty Road
Beltran Road
Ashcombe Street
Narborough Street
Friston Street
Woolneigh Street
South Park Mews
Cranbury Road
Snowbury Road
Oakbury Road
Rosebury Road
Stephendale Road
Querrin Street
Kilkie Street
Charlow Close
Potters Road
Watermeadow Lane
William Morris Way
Edenvale Street
Althea Street
Hamble Street
De Morgan Road
Gurney Road
Hugon Road
Dymock Street
Breer Street
Philpot Square
Bridges Court
Cotton Row
Molasses Row
Cinnamon Row
Calico Row
Rigger Row
Square
Coral Row
Ivory Square
York Place
Gartons Way
York Road
Chatfield Road
0.25 mile
0.25 km

Sands End / Imperial Wharf

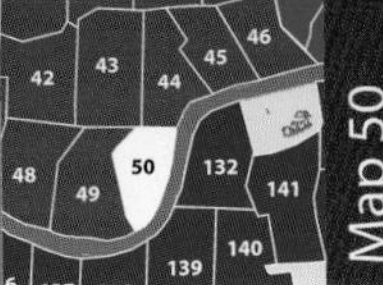

Map 50

Time was, if you asked any Londoner where Sands End is you'd receive a blank look and a bemused 'you wot?' These days the area sees a lot more foot traffic thanks to a newish London Overground stop and the development of Imperial Wharf. Jazz seems to be a major draw to the area with the autumn Jazz Festival and the **606 Club** on Lots Road.

Landmarks

- **Lots Road Power Station** • 27 Lots Rd

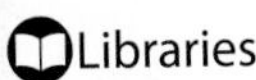

Libraries

- **Sands End Library** • 59 Broughton Rd

Nightlife

- **606 Club** • 90 Lots Rd

Restaurants

- **Sands End** • 135 Stephendale Rd
- **Yamal Alshem** • 5 The Blvd

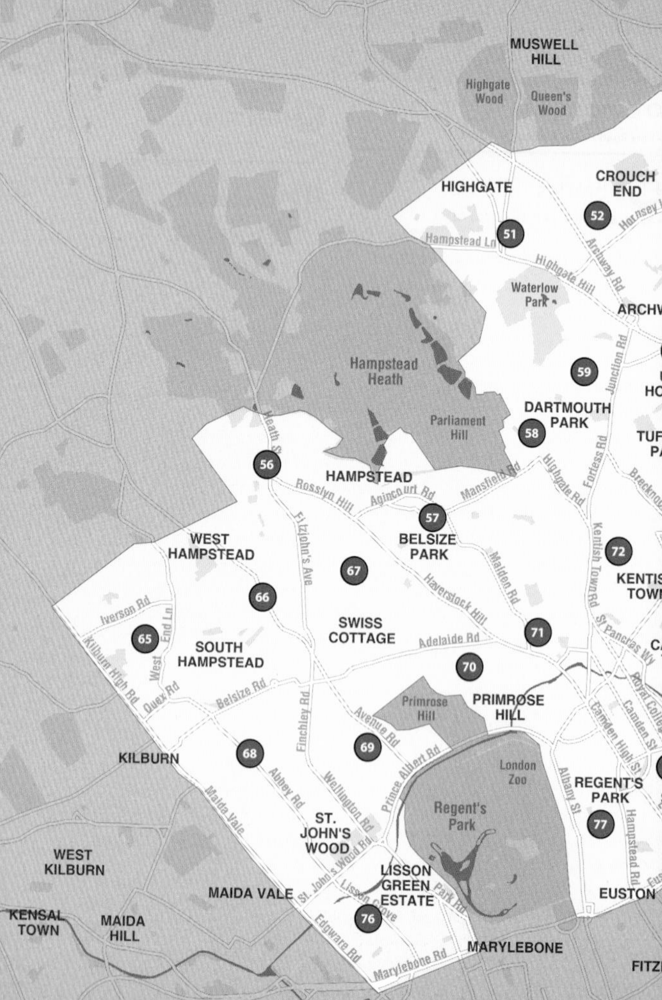

MUSWELL HILL
Highgate Wood
Queen's Wood
HIGHGATE
CROUCH END
52
Hornsey Ln
51
Hampstead Ln
Archway Rd
Highgate Hill
Waterlow Park
ARCHWA
Junction Rd
59
Hampstead Heath
Parliament Hill
DARTMOUTH PARK
58
TUFN PA
Heath St
56
HAMPSTEAD
Rosslyn Hill
Agincourt Rd
Mansfield Rd
Highgate Rd
Fortess Rd
Brecknock
57
BELSIZE PARK
Kentish Town Rd
72
KENTISH TOWN
WEST HAMPSTEAD
Fitzjohn's Ave
67
Maiden Rd
Haverstock Hill
66
Iverson Rd
West End Ln
65
SWISS COTTAGE
71
St Pancras Wy
Kilburn High Rd
SOUTH HAMPSTEAD
Adelaide Rd
70
Quex Rd
Belsize Rd
Finchley Rd
Avenue Rd
Primrose Hill
PRIMROSE HILL
Camden High St
Camden St
Royal College
KILBURN
68
69
Prince Albert Rd
London Zoo
Albany St
REGENT'S PARK
Maida Vale
Abbey Rd
Wellington Rd
Regent's Park
77
Hampstead Rd
ST. JOHN'S WOOD
St. John's Wood Rd
WEST KILBURN
LISSON GREEN ESTATE
MAIDA VALE
Lisson Grove
Park Rd
EUSTON
KENSAL TOWN
MAIDA HILL
76
Edgware Rd
Marylebone Rd
MARYLEBONE
FITZR

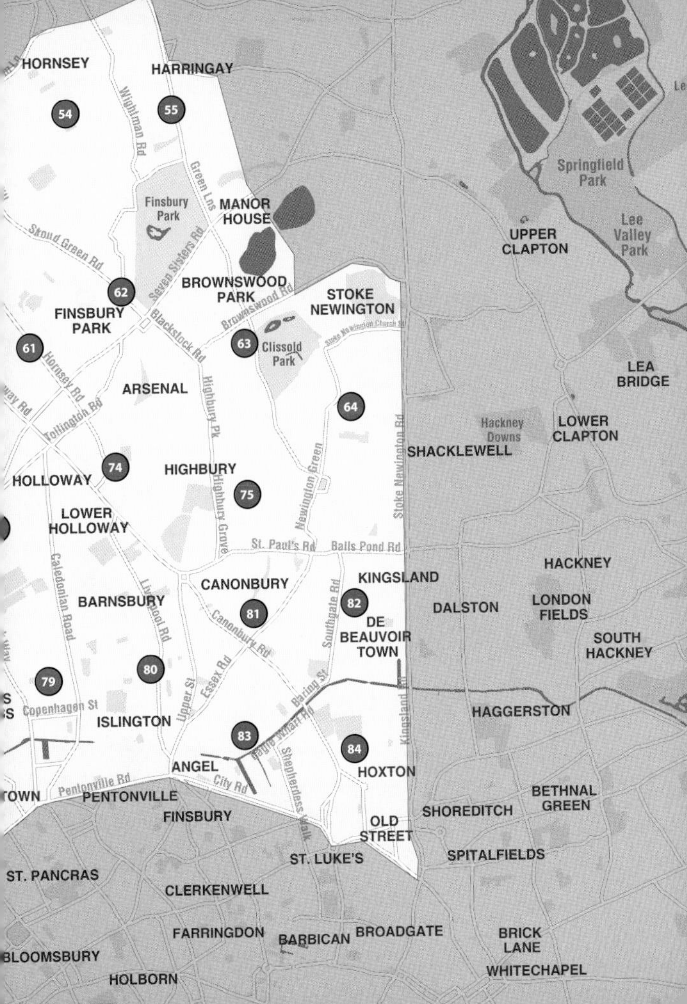
HORNSEY
HARRINGAY
54
55
Wightman Rd
Green Lns
Finsbury Park
MANOR HOUSE
Stroud Green Rd
Seven Sisters Rd
BROWNSWOOD PARK
Brownswood Rd
STOKE NEWINGTON
Stoke Newington Church St
62
FINSBURY PARK
Blackstock Rd
63
Clissold Park
61
Hornsey Rd
ARSENAL
Highbury Pk
64
Tollington Rd
74
HOLLOWAY
HIGHBURY
75
Newington Green
Stoke Newington Rd
LOWER HOLLOWAY
Highbury Grove
St. Paul's Rd
Balls Pond Rd
Caledonian Road
CANONBURY
KINGSLAND
BARNSBURY
Liverpool Rd
81
82
Southgate Rd
Canonbury Rd
DE BEAUVOIR TOWN
80
79
Essex Rd
Upper St
Baring St
Copenhagen St
ISLINGTON
Eagle Wharf Rd
Shepherdess Walk
83
84
Kingsland Rd
ANGEL
HOXTON
City Rd
Pentonville Rd
TOWN
PENTONVILLE
FINSBURY
OLD STREET
ST. LUKE'S
ST. PANCRAS
CLERKENWELL
FARRINGDON
BARBICAN
BROADGATE
BLOOMSBURY
HOLBORN
Springfield Park
Lee
UPPER CLAPTON
Lee Valley Park
LEA BRIDGE
Hackney Downs
LOWER CLAPTON
SHACKLEWELL
HACKNEY
DALSTON
LONDON FIELDS
SOUTH HACKNEY
HAGGERSTON
SHOREDITCH
BETHNAL GREEN
SPITALFIELDS
BRICK LANE
WHITECHAPEL

Map 51 • Highgate

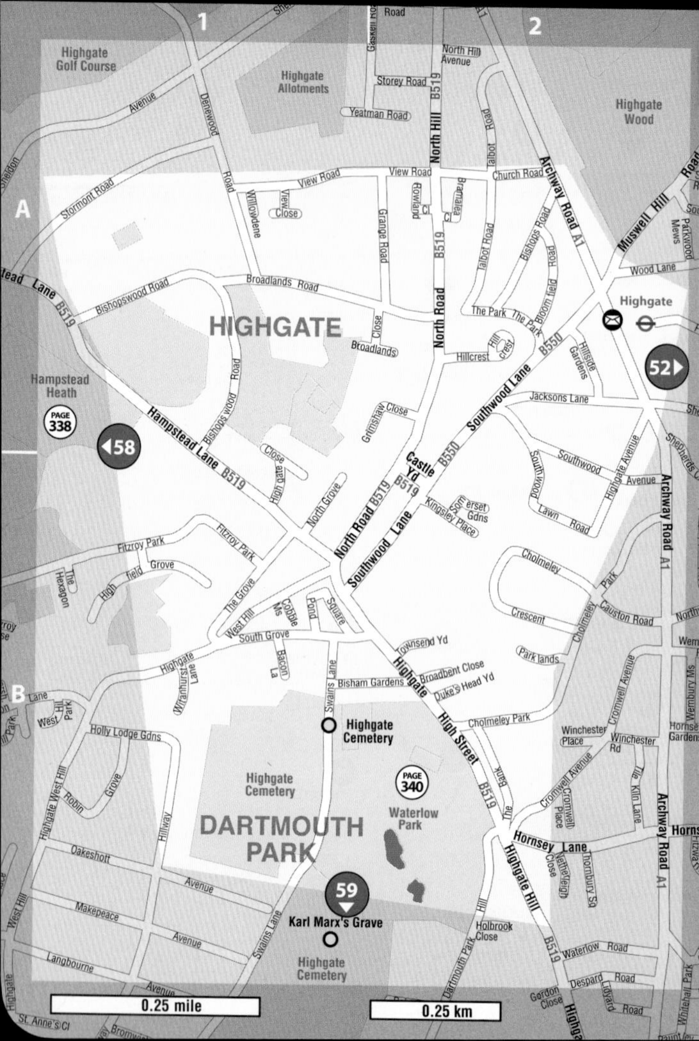

N

1
2
A
B

Highgate Golf Course
Highgate Allotments
Highgate Wood
Road
Storey Road
Yeatman Road
North Hill Avenue
North Hill B519
Avenue
Denewood Road
View Road
Church Road
Talbot Road
Archway Road A1
Muswell Hill Road
Parkwood Mews
Wood Lane
Stormont Road
Willowdene
View Close
Grange Road
Rowland Cl
Bramalea Cl
Talbot Road
Bishops Road
Broadlands Road
Bishopswood Road
Hampstead Lane B519
HIGHGATE
Broadlands Close
North Road B519
The Park
Bloomfield Road
Hill crest
Hillcrest
B550
Hillside Gardens
Highgate
Hampstead Heath
PAGE 338
58
52
Jacksons Lane
Southwood Lane
Grimshaw Close
Bishopswood Road
Shepherds Cl
Southwood Avenue
Highgate Avenue
Southwood Lawn Road
Hampstead Lane B519
Close
Highgate Close
North Grove
Castle Yd
B550
North Road B519
Southwood Lane
Somerset Gdns
Kingsley Place
Archway Road A1
Fitzroy Park
Fitzroy Park
Highfield Grove
The Hexagon
The Grove
Cholmeley Park
Cholmeley Crescent
Causton Road
Cobble Ms
Pond Square
West Hill
South Grove
Highgate West Hill
Witanhurst Lane
Bacon La
Swains Lane
Townsend Yd
Highgate High Street
Broadbent Close
Bisham Gardens
Duke's Head Yd
Park lands
Cromwell Avenue
Cholmeley Park
Winchester Place
Winchester Rd
Wembury Ms
Hornsey Gardens
West Hill Park
Holly Lodge Gdns
Highgate Cemetery
Highgate Cemetery
PAGE 340
Robin Grove
Hillway
Waterlow Park
DARTMOUTH PARK
Bank
The Bank
B519
Cromwell Place
Kiln Lane
Hornsey Lane
Nettleleigh Close
Thornbury Sq
Archway Road A1
Oakeshott Avenue
Makepeace Avenue
59
Karl Marx's Grave
Highgate Cemetery
Swains Lane
Highgate Hill
Hill
Holbrook Close
Dartmouth Park Hill
B519
Waterlow Road
Despard Road
Langbourne Avenue
Gordon Close
Lidyard Road
Whitehall Park
St. Anne's Cl
0.25 mile
0.25 km

Highgate

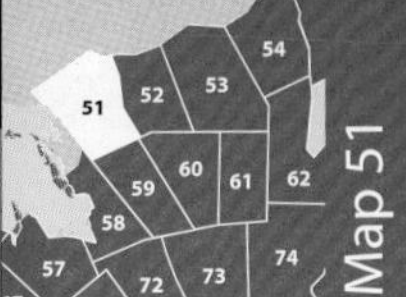

On the cusp of north London you'll find the little suburban gem that is Highgate. Hemmed in by parks, woods and a golf course, the area is an escapist paradise from the chaos of the city, and its well-heeled residents' plush fur is surprisingly—and pleasantly—soft to the touch.

Coffee

- **Caffe Nero** • 62 Highgate High St
- **Costa** • 66 Highgate High St

Landmarks

- **Highgate Cemetery** • 1 Swain's Ln
- **Karl Marx's Grave** • Highgate Cemetry

Nightlife

- **The Angel Inn** • 37 Highgate High St
- **The Boogaloo** • 312 Archway Rd
- **The Flask** • 77 Highgate West Hill
- **Prince Of Wales** • 53 Highgate High St
- **The Woodman** • 414 Archway Rd
- **The Wrestlers** • 98 North Rd

Post Offices

- **Highgate Near Station** • 361 Archway Rd

Restaurants

- **The Bull** • 13 North Hill Ave
- **Papa Del's** • 347 Archway Rd
- **The Red Lion & Sun** • 25 North Rd

Shopping

- **Highgate Butchers** • 76 Highgate High St
- **Hops N Pops** • 389 Archway Rd
- **Mind** • 329 Archway Rd
- **Oxfam** • 47 Highgate High St
- **Walter Castellazzo Design** • 84 Highgate High St
- **Wild Guitars** • 393 Archway Rd

1
2
Wood
Shepherd's Hill Allotments
Highgate
Priory Gardens
Shepherds Hill
Shepherds Hill
Shepherds Cl
Broughton Gardens
Hill Gate Walk
CROUCH END
Jacksons Lane
Holmesdale Rd
Stanhope Road
Hurst Avenue
Stanhope Gardens
Southwood Avenue
Highgate Avenue
Archway Road A1
Orchard Mews
Holmesdale Road
Orchard Road
Claremont Road
Coolhurst Lawn Tennis & Squash Rackets Club
Lawn Road
Northwood Road
Parkland Walk Nature Reseverve
Cholmeley Crescent
Cholmeley Park
Causton Road
Milton Park
Avenue Road
51
53
Cholmeley Crescent
Wembury Road
Langdon Park Road
Milton Avenue
Milton Road
Milton Park
Parkgate Mews
Stanhope Road
Maybury Ms
Wychwood End
Ridgeway Gardens
Roden Court
Cromwell Avenue
Wembury Mews
Parklands
Hornsey Lane Gardens
Hornsey Lane Gardens
Tudor Close
Hornsey Lane Gardens
Ridings Close
Oldfield Mews
Winchester Rd
Tile Kiln Lane
Archway Road A1
Hornsey Lane B540
Ashmount Road
Hazellville Road
Cholmeley Park
Winchester Place
Cromwell Avenue
Cromwell Pl
Hornsey Lane B540
Suicide Bridge
Gresley Road
Dresden Road
Cressida Road
Fitzwarren Gardens
The Bank
High Street B519
Hornsey Lane B540
Thornbury Sq
Netherleigh Cl
Park
Cheverton Road
Highgate Hill B519
Whitehall
Gladsmuir Road
Gladsmuir Road
Cardinals Way
Cardinals Way
Pilgrims Way
Cardinals Way
Cardinals Way
Harberton Road
Archway Road A1
Waterlow Road
60
Parolles Road
Cressida Road
Hillside Park
St. Johns Way
Holbrook Close
Despard Road
Lidyard Road
Whitehall Park
Prospero Road
Dartmouth Park Hill
Gordon Close
Highgate Hill
Pauntley Street
Miranda Road
Lysander Mews
Lysander Grove
Duncombe Road
0.25 mile
0.25 km

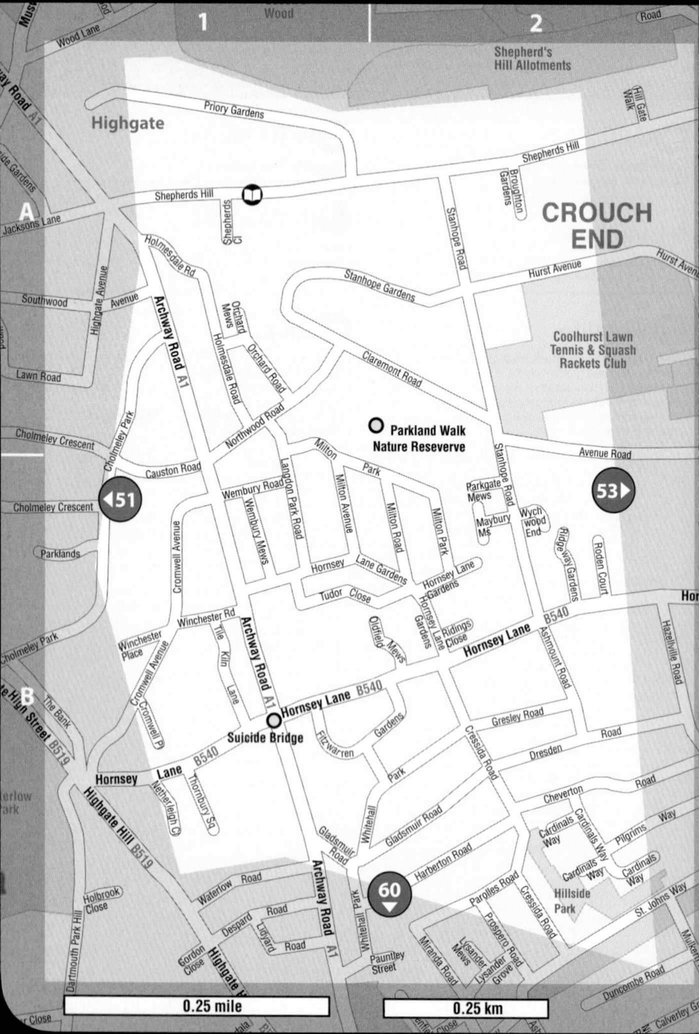

Something unexpected is happening here. Designer boutiques keep popping up; fashion labels we've never even heard of—cafés so fashionably quirky they should really be in Shoreditch. But real change takes time and at night this becomes even more obvious.

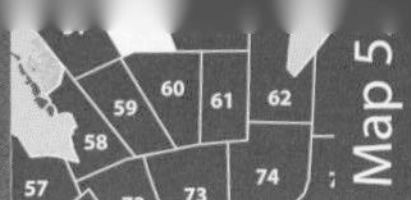

Landmarks

- **Parkland Walk Nature Reserve** • Parkland Walk
- **Suicide Bridge** • Hornsey Ln & Archway Rd

Libraries

- **London Mennonite Centre Library** • 14 Shepherds Hill Heights

Restaurants

- **Bengal Berties** • 172 Archway Rd
- **Tootoomoo Highgate** • 230 Archway Rd

Shopping

- **Pax Guns** • 166 Archway Rd

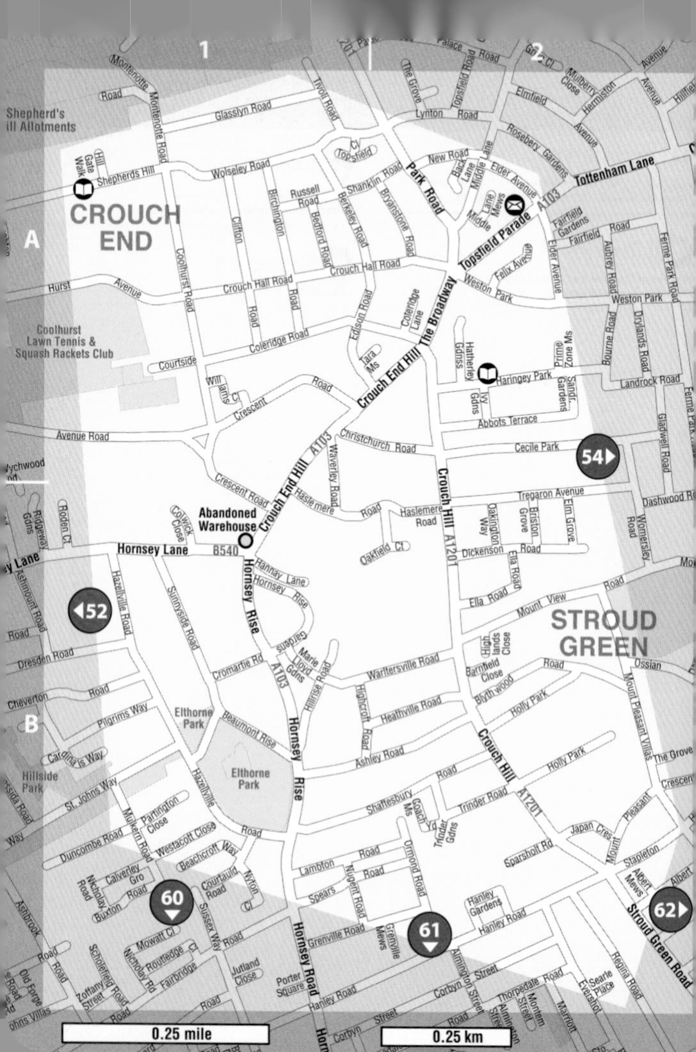

1
2
A
B
CROUCH END
STROUD GREEN
Shepherd's Hill Allotments
Coolhurst Lawn Tennis & Squash Rackets Club
Abandoned Warehouse
Elthorne Park
Hillside Park
Shepherds Hill
Montenotte Road
Glasslyn Road
Tivoli Road
The Grove
Topsfield Road
Lynton Road
Elmfield
Rosebery Gardens
Tottenham Lane
Wolseley Road
New Road
Park Road
Shanklin Road
Russell Road
Birchington Road
Clifton Road
Bedford Road
Berkeley Road
Bryanstone Road
Elder Avenue
Topsfield Parade
Middle Lane
Crouch Hall Road
Coolhurst Road
Hurst Avenue
Coleridge Road
Edison Road
Coleridge Lane
The Broadway
Weston Park
Felix Avenue
Fairfield Gardens
Fairfield Road
Aubrey Road
Ferme Park Road
Bourne Road
Drylands Road
Landrock Road
Courtside
Crescent Road
Crouch End Hill
Hatherley Gdns
Haringey Park
Prime Zone Ms
Abbots Terrace
Cecile Park
Avenue Road
Christchurch Road
Waverley Road
Haslemere Road
Crouch Hill
Tregaron Avenue
Oakington Way
Briston Grove
Elm Grove
Dashwood Rd
Gladwell Road
Womersley Road
Hornsey Lane
B540
A103
A1201
Hornsey Rise
Hannay Lane
Oakfield Ct
Dickenson Road
Ella Road
Mount View Road
Hazellville Road
Sunnyside Road
Cromartie Rd
Warltersville Road
Highlands Close
Barnfield Close
Blythwood
Holly Park
Ossian Road
Mount Pleasant Villas
Dresden Road
Cheverton Road
Pilgrims Way
Beaumont Rise
Highcroft Road
Heathville Road
Hillrise Road
Ashley Road
Cardinals Way
St. Johns Way
Shaftesbury Road
Trinder Road
Japan Cres
Mount Pleasant
Duncombe Road
Mulkern Road
Partington Close
Westacott Close
Beachcroft Way
Courtauld Road
Nyton Cl
Lambton Road
Nugent Road
Ormond Road
Sparsholt Rd
Stapleton
Albert Mews
Calverley Gro
Nicholay Road
Buxton Road
Sussex Way
Hornsey Road
Grenville Road
Grenville Mews
Hanley Gardens
Hanley Road
Stroud Green Road
Mowatt Cl
Routledge Cl
Fairbridge Road
Scholefield Road
Zoffany Street
Jutland Close
Porter Square
Almington Street
Corbyn Street
Thorpedale Road
Montem Street
Marriott
Evershot
Searle Place
Regina Road
Ashbrook
Old Forge Road
Johns Villas
52
54
60
61
62
0.25 mile
0.25 km

rouch End gets a bit of a bad rap. It's boring, people say. Just prams and iiddle-class media types. But, you know, it could be a lot worse. It's safe, with lenty of decent pubs (**The King's Head**), eateries (**Banners**) and a great record hop (**Flashback**). It might be low on the hipster scale, but for plain ol' good vin' it ticks all the boxes.

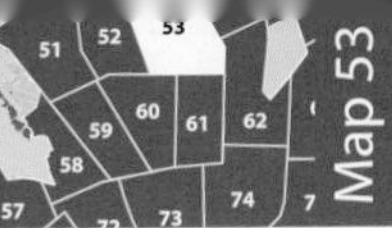

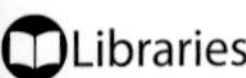

Landmarks

- **Abandoned Warehouse** • Parkland Walk & Crouch End Hill

Libraries

- **Highgate Library** • 1 Shepherds Hill
- **Hornsey Library** • Haringey Park

Nightlife

- **Harringay Arms** • 153 Crouch Hill
- **The King's Head** • 2 Crouch End Hill
- **The Queens Pub & Dining Rooms** • 26 Broadway Parade
- **Stapleton Tavern** • 2 Crouch Hill

Post Offices

- **Crouch End** • 28 Topsfield Parade

Restaurants

- **Banners** • 21 Park Rd
- **Bistro Aix** • 54 Topsfield Parade
- **Jai Krishna** • 161 Stroud Green Rd
- **The King's Head** • 2 Crouch End Hill
- **Wow Simply Japanese** • 18 Crouch End Hill

Shopping

- **Flashback** • 144 Crouch Hill
- **Haelen Centre** • 41 The Broadway
- **Organic Food** • 196 Stroud Green Rd
- **Soup Dragon** • 27 Topsfield Parade
- **Walter Purkis And Sons** • 17 The Broadway

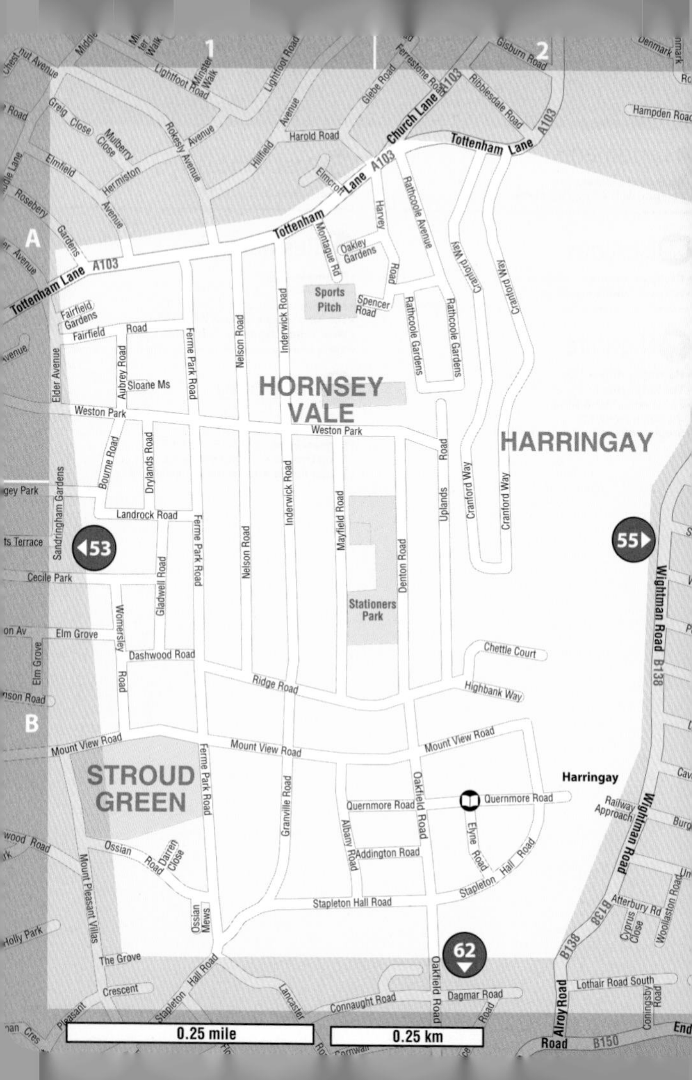

HORNSEY
VALE
HARRINGAY
STROUD
GREEN
Tottenham Lane
A103
Church Lane
Weston Park
Ferme Park Road
Nelson Road
Inderwick Road
Mayfield Road
Denton Road
Uplands Road
Cranford Way
Stationers
Park
Sports
Pitch
Ridge Road
Mount View Road
Quernmore Road
Oakfield Road
Stapleton Hall Road
Wightman Road
B138
Harringay
53
55
62
0.25 mile
0.25 km

Hornsey

Jnless you live in Hornsey, if you're in Hornsey, your bus has probably broken own. In this dystopian residential area you'll be lucky to find a tuft of grass let lone a shop. A modicum of life exist up at Tottenham Lane, but that's pretty nuch Crouch End. **Ridge Cafe** is worth a stop for a cup of coffee and you can vatch sport at the unpretentious **Hope & Anchor**.

Libraries

- **Stroud Green Library** • Quernmore Rd

Nightlife

- **The Hope & Anchor** • 128 Tottenham Ln

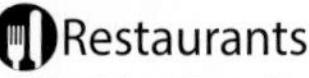

Restaurants

- **Ridge Cafe** • 97 Tottenham Ln
- **Sumak** • 141 Tottenham Ln

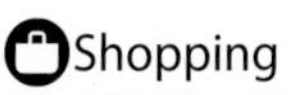

Shopping

- **Micycle N4** • 8 Ferme Park Rd

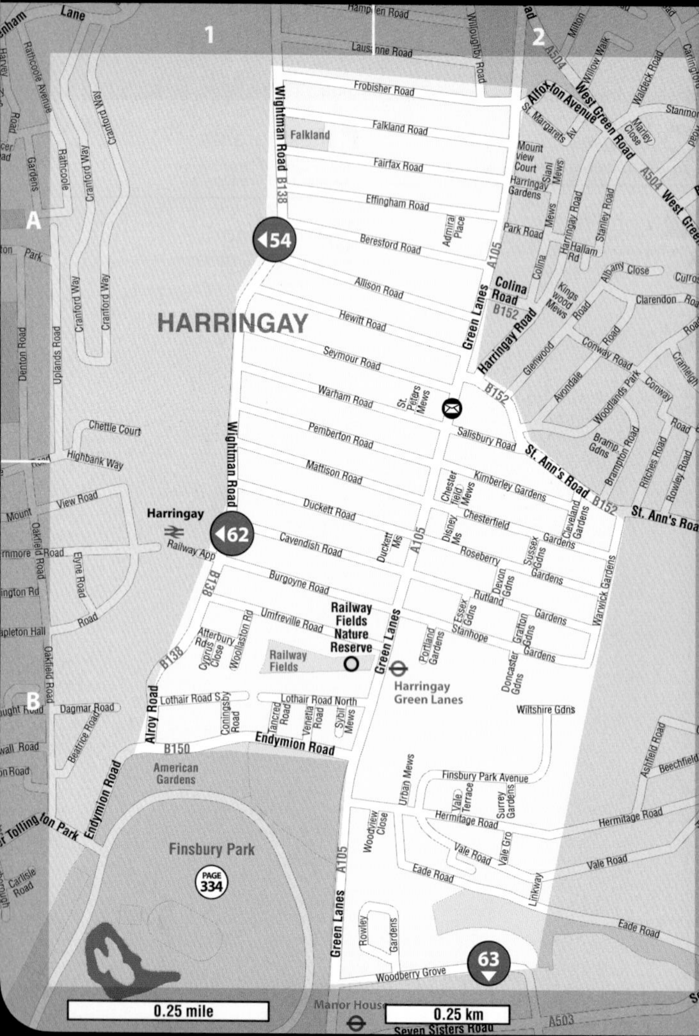

54
62
63
PAGE 334

Harringay

Map 55

reen Lanes was once an endless strip of restaurants which although good, meant that ne only dinner option was Turkish. The last few years have seen so many new openings, 's becoming a bit (dare we say it?) hip. The spirit of the place remains resolutely the same hough and Turkish grocer **Yasar Halim** stands proud in the middle of it all. Get ribs for inner at **Autograf** and indulge in some vodka. Or if beer's more your thing, head to **rouhaha**. Long-standing favourite, **The Salisbury**, is a failsafe choice for a good night nd if you need your organic groceries, **Beans and Barley** will keep you happy.

Coffee

- **Beans and Barley** • 595 Green Lanes
- **Cafe Delight** • 351 Green Lanes
- **Mezzo Shisha Lounge** • 64 Grand Parade

Landmarks

- **Railway Fields Nature Reserve** • 381 Green Lanes

Nightlife

- **Brouhaha** • 501 Green Lanes
- **The Beaconsfield** • 359 Green Lanes
- **Jam In A Jar** • 599 Green Lanes
- **The Salisbury** • 1 Grand Parade, Green Lanes

Post Offices

- **Harringay** • 509 Green Lanes

Restaurants

- **Autograf Grill** • 499 Green Lanes
- **Blend** • 587 Green Lanes
- **Bun & Bar** • 553 Green Lanes
- **Devran** • 485 Green Lanes
- **Gökyüzü** • 26 Grand Parade
- **Hala** • 29 Grand Parade

Shopping

- **Beans and Barley** • 595 Green Lanes
- **Harringay Local Stores** • 581 Green Lanes
- **Yasar Halim** • 495 Green Lanes

Supermarkets

- **Sainsbury's** • 4 Williamson Rd

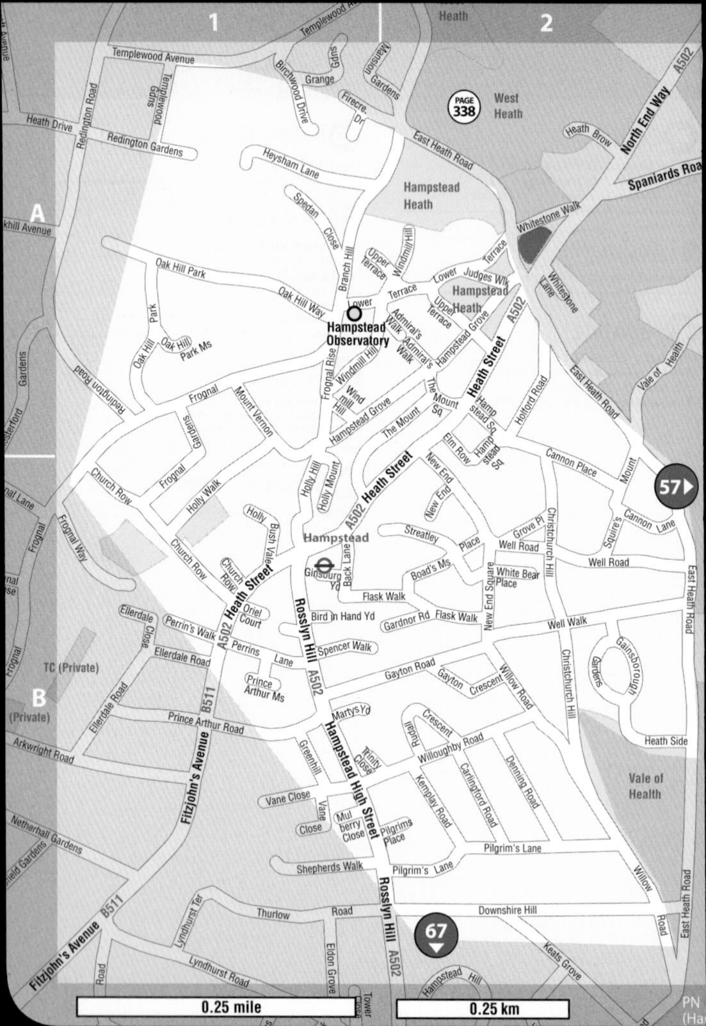
1
2
A
B
West Heath
PAGE 338
Templewood Avenue
Templewood Gdns
Birchwood Drive
Grange Gdns
Mansion Gardens
Firecrest Dr
Heath Drive
Redington Road
Redington Gardens
Heysham Lane
East Heath Road
Heath Brow
North End Way
A502
Spaniards Road
Hampstead Heath
Spedan Close
Whitestone Walk
Whitestone Lane
Oak Hill Park
Oak Hill Way
Branch Hill
Upper Terrace
Windmill Hill
Lower Terrace
Judges Wk
Lower Terrace
Upper Terrace
Hampstead Grove
Hampstead Observatory
Admiral's Walk
Oak Hill Park Ms
Oak Hill Park
Frognal Rise
Heath Street
Holford Road
Vale of Health
Gardens
Frognal
Mount Vernon
Windmill Hill
The Mount Sq
Hampstead Sq
The Mount
Elm Row
Cannon Place
Mount
Frognal Gardens
Church Row
Holly Walk
Holly Hill
Holly Mount
Heath Street
New End
Christchurch Hill
57
Frognal Lane
Frognal Way
Holly Bush Vale
Hampstead
Streatley Place
Grove Pl
Well Road
Squire's Mount
Cannon Lane
Well Road
East Heath Road
Church Row
Ginsburg Yd
Back Lane
Boad's Ms
New End Square
White Bear Place
Flask Walk
Ellerdale Close
Perrin's Walk
Oriel Court
Rosslyn Hill
Bird in Hand Yd
Gardnor Rd
Flask Walk
Well Walk
Ellerdale Road
Perrins Lane
Spencer Walk
Gainsborough Gardens
TC (Private)
Prince Arthur Ms
Gayton Road
Gayton Crescent
Willow Road
(Private)
Ellerdale Road
B511
Martys Yd
Christchurch Hill
Prince Arthur Road
Crescent
Rudall
Willoughby Road
Heath Side
Arkwright Road
Greenhill
Hampstead High Street
Trinity Close
Fitzjohn's Avenue
Kemplay Road
Carlingford Road
Denning Road
Vale of Health
Vane Close
Vane Close
Mulberry Close
Pilgrims Place
Netherhall Gardens
Pilgrim's Lane
Shepherds Walk
Pilgrim's Lane
Willow Road
East Heath Road
Lyndhurst Ter
Thurlow Road
Rosslyn Hill
Downshire Hill
Fitzjohn's Avenue B511
67
Keats Grove
Lyndhurst Road
Eldon Grove
A502
Hampstead Hill
Tower Close
0.25 mile
0.25 km

ıre, leafy Hampstead Village defines posh, but there is still some fun to be had. ead to Flask Walk for cute and eccentric local shops. The **Duke of Hamilton** as good a pub you're likely to find anywhere, and when they kick you out, ıuch like the bankers kicked out the literary-types from the area, there is ways **Tinseltown**.

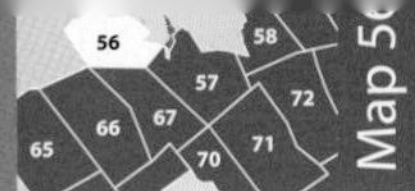

Cinemas

- **Everyman Cinema Club** • 5 Hollybush Vale

Coffee

- **Caffe Nero** • 1 Hampstead High St
- **Ginger & White** • 4 Perrin's Ct

Landmarks

- **Hampstead Observatory** • Lower Terrace & Hampstead Grove

Nightlife

- **The Duke of Hamilton** • 23 New End
- **The Flask** • 14 Flask Walk
- **The Freemasons Arms** • 32 Downshire Hill
- **Holly Bush** • 22 Holly Mount
- **The Horseshoe** • 28 Heath Rd

Restaurants

- **Carluccio's** • 34 Rosslyn Hill
- **La Creperie De Hampstead** • 77 Hampstead High St
- **The Louis Patisserie** • 32 Heath St

Shopping

- **Happy Returns** • 36 Rosslyn Hill
- **Keith Fawkes** • 1 Flask Walk
- **Mystical Fairies** • 12 Flask Walk

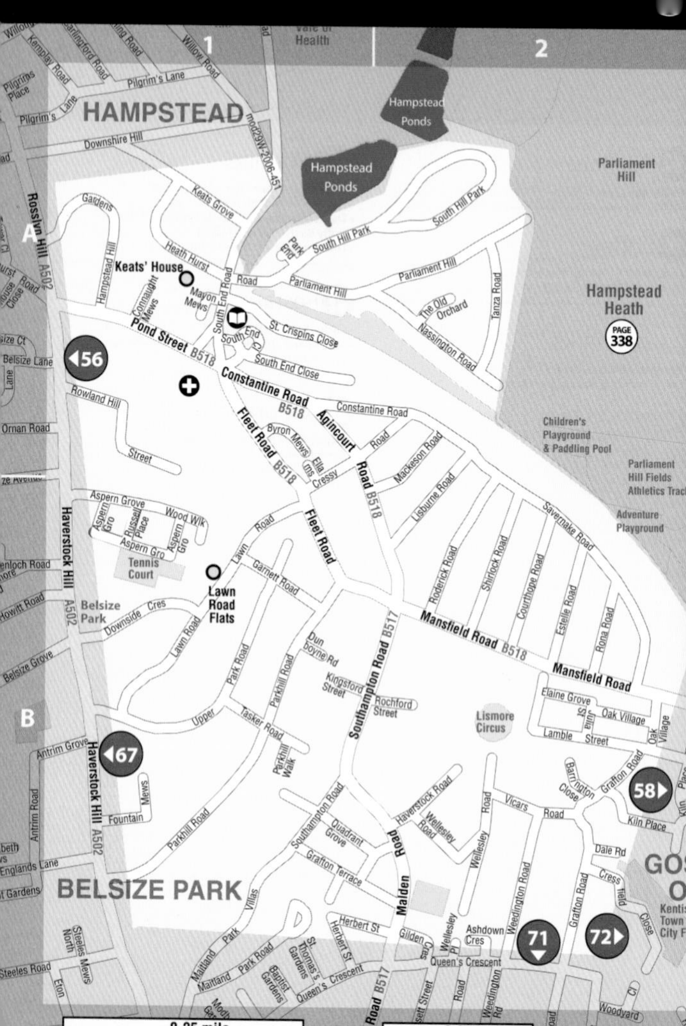

1
2
HAMPSTEAD
Hampstead Ponds
Hampstead Ponds
Parliament Hill
Hampstead Heath
PAGE 338
Keats' House
Pond Street B518
Constantine Road B518
Fleet Road B518
Agincourt Road B518
Mansfield Road B518
Southampton Road B517
Haverstock Hill A502
Rosslyn Hill A502
Lawn Road Flats
Tennis Court
Belsize Park
Lismore Circus
Children's Playground & Paddling Pool
Parliament Hill Fields Athletics Track
Adventure Playground
56
67
58
71
72
BELSIZE PARK
0.25 mile
0.25 km

elieved to be the inspiration for CS Lewis's Narnia, Hampstead Heath was bsorbed into London proper during the Victorian era but still feels more like ne of the Home Counties. With the exception of the blight on the landscape hat is the **Royal Free Hospital**, the area is charming with boutique shops nd restaurants on the South End Road, which cater to a refined and heavy-valleted crowd.

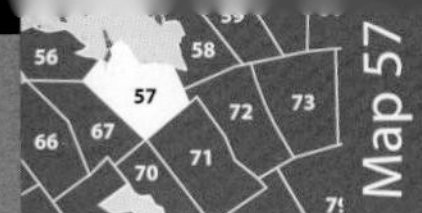

Coffee

- **Starbucks** • 5 South End Rd

Emergency Rooms

- **Royal Free Hospital** • Pond St & Fleet Rd

Landmarks

- **John Keats House** • 10 Keats Grove
- **Lawn Road Flats** • Lawn Rd & Garnett Rd

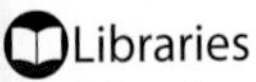

Libraries

- **Heath Library** • Keats Grove

Nightlife

- **The Garden Gate** • 14 S End Rd
- **Roebuck** • 15 Pond St

Restaurants

- **Mimo La Buffala** • 45 South End Rd
- **Paradise** • 49 South End Rd
- **Polly's** • 55 South End Rd
- **The Roebuck** • 15 Pond St

Shopping

- **Daunt Books** • 51 South End Rd
- **Giocobazzi's Delicatessen** • 150 Fleet Rd

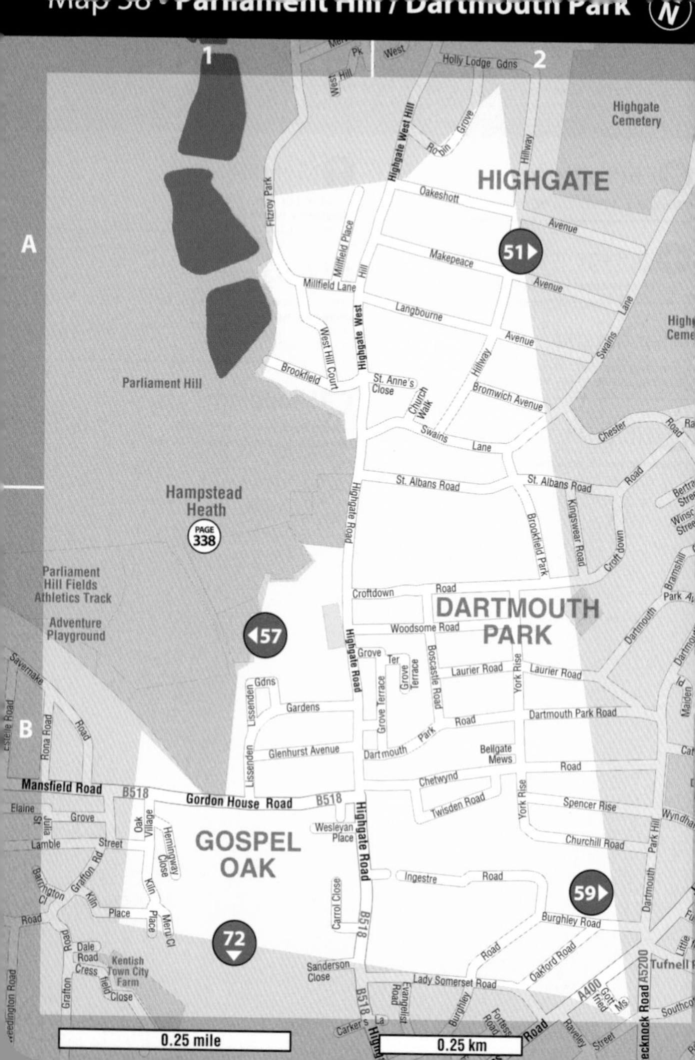
N
1
2
A
B
HIGHGATE
DARTMOUTH PARK
GOSPEL OAK
Highgate Cemetery
Parliament Hill
Hampstead Heath
PAGE 338
Parliament Hill Fields Athletics Track
Adventure Playground
Kentish Town City Farm
51
57
59
72
Holly Lodge Gdns
West Hill Pk
Robin Grove
Hillway
Highgate West Hill
Fitzroy Park
Oakeshott Avenue
Makepeace Avenue
Millfield Place
Millfield Lane
Langbourne Avenue
Swains Lane
West Hill Court
Brookfield
St. Anne's Close
Church Walk
Bromwich Avenue
Chester Road
St. Albans Road
Highgate Road
Kingswear Road
Brookfield Park
Croftdown Road
Woodsome Road
Grove Ter
Grove Terrace
Boscastle Road
Laurier Road
York Rise
Dartmouth Park Road
Dartmouth Park Hill
Lissenden Gdns
Lissenden Gardens
Glenhurst Avenue
Bellgate Mews
Chetwynd Road
Twisden Road
Spencer Rise
Churchill Road
Mansfield Road
B518
Gordon House Road
Savernake Road
Rona Road
Elaine Grove
Julia St
Lamble Street
Oak Village
Hemingway Close
Wesleyan Place
Grafton Rd
Barrington Cl
Kiln Place
Meru Cl
Ingestre Road
Carrol Close
Burghley Road
Oakford Road
Dale Road
Cressfield Close
Grafton Road
Sanderson Close
Lady Somerset Road
Evangelist Road
Fortess Road
Raveley Street
Gotfried Ms
A400
Carker's La
Tufnell Park
Southcote
Leighton Road
0.25 mile
0.25 km

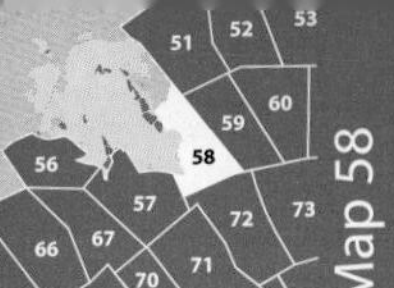

arliament Hill/Dartmouth Park

n area you stumble upon by accident, on your way somewhere else, probably ampstead Heath or Highgate Cemetery. Then you realize how nice it is. Maybe ou should try the little restaurants? Soon you find yourself having pizza at **Al arco** every week and trekking all across London just to find out what new les they're serving at **The Southampton Arms**. You could live here. You really ould.

Nightlife

- **The Southampton Arms** • 139 Highgate Rd

Restaurants

- **Al Parco** • 2 Highgate West Hill
- **Bistro Laz** • 1 Highgate West Hill
- **Carob Tree** • 15 Highgate Rd
- **Kalendar** • 15 Swains Ln
- **Lalibela** • 137 Fortess Rd

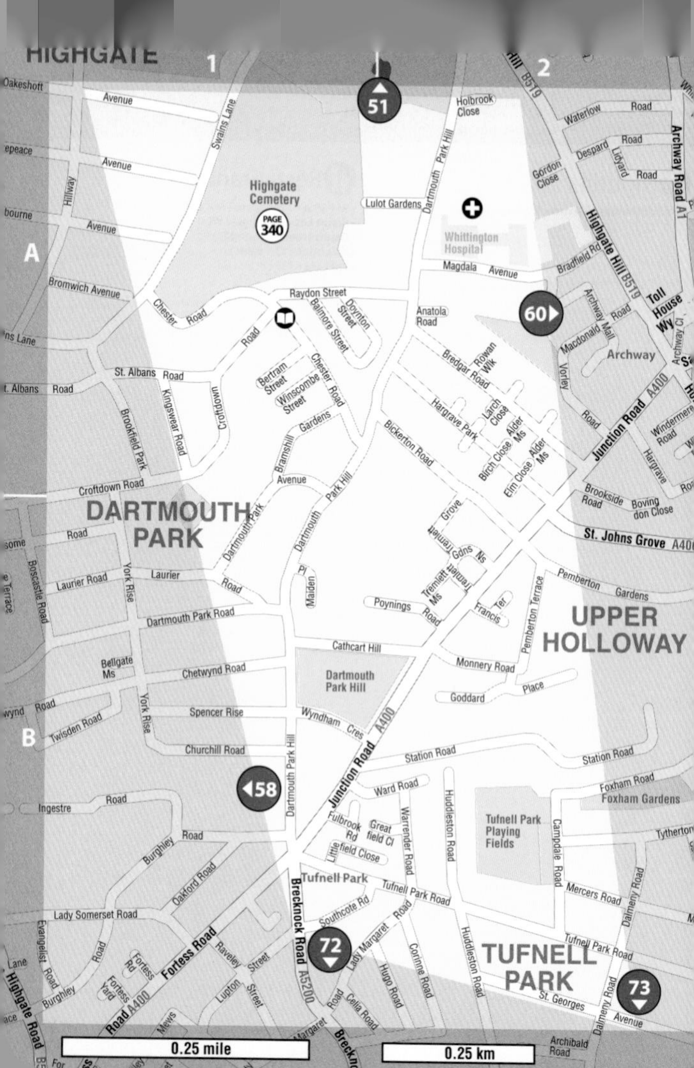

HIGHGATE
1
2
51
60
58
72
73
A
B
Highgate Cemetery
PAGE 340
Whittington Hospital
Archway
DARTMOUTH PARK
UPPER HOLLOWAY
TUFNELL PARK
Dartmouth Park Hill
Tufnell Park Playing Fields
Foxham Gardens
Tufnell Park
Oakeshott Avenue
Avenue
Avenue
Swains Lane
Holbrook Close
Dartmouth Park Hill
Waterlow Road
Despard Road
Lidyard Road
Gordon Close
Archway Road A1
Hillway
Lulot Gardens
Highgate Hill B519
Bradfield Rd
Magdala Avenue
Bromwich Avenue
Raydon Street
Chester Road
Balmore Street
Doynton Street
Anatola Road
Toll House Wy
Archway Mall
Macdonald Road
Rowan Wlk
Bredgar Road
Vorley Road
St. Albans Road
Bertram Street
Winscombe Street
Chester Road
Croftdown
Kingswear Road
Brookfield Park
Hargrave Park
Larch Close
Alder Ms
Birch Close
Elm Close
Junction Road A400
Windermere Road
Hargrave
Bickerton Road
Bramshill Gardens
Avenue
Croftdown Road
Dartmouth Park
Brookside Road
Bovingdon Close
Grove
Tremlett Gdns
St. Johns Grove A400
Road
Boscastle Road
York Rise
Laurier Road
Laurier
Road
Pl
Maiden
Tremlett Ms
Francis Ter
Pemberton Terrace
Pemberton Gardens
Poynings Road
Dartmouth Park Road
Cathcart Hill
Monnery Road
Bellgate Ms
Chetwynd Road
Goddard Place
Twisden Road
York Rise
Spencer Rise
Wyndham Cres
Churchill Road
Station Road
Station Road
Junction Road
Ward Road
Foxham Road
Ingestre Road
Dartmouth Park Hill
Huddleston Road
Warrender Road
Fulbrook Rd
Greatfield Cl
Littlefield Close
Campdale Road
Tytherton
Burghley Road
Oakford Road
Tufnell Park Road
Mercers Road
Dalmeny Road
Lady Somerset Road
Brecknock Road A5200
Southcote Rd
Lady Margaret Road
Corinne Road
Huddleston Road
Tufnell Park Road
Evangelist Road
Road
Fortess Rd
Fortess Road
Fortess Yard
Raveley Street
Lupton Street
Hugo Road
Celia Road
St. Georges Avenue
Dalmeny Road
Highgate Road
Burghley
Lane
Road A400
Mews
Archibald Road
0.25 mile
0.25 km

urrounded by the rougher Archway, Kentish Town, and Holloway and mmortalised by Simon Pegg in cult comedies *Spaced* and *Shaun of the Dead*, ınassuming Tufnell Park has been quietly fashionable for years. Unwind with a ɔook and a coffee at **Rustique**, or hit **Nuraghe Trattoria** for some of the finest talian food in London. **The Dome** hosts everything from the latest cutting-ɘdge electronica to seasoned indie rock acts.

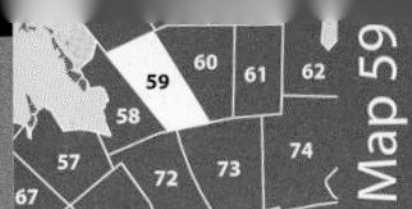

Emergency Rooms

- **Whittington Hospital** •
  Magdala Ave & Dartmouth Park Hill

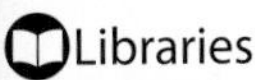

Libraries

- **Highgate Library** • Chester Rd

Nightlife

- **Aces And Eights Saloon Bar** • 156 Fortess Rd
- **Boston Arms** • 178 Junction Rd
- **The Dome** • 178 Junction Rd
- **The Hideaway** • 114 Junction Rd
- **The Lord Palmerston** • 33 Dartmouth Park Hill
- **The Star** • 47 Chester Rd

Restaurants

- **Nuraghe Trattoria** • 12 Dartmouth Park Hill
- **Rustique Cafe** • 142 Fortess Rd
- **The Spice** • 161 Fortess Rd

Shopping

- **North London Adoption Centre** • 135 Junction Rd

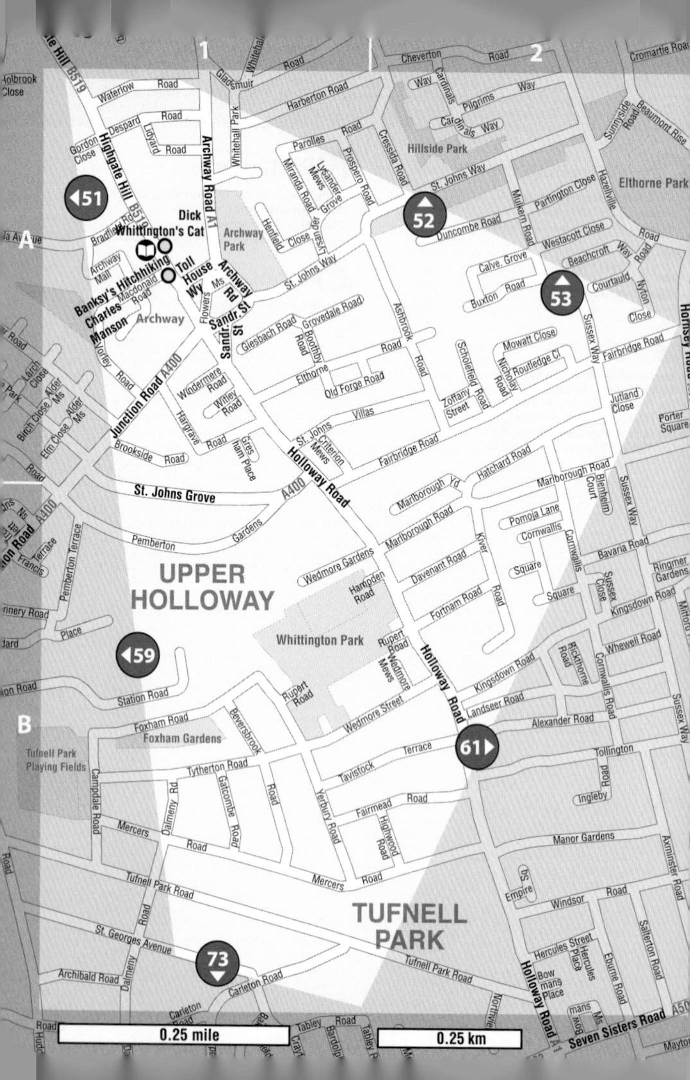

1
2
A
B
51
52
53
59
61
73
UPPER HOLLOWAY
TUFNELL PARK
Dick Whittington's Cat
Banksy's Hitchhiking Charles Manson
Toll House Wy
Archway
Archway Park
Hillside Park
Elthorne Park
Whittington Park
Foxham Gardens
Tufnell Park Playing Fields
Highgate Hill B519
Archway Road A1
Junction Road A400
Holloway Road
Holloway Road A1
St. Johns Way
St. Johns Grove
St. Johns Villas
Pemberton Gardens
Pemberton Terrace
Station Road
Tufnell Park Road
St. Georges Avenue
Seven Sisters Road
Cheverton Road
Harberton Road
Cardinals Way
Pilgrims Way
Duncombe Road
Fairbridge Road
Hatchard Road
Marlborough Road
Kingsdown Road
Alexander Road
Tollington Road
Manor Gardens
Windsor Road
Mercers Road
Tytherton Road
Carleton Road
Archibald Road
0.25 mile
0.25 km

s grey and gritty as ever, Archway could really do with a fresh lick of paint. At ıght, there are enough old man boozers to keep you busy, but bear in mind, icer places are only a short bus ride away.

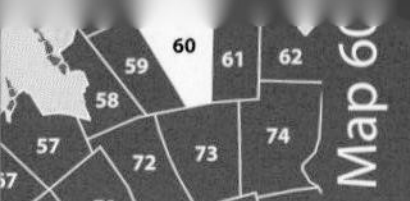

Coffee

- **Cafe Metro** • 4 Junction Rd

Landmarks

- **Dick Whittington's Cat** • 89 Highgate Hill

Libraries

- **Archway Library** • Highgate Hill

Nightlife

- **Mother Red Cap** • 665 Holloway Rd

Restaurants

- **500 Restaurant** • 782 Holloway Rd
- **Il Mio Mosaic** • 24 Junction Rd
- **Nid Ting** • 533 Holloway Rd
- **St Johns Tavern** • 91 Junction Rd

Shopping

- **Second Chance** • 7 St John's Way
- **Super Persia** • 621 Holloway Rd

Supermarkets

- **Co-Op** • 11 Junction Rd
- **Sainsbury's** • 643 Holloway Rd

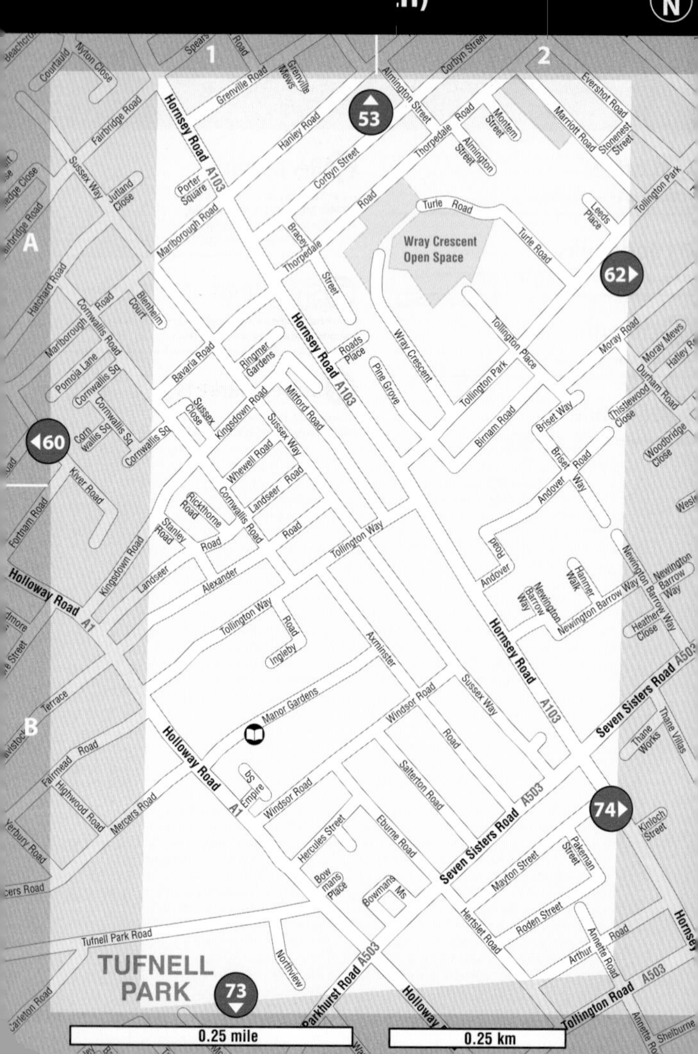

N
1
2
A
B
53
60
62
73
74
Hornsey Road
A103
Grenville Road
Grenville Mews
Hanley Road
Corbyn Street
Almington Street
Thorpedale Road
Montem Street
Marriott Road
Evershot Road
Stonenest Street
Tollington Park
Turle Road
Leeds Place
Wray Crescent Open Space
Bracey Street
Porter Square
Marlborough Road
Fairbridge Road
Courtauld
Nyton Close
Sussex Way
Jutland Close
Hatchard Road
Cornwallis Road
Blenheim Court
Pomoja Lane
Cornwallis Sq
Bavaria Road
Ringmer Gardens
Roads Place
Pine Grove
Wray Crescent
Tollington Place
Moray Road
Moray Mews
Durham Road
Thistlewood Close
Woodbridge Close
Birnam Road
Briset Way
Briset Road
Andover Road
Mitford Road
Kingsdown Road
Sussex Close
Whewell Road
Landseer Road
Rickthorne Road
Stanley Road
Alexander Road
Tollington Way
Kiver Road
Fortnam Road
Holloway Road
A1
Ingleby Road
Axminster Road
Hanmer Walk
Newington Barrow Way
Heather Close
Seven Sisters Road
A503
Thane Works
Thane Villas
Manor Gardens
Windsor Road
Empire Sq
Satterton Road
Terrace
Fairmead Road
Highwood Road
Mercers Road
Yerbury Road
Hercules Street
Eburne Road
Bowmans Place
Bowmans Ms
Pakeman Street
Mayton Street
Roden Street
Kinloch Street
Hertslet Road
Annette Road
Arthur Road
Tollington Road
Tufnell Park Road
TUFNELL PARK
Northview
Parkhurst Road
Carleton Road
Shelburne
0.25 mile
0.25 km

The borough of Islington, in which North Holloway sits, is supposed to be either a byword for liberal middle-class cosiness or else grim inner-city deprivation, depending on who you talk to. This bit has neither, just lots of dull grey streets. Down on Holloway Road, **El Molino** is a great place for tapas.

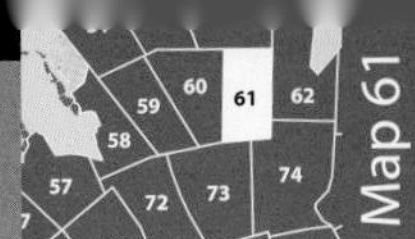

Coffee

• **Caffe Nero** • 400 Holloway Rd

Cinemas

• **Odeon Holloway** • 419 Holloway Rd

Libraries

• **North Library** • Manor Gardens

Nightlife

• **The Owl and Hitchhiker** • 471 Holloway Rd
• **The Swimmer** • 13 Eburne Rd

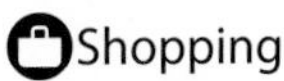

Restaurants

• **El Molino** • 379 Holloway Rd
• **The Landseer** • 37 Landseer Rd
• **North Nineteen** • 194 Sussex Wy

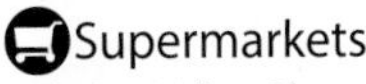

Shopping

• **Holloway Car Boot** •
Opposite Odeon Holloway Cinema, Holloway Rd
• **Michael's Fruiterers** • 56 Seven Sisters Rd

Supermarkets

• **Iceland** • 442 Holloway Rd

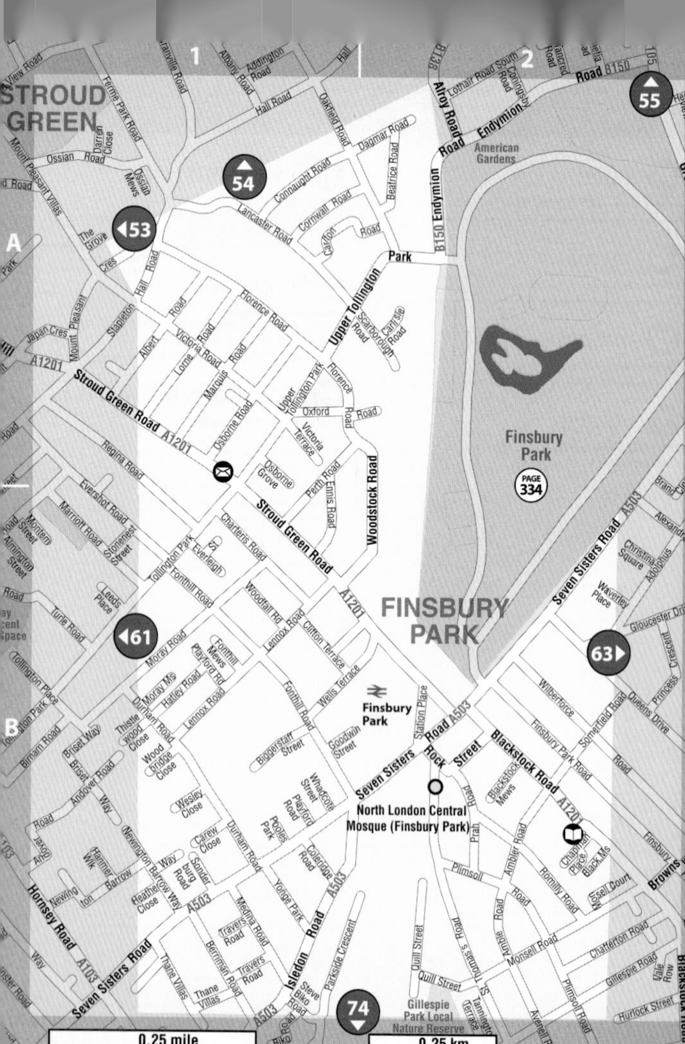

STROUD GREEN
FINSBURY PARK
Finsbury Park
American Gardens
Finsbury Park
North London Central Mosque (Finsbury Park)
Gillespie Park Local Nature Reserve
PAGE 334
53
54
55
61
63
74
1
2
A
B
Stroud Green Road A1201
Seven Sisters Road A503
Blackstock Road A1201
Upper Tollington Park
Endymion Road B150
Alroy Road
Hornsey Road A103
Isledon Road A503
Woodstock Road
Lancaster Road
Florence Road
Victoria Road
Albert Road
Lorne Road
Marquis Road
Osborne Road
Regina Road
Evershot Road
Marriott Road
Stonenest Street
Tollington Park
Fonthill Road
Charteris Road
Woodfall Rd
Lennox Road
Clifton Terrace
Wells Terrace
Station Place
Rock Street
Wilberforce Road
Finsbury Park Road
Somerfield Road
Queens Drive
Gloucester Drive
Brand Close
Alexandra Grove
Christina Square
Adolphus
Waverley Place
Moray Road
Durham Road
Hatley Road
Playford Rd
Biggerstaff Street
Goodwin Street
Whadcote Street
Pooles Park
Coleridge Road
Yonge Park
Medina Road
Travers Road
Berriman Road
Thane Villas
Parkside Crescent
Quill Street
St Thomas's Road
Amble Road
Monsell Road
Chatterton Road
Gillespie Road
Hurlock Street
Plimsoll Road
Romilly Road
Ambler Road
Prah Road
Blackstock Mews
Chapman Place
Black Ms
Monsell Court
Browns
Avenell Road
Tannington Terrace
Steve Biko Road
Newington Barrow Way
Wesley Close
Carew Close
Sonderburg Road
Heather Close
Hanmer Wlk
Andover Road
Briset Way
Birnam Road
Thistlewood Close
Woodbridge Close
Moray Ms
Fonthill Mews
Turle Road
Leeds Place
Monterey Street
Tollington Place
Mount Pleasant Villas
Mount Pleasant Crescent
Japan Cres
Stapleton Hall Road
The Grove
Ossian Road
Ossian Mews
Darren Close
Ferme Park Road
Albany Road
Addington Road
Hall Road
Oakfield Road
Dagmar Road
Connaught Road
Cornwall Road
Carlton Road
Beatrice Road
Scarborough Road
Carlisle Road
Oxford Road
Victoria Terrace
Osborne Grove
Perth Road
Ennis Road
St Everleigh
Lothair Road South
Coningsby Road
Vale Row
0.25 mile
0.25 km

Finsbury Park

Finsbury Park used to be somewhere you passed through rather than lingered but with Stroud Green Road slowly being populated with numerous eating and drinking options and £5 million invested in tarting up the park, it really isn't that bad. You could do worse than have a Sunday roast at **The Old Dairy** or grab a coffee at **The Deli at 80**.

Coffee

- **Boulangerie Bon Matin** • 178 Tollington Park
- **The Deli at 80** • 80 Stroud Green Rd

Landmarks

- **North London Central Mosque (Finsbury Park)** • 7 St Thomas's Rd

Libraries

- **N4 Library** • 26 Blackstock Rd

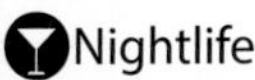

Nightlife

- **The Faltering Fullback** • 19 Perth Rd
- **The Old Dairy** • 1 Crouch Hill
- **WB Yeats** • 20 Fonthill Rd

Post Offices

- **Stroud Green Rd** • 97 Stroud Green Rd

Restaurants

- **Afasika** • 152 Seven Sisters Rd
- **Girasole** • 150 Seven Sisters Rd
- **Hana Sushi** • 150 Seven Sisters Rd
- **Le Rif** • 172 Seven Sisters Rd
- **Lulu's Caribbean Cuisine** • 84 Stroud Green Rd
- **Osteria Tufo** • 67 Fonthill Rd
- **Petek** • 96 Stroud Green Rd
- **Season** • 53 Stroud Green Rd

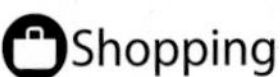

Shopping

- **The Deli at 80** • 80 Stroud Green Rd
- **The Happening Bagel Bakery** • 284 Seven Sisters Rd

Supermarkets

- **Tesco** • 105 Stroud Green Rd

Map 63 • Manor House

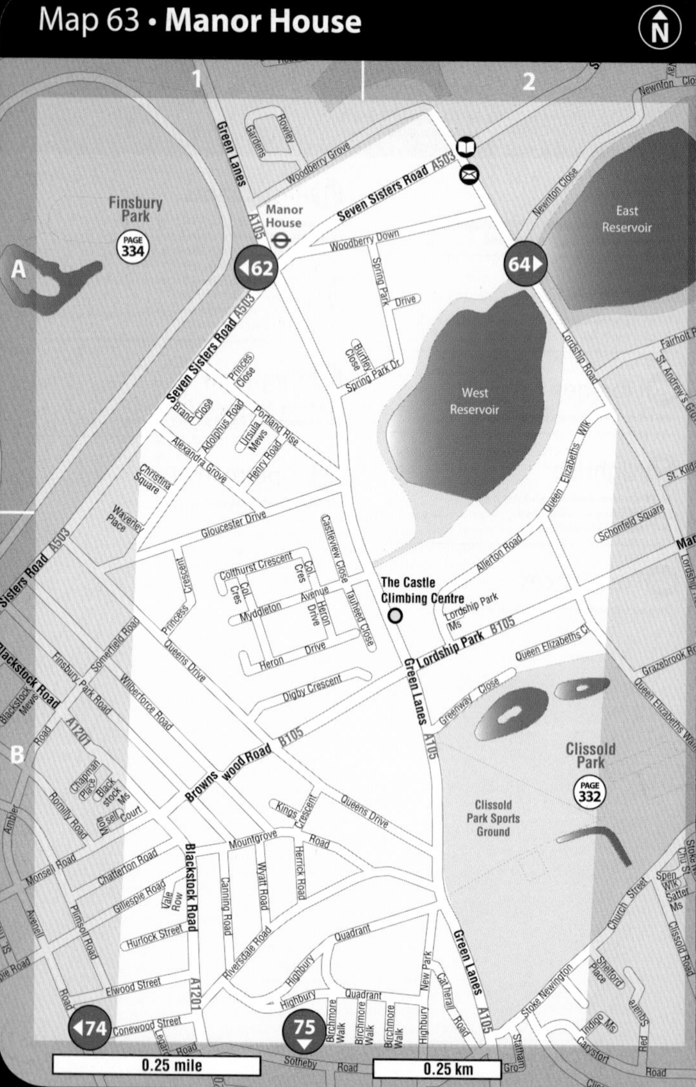

Don't hang out near the 'scummy round the edges' station as it can get pretty gruesome at night. You might chance upon a warehouse party round here, but walk south, dodge the rats around the reservoir, admire the faux turrets of **The Castle Climbing Centre**, and head to the **New River Café** for great fry-ups with views over the leafy oasis of Clissold Park.

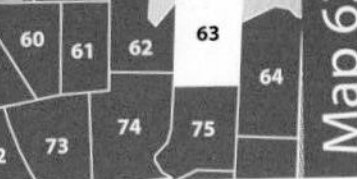

Coffee

- **Boulangerie Bon Matin** • 178 Tollington Park
- **Fink's Salt & Sweet** • 70 Mountgrove Rd
- **Simply Organique** • 316 Green Lanes

Landmarks

- **The Castle Climbing Centre** • Green Lanes & Lordship Park

Libraries

- **Woodberry Down Library** • 440 7 Sisters Rd

Nightlife

- **The Brownswood Park Tavern** • 271 Green Lanes

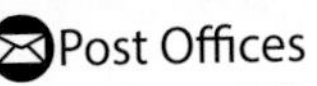

Post Offices

- **Woodberry Grove** • 107 Woodberry Grove

Restaurants

- **Fink's Salt & Sweet** • 70 Mountgrove Rd
- **New River Café** • 271 Stoke Newington Church St

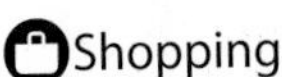

Shopping

- **Bennet & Brown** • 84 Mountgrove Rd
- **Sargent & Co.** • 74 Mountgrove Rd
- **Simply Organique** • 316 Green Lanes
- **Sylvanian Families** • 68 Mountgrove Rd

1
2
A
B
St. Kilda's Road
Manor Road
B105
Royal Close
Collison Place
Margaret Road
Windus
Stamford Hill
Belfast
Schonfeld Square
Lordship Park B105
Allerton Road
Crusoe
Mews
Bouverie Road
Abney Park Cemetery
Martaban Road
Park
Listria
A10
Cazenove Road
Grayling Road
Lordship Park B105
63
85
Queen Elizabeths Close
Grazebrook Road
Chestnut Road
Lordship Road
Lordship Gro
Yoakley Road
STOKE NEWINGTON
Gibson Gardens
Rectory Road
Close
Queen Elizabeths Walk
Lordship Terrace
Lordship Rd
Brett Close
Bouverie Ms
Fleetwood Street
Summerhouse Rd
Wilmer Pl
Abney Gdns
Garnham Street
Clissold Park
PAGE 332
Clissold Park Sports Ground
Lordship Lane
Edward's Lane
Barn Street
Painsthorpe Road
Aysome Road
Oldfield Road
Defoe Road
Dumont Road
Kersley Road
Lancell Street
Brodia Road
Dynevor Road
Stoke Newington High Street
Lawrence Buildings
Smalley Close
Sanford Terrace
Brooke Road
Spensley Walk
Albion Road
Woodlea Road
Hawksley Road
Hawksley Rd
Scolars Pl
Kynaston Road
Chesholm Road
Lavers Road
Manley Ct
Dynevor Road
Bayston Road
Sat.Ms
Park Cres
Stoke Newington Chu St
B104
Woodlea Road
Gatsworthy Terrace
Sandbrook Rd
Sandbrook Road
Harcombe Road
Oldfield Road
Nevill Road
Dynevor Road
Tyssen Road
Leswin Road
Stoke Newington Church Street
Clissold Road
Shelford Place
Carriage Place
Close
Lillian Close
Ormsby Place
Yorkshire Close
Hollar Rd
Bat Place
Batley Road
Uhura Square
Victorian Grove
Victorian Rd
Glading Terrace
Green Lanes
Statham Grove
Red Square
Indigo Ms
Church Walk
Barbauld Road
Evering Rd A10
Carysfort Road
Albion Road
Albion Grove
Knebworth Road
Gunstor Road
Beatty Road
Clissold Crescent
Clissold Cres
Church Walk
Shakspeare Walk
Londesborough Road
Osterley Road
Walford Road
Foulden Terrace
Sydner Mews
Amhurst
A105
Burma Road
Reedholm Villas
Milton Grove
Clonbrock Road
Leonard Place
Allen Road
SHACKLEWELL
Farleigh Place
Brighton Road
Farleigh Road
Foulden
Springdale Road
Grove
Factory Road
Spenser Grove
Butterfield Green
Lynn Mews
Palatine Avenue
Palatine Road
Road A10
Pegasus Close
Lavell Street
Road
Shakspeare Walk
Spenser Grove
Road
Prince George Road
Somerford Grove
75
Green Lanes
Aden
Joiners Place
Bridge Gardens
Lidfield Road
Winston Road
Albion Road
Church Walk
Bennett Road
Belgrade Road
Stoke Newington
Princess May Road
Shacklewell Row
Petherton Road
A105
Newington Green Church
Howard Road
Watson Close
Cowper Road
Wordsworth Road
86
Barretts Grove
Arcola Street
Terrace
Church Walk
Matthias Road
Miller's Square
Chow Square
Dunn St
Gateway Ms
Lane
Poets Road
Leconfield Road
Scarthoe Park
Hedley Row
A105
Pellerin Road
Sal Rd
Ferntower Road
Newington Green
82
Auriga Ms
St Gabriels Lea
Woodville Road
Elton Place
Arundel Grove
King Henry's Walk
Shellgrove Road
Truman's Place
Selsea Place
Road
Shacklewell Lane
Alvington Crescent
Pyrland Road
0.25 mile
Mildmay
Wolsey Road
Arundel
Boleyn Road
Tavistock Cl
Crossway
Street A10
0.25 km
Sandringham

The richer cousin of Dalston and the poorer cousin of Islington, Stoke Newington has an inferiority complex-cum-swagger which explains why 90% of its inhabitants are creative types. The curvy Church Street is the port of call with its boutique shops (**Metal Crumble**) and aptly Nietzsche stacked bookshops. Great beer and atmosphere (**The Shakespeare**), curry (**Rasa N16**), Sunday roast (**Rose and Crown**), and check out the butterflies and bats at Park Cemetery.

Landmarks

- **Newington Green Church** • 39 Newington Green

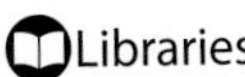

Libraries

- **Stoke Newington Library** • Stoke Newington Church St

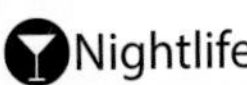

Nightlife

- **The Auld Shillelagh** • 105 Stoke Newington Church St
- **The Dalston Jazz Bar** • 4 Bradbury St
- **Londesborough** • 36 Barbauld Rd
- **Mascara Bar** • 72 Stamford Hill
- **Rose and Crown** • 199 Stoke Newington Church St
- **Ryan's Bar** • 181 Stoke Newington Church St
- **Ruby's** • 76 Stoke Newington Rd
- **The Shakespeare** • 57 Allen Rd
- **White Hart** • 69 Stoke Newington High St

Post Offices

- **Church Street** • 170 Stoke Newington Church St
- **Stoke Newington** • Stoke Newington High St

Restaurants

- **Anglo Asian** • 60 Stoke Newington Church St
- **Blue Legume** • 101 Stoke Newington Church St
- **Rasa N16** • 55 Stoke Newington Church St
- **Sariyer Balik** • 56 Green Lanes
- **Yum Yum** • 187 Stoke Newington High St

Shopping

- **Ark** • 161 Stoke Newington Rd
- **The Beaucatcher Salon** • 44 Stoke Newington Church St
- **Belle Epoque Boulangerie** • 37 Newington Green
- **Bridgewood & Neitzert** • 146 Stoke Newington Church St
- **Church Street Bookshop** • 142 Stoke Newington Church St
- **Metal Crumble** • 13 Stoke Newington Church St
- **Mind** • 11 Stoke Newington Church St
- **Of Cabbages & Kings** • 34 Kersley Rd
- **Pelicans & Parrots** • 81 Stoke Newington Rd
- **Ribbons and Taylor** • 157 Stoke Newington Church St
- **S'graffiti** • 172 Stoke Newington Church St
- **Sacred Art** • 148 Albion Rd
- **The Spence Bakery** • 161 Stoke Newington Church St
- **Stoke Newington Farmers Market** • Stoke Newington Church St & Stoke Newington High St

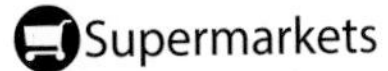

Supermarkets

- **Whole Foods Market** • 32 Stoke Newington Church St
- **Iceland** • 17 Green Lanes

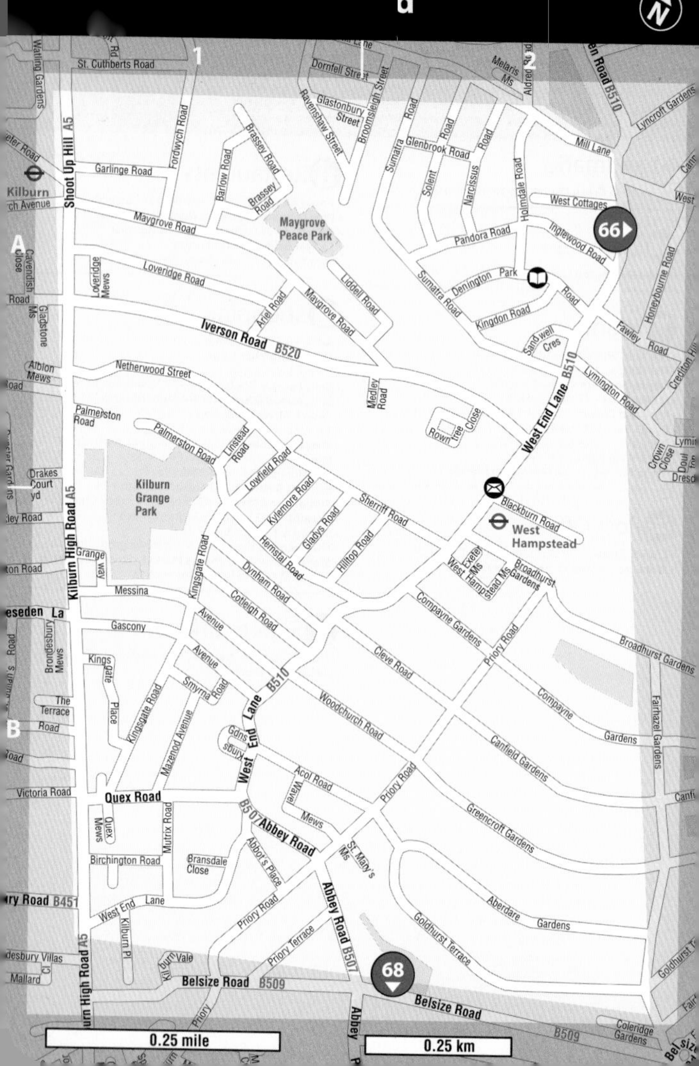

1
2
A
B
St. Cuthberts Road
Kilburn
Shoot Up Hill A5
Garlinge Road
Fordwych Road
Brassey Road
Barlow Road
Maygrove Road
Maygrove Peace Park
Dornfell Street
Glastonbury Street
Ravenshaw Street
Broomsleigh Street
Sumatra Road
Glenbrook Road
Solent Road
Narcissus Road
Holmdale Road
Melaris Ms
Aldred Road
Mill Lane
Lyncroft Gardens
West Cottages
Inglewood Road
Pandora Road
Denington Park Road
Kingdon Road
Sandwell Cres
Fawley Road
Honeybourne Road
Lymington Road
Crediton Hill
66
Loveridge Road
Loveridge Mews
Cavendish Close
Gladstone Ms
Liddell Road
Ariel Road
Iverson Road B520
Albion Mews
Netherwood Street
Medley Road
Rowntree Close
West End Lane B510
Crown Close
Palmerston Road
Linstead Road
Lowfield Road
Kilburn Grange Park
Drakes Court yd
Kylemore Road
Gladys Road
Hilltop Road
Sherriff Road
Blackburn Road
West Hampstead
Exeter Ms
West Hampstead Ms
Broadhurst Gardens
Kilburn High Road A5
Grange way
Kingsgate Road
Hemstal Road
Dynham Road
Cotleigh Road
Compayne Gardens
Priory Road
Messina Avenue
Gascony Avenue
Brondesbury Mews
Kings gate Place
Smyrna Road
Cleve Road
Woodchurch Road
The Terrace
Mazenod Avenue
Kings Gdns
Acol Road
Canfield Gardens
Fairhazel Gardens
Victoria Road
Quex Road
Quex Mews
Mutrix Road
Wavel Mews
Greencroft Gardens
B507 Abbey Road
Birchington Road
Bransdale Close
Abbot's Place
St. Mary's Ms
Aberdare Gardens
West End Lane
Kilburn Pl
Priory Road
Priory Terrace
Abbey Road B507
Goldhurst Terrace
Kilburn Vale
Mallard Cl
Belsize Road B509
68
Coleridge Gardens
0.25 mile
0.25 km

Hampstead's ugly sister, West Hampstead is a leafy suburb that has absorbed some of Kilburn's grittiness. Young urban nomads make up much of the population, as rent is moderate by London standards.

Coffee

- **Costa** • 203 W End Ln
- **Starbucks** • 201 W End Ln

Libraries

- **West Hampstead Library** • Dennington Park Rd

Nightlife

- **The Black Lion** • 274 Kilburn High Rd
- **The Czech and Slovak Bar** • 74 West End Ln

Restaurants

- **Barraco Cafe** • 10 Kingsgate Pl
- **Small & Beautiful** • 351 Kilburn High Rd

Supermarkets

- **Sainsbury's** • 88 Kilburn High Rd
- **Sainsbury's** • 377 Kilburn High Rd

1
2
A
B
WEST HAMPSTEAD
SOUTH HAMPSTEAD
BELSIZE PARK
West Hampstead
Finchley Road
Swiss Cottage
South Hampstead Rail Station
Cumberland Lawn Tennis Club
Hampstead Cricket Club
65
67
68
69
Mill Lane
West Cottages
West End Lane
B510
Inglewood Road
Holmdale Road
Dennington Park Road
Kingdon Road
Sand Well Cres
Fawley Road
Lymington Road
B520
Blackburn Road
Broadhurst Gardens
Priory Road
Compayne Gardens
Canfield Gardens
Fairhazel Gardens
Greencroft Gardens
Aberdare Gardens
Goldhurst Terrace
Belsize Road
B509
Coleridge Gardens
Rowley Way
Boundary Road
Springfield Road
Alexandra Place
Loudoun Road
Alexandra Road
Dorman Way
Hilgrove Rd
Belsize Rd
Cannon Hill
West End Lane
Honeybourne Road
Crediton Hill
Alvanley Gardens
Frognal Lane
Langland Gardens
Lindfield Gardens
Chesterford Gardens
Greenaway Gardens
Frognal Close
Frognal
Frognal Way
Church Row
Holly Walk
Mount Vernon
Ellerdale Cl
Ellerdale Road
Perrins Wlk
Prince Arthur R
Heath Street
Fitzjohn's Avenue
B511
Arkwright Road
Lymington Road
Crown Cl
Doulton Ms
Mint. Ms
Wor. Ms
Bes.Ms
Spode Wlk
Close
Dresden
Lithos Road
Rosemont Road
Finchley Road
A41
Frognal Court
Netherhall Way
Netherhall Gardens
Nutley Terrace
Maresfield Gardens
Akenside Road
Lyndhurst R
Canfield Pl
Broadhurst Close
Sumpter Close
Broadhurst Gardens
Goldhurst Terrace
Naseby Cl
Marston Cl
Fairfax Place
Fairfax Road
Harben Road
Belsize Road
Dobson Close
College Crescent
Belsize Lane
Belsize Park
Buckland Crescent
Eton Avenue
Adamson Road
Crossfield Road
Lancaster Grove
Strathray Gdns
Belsize Square
Daleham Mews
Bay Ms
Bel Pk Ms
Belsize Crescent
Prince Ms
Burdett Ms
Avenue Road
Winchester Road
Fellows Road
Kings College Rd
Hornby Close
Adelaide Road
Merton Rise
0.25 mile
0.25 km

Finchley Road/Swiss Cottage

With so much promise and surrounded by the likes of West Hampstead, Primrose Hill and Camden, the area is still inexplicably in need of resuscitation. A long list of shops not worth mentioning and a few restaurants whose existence defies dignity should not detract from the fact that **The Camden Arts Centre** is a jewel in this battered crown and well worth braving the surrounding boredom to visit.

Cinemas

- **Odeon Swiss Cottage** • 96 Finchley Rd
- **Vue Finchley Road** • Finchley Rd & Blackburn Rd

Coffee

- **Costa** • 98 Finchley Rd
- **Starbucks** • 255 Finchley Rd

Libraries

- **Swiss Cottage Library** • 88 Avenue Rd

Nightlife

- **Ye Olde Swiss Cottage** • 98 Finchley Rd

Restaurants

- **Bradleys** • 25 Winchester Rd
- **Camden Arts Centre** • Arkwright Rd
- **Singapore Garden** • 83 Fairfax Rd

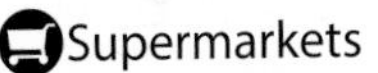

Supermarkets

- **Sainsbury's** • 255 Finchley Rd
- **Waitrose** • 199 Finchley Rd

HAMPSTEAD
BELSIZE PARK
Freud Statue
St. Stephen's
56
57
66
69
70
A
B
1
2
0.25 mile
0.25 km
Hampstead
Belsize Park
Swiss Cottage
Frognal Lane
Frognal Gardens
Langland Gardens
Lindfield Gardens
Frognal Close
Frognal
Frognal Way
Church Row
Holly Mt
Holly Bush Vale
Heath Street
Hamp. High Street
Oriel Court
Perrins Walk
Perrins Lane
Ellerdale Road
Ellerdale Cl
Prince Arthur Ms
Prince Arthur Road
Arkwright Road
Finchley Road A41
Fitzjohn's Avenue B511
Netherhall Gardens
Netherhall Way
Frognal Court
Nutley Terrace
Maresfield Gardens
Daleham Gardens
Daleham Mews
Akenside Road
Lyndhurst Terrace
Lyndhurst Road
Lyndhurst Gdns
Wedderburn Road
Rosslyn Hill A502
Rosslyn Pk Ms
Waterhouse Close
Thurlow Road
Eldon Grove
Tower Cl
Greenhill
Vane Close
Mulberry Cl
Pilgrims Place
Pilgrim's Lane
Shepherds Walk
Downshire Hill
Gayton Road
Gayton Cres
Willow Road
Well Walk
Flask Walk
Gardnor Road
New End Square
Back La
Streatley Place
Christchurch Hill
Gainsborough Gdns
Heath Side
East Heath Road
Rudall Cres
Willoughby Road
Carlingford Rd
Denning Rd
Kemplay Rd
Keats Grove
Hampstead Hill Gdns
Hurst Road
Pond Street B518
South End Rd
Haverstock Hill A502
Belsize Lane
Belsize Court Garages
Princess Ms
Belsize Crescent
Belsize Pl
Ornan Road
Perceval Ave
Rowland Hill Street
Belsize Park Gardens
Belsize Avenue
Belsize Park
Belsize Terrace
Belsize Ms
Burdett Ms
Belsize Square
Tudor Close
Hillfield Ct
Glenloch Road
Glenmore Road
Glenilla Road
Howitt Road
Belsize Grove
Aspern Grove
Russell Pl
Wood Wlk
Downside Cres
Lawn Road
Upper Park Road
College Crescent
Buckland Crescent
Eton Avenue
Adamson Road
Crossfield Road
Lancaster Grove
Lancaster Drive
Lambolle Road
Lambolle Place
Eton Garages
Strathray Gdns
Winchester Road
Kings College Rd
Hornby Close
Fellows Road
Merton Rise
Briary Close
Huson Close
Adelaide Road
Road B509
Primrose Gardens
Antrim Grove
Antrim Road
Elizabeth Mews
England's Lane
Chalcot Gdns
Fountain Mews
Parkhill Road
Steeles Road
Harley Road
Haverstock Road
Lyttelton Close
Brocas Close
Tobin Close

here is a reason that Kate Moss, Jude Law, Chris Martin and Noel Gallagher (to ame a few) all live here. It's less pretentious than neighbouring banker-filled ampstead and far enough away from the Primrose set to be artistically elitist. xtraordinarily expensive shops and restaurants reign over the area but in at ne celebrity-frequented **Washington** pub there's an excellent atmosphere and oodwise, Belsize Lane never disappoints.

Cinemas

- **Everyman Belsize Park** • 203 Haverstock Hill

Coffee

- **The Little One Coffee Shop** • 115 Regent's Park Rd
- **Starbucks** • 57 England's Ln
- **Starbucks** • 202 Haverstock Hill

Landmarks

- **Freud Statue** • Fitzjohn's Ave, opposite Maresfield Gardens Junction
- **St Stephen's** • Rosslyn Hill

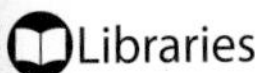

Libraries

- **Belsize Library** • Antrim Rd

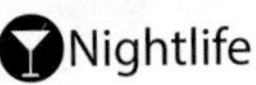

Nightlife

- **The Washington** • 50 England's Ln

Restaurants

- **Retsina** • 48 Belsize Ln
- **Violette Cafe** • 2 England's Ln

Shopping

- **Belsize Village Delicatessen** • 39 Belsize Ln

HAMPSTEAD
1
2
West End Lane
B451
Kilburn Place
Kilburn Vale
Priory Road
Priory Terrace
Aberdare Gardens
Goldhurst Terrace
Fairhazel Gardens
Belsize Road
B509
65
Coventry Cl
Kilburn High Road A5
Springfield Lane
Springfield Walk
Langtry Place
Kilburn Priory
Mortimer Place
Mortimer Crescent
Greville Ms
Manor Ms
Abbey Road B507
Belsize Road B509
Coleridge Gardens
Rowley Way
66
Greville Road
Bolton Road
Ainsworth Way
Alexandra Place
Loudoun Road
Maple Pk Ms
Maida Vale
Road
Boundary Road
Rutland Mews
Belgrave Gardens
Springfield Road
Andover Place
Clifton Hill
Hillside Close
Greville Road
Carlton Vale
Carlton Hill
Blenheim Passage
Ryders Ter
Blenheim Terrace
Blenheim Road
Marlborough Hill
Finchley Road A41
The Marlowes
The Lane
Maida Vale A5
Lanark Road
Hamilton Terrace
Marlborough Place
Aubrey Pl
Abbey Gardens
Violet Hill
Langford Cl
Langford Place
Regents Ms
Queen's Grove
Walpole Mews
Finchley Place
Queen's Terrace
69
Elgin Ms North
Elgin Avenue
Maida Vale
Elgin Ms South
Abercorn Walk
Abercorn Close
Abercorn Place
Waverley Place
Eyre Court
Eyre Ct
St. John's Wood
Alma Square
Hill Road
Acacia Gdns
Acacia Road
27
Hamilton Gdns
ST. JOHN'S WOOD
Grove End Road
Wellington Ct
Kingsmill Terrace
St. Ann's Terrace
Vale Close
Garden Road
Abbey Road Zebra Crossing
Aquila
Grove Hall Court
Circus Road
Cochrane Street
Cochrane Mews
Lanark Mews
Hall Road
Denning Cl
Hall Gate
Elm Tree Road
Elm Tree Close
Cavendish Avenue
Wellington Road A41
Southcott Mews
B507
Randolph Avenue
Melina Place
76
St. John's Wood High Street
Barrow Hill Rd
Cavendish Close
Wellington Place
0.25 mile
0.25 km

‹ilburn High Road/Abbey Road

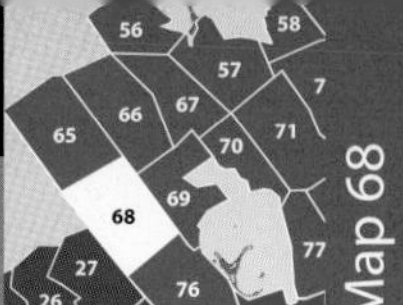

‹FS, "Let it Be!" Indeed, while the area's main attraction is a crosswalk and a ‹ilapidated recording studio once home to the world's greatest band, the ‹rime and urban decay that surround it hardly make it an "Octopus's Garden." ‹ut "Come Together" because "Here Comes the Sun."

Coffee

- **Starbucks** • 79 St John's Wood High St

Landmarks

- **Abbey Road Zebra Crossing** • 3 Abbey Rd

Libraries

- **Kilburn Library** • 12 Kilburn High Rd
- **St John's Wood Library** • 20 Circus Rd

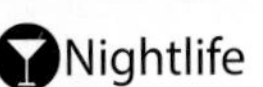

Nightlife

- **The Old Bell** • 38 High Road
- **Raw Brick** • 11 Kilburn High Rd

Post Offices

- **Kilburn** • 79 Kilburn High Rd
- **St Johns Wood** • 32 Circus Rd

Restaurants

- **Little Bay** • 228 Belsize Rd

Supermarkets

- **Tesco** • 115 Maida Vale

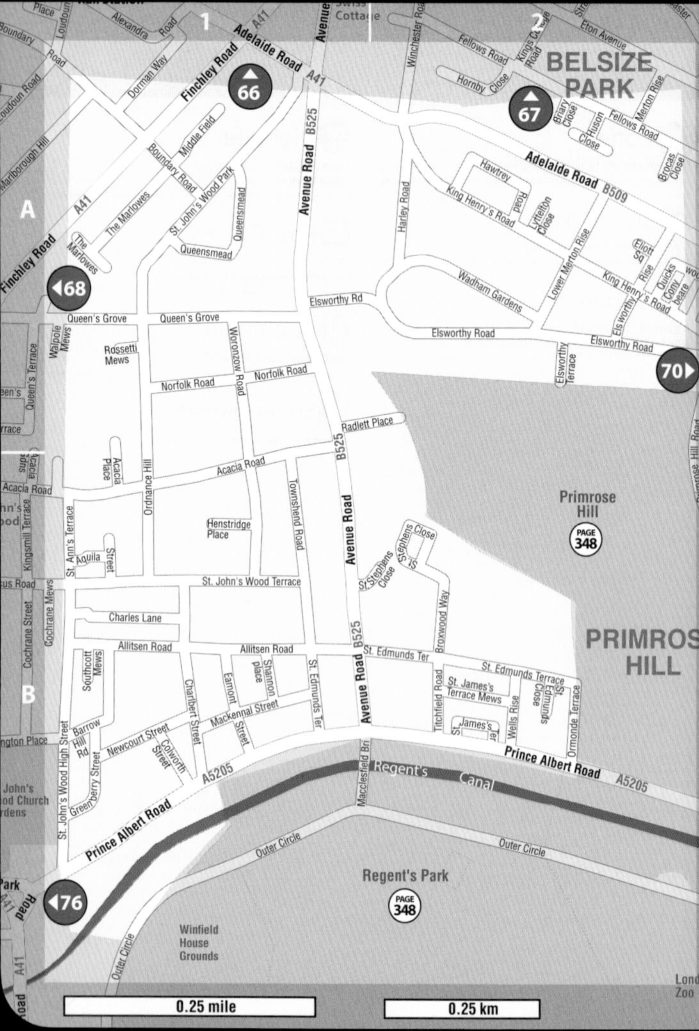

Map 69 • St. John's Wood

1
2
A
B

Swiss Cottage
BELSIZE PARK
PRIMROSE HILL
Primrose Hill
Regent's Park
Winfield House Grounds
Regent's Canal
St. John's Wood Church Gardens
London Zoo

Adelaide Road A41
Finchley Road A41
Avenue Road B525
Adelaide Road B509
Prince Albert Road A5205
Alexandra Road
Boundary Road
Loudoun Road
Marlborough Hill
Dorman Way
Middle Field
St. John's Wood Park
Queensmead
The Marlowes
Winchester Road
Fellows Road
Hornby Close
Kings College Road
Eton Avenue
Merton Rise
Briary Close
Huson Close
Brocas Close
Hawtrey Road
Lyttelton Close
King Henry's Road
Harley Road
Lower Merton Rise
Eliott Sq
Rise
Quickswood
Cony beare
Elsworthy Rise
Wadham Gardens
Elsworthy Rd
Elsworthy Road
Elsworthy Terrace
Queen's Grove
Walpole Mews
Rossetti Mews
Queen's Terrace
Norfolk Road
Woronzow Road
Radlett Place
Acacia Place
Acacia Road
Ordnance Hill
Kingsmill Terrace
St. Ann's Terrace
Henstridge Place
Townshend Road
Aquila Street
St. John's Wood Terrace
St. Stephens Close
Broxwood Way
Charles Lane
Cochrane Street
Cochrane Mews
Allitsen Road
Southcott Mews
Charlbert Street
Eamont Street
Shannon place
St. Edmunds Ter
St. Edmunds Terrace
St. Edmunds Close
St. James's Terrace Mews
St. James's Ter
Titchfield Road
Wells Rise
Ormonde Terrace
Mackennal Street
Newcourt Street
Colworth Street
Barrow Hill Rd
Greenberry Street
St. John's Wood High Street
Macclesfield Bri
Outer Circle

66
67
68
70
76
PAGE 348
PAGE 348

0.25 mile
0.25 km

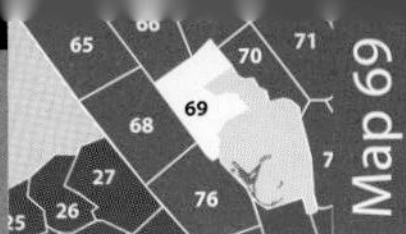

uveau riche and bourgeois mix in this leafy salad of a suburb that, you essed it, reeks of money. Pinned in between Primrose Hill and Regent's Park, ere isn't much to do in this mainly residential area, unless you like to gawk expensive houses.

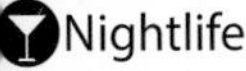

Nightlife

The Duke of York • 2 St Ann's Terrace

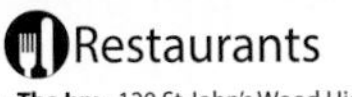

Restaurants

• **The Ivy** • 120 St John's Wood High St

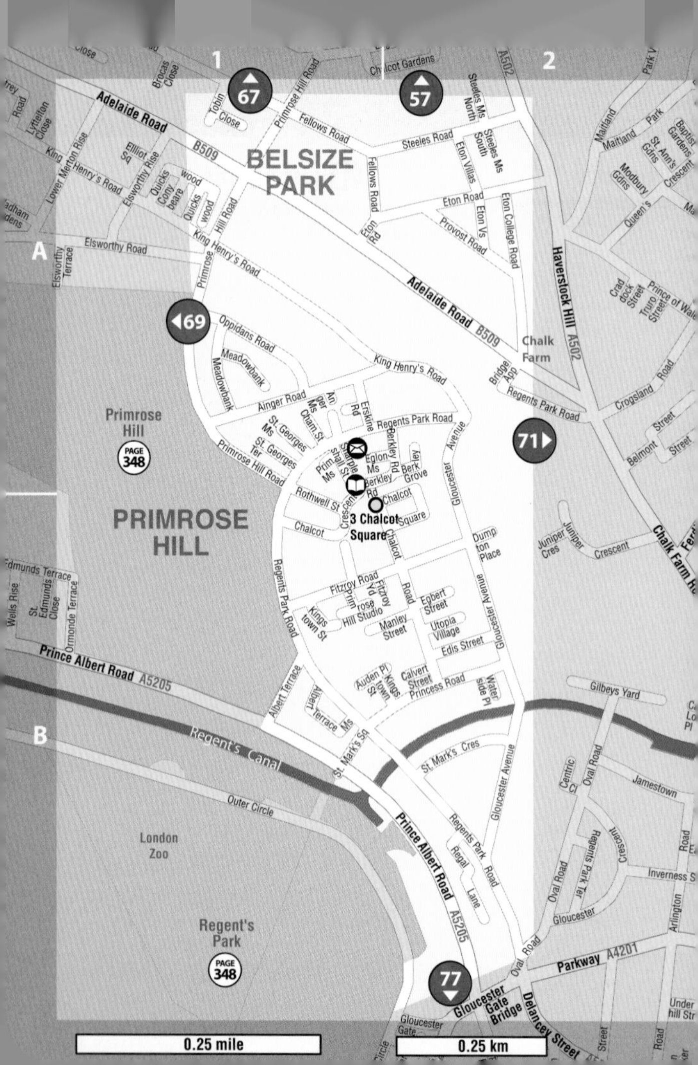

BELSIZE PARK
PRIMROSE HILL
Primrose Hill
PAGE 348
London Zoo
Regent's Park
PAGE 348
Chalk Farm
3 Chalcot Square
Adelaide Road
King Henry's Road
Regents Park Road
Prince Albert Road A5205
Regent's Canal
Outer Circle
Haverstock Hill A502
Chalk Farm Road
Gloucester Avenue
Parkway A4201
Delancey Street
Gloucester Gate Bridge
67
57
69
71
77
0.25 mile
0.25 km

mrose Hill is factory-packed with pretty young things and established actors ıxing with models, designers and artistic types in an area that is London's w-key version of Beverly Hills. If you don't stumble across a celebrity or are sinclined to stalk one you can check out the trendy stores, grab a pint in the ually trendy **Lansdowne** or take in the views of London from the Hill itself.

Landmarks

3 Chalcot Square • 3 Chalcot Sq

Libraries

Chalk Farm Library • 11 Sharples Hall St

Nightlife

Cecil Sharp House • 2 Regent's Park Rd
The Lansdowne • 90 Gloucester Ave
Princess of Wales • 22 Chalcot Rd

Post Offices

Regent's Park Road • 91 Regent's Park Rd

Restaurants

- **The Hill Bar** • 94 Haverstock Hill
- **Lemonia** • 89 Regent's Park Rd
- **Melrose and Morgan** • 42 Gloucester Ave
- **Odette's** • 130 Regent's Park Rd
- **Primrose Bakery** • 69 Gloucester Ave
- **Two Brothers** • 297 Regent's Park Rd

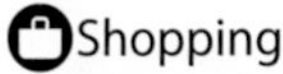

Shopping

- **Judith Michael & Daughter** • 73 Regent's Park Rd
- **Nicolas (off licence)** • 67 Regent's Park Rd
- **Press** • 3 Erskine Rd
- **Primrose Hill Books** • 134 Regent's Park Rd
- **Primrose Newsagent** • 91 Regent's Park Rd
- **Richard Dare** • 93 Regent's Park Rd
- **Shepherd Foods** • 59 Regent's Park Rd
- **Shikasuki** • 67 Gloucester Ave
- **Sweet Pea** • 77 Gloucester Ave
- **Tann Rokka** • 123 Regent's Park Rd

1
2
A
B
57
70
72
77
78
Haverstock Hill
Steeles Mews North
Steeles Mews South
Steeles Road
Eton Villas
Eton Road
Eton Vs
Provost Road
Eton College Road
Adelaide Road B509
Chalk Farm
Haverstock Hill A502
Maitland Park Villas
Maitland Park Road
Maitland Park Rd
Modbury Gardens
Silverbirch Walk
St Ann's Gardens
Queen's Crescent
Baptist Gardens
St. Thomas's Gardens
Herbert Street
Gilden Crescent
Ashdown Cres
Queen's Crescent
Bassett Street
Allcroft Road
Weedington Road
Grafton Road
Spring Place
Woodyard Close
Arctic Street
Browns Lane
Malden Road B517
Coity Rd
Rhyl Street
Warden Road
Marsden Street
Athlone Street
Holmes Road
Regis Road
Craddock Street
Truro Street
St. Silas Place
Prince of Wales Road
St. Leonards Square
Newbury Ms
Talacre Road
Talacre Open Space
Wilkin Street
Wilkin Street Ms
Perren Street
Dalby St
Kentish Town West Rail Station
Rylands Road
Grafton Road
Willes Road
Cathcart Street
Azania Ms
Inkerman Road
Stable Ms
Alma Street
Raglan Street
Henry's Road
Bridge App
Regents Park Road
Crogsland Road
Belmont Street
Malden Cres
Forge Place
Mutton Place
Castle Mews
Angler's Lane
Kentish Town Road
A502 Chalk Farm Road
Ferdinand Street
Powlett Place
Harmood Place
Harmood Street
Hadley Street
Healey Street
Grafton Crescent
Grafton Yd
Juniper Cres
Juniper Crescent
Ferdinand Place
Collard Place
Harmood Grove
Clarence Road
Lewis St
Castlehaven Road
Kelly Street
Church Avenue
Castle Road
Dumpton Place
Gloucester Avenue
Egbert St
Chalcot Road
Utopia Village
Edis Street
Calvert St
Princess Road
Waterside Pl
The Roundhouse
Hartland Way
Hawley Rd
Hawley Ms
Hawley St
Leybourne St
Play Area
Castlehaven Road A502
Lewis Street
Bartholomew Villas
Bartholomew Road
Rochester Road
Gilbeys Yard
Camden Market
Grand Regents Canal
Castlehaven Road
Hawley Rd A502
Haven Street
Leybourne Road
Torbay St
Kentish Town Road
Farrier Street
A5202
Rochester Place
Rochester Terrace
St. Marks Crescent
Gloucester Avenue
Centric Cl
Oval Road
Jamestown Road
Regent's Canal
Water Lane
Jeffreys Street
Jeffreys Pl
Wilmot Place
Rochester Pl
Rochester Mews
Regents Park Road
Regal Lane
Prince Albert Road
Camden High Street A502
Hawley Cres
Kentish Town Road A400
Camden Gardens
Prowse Place
Ivor Street
Royal College Street
St. Pancras Way
Road A503
Rochester Square
Early Mews
Stucley Place
Buck Street
Dewsbury Terrace
Camden Town
Camden Street A400
Bonny Street
Camden
Rousden Street
Inverness Street
Regents Park Terrace
Gloucester Crescent
Arlington Road
A400
Camden Road A503
Randolph Street
A5202
Oval Road
Parkway A4201
Greenland Road
Carol Street
Lyme Street
Baynes Street
Reachview Close
Wrotham Rd
Agar Place
Underhill Street
Greenland Street
A503
St. Martin's Gardens
Georgiana Street
College Street A5202
Glo. Gate Bri
Gloucester Gate Ms
A4201
Park Village East
Albert Street
Delancey Street
Signmaker Yd
A503
Pratt Street
Bayham Street
St. Martins Close
Pratt Street
Barker Drive
Blakeney Ms
Bergholt Ms
Rossendale
St. Pancras Way
0.25 mile
0.25 km

Camden Town/Chalk Farm/Kentish Town (West)

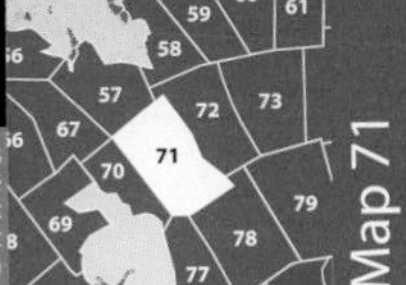

Camden is still the musical heartbeat of London, and while the ratty-tatty venues of the '60s that solidified its reputation are long gone, or surgically modernized, the pavements still reverberate to a constant beat. The area is crowded during the week and jam-packed during the weekend but the cacophony of wacky stores, bric-a-brac stalls, and an eclectic selection of culinary treats mean London wouldn't be London without it.

Cinemas

- **Odeon Camden Town** • 14 Parkway

Coffee

- **Cafe La Cigale** • 41 Heath Road
- **Cafe Metro** • 178 Camden High St
- **Caffe Nero** • 7 Jamestown Rd
- **Caffe Nero** • 11 Parkway
- **Camden Coffee House** • 30 Camden Rd
- **The Coffee Jar** • 83 Parkway
- **Costa** • 181 Camden High St
- **Inhabition** • 15 Chalk Farm Rd
- **Pret A Manger** • 157 Camden High St
- **Pret A Manger** • 261 High St
- **Starbucks** • Parkway Camden & Arlington Rd

Landmarks

- **Camden Market** • Camden Lock Pl
- **Grand Regents Canal** • Grand Regents Canal
- **The Roundhouse** • Chalk Farm Rd & Crogsland Rd

Libraries

- **Queen's Crescent Library** • 165 Queen's Crescent

Nightlife

- **Barfly** • 49 Chalk Farm Rd
- **Dingwalls** • Middle Yard
- **The Dublin Castle** • 94 Parkway
- **Electric Ballroom** • 184 Camden High St
- **The Enterprise** • 2 Haverstock Hill
- **Fiddlers Elbow** • 1 Malden Rd
- **Good Mixer** • 30 Inverness St
- **The Hawley Arms** • 2 Castlehaven Rd
- **Jazz Cafe** • 5 Parkway
- **The Lock Tavern** • 35 Chalk Farm Rd
- **Oxford Arms** • 265 Camden High St
- **Quinn's** • 65 Kentish Town Rd
- **The Underworld** • 174 Camden High St

Post Offices

- **Camden High Street** • 112 Camden High St
- **Queen's Crescent** • 139 Queen's Crescent

Restaurants

- **Andy's Taverna** • 23 Pratt St
- **Anima e Cuore** • 115 Kentish Town Rd
- **Arancini Factory Cafe** • 115 Kentish Town Rd
- **Bar Gansa** • 2 Inverness St
- **Bento Cafe** • 9 Parkway
- **Cotton's** • 55 Chalk Farm Rd
- **Fatburger and Buffalo's** • 10 Jamestown Rd
- **Gilgamesh** • The Stables Market, Chalk Farm Rd
- **Haché** • 24 Inverness St
- **Kim's Vietnamese Food Hut** • Unit D, Camden Lock Palace
- **Marathon Cafe** • 87 Chalk Farm Rd
- **Marine Ices** • 8 Haverstock Hill
- **Muang Thai** • 71 Chalk Farm Rd
- **My Village** • 37 Chalk Farm Rd
- **Thanh Binh** • 14 Chalk Farm Rd
- **Woody Grill** • 1 Camden Rd

Shopping

- **Acumedic** • 101 Camden High St
- **All Ages Records** • 27 Pratt St
- **Black Rose** • The Stables Market, Chalk Farm Rd
- **Cyberdog** • Stables Market, Chalk Farm Rd
- **Eye Contacts** • 10 Chalk Farm Rd
- **Fresh & Wild, Camden** • 49 Parkway
- **General Eyewear** • Chalk Farm Rd & Castlehaven Rd
- **Graham and Green** • 164 Regent's Park Rd
- **Melrose and Morganc** • 42 Gloucester Ave
- **Oi Oi** • 454 Stables Market
- **Ray Man Music** • 54 Chalk Farm Rd
- **Rokit** • 225 Camden High St
- **Traid** • 154 Camden High St
- **Village Games** • 65 The West Yard
- **Whole Foods Market** • 49 Parkway

Supermarkets

- **Whole Foods Market** • 49 Parkway
- **Sainsbury's** • 77 Chalk Farm Rd
- **Sainsbury's** • 17 Camden Rd
- **Sainsbury's** • 10 Camden Rd

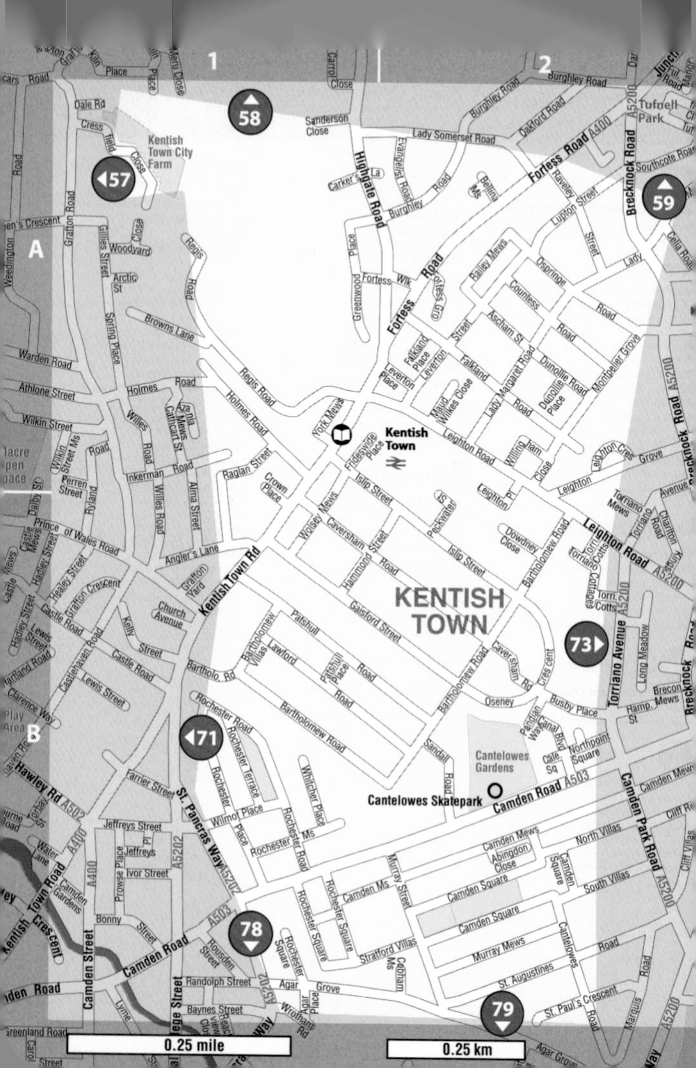

1
2
A
B
58
57
59
73
71
78
79
Kentish Town City Farm
Kentish Town
KENTISH TOWN
Cantelowes Gardens
Cantelowes Skatepark
Highgate Road
Fortess Road
Brecknock Road
Kentish Town Rd
Leighton Road
Camden Road
Camden Park Road
St. Pancras Way
Torriano Avenue
Camden Street
Camden Square
Prince of Wales Road
Castle Road
Hawley Rd
Holmes Road
Regis Road
Caversham Road
Islip Street
Gaisford Street
Patshull Road
Bartholomew Road
Rochester Road
Agar Grove
0.25 mile
0.25 km

ntish Town may be Camden's less-interesting and less-affected neighbour t this isn't necessarily a bad thing. The area is on the up and between the ibby, horrible collection of pound shops, charity shops, and industrial stores re are new venues springing forth that offer some of the most welcoming nospheres in North London. **The Pineapple** is a great little pit-stop pub with infectious atmosphere.

Coffee

Cafe Metro • 180 Camden High St

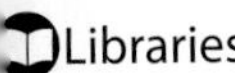

Libraries

Kentish Town Library • 262 Kentish Town Rd

Nightlife

The Abbey Tavern • 124 Kentish Town Rd
The Assembly House • 292 Kentish Town Rd
The Bull & Gate • 389 Kentish Town Rd
HMV Forum • 9 Highgate Rd
Ladies and Gentlemen • 2 Highgate Rd
The Lion and Unicorn • 42 Gaisford St
The Oxford Tavern • 256 Kentish Town Rd
The Pineapple • 51 Leverton St
Rio's Health Spa • 239 Kentish Town Rd

Restaurants

- **The Bengal Lancer**• 253 Kentish Town Rd
- **Cafe Renoir**• 244 Kentish Town Rd
- **Mario's Cafe** • 6 Kelly St
- **The Oxford** • 256 Kentish Town Rd
- **Phoenicia Mediterranean Food Hall** • 186 Kentish Town Rd

Shopping

- **Dots** • 132 St Pancras Way
- **Phoenicia** • 186 Kentish Town Rd
- **Ruby Violet** • 118 Fortress Rd

Supermarkets

- **Co-Op** • 250 Kentish Town Rd
- **EARTH natural foods** • 200 Kentish Town Rd
- **Iceland** • 301 Kentish Town Rd
- **Tesco/Esso** • 196 Camden Rd

TUFNELL PARK
HOLLOWAY
LOWER HOLLOWA
Tufnell Park
Caledonian Road
1
2
A
B
59
60
61
72
74
79
Tufnell Park Road
Mercers Road
St. Georges Avenue
Archibald Road
Anson Road
Carleton Road
Dalmeny Road
Dalmeny Avenue
Huddleston Road
Brecknock Rd
Brecknock Road
Hilldrop Road
Hilldrop Crescent
Camden Road
A503
Parkhurst Road
Hillmarton Road
A5203
Caledonian Road
Hungerford Road
Leighton Rd
A5200
Torriano Avenue
Camden Park Road
York Way
North Road
Market Road
Brewery Road
Caledonian Park
Market Road Gardens
Penn Road
Cardozo Road
Hartham Road
Corporation Street
Surr Street
Camden Square
Camden Mews
North Villas
South Villas
Agar Grove
St. Paul's Mews
Brandon Road
Blundell Street
Wheelwright Street
0.25 mile
0.25 km

Holloway is best known for its women's prison and not much else. To the west of Holloway Road it feels a bit like a sprawling backyard to gentrified Camden, Islington, and King's Cross. Nevertheless, bars like **The Lord Stanley** and **Shillibeer's** have gone all gastro, so it doesn't quite have the gritty vibe that it once had.

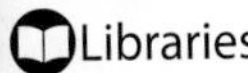

Libraries

- **John Barnes Library** • 275 Camden Rd

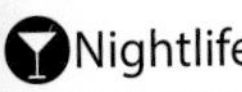

Nightlife

- **Aces and Eights Saloon Bar** • 156 Fortess Rd
- **The Big Red** • 385 Holloway Rd
- **The Lord Stanley** • 51 Camden Park Rd
- **Shillibeer's Bar and Grill** • 1 Carpenter's Mews

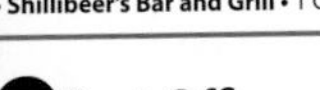

Post Offices

- **Brecknock Rd** • 20 Brecknock Rd

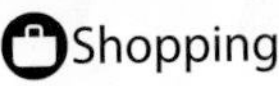

Shopping

- **Bumblebee Natural Foods** • 33 Brecknock Rd

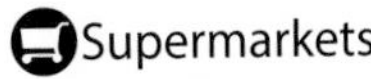

Supermarkets

- **Sainsbury's** • 4 Williamson St
- **Tesco/Esso** • 196 Camden Rd

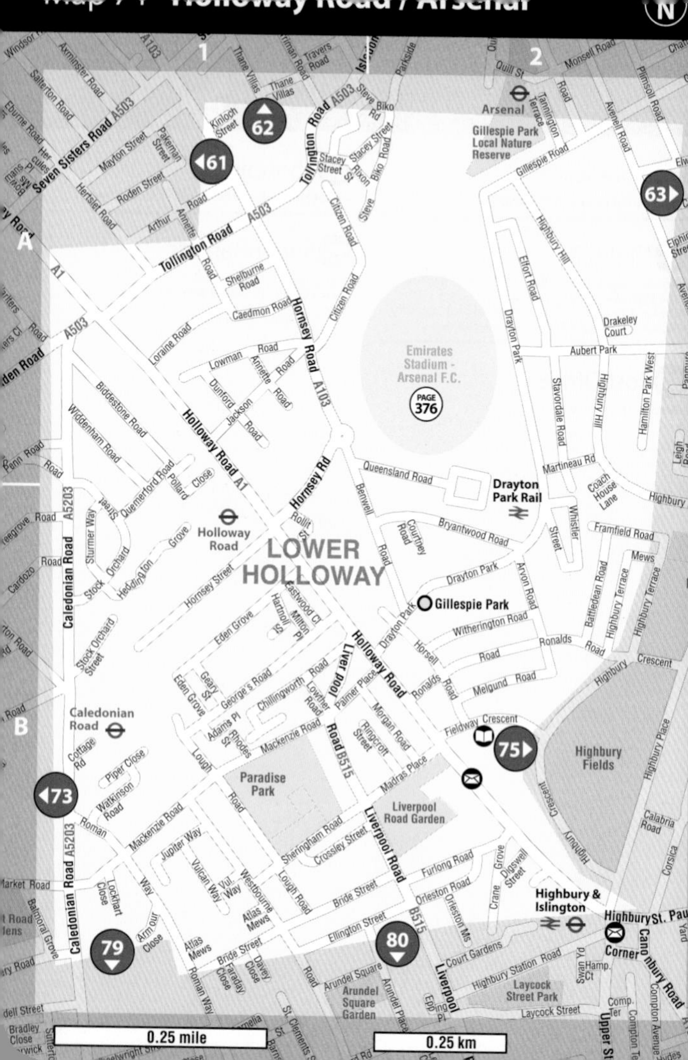

Holloway Road / Arsenal
N
1
2
A
B
62
61
63
73
75
79
80
Seven Sisters Road A503
Tollington Road
Tollington Road A503
Hornsey Road A103
Holloway Road A1
Caledonian Road A5203
Liverpool Road B515
Emirates Stadium - Arsenal F.C.
PAGE 376
Arsenal
Gillespie Park Local Nature Reserve
Drayton Park Rail
Holloway Road
LOWER HOLLOWAY
Gillespie Park
Caledonian Road
Paradise Park
Liverpool Road Garden
Highbury Fields
Highbury & Islington
Highbury Corner
Arundel Square Garden
Laycock Street Park
Citizen Road
Queensland Road
Benwell Road
Bryantwood Road
Drayton Park
Highbury Hill
Aubert Park
Gillespie Road
Avenell Road
Mackenzie Road
Ellington Street
Highbury Station Road
Canonbury Road
Laycock Street
0.25 mile
0.25 km

Holloway Road / Arsenal

uch like the football team the area shares its name with, there is a lot of
otential talent here that just needs some time to come to fruition. On match
ays the streets make a sardine tin look roomy. This area also includes the
otty stretch of Holloway Road. For something different try **Tbilisi** for cheap
astern European eats.

Coffee

- **Cafe Nero** • 348 Holloway Rd
- **Le Peche Mignon** • 6 Ronalds Rd
- **Vagabond N7** • 105 Holloway Rd

Landmarks

- **Emirates Stadium**
- **Gillespie Park** • 191 Drayton Park

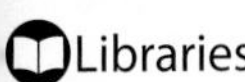

Libraries

- **Central Library** • 2 Fieldway Crescent

Nightlife

- **The Coronet** • 338 Holloway Rd
- **Hen and Chicken Theatre Bar** • 109 St Paul's Rd
- **The Horatia** • 98 Holloway Rd
- **The Relentless Garage** • 20 Highbury Corner

Post Offices

- **Highbury** • 5 Highbury Corner
- **Holloway Rd** • 118 Holloway Rd

Restaurants

- **El Rincon Quiteno** • 235 Holloway Rd
- **Kokeb** • 45 Roman Wy
- **Messi's Kitchen** • 128 Holloway Rd
- **Tbilisi** • 91 Holloway Rd
- **Wolkite Kifto** • 82 Hornsey Rd

Shopping

- **Vivien of Holloway** • 294 Holloway Rd

Supermarkets

- **Waitrose** • 366 Holloway Rd

Map 75 • Highbury

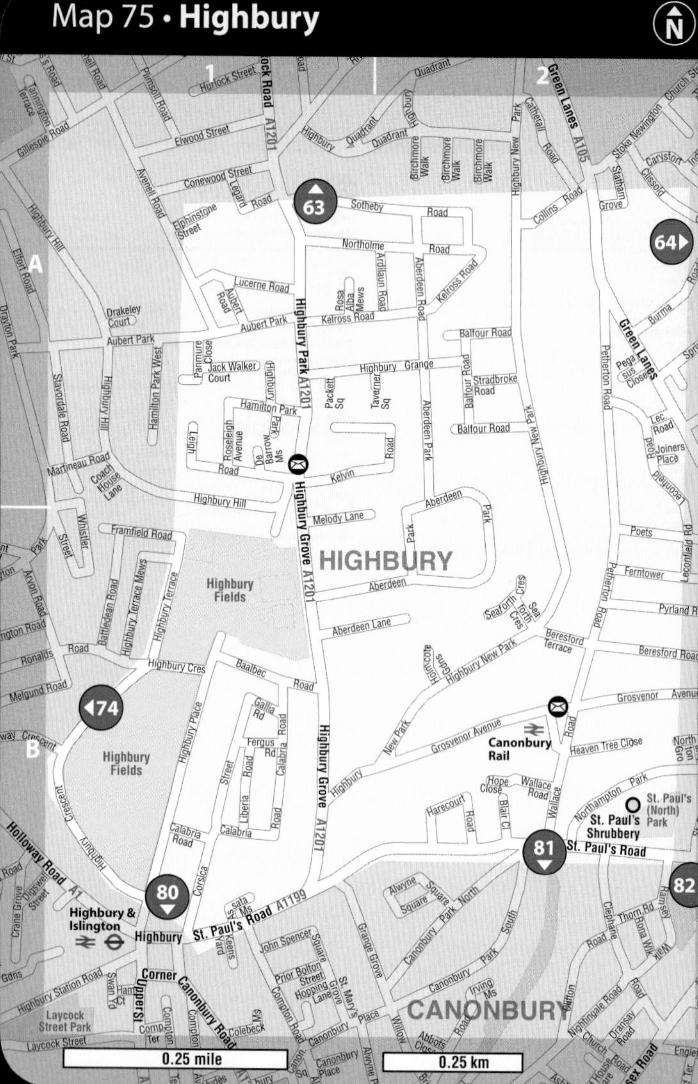

residential area close enough to Upper Street to keep you entertained and far nough away to keep you grounded, Highbury is blessed with the marvellous ighbury Fields, which during the summer is full of pretty things (in varying ates of undress). Bordered by busy St Paul's Road and bustling Green Lanes, ou'll never struggle for something to do here; try the **Snooty Fox** for a quiet rink.

Landmarks

- **St Paul's Shrubbery** • St Paul's Rd & Northampton Park

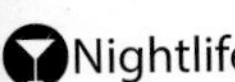

Nightlife

- **Alwyne Castle** • 83 St Pauls Rd
- **The Hen and Chickens Theatre Bar** • 109 St Paul's Rd
- **The Snooty Fox** • 75 Grosvenor Avenue

Post Offices

- **Grosvenor Avenue** • 91 Grosvenor Ave
- **Highbury Park** • 12 Highbury Park

Restaurants

- **Firezza** • 276 St Paul's Rd
- **Highbury Arts Club** • 73 Highbury Park
- **Prawn on the Lawn** • 220 St Paul's Rd
- **Primeur** • 116 Petherton Rd
- **Trullo** • 300-302 St Paul's Rd
- **Ustun** • 107 Green Lanes

Shopping

- **Cabbies Delight Auto Parts** • 9 Green Lanes
- **Highbury Vintners** • 71 Highbury Park
- **La Fromagerie** • 30 Highbury Park
- **Mother Earth** • 282 St Paul's Rd
- **Prawn on the Lawn** • 220 St Paul's Rd

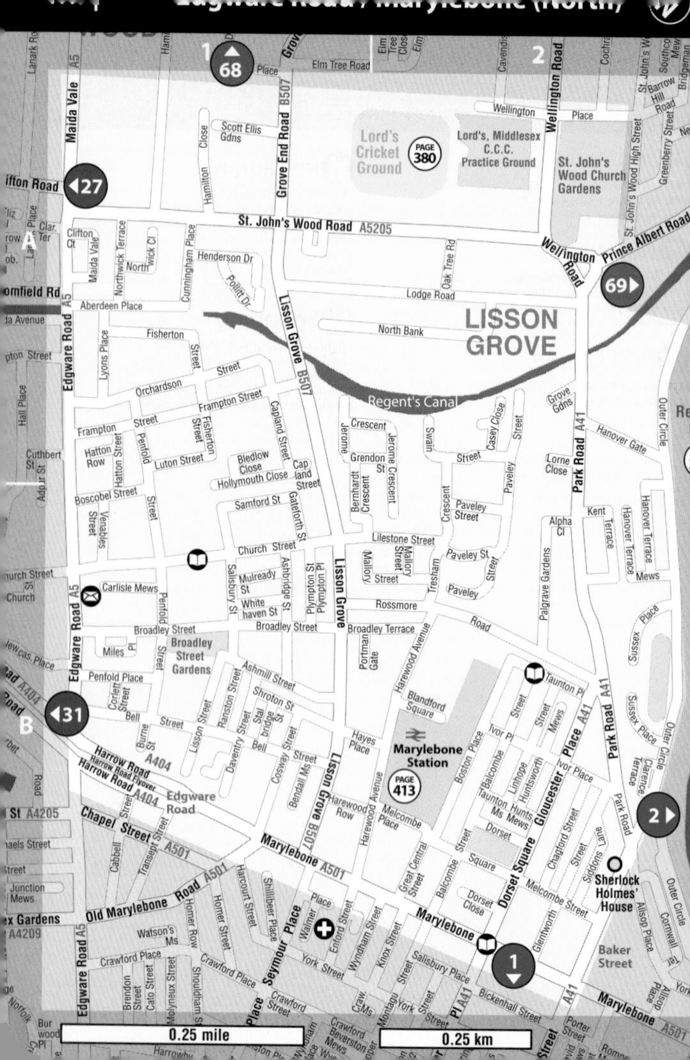

68
Elm Tree Road
Wellington Road
Wellington Place
Scott Ellis Gdns
Hamilton Close
Grove End Road B507
Lord's Cricket Ground
PAGE 380
Lord's, Middlesex C.C.C. Practice Ground
St. John's Wood Church Gardens
St. John's Wood High Street
Greenberry Street
Barrow Hill Road
Maida Vale A5
Clifton Road
27
St. John's Wood Road A5205
Wellington Road
Prince Albert Road
69
Clifton Ct
Maida Vale
Northwick Terrace
North Wick Cl
Cunningham Place
Henderson Dr
Pollitt Dr
Oak Tree Rd
Lodge Road
Aberdeen Place
Edgware Road A5
Lisson Grove B507
North Bank
LISSON GROVE
Fisherton Street
Lyons Place
Orchardson Street
Frampton Street
Regent's Canal
Capland Street
Jerome Crescent
Grendon St
Swain Street
Casey Close
Paveley Street
Grove Gdns
Park Road A41
Hanover Gate
Outer Circle
Frampton Street
Hatton Row
Hatton Street
Penfold Street
Fisherton Street
Luton Street
Bledlow Close
Hollymouth Close
Capland Street
Lorne Close
Cuthbert St
Adpar St
Boscobel Street
Samford St
Gateforth St
Bernhardt Crescent
Crescent
Paveley Street
Kent Terrace
Hanover Terrace
Hanover Terrace Mews
Venables Street
Alpha Cl
Lilestone Street
Mallory Street
Church Street
Salisbury St
Mulready St
Ashbridge St
Plympton St
Plympton Pl
Lisson Grove
Tresham Crescent
Paveley St
Palgrave Gardens
Carlisle Mews
Penfold Street
Whitehaven St
Rossmore Road
Broadley Street
Broadley Terrace
Harewood Avenue
Sussex Place
Broadley Street Gardens
Miles Pl
Portman Gate
Penfold Place
Ashmill Street
Taunton Pl
Corlett Street
Ranston Street
Shroton St
Blandford Square
31
Bell Street
Lisson Street
Daventry Street
Stalbridge St
Cosway Street
Hayes Place
Marylebone Station
Ivor Pl
Boston Place
Balcombe Street
Linhope Street
Huntsworth Mews
Gloucester Place A41
Ivor Place
Park Road A41
Clarence Terrace
Burne St
Bell Street
Harrow Road
Harrow Road Flyover
Harrow Road A404
Edgware Road
Bendall Ms
Lisson Grove B507
Harewood Row
Harewood Avenue
PAGE 413
Melcombe Place
Taunton Ms
Hunts Mews
Dorset Square
Chagford Street
Siddons Lane
Park Road
2
Chapel Street A501
Transept Street
Cabbell Street
Marylebone A501
Great Central Street
Balcombe Street
Dorset Square
Melcombe Street
Sherlock Holmes' House
Old Marylebone Road A501
Homer Row
Homer Street
Harcourt Street
Shillibeer Place
Walmer Place
Enford Street
Wyndham Street
Knox Street
Dorset Close
Marylebone
Glentworth Street
Allsop Place
Outer Circle
Cornwall Ter
Watson's Ms
Edgware Road A5
Crawford Place
Shouldham St
Crawford Place
Seymour Place
York Street
Salisbury Place
1
Baker Street
Brendon Street
Cato Street
Molyneux Street
Crawford Street
Montagu Street
York Street
Gloucester Pl A41
Bickenhall Street
A41
Porter Street
Marylebone A501
0.25 mile
0.25 km

larylebone Road is noisy enough to have you running for the taps of the **wotwentytwo** straight away.

Coffee

- **Pret A Manger** • 120 Baker St

Emergency Rooms

- **Western Eye Hospital** • 173 Marylebone Rd

Landmarks

- **Lord's Cricket Ground** • St John's Wood
- **Sherlock Holmes' House** • 221 Baker St

Libraries

- **Church Street Library** • Church St
- **London Business School Library** • 25 Taunton Pl
- **Marylebone Library** • 109 Marylebone Rd

Nightlife

- **The North London Tavern** • 374 Kilburn High Rd
- **twotwentytwo** • 222 Marylebone Rd
- **Volunteer** • 245 Baker St

Post Offices

- **Edgware Rd** • 354 Edgware Rd

Restaurants

- **Sea Shell of Lisson Grove** • 49 Lisson Grove

Shopping

- **Alfie's Antiques Market** • 25 Church St
- **Archive Secondhand Books & Music** • 83 Bell St
- **Beatles London Store** • 231 Baker St
- **Lord's Cricket Shop** • Lord's Cricket Ground, Lisson Grove

Supermarkets

- **Tesco** • 94 Church St

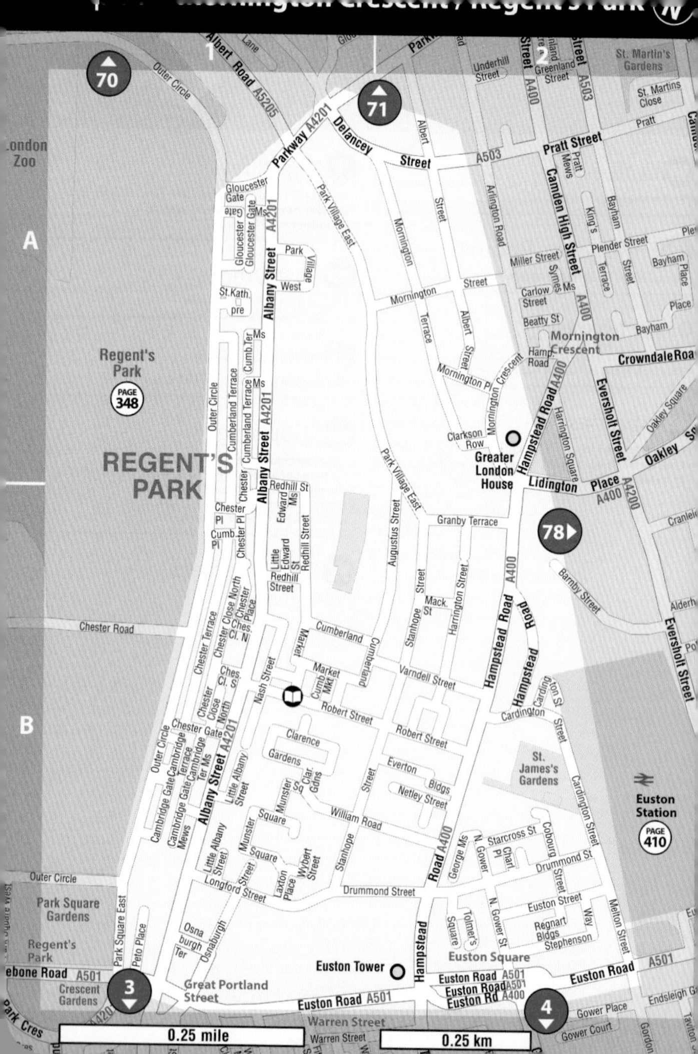

70
71
78
3
4
A
B
1
2
London Zoo
Regent's Park
PAGE 348
REGENT'S PARK
Outer Circle
Albert Road A5205
Parkway A4201
Delancey Street
Pratt Street
Camden High Street
Mornington Crescent
Greater London House
Hampstead Road A400
Lidington Place
Eversholt Street
Oakley Square
Albany Street A4201
Park Village East
Mornington Street
Augustus Street
Granby Terrace
Cumberland Market
Varndell Street
Robert Street
Clarence Gardens
William Road
Drummond Street
Munster Square
Chester Road
Chester Terrace
Cumberland Terrace
Cambridge Terrace
Longford Street
St. James's Gardens
Euston Station
PAGE 410
Cardington Street
Melton Street
Euston Square
Euston Tower
Euston Road A501
Great Portland Street
Park Square Gardens
Park Crescent Gardens
Warren Street
Gower Place
Gower Court
St. Martin's Gardens
Crowndale Road
Arlington Road
Harrington Square
Barnby Street
0.25 mile
0.25 km

Mornington Crescent/Regent's Park

Hemmed in by Regent's Park and Euston, this patch combines pretty streets with tower-block thoroughfares. Skip the din of Euston underpass for Drummond Street, Camden's 'little India'—hit up **Bhel Poori** for decent dosas and visit **Chutneys** for veggies. Wash it all down with mugs of Black Sheep Ale at **The Crown and Anchor** before mingling al fresco with **Edinboro Castle's** yuppier folk.

Landmarks

- **Euston Tower** • 286 Euston Rd
- **Greater London House** • Hampstead Rd

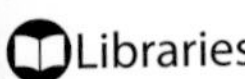

Libraries

- **Regents Park Library** • Robert St

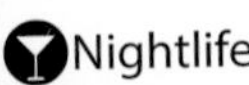

Nightlife

- **The Crown & Anchor** • 137 Drummond St
- **Edinboro Castle** • 57 Mornington Terrace
- **Euston Tap** • 190 Euston Rd
- **Horse & Groom** • 128 Great Portland St

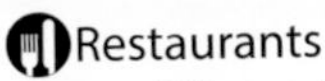

Restaurants

- **Chutneys** • 124 Drummond St
- **Diwana Bhel Poori** • 121 Drummond St
- **The Green Note** • 106 Parkway
- **Mestizo** • 103 Hampstead Rd

Shopping

- **Chess & Bridge** • 369 Euston Rd

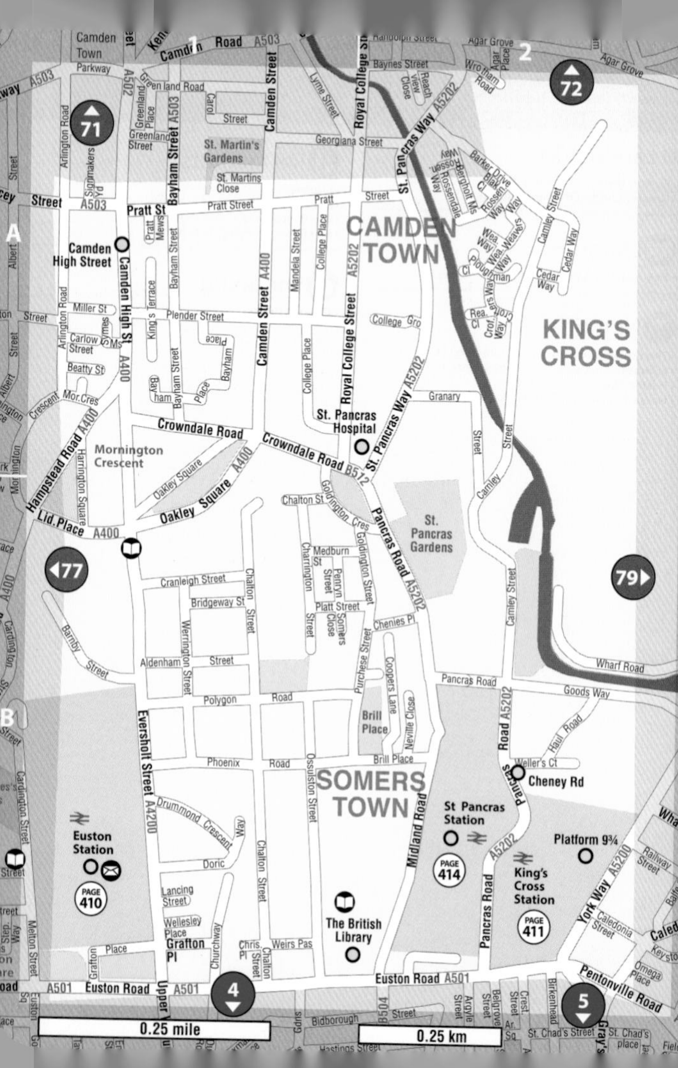

1
2
A
B
4
5
71
72
77
79
Camden Town
Camden Road A503
Parkway
Agar Grove
Baynes Street
Wrotham Road
Agar Place
Randolph Street
Royal College Street
Lyme Street
Greenland Road
Greenland Place
Greenland Street
Carol Street
Camden Street
Georgiana Street
St. Pancras Way A5202
Reach
View Close
St. Martin's Gardens
St. Martins Close
Arlington Road
Signmakers Yd
Bayham Street A503
Pratt St
Pratt Street
Pratt Mews
Street A503
Camden High Street
Camden High St A400
CAMDEN TOWN
KING'S CROSS
Barker Drive
Rossendale Way
Rossendale
Bergholt Ms
Camley Street
Cedar Way
Weavers Way
Ploughman Cl
Crofters Way
College Place
Mandela Street
Camden Street A400
Royal College Street
Miller St
Plender Street
King's Terrace
Bayham Place
Carlow Street
Symes Ms
Beatty St
College Gro
Mor.Cres
Crescent
Hampstead Road A400
Harrington Square
Mornington Crescent
Crowndale Road
Crowndale Road B512
St. Pancras Hospital
St. Pancras Way A5202
Granary Street
Oakley Square
Oakley Square A400
Chalton St
Goldington Cres
Pancras Road A5202
St. Pancras Gardens
Lid.Place A400
Medburn St
Charrington Street
Penryn Street
Goldington Street
Cranleigh Street
Bridgeway St
Chalton Street
Platt Street
Somers Close
Chenies Pl
Werrington Street
Purchese Street
Coopers Lane
Barnby Street
Aldenham Street
Polygon Road
Pancras Road
Goods Way
Wharf Road
Brill Place
Neville Close
Eversholt Street A4200
Phoenix Road
Haul Road
Weller's Ct
Cheney Rd
SOMERS TOWN
Ossulston Street
Midland Road
St Pancras Station
PAGE 414
Platform 9¾
Drummond Crescent
Euston Station
PAGE 410
Doric Way
Chalton Street
Lancing Street
Wellesley Place
Grafton Pl
Churchway
The British Library
King's Cross Station
PAGE 411
York Way A5200
Railway Street
Caledonia Street
Keystone
Omega Place
Pentonville Road
Place
Grafton
Chris. Pl
Weirs Pas
Euston Road A501
A501 Euston Road
Melton Street
Cardington Street
Birkenhead
Crestfield Street
Belgrove Street
Argyle Street
Bidborough Street
B504
St. Chad's Street
St. Chad's place
Gray's
0.25 mile
0.25 km

Euston's the first port of call for thousands of people each day, be it city workers from the Shires or pilgrims to the many erotic bookshops by the railway. Look beyond the station—an ugly grey cube that dominates the area—and you'll find a few gems. Students and bookish types head to the outstanding **library** (British that is) while beer aficionados head to **Euston Tap**.

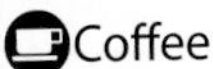

Coffee

- **Bagel Factory** • Euston Station
- **The Espresso Bar** • 96 Euston Rd
- **Pret A Manger** • 296 Pentonville Rd
- **Pret A Manger** • 117 Euston Rd
- **Starbucks** • 296 Pentonville Rd

Landmarks

- **The British Library** • 96 Euston Rd
- **Camden High Street** • Camden High St & Delancey St
- **Central Saint Martins** • 1 Granary Square
- **Cheney Road** • Cheney Rd & Weller's Ct
- **Euston Station** • Eversholt St & Doric Wy
- **Platform 9¾** • King's Cross Station
- **St Pancras**• Pancras Rd & Euston Rd
- **St Pancras Hospital** • 4 St Pancras Way

Libraries

- **The British Library** • 96 Euston Rd
- **Camden Town Library** • 218 Eversholt St
- **Wellcome Library** • 183 Euston Rd

Nightlife

- **The Camden Head** • 100 Camden High St
- **The Champagne Bar at St Pancras** • Pancras Rd
- **The Doric Arch** • 1 Eversholt St
- **Lincoln Lounge** • 52 York Wy
- **The Royal George** • 1 Eversholt St
- **Scala** • 275 Pentonville Rd

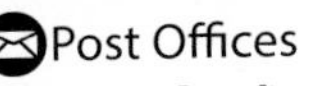

Post Offices

- **Kings Cross** • 21 Euston St

Restaurants

- **Asakusa** • 265 Eversholt St
- **The Booking Office** • St Pancras Renaissance London Hotel, Euston Rd
- **Camino** • 3 Varnisher's Yard
- **Caravan** • 1 Granary Building
- **Chop Chop Noodle Bar** • 1 Euston Rd
- **Dishoom** • 5 Stable St
- **Great Nepalese** • 48 Eversholt St
- **The Somerstown Coffee House** • 60 Chalton St

Shopping

- **All Ages Records** • 27 Pratt St
- **Housmans Bookshop** • 5 Caledonian Rd

Supermarkets

- **Sainsbury's** • 10 Camden High St

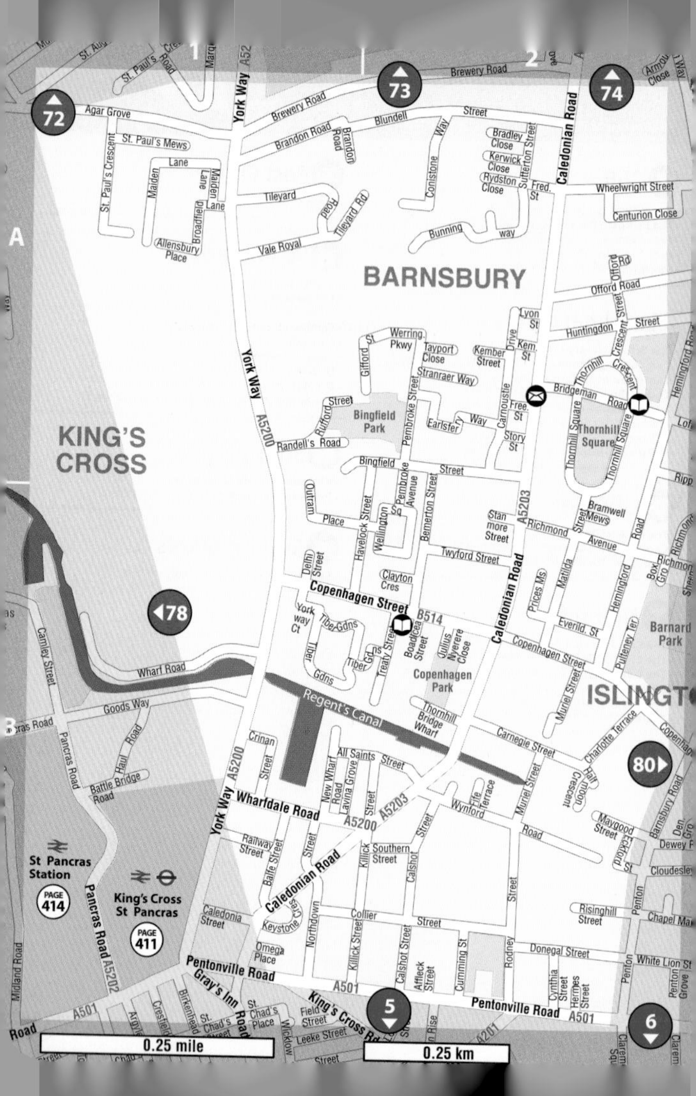

BARNSBURY
KING'S CROSS
ISLINGTON
72
73
74
78
80
5
6
York Way
Caledonian Road
Agar Grove
Brewery Road
Blundell Street
Brandon Road
St. Paul's Crescent
St. Paul's Mews
Maiden Lane
Tileyard Road
Tileyard Rd
Vale Royal
Allensbury Place
Broadfield Lane
Coniston Way
Bradley Close
Kerwick Close
Rydston Close
Sutterton Street
Fred. St
Wheelwright Street
Centurion Close
Bunning Way
Offord Road
Offord Rd
Huntingdon Street
Lyon St
Kem. St
Kember Street
Carnoustie Drive
Werrington St
Tayport Close
Stranraer Way
Gifford St
Rufford Street
Bingfield Park
Pembroke Street
Earlsferry Way
Free. St
Story St
Bridgeman Road
Thornhill Crescent
Thornhill Square
Randell's Road
Bingfield Street
Outram Place
Havelock Street
Wellington Sq
Pembroke Avenue
Bemerton Street
Stanmore Street
Richmond Avenue
Bramwell Mews
Twyford Street
Delhi Street
Clayton Cres
Copenhagen Street
B514
A5200
A5203
York way Ct
Tiber Gdns
Treaty Street
Boadicea Street
Julius Nyerere Close
Copenhagen Park
Prices Ms
Matilda Street
Everild. St
Hemingford Road
Pulteney Ter
Barnard Park
Box Gro
Muriel Street
Wharf Road
Goods Way
Camley Street
Regent's Canal
Thornhill Bridge Wharf
Carnegie Street
Charlotte Terrace
Half moon Crescent
Barnsbury Road
Crinan Street
All Saints Street
New Wharf Road
Lavina Grove
Wharfdale Road
Fife Terrace
Wynford Road
Maygood Street
Eckford St
Railway Street
Balfe Street
Killick Street
Southern Street
Calshot Street
Caledonian Road
Keystone Cres
Caledonia Street
Collier Street
Northdown Street
Omega Place
Risinghill Street
Penton Street
Chapel Market
Donegal Street
White Lion St
Pentonville Road
A501
Gray's Inn Road
Cumming St
Rodney Street
Affleck Street
Cynthia Street
Hermes Street
St. Chad's Place
St. Chad's Street
Field Street
King's Cross Rd
Leeke Street
Wicklow Street
Birkenhead Street
Crestfield Street
Argyle Street
Pancras Road
Battle Bridge Road
Midland Road
A5202
Haul Road
St Pancras Station
PAGE 414
King's Cross St Pancras
PAGE 411
0.25 mile
0.25 km
Brewery Road
Cloudesley
Dewey

No area in North London benefited more from the Olympic games than this crucial commuter hub. The once tawdry Kings Cross Station has a new face and a modern aura while **St Pancras** is as glorious a station as you'll find in Europe. Once London's seediest spot the KC is now full of rakish bars and clubs with excellent live music and some tasty eats up Caledonian Road.

Libraries

- **Lewis Carroll Children's Library** • 166 Copenhagen St
- **West Library** • Bridgeman Rd

Nightlife

- **The Big Chill House** • 257 Pentonville Rd
- **Central Station** • 37 Wharfdale Rd
- **Drake and Morgan** • 6 Pancras Sq
- **Drink, Shop & Do** • 9 Caledonian Rd
- **EGG** • 200 York Wy
- **Hemingford Arms** • 128 Hemingford Rd
- **The Lexington** • 96 Pentonville Rd
- **Lincoln Lounge** • 52 York Wy
- **The Parcel Yard** • Euston Road Kings Cross
- **Simmons** • 32 Caledonian Rd
- **Tarmon** • 270 Caledonian Rd

Post Offices

- **Caledonian Road** • 320 Caledonian Rd

Restaurants

- **Addis** • 42 Caledonian Rd
- **Drink, Shop & Do** • 9 Caledonian Rd
- **Euro Café** • 299 Caledonian Rd
- **Marathon** • 196 Caledonian Rd
- **The New Didar** • 347 Caledonian Rd
- **Oz** • 53 Caledonian Rd

Supermarkets

- **Co-Op** • 303 Caledonian Rd
- **Iceland** • 259 Caledonian Rd

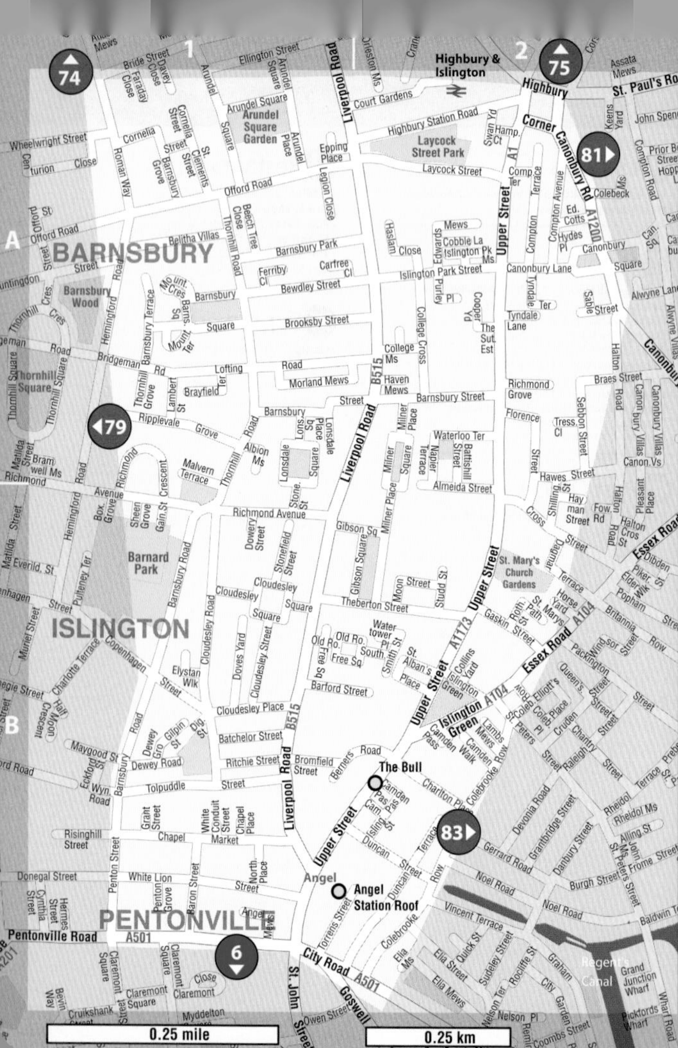

74
75
81
79
83
6
1
2
A
B
Highbury & Islington
Highbury Corner
BARNSBURY
ISLINGTON
PENTONVILLE
Arundel Square Garden
Laycock Street Park
Barnsbury Wood
Thornhill Square
Barnard Park
St. Mary's Church Gardens
The Bull
Angel
Angel Station Roof
Regent's Canal
Grand Junction Wharf
Pickfords Wharf
Wharf Road
Bride Street
Davey Close
Faraday Close
Ellington Street
Arundel Square
Liverpool Road
Orleston Ms
Court Gardens
Highbury Station Road
Swan Yd
Hamp. Ct
Assata Mews
St. Paul's Road
Keens Yard
John Spencer
Canonbury Rd
A1200
Compton Road
Prior Bolton Street
Wheelwright Street
Cornelia Street
Centurion Close
Roman Way
Barnsbury Grove
St. Clements Street
Offord Road
Epping Place
Legion Close
Laycock Street
Upper Street
A1
Compton Terrace
Compton Avenue
Colebeck Ms
Ed. Cotts
Hydes Pl
Canonbury
Offord St
Belitha Villas
Beach Tree Close
Thornhill Road
Barnsbury Park
Haslam Close
Mews
Cobble La
Islington Pk Ms
Edwards
Canonbury Lane
Canonbury Square
Huntingdon Street
Thornhill Cres.
Mount. Cres
Barnsbury Square
Ferriby Cl
Carfree Cl
Bewdley Street
Islington Park Street
Purley Pl
Cooper Yd
Tyndale Ter
Tyndale Lane
Sable Street
Alwyne Lane
Alwyne Villas
Hemingford Road
Barnsbury Terrace
Brooksby Street
College Cross
The Sut. Est
Bridgeman Rd
Lofting Road
Morland Mews
College Ms
Haven Mews
B515
Halton Road
Braes Street
Richmond Grove
Thornhill Square
Thornhill Grove
Lambert St
Brayfield Ter
Barnsbury Street
Lonsdale Place
Lonsdale Square
Milner Place
Milner Square
Florence Street
Tress. Cl
Sebbon Street
Canonbury Villas
Canon.Vs
Ripplevale Grove
Albion Ms
Waterloo Ter
Napier Terrace
Battishill Street
Matilda Street
Bramwell Ms
Richmond Crescent
Malvern Terrace
Richmond Avenue
Stonefield Street
Almeida Street
Hawes Street
Shillingford St
Hayman Street
Fowler Rd
Pleasant Place
Halton Cros St
Essex Road
Dibden
Box. Grove
Sheen Grove
Gain.St
Barnsbury Road
Dowery Street
Gibson Sq
Gibson Square
Cross Street
Dagmar Terrace
Everild St
Pulteney Ter
Cloudesley Road
Cloudesley Square
Cloudesley Street
Moon Street
Studd St
Theberton Street
Piker St
Elder Wlk
Popham Street
Copenhagen Street
Muriel Street
Charlotte Terrace
Elystan Wlk
Doves Yard
Old Royal Free Sq
Water tower Pl
South. Smith St
St. Alban's Place
A1173
Collins Yard
Islington Green
Gaskin Street
Roth. St
St. Marys Path
Horse Yard
A104
Britannia Row
Packington Street
Windsor Street
Queen's Street
Carnegie Street
Half Moon Crescent
Barford Street
Cloudesley Place
Colebrooke Row
St. Peters Street
Coleb. Place
Elliott's Row
Cruden Street
Chantry Street
Lambs Mews
Maygood St
Dewey Road
Dewey Gro
Gilpin St
Batchelor Street
Ritchie Street
Bromfield Street
Berners Road
Camden Walk
Camden Pass
Raleigh Street
Prebend Street
Eckford St
Wyn. Road
Tolpuddle Street
Charlton Place
Camden Pas
Rheidol Terrace
Rheidol Ms
Devonia Road
Grantbridge Street
Danbury Street
Alling. St
Grant Street
White Conduit Street
Chapel Place
Chapel Market
Risinghill Street
Islington St
Duncan Terrace
Duncan Street
Gerrard Road
John Ms
St Peters Street
Frome Street
Donegal Street
Penton Street
White Lion Street
Penton Grove
Baron Street
North. Place
Noel Road
Burgh Street
Cynthia Street
Hermes Street
Angel Mews
Torrens Street
Vincent Terrace
Baldwin Terrace
Pentonville Road
A501
Claremont Square
Claremont Close
St. John Street
City Road
Colebrooke Row
Elia Ms
Elia Street
Elia Mews
Quick St
Sudeley Street
Rocliffe St
Graham Street
City Garden Row
Bevin Way
A201
Cruikshank Street
Claremont Square
Myddelton
Owen Street
Goswell
Nelson Ter
Nelson Pl
Coombs Street
0.25 mile
0.25 km

A purpose-built playground for a twenty-somethings crowd that has to wake up for work in the morning. Whether it's the boutique shops, bars and restaurants that cater to any and all taste preoccupying Upper Street, the antique shops along **Camden Passage**, or an eclectic and vivid live music and theatre scene (Head to the **Kings Head Pub** for both), Angel has it all, and much more.

Cinemas

- **Everyman Screen on the Green** • 83 Islington Green
- **Vue Islington** • 36 Parkfield St

Coffee

- **Estorick Gallery** • 39 Canonbury Sq
- **Euphorium Bakery** • 202 Upper St
- **Pret A Manger** • 27 Islington High St
- **Starbucks** • 7 Islington High St

Landmarks

- **Angel Station Roof**
- **The Bull** •100 Upper St

Nightlife

- **69 Colebrooke Row** • 69 Colebrooke Row
- **The Angel** • 3 Islington High St
- **The Angelic** • 57 Liverpool Rd
- **Camden Head** • 2 Camden Walk
- **The Castle** • 54 Pentonville Rd
- **Colebrookes** • 69 Colebrooke Row
- **Compton Arms** • 4 Compton Ave
- **The Crown** • 116 Cloudesley Rd
- **Dead Dolls House** • 181 Upper St
- **The Drapers Arms** • 44 Barnsbury St
- **The Garage** • 20 Highbury Corner
- **Hope And Anchor** • 207 Upper St
- **Islington Academy** • 16 Parkfield St
- **King's Head Theatre & Pub** • 115 Upper St
- **Little Bat** • 54 Islington Park St
- **Lucky Voice** • 173 Upper St
- **Old Red Lion** • 418 St John St
- **The Regent** • 201 Liverpool Rd
- **Round Midnight: Jazz and Blues Bar** • 13 Liverpool Rd
- **Union Chapel** • Compton Terrace

Restaurants

- **Afghan Kitchen** • 35 Islington Green
- **The Albion** • 10 Thornhill Rd
- **Alpino** • 97 Chapel Market
- **The Breakfast Club** • 31 Camden Passage
- **Candid Café** • 3 Torrens St
- **Dead Dolls House** • 181 Upper St
- **Fig and Olive** • 151 Upper St
- **Fredericks** • Camden Passage
- **Gem** • 265 Upper St
- **Indian Veg Bhelpoori House** • 93 Chapel Market
- **Isarn** • 119 Upper St
- **Le Mercury** • 140 Upper St
- **Masala Zone** • 80 Upper St
- **Mem & Laz** • 8 Theberton St
- **Oldroyd** • 344 Upper St
- **Ottolenghi** • 287 Upper St
- **Pizzeria Oregano** • 19 St Alban's Pl
- **Rodizo Rico** • 77 Upper St
- **Tortilla** • 13 Islington High St
- **Zaffrani** • 47 Cross St

Shopping

- **After Noah** • 121 Upper St
- **Annie's Vintage Costume and Textiles** • 12 Camden Passage
- **Camden Passage** • Camden Passage
- **Cass Art** • 66 Colebrooke Row
- **Gill Wing Kitchen Shop** • 194 Upper St
- **Micycle N1** • 47 Barnsbury St
- **Monte's Deli** • 23 Canonbury Ln
- **Paul A Young Fine Chocolates** • 33 Camden Passage
- **Twentytwentyone** • 274 Upper St

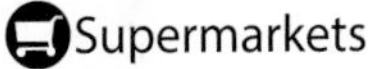

Supermarkets

- **Iceland** • 62 Chapel Market

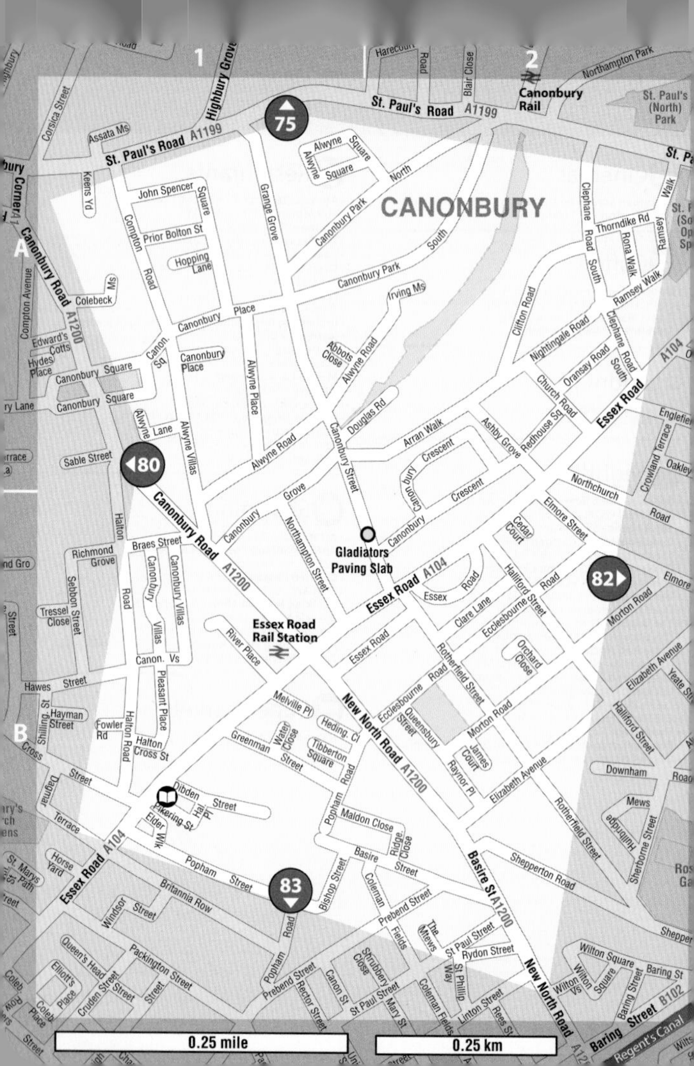

CANONBURY
Canonbury Rail
St. Paul's Road A1199
St. Paul's (North) Park
Northampton Park
Harecourt Road
Blair Close
Highbury Grove
Corsica Street
Assata Ms
Keens Yd
Canonbury Corner A1
Canonbury Road A1200
Compton Avenue
Colebeck Ms
Edward's Cotts
Hydes Place
Canonbury Square
Canonbury Lane
Sable Street
Halton Road
Richmond Grove
Braes Street
Canonbury Villas
Canon. Vs
Sebbon Street
Tressel Close
Hawes Street
Shillingford St
Hayman Street
Fowler Rd
Halton Cross St
Pleasant Place
Cross Street
Dagmar Terrace
Elder Wlk
Pickering St
Dibden Street
Hal. Pl
Essex Road A104
Horse Yard
St. Marys Path
Popham Street
Britannia Row
Windsor Street
Queen's Head Street
Elliott's Place
Coleb. Row
Coleb. Place
Cruden Street
Packington Street
Popham Road
Prebend Street
Rector Street
Canon St
Shrubbery Close
St Paul Street
Mary St
Coleman Fields
St Phillip Way
Linton Street
Rees St
Rydon Street
The Mews
New North Road
Basire St A1200
Wilton Vs
Wilton Square
Baring Street B102
Regent's Canal
John Spencer Square
Prior Bolton St
Hopping Lane
Compton Road
Canonbury Place
Canon. Sq
Alwyne Lane
Alwyne Villas
Alwyne Place
Alwyne Road
Alwyne Square
Grange Grove
Canonbury Park North
Canonbury Park South
Irving Ms
Abbots Close
Douglas Rd
Canonbury Street
Canonbury Grove
Northampton Street
Arran Walk
Canonbury Crescent
Canon bury
Gladiators Paving Slab
Essex Road Rail Station
River Place
Melville Pl
Greenman Street
Water Close
Heding. Cl
Tibberton Square
Popham Road
Maldon Close
Ridge. Close
Basire Street
Bishop Street
Coleman Street
Prebend Street
New North Road A1200
Ecclesbourne Road
Queensbury Street
Rotherfield Street
Raynor Pl
James Court
Morton Road
Elizabeth Avenue
Shepperton Road
Essex Road
Clare Lane
Ecclesbourne Street
Orchard Close
Halliford Street
Cedar Court
Elmore Street
Northchurch Road
Ashby Grove
Redhouse Sq
Church Road
Oransay Road
Nightingale Road
Clifton Road
Clephane Road South
Thorndike Rd
Rona Walk
Ramsey Walk
Crowland Terrace
Oakley
Englefield
Morton Road
Elizabeth Avenue
Yeate St
Halliford Street
Downham Road
Mews
Hullbridge
Sherborne Street
Shepperton
A104
75
80
82
83
1
2
A
B
0.25 mile
0.25 km

he Canonbury area is a delicious cocktail of diversity with a heady mix of leafy pacious streets, multi-million-pound mansions, a dollop of tempered hipster bodes and some of London's poorest estates. Essex Road has a Banksy and uirky shops including the notable **Get Stuffed** for all your taxidermy needs. oodies are well catered for with real butchers (**James Elliot**), bakers (**Raab's**), nd great ethnic eateries.

Landmarks

- **Gladiators Paving Slab** • 10 Canonbury St

Libraries

- **South Library** • 115 Essex Rd

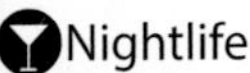

Nightlife

- **The Canonbury Tavern** • 21 Canonbury Pl
- **Marquess Tavern** • 32 Canonbury St
- **Myddleton Arms** • 52 Canonbury Rd
- **The Lord Clyde** • 342 Essex Rd

Restaurants

- **Raab's Bakery** • 136 Essex Rd
- **Tierra Peru** • 164 Essex Rd

Shopping

- **Get Stuffed** • 105 Essex Rd
- **James Elliot Butchers** • 96 Essex Rd
- **Planet Organic** • 64 Essex Rd
- **Steve Hatt** • 88 Essex Rd

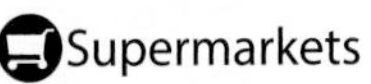

Supermarkets

- **Co-Op** • 132 Essex Rd

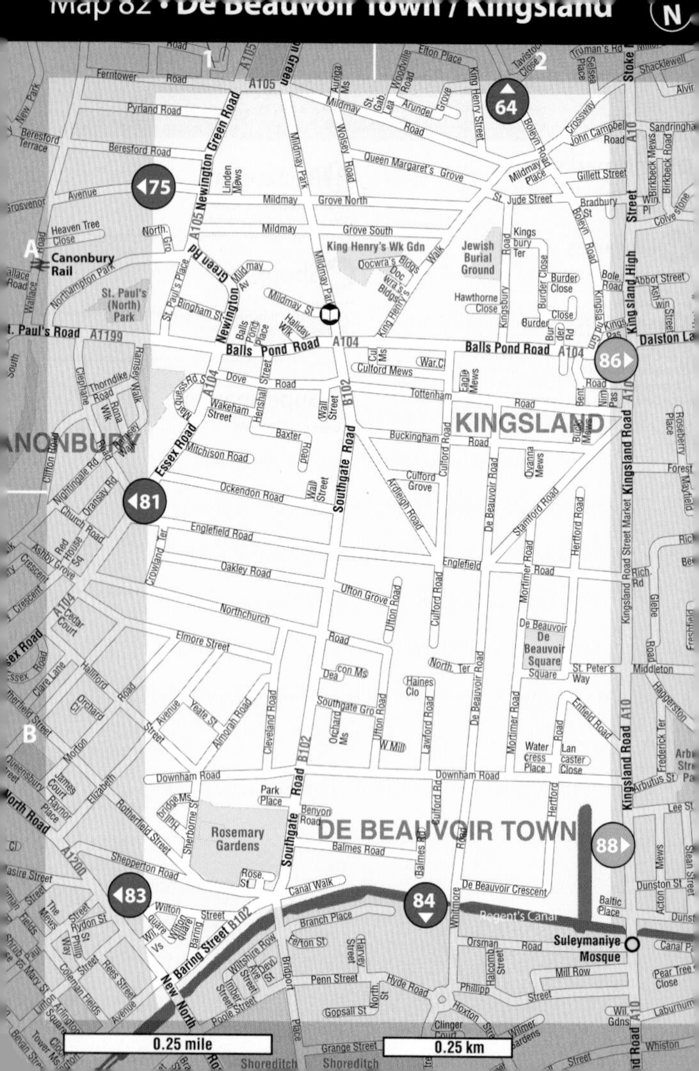

Map 82 • De Beauvoir Town / Kingsland
N
KINGSLAND
DE BEAUVOIR TOWN
CANONBURY
Canonbury Rail
St. Paul's (North) Park
King Henry's Wk Gdn
Jewish Burial Ground
De Beauvoir Square
Rosemary Gardens
Regent's Canal
Suleymaniye Mosque
64
75
81
83
84
86
88
Ferntower Road
Pyrland Road
Beresford Road
Beresford Terrace
Newington Green Road
Mildmay Road
Mildmay Park
Mildmay Grove North
Mildmay Grove South
Queen Margaret's Grove
Wolsey Road
Boleyn Road
King Henry Street
St. Jude Street
Balls Pond Road
St. Paul's Road
Dove Road
Tottenham Road
Culford Mews
Culford Road
Buckingham Road
Southgate Road
Essex Road
Mitchison Road
Ockendon Road
Englefield Road
Oakley Road
Northchurch Road
Elmore Street
Ufton Grove
Ufton Road
De Beauvoir Road
Stamford Road
Hertford Road
Mortimer Road
Kingsland Road
Kingsland High Street
Downham Road
Balmes Road
De Beauvoir Crescent
Canal Walk
Baring Street
New North Road
Branch Place
Orsman Road
Hyde Road
Penn Street
Mill Row
Dalston Lane
Stoke Newington
0.25 mile
0.25 km
Shoreditch

De Beauvoir Town / Kingsland

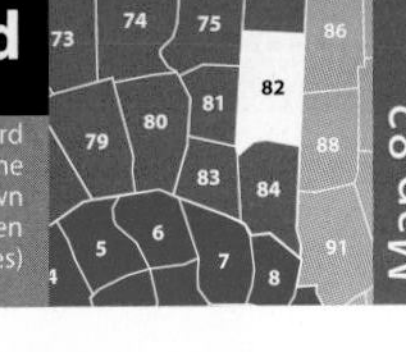

)e Beauvoir is the buffer zone where swanky Islington meets the self-regard)f Dalston. As such it's an ideal place to get a reprieve from either side. To the vest are quiet squares and gastropubs. Venture east and you'll be up-'til-dawn)oozing, talking to individuals comic book writers couldn't dream up. When 'ou're sick of both, sit in De Beauvoir Square (with its thousands of palm trees) nd ponder life.

Coffee

- **2&4** • 4 Southgate Rd
- **Tina, We Salute You** • 47 King Henry's Walk

Landmarks

- **Suleymaniye Mosque** • 212 Kingsland Rd

Libraries

- **Mildmay Library** • 21 Mildmay Park

Nightlife

- **Dalston Boys Club** • 68 Boleyn Rd
- **Dalston Jazz Bar** • 4 Bradbury St
- **The Duke of Wellington** • 119 Balls Pond Rd
- **The Hunter S** • 194 Southgate Rd
- **Rosemary Branch Theatre** • 2 Shepperton Rd
- **The Vortex** • 11 Gillett Sq

Restaurants

- **Mother Earth** • 101 Newington Green Rd
- **Peppers and Spice** • 40 Balls Pond Rd
- **Stone Cave** • 111 Kingsland

Shopping

- **2&4** • 4 Southgate Rd
- **Mother Earth** • 101 Newington Green Rd
- **North One Garden Centre** • 25 Englefield Rd

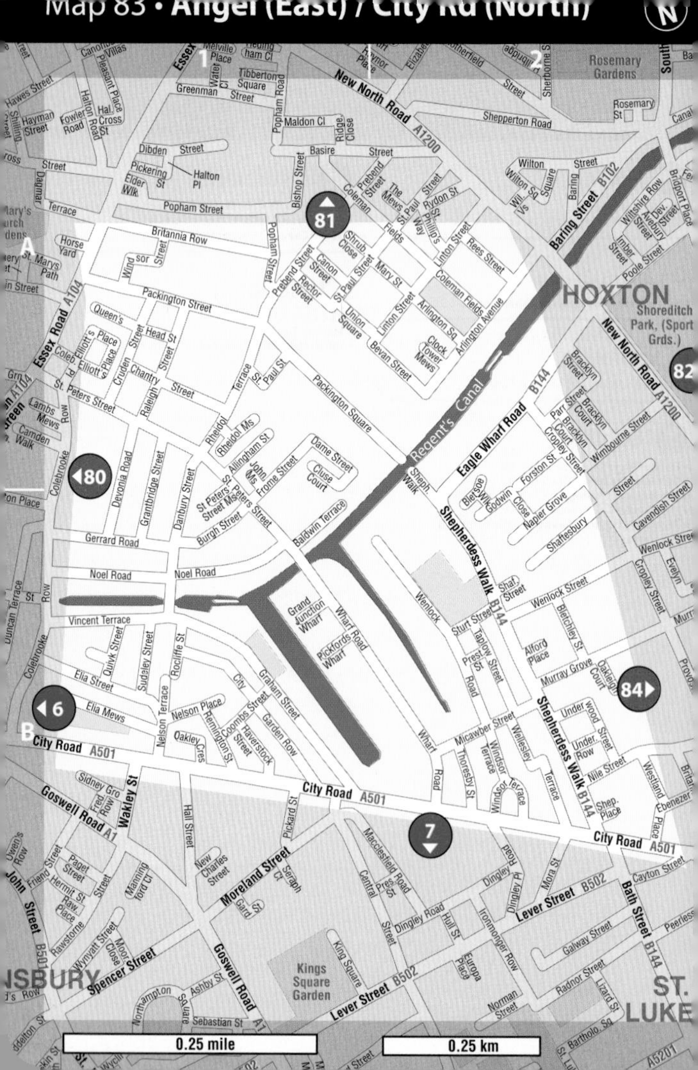

N
1
2
A
B
Rosemary Gardens
Rosemary St
Melville Place
Tibberton Square
Greenman Street
New North Road A1200
Shepperton Road
Popham Road
Maldon Cl
Ridge Close
Basire Street
Dibden Street
Pickering St
Halton Pl
Elder Wlk
Popham Street
Bishop Street
Prebend Street
The Mews
St Paul Street
Rydon St
St Philip's Way
Coleman Fields
Wilton Square
Wilton Sq
Wil. Vs
Baring Street B102
Canonbury Villas
Pleasant Place
Hawes Street
Shillingford Street
Hayman Street
Fowler Road
Halton Road
Hal. Cross St
Dagmar Terrace
Cross Street
81
Britannia Row
Horse Yard
St. Marys Path
Windsor Street
Shrub Close
Canon Street
Rector Street
Union Square
Mary St
Linton Street
Rees Street
Coleman Fields
Arlington Sq
Arlington Avenue
Clock Tower Mews
Bevan Street
HOXTON
Shoreditch Park, (Sport Grds.)
New North Road A1200
82
Wiltshire Row
Bridport Place
Imber Street
Poole Street
Packington Street
Queen's Head St
Essex Road A104
Elliott's Place
Coleb. Elliott's Place
Cruden Street
Chantry Street
Raleigh Street
Terrace
St. Paul St
Packington Square
St. Peters Street
Lambs Mews
Camden Walk
Rheidol Ms
Allingham St
John Ms
Frome Street
Dame Street
Cluse Court
Regent's Canal
Eagle Wharf Road
B144
Brackley Street
Parr Street
Brackyn Court
Cropley Street
Wimbourne Street
Forston St
Bletsoe Wlk
Godwin Close
Napier Grove
Shaftesbury Street
Cavendish Street
Colebrooke Row
80
Devonia Road
Grantbridge Street
Danbury Street
St Peters Street Ms
St. Peters Street
Burgh Street
Baldwin Terrace
Sheph. Walk
Shepherdess Walk
Gerrard Road
Noel Road
Wenlock Street
Cropley Street
Evelyn
Duncan Terrace
St Row
Vincent Terrace
Grand Junction Wharf
Wharf Road
Rickfords Wharf
Wenlock
Shaf. Street
Sturt Street
B144
Taplow Street
Prest St
Road
Bletchley St
Alford Place
Murray Grove
Oakley Court
84
Quick Street
Sudeley Street
Rocliffe St
Colebrooke
Elia Street
Elia Mews
6
Nelson Terrace
Nelson Place
Remington St
Coombs Street
City Graham Street
Garden Row
Haverstock Street
Oakley Cres
City Road A501
Wharf Road
Micawber Street
Thoresby St
Windsor Terrace
Wellesley Terrace
Shepherdess Walk B144
Underwood Street
Under. Row
Nile Street
Shep. Place
Westland Place
Ebenezer
Sidney Gro
Fred. Row
Wakley St
Goswell Road A1
Hall Street
Pickard St
7
City Road A501
Owen's Row
John Street B501
Friend Street
Paget Street
Hermit St
Raw. Place
Rawstorne
Manningford Cl
New Charles Street
Moreland Street
Gard St
Seraph Ct
Macclesfield Road
Central Street
Pres. St
Dingley Road
Hull St
Dingley Pl
Mora St
Lever Street B502
Bath Street B144
Cayton Street
Peerless
Galway Street
Wynyatt Street
Moor Close
Spencer Street
ISBURY
Ashby St
Northampton Square
Goswell Road
Sebastian St
Kings Square Garden
King Square
Lever Street B502
Ironmonger Row
Europa Place
Norman Street
Radnor Street
Lizard St
ST. LUKE
St. Bartholo. Sq
A5201
0.25 mile
0.25 km

Angel (East) / City Rd (North)

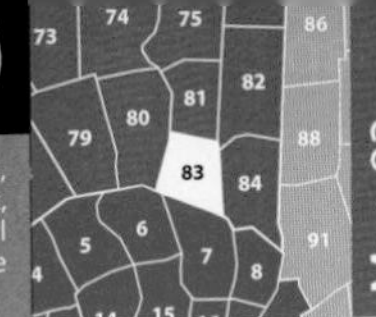

f you're bored of the bars on Upper Street or the ironic chic of Hoxton, he streets in between (along Essex Road or by the canal) are a better bet, vith a more laidback atmosphere. The **Island Queen** (NFT London's official irthplace!) is a cosy local pub and well worth a visit. One day they'll just have o give us one of those blue plaques.

Nightlife

- **Barrio North** • 45 Essex Rd
- **The Bill Murrary** • 39 Queen's Head St
- **The Charles Lamb** • 16 Elia St
- **The Duke of Cambridge** • 30 St Peter's St
- **Earl of Essex** • 25 Danbury St
- **The Narrow Boat** • 119 St Peters St
- **The Island Queen** • 87 Noel Rd
- **The New Rose** • 84 Essex Rd
- **The Old Queenís Head** • 44 Essex Rd
- **The Wenlock Arms** • 26 Wenlock Rd

Restaurants

- **The Charles Lamb** • 16 Elia St
- **Shepherdess Cafe** • 221 City Rd
- **William IV** • 7 Shepherdess Walk

Shopping

- **Flashback** • 50 Essex Rd
- **Past Caring** • 54 Essex Rd

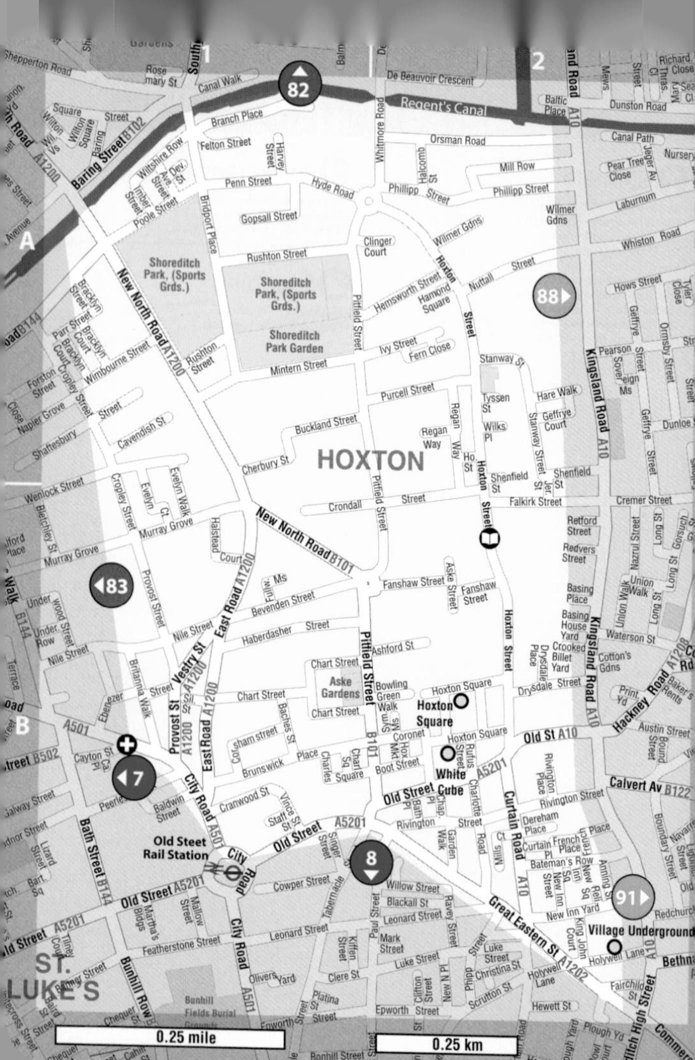
HOXTON
ST. LUKE'S
1
2
A
B
82
83
88
7
8
91
0.25 mile
0.25 km
Shepperton Road
Rosemary St
Canal Walk
De Beauvoir Crescent
Regent's Canal
Baltic Place
Dunston Road
Canal Path
Nurser
Orsman Road
Mill Row
Phillipp Street
Pear Tree Close
Laburnum
Whiston Road
Wilmer Gdns
Branch Place
Felton Street
Harvey Street
Whitmore Road
Halcomb St
Baring Street B102
Wiltshire Row
Dev. St
Penn Street
Hyde Road
Imber Street
Poole Street
Bridport Place
Gopsall Street
Clinger Court
Wilmer Gdns
Rushton Street
Shoreditch Park, (Sports Grds.)
Shoreditch Park Garden
Hoxton Street
Nuttall Street
Hemsworth Street
Hamond Square
Pittfield Street
Hows Street
Tyler Close
Geffrye Street
Ormsby Street
New North Road A1200
Brackly Street
Parr Street
Bracklyn Court
Wimbourne Street
Forston Street
Cropley Street
Napier Grove
Shaftesbury
Cavendish St
Rushton Street
Mintern Street
Ivy Street
Fern Close
Stanway St
Pearson Street
Sovereign Ms
Kingsland Road A10
Purcell Street
Tyssen St
Hare Walk
Geffrye Court
Buckland Street
Regan Way
Wilks Pl
Stanway Street
Dunloe
Cherbury St
Ho. St
Shenfield St
Jer. St
Wenlock Street
Bletchley St
Evelyn Walk
Evelyn Ct
Murray Grove
Halstead Court
Crondall Street
Falkirk Street
Cremer Street
Retford Street
Redvers Street
Nazrul Street
Long St
Gorsuch
New North Road B101
Fanshaw Street
Aske Street
Basing Place
Basing House Yard
Union Walk
Provost Street
Fullwood Ms
Bevenden Street
East Road A1200
Under wood Street
Under. Row
Nile Street
Haberdasher Street
Waterson St
Drysdale Place
Crooked Billet Yard
Cotton's Gdns
Ashford St
Chart Street
Vestry St
Britannia Walk
Aske Gardens
Bowling Green Walk
Hoxton Square
Drysdale Street
Hackney Road A1208
Print. Yd
Baker's Rents
Ebenezer Street
Sil. St
Provost St
Baches St
Sym. Ms
Coronet
Old St A10
Austin Street
Bound. Street
A501
Cayton St
Ca. Pl
Corsham street
Brunswick Place
Charles Square
Charl. Sq
Hox Mkt
Rufus Street
Boot Street
White Cube
A5201
Rivington Place
Calvert Av B122
Peerless
Baldwin Street
City Road A501
Cranwood St
Vince St
Staff St
Old Street Pl
Bath Pl
Chap. Pl
Charlotte Road
Curtain Road
Rivington Street
Dereham Place
Boundary Street
Navarre
Galway Street
Bath Street B144
Old Steet Rail Station
Old Street
Singer Street
Rivington Street
Garden Walk
Mills Ct
Curtain Pl
French Place
Bateman's Row
Anning St
Lizard Street
Bart. Sq
Old Street A5201
Mallow Street
Martha's Bldgs
Cowper Street
Tabernacle
Willow Street
Blackall St
Leonard Street
Ravey Street
Great Eastern St A1202
New Inn Sq
New Inn Street
New Inn Yard
New Reil Sq
Redchurch
Village Underground
Featherstone Street
Tilney Court
Paul Street
Mark Street
Kiffen Street
Luke Street
Christina St
King John Court
Holywell Lane
Bunhill Row
Banner Street
Olivers Yard
Clere St
Platina St
Clifton Street
New N Pl
Phipp Street
Scrutton St
Holywell Lane
Fairchild St
Shoreditch High Street
Bunhill Fields Burial Grounds
Chequer St
Epworth Street
Hewett St
Plough Yd
Bonhill Street
Commerc
Ironmonger
Baird Street

The only constant in Hoxton is change: what passes as monthly rent now was a deposit on a pad a decade earlier. The vibe is special and the pulse of the area radiates out of Hoxton Square and its bedfellow Curtain Road. Shop at **Hoxton Monster Supplies**, check modern art at **White Cube**, drink at **Zigfrid**, and finish on the floor at **Cargo**.

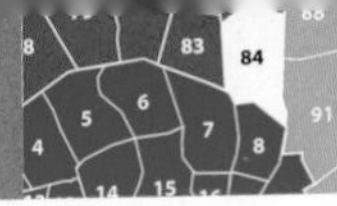

Coffee

- **Eat.** • 59 Great Eastern St
- **Tre Era Cafe** • 30 Whitmore Rd

Emergency Rooms

- **Moorfields Eye Hospital** • 162 City Rd

Landmarks

- **Hoxton Square** • Hoxton Sq
- **Village Underground** • 54 Holywell Ln
- **White Cube** • 48 Hoxton Sq

Libraries

- **Shoreditch Library** • 80 Hoxton St

Nightlife

- **Cargo** • 83 Rivington St
- **Charlie Wright's International Bar** • 45 Pitfield St
- **Club Aquarium** • 256 Old St
- **Happiness Forgets** • 9 Hoxton Sq
- **Howl at the Moon** • 178 Hoxton St
- **Hoxton Square Bar and Kitchen** • 2 Hoxton Sq
- **The Macbeth** • 70 Hoxton St
- **The Old Blue Last** • 38 Great Eastern St
- **Red Lion** • 41 Hoxton St
- **The Stag's Head** • 55 Orsman Rd
- **Strongroom** • 120 Curtain Rd
- **Troy Bar** • 10 Hoxton St
- **Zigfrid** • 11 Hoxton Sq

Restaurants

- **100 Hoxton** • 100 Hoxton St
- **The Barrel Boulangerie** • 110 Hoxton St
- **Big Apple Hot Dogs** • 239 Old St
- **The Clove Club** • 380 Old St
- **Cocotte Shoreditch** • 8 Hoxton Sq
- **The Diner** • 128 Curtain Rd
- **The Jones Family Project** • 78 Great Eastern St
- **Meat Mission** • 15 Hoxton Market
- **Rivington Bar and Grill** • 28 Rivington St
- **Tramshed** • 32 Rivington St
- **Visions Canteen** • 31 New Inn Yard

Shopping

- **Good Hood** • 151 Coronet St
- **Hoxton Street Monster Supplies** • 159 Hoxton St
- **SCP** • 135 Curtain Rd
- **Sh!** • 57 Hoxton Sq

Supermarkets

- **Co-Op** • 136 New North Rd
- **Iceland** • 209 Hoxton St

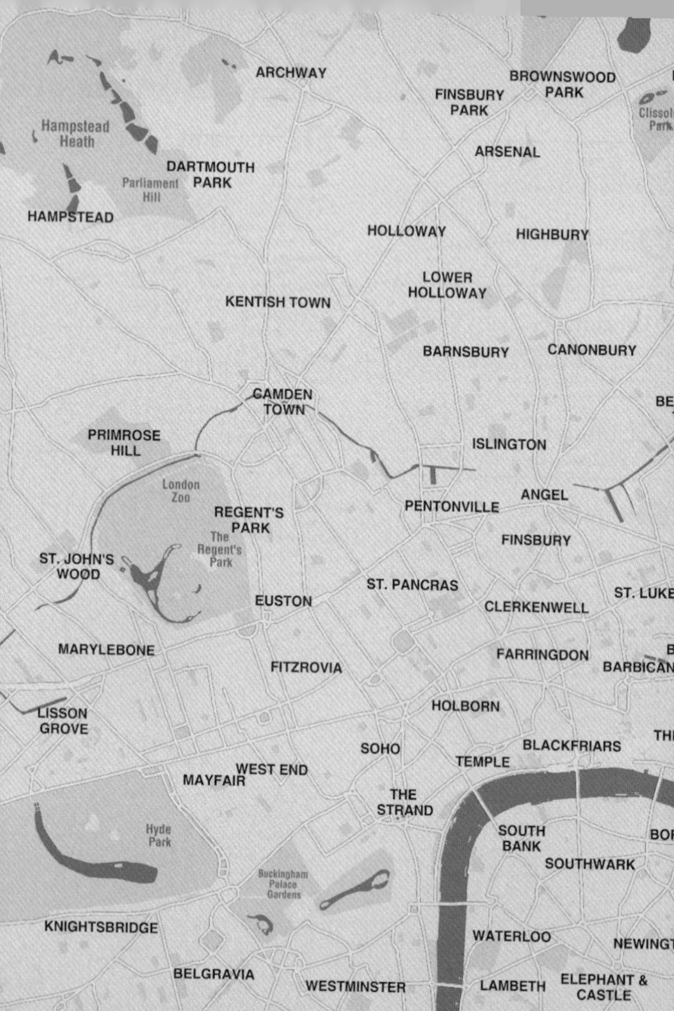

ARCHWAY
BROWNSWOOD PARK
FINSBURY PARK
Hampstead Heath
ARSENAL
DARTMOUTH PARK
Parliament Hill
HAMPSTEAD
HOLLOWAY
HIGHBURY
LOWER HOLLOWAY
KENTISH TOWN
BARNSBURY
CANONBURY
CAMDEN TOWN
PRIMROSE HILL
ISLINGTON
London Zoo
ANGEL
PENTONVILLE
REGENT'S PARK
The Regent's Park
FINSBURY
ST. JOHN'S WOOD
ST. PANCRAS
EUSTON
CLERKENWELL
MARYLEBONE
FARRINGDON
BARBICAN
FITZROVIA
HOLBORN
LISSON GROVE
BLACKFRIARS
SOHO
TEMPLE
WEST END
MAYFAIR
THE STRAND
Hyde Park
SOUTH BANK
SOUTHWARK
Buckingham Palace Gardens
KNIGHTSBRIDGE
WATERLOO
BELGRAVIA
WESTMINSTER
LAMBETH
ELEPHANT & CASTLE

UPPER CLAPTON
Stamford Hill
85
Rectory Rd
Lee Valley Park
LEA BRIDGE
LOWER CLAPTON
Hackney Downs
Stoke Newington High St
L. Clapton Rd
Pembury Rd
87
Urswick Rd
86
HOMERTON
Hackney Marsh
Dalston Ln.
Amhurst Rd
HACKNEY WICK
Graham Rd
90
Wick Rd
Cassland Rd
HACKNEY
Victoria Park
Queensbridge Rd
Mare St
ALSTON
LONDON FIELDS
89
Well St
Victoria Park Rd
OLD FORD
SOUTH HACKNEY
Kingsland Rd
88
Old Ford Rd
HAGGERSTON
Haggerston Park
Hackney Rd
Bishops Way
Cambridge Heath Rd
Roman Road
94
GLOBE TOWN
BOW
Grove Rd
BETHNAL GREEN
Mile End Rd
BROMLEY
93
MILE END
91
92
SPITALFIELDS
Globe Rd
Dunbridge St
Cheshire St
BOW COMMON
Mile End Park
BRICK LANE
Brick Ln
Vallance Rd
Whitechapel Rd
St. Pauls Way
STEPNEY
Ben Jonson Rd
99
97
98
WHITECHAPEL
Burdett Rd
96
RATCLIFF
New Rd
Commercial St
SHADWELL
Commercial Rd
POPLAR
Mansell St
Cable St
Westferry Rd
LIMEHOUSE
The Highway
Aspen Way
100
95
Tower of London Park
101
CANARY WHARF
WAPPING
DOCKLANDS
Thames River
ISLE OF DOGS
Westferry Rd
Manchester Rd
ROTHERHITHE
103
102
CUBITT TOWN
BERMONDSEY
Southwark Park
MILLWALL
Millwall Park

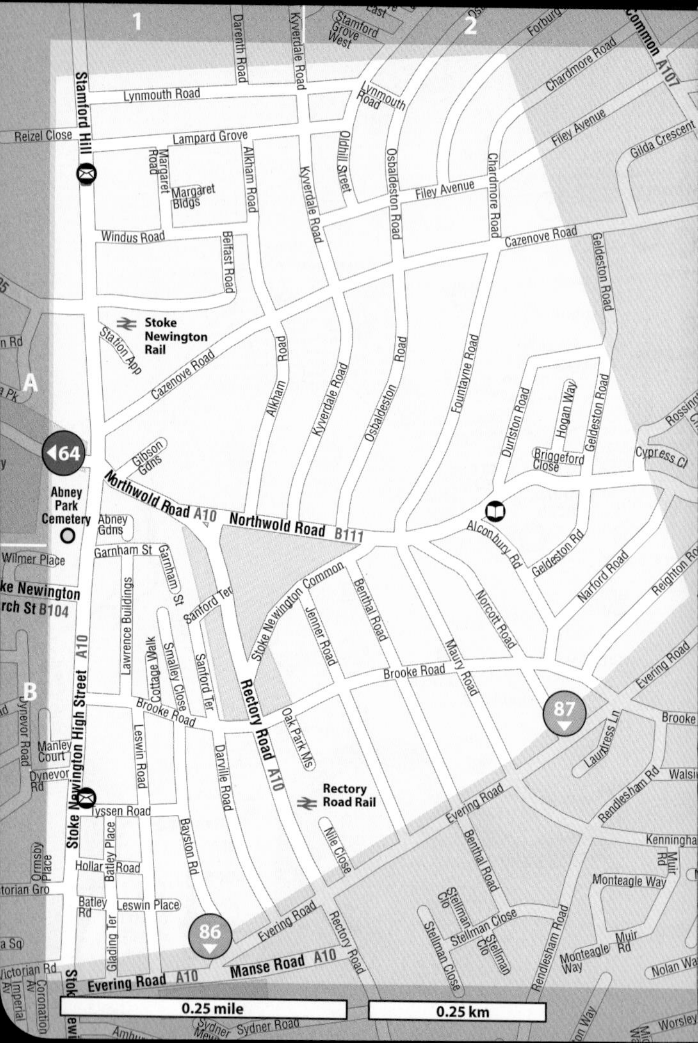

1
2
A
B
Stamford Hill
Lynmouth Road
Reizel Close
Lampard Grove
Darenth Road
Kyverdale Road
Stamford Grove West
Lynmouth Road
Margaret Road
Margaret Bldgs
Alkham Road
Oldhill Street
Osbaldeston Road
Filey Avenue
Chardmore Road
Cazenove Road
Forburg
Chardmore Road
Common A107
Filey Avenue
Gilda Crescent
Windus Road
Belfast Road
Geldeston Road
Stoke Newington Rail
Station App
Cazenove Road
Alkham Road
Kyverdale Road
Osbaldeston Road
Fountayne Road
Durlston Road
Hogan Way
Geldeston Road
Briggeford Close
Cypress Cl
64
Gibson Gdns
Abney Park Cemetery
Abney Gdns
Northwold Road A10
Northwold Road B111
Alconbury Rd
Geldeston Rd
Narford Road
Reighton Rd
Wilmer Place
Garnham St
Garnham St
Stoke Newington Church St B104
Lawrence Buildings
Cottage Walk
Smalley Close
Sanford Ter
Sanford Ter
Stoke Newington Common
Jenner Road
Benthal Road
Norcott Road
Maury Road
Brooke Road
Evering Road
Stoke Newington High Street A10
Brooke Road
Rectory Road A10
Oak Park Ms
87
Brooke
Dynevor Road
Manley Court
Leswin Road
Darville Road
Laudress Ln
Dynevor Rd
Rectory Road Rail
Rendlesham Rd
Walsi
Tyssen Road
Bayston Rd
Nile Close
Evering Road
Benthal Road
Kenningha
Muir Rd
Ormsby Place
Batley Place
Hollar Road
Monteagle Way
Victorian Gro
Batley Rd
Leswin Place
Stellman Clo
Stellman Close
Stellman Clo
Rendlesham Road
Muir Rd
Monteagle Way
Nolan Wa
86
Evering Road
Rectory Road
Stellman Close
Gladling Ter
Manse Road A10
Victorian Rd
Evering Road A10
Imperial Av
Coronation Av
0.25 mile
0.25 km
Sydner Mews
Sydner Road
Worsley

Stoke Newington (East)

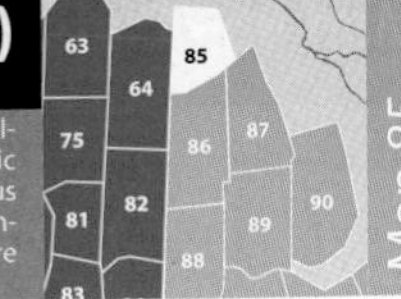

›key has turned into something of a Notting Hill of the east with all-rain buggies taking up the pavement while the MILFs do their organic ›cery shopping. It's resplendent in dining options but try **Testi** first. Various olitionists and Salvation Army veterans are interred at the nineteenth-ntury **Abney Park Cemetery**, which doubles as an overgrown nature eserve and cruising spot.

Landmarks

Abney Park Cemetery • Stoke Newington High St & Rectory Rd
Kynaston Gardens • 2 Kynaston Ave

Libraries

• **Clapton Library** • Northwold Rd

Nightlife

• **The Jolly Butchers** • 204 Stoke Newington High St
• **Royal Sovereign** • 64 Northwold Rd
• **White Hart** • 69 Stoke Newington High St

Post Offices

• **Stamford Hill** • 82 Stamford Hill
• **Stoke Newington** • 138 Stoke Newington High St

Restaurants

• **19 Numara Bos Cirrik** • 34 Stoke Newington Rd
• **Bagel House** • 2 Stoke Newington High St
• **Café Z Bar** • 58 Stoke Newington High St
• **Testi** • 38 Stoke Newington High St
• **Thai Cafe** • 3 Northwold Rd
• **Three Crowns** • 175 Stoke Newington Church St

Shopping

• **Bargain Bookshop** • 153 Stoke Newington High St
• **Hamdys** • 167 Stoke Newington High St
• **Stoke Newington Bookshop** • 159 Stoke Newington High St
• **Rouge** • 158 Stoke Newington High St

1
2
85
64
87
82
89
88
A
B
Scolars Place
Lavers Road
Manley Court
Stoke Newington High Street
Dynevor Road
Chesholm Road
Nevill Road
Oldfield Road
Harcombe Road
Sandbrook Road
Tyssen Road
Ormsby Place
Batley Place
Leswin Rd
Victorian Grove
York shire Clo
Batley Rd
Leswin Place
Uhura Sq
Barbauld Road
Victorian Rd
Glading Ter
Hollar Road
Darville Road
Rectory Rd
Nile Close
Oak Park Ms
Jenner Road
Benthal Road
Maury Road
Norcott Road
Laundress Lane
Rectory Road
Evering Road
Evering Road A10
Manse Road A10
A10
Knebworth Road
Londesborough Road
Gunstor Road
Victorian Grove
Imperial Avenue
Coronation Avenue
Osterley Road
Beatty Road
Sydner Ms
Sydner Road
Stellman Close
Monteagle Way
Rendlesham Road
Muir Road
Della
Nolan Way
Walford Road
Foulden Terrace
Foulden Road
Vine Cl
Clapton Way
Abbey Cl
Worsley Grove
Midhurst Way
Monro Way
Brighton Road
Farleigh Place
Downs Road
Lyn Ms
Palatine Avenue
Farleigh Road
Rectory Road
Forman Pl
Palatine Road
Wordsworth Rd
Amhurst Ter
Hackney Downs
Scoble Pl
Shacklewell Road
Prince George Road
Bennett Road
Somerford Grove
Shacklewell Lane
Belgrade Road
April St
Perch St
Amhurst Road
Princess May Road
Shacklewell Row
Seal Street
Cressington Close
Cowper Road
Barretts Grove
Stoke Newington Road
Miller's Ave
Shacklewell Green
Charterhouse Road
Blundell Clo
Rusbridge Clo
Arcola Street
Chow Sq
Pellerin Road
Miller's Ter
Gateway Ms
Dunn St
Independent Place
Downs Park Road
Sal. Rd
Truman's Road
Millard Close
Andre St
Selsea Place
Boleyn Road
King Henry Street
Tavistock Close
Crossway
Centreprise
Alvington Cres
Spenser Mews
Abersham Road
Langford Close
Foxley Close
Amton Street
Mildmay Road
Kingsland High Street A10
John Campbell Road
Birkbeck Mews
Birkbeck Road
Pendulum Ms
Sandringham Road
Fernclif Road
Mildmay Pl
Gillett Street
Time Sq
St. Jude Street
Brad. St
Colvestone Crescent
Cecilia Road
Montague Road
Wayland Ave
Sigdon Road
Sigdon Pass
Bodney Road
Brad. Ms
Win. Place
St. Marks Rise
Kreedman Walk
Hermitage Row
Lushington Terrace
Jewish Burial Ground
Kingsbury Road
Kingsbury Terrace
Ridley Road
Chester Cres.
Dalston Kingsland Rail
Hackney Downs Rail
Burder Close
Burder Clo
Kingsland Green
Abbot Street
Martel Pl
Victoria Mews
Madinah Road
Carrara Mews
Stanford Mews
Spurstowe Terrace
Navarino Road
Tyssen St
Ritson Rd
Kingsland Pass
Ashwin St
Hartwell St
Ramsgate St
Ghent Way
Atlas Ms
Fassett Sq
Cottrill Gdns
Balls Pond Road A104
Dalston Lane A104
Woodland St
Stannard Rd
Stannard Mews
Clifton Gro
Fassett Rd
Navarino Gro
Holy Trinity, The Clowns Church
Graham Road A1207
Anchor Ms
Bentley Rd
Crosby Walk
Laurel St
Fenton Clo
B108
Massie Road
Tottenham Road
Nimrod Pas
Buckingham Mews
Dalston Junction
Walkers Ct
Royal Oak Road
Buckingham Rd
Kingsland Road A10
Beechwood Road
Sokway Clo
Skelton Clo
Buttermere Walk
Camerton Clo
Houghton Clo
Queensbridge Road
Sanctuary Mews
Parkholme Road
Wilton Way
Stamford Road
Roseberry Pl
Cumberland Close
St. Philip's Rd
Elrington Rd
Lansdowne Dr
Greenwood Rd
Eleanor Road
Hertford Road
Forest Rd
Mayfield Clo
Forest Grove
Grace Jones Close
Blanchard Way
Englefield Road
Beehive
0.25 mile
0.25 km

Dalston / Kingsland

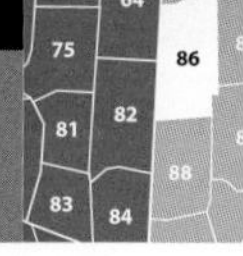

stling Ridley Road market is still the beating heart of Dalston, while Kingsland ad is like a Vice mag shoot with Nathan Barleys stalking up and down as ugh it were a catwalk. With hip bars like **Dalston Superstore** and **Ridley ad Bar**, it's no wonder. **Cafe Oto** is the experimental music cafe de jour.

Cinemas

- **Lux** • 18 Shacklewell Ln
- **Rio Cinema** • 107 Kingsland High St

Coffee

- **Dalston Eastern Curve Garden** • 13 Dalston Ln

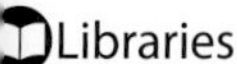

Landmarks

- **Holy Trinity, The Clowns Church** • Beechwood Rd & Kirkland Walk

Libraries

- **CLR James Library** • 30 Dalston Ln

Nightlife

- **Café Oto** • 18 Ashwin St
- **Dalston Superstore** • 117 Kingsland High St
- **The Haggerston** • 438 Kingsland Rd
- **High Water London** • 23 Stoke Newington Rd
- **The Moustache Bar** • 58 Stoke Newington Rd
- **The Prince George** • 40 Parkholme Rd
- **Ridley Road Market Bar** • 49 Ridley Rd
- **The Shacklewell Arms** • 71 Shacklewell Ln
- **VFD** • 66 Stoke Newington Rd

Post Offices

- **Kingsland High Street** • 118 Kingsland High St

Restaurants

- **Arancini Brothers** • 592 Kingsland Rd
- **The Best Turkish Kebab** • 125 Stoke Newington Rd
- **Dalston Eastern Curve Garden** • 13 Dalston Ln
- **Evin Bar and Café** • 115 Kingsland High St
- **Mangal 1** • 10 Arcola St
- **Mangal 2** • 4 Stoke Newington Rd
- **Peppers and Spice** • 20 Kingsland High St
- **Somine** • 131 Kingsland High St
- **Stone Cave** • 111 Kingsland High St

Shopping

- **Centre Supermarket** • 588 Kingsland Rd
- **Dalston Mill Fabrics** • 69 Ridley Rd
- **Hackney Downs Studios** • 17 Amhurst Terrace
- **Healthy Stuff** • 168 Dalston Ln
- **LN-CC** • 18 Shacklewell Ln
- **Oxfam** • 514 Kingsland Rd
- **Party Party** • 9 Ridley Rd
- **Ridley Road Food Market** • Ridley Rd
- **St Vincent's** • 484 Kingsland Rd
- **Turkish Food Centre** • 89 Ridley Rd

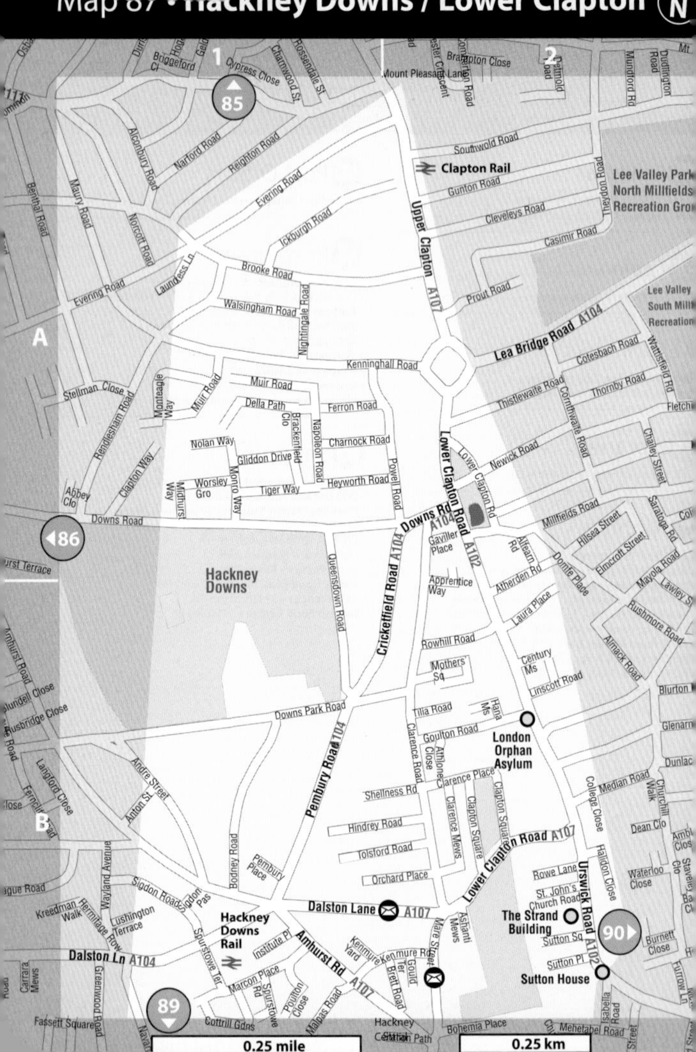
Clapton Rail
Lee Valley Park North Millfields Recreation Ground
Lee Valley South Millfields Recreation
Upper Clapton A107
Lower Clapton Road A102
Lea Bridge Road A104
Downs Rd A104
Cricketfield Road A104
Pembury Road A104
Amhurst Rd A107
Dalston Lane A107
Dalston Ln A104
Urswick Road A102
Hackney Downs
Hackney Downs Rail
London Orphan Asylum
The Strand Building
Sutton House
Hackney Central
0.25 mile
0.25 km

ackney Downs/Lower Clapton

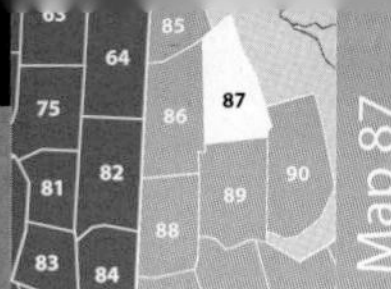

ew years ago you couldn't move for house gigs and secret raves around the wns, but these days the area is devolving into the moody gangland it used be whilst breeding the rioters of tomorrow. Lower Clapton, on the other nd, is ever on the up. Shop at **Umit's** for rare films and sweets. Food and fee can be found at vegan punk paradise **Pacific Social Club**.

Coffee

Organic & Natural • 191 Lower Clapton Rd
Pacific Social Club • 8 Clarence Rd

Landmarks

London Orphan Asylum •
Lower Clapton Rd & Linscott Rd
The Strand Building • 29 Urswick Rd
Sutton House • 2 Homerton High St

Nightlife

Biddle Brothers • 88 Lower Clapton Rd
The Crooked Billet • 84 Upper Clapton Rd
The Pembury Tavern • 90 Amhurst Rd
Star by Hackney Downs • 35 Queenstown Rd

Post Offices

Dalston Lane • 244 Dalston Ln
Hackney • 382 Mare St

Restaurants

• **Mess Café** • 38 Amhurst Rd

Shopping

• **Kate Sheridan** • 112 Lower Clapton Rd
• **Oslo** • 1 Amhurst Rd
• **Palm 2** • 152 Lower Clapton Rd
• **The Pet Shop** • 40 Amhurst Rd
• **Salvation Army Clapton** • 122 Lower Clapton Rd
• **Umit & Son** • 35 Lower Clapton Rd

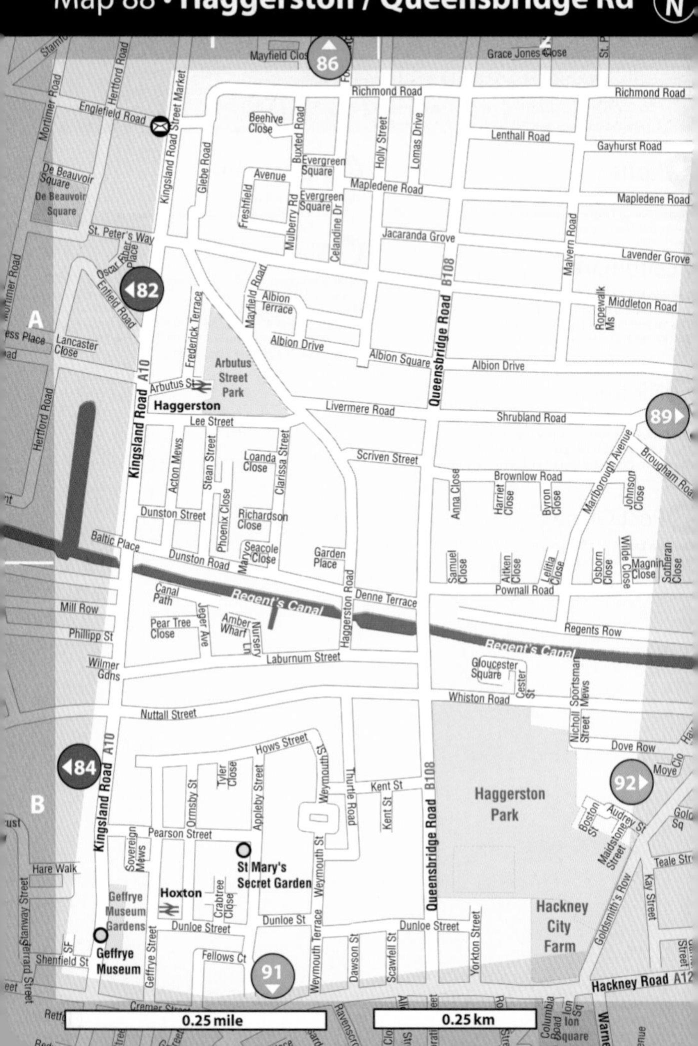

Haggerston
Arbutus Street Park
Arbutus St
Kingsland Road A10
Queensbridge Road B108
Richmond Road
Mayfield Close
Grace Jones Close
Englefield Road
Hertford Road
Mortimer Road
Kingsland Road Street Market
Beehive Close
Buxted Road
Holly Street
Lomas Drive
Lenthall Road
Gayhurst Road
Evergreen Square
Avenue
Mapledene Road
Glebe Road
De Beauvoir Square
Freshfield
Mulberry Rd
Celandine Dr
Jacaranda Grove
Malvern Road
Lavender Grove
St. Peter's Way
Oscar Faber Place
Enfield Road
Mayfield Road
Albion Terrace
Albion Drive
Albion Square
Ropewalk Ms
Middleton Road
Frederick Terrace
Lancaster Close
Livermere Road
Shrubland Road
Lee Street
Loanda Close
Clarissa Street
Scriven Street
Acton Mews
Stean Street
Brownlow Road
Anna Close
Harriet Close
Byron Close
Marlborough Avenue
Johnson Close
Brougham Road
Dunston Street
Phoenix Close
Richardson Close
Baltic Place
Dunston Road
Seacole Close
Garden Place
Samuel Close
Aitken Close
Lelitia Close
Osborn Close
Wilde Close
Magnin Close
Sotheran Close
Pownall Road
Canal Path
Regent's Canal
Denne Terrace
Haggerston Road
Mill Row
Phillipp St
Pear Tree Close
Jeger Ave
Amber Wharf
Nursery Ln
Regents Row
Laburnum Street
Gloucester Square
Cester St
Sportsman Mews
Wilmer Gdns
Whiston Road
Nuttall Street
Nicholl Street
Dove Row
Hows Street
Tyler Close
Appleby Street
Weymouth St
Thurtle Road
Kent St
Moye Clo
Haggerston Park
Ormsby St
Boston St
Audrey St
Maidstone Street
Pearson Street
Sovereign Mews
St Mary's Secret Garden
Hare Walk
Teale Str
Geffrye Museum Gardens
Hoxton
Crabtree Close
Weymouth Terrace
Hackney City Farm
Goldsmith's Row
Kay Street
Dunloe St
Dunloe Street
Yorkton Street
Stanway Street
Shenfield St
Geffrye Museum
Geffrye Street
Fellows Ct
Dawson St
Scawfell St
Gerrard Street
Hackney Road A12
Columbia Road
Cremer Street
Ravenscroft
0.25 mile
0.25 km
86
82
89
84
92
91
A
B
N

Haggerston/Queensbridge Rd

Vith the opening of Haggerston Station and the Ginger Line, it seems ihoreditch is merging with Dalston to form one sprawling kingdom of hipdom. itroll down to the gardens at the **Geffrye Museum** or Haggerston Park for ome people-watching with a flat white from **Long White Cloud**.

Coffee

- **Long White Cloud** • 151 Hackney Rd

Landmarks

- **Geffrye Museum** • 136 Kingsland Rd
- **St Mary's Secret Garden** • 30 Pearson St

Nightlife

- **Brilliant Corners** • 470 Kingsland Rd
- **The Jago** • 440 Kingsland Rd

Post Offices

- **Kingsland Road** • 416 Kingsland Rd

Restaurants

- **Berber & Q** • Arch 338, Acton Mews
- **Chicks n Sours** • 390 Kingsland Rd
- **Fabrique Bakery** • 385 Geffrye St
- **Faulkner's** • 424 Kingsland Rd
- **Hackney City Farm** • 1 Goldsmiths Row
- **Uludag** • 398 Kingsland Rd
- **Song Que** • 134 Kingsland Rd
- **Viet Hoa Café** • 70 Kingsland Rd

Shopping

- **KTS The Corner** • 415 Kingsland Rd

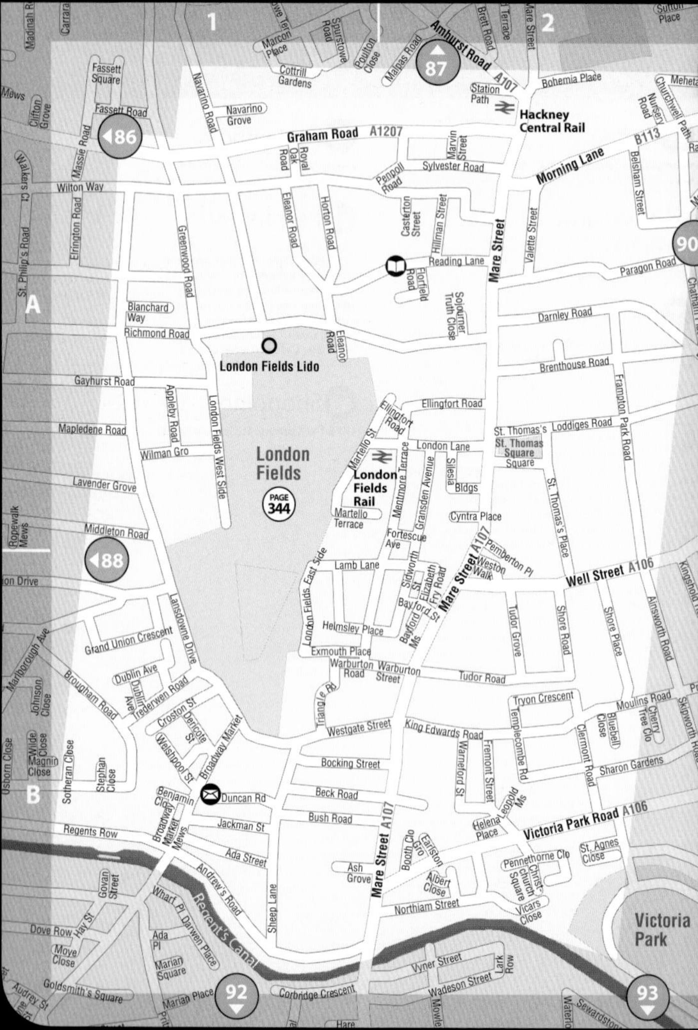

Map 89 • London Fields / Hackney Central

ondon Fields/Hackney Central

Map 89

ip through London Fields, dip your toe in the **Lido**, and attempt to make your ay through the throngs checking out their reflections in the shop windows Broadway Market.

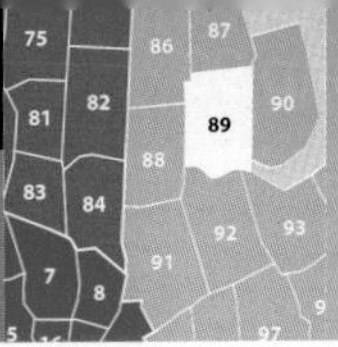

Coffee

- **Climpson & Sons** • 67 Broadway Market
- **The Corner Deli** • 121 Mare St
- **Donlon Books** • 77 Broadway Market
- **Violet** • 47 Wilton Wy
- **Wilton's** • 63 Wilton Way

Landmarks

- **London Fields Lido** • London Fields Westside

Libraries

- **Hackney Central Library** • 1 Reading Ln

Nightlife

- **Baxter's Court** • 282 Mare St
- **The Dolphin** • 165 Mare St
- **The Dove** • 24 Broadway Market
- **Draughts** • 337 Acton Mews
- **The Old Ship** • 2 Sylvester Path
- **Pub on the Park** • 19 Martello St

Post Offices

- **London Fields** • 39 Broadway Market

Restaurants

- **Buen Ayre** • 50 Broadway Market
- **Cat and Mutton** • 76 Broadway Market
- **Corner Deli** • 121 Mare St
- **Hai Ha** • 206 Mare St
- **Okko** • 49 Broadway Market
- **Ombra** • 1 Vyner St
- **Pidgin** • 52 Wilton Wy
- **The Spurstowe Arms** • 68 Greenwood Rd

Shopping

- **Broadway Market** • Broadway Market
- **Burberry Factory Shop** • 29 Chatham Pl
- **Candle Factory** • 184 Mare St
- **E5 Bakehouses** • 395 Mentmore Terrace
- **L'eau a la Bouche** • 49 Broadway Market London
- **Viktor Wynd's Shop of Horrors** • 11 Mare St

Supermarkets

- **Iceland** • 150 Mare St
- **Tesco** • 55 Morning Ln

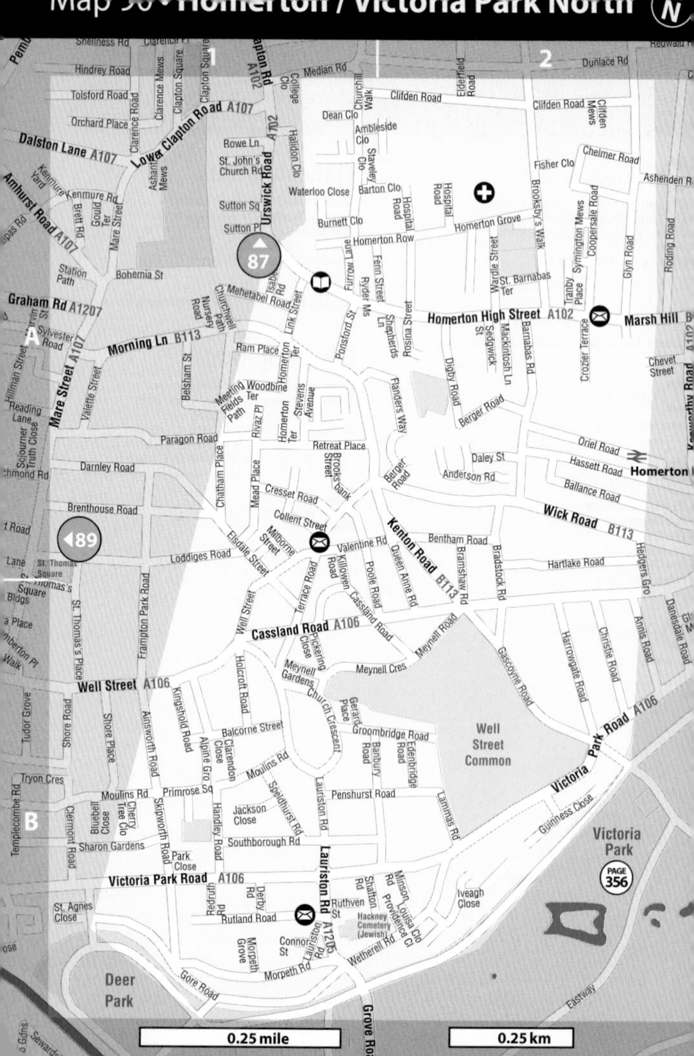

N
1
2
A
B
Shellness Rd
Clarence Pl
Hindrey Road
Tolsford Road
Orchard Place
Clarence Road
Clarence Mews
Clapton Square
Clapton Square
Lower Clapton Road A107
Clapton Rd A102
Median Rd
College Clo
Churchill Walk
Clifden Road
Elderfield Road
Dunlace Rd
Clifden Road
Clifden Mews
Dean Clo
Ambleside Clo
Dalston Lane A107
Ashanti Mews
Rowe Ln
A102
St. John's Church Rd
Halidon Clo
Staveley Clo
Chelmer Road
Fisher Clo
Ashenden Rd
Amhurst Road A107
Kenmure Yard
Kenmure Rd
Brett Rd
Gould Ter
Mare Street
Urswick Road
Sutton Sq
Sutton Pl
Waterloo Close
Barton Clo
Hospital Road
Hospital Road
Burnett Clo
Homerton Row
Homerton Grove
Brooksby's Walk
Symington Mews
Coopersale Road
Glyn Road
Roding Road
Station Path
Bohemia St
87
Mehetabel Road
Isabella Rd
Furrow Lane
Fenn Street
Ryder Ms
Wardle Street
St. Barnabas Ter
Tranby Place
Graham Rd A1207
Churchwell Path
Nursery Road
Link Street
Ponsford St
Shepherds Ln
Rosina Street
Homerton High Street A102
Marsh Hill
Sylvester Road
Morning Ln B113
Ram Place
Homerton Ter
Sedgwick St
Mackintosh Ln
Barnabas Rd
Crozier Terrace
Chevet Street
Hillman Street
Mare Street A107
Valette Street
Belsham St
Meeting Fields Path
Woodbine Ter
Stevens Avenue
Flanders Way
Digby Road
Berger Road
Reading Lane
Sojourner Truth Close
Rivaz Pl
Homerton Ter
Paragon Road
Retreat Place
Brooksbank Street
Oriel Road
Hassett Road
Homerton
Daley St
Anderson Rd
Berger Road
Darnley Road
Chatham Place
Mead Place
Cresset Road
Ballance Road
Wick Road B113
Brenthouse Road
Collent Street
89
Elsdale Street
Milborne Street
Kenton Road B113
Bentham Road
Valentine Rd
Loddiges Road
Killowen Road
Poole Road
Queen Anne Rd
Bramshaw Rd
Bradstock Rd
Hartlake Road
Hedgers Gro
St. Thomas Square
St. Thomas's Square
Frampton Park Road
Terrace Road
Cassland Road
Well Street
St. Thomas's Place
Cassland Road A106
Pickering Close
Meynell Road
Gascoyne Road
Harrowgate Road
Christie Road
Annis Road
Danesdale Road
Meynell Gardens
Meynell Cres
Holcroft Road
Kingshold Road
Well Street A106
Church Crescent
Gerard Place
Tudor Grove
Shore Road
Shore Place
Ainsworth Road
Balcorne Street
Groombridge Road
Well Street Common
Alpine Gro
Clarendon Close
Banbury Road
Edenbridge Road
Victoria Park Road A106
Moulins Rd
Speldhurst Rd
Tryon Cres
Moulins Rd
Primrose Sq
Lauriston Rd
Penshurst Road
Templecombe Rd
Bluebell Close
Cherry Tree Clo
Skipworth Road
Handley Road
Jackson Close
Lammas Rd
Guinness Close
Clermont Road
Sharon Gardens
Southborough Rd
Victoria Park
PAGE 356
Park Close
Victoria Park Road A106
Redruth Rd
Derby Rd
Lauriston Rd A1205
Ruthven St
Shafton Rd
Minson Rd
Providence Cl
Louisa Clo
Iveagh Close
St. Agnes Close
Rutland Road
Hackney Cemetery (Jewish)
Morpeth Grove
Connor St
Lauriston Rd
Wetherell Rd
Morpeth Rd
Deer Park
Gore Road
Grove Road
Eastway
0.25 mile
0.25 km

Homerton/Victoria Park North

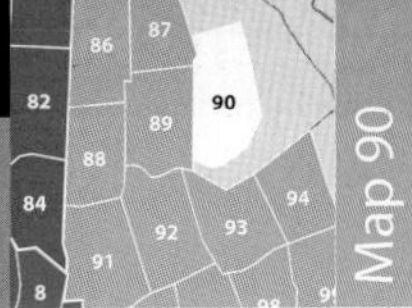

ah, Hackney Village: leafy Lauriston Road and its surrounds would make a ice retreat from the madding crowd if everyone else didn't have the same lea. Nevermind, have a Sunday Roast at the **Royal Inn on The Park**. Whereas nce one would only be seen in Homerton if one was going to the hospital (or oing to the hospital because one was in Homerton), Chatsworth Road (just ff map) is now the place du jour.

Emergency Rooms

- **Homerton University Hospital** • Homerton Row

Libraries

- **Homerton Library** • Homerton High St

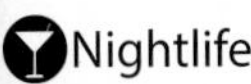

Nightlife

- **Chats Palace Arts Centre** • 42 Brooksby's Walk
- **The Kenton** • 38 Kenton Rd
- **The Lauriston** • 162 Victoria Park Rd
- **Royal Inn on the Park** • 111 Lauriston Rd

Post Offices

- **High Street** • 226 Homerton High St
- **Victoria Park** • 112 Lauriston Rd
- **Well Street** • 188 Well St

Restaurants

- **Eat 17** • 64–66 Brooksby's Walk
- **The Empress of India** • 130 Lauriston Rd
- **The Fish House** • 126 Lauriston Rd
- **Well Street Kitchen** • 203 Well St

Shopping

- **The Ginger Pig** • 99 Lauriston Rd
- **House of Pets** • 135 Well St
- **Perlie Rides** • 137 Well St
- **Sublime** • 225 Victoria Park Rd
- **Work Shop** • 77 Lauriston Rd

Supermarkets

- **Tesco** • 180 Well St

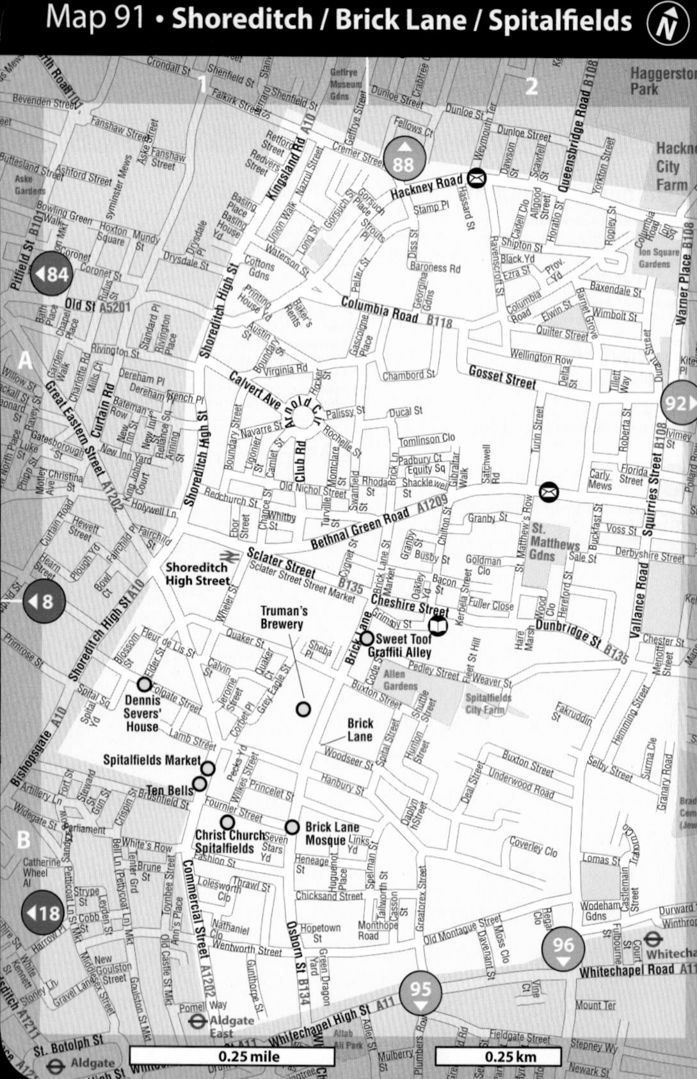

Map 91 • Shoreditch / Brick Lane / Spitalfields
1
2
A
B
88
84
92
8
18
96
95
Haggerston Park
Hackney City Farm
Geffrye Museum Gdns
Aske Gardens
Ion Square Gardens
Allen Gardens
Spitalfields City Farm
St. Matthews Gdns
Shoreditch High Street
Truman's Brewery
Sweet Toof Graffiti Alley
Dennis Severs' House
Brick Lane
Spitalfields Market
Ten Bells
Christ Church Spitalfields
Brick Lane Mosque
Aldgate East
Aldgate
Whitechapel
Crondall St
Shenfield St
Falkirk Street
Dunloe Street
Fellows Ct
Cremer Street
Kingsland Rd
Hackney Road
Stamp Pl
Hassard St
Weymouth Ter
Dawson St
Scawfell St
Queensbridge Road B108
Yorkton Street
Cadell Clo
Allgood Street
Horatio St
Ropley St
Shipton St
Black Yd
Ezra St
Prov. Yd
Baxendale St
Barnet Grove
Wimbolt St
Elwin St
Columbia Road
Quilter Street
Warner Place B108
Columbia Road B118
Baroness Rd
Georgina Gdns
Diss St
Peltier St
Ravenscroft St
Wellington Row
Gosset Street
Delta St
Tillett Way
Durant Street
Chambord St
Gascoigne Place
Calvert Ave
Arnold Cir
Virginia Rd
Boundary St
Palissy St
Ducal St
Hocker St
Rochelle St
Navarre St
Tomlinson Clo
Padbury Ct
Equity Sq
Shacklewell St
Gibraltar Walk
Satchwell Rd
Turin Street
Roberta St
Carly Mews
Florida Street
Squirries Street B108
Club Rd
Camlet St
Ligonier St
Montclare St
Swanfield St
Rhoda St
Old Nichol Street
Redchurch St
Chance St
Whitby St
Ebor Street
Turville St
Bethnal Green Road A1209
Granby St
Chilton St
St. Matthew's Row
Buckfast St
Voss St
Derbyshire Street
Sale St
Sclater Street
Sclater Street Street Market
Cygnet St
Brick Lane St Market
Busby St
Oakley Yd
Bacon St
Goldman Clo
Kerbela Street
Fuller Close
Hereford St
Wood Clo
Vallance Road
Cheshire Street B135
Grimsby St
Dunbridge St B135
Hare Marsh
Chester St
Menotti Street
Quaker St
Sheba Pl
Code St
Pedley Street
Fleet St Hill
Weaver St
Buxton Street
Shuttle Street
Fakruddin St
Hemming Street
Wheler St
Fleur de Lis St
Blossom St
Elder St
Calvin St
Quaker Ct
Grey Eagle St
Jerome Street
Corbet Pl
Folgate Street
Spital Sq
Spital Yd
Lamb Street
Woodseer St
Spital Street
Hunton Street
Buxton Street
Underwood Road
Selby Street
Surma Clo
Granary Road
Hanbury St
Deal Street
Peck's Yd
Wilkes Street
Princelet St
Fournier Street
Brushfield St
Daplyn Street
Seven Stars Yd
Links Yd
Heneage St
Spelman St
Coverley Clo
Lomas St
Fashion St
Thrawl St
Huguenot Place
Chicksand Street
Tailworth St
Casson St
Greatorex Street
Castlemain Street
Wodeham Gdns
Durward St
Lolesworth Clo
Nathaniel Clo
Wentworth Street
Hopetown St
Monthope Road
Old Montague Street
Davenant St
Moss Clo
Regal Clo
Fulbourne St
Court St
Whitechapel Road A11
Osborn St B134
Commercial Street A1202
Gunthorpe St
Green Dragon Yard
Vine Ct
Mount Ter
Pomell Way
Whitechapel High St A11
Altab Ali Park
Adler St
Plumbers Row
Fieldgate Street
Stepney Wy
Newark St
Mulberry St
Bevenden Street
Fanshaw Street
Aske Street
Fanshaw Street
Buttesland Street
Ashford Street
Symister Mews
Bowling Green Walk
Hoxton Square
Mundy St
Drysdale Pl
Drysdale St
Pitfield St B101
Coronet St
Rufus St
Old St A5201
Bath Place
Chapel Place
Standard Pl
Rivington Place
Rivington St
Garden Walk
Charlotte Rd
Mills Ct
Curtain Rd
Dereham Pl
Bateman's Row
Bench Pl
Great Eastern Street A1202
Willow St
Gatesborough St
Luke St
New Inn Yard
New Inn St
Reliance Sq
Anning St
Christina St
Holywell Ln
Fairchild St
Hewett Street
Plough Yd
Bowl Ct
Shoreditch High St A10
Primrose St
Bishopsgate A10
Artillery Ln
Steward St
Gun St
Crispin St
Widegate St
Parliament
White's Row
Bell Ln
Tenter Grd
Brune St
Toynbee Street
Catherine Wheel Al
Strype St
Leyden St
Cobb St
Petticoat Ln St
Harrow Pl
Old Castle St
New Goulston Street
Goulston St Mkt
Middlesex Street
Gravel Lane
Stoney Ln
White Kennett St
St. Botolph St
0.25 mile
0.25 km

Shoreditch/Brick Lane/Spitalfields

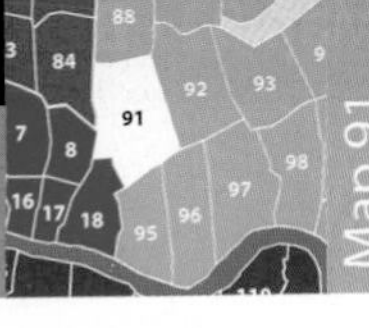

hrobbing with trend-lords on single-speed bikes, great curry houses, and lternative-lifestyle vomit, the trick is to sample Brick Lane and Shoreditch n market days for pure colour and bustle, but to avoid it on weekend eves. hopping is abundant: **Beyond Retro**, and oodles of great little rag shacks. ead towards **Catch** for booze. For a dash of authenticity, leave your £1000 bike nlocked and see what happens.

Cinemas

- **Rich Mix Centre** • 34 Bethnal Green Rd
- **Short & Sweet** • 91 Brick Ln

Coffee

- **Allpress** • 58 Redchurch St
- **Cafe 1001** • 91 Brick Ln
- **Lanark** • 262 Hackney Rd
- **Leila's Shop** • 17 Calvert Ave
- **Nude Espresso** • 26 Hanbury St
- **Prufrock** • 140 Shoreditch High St
- **Time For Tea** • 110 Shoreditch High St

Landmarks

- **Brick Lane Mosque** • 59 Brick Ln
- **Christ Church Spitalfields** • 2 Fournier St
- **Dennis Severs' House** • 18 Folgate St
- **Spitalfields Market** • 105 Commercial St
- **Sweet Toof Graffiti Alley** • Pedley St & Brick Ln
- **Ten Bells** • 84 Commercial St
- **Truman's Brewery** • Brick Ln

Libraries

- **Dorset Library** • Ravenscroft St

Nightlife

- **93 Feet East** • 150 Brick Ln
- **Bar Kick** • 127 Shoreditch High St
- **The Birdcage** • 80 Columbia Rd
- **Browns** • 1 Hackney Rd
- **The Big Chill Bar** • Dray Walk off Brick Ln
- **Café 1001** • 91 Brick Ln
- **The Carpenters Arms** • 73 Cheshire St
- **Catch** • 22 Kingsland Rd
- **The Cocktail Trading Co.** • 68 Bethnal Green Rd
- **The Commercial Tavern** • 142 Commercial St• Comedy Cafe • 66 Rivington St
- **The Culpeper** • 40 Commercial St
- **The George & Dragon** • Hackney Rd
- **The Golden Heart** • 110 Commercial St
- **Jaguar Shoes** • 32 Kingsland Rd
- **The Love Shake** • 5 Kingsland Rd
- **The Old Shoreditch Station** • 1 Kingsland Rd
- **Owl & Pussycat** • 34 Redchurch St
- **Prague** • 6 Kingsland Rd
- **Pride of Spitalfields** • 3 Heneage St
- **The Redchurch** • 107 Redchurch St
- **The Royal Oak** • 73 Columbia Rd
- **Sager + Wilde** • 193 Hackney Rd
- **Shoreditch House** • Ebor St
- **The Water Poet** • 9 Folgate St
- **Ye Olde Axe** • 69 Hackney Rd

Post Offices

- **Bethnal Green** • 223 Bethnal Green Rd
- **Hackney Road** • 198 Hackney Rd

Restaurants

- **Andina** • 1 Redchurch St
- **Beigel Bakery** • 155 Brick Ln
- **Boundary** • 2 Boundary St
- **Brawn** • 49 Columbia Rd
- **Brick Lane Clipper Restaurant** • 104 Brick Ln
- **Chez Elles** • 45 Brick Ln
- **The Culpeper** • 40 Commercial St
- **Dishoom** • 7 Boundary St
- **Ethiopian Food Stall** • Brick Ln
- **Frizzante** • 1 Goldsmith's Row
- **Hanoi Cafe** • 98 Kingsland Rd
- **Hawksmoor** • 157 Commercial St
- **Lyle's** • 56 Shoreditch High St
- **Marksman Public House** • 254 Hackney Rd
- **Mein Tay** • 122 Kingsland Rd
- **The Premises** • 209 Hackney Rd
- **Rosa's** • 12 Hanbury St
- **St John Bread and Wine** • 94 Commercial St
- **Tay Do** • 60 Kingsland Rd
- **Tay Do Cafe** • 65 Kingsland Rd
- **Troy Cafe** • 124 Kingsland Rd
- **Viet Grill** • 58 Kingsland Rd

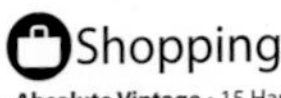

Shopping

- **Absolute Vintage** • 15 Hanbury St
- **Beyond Retro** • 112 Cheshire St
- **Blackmans** • 44 Cheshire St
- **Blackman's Shoes** • 42 Cheshire St
- **Brick Lane** • Brick Ln
- **Caravan** • 3 Redchurch St
- **A Child of The Jago** • 10 Great Eastern St
- **Columbia Road Flower Market** • Columbia Rd
- **Columbia Road Market** • Columbia Rd
- **Duke of Uke** • 22 Hanbury St
- **Dum Dum Donutterie** • 2–4 Bethnal Green Rd
- **FairyGothMother** • 15 Lamb St
- **The Grocery** • 54 Kingsland Rd
- **Labour & Wait** • 18 Cheshire St
- **Lily Vanillie** • 6 Ezra St
- **Luna and Curious** • 198 Brick Lne
- **A Portuguese Love Affair** • 142 Columbia Rd
- **Present** • 140 Shoreditch High St
- **Rough Trade East** • 91 Brick Ln
- **Ryantown** • 126 Columbia Rd
- **Sunday (Up)Market** • Brick Ln
- **Taj Stores** • 112 Brick Ln
- **Tatty Devine** • 236 Brick Ln
- **Taylor Taylor** • 12 Cheshire St
- **Taylor Taylor** • 137 Commercial St

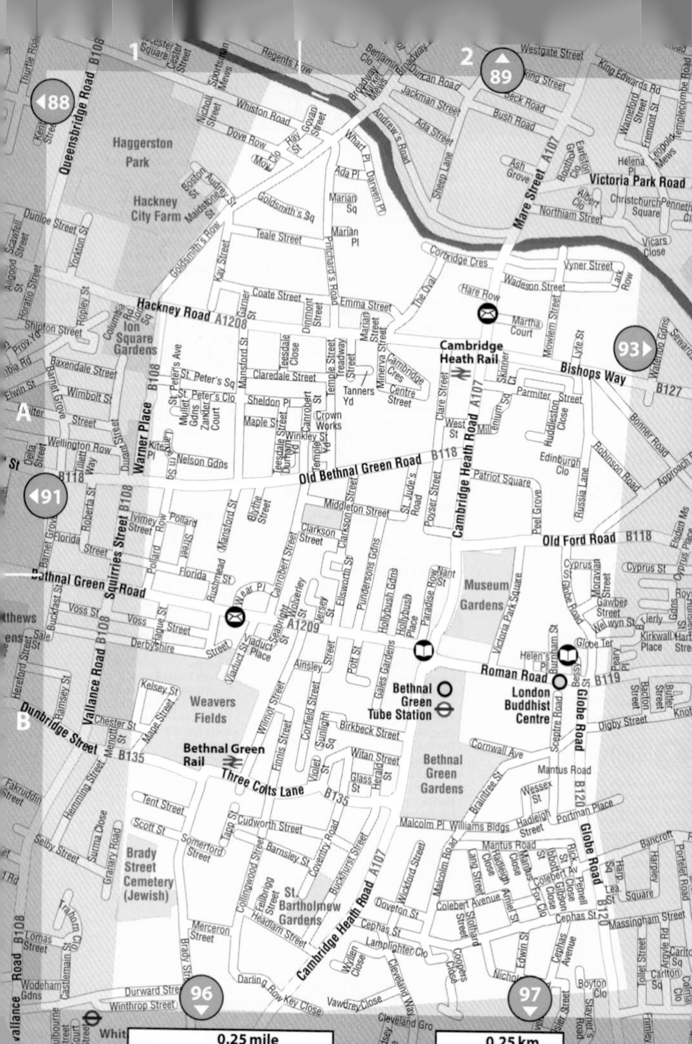

1
2
88
89
91
93
96
97
A
B
Regents Row
Westgate Street
King Edwards Rd
Queensbridge Road B108
Haggerston Park
Hackney City Farm
Sportsman Mews
Whiston Road
Dove Row
Nicholl Street
Hay St
Govan Street
Broadway Market Mews
Benjamin Clo
Broadway
Duncan Road
Jackman Street
Ada Street
Beck Road
Bush Road
King Street
Andrew's Road
Wharf Pl
Ada Pl
Darwen Pl
Sheep Lane
Marian Sq
Marian Pl
Goldsmith's Sq
Goldsmith's Row
Boston St
Audrey St
Maidstone St
Dunloe Street
Yorkton St
Scawfell Street
Allgood St
Horatio Street
Teale Street
Pritchard's Road
Kay Street
Coate Street
Garner St
Emma Street
Dinmont Street
The Oval
Corbridge Cres
Hare Row
Mare Street A107
Ash Grove
Boothby Clo
Earlston Grove
Victoria Park Road
Albert Clo
Northiam Street
Christchurch Square
Helena Pl
Leopold Mews
Templecombe Road
Warneford Street
Fremont St
Pennethorne Cl
Vicars Close
Vyner Street
Wadeson Street
Lark Row
Martha Court
Mowlem Street
Lyte St
Cambridge Heath Rail
Bishops Way
B127
Seward
Waterloo Gdns
Hackney Road A1208
Columbia Rd
Ion Square Gardens
Shipton Street
Ropley St
Baxendale Street
Barnet Grove
Wimbolt St
Elwin St
Street
Wellington Row
Delta Street
Tillett Way
Durant Street
Warner Place B108
St. Peter's Ave
St. Peter's Sq
St. Peter's Clo
Mullet Gdns
Zander Court
Kite Pl
Nelson Gdns
Mansford St
Teesdale Close
Claredale Street
Sheldon Pl
Maple St
Canrobert St
Winkley St
Crown Works
Temple Yd
Teesdale Yd
Temple Street
Treadway Street
Tanners Yd
Marian Street
Minerva Street
Cambridge Cres
Centre Street
Clare Street
West St
Mill
Skinner Ct
Parmiter Street
Huddleston Close
Edinburgh Clo
Bonner Road
Robinson Road
Approach Rd
Old Bethnal Green Road B118
Cambridge Heath Road A107
Patriot Square
Russia Lane
B118
Roberta St
Squirries Street B108
Ivimey Street
Pollard Row
Pollard Street
Mansford St
Blythe Street
Middleton Street
Clarkson Street
St. Jude's Road
Poyser Street
Peel Grove
Old Ford Road B118
Elsden Ms
Cyprus Place
Cyprus St
Florida Street
Barnet Grove
Bethnal Green Road
Florida St
Rushmead
Wear Pl
Canrobert Street
Wolverley St
Jersey St
Ellsworth St
Pundersons Gdns
Hollybush Gdns
Hollybush Place
Paradise Row
Nant St
Museum Gardens
Victoria Park Square
Moravian Street
Globe Road
Gawber Street
Welwyn St
Kirkwall Place
Buckfast St
Voss St
Voss Street
Hague St
Derbyshire Street
Viaduct St
Viaduct Place
Seabright St
A1209
Ainsley Street
Pott St
Gales Gardens
Burnham St
Globe Ter
Helen's Pl
Peary Pl
Roman Road B119
Bessy St
Bethnal Green Tube Station
London Buddhist Centre
Sceptre Road
Globe Road
Bacton Street
Butler Street
Knot
Digby Street
Hereford Street
Ramsey St
Vallance Road B108
Kelsey St
Mape Street
Chester St
Menotti St
Weavers Fields
Dunbridge Street
B135
Bethnal Green Rail
Wilmot Street
Corfield Street
Sunlight Sq
Birkbeck Street
Witan Street
Violet St
Glass St
Herald St
Finnis Street
Three Colts Lane
B135
Bethnal Green Gardens
Cornwall Ave
Mantus Road
Wessex St
Braintree St
B120
Portman Place
Hadleigh Street
Malcolm Pl
Williams Bldgs
Fakruddin Street
Hemming Street
Tent Street
Scott St
Somerford Street
Tapp St
Cudworth Street
Barnsley St
Coventry Road
Buckhurst Street
Wickford Street
Malcolm Road
Mantus Road
Lang Street
Hadleigh Close
Mantus Close
Fox Clo
Colebert Av
Gibson Close
Pemell Close
Bancroft
Harpley Sq
Lea Sq
Portelet Road
Selby Street
Surma Close
Granary Road
Brady Street Cemetery (Jewish)
Collingwood Street
Felbrigg Street
St. Bartholmew Gardens
Headlam Street
Cambridge Heath Road A107
Doveton St
Colebert Avenue
Stothard Street
Cephas St
Cephas Avenue
Massingham Street
Trahorn Clo
Lomas Street
Castlemain St
Wodeham Gdns
Vallance Road B108
Mercerton Street
Brady St
Lamplighter Clo
Wyllen Close
Cleveland Way
Coopers Close
Edwin St
Nichol
Boyton Clo
Carlton Sq
Argyle Rd
Tollet Street
Durward Street
Winthrop Street
Darling Row
Key Close
Vawdrey Close
Cleveland Gro
Fulbourne Street
Court Street
Stayner's Road
Fremley W
0.25 mile
0.25 km

Beth

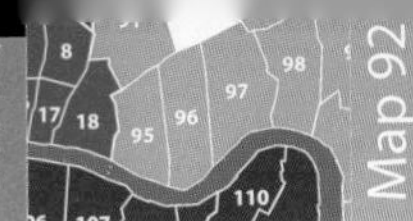

o longer the inner-city ghetto from days of yore, but you can still find some of ne gor-blimey-lor-love-a-duck cockney cheekiness that one would expect in nis hood. **E. Pellicci** is one of the oldest remaining greasy spoons in London, o head in for a Full Monty and a cuppa. If a lager and a burger down the **ebright Arms** is not your thing, head down to the **Buddhist Centre** for a it of instant karma.

Coffee

- **Hurwundeki Cafe** • 298 Cambridge Heath Rd

Landmarks

- **Bethnal Green Tube Station** • Bethnal Green Tube Station
- **London Buddhist Centre** • 51 Roman Rd

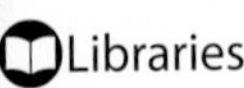

Libraries

- **Bethnal Green Library** • Cambridge Heath Rd
- **Idea Store Bow** • Roman Rd

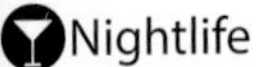

Nightlife

- **Bethnal Green's Working Men's Club** • 44 Pollard Row
- **The Florist Arms** • 255 Globe Rd
- **Sebright Arms** • 31 Coate St
- **Satan's Whiskers** • 343 Cambridge Heath Rd
- **The Star Of Bethnal Green** • 359 Bethnal Green Rd
- **The Virgin Queen** • 94 Goldsmiths Row

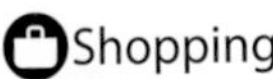

Post Offices

- **Bethnal Green Road** • 365 Bethnal Green Rd
- **Cambridge Heath** • 481 Cambridge Heath Rd

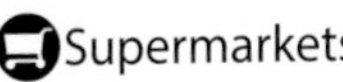

Restaurants

- **Bistrotheque** • 23 Wadeson St
- **E Pellicci** • 332 Bethnal Green Rd
- **The Gallery Cafe** • 21 Old Ford Rd
- **Little Georgia** • 87 Goldsmiths Row
- **Mission** • 250 Paradise Row

Shopping

- **AP Fitzpatrick** • 142 Cambridge Heath Rd

Supermarkets

- **Tesco** • 361 Bethnal Green Rd

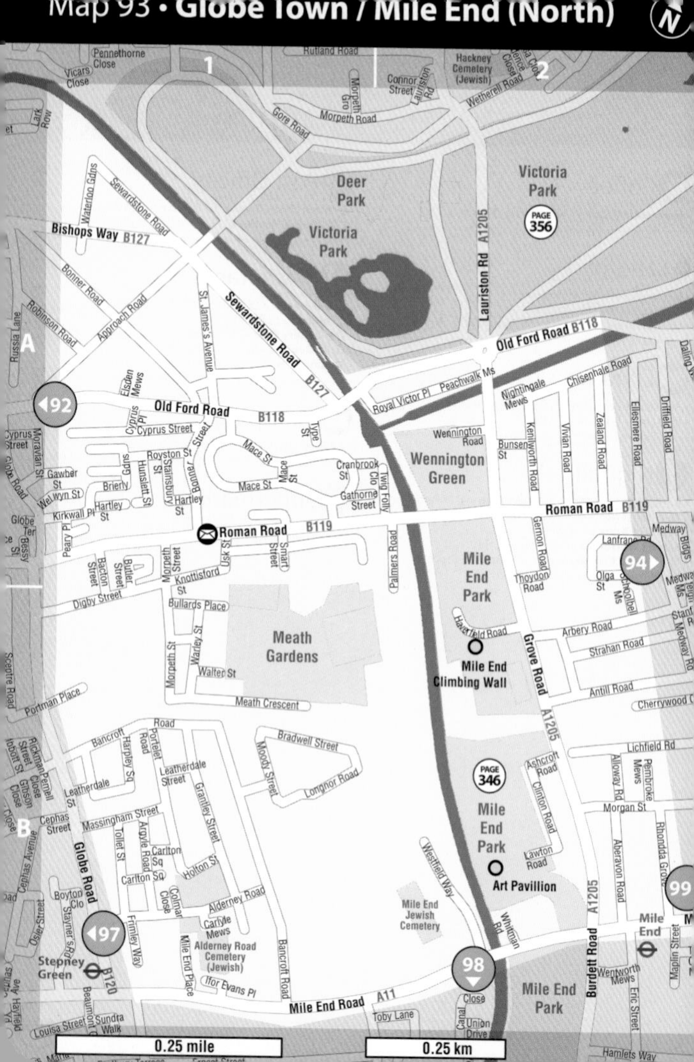
Map 93 • Globe Town / Mile End (North)
N
1
2
A
B
Pennethorne Close
Vicars Close
Rutland Road
Hackney Cemetery (Jewish)
Morpeth Gro
Connor Street
Lauriston Rd
Wetherell Road
Gore Road
Morpeth Road
Lark Row
Deer Park
Victoria Park
Victoria Park
PAGE 356
Waterloo Gdns
Sewardstone Road
Bishops Way B127
Bonner Road
Approach Road
Robinson Road
Russia Lane
St. James's Avenue
Sewardstone Road
B127
Lauriston Rd A1205
Old Ford Road B118
Royal Victor Pl
Peachwalk Ms
Nightingale Mews
Chisenhale Road
Ellesmere Road
Driffield Road
92
Elsden Mews
Old Ford Road
B118
Cyprus Pl
Cyprus Street
Cyprus Street
Moravian St
Globe Road
Gawber St
Welwyn St
Kirkwall Pl
Hartley St
Brierly Gdns
Royston St
Hunslett St
Stainsbury St
Bonner Street
Hartley St
Mace St
Mace St
Mace St
Type St
Cranbrook St
Clo
Twig Folly
Gathorne Street
Wennington Road
Wennington Green
Bunsen St
Kenilworth Road
Vivian Road
Zealand Road
Roman Road B119
Globe Ter
Bessy St
Peary Pl
Roman Road
B119
Usk St
Smart Street
Palmers Road
Gernon Road
Mile End Park
Medway Bldgs
Lanfranc Rd
94
Bacton Street
Butler Street
Morpeth Street
Knottisford St
Thoydon Road
Olga St
Schoolbell Ms
Medway Ms
Digby Street
Bullards Place
Meath Gardens
Wadley St
Morpeth St
Walter St
Haverfield Road
Mile End Climbing Wall
Grove Road
Arbery Road
Strahan Road
Medway Rd
Sceptre Road
Portman Place
Meath Crescent
Antill Road
Cherrywood C
A1205
Road
Bancroft Road
Harpley Sq
Portelet Road
Leatherdale Street
Bradwell Street
Moody Street
Longnor Road
Ashcroft Road
Lichfield Rd
Allonby Rd
Pembroke Mews
Rickman Street
Pennell Close
Gibson Close
Leatherdale St
Cephas Street
Cephas Avenue
Massingham Street
Globe Road
Tollet St
Argyle Road
Grantley Street
PAGE 346
Clinton Road
Morgan St
Mile End Park
Aberavon Road
Rhondda Grove
Carlton Sq
Carlton Sq
Holton St
Westfield Way
Lawton Road
Art Pavillion
99
Boyton Clo
Stayner's Rd
Osier Street
Colmar Close
Alderney Road
Carlyle Mews
Alderney Road Cemetery (Jewish)
Mile End Jewish Cemetery
Frimley Way
97
Mile End Place
Bancroft Road
Whitman Rd
Burdett Road A1205
Mile End
Stepney Green
B120
Ifor Evans Pl
98
Wentworth Mews
Maplin Street
Mile End Road A11
Toby Lane
Close
Canal
Union Drive
Mile End Park
Eric Street
Beaumont
Louisa Street
Sundra Walk
Hayfield Yd
0.25 mile
0.25 km
Hamlets Way

Globe Town / Mile End (North)

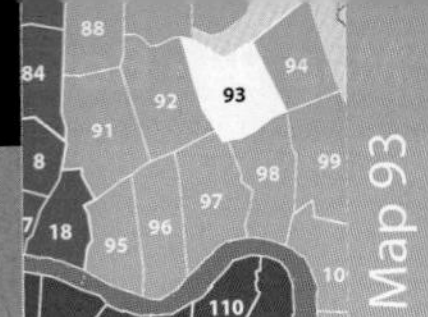

eah Victoria Park is nice and all, but it's just a bunch of trees and grass innit? outh of all that green sh** is an up-and-coming nabe with so many great little ems. So, **The Palm Tree** is the best pub in Britain. **The Victoria** is becoming a rilliant gig spot. We'd move here if we had the balls, in fact.

Landmarks

- **Art Pavilion** • 221 Grove Rd
- **Mile End Climbing Wall** • Haverfield Rd & Grove Rd

Nightlife

- **The Approach** • 47 Approach Rd
- **The Lord Tredegar** • 50 Lichfield Rd
- **Morgan Arms** • 43 Morgan St
- **Palm Tree** • 127 Grove Rd
- **The Victoria** • 110 Grove Rd

Post Offices

- **Roman Road** • 138 Roman Rd

Restaurants

- **Greedy Cow Burgers & Steaks** • 2 Grove Rd
- **Morgan Arms** • 43 Morgan St

1
2
Victoria Park
PAGE 356
River Lee or Lea
Jodrell Road
Ollerton Grn
Waterside Close
Parnell Road
Candy Street
Cedar Clo
Ruston Street
Old Ford Road
Ruston Street
Sycamore Avenue
Hawthorn Ave
Hornbeam Square
Birdsfield Ln
Barge Lane
Willow Tree Cl
Gunmakers Lane
Printers Mews
Saw. Yard
Old Ford Road
B118
Empire Wharf
B118
A
Chisenhale Rd
Ford Street
Ford Road
St. Stephen's Road
Ranwell Street
Beale Road
Beale Road
Alice Lane
Daling Way
Pulteney Clo
Annie Besant Close
Lea Sq
Legion Terrace
Chariot Clo
Tamar Clo
Garrison Road
Hadrian Clo
Zealand Road
Ellesmere Road
Driffield Road
Hewlett Road
Allen Road
McCullum Rd
Wrights Road
Armagh Road
Beale Place
McCullum Road
Libra Road
Forum Clo
Hitchin Sq
Daling Way
Roman Sq Market
Ford Clo
Ford Rd
Usher Road
Parnell Road
Tiber Clo
Roman Road
B119
Roman Road
Dane Pl
St. Stephen's Road
Ewart Place
Gladstone Place
Cardigan Road
Hewison Street
Usher Road
B142
Lanfranc Road
93
Medway Bldgs
Medway Road
Lyal Road
Norman Grove
Rosebank Gdns
Anglo Road
Vernon Road
Saxon Road
Stafford Road
Shetland Road
Stanfield Road
Selwyn Road
Tredegar Road
B142
Four Seasons Close
Strahan Road
Athelstane Grove
Lacey Wk
Matilda Gdns
Morville Street
Redwood Close
Carlile Clo
Ordell Road
Mostyn Grove
Eastern Mews
Primrose Close
Antill Road
Tredegar Road
Hereford Road
Springwood Close
Cherrywood Close
Lichfield Road
Malmesbury Road
B
Alloway Rd
Pembroke Mews
Tredegar Terrace
Tredegar Mews
Morgan Street
Lawrence Close
Benworth Street
Caxton Grove
Aberavon Road
Rhondda Grove
Tredegar Sq
Coborn Road
Coborn Street
Harley Grove
Alfred Street
Addington Road
Kitcat Terrace
Denmark Place
A1205
Lyn Mews
Regal Place
98
99
Mile End
Bow Road
A11
Bow Road
0.25 mile
0.25 km

/hat have the Romans ever done for us? Not much, you might think, walking own Roman Road. But look closer and you'll find not only one of the oldest, nost authentically East End jellied eels and mash eateries of the city, but also market so cheap it'll knock even the most die-hard bargain hunters right out f their Centurion sandals. Pint? The haughty-sounding combo of **The Young rince** or **The Lord Morpeth**.

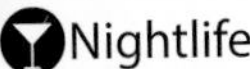

Nightlife

- **Coborn Arms** • 8 Coborn Rd
- **Lord Morpeth** • 402 Old Ford Rd
- **The Lord Tredegar** • 50 Lichfield Rd
- **Young Prince** • 448 Roman Rd

Post Offices

- **Roman Road (603)** • 603 Roman Rd

Restaurants

- **Chicchi** • 516 Roman Rd
- **The EggFree Cake Box** • 449 Roman Rd
- **G. Kelly Noted Eel & Pie Shop** • 526 Roman Rd
- **Pavilion Victoria Park** • Old Ford Rd

Shopping

- **Roman Road Market** • Roman Rd
- **Sew Amazing** • 80 St Stephens Rd
- **South Molton Drug Store** • 583 Roman Rd

1
2
A
B
WHITECHAPEL
WAPPING
Aldgate East
Aldgate
Tower Gateway
Tower Hill
Tower Gardens
Tower Of London
St. Katharine's Dock
Commodity Quay
River Thames
Altab Ali Park
The Sun HQ
John Orwell Sports Centre
91
96
18
Whitechapel Road A11
Whitechapel High Street A11
Commercial Road A13
Commercial Street A1202
Brick Lane B134
Osborn Street B134
Princelet Street
Heneage Street
Chicksand St
Fashion Street
Flower&Dean Wlk
Gunthorpe Street
Old Castle Street
Old Montague Street
New Road B108
Stepney Way
Ashfield Street
Fieldgate Street
Plumbers Row
Greenfield Road
Settles Street
Parfett Street
Myrdle Street
Romford Street
Fordham Street
Nelson Street
Mulbery St
Adler Street
Coke Street
White Lane
Assam Street
Plough St
Buckle St
Drum St
Braham Street
Camperdown Street
Mansell St A1211
Alie Street
Leman St A1202
Gower's Walk
Back Church Lane
Fairclough Street
Henriques Street
Batty Street
Christian Street
Boyd Street
Ellen Street
Stutfield Street
Philchurch Place
Forbes St
Pinchin Street
Golding Street
Burslem St
Ponler Street
Cannon Street Road
Bigland Street
Chapman Street
Cable Street
B126
B108
Crowder Street
Swedenborg Gdns
Hindmarsh Cl
North Tenter St
East Tenter Street
West Tenter Street
S Tenter St
Scar. St
St. Mark St
Prescot Street A1202
Chamber Street
Portsoken Street
Haydon Street
Minories A1211
Goodman's Yd
Royal Mint Street B126
Dock Street A1202
Blue Anchor Yard
John Fisher Street
Cartwright Street
Croft Street
Ensign Street
Wellclose Square
Well St
The Highway A1203
Pennington Street
Breezers Hill
Virginia Street
East Smithfield A1203
Thomas More Street B107
Vaughan Way
Asher Way
Nesham St
Star Place
Sun Walk
St. Katharine's Way
Marble Qa.
Mews
St. Anthonys Close
Burr Cl
Hermitage Wall
Wapping High Street
Sampson St
Knighten Street
Lilley Close
Smeaton Street
Tower Bridge Approach A100
Tower Bridge A100
Tower Hill A3211
Mansell Street A100
0.25 mile
0.25 km

Whitechapel (West) / St Katharine's Dock

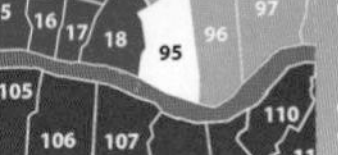

ead to **Wilton's Music Hall** for crumbling decadence and table tennis.

Coffee

- **Black Sheep Coffee** • 2 Leman St
- **Starbucks** • 45 Whitechapel Rd
- **Vagabond E1** • 59–63 Whitechapel High St
- **White Mulberries** • 3 Ivory House

Landmarks

- **The Sun HQ** • 1 Virginia St

Nightlife

- **The Dickens Inn** • 1 St Katherine Docks
- **Simmons** • 61 Mint St
- **Wilton's Music Hall** • Graces Alley & Ensign St

Restaurants

- **Cafe Spice Namaste** • 16 Prescot St
- **The Empress** • 141 Leman St

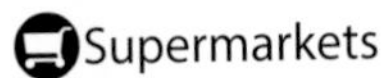

Supermarkets

- **Waitrose** • Thomas More St & Nesham St

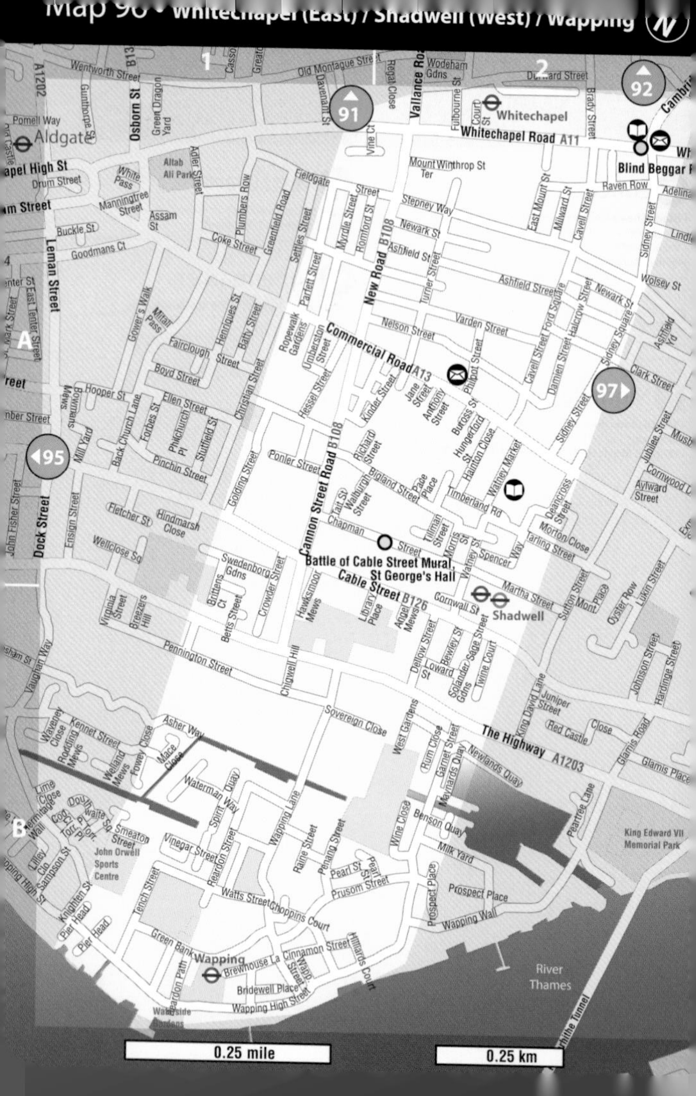
Aldgate
Whitechapel
Whitechapel Road A11
Blind Beggar
Commercial Road A13
New Road B108
Cannon Street Road B108
Battle of Cable Street Mural, St George's Hall
Cable Street B126
Shadwell
The Highway A1203
Wapping
King Edward VII Memorial Park
River Thames
Leman Street
Dock Street
91
92
95
97
0.25 mile
0.25 km

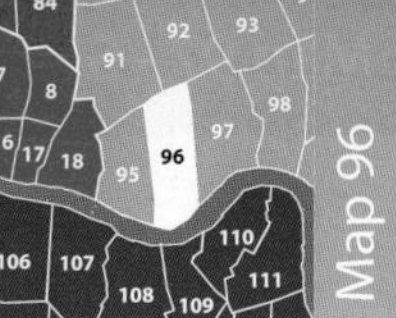

x-dockland Wapping now imports yuppies into its converted warehouses, ss-gleaming Shadwell and Whitechapel keep more of the East End spirit live. Wapping High Street is mainly residential, Whitechapel Road is more vely. **Tayyab's** is cracking—stick out the queues, or if curry's not your thing ead to **Il Bordello**.

Emergency Rooms

- **Royal London Hospital** • Whitechapel Rd & Vallance Rd

Landmarks

- **Battle of Cable Street Mural, St George's Hall** • 236 Cable St
- **Blind Beggar Pub** • 337 Whitechapel Rd

Libraries

- **Idea Store Whitechapel** • 321 Whitechapel Rd
- **Watney Market Library** • 30 Watney Market

Nightlife

- **Captain Kidd** • 108 Wapping High St
- **Town of Ramsgate** • 62 Wapping High St

Post Offices

- **Eastern** • 206 Whitechapel Rd
- **Philpot Street** • 12 Philpot St

Restaurants

- **Il Bordello** • 81 Wapping High St
- **Lahore Kebab House** • 2–10 Umberston St
- **Needoo Grill** • 87 New Rd
- **Tayyabs** • 83 Fieldgate St

Supermarkets

- **Iceland** • Watney St & Tarling St
- **Sainsbury's** • 1 Cambridge Heath Rd

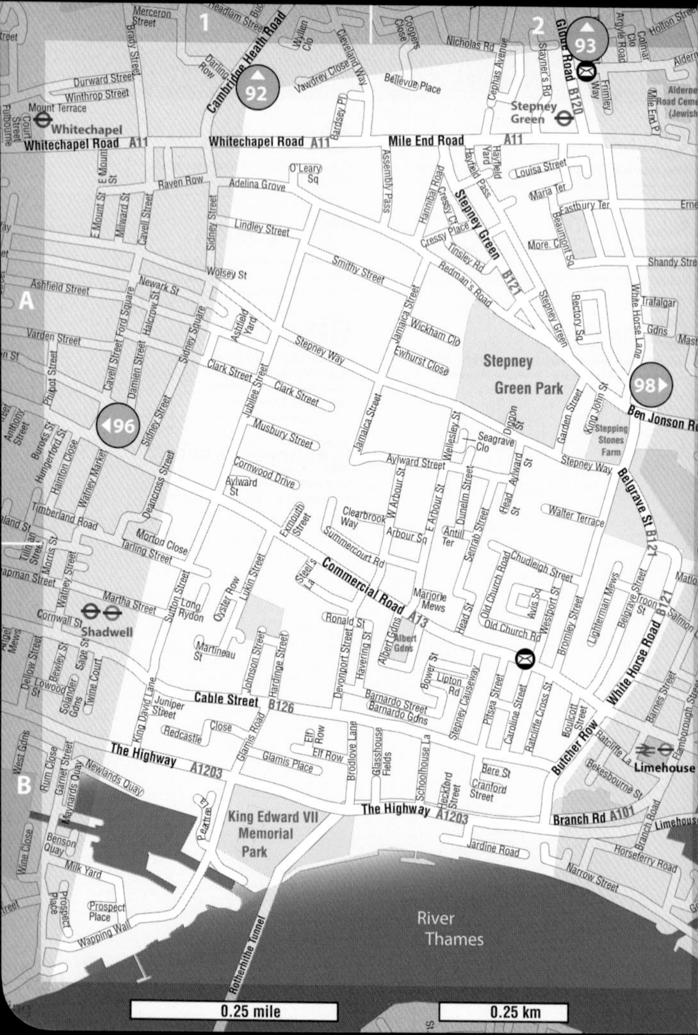

Map 97 • Stepney / Shadwell (East)

Whitechapel Road A11
Mile End Road A11
Commercial Road A73
Cable Street B126
The Highway A1203
Branch Rd A101
Stepney Green B121
Globe Road B120
Belgrave St B121
White Horse Road B121
Ben Jonson Rd
Stepney Green Park
King Edward VII Memorial Park
Stepping Stones Farm
River Thames
Whitechapel
Stepney Green
Shadwell
Limehouse
Rotherhithe Tunnel

0.25 mile

0.25 km

Stepney / Shadwell (East)

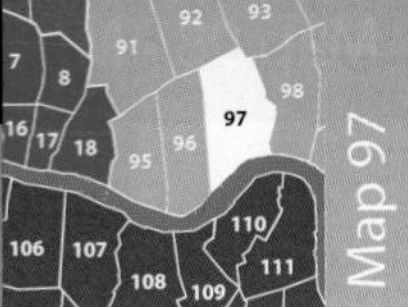

Cockney geezers run into hipsters and smart new developments sit next to rundown estates. No one quite knows where this area is going. We know where we're going, though—to **The George Tavern**, mainly, for impromptu theatre, blue-collar poetry and other arty madness, or **The Prospect of Whitby**, if we're feeling nostalgic.

Cinemas

- **Genesis Mile End** • 93 Mile End Rd

Coffee

- **Popular Café** • 536 Commercial Rd

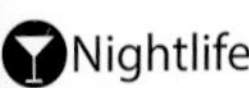

Nightlife

- **The Blind Beggar** • 337 Whitechapel Rd
- **Cable Street Studios** • 566 Cable St
- **The George Tavern** • 373 Commercial Rd
- **The Prospect of Whitby** • 57 Wapping Wall
- **Troxy** • 490 Commerical Rd

Post Offices

- **Globe Road** • 34 Globe Rd
- **Stepney** • 502 Commercial Rd

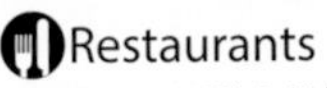

Restaurants

- **Dirty Burger** • 27 Mile End Rd

Shopping

- **East End Thrift Store** • 1 Assembly Passage

Supermarkets

- **Co-Op** • 193 Mile End Rd

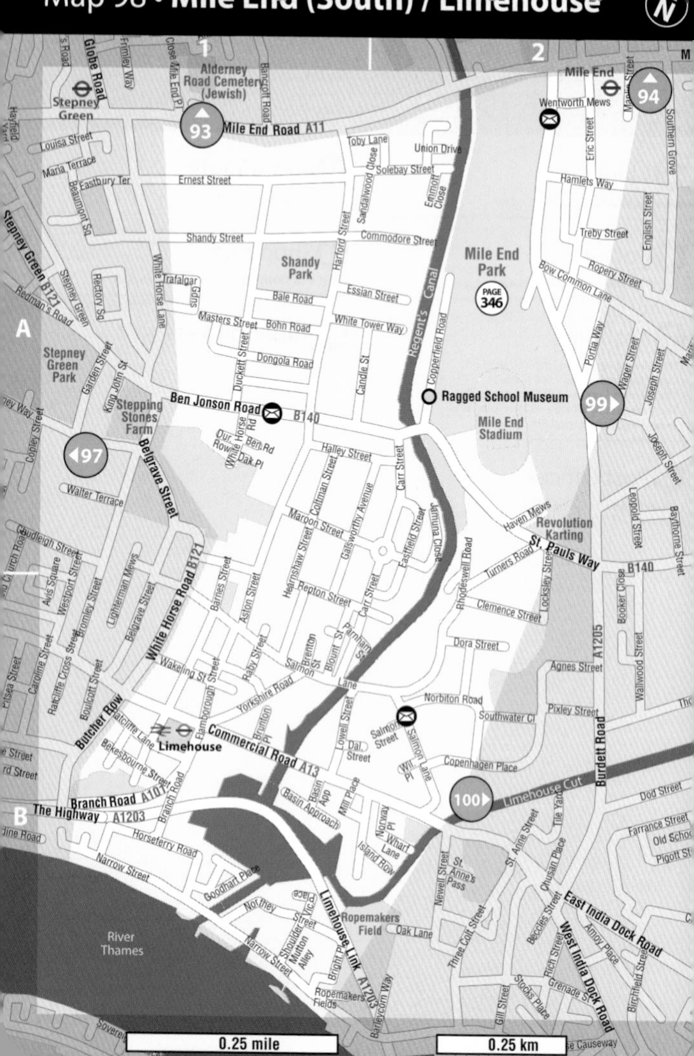

Alderney Road Cemetery (Jewish)
Stepney Green
Mile End
Mile End Road A11
Globe Road
Frimley Way
Close Mile End Pl
Bancroft Road
Wentworth Mews
Eric Street
Southern Grove
Louisa Street
Maria Terrace
Eastbury Ter
Beaumont Sq
Ernest Street
Toby Lane
Union Drive
Sandalwood Close
Solebay Street
Emmott Close
Hamlets Way
Treby Street
English Street
Shandy Street
Commodore Street
Shandy Park
Harford Street
Mile End Park
PAGE 346
Ropery Street
Bow Common Lane
Stepney Green B121
Redman's Road
Rectory Sq
White Horse Lane
Trafalgar Gdns
Bale Road
Essian Street
Regent's Canal
Copperfield Road
Masters Street
Bohn Road
White Tower Way
Portia Way
Wager Street
Joseph Street
Stepney Green Park
Garden Street
King John St
Duckett Street
Dongola Road
Candle St
Stepping Stones Farm
Ben Jonson Road
B140
Ragged School Museum
Mile End Stadium
Our Rowie
White Horse Rd
Ben Rd
Oak Pl
Halley Street
Copley Street
Belgrave Street
Walter Terrace
Carr Street
Coltman Street
Galsworthy Avenue
Maroon Street
Eastfield Street
Jamuna Close
Haven Mews
Revolution Karting
St. Pauls Way
Turners Road
Leopold Street
Baythorne Street
Caudleigh Street
Church Road
Avis Square
Westport Street
Bromley Street
Lighterman Mews
Belgrave Street
White Horse Road B121
Barnes Street
Aston Street
Hearnshaw Street
Repton Street
Carr Street
Rhodeswell Road
Locksley Street
Clemence Street
Booker Close
B140
Caroline Street
Ratcliffe Cross Street
Boulcott Street
Wakeling St
Raby Street
Brenton St
Blount St
Parnham St
Salmon Lane
Dora Street
A1205
Agnes Street
Wallwood Street
Pitsea Street
Flamborough Street
Yorkshire Road
Norbiton Road
Southwater Cl
Pixley Street
Butcher Row
Ratcliffe Lane
Limehouse
Commercial Road A13
Brunton Pl
Lowell Street
Dal Street
Salmon Street
Salmon Lane
Wil Pl
Copenhagen Place
Burdett Road
Bekesbourne Street
Branch Road A101
Branch Road
Basin App
Basin Approach
Mill Place
Limehouse Cut
Dod Street
The Highway A1203
Norway Pl
Wharf Lane
Island Row
Tile Yard
St. Anne Street
Farrance Street
Old School
Pigott St
Horseferry Road
Narrow Street
Goodhart Place
Newell Street
St. Anne's Pass
Chusan Place
East India Dock Road
Northey Street
Vicar Place
Limehouse Link A1203
Ropemakers Field
Oak Lane
Three Colt Street
Beccles Street
Amoy Place
West India Dock Road
Birchfield Street
River Thames
Narrow Street
Shoulder Mutton Alley
Bright Pl
Ropemakers Fields
Barleycorn Way
Rich Street
Grenade St
Gill Street
Stocks Place
0.25 mile
0.25 km
93
94
97
99
100
A
B
1
2

Mile End (South) / Limehouse

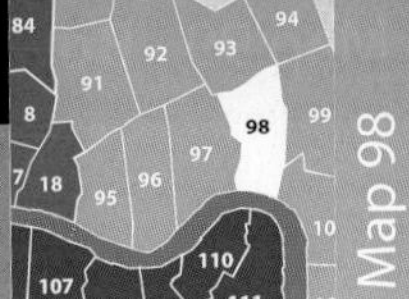

cary desolate landscapes and urban decay? Cool! Authenticity and Edge go and-in-hand 'round here until you get to the water, where it livens up and ırns into a Foxtons wank fantasy. Still, **The Grapes**, **The Narrow** and **La Figa** re eats and drinks havens while the **Ragged School Museum** offers a glimpse f what it was like when it was really grim round 'ere.

Landmarks

- **Ragged School Museum** • 46 Copperfield Rd

Nightlife

- **The Grapes** • 76 Narrow St

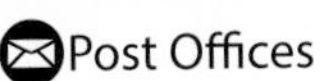

Post Offices

- **Ben Jonson Road** • 52 Ben Jonson Rd
- **Mile End** • 1 Burdett Rd
- **Salmon Lane** • 127 Salmon Ln

Restaurants

- **Ariana** • 2 Midlothian Rd
- **La Figa** • 45 Narrow St
- **The Narrow** • 44 Narrow St
- **The Orange Room** • 63 Burdett Rd

Morgan Street
Tredegar Sq
Lyn Ms
Coborn Road
Coborn Street
Harley Grove
Alfred St
Bow Road A11
Bow Road
Bow Church
Bromley Hi
Arnold Road
Tomlins Grove
Campbell Road
Aberavon Road
Rhondda Grove
1
2
94
93
Mile End
Maplin St
Went. Ms
Wentworth Mews
Eric Street
Southern Grove
Brokesley Street
British Street
Merchant St
Eleanor Street
Archibald Street
Wellington Way
Ireton Street
Tidworth Road
Holyhead Close
Rainhill Way
Stroudley Walk
Devons Road
Hamlets Way
English Street
Treby St
Tower Hamlets Cemetery Park
Fairfoot Road
Swaton Road
Rounton Road
Chiltern Road
Purdy Street
Reeves Road
A
Mile End Park
98
Mile End Stadium
Revolution Karting
Ropery Street
Bow Common Lane
Portia Way
Wager Street
Joseph Street
Maritime St
Cantrell Rd
Corby Way
Spanby Rd
Knapp Road
Devons Road
Fern Street
Blackthorn St
Brock Place
Cranwell Close
St. Andrews Way
Robeson Street
Ackroyd Dr
Whitethorn Street
Tidey St
B140
Maddams Street
Watts Grove
Glaucus Street
Violet Road
Weatherley Close
Shelmerdine Cl
Belton Way
Devons Road
Gale Street
Copton Close
Yeo Street
Leopold St
Baythorne Street
Huddart Street
Bellmaker Ct
Celandine Cl
Furze Street
Hawgood Street
Haven Mews
Turners Road
St. Paul's Way B140
Locksley Street
Burdett Road
Booker Cl
Calling Cl
Wallwood Street
Burgess Street
Selsey Street
Kilner Street
Bow Common Lane
Balladier Walk
Barchester St
Locksons Clo
Metro Cl
Broomfield Street
Morris Road
Rhodeswell Road
Clemence Street
Dora Street
Agnes Street
Thomas Road
Cotall Street
Upper North Street
Brabazon Street
Chrisp Street
Rifle Str
Pixley Street
Limehouse Cut
Stainsby Road
Bartlett Park
Arcadia Street
Ellesmere Street
Godalming Road
Cording St
Norbiton Rd
Southwater Cl
A1205
Northumbria St
Carmen St
Augusta Street
B
Salmon Lane
Copenhagen Pl
Dod Street
Giraud St
Carron Close
Hay Currie Street
Farrance Street
Old School Sq
Pigott Street
Lindfield Street
Hind Grove
Cordelia Street
Tile Yard
St. Anne Street
Chusan Place
Upper North Street
Flora Close
Ricardo Street
Kerbey Street
Southill Street
Willis St
100
Canton Street
Newell Street
Beccles Street
Rich Street
Amoy Place
East India Dock Road A13
Saracen Street
Pekin Street
Nankin St
Grundy Street
Annabel Close
Jeremiah Street
Duff Street
Plimsoll Close
Sturry Street
101
Oak Lane
Three Colt Street
Gill Street
Grenade Street
West India Dock Road
East India Dock Road A13
0.25 mile
0.25 km
Morant Street
All Saints

Bow Common

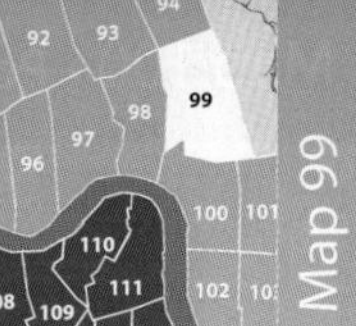

Desolation Row pretty much. For hardy explorers kitted out with knives and/or chastity belts, the wonderfully overgrown and sh**-your-pants scary **Tower Hamlets Cemetery Park** is great. In fact, keep the afore-mentioned kit on if you intend creeping through the boarded-up council estates and general doom.

Post Offices

• **Poplar** • 22 Market Sq

Map 100 • Poplar (West) / Canary Wharf (West)

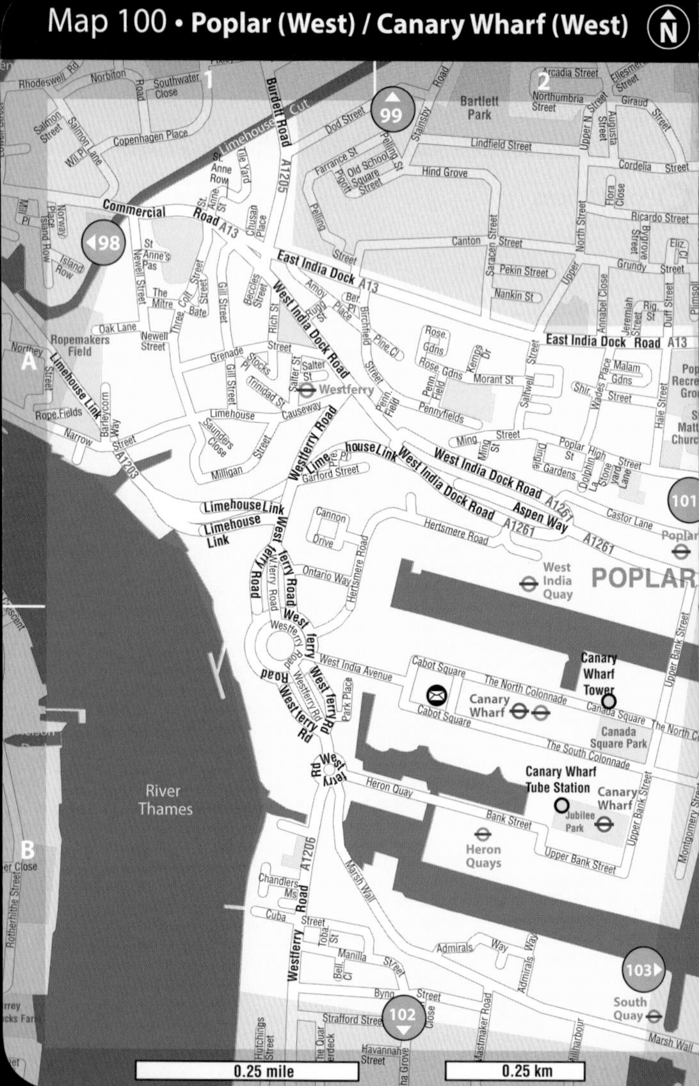

Poplar (West) / Canary Wharf (West)

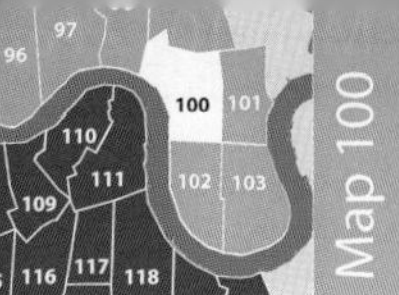

ow that we're officially out of the recession you can wander the wharf arveling at the 'scrapers without pesky ruined bankers landing on you. Ah es, the smell of money has resurfaced around finance's engine room and the rilliantly futuristic landscape is once again replete with suits shopping at the and mall under Cabot Square. They never left of course, they just got used to acked lunches like the rest of us.

Cinemas

- **Cineworld West India Quay** • 11 Hertsmere Rd

Coffee

- **Bagel Factory** • 7 Westferry Circus
- **Café Brera** • 45 Bank St
- **Café Brera** • 12 Cabot Sq
- **Café Brera** • 31 Westferry Circus
- **Starbucks** • 1 Canada Sq

Landmarks

- **Canary Wharf Tower** • 1 Canada Sq
- **Canary Wharf Tube Station** • Canary Wharf

Nightlife

- **Davy's** • 31 Canary Wharf
- **The Parlour** • 40 Canada Sq Pk
- **Via Fossa** • 18 Hertsmere Rd

Post Offices

- **Canary Wharf** • 5 Chancellor Passage

Restaurants

- **Browns** • Hertsmere Rd
- **Plateau** • Canada Pl
- **Royal China** • 30 Westferry Circus

Supermarkets

- **Tesco** • 15 Cabot Sq
- **Waitrose** • N Colonnade & Canada Sq

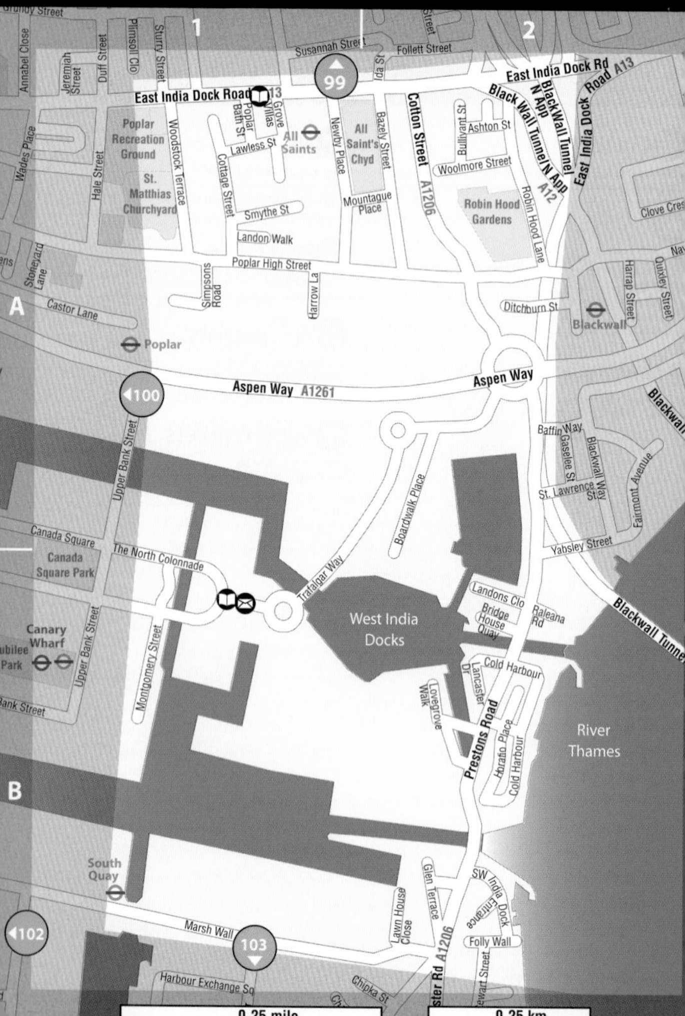

Granby Street
1
2
Annabel Close
Jeremiah Street
Duff Street
Plimsoll Clo
Sturry Street
Susannah Street
99
Ida St
Street
Follett Street
East India Dock Rd
A13
East India Dock Road
A13
Poplar Bath St
Grove Villas
Black Wall Tunnel N App
BlackWall Tunnel N App
East India Dock Road
Wades Place
Hale Street
Poplar Recreation Ground
St. Matthias Churchyard
Woodstock Terrace
Lawless St
All Saints
Cottage Street
Newby Place
All Saint's Chyd
Bazely Street
Cotton Street
A1206
Bullivant St
Ashton St
Woolmore Street
Black Wall Tunnel N App
A12
Clove Cres
Smythe St
Mountague Place
Robin Hood Gardens
Robin Hood Lane
Landon Walk
Stoneyard Lane
Poplar High Street
Simpsons Road
Harrow La
Harrap Street
Quixley Street
Nav
A
Castor Lane
Ditchburn St
Blackwall
Poplar
Aspen Way
A1261
Aspen Way
100
Blackwall
Baffin Way
Gaselee St
Blackwall Way
Fairmont Avenue
Upper Bank Street
Boardwalk Place
St. Lawrence St
Yabsley Street
Canada Square
Canada Square Park
The North Colonnade
Trafalgar Way
Landons Clo
Bridge House Quay
Raleana Rd
Blackwall Tunnel
West India Docks
Canary Wharf
Jubilee Park
Upper Bank Street
Montgomery Street
Cold Harbour
Lancaster Dr
Lovegrove Walk
Bank Street
Prestons Road
Horatio Place
Cold Harbour
River Thames
B
South Quay
Glen Terrace
SW India Dock Entrance
Lawn House Close
102
Marsh Wall
103
A1206
Folly Wall
Harbour Exchange Sq
Chipka St
ster Rd
ewart Street
0.25 mile
0.25 km

Poplar (East) / Canary Wharf (East)

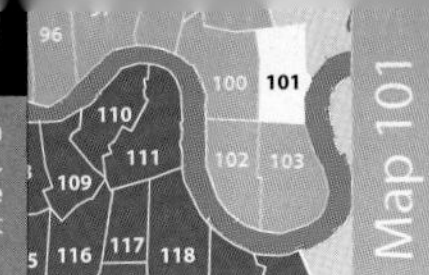

ne day NFT lay down in the shadow of the Tower after a few in **The Greenwich ensioner** and gazed up at the 'scraper, admiring its Philip K. Dickian splendour. small plane buzzed by. Well-heeled bankers stuffed with pub grub from **The un** strode by us. Then we got pulled up by the dreadlocks by a rozzer and got oofed out for not reading the *Financial Times*. Serves us right.

Libraries

- **Idea Store Canary Wharf** • Churchill Pl
- **Idea Store Chrisp Street** • East India Dock Rd • 1 Vesey Path

Nightlife

- **Bar Salento** • 3 Clove Cres
- **The Greenwich Pensioner** • 28 Bazely Street

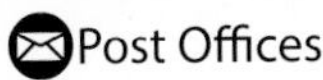

Post Offices

- **Churchill Place** • 2 Churchill Pl

Restaurants

- **The Gun** • 27 Coldharbour

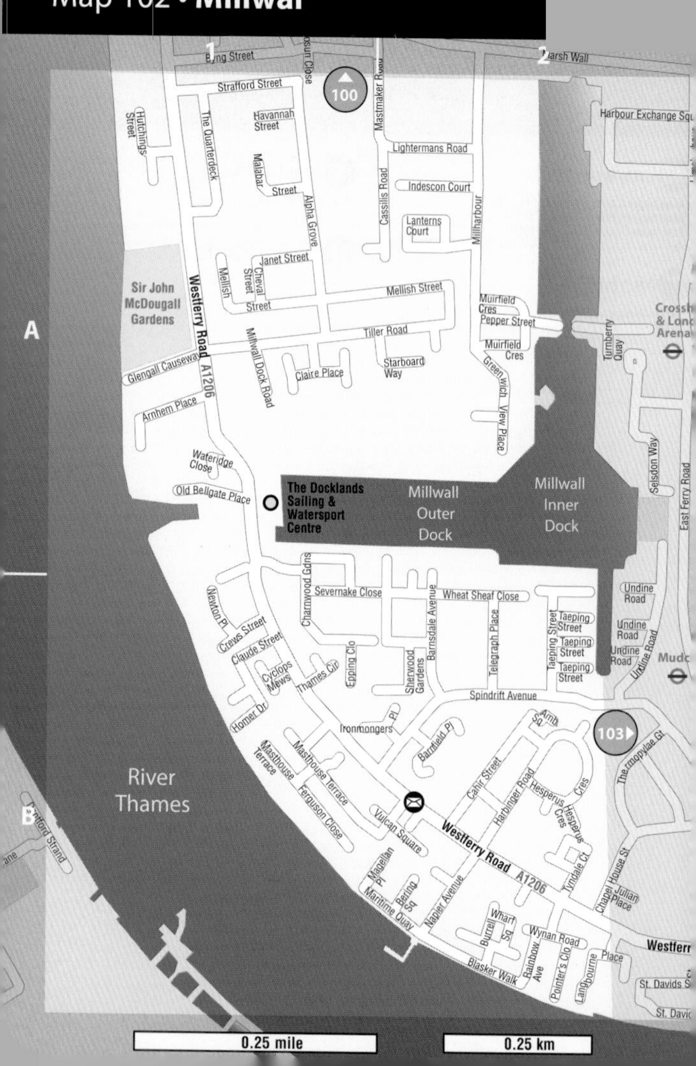

Byng Street
Marsh Wall
Strafford Street
100
Havannah Street
Hutchings Street
The Quarterdeck
Malabar Street
Alpha Grove
Mastmaker Road
Lightermans Road
Indescon Court
Cassilis Road
Lanterns Court
Millharbour
Harbour Exchange Sq
Janet Street
Mellish Street
Cheval Street
Mellish Street
Sir John McDougall Gardens
Westferry Road
Tiller Road
Muirfield Cres
Pepper Street
Muirfield Cres
Turnberry Quay
A
Glengall Causeway
A1206
Millwall Dock Road
Claire Place
Starboard Way
Greenwich View Place
Arnhem Place
Wateridge Close
Selsdon Way
East Ferry Road
Old Bellgate Place
The Docklands Sailing & Watersport Centre
Millwall Outer Dock
Millwall Inner Dock
Charnwood Gdns
Severnake Close
Barnsdale Avenue
Wheat Sheaf Close
Undine Road
Undine Road
Undine Road
Undine Road
Newton Pl
Crews Street
Claude Street
Cyclops Mews
Thames Cir
Epping Clo
Sherwood Gardens
Telegraph Place
Taeping Street
Taeping Street
Taeping Street
Taeping Street
Spindrift Avenue
Homer Dr
Ironmongers Pl
Barnfield Pl
Amb Sq
103
Thermopylae Gt
Masthouse Terrace
Masthouse Terrace
Cahir Street
Harbinger Road
Hesperus Cres
Hesperus Cres
Hesperus Cres
River Thames
Ferguson Close
Vulcan Square
Westferry Road
A1206
Tyndale Ct
B
Chapel House St
Julian Place
Magellan Pl
Bering Sq
Maritime Quay
Napier Avenue
Wharf
Burrell
Sq
Wynan Road
Westferr
Blasker Walk
Rainbow Ave
Pointer's Clo
Langbourne Place
St. Davids S
St. David
0.25 mile
0.25 km

ough Millwall has award-winning **Docklands Sailing Centre**, it doesn't really ve much else. Bereft of tube, overground, or DLR, it doesn't even have Millwall anymore. Despite the potential of Canary Wharf on the doorstep and flush of xury riverside apartments, it's still tainted with the whiff of BNP and football oliganism. Buy now.

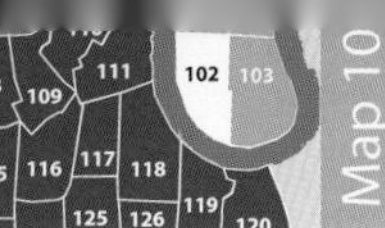

Landmarks

- **The Docklands Sailing & Watersport Centre** • 235 Westferry Rd

Nightlife

- **Hubbub** • 269 Westferry Rd

Post Offices

- **Westferry Rd** • 367 Westferry Rd

Meridian Place
1
2
Marsh Wall
101
Folly Wall
East Ferry Road
Harbour Exchange Sq
Chipka Street
Capstan Sq
Aste Street
Roserton Street
River Barge Close
Limeharbour
Roffey Street
Ovex Close
Millwall Inner Dock
Stewart Street
Plevna Street
Manchester Road
Launch Street
New Union Close
Crossharbour & London Arena
Strattondale St
Pepper Street
Marshfield Street
A
Turnberry Quay
Glengall Grove
A1206
Amsterdam Road
102
Leerdam Dr
Rotterdam Drive
Rembrandt Close
Friars Mead
Millennium Drive
Schooner Close
Selsdon Way
East Ferry Road
Jubilee Circle
Sambard Mews
James Mews
Olliffe Street
Millwall Inner Dock
Mudchute Park
Chichester Way
Pier Street
Blyth Close
Sextant Avenue
Undine Road
Mudchute Farm
Plymouth Wharf
Taeping Street
Seyssel Street
Telegraph Place
Mudchute
Storers Quay
Kingfield Street
Saunders Ness Road
Billson Street
Caledonian Wharf
Spindrift Avenue
Sonage Street
Empire Wharf
Stebondale Street
Thermopylae Gate
Macquarie Way
Millwall Park
Glengarry St
Glenaffric Ave
Grosvenor Wharf
Harbinger Road
B
House Street
Island Gardens
Cumberland Mills Sq
Chapel
Tyndale Court
Manchester Road
A1206
Westferry Road
A1206
Lockesfield Place
Julian Place
Manchester Grove
Island Gardens
Saunders Ness Road
Luralda Gdns
Wynan Road
East Ferry Road
Horseshoe Cl
Langbourne Pl
Ferry Street
Midland Plvv
Pointer Cl
Livingstone Gdns
Felstead Gdns
River Thames
Blasker Walk
St. Davids Square

Cubitt Town / Mudchute

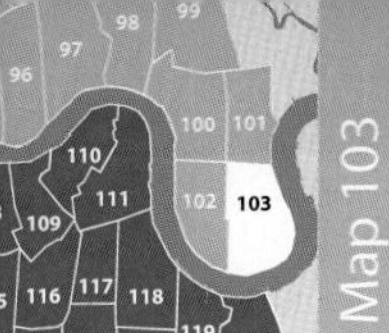

hough shaded by the skyscrapers of Canary Wharf and a rash of luxury evelopments, this corner of the Island is blessed by the marvellous **Mudchute rm and Park** (with the standout **Mudchute Kitchen** and equestrian centre), ot one, not two, but three DLR stations, and a number of down-to-earth oozers like **Lord Nelson**. Who let the Isle of Dogs out?

Landmarks

- **Mudchute Farm** • Pier St

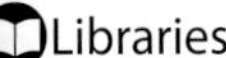

Libraries

- **Cubitt Town Library** • Strattondale St

Nightlife

- **The Ferry House** • 26 Ferry St
- **The Lord Nelson** • 1 Manchester Rd

Post Offices

- **Cubitt Town** • 15 Castalia Sq
- **Isle Of Dogs** • 159 Manchester Rd

Restaurants

- **Mudchute Kitchen** • Pier St

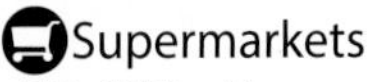

Supermarkets

- **ASDA** • 151 E Ferry Rd

THE STRAND
SOUTH BANK
SOUTHWARK
BOROUGH
BERMONDSEY
WATERLOO
NEWINGTON
ELEPHANT & CASTLE
LAMBETH
WALWORTH
KENNINGTON
VAUXHALL
CAMBERWELL
SOUTH LAMBETH
STOCKWELL
BRIXTON
HERNE HILL
EAST DULWICH
Tower of London Park
Burgess Park
Kennington Park
Ruskin Park
Stamford St
Southwark St
Thrale St
Tooley St
St. Thomas St
Union Street
The Cut
York Rd
Waterloo Rd
Blackfriars Rd
Baylis Rd
Borough Rd
Long Ln
Bermondsey St
Tower Bridge Rd
Druid St
Abbey St
Harper Rd
Great Dover St
Grange Rd
St. Georges Rd
London Rd
New Kent Rd
Kennington Rd
Old Kent Rd
Dunton Rd
Rolls Rd
Walworth Rd
Kennington Park Rd
Albany Rd
Trafalgar Ave
Camberwell New Rd
Camberwell Rd
Peckham Rd
Denmark Hill
Coldharbour Ln
Grove Ln
Dog Kennel Hill
Hinton Rd
Milkwood Rd
Herne Hill
Railton Rd
E Dulwich Gro
Lordship Ln
Dulwich Rd
Half Moon Ln
104
105
106
107
108
112
113
114
121
122
123
127
128
129

CANARY WHARF
DOCKLANDS
Salter Rd
Brunel Rd
110
111
ROTHERHITHE
ISLE OF DOGS
CUBITT TOWN
Redriff Rd
109
Southwark Park
Hawkstone Rd
Mudchute Park
MILLWALL
Millwall Park
Lower Rd
Grove St
Evelyn St
Trundley Rd
117
Deptford Park
116
118
Thames River
DEPTFORD
119
Creek Rd
GREENWICH
Sanford St
Deptford Church St
Greenwich High Rd
Greenwich Park
New Cross Road
125
120
New Cross Rd
126
Pomeroy St
Besson St
P.O.S.
Blackheath Hill
124
Queens Rd
Florence Rd
NEW CROSS
Evelina Rd
NUNHEAD
LEWISHAM
BROCKLEY

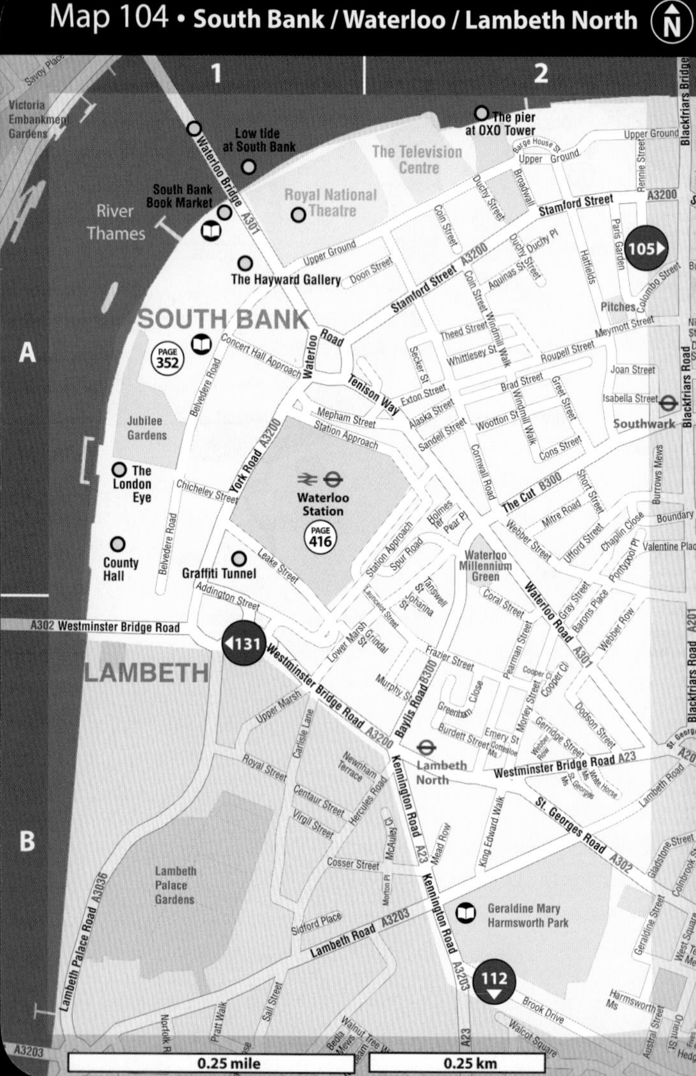

The pier at OXO Tower
Low tide at South Bank
South Bank Book Market
The Television Centre
Royal National Theatre
The Hayward Gallery
River Thames
SOUTH BANK
Jubilee Gardens
The London Eye
County Hall
Graffiti Tunnel
Waterloo Station
Waterloo Millennium Green
Southwark
Lambeth North
LAMBETH
Lambeth Palace Gardens
Geraldine Mary Harmsworth Park
Waterloo Bridge A301
Stamford Street A3200
Waterloo Road
York Road A3200
Westminster Bridge Road A3200
Kennington Road A23
Lambeth Road A3203
St. Georges Road A302
The Cut B300
Baylis Road B300
Blackfriars Road
0.25 mile
0.25 km

outh Bank / Waterloo / Lambeth North

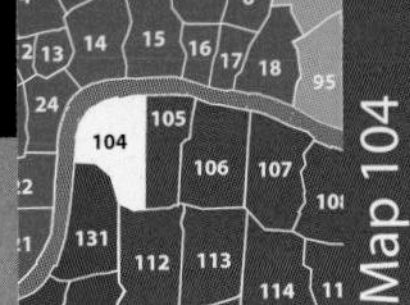

g the riverbank and you can culture 'til you puke. But you'll need stamina survive; with such densely populated institutions your brain will give up g before your body. When it does, head for the cafe by day/bar by night, **ncrete**, tucked away behind the **Southbank Centre**, where the art tallation du jour promises to have you wetting your pants in no time.

Cinemas

BFI London IMAX • 1 Charlie Chaplin Walk
BFI Southbank • Belverdere Rd & Waterloo Rd

Coffee

Bagel Factory • Waterloo Station
Benugo Bar & Kitchen • Belvedere Rd
Four Corners Cafe • 12 Lower Marsh
ScooterCaffe • 132 Lower Marsh
Starbucks • 3 Belvedere Rd

Landmarks

County Hall • Westminster Bridge Rd & Belvedere Rd
The Hayward Gallery • Southbank Centre
The London Eye • Westminster Bridge Rd
Low Tide at South Bank • Waterloo Rd & Upper Ground
National Theatre • South Bank
The Pier at OXO Tower • Barge House St & Upper Ground
South Bank Book Market • Under Waterloo Bridge
Waterloo Bridge • Waterloo Bridge

Libraries

Imperial War Museum • Lambeth Rd
Poetry Library • Royal Festival Hall
Waterloo Library • 114 Lower Marsh

Nightlife

The Anchor & Hope • 36 The Cut
Benugo Bar & Kitchen • Belvedere Rd
Concrete • Southbank Centre
Cubana • 48 Lower Marsh
The Cut Bar • 66 The Cut
The Pit Bar at the Old Vic • The Cut
Royal Festival Hall • Belvedere Rd
Skylon • Belvedere Rd

Restaurants

- **The Anchor & Hope** • 32 The Cut
- **Canteen** • Royal Festival Hall, Belvedere Rd
- **Concrete** • Southbank Centre
- **The Cut Bar** • 66 The Cut
- **Giraffe** • Riverside Level 1
- **Marie's Cafe** • 90 Lower Marsh
- **Oxo Tower Wharf** • Barge House St
- **RSJ** • 33 Coin St
- **Skylon** • Belvedere Rd
- **Studio 6** • 56 Upper Ground
- **Tas Cut** • 33 The Cut

Shopping

- **Calder Bookshop** • 51 The Cut
- **Calder Bookshop Theatre** • 51 The Cut
- **Greensmiths** • 27 Lower Marsh
- **Konditor & Cook** • 22 Cornwall Rd
- **Oasis** • 84 Lower Marsh
- **ScooterCaffe** • 132 Lower Marsh
- **Silverprint** • 12 Valentine Pl
- **Southbank Book Market** • Under Waterloo Bridge
- **Top Wind** • 2 Lower Marsh

Supermarkets

- **Iceland** • 112 Lower Marsh
- **Marks & Spencer** • Waterloo Station
- **Sainsbury's** • 101 Waterloo Rd

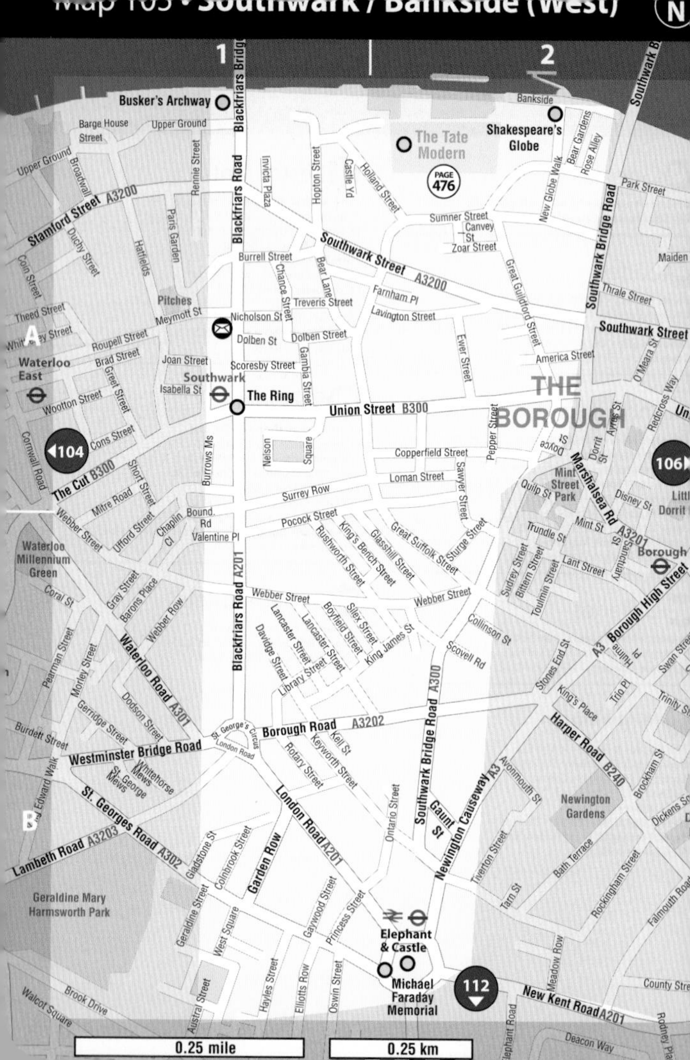

N
1
2
A
B
Busker's Archway
Blackfriars Bridge
Bankside
The Tate Modern
Shakespeare's Globe
PAGE 476
Southwark Bridge
Barge House Street
Upper Ground
Rennie Street
Blackfriars Road
Invicta Plaza
Hopton Street
Castle Yd
Holland Street
Bear Gardens
Rose Alley
New Globe Walk
Park Street
Southwark Bridge Road
Upper Ground
Broadwall
Stamford Street A3200
Duchy Street
Coin Street
Hatfields
Paris Garden
Sumner Street
Canvey St
Zoar Street
Southwark Street A3200
Maiden
Burrell Street
Chance Street
Bear Lane
Treveris Street
Farnham Pl
Lavington Street
Great Guildford Street
Thrale Street
Southwark Street
Pitches
Theed Street
Whittlesey Street
Meymott St
Nicholson St
Roupell Street
Dolben St
Dolben Street
Waterloo East
Brad Street
Joan Street
Scoresby Street
Gambia Street
Ewer Street
America Street
O'Meara St
Greet Street
Southwark
Isabella St
The Ring
THE BOROUGH
Redcross Way
Wootton Street
Union Street B300
Pepper Street
Doyce St
Ayres St
Dorrit St
Cornwall Road
104
Cons Street
Nelson Square
Copperfield Street
106
The Cut B300
Short Street
Burrows Ms
Sawyer Street
Loman Street
Mint Street Park
Marshalsea Rd
Quilp St
Disney St
Little Dorrit
Mitre Road
Surrey Row
Webber Street
Ufford Street
Chaplin Cl
Bound. Rd
Valentine Pl
Pocock Street
Rushworth Street
King's Bench Street
Glasshill Street
Great Suffolk Street
Sturge Street
Mint St
Trundle St
A3201
Sanctuary St
Borough
Waterloo Millennium Green
Lant Street
Sudrey Street
Bittern Street
Toulmin Street
Coral St
Gray Street
Barons Place
Webber Row
Blackfriars Road A201
Webber Street
Webber Street
Lancaster Street
Boyfield Street
Silex Street
King James St
Collinson St
Scovell Rd
Borough High Street
A3
Hulme Pl
Swan Street
Pearman Street
Morley Street
Waterloo Road A301
Davidge Street
Lancaster Street
Library Street
Stones End St
Trio Pl
King's Place
Trinity St
Gerridge Street
Dodson Street
Southwark Bridge Road A300
Harper Road B240
Burdett Street
St. George's Circus
London Road
Borough Road A3202
Keil St
Keyworth Street
Rotary Street
Brockham St
Westminster Bridge Road
Whitehorse Mews
St. George Mews
Avonmouth St
Newington Gardens
Dickens Sq
King Edward Walk
St. Georges Road A302
London Road A201
Ontario Street
Gaunt St
Newington Causeway A3
Lambeth Road A3203
Gladstone St
Colnbrook Street
Garden Row
Tiverton Street
Bath Terrace
Rockingham Street
Falmouth Road
Geraldine Mary Harmsworth Park
Geraldine Street
West Square
Gaywood Street
Princess Street
Tarn St
Elephant & Castle
Meadow Row
Brook Drive
Walcot Square
Austral Street
Hayles Street
Elliotts Row
Oswin Street
Michael Faraday Memorial
112
New Kent Road A201
County Street
Elephant Road
Deacon Way
Rodney Place
0.25 mile
0.25 km

Southwark / Bankside (West)

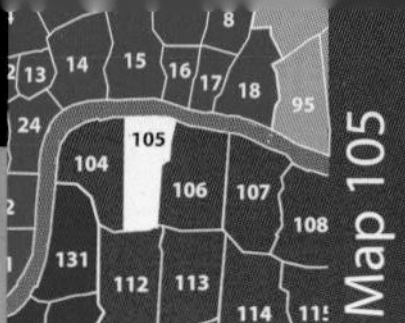

he **Tate Modern**, ladies and gents. It deserves all the praise it gets. And next door ere's **Shakespeare's Globe**, the modern reconstruction of the Elizabethan playhouse here the Bard of Avon's works were contemporaneously produced. Both make this oked-after stretch of the Thames embankment a treasure for those hungry for culture. or those hungry for something else, you're spoilt with quirky options: Try **Baltic** for olish Hunters' Stew, **The Table** for award-winning brunches, or **Laughing Gravy** for a staurant named after Laurel & Hardy's dog.

Coffee

- **Pret A Manger** • 2 Canvey St
- **Starbucks** • Emerson St (Units 1–3 Benbow House)

Landmarks

- **Buskers' Archway** • Southbank
- **Elephant & Castle** • Elephant & Castle
- **Michael Faraday Memorial** • Elephant & Castle
- **The Ring** • 72 Blackfriars Rd
- **Shakespeare's Globe** • 21 New Globe Walk
- **Tate Modern** • Bankside

Nightlife

- **Albert Arms** • 1 Gladstone St
- **The Libertine** • 125 Great Suffolk St
- **The Lord Nelson** • 243 Union St
- **Ministry of Sound** • 103 Gaunt St
- **The Prince of Wales** • 51 St George's Rd
- **Union Theatre** • 229 Union St

Post Offices

- **Blackfriars Road** • 52 Blackfriars Rd

Restaurants

- **Baltic** • 74 Blackfriars Rd
- **El Vergel** • 132 Webber St
- **Laughing Gravy** • 154 Blackfriars Rd
- **Mercato Metro** • 42 Newington Causeway
- **The Table** • 83 Southwark St
- **Tate Modern Restaurant** • Bankside
- **Terry's Cafe** • 158 Great Suffolk St

Shopping

- **Elephant & Castle Market** • Elephant & Castle

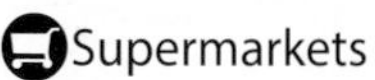

Supermarkets

- **Tesco** • Elephant & Castle Station

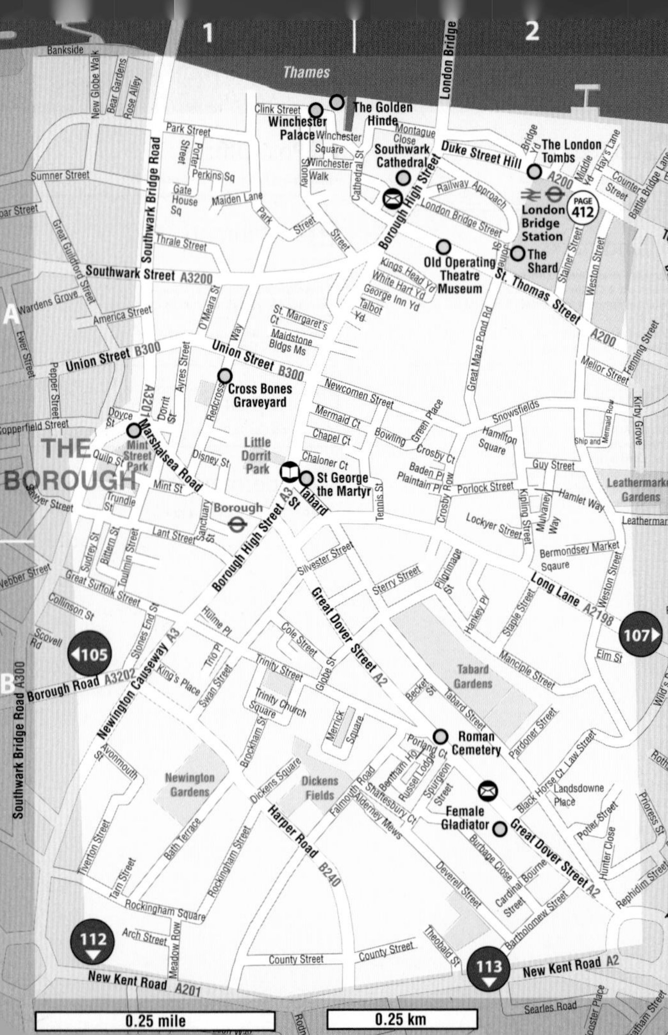

Thames
THE BOROUGH
The Golden Hinde
Winchester Palace
Southwark Cathedral
The London Tombs
London Bridge Station
The Shard
Old Operating Theatre Museum
Cross Bones Graveyard
Little Dorrit Park
St George the Martyr
Borough
Tabard Gardens
Roman Cemetery
Female Gladiator
Newington Gardens
Dickens Fields
Leathermarket Gardens
0.25 mile
0.25 km

Bankside (East) / Borough / Newington

Shoreditch for grown-ups, these parts have become a bit suitified lately—specially now that it's been reborn as 'London Bridge Quarter' under the Shard. till, there's plenty of fun to be had. Gourmet-minded **Borough Market** draws he crowds on Saturdays, while the pubs and bars lining Borough High Street eep the party-minded happy throughout the week. Don't miss **The Rake** if you ke (unusual) beer, **Brindisa** for Spanish tapas, and **Roast** if meat's your thing.

Coffee

- **Caffe Nero** • 3 Cathedral St
- **Costa** • 134 Borough High St
- **Pret A Manger** • 8 London Bridge St
- **Pret A Manger** • 49 Tooley St

Landmarks

- **Cross Bones Graveyard** • Red Cross Way & Union St
- **Female Gladiator** • 159 Great Dover St
- **The Golden Hinde** • Clink St & Stoney St
- **The London Tombs** • 2 Tooley St
- **Mint Street Park** • Southwark Bridge Rd & Marshalsea Rd
- **Old Operating Theatre Museum** • 9 St Thomas St
- **Roman Cemetery** • 165 Great Dover St
- **The Shard** • 32 London Bridge St
- **Southwark Cathedral** • Cathedral St & Montague Close
- **St George the Martyr** • Borough High St & Tabard St
- **Winchester Palace** • Clink St & Storey St

Libraries

- **John Harvard Library** • 211 Borough High St

Nightlife

- **The Anchor** • 34 Park St
- **Belushi's** • 161 Borough High St
- **Bunch of Grapes** • 2 St Thomas St
- **The Blue-Eyed Maid** • 173 Borough High St
- **The George Inn** • 77 Borough High St
- **The Globe** • 8 Bedale St
- **Number 1 Bar** • 1 Duke St Hill
- **The Market Porter** • 9 Stoney St
- **The Rake** • 14 Winchester Walk
- **The Roebuck** • 50 Great Dover St
- **The Rose** • 123 Snowfields
- **The Royal Oak** • 44 Tabard St
- **Southwark Tavern** • 22 Southwark St

Post Offices

- **Great Dover Street** • 159 Great Dover St
- **London Bridge** • 19 Borough High St

Restaurants

- **Arabica Bar & Kitchen** • 3 Rochester Walk
- **Boot and Flogger** • 10 Redcross Wy
- **Champor-Champor** • 62 Weston St
- **Feng Sushi** • 13 Stoney St
- **Fish!** • Cathedral St
- **Nando's** • 215 Clink St
- **Roast** • The Floral Hall, Stoney St
- **Silka** • Southwark St
- **Tapas Brindisa** • 18 Southwark St
- **Tas Borough High Street** • 72 Borough High St
- **Wright Bros Oyster Bar** • 11 Stoney St

Shopping

- **Borough Market** • 8 Southwark St
- **Brindisa Retail** • Borough Market
- **Paul Smith** • 13 Park St

Supermarkets

- **Marks & Spencer** • London Bridge Station
- **Sainsbury's** • 116 Borough High St

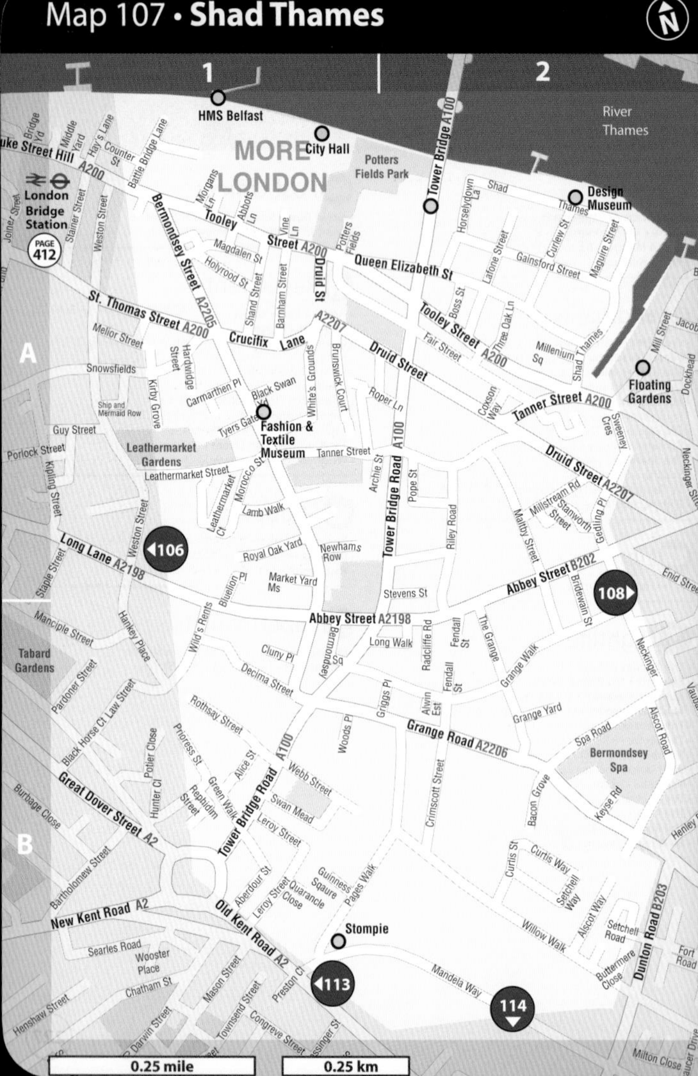

1
2
A
B
HMS Belfast
City Hall
MORE LONDON
Potters Fields Park
River Thames
Design Museum
London Bridge Station
PAGE 412
Tower Bridge A100
Tooley Street A200
Queen Elizabeth St
St. Thomas Street A200
Crucifix Lane
Druid St
Druid Street
Bermondsey Street A2205
Fashion & Textile Museum
Leathermarket Gardens
Floating Gardens
Tanner Street A200
Tower Bridge Road A100
Long Lane A2198
Abbey Street A2198
Abbey Street B202
Grange Road A2206
Bermondsey Spa
Great Dover Street A2
New Kent Road A2
Old Kent Road A2
Tabard Gardens
Stompie
Mandela Way
Dunton Road B203
106
108
113
114
0.25 mile
0.25 km

Shad Thames

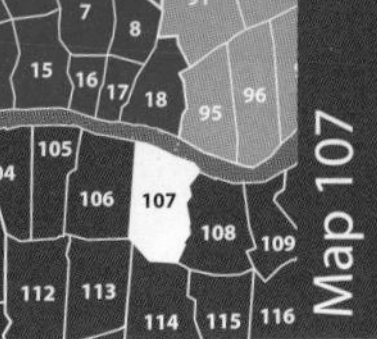

Map 107

The elitist's Bermondsey, Shad Thames is home to ultra-hip boutiques, glass balconies, and converted warehouses. No café dares exist without its own gallery. Bermondsey Street blossoms as an epicentre of creatives knocking out their latest bestseller over brunch, while the More London space by the Thames is an invigorating crowd-pleaser. Head to so-new-its-still-burping-formula **Shortwave** for indie flicks, and **The Scoop** for top free events.

Cinemas

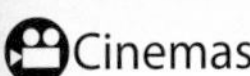

- **Shortwave** • 10 Bermondsey Sq

Coffee

- **Caffe Nero** • 6 More Pl
- **Caphe House** • 114 Bermondsey St
- **Coffee @ Bermondsey** • 163 Bermondsey St
- **Hej** • 1 Bermondsey St

Landmarks

- **City Hall** • Queen's Walk, More London Development
- **Design Museum** • Shad Thames
- **Fashion and Textile Museum** • 83 Bermondsey St
- **Floating Gardens** • 31 Mill St
- **HMS Belfast** • Morgan's Lane & Tooley St
- **Stompie** • Mandela Way & Page's Walk
- **Tower Bridge** • Tower Bridge Road

Nightlife

- **Cable** • 33 Bermondsey St
- **The Garrison Public House** • 99 Bermondsey St
- **The Hide** • 39 Bermondsey St
- **Hilton London Tower Bridge** • 5 Tooley St
- **Loyal Tavern** • 171-173 Bermondsey St
- **The Woolpack** • 98 Bermondsey St

Restaurants

- **Butlers Wharf Chop House** • 36 Shad Thames
- **Casse-Croute** • 109 Bermondsey St
- **Le Pont de la Tour** • 36 Shad Thames
- **Loyal Tavern** • 171-173 Bermondsey St
- **M Manze Pie and Mash** • 87 Tower Bridge Rd
- **Pizarro Tapas** • 104 Bermondsey St

Shopping

- **Fine Foods** • 218 Long Ln
- **The Design Museum Shop** • 28 Shad Thames
- **Long Lane Deli** • 218 Long Ln
- **Maltby Street Market** • Maltby St

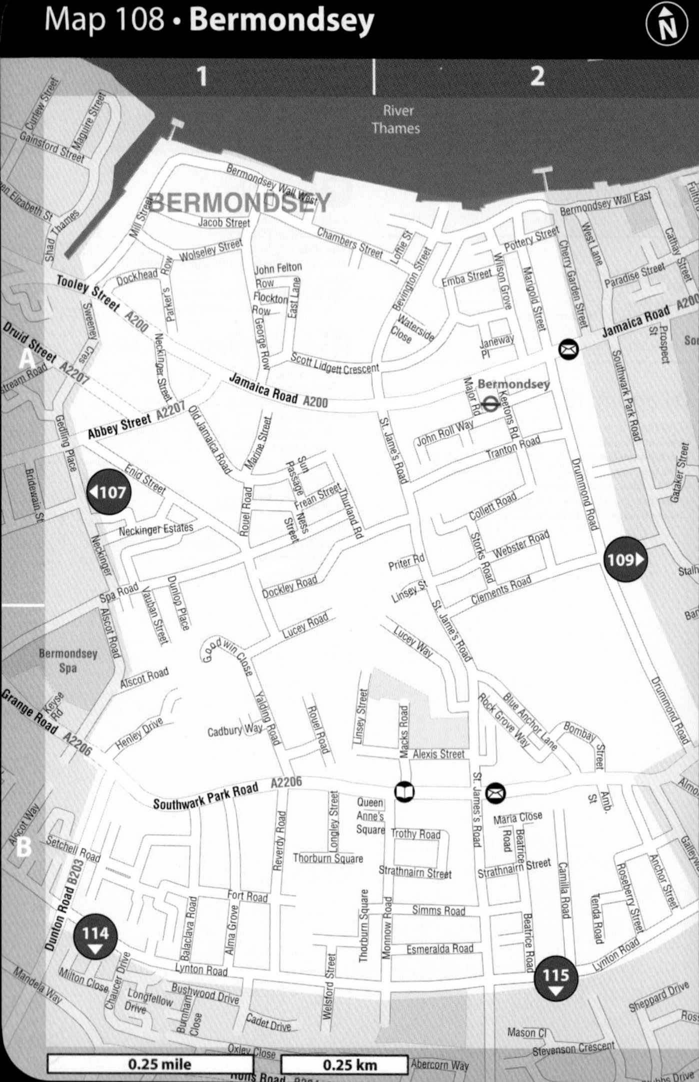

Map 108 • Bermondsey
N
1
2
A
B
River Thames
BERMONDSEY
Bermondsey Wall West
Bermondsey Wall East
Jacob Street
Chambers Street
Mill Street
Wolseley Street
Dockhead
Parker's Row
John Felton Row
Flockton Row
East Lane
George Row
Loftie St
Bevington Street
Waterside Close
Emba Street
Wilson Grove
Pottery Street
Marigold Street
Cherry Garden Street
West Lane
Cathay Street
Paradise Street
Jamaica Road A200
Prospect St
Southwark Park Road
Janeway Pl
Bermondsey
Major Rd
Keetons Rd
John Roll Way
Tranton Road
Scott Lidgett Crescent
Tooley Street A200
Curlew Street
Maguire Street
Gainsford Street
Queen Elizabeth St
Shad Thames
Druid Street A2207
Sweeney Cres
Neckinger Street
Old Jamaica Road
Marine Street
Abbey Street A2207
Gedling Place
Bridewain St
Enid Street
107
Neckinger Estates
Neckinger
Rouel Road
Sun Passage
Frean Street
Ness Street
Thurland Rd
St. James's Road
Collett Road
Storks Road
Webster Road
Drummond Road
109
Gataker Street
Priter Rd
Linsey St
Clements Road
Dockley Road
Spa Road
Vauhan Street
Dunlop Place
Alscot Road
Lucey Road
Lucey Way
Goodwin Close
Bermondsey Spa
Alscot Road
Grange Road A2206
Keyse Rd
Henley Drive
Cadbury Way
Yalding Road
Rouel Road
Linsey Street
Macks Road
Alexis Street
Rock Grove Way
Blue Anchor Lane
Bombay Street
Drummond Road
Southwark Park Road A2206
Queen Anne's Square
Longley Street
Reverdy Road
Trothy Road
Thorburn Square
Strathnairn Street
Maria Close
Beatrice Road
Strathnairn Street
Camilla Road
Amb. St
Alscot Way
Setchell Road
Dunton Road B203
Fort Road
Balaclava Road
Alma Grove
Simms Road
Thorburn Square
Monnow Road
Esmeralda Road
Beatrice Road
Tenda Road
Roseberry Street
Anchor Street
Lynton Road
114
115
Lynton Road
Milton Close
Chaucer Drive
Longfellow Drive
Bushwood Drive
Burnham Close
Cadet Drive
Welsford Street
Mandela Way
Mason Cl
Stevenson Crescent
Sheppard Drive
Oxley Close
Abercorn Way
0.25 mile
0.25 km

Bermondsey

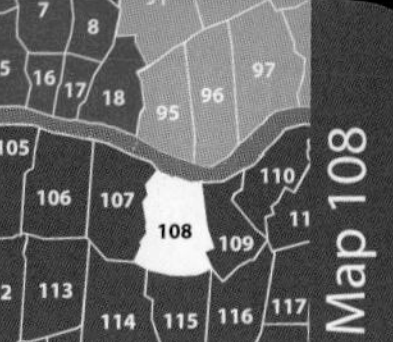

Map 108

With its mixed bag of winding cobbled streets, council estates, and posh new builds, you can imagine the awkwardness when the new-to-the-neighbourhood clean shirt steps into the the adamantly local Bermondsey boozer. The old-timers are sticking to their guns, and there is a definite dirty side to this on-the-cusp part of town. For quaint Japanese try **Poppy Hana** on Jamaica Road.

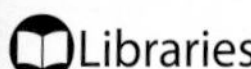

Libraries

- **Blue Anchor Library** • Southwark Park Rd

Post Offices

- **Jamaica Road** • 158 Jamaica Rd
- **Southwark Park Road** • 200 Southwark Park Rd

Restaurants

- **Brew by Numbers** • 79 Enid St
- **Poppy Hana** • 169 Jamaica Rd

Shopping

- **The Kernel Brewery** • 11 Dockley Road Industrial Estate

Supermarkets

- **Co-Op** • 193 Southwark Park Rd
- **Iceland** • 222 Southwark Park

Map 109 • Southwark Park

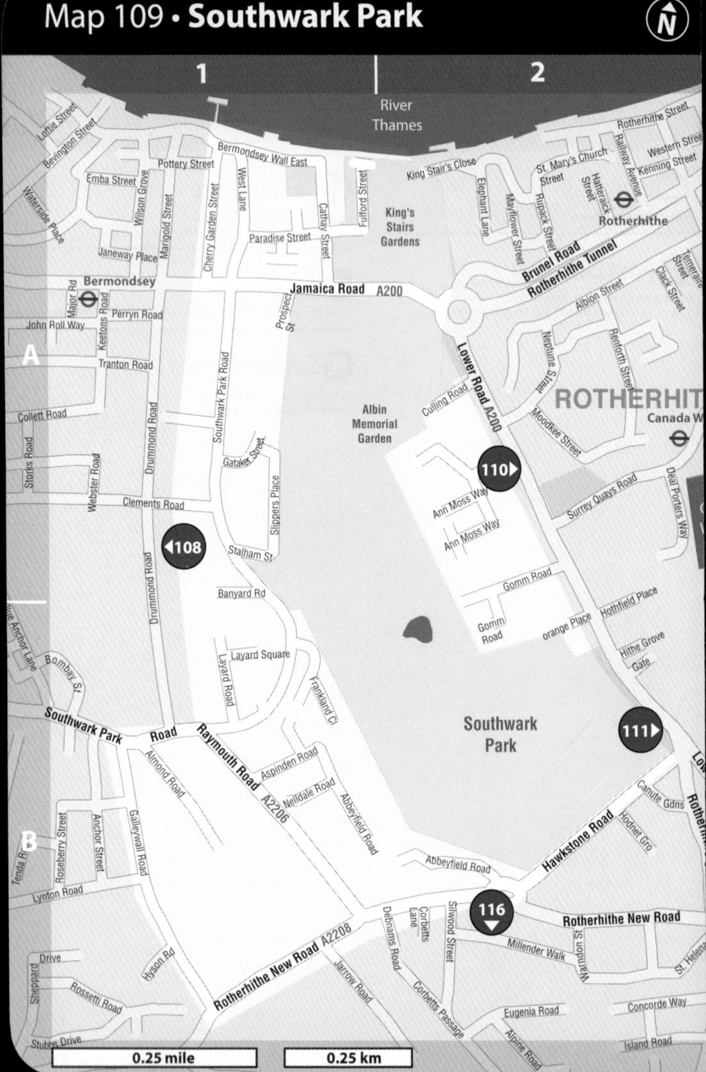

Southwark Park

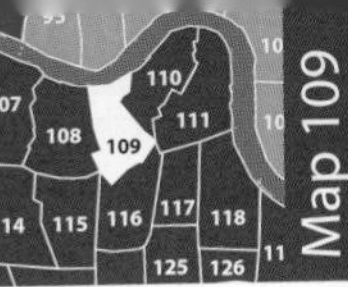

Bordered by tower blocks and the unfortunate juxtaposition of a nursing home and undertaker's, you might toy with taking your picnic elsewhere. But step inside, because it's every bit the oasis that local hero Dr Salter hoped it would be. Well-spent investment has given it a boating lake, rose garden, wildlife area, and the inspired Café Gallery Projects. Nip to **The Angel** afterwards for cheap beers and river views.

Nightlife

- **Ancient Foresters** • 282 Southwark Park Rd
- **The Angel** • 101 Bermondsey Wall E

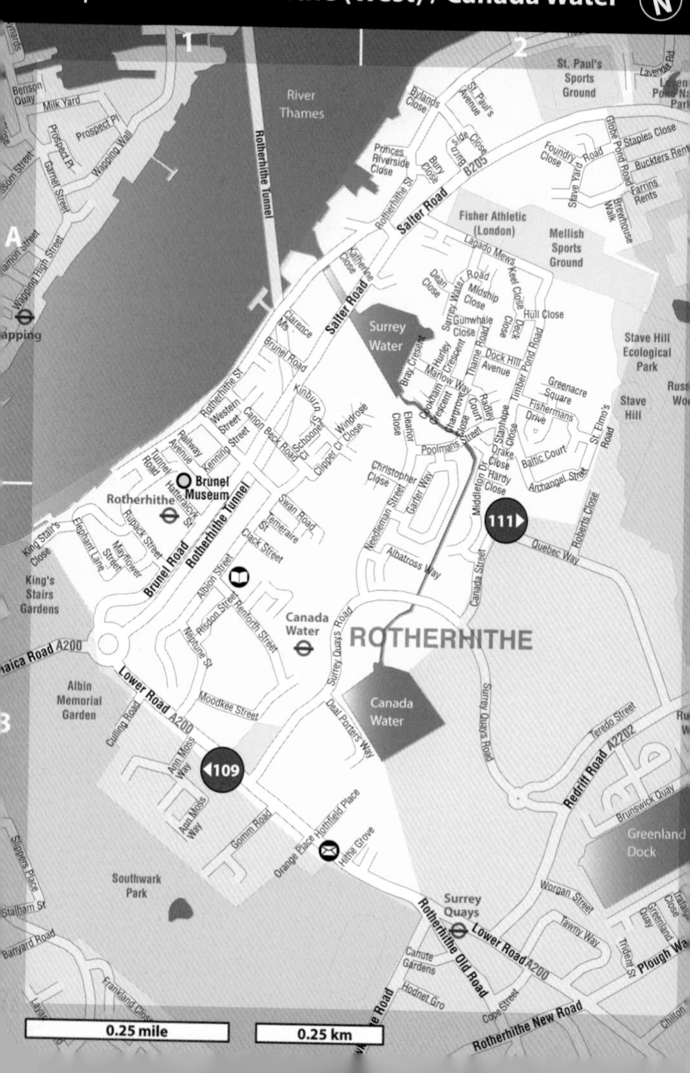
Rotherhithe (West) / Canada Water
N
1
2
A
B
River Thames
Rotherhithe Tunnel
Benson Quay
Milk Yard
Prospect Pl
Prospect Pl
Wapping Wall
Garnet Street
Wapping High Street
Wapping
St. Paul's Sports Ground
Lavender Rd
Bylands Close
St. Paul's Avenue
Princes Riverside Close
Bury Close
Burnside Close
B205
Rotherhithe St
Salter Road
Foundry Close
Stave Yard Road
Globe Pond Road
Staples Close
Buckters Rents
Farrins Rents
Brewhouse Walk
Fisher Athletic (London)
Mellish Sports Ground
Lagado Mews
Katherine Close
Dean Close
Road
Midship Close
Keel Close
Surrey Water Road
Hull Close
Gunwhale Close
Deck Close
Timber Pond Road
Surrey Water
Clarence Ms
Salter Road
Brunel Road
Bray Crescent
Hurley Crescent
Marlow Way
Thame Road
Dock Hill Avenue
Stave Hill Ecological Park
Greenacre Square
Fishermans Drive
Stave Hill
Cookham Crescent
Shargrove Close
Radley Court
Stanhope Close
Gloucester Close
St. Elmo's Road
Rotherhithe St
Western Street
Canon Beck Road
Kinburn St
Schooner Cl
Windrose Close
Clipper Cl
Eleanor Close
Poolmans Street
Drake Close
Baltic Court
Railway Avenue
Kenning Street
Tunnel Road
Brunel Museum
Christopher Close
Carter Way
Hardy Close
Archangel Street
Middleton Dr
Rotherhithe
Hatteraick St
Rotherhithe Tunnel
Swan Road
Temeraire St
111
Roberts Close
Quebec Way
King Stairs Close
Elephant Lane
Rupack Street
Mayflower Street
Brunel Road
Clack Street
Needleman Street
Albatross Way
Canada Street
King's Stairs Gardens
Albion Street
Riston Street
Renforth Street
Canada Water
Surrey Quays Road
ROTHERHITHE
Jamaica Road A200
Neptune St
Albin Memorial Garden
Lower Road A200
Culling Road
Moodkee Street
Canada Water
Deal Porters Way
Surrey Quays Road
Teredo Street
Redriff Road A2202
Ann Moss Way
109
Brunswick Quay
Ann Moss Way
Gomm Road
Orange Place
Hothfield Place
Hithe Grove
Greenland Dock
Slippers Place
Southwark Park
Worgan Street
Surrey Quays
Stalham St
Tawny Way
Greenland Quay
Trafalgar Close
Banyard Road
Rotherhithe Old Road
Lower Road A200
Canute Gardens
Trident St
Plough Way
Frankland Close
Hodnet Gro
Cope Street
Rotherhithe New Road
Chilton
0.25 mile
0.25 km

Rotherhithe (West) / Canada Water

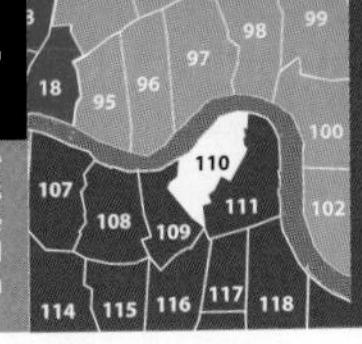

If residential flats are your thing, you'll love Rotherhithe West. Not if bars are your thing though. Or shops. Or life. But among the warren of apartments is **The Mayflower**, one of the greatest historical pubs in London, with the grave of the Mayflower ship's captain in the churchyard opposite. Entertain your dad at the **Brunel Museum**, and jog or snog your way along this serene stretch of Thames path.

Coffee

- **Brunel Museum Café** • Railway Ave

Landmarks

- **Brunel Museum** • Railway Ave & Rotherhithe St

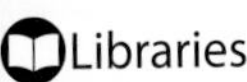

Libraries

- **Rotherhithe Library** • Albion St

Nightlife

- **The Mayflower** • 117 Rotherhithe St
- **Old Salt Quay** • 163 Rotherhithe St
- **The Ship** • 39 St Marychurch St

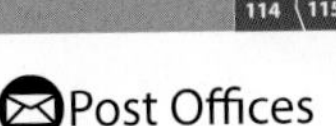

Post Offices

- **Lower Road Rotherhithe** • 142 Lower Rd

Restaurants

- **Mayflower** • 117 Rotherhithe St
- **The Rainbow** • 33 Brunel Rd
- **Simplicity** • 1 Tunnel Rd

N

River Thames
1
2
A
B

Sovereign Crescent
Rotherhithe Street
Road
Edward Square
St. Paul's Sports Ground
Lavender Road
Pageant Crescent
Lavender Pond Nature Park
Bywater Place
Heron Place
Bylands Close
St. Paul's Ave
Burn side Cl
Rotherhithe Street
Rotherhithe Tunnel
Salter Road B205
Foundry Close
Stave Yard Road
Globe Pond Road
Staples Close
Buckters Rents
Farrins Rents
Acorn Walk
Fisher Athletic (London) Football Club Ground (Surrey Docks Stadium)
Lagado Mews
Timber Pond Road
Katherine Close
Clarence Mews
Brunel Road
Surrey Water
Dean Close
Surrey Water Road
Midship Close
Brewhouse Walk
Fir Trees Close
Capstan Way
Silver Walk
Russia Dock Road
Mellish Sports Ground
Gunwhale Close
Hull Close
Deck Close
Pond Road
Teak Close
Redwood Close
Kinburn St
Marlow Way
Hurley Crescent
Thame Road
Dock Hill Avenue
Timber
Canon Beck Road
Windrose Close
Schooner Cl
Clipper Cl
Cookham Crescent
Chargrove Close
Court
Radley
Greenacre Square
Stave Hill Ecological Park
Byfield Close
Sandpiper Close
Salter Road
Rotherhithe Street
Stanhope Close
Fishermans Drive
Christopher Close
Poolmans Street
Stave Hill
Swan Road
Street
Middleton Dr
Holyoake Court
Bryan Road
Garter Way
Needleman Street
Baltic Ct
Russia Dock Woodland
Archangel Street
Somerford Way
Downtown Road
Hamilton Close
Steers Way
Albatross Way
110
Roberts Close
Howland Way
Victory Way
Surrey Docks Farm
Canada Street
Surrey Quays Road
Shipwright Road
Vaughan Street
Spence Close
Wyatt Close
Lovell Place
Redriff Est
Canada Water
ROTHERHITHE
Quebec Way
Oslo Square
Elgar Street
Odessa Street
Norway Gate
Bergen Square
Gullivar Street
Plover Way
Norway Dock
Onega Gate
Teredo Street
109
Redriff Road A2202
Finland Street
Helsinki Square
South Sea Street
Brunswick Quay
A200
Greenland Dock
Surrey Quays
Worgan Street
Trundleys Road
118
Rope Street
Sweden Gate
South Dock
Canute Gardens
Lower Road A200
Tawny Way
Greenland Quay
117
Calypso Way
116
Cl
Trident St
Mayflower
Boat Lifter Way
Dunnage Crescent
Transom Close
Cope Street
Plough Way
Yeoman Street B206
Lighter Close
Plough Way
B206
St. Georges Mews
St. Georges Square

0.25 mile
0.25 km

Rotherhithe (East) / Surrey Quays

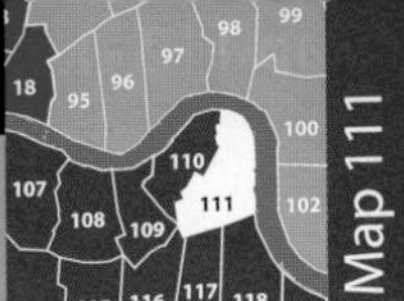

It still has some dodgy estates, but Rotherhithe East is blossoming in a clean-cut city-worker kind of way. The docks are delightful and have resisted the chain bars, instead allowing great little independents like **Wibbley Wobbley** and **The Moby Dick** to flourish. Trying to be healthy? Enjoy lunch among the goats at wholesome **Surrey Docks Farm Café**, and visit **Decathlon** for sport equipment paradise.

Cinemas

- **Odeon Surrey Quays** • Redriff Rd & Surrey Quays Rd

Landmarks

- **Surrey Docks Farm** • Rotherhithe St

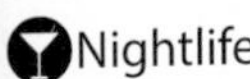

Nightlife

- **Blacksmith's Arms** • 257 Rotherhithe St
- **Moby Dick** • 6 Russell Place, off Greenland Dock
- **Ship & Whale** • 2 Gulliver St
- **Whelan's** • 11 Rotherhithe Old Rd
- **Wibbley Wobbley** • South Dock Marina, Rope St

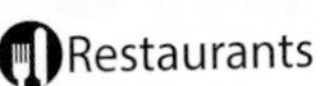

Restaurants

- **Café East** • 100 Redriff Rw
- **Café Nabo** • Surrey Docks Farm, Rotherhithe St
- **Mao Po** • 176 Lower Rd

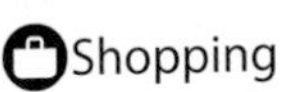

Shopping

- **Decathlon** • Surrey Quays Rd

Supermarkets

- **Tesco** • Redriff Rd

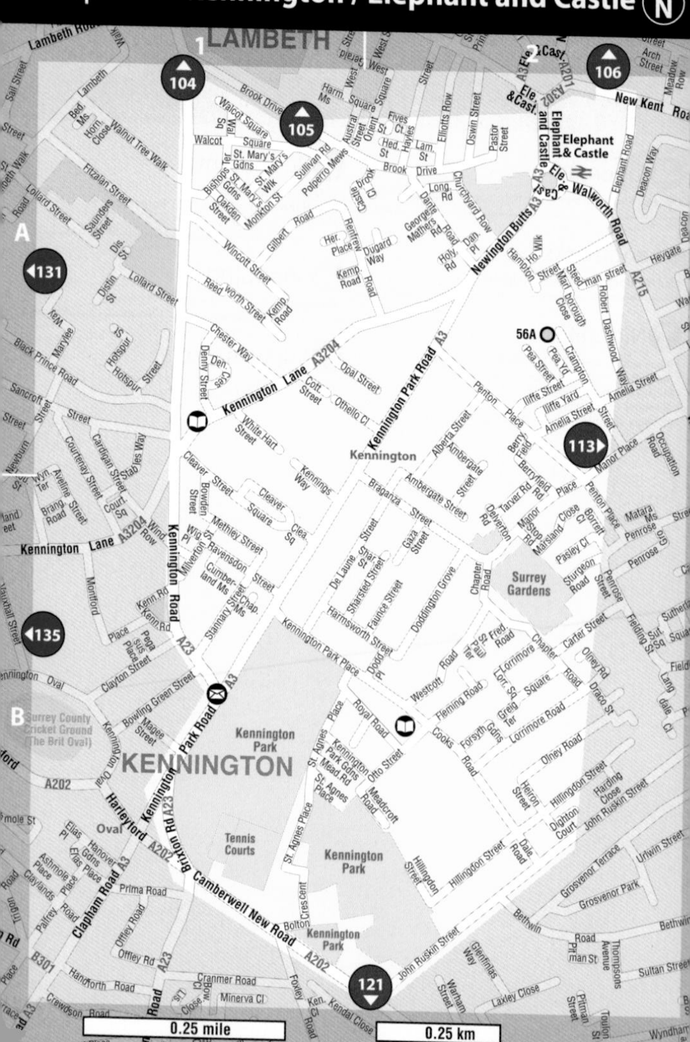
Kennington / Elephant and Castle
N
LAMBETH
1
2
104
105
106
131
135
113
121
A
B
Lambeth Road
Brook Drive
Walcot Square
Walnut Tree Walk
Fitzalan Street
Lollard Street
Saunders Street
Reedworth Street
Wincott Street
Gilbert Road
Renfrew Road
Dugard Way
Kemp. Road
George Mathers Rd
Dante Road
Churchyard Row
Elliotts Row
Oswin Street
Pastor Street
Elephant & Castle
Elephant and Castle
Elephant Road
New Kent Road
Walworth Road
Newington Butts A3
Heygate Street
Deacon Way
Hampton Street
Marlborough Close
Robert Dashwood Way
56A
Crampton Street
Pea Yd
Iliffe Street
Iliffe Yard
Amelia Street
Penton Place
Manor Place
Occupation Road
Kennington Lane A3204
Kennington Park Road A3
Kennington Road
Chester Way
Denny Street
Opal Street
Cott. Street
Othello Cl
White Hart Street
Kennington
Alberta Street
Ambergate Street
Berryfield Rd
Braganza Street
Cleaver Street
Cleaver Square
Kennings Way
Bowden Street
Methley Street
Ravensdon Street
Milverton St
Cumberland Ms
Stannary Street
De Laune Street
Sharsted Street
Faunce Street
Gaza Street
Doddington Grove
Harmsworth Street
Chapter Road
Delverton Rd
Tarver Rd
Manor Place
Marsland Close
Borrett Cl
Pasley Cl
Sturgeon Road
Surrey Gardens
Penrose Street
Penrose Gro
Fielding St
Carter Street
Kennington Park Place
Westcott Road
Fleming Road
Lorrimore Road
Lorrimore Square
Olney Rd
Olney Road
Draco St
Langdale Cl
Royal Road
Otto Street
Cooks Road
Forsyth Gdns
Greig Ter
Meadcroft Road
Hillingdon Street
Heiron Street
Harding Close
John Ruskin Street
Dighton Court
Dale Road
Grosvenor Terrace
Grosvenor Park
Urlwin Street
Bethwin Road
Pitman St
Thompsons Avenue
Sultan Street
Kennington Park
Tennis Courts
St. Agnes Place
Kennington Park Gdns
Mead Rd
Bolton Crescent
Camberwell New Road A202
Brixton Rd A23
Clapham Road A3
Harleyford A202
Kennington Oval
Oval
Surrey County Cricket Ground (The Brit Oval)
KENNINGTON
Kennington Lane
Black Prince Road
Sancroft Street
Newburn St
Courtenay Street
Cardigan Street
Stables Way
Aveline Street
Brang. Road
Wind. Row
Montford Place
Kenn Rd
Pegasus Place
Clayton Street
Bowling Green Street
Magee Street
Vauxhall Street
Hotspur Street
Marylee Way
Distin St
Elias Pl
Hanover Gdns
Ashmole Place
Claylands Place
Palfrey Place
Prima Road
Offley Road
Offley Rd
B301
Handforth Road
Crewdson Road
Cranmer Road
Minerva Cl
Foxley Road
Ken. Kendal Close
Glenfinlas Way
Warham Street
Laxley Close
Pitman Street
Toulon St
0.25 mile
0.25 km

Massive change is being promised in Elephant and Castle, although when and for whom is quite debatable. With masses of social housing lost with the closure of the Heygate Estate, the area could be set to become another drab luxury development a la Docklands.

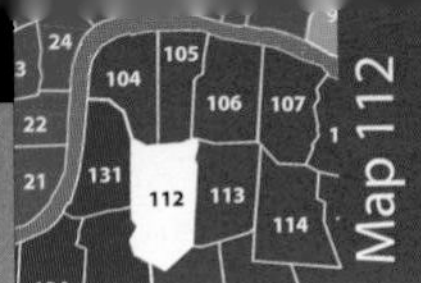

Landmarks

- **56A** • 56 Crampton St

Libraries

- **Brandon Library** • Cooks Rd
- **Durning Library** • 167 Kennington Ln

Nightlife

- **Brasserie Tolouse Lautrec** • 140 Newington Butts
- **Corsica Studios** • 5 Elephant Rd
- **Dog House** • 293 Kennington Rd
- **The Old Red Lion** • 42 Kennington Park Rd
- **Prince of Wales** • Cleaver Sq
- **South London Pacific** • 340 Kennington Rd

Post Offices

- **Kennington Park** • 410 Kennington Park Rd

Restaurants

- **Brasserie Tolouse Lautrec** • 140 Newington Butts
- **Dragon Castle** • 114 Walworth Rd
- **La Bodeguita** • Elephant & Castle Shopping Centre

Shopping

- **Recycling** • 110 Elephant Rd

Supermarkets

- **Iceland** • 300 Elephant & Castle Shopping Centre

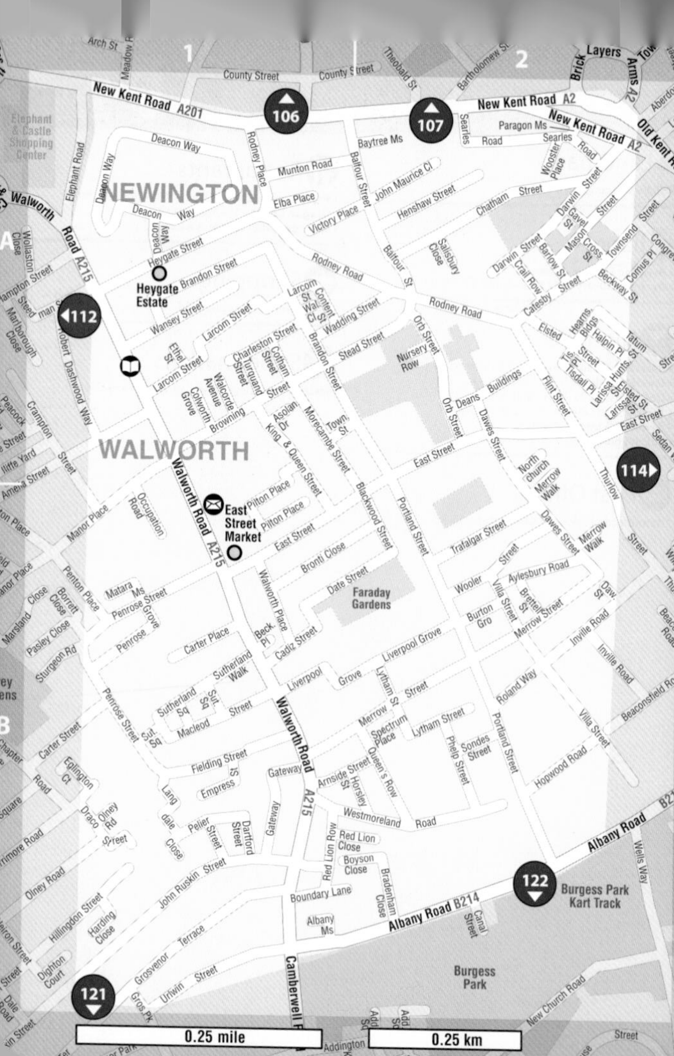

1
2
A
B
NEWINGTON
WALWORTH
Elephant & Castle Shopping Center
Heygate Estate
East Street Market
Faraday Gardens
Burgess Park
Burgess Park Kart Track
106
107
112
114
121
122
New Kent Road A201
New Kent Road A2
Old Kent Road
Arch St
Meadow Row
County Street
Theobald St
Bartholomew St
Brick Layers Arms A2
Deacon Way
Rodney Place
Baytree Ms
Balfour Street
Searles Road
Paragon Ms
Wooster Place
Munton Road
John Maurice Cl
Elba Place
Victory Place
Henshaw Street
Chatham Street
Darwin Street
Gaywood St
Mason St
Cross St
Townsend Street
Congreve Street
Elephant Road
Walworth Road A215
Wollaston Close
Hampton Street
Heygate Street
Brandon Street
Rodney Road
Salisbury Close
Crail Row
Barlow St
Catesby Street
Beckway St
Comus Pl
Larcom Street
Content St
Wadding Street
Wansey Street
Ethel St
Charleston Street
Cotham Street
Turquand Street
Stead Street
Orb Street
Nursery Row
Elsted
Hearns Bldgs
Halpin Pl
Tatum Street
Tisdall Pl
Larissa Street
Flint Street
Dean's Buildings
Dawes Street
East Street
Sedan Way
Marlborough Close
Robert Dashwood Way
Crampton Street
Peacock St
Iliffe Yard
Amelia Street
Colworth Grove
Walcorde Avenue
Browning Street
Asolando Dr
King & Queen Street
Morecambe Street
Townsley St
North church
Merrow Walk
Thurlow Street
Manor Place
Occupation Road
Pilton Place
Blackwood Street
Portland Street
Trafalgar Street
Penton Place
Matara Ms
Penrose Street
Penrose Grove
Borrett Close
Marsland Close
Pasley Close
Sturgeon Rd
Bronti Close
Date Street
Wooler Street
Aylesbury Road
Villa Street
Brettell St
Burton Gro
Merrow Street
Inville Road
Beaconsfield Road
Walworth Place
Beck. Pl
Cadiz Street
Carter Place
Liverpool Grove
Sutherland Walk
Sutherland Sq
Sut. Sq
Macleod Street
Lytham St
Lytham Street
Spectrum Place
Roland Way
Phelp Street
Sondes Street
Carter Street
Chapter Road
Eglington Ct
Fielding Street
Empress St
Gateway
Arnside Street
Horsley St
Queen's Row
Hopwood Road
Westmoreland Road
Albany Road B214
Wells Way
Langdale Close
Draco St
Olney Rd
Pelier Street
Dartford Street
Red Lion Row
Red Lion Close
Boyson Close
Bradenham Close
Olney Road
John Ruskin Street
Boundary Lane
Albany Ms
Canal Street
Hillingdon Street
Harding Close
Heiron Street
Dighton Court
Grosvenor Terrace
Urlwin Street
Camberwell Road
New Church Road
Addington Sq
0.25 mile
0.25 km

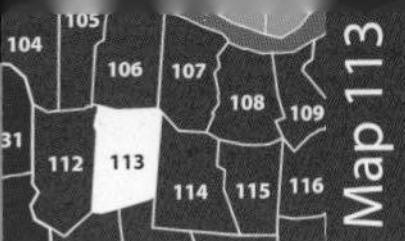

ı, Walworth. With all this about the Elephant and Castle redevelopment, why
› we get the funny feeling you will never change? From the excessive amount
Gregg's bakeries along Walworth Road, to the 'who really buys these things?'
t at **East Street Market**, Walworth's lack of motivation is somehow endearing.
Luna for pizza is a find, as is **The Beehive** pub.

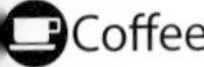

Coffee

- **Ranya Café** • 314 Walworth Rd

Landmarks

- **East Street Market** • Walworth Rd & East St
- **Heygate Estate** • Deacon Way & Heygate St

Libraries

- **Newington Library** • 157 Walworth Rd

Nightlife

- **The Beehive** • 60 Carter St
- **Red Lion** • 407 Walworth Rd

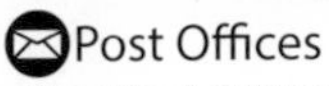

Post Offices

- **Walworth Road** • 234 Walworth Rd

Restaurants

- **La Luna** • 380 Walworth Rd

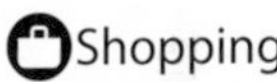

Shopping

- **G Baldwin & Co** • 171 Walworth Rd
- **Threadneedleman Tailors** • 187 Walworth Rd
- **Walworth Surplus Stores** • 211 Walworth Rd

Supermarkets

- **Iceland** • 332 Walworth Rd

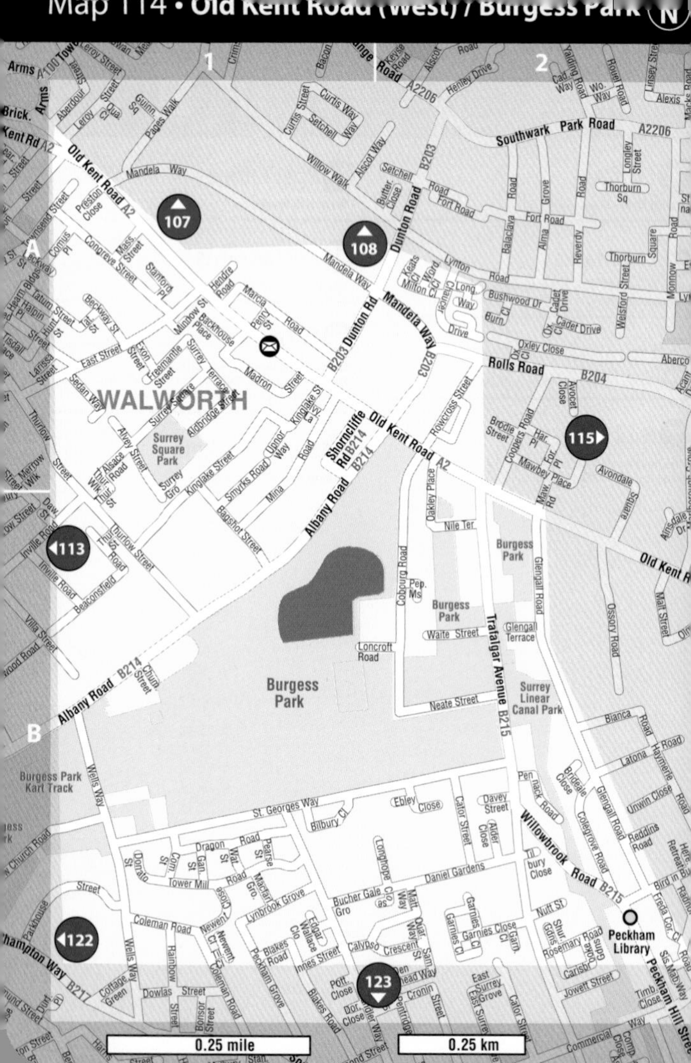
N
1
2
A
B
WALWORTH
Old Kent Road A2
Mandela Way
Dunton Road
B203 Dunton Rd
Southwark Park Road A2206
Rolls Road B204
Albany Road B214
Shorncliffe Rd B214
Trafalgar Avenue B215
Willowbrook Road B215
Burgess Park
Burgess Park Kart Track
Surrey Square Park
Surrey Linear Canal Park
Peckham Library
Peckham Hill Street
St. Georges Way
Wells Way
Coleman Road
Daniel Gardens
Calypso Crescent
Commercial Way
Camberwell
Willow Walk
Setchell Way
Curtis Way
Curtis Street
Pages Walk
Congreve Street
Preston Close
East Street
Freemantle Street
Surrey Square
Kinglake Street
Smyrks Road
Bagshot Street
Thurlow Street
Inville Road
Beaconsfield Road
Villa Street
Cobourg Road
Oakley Place
Nile Ter
Waite Street
Loncroft Road
Neate Street
Glengall Road
Glengall Terrace
Ossory Road
Avondale Square
Mawbey Place
Coopers Road
Lynton Road
Fort Road
Thorburn Square
Oxley Close
Cator Street
Bird in Bush Road
Latona Road
Rosemary Road
Jowett Street
Blakes Road
Peckham Grove
Lynbrook Grove
Tower Mill Road
Dragon Road
Ebley Close
Bilbury Cl
Longhope Close
Garnies Close
East Surrey Grove
Dowlas Street
Rainbow Street
Camberwell Church Road
Parkhouse Street
Cottage Green
107
108
113
115
122
123
0.25 mile
0.25 km

Old Kent Road (West) / Burgess Park

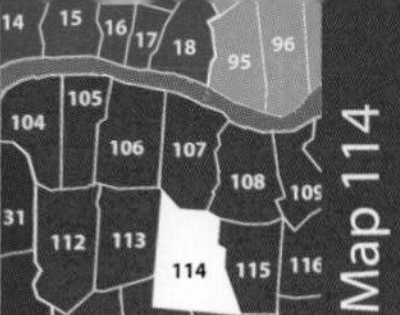

ow that the 51-acre Burgess Park has been given an £8 million facelift (due to eless community campaigning), locals have good reason to be smug as they njoy the 30ft water fountains, 5k running track, or any of the other many new lditions on their doorstep. For something different, stroll along the old canal nd connect with ghosts of Peckham past.

Landmarks

- **The Animatronic Fireman** • Old Kent Rd
- **Peckham Library** • 122 Peckham Hill St

Post Offices

- **Old Kent Road** • 240 Old Kent Rd

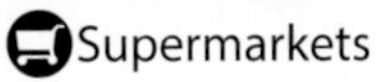

Supermarkets

- **Tesco** • 107 Dunton Rd

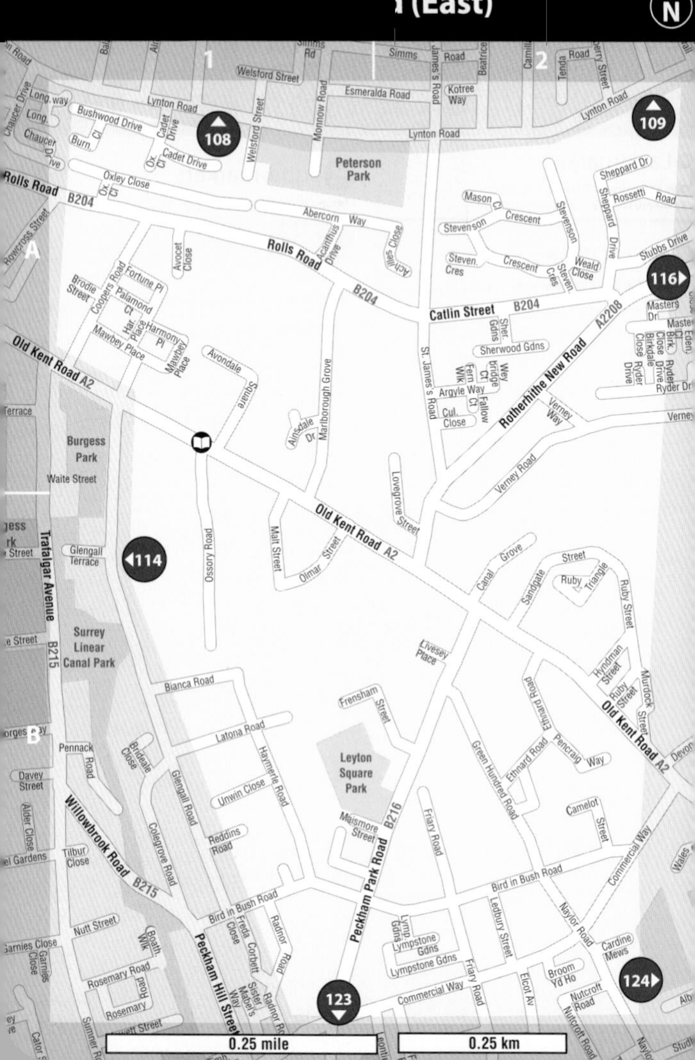
N
1
2
A
B
108
109
116
114
123
124
Peterson Park
Burgess Park
Surrey Linear Canal Park
Leyton Square Park
Rolls Road B204
Old Kent Road A2
Catlin Street B204
Rotherhithe New Road A2208
Trafalgar Avenue B215
Willowbrook Road B215
Peckham Park Road B216
Peckham Hill Street
Lynton Road
Welsford Street
Esmeralda Road
Monnow Road
Simms Road
James's Road
Kotree Way
Tenda Road
Bushwood Drive
Cadet Drive
Chaucer Drive
Oxley Close
Abercorn Way
Acanthus Drive
Achilles Close
Avocet Close
Brodie Street
Coopers Road
Fortune Pl
Palamond Ct
Harmony Pl
Mawbey Place
Avondale Square
Marlborough Grove
Ainsdale Dr
St. James's Road
Mason Cl
Stevenson Crescent
Weald Close
Sheppard Dr
Rossetti Road
Stubbs Drive
Sherwood Gdns
Argyle Way
Cul. Close
Verney Way
Verney Road
Lovegrove Street
Ossory Road
Malt Street
Olmar Street
Canal Grove
Sandgate Street
Ruby Triangle
Ruby Street
Livesey Place
Hyndman Street
Murdock Street
Ethnard Road
Pencraig Way
Green Hundred Road
Camelot Street
Commercial Way
Bird in Bush Road
Naylor Road
Friary Road
Ledbury Street
Lympstone Gdns
Elcot Av
Cardine Mews
Nutcroft Road
Maismore Street
Frensham Street
Haymerle Road
Latona Road
Bianca Road
Unwin Close
Reddins Road
Glengall Road
Glengall Terrace
Colegrove Road
Bridale Close
Pennack Road
Davey Street
Alder Close
Tilbury Close
Nutt Street
Boath. Wlk
Rosemary Road
Garnies Close
Radnor Road
Freda Corbett Close
Sister Mabel's Way
Waite Street
0.25 mile
0.25 km

Old Kent Road (East)

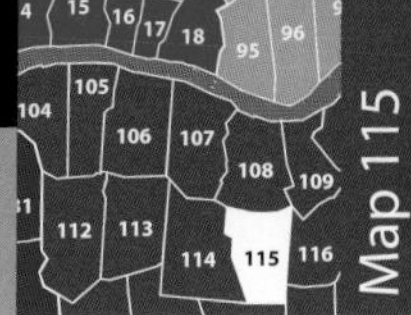

here must be something to this portion of Old Kent Road, as the Pearly Kings nd Queens won't shut up about the whole thing. As far as we can tell, it's not hat much more than a giant Asda. Walk along Bird In Bush Road to laugh at its ame and over to Peckham Park Road for a damn good fry-up at **Roma Café**.

Libraries

- **East Street Library** • 168 Old Kent Rd

Restaurants

- **Roma Café** • 21 Peckham Park Rd

Supermarkets

- **ASDA** • Old Kent Rd & Ossory Rd

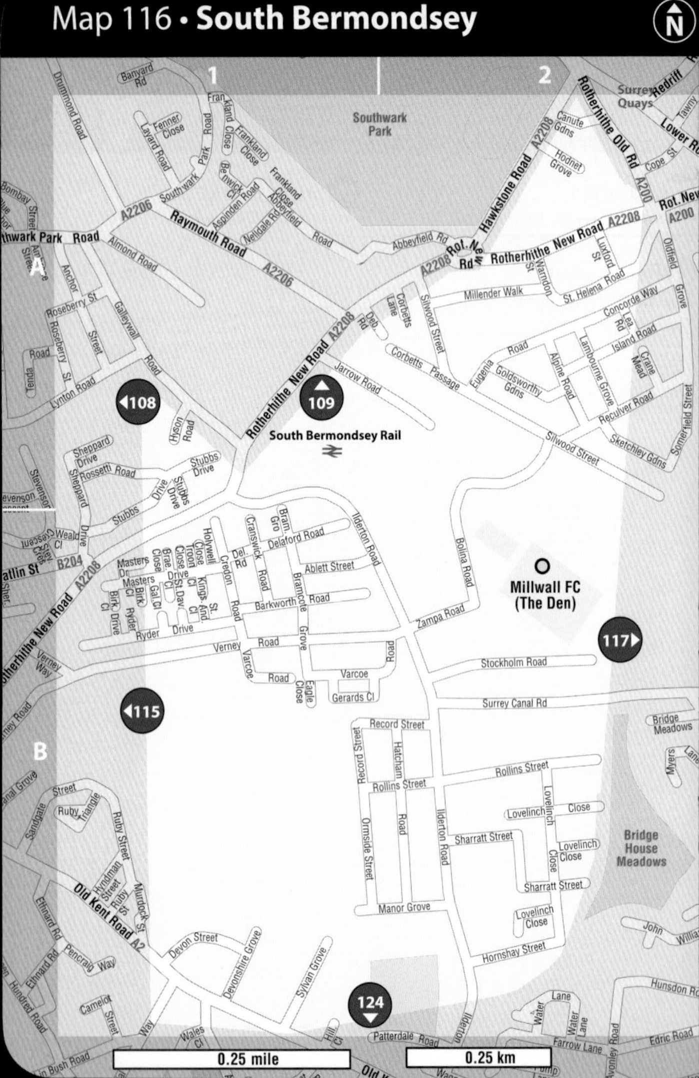

Southwark Park
South Bermondsey Rail
Millwall FC (The Den)
Bridge House Meadows
108
109
115
117
124
Rotherhithe New Road
Raymouth Road
Southwark Park Road
Hawkstone Road
Rotherhithe Old Rd
Ilderton Road
Bolina Road
Zampa Road
Stockholm Road
Surrey Canal Rd
Rollins Street
Record Street
Hatcham Road
Ormside Street
Manor Grove
Sharratt Street
Lovelinch Close
Hornshay Street
Old Kent Road A2
Devon Street
Devonshire Grove
Sylvan Grove
Silwood Street
Corbetts Passage
Jarrow Road
Millender Walk
Verney Road
Varcoe Road
Gerards Cl
Eagle Close
Delaford Road
Ablett Street
Barkworth Road
Bramcote Grove
Cranswick Road
Credon Road
Galleywall Road
Stubbs Drive
Sheppard Drive
Rossetti Road
Hyson Road
Lynton Road
Almond Road
Abbeyfield Road
Frankland Close
Layard Road
Fenner Close
Banyard Rd
Drummond Road
Surrey Quays
Lower Rd
Patterdale Road
Farrow Lane
Avonley Road
Hunsdon Rd
Edric Road
Ruby Street
Murdock St
Camelot Street
0.25 mile
0.25 km

South Bermondsey

ere may be more to this area than we've listed, but the fact is we like you. want to see you live to enjoy our favourite picks among these pages. If ı make the wrong kind of eye contact as you tremble past the Millwall flags ttering menacingly from the balconies, then we're worried we'll lose a much-ed reader. Swallow your valuables and back slowly away.

Landmarks

Millwall FC Stadium • Zampa Rd & Bolina Rd

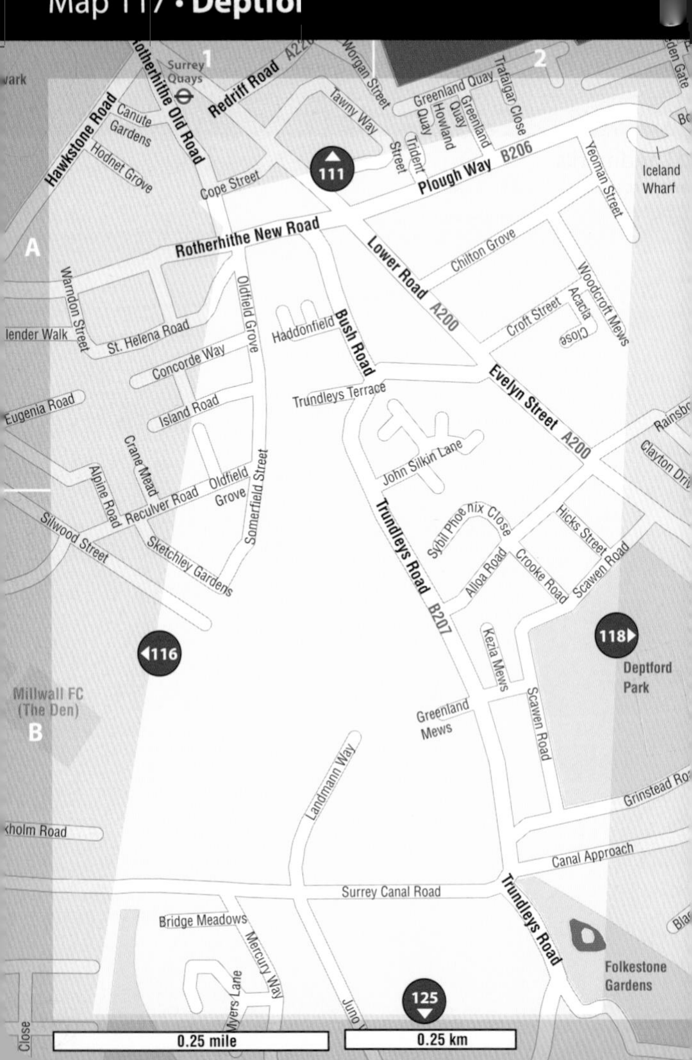

1
2
A
B
Surrey Quays
Redriff Road
Rotherhithe Old Road
Hawkstone Road
Canute Gardens
Hodnet Grove
Worgan Street
Tawny Way
Greenland Quay
Howland Quay
Greenland Quay
Trafalgar Close
Trident Street
Plough Way B206
Yeoman Street
Iceland Wharf
Cope Street
111
Rotherhithe New Road
Lower Road A200
Chilton Grove
Woodcroft Mews
Acacia Close
Croft Street
Warndon Street
St. Helena Road
Oldfield Grove
Haddonfield
Bush Road
Concorde Way
Island Road
Trundleys Terrace
Evelyn Street A200
Eugenia Road
Crane Mead
Somerfield Street
John Silkin Lane
Clayton Drive
Alpine Road
Reculver Road
Oldfield Grove
Trundleys Road B207
Sybil Phoenix Close
Hicks Street
Scawen Road
Silwood Street
Sketchley Gardens
Alloa Road
Crooke Road
116
118
Deptford Park
Kezia Mews
Millwall FC (The Den)
Greenland Mews
Scawen Road
Landmann Way
Grinstead Road
Canal Approach
Surrey Canal Road
Trundleys Road
Bridge Meadows
Mercury Way
Myers Lane
Juno
125
Folkestone Gardens
0.25 mile
0.25 km

Deptford (West)

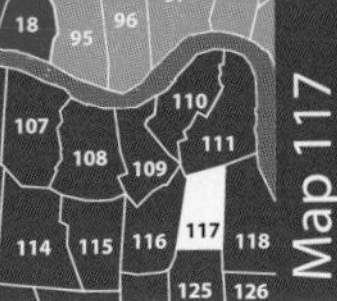

pparently, developers have their eye on Deptford West. You've really got to ope so. The Blitz did its best, but the area came back with hastily built and harmless '60s tower blocks. Still, like the rest of Deptford it's going through a radual regeneration as young buyers move in to make their money stretch.

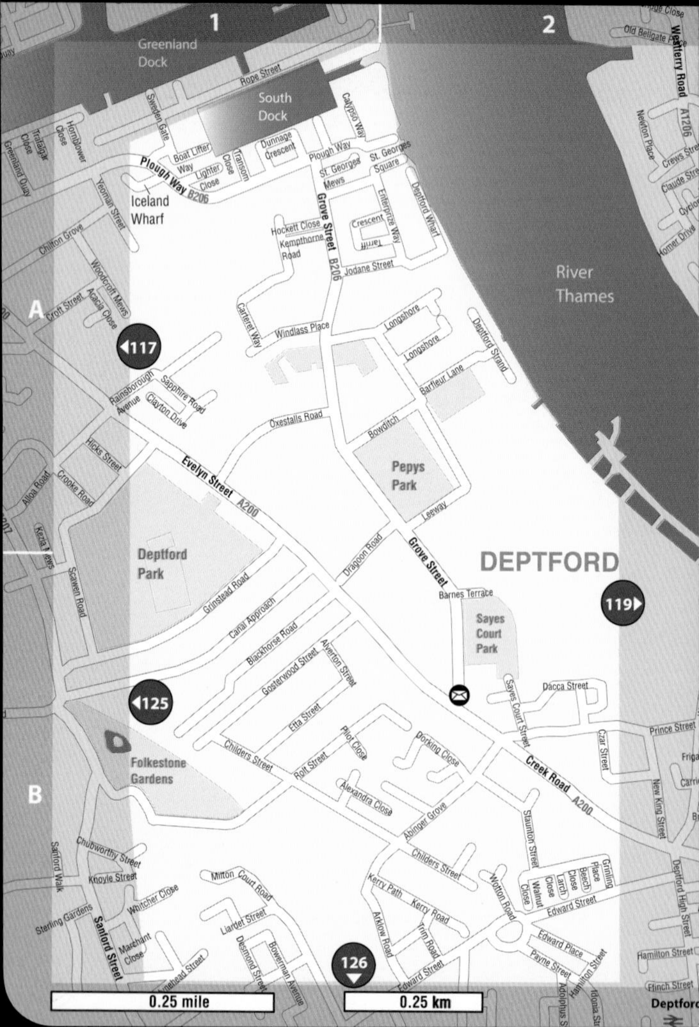

N
1
2
Greenland Dock
South Dock
Rope Street
Sweden Gate
Calypso Way
Hornblower Close
Trafalgar Close
Greenland Quay
Boat Lifter Way
Lighter Close
Transom Close
Dunnage Crescent
Plough Way
St. Georges Mews
St. Georges Square
Plough Way B206
Iceland Wharf
Yeoman Street
Grove Street B206
Enterprize Way
Deptford Wharf
Hockett Close
Kempthorne Road
Crescent
Tarriff
Jodane Street
Chilton Grove
Woodcroft Mews
Acacia Close
Croft Street
A
117
Carteret Way
Windlass Place
Longshore
Longshore
Deptford Strand
River Thames
Old Bellgate Place
Westferry Road
A1206
Newton Place
Crews Street
Claude Street
Homer Drive
Barfleur Lane
Rainsborough Avenue
Sapphire Road
Clayton Drive
Oxestalls Road
Bowditch
Pepys Park
Hicks Street
Evelyn Street A200
Alloa Road
Crooke Road
Leeway
Keziah Mews
Scawen Road
Deptford Park
Grinstead Road
Dragoon Road
Grove Street
DEPTFORD
Barnes Terrace
Sayes Court Park
119
Canal Approach
Blackhorse Road
Alverton Street
Gosterwood Street
125
Folkestone Gardens
Etta Street
Dacca Street
Sayes Court Street
Prince Street
Czar Street
Childers Street
Pilot Close
Dorking Close
Rolt Street
Creek Road A200
Alexandra Close
B
Abinger Grove
Staunton Street
New King Street
Childers Street
Sanford Walk
Chubworthy Street
Knoyle Street
Milton Court Road
Kerry Path
Kerry Road
Wotton Road
Grinling Place
Beech Close
Larch Close
Walnut Close
Edward Street
Deptford High Street
Whitcher Close
Sterling Gardens
Sanford Street
Marchant Close
Liardet Street
Arklow Road
Trim Road
Edward Place
Hamilton Street
Payne Street
Hamilton Street
Desmond Street
Bowerman Avenue
126
Edward Street
Finch Street
Adolphus Street
Deptford
0.25 mile
0.25 km

hen Christopher Marlowe was murdered in a Deptford tavern, Deptford t its nightlife peak. That was 1593. Today, while the rest of London turns erything into a pub, Deptford turns its pubs into churches. Without beer, u may want to drown your sorrows in the Thames, but even that is thwarted: re the Thames path breaks to take you through neglected residential areas stead. Escape!

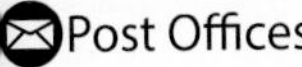

Post Offices

- **Evelyn Street** • 301 Evelyn St

1
2
A
B
River Thames
Glaisher Street
Glaisher Street
Twinkle Park
Borthwick Street
Watergate Street
Trevithick Mews
Caravel Mews
Benbow Street
Henrietta Close
Hamilton Cresent
Glaisher Street
Basevi Way
Basevi Way
Glaisher Street
Greenwich Quay
Dacca Street
Prince Street
Prince Street
Czar Street
New King Street
Frigate Mews
Carrick Mews
Brig Mews
Deptford Green
House
St. Nicholas
Stowage
Creek Road A200
118
Evelyn Street A200
McMillan Street
Bruford Court
Copperas Street
Deptford Creek
Staunton Street
Larch Close
Beech Close
Grinling Place
Lamerton Street
Albury Street
Deptford Church Street
Berthon Street
Berthon Street
Walnut Close
Edward Street
Hyde Street
Mary Ann Gardens
St. Paul's Churchyard Gardens
Bronze Street
Wotton Road
Hamilton Street
Crossfield Street
Sue Godfrey Local Nature Reserve
Edward Place
Payne Street
Hamilton Street
Ffinch Street
A2209
Deptford Rail
Resolution Way
Adolphus Street
Adolphus Street
Idonia Street
Octavius Street
Rochdale Way
Giffin Square Market
Creekside
Napier Close
Giffin Street
Frankham Street
Amersham Vale
Turnpike Close
Douglas Way Street Market
Margaret McMillan Park
Vaughn Williams Close
Margaret McMillan Park
Comet Place
Deptford High Street Street Market
Watson's Street
Elgar Close
Reginald Road
New Butt Lane
Reginald Square
Fletcher Path
Ravensbourne River
Mumford Mills
Greenwich High Road
Douglas Way
Stanley Street
Mornington Road
Glenville Grove
Glenville Grove
Baildon Street
Comet Street
Admiralty Close
126
New Cross
Deptford Broadway
Deptford Bridge A2
Blackheath
New Cross Road A2
Deptford Broadway
Deptford Bridge
0.25 mile
0.25 km

ou're one for a bargain, then this is your place. Browse the charity shops for ɛsses rumored to be donated by local prostitutes, pick up all manner of junk m the market or visit one of the many fishmongers, who have been known sell live eels and sharks. And if you want to fit in with the countless old punks nking cider get yourself a face tattoo on Church Street.

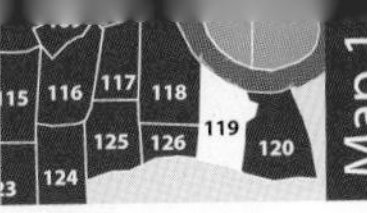

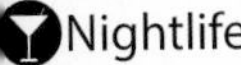

Nightlife

The Bird's Nest • 32 Deptford Church St
Bunker Club • 46 Deptford Broadway
Dog & Bell • 116 Prince St

Post Offices

New Cross • 500 New Cross Rd

Restaurants

- **The Big Red Pizza Bus** • 30 Deptford Church St
- **Chaconia Roti** • 26 Deptford High St
- **Manzes** • 204 Deptford High St
- **The Waiting Room** • 134 Deptford High St

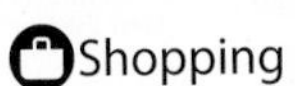

Shopping

- **Deptford Market** • Deptford High St

Supermarkets

- **Iceland** • 112 Deptford High St

1
2
River Thames
Cutty Sark Gardens
Greenwich Foot Tunnel
Naval College Gardens
Thames Street
Woodwharf
Norway Street
Clavell Street
Welland Street
Cutty Sark
Creek Road A200
College Approach
Durnford Street
Romney Road A206
Nelson Road A206
King William Walk
Greenwich Church Street
National Maritime Museum Ga
Bardsley Lane
Haddo Street
Norman Road B208
Thornham Street
Claremont Street
Roan Street
Randall Place
Churchfields
Straightsmouth
Stockwell Street
Greenwich Park
PAGE 336
Deptford Creek
Tarves Way
Greenwich
Greenwich High Road
Burney Street
Crooms Hill
Gloucester Circus
Crooms Hill Grove
King George Street
Royal Hill B209
Peyton Place
Circus Street
Prior Street
Brand Street
Waller Way
Kay Way
Maitland Close
Langdale Road
Greenwich South Street A2211
119
Greenwich High Road A206
Ashburnham Place
Ashburnham Grove
Ashburnham Retreat
St. Marks Close
Arlington Place
Royal Place
Georgette Place
Hawks Mews
Royal Hill
Glaisher Street
Basevi Way
Greenwich Quay
Stowage
Bruford Court
Copperas Street
Berthon Street
Bronze Street
Creekside
A
B
Mumford Mills
Burgos Grove
Catherine Grove
Egerton Drive B208
Devonshire Drive
Peabody Close
Guildford Grove
Admirals Gate
Bissett Street
Winforton Street
Cable Place
Diamond Terrace
Hyde Vale B209
Chesterfield
Rangers Square
Clayton Mews
Maidenstone Hill
Point Hill
Westgrove Lane
West Grove
Point Close
Lindsell Street
Trinity Grove
Dutton Street
Plumbridge Street
Dabin Cresent
Hollymount Close
Blackheath Road A2
Crosslet Vale
Franklin Place
Friendly Place
Robinscroft Mews
Blackheath Hill A2
Dartmouth Hill
Allison Close
Dartmouth Terrace
Cade Road
Shooters Hi
Deals Gateway
Franklin Close
John Penn Street
Morden Street
Lewisham Road A21
Dartmouth Row
Dartmouth Grove
Wat Tyler Road
Hare & Billet Road
Beck Close
Bennett Grove
Sparta Street
Brookmill Park
0.25 mile
0.25 km

Greenwich

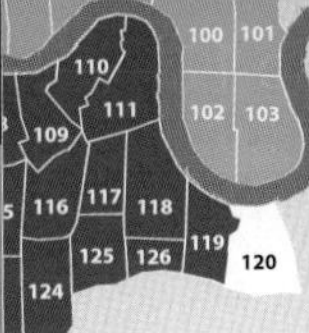

th the **Cutty Sark** magnificently restored and Greenwich's status as an ympic Borough, the area has been given a new, touristy lease of life recently. ere's still plenty of quirky pubs and shops to let you escape the crowds ɔugh, from vintage clothes and dusty vinyl at **The Beehive** to artisan beer at **eenwich Union**. And anyway, if you do want to do some proper sightseeing, ıat better place to do it?

Cinemas

Greenwich Picturehouse • 180 Greenwich High Rd

Coffee

Rhodes Bakery • 37 King William Walk
Starbucks • 54 Greenwich Church St

Landmarks

- **Cutty Sark** • King William Walk & Romney Rd
- **Greenwich Foot Tunnel** • Greenwich Church St & Thames St

Libraries

- **West Greenwich Library** • Greenwich High Rd

Nightlife

- **The Beehive** • 60 Carter St
- **The Greenwich Union** • 56 Royal Hill
- **North Pole Bar and Piano** • 131 Greenwich High Rd
- **O2** • O2 Arena
- **Up The Creek** • 302 Creek Rd

Post Offices

- **Greenwich** • 261 Greenwich High Rd

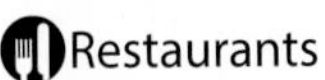

Restaurants

- **Craft London** • 1 Greenwich Pl
- **Goddard's Pie Shop Booth** • Fountain Court (off Greenwich Church St)
- **The Hill** • 89 Royal Hill
- **Piano Restaurant** • 131 Greenwich High Rd
- **Rivington Grill** • 178 Greenwich High Rd

Shopping

- **Cheeseboard** • 26 Royal Hill
- **Johnny Rocket** • 10 College Approach
- **Meet Bernard** • 23 Nelson Rd
- **Mr Humburg** • Greenwich Market
- **Music & Video Exchange** • 23 Greenwich Church St

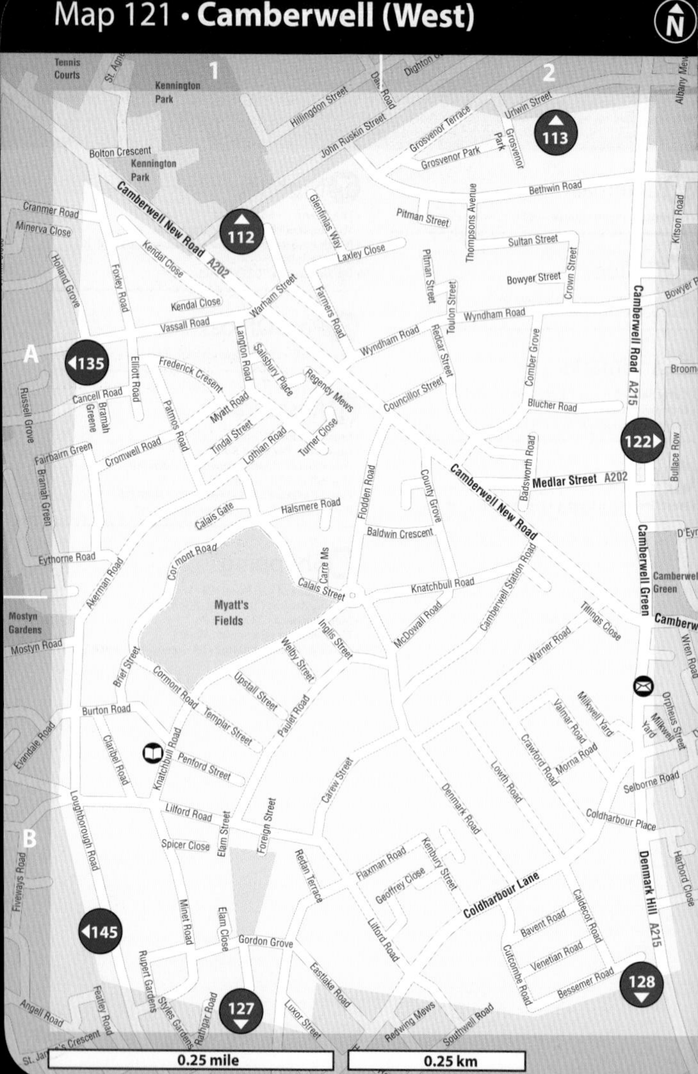
N
1
2
A
B
Tennis Courts
Kennington Park
Bolton Crescent
Kennington Park
Hillingdon Street
John Ruskin Street
Grosvenor Terrace
Urlwin Street
Grosvenor Park
Grosvenor Park
113
112
135
122
145
127
128
Cranmer Road
Minerva Close
Holland Grove
Camberwell New Road A202
Kendal Close
Kendal Close
Foxley Road
Vassall Road
Warham Street
Glenfinlas Way
Laxley Close
Farmers Road
Pitman Street
Pitman Street
Thompsons Avenue
Bethwin Road
Sultan Street
Bowyer Street
Crown Street
Toulon Street
Wyndham Road
Wyndham Road
Redcar Street
Comber Grove
Camberwell Road A215
Kitson Road
Bowyer Place
Broom
Frederick Cresent
Elliott Road
Langton Road
Salisbury Place
Regency Mews
Councillor Street
Blucher Road
Russell Grove
Cancell Road
Bramah Greene
Myatt Road
Patmos Road
Tindal Street
Lothian Road
Turner Close
Fairbairn Green
Cromwell Road
Bramah Green
Flodden Road
County Grove
Badsworth Road
Medlar Street A202
Camberwell New Road
Bullace Row
Halsmere Road
Calais Gate
Baldwin Crescent
Camberwell Green
D'Eyn
Camberwell Green
Eythorne Road
Akerman Road
Cormont Road
Carre Ms
Myatt's Fields
Calais Street
Knatchbull Road
Camberwell Station Road
Tillings Close
Camberw
Mostyn Gardens
Mostyn Road
Brief Street
Inglis Street
Welby Street
McDowall Road
Warner Road
Wren Road
Cormont Road
Upstall Street
Templar Street
Paulet Road
Milkwell Yard
Valmar Road
Orpheus Street
Milkwell Yard
Burton Road
Evandale Road
Claribel Road
Knatchbull Road
Penford Street
Crawford Road
Morna Road
Lowth Road
Carew Street
Denmark Road
Selborne Road
Coldharbour Place
Loughborough Road
Lilford Road
Elam Street
Foreign Street
Spicer Close
Redan Terrace
Flaxman Road
Kenbury Street
Geoffrey Close
Coldharbour Lane
Denmark Hill A215
Harbord Close
Fiveways Road
Minet Road
Elam Close
Lilford Road
Caldecot Road
Bavent Road
Gordon Grove
Venetian Road
Cutcombe Road
Bessemer Road
Rupert Gardens
Eastlake Road
Angell Road
Featley Road
Styles Gardens
Rathgar Road
Luxor Street
Redwing Mews
Southwell Road
0.25 mile
0.25 km

'his slowly reviving segment of Camberwell brings together a minority of polite ırty types in the crumbling-yet-quaint town houses of Camberwell New Road with ake-no-prisoners urbanites as seen in the chaos of Denmark Hill and its pointless **3utterfly Walk** (why?). The neighbourhood good stuff includes music bargains (**Rat Records**), killer Indian (**New Dewaniam**), and the unpronounceable Central Asian ·atery at the Pasha Hotel: **Kazakh Kyrgyz Restaurant.**

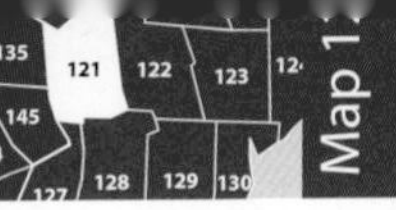

Libraries

- **Minet Library** • 52 Knatchbull Rd

Nightlife

- **The Joiners Arms** • 35 Denmark Hill
- **The Sun of Camberwell** • 61-63 Coldharbour Ln

Post Offices

- **Camberwell Green** • 25 Denmark Hill

Restaurants

- **Kazakh Kyrgyz** • 158 Camberwell Rd
- **New Dewaniam** • 225 Camberwell New Rd
- **Rock Steady Eddie's** • 2 Coldharbour Ln
- **Viet Cafe** • 75 Denmark Hill
- **Zeret Kitchen** • 216 Camberwell Rd

Shopping

- **Butterfly Walk Shopping Centre** • Denmark Hill
- **Rat Records** • 348 New Camberwell Rd

Supermarkets

- **Co-Op** • 177 Camberwell New Rd
- **Iceland** • 120 Camberwell Rd

1
2
A
B
Burgess Park Kart Track
Burgess Park
Burgess Park
CAMBERWELL
Camberwell Green
Lucas Gardens
Warwick Gardens
Denmark Hill
113
114
121
123
128
129
Boundary Lane
Red Lion R
Bradenham Close
Albany Mews
Albany Road
B214
Canal Street
Wells Way
St. Georges Way
Bibury Close
Ebley Close
Dragon Road
Gandolfi Street
Comfort Street
Watling Street
Pearse Street
Tower Mill Road
Newent Close
Longhope Close
Daniel Garde
Lynbrook Grove
Coleman Road
Tilman Close
Blakes Road
Innes Street
Calypso Crescent
Samuel Street
Garnies Close
Potters Close
Cinnamon Close
New Church Road
Southampton Way
Parkhouse Street
Rust Square
Kitson Road
Bowyer Place
Sears Street
Edmund Street
Caspian Street
Notley Street
Durfey Place
Cottage Green
Camberwell Road
A215
Draycott Close
Picton Street
Harris Street
Rainbow Street
Bonsor Street
Coleman Road
Peckham Grove
Chandler Way
Pentridge Street
Cronin Street
East Surrey Grove
Broome Way
Jago Walk
Hopewell Street
Bantry Street
Owgan Close
Havil Street
Melbury Drive
Diamond Street
Blucher Road
Lomond Grove
Brisbane Street
Houseman Way
Elmington Road
Ada Road
St. Giles Road
Stanswood Gardens
Sedgmoor Place
Southampton Way
Lidgate Road
Bullace Row
Don Phelan Close
Mary Datchelor Close
Sansom Street
Benhill Road
Brunswick Villas
Redbridge Gardens
Muscatel Place
Moody Road
Kelly Avenue
D'Eynsford Road
Kimpton Road
Gables Close
Dalwood Street
Camberwell Green
Vicarage Grove
Brunswick Park
Crane Street
Camberwell Glebe
Tilings Close
Wren Road
Camberwell Church Street
A202
Peckham Road
Peckham Road
Grummant Road
Jephson Street
Milkwell Yard
Orpheus Street
Daneville Road
Cuthill Walk
Vestry Mews
Shenley Road
Crofton Road
Valmar Road
Kerfield Place
Camberwell Grove
Wilson Road
Dagmar Road
Bushey Hill Road
Talfourd Place
Morna Road
Allendale Close
Evelina Walk
Maude Road
Selborne Road
Denman Road
Love Walk
Graces Mews
Graces Road
Linnell Road
Coldharbour Place
Talfourd Road
Vestry Road
Oswyth Road
Cross Road
De Crespigny Park
Grove Lane
Lettsom Street
Harbord Close
Denmark Hill
A215
Gairloch Road
Caldecot Road
Azenby Road
Lyndhurst
Cactus Close
Fowler
McNeil Road
Venetian Road
Grovelands Close
Windsor Walk
Linwood Close
Bessemer Road
Canning Cross
Camberwell Grove
Camberwell Grove
Linwood Close
Draymans Close
Champion Park
A2216
Grove Park
Chadwick Road
Champion Grove
Stories Mews
Pelham Close
Stories Road
Copleston Mews
Choumert Ro
0.25 mile
0.25 km

aybe it was Kevin Spacey moving to the Grove, maybe something else ntirely, but this area of Camberwell, in particular Church Street, has become omething of an eating and drinking mecca in recent years. Work through e mammoth selection of craft beers in **Stormbird** before soaking it up with xcellent kebabs from **FM Mangal** or regional Chinese from **Silk Road**.

Coffee

- **Daily Goods** • 36 Camberwell Church St
- **Fowlds Cafe** • 3 Addington Square

Libraries

- **Camberwell Library** • 17 Camberwell Church St

Nightlife

- **Grand Union** • 26 Camberwell Grove
- **The Flying Dutchman** • 156 Wells Wy
- **Hermit's Cave** • 28 Camberwell Church St
- **Stormbird** • 25 Camberwell Church St

Post Offices

- **Southampton Way** • 156 Southampton Wy

Restaurants

- **Caravaggio** • 47 Camberwell Church St
- **Crooked Well** • 16 Grove Ln
- **Falafel** • 27 Camberwell Church St
- **FM Mangal** • 54 Camberwell Church St
- **Silk Road** • 49 Camberwell Church St
- **Theo's** • 2 Grove Ln
- **Wuli Wuli** • 15 Camberwell Church St

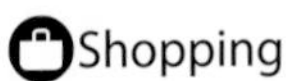

Shopping

- **Architectural Rescue** • 1-3 Southampton Way
- **Cowling and Wilcox** • 8-12 Orpheus St

PECKHAM
Peckham Rye Rail
Peckham High Street
Peckham Road A202
Queens Road A202
Hanover Park A202
Rye Lane A2215
Peckham Rye A2215
Peckham Park Road B216
Willowbrook Road B215
Surrey Linear Canal Park
Central Venture Park
Warwick Gardens
114
115
122
129
130
0.25 mile
0.25 km

Peckham

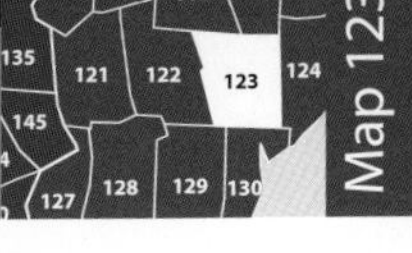

As old pubs, pool halls, telephone boxes, and coal bunkers are converted into galleries faster than you can say 'fixed gear bicycle', it's safe to say Peckham is the epicenter of the new(ish) South London art scene. But don't be scared off—get the cheapest lunch for miles at **Manze's** or pay a visit to the art/music/religion/theatre behemoth that is **The Bussey Building**.

Coffee

- **Petitou** • 63 Choumert Rd

Libraries

- **Peckham Library** • 122 Peckham Hill St

Movie Theaters

- **Peckham Multiplex** • 95 Rye Ln

Nightlife

- **Bar Story** • 213 Blenheim Grove
- **The Bussey Building** • 133 Rye Ln
- **Canavan's Peckham Pool Club** • 188 Rye Ln
- **The Four Quarters** • 187 Rye Ln
- **Frank's Cafe** • 95 Rye Ln
- **The Montpelier** • 43 Chomert Rd

Post Offices

- **Peckham** • 121 Peckham High St
- **Rye Lane** • 199 Rye Ln

Restaurants

- **Agrobeso African Cuisine** • 139 Peckham High St
- **Ganapati** • 38 Holly Grove
- **M. Manze Pie and Mash** • 105 Peckham High St
- **Miss Tapas** • 45 Choumert Road
- **Obalende Suya Express** • 43 Peckham High St

Shopping

- **Persepolis** • 30 Peckham High St
- **Primark** • 51 Rye Ln

Supermarkets

- **Iceland** • 74 Rye Ln

Map 124 • Peckham East (Queen's Road)

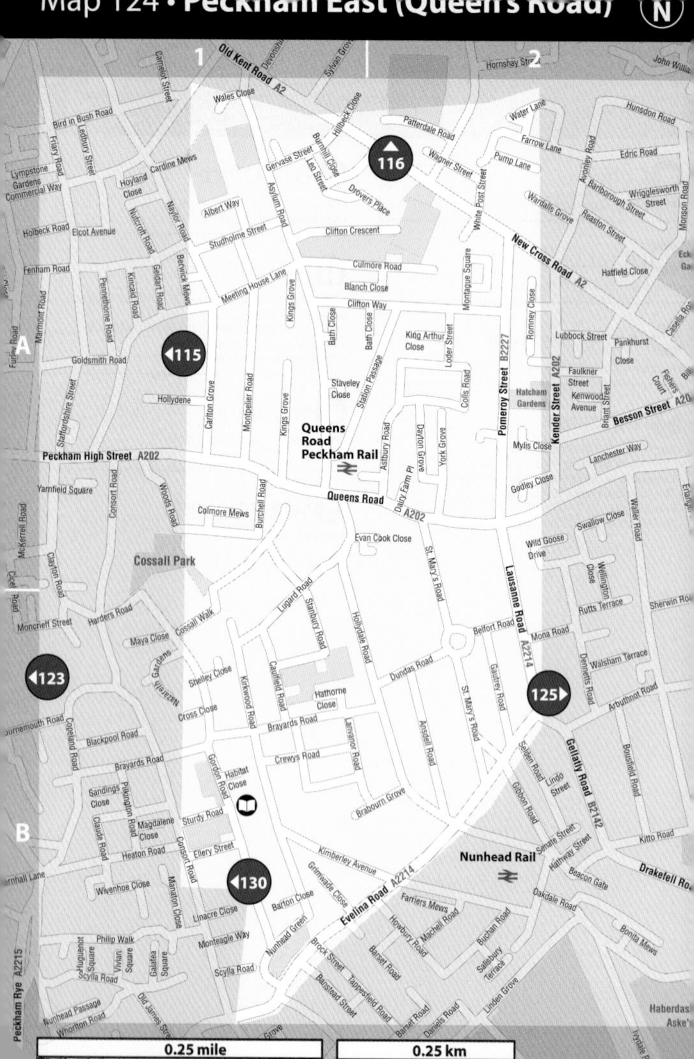

Peckham East (Queen's Road)

Although the local halfway house ensures the streets are filled with beggars, and the buses passing through en route to the continent make you wish you were somewhere else, this small pocket of Peckham isn't really so bad. Head for great African food at **805** or take a short walk to the incredible Victorian **Nunhead Cemetery**.

Libraries

- **Nunhead Library** • Gordon Rd

Restaurants

- **805** • 805 Old Kent Rd
- **Tops Carribean Takeaway** • 173 Queens Rd

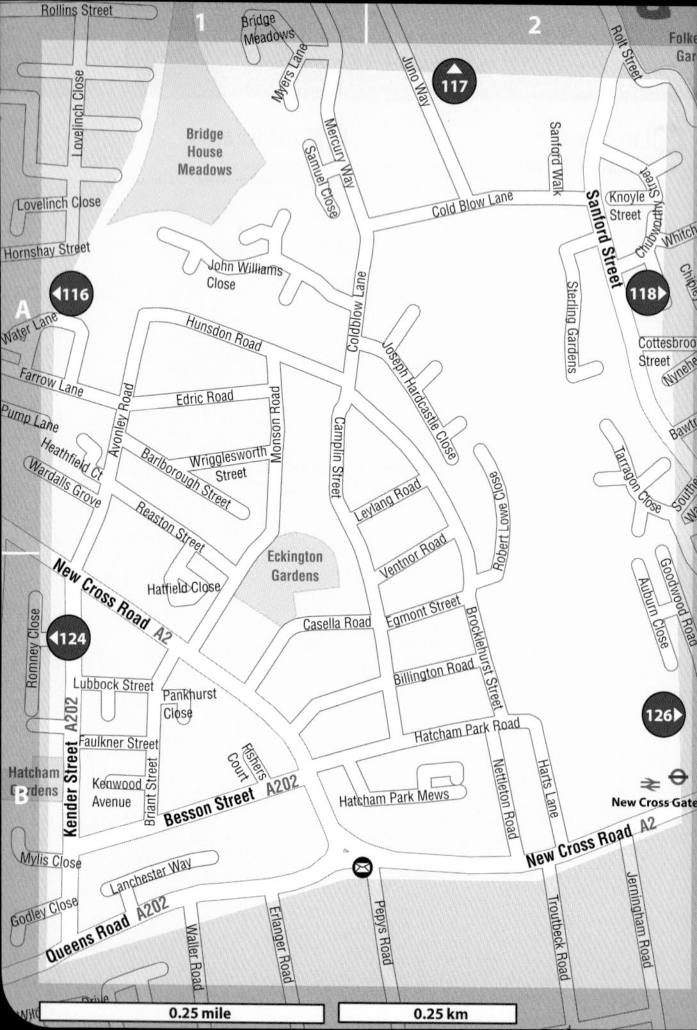

N

1
2
A
B

117
116
118
124
126

Rollins Street
Bridge Meadows
Myers Lane
Juno Way
Rolt Street
Lovelinch Close
Bridge House Meadows
Mercury Way
Samuel Close
Sanford Walk
Lovelinch Close
Cold Blow Lane
Sanford Street
Knoyle Street
Chubworthy Street
Hornshay Street
John Williams Close
Sterling Gardens
Coldblow Lane
Water Lane
Hunsdon Road
Joseph Hardcastle Close
Cottesbrook Street
Farrow Lane
Edric Road
Avonley Road
Monson Road
Camplin Street
Pump Lane
Heathfield Ct
Barlborough Street
Wrigglesworth Street
Wardalls Grove
Leylang Road
Robert Lowe Close
Tarragon Close
Reaston Street
Eckington Gardens
Ventnor Road
New Cross Road A2
Hatfield Close
Goodwood Road
Auburn Close
Romney Close
Casella Road
Egmont Street
Brocklehurst Street
Billington Road
Lubbock Street
Pankhurst Close
Kender Street A202
Faulkner Street
Hatcham Park Road
Fishers Court
Nettleton Road
Harts Lane
Hatcham Gardens
Kenwood Avenue
Briant Street
Besson Street A202
Hatcham Park Mews
New Cross Gate
New Cross Road A2
Mylis Close
Lanchester Way
Godley Close
Queens Road A202
Waller Road
Erlanger Road
Pepys Road
Troutbeck Road
Jerningham Road

0.25 mile
0.25 km

Since the sad demise of the Montague Arms this strip has become even more of a no man's land—not quite New Cross but not quite Peckham. Apart from a semi-decent junk shop and a not-so-great retail park, there's not much to see. Do yourself a favor and stroll on into one of the aforementioned neighborhoods—or jump on the brilliant London Overground and be in Dalston in no time.

Post Offices

- **New Cross Gate** • 165 New Cross Rd

Restaurants

- **Hong Kong City** • 43 New Cross Rd

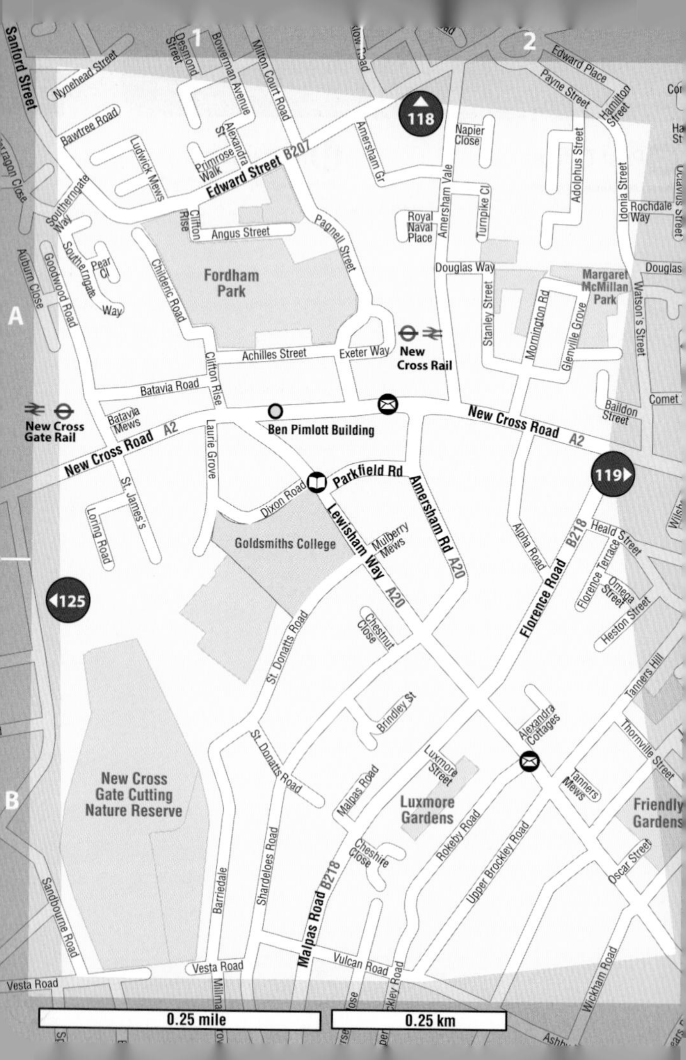

1
2
A
B
Sanford Street
Nynehead Street
Desmond Street
Bowerman Avenue
Milton Court Road
Edward Place
Payne Street
Hamilton Street
Bawtree Road
Ludwick Mews
Primrose Walk
Alexandra St
Edward Street B207
Amersham Gr
118
Napier Close
Adolphus Street
Idonia Street
Rochdale Way
Southerngate Way
Clifton Rise
Angus Street
Pagnell Street
Royal Naval Place
Amersham Vale
Turnpike Cl
Auburn Close
Goodwood Road
Southerngate Way
Pear Cl
Childeric Road
Fordham Park
Douglas Way
Stanley Street
Mornington Rd
Glenville Grove
Margaret McMillan Park
Watson's Street
Achilles Street
Exeter Way
New Cross Rail
Batavia Road
Clifton Rise
Comet
Batavia Mews
New Cross Gate Rail
Ben Pimlott Building
New Cross Road A2
Baildon Street
New Cross Road A2
Laurie Grove
Parkfield Rd
Amersham Rd A20
119
Dixon Road
St. James's
Loring Road
Lewisham Way A20
Goldsmiths College
Mulberry Mews
Alpha Road
Florence Road B218
Heald Street
Florence Terrace
Omega Street
Heston Street
125
St. Donatts Road
Chestnut Close
Tanners Hill
Brindley St
Alexandra Cottages
Thornville Street
St. Donatts Road
Luxmore Street
Tanners Mews
New Cross Gate Cutting Nature Reserve
Malpas Road
Luxmore Gardens
Friendly Gardens
Cheshire Close
Rokeby Road
Upper Brockley Road
Oscar Street
Sandbourne Road
Barriedale
Shardeloes Road
Malpas Road B218
Wickham Road
Vulcan Road
Vesta Road
Vesta Road
0.25 mile
0.25 km

Once hailed as the new Shoreditch, this corner of Lewisham has managed to provide us with all the good stuff about hipsterville, while avoiding everything bad.

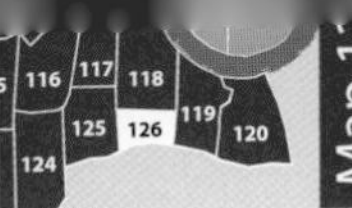

Landmarks

- **Ben Pimlott Building** • University of London, New Cross

Libraries

- **Goldsmiths Library** • Lewisham Wy

Nightlife

- **Amersham Arms** • 388 New Cross Rd
- **Marquis of Granby** • 322 New Cross Rd
- **New Cross Inn** • 323 New Cross Rd

Post Offices

- **Lewisham Way** • 150 Lewisham Wy
- **New Cross Road** • 500 New Cross Rd

Restaurants

- **Birdie Num Nums** • 11 Lewisham Wy
- **The London Peculiar** • 399 New Cross Rd

Supermarkets

- **Iceland** • 277 New Cross Rd
- **Sainsbury's** • 263 New Cross Rd

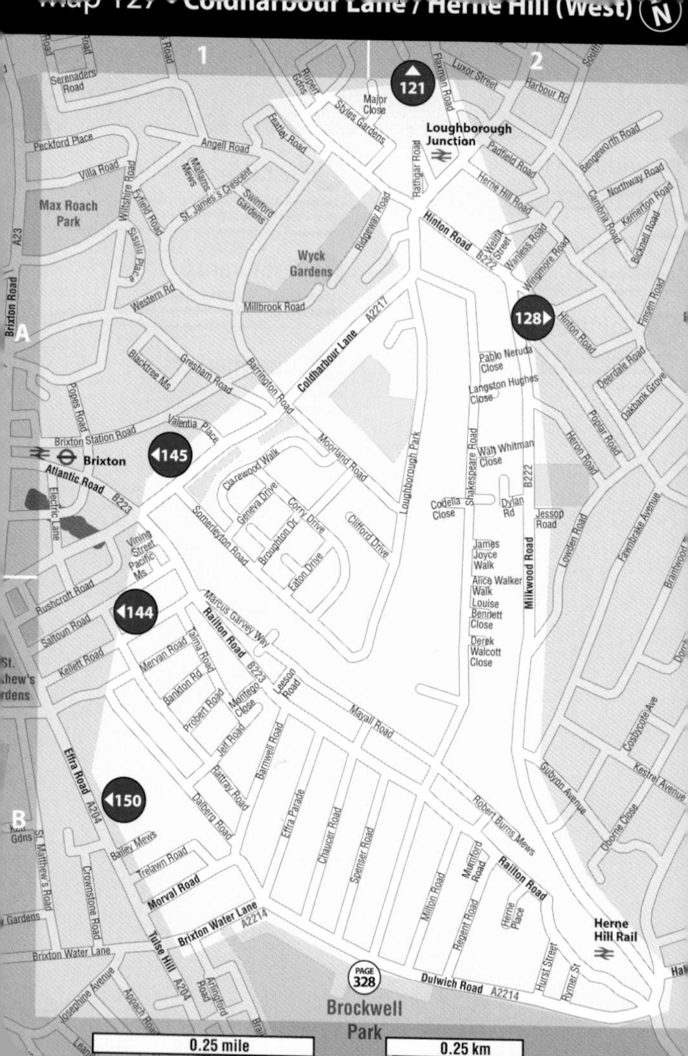

Coldharbour Lane / Herne Hill (West)
N
1
2
121
128
145
144
150
A
B
Serenaders Road
Peckford Place
Villa Road
Angell Road
Max Roach Park
A23
Brixton Road
Wiltshire Road
Fyfield Road
Mallams Mews
St. James's Crescent
Swinford Gardens
Sisulu Place
Western Rd
Rupert Gdns
Styles Gardens
Major Close
Featley Road
Flaxman Road
Luxor Street
Harbour Rd
Loughborough Junction
Rathgar Road
Padfield Road
Herne Hill Road
Bengeworth Road
Northway Road
Cambria Road
Kemerton Road
Bicknell Road
Hinton Road
B222
Wellfit Street
Wanless Road
Wingmore Road
Ridgeway Road
Wyck Gardens
Millbrook Road
Coldharbour Lane
A2217
Finsen Road
Pablo Neruda Close
Langston Hughes Close
Deerdale Road
Oakbank Grove
Blacktree Ms
Gresham Road
Barrington Road
Popes Road
Valentia Place
Brixton Station Road
Brixton
Atlantic Road
B223
Electric Lane
Moorland Road
Clarewood Walk
Geneva Drive
Corry Drive
Somerleyton Road
Broughton Dr
Eaton Drive
Clifford Drive
Loughborough Park
Shakespeare Road
Walt Whitman Close
Codella Close
Dylan Rd
B222
Jessop Road
Heron Road
Poplar Road
Lowden Road
Fawnbrake Avenue
Brantwood
Milkwood Road
James Joyce Walk
Alice Walker Walk
Louise Bennett Close
Derek Walcott Close
Vining Street
Pacific Ms
Rushcroft Road
Saltoun Road
Kellett Road
Marcus Garvey Way
Railton Road
B223
Meryan Road
Talma Road
Bankton Rd
Probert Road
Montego Close
Leeson Road
Jelf Road
Mayall Road
Barnwell Road
Rattray Road
Effra Road
A204
Dalberg Road
Effra Parade
Chaucer Road
Spenser Road
Milton Road
Mumford Road
Regent Road
Robert Burns Mews
Railton Road
Herne Place
Gubyon Avenue
Cosbycote Ave
Kestrel Avenue
Oborne Close
Bailey Mews
Trelawn Road
Morval Road
Brixton Water Lane
A2214
St. Matthew's Road
Crownstone Road
Gardens
Brixton Water Lane
Tulse Hill
A204
Arlingford Road
Josephine Avenue
Appach Road
Dulwich Road
A2214
Hurst Street
Rymer St
Herne Hill Rail
PAGE 328
Brockwell Park
0.25 mile
0.25 km

Coldharbour Lane / Herne Hill (West)

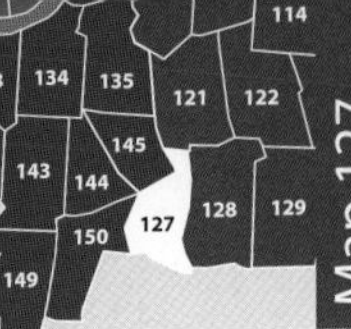

'here don't seem to be as many shootings on Coldharbour Lane as there used o be. Maybe the crack dealers are just quietly selling the stuff, as somebody n The Wire once sensibly advised. Or maybe they've all been converted by the leasant conservatory at **The Florence**, invigorating swims at the **Brockwell .ido**, and handmade jams from the **Blackbird Bakery**. Yes, that's probably it.

Nightlife

- **The Commercial** • 210 Railton Rd
- **The Florence** • 133 Dulwich Rd
- **The Prince Regent** • 69 Dulwich Rd

Restaurants

- **Café Prov** • 2 Half Moon Ln
- **Ichiban Sushi** • 58 Atlantic Rd
- **Naughty Piglets** • 28 Brixton Water Ln

Shopping

- **Blackbird Bakery** • 208 Railton Rd

Coffee

- **The Parlour** • 19 Norwood Rd

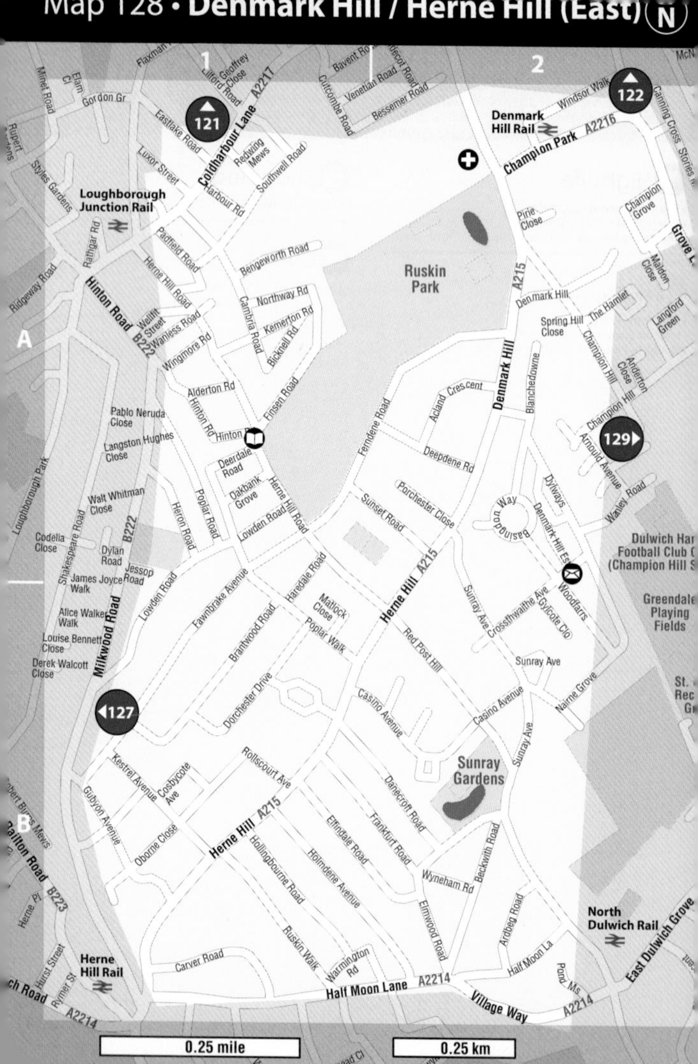
N
1
2
A
B
121
122
127
129
Loughborough Junction Rail
Denmark Hill Rail
Herne Hill Rail
North Dulwich Rail
Ruskin Park
Sunray Gardens
Dulwich Hamlet Football Club (Champion Hill)
Greendale Playing Fields
Coldharbour Lane A2217
Champion Park A2216
Denmark Hill
A215
Herne Hill A215
Hinton Road B222
Milkwood Road
Half Moon Lane A2214
Village Way A2214
East Dulwich Grove
Gordon Gr
Eastlake Road
Luxor Street
Harbour Rd
Redwing Mews
Southwell Road
Padfield Road
Herne Hill Road
Bengeworth Road
Northway Rd
Kemerton Rd
Bicknell Rd
Cambria Road
Wellfit Street
Wanless Road
Wingmore Rd
Alderton Rd
Hinton Rd
Finsen Road
Deerdale Road
Oakbank Grove
Lowden Road
Poplar Road
Heron Road
Pablo Neruda Close
Langston Hughes Close
Walt Whitman Close
Codelia Close
Dylan Road
Jessop Road
James Joyce Walk
Alice Walker Walk
Louise Bennett Close
Derek Walcott Close
Shakespeare Road
Loughborough Park
Ridgeway Road
Rathgar Rd
Styles Gardens
Minet Road
Elam Cl
Flaxman
Geoffrey Close
Lilford Road
Bavent Road
Venetian Road
Bessemer Road
Cutcombe Road
Windsor Walk
Canning Cross
Pirie Close
Champion Grove
Grove La
Maldon Close
The Hamlet
Langford Green
Spring Hill Close
Champion Hill
Anderton Close
Blanchedowne
Acland Crescent
Deepdene Rd
Ferndene Road
Porchester Close
Sunset Road
Arnould Avenue
Dylways
Wanley Road
Basingdon Way
Denmark Hill Est
Woodfarrs
Gylcote Clo
Crossthwaite Ave
Sunray Ave
Nairne Grove
Casino Avenue
Red Post Hill
Haredale Road
Matlock Close
Poplar Walk
Fawnbrake Avenue
Brantwood Road
Dorchester Drive
Rollscourt Ave
Danecroft Road
Frankfurt Road
Effingdale Road
Holmdene Avenue
Hollingbourne Road
Kestrel Avenue
Cosbycote Ave
Gubyon Avenue
Oborne Close
Beckwith Road
Wyneham Rd
Elmwood Road
Ardbeg Road
Half Moon La
Pond Ms
Ruskin Walk
Warmington Rd
Carver Road
Robert Burns Mews
Railton Road B223
Herne Pl
Hurst Street
Rymer St
A2214
0.25 mile
0.25 km

Denmark Hill / Herne Hill (East)

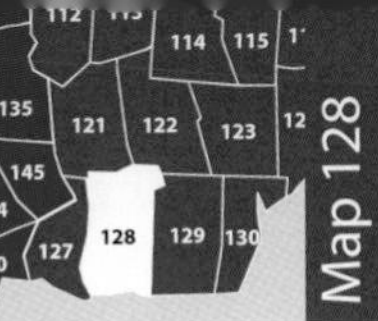

There's something quaintly grounded about the leafy Victorian suburb of Herne Hill, where funky neo-hippies settle into dreadlocked nuclear families. Denmark Hill sits at its top, with its imposing Salvation Army training grounds, following on to Ruskin Park for ornamental ponds and Edwardian ruins. Half Moon Lane plays main drag—get lost in a book at **Tales on Moon Lane** and lost in a bowl of noodles at **Lombok**.

Emergency Rooms

- **King's College Hospital** • Denmark Hill & Champion Park

Libraries

- **Carnegie Library** • 188 Herne Hill Rd

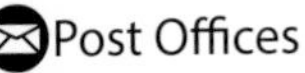

Post Offices

- **Crossthwaite Avenue** • 6 Crossthwaite Ave

Restaurants

- **Lombok** • 17 Half Moon Ln
- **Number 22** • 22 Half Moon Ln

Shopping

- **Tales on Moon Lane** • 25 Half Moon Ln

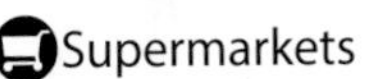

Supermarkets

- **Sainsbury's** • 132 Herne Hill

1
2
A
B
122
123
130
128
Champion Park
Stories Mews
Stories Road
Camberwell Grove
Pelham Close
Copleston Mews
Choumert Road
Danby Street
Ivanhoe Road
Grove Hill Road
Malfort Rd
Champion Grove
Grove Lane A2216
Avondale Rise
Bellenden Road
Bromar Road
Albrighton Road
Soames Street
The Hamlet
Langford Grn
Champion Hill
Anderton Close
Pytchley Road
Oglander Road
Adys Road
Muschamp Road
Maxted Road
Oxenford Street
Marsden Road
Everthorpe Road
Dog Kennel Hill
Quorn Road
Hayes Gr
Copleston Road
Ondine Road
Arnould Avenue
Kings College Sports Ground
Abbotswood Road
St. Francis Road
A2216
Vale End
Besant Place
Grove Vale
East Dulwich Road
Goose Green
Wanley Road
Dylways
Dulwich Hamlet Football Club Ground (Champion Hill Stadium)
East Dulwich Rail
Derwent Grove
Elsie Road
Zenoria Street
Spurling Road
Worlingham Road
Burrow Road
Talbot Road
Jarvis Rd
Melbourne Grove
East Dulwich Grove A2214
Matham Grove
Frogley Road
Crawthew Grove
Greendale Playing Fields
Woodfarrs
Gylcote Close
Shaw Road
Tell Grove
Nutfield Road
Archdale Road
Ashbourne Grove
Nairne Grove
North Cross Road
St. Olave's Recreation Ground
Trossachs Road
Chesterfield Grove
Tarbert Road
Shawbury Road
Dudrich Mews
Sage Mews
Thorncombe Road
Glengarry Road
Bassano St
Lordship Lane
Hansler Road
Lytcott Grove
Fellbrigg Road
Bawdale Road
Hillsboro Road
Green Dale Close
Green Dale
Playfield Crescent
Whateley Road
Silvester Road
Colwell Road
Great Spilmans
Pellatt Road
North Dulwich Rail
Village Way A2214
Calton Avenue
Landcroft Road
Woodside Mews
Rodwell Road
Ardbeg Road
Half Moon La
Townley Road
Heber Road
Gilkes Crescent
Jennings Road
Pond Mead
Dovercourt Road
Beauval Road
Goodrich Road
0.25 mile
0.25 km
Thompson Road

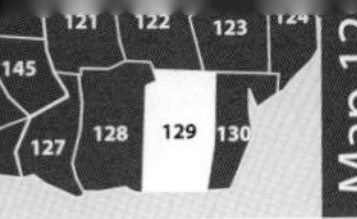

ˌst Dulwich is where your ex-flatmate finally settled down and now won't shut
› about taramasalata, babies, and how he's only fifteen minutes from London
idge by train over perfect cocktails. Dodge baguettes, pushchairs, and delis
ong Lordship Lane, just don't get sucked in.

Coffee

- **Caffe Nero** • 8 Lordship Ln

Libraries

- **Grove Vale library** • 25 Grove Vale

Nightlife

- **East Dulwich Tavern** • 1 Lordship Ln
- **House of Tippler** • 123 Lordship Ln

Restaurants

- **Anderson & Co** • 139 Bellenden Rd
- **The Palmerston** • 91 Lordship Ln

Supermarkets

- **Iceland** • 84 Lordship Ln
- **Sainsbury's** • 80 Dog Kennel Hill

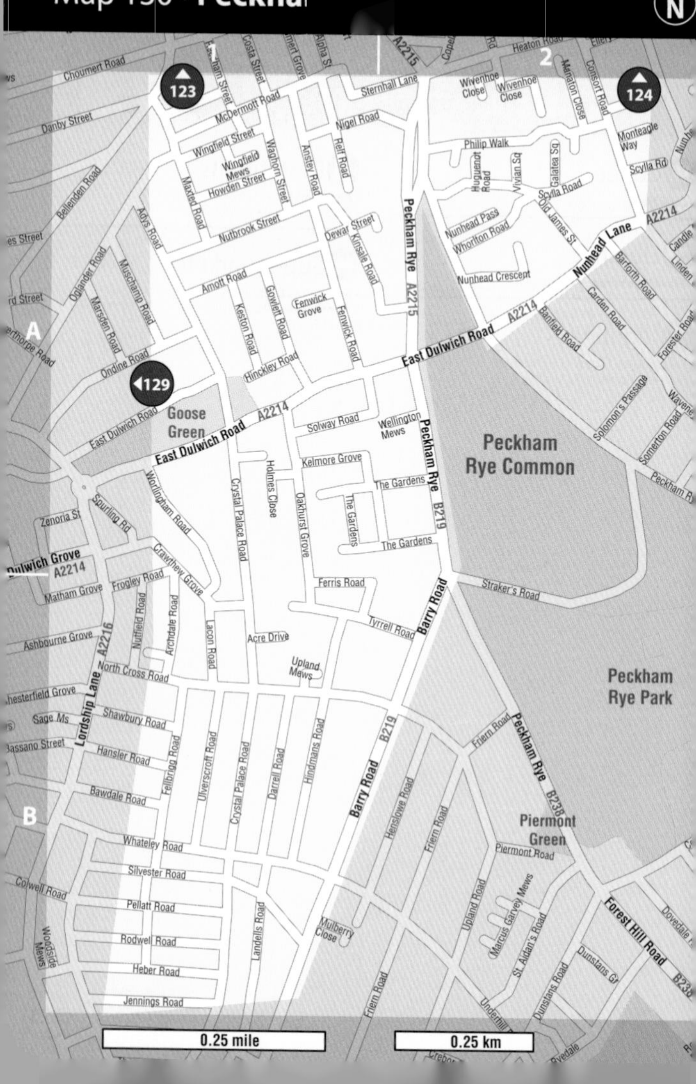
123
124
129
Choumert Road
Danby Street
Bellenden Road
McDermott Road
Wingfield Street
Wingfield Mews
Howden Street
Nutbrook Street
Sternhall Lane
Nigel Road
Philip Walk
Scylla Road
Scylla Rd
Monteagle Way
Nunhead Pass
Whorlton Road
Nunhead Crescent
Nunhead Lane
A2214
Peckham Rye
A2215
East Dulwich Road
Amott Road
Fenwick Grove
Hinckley Road
Ondine Road
Goose Green
Solway Road
Wellington Mews
Kelmore Grove
The Gardens
Peckham Rye Common
Straker's Road
Ferris Road
Tyrrell Road
Barry Road
B219
Acre Drive
Upland Mews
Peckham Rye Park
North Cross Road
Shawbury Road
Hansler Road
Bawdale Road
Lordship Lane
A2216
Dulwich Grove
Matham Grove
Frogley Road
Ashbourne Grove
Whateley Road
Silvester Road
Pellatt Road
Rodwell Road
Heber Road
Jennings Road
Colwell Road
Piermont Green
Piermont Road
Forest Hill Road
B238
0.25 mile
0.25 km
A
B
1
2

Peckham Rye

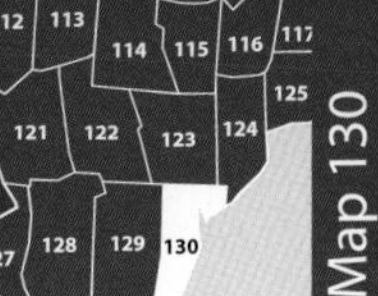

\ noticeboard on Peckham Rye Common alleges that ancient British Queen 3oudicca was finally defeated by the Romans here. Anyone suggesting that the ery middle class streets around North Cross Road—with its market and lazy unday lunches at **The Rye**—have anything to do with Peckham as we know it night get the same treatment.

Coffee

- **Old Spike Roastery** • 54 Peckham Rye

Nightlife

- **The Gowlett** • 62 Gowlett Rd
- **The Rye** • 31 Peckham Rye

Restaurants

- **Artusi** • 161 Bellenden Rd
- **Pedler** • 58 Peckham Rye
- **Thai Corner Cafe** • 44 Northcross Rd
- **The Rye** • 31 Peckham Rye

Shopping

- **Flock and Herd** • 155 Bellenden Rd

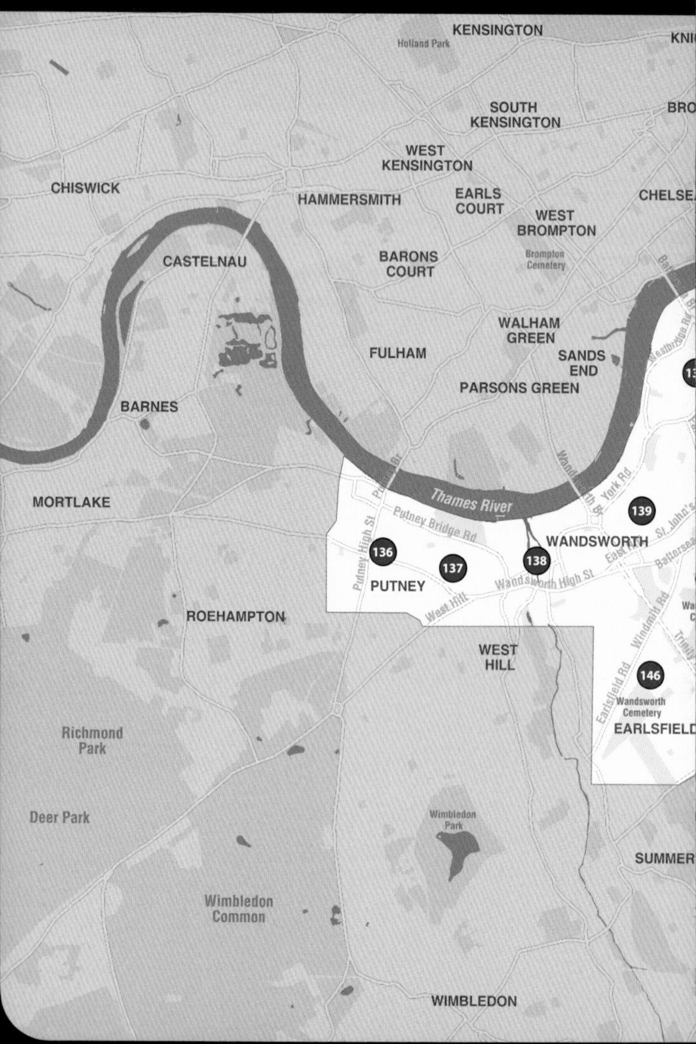
KENSINGTON
Holland Park
SOUTH KENSINGTON
WEST KENSINGTON
CHISWICK
HAMMERSMITH
EARLS COURT
WEST BROMPTON
CHELSE
BRO
KNI
CASTELNAU
BARONS COURT
Brompton Cemetery
WALHAM GREEN
FULHAM
SANDS END
PARSONS GREEN
BARNES
MORTLAKE
Thames River
Putney Bridge Rd
Putney High St
136
137
138
139
WANDSWORTH
PUTNEY
Wandsworth High St
West Hill
York Rd
ROEHAMPTON
WEST HILL
146
Earlsfield Rd
Windmill Rd
Wandsworth Cemetery
EARLSFIELD
Richmond Park
Deer Park
Wimbledon Park
SUMMER
Wimbledon Common
WIMBLEDON

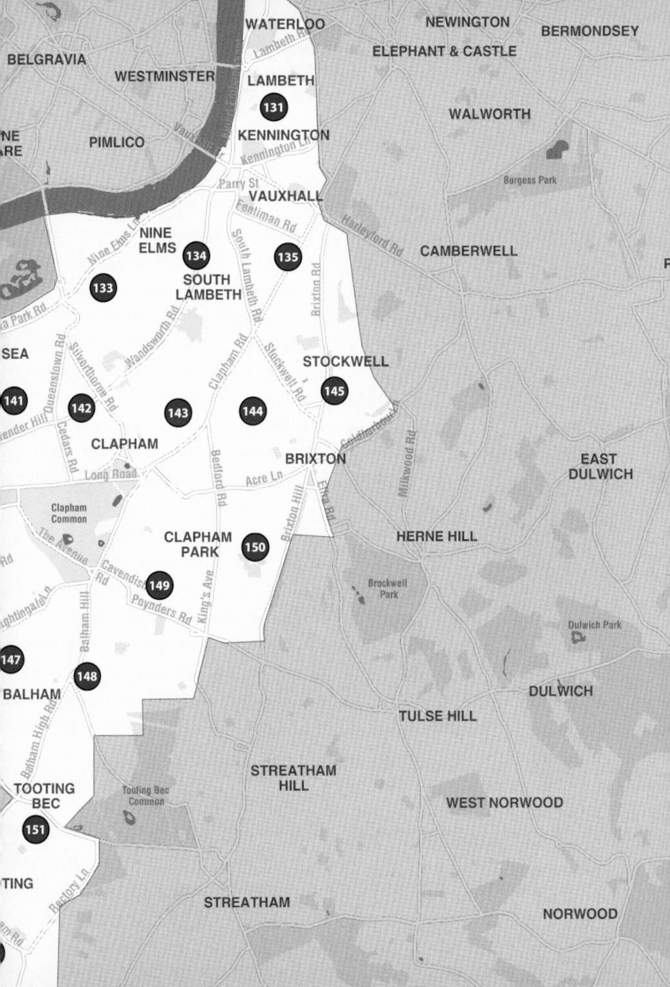
WATERLOO
NEWINGTON
BERMONDSEY
BELGRAVIA
ELEPHANT & CASTLE
WESTMINSTER
LAMBETH
131
WALWORTH
PIMLICO
KENNINGTON
Kennington Ln
Parry St
VAUXHALL
Burgess Park
Fentiman Rd
Harleyford Rd
NINE ELMS
134
135
CAMBERWELL
Nine Elms Ln
133
SOUTH LAMBETH
South Lambeth Rd
Brixton Rd
Wandsworth Rd
Clapham Rd
Stockwell Rd
STOCKWELL
145
141
142
143
144
Queenstown Rd
Silverthorne Rd
Cedars Rd
CLAPHAM
BRIXTON
EAST DULWICH
Long Road
Acre Ln
Bedford Rd
Milkwood Rd
Clapham Common
CLAPHAM PARK
150
Brixton Hill
Effra Rd
HERNE HILL
The Avenue
Cavendish Rd
149
Brockwell Park
Poynders Rd
King's Ave
Balham Hill
Dulwich Park
147
148
BALHAM
DULWICH
TULSE HILL
Balham High Rd
STREATHAM HILL
TOOTING BEC
Tooting Bec Common
WEST NORWOOD
151
Rectory Ln
STREATHAM
NORWOOD

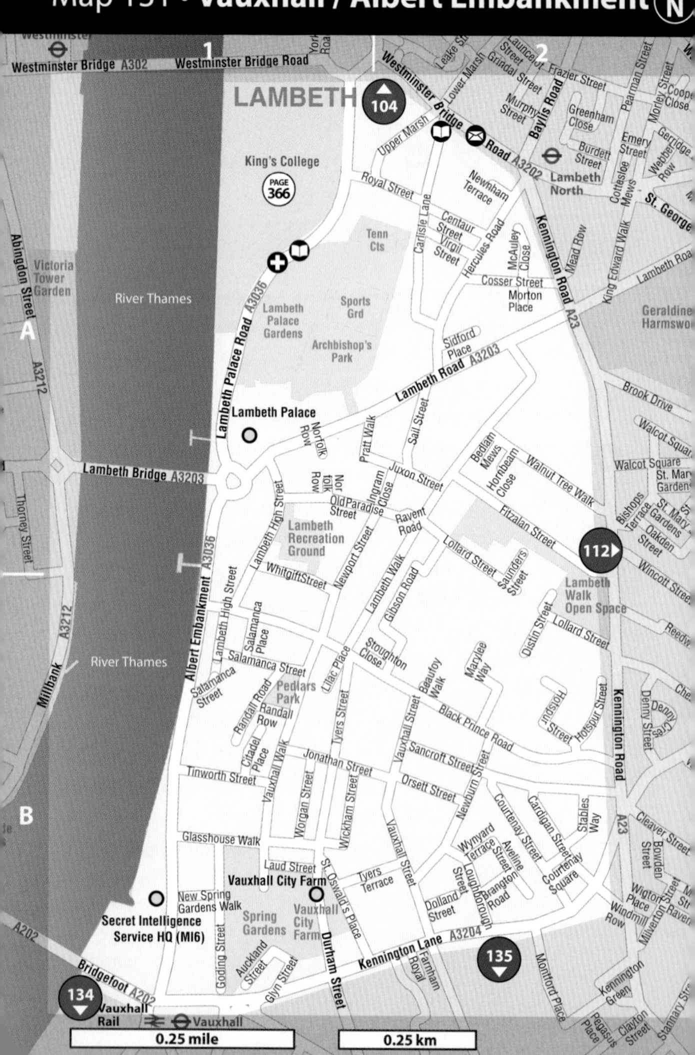
N
1
2
A
B
Westminster Bridge A302
Westminster Bridge Road
York Road
Westminster Bridge Road A3202
LAMBETH
104
King's College
PAGE 366
Leake Street
Lower Marsh
Launcelot Street
Grindal Street
Frazier Street
Pearman Street
Morley Street
Cooper Close
Murphy Street
Baylis Road
Greenham Close
Emery Street
Gerridge Street
Burdett Street
Webber Row
Lambeth North
Cottesloe Mews
St. George's
Upper Marsh
Royal Street
Newnham Terrace
Centaur Street
Virgil Street
Carlisle Lane
Hercules Road
McAuley Close
Kennington Road A23
Mead Row
King Edward Walk
Lambeth Road
Tenn Cts
Cosser Street
Morton Place
Geraldine Harmsworth
Abingdon Street
Victoria Tower Garden
River Thames
Lambeth Palace Road A3036
Lambeth Palace Gardens
Sports Grd
Archbishop's Park
Sidford Place
Lambeth Road A3203
A3212
Brook Drive
Lambeth Palace
Norfolk Row
Pratt Walk
Sail Street
Walcot Square
Lambeth Bridge A3203
Bedlam Mews
Hornbeam Close
Walnut Tree Walk
Juxon Street
St. Mary's Gardens
Thorney Street
Norfolk Row
Ingram Close
Old Paradise Street
Ravent Road
Bishops Terrace
Oakden Street
Lambeth High Street
Lambeth Recreation Ground
Fitzalan Street
112
Newport Street
Lollard Street
Saunders Street
Wincott Street
Whitgift Street
Lambeth Walk
Gibson Road
Lambeth Walk Open Space
Albert Embankment A3036
Lambeth High Street
Salamanca Place
Distin Street
Lollard Street
A3212
River Thames
Salamanca Street
Lilac Place
Stoughton Close
Beaufoy Walk
Marylee Way
Millbank
Salamanca Street
Pedlars Park
Randall Road
Randall Row
Tyers Street
Vauxhall Street
Black Prince Road
Hotspur Street
Kennington Road
Denny Street
Denny Cres
Citadel Place
Vauxhall Walk
Jonathan Street
Sancroft Street
Newburn Street
Tinworth Street
Orsett Street
Worgan Street
Wickham Street
Courtenay Street
Cardigan Street
Stables Way
A23
Cleaver Street
Bowden Street
Glasshouse Walk
Vauxhall Street
Wynyard Terrace
Aveline Street
Laud Street
St. Oswald's Place
Courtenay Square
Vauxhall City Farm
Tyers Terrace
Loughborough Street
Brangton Road
Wigton Place
Milverton Street
Windmill Row
New Spring Gardens Walk
Dolland Street
Secret Intelligence Service HQ (MI6)
Spring Gardens
Vauxhall City Farm
Durham Street
Kennington Lane A3204
135
A202
Goding Street
Auckland Street
Glyn Street
Royal Street
Farnham Royal
Montford Place
Kennington Green
Bridgefoot A202
134
Vauxhall Rail
Vauxhall
Pegasus Place
Clayton Street
0.25 mile
0.25 km

/auxhall / Albert Embankment

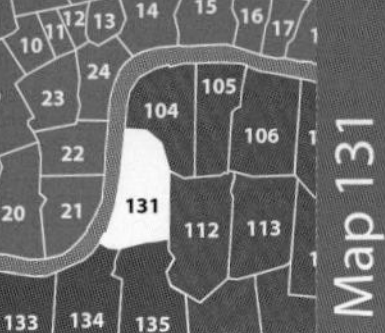

el like doin' the Lambeth Walk? You can. Right here. On Lambeth Walk, incidentally. ough nowadays 'doing the Lambeth Walk' is likely to have an entirely less innocent nnotation if some of the area's kinkier gay clubs are anything to go by. This part of uxhall, under the watchful eye of MI6, is slightly less that way inclined, but maintains share of hot spots. If you're after a sausage fest of another kind, get stuffed at **itgeist at the Jolly Gardeners**.

Emergency Rooms

- **St Thomas' Hospital** • Westminster Bridge Rd & Lambeth Palace Rd

Landmarks

- **Lambeth Palace** • Lambeth Palace Rd & Lambeth Rd
- **Secret Intelligence Service HQ (MI6)** • 85 Vauxhall Cross
- **Vauxhall City Farm** • 165 Tyers St

Libraries

- **CILT Resources Library** • 111 Vauxhall Bridge Rd
- **Lambeth Palace Library** • Lambeth Palace Rd

Nightlife

- **Area** • 67 Albert Embankment
- **Eagle London** • 349 Kennington Ln
- **The Royal Vauxhall Tavern** • 372 Kennington Ln
- **Zeitgeist at the Jolly Gardeners** • 49–51 Black Prince Rd

Post Offices

- **Westminster Bridge Road** • 125 Westminster Bridge Rd

Supermarkets

- **Tesco** • Kennington Ln

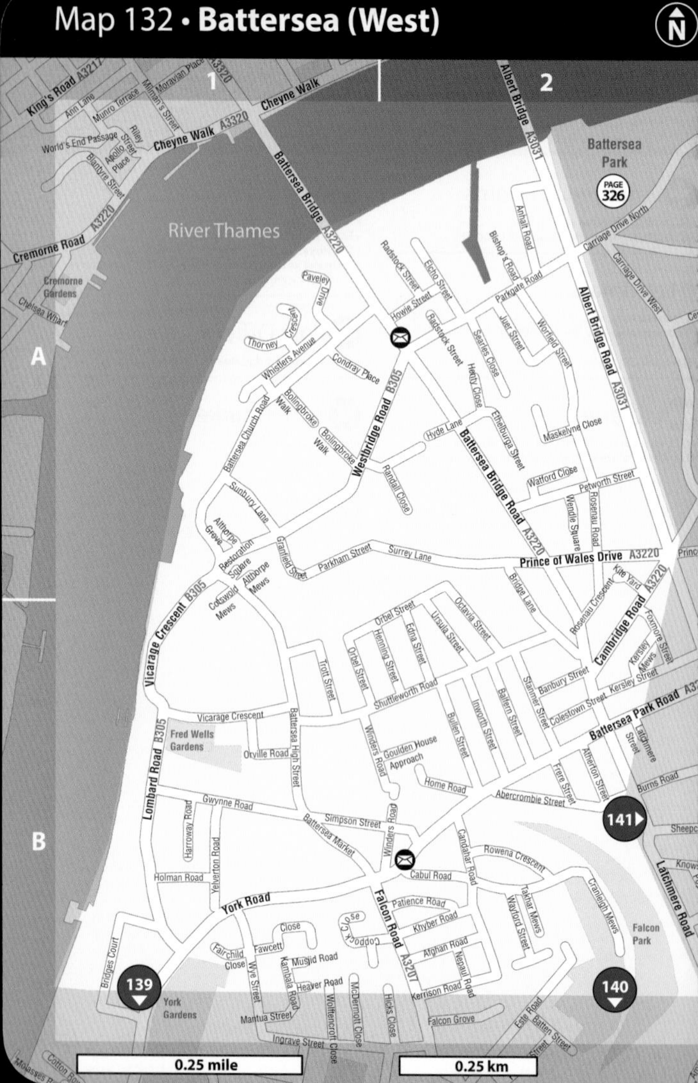
Map 132 • Battersea (West)
N
1
2
A
B
King's Road A3217
Ann Lane
Munro Terrace
Milman's Street
Moravian Place
A3320
Cheyne Walk
Cheyne Walk A3320
World's End Passage
Riley Street
Apollo Place
Blantyre Street
Cremorne Road A3220
Cremorne Gardens
Chelsea Wharf
River Thames
Battersea Bridge A3220
Albert Bridge A3031
Battersea Park
PAGE 326
Carriage Drive North
Carriage Drive West
Anhalt Road
Bishop's Road
Parkgate Road
Radstock Street
Elcho Street
Howie Street
Paveley Drive
Thorney Crescent
Whistlers Avenue
Condray Place
Juer Street
Searles Close
Worfield Street
Albert Bridge Road A3031
Henty Close
Maskelyne Close
Bolingbroke Walk
Battersea Church Road
Westbridge Road B305
Hyde Lane
Battersea Bridge Road A3220
Ethelburga Street
Randall Close
Watford Close
Petworth Street
Wendle Square
Rosenau Road
Sunbury Lane
Althorpe Grove
Restoration Square
Granfield Street
Parkham Street
Surrey Lane
Prince of Wales Drive A3220
Kite Yard
Bridge Lane
Rosenau Crescent
Cambridge Road A3220
Foxmore Street
Kersley Mews
Kersley Street
Althorpe Mews
Cotswold Mews
Vicarage Crescent B305
Orbel Street
Henning Street
Edna Street
Ursula Street
Octavia Street
Trott Street
Shuttleworth Road
Banbury Street
Colestown Street
Battersea Park Road
Stanmer Street
Balfern Street
Inworth Street
Bullen Street
Vicarage Crescent
Fred Wells Gardens
Orville Road
Battersea High Street
Winders Road
Goulden House Approach
Home Road
Latchmere Street
Atherton Street
Frere Street
Abercrombie Street
Burns Road
Lombard Road B305
Gwynne Road
Harroway Road
Yelverton Road
Simpson Street
Battersea Market
Winders Road
141
Candahar Road
Rowena Crescent
Holman Road
Cabul Road
York Road
Falcon Road A3207
Patience Road
Khyber Road
Coppock Close
Takhar Mews
Wayford Street
Cranleigh Mews
Latchmere Road
Falcon Park
Afghan Road
Nepaul Road
Close
Fawcett
Fairchild Close
Musjid Road
Kambala Road
Wye Street
Heaver Road
Kerrison Road
Bridges Court
139
York Gardens
140
Mantua Street
Wolftencroft Close
McDermott Close
Hicks Close
Falcon Grove
Este Road
Batten Street
Ingrave Street
0.25 mile
0.25 km

Battersea (West)

ı no tubes or trains to attract the hoi polloi, Battersea West sits smugly hugging the ɛr Thames, happily cut off from the hustle and bustle of the rest of London. However, ı the Imperial Wharf Overground not far away, the commute isn't as bad as it used ɔe and the masses flock—mostly for the spacious floor-to-ceiling glass apartments ı killer river views. Take in a Sunday lunch at **The Prince Albert**.

Nightlife

Barrio • 14 Battersea Sq
The Draft House • 74 Battersea Bridge Road
Le QuecumBar • 42 Battersea High St
The Prince Albert • 85 Albert Bridge Rd
The Woodman • 60 Battersea High St

Post Offices

Battersea Bridge Road • 72 Battersea Bridge Rd
York Road • 583 Battersea Park Rd

Restaurants

• **Ransom's Dock** • 35 Parkgate Rd

Supermarkets

• **Sainsbury's** • 326 Battersea Park Rd

1
2
River Thames
Battersea Power Station
Kirtling Street
Cringle Street
NINE ELMS
Nine Elms Lane
Kirtling St
Millennium Arena
Queenstown Road
A3216
Sopwith Way
A
Battersea Park
PAGE 326
Battersea Park Gasometers
Battersea Dogs Home
Battersea Park Road
A3205
Sleaford Street
Thessaly Road
Savona Street
Prince of Wales Drive
Queen's Circus
Battersea Park
Palmerston Way
Bradmead
Havelock Terrace
Pagden Street
Lockington Road
Gladstone Terrace
St. Joseph's Street
Patcham Terrace
Meath Street
Lurline Gardens
Cupar Road
Stewart's Road
Ascalon Street
Wadhurst Road
Corunna Road
Patmore Street
St. George's Close
Condell Road
Corunna Street
Linford Street
141
Alfreda Street
Strasburg Road
Rawson Street
Ravenet Street
Newtown Street
Southolm Street
Queenstown Road (Battersea)
Ingate Place
B
Queenstown Mews
Silverthorne Road
B224
142
Heathbrook Park
Crichton Street
Westbury Street
Portslade Road
Pensbury Street
Pensbury Place
Wandsworth Road
Clyston Street
Broughton Street
St. Philip Square
Dickens Street
Coleridge Close
Motley Street
0.25 mile
0.25 km
Wandsworth Road

Battersea (East)

odd slice of post-industrial London dominated by the derelict Battersea wer Station, there's naff-all here until someone decides what to do with e old hulk and its surrounding domain. In the meantime, try cycling around arby Battersea Park. **The Mason's Arms** serves a decent beer.

Landmarks

- **Battersea Dogs' Home** • 4 Battersea Park Rd
- **Battersea Park Gasometers** • Queenstown Rd & Prince of Wales Dr
- **Battersea Power Station** • 188 Kirtling St

Libraries

- **Battersea Park Library** • 309 Battersea Park Rd

Nightlife

- **The Mason's Arms** • 169 Battersea Park Rd

Post Offices

- **Battersea Park Road** • 20 Battersea Park Rd

Shopping

- **London Recumbents** • Battersea Park

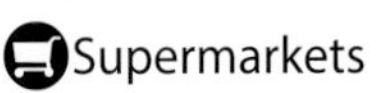

Supermarkets

- **Sainsbury's** • 326 Queenstown Rd

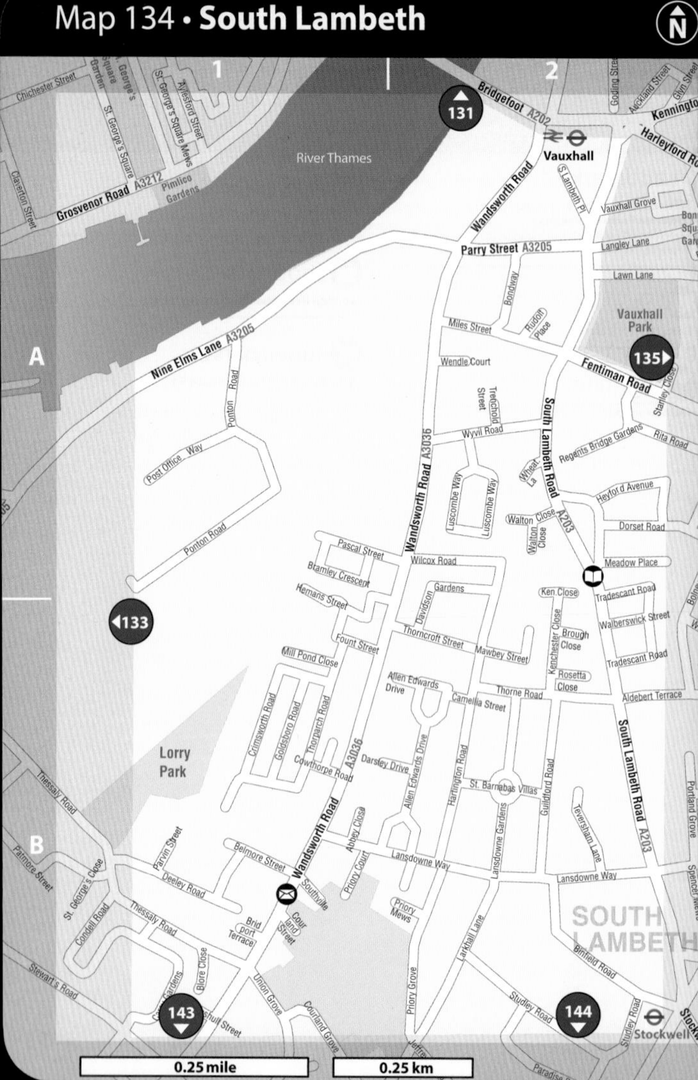

131
133
135
143
144

ɦ an overground, tube, and extensive bus station, Vauxhall's southern counterpart is ɪarkably well connected. But it offers a mixed bag. Gritty backwater estates intermix n middle class townhouses and no-nonsense gay clubs. For pastel de nata like ɔody's business, hit up Little Portugal on South London Road. Bite into a fois gras stie at the **Canton Arms** and wash it down with beer and amateur comedy at **The ʼendish Arms.**

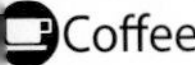

Coffee

Starbucks • 2 S Lambeth Rd

Libraries

South Lambeth Library • 180 S Lambeth Rd

Nightlife

Bar Estrela • 113 S Lambeth Rd
The Battersea Barge • Nine Elms Ln
The Cavendish Arms • 128 Hartington Rd
Fire • 38 Parry St
The Priory Arms • 83 Lansdowne Wy
The Vauxhall Griffin • 8 Wyvil Rd

Post Offices

South Lambeth • 347 Wandsworth Rd

Restaurants

- **A Toca** • 343 Wandsworth Rd
- **Bar Estrela** • 113 S Lambeth Rd
- **Brunswick House** • 30 Wandsworth Rd
- **Canton Arms** • 177 S Lambeth Rd
- **Hot Stuff** • 19 Wilcox Rd
- **O Moinho** • 355 Wandsworth Rd
- **Tia Maria** • 126 S Lambeth Rd

Shopping

- **Fetish Freak** • 76 Bolton Crescent
- **LASSCO** • 30 Wandsworth Rd
- **New Covent Garden Market** • Nine Elms Ln
- **The Nine Elms Sunday Market** • New Covent Garden

Supermarkets

- **Sainsbury's** • 62 Wandsworth Rd

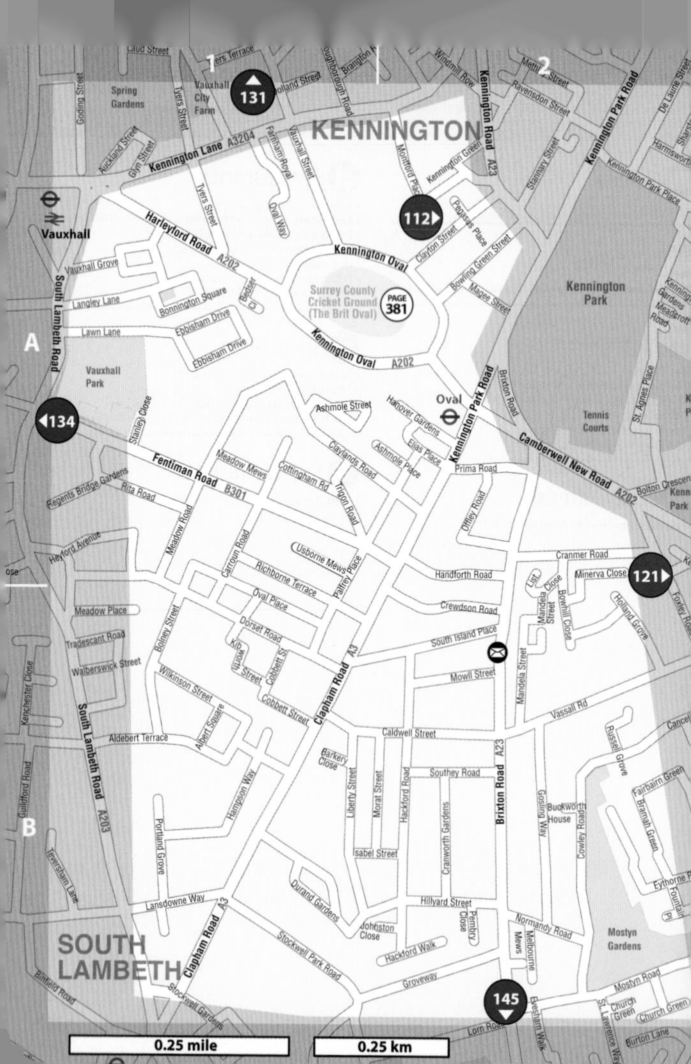

KENNINGTON
SOUTH LAMBETH
Vauxhall
Vauxhall City Farm
Spring Gardens
Vauxhall Park
Kennington Park
Tennis Courts
Surrey County Cricket Ground (The Brit Oval)
PAGE 381
Oval
Mostyn Gardens
Buckworth House
131
112
134
121
145
A
B
1
2
Kennington Lane A3204
Harleyford Road A202
Kennington Oval
Kennington Oval A202
Kennington Road A23
Kennington Park Road
Camberwell New Road A202
South Lambeth Road
South Lambeth Road A203
Fentiman Road B301
Clapham Road A3
Brixton Road A23
Vauxhall Grove
Langley Lane
Lawn Lane
Bonnington Square
Ebbisham Drive
Stanley Close
Regents Bridge Gardens
Rita Road
Meadow Road
Meadow Mews
Heyford Avenue
Meadow Place
Tradescant Road
Walberswick Street
Kenchester Close
Aldebert Terrace
Guildford Road
Teversham Lane
Binfield Road
Stockwell Gardens
Stockwell Park Road
Lansdowne Way
Portland Grove
Hampson Way
Albert Square
Wilkinson Street
Bolney Street
Cobbett Street
Kibworth Street
Dorset Road
Oval Place
Richborne Terrace
Carroun Road
Usborne Mews
Palfrey Place
Trigon Road
Cottingham Rd
Claylands Road
Ashmole Street
Ashmole Place
Hanover Gardens
Elias Place
Prima Road
Offley Road
Handforth Road
Crewdson Road
South Island Place
Mowll Street
Caldwell Street
Southey Road
Barkery Close
Liberty Street
Morat Street
Hackford Road
Cranworth Gardens
Isabel Street
Durand Gardens
Hillyard Street
Pembry Close
Johnston Close
Hackford Walk
Groveway
Lorn Road
Normandy Road
Melbourne Mews
Gosling Way
Cowley Road
Vassall Road
Mandela Street
Mandela Close
Bowhill Close
Minerva Close
Cranmer Road
Holland Grove
Russell Grove
Fairbairn Green
Bramah Green
Eythorne
Fountain Pl
Mostyn Road
Church Green
St. Lawrence Way
Burton Lane
Evesham Walk
Foxley Road
Bolton Crescent
Kennington Park Place
Kennington Gardens
Meadcroft Road
St. Agnes Place
Brixton Road
Harmsworth
De Laune Street
Ravensdon Street
Methley Street
Windmill Row
Kennington Green
Montford Place
Clayton Street
Pegasus Place
Bowling Green Street
Magee Street
Stannary Street
Farmham Royal
Vauxhall Street
Oval Way
Tyers Street
Tyers Terrace
Laud Street
Goding Street
Auckland Street
Glyn Street
Bedser Cl
Holland Street
Loughborough Road
Brangton Road
0.25 mile
0.25 km

h town houses rub shoulders somewhat uneasily with housing estates here, there's no denying the walk from Oval Station can be dodgy, but if you're a of cricket, the presence of the Oval cricket ground more than makes up for /hen there's a match on, the area fills to the brim, but normally it's a modest unimposing neighbourhood. Organic foodies delight in vegan ex-squat **Bonnington Café**.

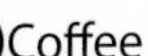

Landmarks

The Oval • Kennington

Coffee

Bonnington Cafe • 11 Vauxhall Grove

Nightlife

The Brown Derby • 336 Kennington Park Rd
The Fentiman Arms • 64 Fentiman Rd

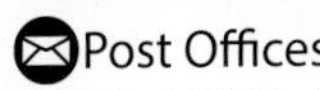

Post Offices

• **Brixton Road** • 82 Brixton Rd

Restaurants

• **Adulis** • 44 Brixton Rd
• **Bonnington Café** • 11 Vauxhall Grove

1
2
A
B
River Thames
Putney Bridge Approach A219
Putney Bridge A219
Prior Bank Gardens
Gonville Street
Station Approach
Ranelagh Gardens
Willow Bank
Embankment
Lower Richmond Road B306
Felsham Road B306
Upper Richmond Road A205
Upper Richmond Road
Putney Bridge Road
Putney High Street A219
Putney Hill A219
Putney
East Putney
PUTNEY
137
Ashlone Road
Festing Road
Rotherwood Road
Gladwyn Road
Bendemeer Road
Spring Passage
Glendarvon Street
Ruvigny Gardens
Farlow Road
Roskell Road
Salvin Road
Henry Jackson Road
Biggs Row
Weiss Road
Ardshiel Cl
Bemish Road
Thames Pl
Waterman Street
Kenilworth Court
Kingsmere Close
Mount Court
Darfur Street
Dryad Street
Bangalore Street
Blackett Street
Charlwood Road
Redgrave Road
Princeton Court
Gwalior Road
The Platt
Mascotte Road
Walkers Place
Weimar Street
Lacy Road
Rossdale Road
Gamlen Road
Carlyle Place
Glegg Place
Cardinal Place
Charlwood Terrace
Lifford Street
Stratford Grove
Clarendon Drive
Spencer Walk
Chelverton Road
Norroy Road
Deodar Road
Brewhouse Lane
Merivale Road
Florian Road
Token Yard
Burstock Road
Atney Road
Montserrat Road
Archway Mews
Esmond Street
Oxford Road
Winthorpe Road
Werter Road
Rockland Road
Wadham Road
Bective Road
Disraeli Road
Carmalt Gardens
Howards Lane
Gwendolen Avenue
Tideswell Road
Ravenna Road
Burston Road
Nursery Close
Ulva Road
Crescent Stables
Grand Ms
Hazlewell Road
St. John's Avenue
Burleigh Place
Ernshaw Place
Keswick Road
Gwendolen Close
Cambalt Road
Cedar Ms
St Simon's Avenue
Cherrywood Drive
Chartfield Sq
Rayners Road
Fairburn Court
Mercier Road
Carlton Drive
Buttermere
Portinscale Road
Askill Drive
Chartfield Avenue
Whitnell Way
Balmoral Close
Winchelsea Close
Rye Walk
Lodge Close
Evenwood Close
Penrith Close
Lytton Grove
Redgate Terrace
Tintern Close
Ardesey Close
Chepstow Close
Clockhouse Place
Westleigh Avenue
0.25 mile
0.25 km

Putney

Putney has a bit of a bipolar personality disorder. On the one side, it's suburban middle England with its rugby and rowing types, on the other, it's increasingly vibrant and hip. The High Street's a bit genteel by day and young-and-up-for-it at night. Try **Ma Goa** for authentic Goan cuisine.

Coffee

- **Artisan Coffee** • 203 Upper Richmond Rd
- **Caffe Nero** • 112 Upper Richmond Rd
- **Costa** • 132 Putney High St
- **Grind** • 79 Lower Richmond Rd
- **Pret A Manger** • 121 Putney High St

Libraries

- **Putney Library** • 5 Disraeli Rd

Movie Theaters

- **Odeon Putney** • 26 Putney High St

Nightlife

- **The Boathouse** • Brewhouse Ln
- **Duke's Head** • 8 Lower Richmond Rd
- **The Jolly Gardeners** • 61 Lacy Rd
- **Star & Garter** • 4 Lower Richmond Rd

Post Offices

- **Putney** • 214 Upper Richmond Rd

Restaurants

- **Ma Goa** • 242 Upper Richmond Rd

Supermarkets

- **Sainsbury's** • 2 Werter Rd
- **Talad Thai** • 320 Upper Richmond Rd
- **Waitrose** • Putney High St & Lacy Rd

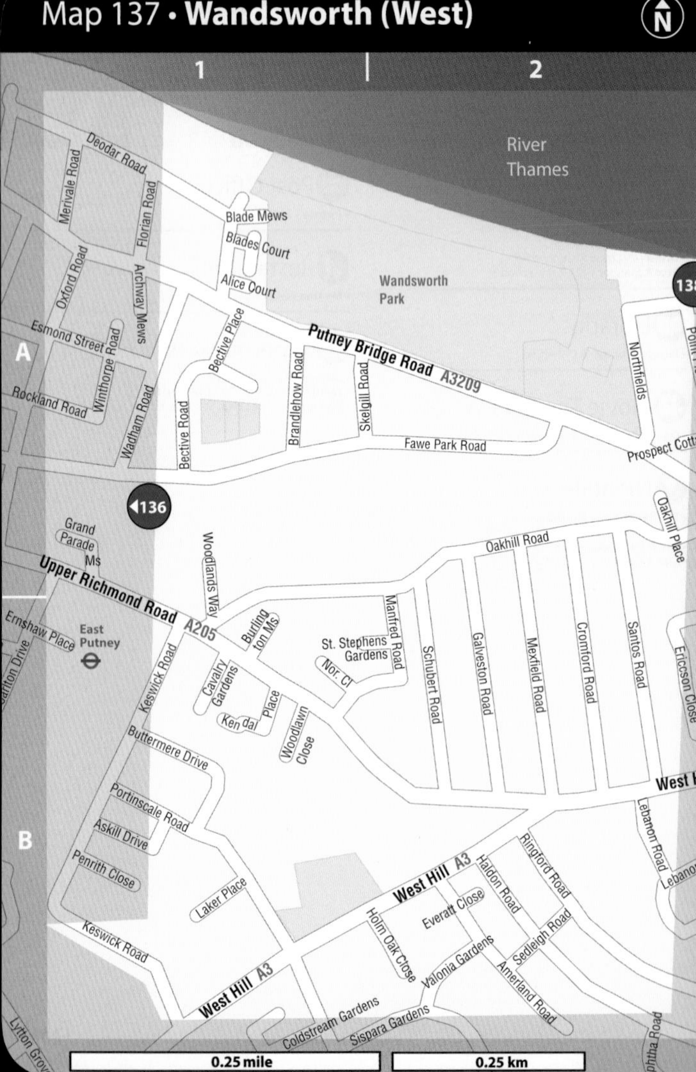
N
1
2
River Thames
Deodar Road
Merivale Road
Florian Road
Blade Mews
Blades Court
Alice Court
Wandsworth Park
Oxford Road
Archway Mews
Esmond Street
Winthorpe Road
Bective Place
Putney Bridge Road A3209
Northfields
A
Rockland Road
Wadham Road
Bective Road
Brandlehow Road
Skelgill Road
Fawe Park Road
Prospect Cott
136
Grand Parade Ms
Woodlands Way
Oakhill Road
Oakhill Place
Upper Richmond Road A205
Burlington Ms
Manfred Road
Ernshaw Place
East Putney
Keswick Road
Cavalry Gardens
St. Stephens Gardens
Nor. Cl
Schubert Road
Galveston Road
Mexfield Road
Cromford Road
Santos Road
Ericcson Close
Kendal Place
Woodlawn Close
Buttermere Drive
West H
Portinscale Road
Lebanon Road
B
Askill Drive
Ringford Road
Penrith Close
West Hill A3
Haldon Road
Laker Place
Everatt Close
Holm Oak Close
Sedleigh Road
Keswick Road
Valonia Gardens
Amerland Road
West Hill A3
Coldstream Gardens
Sispara Gardens
Lytton Grove
0.25 mile
0.25 km

Wandsworth (West)

Dissected by the busy Upper and Lower Richmond Roads, this bit of Wandsworth is a bit lifeless though pleasant enough. The pretty, riverside Wandsworth Park is a huge plus and heaves with locals with the first sniff of sunshine.

Restaurants

- **Miraj** • 123 Putney Bridge Rd
- **Putney Fire Bar & Grill** • 40 Upper Richmond Rd

Map 138 • Wandsworth (Central)

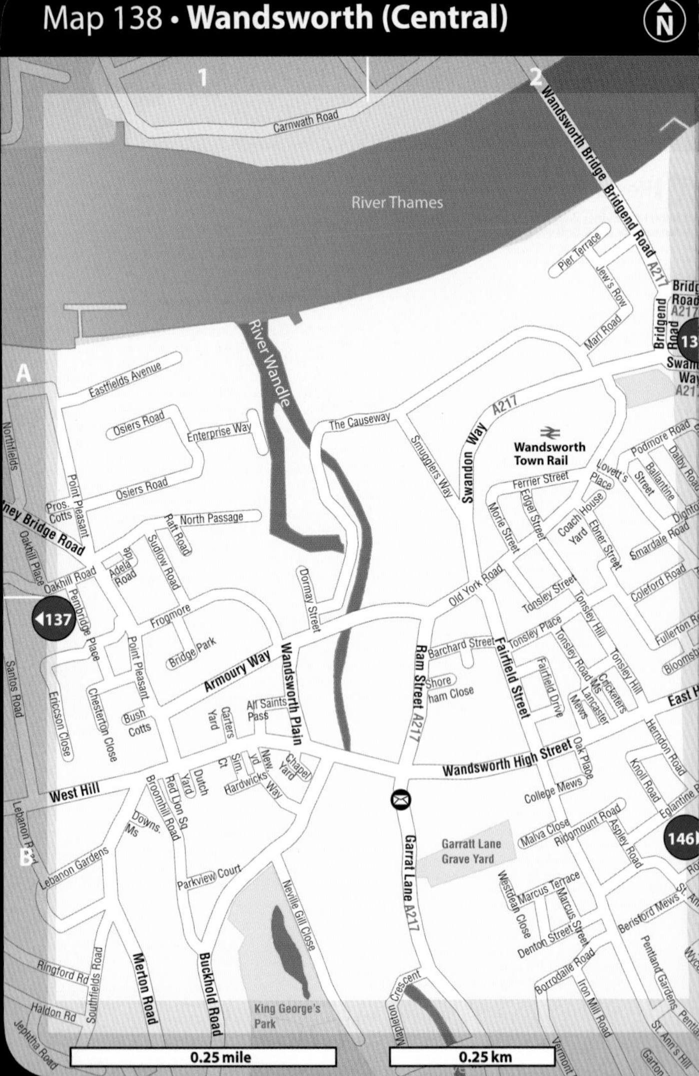

Wandsworth (Central)

s is East Wandsworth's poorer, uglier cousin—and you've got to feel sorry it. It's got a drab shopping centre and a four-lane traffic system brings noise 1 air pollution. On the plus side, plenty of chain stores (Gap, Uniqlo etc.) and **ineworld** make life a little easier. To get away from it all, hibernate in the 1 York Road. For the best Nepalese food in London, hit **Kathmandu Valley**.

Cinemas

Cineworld Wandsworth • Wandsworth High St & Ram St

Coffee

Caffe Nero • Southside Shopping Centre

Nightlife

The Cat's Back • 88 Point Pleasant
GJ's • 89 Garratt Ln
The Queen Adelaide • 35 Putney Bridge Rd

Post Offices

• **Wandsworth** • 1 Arndale Walk

Restaurants

• **Kathmandu Valley** • 5 West Hill

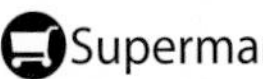

Supermarkets

• **Iceland** • Wandsworth High St & Buckhold Rd
• **Sainsbury's** • 45 Garratt Ln
• **Waitrose** • 66 Wandsworth High St

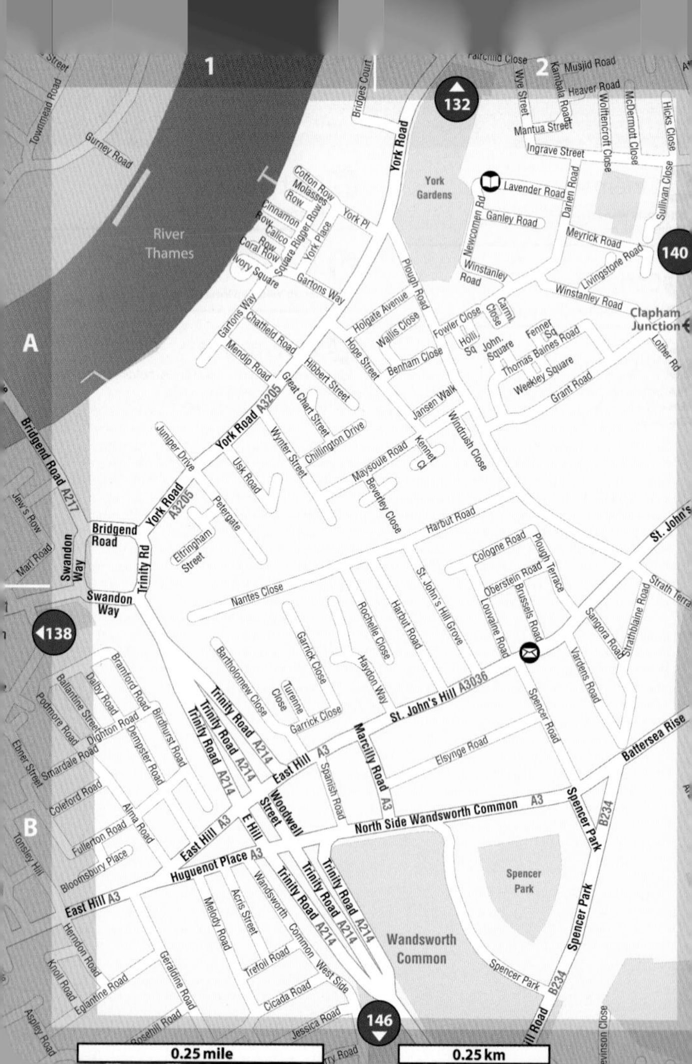

1
2
A
B
132
140
138
146
River Thames
York Gardens
Spencer Park
Wandsworth Common
Clapham Junction
York Road
York Road A3205
Trinity Road A214
East Hill A3
North Side Wandsworth Common A3
St. John's Hill A3036
Battersea Rise
Spencer Park B234
Bridgend Road A217
Swandon Way
Huguenot Place A3
Marcilly Road A3
Lavender Road
Plough Road
Harbut Road
0.25 mile
0.25 km

Wandsworth (East)

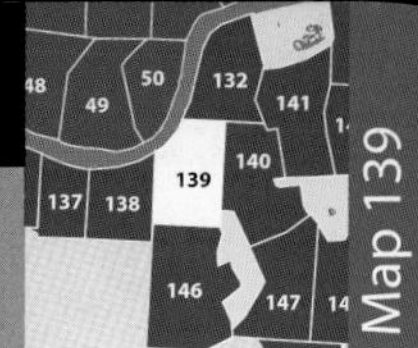

ith London's new Overground network and Clapham Junction on its doorstep, this corner Wandsworth, including what locals call 'the Toast Rack' on East Hill, is becoming more entrified everyday. You'll hear your share of 'rah's at **Powder Keg Diplomacy**, with its oscale gastro fare and nod to colonial Britain, while yummy mummies stuff their cake oles at **Cake Boy** and practice their French at **Gazette**. Stay true to the neighbourhood's ots with a less than picturesque view of the Thames at **The Waterfront**.

Coffee

- **Birdhouse** • 123 St John's Hill
- **Caffe Nero** • Southside Shopping Centre
- **Story Coffee** • 115 St John's Hill

Libraries

- **York Gardens Library** • 34 Lavender Rd

Nightlife

- **Powder Keg Diplomacy** • 147 St Johns Hill
- **The Waterfront** • Juniper Dr

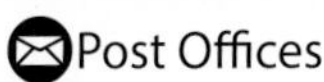

Post Offices

- **St Johns Hill** • 7 St John's Hill

Restaurants

- **Gazette** • 79 Chatfield Rd

Shopping

- **Cake Boy** • 2 Kingfisher House, Battersea Reach

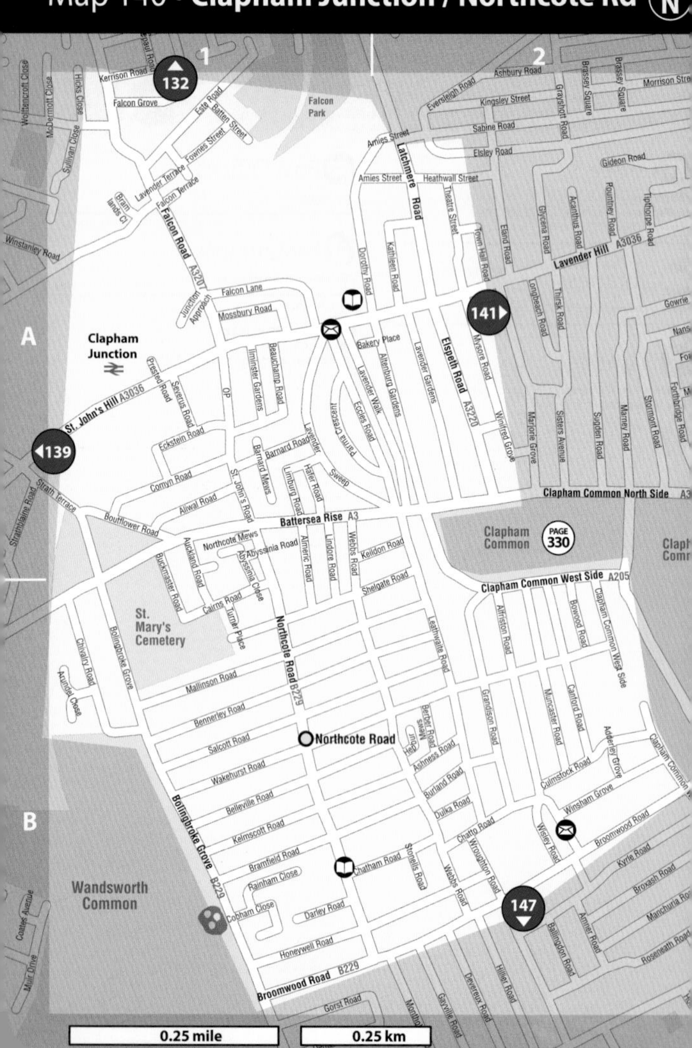
N
1
2
A
B
132
139
141
147
PAGE 330
Clapham Junction
Falcon Park
Clapham Common
St. Mary's Cemetery
Wandsworth Common
Northcote Road
Kerrison Road
Falcon Grove
Este Road
Batten Street
Fownes Street
Lavender Terrace
Falcon Terrace
Bramlands Cl
Falcon Road
A3207
Winstanley Road
Wolftencroft Close
McDermott Close
Hicks Close
Sullivan Close
Ashbury Road
Eversleigh Road
Kingsley Street
Sabine Road
Elsley Road
Grayshott Road
Brassey Square
Morrison Street
Gideon Road
Amies Street
Latchmere Road
Heathwall Street
Theatre Street
Dorothy Road
Kathleen Road
Town Hall Road
Eland Road
Glycena Road
Acanthus Road
Pountney Road
Tipthorpe Road
Lavender Hill
A3036
Falcon Lane
Junction Approach
Mossbury Road
Bakery Place
Longbeach Road
Thirsk Road
Gowrie
Mysore Road
Elspeth Road
A3220
Lavender Gardens
Altenburg Gardens
Lavender Walk
Eccles Road
Parma Crescent
Beauchamp Road
Ilminster Gardens
OP
Severus Road
Prested Road
St. John's Hill
A3036
Eckstein Road
Barnard Road
Barnard Mews
Lavender Sweep
Limburg Road
Hafer Road
Winifred Grove
Marjorie Grove
Sisters Avenue
Sugden Road
Marney Road
Stormont Road
Forthbridge Road
Comyn Road
Aliwal Road
St. John's Road
Strath Terrace
Strathblaine Road
Boutflower Road
Battersea Rise
A3
Clapham Common North Side
Northcote Mews
Abyssinia Road
Abyssinia Close
Almeric Road
Lindore Road
Webbs Road
Keildon Road
Shelgate Road
Auckland Road
Buckmaster Road
Cairns Road
Turner Place
Clapham Common West Side
A205
Alfriston Road
Bowood Road
Leathwaite Road
Chivalry Road
Arundel Close
Bolingbroke Grove
Mallinson Road
Bennerley Road
Northcote Road
B229
Salcott Road
Wakehurst Road
Belleville Road
Kelmscott Road
Bramfield Road
Rainham Close
Cobham Close
Darley Road
Honeywell Road
Broomwood Road
Gorst Road
Grandison Road
Muncaster Road
Canford Road
Adderley Grove
Berber Road
Hebdon Road
Ashness Road
Burland Road
Dulka Road
Chatto Road
Wroughton Road
Stonells Road
Chatham Road
Webbs Road
Culmstock Road
Winsham Grove
Wisley Road
Broomwood Road
Kyrle Road
Broxash Road
Manchuria Road
Roseneath Road
Amner Road
Ballingdon Road
Hillier Road
Devereux Road
Gayville Road
Coalecroft Avenue
Muir Drive
0.25 mile
0.25 km

Clapham Junction / Northcote Rd

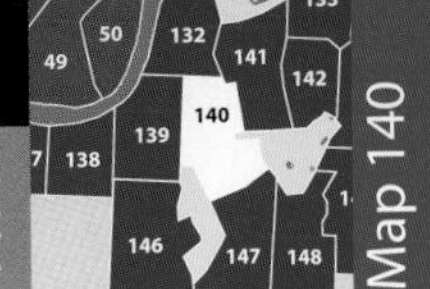

have a newfound sense of respect for Clapham Junction after it rose like a termined phoenix from the ashes of the summer 2011 riots. Suffering extensive vastation from looters, the neighbourhood dusted itself off with help of volunteers m across the capital and was back in business almost instantly. Seeing the **Party perstores** open again after nearly burning to the ground is a particular sight for sore es. All fancy dress party goers can breathe a sigh of relief.

Coffee

- **Caffe Nero** • 20 St John's Rd
- **Caffe Nero** • 21 Battersea Rise

Landmarks

- **Northcote Road** • Northcote Rd

Libraries

- **Battersea Library** • 265 Lavender Hill
- **Northcote Library** • 155 Northcote Rd

Nightlife

- **Adventure Bar and Lounge** • 91 Battersea Rise
- **B@1 Cocktail Bar** • 85 Battersea Rise
- **Humble Grape** • 2 Battersea Rise

Post Offices

- **Alfriston Road** • 99 Alfriston Rd
- **Battersea** • 202 Lavender Hill

Restaurants

- **Gail's Bread** • 64 Northcote Rd
- **Jack's At The Junction** • 252 Lavender Hill
- **Mien Tay** • 180 Lavender Hill
- **Parisienne** • 225 Lavender Hill
- **Pizza Metro** • 64 Battersea Rise

Shopping

- **Huttons** • 29 Northcote Rd
- **Party Superstores** • 268 Lavender Hill
- **Space NK Apothecary** • 46 Northcote Rd
- **Sweaty Betty** • 136 Northcote Rd
- **TK Maxx** • St John's Rd & Barnard Rd
- **TRAID** • 28 St John's Rd
- **Vintage Market Place** • Battersea Arts Centre
- **Whole Foods Market** • 305 Lavender Hill

Supermarkets

- **ASDA** • 204 Lavender Hill
- **Whole Foods Market** • 305 Lavender Hill
- **Sainsbury's** • Clapham Junction Shopping Centre

ɔart from the occasional house party, few have reason to go to Battersea ·uth. You either live there, congratulating yourself on your nice Victorian nversion, or you pass through on the way to Clapham or one of the livelier ts of Battersea. The 'action' happens around Lavender Hill.

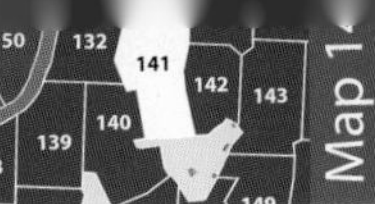

Coffee

- **Captain Corelli** • 132 Battersea Park Rd

Nightlife

- **Lost Society** • 339 Battersea Park Rd

Shopping

- **Battersea Car Boot Sale** • 401 Battersea Park Rd
- **Comet Miniatures** • 44 Lavender Hill
- **Get A Grip Bicycle Workshop** • 19 Lavender Hill

Town
N
1
2
A
B
133
141
143
PAGE 330
Queenstown Road
A3216
Broughton Street
St. Philip Sq
Prairie Street
Emu Road
Ingelow Road
St. Philip Street
Tennyson Street
Montefiore Street
Gambetta Street
Thackeray Road
Bewick Street
Silverthorne Road
Dickens Street
Froude Street
Coleridge Close
Robertson Street
St. Rule Street
Motley Street
Heathbrook Park
Crichton St
Westbury Street
Portslade Road
Pensbury Place
Brayburne Avenue
Heath Road
B224
Wandsworth Road
St. Paul's Churchyard
Netherford Road
Turret Grove
Stone Close
Iveley Road
Stephen Place
Charles Barry Close
North Street
Rozel Road
Rash. Street
Peardon Street
Daley Way
Keith Connor Close
Bev Call. Way Close
Daley Thompson
Newby Street
Heather Close
Heather Cl
Robertson Street
Stanley Grove
Caroline Place
Dunston Road
Evesham Way
Audley Close
Beaufoy Road
Basnett Road
Lavender Hill A3036
Willard Street
Mackay Road
Redwood Mews
Lambourn Road
Hannington Road
Broadhinton Road
Bobbin Close
Lilleshall Road
Charlotte Row
Floris Place
Rectory Grove
Fitzwilliam Road
Liston Road
Offerton
Abberley Mews
Turn chapel Mews
Garfield Mews
Garfield Road
Crosland Place
CLAPHAM
Cedars Road
Victoria Rise
Macaulay Road
Orlando Road
Lydon Road
Sycamore Ms
Scout Lane
Prin. Cl
Slater Mews
Grafton Square
Old Town
Downers Cottages
The Polygon
The Pavement B303
B224 The Pavement
Freke Road
Taybridge Road
Wixs Lane
Lyncott Crescent
Wilderness Mews
Macaulay Square
The Chase
Clapham Common
Cock Pond
Willoughby Mews
Cedars Mews
Victoria Mews
Barker Mews
Clapham Common North Side B303
Clapham Common North Side A3
Jedburgh Street
Long Road A3
Bromell's Road
Clapham Common
0.25 mile
0.25 km

The more genteel side of Clapham, Old Town hosts some fine restaurants (**Trinity**), good watering-holes **(The Prince of Wales)**, and one of London's best butchers (**Moen's**), all bordered by the green of Clapham Common. If you need more, head to Queenstown Road for further classy dining establishments.

Coffee

- **Maiolica Cafè** • 789 Wandsworth Rd
- **Starbucks** • 40 Old Town

Libraries

- **Clapham Library** • 1 Clapham Common North Side

Nightlife

- **Prince of Wales** • 38 Clapham Old Town
- **The Sun** • 47 Old Town

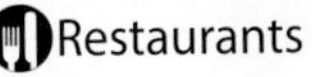

Restaurants

- **Nardullis Ice Cream** • 29 The Pavement
- **The Sun** • 47 Old Town
- **Trinity** • 4 The Polygon

Shopping

- **Cult Furniture** • 811 Wandsworth Rd
- **M. Moen & Sons** • 24 The Pavement
- **Puppet Planet** • 787 Wandsworth Rd

Supermarkets

- **Sainsbury's** • 646 Wandsworth Rd

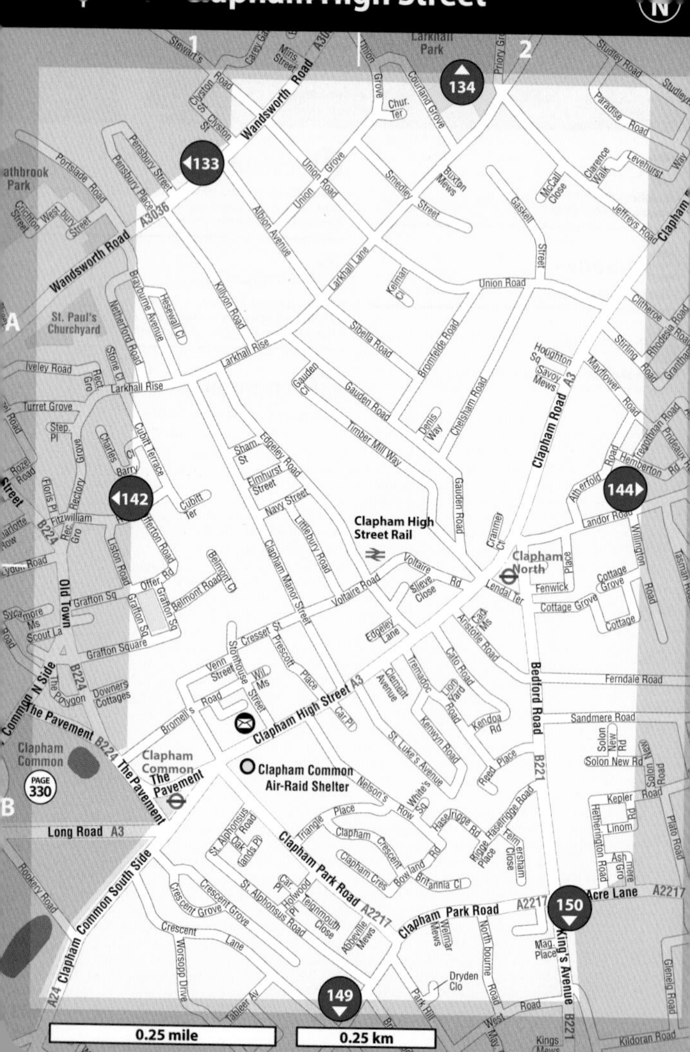

1
2
A
B
Larkhall Park
134
133
142
144
150
149
PAGE 330
Stewart's Road
Mins. Street
A3036
Clyston Road
Clyston St
Wandsworth Road
Grove
Chur. Ter
Courland Grove
Priory Gro
Studley Road
Paradise Road
Clarence Walk
Levehurst Way
Jeffreys Road
Clapham Road
McCall Close
Gaskell Street
Buxton Mews
Smedley Street
Union Grove
Union Road
Albion Avenue
Larkhall Lane
Kelman Cl
Union Road
Pensbury Street
Pensbury Place
Portslade Road
Crichton Street
Westbury Street
Wandsworth Road
A3036
St. Paul's Churchyard
Brayburne Avenue
Hesewall Cl
Netherford Road
Killyon Road
Larkhall Rise
Sibella Road
Bromfelde Road
Clitheroe Road
Rhodesia Road
Stirling Road
Grantham
Mayflower Road
Houghton Sq
Savoy Mews
Clapham Road A3
Chelsham Road
Denis Way
Iveley Road
Rect. Gro
Stone Cl
Larkhall Rise
Gauden Cl
Gauden Road
Timber Mill Way
Turret Grove
Step. Pl
Charles Cl
Cubitt Terrace
Barry
Sham. St
Edgeley Road
Elmhurst Street
Navy Street
Rozel Road
Floris Pl
Rectory Grove
Cubitt Ter
Littlebury Road
Clapham High Street Rail
Gauden Road
Cranmer Ct
Trevithan Road
Prideaux Rd
Hemberton Rd
Atherfold Road
Landor Road
Street
Fitzwilliam
B224
Rec. Gro
Liston Road
Offerton Road
Belmont Cl
Clapham Manor Street
Voltaire Rd
Voltaire Road
Sleeve Close
Clapham North
Lendal Ter
Place
Fenwick
Willington Road
Tasman Road
Cottage Grove
Cottage Grove
Cottage
Old Town
Grafton Sq
Offer. Rd
Grafton Sq
Belmont Road
Grafton Sq
Sycamore Ms
Scout La
Grafton Square
Cresset St
Stonhouse Street
Prescott Place
Edgeley Lane
Cadi Ms
Aristotle Road
Common N Side
B224
The Polygon
Downers Cottages
Venn Street
Road
Wil. Ms
Clapham High Street A3
Car Pl
Clement Avenue
Tremadoc Road
Cato Road
Lion Yard
Kenwyn Road
Kendoa Rd
Bedford Road
Ferndale Road
Sandmere Road
Solon New Rd
Solon New Rd
Solon New Road
The Pavement B224
Bromell's Road
Clapham Common
Clapham Common
The Pavement
The Pavement
Clapham Common Air-Raid Shelter
St. Luke's Avenue
Reed Place
B221
Nelson's Row
White's Sq
Haselrigge Rd
Haselrigge Road
Ridge Place
Fenn Close
Elmhurst
Kepler Rd
Hetherington Road
Linom
Ash Gro
Plato Road
Long Road A3
Triangle Place
Clapham Crescent
Clapham Cres
Bowland Rd
Britannia Cl
St. Alphonsus Road
Oaklands Pl
Clapham Park Road A2217
Rookery Road
Clapham Common South Side
Crescent Grove
Crescent Grove
St. Alphonsus Road
Car. Pl
Holwood Pl
Teignmouth Close
Abbeville Mews
Clapham Park Road
A2217
Acre Lane
A2217
Weimar Mews
Northbourne Road
Mag. Place
King's Avenue
Crescent Lane
Worsopp Drive
Tableer Av
Dryden Clo
Park Hill
Road
West
Glenelg Road
A24
B221
Kings Mews
Kildoran Road
0.25 mile
0.25 km

Clapham High Street

Clapham is a microcosm of Cath Kidston mummies and their token gay best friends—watch them jog and brunch around the common in all weather. Whatever you do, do not—we repeat, DO NOT—set foot in **Infernos.** We will find out and we will judge you.

Cinemas

- **Clapham Picturehouse** • 76 Venn St

Coffee

- **The Black Lab** • 18 Clapham Common South Side
- **Brickwood** • 16 Clapham Common South Side
- **Café Delight** • 19 Clapham High St
- **Caffe Nero** • 186 Clapham High St

Landmarks

- **Clapham Common Air-Raid Shelter** • Clapham High St

Nightlife

- **The Alexandra** • 14 Clapham Common South Side
- **Bread & Roses** • 68 Clapham Manor St
- **The Clapham North** • 409 Clapham Rd
- **The Coach and Horses** • 173 Clapham Park Rd
- **The Falcon** • 33 Bedford Rd
- **Infernos** • 146 Clapham High St
- **Inn Clapham** • 15 The Pavement
- **The Railway** • 18 Clapham High St
- **Two Brewers** • 114 Clapham High St

Post Offices

- **Clapham Common** • 161 Clapham High St

Restaurants

- **Brickwood** • 16 Clapham Common South Side
- **The Dairy** • 15 The Pavement
- **The Pepper Tree** • 19 Clapham Common South Side
- **Roti Joupa** • 12 Clapham High St
- **San Marco Pizzeria** • 126 Clapham High St
- **Tsunami** • 5 Voltaire Rd

Shopping

- **Apex Cycles** • 40 Clapham High St
- **Esca** • 160 Clapham High St
- **M. Moen & Sons** • 24 The Pavement
- **Today's Living Health Store** • 92 Clapham High St

Supermarkets

- **Iceland** • 4 The Pavement
- **Sainsbury's** • 133 Clapham High St
- **Sainsbury's** • 33 Clapham High St

1
2
A
B
134
143
145
150
Larkhall Park
Stockwell
Slade Gardens
Brixton
Brixton Market
Electric Ave
Electric Lane
Courtland Grove
Priory Grove
Binfield Road
South Lambeth Road
Lansdowne Way
A3
Clapham Road
Durand Gardens
Liberty Street
Johnston Close
Hackford
Grove
Buxton Mews
Smedley Street
Gaskell Street
McCall Close
Clarence Walk
Studley Road
Paradise Road
Levehurst Way
Clapham High Street
Stockwell Terrace
Stockwell Gardens
Stockwell Road
A203
St. Michael's Road
St. Martin's Road
Stockwell Park Crescent
Stockwell Park Road
Lorn Road
Jeffreys Road
Union Road
Chelsham Road
Lingham Street
Grantham Road
Crossford Street
Burnley Road
Irving Grove
Stockwell Lane
Park View Mews
Ingle. St
Robsart St
Gdns
Lidcote
Clitheroe Road
Rhodesia Road
Savoy Mews
Mayflower Road
Sidney Road
Aytoun Place
Aytoun Road
Edithna Street
Kimberley Road
Kay Road
Landor Road
Broomgrove Road
Stockwell Green
Atherfold Road
Tregothnan Road
Prideaux Road
Arlesford Road
Argyll Close
Moat Place
Winans Walk
Nealden Street
Combermere Road
Burgoyne Rd
Romero Close
Rumsey Road
Benedict Road
Fenwick Place
B221
Bedford Road
Cottage Grove
Willington Road
Tasman Road
Andalus Road
Hubert Grove
Hargwyne Street
Mordaunt Street
Dalyell Road
Stansfield Road
Chantrey Road
Gateley Road
Stockwell Park Walk
St. John's
Stockwell Avenue
Astoria Walk
Brixton Road
Western Road
Pulross Road
Bellefields Road
Canterbury Crescent
Ferndale Road
Sandmere Road
Dolman Street
Glendall Street
Bythorn Street
Beehive Place
Solon New Road
Solon New Rd
Medwin Street
Ducie Street
Tintern Street
Nursery Road
Dorrell Place
Popes Road
Brixton Station Road
Kepler Road
Santley Street
Shannon Grove
Tunstall Road
Bernay's Grove
Atlantic Road
Hetherington Road
Ashmere Grove
Plato Road
Solon Road
Corrance Road
Ballater Road
Raeburn Street
Concanon Road
Marlborough Ms
Belvedere Place
Bucknell Close
Trinity Gardens
Brighton Terrace
Valentia Place
Coldharbour Lane
A2217
Acre Lane
Horseshoe Mews
Regis Place
Porden Road
Buckner Road
Brixton Hill
A23
Rushcroft Road
Vining Street
Saltoun Road
Baytree Road
Kellett Road
Sudbourne Road
Glenelg Road
0.25 mile
0.25 km

Stockwell / Brixton (West)

up the roof of **Brixton Market** on Thursday, Friday, and Saturday nights and erneath you will find rows of arcades teaming with all species of hipster. After years lmost being cool, this microcosmic neighbourhood beneath the train tracks has cially earned Brixton the title of hippest place in town.

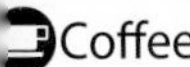

Coffee

Federation Coffee • 77–78 Brixton Village Market

Landmarks

Brixton Market • Electric Ave & Electric Ln
Brixton Village Market • Coldharbour Ln
Electric Avenue • Electric Ave

Nightlife

The Duke of Edinburgh • 204 Ferndale Rd
Marquis of Lorne • 49 Dalyell Rd
The Prince of Wales • 469 Brixton Rd
The Queen's Head • 144 Stockwell Rd
Seven at Brixton • 7 Market Row
The Swan • 215 Clapham Rd

Post Offices

Stockwell • 225 Clapham Rd

Restaurants

- **Agile Rabbit** • 24–25 Coldharbour Ln
- **Brixton Cornercopia** • 65 Coldharbour Ln
- **Falafel Van** • Station Rd
- **Honest Burgers** • 12 Brixton Village
- **Jeff the Chef** • Station Rd
- **Mama Lan** • 18 Brixton Village Market
- **SW9 Bar Cafe** • 11 Dorrell Pl

Shopping

- **A&C Co Continental Grocers** • 3 Atlantic Rd
- **Funchal Bakery** • 141–143 Stockwell Rd
- **The Old Post Office Bakery** • 76 Landor Rd

Supermarkets

- **Iceland** • 441 Brixton Rd
- **Iceland** • 314 Clapham Rd
- **Sainsbury's** • 425 Brixton Rd
- **Tesco** • 330 Brixton Rd

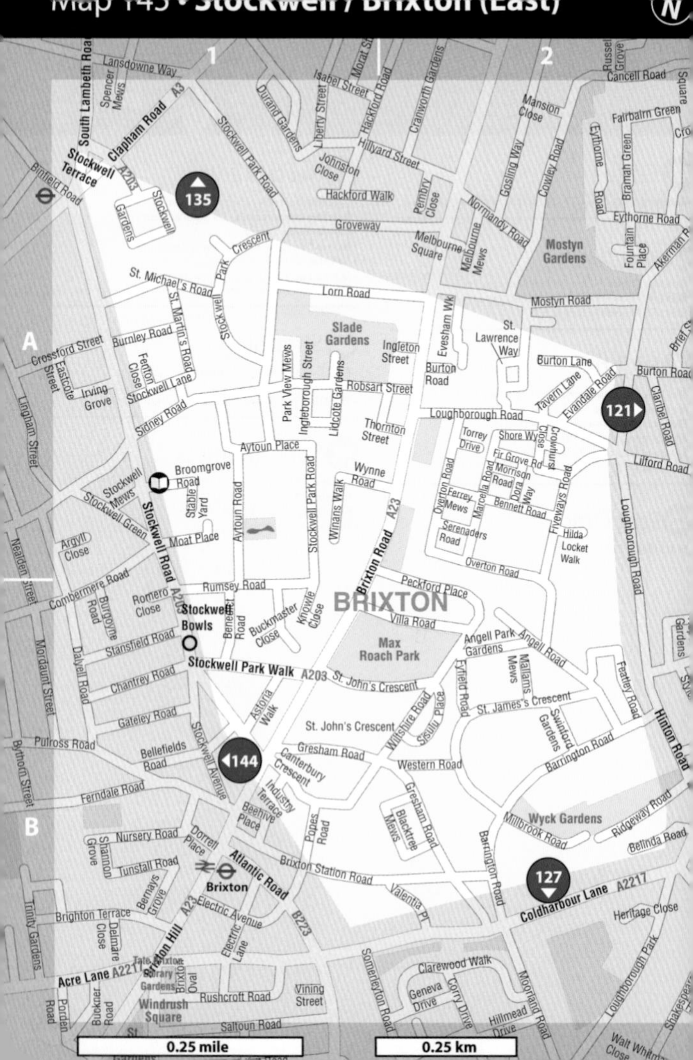

Map 143 • Stockwell / Brixton (East)
N
1
2
A
B
135
121
144
127
BRIXTON
Lansdowne Way
South Lambeth Road
Spencer Mews
Clapham Road
A3
Stockwell Terrace
A203
Binfield Road
Stockwell Gardens
Stockwell Park Road
Durand Gardens
Isabel Street
Morat St
Liberty Street
Hackford Road
Cranworth Gardens
Hillyard Street
Johnston Close
Hackford Walk
Pembry Close
Mansion Close
Gosling Way
Cowley Road
Russell Grove
Cancell Road
Square
Fairbairn Green
Eythorne Road
Bramah Green
Eythorne Road
Fountain Place
Akerman Road
Mostyn Gardens
Normandy Road
Melbourne Mews
Melbourne Square
Groveway
Stockwell Park Crescent
St. Michael's Road
St. Martin's Road
Lorn Road
Mostyn Road
Slade Gardens
Ingleton Street
Evesham Wk
Burton Road
St. Lawrence Way
Burton Lane
Burton Road
Tavern Lane
Evandale Road
Claribel Road
Crossford Street
Burnley Road
Fenton Close
Stockwell Lane
Eastcote Street
Irving Grove
Sidney Road
Lingham Street
Park View Mews
Ingleborough Street
Lidcote Gardens
Robsart Street
Thornton Street
Loughborough Road
Torrey Drive
Shore Way
Crowhurst Close
Fir Grove Rd
Morrison Road
Dora Way
Lilford Road
Aytoun Place
Wynne Road
Broomgrove Road
Stable Yard
Stockwell Mews
Stockwell Green
Stockwell Road
Aytoun Road
Stockwell Park Road
Winans Walk
A23
Overton Road
Ferrey Mews
Marcella Road
Bennett Road
Fiveways Road
Loughborough Road
Serenaders Road
Hilda Lockett Walk
Overton Road
Argyll Close
Moat Place
Nealden Street
Brixton Road
Peckford Place
Combermere Road
Burgoyne Road
Romero Close
Stockwell Bowls
Rumsey Road
Benedict Road
Buckmaster Close
Knowle Close
Villa Road
Max Roach Park
Angell Park Gardens
Angell Road
Gardens
Stansfield Road
Dalyell Road
Mordaunt Street
Chantrey Road
Stockwell Park Walk
A203
St. John's Crescent
Eythfield Road
Mallams Mews
Featley Road
Gateley Road
Astoria Walk
Wiltshire Road
Sisulu Place
St. James's Crescent
Swinford Gardens
Hinton Road
Pulross Road
Stockwell Avenue
St. John's Crescent
Gresham Road
Western Road
Barrington Road
Bellefields Road
Canterbury Crescent
Bythorn Street
Ferndale Road
Industry Terrace
Beehive Place
Gresham Road
Blacktree Mews
Wyck Gardens
Millbrook Road
Ridgeway Road
Belinda Road
Nursery Road
Shannon Grove
Dorrell Place
Popes Road
Barrington Road
Tunstall Road
Atlantic Road
Brixton Station Road
Brixton
Bernays Grove
Valentia Pl
Coldharbour Lane
A2217
Heritage Close
Trinity Gardens
Brighton Terrace
Delmare Close
Electric Avenue
B223
Brixton Hill
Electric Lane
Loughborough Park
Tate Brixton Library Gardens
Brixton Oval
Somerleyton Road
Clarewood Walk
Geneva Drive
Corry Drive
Moorland Road
Acre Lane
A2217
Windrush Square
Rushcroft Road
Vining Street
Hillmead Drive
Porden Road
Buckner Road
Saltoun Road
Shakespeare
Walt Whitman Close
0.25 mile
0.25 km

Stockwell / Brixton (East)

ngs have changed a bit since The Clash sang 'The Guns of Brixton' in '79 and e riots were a regular occurrence. While the middle classes have infiltrated ıst parts of Brixton, this neighbourhood still retains a defiant edge. Community rit and close-knit neighbourhoods take precedence over trendy bars and pricey taurants. Live music rules here; the legendary **Brixton Academy** still draws the ·des, while **Jamm** offers an eclectic and worthy alternative.

Landmarks

Stockwell Bowls • Stockwell Rd & Stockwell Park Walk

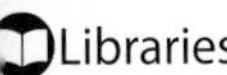

Libraries

Anti-Slavery International Library • Broomgrove Rd

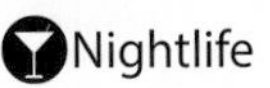

Nightlife

• **Brixton Academy** • 211 Stockwell Rd
• **Jamm** • 261 Brixton Rd

1
2
A
B
138
139
147
Wandsworth Common
Wandsworth Common
Wandsworth Common
Wandsworth Common
Wandsworth Cemetery
Magdalen Park Tennis Club
Central London Golf Centre
Earlsfield Rail
Trinity Road A214
Windmill Road
Earlsfield Road B234
Burntwood Lane B229
Magdalen Road
St. Ann's Hill
Heathfield Road
Heathfield Square
Heathfield Avenue
Heathfield Gardens
John Archer Way
Nevinson Close
Stott Close
Coates Avenue
Muir Drive
Fitzhugh Grove
Dorlcote Road
Henderson Road
Baskerville Road
Nicosia Road
Patten Road
Routh Road
Lyford Road
Burcote Road
Multon Road
Loxley Road
Frewin Road
Herondale Avenue
Burntwood Grange Road
Burntwood Close
Collamore Avenue
Lyminge Gardens
Marham Gardens
Bennett Rd
Gunners Road
Sandgate Lane
Beechcroft Road
St. Hildas Close
St. Peters Close
St. Edmunds Close
Titchwell Road
Ellerton Road
Tilehurst Road
Godley Road
Fieldview
Brightman Road
Openview
Headington Road
Leckford Road
Aldrich Terrace
Lidiard Road
Dawnay Road
Victoria Mews
Swaby Road
Tranmere Road
Townsend Mews
St. Andrew's Court
Wayneflete Street
Isis Street
Skelbrook Street
Summerley Street
Smiths Yard
Groton Road
Thornsett Road
Heritage Place
Garratt Lane
Capern Road
Cargill Road
Willow Tree Close
Vanderbilt Road
Atheldene Road
Farlton Road
Oakshaw Road
Waverton Road
Wilna Road
Inman Road
Mountbatten Mews
Winfrith Road
Dingwall Road
Wells Place
Whitehead Close
Shire Place
Kingham Close
Brocklebank Road
Bucharest Road
Bassingham Road
Swaffield Road
Aslett Street
Crealock Street
Daphne Street
Garton Place
Alfarthing Lane
St. Ann's Park Road
Cader Road
Galesbury Road
Jeypore Road
Barmouth Road
Swanage Road
Westover Road
Killarney Road
Crieff Road
Marshall Close
Pentland Street
Pentland Gardens
Wycombe Place
Berisford Mews
St. Ann's Crescent
Dault Road
Cicada Road
Rosehill Road
Geraldine Road
Eglantine Road
Knoll Road
Trefoil Road
Cicada Road
Jessica Road
Quarry Road
Melody Road
Wandsworth Common West Side
Kershaw Close
Groom Crescent
Strickland Row
Wilde Place
Alma Terrace
Carmichael Mews
Spencer Park
A214
A214 A3
0.25 mile
0.25 km

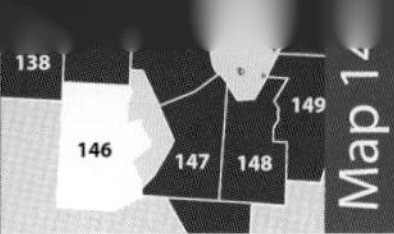

eepy little Earlsfield tends to mind its own business. It's a pretty sedate kind place, slightly cut off by the lack of a tube stop. The well-heeled locals seem ppy enough and make the most of what's on offer. Try **Amaranth** for great oodles.

Coffee

- **Caffe Nero** • 529 Garratt Ln

Libraries

- **Alvering Library** • 2 Allfarthing Ln
- **Earlsfield Library** • 276 Magdalen Rd

Nightlife

- **Halfway House** • 521 Garratt Ln
- **Le Gothique** • Windmill Rd & John Archer Wy

Restaurants

- **Cafe Amaranth** • 346 Garratt Ln

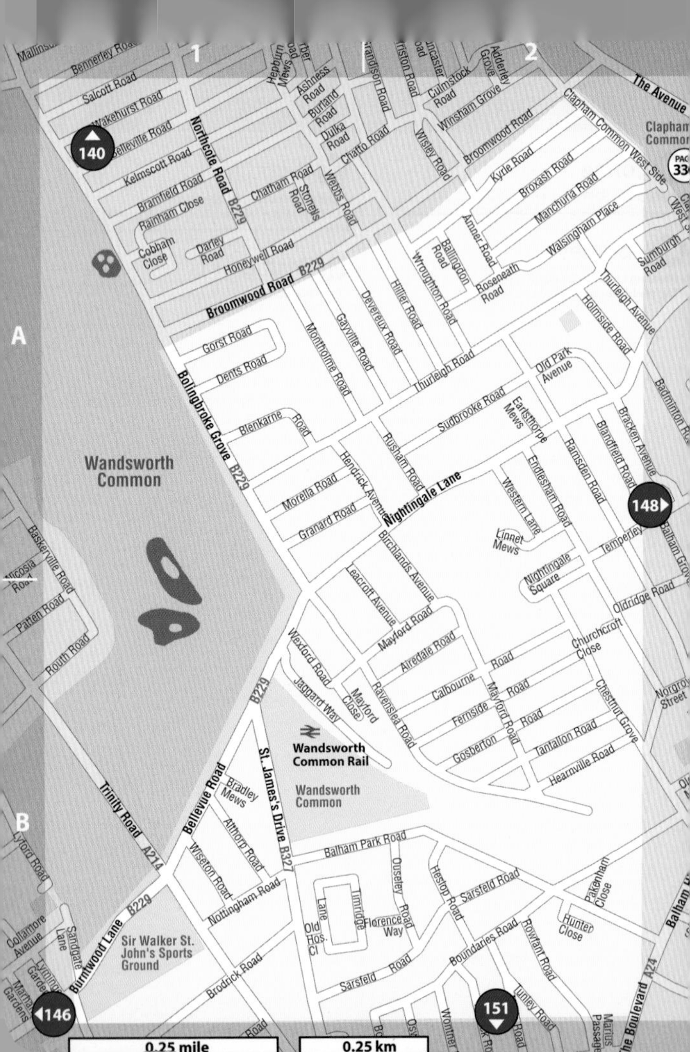
1
2
A
B
Bennerley Road
Salcott Road
Wakehurst Road
Belleville Road
Kelmscott Road
Bramfield Road
Rainham Close
Cobham Close
Darley Road
Honeywell Road
Northcote Road B229
Hepburn Mews
Ashness Road
Burland Road
Dulka Road
Chatham Road
Stonells Road
Webbs Road
Chatto Road
Wisley Road
Culmstock Road
Winsham Grove
Adderley Grove
Broomwood Road
Clapham Common West Side
The Avenue
Clapham Common
Kyrle Road
Broxash Road
Manchuria Road
Walsingham Place
Amner Road
Ballingdon Road
Roseneath Road
Sumburgh Road
Thurleigh Avenue
Holmside Road
Broomwood Road B229
Montholme Road
Gayville Road
Devereux Road
Hillier Road
Wroughton Road
Thurleigh Road
Old Park Avenue
Gorst Road
Dents Road
Bolingbroke Grove B229
Blenkarne Road
Sudbrooke Road
Earlsthorpe Mews
Badminton Road
Bracken Avenue
Blandfield Road
Ramsden Road
Endlesham Road
Western Lane
Rusham Road
Hendrick Avenue
Nightingale Lane
Morella Road
Granard Road
Wandsworth Common
148
140
Linnet Mews
Temperley
Balham Grove
Nightingale Square
Oldridge Road
Birchlands Avenue
Leacroft Avenue
Mayford Road
Airedale Road
Churchcroft Close
Baskerville Road
Patten Road
Routh Road
Wexford Road
Jaggard Way
Mayford Close
Ravenslea Road
Calbourne Road
Fernside Road
Gosberton Road
Tantallon Road
Hearnville Road
Chestnut Grove
Norgrove Street
B229
St. James's Drive B327
Wandsworth Common Rail
Wandsworth Common
Bradley Mews
Bellevue Road
Althorp Road
Wiseton Road
Trinity Road A214
Balham Park Road
Ouseley Road
Heslop Road
Sarsfeld Road
Pakenham Close
Nottingham Road
Old Hos. Cl
Lane
Timbridge
Florence Way
Hunter Close
Boundaries Road
Rowfant Road
Lyford Road
Collamore Avenue
Sandgate Lane
Lyminge Gardens
Marmion Gardens
Burntwood Lane B229
Sir Walker St. John's Sports Ground
Brodrick Road
Sarsfeld Road
Tunley Road
Marius Passage
The Boulevard A24
Balham
146
151
0.25 mile
0.25 km

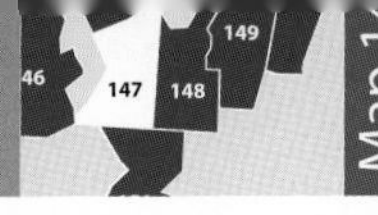

ıscnced between the livelier Clapham and Tooting, this is a gentle slice of ·sidential Southwest London. Bellevue Road offers a number of places to eat ıd drink overlooking Wandsworth Common, climaxing with the stupendous **ıez Bruce**. Nightingale Lane is terribly twee and hosts a few opportunities to ıop organically and **The Hope** serves up a healthy pint of Tribute.

Coffee

- **Caffe Nero** • 137 Balham High Rd

Nightlife

- **The Hope** • 1 Bellevue Rd
- **The Nightingale** • 97 Nightingale Ln

Restaurants

- **Chez Bruce** • 2 Bellevue Rd

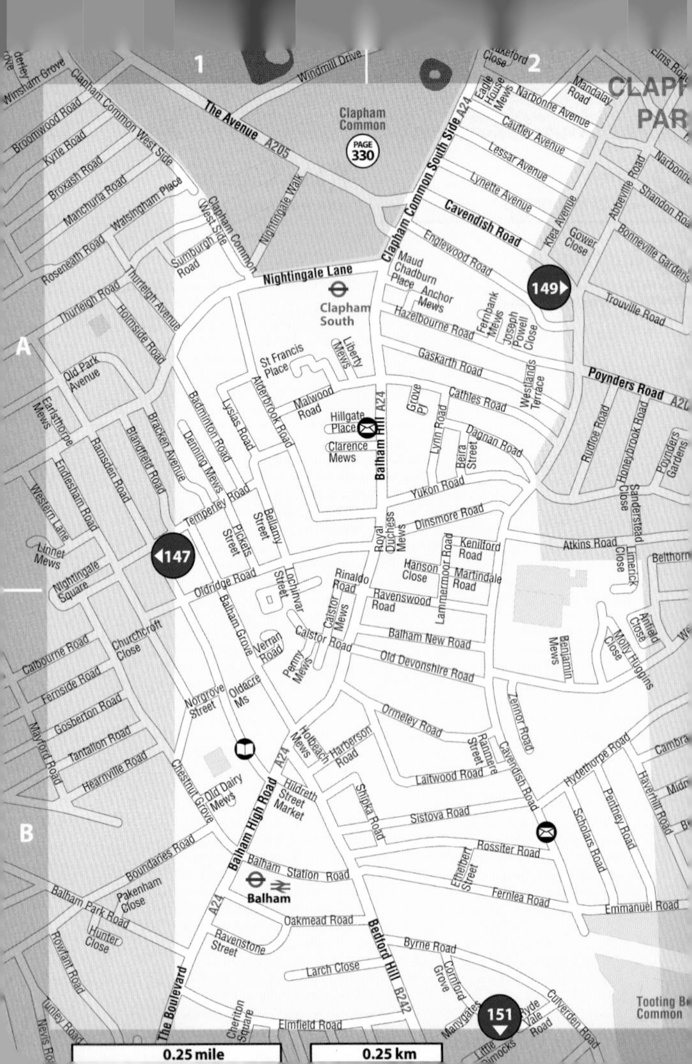

1
2
A
B
Windmill Drive
The Avenue A205
Clapham Common
PAGE 330
CLAPHAM PARK
Winsham Grove
Clapham Common West Side
Broomwood Road
Kyle Road
Broxash Road
Manchuria Road
Walsingham Place
Roseneath Road
Sumburgh Road
Clapham Common West Side
Nightingale Walk
Clapham Common South Side A24
Eagle House Mews
Narbonne Avenue
Mandalay Road
Cautley Avenue
Lessar Avenue
Lynette Avenue
Cavendish Road
Klea Avenue
Gower Close
Abbeville Road
Shandon Road
Bonneville Gardens
Englewood Road
Maud Chadburn Place
Anchor Mews
Nightingale Lane
Clapham South
Thurleigh Road
Thurleigh Avenue
Holmside Road
Hazelbourne Road
Fernbank Mews
Joseph Powell Close
149
Trouville Road
Old Park Avenue
St Francis Place
Liberty Mews
Gaskarth Road
Westlands Terrace
Poynders Road A205
Earlsthorpe Mews
Badminton Road
Lysias Road
Alderbrook Road
Malwood Road
Hillgate Place
Clarence Mews
Balham Hill A24
Grove Pl
Cathles Road
Lynn Road
Dagnan Road
Beira Street
Rudloe Road
Honeybrook Road
Poynders Gardens
Bracken Avenue
Blandfield Road
Ramsden Road
Endlesham Road
Western Lane
Denning Mews
Temperley Road
Bellamy Street
Yukon Road
Dinsmore Road
Royal Duchess Mews
Sanderstead Close
Linnet Mews
147
Nightingale Square
Pickets Street
Oldridge Road
Kenilford Road
Atkins Road
Limerick Close
Belthorn
Hanson Close
Lammermoor Road
Martindale Road
Rinaldo Road
Lochinvar Street
Ravenswood Road
Balham Grove
Caistor Mews
Calbourne Road
Churchcroft Close
Verran Road
Caistor Road
Balham New Road
Anfield Close
Benjamin Mews
Molly Huggins Close
Fernside Road
Old Devonshire Road
Penny Mews
Gosberton Road
Norgrove Street
Oldacre Ms
Zennor Road
Mayford Road
Tantallon Road
Ormeley Road
Holbeach Mews
Harberson Road
Hearnville Road
Chestnut Grove
Ranmere Street
Cavendish Road
Hydethorpe Road
Cambray
Old Dairy Mews
A24
Hildreth Street Market
Laitwood Road
Haverhill Road
Balham High Road
Shipka Road
Sistova Road
Scholars Road
Penfrey Road
Boundaries Road
Rossiter Road
Balham Station Road
Pakenham Close
Balham
Ethelbert Street
Fernlea Road
Balham Park Road
Emmanuel Road
A24
Hunter Close
Oakmead Road
Ravenstone Street
Bedford Hill B242
Byrne Road
Rowfant Road
Larch Close
Grove
Cornford
Tooting Bec Common
Culverden Road
Hyde Vale Road
151
Manygates
Tunley Road
Nevis Road
The Boulevard
Cheriton Square
Elmfield Road
Little Dimocks
0.25 mile
0.25 km

alham is growing up to become the cooler, decidedly more understated little other to nearby Clapham. Although it still oozes its own sense of character, vident in quirky mainstays like the **Balham Bowls Club**, the draw of its aitrose risks losing its hip factor.

46 147 148 149

Coffee

- **Brickwood** • 11 Hildreth St
- **Camden Coffee House** • 208 Balham High Rd
- **M1LK** • 20 Bedford Hill

Libraries

- **Balham Library** • 16 Ramsden Rd

Nightlife

- **The Avalon** • 16 Balham Hill
- **Balham Bowls Club** • 7 Ramsden Rd
- **The Bedford** • 77 Bedford Hill
- **The Exhibit** • 12 Balham Station Rd
- **Hagen & Hyde** • 157 Balham High Rd

Post Offices

- **Balham Hill** • 92 Balham Hill
- **Cavendish Road** • 273 Cavendish Rd

Restaurants

- **Brickwood** • 11 Hildreth St
- **The Exhibit** • 12 Balham Station Rd
- **Hagen & Hyde** • 157 Balham High Rd

Shopping

- **Moxon's Fishmongers** • Westbury Parade

Supermarkets

- **Sainsbury's** • 149 Balham High Rd
- **Sainsbury's** • 21 Balham Hill
- **Waitrose** • Balham High Rd & Ramsden Rd

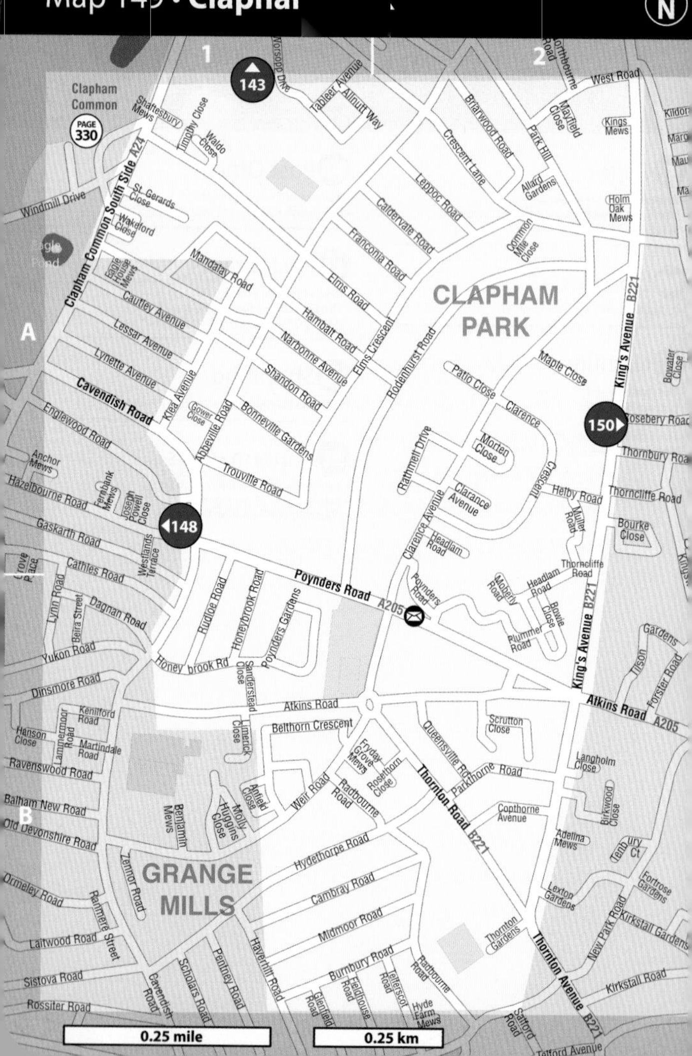
N
1
2
A
B
143
148
150
PAGE 330
Clapham Common
CLAPHAM PARK
GRANGE MILLS
Clapham Common South Side A24
Windmill Drive
Shaftesbury Mews
Timothy Close
Waldo Close
Worsopp Drive
Tableer Avenue
Allnutt Way
Northbourne Road
West Road
Briarwood Road
Crescent Lane
Mayfield Close
Park Hill
Kings Mews
Allard Gardens
Holm Oak Mews
Leppoc Road
Caldervale Road
Franconia Road
Elms Road
Hambalt Road
Narbonne Avenue
Shandon Road
Bonneville Gardens
Elms Crescent
Rodenhurst Road
Common Mile Close
St. Gerards Close
Wakeford Close
Eagle House Mews
Mandalay Road
Cautley Avenue
Lessar Avenue
Lynette Avenue
Cavendish Road
Kyrle Avenue
Gower Close
Abbeville Road
Trouville Road
Englewood Road
Anchor Mews
Hazelbourne Road
Fernbank Mews
Joseph Powell Close
Gaskarth Road
Westlands Terrace
Grove Place
Cathles Road
Lynn Road
Beira Street
Dagnan Road
Yukon Road
Rudloe Road
Honeybrook Road
Poynders Gardens
Poynders Road A205
Honeybrook Rd
Sandersted Close
Maple Close
Patio Close
Clarence Crescent
Morten Close
Rathmell Drive
Clarance Avenue
Clarence Avenue
Headlam Road
Poynders Road
Helby Road
Muller Road
Thorncliffe Road
Moberly Road
Bowie Close
Plummer Road
King's Avenue B221
Bowater Close
Rosebery Road
Thornbury Road
Thorncliffe Road
Bourke Close
Gardens
Tilson
Forster Road
Atkins Road A205
Dinsmore Road
Kenilford Road
Lammermoor Road
Hanson Close
Martindale Road
Ravenswood Road
Balham New Road
Old Devonshire Road
Atkins Road
Belthorn Crescent
Limerick Close
Queensville Road
Scrutton Close
Parkthorne Road
Langholm Close
Fryday Grove Mews
Rosethorn Close
Thornton Road B221
Copthorne Avenue
Birkwood Close
Adelina Mews
Tenbury Ct
Anfield Close
Weir Road
Radbourne Road
Benjamin Mews
Molly Huggins Close
Zennor Road
Hydethorpe Road
Cambray Road
Midmoor Road
Ormeley Road
Ramsmere Street
Laitwood Road
Sistova Road
Rossiter Road
Cavendish Road
Scholars Road
Pentney Road
Haverhill Road
Burnbury Road
Glenfield Road
Fieldhouse Road
Telferscot Road
Radbourne Road
Hyde Farm Mews
Thornton Gardens
Lexton Gardens
Fortrose Gardens
New Park Road
Kirkstall Gardens
Kirkstall Road
Thornton Avenue B221
Salford Road
Telford Avenue
0.25 mile
0.25 km

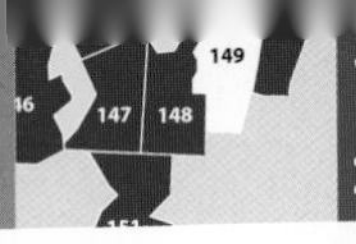

his is where all the Claphamites settle down, have kids, move into their dream
own house, and one-up their friends with dinner parties and barbecues every
ther weekend. All this domesticity has left the locals' only restaurant options
orth on Clapham High Street or south in Balham. Still, you need fodder for your
iends, so gourmet food shopping is where it's at at **MacFarlane's**.

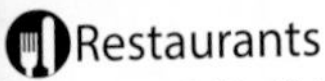

Restaurants

- **Bistro Union** • 40 Abbeville Rd

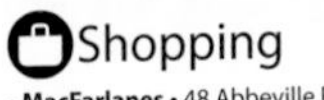

Shopping

- **MacFarlanes** • 48 Abbeville Rd

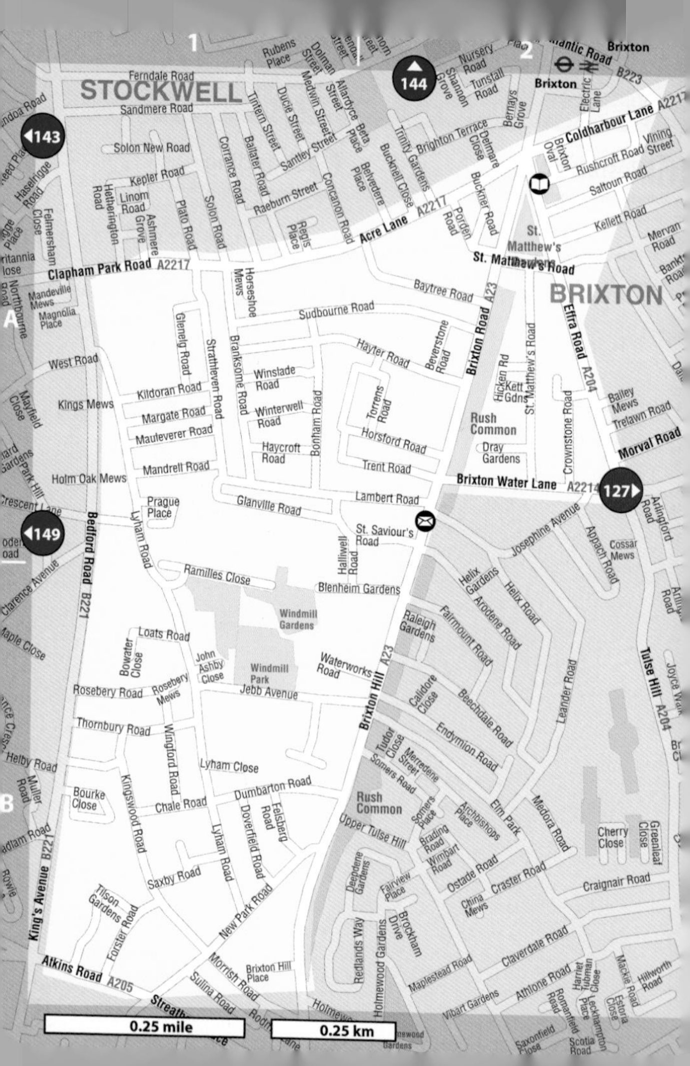

STOCKWELL
BRIXTON
Brixton
143
144
149
127
Ferndale Road
Sandmere Road
Solon New Road
Kepler Road
Clapham Park Road A2217
Acre Lane A2217
Coldharbour Lane A2217
Atlantic Road
Brixton Road A23
Brixton Hill A23
Brixton Water Lane A2214
St. Matthew's Road
Effra Road A204
Tulse Hill A204
Bedford Road B221
King's Avenue B221
Atkins Road A205
Sudbourne Road
Baytree Road
Hayter Road
Horsford Road
Trent Road
Lambert Road
Glanville Road
St. Saviour's Road
Blenheim Gardens
Ramilles Close
Windmill Gardens
Windmill Park
Jebb Avenue
Waterworks Road
Lyham Road
Lyham Close
Dumbarton Road
New Park Road
Morrish Road
Brixton Hill Place
Josephine Avenue
Rush Common
St. Matthew's Gardens
Upper Tulse Hill
Elm Park
Craster Road
Claverdale Road
Athlone Road
Mandrell Road
Kildoran Road
Margate Road
Mauleverer Road
Rosebery Road
Thornbury Road
Chale Road
Saxby Road
Kingswood Road
Wingford Road
Loats Road
Helix Road
Arodene Road
Fairmount Road
Beechdale Road
Endymion Road
Leander Road
Medora Road
Craignair Road
0.25 mile
0.25 km

ton is where it's at. Shoreditch: old news. Dalston: yawn. Any self-respecting hipster ldn't be caught dead around these hot spots (too many hipsters) and so they've itated south of the river. For Brixton Village's other half, check out Market Row, with ller katsu (Curry Ono) and flavourful vegan baked goods (**Ms Cupcake**). For culture, in an exhibition at **Photofusion** and a flick at stalwart **The Ritzy.**

Cinemas

Ritzy Picturehouse • Coldharbour Ln & Brixton Oval

Libraries

Brixton Library • Brixton Oval

Nightlife

The Dogstar • 389 Coldharbour Ln
The Effra • 38 Kellet Rd
Effra Social • 89 Kellet Rd
Electric Brixton • Town Hall Parade
Grand Union • 123 Acre Ln
Gremio de Brixton • St Matthew's Rd
Hootananny • 95 Effra Rd
Prince Albert • 418 Coldharbour Ln
Satay • 447 Coldharbour Ln
St Matthews Church • Brixton Hill
Upstairs at the Ritzy • Ritzy Picturehouse • Brixton Oval, Coldharbour Ln
The Windmill • 22 Blenheim Gardens

Post Offices

• **Brixton Hill** • 104 Brixton Hill

Restaurants

• **Asmara** • 386 Coldharbour Ln
• **Boqueria** • 192 Acre Ln
• **Curry Ono** • 14 Market Row
• **Franco Manca** • 4 Market Row
• **KaoSarn** • Coldharbour Ln
• **Khan's of Brixton** • 24 Brixton Water Ln
• **Lounge** • 56 Atlantic Rd
• **Negril** • 132 Brixton Hill
• **Refill** • 500 Brixton Rd

Shopping

• **Bookmongers** • 439 Coldharbour Ln
• **Ms. Cupcake** • 408 Coldharbour Ln
• **Supertone Records** • 110 Acre Ln
• **Tasty Rich Bakery** • Brixton Village Market
• **Traid** • 2 Acre Ln

Supermarkets

• **Iceland** • 13 Winslade Rd

1
2
A
B
147
148
152
UPPER TOOTING
Tooting Bec
Tooting Broadway
Tooting Graveney Common
Furzedown Recreation Ground
St. James's Drive B327
Trinity Road A214
Balham High Road A24
Upper Tooting Road A24
Tooting Bec Road A214
Mitcham Road A217
Rectory Lane B241
Church Lane B241
Sarsfeld Road
Wandle Road
Hendham Road
Dalebury Road
Crockerton Road
Brenda Road
Pavilion Square
Langroyd Road
St. James's Close
Appledore Close
Boundaries Road
Oswald Road
Wontner Road
Hosack Road
Nevis Road
Tunley Road
Rowfant Road
Marius Passage
Marius Road
Upper Tooting Park
Eatonville Villas
Eatonville Road
Ashdown Way
Flowersmead Estate
Trinity Crescent
Adams Mews
Holderness Road
Chetwode Road
Brook Close
Cheriton Square
Elmfield Road
Bedford Hill
Cloudesdale Road
Childebert Road
Carminia Road
Foxbourne Road
Sainfoin Road
Brandreth Road
Ritherdon Road
Manville Road
Manville Gardens
Bushnell Road
Huron Road
Carnie Lodge
Streathbourne Road
Drakefield Road
Louisville Road
Noyna Road
Fircroft Road
Mandrake Road
Beechcroft Road
Bevin Square
Glenburnie Road
Morven Road
Gateside Road
Beeches Road
Park Hill Court
Holmbury Court
Price Close
Wheatlands Road
Stapleton Road
Netherfield Road
Dafforne Road
Foulser Road
Romberg Road
Topsham Road
Montana Road
Avoca Road
Ravenfield Road
Brudenell Road
Lynwood Road
Hillbrook Road
Ansell Road
Fishponds Road
Hebdon Road
Hertwyn Gardens
Defoe Place
Ruislip Street
Treherne Court
Barringer Square
Macmillan Way
Hereward Road
Moffat Road
Cowick Road
Blakenham Road
Bruce Hall Mews
Franciscan Road
Gearing Close
Henry Doulton Dr.
Molyneux Drive
Massingberd Way
Lisle Close
Broadwater Road
Letchworth Street
Derinton Road
Groomfield Close
Gatton Road
Kellino Street
Lessingham Avenue
Coteford Street
Mantilla Road
Moring Road
Elderfield Place
Massingberd Way
Selkirk Road
St. Cyprian's Street
Chasefield Road
Cowick Road
Lucien Road
Gassiot Road
Angel Court
Longmead Road
Eswyn Road
Ashvale Road
Totterdown Street
Okeburn Road
Furzedown Road
Birchwood Road
Undine Street
Valnay Street
Chertsey Street
Church Lane
Abbey Drive
Franciscan Road
St. Benedict's Close
Crowborough Road
Chillerton Road
Furzedown Drive
Laurel Close
Dewey Street
Carlisle Way
Ramsdale Road
Bickley Street
Vant Road
Church Lane
Hawthorn Crescent
0.25 mile
0.25 km

quite the Bec of beyond, this Tooting is the home of Europe's largest lido has a plethora of Asian grill bars for post-pub munchies. The best of the houses has to be **Al Mirage**, despite a popular following at **Mirch Masala**. airy cakes head to **Bertie and Boo** (we boo the name).

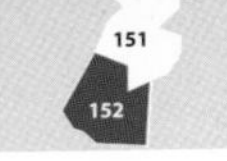

Coffee

- **ertie and Boo** • 162 Balham High Rd
- **affe Moka** • 243 Balham High Rd
- **ee Light Bakery** • 14 Ritherdon Rd

Nightlife

- **he King's Head** • 84 Upper Tooting Rd

Post Offices

- **Jpper Tooting** • 63 Trinity Rd

Restaurants

- **Al Mirage** • 215 Upper Tooting Rd
- **Masaledar Kitchen** • 121 Upper Tooting Rd
- **Meat and Shake** • 47 Upper Tooting Rd
- **Mirch Masala** • 213 Upper Tooting Rd
- **Spice Village** • 32 Upper Tooting Rd

Shopping

- **Crazy Horse Bike Workshop** • 275 Balham High Rd
- **Russell's Trade & DIY** • 46 Upper Tooting Rd
- **Wandsworth Oasis HIV/AIDS Charity Shop** • 40 Trinity Rd

N
1
2
A
B
Fishponds Playing Field
Tooting Broadway
Gala Bingo Hall
151
COLLIER'S WOOD
Tooting
Colliers Wood Recreation Ground
Figge's Marsh
Upper Tooting Road
A24
Garratt Lane
A217
Mitcham Road
London Road
Rectory Lane
Tooting High Street
Church Lane
Broadwater Road
Rogers Road
Gatton Road
Selkirk Road
Graveney Road
Khama Road
Greaves Place
Gambole Road
Castle Mews
Garratt Terrace
Gilbey Road
Coverton Road
Ivy Road
Laurel Close
Hoyle Road
Effort Street
Recovery Street
Tooting Grove
Woodbury Street
Nutwell Street
Mayburg Street
Aldis Street
Aldis Mews
Carlwell Street
Fishponds Road
Herlwyn Gardens
Hebdon Road
Hereward Road
Moffat Road
Defoe Place
Ruislip Street
Letchworth Street
Cowick Road
Kellino Street
St. Cyprian's Street
Angel Court
Longmead Road
Ashvale Road
Totterdown Street
Undine Street
Vainay Street
Franciscan Road
Bickley Street
Mellison Road
Rookstone Road
Dewey Street
Vant Road
Blakenham Road
Lynwood Road
Hillbrook Road
Rudenell Road
Avoca Road
Barringer Square
Bruce Hall Mews
Groomfield Close
Derinton Road
Lessingham Avenue
Coteford Street
Chasefield Road
Gassiot Road
Eswyn Road
Okeburn Road
Lucien Road
Chertsey Street
Abbey Drive
St. Benedict's Cl
Hawthorn Crescent
Carlisle Way
Rame Cl
Southview Close
Crowborough Road
Idlecombe Road
Bevill Allen Close
St. Nicholas Glebe
Himley Road
Charlmont Road
Brightwell Crescent
Avarn Road
Byton Road
Stella Road
Knapton Mews
Southcroft Road
Sellincourt Road
Trevelyan Road
Longley Road
Loubet Street
Otterburn Street
Bickersteth Road
Glasford Street
Renmuir Street
Seely Road
Ascot Road
Boscombe Road
Cromer Road
Deal Road
Eastbourne Road
Links Road
Waterfall Terrace
West Gardens
East Gardens
Daniel Close
Defoe Close
Clive Road
Birdhurst Road
Warren Road
Robinson Road
Lyveden Road
Marlborough Road
Marlborough Close
Rutland Close
Rutland Road
Norfolk Road
Harewood Road
Watson Close
Devonshire Road
Singleton Close
Flanders Crescent
Shrewton Road
Finborough Road
Woodley Close
Grenfell Road
Sirdar Road
Stanley Gardens
Ashbourne Road
Inglemere Road
Arnold Road
Swains Road
Pitcairn Road
Wilton Road
Cavendish Road
North Place
Holmbury Court
Bruce Road
Heaton Road
Tynemouth Road
Thirsk Road
Stanley Road
St. Barnabas
Gorringe Park Avenue
Crusoe Road
Myrna Close
Fleming Mead
Clarendon Road
Taylor Road
Island Road
Friday Road
Kenmare Drive
Dovedale Rise
Figges Road
St. James Road
0.25 mile
0.25 km

Tooting Broadway

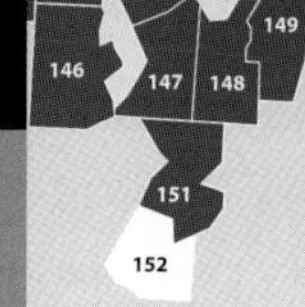

ecent rent, a Northern Line station and a grade one listed bingo hall: there's lot here to like. Hit the High Street for curries and halal it all. Need anything lse? Mitcham Road has the ticket.

Coffee

- **Caffee Manal** • 984 Garratt Ln

Landmarks

- **Gala Bingo Hall** • 50 Mitcham Rd

Libraries

- **Tooting Library** • 75 Mitcham Rd

Nightlife

- **The Ramble Inn** • 223 Mitcham Rd
- **The Secret Bar** • Totterdown St
- **Tooting Tram and Social** • 46 Mitcham Rd
- **Unwined** • 21 Tooting High St

Post Offices

- **London Road** • 47 London Rd
- **Tooting** • 2 Gatton Rd

Restaurants

- **Dosa n Chutny** • 68 Tooting High St
- **Jaffna House** • 90 Tooting High St
- **Radha Krishna Bhavan** • 86 Tooting High St
- **Rick's Restaurant** • 122 Mitcham Rd

Shopping

- **Tooting Market** • 21 Tooting High St

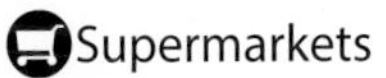

Supermarkets

- **Iceland** • 27 Tooting High St

General Information

Website: www.alexandrapalace.com
Phone: 020 8365 2121

Overview

If you fancy panoramic London views, exemplary Victorian architecture and an unrelenting stiff breeze to the face, the heights of Alexandra Park could be your cup of tea. With a fraction of the visitors of North London neighbours Hampstead Heath and Primrose Hill, Alexandra Park is nonetheless home to Ally Pally—Alexander Mackenzie's magnificent 1873 exhibition centre once renowned as the home of television after the BBC used it to broadcast the world's first high def transmissions in '36. It also boasts 196 acres of pristine, Green Flag-winning parkland, a two-hectare conservation area, and a fully functioning ice rink to boot.

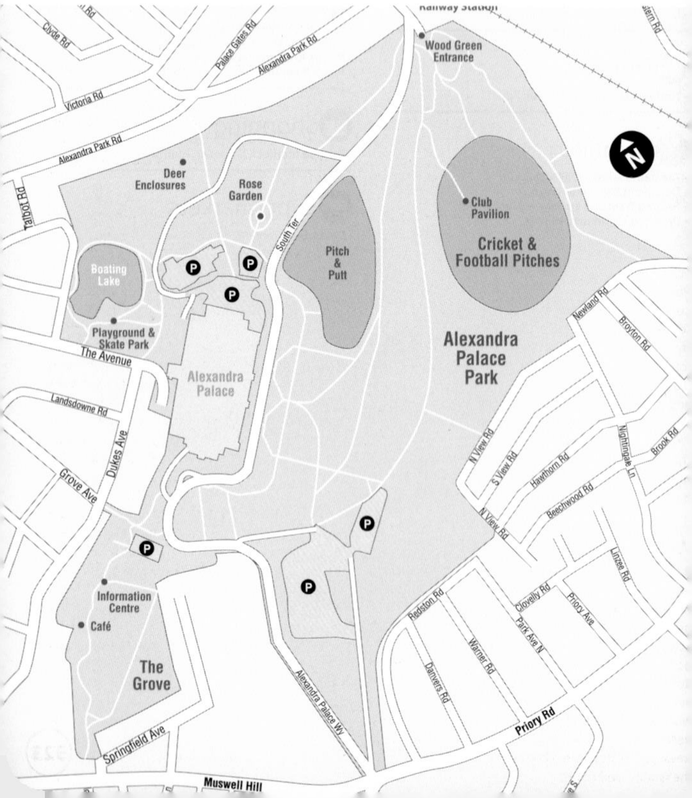

Practicalities

Alexandra Park is well served by public transport: Alexandra Palace railway station is a short ride from King's Cross and Moorgate and sits directly next to the park's Wood Green entrance. You can also take the underground to Wood Green, catch the W3 direct to Ally Pally from just outside. You could also take advantage of the 2000 free parking spaces in the park itself if driving, though it's only a short walk from Muswell Hill town centre.

Nature

No doubt tempted by the reservoirs, 155 species of birds have been spotted in the park over the last 30 years. Nature fetishists should take in the two-hectare conservation area, which includes a wide array of animals including deer, donkeys, foxes and rabbits. In 1998, there was even a rare water vole sighting. There he was, large as life, like he owned the bloody place.

Architecture

For most Alexandra Park visitors it's all about the Palace, these days a thriving hub for exhibitions, concerts, farmer's markets and, uh, world darts tournaments. The Palace building itself was ravaged by fire in the 80s and has since been restored to its former glory, though nearby banqueting venue Blandford Hall succumbed to the same fate in 1971 and was completely destroyed. No matter: Ally Pally remains an impressive, domineering building well worth a nose-around. For the less active, admiring the view from sedentary perspective from the underrated Phoenix Bar (located in the south wing) is just as good.

Open Spaces

It's safe to say that Alexandra Park has more than enough grass to keep Cheech & Chong happy, being typified by the diverse range of landscaped grounds that can be found within. The Grove Garden actually pre-dates the park itself and there's also a good little café here if you fancy a quick bite. The Rose Garden is to the east side of the Palace and is even more aesthetically pleasing. Many newer small woodlands have been developing over the last few decades owing to the planting of large numbers of trees, producing an environment pleasing to both the rambler and runner.

Performance

The park often plays host to funfairs and circuses, but the Palace itself will usually be used at night for concerts. Its revival over recent years as a gig venue has led to the likes of the Arctic Monkeys and Paul Weller playing there, with its capacity being around 8,500, making it ideal for bands who've outgrown the Brixton Academy. Other parts of the Palace, such as the Great Hall, are used for classical music recitals.

More recently 'The Secret Cinema' took over the Palace for a screening of *Lawrence of Arabia*, attracting thousands of filmgoers clad in Bedouin attire. Some even brought a camel.

The Palace also houses a theatre, which was dormant for over sixty-five years until a performance took place in 2004. It is still being restored and should be re-opened to the public for performances in the near future.

Check out Ally Pally's informative website (listed above) for a full calendar of upcoming events.

Sports

An indoor ice rink is housed within the Palace with a capacity of 1,250, with all manner of ice sports catered for (you can get further information by ringing 020 8365 4386). There is also a large boating lake with its own islands and fishing area (and even a smaller area for kids to boat on their own), with pedalos and rowing boats available for hire; being a seasonal facility, it's best to ring the operators Bluebird Boats Ltd. (020 7262 1330) beforehand. The boating pond is adjacent to a children's playground as well. For those who like golf with a view, the popular ten-hole pitch and putt course was recently revamped with an injection of Heritage Fund money: for prices and booking info see www.pitchnputt.co.uk or call 01245 257682. Alexandra Palace Park is also popular with cyclists, with the Parkland Walk a particular favourite, being a disused railway line that links up with Finsbury Park. In summertime the park is also a great place to get embroiled in countless spontaneous games of football and Frisbee, or to gawp/hurl insults at joggers

General information

NFT Map: 7
Address: Barbican Centre, Silk St, London, EC2Y 8DS.
Phone: Box Office & Membership: 020 7638 8891 (9 am-8 pm daily); Switchboard: 020 7638 4141
Centre opening times: Mon-Sat: 9 am-11 pm; Sun & Public Holidays: 11 am-11 pm (although different parts of the centre may open at different times)
Website: www.barbican.org.uk

Overview

As terrifying as it is impressive, the Barbican Centre is a one-stop shop for all things cultural. At its best, the Barbican is utterly brilliant: a rambling collection of cinemas, galleries, bars, theatres, even a housing estate and a school. But stay after dark, when the culture vultures have left, and you can find yourself alone and lost in this city-within-a-city.

That the centre is brutally ugly makes what's inside even more splendid. The gallery space hosts world-class exhibitions and the cinemas show both mainstream and arthouse films. There's a world, classical and jazz music programme catering for everyone from scruffy backpackers to bearded professors. Most are sensible enough to leave before it gets too spooky. But plan your exit route in advance just in case.

Music

The heart of the Barbican monster is its music hall. A mecca for lovers of cerebral music, the centre's resident band is the London Symphony Orchestra: classical heavyweights who play year-round. The BBC Symphony Orchestra also has a base here, and the stage attracts biggies from around the world, including performances from Yo-Yo Ma, the Vienna Philharmonic and Cesaria Evora. But you don't need a high brow to find something to like: a flick through their listings—which last year included Sufjan Stevens, Sparks

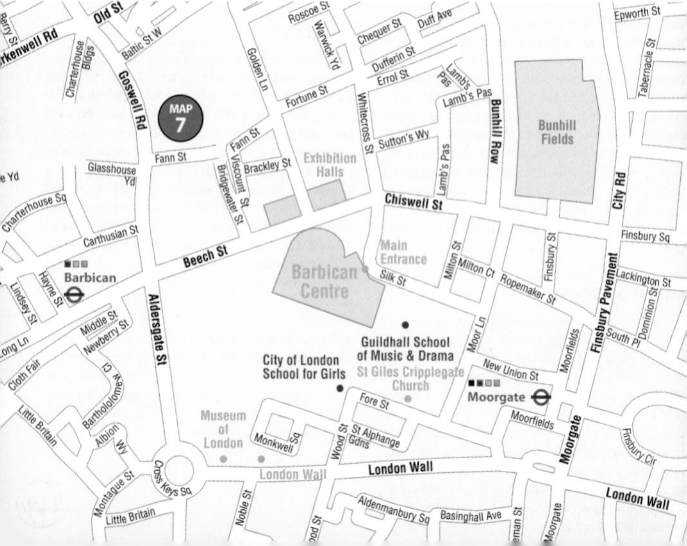

The Africa Express and Micachu—will soon have you clicking Book Now.

Festivals are another key draw: not the pot-and-portacabin type, but impassioned celebrations. The Mostly Mozart festival reaches sci-fi convention levels of fanaticism; the Great Performers Festival is an orgy of some of the world's most spectacular musicians; and the Jazz Festival will have you feeling über hip (then perhaps a bit perplexed. And then, if you're 100% honest, rather wishing it was over). African, Latin, Contemporary and Opera festivals also sell out the near-2000 capacity venue.

Film

The programme has an arty bias but is so diverse that you're bound to find something inviting on one of the three screens. Rule of thumb: silent films, in. J-Lo, out. Subtitles, in. Mighty Duck trilogy, out. But they do offer the screens for private hire, so if you really want you can stick it to 'em and have your own showing of Snakes on a Plane. The Barbican also hosts the annual Australian Film and London Children's Film Festivals, and runs constantly changing series. Recent favourites include the Bad Film Club for fans of the most reviled films, and Second Chance Sunday so you can see on the big screen films which you missed first time around.

Theatre and Dance

Don't be fooled by the Barbican's hulking exterior—the centre dabbles in the more delicate arts rather well. Its two theatres cater for both ends of the performance spectrum. The main room, a shared home for acting and dance, seats over 1,000 punters and attracts some of the biggest names in high culture. Deep in the Barbican's bowels the smaller Pit theatre is home to experimental and new acts. But be warned: with just 200 seats the Pit is small enough for anyone dozing off to be highly visible.

Art

Nowhere else at the Barbican is the idea of making culture accessible for all more apparent than their art spaces. The main gallery hosts temporary exhibitions, mixing all types of art into one cultural hot pot. In 2007, under the umbrella of Art and Sex from Antiquity to Now, erotic Roman cutlery—that's right: erotic cutlery—shared a stage with impressionist paintings and an 11-minute film of someone's face as she was, ahem, attended to. Every first Thursday of the month the gallery opens for a nocturnal viewing, with talks, performances—burlesque dancers for the art and sex exhibition—and a themed bar. A second space, The Curve, winds its way round the ground floor where the exhibitions are generally free.

The Library

Libraries often get a bad press. They've got stuck with an image of frumpy, middle-aged women peering down their spectacles and telling youths to be quiet. But this couldn't be further removed from the reality of the Barbican Library. Alongside a decent array of books, there's a dazzling collection of live musical recordings. Some of these tracks are so rare that they can't be heard anywhere else in the world. Put some headphones on and rock out. Just don't get carried away and smash up the children's section.

How to Get There

By car: Parking is pricey with two hours costing £6.50 and each hour thereafter costing two or three quid more, though there's a flat weekend fee of £7.50 per day.

By bus: The 153 (which runs from Liverpool Street to Finsbury Park) stops directly outside the Barbican at Silk Street; the following buses run nearby: 8, 11, 23, 26, 35, 42, 43, 47, 48, 55, 56, 76, 78, 100, 133, 141, 149, 172, 214, 242, 243, 271, 344 (seven days a week); 4, (Mon-Sat); 21, 25, 521 (Mon-Fri). If none of these buses can take you home then consider yourself extremely unlucky. By tube: Barbican stations runs on the Circle, District and Hammersmith & City lines. Other stations nearby are Moorgate, St Paul's, Bank, Liverpool Street and Mansion House.

By train: The nearest overland stations are Liverpool Street, Farringdon and Blackfriars. City Thameslink services run through Barbican, Moorgate and Cannon Street.

Practical Information

NFT Map: 132, 133, & 141

Official opening time is 8 am, although the gates are usually unlocked a little earlier than this. The park closes at dusk.

Friends of Battersea Park:
www.batterseapark.org

Zoo: www.batterseaparkzoo.co.uk

Local council: www.wandsworth.gov.uk (see also for information on the Pump House Gallery)

Cycle hire:
www.londonrecumbents.co.uk

BlueBird boat hire:
www.solarshuttle.co.uk

Overview

Opened in 1858 with the aim of giving the Victorian working classes something to do other than drinking gin, Battersea Park has developed to become one of London's prettiest, most popular and most usable parks. Squeezing a range of gardens, cafes, animals, sports, cultural facilities and even a peace pagoda into its diminutive 200 acres, the park is popular with everyone from hordes of snotty little kids to wandering dog-walkers. It is also centrally located enough to be easy to get to but still far enough from Central London to retain a local feel.

The park is about two miles southwest from Westminster and occupies the spot on the south bank of the Thames between Albert and Chelsea bridges. Originally used for duelling, the Duke of Wellington famously discharged upon the Earl of Winchelsea on the site in 1829. Rather than the vast open and flat spaces that many London parks offer, Battersea is neatly divided into a number of features and sections, making it feel much larger than it is.

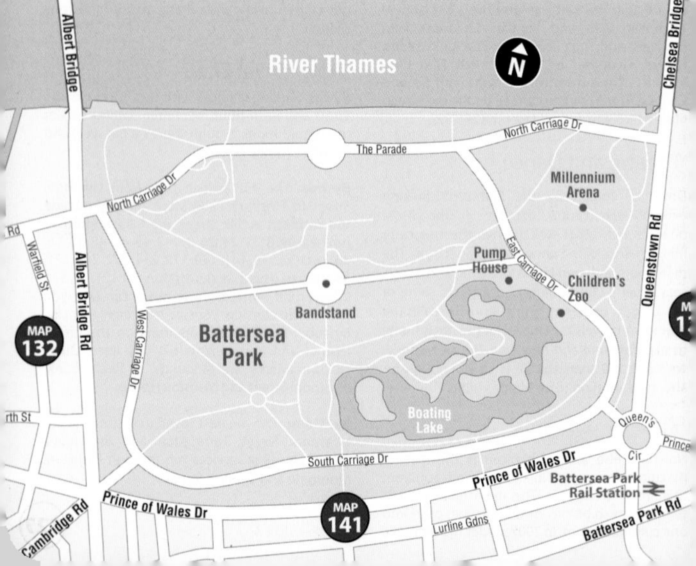

Sporting Activities

Battersea has an incredibly good array of sporting facilities. The 'Millennium Arena' is a 400m 8-lane running track situated in the northeast corner of the park; it hosts athletic meets and training sessions and it benefited from an expensive overhaul in, you guessed it, 1999. Next to the arena are ten tennis courts and an all-weather football pitch whilst there are further all-weather astro-turf pitches in the southeast corner of the park marked for both hockey and football. The park also boasts cricket pitches and practice nets, a bowling green, smooth wide paths for skating and enough open spaces to invite impromptu sessions of pretty much any other sport. If you consider attacking fish a sport, and have a permit and rod licence, the park's lake offers fishing for nine months of the year. Rowing boats and pedaloes can also be taken out on to the lake during July and August (adults £4.50/hour, children £2). Bicycles can be hired from the London Recumbents shop, which is next to the Millennium Arena on the park's East Carriage Drive—but be warned: bikes can only be used in the park itself, and as it takes just 15 minutes for a leisurely pedal around the parameter, an hour's hire can become a little Groundhog Day.

Art

Battersea has fostered a creative relationship with the arts and has a number of sculptures dotted about, its own public gallery and a biannual art fair. Taking pride of place next to the lake are two large Henry Moore and Barbara Hepworth sculptures, both of which are well worth rooting out. The Pumphouse Gallery is a grade II-listed building, originally used to power the park's water works, which has been restored and converted into a gallery and information centre with six exhibitions throughout the year. The Gallery, located northeast of the lake, is also available for private hire and even has a licence to hold civil weddings. The park has hosted the Affordable Art Fair since 1999, which has become a leading showcase for art priced under £3,000.

Performance

In summer music aficionados should head down to La Gondola al Parco, the café by the lake, for free live concerts every Tuesday and Friday from 7 pm. Entrance is free and there's also a BBQ and refreshments aplenty.

Nature and Children's Zoo

Battersea's varied landscapes ensure you stand a decent chance of seeing more than a rat or a pigeon while you saunter round. Squirrels, ducks and Canada geese are all too plentiful. More interesting potential sightings include woodpeckers, cormorants, Peregrine falcons, terrapins and, according to the RSPB, Pochards (whatever they are). If you don't come across any interesting wildlife, your only option is to cheat and visit the park's zoo. A five-minute stroll from the Chelsea Gate entrance, the zoo is aimed at children and has a cool collection of small mammals, including lemurs, as well as small farm animals and some excitingly named birds, such as some 'Peach-faced Love birds'. In case you do fall in love with any of the zoo's inhabitants, most are available for adoption. Mice start at £10 for six months, pay-up and claim it's for your kid. The zoo is open throughout the year and entry costs £8.75 for adults, £6.50 for children.

How to Get There

By tube: Sloane Square (on the Circle and District lines) is the nearest Underground station at just under a mile away. From the station walk down Lower Sloane Street, which becomes Chelsea Bridge Road and leads to the Thames. Walk over Chelsea Bridge and you will see the park on your right. Alternatively take bus no 319.

By bus: From central London, buses run to the park from Liverpool Street (number 344), Notting Hill (452), Oxford Circus (137), Sloane Square (319, 137), Victoria Station (44) and Vauxhall (344).

By train: Battersea Park station is within sight of the park, trains run to both Clapham Junction and Victoria at high frequency. Queenstown Road is around 300m from the park. Trains from this station run to Waterloo and Clapham Junction and depart less often than from Battersea Park.

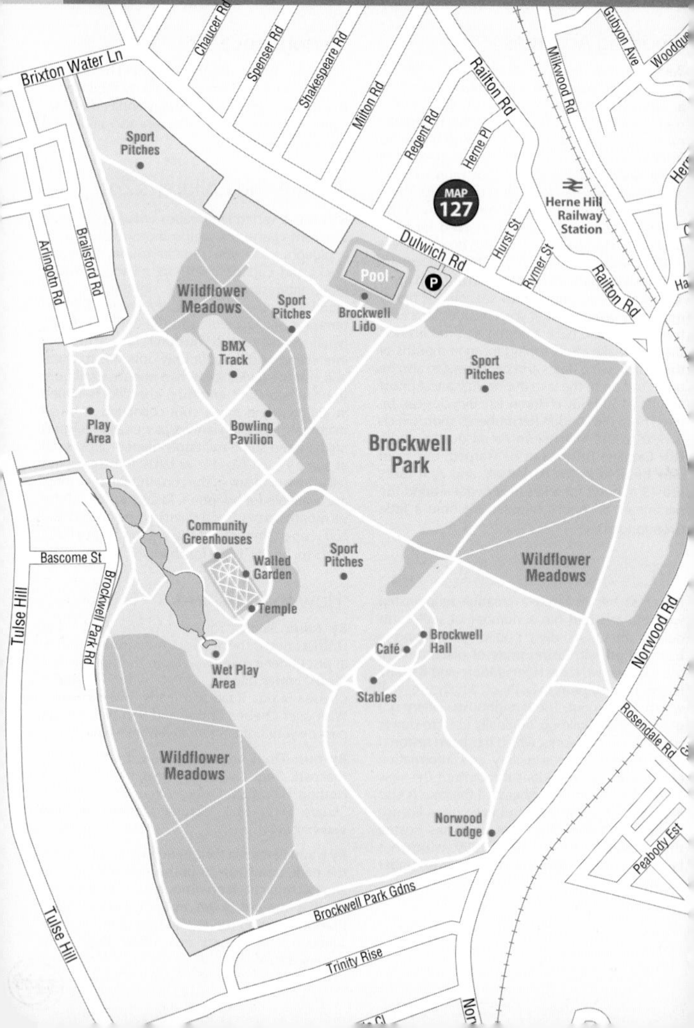

Brixton Water Ln
Chaucer Rd
Spenser Rd
Shakespeare Rd
Milton Rd
Regent Rd
Herne Pl
Railton Rd
Milkwood Rd
Gubyon Ave
MAP 127
Herne Hill Railway Station
Hurst St
Rymer St
Dulwich Rd
Railton Rd
Sport Pitches
Arlingotn Rd
Brailsford Rd
Wildflower Meadows
Sport Pitches
Pool
Brockwell Lido
BMX Track
Sport Pitches
Play Area
Bowling Pavilion
Brockwell Park
Community Greenhouses
Walled Garden
Sport Pitches
Temple
Wildflower Meadows
Bascome St
Brockwell Park Rd
Tulse Hill
Brockwell Hall
Café
Wet Play Area
Stables
Norwood Rd
Rosendale Rd
Wildflower Meadows
Norwood Lodge
Peabody Est
Brockwell Park Gdns
Tulse Hill
Trinity Rise

General Information

NFT Map: 127
Brockwell Park: www.brockwellpark.com
Brockwell Park Lido: www.brockwelllido.com
020 7274 3088

Overview

Brockwell Park may not be a household name when it comes to London Parks but for many South Londoners—not least residents of neighbouring Herne Hill—it's the pick of the bunch, all the lovelier for its unconventionality, tattiness and relative anonymity. It's eclectic, it's quirky, and it's impossible not to fall in love with.

History

By the end of the 19th century the local population was large, growing and in need of a serious park. Brockwell was secured for use by the public after MP Thomas Bristowe got wind of a private country estate that seemed just the ticket. Still, he might have over-exerted himself in the process: having taken a Bill through Parliament to convert the land, led a committee to negotiate the price, and raised funds from across the community, Bristowe himself promptly collapsed and died on the steps of Brockwell Hall, moments after the opening ceremony in 1892.

Café

If that doesn't put you off your scones, nowadays, the ground floor of Brockwell Hall is a café where refreshments have been served ever since. Located at the top of the hill, it's a great place to stop for inexpensive cake, drinks etc. after some…

Activities!

There's heaps to do. A BMX track, tennis courts, bowling green, football and cricket pitches, basketball courts, outdoor theatre club, a children's play area and a paddling pool. Or you could chill by the ponds, in the walled garden, under the clock tower, at the picnic area, near the flower gardens, etc.

Brockwell Lido and Greenhouses

Built in 1937, Brockwell Lido is essentially an (unattractive) art deco building that replaced an old bathing pond. After experiencing financial difficulty it was restored and reopened in 2007. As well as a large outdoor pool, there is a gym and classes are held in yoga, pilates, tai-chi and meditation. For the under 5s, Whippersnappers have everything from acrobatics to puppets and African drumming. A Miniature Railway runs between Herne Hill Gate and the Lido. Run by a local enthusiast on a not-for-profit basis; it's only £1 for a round trip. May–Sept, Sat–Sun, 11am–5pm.

Brockwell also boasts a superb community greenhouse project open to volunteers. The greenhouses are open Sunday afternoons and give Londoners a rare chance to get green fingers and grow their own produce. Contact the greenhouse secretary on bpcgsecretary@gmail.com to get involved.

Annual Events

July: Lambeth Country Show is always good fun and involves medieval jousting, farm animals, live reggae/dub and rides, and there are homemade cake and jam contests, too. The Alternative Vegetable Animal Competition requires fruit and veg be crafted into a famous person or building with a very entertaining adult category.
September: The annual Urban Green Fair helps teach London to become more sustainable.
November: The big fireworks show on Guy Fawkes Night is worth braving the cold for.

How to Get There

By rail/tube/foot: The park is a short walk from the following overland and underground stations:

Herne Hill Rail Station—5 mins
Tulse Hill Rail Station—15 mins
Brixton Tube—20 mins
Clapham North Tube—30 mins

By bus: The following all stop at Brockwell Park—2, 3, 37, 68, 196, 322, 468, P15

Overview

Lively and happening; youngish, professional, and trendy (in a safe way). Clapham Common reflects the area well.

Popular all year round, the Common truly comes alive in summer. On a warm weekend you'll find the park overflowing with picnickers sipping champagne and just plain lookin' good. It's a lovely scene made better by the relaxed, friendly atmosphere. And, when the sun finally sets, you're left with a seriously impressive choice of bars close by.

As well as drawing the usual funky sophisticates, the park is also family-friendly with lots of little ones enjoying the space.

Plenty of organised (or not) sport, kite flying, model boating, Ultimate Frisbee, and even fishing happens here too, but while the common is safe as houses during the day, at night time it is best avoided.

History

Clapham began as a Saxon village. Back then it was called Clopp Ham, meaning the village (ham) by the short hill (clopp). The common was used by villagers to graze their livestock and as a source of firewood.

In the late 17th century the population began to grow as refugees arrived from the Great Plague of London (1665) and the fire of 1666. During this time, the rich gentry of London built a number of fine country houses around the common. When the railways were developed there was a sudden influx of commuters, driving the upper class away to somewhere less, um, common.

Today, the surrounding area is one of the more expensive in South London, partly because of its excellent transport links.

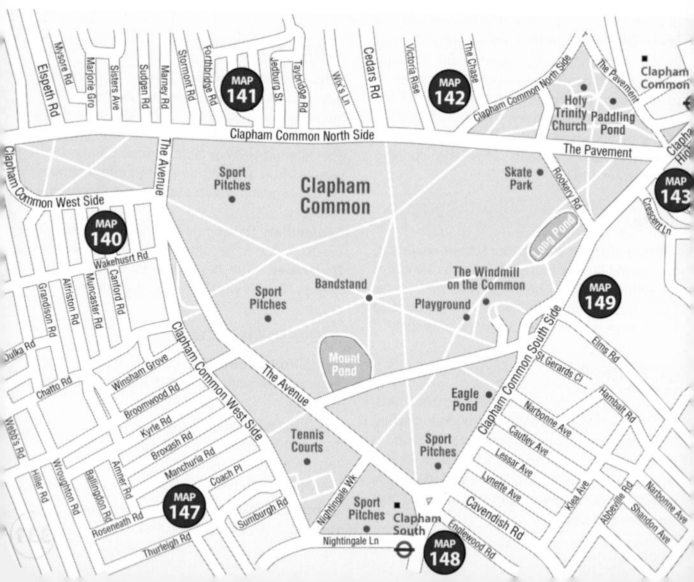

Clapham Sect

On the common is the Holy Trinity Church. This was a meeting place of the Clapham Sect, a group of 19th-century Evangelical Anglicans who fought for social reform. "Ugh" you say, but wait…

The Clapham Sect played a significant part in the abolition of slavery in England. They didn't stop there, going on to campaign for the eradication of slavery worldwide. They also fought for reform in the penal system, focusing on unjust sentencing and the dire prison conditions of the time.

Eateries

Cicero's on the Common (vegetarian)
2 Rookery Road, SW49QN, 020 7498 0770

Three ponds

Mount Pond—is a fishing park pond about three acres in size. It contains carp, roach, gudgeon and eels. Suggested baits include pellet, maggot, meat, and boilies, it says here.

Eagle Pond—is a smaller pond with a little island. This one is also fishable. Stocks include carp, tench, bream, roach, rudd, perch, chub and gudgeon. Best baits are bread, pellet, maggot, hemp and castor, it goes without saying.

Long Pond—has a century-old tradition of use for model boating.

Activities

These days there are still some nice leafy pathways lined by mature trees left for the strollers to enjoy.

Sporty types can go for the football, rugby, cricket, softball, tennis, basketball, Aussie rules football, croquet (!) or bowling.

Events

Some of the annual highlights include:

Race For Life—Throughout the year: Race For Life—The girls take on the common in pink to raise awareness of cancer. One of the biggest Race For Life running events.

July: Ben 'n Jerry's Sundae On The Common—also goes down well. If it sounds horribly corporate, it's worth noting that a full restoration of the bandstand in '05/'06 was partly funded by proceeds from this festival. Or, just think of the free ice-cream…

August: The Clapham Common Metro Weekender—Two successful, quality festivals have joined forces. South West Four (progressive house, trance, and breaks) and Get Loaded In the Park (indie/dance) now happen side by side at the end of August.

November: The Bonfire Night Fireworks—it's as good as it gets here.

How to Get There

By train: Wandsworth Road Station (12 minutes), Clapham High Street Station (12 minutes)

By tube: Clapham Common (4 minutes), Clapham South (13 minutes)

By bus: 4, 35, 37, 88, 137, 155, 255, 345, 355, 417, G1

Overview

A lot is packed into this 54-acre park—mostly people. On a sunny day Clissold throngs with Stokenewingtonites; yummy mummies and three-wheeled buggies; gaggles of youths, with or without hoods; lads playing football; and assorted dog walkers. Visitors can see deer and goats in the animal enclosure, diamond doves and love birds in the aviary, and coots and moorhens in the nature ponds. Parents take little ones to the paddling pool (summer months only), toddlers group at the One O'clock Club or the well-equipped children's playground. The park hosts the usual hodgepodge of circuses and steam fairs as well as the famous arts festival, StokeFest, in the summer. On grey days, chilly days, or in the early hours, peace can be found—in the rose garden perhaps, or underneath one of the ancient trees.

Clissold House and Café

Phone:	0207 923 9797
Email:	info@clissoldparkcafe.com
Website:	www.hackneyvenues.com/clissold-house
Hours:	Open daily.
Admission:	FREE

Clissold Mansion, the Grade II listed building just visible from Stoke Newington Church Street, is home to a large, child-friendly cafe. Herbal tea drinkers jostle with dripping ice-cream cone lickers on the sun trap front veranda and circular lawn. The large inside rooms are best avoided if you find children's chatter grating, but otherwise a lively spot to tuck into a plate of egg and chips. The building was constructed in the late 18th century on behalf of a Quaker family whose daughter was courted by a local reverend—Augustus Clissold. He wooed, then married her, and swiftly changed the name of the estate to Clissold Place. Where is Catherine Cookson when you need her?

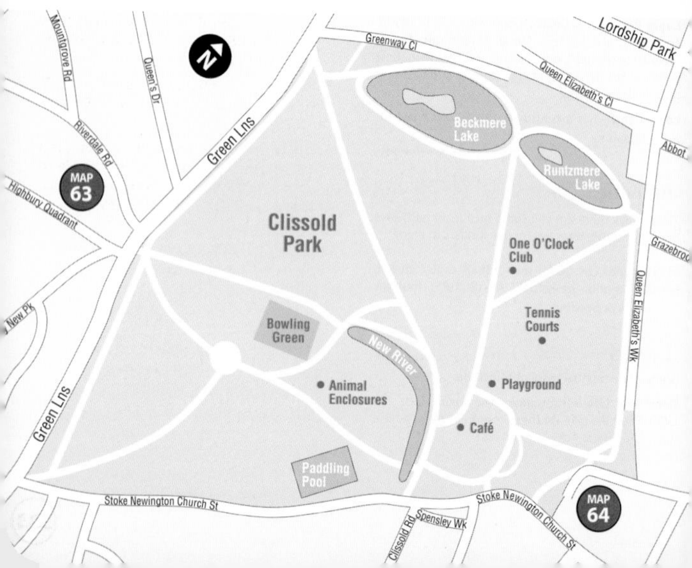

A hundred years later when the land was up for redevelopment, two influential campaigners persuaded the Metropolitan Board of Works to create a public space, and Clissold Park was born on 24 July 1889. Now run by the London Borough of Hackney, Clissold is kept in check by the Clissold Park User Group, who recently secured a multi-million pound lottery bid to spruce the place up a bit and return it to its former 19th century splendour.

Sport in the Park

Year round you can hear the yells of football players churning up mud, the whine of iPods as joggers run in ever decreasing circles, the thwack of cricket ball against cricket bat, and the crunch of misthrown Frisbees hitting the litter bins. There is a basketball court and 10 tennis courts (two kiddies' sized) which are bookable by contacting the Park rangers (020 7254 4235) though they are impossible to get your hands on around Wimbledon—and they say TV doesn't affect our behaviour.

But one of the delights of this park is the more unusual sport that takes place. On misty mornings you can watch cotton-clad figures practice tai chi, and on warm weekends you can nearly always spot a group of hotties from the London School of Capoeira circling around each other. Then there is the occasional father/ daughter pair practising Taekwondo, or two dreadlocked crusties slinging up a line to get some tightrope practice in. Most recent addition to watchable sports in the park is run by 'Pushy Mothers'—groups of mums exercising with buggies. The buggy, with child on board, is pushed hither and thither by the panting parent. It's the ultimate in resistance training.

Nature and the Ponds

Hackney is one of the greenest inner-city boroughs and though relatively small, Clissold Park is still an important green, shady and watery spot for local wildlife, particularly waterfowl. The two nature ponds are named Beckmere and the Runtzmere in honour of the two principal founders (Beck and Runtz, in case you were wondering). The third pond in front of the cafe is more of a 'canalette' and actually used to be part of the New River built in the early 1600s to supply drinking water to London.

The animal enclosure with its fuzzy-nosed deer, fluffy rabbits and bearded mini-goats are popular with visitors who stand stuffing chips and handfuls of poisonous leaves from nearby bushes through the fence directly under the signs saying: 'Please don't feed the animals—it will make them ill.'

Note: the paddling pool is not a nature pond and though you still can't let your dog in, hours spent gazing at its inhabitants are not looked on kindly.

How to Get There

By car: Don't. There isn't much in the way of parking. But if you really need to, from Newington Green head north along Green Lanes until you see a large green space with trees on your right. Or from the A10 turn left onto Stoke Newington Church St past all the cute shops and inviting pubs, until you get to the large church on your left. The park is on your right.

By tube: From Manor House, take exit 4 and walk south down Green Lanes for 10 minutes. The park is on your left.

By train: From Stoke Newington station, head south down the High St and turn right up Stoke Newington Church St, walk for 10 minutes until you see the park on your left just past Stoke Newington Town Hall.

By bus: The 341, 141, 73, 393, and 476 all stop at various entrances to the park

Additional Information

London Borough of Hackney
www.hackney.gov.uk/clissold-park.htm

Clissold Park User Group
www.clissoldpark.com

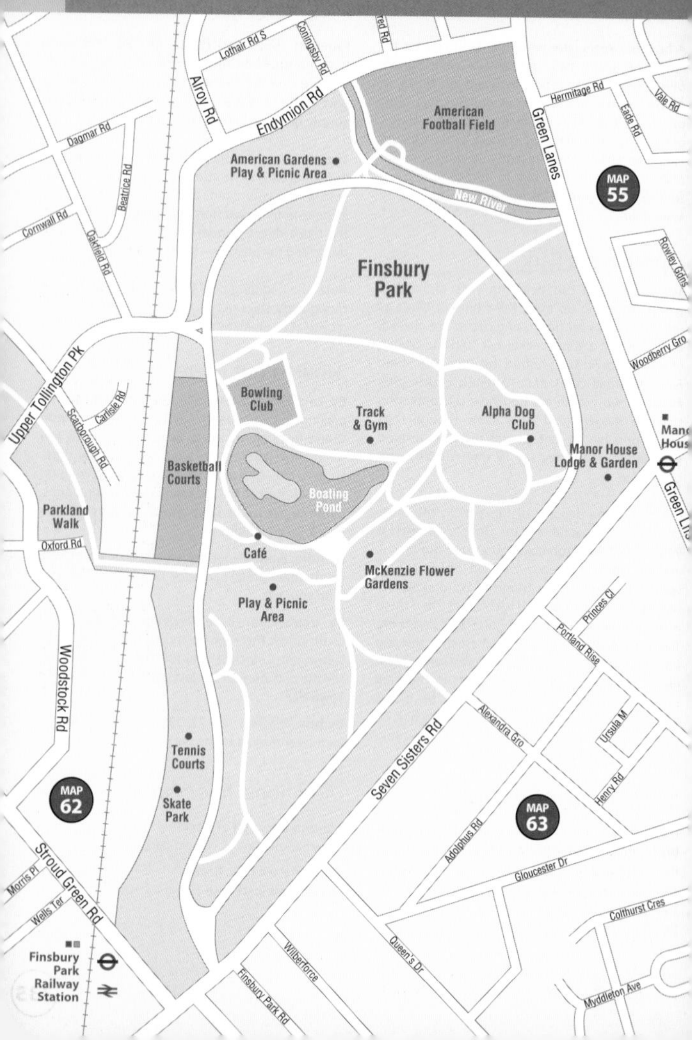

Lothair Rd S
Coningsby Rd
Alroy Rd
Endymion Rd
American Football Field
Hermitage Rd
Vale Rd
Eade Rd
Green Lanes
Dagmar Rd
American Gardens Play & Picnic Area
MAP 55
New River
Beatrice Rd
Cornwall Rd
Oakfield Rd
Finsbury Park
Rowley Gdns
Woodberry Gro
Upper Tollington Pk
Carlisle Rd
Scarborough Rd
Bowling Club
Track & Gym
Alpha Dog Club
Manor House Lodge & Garden
Basketball Courts
Boating Pond
Green Lns
Parkland Walk
Oxford Rd
Café
McKenzie Flower Gardens
Play & Picnic Area
Princes Cl
Portland Rise
Woodstock Rd
Alexandra Gro
Ursula M
Seven Sisters Rd
Tennis Courts
Skate Park
Henry Rd
MAP 62
MAP 63
Adolphus Rd
Stroud Green Rd
Gloucester Dr
Morris Pl
Wells Ter
Colthurst Cres
Finsbury Park Railway Station
Wilberforce
Queen's Dr
Finsbury Park Rd
Myddleton Ave

General Information

NFT Map: 55, 62, & 63
Website: www.haringey.gov.uk/finsbury_park_leaflet.pdf

Overview

Sculpted from what was once a large woodland area on the fringes of London, Finsbury Park was baptized officially in the mid 19th century as a green escape for increasingly urbanized North Londoners. Today's Finsbury Park has been revamped to the tune of £5 million in an attempt to shake off the cloak of urban grime which descended during the 1970s. Though it certainly has cleaned up its act, the park is still a barren tundra-esque plain compared to Hyde or Regent's Park. More of a green scab on the city landscape that surrounds it, the sparse shrubbery and token trees are more suitable for football or running away from Staffordshire Terriers. Delve a little deeper, however and there are quaint eccentricities and little gems dotted around.

Practicalities

You can enter this veritable urban Oz at Endymion Road, Seven Sisters Road, Green Lanes and Stroud Green Road. Two tube stops serve Finsbury Park: Manor House and the eponymous Finsbury Park. There are also overland trains at Harringey Green Lanes (grab an opulent Turkish meal on the way) and at Finsbury Park Stroud Green Road. Buses 4, 19, N19, 29, N29, 106, N106, 253, N253, 254, N279, W3 and W7 all touch the park at some point. Bear in mind that if you wish to travel in the area during an Arsenal match day you'd better take a stun gun and a red scarf to navigate the crowds!

Attractions

Quaint Englishness and sweaty sporting pursuits abound within the perimeters of Finsbury Park. There are many activities you can partake in from tennis (seven courts are available on a turn up and play basis) to running in the London Heathside Athletics Club (020 8802 9139). There are even two American Football pitches. For a more twee time stroll up to the tiny boating pond and spend an hour in a beat-up boat circling the aviary island—home to exotic birds like ducks, some swans and, uh, ducks again. The kidz are catered for in the form of a skate park. Best of all is the amazing Parkland Walk, which snakes out from Finsbury Park to Alexandra Palace via Highgate.

Nature

The Arboretum and the Avenue of Mature Trees are the two main spots for tree watching. Granted, experienced botanists may find little to fire them up here, but on a mild Autumn day there are plenty of rich colours and textures that enrich any stroll through the park. There are no real 'wild' areas in the park, unlike Hampstead Heath, but there are some lovely quiet spots in the American Gardens which have been landscaped according to the original 19th century plans, with added kiddie play areas. There are some shrubs planted around the boating pond which Harringey Council calls the 'McKenzie Flower Garden' with capital letters which are barely merited.

Festivals

Recently the vast open spaces of the park have been used for music festivals and various other fairs. The Rise, Fleadh, and FinFest festivals are all fairly regular events. The park is also a popular venue for one off special music events—both the Sex Pistols and Morrissey have played controversial shows here. The steam and fun fairs are also worth going to for nostalgic or regressive fun.

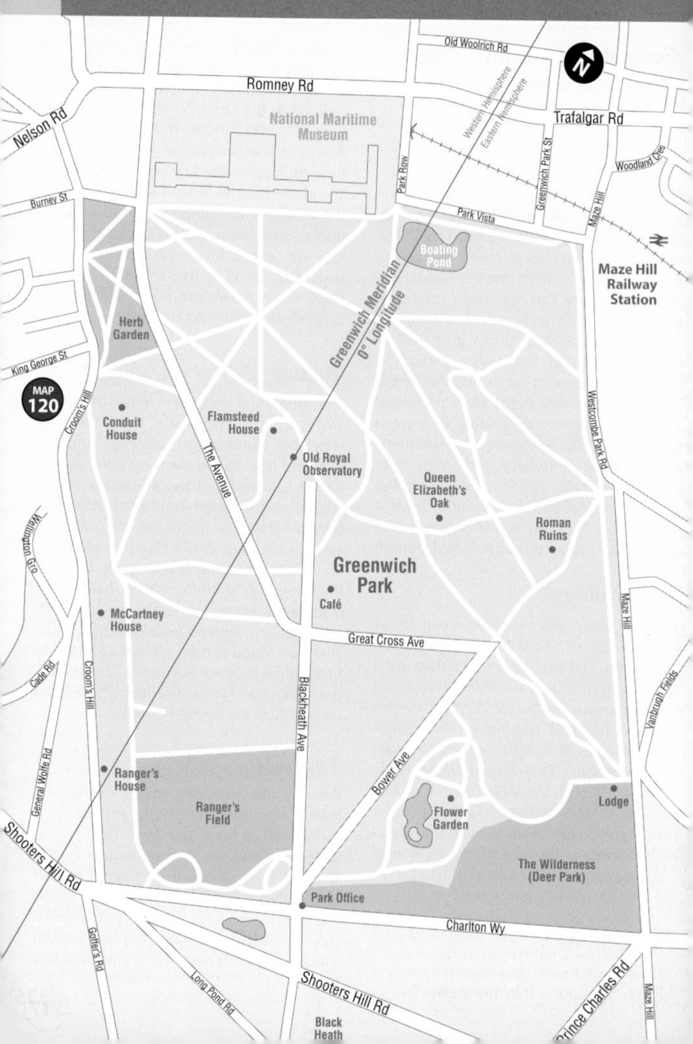
Old Woolrich Rd
Romney Rd
Trafalgar Rd
Nelson Rd
National Maritime Museum
Western Hemisphere
Eastern Hemisphere
Woodland Cres
Park Row
Greenwich Park St
Maze Hill
Burney St
Park Vista
Boating Pond
Maze Hill Railway Station
Greenwich Meridian 0° Longitude
Herb Garden
King George St
MAP 120
Croom's Hill
Conduit House
Flamsteed House
Old Royal Observatory
The Avenue
Westcombe Park Rd
Queen Elizabeth's Oak
Roman Ruins
Wellington Gro
Greenwich Park
Café
McCartney House
Great Cross Ave
Maze Hill
Cade Rd
Croom's Hill
Blackheath Ave
Vanbrugh Fields
General Wolfe Rd
Bower Ave
Ranger's House
Ranger's Field
Flower Garden
Lodge
Shooters Hill Rd
The Wilderness (Deer Park)
Park Office
Charlton Wy
Goffer's Rd
Long Pond Rd
Shooters Hill Rd
Prince Charles Rd
Maze Hill
Black Heath

Overview

Greenwich Park is the oldest enclosed Royal Park in Britain and has been an integral part of London life for centuries. Saxons built mounds here; Romans worshipped here; King Henry VIII and Anne Boleyn flirted here, and Charles II even built an observatory here. Then the modern day caught up and 2012 brought it to the world as an Olympic venue. It's now a playground for ageing eccentrics escaping London, yuppie families with new puppies, and heaps of tourists trekking up the staggeringly steep hill towards the iconic Royal Observatory.

And it's worth the trek. The sweeping views from the highest point are spectacular and beat the London Eye hands down. London is revealed in all its glory, from the jutting skyline of Canary Wharf, to the sinuous turns of the Thames and the seemed-like-a-good-idea-at-the-time Millennium Dome. All in stark contrast with the neoclassical architecture of the Old Royal Observatory, Royal Naval College, National Maritime Museum and the Queen's House in the immediate foreground.

A well sought-after spot throughout history, the park has belonged to the Royal Family since 1427, and in the early 1600s, under James I, the park was given a makeover in the French style, which gave it its well-groomed tree-lined pathways. He then had Inigo Jones build the missus the stately Queen's House.

The Royal Observatory and Flamsteed House

Address:	Greenwich Royal Park, Greenwich, London SE10
Phone:	020 8858 4422
Website:	www.rmg.co.uk/royal-observatory
Hours:	10 am-5 pm daily
Admission:	Flamsteed House & Meridian Courtyard—£14.40 adults, £7.20 Children

Time begins, rather arbitrarily, here—on the Prime Meridian of the World, or Longitude 0°. Time all over the earth is based on a place's distance east or west from this imaginary line, outlined in metal so throngs of tourists can gawp at it. Thanks to Charles II's interest in science, Sir Christopher Wren was commissioned to build the Royal Observatory and Flamsteed House, the living quarters for the first Royal Astronomer. Time your visit to catch a workshop, talk, exhibition or planetarium show, which seek to give visitors a richer experience than simply straddling the Meridian with thumbs up.

Also notable is the Camera Obscura, which sits in a small building next to Flamsteed House. A predecessor to the modern camera, this small dark room displays a live image of the distant National Maritime Museum, projected using only a small hole in the roof.

National Maritime Museum

Address:	Greenwich, London SE10 9NF
Phone:	020 8858 4422
Website:	www.rmg.co.uk/national-maritime-museum
Hours:	10 am-5 pm daily
Admission:	Free

Adjacent to the park's boundaries, this is a museum dedicated to all things nautical. It comprises the Royal Observatory, as well as the Queen's House, but its main components are the Maritime Galleries. Highlights include a collection of ships' figureheads, navigational charts, maps, medals, flags and models. They also host relics from Sir John Franklin's ill-fated Northwest Passage expedition (1845-1848) including a pair of his very old-school sunglasses.

Nature

Amongst the well-mowed green are trees of infinite varieties. The scented herb garden is best enjoyed in the summer time. The fallen remains of the 900 year-old Queen Elizabeth Oak can still be viewed and lie as proof of Henry VIII's passion for these grounds, he was said to have danced around the younger tree with Anne Boleyn (before he had her executed, obviously).

How to Get There

The nearest DLR station is Cutty Sark. It's fun too: push the excitable children out the way so you can sit in the front and pretend to be the driver—always a winner with the ladies. By bus, the 53, 177, 180, 188, 199 and 286 will all get you to points of suitable proximity.

You can also take the Greenwich foot tunnel from the Isle of Dogs, which runs beneath the Thames and is open 24 hours a day. Ignore the ominous drips: it's been sturdy for over 110 years, and even if it does at last succumb to the pressure of 50 ft of river above it, then you'll not have time to worry about it. So relax and enjoy!

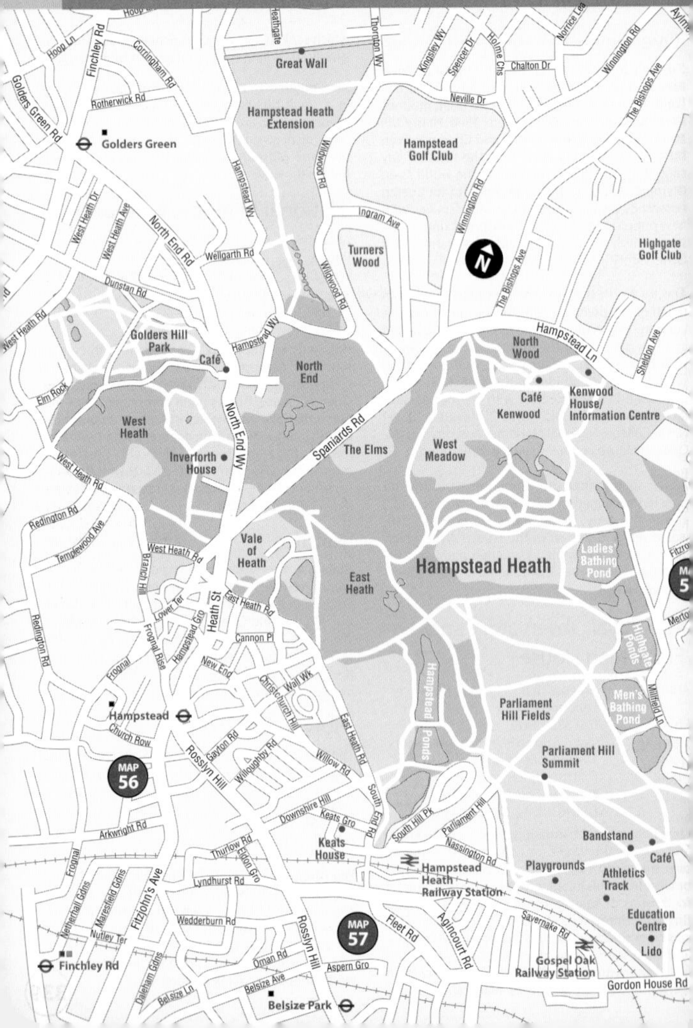
Great Wall
Hampstead Heath Extension
Hampstead Golf Club
Golders Green
Turners Wood
Highgate Golf Club
Golders Hill Park
Café
North End
North Wood
Café
Kenwood
Kenwood House/ Information Centre
West Heath
Inverforth House
The Elms
West Meadow
Vale of Heath
East Heath
Hampstead Heath
Ladies' Bathing Pond
Highgate Ponds
Men's Bathing Pond
Hampstead Ponds
Parliament Hill Fields
Parliament Hill Summit
Hampstead
MAP 56
Keats House
Hampstead Heath Railway Station
Bandstand
Café
Playgrounds
Athletics Track
Education Centre
Lido
MAP 57
Gospel Oak Railway Station
Finchley Rd
Belsize Park
Hoop Ln
Finchley Rd
Corringham Rd
Golders Green Rd
Rotherwick Rd
Heathgate
Thornton Wy
Kingsley Wy
Spencer Dr
Holme Chs
Chalton Dr
Norrice Lea
Winnington Rd
The Bishops Ave
Neville Dr
Wildwood Rd
Hampstead Wy
Ingram Ave
Winnington Rd
West Heath Dr
West Heath Ave
North End Rd
Wellgarth Rd
Dunstan Rd
West Heath Rd
Hampstead Wy
Hampstead Ln
Sheldon Ave
Elm Rock
North End Wy
Spaniards Rd
West Heath Rd
Redington Rd
Templewood Ave
West Heath Rd
Branch Hill
Lower Ter
East Heath Rd
Heath St
Cannon Pl
Hampstead Gro
Frognal Rise
Redington Rd
Frognal
New End
Christchurch Hill
Wall Wk
East Heath Rd
Millfield Ln
Church Row
Gayton Rd
Willoughby Rd
Willow Rd
Rosslyn Hill
Downshire Hill
Keats Gro
South End Rd
South Hill Pk
Parliament Hill
Arkwright Rd
Thurlow Rd
Eldon Gro
Nassington Rd
Frognal
Lyndhurst Rd
Netherhall Gdns
Maresfield Gdns
Fitzjohn's Ave
Wedderburn Rd
Nutley Ter
Rosslyn Hill
Fleet Rd
Agincourt Rd
Savernake Rd
Daleham Gdns
Oman Rd
Aspern Gro
Belsize Ave
Belsize Ln
Gordon House Rd
Merton
Fitzroy

Overview

Hampstead Heath is 791 acres of rambling woods and idyllic meadows worthy of much frolicking. It's the fact that its wilderness seems so, well, wild that makes this London park deceptive. You can be merrily re-enacting the Brothers Grimm, only to be spat out rather rudely onto Parliament Hill and confronted with gob-smacking views of St Paul's and the Gherkin. The Heath is truly nothing short of heaven—until you stumble over George Michael up to no good in the bushes. You can swim naked in its ponds, stroll amongst its tall grasses without seeing another living soul for twenty minutes or more and engage in a little sex scandal amongst the greenery. The park's common theme is one of a hidden countryside retreat right in the middle of it all.

Most likely because it *is* countryside. It's just the rest of London that's gone all urban around it. Long-established hedgerows and ancient trees attest to its lengthy history. The range of wildlife on show is impressive—kingfishers, parakeets, 300 species of fungi and several types of bat, to name a few. All sorts of famous people have enjoyed its leafy company through the years. Boudicca's Mound near the men's bathing pond (hmm... sounds dirty), is said to mark the ancient queen's burial chamber. Karl Marx and his family had a picnic here every Sunday while he lived in London and writer Wilkie Collins used the park as a backdrop for The Woman in White. All in all, the Heath has been a much-loved place of social gathering and strolling for centuries, a place of peace and perspective amongst the greater hustle and bustle of the Big Smoke.

Ponds, Ponds and…Oh Yeah, More Ponds…

It might be argued that losing your Heath virginity consists of swimming in one of its famous outdoor bathing ponds. These are open throughout the year and attract throngs of dedicated swimming fans. On the eastern side—closer to Highgate—are a series of eight 17th and 18th century reservoirs dotted between Parliament Hill Fields and Kenwood House. Amongst these is one swimming pond for guys, another for gals, a toy boat pond, a wildlife reserve pond, and a lake for fishing. On the western side of the Heath are three more, including the 'mixed pond', where you can have some underwater flirtations, should you wish.

Kenwood House

Kenwood House is closed for refurbishment until Autumn 2013. However, the Brewhouse Café remains open and can be visited between 9am-5pm. Kenwood House, a 17th century manor in the middle of the park, adds very nicely to the Heath's countryside effect. Its striking classically white walls and landscaped grounds play backdrop to summer jazz festivals as well as a few scenes in the movie Notting Hill. Purchased by brewing magnate Edward Cecil Guinness in 1925, Kenwood House is more than just a pretty façade. Thanks to Guinness's fortune and interest in art, the manor house is also a very noteworthy art gallery featuring works by the likes of Rembrandt, Turner and Gainsborough.

Golders Hill Park

Golders Hill Park is the younger brother to the bigger Hampstead Heath, adjoining it on the western side. Where the latter is an icon of epic proportions, the former is more of a good ol' neighbourhood park. Its large expanse of grass was created rather suddenly when a house that stood on the grounds was bombed during the Blitz. It has a lot to offer for its size though, with a formal flower garden, a deer park and a small zoo (with alpacas no less). If you're feeling sporty, there are tennis courts, putting greens and plenty of jogging paths.

How to Get There

The closest tube stations are Hampstead, Golder's Green and Archway on the Northern Line. Nearby overland stations include Hampstead Heath and Gospel Oak. Bus numbers running to the park are the 168, 268 and 210, which cuts through on Spaniard's Road (where you may want to stop for a pint at the historic Spaniard's Inn).

Additional Information

City of London
www.cityoflondon.gov.uk

Information and booking tickets for swimming:
020 7485 5757

Heath and Hampstead Society:
www.heathandhampsteadsociety.org.uk

Highgate Cemetery General Info

NFT Map: 51 & 59
Web: www.highgate-cemetery.org
Phone: 020 8340 1834

West Cemetery

The West Cemetery opened in 1839 and most of the original pathways and structures still exist. This part of the cemetery is a wild wonderland of creeping vines and eerie Victorian tombs. On weekdays, tours take place daily at 1:45 pm from March to November. There's a limit of 15 people so you'll need to book in advance on the number above. The weekends are a free-for-all with tours taking place hourly from 11 am until 4 pm April to November and until 3 pm December to March.

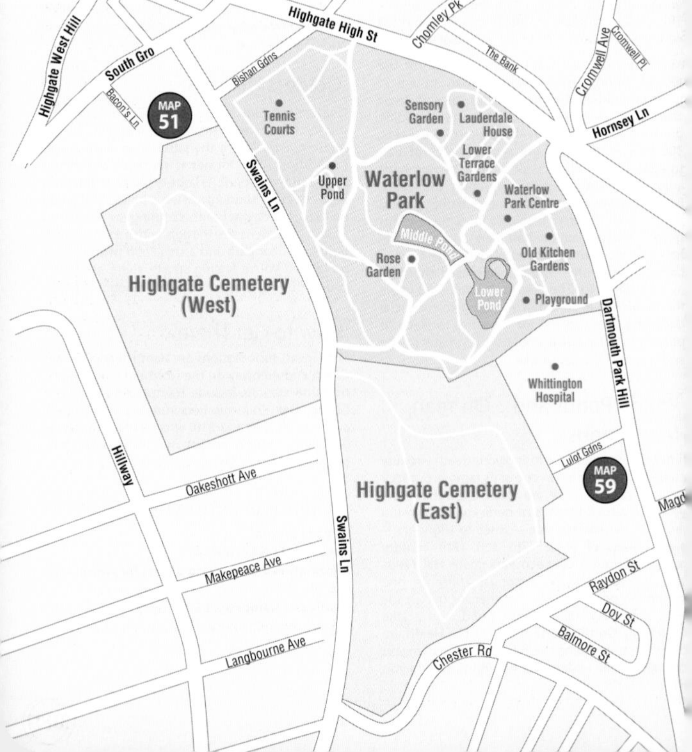

East Cemetery

The newer East Cemetery is located on the opposite side of the road to the West entrance. This side is open daily and for four pounds you get to roam unsupervised for as long as you please. It may not be as impressive as the West side, but it's still a place of breathtaking beauty. Although there are some well-trodden paths and proper walkways, large parts of the cemetery are almost completely overgrown, making it a wonderful place to go for a stroll.

Opening Hours
1st April to 31st October
Mon-Fri: 10 am-5 pm
Sat-Sun: 11 am-5 pm

1st November to 31st March
Mon-Fri: 10 am-4 pm
Sat-Sun: 11 am-4 pm

Famous Occupants

Quite a few notable people are buried here. The caretakers will be more than willing to inform you of the whereabouts of the following graves and plenty of others.

Douglas Adams, author. Most famous for the *Hitchhiker's Guide To The Galaxy* series of books.

George Eliot, English author and poet; also actually a woman.

Christina Rossetti, English poet.

Karl Marx. Philosopher; considered the father of communism.

Alexander Livinenko, Russian ex-spy, famously murdered by radiation poisoning in a Soho sushi restaurant in 2006.

A whole load of Charles Dickens' clan but not the man himself.

The Highgate Vampire

There have been numerous accounts of shapes, ghosts and supernatural figures seen on the cemetery grounds, and in the early 70s the media picked up on a theory involving a vampire and the legend of The Highgate Vampire was born. It caused quite a stir and soon mobs of 'vampire hunters' descended on the place (imagine something like the Thriller video, but with flares and tank tops). Finally, Sean Manchester, president and founder of the Vampire Research Society, claimed to have killed the fiend in 1973, when he tracked it to a nearby house. Manchester was also, in his spare time, patron of the Yorkshire Robin Hood society, and remains, in this publication's estimation, the single most compelling reason not to wander around Highgate Cemetery after dark.

Waterlow Park Overview

Waterlow Park is a beautifully landscaped park located just next to the cemetery, making it a perfect spot for a pre- or post-gravespotting picnic. Often overlooked and overshadowed by nearby Hampstead Heath it is a charming and peaceful alternative. You can feed the ducks in one of the three ponds, hire tennis courts by the hour, admire the awesome view of London, wander in the rose garden, or just go and look at the cool hollow tree at the bottom of the park.

Lauderdale House

Address: Highgate Hill, Waterlow Park
London N6 5HG
Tel: 020 8348 8716
Web: www.lauderdalehouse.co.uk

Lauderdale House operates independently from the park, but is located on its grounds. The original house was built in 1582, but has gone through major alterations and restorations since then. In 1963 a major fire destroyed much of the old building and it was left untouched and unoccupied for 15 years. In 1978 it was finally repaired and reopened in its current incarnation. The house runs classes, concerts and exhibitions by local artists. There's also a small café. The House and the galleries are usually open Tue-Fri 11 am-4 pm, Sat 1.30 pm-5 pm & Sun 12 pm-5 pm, but you can always phone in advance to avoid disappointment.

How to Get There

Nearest tube station is Archway. Exit the station and turn left up Highgate Hill. Waterlow Park is about five minutes walk on your left hand side. To get to the cemetery, cross the park down to the Swain's Lane exit, which is adjacent to the East Cemetery gates.

General Information

Website:	http://www.royalparks.org.uk/parks/hyde-park parks/hyde_park
Phone:	030 0061 2000

Overview

For over 370 years Hyde Park has been the 'Lungs of London'—the place to go for oxygen-starved Londoners to take a breath of fresh air. This park remains an essential part of the beating heart of London. As the city's grown, so has the desire to preserve this 350-acre mass of parkland and thankfully, Hyde Park has never been in better shape.

Eating

Perambulating through the park is bound to get that metabolism going, so stop off at one of the numerous food stalls to quench your thirst or down a plasticky hot-dog. Yum. For a more civilised affair check out one of the park's seated joints: the **Lido Café** (whic also has a paddling pool) or **The Serpentine Bar & Kitchen**.

Nature, Architecture & Sculpture

The Serpentine Lake attracts the usual assortmer of ducks as well as some exotic additions, such a Egyptian Geese. **The Lookout Education Centr** holds informative talks about the park's wildlif **The Grand Entrance** at Hyde Park Corner is an awe inspiring arched construction of Greek influenc whilst the **Albert Memorial**, erected by Quee Victoria after her husband's death, is a true shov of love. The **Diana, Princess of Wales Memoria Fountain**, remains one of the most visited areas i Hyde Park and is worth a look to satisfy curiosity, as the **Peter Pan Memorial**. And pause to reflect at th heartbreaking 7 July Memorial, which pays tribute t each of the victims of the 2005 London Bombings.

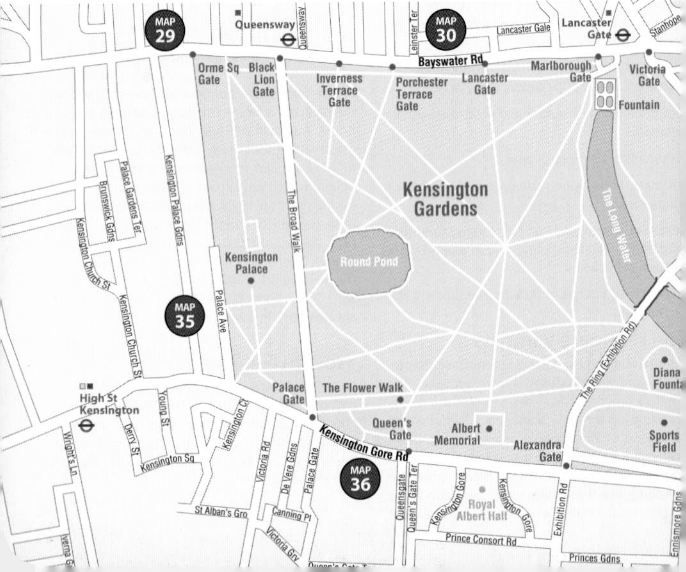

Performance

The park attracts big musical events, and by big we mean Live 8 big. It's only the musical deities that get their own special Hyde Park treatment—Bruce Springsteen, Paul McCartney and Blur, but summer means festival time and the annual Wireless Festival and Hard Rock Calling. Brass band concerts are held throughout the summer at **The Bandstand**. **Speakers' Corner** is guaranteed to entertain. Since 1872 it's been the site of a verbal free-for-all stemming from the activities of the Reform League who marched for manhood suffrage in 1866. These days the topics aren't quite as revolutionary. Heather Mills sounded off here recently…ah, the injustice of having too much cash.

Sports

There are ample jogging paths, designated bike routes (see www.companioncycling.org.uk) and great paths for roller-blading and walking. Even more fun is boating on **The Serpentine Lake** from March to October. Informal games of rugby, football or cricket can be played on the **'Sports Field'** while **Hyde Park Tennis & Sports Centre** does exactly what it says on the tin. There's also a bowling green and horse riding at the **Manege.**

Kensington Gardens

The 111 hectares west of the Western Carriage Drive are known as Kensington Gardens. Annexed from the main park in 1689, the area retains a slightly more formal air, with regular tree-lined avenues to stroll down and less spaces for rambunctious sporting displays. This makes the Gardens an ideal spot for a picnic or a quiet ponder. Kensington Gardens also boasts the **Serpentine Gallery** (in between the Diana Fountain and the Albert Memorial), a toy-sized venue for renowned modern and contemporary art exhibitions, and the rather stunning **Kensington Palace**. Still a royal residence, the palace majestically overlooks some of the most well ordered green spaces London has to offer.

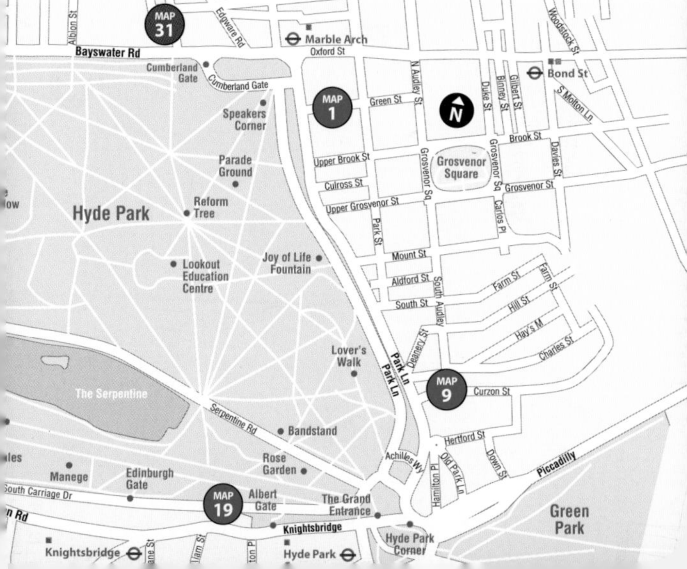

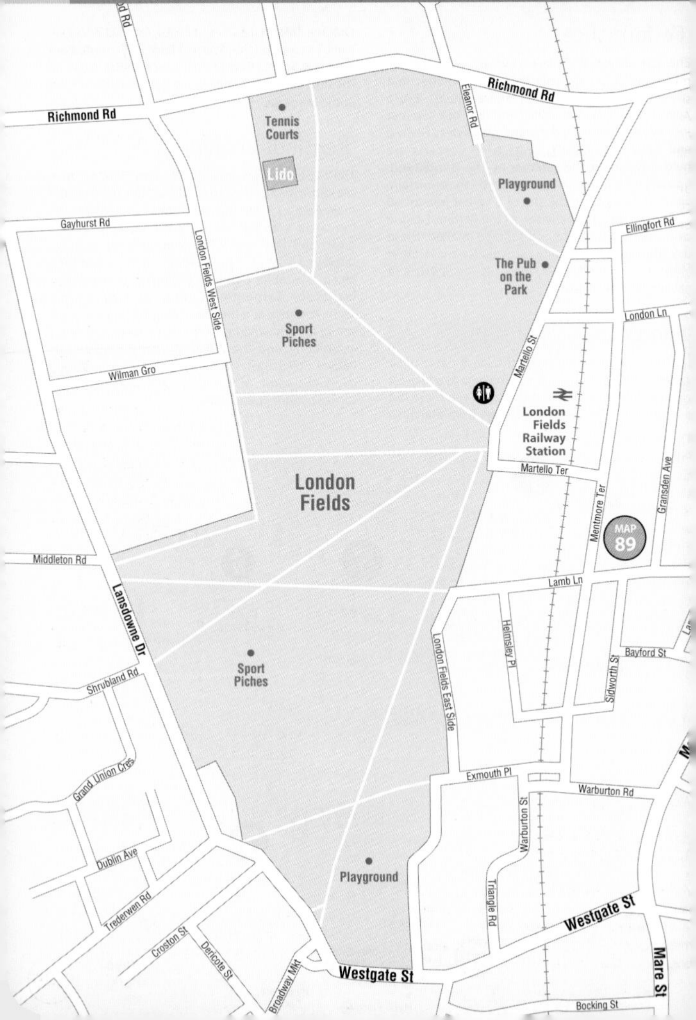

Richmond Rd
Richmond Rd
Tennis Courts
Lido
Eleanor Rd
Playground
Gayhurst Rd
London Fields West Side
Ellingfort Rd
The Pub on the Park
Sport Piches
London Ln
Martello St
Wilman Gro
London Fields Railway Station
Martello Ter
London Fields
Gransden Ave
Mentmore Ter
MAP 89
Middleton Rd
Lamb Ln
Lansdowne Dr
Helmsley Pl
Bayford St
Sport Piches
Shrubland Rd
Sidworth St
London Fields East Side
Grand Union Cres
Exmouth Pl
Warburton Rd
Warburton St
Dublin Ave
Playground
Trederwen Rd
Triangle Rd
Westgate St
Croston St
Dericote St
Broadway Mkt
Westgate St
Mare St
Bocking St

Overview

Best green space of the northeast? Victoria Park might still bag the accolade, but this relaxed, mid-sized park in the middle of Hackney is catching up. And quickly. It's lush and it's spacious and its latest addition, a smashing 50-metres Lido (see below), is hard to beat. Just off busy Mare Street and minutes from Regent's Canal, the park is easily reachable and easily manageable. There are two tennis courts, football, basketball and cricket pitches, and two well-equipped and well-maintained playgrounds, if you have kids in tow. London Fields does a nice job of attracting a pleasantly diverse mix of people, from Hoxton-refugee artists and rollie-smoking would-be philosophers, to pram-pushing mums and East End geezers with no teeth and big dogs. The architecture framing the tree-studded space is just as varied: bland high rises, pretty Victorians, depressing brick estates and fancy new developments, all modern Hackney is there.

The park's own drinking spot, imaginatively called Pub on the Park, is good for a relaxed outside pint, simple pub food or the footie. If you're after a slightly more refined meal, check the gastropub-ish Cat and Mutton at the park's bottom. This is also where Broadway Market begins, a traditional East End market street, now brimming with nice little shops, several pubs and original eateries. If the red wine you shared with your painter friends on their picnic blanket got you into serious party mood, head to the close-by (and late-night) Dolphin on Mare Street. Or just fall asleep in the shadows of those massive oak trees. Chances are, one of the dogs will lick you back to reality.

London Fields Lido

Address: London Fields Westside, London E8 3EU
Phone: 020 7254 9038
Website: http://www.hackney.gov.uk/c-londonfields-lido.htm
Hours: Mon-Fri 6:30am—8pm
Admission: £3.65 for adults, £2.10 for kids

You might say that in a city where, essentially, you have the choice between stomach-turningly grotty leisure centre pools and hopelessly overpriced member gym versions, any new public swimming basin would be a winner. Fair enough. But WHAT a winner. Having mouldered closed for almost two decades, a £2.5m effort has restored this art deco gem to its former glory. In fact, it's probably better than ever: the 50-metre basin is nicely heated all year round (25C when we last checked), the changing rooms are modern and clean, admission's okay. Come during the week for a few pre-work lanes, when steam mysteriously hangs over the water, or jump in on the weekend, followed by a Sunday roast in one of the pubs close-by or a picnic in the park. Sounds nice? We know.

Sports

There's no shortage of things to do. The park's two tennis courts can be booked for hourly slots (open 8.30 am-dusk; £6.00/h during peak times, £4.00/h off-peak; call 020 7254 4235 for more info). The Hackney Tennis Club (www.hackneycitytennisclubs.co.uk) also offers classes and joint sessions. The football pitch (just come and play) is located in the middle, the basketball space (ditto) towards the south. Follow the sound of children for the playgrounds, one in the north, one in the south. If cricket is your cup of tea, get in touch with the London Fields Cricket Club (londonfieldscc@gmail.com), who keep the park's long-standing tradition as a cricket pitch alive (which, incidentally, is said to go back to 1800).

How to Get There

By bus: Most buses stop on Mare Street (get off at the London Fields stop), a few minutes walk from the actual park. From Liverpool Street Station, take 48 and 55, from Mile End or Bethnal Green grab the D6. The 106 takes you here from Finsbury Park, the 277 from Highbury & Islington. Two buses stop directly at the bottom of the park: the 236 (connecting to Dalston, Newington Green, Finsbury Park) and the 394 (Hackney Central, Homerton Hospital, Hoxton, Angel).

By train: The train is a great option, since London Fields station is located right next to the park. Train operator National Express East Anglia (formerly known as One Railway) serves the central Liverpool Street Station (via Cambridge Heath and Bethnal Green) and connects the Victoria Line tube stations Seven Sisters and Tottenham Hale further north. You can travel using your Oyster Card, for timetables check www.greateranglia.co.uk.

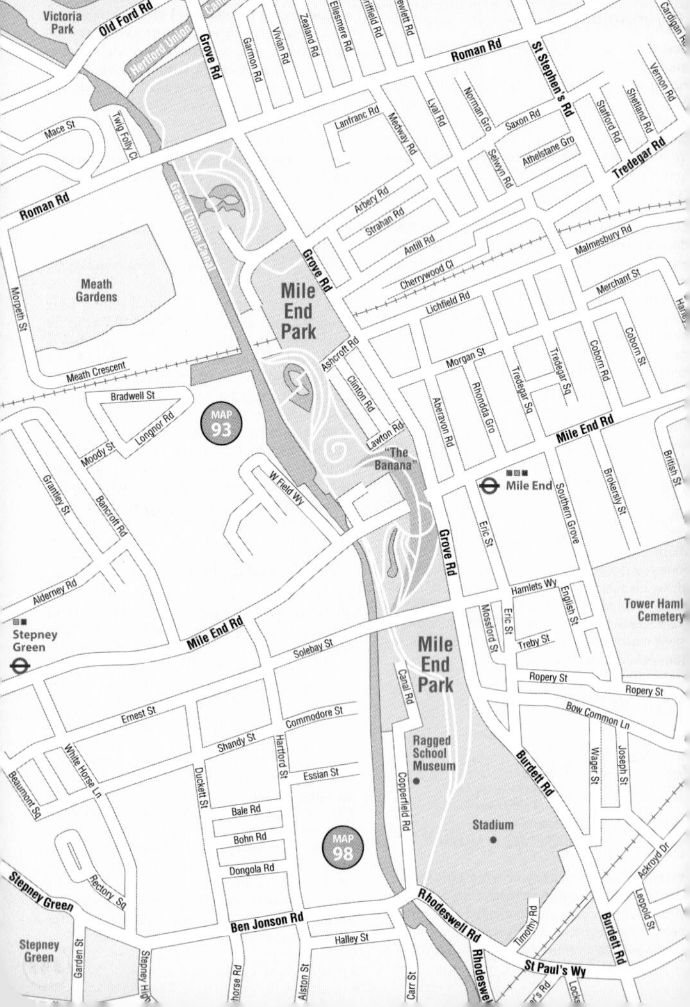

Victoria Park
Old Ford Rd
Hertford Union Canal
Grove Rd
Garmon Rd
Vivian Rd
Zealand Rd
Ellesmere Rd
Driffield Rd
Hewlett Rd
Roman Rd
St Stephen's Rd
Cardigan Rd
Vernon Rd
Shetland Rd
Stafford Rd
Tredegar Rd
Mace St
Twig Folly Cl
Lanfranc Rd
Medway Rd
Lyal Rd
Norman Gro
Saxon Rd
Selwyn Rd
Athelstane Gro
Roman Rd
Grand Union Canal
Arbery Rd
Strahan Rd
Antill Rd
Malmesbury Rd
Cherrywood Cl
Merchant St
Meath Gardens
Mile End Park
Lichfield Rd
Morpeth St
Ashcroft Rd
Coborn Rd
Coborn St
Morgan St
Tredegar Sq
Meath Crescent
Clinton Rd
Bradwell St
Aberavon Rd
Rhondda Gro
Longnor Rd
MAP 93
Lawton Rd
Mile End Rd
British St
Moody St
"The Banana"
W Field Wy
Mile End
Southern Grove
Brokersly St
Grantley St
Bancroft Rd
Eric St
Grove Rd
Alderney Rd
Hamlets Wy
English St
Tower Haml Cemetery
Stepney Green
Mile End Rd
Mossford St
Eric St
Treby St
Solebay St
Mile End Park
Canal Rd
Ropery St
Ropery St
Bow Common Ln
Ernest St
Commodore St
Shandy St
Hartford St
Ragged School Museum
Wager St
Joseph St
White Horse Ln
Essian St
Burdett Rd
Beaumont Sq
Duckett St
Copperfield Rd
Bale Rd
Stadium
Bohn Rd
MAP 98
Ackroyd Dr
Dongola Rd
Stepney Green
Rectory Sq
Rhodeswell Rd
Leopold St
Timothy Rd
Burdett Rd
Ben Jonson Rd
Halley St
St Paul's Wy
Stepney Green
Garden St
Alston St
Carr St

Overview

Bordered at the north by the chain-ridden fake-a-rama, Bow Wharf, to the east and south by rat runs, and to the west by the dank waters of the Regent's Canal, this strange elongated park doesn't appear to have a lot going for it. However, this 32-hectare wiggle of green is more a string of mini parks—divided up by roads and railway lines—and each segment has hidden treasures worth digging for. There is an adventure playground, an arts pavilion with weird orange-and-white sculptural seats by Leona Matuszczak, an ecology park with moths and all sorts, a terraced garden and a sheltered children's playground. Clever landscaping and inventive use of space creates pockets of peace, and when the sun comes out, sparkling on the canal, bouncing off of the reflective jackets of the cyclists bombing past or laying its beams on giggling young couples, the park of many parks comes into its own.

It was created following the Second World War after the area was destroyed in the Blitz. The idea of Lord Abercombie, who envisioned a creepy-sounding 'finger of green' in amongst the rubble, Mile End really came into being in 1999 with Millennium Commission funding providing new areas, strange metal cross signage and an amazing green bridge—known by locals as the Banana. It actually has grass and shrubs taking walkers and cyclists over Mile End Road.

The remains of the Victorian terraces sit on the west side of the park, and one resilient pub, The Palm Tree, squats alone in the middle of a grey car park, a testament to the rows of two-up-two-downs which no longer flank the pub. This great local boozer is filled most nights with a mix of climbers and locals tucking into doorstep sandwiches and draft beer.

For those who want a bit more local history, The Ragged School Museum (www.raggedschoolmuseum.org.uk) on Copperfield St overlooks the southern tip of the park: a canal side slum that was transformed into a school for the local urchins by philanthropist Dr Barnado. It now has a mocked-up Victorian classroom and clunky little cafe. Only open Wednesday and Thursday and the occassional Sunday—check before you go.

Sports in the Park

The southern end of the park is a haven for sporty types with a refurbished stadium and ten all-weather pitches made from recycled car tyres, a go-kart track and the large Ikea-like Mile End Leisure Centre with all the usual sauna, gym, pool and verruca-infested changing rooms.
Mile End Climbing Wall is housed in an old pipe engineering works in the middle of the park, and is one of London's 'big three' (The Castle and the Westway are the others). It was opened in the 80s and some of its users seem unaware of time's passage, judging by their fetching leggings.

How to Get There

By tube: Turn left out of Mile End station, cross Grove Rd and you'll find yourself at one of the entrances to the middle section of the park.

By car: The park can be easily accessed from Bow Road, Grove Rd, or Mile End Rd, though according to London Borough of Tower Hamlets, 'The local streets operate a resident's parking permit system and are regularly patrolled by traffic wardens. Limited parking is available at Bow Wharf.'

By bus: The, D6, D7, 25, 205, 277, 323, 339 and all take you to various entrances around the park.

Additional Information

London Borough of Tower Hamlets
www.towerhamlets.gov.uk/default.aspx?page=12599

Mile End Climbing Wall
www.mileendwall.org.uk

General Information

Website:	www.royalparks.org.uk/parks/the-regents-park
Park Tel:	030 0061 2300
London Zoo:	www.zsl.org
Open Air Theatre:	www.openairtheatre.org

Overview

Whenever your quaint and backward country-dwelling friends are telling you the virtues of rural life, you can silence them with two words: Regent's Park. Let the yokels have their cleaner lungs, their maypoles and their children running barefoot and feral, because London may have its city drawbacks but it knows how to do a good park. When you stroll in Regent's Park, you're strolling on nothing less than Property of the Crown—you can see tigers and gorillas, play on the largest outdoor sports area in London, take in some Shakespeare, or, on a very good day, watch girls playing volleyball in bikinis. With 410 acres of parkland, you will always find a spot away from the (many thousands of) fellow visitors. It is the perfect space to take stock, step back and refresh, to sit in a deckchair with a good book, picnic with friends, breathe better air. Moreover, the same obnoxious people who wouldn't move down the tube to let you on or

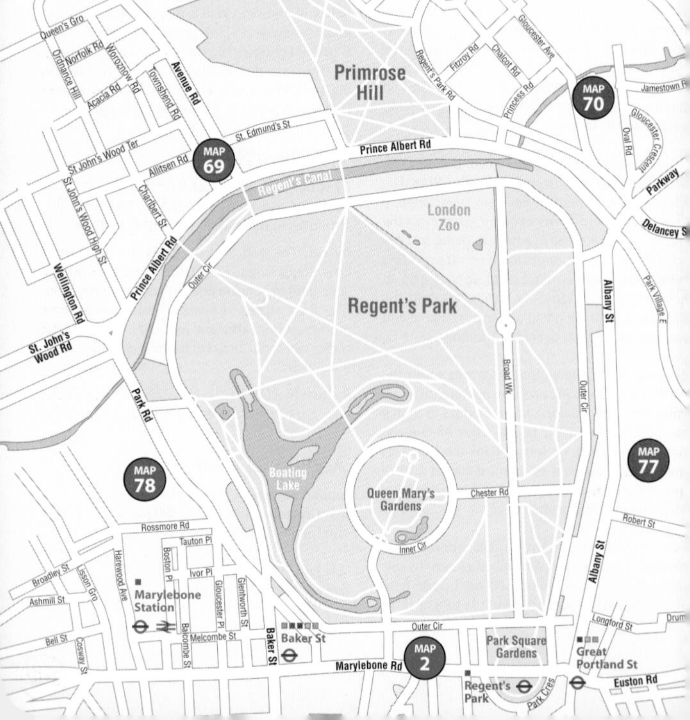

who pushed in the sandwich queue, are here relaxing with their families, lazing over a paper in a patch of sun, falling in love, throwing a Frisbee: it can be just what you need to re-bond with London when you're becoming jaded, and to get away from it all without leaving Zone One.

How to Get There

By tube:
Regent's Park—Bakerloo.
Great Portland St—Hammersmith & City, Circle, Metropolitan.
Baker St—Hammersmith & City, Jubilee, Metropolitan, Bakerloo.
St John's Wood—Jubilee.
Camden Town—Northern.

The Park is served by bus routes 2, 13, 18, 27, 30, 74, 82, 113, 139, 189, 274, 453 and C2.

Nature

The Park is a haven for the city's wildlife, thanks to a biodiversity which includes grassland, woodland, wetland, lakes and scrubs, as well as beautifully tended and fragrant gardens. Over 200 species of birds have been spotted in the Park, along with favourite garden mammals such as hedgehogs, squirrels and foxes. But if that's all just a bit too Beatrix Potter, you can get your fix of the more badass species at London Zoo in the Park's north-east end, where in addition to the normal enclosures, visitors can get closer to some of the animals with events like "Meet the Monkeys" or even help as a volunteer.

The Park's size and calm makes it a choice hangout for celebrities (not strictly nature, but dandelion schmandelion: spotting A-Listers doing tai chi in oversized sunglasses will impress more down the pub, and can there be a nobler calling?).

Performances and Events

The Park's permanent outdoor theatre is an absolute treat. The shows have a Shakespearian bias, but the venue also puts on non-bard performances, comedy nights and concerts. It is the experience more than the performance which will likely stay in your memory. Among the atmospheric trees of the park in the evening, with a bottle of wine and a blanket to snuggle up in (it is Britain after all—how many other theatres have an official "weather policy"?), it is a magical way to spend an evening. Outdoor does not mean free however: prices range from £10–£50 (Saturdays are the most expensive), and you pay theatre prices for food and drink. Cheaper to bring a picnic to enjoy in front of the theatre before the performance.

Regent's Park also hosts a number of big outdoor events. Notable regulars include Taste of London and the Frieze Art Fair London. Check the website for one-off listings.

Primrose Hill

To the north of Regent's Park sits Primrose Hill, which is a rather large hill, boasting corking views of much of Central and East London. It's also surrounded by some rather lovely eateries.

The former hunting ground for playboy king Henry VIII has a murky history, becoming the scene of a political feud in 1678, when magistrate Edmund Berry Godfrey was found dead there after being implicated in a plot to kill Charles II. In later generations Primrose Hill became the setting for duels: London lovers fought there over their ladies, while fops found it a good place to settle literary disagreements ("I say Dryden is naught but a one-trick satirist sir!" "Well then I say you are a cad and a scoundrel! Die you maggot!").

Celebrity voyeurs should keep 'em peeled for the likes of Kate Moss, old bumbles himself Mr Boris Johnson, and writer Alan Bennett, while Primrose Hill in winter is the ideal spot to check out panoramic views of fireworks across the city on Guy Fawkes Night (5 November).

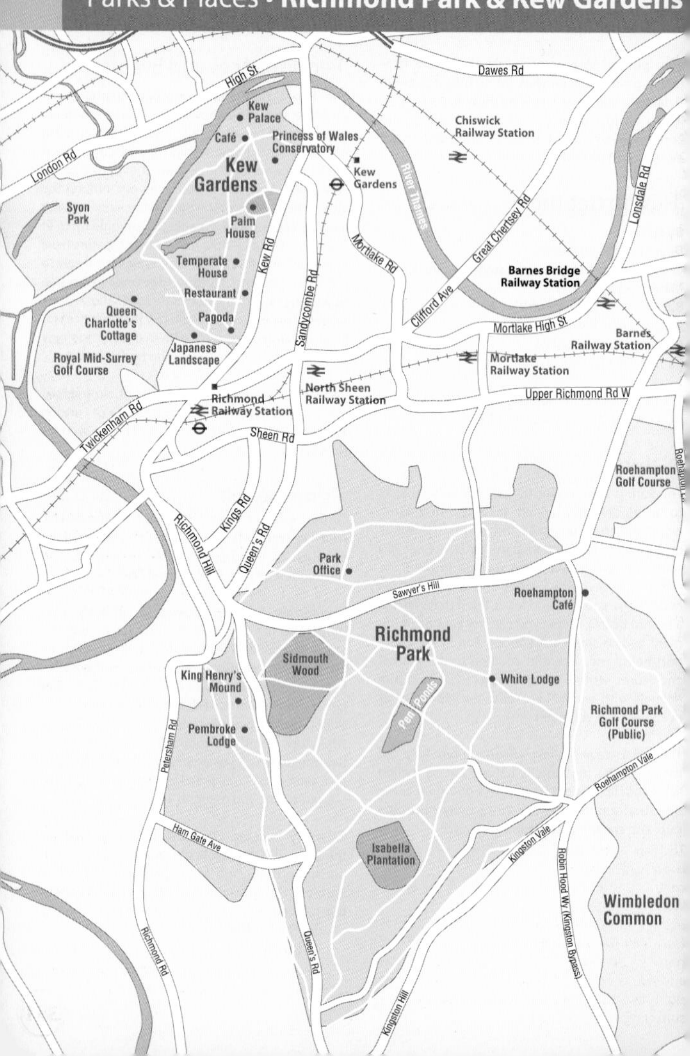

High St
Dawes Rd
Kew Palace
Café
Princess of Wales Conservatory
Chiswick Railway Station
London Rd
Kew Gardens
Kew Gardens
River Thames
Syon Park
Palm House
Great Chertsey Rd
Lonsdale Rd
Mortlake Rd
Temperate House
Kew Rd
Barnes Bridge Railway Station
Sandycombe Rd
Restaurant
Clifford Ave
Queen Charlotte's Cottage
Pagoda
Mortlake High St
Barnes Railway Station
Japanese Landscape
Royal Mid-Surrey Golf Course
Mortlake Railway Station
North Sheen Railway Station
Richmond Railway Station
Upper Richmond Rd W
Twickenham Rd
Sheen Rd
Roehampton Golf Course
Kings Rd
Richmond Hill
Queen's Rd
Park Office
Sawyer's Hill
Roehampton Café
Richmond Park
Sidmouth Wood
King Henry's Mound
White Lodge
Pen Ponds
Richmond Park Golf Course (Public)
Pembroke Lodge
Petersham Rd
Roehampton Vale
Ham Gate Ave
Isabella Plantation
Kingston Vale
Robin Hood Wy (Kingston Bypass)
Wimbledon Common
Richmond Rd
Queen's Rd
Kingston Hill

Overview

In 1625 Charles I brought his court to Richmond. He subsequently, with quite heroic selfishness, built a wall 'round a large expanse of open grassland, and created Richmond Park. These days the park is thankfully accessible to the public, opening at 7 am (or 7.30 in the winter) and closing at dusk every day. It's the biggest of the Royal Parks in London, and is an obvious choice for long bike rides, picnics, informal sports and other wholesome pursuits for your golden, happy days of youth. Oh, and there's deer.

Attractions

The park has a number of gardens and wooded areas, the most beautiful of which is probably the Isabella Plantation, an organic woodland garden that blooms with azaleas and rhododendrons. The Pen Ponds is another popular feature, as is Pembroke Lodge, the park's Georgian mansion, which can be rented out for weddings and conferences (www.pembroke-lodge.co.uk or call 020 8940 8207). The adjacent café also does a mean cream team.

Sports

There are three rugby pitches near the Roehampton Gate that are available for rental on weekdays during winter (contact the Rosslyn Park Rugby Club at 020 8948 3209), and two eighteen hole, pay and play golf courses (call 020 8876 1795 for info. and booking). Between 16 June and 14 March you can purchase a fishing permit for the Pen Ponds (call 020 8948 3209 for information). Or for more extreme park-goers there is the option of Power Kiting, whatever the hell that is (www.kitevibe.com), and military-led Boot Camps to shape you up fast and mercilessly.

Kew

The Royal Botanic Gardens, Kew, begun in 1660, is not only easy on the eyes but is an important centre for horticultural research and a UNESCO World Heritage Site. Guaranteed to take place every year are the summer festival 'Kew the Music' (July) and ice-skating (Nov-Feb). Kew is a hugely popular day trip destination for schoolchildren and adults alike and contains such a surplus of sights and attractions that repeat visits are always surprising.

Attractions

Of course the main attractions here are the Gardens themselves. Between the formal gardens, smaller themed collections of plants and wildlife and conservation areas, there is enough walking and cooing to be done to justify any length of cake and sandwich sessions at one of the Gardens' eateries. There are also 39 Grade I and II listed buildings, all of which have some kind of historic significance. The 17th century Kew Palace (www.hrp.org.uk), is one of the most interesting of these, having previously been home to the notoriously 'mad' King George III. Other buildings in the gardens include the Chinese Pagoda of 1762, a traditional Japanese 'Minka' house and a number of museums. Decimus Burton's glasshouses (The Palm House and the Temperate) are iconic examples of this quintessentially Victorian architectural theme, and an essential part of any visit to Kew.

Events

Kew Gardens is run with great enthusiasm and has a packed programme of events throughout the year. These occur and change frequently so it's best to check the Kew website, which has comprehensive listings of everything that is going on in the Gardens, down to the blooming or blossoming of individual plant species: www.kew.org.

Several of the historic buildings, most spectacularly the Temperate Glasshouse, are available to rent for corporate and private parties.

How to Get There

Richmond station (overland trains, District Line) is a 20 minute walk from Richmond Park, or buses 371 and 65 both go from the station to the pedestrian gate at Petersham. Kew Gardens is (surprisingly) the closest station for Kew Gardens, London Overground trains stop here from across North and North West London. Trains from Waterloo stop at Kew Bridge station, a ten- minute walk from the gardens.

A large number of buses go from Hammersmith, Fulham, Clapham Junction, Wandsworth and Ealing to Richmond Park and to Kew Gardens.

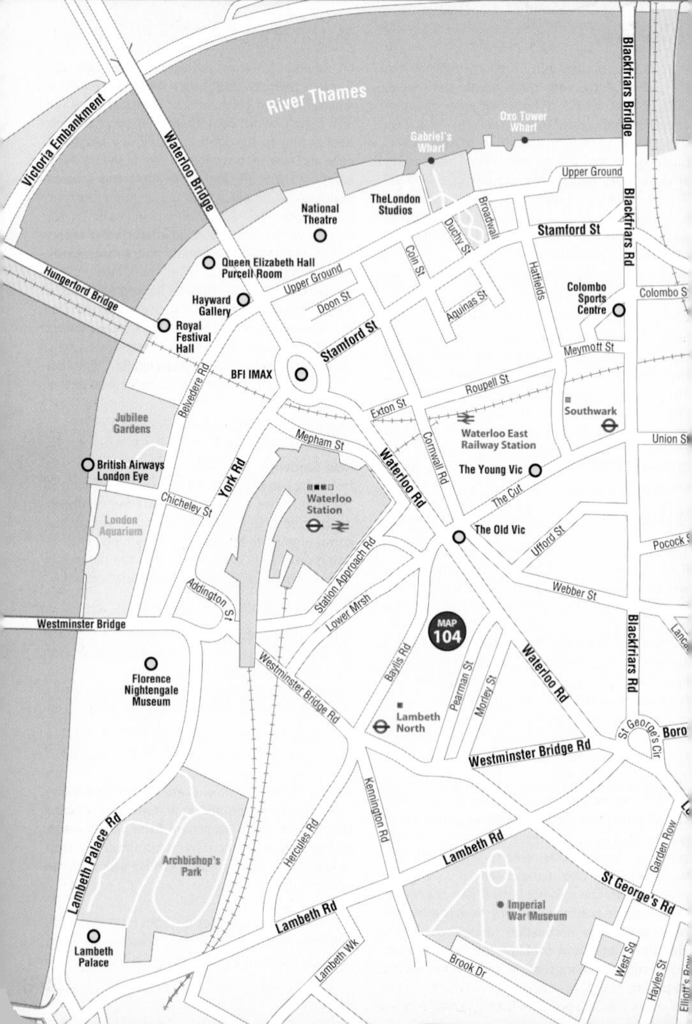
River Thames
Victoria Embankment
Waterloo Bridge
Blackfriars Bridge
Oxo Tower Wharf
Gabriel's Wharf
Upper Ground
National Theatre
TheLondon Studios
Broadwall
Duchy St
Blackfriars Rd
Stamford St
Hungerford Bridge
Queen Elizabeth Hall
Purcell Room
Upper Ground
Coin St
Hatfields
Colombo Sports Centre
Colombo St
Hayward Gallery
Doon St
Aquinas St
Royal Festival Hall
Stamford St
Meymott St
BFI IMAX
Belvedere Rd
Roupell St
Exton St
Southwark
Jubilee Gardens
Waterloo East Railway Station
Mepham St
Union St
Cornwall Rd
British Airways London Eye
York Rd
Waterloo Rd
The Young Vic
Waterloo Station
The Cut
Chicheley St
London Aquarium
The Old Vic
Ufford St
Station Approach Rd
Pocock St
Webber St
Addington St
Lower Mrsh
MAP 104
Westminster Bridge
Baylis Rd
Blackfriars Rd
Waterloo Rd
Westminster Bridge Rd
Pearman St
Morley St
Florence Nightengale Museum
Lambeth North
St George's Cir
Westminster Bridge Rd
Kennington Rd
Lambeth Palace Rd
Hercules Rd
Lambeth Rd
Garden Row
Archbishop's Park
St George's Rd
Imperial War Museum
Lambeth Rd
Lambeth Palace
Lambeth Wk
Brook Dr
West Sq
Hayles St

Overview

A pedestrianised quarter formed of venues for theatre, music, cinema, art and various other artistically orientated entities, the South Bank is the realisation of a post-war dream of an arts-for-all hub in London. The area has its roots in 1951's Festival of Britain, a technicoloured marvel designed to showcase an optimistic future for Britons used to coal, Spitfires and fake mashed potato. The legacy of the Festival ensured that the surrounding area went on to grow into the playground that it has become today.

The South Bank Centre

The actual 'South Bank Centre' is officially formed of the Royal Festival Hall, the Queen Elizabeth Hall, the Purcell Room, the Hayward Gallery and the Saison Poetry Library, which are all concentrated in the centre of the South Bank. The Royal Festival Hall hosts a variety of musical and dance performances from its auditorium, whilst the Hall's foyer is an enormous and relaxed open-plan area with a bar, performance spaces and shop. The Queen Elizabeth Hall and Purcell Room offer further stages for musical recitals whilst the Saison Poetry Library houses a vast collection of poetry dating from 1912 onwards. The Hayward Gallery has an exterior of frightening ugliness, which shields a surprisingly spacious interior, devoted to exhibitions of the visual arts.

The National Theatre

The National Theatre is next-door to the South Bank Centre complex and is another gaping example of uncompromising architecture. Opened in 1963, it still looks slightly unhinged. The building consists of three theatres and puts on a range of productions from the established to the experimental. It also features an inviting foyer, and in the open spirit of the South Bank, offers back-stage tours, workshops, talks and costume and prop hire to Joe Schmo.

British Film Institute and IMAX

Nestling under Waterloo Bridge, the BFI promotes film and television through its archives, cinema screens, talks and festivals. It's a great alternative to the disgustingly over-priced and sticky-floored chain cinemas of central London and promotes an all-encompassing program from its three screens. The Film Café and Benugo Bar & Kitchen do good pre- and post-flick munch. The BFI IMAX is the separate, rotund glass building situated around 200m south of the BFI. It shows films on Britain's biggest cinema screen accompanied by sound pumped from a gargantuan 11,600-watt sound system.

Everything Else

Beyond its theatres, music halls, galleries and cinemas, the South Bank has spawned a number of other attractions. The London Eye is an enormous Ferris wheel built in 2000 on the banks of the Thames adjacent to Westminster Bridge, it revolves at a leisurely 0.5 mph and offers brilliant views from its 135m-high peak. The London Aquarium is just opposite but with ticket prices roughly similar to the Eye, seeing big fish in small tanks starts to look a distinctly lame option. Less expensive attractions around South Bank include the open-air book market tucked under Waterloo Bridge and Gabriel's Wharf, a dinky enclave of small shops, bars and restaurants that offer succour to those cultured-out. Or you can ogle at the cool kids doing half pipes at the South Bank Skate Park..

Getting There

By tube: Nearest stations are Waterloo (Northern, Bakerloo, Jubilee and Waterloo & City lines) and Embankment (Circle, District, Northern & Bakerloo lines). From Waterloo, head 50m towards the river. Embankment station is at the northern foot of Hungerford footbridge.

By train: Nearest stations are Waterloo & Charing Cross. For directions from Waterloo, see 'By Tube'. From Charing Cross, walk 100m down Villiers Street towards the river and then walk across the Hungerford footbridge.

By bus: The South Bank is on numerous bus routes. Buses stop on nearby Waterloo Bridge, York Road, Belvedere Road, Stamford Street and Waterloo Station. Most coming from the North get to South Bank via Holborn, The Strand or Victoria. From the South they come via Elephant and Castle or Lambeth North.

By boat: Festival Pier is adjacent to the London Eye. Pleasure boats dock here on cruises, as do riverboat services which sail west as far as Tate Britain and east as far as Woolwich Arsenal.

General Information

NFT Map: 9 & 23
Website: www.royalparks.org.uk/parks/st-jamess-park
www.royalparks.org.uk/parks/green-park
Free guided walks: 020 7930 1793
Inn the Park Café and Restaurant (St. James's Park): 020 7451 9999

Overview

With Trafalgar Square at one end and Buck Palace at the other, both St. James's and Green Park are slap-bang in the heart of picture-postcard London. When the belching fumes of the Hackney cab and hordes of Oxford Street shoppers threaten both health and sanity, there's only one place to go. Zip past the crowds and pigeons in Trafalgar Square and head under the grand curve of Admiralty Arch into the stately calm of St. James's Park. Stand yourself on the bridge that crosses the lake, take a deep breath and marvel at the history surrounding you in the city's oldest Royal Park, dating back to the days of Henry VIII.

The views: fairytale Buckingham Palace to the west, Downing Street, the seat of Parliament and Big Ben jutting out over Horse Guards' Parade to the east and the towers of Westminster Abbey to the south. There ain't nowhere else in London where you can view the icons of Church, State and Monarchy in one quick spin on your heels. Impressive. And when you're done marvelling, join the families, office workers, joggers and tourists in taking a stroll round the lake for pelican-spotting, duck-feeding, lunching and romancing.

A hop across the Mall and you'll find yourself in the rolling green of, yup, Green Park. Flowerbed free, this 53-acre patch of park with its aged plane trees is the more meditative of the two. A refuge from the noisy thoroughfare of Piccadilly and Hyde Park corner, its grounds soon fill with picnicking office-workers at the slightest suggestion of sun while the tree-lined Mall is the nearest you'll get to a Parisian boulevard.

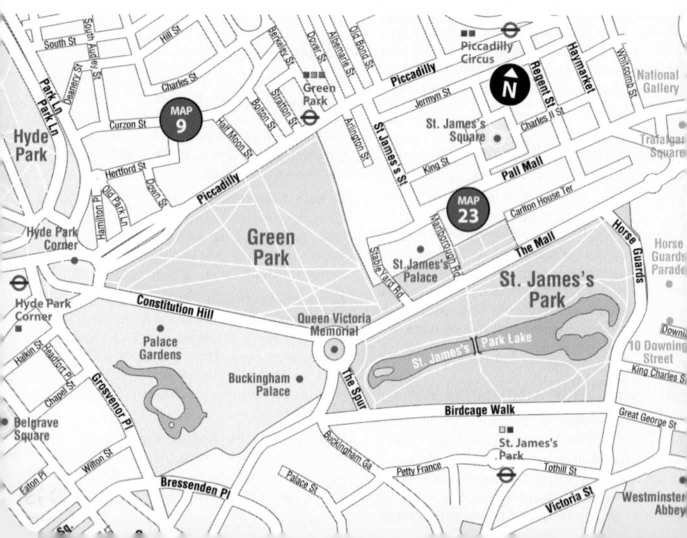

Nature

The curving lake of St. James's park runs the length of the grounds and is perfect for indulging in some casual bird-spotting. Ever since the days of James I, the park has been home to an exotic menagerie, once including elephants, camels and even crocs.

While the crocs and ellies might be long gone, both Duck Island and the smaller West Island remain home to an impressive array of water birds. Beyond the humble duck and gulls, there are suitably stately black swans, rare golden eyes and the rather less-illustrious sounding shovelers, a close relative of the time-starved office-worker on lunch, we believe. But, with their gentlemanly swagger and mighty beaks, the five resident pelicans unquestionably steal the show. A gift from the Russian Ambassador in 1664, feeding time is worth a gander at 3pm daily. Known for their entertaining antics—like flying to Regent's Park Zoo on fish-stealing sprees—one caused a media storm when, clearly lusting after a menu change, it swallowed a live pigeon whole, flapping feathers 'n' all.

Take some old bread and the park's tame, tubby squirrels will feast from your hand. Hang around 'til dusk and the bats come out to play.

Architecture & Sculpture

As if housing ol' Queenie's Buckingham Palace wasn't enough, the parks are surrounded by two more palaces—Westminster, now the Houses of Parliament, and St. James's. From the Regency elegance of the Mall's Carlton House, home to the Institute of Contemporary Arts (ICA), to the impressive frontage of Horse Guard's Parade, the parks are hemmed in by grandeur.

Once a swampy wasteland for grazing pigs, it's a tale with humble beginnings for London's most royal park. While each passing King and Queen slowly improved St. James's Park, it was Charles II that really put the work in, getting trees planted, lawns laid and then opening it up for the first time to us commoners.

Sobering war memorials in St. James's Park abound, including world war icons Mountbatten and Kitchener in Horse Guards' Parade, and an overblown marble statue of Queen Victoria complete with glitter and gates. Oh, and that grand old Duke of York, best-known for marching his men up and down some hill? He's here too, in bronze atop a mighty pillar by the ICA.

The Parks in Season

St. James's in spring is carpeted with crocuses and daffodils. Come summer, they're quickly replaced with a carpet of sun-starved Tom, Dick and Sallys, laid bare as they dare to catch some rays. For an instant upgrade from the rabble, head to Green Park by the tube and hire a stripy deck-chair at £1.50 a pop from April to September.

Between May and August, add a dash of high-brow culture to your day with free concerts at the bandstand every lunchtime and early evening.

Autumn days might be chilly but clear skies make for impressive sunsets while wintry strolls are all the more head-clearing, especially after a night on the Soho tiles.

Sports

With cycling and ball-games banned—*entirely* inappropriate in such stately surrounds!—jogging, morning tai chi, leisurely strolls and pigeon chasing are as energetic as it gets. Sundays are best for strolling when Constitution Hill is closed to traffic.

The Mall and Constitution Hill are cycle-friendly and make a pleasant cut through the West End. Join the Serpentine running club for regular jaunts through St. James's. (www.serpentine.org.uk).

Enjoy the sedate pace with free lunch-time guided walks twice a month, discussing anything from horticulture to royalty (booking line: 020 7930 1793).

General info

NFT Map: 90, 93, & 94
Website: www.towerhamlets.gov.uk/default.aspx?page=12670
Information: 020 7364 2494

Overview

Look at all the joggers, skaters, cricketers and picnickers swarming in Victoria Park on any given weekend, and it seems hard to continue calling this 218-acres green space one of London's best-kept secrets. Yet, to many Londoners not living east, it still is. Lined by Regent's Canal in the south, London's third-largest cultivated green space is a nice blend of Regent's Park's beauty and the wilderness found in Hampstead Heath. It's also far enough off the Central London map to stay virtually tourist-free, while, at the same time, feeling reassuringly inner city urban, with the Gherkin and Canary Wharf's skyscrapers all in sight.

Divided into two handy bits by Grove Road, Victoria Park has much of what makes a park more than just grass and trees: excellent sporting facilities, ranging from athletics to rugby, several lakes, a deer enclosure, a secret garden—and plenty of decent drinking holes nearby. Designed in the 1840s to bring much needed greenery and breathing space to a soul-destroyingly grim East End, the "people's park" can also look back on an intriguing past of dissent, non-conformist rallying and all sorts of political mischief-making. And it's home to the oldest model boat racing club in the country. Come now, before the Olympics do. Once the squirrels start digging out amphetamines, the secret will be gone forever.

Nature

Ducks, swans, birds and god knows what else live around The Lake in the west, while deer and goats graze slightly further north. You're allowed to fish in the Old Lake, although we're not at all sure that there are really many fish in there. Pretty oak trees and hawthorns stud the whole place; colourful flowers and perfectly-groomed shrubs grow in the Old English Garden. It's a beautifully landscaped gem of a garden and one of this city's most peaceful spots—if you don't mind the odd greying philosopher, mumbling to himself.

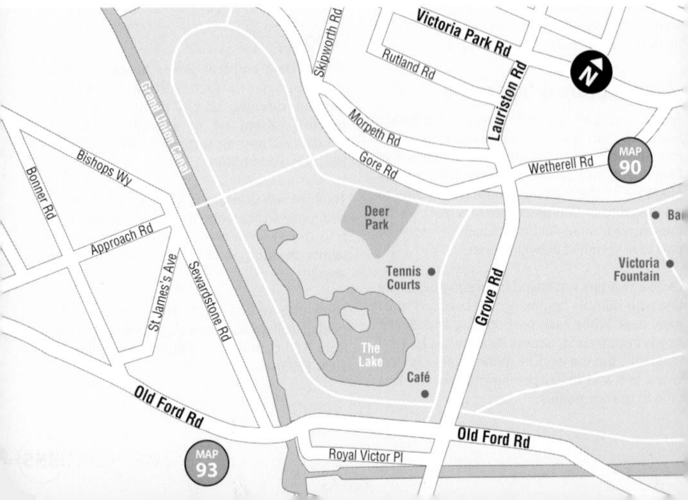

Sports

Jogging and skating are popular and, thanks to wide pathways, possible throughout the park. There's a rugby pitch, a large dedicated football area, four tennis courts (call 020 8986 5182) and three all-weather cricket pitches, run by the esteemed Victoria Park Community Cricket League (www.vpccl.co.uk). The children's playgrounds are decent enough, and the athletic field is excellent. Get in touch with the park's own athletics association (www.vphthac.org.uk) for access to changing rooms, showers and its indoor training hall.

Architecture & sculpture

Rising in the middle of the park is a Grade-II listed drinking fountain erected by Baroness Angela Burdett-Coutts (England's wealthiest woman at some point, we're told), adorned by several half-naked marble boys, smiling cheekily. The Hackney Wick Great War Memorial, in the east part of the park, is a reminder that this part of London was hit especially hard by the bombings of the Second World War. Close-by, you'll find two alcove-type fragments that survived the demolition of the old London Bridge Station. Fairly unremarkable, but good shelter when it's raining. Let's face it, no one comes here for architecture.

Festivals

The hazy days when The Clash whipped up a beer-can-throwing frenzy in the park—heralding a new era called punk along the way—might be over, but Victoria Park has kept its musical tradition alive. Slightly more tamed and organised, the festivals taking place these days range from the trendy, village-feel Field Day to the indie-and-electro-blending Lovebox Weekender, while big names (Radiohead for one) have also discovered a liking for the park's scenery and music-appreciating attitude.

Eat & Drink

The park's café, next to The Lake, is tiny, but the organic cakes are a tasty lot. That aside, you have to venture to the park's fringes for food and drink, but fear not: a tap is never far. Leave behind the bog-standard, soulless pub that is The Victoria and opt for the East End earthiness of the Top of the Morning instead, near the Cadogan Gate. Good Ales, a real fireplace, and up-marketish pub food make The Royal Inn on the Park, near the Royal Gates, the usually busy favourite. The Fat Cat, a few minutes south of the park along Grove Road, is more restaurant than pub, a bit pricey but a good choice for high-quality pasta, burgers and steaks.

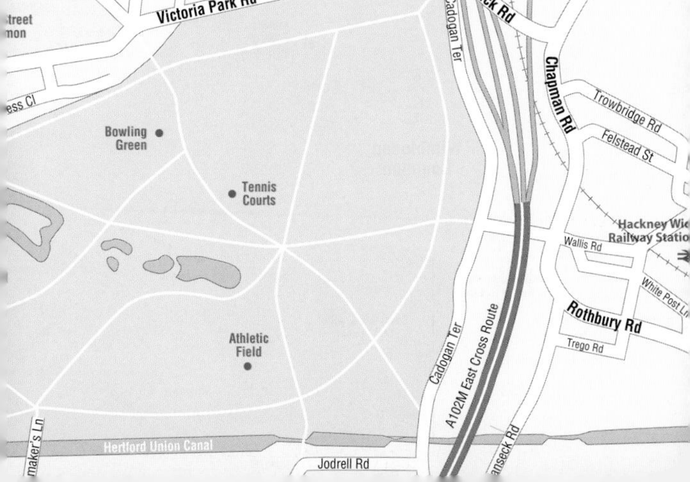

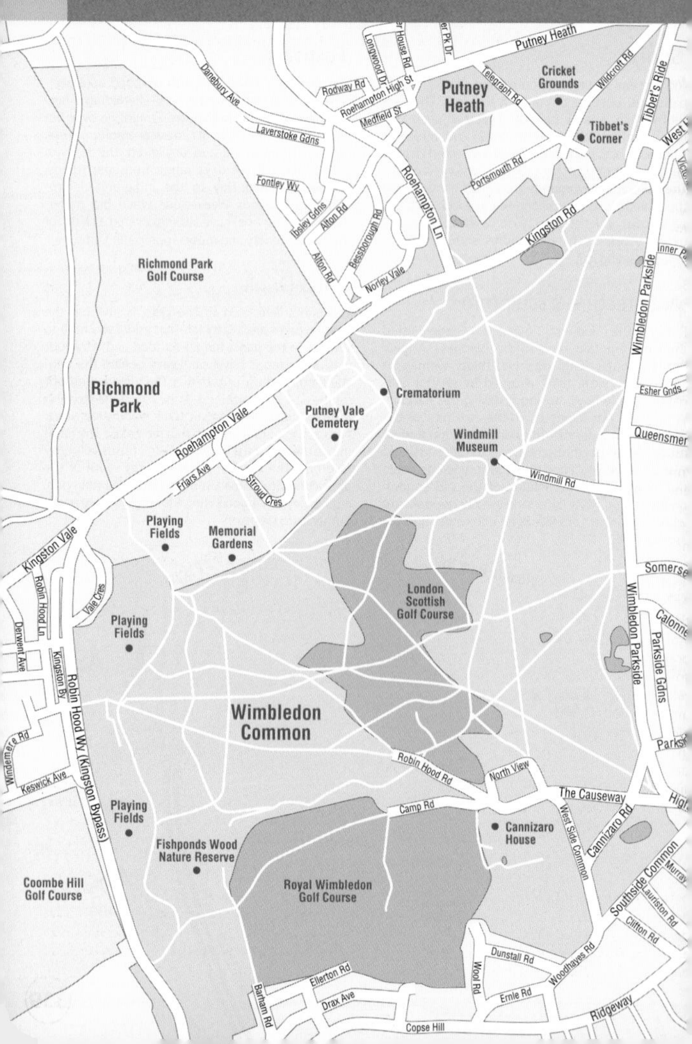
Putney Heath
Danebury Ave
Longwood Dr
Rodway Rd
Roehampton High St
Medfield St
Laverstoke Gdns
Telegraph Rd
Cricket Grounds
Wildcroft Rd
Tibbet's Ride
Putney Heath
Tibbet's Corner
Portsmouth Rd
Roehampton Ln
Fontley Wy
Ibsley Gdns
Alton Rd
Bessborough Rd
Norley Vale
Kingston Rd
Inner Pk
Wimbledon Parkside
Richmond Park Golf Course
Richmond Park
Crematorium
Esher Gdns
Putney Vale Cemetery
Roehampton Vale
Windmill Museum
Queensmer
Friars Ave
Stroud Cres
Windmill Rd
Kingston Vale
Playing Fields
Memorial Gardens
Somerse
Robin Hood Ln
Vale Cres
London Scottish Golf Course
Calonne
Derwent Ave
Playing Fields
Kingston By
Wimbledon Parkside
Parkside Gdns
Robin Hood Wy (Kingston Bypass)
Wimbledon Common
Windermere Rd
Keswick Ave
Robin Hood Rd
North View
The Causeway
Camp Rd
West Side Common
Cannizaro Rd
Playing Fields
Cannizaro House
Fishponds Wood Nature Reserve
Southside Common
Murray
Lauriston Rd
Coombe Hill Golf Course
Royal Wimbledon Golf Course
Clifton Rd
Dunstall Rd
Woodhayes Rd
Wool Rd
Ellerton Rd
Barham Rd
Drax Ave
Ernle Rd
Ridgeway
Copse Hill

General Information

Website: www.wpcc.org.uk

Overview

If London life starts to get you down, but trekking to the countryside is too much hassle, then Wimbledon Common provides the best of both worlds. Incorporating Putney Heath to the north, Wimbledon Common offers over 1000 acres of wild woodland, scrubland, heathland, ponds and well-tended, mown areas for sports and recreation. Bordered by the urban sprawls of Wimbledon, Putney and Richmond, the common has offered Londoners an escape from city life for centuries. Although thousands visit every weekend, the scale of the place is so vast that you can easily find a private haven for reading a book or a romantic picnic.

Unlike the micro-managed and perfectly structured central London parks, Wimbledon feels much more natural and random. Paths are unpaved and often little more than a muddy track leading off in unlikely directions. The untamed beauty of the common and the lack of traffic noise, or any noise for that matter, make it hard to believe you are still in London.

After a hard day of outdoor activity, or sunbathing, there are plenty of historic pubs to retire to in Wimbledon village. If you prefer your nature tamed or don't want to get your shoes dirty, head to the southeast corner of the common for Cannizaro House and gardens, a grand mansion converted into a boutique hotel and restaurant, with elegantly manicured gardens open to the public. In the summer, the friendly hotel bar opens onto a patio overlooking the grounds and makes a good spot for a sun-downer as you imagine being Lord or Lady of the Manor for the day.

Nature

The common is home to many animals including bats, badgers, and muntjac deer. It's also an important breeding ground for dragonflies and damselflies. For anyone wanting to find out more about the flora and fauna, the London Bat Group organises 'bat walks' while the London Wildlife Trust organises guided walks. You can also take a self-guided wander along The Windmill Nature Trail. 800 metres long, the trail has been created with accessibility in mind and begins right next to the Windmill car park. The visitors' centre behind the Windmill has wildlife exhibits and also tells the history of the common. It also sells maps and booklets giving the low down on the nature on offer.

Recreation

There is loads of space on the common for pick-up games of rugby, football, Frisbee and cricket. If you fancy a 'real game', you can hire tennis courts by the hour, cricket pitches by the day (from as little as £150) or enjoy a round of golf on the two available courses. The common is very popular with runners and steeplechase events have been held here since 1867. Various running clubs such as the South London Harriers and Hercules Wimbledon use the Common. If you've ever fancied trying horse riding, there are a number of stables that make use of the 16 miles of trails—or bring your own nag with you.

Golf
www.wcgc.co.uk
www.londonscottishgolfclub.co.uk

Horse Riding
Wimbledon Village Stables: 020 8946 8579
Ridgway Stables: 020 8946 7400

Rugby, Football and Cricket Pitch Hire
020 8788 7655

How to Get There

By public transport:
The Northern Line goes to South Wimbledon where you can take a bus to central Wimbledon then change or walk to the village and common. Wimbledon station is much closer. Take the District Line from central London or over ground trains from Waterloo or London Bridge. If you are feeling fit, a ten-minute walk up Wimbledon Hill takes you to Wimbledon village and beyond that, the edge of the common. Regular buses serve the village. Alternatively, you can access Putney Heath which joins up with Wimbledon Common. To do this, take the District Line to Putney Bridge or East Putney overground to Putney mainline station and take a bus up Putney Hill.

It's likely that at some point during your London residence, you've been seized with the romantic notion of floating your way round a London market—savouring the smells, laughing with a vendor, flirting your way to some freebies. If you have, then your attempts to live that dream almost certainly resulted in you silently fuming as you crawled among a crowd of thousands, trekking for a cashpoint because you forgot that stalls don't accept cards, and getting crapped on by a pigeon. Don't be put off!

At the markets you can buy some of the most unique, quirky, fresh, stylish, grungy, exquisite, unusual items in London. Sometimes you'll get brilliant bargains, sometimes you'll pay high for something you fall in love with. And sometimes, yes, you'll be driven near to homicidal rampage. But they're one of London's great strengths: use them while you can, because the developers have their evil, dollar-signed eyes on them.

For Groceries

The food in markets isn't necessarily locally grown, but you get a much more tempting choice than in most supermarkets. Expect fruit, veg, breads, cheeses, meats, spices and pastries, as well as stalls concocting irresistible snacks from around the world.

Borough (Map 106)

You don't come here for bargains: you come for ambiance, exquisite international foods, and to impress the person you woke up with. If you're rich and like the finer things in life, then here your weekly shop can consist of some of the freshest vegetables, plumpest fruit, sweetest patisseries and sockiest cheeses in London. If you're poor and just fancy a change from Saturday morning repeats of *Friends*, then head here for a hearty hog roast sandwich and to snaffle some free samples.

Broadway (Map 89)

As gorgeous as Borough, for a third of the price and a fifth of the crowds. It's a pain to get to, stuck in one of the city's remaining quaintly retro spots not closely served by the tube (London Fields), but you'll want to move here by the end of your visit.

Ridley Road (Map 86)

If the gourmet markets are too poncey for you, with their Bavarian organic rye bread and Malaysian honey from breast-fed bees, then get down the Ridley Road. Here, in a market which is bright, chaotic, grubby and bouncing to reggae, you can pick up an incredible array of Jamaican, Turkish, African, Indian and Chinese foodstuffs (and possibly e-coli).

For Market-Chic

You won't necessarily pay less than at the high street, but you will have a choice of original and irresistible items sold with passion and knowledge. Expect to leave these markets with a lighter pocket (though try to make sure it's not because of the pickpockets…).

Spitalfields (Map 91)

Mecca for anyone looking for ethnic-hip and well-priced clothes, bags and jewellery. Here you can often chat to the maker of the clothes you're eyeing up and learn the story behind their designs. Which is all very inspiring, until you try on their beloved creations, realise you're too fat for it, and reject it having slightly stretched it. Because then it's just awkward.

Greenwich (Map 120)

Craft-tastic: a great place to go for beautiful handmade gifts which people love to receive and then put in a cupboard for the rest of their useful life. Here you'll find a gorgeous range of items for home and lifestyle: pictures, antiques, candles, pottery, soft furnishings and clothes, as well as some great food stalls, and an above-average number of beautiful rich people than at most markets.

Portobello Road (Map 29)

Although famed for being the World's Largest Antiques Market, Portobello Road seems to sell *everything*. You'll need patience to work around its sprawling size and the crowds, but just about anything you're looking for is there somewhere or can be sourced by speaking to the right vendor. Stalls include clothes (from classy-vintage to student-cheap), jewellery, fabric, food, as well as 1500 antique stalls selling maps, medals, silverware, and things you never thought you needed (and which, after you've got them home, you realise you didn't).

Camden (Map 71)

Camden is actually home to six markets, though "chic" doesn't do any of them justice. Here you'll find a purse-emptying range of alternative fashions, vintage clothes, accessories, gifts, t-shirts, comedy hot water bottle covers, tie-dyed hippies, teeny-punks and chaps asking if you'd care for a nice bit of crack. Anything goes, and this open, free atmosphere makes it a major and exciting draw. Hit Camden Stables for brilliant international food stalls.

Fer Findin a Bit o' Laaandon Prop'a

If you're a Londoner who "just adores the city! But oh dear *no,* wouldn't *dream* of bringing kids up here", then chances are you don't mingle much with the Prop'a Laandoner. This hardy breed whose family history is a Dickensian yarn of blitzes, TB and chimney sweeps are the core of this city, and the gradual nudging out of their jellied eels and pub sing-songs is tantamount to ethnic cleansing. Find them at London's Propa Markets before they vanish.

Smithfield (Map 15)

Smithfield Market is in full swing at 4 am, which makes it the perfect place to stumble into on your way home from clubbing. Unless you're vegetarian, because while frying bacon may have you yearning for looser morals, the smell of this 800 year old meat market will have you retching over your recycled sandals. It's the best place in London to pick up any meat you could hope for, including, in the 1500s, a barbecued Protestant or a topside of William Wallace, this being the site of hundreds of executions in its time. Some of the local pubs hold special early licenses, so on your way to the office you can swing in for breakfast over a pint with some of the meat porters: they'd just *love* it if you did.

Columbia Road (Map 91)

There's something deeply touching about an exquisite flower market being manned by some of the burliest Cockneys you'll see outside a Guy Ritchie film. Get there first thing on Sundays for the best choice, or in a low-cut top for the best bargains. And if the crowds and cries of the "daffs, dahlin'?" become too much, just slip into the enchanting boutiques lining Columbia Road.

Billingsgate (Map 101)

For the largest selection of fish in London, outside the London Aquarium (where they frown on you if you try to fry the fish. Bloody bureaucracy.), head to Billingsgate. People were buying their fish here long before London went all yuppie, and much the same stock is available—winkles, cockles, potted shrimp and things which smell ungodly. Today you'll find alongside them almost any fish you could hope for (though don't ask for goldfish), as well as poultry, oils and snacks.

General Information

King's Cross Address: Granary Building, 1 Granary Square, London, N1C 4AA

Phone: 020 7514 7000

Website: www.arts.ac.uk/csm or @CSM_news

Overview

Though hyped to infinity, and often lazily editorialised as the one vital source of all things up-and-coming in London, Central St Martins nevertheless has an undeniable history of producing graduates that tend to rocket to international fame upon leaving. The frequently cited list of alumni reads like a Who's Who of European art-and-design talent, and includes past superstars such as Alexander McQueen, Gilbert and George, and Anthony Gormley, as well as recent fashion darlings Christopher Kane, Gareth Pugh and Kim Jones, to name a few.

Central St Martins is part of the much larger University of the Arts London, made up of CSM, Chelsea College of Art, Camberwell College of Art, London College of Fashion, London College of Communication and Wimbledon College of Art. The school as it is today was formed in 1989 through the amalgamation of two prestigious 19th century institutions, the Central School of Arts and Crafts and St Martins School of Art. Since then it has annexed the Byam Shaw School of Art in Archway, and as a result offers a huge range of courses covering most areas of the visual and performing arts. St Martins has a particularly formidable reputation for fashion design—it is the only university to show student collections as part of London Fashion Week—but it is well respected in all departments for its hyper-progressive ethos (expect to hear words like 'challenging,' and 'risk-taking' liberally thrown around on open days). Whether you find the whole thing pretentious and overrated or are waiting in breathless anticipation for the next St Martins wunderkind, CSM is very difficult to ignore.

Campuses

The swish renovated warehouse building in Kings Cross, opened in 2011, centralises programs and student life in a way that was once difficult. The massive campus anchors the redevelopment of Kings Cross, formerly known for its transport links and general seediness. The facility allows students of art, fashion, design, and drama to be in one location, to interact cross-discipline, and form more of a united front rather than being scattered across the capital. Anyone who has walked the corridors of the old Charing Cross Road building will tell you that however charming the decaying archaic halls of academia may be, a brand spanking new building with technology to match is more than welcome. Occupying the Grade II listed Granary Building, architects Stanton Williams have integrated such wonders as an internal street, the Platform Theatre performance space, and an open-air terrace.

The Byam Shaw School of Art in Archway is a relatively recent addition (2003) to Central St Martins. Devoted solely to fine art, it runs a BA and a more skills-based 2 year FdA as well as a variety of short and post-graduate courses. CSM also has facilities in Richbell Place, Holborn.

College Culture

As is the case with most London institutions, the university community is massively subsumed by the bright lights of the city itself, but this is no bad thing. Though the college puts on frequent exhibitions, talks and events, there is no independent bar or central hub. The Student Union is not particular to Central St Martins but provides services for and represents all the art colleges in London (University of the Arts London) as a whole, and various services and societies (such as sports clubs) are run at this level. As far as the education part goes, it's not always easy being in the midst of the constant search for the next-big-thing, but at the same time the idiosyncratic slant of the teaching makes for a unique experience, and the generally high talent level of the students fosters a fantastic creative and social atmosphere.

Tuition

Fees are £9,000 a year for UK/EU applicants taking an undergraduate or Foundation level degree. Some courses require payment of an additional course fee for materials. International students can expect to pay approximately £16,000 depending upon the type of course taken.

Short Courses

Central St Martins also runs a large number of short courses for all aspirational (and rich) non-students wanting a piece of the action. Prices are high but the courses very popular, partly because of the college's reputation and partly because there are many interesting options to choose from. The courses run in evenings, weekends, or can be taken intensively as a Summer, Easter or Christmas school.

Phone Numbers:

Reception (Granary Building): 020 7514 7444

Drama Centre London: 020 7514 8760

Admissions—Degree Courses: 020 7514 7023

Admissions—Short Courses: 020 7514 7015

International Office: 020 7514 7027

Lethaby Gallery: 020 7514 9897

University of the Arts Students' Union: 020 7514 6270

Press Office: 020 7514 8098

General Info

Address: Northampton Square, London, EC1V 0HB
Phone: 020 7040 5060
Website: www.city.ac.uk or @CityUniLondon

Overview

In London, a place rich with academia, City University often gets overlooked. Unlike King's or LSE it has no grand halls, secret-handshakes or old-boys' networks. Its facilities are modest and its library short on fusty books. But it has carved out a reputation as a supplier of professionals, cementing its place in the top five for graduate employment.

Located on a pretty park on the edge of the City of London—the 'Square Mile' that itself has emerged at the centre of the global economy—the university is overwhelmingly diverse, with many coming from abroad to study at the Cass Business School. It's that section of the university that churns out workers for the finance industry—students who are so hell-bent on business success that they go to school in suits. The other five schools comprising City are the School of Arts & Social Sciences, School of Health Sciences, School of Mathematics, Computer Science & Engineering, School of Informatics, and The City Law School.

The university's first incarnation came in 1894 as an industrial college for the working classes. The on-site swimming pool was used when London hosted the 1908 Olympics, although it wasn't until 1966 that it gained full university status. It has maintained strong links with industry, with alumni including the founding father of budget Euro-travel, easyJet's Stelios (like Sting and Madonna he chooses to use only one name). Students at City may be lined up for good jobs when they graduate, but it comes at the cost of having to explain what their less well-known university is whenever they mention it.

Tuition

Annual undergraduate fees are £9,000. International undergraduate fees can be upward of £15,000.

Student Life

City offers on-campus housing, including a guarantee scheme for first-year undergraduates. The uni hosts some heavyweight lectures. The Students' Union offers limited clubs and societies with all the usual fare—tennis, chess, Christian Union. CitySport is City's state-of-the-art sports and fitness centre. 'Ten' (10 Northampton Square) is where the kids hang out, the social hub of City.

Departments

Cass Business School: 020 7040 8600
Admissions office (undergrad and postgrad): 020 7040 8716
Library: 020 7040 8191
CitySport: 020 7040 5656
Students' Union: 020 7040 5600

General Information

Address: Imperial College London,
South Kensington Campus, London SW7 2AZ
Phone: 020 7589 5111
Website: www.imperial.ac.uk or @imperialcollege

Overview

Imperial College really did have imperial beginnings with Prince Albert setting up the college as a research and learning centre of science, maths, medicine and engineering to enhance the image of the British Empire in 1887. In the Victorian age, and to this day, the college attracted the most enquiring of minds and was the central feature of what was once Prince Albert's successful push to create a centre of culture and learning, encompassing the nearby museums, Royal College of Music, Royal Geographical Society and the Royal Albert Hall. The university remains one of the best in the world, and as such remains one of the most selective institutions in the UK with the application to admissions ratio hovering around 7:1. Famous alumni include clever clogs Brian May (Queen), HG Wells and Alexander Fleming. In 2007 Imperial College became independent from the University of London and now awards its own degrees.

Departments

The pride and soul of the college are three faculties, each headed by a principal: engineering, medicine and natural sciences. Imperial also has a business school with Departments of Finance, Innovation & Entrepreneurship, and Management. The main purpose of the Humanities department is to provide elective subjects and language courses for the science students. For medical students Imperial is also associated with various London hospitals including St Mary's Hospital and Charing Cross Hospital.

Campus Culture

Imperial may have a 'heads down' atmosphere but there is still that unwritten rule that if you work hard you play hard. Imperial College Union (www.imperialcollegeunion.org) offers numerous clubs and societies from belly dancing to wakeboarding to backgammon. The Union Bar is also well used, and is particularly lively on an afternoon when a football or rugby match is screened. The free student paper, Felix (felixonline.co.uk), is a popular and useful resource for keeping up to date with campus life and aims to be independent from the College itself. Imperial also has its own student TV station, Stoic, and radio station ICRadio (www.icradio.com). There are also regular public lectures on a variety of subjects.

Facilities

Imperial's main campus in South Kensington is surrounded by many of London's best museums including the Natural History Museum, Science Museum and Victoria & Albert Museum. Being in the thick of it also means a close proximity to the shops and cafes of South Ken and High Street Kensington and being a stone's throw from Hyde Park.

The main campus boats some of the best facilities of the London universities. As well as the usual on-campus shops (including bookshop, cafes, travel agents and bank) there are some impressive sports facilities on offer. The Ethos sports centre contains not only a fully equipped gym but also an inside climbing wall, swimming pool, squash courts, sports hall and a treatment room offering massages and physiotherapy. On top of that there's a boathouse and a 60-acre athletic ground. Naturally, there's a well-stocked central library and various smaller departmental libraries.

Tuition

Home students' (UK/EU) annual fees are £9,000 for undergraduate programmes. International students pay upward of £25,000.

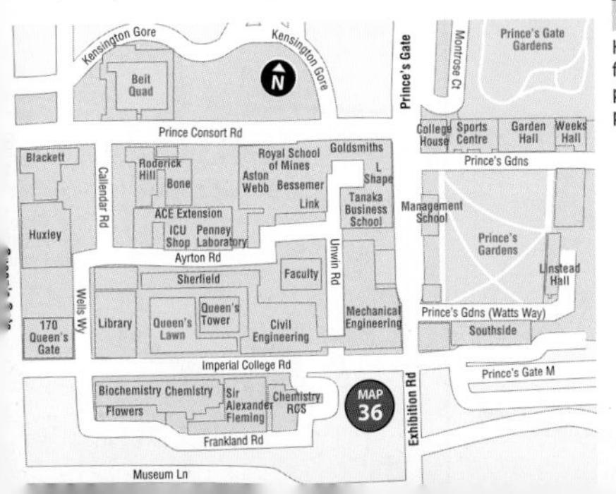

General Information

Address: King's College London, Strand, London, WC2R 2LS
Phone: 020 7836 5454
Website: www.kcl.ac.uk or @KingsCollegeLon

Overview

Although it grants its own degrees, Kings College is one of the 18 colleges that make up the colossus that is the University of London. King's (or KCL, as otherwise known) has nearly 20,000 students and five campuses—the Strand, Guy's, Waterloo, St. Thomas' and Denmark Hill. In 2011 the school of law moved into the East Wing of the magnificent Somerset House. It has an excellent academic reputation and ranks among the top UK universities. Unlike some of the other University of London colleges, King's is equally well known for its arts and science courses.

Its religious affiliation is now less central, but back in 1829 King's was founded as a Church of England institution to counter University College London, or "the godless college in Gower Street." The beautifully designed chapel at the Strand campus testifies to its pious beginnings, though few students would consider it a motivation for attending the college. The student body is diverse, as the societies list reflects—it includes a Catholic society, a Christian Union, a Krishna Consciousness group, and a Nomads society, among a myriad of others.

King's boasts a number of famous alumni. Keats studied apothecary there (he didn't like it much), and Florence Nightingale set up the world's first school of nursing at St. Thomas' Hospital, now the Florence Nightingale School of Nursing and Midwifery. In the 1960s, Archbishop Desmond Tutu spent time in its halls.

London prices may take their toll on the student purse, but King's students at least benefit from a prime location. As well as the nightclub, the college has two bars, one at Guy's Campus and one at the Strand. The Waterfront bar at the Strand looks directly onto the Thames, giving a view of everything from Westminster to the OXO Tower. It's also a great gig venue.

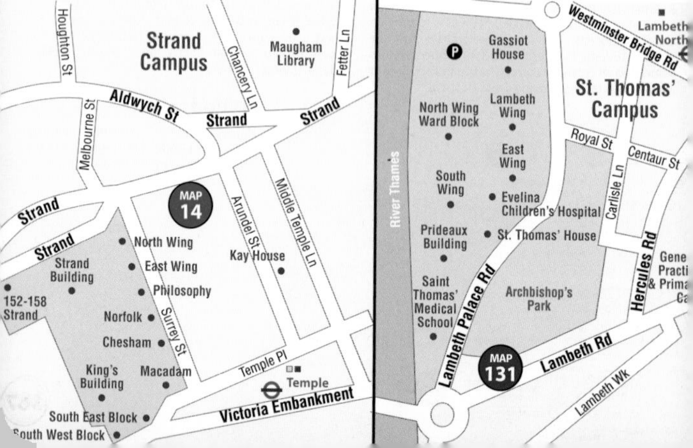

Sports

The college's sports facilities are impressive. It caters to almost anything—it has a swimming pool, gym, and even rifle range. Although King's cannot rival the Oxbridge rowing tradition, its sports do have a history—two of the men's rugby clubs, Guy's and St. Thomas', are the oldest in the world. To access the sports grounds students must leave Zone 1; the grounds are in Dulwich, Surrey, and South London.

Culture

Kings has numerous dramatic societies where amateur thespians can hone their skills. More unusually, its classics department stages a play in ancient Greek every year, and is the only classics department in the UK to do so. The college's religious origins are evident in its wonderful choral music. 25 choral scholars uphold this tradition.

Tuition

Annual undergraduate fees are £9,000. International undergraduate fees are upward of £15,000.

Contact Details

Admissions: 020 7848 7000
International Students: 020 7848 3388
Students' Union: 020 7848 1588

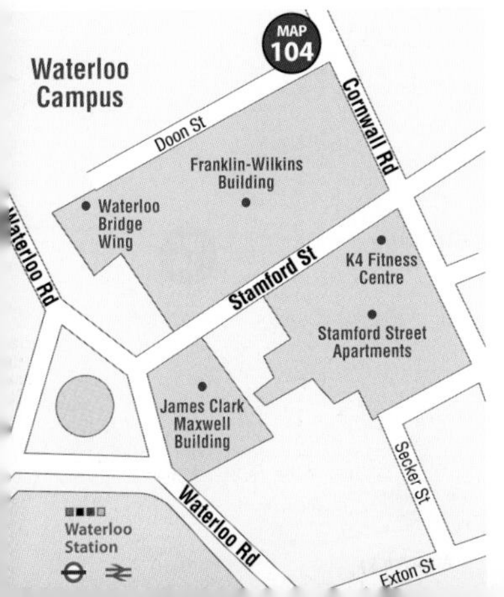

General Information

Address: Houghton Street,
London WC2A 2AE
Phone: 020 7405 7686
Website: www.lse.ac.uk or @LSEnews

Overview

The London School of Economics and Political Science, or LSE as it is commonly known, is a single faculty college focused on the social sciences, world renowned for its highly prestigious programmes and distinguished alumni. Located amidst a hub of academic activity with UCL, King's College, SOAS and Birkbeck nearby, the college is affiliated with the University of London and stands apart due to its high proportion of postgraduate students.

LSE was founded in 1895 by the intellectual socialist movement the Fabian Society with the aim of bettering society through the education of Britain's business and political elite. Today it remains a strongly political institution, with considerable influence in government through both its research programmes and campaigns. Its alumni are also highly represented in business and law spheres. While best known for its economics and politics degrees, the broad range of social science programmes offered complements the international ethos of the school and it remains at the cutting edge in terms of research.

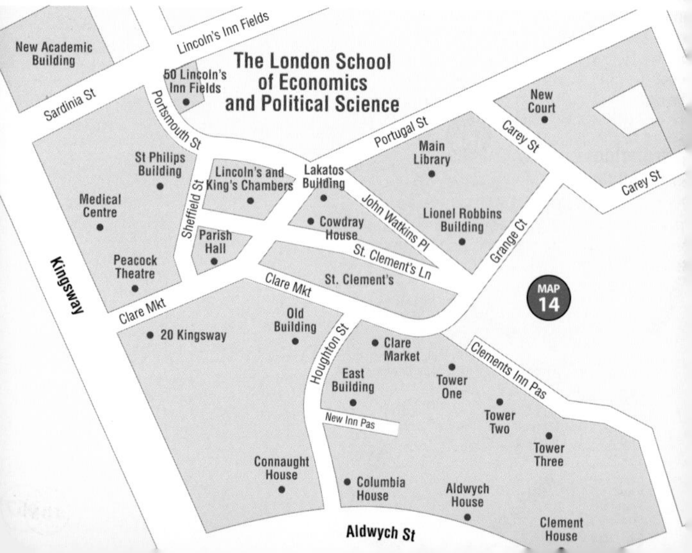

The college enrolls around 9,500 students from over 140 different countries; over half of these are postgraduates who rarely leave the library unless attending high-brow seminars on globalization and inequality. Its starry alumni includes Nobel laureates, International Heads of State, outstanding academics, and a notable proportion of British MP's. And of course Mick Jagger.

Campus Culture

Despite its reputation for academic excellence, LSE's social activities are mainly fuelled by a lively undergraduate population who also know how to enjoy themselves. With over 170 eclectic student societies ranging from Anime to Beekeeping to Catalan to Philosophy to Swing Dance, the broad international and diverse facets of the student population is encompassed. An atmosphere of work hard/play hard prevails and nightly events lure the undergraduates from the libraries and keep the campus buzzing. The large postgraduate population tends to shuffle by, however, books in hand; the days of cheesy music, luminous drinks in shot glasses and ill-conceived experimental fashions behind them while they actually do some work. LSE also hosts numerous public lectures with acclaimed speakers at the forefront of the subject discussed. Past speakers have included Noam Chomsky, Kofi Annan, David Cameron and architect Richard Rogers.

Sports

Not to be let down by its central, and somewhat geographically limited campus, LSE manages to maintain a thriving sports culture through the Athletics Union. Football and rugby seem to top the bill, with provision for some of the less mainstream athletic pursuits such as capoeira and Ultimate Frisbee. The college makes use of its affiliation with the University of London Union, which broadens the scope for sports participation alongside students of other universities.

Tuition

2015/16 undergraduate fees are £9,000 and international undergraduate fees are upward of £17,040.

Contact

Undergraduate Admissions: 020 7955 7125
Graduate Admissions: 020 7955 7160
Library: 020 7955 7229
Students' Union: 020 7955 7158

General Information

Address: Gower Street, London WC1E 6BT
Phone: 020 7679 2000
Website: www.ucl.ac.uk or @uclnews

Overview

UCL, a constituent college of the University of London, has been a place of diversity from the word go—living very much up to its status as "London's Global University." University College London was founded in 1826 as a progressive alternative to Oxford and Cambridge's social exclusivity and religious restrictions. Thus, it was the first university in England to admit students of any race, class or religion and welcome women on equal standing with men. International students have been a part of the college's fabric since day one and it was the first English university to offer the systemati teaching of law, architecture and medicin UCL is strongly associated with philosophe Jeremy Bentham, the university's so-calle "spiritual father," perhaps in part becaus Bentham's clothed skeleton is on display i UCL's South Cloisters.

UCL consistently ranks among the to universities not only in the UK but als worldwide. The science, law and medic departments remain some of its stronges 29 Nobel prizes have been awarded to UC academics and students, a large portion c which in Physiology & Medicine. That sai UCL degrees in anthropology, history an the arts are also very highly regarded in the fields.

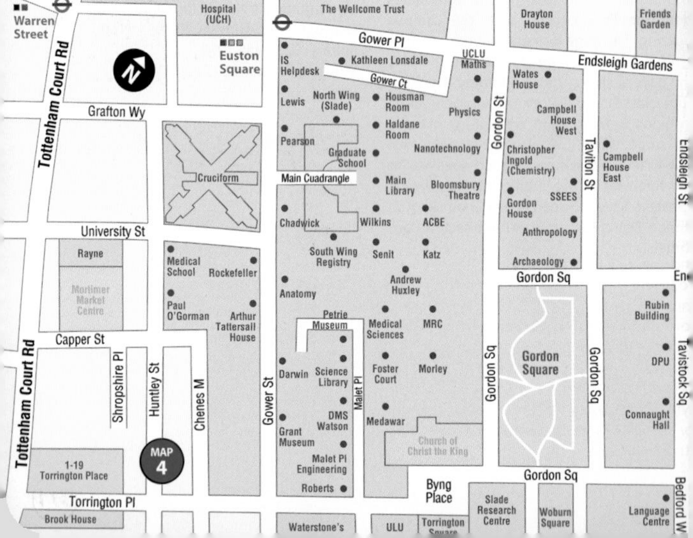

'CL's many networks of libraries are npressive and an easy place to get lost. The lain Library, designed by William Wilkins, /ho also designed the similar National iallery building, focuses on arts and umanities, history, economics, public policy nd law. The Special Collections include ıedieval manuscripts and first editions f works by George Orwell, James Joyce's *'lysses*, Newton's *Principia* and Darwin's *'rigin of the Species*.

here's no such thing as a typical UCL :udent, as it's such a diverse place. The nly thing students have in common is ıeir intelligence and London. Because it's university with great academics right in ıe heart of Bloomsbury, it makes for some retty interesting alums. Where else can you ave such diverse graduates as Alexander raham Bell, Mahatma Gandhi, Ricky ervais, and all four members of Coldplay?

Tuition

ndergraduate home student (UK/EU) fees 'e £9,000 per year while International :udents should expect to pay upward of 15,000 (or upward of £20,000 for science-elated programmes).

Sports

CL's sports are as diverse as its students—verything from hockey, rowing and /omen's rugby to Kung Fu, skateboarding nd water polo. The UCLU (University ollege London Union) is your one-stop ıop for campus sports teams and clubs. If ɔu're looking for football, The 90-acre UCL ɔorts ground at Shenley, Hertfordshire, ıs very high quality pitches. Watford otball club even train there. The Union /m (Bloomsbury Fitness) offers facilities r activities such as basketball and personal tness programmes.

Culture

Being right in the centre of London means that you're never short of something cultural to do. However, UCL stands up quite well. It even has its own museum—the Petrie Museum of Egyptian Archaeology—accessible from the Science Library. Here you're even given your own torch to explore the collection of over 80,000 rare objects DIY (or Indiana Jones) style. UCL also has its own West End theatre, the Bloomsbury Theatre, wedged into the maze of main buildings. It's a must-stop for top comedian tours. Jimmy Carr and Ricky Gervais have been known to shoot their stand-up DVDs there. The UCL Union has access to the theatre for at least ten weeks a year, where it is dedicated to student drama and music society performances. Although neither drama, music nor dance are formally taught at UCL, this does not stop the Union's drama club from making it to the Edinburgh Fringe Festival. At UCL, despite the fact that students can really go out just about anywhere in London, many stay loyal to the bars within the Union, and it's usually a great place to meet before a bigger night out.

Contact

Admissions: 020 7679 7742
UCL Union: 020 7679 2500 or uclu.org
Bloomsbury Theatre: 020 3108 1000
Petrie Museum: 020 7679 2884

General Information

Address: Thornhaugh Street, Russell Square, London WC1H 0 XG
Phone: 020 7637 2388
Website: www.soas.ac.uk or @SOAS

Overview

School of Oriental and African Studies is a specialist college which focuses on the languages, cultures, law and social studies of Africa, Asia, and the Near and Middle East. SOAS, as it is commonly known, is part of the University of London and is the only institution of its kind in the United Kingdom. It has an excellent reputation as one of the leading authorities on African and Asian studies in the world and ranks highly in university charts on the strength of its programmes. Originally founded in 1916 to educate and inform British citizens bound for overseas postings, the school began with an Oriental studies' focus and later incorporated African studies. SOAS is nestled in the corner of Russell Square, with another campus up close to King's Cross; its diversity complements the hotbed of academic activity that makes up this part of London.

The college enrolls over 5,000 students, with more than half coming from countries outside of the UK. They are often seen sitting in Russell Square eating their organic lunch, and chatting (in Swahili or Taiwanese) about their UNICEF internships. SOAS's alumni include members of parliament and royalty of a range of countries from Ghana to Burma. The Crown Princess of Norway went here. Well of course she did. The Norwegians are so PC. Except for whale hunting.

Culture On Campus

One thing to be said about SOAS students is they are serious. The Students' Union has a reputation of leaning heavily to the left and is very politically active. SOAS students have been a notable presence at anti-war protests and they are also now rather concerned with environmental causes—campaigning for the reduction of carbon footprints, among other issues. Societies at the college, unsurprisingly have a very international, 'right-on' flavour: the Decolonising Our Minds Society, Student Action for Global Internationalist Justice Society, Urdu Conversation Society are just a few.

Tuition

Undergraduate home (UK/EU) fees are £9,000. International undergraduate students can expect to pay £16,090 per year.

Contacts

Undergraduate Admissions: 020 7898 4301
Masters Admissions: 020 7898 4361
Research Admissions: 020 7074 5117
Library: 020 7898 4163
Students' Union: 020 7898 4992
or soasunion.org

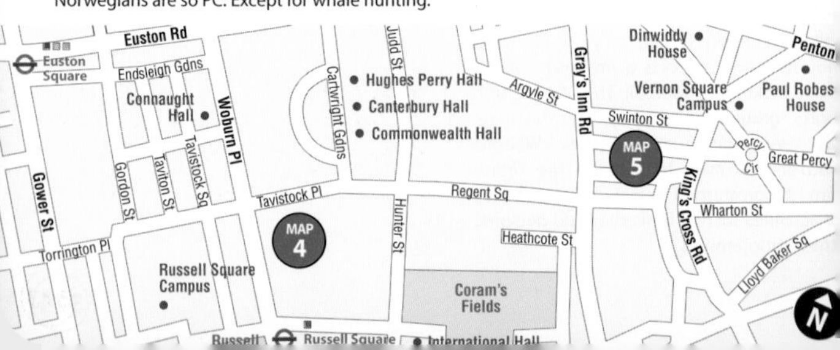

General Information

Address: Student Central,
Malet Street, WC1E 7HY
Phone: 020 7664 2000
Website: www.studentcentral.london or @UoLondonSC

Overview

Students are the same the world over and in London they ain't no different. In amongst the banter over Bronte and misunderstandings about Marx stands beer, boogeying and burgers. Luckily, for over 120,000 of the University of London's students there's a central place to go to make your university years active and sociable—Student Central.

Formerly the student-run University of London Union, or ULU, in 2014 the University of London took over the entity and renamed it Student Central. You will need to be a member of to get into some of the events, although grabbing a cheeky cheap sarnie in the café shouldn't pose too much of a problem for clued-up Londoners. There are 18 University of London colleges that are eligible for membership including Kings College and UCL, as well as ten other smaller institutions.

Practicalities

You cannot really get more central. There is a plethora of tube stations and lines within a five – to ten-minute walk, not to mention Oxford Street. The nearest tube, however, is Russell Square (Piccadilly Line) or Goodge Street (Northern Line).

Clubs & Societies (non-sport)

The range of clubs and societies on offer change more often than Europe's borders. Reason being the turnover of students and the lure from students' own colleges—all the more reason to get down there and sign up now! You've got the usual suspects such as Drama club but it would not be Londontown without a few obscure offerings—Revelation Rock Gospel Choir anyone? Hell, yeah.

Sports

Student Central has to cater to thousands of students, but also attract students away from sports clubs in their particular college. Sports, and the bar afterward, is the place to mix with students from the other colleges. Sportswise there's the usual fare—tennis, football, swimming and martial arts. There's also Energybase which contains a gym and pool. Amongst other things take your pick from salsa, breakdancing, fencing or rifle club. Now there's one for the CV…

Food & Bars

Lunch Box is Student Central's coffee shop, conveniently located on the ground floor for those who want to grab a quick (fair trade) coffee or a bargain meal deal. The Library is the main bar, with a lively atmosphere and live acts. The Gallery Bar is a low-key alternative to The Library, and also serves food. The Venue hosts a club night on Fridays, live music acts (up-and-coming unsigned bands as well as the odd better-known act) and cinema events during the week. For gigs enter Student Central on Byng Place.

Facilities

Copycats Print Centre will resolve all your reprographics and binding troubles. The Student Shop carries everything from lab coats to University of London-branded gear.

Learning in the capital has a long and venerable history. University College London (UCL) was the third university founded in England after Cambridge and Oxford and the first to admit students of any race or religion. Now there are hundreds of universities, colleges and adult education centres offering a mindboggling array of courses.

The first port of call for those with a lust for learning or even an empty Tuesday night to fill is Floodlight (london.floodlight.co.uk), which lists tens of thousands of courses. Fancy brushing up your motorbike maintenance skills at Hackney Community College, getting an NVQ in sugar modelling at the National Bakery School, learning how to create the ultimate kitchen garden at the English Gardening School or studying the nonsense verse of Lear and Carroll at City Lit? The sky is your oyster.

Continuing Education and Professional Development

University College London
Gower Street, WC1E 6BT
020 7679 2000
www.ucl.ac.uk or @uclnews

City University
Northampton Square, EC1V 0HB
020 7040 5060
www.city.ac.uk or @CityUniLondon

London South Bank University
103 Borough Road, SE1 0AA
020 7815 7815
www.lsbu.ac.uk or @LSBU

London Metropolitan University
166-220 Holloway Road, N7 8DB
020 7423 0000
www.londonmet.ac.uk or @LondonMetUni

University of East London
University Way, E16 2RD
020 8223 3000
www.uel.ac.uk or @UEL_News

University of Greenwich
Park Row, SE10 9LS
020 8331 8000
www.gre.ac.uk or @UniGreenwich

A Little Bit of Everything…

Birkbeck
Malet Street, WC1E 7HX
020 7631 6000
www.bbk.ac.uk or @BirkbeckNews

Open University
0300 303 5303
www.open.ac.uk

Bishopsgate Institute
230 Bishopsgate, EC2M 4QH
020 7392 9200
www.bishopsgate.org.uk or @BishopsgateInst

Arts and Lifestyle

University of the Arts London
272 High Holborn, WC1V 7EY
020 7514 6000
www.arts.ac.uk or @UniArtsLondon

Leiths School of Food and Wine
16-20 Wendell Road, W12 9RT
020 8749 6400
www.leiths.com or @Leithscooking

The London School of Journalism
126 Shirland Road, W9 2BT
020 7432 8140
www.lsj.org or @LSJournalism

English Gardening School
66 Royal Hospital Road, SW3 4HS
020 7352 4347
www.englishgardeningschool.co.uk

London School Of Beauty & Make-Up
18-19 Long Lane, London EC1A 9PL
020 7776 9767
www.beauty-school.co.uk or @londest

Institute Francais
17 Queensberry Place SW7 2DT
020 7871 3515
www.institut-francais.org.uk or @ ifru_london

London Buddhist Centre
51 Roman Road, E2 0HU
020 8981 1225
www.lbc.org.uk or @LDNBuddhist

The School of Life
70 Marchmont Street, WC1N 1AB
020 7833 1010
www.theschooloflife.com or @ TheSchoolOfLife

Athletics and Dance

National Centre for Circus Arts
Coronet Street, London, N1 6HD
020 7613 4141
www.nationalcircus.org.uk or @ NationalCircus

Tokei Martial Arts
28 Magdalen Street, SE1 2EN
020 7403 5979
www.tokeicentre.org

The Basement Dance Studio
400 York Way, N7 9LR
020 7700 7722
www.thebasementdancestudio.com or @basement_studio

Regents Canoe Club
Regents Canal, 6-34 Graham Street, N1 8JX
www.regentscanoeclub.co.uk

Docklands Sailing & Watersport Centre
235a Westferry Road, E14 3QS
020 7537 2626
www.dswc.org or @dswcofficial

London School of Capoeria
1 & 2 Leeds Place, N4 3RF
020 7281 2020
www.londonschoolofcapoeira.com or @ londoncapoeira

General Information

NFT Map: 74
Website: www.arsenal.com or @Arsenal
Phone: 020 7619 5000
Box office: boxoffice@arsenal.co.uk
Location: Highbury House, 75 Drayton Park, London N5 1BU

Overview

Regardless of how many years may have passed since Arsenal last stuffed another piece of silverware into their full trophy cabinet, Arsene Wenger continues to avoid splashing the cash on top names, instead building a young thriving team out of foreign talent and an exciting new crop of home-grown kids. The problem with this is that during the start of every new season at the Emirates it is inevitable that a pundit will proclaim this will be the year Arsenal's young side realize their full potential, but just as equally inevitable, a big money club will breeze in and buy out marquee players adding to the fans dismay and Wenger's greys. However, Arsenal is historically London's greatest club and holds numerous national records with a trophy room packed with more silver than any other, save Manchester United and Liverpool. T'was not always thus of course. From humble beginnings south of the river, Arsenal built themselves up from roots level, with glory years seeming to come in waves. The mid-80s saw the instatement of George Graham, a hugely popular former player, who begat a powerful, muscular side captained by local hero Tony Adams. Wenger brought a continental flavour to the team and an invigorating playing style—the once "boring, boring Arsenal" started playing "sexy football" which reached its zenith with the 2003–04 "Invincibles" who went the entire season without losing a game. Following Arsenal is not always an easy ride. It's surprising that so many people still flock to the Emirates stadium in Holloway given the stupendous ticket prices. If you're lucky enough to have the £1000s needed for a decent season ticket then you get to sit in a huge, soulless stadium named after an airline company to watch what are ostensibly a bunch of bloody foreigners. On the plus side, those bloody foreigners play some of the most dazzling football in Europe and you never know, this just could be the year Arsenal's young team realizes their full potential (groan).

How to Get There

By Car: Unless you have a resident's permit to get around the Event Day Parking Scheme always in effect, it's impossible to park on-street. Which is to say, don't bother bringing a car.

By Public Transport: Arsenal (Piccadilly Line) is the nearest tube station, around three minutes walk from the ground. Finsbury Park (Victoria, Piccadilly Lines and Great Northern rail) and Highbury & Islington (Victoria Line, North London Line and Great Northern rail) stations are around a 10-minute walk—these should be slightly less crowded.

How to Get Tickets

As Arsenal play some damn sexy football, tickets are not easy to come by. However, in the new, swanky Emirates Stadium there is always going to be one or two no-shows or corporate tickets that have slipped into the wrong hands. Members have first dibs on tickets and snap them up but the less scrupulous ones sell them on to make a fast buck. Try Gumtree or matchday touts if you really must. To be honest, it's probably one of the rare instances where it really is worth the hassle.

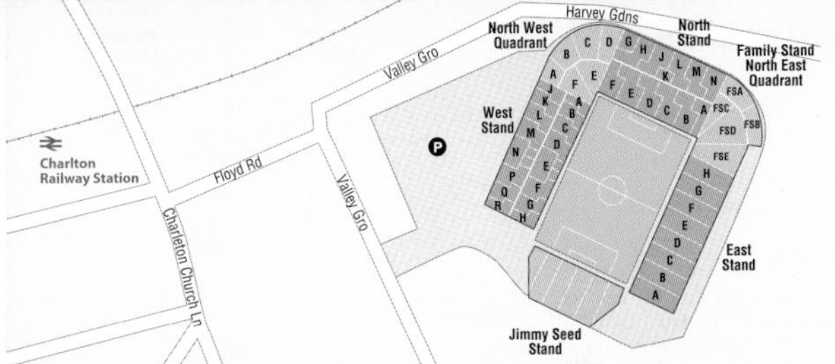

General Information

Phone: 020 8333 4000
Website: www.cafc.co.uk or @CAFCofficial
Location:The Valley, Floyd Road,
Charlton, London SE7 8BL

Overview

Supporting Charlton is like being a drug addict without a healthy bank balance, the highs are amazing (when they come) but the lows are dark and lonely days. Back in 2007, The Addicks were mixing it with the big boys in the Premier League. But after several seasons in freefall, Charlton found themselves in football's third tier. During the dark days football's ugliest man, Iain Dowie took control and drunkenly drove the team off a bridge. He played a brand of football, which matched his grotesque looks, and got the boot (no, not to his face, that's just how he looks). Inexplicably, Les Reed got the job next—a man with no managerial experience. He lasted a month. That year they went down to the Championship. And guess what? They were relegated again, and finished 13th in League 1 (Third Division). In 2009 Phil Parkinson took over and things remained more or less the same. But during 2010 new ownership meant big changes, the effective but unremarkable Parkinson was given the boot in place of Charlton legend Chris Powell. After the 2010-11 season ended with mixed results the team had a spring clean, literally, Powell bought 19 new players and 2011-12 season ended with Charlton winning the Third Division and earning promotion to the Championship. Subsequent seasons saw the club underperform and under new ownership Powell was sacked. Perhaps coming years should see the darkness lifted from the club and the ground reflect Charlton's reputation as a family club, rather than a stadium full of recovering addicts.

How to Get There

By Car: You can leave the M25 at Junction 2 in order to access the A2, heading towards London. When the A2 becomes the A102 (M), take the right hand exit at the roundabout into the A206 Woolwich Road. After passing the major set of traffic lights at the junction of Anchor and Hope Lane and Charlton Church Lane, turn right at the second roundabout into Charlton Lane. Go over the railway crossing then take the first right into Harvey Gardens, with the road leading to the ground. From central London, travel along the A13 until it becomes the East India Dock Road, then take the A102 through the Blackwall Tunnel. Come off at the second junction and take the first exit at the roundabout, then go along the A206 Woolwich Road into Charlton Lane as detailed above. Thanks to the local residents' parking scheme, you'll be hard pushed to find a parking space; try Westmoor Street, Eastmoor Street, Warspite Road and Ruston Road.

By Public Transport: The ground is within walking distance of Charlton railway station, with the Southeastern line running services from mainline stations Charing Cross and London Bridge and services from Cannon Street on Saturdays. You can also take the Jubilee Line to North Greenwich, and then take a short ride on buses 161, 472 or 486 to get to the Valley. Moderate masochists can walk from the tube station.

How to Get Tickets

For years Charlton couldn't give their tickets away. Now, interest ebbs and flows depending on how close the club is to being relegated, but seeing a match is by no means impossible. Tickets can be ordered by phone from the Box Office, via the internet at the club's website or in person at The Valley.

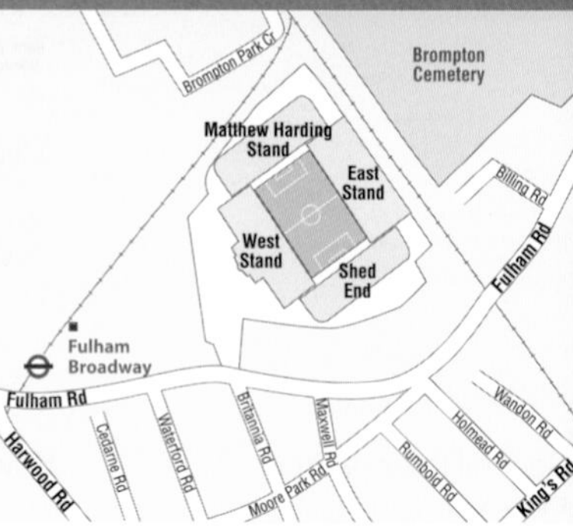

General Information

NFT Map: 43
Phone: 020 7958 2190
Website: www.chelseafc.com
or @ChelseaFC
Location: Stamford Bridge,
Fulham Road, London, SW6 1HS

Overview

Stamford Bridge, home to one of the Premiership's 'big four' clubs, is now one of Europe's most glamorous stadiums. However, 'The Bridge' was once an unappealing and daunting shit-hole more used to hosting pitch invasions and fighting hooligans than the well-heeled city types and Russian oligarchs of today. In the '70s and '80s, it was the violent 'headhunters' that made the club unpopular, but as 'The Blues' never won anything, no one took much notice. In recent years, Chelsea have succeeded in wrestling the mantle of most-hated team in England away from Manchester United, largely due to winning things with the never-ending supply of money from Roman Abramovich. The hooligans have all but gone, either priced out or grown up, but the antics of Prima Donna players and their sitcom private lives have been placing cement shoes on the club's image of late. While Chelsea's coffers have meant they've been able to import expensive foreign players, leading to back-to-back title wins in 2004–2006, their homegrown players have spent more time on tabloid front covers than on football pitches. John Terry and Ashley Cole's bed-hopping adventures will make a great airport novel one day but they've left a lot of fans disappointed in the meantime. These are troubling times indeed for the Blues; after the departure of celebrated manager Mourinho (his first stint with the club) the top position saw its own share of turbulence. With superstar coach Scolari sacked and the silverware drying up it seems money can't buy you everything. However, after two seasons of relative anonymity and a parade of failed managers, unlikely hero Roberto Di Matteo took over the reins of the club during 2012, managed to win both the FA Cup and the Champions League final (and then was sacked as well). Mourinho returned in 2013 and whatever the club's future, one thing is for sure: money will be thrown to the boys at the bridge, silverware or not.

How to Get There

By Car: It is possible to drive to Stamford Bridge on match days but it's pretty pointless to do so. Traffic snarls up badly and the effects are felt throughout Southwest London. If you do brave the traffic, remember that Fulham Road is closed off on match days. Parking is a nightmare with most zones given over to residents. Gangs of eager traffic wardens are on hand to make your Saturday afternoon miserable.

By Public Transport: Stamford Bridge is a two-minute stroll from Fulham Broadway tube station. Regular district line underground trains deliver the hordes from central London in a matter of minutes. If the idea of a packed train full of sweaty football fans isn't your idea of heaven, many fans descend at Ealing Broadway and take the ten-minute walk to the stadium instead.

How to Get Tickets

With so many competitions and cups, getting tickets is easier than you might think. The 'big' fixtures—London derby's, Man U, Liverpool and the later cup stages are either impossible to get or crazily priced, but tickets for the less glamorous ties can be picked up from the Chelsea website or box office. Otherwise, cheeky geezers will be on hand to fleece you on match day. You will probably end up in the West Stand alongside Japanese and American tourists, but that might be preferable to a fat skinhead in the 'Shed.

General Information

NFT Map: 47
Tickets: 0843 208 1222
Website: www.fulhamfc.com or @FulhamFC
Location: Craven Cottage, Stevenage Road, London SW6 6HH

Overview

Fulham like to think of themselves as a family club. They have a quaint little stadium by the Thames and they play in Fulham for God's sake. (Now about that "Cottagers" nickname…easily the most off-color in all of football.) When Roy Hodgson took the reins in 2008 they were doomed. But he rescued The Cottagers from relegation and in 2009 guided them into Europe, before taking over football's worst job (England manager) in 2012. Mark Hughes took over the team and inexplicably quit before the season finished which, tossed Fulham into turmoil, until the steady hand of Martin Jol took control and ensured business as usual. The club is owned by Shahid Khan, the Pakistani-born embodiment of the American Dream who also owns the NFL Jacksonville Jaguars franchise. (Mohamed Al-Fayed, the club's previous owner, once owned Harrods; he's the father of Dodi Fayed, who died with Princess Diana in Paris in 1997.) The club has been in flux in recent years, and was relegated to the Championship in 2014. All that aside, Craven Cottage is still one of the nicest grounds in London and tickets are relatively easy to come by. Just be wary of that hole in the gents.

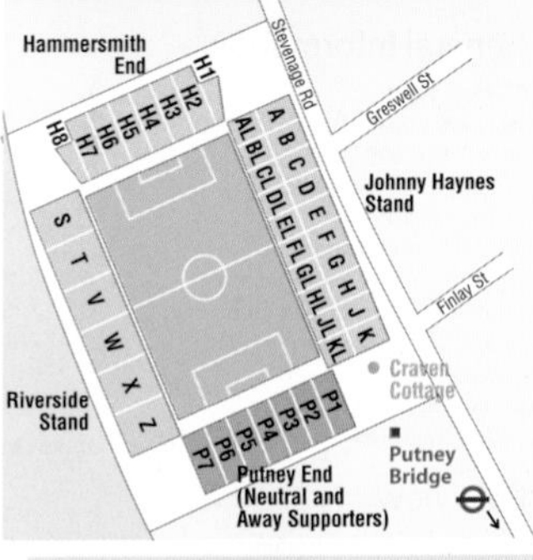

How to Get There

By Car: Craven Cottage sits in a leafy, riverside suburb of Fulham. Parking is relatively easy around the ground with plenty of parking meters, although reaching the ground could be difficult as weekend traffic in London is never fun to negotiate.

By Public Transport: Putney Bridge on the District Line is your best bet. Putney also has a mainline station with connections from Clapham Junction and direct trains from Waterloo. Cross the road opposite Putney station and hop on any passing bus. Alternatively, a ten-minute walk down the high street and over the river will get you to the ground.

How to Get Tickets

One of the 'joys' of watching Fulham is that tickets are easy to get your hands on. Many games are available on general sale through the club website. For the biggest matches, priority is given to members but persevere and you should be rewarded. If you can't get a ticket legitimately, you can always take your chance with a tout on match day. Try haggling; due to Fulham's fortunes, you could get lucky.

General Information

NFT Map: 76
Main switchboard: 020 7616 8500
Ticket Office: 020 7432 1000
Lord's website: www.lords.org
or @HomeOfCricket
England Cricket Board:
www.ecb.co.uk or @ECB_cricket
Middlesex County Cricket Club:
www.middlesexccc.com
or @Middlesex_CCC
Location: St John's Wood,
London NW8 8QN.

Overview

Even if you know nothing about cricket, don't be put off coming to Lord's. Yes, some games last for five days, and yes, it can still be a draw at the end of it. But as much as anything else Lord's is a fabulous place to come and have a drink. On a hot day the ground is paradise. The sunburnt crowd get slowly boozed up and by the time the players break for tea—yes, tea—few people are concerned at what's going on in the middle. With the polite hum of chatter building up to full-blown drunken singing, it's worth going to Lord's for the atmosphere alone. But when the rabble have calmed down, Lord's is a very genteel place. It's widely seen as the Home of Cricket, and used to house the international governing body. It hosts a heap of England games every year and it's the home ground of county side Middlesex. There's also a year-round gym—you don't even have to be posh to use it—and an indoor training centre. There's even a museum to amuse you when rain stops play. And, rest assured, at some point rain WILL stop play. At the moment, Lord's holds two Test matches (the marathon international five-dayers) and occasional England one-day games. These are the ground's showpiece events, where the crowd are at their most boisterous. Middlesex games rarely attract many spectators, and unless you're an old man or a dog you may be in a minority.

How to Get There

By Car: There's little parking around Lord's so, as you'll be parked up all day, public transport will always be cheaper. If you must drive, the ground is off the A4, which turns into the M4.

By Public Transport: The nearest station is St John's Wood (Jubilee Line). Marylebone (Bakerloo) and Baker Street (Bakerloo, Jubilee, Hammersmith and City, Metropolitan and Circle) are both nearby. Marylebone mainline station serves the north and west of the country. London Paddington is a short bus ride away. Dozens of buses run to Baker Street, and many of which stop right outside the ground.

How to Get Tickets

Getting your hands on England tickets can be tricky. The first few days of a Test match tend to sell out months in advance, though tickets for the last day never go on pre-sale (as the game could be over by then). Similarly, One Day Internationals are normally sell-outs, so it does take a little planning to get in. Check the website over the preceding winter and you might get lucky. If there are less than ten overs in a day due to rain, or if the game's already over, you can claim the full ticket price back. If the weather limits play to between 10.1–24.5 overs (in English, that's up to 149 balls played) you get a 50 per cent refund. Any more than that and you're deemed to have got your money's worth. Middlesex games rarely sell out, however, so you can just rock up on the day, beers in hand, and enjoy the Lord's village.

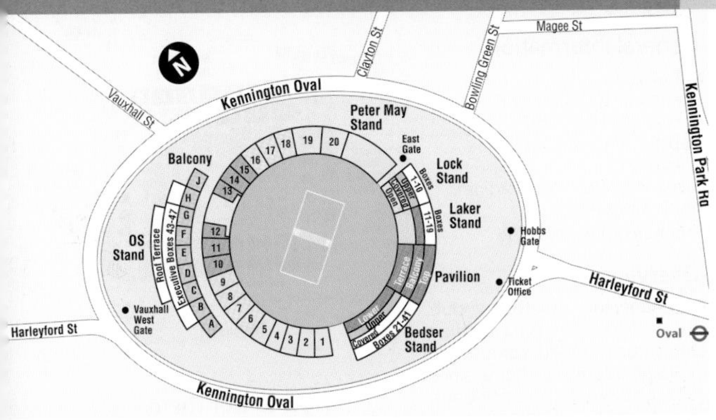

General Information

NFT Map: 135
Telephone: 0844 375 1845
Website: www.kiaoval.com or @surreycricket
Location: The Kia Oval,
Kennington, London, SE11 5SS

Overview

What better way to while away a sunny summer's day than at The Oval cricket ground, typically alongside hundreds of other shirkers who also called in sick? The Oval is one of London's twin icons of the game, alongside Lord's in North London, and boasts a rich history stretching all the way back to 1846, when it was converted from cabbage patch to cricket pitch. It now plays host to Surrey County and international test matches, including the biennial England-Australia slugfest "The Ashes." Live international cricket remains a boozy, good natured affair with English fanbase 'The Barmy Army' typically belting out salty chants and cheering occasional streakers. County cricket is a mellower, no less enjoyable event, with readily available tickets and a good portion of the crowd more interested in today's paper than the action in front of them. Taxing it ain't.

How to Get There

By Car: Driving to the Oval is not ideal, because parking is near impossible. Should you be willing to risk it, it's situated on the A202, near the junction with the A3 and A24, south of Vauxhall Bridge. As ever with London driving, you'll need your A to Z and nerves of steel.

By Public Transport: The Oval boasts its own, eponymous tube stop on the Northern Line, from which the stadium is a few hundred yards walk. Determinedly overground travellers should alight at Vauxhall, from which Oval is a ten-minute jaunt, tops. Buses 36, 185 and 436 stop right outside the ground, too.

How to Get Tickets

Tickets for Surrey county matches are relatively easy to get hold of, though seats for some fixtures can only be bought on site on the day of the match. International matches tend to sell out very quickly indeed—touts or online sales sites like eBay and Gumtree are usually the best option, at a price.

General Information

NFT Map: 32
Telephone: 020 8743 0262
Tickets: 0844 477 7007
Website: www.qpr.co.uk
or @QPRFC
Location: Loftus Road Stadium,
South Africa Road,
Shepherd's Bush, W12 7PJ

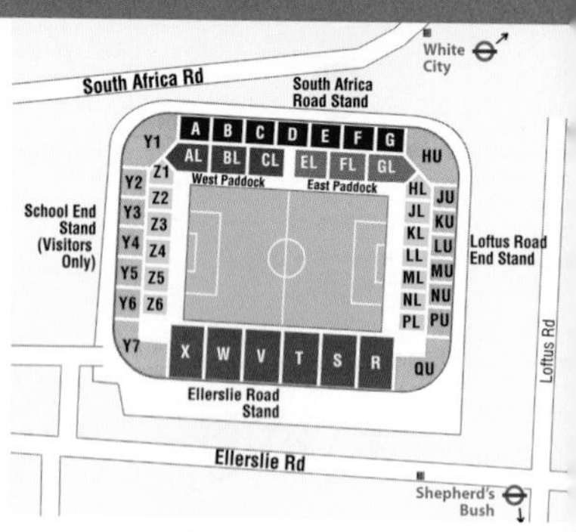

Overview

Once-itinerant football club Queens Park Rangers have called Loftus Road—based, confusingly, in Shepherd's Bush—home since 1917, give or take a few seasons. Their footballing fortunes have yo-yoed through the decades: once a whisker away from winning Division One in the years before it became the Premiership; they finished the 2011-12 season just above the relegation zone, but gave us what undoubtedly was the game of the season after losing a 2–0 lead in stoppage time to gift moneybags Man City the Premier League title. New ownership, including pint-sized F1 oligarch Bernie Ecclestone, injected some much needed glamour into the club (prior to the takeover, Pete Doherty was the Hoops' most famous fan). But, amid wacky boasts of Euro domination, Bernie was cut down to size; Ecclestone has since sold his stake in the team, and at a healthy profit. The years following the sacking of their Italian boss De Canio has seen the Hoops' top spot resemble a revolving door in a busy brothel. Though different managers and caretakers have come and gone, resulting in turmoil on and off the pitch, the erratic QPR are definitely and defiantly worth watching live.

How to Get There

By Car: Whether you're approachin[g] Loftus Road from the North (from the M through the A406 and A40), East (via th[e] A40(M)), South (from the A3 and A219) o[r] West (up the M4 via the A315 and A40. on a wing and a prayer), all routes lea[d] through White City. Once there, tur[n] right off Wood Lane into South Afric[a] Road. Don't even set off without prope[r] navigation tools, or emergency rations.

By Public Transport: The majority o[f] QPR fans are local and rely either o[n] nearby tube stops (White City on th[e] Central Line, Shepherd's Bush on th[e] the Hammersmith and City Line), any o[f] buses 72, 95, or 220 to White City Station or overground train to Acton Central followed by a quick bus ride.

How to Get Tickets

Getting tickets for a QPR game is harder than you might expect. The team has a loyal fan base and is quickly becoming a guilty pleasure (due mainly to moments of madness) for casual spectators. However, getting tickets for a run-of-the-mill mid-season game should be a cinch, either via the Rangers' ticket website or by phone. You can also visit the Loftus Road box office on match days.

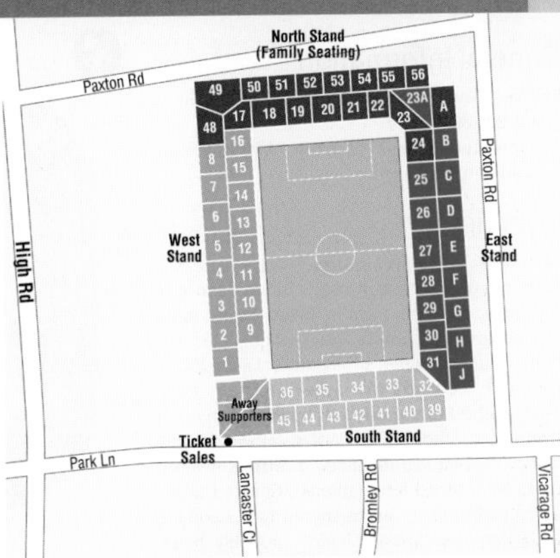

General Information

Telephone: 0344 499 5000
Tickets: 0344 844 0102
Website: www.tottenhamhotspur.com or @SpursOfficial
Location: Bill Nicholson Way, 748 High Road, London, N17 OAP

Overview

The times they are a-changin at Tottenham, the blaggers at Stamford Bridge robbed them of a deserved Champion's League place and the country's favourite tax dodger Harry Redknapp didn't get the England job and then, to add insult to injury, was let go by the club. The scruffy but (for some reason) adored century-old White Hart Lane is on its last legs as a new mega-development is heading into the building phase. This isn't a bad thing, because nostalgia aside, few grounds in the capital are located further from a tube stop and closer to a corner of London where even police dogs walk in pairs. More than most fans, the Spurs faithful have a tight grasp of history (which could be because there's been no league title there since 1961). And it shows at the stadium—supporters even chant about what a grand old team Spurs are. But that song only gets sporadic outings. Most of the chants that ring around White Hart Lane are about how much the fans hate Arsenal. It's a rivalry that's as intense as any in football—and as Arsenal started out in the south of the city, only moving across the river in 1913, Spurs claim of being Kings of North London isn't such a wild one. This division grew deeper during Arsenal's years of success, their American ownership, snooty fans, and their new corporate-branded Emirates Stadium just added fuel to the fire. But Spurs are contenders now, they have a new stadium of their own in the pipeline and the days of old ladies selling bagels inside the ground will soon be replaced by £400 million hotel-cum-shopping-centre-cum-football-ground.

How to Get There

By Car: The area's congested at the best of times; on match days, traffic can grind to a standstill. But if you don't mind a bit of gridlock, White Hart Lane is on the Tottenham High Road (A1010) a mile south of the North Circular (A406). This is easily accessible from junction 25 of the M25, in itself a temple to traffic.

By Public Transport: The nearest tube is Seven Sisters (Victoria Line), which is a 25-minute walk away. But at least if you work up a hunger from all that walking there's hundreds of kebab shops en route. White Hart Lane overland station, which runs from Liverpool Street through Seven Sisters, is a five-minute walk from the ground. Bus routes 279, 349, 149, 259 run closest to the stadium, but many more pass nearby.

How to Get Tickets

Although home games normally sell out, tickets are fairly easy to get hold of. Club members get first refusal at tickets, ten days before going on sale to the public. To get on the season ticket waiting list, you have to become a One Hotspur Bronze Member, but as the club's fortunes are on the rise, the wait could be some time.

General Information

Website: www.englandrugby.com/twickenham
Phone: 020 8892 8877
Location: Twickenham Stadium, Whitton Road, Twickenham, TW2 7BA

Overview

The home of English rugby, Twickenham is a behemoth of a stadium. An ugly chunk of concrete seemingly dumped from a great height onto a quiet London suburb, Twickenham lacks the charm and character of Ireland's Landsdowne Road and Scotland's Murrayfield, and has been all but pushed to the sidelines by the magnificent Millennium Stadium in Wales. However, the stadium has largely remained a fortress when it comes to England Internationals. Cheered on by 82,000 well-spoken, white-shirted fans booming out 'Swing Low Sweet Chariot' probably helps. Maybe the England players absorb the unfussy and uncompromising nature of their surroundings into their psyche on match days. Critics would argue that their style of rugby is as ugly and bland as the stadium they play in. This would be harsh if England hadn't consistently underperformed after carrying off the Rugby World Cup in 2003. Twickenham also hosts a series of Rugby tournaments and exhibition matches, including the famous 'Sevens', in addition to the occasional Premiership fixture. Outside the Rugby season, the stadium is given over to rock concerts for international bands like U2, Bon Jovi and Lady Gaga. The World Rugby Museum, located in the East Stand at the stadium, is a collection of over 25,000 items related to the history of the sport. Tours of Twickenham are also available.

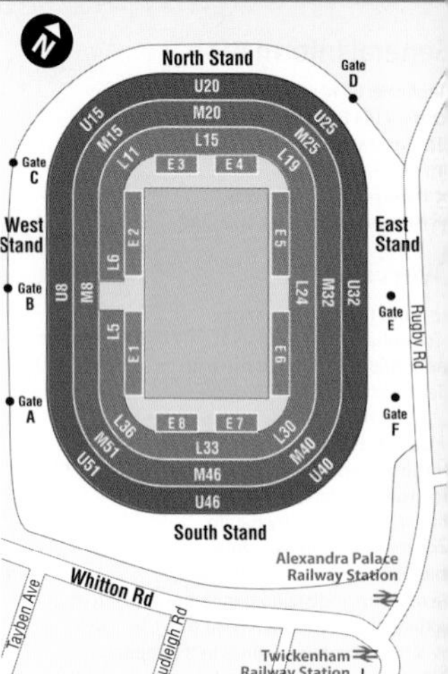

By Public Transport: Mainline trains run t Twickenham station from Waterloo and Readin London Underground runs to Richmond on th District Line where shuttle buses will take fans t the stadium (50p outbound, free return) Hounslo is an alternative Underground station but shutt buses only run from Twickenham to Hounslo station so you will have to make it to the stadiur under your own steam. Bus numbers 281, 267, 48 681 and H20 all have regular services passing clos to the stadium.

How to Get There

By Car: Twickenham is very accessible by road—if you live in the South. The M3 motorway turns into the A316 that passes the stadium, carrying on into central London. Certain roads get closed down on match days so drivers should allow plenty of time. Parking at the stadium is extremely limited and should be booked in advance. Resident permits are helpfully required for all roads bordering the stadium so the best thing to do is park in the general vicinity and walk the rest of the way.

How to Get Tickets

England rugby tickets are hot propert commanding higher prices than top footba games. As competition games are relative infrequent, tickets sell out well in advance s keep checking the website for updates o ticket releases. Premiership tickets and friend matches are easier to come by but will general sell out. If you don't get lucky in advance, rugb touts (slightly less aggressive than their footba cousins) will happily make your wallet lighter fc you. Ticketmaster is the best option for concer or Gumtree and Craigslist for re-sales and swaps.

General Information

Website: www.whufc.com or @whufc_official
Telephone: 020 8548 2748
Tickets: www.whufcboxoffice.com or 0871 529 1966
Location: Boleyn Ground, Green Street, London E13 9AZ

Overview

When bald biscuit king Eggert Magnusson bought the Hammers everything looked rosy. But then the world went tits up. The recession meant Icelander Eggert's companies were suddenly worth nothing. He went bankrupt—and West Ham became a Scandinavian IOU. While boss Gianfranco Zola was leading a revolution on the pitch—shepherding a young team to the brinks of Europe—there were real dangers the club would fold.

Since the Icelandic money troubles, West Ham has been owned by an ever-changing cast of consortiums and moneyed men. Not really where you want your money right now. But if they survive, the Irons are on the way up. If you can find the ground in deepest East London they're well worth a look.

Over the years, West Ham has been unfairly tainted by association with the ICF hooligan firm. Largely active in the '70s and '80s, a 2005 film, <i>*Green Street*</i> did its best to rekindle unwanted memories. The drama was undermined slightly by giving the lead role to a hobbit. They finished the 2011 season at the bottom of the Premiership and were relegated—but during 2012 they proved they were too good for the Championship and are back with the big boys. Let's hope they keep doing better, we don't want to give them any excuse to get angry.

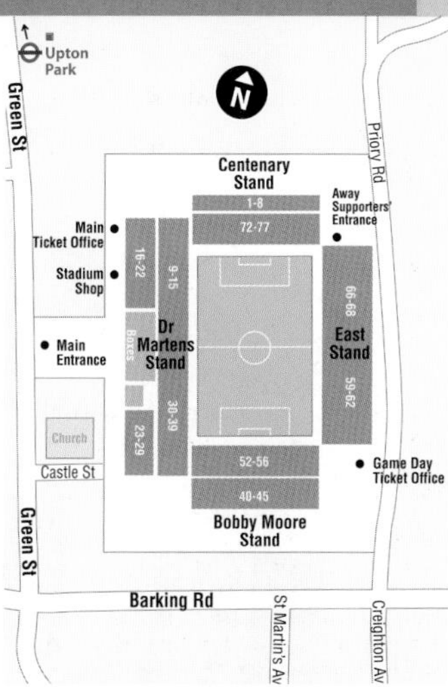

How to Get There

By Car: Driving in London is a waste of time even on the best of days, but try it on match days and you are asking for trouble. East London is a warren of one way streets, dead ends and no through roads. You are likely to either miss kick-off or get a parking ticket or both.

By Public Transport: The District line will 'whisk' you from central London to Upton Park in half an hour or so. The Boleyn Ground is five minutes walk from the underground station.

How to Get Tickets

Unless you want to pay through the nose for tickets against the big clubs, you should be able to find spares for the smaller fixtures. West Ham is a relatively small ground with a dedicated, hardcore following. Being less glamorous than Chelsea, et al. means that casual fans have a better chance of watching a game for a decent price.

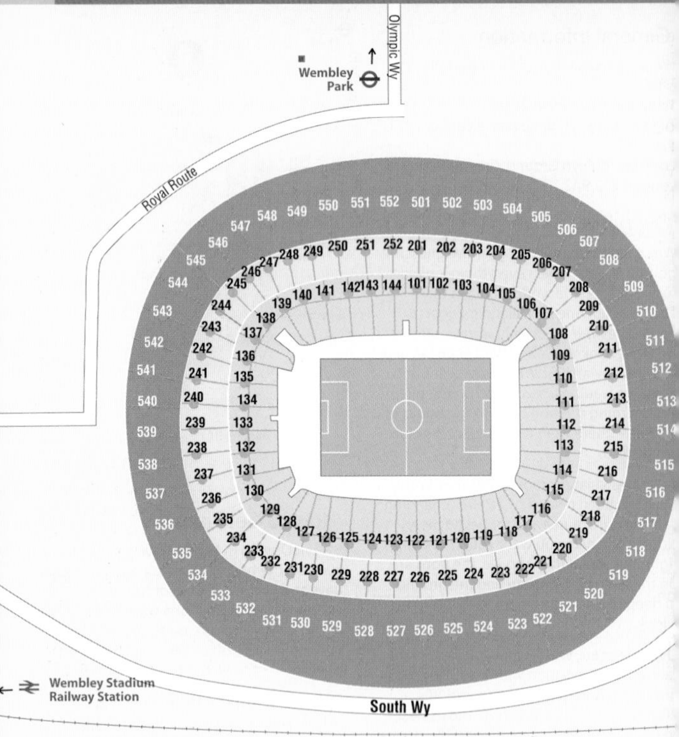

General Information

Phone: 0800 169 2007
Website: www.wembleystadium.com or @wembleystadium
Location: Wembley Stadium, Wembley HA9 0WS

Overview

Wembley Stadium enjoys a strange position in the British psyche. For football fans it's most significant as the scene of England's only World Cup win back in 1966, as well as numerous pitch invasions by angry/jubilant Scottish fans whenever their national team came down to play. Plus, a generation of British bands have grown up dreaming of the day they'd bellow: "hello Wem-ber-ley, are you ready to rock?!!" to tens of thousands of people who've just paid a fiver for a chewy patty of minced spleen 'n' testicles in a dry bun. For these sentimental reasons, then, very few people complained that the National Stadium was a bit of a crap-hole stuck in an inaccessible suburb of West London. By the late '90s the place was looking a bit battered, so they knocked it down and then very, very slowly, and at tremendous, tabloid-scandalising expense, built a replacement on the same site. The result is, just about, worth it. There are none of the blind spots for spectators that the old stadium used to have, plus it has far greater leg-room for 90-thousand-plus people and much more comfortable seating. It also looks fantastically imposing as you walk out of Wembley Park tube with its massive arch curving into the sky. A trip here might not make your knees go "all trembly" as fans used to sing but for football lovers it's one of the world's great venues. They also have a special removable running track for athletics and, to the disgust of "soccer" purists, they've even let American "football" teams play here, too.

How to Get There

By Car: Short of hiring snipers to pick drivers off as they approach the mighty arch, the Stadium could hardly do more to discourage visitors from driving. "Wembley Stadium is a public transport destination. Please leave your car behind," the website primly advises. However, if you are some kind of die-hard, planet-raping petrol-head you'll see signs pointing to the stadium from Great Central Way onwards. There are very few parking spaces at the Stadium itself and these need to be booked in advance. On match days, or when there's anything else happening, the local area becomes residents' parking only, too. Yes, they really don't want you to bring your car.

By Public Transport: The nearest Tube is Wembley Park on the Metropolitan and Jubilee line. Wembley Central (on the Bakerloo line) is about 10–15 minutes walk and there's also Wembley Stadium mainline train station with links all over the country. If you're travelling from outside London there are National Express coaches from 43 different towns and cities.

How to Get Tickets

Easier said than done. 'Club Wembley' have kindly created a 'ten year seat licence'—no doubt to re-coup the massive overspend that accompanied completion of the stadium. These licences give owners access to all major events hosted at Wembley and its worth going on the website to laugh at the ridiculous prices. A 'one-off licence fee' starts at £172 per person per event. Annual season tickets are on top of that. Cloud Cuckoo Land. 'Normal' people can buy tickets to England games through the FA (you need to be a member), for football and rugby cup games through the respective clubs and tickets for one off events and shows through Ticketmaster. It's always worth checking Gumtree.com as you never know who might be flogging off a golden ticket to the highest bidder.

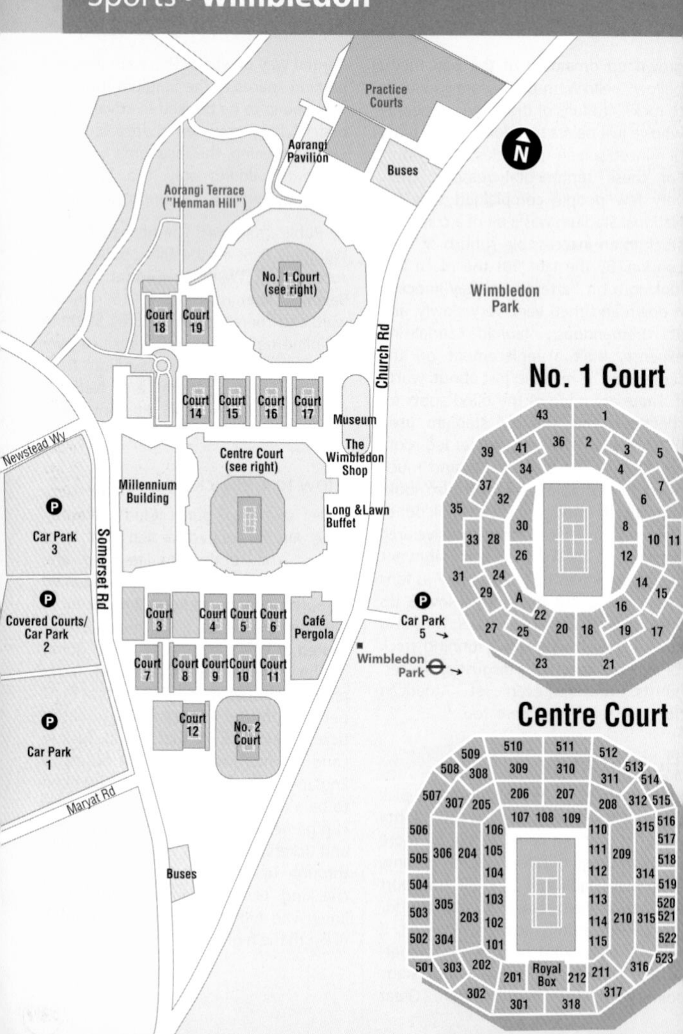
Practice Courts
Aorangi Pavilion
Buses
Aorangi Terrace ("Henman Hill")
No. 1 Court (see right)
Wimbledon Park
Court 18
Court 19
Church Rd
Court 14
Court 15
Court 16
Court 17
Museum
The Wimbledon Shop
Newstead Wy
Centre Court (see right)
Millennium Building
Long &Lawn Buffet
Car Park 3
Somerset Rd
Covered Courts/ Car Park 2
Court 3
Court 4
Court 5
Court 6
Café Pergola
Car Park 5
Court 7
Court 8
Court 9
Court 10
Court 11
Wimbledon Park
Court 12
No. 2 Court
Car Park 1
Maryat Rd
Buses
No. 1 Court
Centre Court
Royal Box

General Information

Telephone: 020 8944 1066
Website: www.wimbledon.com
or @Wimbledon
Location: The All England Lawn Tennis and Croquet Club, Church Road, Wimbledon, SW19 5AE

Overview

New balls please! If it's not pissing it down—which is a big if—Wimbledon's All England Tennis and Croquet Club is the place to witness the world's finest tennis players do battle on rye grass courts, home as it is to the oldest major Championship in the game each June/July. But this is also a place to be seen and to be merry—sure, it's about the tennis, but it's also about strawberries and cream (of which 62,000 pounds and 1,540 gallons worth are sold each year respectively), the free-flowing champagne, the celebrity crowd, and the Ralph Lauren-designed ballboy and ballgirl outfits. If you can't actually get a ticket for the tournament—the All England Club makes approximately 1,500 of them available each day, and more importantly, if you're not prepared to camp out overnight in the queue—you can always sit yourself on Murray Mound (formerly Henman Hill) at the northern end of the complex, where a vast television screen allows you to watch British players systematically eliminated in typically heartbreaking fashion. Really, we should stick to darts.

How to Get There

By Car: During the tournament, traffic and parking are nightmarish propositions, and you're better off using public transport. Nonetheless, the determined will need to take the A219 from the A3, and turn off left onto Church Road once in Wimbledon itself.

By Public Transport: Wimbledon railway station is a short journey from both Waterloo and Clapham Junction, and is otherwise serviced (Vicar!) by trains from towns right across the South of England. From here, board the London General shuttle bus straight to the grounds; they depart every five minutes or so during the tournament. Tube users should head for Southfields on the District line, from where a London General shuttle also operates. Those who prefer to saunter can mosey on down Wimbledon Park Road heading south for ten minutes or so, and you can also walk it from Wimbledon Park tube station, heading north-west.

How to Get Tickets

You can (legally) come by tickets to Wimbledon in two ways—one, apply in advance to the public 'ballot', via the website, in the hope you are selected at random to purchase tickets (closing date end of December). Two, join the serpentine, overnight queues for on-the-day tickets, of which five hundred are usually made available for each of Centre, Number One and Number Two Courts. Then, of course, there are all the other methods of which you're already no doubt aware.

Any bowling buff will tell you that there are two types of bowling in this country. Ten-pin bowling, the ghastly Americanized import, is by far the most popular among Londoners and the generally disrespectful Youth Of Today. Crown Green Bowling is a far more serene, (elderly) gentlemanly pursuit complete with its own rules and rituals.

London's ten pin bowlers are spoiled rotten. As it's now a trendy pastime shot through with irony, there are plenty of old, large basements converted into pristine bowling alleys designed to look retro. There's no chavs in tracksuits on speed around here: the **All Star Lanes** franchises **(Map 4, 30, 91)** are heaving with immaculately dressed trendos and hen/stag nights drunkenly bowling and singing in the karaoke booths. However, at a peak rate of £8.95 per person per game (your average game is a mere 10 minutes) and an off-peak rate of a laughably similar £6.95 per game, you'll have to access whether it's worth blowing the rent money on one night of fun. **Bloomsbury Bowling Lanes (Map 4)** does the American chic thing a bit better and its lanes are £39 an hour, which works out cheaper in a group. They also host cool gigs and DJs occasionally.

For families and the penniless, London has plenty of more 'traditional' British bowling lanes. By this, of course, we mean cavernous warehouses with pumping chart music, scary underage drinkers and sticky air hockey tables. Try the classic **Rowans (Map 62)** which at its priciest is a mere £5.20 per person per game or **Queens Ice & Bowl (Map 30)** which has also has an ice rink to cool off those skittle blues.

And what of Green Bowling? Well, being an outdoor pursuit in Britain, it's safe to say it is primarily a summer affair. When the sun is out you'll find bowling greens in all the major parks; Hyde Park offers lanes for £7.50 an hour.

After suffering at the hands of boho and cheapo ten-pin bowling facilities you may find that there can be no better way to waste an afternoon than to sit around a bowling green in Finsbury Park with a beer in hand, laughing at your idiot friends' attempts to hit the 'jack'. Maybe those elderly gentlemen are on to something…

Bowling	*Address*	*Phone*	*Map*
All Star Lanes	95 Brick Ln	020 7426 9200	91
All Star Lanes	Victoria House, Bloomsbury Pl	020 7025 2676	4
All Star Lanes	6 Porchester Gardens	020 7313 8363	30
Bloomsbury Bowling Lanes	Bedford Way	020 7183 1979	4
Hyde Park	Hyde Park	020 7262 3474	n/a
Palace Superbowl	First Floor, Elephant &	020 7277 0001	112
Castle Shopping Centre			
Queens	17 Queensway	020 7229 0172	30
Rowans	10 Stroud Green Rd	020 8800 1950	62

Nothing combines relaxation and hypertension quite like golf, nor indeed knee-length socks, spats and flat caps. For golfing Londoners, opportunities to play must be sought towards the outskirts of the capital, where the city shore is lapped once more by greenery and open space. You can, of course, take your one wood out onto London's pavements and practise your fade drive there, but you're odds on to be arrested if you do.

You'll be better received moving clockwise around London from the north, at establishments such as the **Highgate Golf Club** and **Muswell Hill Golf Club**. Both are highbrow member institutions with epic fairways, open nonetheless to the public, as long as that public is wearing a decent shirt. Eighteen holes at each are in the £30-45 range, which is also the case at the **Hampstead Golf Club**, home of one of England's toughest front nines. Nearby **Finchley Golf Club** is similarly priced for visitors but also offers some neat specials such as winter green fees under £30 and knockdown prices for twelve holes of 'twilight golf'. A little farther north, **Mill Hill Golf Club** is a shade cheaper though no less satisfying.

In the south-east, the **Royal Blackheath Golf Club** positions itself as the oldest in the world, which might be why playing eighteen holes as a visitor requires a small trust fund, at £60 during summer. Moving farther west, the **Central London Golf Centre** is a no-nonsense 'pay-and-play' establishment offering nine full-length holes to golfers of all standards for little more than a tenner. The **Wimbledon Park Golf Club** is another quality members club open to visitors, while nearby **Royal Wimbledon Golf Club** terms itself a 'very private' club—visitors are welcome but will be required to apply in writing, prove handicap and, in all likelihood, undergo some kind of permanently scarring initiation ritual. Access to each of these Wimbledon clubs kicks off at a chokingly high £70 for eighteen holes. You could buy a second-hand Playstation for that. The **London Scottish Golf Club** on Wimbledon Common is much more like it, in the range of £20-30 a round, though a pillar-box red top is compulsory for all. Out west, **Dukes Meadows Golf Club** in Chiswick offers nine three-par holes, a driving range and function rooms, all at a reasonable price.

For golfers who really are determined not to leave Zone One, there is one option after all. **Urban Golf (Map 10)** in Soho and the **Urban Golf (Map 15)** Smithfield location is the last word in golf simulation, with the chance to play, virtual-style, some of the world's top courses. It also boasts well-stocked bars and chic lounge areas. You just know the purists will loathe it.

Golf Clubs	*Address*	*Phone*	*Map*
Central London Golf Centre	Burntwood Ln	020 8871 2468	n/a
Dukes Meadows Golf Club	Dukes Meadow	020 8995 0537	n/a
Finchley	Frith Ln	020 8346 1133	n/a
Hampstead Golf Club	82 Winnington Rd	020 8455 0203	n/a
Highgate Golf Club	Denewood Rd	020 8340 3745	n/a
Holland Park	Ilchester Pl	020 7602 2226	34
London Scottish Golf Club	Windmill Rd	020 8788 0135	n/a
Mill Hill Golf Club	100 Barnet Way	020 8959 2339	n/a
Muswell Hill Golf Club	Rhodes Ave	020 8888 1764	n/a
Royal Blackheath Golf Club	Court Rd	020 8550 1795	n/a
Urban Golf	33 Great Pulteney St	020 7434 4300	10
Urban Golf	12 Smithfield St	020 7248 8600	15
Wilbledon Park Golf Club	Home Park Rd	020 8946 1250	n/a

Remember the Levi's ad in the pool hall? The one which had The Clash's "Should I Stay Or Should I Go?" as the soundtrack? Yeah, that one. It conjured up a pretty cool image, right? Unfortunately London's pool halls have not had the retro revamp (is that an oxymoron?) that bowling is currently enjoying (**All Star Lanes**, **Bloomsbury Bowling**) so it's rare to actually find a place where you can stand around looking like James Dean, kissing your teeth, chewing on a tooth pick, and generally inviting any hustler to take you on without like, really being taken on by someone from the Russian/Turkish mafia. We also inextricably link shooting some pool with having a drink or two, but it is often the lesser red and yellow-balled "pub" pool table (funnily enough) rather than the greater spotted (and striped) genuine American pool table which is found within the confines of the few remaining non-chain traditional pubs in London. **19:20 (Map 6)** in Clerkenwell has more of a pool hall feel with media types taking their game a little more seriously at the end of the working day. If you do fancy something a little more louche, there are many a pool and snooker hall to be found on the edges of central London which can offer a grittier atmosphere. **Efes (Map 86)** used to be a bit of a no-go for middle-class hipster kids until the owners realised that they were sitting on a goldmine what with having a long-standing late licence and being slap bang in the middle of the action. Now the place hosts gigs and is a regular fixture for anyone doing a Kingsland crawl. Oh yeah, and has pool tables.

Pool & Snooker	*Address*	*Phone*	*Map*
19:20	20 Great Sutton St	020 7253 1920	6
Efes Pool Club & Bar	17 Stoke Newington Rd	020 7249 6040	86
The Elbow Room	97 Curtain Rd	020 7613 1316	84
The Elbow Room	89 Chapel Market	020 7278 3244	80
The Elbow Room	103 Westbourne Grove	020 7221 5211	30
Number 1 Bar	1 Duke Street Hill	020 7407 6420	106
Riley's	638 Wandsworth Rd	020 7498 0432	142
Riley's	16 Semley Pl	020 7824 8261	19
Rowans	10 Stroud Green Rd	020 8800 1950	62
The Westbury	34 Kilburn High Rd	020 7625 7500	68

Tennis

Ah…the other beautiful game, beloved of park fence jumpers and upper class grunters alike. Like many popular sports, tennis may have originated in Britain, but we're pretty consistent in our ineptitude at it. This is not for the lack of trying: the country's capital is packed full of tennis clubs, outdoor park courts and large sports complexes.

Tennis is certainly not as exclusive as it once was, with an hour's playing a lot cheaper than ten-pin bowling, for example. You can mince about amidst leafy surroundings in Hyde Park (Hyde Park Tennis and Sports Centre, 020 7262 3474), flail in the dark depths of Finsbury Park on a turn-up-and-play basis, or in the luxury of the historic Queens Club (www.queensclub.co.uk, 020 7386 3429 for membership information). Also commendable are the Paddington Sports Club (psclondon.com or 020 7286 8448) in Maida Vale and the courts in Regent's Park: go to www.tennisintheparks.co.uk for information on, uh, playing tennis in parks. Indicative of the new equalitarian nature of the game are Tennis London International (www.tennislondon.com) who take pride in being 'the largest gay and lesbian tennis group in the UK.' But it's not all democratic: there's always Wimbledon (www.wimbledon.org, which due to the jaw-dropping ticket prices, still is as exclusive as it's always been. If you still want to get caught up in the annual tennis frenzy, head to Henman Hill, or Murray Mound, or whatever it's called these days. Essentially a hill outside Centre Court, here you can sit on the grass and watch the action on video screens with all the other poor proles who don't have any kidneys left to trade for a ticket.

Squash

Like some weird secret society, squash players spend their time locked indoors, organised into little private clubs and engaged in an activity which will eventually mess them up. Squash is hard—just ask your poor knees. The squash court is a high-octane containment tank swimming in adrenalin, which explains why Londoners have taken to it with such gusto. A court at Sobell Leisure Center (020 7609 2166) in Finsbury Park for example, is near impossible to book at peak times. Be warned—a lot of sports centres don't have squash facilities, but somewhere like the Oasis Sports Centre (020 7831 1804) in Tottenham Court Road is a church to all things sweaty and squashy…and you can go for an outdoor swim afterwards, too. For a quirkier court try Maiden Lane Youth Club (020 7267 9586)—a community centre in a housing estate, which has one beat-up court for an hourly fee. If there isn't a yoga class in progress, that is.

Badminton/Table Tennis

They may be worlds apart in many ways, but badminton and table tennis are usually offered in the same place, and both are 'genteel' sports in which it is almost acceptable to be beaten by the opposite sex (whichever sex you are). Badminton is especially popular across the board, with almost all sizeable sports centres offering courts and equipment. However, if you've any experience in attempting to book a court at most public sports complexes you'll know of the often depressing amount of phone wrangling and frustration that arises from these exchanges. Chief perpetrator is Kings Hall Leisure Centre (020 8985 2158) in Lower Clapton, who will test your patience to inhumane limits. The Brixton Recreation Centre (020 7095 5100) caters to badminton and squash players but always sound like they can't wait to get you off the phone; their rates are £6.25-£8.50 for badminton, which is pretty competitive. The Sobell Centre, as mentioned above, also caters for table tennis (doesn't "ping pong" sound nicer?) and badminton. The best strategy is to phone your local centre to ascertain which racquet sports they cater for and then prepare yourself to be either double-booked, misinformed or given a free session depending on the ability of the desk assistant!

Overview

As the nascent city of 'Londinium' was being named by the Romans in AD 43, in Asia the practice of yoga was entering its third or fourth millennium. Nineteen hundred years on, at last it found its way out west, and London's yoga establishments have flourished ever since. Essentially, the capital's schools can be divided into those concerned primarily with physical fitness—often the larger institutions offering a range of styles—and those with a more spiritual bent. Of the former, Go Yoga in Shepherd's Bush is a fine example, offering yoga and pilates for adults and kids alike, while the popular Triyoga centres in Primrose Hill and Covent Garden are one-stop holistic shops for the upwardly mobile set. More specialised centres include Bikram Yoga College of India in Kentish Town, and its partner Bikram Yoga City—bring water and a towel for hard wearing, specially heated sessions—and the Iyengar Yoga Institute in Maida Vale, which offers a free introductory class. Special mention also goes to Fulham Yogashala, a newish venture offering all sorts including, unnervingly, 'power yoga'. Still, entering the peaceful surroundings of Yogashala is, according to one client, like getting a hug. Those more spiritual schools include the wonderful Sivanada Yoga Centre, an oasis of serenity in the midst of Putney boasting resident yogi teachers, and the Satyananda Yoga Centre in Clapham with its deep focus on yoga-meditation techniques. Shanti Sadam, out west, is also more concerned with inner stillness than downward dogs. And hidden away in Archway, the Kriya Centre runs a series of kundalini yoga classes in humble but hospitable surroundings—Ohm tastic!

There's nothing quite like an obesity epidemic to make a city sporty. We're constantly being told that we're swelling to huge new levels. The message is worrying: buck up fatties, or you won't even fit into your own coffin. Unlike the majority of celebrations that take place in the capital, the 2012 Olympic Games didn't leave us dry mouthed and heaving on the floor with a national hangover. Instead the summer games littered our fair city with a legacy of leading sports venues, and lower-level sport has benefited the most with increased involvement citywide. London's sizeable ethnic communities have also brought weird and wonderful games with them (American Football? In London? They keep threatening…). Dozens of leagues, in dozens of sports, gather every evening to try and beat the bulge.

General Tips

A good starting point is the Gumtree website (www.gumtree.com). Their sports and community section is full of ads trying to fills gaps in sports teams. And as it was started by born-to-sweat Aussies, it never lets up in sheer quantity of athletic opportunities. The local press is also a decent bet. All London boroughs have their own newspapers, who cover amateur sports with as much enthusiasm as the professionals. You may never make it in the big leagues, but at least you can be a hero in Camden. But one area where London struggles is with the concept of pick-up games. Perhaps it's part of our reserved nature, but it's unusual to just rock up at a park and challenge whoever's there. By all means try, but you may get rebuked by a stiff upper lip.

Football

Sunday league football in London used to have a reputation of being rough. For many years it was the preserve of hungover builders, who wanted ninety minutes letting off steam by kicking people around. But it's moved on slightly from those days, with a more general acceptance of skill and less emphasis placed on pain. The spiritual home of recreational football is Hackney Marshes. The East London site has a whopping 80-plus pitches—so many leagues and teams play there that it's worth just turning up and asking around. If you draw a blank there, then the FA website (www.thefa.com) has a club locator search. Regardless of where you live, you'll get a mammoth list of clubs. The hardest part of finding a team in London is narrowing down who it is you want to play for. Five-a-side football is also booming in London. In the city centre, where space is at a premium, it's often the only way of getting in a game. Powerleague (www.powerleague.co.uk) organise leagues around the capital, though these can be pricey. A cheaper option is to head to a leisure centre with a five-a-side pitch. They often run leagues and are less profit-driven than the private companies. Lists of leisure centres can be found on specific borough's website (such as Islington's www.islington.gov.uk).

Rugby

Don't mind drinking pints of your team-mates' urine? Enjoy a good eye-gouging? Then you must be a rugby fan! The Rugby in London website (www.rugbyinlondon.co.uk) is a Bible for lovers of casual violence, as it lists hundreds of clubs, contact details and even training venues and times. Female fans of egg chasing are also well represented. Most teams play around Southwest London, though there's a few more dotted around the city. A full list is on the RFU Women's website (www.rfuwlonse.co.uk). If you don't fancy the full-on ear-biting code of the sport there's a flourishing touch rugby scene in London. In this form of the game tackling is represented by tagging your opponent. It's an altogether less bloody type of rugby, although you're still allowed to indulge in the booze-fuelled rituals that the contact players enjoy. In2Touch (www.in2touch.com) lists a few of these leagues.

Cricket

As a sport that takes up plenty of space, you have to head to the leafier parts of London such as Hampstead, Putney, and Dulwich to find cricket clubs at play. But with more green space than any other London borough, Hackney has embraced the gentleman's game, and the thwack of leather on willow can oft be heard on London Fields during the summer months where the North East London Cricket League (nelcl.leaguerepublic.com) has established itself. Victoria Park also has a Community Cricket League (www.vpccl.co.uk). The Play-Cricket website (www.play-cricket.com) has a full rundown on London clubs

Athletics and the London Marathon

Every spring, London's runners dust down their gorilla costumes and tackle the London Marathon. If you feel up to it then you have to plan ahead; places are limited and dished out via a ballot. If you need a helping hand in the run up to the race, consider a jogging and/or roadrunning club associated with British Athletics (www.britishathletics.org.uk): as well as getting you in shape, so you don't die after 20 miles, they can help you get a spot in the starting line-up. And if you catch the bug of competitive athletics, there are six clubs who compete in the London Inter Club Challenge (see London Athletcis at www.londonathletics.org).

Miscellaneous

For fans of all things Irish, there's the London Gaelic Sports Association (www.londongaa.org); American footballers can get their fix with the British American Football League (www.britishamericanfootball.org); and if tight shorts and sleeveless shirts are your thing there's the British Aussie Rules Association (www.aflengland.org; or you could just join the navy).

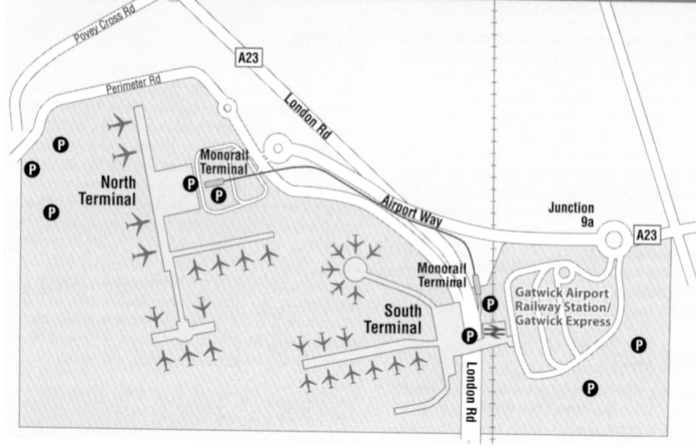

General Information

Address: Gatwick Airport,
West Sussex, RH6 0NP

Airport Code: LGW

General Information: 0844 892 0322

Lost Property: 01293 503162
or gatwick.lostproperty@excess-baggage.com

Website: www.gatwickairport.com
or @Gatwick_Airport

Overview

The UK's second-largest airport (behind Heathrow) and "the most efficient single-runway airport in the world" (seems to repeat the negative, that), Gatwick is not terribly flashy, but not so bad to deal with, and getting better and better. Located 28 miles south of London, Gatwick is not linked by the Tube, but the airport is served by a mostly painless 30-minute train ride from Victoria Station. Gatwick is a much nicer place than it once was ("high-summer sweat-filled free-for-all check-in zones for budget flights to Spain" sounds about right) but after BAA sold the airport to Global Infrastructure Partners (of London City Airport fame), GIP undertook an initial £1.2 billion overhaul of the airport and its services to better position itself as a go-to European hub. And there is even talk of a second runway—good news for Gatwick and especially whichever single-runway airport is the second-most efficient in the world.

Gatwick has two terminals: the South Terminal and the North Terminal. Trains arrive at the South Terminal, and there are more shops there, but if your flight is out of the North Terminal, a free automated train will take you on the five-minute transfer.

As far as amenities go, the usual suspects are all present, with convivial times available at Britain's premier diluting station, J.D. Wetherspoons, and the glamour of Knightsbridge miraculously squeezed into one of those little airport branches of Harrods—just in case you feel the need to inflict one of their god-awful teddy bears on another country. As far as eating's concerned, there are several Jamie Oliver outlets, a Comptoir Libanais and other spots catering to varied tastes and dietary restrictions, including vegetarian and gluten-free options. For shopping there are the usual wide range of shops befitting an airport as destination: Boots but also outlets like Zara, Ray-Ban, and BOSS.

Getting There

The Gatwick Express (www.gatwickexpress.com) runs from Victoria Station in London to the South Terminal at Gatwick in 30 minutes. First trains run at 3:30, 4:30 and then every fifteen minutes thereafter with the last trains at 00:01 and 00:32. If you're near the rail hubs it is by far the most pleasant way to get there—though a single journey is going to set you back around £20. Thameslink (www.thameslinkrailway.com) run trains to Gatwick from Blackfriars, City Thameslink, Farringdon and St Pancras International stations for £19. Easybus (www.easybus.co.uk) coaches offer service to London with prices starting from £2 each way; travel takes about an hour.

To drive to Gatwick from the M25 you need to leave at Junction 7 and carry on southwards along the M23, following the signs. Leave the M23 at Junction 9 and again, follow those handy signs to get to the appropriate terminal.

Parking

Short stay car park rates start at £3 for the first half hour, £6 up to one hour, £10 up to two hours, £12 up to three hours, and climb steadily toward £35 for a 24-hour period. For long stays there are several parks located 5-15 minutes away (via bus transfers) from the airport. These are best booked in advance. For the official Gatwick car park, charges are £20 for the first day and £15 per day thereafter, and may be booked in advance online at www.gatwickparking.com.

Car Hire

The Gatwick on-airport car rental partners are Hertz, Avis, Europcar, Sixt, National, Alamo, Enterprise and Budget. The Gatwick Airport website also offers its own online car rental feature, with special rates.

Hotels

Gatwick has several hotels on site with varying levels of service. Keep in mind that the North and South Terminals are connected via a free five-minute transfer. In the South Terminal there is the 245-room BLOC hotel, the Hilton London Gatwick, and the economical YOTEL, which offers 46 cabins (available for four hour blocks or overnight) in a choice of premium (full-size double bed) or standard (large single). In the North Terminal, there is a Hampton by Hilton close to the airport check-in desks, the Premier Inn directly opposite the main entrance, and a four-star Sofitel. The full-service hotels feature amenities such as salons, restaurants, business facilities, and 24-hour gyms.

Airline/Terminal

Aegean Airlines: South
Aer Lingus: South
Afriqiyah Airways: South
Air Arabia Maroc: South
Air Baltic: South
Air Dolomiti: South
Air Europa: South
Air Malta: South
Air Transat: South
Aurigny: South
Belavia Belarusian: South
British Airways: North
Caribbean Airlines: North
easyJet: North/South
Emirates: North
Flybe: South
Freebird: South
Gambia Bird: South
Garuda Indonesia: North
Germania: South
Icelandair: North
Iraqi Airways: South
Meridiana Airlines: North
Monarch: South
Norwegian: South
Royal Air Maroc: North
Ryanair: South
Swiss International Air Lines: South
TAP Air Portugal: South
Thomas Cook: South
Thomson Airways: North
Titan Airways: South
Tunis Air: South
Turkish Airlines: North
Ukraine International Airlines: South
Vietnam Airlines: North
Virgin Atlantic: South
Vueling: North
WOW Air: South

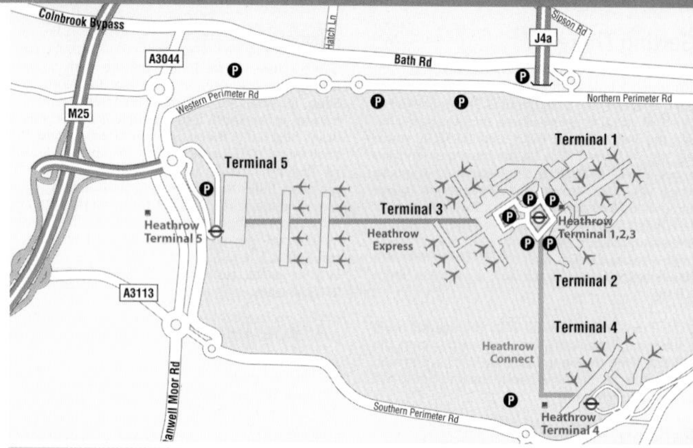

General Information

Address: Hounslow, Middlesex, TW6
Airport Code: LHR
General Information: 0844 335 1801
Lost Property: 0844 824 3115 or missingx.com
Website: www.heathrowairport.com or @HeathrowAirport

Overview

Ah, Heathrow—London's main link to the outside world, resplendent in all the main airport offenders: infinite queues, bad food, draconian security and the acrid scent of 'the British on holiday.' Or as PM Hugh Grant once noticed, "Whenever I get gloomy with the state of the world, I think about the arrivals gate at Heathrow Airport." Or something like that.

Indeed, ex-London mayor Ken Livingstone once accused Heathrow of keeping people "prisoner" in its "ghastly shopping mall" but there does seem to be slow, gradual improvement. Heathrow has undergone years of seeming perpetual change, resulting in vastly improved transport services and upgraded motorway access. Terminal 1 is a thing of the past and the new Terminal 2 has eclipsed the old Terminal 2 in people's memory. Terminal 5 picked up the baton following a chaotic opening in 2008, taking the annual passenger count to upward of 70 million, and placing the airport in contention for busiest in the world. For years Heathrow has been stretched beyond its capacity, which has resulted in a campaign for a controversial third runway. The local residents might not like it but at least they don't have to suffer an hour on the tube to catch a flight.

Terminals

The terminals are organised around airline networks: Star Alliance, Oneworld, SkyTeam, with the non-aligned airlines wedged in where possible. Terminal 5 is the domain of British Airways.

Departures

Busy and security conscious, Heathrow demands travelers get there early—they suggest three hours before departure for long-haul and El Al flights, two hours for European flights, and a full 90 minutes for flights to the UK and Ireland. Makes you appreciate coach travel. Check-in is on the first floor of Terminal 4, the ground floor in Terminal 3, and the top floor of Terminals 2 and 5. When you arrive look for your check-in zone on the information screens near the entrance; check-in zones are marked by illuminated yellow cubes. If you are travelling through Heathrow, transfers are available between Heathrow Airport's four terminals. Terminals 2 and 3 are a short walk from each other (10–20 minutes) while Terminals 4 and 5 are served by free trains and buses.

Arrivals

As for the romance of the arrivals gate at Heathrow, arrivals areas are located on Level 1 at Terminal 2, the ground level of the Arrivals building at Terminal 3, and the ground levels of both Terminals 4 and 5. Official airport meeting points are marked. There are information screens in the arrivals area with flight status information and status codes: 'Expected' means the flight hasn't landed yet and Heathrow Airport Holdings Limited encourages you to indulge in a spot of shopping, 'Landed' means that you should expect 30–40 minutes for passengers to clear passport control, baggage reclaim and customs (longer at busy periods), and 'Baggage in hall' means that passengers should be in the arrivals area shortly. The Heathrow website also has live flight status information.

Hotels

In addition to the handful of area hotels that cater to Heathrow travellers, there are several hotels at the terminal, accessible by foot. The 605-room luxury Sofitel London Heathrow is located at Terminal 5 and the four-star Hilton London Heathrow Airport is located at Terminal

4. Both hotels offer requisite hotel amenities such as restaurants and business and fitness centres. Terminal 4 also has a YOTEL, the Japanese-style low-budget mini pod chain that offers sleeping cabins for several hours. The No.1 Traveller Lounge after the security lines in Terminal 3 offers day rooms, both twin bunks and singles.

Getting There

The cheapest option is London Underground's Piccadilly Line, which gets you to central London in less than an hour for £5.70. The wait time for a train is generally no more than 10 minutes. Heathrow has three underground stations; one serving both Terminals 2 and 3, and one each for Terminals 4 and 5.

The fastest option is Heathrow Express (www.heathrowexpress.com), a non-stop train between the airport and Paddington station—"in 15 minutes, every 15 minutes." It stops at Heathrow Central Station near Terminals 2 and 3, and also at Terminal 5. On-board fares are £26.50 one way and £40 for a return (£5 less if bought online, from ticket offices or ticket machines). Heathrow Connect follows the same route into west London, but serves intermediate stations making its journey time 25 minutes. At half the price of the Express though, it's probably worth the added minutes. Heathrow Connect trains depart Paddington every 30 minutes from Terminals 2 and 3 (travellers from Terminal 4 and 5 should use the free transfer). Fare is £10.10 one way to Paddington Station, less to intermediate stations. Both these trains run between approx 5 am–12 am.

National Express (www.nationalexpress.com) offers coach service from points around London to Heathrow. Tickets start at £12.

Driving from Central London takes about 45-60 minutes depending on traffic. To Terminals 2 and 3, exit the M4 (Junction 4) or M25 (Junction 15) and follow signs. When leaving Terminals 2 and 3, follow exit signs to the access/exit tunnel. Then follow signs to the M4 motorway, which will eventually bring you into London. Terminals 4 and 5 have separate entrances. If driving, exit M25 at Junction 14 and follow signs (if coming from the M4, leave at Junction 4B and follow the M25 south to Junction 14). A taxi to central London takes 45-60 minutes and costs £35-plus; note that there is no set fare from the airport.

Car Parking

There are short-term and long-term car parks, and both are expensive. Up to 30 minutes at the short stay is £3.50 (£4 for Terminal 4). An hour at the short stay is £6.50 (£7 at Terminal 4), two hours is £10.50 (£11 at Terminal 4), then rising steadily to £56 for 24 hours. The long stay car park is about 10 minutes away by courtesy bus and the standard drive-up price is £26 for the first day, then £20.50 each day thereafter. A peak surcharge is in effect for Easter, Christmas and some summer weeks.

Airline/Terminal

Aegean Airlines: 2
Aer Lingus: 2
Aeroflot: 4
Aeromexico: 4
Air Algerie: 4
Air Astana: 4
Air Canada: 2
Air China: 2
Air France: 4
Air India: 4
Air Malta: 4
Air Mauritius: 4
Air New Zealand: 2
Air Serbia: 4
Alitalia: 4
American Airlines: 3
ANA: 2
Arik Air: 4
Asiana Airlines: 2
Austrian: 2
Avianca: 2
Azerbaijan Airlines: 4
Biman Bangladesh Airlines: 4
British Airways: 5 (some 3)
Brussels Airlines: 2
Bulgaria Air: 4
Cathay Pacific Airways: 3
China Eastern: 4
China Southern: 4
Croatia Airlines: 2
Delta Air Lines: 3 & 4
Egypt Air: 2
El Al: 4
Emirates: 3
Ethiopian Airlines: 2
Etihad Airways: 4
EVA Air: 2
Finnair: 3
Germanwings: 2
Gulf Air: 4
Iberia: 5
Icelandair: 2
Iran Air: 3
Japan Airlines: 3
Jet Airways (India): 4
Kenya Airways: 4
KLM-Royal Dutch Airlines: 4
Korean Air: 4
Kuwait Airways: 4
Libyan Airlines: 4
LOT Polish Airlines: 2
Lufthansa: 2
Malaysia Airlines: 4
MEA: 3
Oman Air: 3
Pakistan International Airlines: 3
Philippine Airlines: 4
Qantas: 3
Qatar Airways: 4
Royal Air Maroc: 4
Royal Brunei Airlines: 4
Royal Jordanian: 3
SAS-Scandinavian Airlines: 2
Saudia: 4
Singapore Airlines: 2
South African Airways: 2
Sri Lankan Airlines: 3
Swiss International Airlines: 2
TAM: 3
TAP Portugal: 2
Tarom: 4
Thai Airways: 2
Transaero: 4
Tunisair: 4
Turkish Airlines: 2
Turkmenistan Airlines: 3
United Airlines: 2
US Airways: 3
Uzbekistan Airways: 4
Vietnam Airlines: 4
Virgin Atlantic: 3
Virgin Atlantic Little Red: 2
Vueling: 3

General Information

Address: Hartmann Road,
London, E16 2PX

Airport Code: LCY

General Enquiries: 020 7646 0088/0000

Website: www.londoncityairport.com
or @LondonCityAir

Overview

With its one wee runway squeezed over the water between the old George V and Royal Albert Docks, City is London's smallest and most central airport (six miles from the City of London, 22 minutes from Bank station). Where once stevedores ate pie and mash, stockbrokers are now whisked off to lunchtime meetings on dinky short takeoff jets. Primarily used by business types, its small size and short runway means city serves mainly European destinations, with BA's New York service (including a stop off) being the one exception. Still, this means much faster check-in times and fewer delays than at the comparative behemoths of Heathrow and Gatwick.

Amenities at London City Airport include some above-average food options and complimentary WiFi. LCY also has a "silent airport policy," meaning no announcements are made, which also means you definitely shouldn't zone out too far away from your gate (you've been warned).

Getting There

In 2005 someone, somewhere, saw the light and extended the DLR (Docklands Light Railway) to City. The airport now couldn't be simpler to get to by public transport: get on the DLR at Bank; make sure you take a train destined for the King George V branch (these are marked "via City Airport"); and you'll arrive at the airport's station in under 25 minutes. A slightly quicker route is to take the Jubilee Underground line to Canning Town and take the DLR a mere three stops westbound from there. There is a taxi rank directly outside the terminal exit, expect to pay at least £40 for a black cab to go to or from the West End. Don't expect the journey to be much faster than on the DLR/Underground. Pre-booked cabs should be a little cheaper; bookings are available via www.minicabit.com.

If you're driving, given its central location there's no obvious route to City. A useful general rule is to point your wheels at the eastern end of Central London and then keep going that way from Tower Hill on the A1203 (East Smithfield/The Highway). The airport is signposted from this road. If you're getting there from the South East, head through the Blackwall tunnel and follow signs once you emerge into the daylight. If you're near the M25 and like traffic jams, crawl your way to junction 30 and take the Thames Gateway to the airport from there.

Parking

Short stay is directly next to the terminal and rates start at £6 for the first 30 minutes, £11 for one hour, £15 for two hours, and steadily increasing up to £55 for 24 hours. The long stay carpark is a short walk from the terminal and costs £45 per day. Pre-booking long stay parking results in drastically reduced rates; check online for more. All of which is to say, parking is expensive. If you still feel the need to park and can book in advance, get in touch with BCP airport parking for a (slightly) cheaper option at www.parkbcp.co.uk.

Car Hire

On-site car hire desks for Avis, Europcar and Hertz are located next to the terminal. Travellers can book cars through the London City Airport website.

Airlines

Air France
Alitalia
British Airways
Blue Islands
CityJet
Flybe
KLM Royal Dutch Airlines
Lufthansa
Luxair
Sky Work
Sun-Air
Swiss International Airlines (SWISS)

General Information

Address: Navigation House, Airport Way, Luton, Bedfordshire LU2 9LY

Airport Code: LTN

General Enquiries: 01582 405100

Lost Property: 01582 395219 or lostproperty@ltn.aero

Website: www.london-luton.co.uk or @LDNLutonAirport

Overview

You have to admire branding at work: appending "London" to "London Luton Airport" is perhaps slightly wishful thinking, seeing as the facility is located 35 miles north of Central London. That said, it's not impossible to get to the airport and parking is reasonable, but everyone knows why they're flying out of Luton: those ridiculously cheap budget tickets to the Spanish coast.

Luton debuted in 1938, was put to good use during WWII and quickly became a top airport for package holiday travel. Charter trips comprised the majority of flights in and out of Luton until the 1980s, when Ryanair began using Luton for short-haul flights. In the 1990s Luton was reborn as the go-to for no-frills budget air carriers flying in and out of the London area. Thus, the £2.99 flight to the Canary Islands with every other stag or hen party travelling that weekend.

Luton features the requisite airport amenities: Boots, Dixons, et al. plus light meals. For assistance in leaving the airport to wherever it is you're headed, the Onward Travel Centre is located on the main concourse in the terminal building and is open 24 hours a day, seven days a week.

Getting There

Unless you live in North London, getting to and from Luton by public transport isn't quite seamless. It consists of taking a half-hour train service from St Pancras or London Bridge to Luton Parkway. After your train journey you'll be met at Luton Parkway by a shuttle bus. Be sure to purchase your rail tickets with London Luton Airport as your final destination.

Luton is served by rail via the Luton Airport Parkway Station. From there a ten-minute shuttle bus takes you to the terminal. Keep in mind that while rail service from Luton Airport Parkway Station to central London is frequent (and through the night via Thameslink service), the shuttle only operates between 5 a.m. and midnight. Which is to say, if your plane is delayed past midnight—not out of the question with budget carriers—consider coach alternatives.

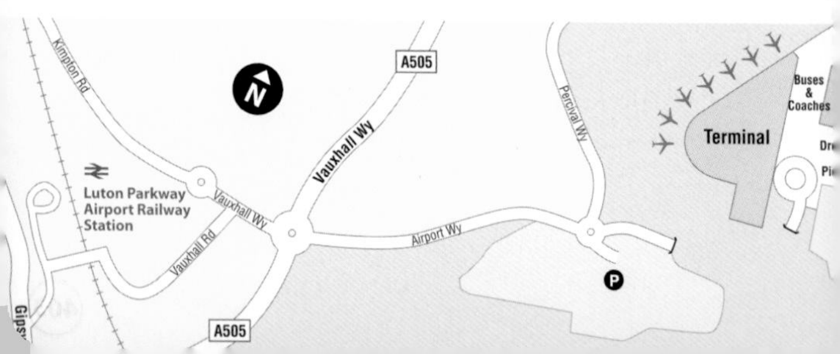

Coach services, such as the 757 Greenline, easyBus and National Express are good alternatives that will at least get you home if your flight comes in late. Greenline (www.greenline.co.uk/757 or 0844 801 7261) is probably your best bet, and it offers pick-up and drop-off points on Buckingham Palace Road, Marble Arch and Baker Street, as well as free WiFi. Fares to London Victoria are £10 and it takes about an hour, but it runs pretty regularly through the night. The National Express service A1 operates 60 departures a day between Luton and London Victoria, with free WiFi as well.

London Luton Airport is somewhat accessible from both the M1 and M25. If you have a choice, go for the M1, as the airport is only about five minutes from Junction 10. Without traffic, it can take about 45 minutes from central London. This can sometimes be longer when there are extensive road works, which tends to be always. When using Sat Nav systems, use the postcode LU2 9QT.

How to Get There—Really

Seriously. You've paid next to nothing for your airfare, splash out on a private cab. If you book a licensed mini-cab ahead of time, the service is often cheaper than the equivalent black cab fare and definitely easier, as they'll meet you at the arrivals hall. A consistently cheap company is Simply Airports (www.simplyairports.co.uk or 020 7701 4321) which is usually under £55, but you may want to get a quote from your own local company. If you leave it to the last minute, and must take a black cab, get ready to shell out at least £85 (with their meters, this can increase with traffic) plus a meeting fee if you want them to wait for you. Cab rides from central London usually take about an hour.

Parking

Short Term Parking is pricier but situated closest to the terminal, with prices ranging from £4 for 30 minutes or £37 per day drive-up. Mid-term parking is ideal for stays of around five days and is about a five-minute transfer by bus. Mid term is £21 per day drive-up with significant savings if booked well in advance. Long-term parking is about 10 minutes from the terminal by bus, and costs £19 per day, with hefty discounts for booking in advance.

Rental Cars

Car hire desks are located at the Onward Travel Centre on the main concourse in the terminal building. Lots are connected to the airport via free shuttle service. On-site companies are Avis, Europcar/National/Alamo, Hertz and Enterprise.

Hotels

There is no hotel at Luton but there are four hotels near the airport: Ibis Hotel (01582 424488), Holiday Inn Express (01582 589100), Ramada Encore Hotel (01582 218132) and Hampton by Hilton (01582 798477).

Airlines

Air Nostrum
AtlasGlobal
Blue Air
easyJet
El Al
La Compagnie
Monarch
Ryanair
SunExpress
TAROM
Thomson
Wizz Air

General Information

Address: Stansted Airport, Essex CM24 1QW

Airport Code: STN

General Enquiries: 0844 335 1803

Lost Property: 0844 824 3109
or stn.lostproperty@bagport.co.uk

Website: www.stanstedairport.com
or @STN_Airport

Overview

It might be tucked away on a former Roman burial site in the middle of the dull Essex countryside, but Stansted Airport has one thing going for it—it's amazingly simple. One terminal (and quite a nice one too, Norman Foster saluted), one check-in area, one security gate. Take that, Heathrow. Nearly 20 airlines, most of them budget, fly nearly 18 million passengers per year from here to a growing list of mainly domestic and short-haul destinations.

Stansted dates to WWII, and was a base for the RAF and the US Air Force during the war. Post-war Stansted was used for charter flights, then eventually scheduled flights. The Norman Foster-designed main terminal opened in 1991, considered one of the most modern airports at the time. During the 2000s annual passenger traffic doubled from about 12 million to nearly 24 million by 2007 before leveling off to about 17-18 million per year.

A word about amenities. As far as shopping is concerned, Stansted offers Boots and Dixon outlets plus the usual selection of 'small airport shops' more aimed at passing the time than serious purchases. Stansted, like the other area airports, has made efforts to provide nicer dining options (then there's the Burger King); feel free to settle in for a few pints and then grab a sandwich on the run once you hear your name being called for the third time; gingerly avoid screaming children and/or singing hen-night crowds on the way. You could also try the Escape Lounge where, for about the price of an easyJet fare, one can enjoy an open bar, complimentary dishes and free WiFi. Speaking of WiFi, travellers get 60 free minutes per device throughout the airport.

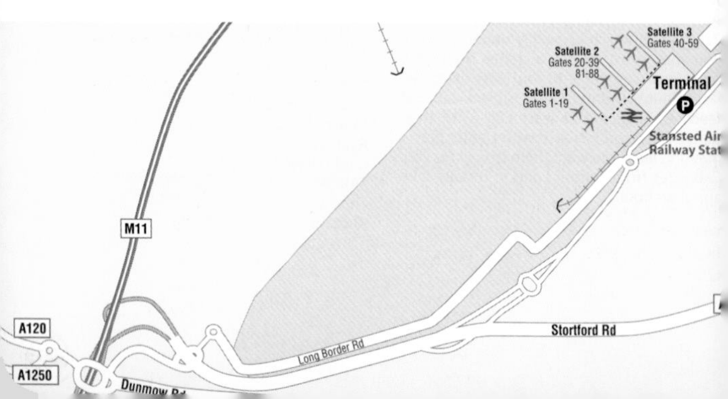

Getting There

Stansted might seem a long way from London, but getting there by public transport is surprisingly easy. All you have to do is choose between the train (fast) and the bus (cheap). Several train operators serve the airport from Liverpool Street Station. But before you start struggling with too many timetables for trains that stop at too many stops, opt for the dedicated Stansted Express (www.stanstedexpress.com). The service runs every 15 minutes and takes you to the airport in just over 45 minutes. Tickets start at £19 for a standard single ride between Stansted and London Liverpool Street. Buses will take an hour to take you to the airport, and longer if there's a lot of traffic, but single tickets go for between £8 and £10.50 (potentially even less for easyBus). A number of operators fight for your custom, the main ones are: Terravision (www.terravision.eu), which leaves from Liverpool Street Station and Victoria Station; the slightly more expensive National Express (www.nationalexpress.com) connects to the same stations but some buses also stop in Stratford and Golders Green; and easyBus (www.easybus.co.uk) gives you the intimacy of a small mini-van, stopping in Baker Street and Old Street in the City. If you're traveling during the rush hour, take a book. Whitechapel Road is one of London's most bustling streets, but it will get boring at some point.

Driving

f you're fortunate enough to have a car, or managed to convince your dad-in-law to lend you his, find your way out of the city via Stratford and hit the M11. It's a straight drive from here and amid Essex' greenery, the airport is hard to miss. Cab drivers will know how to get you to the airport, but will probably charge you a small fortune for it.

Parking

Short-term parking rates start at £3 for the first 30 minutes and rise in steps to £39 for 24 hours. Long-stay will cost you £19 a day. If you're in for a weekend trip, opt for the mid-stay car park, which is closer to the terminal than the long-stay option and charges £21/day drive-up. Valet parking is available and can be pre-booked. Once there, drop your car at the end of Set Down Lane; the pickup point is next to the Fast Track car park. Book online before you head off for discounts on all Stansted parking options.

Car Rental

Hertz, Avis, Europcar, Budget, National, Alamo, Enterprise and Sixt all have desks at Stansted.

Hotels

There are three hotels either next to or within the perimeter of the airport. The four-star Radisson Blu (01279 661 012) is connected to the airport via a covered walkway. The Premier Inn (0871 527 9352) and Hilton London Stansted Airport (01279 680 800) are both located within the perimeter of the airport and connected by a short shuttle bus ride.

Airlines

Aegean Airlines
Air Berlin
Air Moldova
Atlantic Airways
Atlasjet
Aurigny
Belle Air
Cyprus Airways
easyJet
FlyBe
Freebird Airlines
Germanwings
Pegasus Airlines
Ryanair
Tangney-Tours
Thomas Cook
Thomson Airways

General Information

TfL Customer Services: 4th Floor,
14 Pier Walk, London SE10 0ES

Phone: 0343 222 1234

Website: www.tfl.gov.uk/modes/tube
or @TfLTravelAlerts

Overview

If the Underground had a motto it wouldn't be "Mind the gap" but "Sorry for any inconvenience caused." But as we grumble and ponder if anyone is ever actually sorry for squeezing you 30m below the surface, in a sweat-box held together by dust, rust and expensive fares, the magnificence of the 'Tube' network should really be appreciated. Across its 250-odd miles of track the Underground will take you to 270 stations spread the length and breadth of London (although with disproportionately few lines reaching into south London). The system is well integrated with the bus and overground train networks which share a common ticketing system with the Oyster card.

When fully functioning, the Underground will get you across town quicker than the bus and without the complicated timetables and schedules of overground trains. When it is struck by signal failures and breakdowns, which is very often, it can be excruciatingly slow and get very overcrowded, very quickly. In conclusion: the Underground won't necessarily get you anywhere on time, in style or in comfort, but it will (eventually) get you pretty much anywhere.

Fares

The vast majority of the network is divided into concentric fare rings or zones (1-6). Zone 1 covers central London, zone 6 covers the outskirts of London. Fares are dependent on how many zones your journey includes and there's a premium for travelling in zone 1. Peak fares (Monday to Friday from 6.30-9.30 am and 4-7 pm) are from 50p to a few pounds more than off-peak, although journeys limited to zone 1 do not benefit from the off-peak discount. Your best bet is to get an Oyster Card—lowest zone 1 single fare is £2.30 instead of £4.80 if you pay by cash. Oyster cards are available for just £5 from vending machines. It's a total no-brainer: the total amount that can be deducted from your Oyster card is also capped over a 24-hour period to match the equivalent cost of a one day travel card. So the fare system is complicated, but if you take £2.30 (which will get you a single journey within zone 1 with an Oyster card) as a base rate, and add to this the further out of zone 1 you travel, things become clearer. If you feel the need to marvel at the full intricacy of the fares and ticketing system, give yourself eye-strain at Transport for London's website.

Frequency and Quality of Service

The vast majority of centrally located stations will have a train at least every three minutes most of the day. At the very beginning and end of the day service frequency tails-off and can get as low as eight minutes between trains. Trains are also much less frequent at the farther reaches of some lines—the Metropolitan line has trains only every 20 minutes from its most north-western stations, even during peak times. Almost all lines have a reduced frequency on Sundays. First trains are 05:00-05:30, last trains are between midnight and 12.30. Last trains are generally safe; expect a slightly raucous mix of pickled after-workers and overly obsequious rough-sleepers rather than any real troublemakers, especially after booze was banned in 2008. The whole network had £5bn thrown at it for the 2012 Olympics, but the only noticeable improvement was increased cleanliness in many of the stations.

Lines

Bakerloo: (Brown coloured on maps) Runs from Harrow & Wealdstone in the north west to Elephant & Castle in the south east.

Central: (Red) Runs from West Ruislip in the west to Epping in the far north east. The central section is buried under Oxford Street and has four stops on the street, the quietest usually being Bond Street.

Circle: (Yellow) Notoriously slow, unreliable, and not strictly a circle—even more so now that a tail reaches down to Hammersmith. For this reason Edgware Road is now the end of the line. Shares almost all of its track and stations with other lines so don't necessarily bother waiting specifically for a dedicated Circle Line train. Look out for the 'Platform for Art' as you pass Gloucester Road station.

District: (Green) One of the few lines to serve deepest south London, branches run into Richmond and Wimbledon in the southwest and also to Ealing. The line continues up to Upminster in the northeast. Almost all of the branches of this fragmented line come together at Earls Court station into an infuriating mess, so plan ahead if changing there.

Hammersmith & City: (Pink) Starts at Hammersmith in the west of the city before heading north to Paddington and continuing east to Barking. Take it to Ladbroke Grove if heading to the Portobello market.

Jubilee: (Silver) Silver coloured as it opened in the year of the Queen's Silver Jubilee in 1977, the line serves northwest, central and east London, including the Canary Wharf business district. The section east of Green Park is the most recent addition to the network (it opened in 1999) and has a number of architecturally exemplary stations.

Metropolitan: (Dark Purple) The oldest of all the lines, this granddaddy of metropolitan underground railways strikes far out in the suburbs and countryside northwest of the city from its central root at Aldgate.

Northern: (Black) Presumably given black as its colour to reflect the dark mood of anyone unlucky enough to have to commute on it, the Northern line is the overcrowded spine of London, covering vast swathes of the city centre, the north and the south.

Piccadilly: (Dark Blue) From Cockfosters in the far northeast this line trundles all the way to Heathrow airport, with some of the most popular tourist spots in between. It's a very cheap way to the airport but is also the slowest. Southgate and Arnos Grove stations are both 1930s modernist brilliance.

Victoria: (Light Blue) Runs from Walthamstow in the north to Brixton in the south. This musty line is currently undergoing refurbishment and will feature new trains and track by 2011. In the meantime, check for early closing and shutdowns, particularly during weekends.

Waterloo & City: (Turquoise) No-one has ever met anyone who has been on this line. Erm, it has two stations, Waterloo and Bank, and is designed for suited and booted commuters coming in by train from Waterloo. No trains on Sundays.

London Overground: (Orange) TfL took over part of the overground rail network, notably the somewhat shabby and North London Line which runs from Richmond to Stratford This has now been merged with what was the East London Line, which connects East, Southeast and Northeast London. Just think of it as an extension to the tube network.

Bicycles

Bicycles are generally only allowed on the tube outside peak hours and only from stations outside central London. They are not permitted on the Victoria or Waterloo and City lines at all. Folding bicycles can be taken on all sections of the Tube free of charge.

General Info

TfL Customer Services: 4th Floor, 14 Pier Walk, London SE10 0ES

Phone: 0343 222 1234

Website: www.tfl.gov.uk/modes/dlr/ or @LondonDLR

Overview

Not quite a tram, tube or train, it's simply the Docklands Light Railway, a nifty little thing that makes getting to places like Greenwich Village and City Airport easy and cheap. Launched in 1987 with a modest 11 trains and only 15 stations, the regeneration of the Docklands area has seen it grow to seven lines covering 45 stations and counting, serving over 100 million passengers a year. Serving the east and Southeast of the city, it is pretty much as pleasant as London public transport gets. It's reliable, less noisy than the tube, generally less crowded and it's pretty well air-conditioned. The DLR is also fully automated and most of the time there is no driver, meaning that you can take the front seat and pretend that you're actually driving the thing.

The DLR provides a key service for London's suits, with the Bank to Canary Wharf journey taking just over ten minutes. For normal people, Canary Wharf also makes an interesting/unusual weekend destination. Almost completely deserted, a stroll amongst the abandoned skyscrapers is a strangely satisfying way to spend a Sunday afternoon.

Fares

As on the rest of London's public transport you're best off with an Oyster card. One thing to remember is that there are no barriers at DLR stations and instead Oyster readers are located at station exits and entrances. To avoid getting slapped with a fine and to ensure you're charged the right amount, remember to touch in and out correctly. The prices are similar to the tube, so cash works out more expensive (though not as expensive as the tube's cash single).

Hours

The DLR runs 5.30 am–12.30 am (Sundays 7.00 am–11.30 pm), with train frequencies depending on the time of day. On weekdays, trains run as often as every three-and-a-half minutes during peak times, and every five to ten minutes during off-peak times and weekends. The DLR is closed Christmas.

General Information

National Rail: www.nationalrail.co.uk
or @nationalraileng
Eurostar: www.eurostar.com or @Eurostar
TfL London Overground:
www.tfl.gov.uk/modes/london-overground/

Overview

The railways are one of the great British inventions but, unfortunately, the Victorians who built the network in this country did slightly too good a job. Every generation since has taken one look at the massively expensive task of modernising them and scuttled back into their Ford Fiestas. So, while France, Germany and Japan got on with building super-speed bullet trains Britain was stuck with an uneasy compromise between the technologies of 1950 and 1850. This doesn't mean that you shouldn't use trains. It just means that it's probably best to avoid them at peak times. That's when London plays a cruel trick on people who choose to live in places with names like 'Gravesend' and 'Slough' by making them lurch home slowly with less personal space than the legal minimum for cattle. During off-peak times train travel can, in contrast, be positively pleasant. It's a great way to see the countryside, every city and major town in the country is connected, and, if you book far enough in advance and shop around on sites like www.megatrain.com or www.thetrainline.com it can be less expensive than you'd think. In London itself, Transport for London manages four suburban rail routes that use the pay as you go Oyster system.

Stations

Broadly speaking, Euston and King's Cross stations serve the north of the country, Liverpool Street the east, Victoria the south, Paddington and Marylebone the west.

Eurostar

The King's Cross area is also home to the splendid St Pancras—the terminal for the Eurostar train service which connects Britain with the rest of Europe. Since November 2007 it's been possible to get from here to Paris or Brussels in around two hours—with connecting trains to Siberia and beyond.

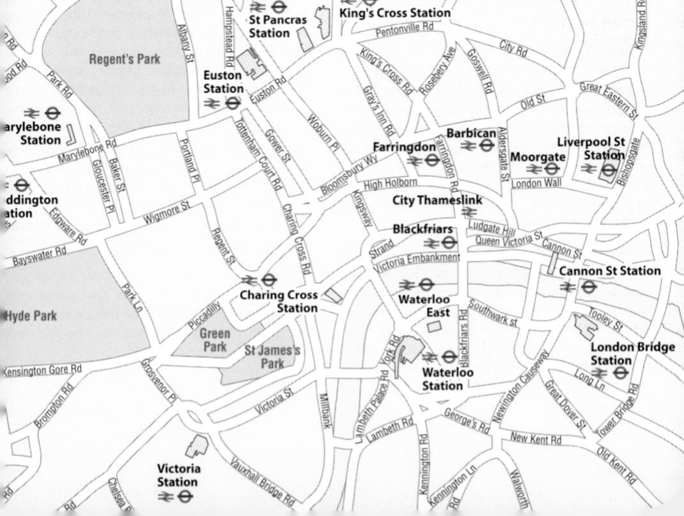

Charing Cross Station

NFT Map: 24

Address: The Strand, London, WC2N 5HF

Station Code: CHX

General Station Enquiries: 03457 11 41 41

Lost Property: 020 7930 5444

Southeastern: www.southeasternrailway.co.uk or @Se_Railway

Overview

Perched at the top of the Strand amidst popular tourist attractions such as Trafalgar Square and with the majestic 1865 Charing Cross Hotel being part of the station, you may presume that a cornucopia of ornate delights lies within. Well, it's a dump; the chances of *Brief Encounter* being remade here are pretty slim. But your chances of being barged by a curmudgeonly office worker are very good, what with it being one of the busiest rail terminals in London. Still, can you blame them for wanting to get out of the place so quickly?

Tickets

There is a small ticket office open some 20 hours per day, and three banks of ticket machines on or around the concourse.

Services

If you're in need of a quick bite, there's a decent variety of food outlets to cater for all tastes, from Burger King to a M &S Simply Food outlet. Indulge your Schadenfreude by watching the beleaguered information guy having to dispense a plethora of poor excuses as to why the 17.34 to Margate was cancelled. There is both a Boots and a WHSmith and cash machines can be found on the concourse and in the front entrance.

Public Transport

The station is easily accessible by Charing Cross station (Northern & Bakerloo lines) and also the adjoining Embankment station (Circle & District lines). The nearby Trafalgar Square is a major hub for buses—especially night buses for post-West End madness—which inch their way out to places as far apart as Harrow and Crystal Palace.

Euston Station

NFT Map: 78

Address: Euston Road, London, NW1 2RT

Station Code: EUS

General Station Enquiries: 03457 11 41 41

Lost property: 0207 387 8699

Website: www.networkrail.co.uk/EUS or @NetworkRailEUS

Overview

Easily the ugliest station in London, Euston creeps up as you nervously edge along Euston Road. The first inter-city terminal built in London, it was originally constructed in 1837, but the lovely original was demolished to make way for the monstrous concrete-and-glass coffin which now squats next to the mail depot. Since privatisation the interior has become an identi-kit British rail station with more chain businesses per head than is morally decent.

It's not all doom and gloom, however. Within this architectural eyesore you'll find a scarily concise summation of human nature. Like most busy stations, there's plenty of eccentricity and electricity here: abandoned Tube tunnels, stressed-out coffee-guzzling power-commuters, fresh-faced backpackers sprawled out on the floor; and the infamous beggar who—to the delight of football lovers everywhere except in Manchester—was arrested for punching Manchester Utd manager Sir Alex Ferguson.

The station is London's gateway to the north west of England and Scotland, and also North Wales. As such it is the point of entry for Scousers, Mancunians, Glaswegians and more. Virgin trains (www.virgintrains.co.uk) to Glasgow can take as little as 4 hrs 10 mins.

Tickets

The ticket cashiers may have the glazed look of Kafka-esque zombies but the cleaning staff are often more helpful. Just use the Fasttrack machines!

Services

There's plenty of eating and drinking options, all of the 'chain' variety. If you're an aficionado and determined to hang around, check out the Doric Arch (1 Eversholt St; 020 7383 3359), a little boozer with train memorabilia lining the walls. The left luggage office is at the top of the ramp to platforms 16–18 and is open between 7 am–11 pm.

Public Transport

As an actual railway station it is adequate. Served by two Tube lines and nine bus routes, it's nothing if not convenient.

King's Cross Station

NFT Map: 78

Address: Euston Rd & Pancras Rd, London, N1 9AL

Station Code: KGX

General Station Enquiries: 03457 11 41 41

Lost property: 020 7278 3310

Website: www.networkrail.co.uk/kingscross

Overview

Previously a dingy playground for prostitutes, drug dealers, and all sorts of similarly bad kids, King's Cross Station scrubbed up a bit, thanks to lots of chin scratching and typically panicked spending on the government's part. Built in 1852 on the site of a former smallpox hospital, it is one of the busiest and most well-connected stations in the country: running trains to Edinburgh; Newcastle; the East coast; as well as six Tube lines. Zany trivia about the station includes the fact that it is supposedly built on top of legendary Fembot-Queen Boudicea's grave (most probably a total lie) and that it has a tacky little shrine to Harry Potter at what has been designated 'Platform 9 3/4' (oh God).

Nearly all long distance train services leave from the overground platforms under the arches straight ahead of you as you enter from Euston Road. The Tube is also accessible from steps at this entrance and at what used to be the Thameslink station next to the Scala on Pentonville Road. From the main Tube entrance there is a pedestrian subway that comes up on the other side of Euston Road just outside Macdonald's. This is handy for crossing the road at busy times, and of course for getting chips.

Tickets

Tube tickets, including Oyster top ups and season tickets, can be purchased from the machines in front of the Tube entry gates, located just at the bottom of both sets of stairs at the station. For railcard discounts and more specific enquiries you'll have to queue at the manned ticket desks next to the machines. For all other tickets go to the upstairs ticket hall which is to the left of the main Euston Road entrance.

Services

With the renovations, the quality of services has significantly improved. But with the excellent Eat St literally round the corner, ditch the station completely and sample the wares of London's best street food traders. And for the basics, the trusty newspaper kiosk underneath the awning is still going strong.

Public Transport

King's Cross crosses more Tube lines (six) than any other station, and is serviced by at least twice as many buses, many of which run all night.

Liverpool Street Station

NFT Map: 8

Address: Liverpool St, London, EC2M 7PY

Station Code: LST

General Station Enquiries: 03457 11 41 41

Lost property: 020 7247 4297

Website: www.networkrail.co.uk/liverpoolstreet

Overview

It's not that Liverpool Street is particularly ugly, but if it's architectural beauty you're after, you're much better off heading to Paddington or the new, improved St. Pancras International. In comparison to these two icons of British station design, Liverpool Street is extremely modest, boring even. Clean, modern and easy to navigate around, it is simply a good train station. With the markets, bars and restaurants of Spitalfields and Brick Lane just around the corner, the station is the perfect starting point to explore east London. First opened to the public in 1874, it is one of the busiest stations in London. With 18 platforms, the station mainly serves destinations in the east of England, including daytrip favourites such as Cambridge and Southend on Sea.

It is also the home of the Stansted Express, providing easy airport access with departures every 15 minutes. If you're travelling with a group of people a taxi might work out slightly cheaper, but the train is much quicker and more reliable. The Tube station, with its main entrance centrally located on the main concourse, makes all of London easily accessible with the Central, Hammersmith & City, Circle and Metropolitan lines all passing through. Being one of the busiest stations on the underground network, rush hour can get nasty and is best avoided.

Tickets

The ticket office is located on the main concourse, on your left hand side if entering from Bishopsgate. Ticket windows are open during station opening hours. There are also several express ticket machines scattered throughout the station. Tickets for the Stansted Express can be purchased from designated ticket machines opposite platforms 5-6. A cluster of cash machines can be found by the stairs leading up to the Old Broad Street exit. There are payphones on both levels and most are located on the Bishopsgate side of the station.

Services

With Brick Lane just around the corner, eating, drinking and shopping here should really be a last resort. The regular big-chain fast food joints are scattered (some of them repeatedly) throughout the station with the usual selection of coffee, burgers, sandwiches and sweets. The main shopping area is on the lower level around the Broadgate and Exchange Square exits, offering everything from toiletries and birthday cards to Italian silk ties and double-glazed windows.

Passengers are invited to wait for their trains in the so-called "food court," which really isn't much more than a few cramped tables near the Burger King. There's a small but nicer waiting lounge located adjacent to platform 10. Here you also find the left luggage, a bureau de change, a less busy cash machine and access to the main taxi rank. Smoking is prohibited at all times throughout the station.

Public Transport

The main bus station is located on the upper level of the station (Broadgate end), and provides a large number of services to destinations throughout London. Plenty of buses also stop on the street just outside the Bishopsgate exit.

London Bridge Station

NFT Map: 106

Address: Station Approach Road, London, SE1 9SP

Station Code: LBG

General Station Enquiries: 03457 11 41 41

Lost property: 03451 27 29 20 (Southern Railway)

Website: www.networkrail.co.uk/londonbridge

Overview

Around in one form or other since 1836, when steam trains filled the air with smoke, London Bridge is the city's oldest station. It's a good starting point for weekend trips to Kent's countryside or days on Brighton's beach. Operators Southeastern and Southern cover the south east, while Thameslink operates (little-known) connections to the airports Gatwick and Luton. The station couldn't be better connected to public transport, with two Tube lines and a plethora of buses at the doorstep. The catacombs underneath the station—said to be haunted—have been turned into the museum-cum-gore-fest London Bridge Experience, adding to the spooky entertainment already provided by the London Dungeon next door—just in case a cancelled or delayed train leaves you with too much time on your hands. Does happen, we're told.

Tickets

The main office is located next to the main entrance (London Bridge Street) or there are machines situated throughout the station.

Services

The main concourse is lined with eating and shopping options. Grab Cornish pasties, sandwiches, donuts; and the usual burgers from the usual chains, with Borough Market just over the road though, you'd be mad to waste your money on these. M &S and WH Smith lead the list of practical, but terribly unexciting shop names. The caverns connecting the Underground station with the national trains is teeming with better food options however—some even non-chain.

Public Transport

Connections are excellent. London Bridge Station is served by the Jubilee Line and the Bank branch of the Northern Line. Escalators take you down from the main concourse. Step outside the main entrance for the massive bus station, where buses leave in all directions of the city, except its far western reaches.

Marylebone Train Station

NFT Map: 76

Address: Great Central House, Melcombe Place, London, NW1 6JJ

Station Code: MYB

Lost Property: 08456 005 165

Overview

Despite Monopoly-board notoriety, Marylebone railway station fell into neglect in the mid – to late-twentieth century, spurned as a rundown piggy-in-the-middle wedged haplessly between neighbours Paddington and Euston. But it's an aimless drifter no more. A refurb' in the 90s and again in 2006 saw Marylebone reinvigorated, with a thorough sprucing up and two new platforms. Servicing the Midlands, it now threads as far as Birmingham, Shakespeare's Stratford-Upon-Avon, Leamington Spa, Aylesbury, and High Wycombe, amongst others. It remains the runt of the London train station litter, but is a popular location for television filming (Doctor Who; Magnum PI; Green Wing; Peep Show) at a fraction of the price of King's Cross. In its bowels, Bakerloo Line trains rumble through an underground station of the same name.

Tickets

Rail ticket windows are to the north of Marylebone's relatively petite concourse and open Monday-Saturday 06.30–22:10 or Sunday 07.30–21.40. As with all mainline train stations, self-service ticket machines are in abundance should ticket offices be closed or queues too long. Sturdy padded-barriers ensure buying tickets on board the train, or getting away without them, is not an option. Underground tickets can be purchased from windows or machines alike within the Tube station itself.

Services

The usual plethora of railway station chains are on hand: newsagent WH Smith, baguette bakers Upper Crust, supermarket Marks & Spencer, and pasty purveyors the West Cornwall Company among them. More individually, Marylebone also hosts AMT Coffee, a cafe with a seating area at the centre of the concourse, the nifty flower stand on the south wall, and The V &A free house in the west passageway—an old man's boozer in the classic, wood panelled style. Cash points and payphones are in this same walkway, and toilets are situated on the south wall.

Public Transport

Marylebone underground station lies directly beneath Marylebone overground, and is serviced (Matron!) by the Bakerloo Line, while buses 2 and 205 stop directly outside the main entrance. A taxi stand is also situated out front. Baker Street and Edgware tube stations are a short walk away.

Paddington Station

NFT Map: 31

Address: Praed Street, London, W2 1HQ

Station Code: PAD

General Station Enquiries: 03457 11 41 41

Lost property: 020 7262 0344

Website: www.networkrail.co.uk/paddington or @NetworkRailPAD

Overview

If you're in that small minority of people who love stations, then Paddington's paradise. Designed by engineering legend Isambard Kingdom Brunel—his middle name is Kingdom for God's sake, of course his work's going to be magnificent—this barn-like structure harks back to an era when train travel retained a little glamour. If it wasn't for the on-site Burger King you could easily imagine tearful ladies waving silk handkerchiefs at dapper gents.

The station also occupies a unique place in literary heritage. Every British child in the last half-century knows the tales of Paddington Bear. From "deepest darkest Peru", he was left unattended at the station; but a kind family picked him up, took him in, and named him after it. No other station name can inspire such genuine warmth. It certainly wouldn't have worked if he'd been found at Clapham Junction.

Heathrow Express

The super-fast link to Heathrow from Paddington takes just 15 minutes to Terminals 1, 2 and 3. Be warned, though; it's far from cheap (www.heathrowexpress.com).

Tickets

A ticket office and machines are located near platforms 9-10, and there are other machines and an information point near the Eastbourne Terrace entrance and also underneath the mezzanine.

Services

If you have any money left from your ticket—unlikely at today's prices—there are plenty of sharks who can take it off you. Burger King and Upper Crust will overcharge you for burgers or baguettes and there's an 'offie' (off-license) for expensive booze. There are also other ways of staying amused; as it's the main portal for commuters entering London from the west and Wales) there's WiFi, a supermarket, a bookshop and curiously, a lingerie shop. Just what sort of a job do you have if you get to the station and realise: "Bollocks! No suspenders!"? Certainly not one compatible with Paddington's place in children's lit, that's for sure.

Public Transport

The Bakerloo, Circle, District, and Hammersmith & City Tube lines all stop at Paddington. Buses serve west and north west London.

St Pancras International

NFT Map: 78

Address: Euston Road, London, N1C 4QP

Station Reception: 020 7843 7688

Lost Property: 020 7837 4334

Website: stpancras.com or @StPancrasInt

Overview

St Pancras station has been generating waves of breathless excitement ever since its opening ceremony in 2007, which was by all accounts a pretty histrionic affair. This "Cathedral of Transport" situated next door to King's Cross station is now home to the Eurostar international train service and has domestic connections (via Thameslink trains) to Luton Airport, Bedford and Brighton; as well as Midland Mainline connections to places like Leicester and Sheffield. As the first major project of a huge scheme to redevelop the area, St Pancras has been marketed as so-much-more-than-a-station. Alongside its rail platforms it features Europe's longest Champagne bar, a farmers market, and an arcade of pointedly classy shops. All this is housed within beautiful listed buildings dating from 1868, with an extension for the long Eurostar trains designed by British starchitect Norman Foster.

Tickets

The Eurostar ticket office and travel centre is located at the Euston Road end of the long arcade, while self-service machines (for collecting pre-booked tickets) can be found outside the Eurostar departure lounge further along the arcade and to the right. For National Rail services, you will need to buy tickets from machines, or a manned ticket desk at the designated area at the far end of the Arcade, next to that horrific kissing statue.

Services

At St Pancras International there are dozens of places to eat, drink and shop, with a fair number of chain stores as well as some exclusives. Best of all is the Booking Office bar, which serves some of the best cocktails in the city. The station has its own dedicated shopping arcade with branches of classic London stores like Hamleys, as well as a market area and another brace of shops at the north end of the station ('The Circle'). Everything is shiny, new and upmarket, so expect your money to vanish pretty damn quickly. The Betjeman Arms pub—named after the famous poet whose petition saved the listed buildings from the same fate as Euston's arch—hosts beer festivals and music/literature events.

Public Transport

St Pancras can be reached by Tube (via adjacent King's Cross station) on the Victoria, Hammersmith & City, Circle, Piccadilly, Northern and Metropolitan Lines. A large number of buses also stop along Euston Road day and night.

Victoria Station

NFT Map: 20

Address: Buckingham Palace Road, London, SW1E 5ND

Station Code: VIC

General Station Enquiries: 03457 11 41 41

Lost property: 020 7963 0957

Website: www.networkrail.co.uk/victoria or @NetworkRailVIC

Overview

80 million people use London Victoria per year, making it one of the UK's busiest stations. Hit it at rush hour and it will feel like those 80 million are all there with you. Built a century ago for a less populous, less rushed and less demanding city, it struggles with crowds of commuters who jostle for platform space. Now it enforces crowd-control measures at peak times: prepare to be patient. Nevertheless, it is well laid-out with services clearly sign-posted, and a major upgrade is planned to improve its capacity.

Victoria's main train operators are Southeastern, Southern and Gatwick Express, who between them will whisk you to Brighton, Portsmouth, Hastings and Gatwick, among other Southeastern towns. Or if you're looking for a romantic break and the Victoria route to Bognor Regis is just a little too obvious for you, you can earn yourself brownie points and a hefty overdraft by taking the Orient Express from this station.

The building itself is impressive: look above the modern shop fascias to enjoy century-old architecture. But if that is all a little too high-brow, look up anyway, as the entrance to the South East building sports four caryatids: columns shaped like women, whose tunics saucily hang open so a gratuitous nipple can pop out to cheer the commuters. Rule Britannia!

Tickets

If you haven't booked in advance (why? Why?!), then head for the 24 hour ticket office in the central concourse, where you will queue for anything up to a year to buy your journey for much more money than you'd have paid online a week earlier. If you don't require assistance from a ticket officer, use the automated machines dotted round the concourse: their queues always move faster (unless the person in front of you is a newbie who can't figure out the buttons, which is guaranteed if you have less than five minutes to catch your train). Keep your ticket handy as all platforms are guarded by ticket barriers, and add a few extra minutes to reach platforms 15–19.

Services

All the predictable station fare is available in the main concourse for your journey's usual sandwich, loofah and tie needs. Food options have mercifully diversified so in addition to the obligatory artery-cloggers you can now grab sushi from the Wasabi stand or maintain your body's temple-status at the Camden Food Co. If it's a meal you're after and you must remain at the station, head up to the food court via Victoria Place for a choice of what could charitably be described as restaurants. Victoria Place itself boasts the ubiquitous high street shops to help you kill time or for any last minute gifts (as long as you don't really like the person you're buying for). Station loos are 30p—even up in the food court you can't pee for free—and showers are available if you're getting a bit ripe. Victoria also has a left luggage service, WiFi (charged) and photo booths.

Public Transport

Victoria is on the Victoria, Circle and District lines: entrance to the underground is opposite platform 7. The bus terminus is just outside the main entrance. It is also next door to London's national bus depot for cheapo travel to/from other parts of the UK. The main taxi rank is outside the main entrance, but if it has a heart-sinking queue then head up to the Plaza exit for an alternative rank.

Waterloo Station

NFT Map: 104

Address: Station Approach Road,
London, SE1 8SW

Station Code: WAT

General Station Enquiries: 03457 11 41 41

Lost property: 020 7401 7861

Website: www.networkrail.co.uk/waterloo

Overview

Until 2007, Waterloo was the first port of call for 'Europeans' arriving by train. Thousands of chic foreigners, clutching manbags and sporting huge sunglasses, would arrive at the station every week. But not any more. Nearly 200 years after the British triumphed in the first battle of Waterloo—a town in Belgium—the French got their revenge. Last November Eurostar gave the two fingers to the British Waterloo and promiscuously buggered off to St Pancras. Rumour has it that ex-PM Margaret Thatcher had specifically ordered that Eurostar terminate at a station named after a famous French defeat; but things have moved on a little since the "Iron Lady" left office. We're all Europeans now…

In truth, perhaps it's not that bad a thing. Even though no other British station covers as much space, Waterloo feels like it's at its bursting point. Even without the Eurostar it has a whopping 19 platforms—in almost constant use—and four Tube lines; it's the busiest station in Britain. It's calmed down slightly since the international terminal was put out to stud, but it's still pretty manic.

The station services London's south western suburbs (as can be seen by the swathes of well-dressed commuters) and, farther afield, the towns south west of the capital.

Waterloo East

NFT Map: 104

Address: Sandell St, SE8 8H

General Station Enquiries: 0 800 405 040

Overview

If the south west isn't your bag, you can disappear to England's south east—Kent, Sussex and SE London—from Waterloo East (station code: WAE). There's an escalator next to Burger King, opposite platform 12, that makes a trip to the south east look far more alluring than it really is; an elevated walkway over Waterloo Road connects Waterloo East with its larger cousin. The facility, considered its own terminal, is operated by Southeastern. The main entrance is on Sandell St.

Tickets

The main office is opposite platforms 16–17. And it's open 24 hours—so why not charm them into giving you a free ticket after a few drinks? They can't have heard it before, right?

Services

A delay is just unplanned "me time", so make the most of it by buying a newspaper, eating your own weight in overpriced pasties and cookies; then wash it down with a few pints of generic football-sponsorlager in the pub before buying your loved-one a novelty tie/'cute' socks to make for up being late. And drunk. And flatulent. And tasteless. There's a left luggage office between platforms 11-12.

Public Transport

Waterloo is served by four underground lines: Bakerloo, Jubilee, Northern, Waterloo & City; and numerous bus routes.

Overview

If there's one thing that screams London, it's big red buses—loads of 'em—preferably passing beneath Big Ben for maximum iconic impact. There was an almighty roar from Londoners when the Routemaster was scrapped: panoramas viewed from the Oxo tower were dotted with fists clutching rolled-up Time Outs shaking at the mayoral offices. The accordion buses which replaced them were met with similar anger but they've now been phased out: one can only guess at the amount of revenue lost by fare dodgers.

Whatever you think of the death of the bendy bus and Boris' reinvention of the Routemaster (also known as the "New Routemaster") one thing is certain: you're going to spend a lot of time on buses, around them, dodging them or moaning about them. Let's have a quick rundown of things to drop in a London bus convo: 'Drivers take pleasure in driving off just as you get to the stop,' 'Why do they always drive so fast/slow?' 'They're earning up to £500 a week? Why are they so grumpy all the time?' ad infinitum. As a Londoner, your list of hobbies and interests now includes transport: deal with it.

There are a variety of different operating companies, but to us they're all the same, all the way out to the frontiers of Zone 6. Get on at the front, get off at the middle. After the old double-decker buses were retired in 2005, Thomas Heatherwick's all-new Routemaster launched in Spring 2012. Just like the classic version there is an open rear platform for hopping on and hopping off. If you do want to live out your 1940s film fantasies, you can still catch the quaint old Routemasters doddering along the Heritage Route 15 during the day, a shorter version of the full route.

Fares

In a further move towards the cashless society, cash is not accepted on buses. A single fare costs £1.50 with an Oyster card, contactless card or one-day paper Travelcard. A bus and tram pass costs £21 per week. The Oyster ("The world's your..."—geddit?) is an electronic swipe card that can be bought at all Tube stations and thousands of other outlets such as newsagents and corner shops. The card can carry a mixture of travel passes (travelcards) and pay-as-you-go cash value. Note that if you choose pay-as-you-go, and you end up making more journeys than you anticipated; once it reaches the equivalent cost of a one-day travelcard, it will cap itself so you don't spend more. When you get on, don't forget to push your card against the scanner by the drivers' window. Sure, you're on camera 300 times per day, and every journey you make is recorded. But if you're paranoid, try another city, because they are watching you here.

24-Hour Services

You'll not hear London referred to as "the other city which never sleeps". Partly because it's unwieldy, but mostly because it's not true. After a hard night's binge-drinking and fighting in taxi ranks, we like our kip. But for those of you that are hardcore no-sleep-till-Brockley types, there is a network of 24-hour services. There are also a large number of night buses. They're just like day buses, except the route number is prefixed by a large 'N' and the view is less interesting.

Information

TfL's website (tfl.gov.uk) is an essential reference. Fare information and travel updates are available, plus PDFs of routes and timetables. As you get closer to central London, many routes operate on a frequency-basis rather than at fixed times. The main reason to visit TfL's site is the useful Journey Planner: enter your start and end points and it will (usually) calculate the best options. A word of warning though, computers are fallible and some route maps are schematics—so do check your own map and use common sense. Like those idiots that follow their GPS even when it tells them to drive into a river, it's frustrating to take three buses in a big circuit then realise you could have walked it in five minutes…

Safety

Like all big cities, London has its fair share of oddballs and criminals. And then a few institution-loads more in case things ever get boring. But CCTV in every bus and the creation of Safer Transport teams is having an effect—and not just on the share price of video camera manufacturers. Also, bus crime is concentrated in particular areas on particular routes. And you'll soon get to know the 'usual suspects' so don't worry. Night buses can get a bit lairy, so follow a few tips to make sure the only stress you suffer is traffic-related. Gangsters may wish to laugh at the following; Mother Theresas may wish to tattoo it on the inside of their eyelids: Avoid top decks where necessary. Sit on the left so the driver can see you (he has a radio link to base). Don't fall asleep. Use the same stop at night and know your surroundings so you can be confident. Keep your belongings close to you and be switched on. Get to know the 'hot spots' so you can be aware.

Overview

Although convenient and cost effective, coaches are traditionally associated with the grimier side of travel. But when it comes to budget travel, grime is in the eye of the beholder. So if your impression of coaches includes cold turkey junkies showering sick on unsuspecting passengers or if you maintain a general aversion to getting within three coach lengths of the portal of hell that is the coach toilet, then perhaps this mode of travel is not for you. That said, coach travel enjoys a long tradition across the UK, and it's much, much better here than many other places.

For years, National Express (www.nationalexpress.com), the UK's biggest coach company, has been trying to shake its image as a purveyor of seedy transport. Having rebranded itself as quick, comfortable and green, their fleet of coaches are shiny and the drivers slightly less grumpy than they used to be. National Express' nemesis is Megabus (www.megabus.co.uk), the £1 people (of course they release only a handful of these tickets for each journey and then the fare rises the closer you get to your preferred date). It hasn't always been this way, but Megabus coaches are now pretty much as good as National Express. Megabus Plus (www.megabusplus.com) combines bus and rail travel for selected destinations. At the same time, National Express started its own super cheap ticket campaign. Eurolines (www.eurolines.co.uk) is National Express' low-cost option to Europe.

Victoria Coach Station (Buckingham Palace Road, London, SW1W 9TP) is the main coach hub is near Victoria train station. You can buy tickets for both Megabus and National Express—the two main operators who run from Victoria Coach Station—from the same booths just inside the station. But, like plane tickets, (only without that last shred of glamour that air travel still has) if you buy in advance, you can get some super-cheap prices. National Express has an office on the road between the train and bus stations. Victoria Coach Station is also a hub for other bus companies serving the continent, some of which can be very cheap.

London's other main hub is Golder's Green. This is the last stop for services heading north (or the first stop for buses coming down into London). If you live in north London, it's worth jumping off here, as it's on the Northern Line and can shave an hour off the trip.

There's also a healthy trade in coaches to Oxford. The Oxford Tube (www.oxfordtube.com) competes with National Express on the route from Victoria; travelling via Marble Arch, Notting Hill and Shepherd's Bush. Tickets normally cost about £15 and you can buy on board. They also run through the night—so if you get drunk and have the urge to go on an impromptu holiday—well, Oxford it is.

Beyond Tooting, Croydon's trams will take you from places like Wimbledon to shop—lemming-like with the locals—at the Ampere Way IKEA. The trams accept Oyster and use a similar charging scale to buses. Once you get back on the map, your flatpacked sideboard will win admiring glances but few friends as you trail home on busy tubes.

General Information

Transport for London: www.tfl.gov.uk

London Cycling Campaign: lcc.org.uk or @london_cycling

Overview

There's a war going on out there, one with real casualties and collateral damage. When David Cameron was spotted going through a red light on his bicycle, it threw into sharp relief a low-level conflict which has been going on for decades. Bikes v. Cars: with hapless pedestrians caught in the middle.

Cycling around London is not for the faint-hearted, but municipal improvements (especially during Boris Johnson's tenure) and the hard work of the London Cycling Campaign, are encouraging people to drop their Oyster cards and jump on their bikes. London continues to implement its system of Cycle Superhighways providing safer routes (and some dedicated lanes) into Central London and across the city. The city's cyclehire program, Santander Cycles (formerly sponsored by Barclays and also known as 'Boris Bikes'), is a brilliant system based on European models in which users pick up a bike and then drop it off when finished at a suitable point in the city. If you want to explore London this way, note that Transport for London has some fun leisure routes detailed on its website. Transport for London offers great free cycling maps (order via the TfL website); some of the 14 routes have become so popular, cycling along them is like taking part in the Tour de France (albeit slower and with slightly fewer drugs). The maps give colour-coded help; look for the brown routes (separate from the traffic) or even better the green routes (separate from the traffic and passing through parks, beside canals or rivers.)

But cycling does hold some risks. As well as the nightmare of walking around all day with 'helmet hair' you've got accidents and theft. LCC's website has details of road-confidence training and lists local cycling groups who run social events and cycle maintenance classes. They will sometimes cycle your new route to work with you to help you negotiate the difficult bits. Aren't they nice?

For those new to cycling on London's roads, basic rules include: stay a door length (or stride) away from the pavement or parked cars; watch out for distracted office drones leaping into the road and into black cabs; don't undertake bendy-buses or HGVs; don't use your phone while moving; and if in doubt on a tricky junction, transform yourself into a pedestrian—get off and push your bike wherever you need to go.

Bolt-cutting 'tea-leaves' steal thousands of bikes every year. You have three options to reduce this particular risk. One, buy a rubbish bike that no-one would want to steal and lock it with one lock. Two, get a decent bike, carry around a D-lock and two other locks and spend 20 mins each time you stop. Three, get a shit-hot bike and never take it out.

Where to Ride Bikes

There are plenty of great rides around town and a happy cyclist is one who has been able to incorporate one into their commute. Good options are the short but scenic Parkland Walk Nature Reserve, which links Finsbury Park to Highgate via an abandoned railway line; a Saturday morning cycle takes you to one of Highgate's wonderful pubs for lunch and a lazy pint. The City, normally snarled with cabs, buses and kamikaze pedestrians, is a dream on a Sunday morning.

Though not continuous, the path along the Regent's Canal linking Paddington with Canary Wharf takes cyclists away from traffic and along some surprisingly gorgeous stretches of canal (which also sport some top-notch graffiti)—as well as some godawful, festering dumps. A useful section of the canal links the west side of Regent's Park with Paddington via Lisson Grove and Warwick Avenue. Watch out for super-fast cyclists determined to slice a second off their PB, especially where the path narrows under bridges or around ramps.

A jaunt through any of the capital's great parks seems an obvious choice, but beware, some parks (notably Hampstead Heath) ban bikes on almost all paths, thanks to selfish cyclists of the past who went too fast and frightened the jumpy pedestrians.

RideLondon (www.prudentialridelondon.co.uk) is a fun two-day riding festival built on the success of the earlier FreeWheel. Events include a family ride along closed central London roads, a 100-mile ride, and a Grand Prix for pros.

Bike Shops	*Address*	*Phone*
Apex Cycles	40-42 Clapham High St, SW4 7UR	020 7622 1334
Archway Cycles	183 Archway Rd	020 8340 9696
Bikefix	48 Lamb's Conduit St, WC1N 3LJ	020 7405 1218
Brick Lane Bikes	118 Bethnal Green Rd, E2 6DG	020 7033 9053
Bobbin Bicycles	397 St John St	020 7837 3370
Brixton Cycles	145 Stockwell Rd, SW9 9TN	020 7733 6055
Cheech Miller	227 Victoria Park Rd	020 8985 9900
Condor Cycles	51 Gray's Inn Rd, WC1X 8PP	020 7269 6820
Decathlon	Surrey Quays Rd	020 7394 2000
Evans (Spitalfields)	The Cavern, 1 Market St, E1 6AA	020 7426 0391
Holloway Cycles	290 Holloway Rd, N7 6NJ	020 7700 6611
London Fields Cycles	281 Mare St, E8 1PJ	020 8525 0077
London Recumbents	Battersea Park	020 7498 6543
Mosquito	123 Essex Rd, N1 2SN	020 7226 8765
ReCycling	110 Elephant Rd, SE17 1LB	020 7703 7001

To consider taking a taxi in London you either need (a) a trust fund, or (b) to be drunk. If you are both, congratulations: prepare to be taken for a ride in more ways than one.

Dating back to the mid-17th Century (kind of), London's 'black cabs', or 'Hackneys', are the world's oldest taxi service and are as representative of London as Routemasters, Big Ben and robbery. They are the most visible, the most iconic and probably the most expensive taxi service in London. While this flag-down option is great (they are the only company licensed to pick up on the street) budgeting for a black cab is tricky. Their prices are designed to confuse passengers into parting with huge wads for what often feels like a round-the-block trip. A whole range of metaphysical problems contribute to that huge sum waiting to be paid at journey's end; all fares start at £2.40 and are based on three types of tariffs—higher tariffs apply on evenings, weekends and late nights. Fares are also affected by traffic. In general, as a very broad guideline, expect to pay around £9 for up to one mile, £14 for up to two miles, and £22 for up to four miles. Fares between Heathrow and Central London are anywhere between £45–£85. A £4 surcharge applies during the days around Christmas and New Year. There's also a 'puke charge' of £40 if you soil the cab and the driver has to take it out of service to clean it; keep it in!

Black cabs are operated by many different companies who are all regulated and licensed by the Public Carriage Office (PCO). Generally speaking, the service you receive doesn't vary much from company to company, though some boast little add-ons to capture your fare. Big, well organized companies like Dial-A-Cab (www.dialacab.co.uk; 020 7253 5000) and Radio Taxis (www.radiotaxis.co.uk; 020 7272 0272) offer online booking, carbon neutral trips, and friendly service. All black cab drivers must pass 'The Knowledge' test to get their license, so every driver will have a labyrinthine understanding of London and most will not be shy in sharing this with you.

Though a cheaper option, going private can be a minefield. Since 2001 all taxi services in London are required by law to be licensed by the PCO: this includes the city's thousands of private-hire minicabs. Private hire companies are everywhere you look and often take the form of nicotine-stained, shoddily built little offices with lots of bored men milling about. Every neighbourhood has plenty of local services and it's really trial and error to find one that doesn't rip you off or drive barely roadworthy chariots of rust. The drivers of these little companies can be pretty eccentric—you can be regaled by tales of times past, given essential life advice or simply receive the disdainful silent treatment. The 'private taxi sector' does do upmarket, however. By far the most efficient and elegant service is that offered by Addison Lee, (www.addisonlee.com; 020 7407 9000) who text you twice, have huge gleaming six-seaters, and perfectly-manicured drivers. Fares are pretty cheap over longer distances but the minimum is around £10. Transport for London (tfl.gov.uk) has a useful online tool for locating licensed black cabs and minicabs, as well as an app (Cabwise). Another option is Uber (www.uber.com/cities/london), with its handy app and account-based system.

A word of warning: London is awash with rogue taxi-drivers who are not licensed and who will attempt to pick you up from outside a club or theatre. These guys will either charge you more than you agreed upon, not know where they are going, or they will be driving beat-up death-traps. If a ride hasn't been booked with a licensed minicab company, then there is no record of your journey, meaning also that if there is a problem, your driver cannot be traced. There are also many stories of attacks on women, so if in doubt, don't get in!

London Heliport
020 7228 0181
www.londonheliport.co.uk or @LondonHeliport

SW11's very own heliport! Includes aerial tours of London and airport transfers (Heathrow in ten minutes). The nearest tube is Clapham Junction.

EBG Helicopters
01737 823 282
www.ebghelicopters.co.uk or @ebgheli

Running helicopter tours of London and charter flights from Redhill Airport in Surrey, 10 minutes by car from Gatwick Airport. £140 will get you 35 minutes over London, the only downside is getting to Surrey. Also offers charters for weddings and corporate events and air taxi service starting from £650 for up to three passengers.

Helicopter Days
0844 815 0952
www.helicopterdays.co.uk or @Helicopterdays

London sightseeing trips starting from £900.

Elstree Aerodrome
www.londonelstreeaerodrome.com

A variety of charters operate out of Elstree offering sky tours, as well as flight academies for those who want to take the wheel. On site is a restaurant, plus it's close to the M1.

Ferries/Boat Tours, Rentals & Charters

London River Services (LRS)
020 7941 2400
www.tfl.gov.uk/gettingaround

Provides commuter river transportation on the Thames. This runs in the East from Masthouse Terrace Pier to Savoy Pier at Embankment. In peak hours services run to Woolwich Arsenal with a further service from Blackfriars Millenium Pier in the City to Putney Pier in the west costing £15 return. WiFi is available on boats serving Woolwich. Services run every 20 minutes. All are wheelchair friendly.

Thames Clippers
0870 7815049
www.thamesclippers.com

London's answer to the NYC water taxis, primarily serving the O2 stadium from Waterloo, Embankment and Tower Bridge. Conveniently runs later than the Tube meaning you can actually stay right to the end of a show without the worry of being stranded on the south side of the river. Single tickets cost between £3-5 with Oyster Card holders getting 1/3 off. Boats leave every 15 minutes.

Bateux London
020 7695 1800
www.bateuxlondon.com.

Dinner, lunch and charter cruises from Embankment Pier. Yes, there's even a jazz cruise.

Westminster Passenger Services Association
020 7930 2062
www.wpsa.co.uk

One of the only popular charters to offer services upriver to Kew, Richmond and Hampton Court.

City Cruises
020 7488 0344
www.citycruises.com.

Hop on hop off services primarily aimed at tourists and with tourist prices. Tickets start from £11 return for adults from Greenwich to Westminster/Waterloo Pier.

Heritage Boat Charters
01932 224 800
www.heritageboatcharters.com

For something different, try messing about on the river in one of these historic wooden numbers. On offer are skippered cruises down the Thames starting at £825. Formal dinner on board is available.

Silver Fleet Woods River Cruises
020 7759 1900
www.silverfleet.co.uk

Luxury chartered boats. Particularly good at putting on top-notch corporate events.

Thames Cruises
020 7928 9009
www.thamescruises.com

Two words—disco cruise. Hot pants are not required for dinner cruises.

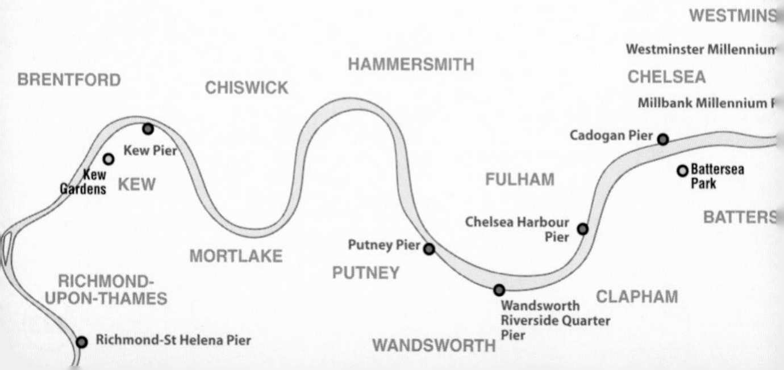

Marinas/Passenger Ship Terminal

Chelsea Marina
07770 542 783
www.chelseaharbourmarina.com

Despite being in upmarket Chelsea, the prices for mooring your boat here are incredibly generous—£2 per metre a night or £300 a year with space for 60 boats. Secure subterranean parking also available.

Chiswick Quay Marina
020 8994 8743
www.chiswickquay.com/marina

Great, secluded spot for West Londoners near Chiswick Bridge. A little far from a tube station, yet Chiswick overland station is within walking distance with services to Waterloo. Prices are on an annual basis at £162 per metre including a resident harbourmaster, shower block, mains water and electricity.

Gallions Point Marina
020 7476 7054
www.gallionspointmarina.co.uk

In London's Docklands and therefore perfect for those working in the city.

St Katharine Haven
020 7264 5312
skdocks.co.uk

One of London's best marinas. Great location by Tower Bridge, close to the quayside bars and restaurants and reasonable London prices—£3.60 per metre, per day.

Welcome Floating Terminal in Greenwich
01474 562 200
www.portoflondon.co.uk

Built in 2004 and believed to be the world's first floating terminal. Welcome has on-site immigration and custom services for cruise ship passengers entering or leaving London.

London Cruise Terminal at Tilbury
01375 852 360
www.londoncruiseterminal.com

The most popular regional departure point for passenger liners is 25 miles from Central London in Essex. Its close proximity to the M25 makes it easy for Londoners to get to. Current destinations from here include Scandinavia and continental Europe.

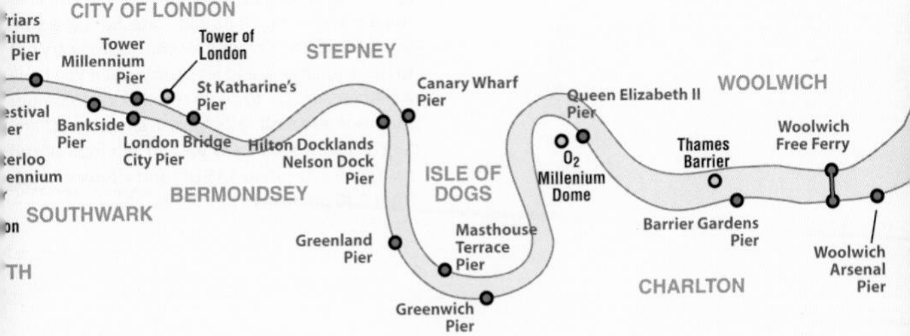

General Information

TfL Traffic News: tfl.gov.uk/trafficnews or @TfLTrafficNews

Parking Information for Cars: www.park-up.com

Parking Information for Motorbikes and Scooters: www.parkingforbikes.com

AA Route Planner: www.theaa.com/route-planner

Overview

With London's Congestion Charge, Low Emission Zone, pricey parking, kamikaze bus drivers, dreaded speed bumps, 20 mph limits, speed cameras and a road layout that would give Spock the night terrors—"it's so illogical Captain"—driving around town is something to be avoided. Combine this with over 7.5 million people who just want to get from A to B without anyone getting in their frickin' way, and you can see where problems arise.

That said, there are times when a four-wheeler is the only option, in which case the more you know... To start, pedestrians can become an infuriating lot, at least those who love striding purposefully into the road with nary a thought for their safety; keep a weather eye out, one foot over the brake and one hand over the horn. Then there are the cyclists, an ever-increasing number—give them plenty of space and remember for the one speedhound jumping the lights there are hundreds of law abiders that you just don't notice; for your own sanity, try to focus on them. As for the mechanized obstacles, remember that motorbikes and scooters are not all ridden by leather-clad Hells Angels or Jamie Oliver clones—most just want to get about and avoid the Congestion Charge; as with cyclists, give plenty of space and check your blind spots. A special danger are the black cabs, those roving London landmarks that have been known, on occasion, to pull up to the curb, do a 'U-ie' and even advertise the FT without sufficient warning. And finally, a word about traffic wardens, which are also known as 'council revenue generating units': make sure you avoid illegal parking—unless you are an ambassador. Fines are not cheap.

Indeed, most of the stress caused by driving in London, apart from the sheer volume of traffic, is caused by lack of consideration for others—usually as drivers are running late. So make sure you leave PLENTY of time for your journey, try not to block junctions, and let people out if you have a chance. And try to avoid rush hour: remember that morning rush lasts from 7 am to 10.30 am, lunch rush from 11 am to 2.30 pm, school run rush from 2.45 pm to 4.15 pm and afternoon rush from 4.30 pm to 8.45 pm. Bonne chance...

Driving in the Congestion Charge Zone and the Low Emission Zone

The Congestion Charge Zone, introduced in 2003, is a surcharge for driving in Central London between 7 am and 6 pm Monday through Friday (except Bank Holidays). Huge red Cs in circles alert drivers to the start of the zone, if you miss them you should consider a swift visit to your optician. There is ongoing debate over the actual impact of the charge, although it has raised money for public transport.

The charge is £11.50 and there is no extra charge for driving in and out of the zone. Drivers who use the Congestion Charge Auto Pay (CCAP) system receive a £1 discount; Auto Pay keeps a tally of how many days a car was driven and charges your card at the end of the month. Drivers can pay in advance or by midnight on the day of travel. For £14 you have until midnight the following day to pay the charge. Payments are accepted by phone, online, by regular mail, and by text. Exemptions and discounts exist for motorbikes and residents living in or near the charge zone. Penalty charges are steep: £130 penalty charge (reduced to £65 if paid within 14 days).

The Low Emission Zone (LEZ) was introduced in February 2008 to deter everything from pickup trucks and van to buses, coaches and large lorries from dragging their belching exhausts through town. It covers a much larger area than the Congestion Charge: almost all of London within the M25 and applies 24/7. The charge varies between £100 and £200 a day. Best leave your concrete mixer at home.

Red Routes

The red double lines along a roadway indicate a "red route," part of the Transport for London Road Network (TLRN), and amounting to a special enforcement zone patrolled by Transport for London agents. No stopping rules are strictly enforced, as are yellow box junction infractions, banned turns, and unauthorized use of bus lanes. Although only five percent of London's roadways, the TLRN carries 30 percent of the city's traffic. As such the point of the oversight is to keep traffic moving. The rest of the roads are managed by local councils.

Key Roads

A1

Running straight north from St Paul's Cathedral in the City through Islington, Archway, Highgate and beyond, this old Roman Road has some freer stretches allowing the frustrated drive to accelerate to 43 mph for 3 seconds, get a speeding ticket and then slam on the brakes. Ends (eventually) in Princes Street, Edinburgh, Scotland.

North Circular/South Circular (A406)

This is the M25's angrier and twisted little brother. Circling Outer London it has some of the busiest stretches of road in London and even includes a ferry across the river at Woolwich. The way dwindles to one exhausted lane in certain sections, causing great clots of traffic every day in rush hour. See left for rush hour times.

Euston Rd/Marylebone Road (A501)

Running east-west past King's Cross and Euston, this wide road skirts the northern edge of the congestion zone. It gets very crowded, because it's a feeder road to the relatively breezy start of the A40 heading out of London.

Embankment

The view as you drive along the Embankment along the north bank of the Thames is breathtaking. It needs to be to keep you occupied as you inch forward for hours. Runs from Chelsea (A4) to Tower Bridge.

Vauxhall Bridge Rd/Grovesnor Place/Park Lane/Edgware Rd (A5)

Running roughly north-west from Vauxhall Bridge Rd, around Victoria, past Hyde Park Corner and Marble Arch and out to join the A40, this route is a free corridor through the Congestion zone—free from charge rather than free from traffic. Be prepared—it's rammed.

Old Kent Rd/New Cross Rd/ Lewisham Way/etc. (A2/A20)

Running south-west from The Bricklayers Arms roundabout and eventually down to Dover, where you catch the ferry to France; the Old Kent Rd, despite being the cheapest Monopoly property, is totally free from traffic at all times. No wait—that can't be right.

A3

Starting at London Bridge, this road eventually ends up in Portsmouth, but you have to struggle past Elephant and Castle, Clapham Common and Wimbledon Common along with everyone else trying to get to Guildford.

Traffic Hot Spots

Angel, Elephant and Castle, Hanger Lane Gyratory, Vauxhall Gyratory, Trafalgar Square, Parliament Square, Hammersmith Gyratory, everywhere else.

Car Share

The great thing about being a Londoner is there's really no need to have a car. Except on those few occasions where you're cursing yourself for hauling a flat-packed Ikea coffee table on the shitty Croydon tram service. This is where joining a membership-based carsharing company, such as such as Zipcar (www.zipcar.co.uk or @ZipcarUK), Enterprise CarShare (www.enterprisecarshare.com or @carshare) or Hertz 24/7 (www.hertz247.com or @Hertz247). When you need to move the band, there's also Zipvan (www.zipvan.com).

The membership services are convenient and easy: self-service cars and vans billable by the hour, day, week or month. The vehicles are parked in town, which means you don't have to hike to a car rental centre, stand in a queue or deal with annoying upselling at a counter. Plus, if you get thrown out of your girlfriend's flat at 2 am and need a ride, you're in luck. After signing up for a modest membership fee (less than £100 a year), all you have to do is unlock the car with an entry card or fob, grab the keys from the glovebox and away you go. Cars have hourly rates (in general between £5–10 depending on the plan and type of vehicle) on top of the membership fee. Fuel and insurance are included.

January

- **New Year's Day Parade** • Big Ben to Piccadilly Circus • Marching band and thousands of kids. How better to cure a hangover?
- **London Boat Show** • ExCel Exhibition Centre • Like we always say: you can never have too many yachts.
- **Russian Winter Festival** • Trafalgar Square • Magical Russian Winterland replaces the normal Pigeon-Crap Land.
- **London Art Fair** • Over 100 galleries and thousands of artists under one roof.
- **The London Bike Show** • ExCel Exhibition Centre • The best of the best of modern cycling equipment pandering to over-indulged cyclists.
- **London International Mime Festival** • Southbank Centre • Even weirder when you see it for real.
- **The London Outdoors Show** • ExCel Exhibition Centre • The country's biggest collection of outdoor goods—ironically hosted indoors.
- **Charles I Commemoration Ceremony** • Trafalgar Sq • St James' Palace • Thousands of uniformed Cavaliers confuse the tourists.
- **TNA Wrestling** • Wembley Arena • Strange men in spandex faux-fighting in front of drunken man-children.
- **Walking with Dinosaurs** • The O2 • Get your prehistoric freak on with twenty life-size dinosaurs (not literally) freaks!

February

- **British Academy Film Awards (BAFTA)** • Royal Opera House • Britain's finest film and television talent take a bow.
- **Chinese New Year** • West End • Party like it's 4707.
- **Destinations: Holiday and Travel Show** • Earls Court Exhibition Centre • Chase away the Winter Blues.
- **Live Tudor Cookery** • Hampton Court Palace • Glutinous Tudor food prepared in classic Tudor fashion. It's OK the New Year's resolutions will be long dead by now.
- **London Fashion Week** • Somerset House• Far Too Thin.
- **National Wedding Show** • Olympia • Perfect day out for a first date.
- **Professional Beauty** • ExCel Exhibition Centre • Pay to get pretty with the latest developments in modern cosmetics.
- **Lifted** • Harrods • A bizarre annual exhibition inside Harrod's lifts.
- **The Great Spitalfields Pancake Race** • Old Truman Brewery • Pancake race in wacky clothes. No, London. Just, no.
- **Blessing the Throats** • St Ethelreda's Church, Ely Place • Lemsip not working? Sore throats cured by holy candle.
- **Clowns' Service** • Holy Trinity, Dalston • Because God likes clowns too.
- **Kinetica Art Fair**• P3• Carnivorous lampshades and pole-dancing robots? We're there.
- **BAFTAs** • London Palladium • Ten points per autograph.

March

- **Affordable Art Fair** • The Marquee, Battersea Park • Now even The Great Unwashed can buy art!
- **Affordable Art Fair** • The Marquee, Battersea Park • Now even The Great Unwashed can buy art!
- **Easter Egg Hunt** • Kew Garden's • Delightful Easter affair, perfect for the kids, don't forget to check out the animal farm.
- **Ideal Home Show** • Earls Court Exhibition Centre • Make your home ideal (or a bit less grotty).
- **St Patrick's Day Parade** • Park Lane • Shamrocks, river-dancing, big fluffy Guinness hats: true Irish tradition.
- **London Drinker Beer & Cider Festival** • The Camden Centre • Get rat-arsed on Pressed Rat & Warthog.
- **La Dolce Vita** • Business Design Centre • Get your sampling face on
- **Men's Afternoon Tea** • Mandeville Hotel • Because nothing is manlier than an exclusive tea, champagne and cake afternoon.
- **Move It** • Olympia • Put on your dancing shoes.
- **The International Food & Drink Event** • Olympia • This gorge-fest happens biannually, so start starving yourself now.
- **The Country Living Spring Fair** • Business Design Centre • For those with time for wooden chicken eggs
- **JobServe Live!** • Olympia • Career ideas and thousands of vacancies.

April

- **Cake International** • ExCel Exhibition Centre • Decorate and glutinously devour delicious cakes.
- **Oxford & Cambridge Boat Race** • River Thames • Hole up in a pub by the river and cheer over a beer.
- **Virgin London Marathon** • Greenwich – The Mall • 35,000 pairs of bleeding nipples.
- **London Book Fair** • Earl's Court • The publishing industry's main event. Occasionally stuff for free.
- **Alternative Fashion Week** • Old Spitalfields Market • Huge range of cutting edge fashion. And fetishwear.
- **Queen's Birthday Gun Salute** • Hyde Park • Who said the monarchy is archaic?
- **St George's Day** • Covent Garden / Cenotaph / Shakespeare's Globe • Brush up your Morris dancing skills.
- **The Real Food Festival** • Earl's Court Exhibition Centre • Real Food: much nicer than fake food.
- **Hot Cross Bun Service** • St Bartholomew-the-Great, Smithfield • Widows get a free hot cross bun. Worth losing the husband.
- **London Independent Film Festival** • Various West and Central Cinemas • Cool celebration of cinematographic indieness without The Man. Or something.

May

- **Freedom of the City** • Central London • Frequently awesome improv and experimental festival attracting top names.
- **Baishakhi Mela** • Brick Lane • Celebrate the Bengali New Year in the British tradition: vindaloo.
- **Bathing the Buddha** • Leicester Square • Buddha gets a birthday bath.
- **Mind, Body, Spirit Festival** • Royal Horticultural Halls • Make up for all the time in the pub.
- **Camden Crawl** • Throughout Camden • If you're not crawling by the end, you haven't done it right.
- **Chelsea Flower Show** • Royal Hospital Chelsea • You'll go for the flowers. You'll stay for the Pimms.
- **Chelsea Flower Show** • Royal Hospital Chelsea • You'll go for the flowers. You'll stay for the Pimms.
- **Greenwich Beer & Jazz Festival** • Old Royal Naval College • An odd paring that somehow works.
- **London Pet Show** • Earls Court Two – The cute, odd, scary and weird bring their pets and show them off.
- **Sci-Fi Festival** • London Apollo • The UK's only Sci-Fi Festival. Thank god.
- **Interiors London** • ExCel Centre • For those rich enough to treat their homes like art.
- **The Drag Olympics** • The Way Out Club • Drag Queens are put through their pedicured, high-heeled paces.

June

- **City of London Festival** • The City • Bringing High Culture to a bunch of bankers.
- **Field Day** • Victoria Park • A pseudo hippy music festival with a lighthearted vibe.
- **Start of Open Air Theatre season** • Regent's Park • Ignore the climate and take in an outdoor play.
- **Taste of London** • Regent's Park • The best picnic in the world.
- **Wimbledon** • All England Lawn Tennis and Croquet Club • Short skirts and grunting. Marvellous.
- **Trooping the Colour** • Horse Guard's Parade • Hundreds of chaps in uniforms. Ohhhhh yes.
- **Meltdown Festival** • Southbank Centre • Eclectic music festival curated by major musicians.
- **Royal Academy Summer Exhibition** • Royal Academy • Lots and lots and LOTS of art.
- **Arts Festival Chelsea** • Chelsea • The artists formerly known as 'The Chelsea Festival'.
- **Naked Bike Ride** • Hyde Park • Don't think about the bums on seats.
- **Polo in the Park** • Hurlingham Park • Its turbo-rah dahhling, pass the Pimms.
- **Shakespeare Globe Season**• Bankside • To go, or not to go, that is the question.

July

- **Dogget's Coat & Badge Race** • Thames: London Bridge to Chelsea • Intense boat race to win a badge. Hardly seems worth it.
- **Pimms Urban Regatta** • Finsbury Square • People full of Pimms race on land in bottomless boats. Bloody Ozzies.
- **Pride London** • Trafalgar Square • One of Britain's biggest, funnest street parties.
- **The British 10k London Run** • Hyde Park • Whitehall • Work off the pies.
- **Hampton Court Palace Show** • Hampton Court • Stock up your garden / flowerpot / imagination.
- **The Chap Olympiad**• Bedford Square Gardens • Olympics for gentleman—no sportswear please.
- **Uprise Festival** • Islington • Celebrating the best of multicultural London, for free.
- **Swan Upping** • River Thames • Census of swans. For goodness sake.
- **Opening of Buckingham Palace** • Buckingham Palace • The Plebeians allowed in to see how their taxes (and steep entrance fees) are spent.
- **Wireless Festival** • Hyde Park • Big names vibrate the Serpentine.
- **Shoreditch Festival** • Shoreditch. • Because you can never have too many local festivals. Apparently.

August

- **Innocent Smoothies Festival** • Regent's Park • You wouldn't think fun could be this wholesome.
- **Great British Beer Festival** • Earls Court Exhibition Centre • A festival that puts the Great in Britain.
- **Trafalgar Square Festival** • Trafalgar Square • 3 weeks of music, theatre, dance and art.
- **Carnaval del Pueblo** • Royal Victoria Docks • Thousands of Latino lovelies. That's all you need to know, right?
- **Camden Fringe** • Camden People's Theatre • Wonderfully weird, hilariously funny and light on the wallet.
- **London Triathlon** • Docklands • Marathons are for pussies.
- **London Mela** • Gunnersbury Park • Partaaaay, Asia-style.
- **Metro Weekender** • Clapham Common • Dance music Saturday, bands on Sunday, chilled all weekend.
- **Notting Hill Carnival** • Ladbroke Grove • Party till your wallet gets nicked.
- **Parliament Tour Season** • Westminster • Go see first hand where it all goes so wrong.
- **Kids Week** • West End • West End shows free for kids. Soooo unfaaaaiiiiir.
- **Tiger Beer Singapore Chilli Crab Festival** • Truman Brewery • Cold beer, hot food and cool sounds.

September

- **The Great British Duck Race** • The Thames • Like the Oxbridge boat race. But with 165,000 rubber ducks.
- **Horseman's Sunday** • Hyde Park Crescent • London's horses say their Hail Maries. Yes, really.

- **Oyster & Seafood Fair** • Hays Galleria • The romance of oysters with the unholy stink of kippers.
- **Thames Festival** • Tower Bridge • Westminster • Fireworks, costumes, river races, carnivals. Kids like it.
- **Last Night of the Proms** • Royal Albert Hall • Camp overnight if you want tickets.
- **London Duathlon** • Richmond Park • It's like a triathlon… for people who can't swim.
- **London Tattoo Convention** • Old Truman Brewery • Who cares if it looks crap when you're 80?
- **Spitalfields Show & Green Fair** • Buxton Street • Who has the biggest marrow?
- **Open House Weekend** • Various around London • Over 600 architectural landmarks open for a nosey.
- **Fashion Week** • Summerset House • the September instalment of the famous frockfest.
- **Great Gorilla Run** • Start at London Underwriting Centre • Raise £400 for the Gorilla Organisation and the costume's yours.
- **Vintage Fashion Fair** • Primrose Hill • For those with a passion for vintage fashion.

October

- **The Big Draw** • Museum of Childhood • Pencils, not guns. Unfortunately.
- **Down Under Live** • Olympia • For those contemplating emigrating to warmer climes.
- **'Original Pearly Kings & Queens Association Harvest Festival** • Church of St Martin-in-the-Fields Affordable Art Fair.
- **International Halloween Festival** • Queen Mary College • Witches, druids and shamans unite for Europe's biggest Pagan festival.
- **Halloween** • London Dungeon • Trick Or Treating is for pussies.
- **Frieze Art Fair** • Regent's Park • Air kisses all round.
- **London Film Festival** • BFI Southbank • Two weeks of the best new films and lectures from A-Listers.
- **Metro Ski & Snowboard Show** • Olympia • London hosts the world's biggest winter sport show. Naturally.
- **Veolia Entertainment Wildlife Photographer of the Year (exhibition opens, for 6mths)** • Natural History Museum Puts your arty market photos to shame.
- **The Yoga Show** • Olympia • Bendy people upon bendy people. Literally.
- **Turner Prize Exhibition** • Tate Britain • Get to know the next Hirst or Emin.

November

- **London's Christmas Ice Rinks** • Venues across London • Much more romantic in your head than in reality.
- **Brighton Veteran Car Run** • Starts Hyde Park • Century-old bangers potter their way to Brighton.
- **Erotica Show** • Olympia • 31,000 horny adults pretend they're just browsing.
- **Barclays ATP World Tour Finals** • O2 Arena • Very rich tennis players make more money at this entertaining but unimportant tournament.
- **Bonfire Night** • Venues across London • Hundreds of thousands of pounds go pop.
- **Country Living Christmas Fair** • Business Design Centre • For those dreaming of a posh Christmas.
- **Royal British Legion Festival of Remembrance** • Royal Albert Hall • Take tissues.
- **Lord Mayor's Show** • Central London • Running for over 800 years and yet still a bit crap.
- **London Jazz Festival** • South Bank Centre • Start practising your jazz hands.
- **Winter Wonderland** • Hyde Park Grottos and Glühweins galore.

December

- **Satan's Grotto** • London Dungeon • Tortured elves and spit-roasting robins.
- **Trafalgar Square Christmas Tree** • Trafalgar Square • The only thing everyone knows about Oslo.
- **Aegon Masters Tennis** • Royal Albert Hall • Former World No.1s wheeze their way through a tournament.
- **Peter Pan Cup** • Serpentine Lido, Hyde Park • Freeze your nipples off on Christmas morning.
- **Great Christmas Pudding Race** • Covent Garden • We're mad, us! What are we like? Crazy!
- **Christmas Carol Sing-along** • Royal Albert Hall • Belt out your favourites and get in the mood.
- **Christmas Carol Sing-along** • Royal Albert Hall • Belt out your favourites and get in the mood.
- **Taste of Christmas** • ExCel Exhibition Centre • Tasty tips for making Christmas that little merrier.
- **Midnight Mass at St Paul's** • St Paul's • Eats the other Midnight Masses for breakfast.
- **New Year's Eve Fireworks** • Jubilee Gardens • Oooooh. And, of course, aaaaaaah.

Tactics

Finding somewhere to live in London is a ruthless and cutthroat business. Make sure you have plenty of red bull, cigarettes and patience. However, places go in the blink of an eye so it's important to move quick. Take a week off and hire a driver, if you can.

Ok, so these precautions aren't completely necessary, but you will have to work in mysterious and multifarious ways if you don't want to spend the next six months paying through your gullible nose for mice and verrucas. A good place to start by harassing your friends, your friends' friends, and your friends' friends' friends. Send out a group email and hope it gets passed around, and make sure you Tweet like mad about it. Twitter is a great place to get your request passed around. Who knows? Stephen Fry might have a room to let. Estate agents (see below for a list) will invariably try and rip you off but, then again, so will everyone else, so it's worth registering with all the big ones, as well as any whose office you see in the street, or you spot in newspapers, on TV or the internet. After uncovering a fair few completely brazen lies in the property listings on www.gumtree.com you will find that many of the smaller businesses place adverts for (sometimes fake) properties here. Don't be put off by the lies though, because this can be a good way of finding an agent (or getting in direct contact with a landlord) who is keen to make a deal with you, or who will try and match the prices advertised, even if they have nothing that fits the bill at the exact moment of lying. Of course, some of these listings are also genuine, and a good way to find rooms/apartments at lower than usual rates. Just bare in mind that a LOT of people use this site.

General sites

www.gumtree.com
www.craigslist.org
www.rightmove.co.uk
www.roombuddies.com
www.zoopla.co.uk

Estate Agents

There are hundreds of Estate Agents and Letting Agents across the city, some of the larger players (good and bad) include:

www.keatons.com - Offices all over London.
www.keatons.co.uk - Bow, Hackney, Harringey, Kentish Town, Stratford.
www.blackkatz.com - Lettings only agency, numerous offices.
www.fjlord.co.uk - Numerous offices, specialise in uncooperative staff.
www.nelsonslettings.com - South and central London.
www.atkinsonmcleod.com - City and Docklands.

If you do end up using an agent, they will of course want to charge you an additional fee beyond any deposits or advance rent required by the landlord. But, as many of the agents in central London are close together, it's possible that they may be competing with each other to sell/rent the same properties. This will enable you to get a better deal. So shop around, be devious, and backstab as much as possible.

Council Tax

Council Tax is an annoying hidden cost that always comes as a bit of a surprise. It is worked out by your local council and is based on the value of your house/flat, which the council will already have placed in to one of 8 tax bands (bands are A–G, G covering the most valuable properties).There are several ways to determine the value of a property, but the easiest is probably to go to the website of the valuation office at www.voa.gov.uk. Having done that, it's possible to weigh up the benefits of different areas by comparing the council tax in equivalent bands charged by different local councils. It's fairly laborious, but worth it in the long run, if you can be bothered.

Because council tax is based on the property, not the people inside it, the rate is constant no matter how many people live in the house. This means that it's much cheaper to live in a big house with lots of people to split the tax with, than on your own, when you are liable for the full amount. Students do not have to pay council tax at all, but if they are sharing with one or more non-students then there will still be council tax to pay. A single non-student in a house full of students receives a 25% discount on his/her council tax bill, but if there is more than one non-student then all non-students are liable to pay full whack.

Deposit Information

The deposit is the necessary bank drain of every new tendency agreement. Typically deposits range from one – three months rent in advance, but if you pay over a two-month deposit you are entitled to special privileges including the right to sublet your space. If you can't afford the financial outlay there are other options available to you; it is possible to get involved with the Deposit Guarantee Scheme (you will need to contact your local council for more information), or independent agencies offer a similar service for a 10% - 20% fee. While not all landlords in London are Ebenezer Scrooge pre hallucination-esque you'll still hear your fair share of horror stories. Make sure you use the Deposit Protection Scheme (DPS) www.depositprotection.com to protect your cash. For a comprehensive overview on deposit information and your rights visit the Direct Gov website at www.direct.gov.uk.

Alternative Options

In a city where house prices have been soaring through the roof for some time now (although it's calmed down somewhat recently), of course people do things like squat, have dreadlocks and go vegan. If you're not willing to go the whole way but fancy an adventure, or simply don't have much money, then it might be worth taking a look at being a guardian for Camelot. This company aims to fill vacant properties with responsible people who will prevent them from being abused. You must have goo references, a job, and be over eighteen as well as be ok with sharing with a indeterminate number of strangers, but th benefits are the unusual properties (e.g schools, disused churches), the often larg spaces and the ridiculously cheap rent (£25-60 pw inclusive of all bills). Of course load of people want to do this and propertie in London are not always available, but it' nevertheless a good idea to keep an ey on their site if the idea excites you: website uk.cameloteurope.com.

WAREHOUSES

As with Starbucks and obesity, us Brits hav finally caught on to the American craz for warehouse 'live/work' spaces. Okay w may have had the likes of Tracey Emin an other artists living in old carpet factorie since the YBA days, but recently a whol crop of established estate agents have beer refurbishing lofts and factories for lettin at a premium. Any established warehouse will tell you the way to go is independent through enthusiastic urban explorers wh renovate and convert these old building for love and enjoyment. Often the only wa into this secret brotherhood of the leak roof is by simply ending up at a huge part at 4am in one of these spaces and askin the residents politely. The freedom of livin in these places can be exhilirating if you'v spent years toeing the line with grump neighbours and grumpier landlords.

CANAL-BOATS

If all this land lubbing is bringing you down there's always the option of dropping ancho at Little Venice or the Lea Valley Harbour an sampling London's canal networks. Mor and more skint artsy fartsy folk are squeezin their possessions into canal boats and livin a romantic life on the water. A casual stro down Regent's Canal may convince yo this is the way to live, but bare in mind th hidden cons of London nautical life: moorin fees, fuel, unlit walks down leafy path frequented by degenerates…Don't say w didn't warn you!

The Best of the Best

London is full of interactive children's pursuits, and nothing beats discovering all the joys that the city has to offer to the little ones, so we thought we'd give you some inside tips on what there is!

- **Best Rainy Day Activity:** The Science Museum (Exhibition Road, SW7 2DD, 0870 870 4868) is great fun and one of London's most interactive museums. Don't miss the Launchpad gallery, which is full of hands-on exhibits to tinker with, simulators and a face morphing machine. The museum's occasional Science Nights are activity filled, with overnight camping in the building included. Entry is free. Open 7 days a week from 10am to 6pm.
- **Coolest Cinema:** The BFI London IMAX Cinema (1 Charlie Chaplin Walk, SE1 8XR, 020 7902 1234) has the largest screen (20 metres) in the country, as well as an 11,600-watt digital surround sound system with which to deafen your children. With most of the cinema's 3D programming dedicated to children's films, they'll be spoilt rotten by the whole experience; even the entrance to the place is cool, with futuristic blue lighting paving your way through the tunnels.
- **Goriest Tourist Haunt:** The London Dungeon (28-34 Tooley Street, SE1 2SZ, 020 7403 7221) specialises in the darker side of English history and has a preponderance of gruesome waxworks, theme rides and costumed staff to scare the bejesus out of your children, which they'll love (unless you've brought them up to be soft). Open all week from 11am to 5pm.
- **Best Tour For Budding Media Moguls:** The BBC Television Centre Tour (Wood Lane, W12 7RJ, 0870 603 0304) provides a chance for children 9 and over to take a behind the scenes look at the world of TV, as well as a chance to play in an interactive studio. A separate tour (ages 7 and over) entitled "The CBBC Experience" is based on the BBC's kids' channel and offers visitors the chance to roam around the Blue Peter garden, amongst other things. Regular tours are conducted every day except Sunday.

Best Ice Cream: It's no secret that kids love ice cream, but the plethora of dodgy "Mr Whippy" vans selling their frozen wares in London can be improved upon. For outstanding homemade gourmet sorbets and exotic ice cream cones, there is no better place than the kiosk to the side of Golders Hill Park Refreshment House (North End Road, NW3 7HD, 020 8455 8010); prices are very reasonable and the park is a gorgeous setting within which to consume such tasty delights.

- **Best Inner City Farm:** Hackney City Farm (1a Goldsmiths Row, E2 8QA, 020 7729 6381). You don't want your child to be the one hiding on the bus on their first fieldtrip because they've never seen a cow. Hackney City Farm gives children and adults alike the chance to experience farming first-hand, interact with the animals and understand sustainable living, all of this in the heart of Hackney.
- **Best For Halloween Costumes:** Escapade (45-46 Chalk Farm Road, NW1 8AJ, 020 7485 7384) has been kitting kids out in all manner of costumes since 1982, and offers wigs (maybe one for Dad?), hats, masks, make-up, jokes and magic tricks. Perfect for trick or treat, or for those already bored of their child's ugly face.
- **Best Eatery For Families:** Maxwell's (8-9 James Street, WC2E 8BH) lies deep in the heart of Covent Garden and specialises in burgers (does any child not like burgers?) which won't break parents' banks. A kids' menu is provided, as well as activities and games.

Rainy Day Activities

Especially for when the infamous London weather puts a dampener on outdoor activities…

- **Cartoon Museum** (35 Little Russell Street, WC1A 2HH, 020 7580 8155) This fascinating place archives the development of cartoon art in Britain, from the 18th century through to the present day; best of all, the Young Artists' Gallery lets children try their hands at animation and claymation.
- **London Aquarium** (County Hall, Westminster Bridge Road, SE1 7PB, 020 7967 8000) One of the largest aquariums in the world, over 400 species of aquatic life (including the only zebra sharks in the U.K.) can be found within this building. With three floors, piranhas, and pools where you can prod things, there's more than enough to keep even the most jaded parent happy.

- **London Eye** (Jubilee Gardens, South Bank, SE1 7PB, 0870 500 0600) This 135-metre high riverside Ferris wheel offers breathtaking views of London in up to 25 miles in each direction, all from the vantage point of an air-conditioned glass pod. Book online to beat the queues.
- **Natural History Museum** (Cromwell Road, SW7 5BD, 020 7942 5000) Ever wanted to see a replica skeleton of a 26-metre long Diplodocus dinosaur? It's one of the 70 million items housed within this excellent museum, which also includes the Darwin Centre, a must for any budding paleontologists; non-nerds should love it too.
- **Madame Tussaud's** (Marylebone Road, NW1 5LR, 0870 999 0046) Infamous exhibition of waxworks, with recently introduced interactive exhibits giving you the chance to score a goal for England or sing with Britney Spears (she'll be the one lip-syncing). Worth booking online to avoid the often long queues.
- **Museum Of London** (150 London Wall, EC2Y 5HN, 0870 444 3852, some galleries undergoing renovation and due to re-open late 2009) Explains the history of London in vivid detail; the innovative layout consists of a chain of chronological galleries (no skipping to 1945, OK?) Also has fragments of the old London Wall in the grounds.
- **Peter Harrison Planetarium** (Royal Observatory Greenwich, Greenwich Park, SE10 9NF, 020 8312 8565) Open since 2007 and the only planetarium in London seats 120 and uses the latest technology to take you on an armchair tour of the universe. Children aged 4 and under will not be admitted.
- **Queens Ice And Bowl** (17 Queensway, W2 4QP, 020 7229 0172) An ice rink, ten pin bowling alleys and a pizza restaurant, it's the perfect opportunity for kids to stuff their faces whilst watching their Dad break a bone on the rink. Children's skating classes available.
- **Topsy Turvy World** (Brent Cross Shopping Centre, Prince Charles Drive, NW4 3FP, 020 8359 9920) A huge indoor playground in the middle of one of London's busiest shopping centres. There's more to this place than just bouncy things and over-excitement, it also offers baking activities (might as well get your children cooking for you early) and various classes.
- **Tower Of London** (Tower Hill, EC3N 4AB, 0870 756 7070) A cornucopia of royal history and English culture lies within the Tower's ancient walls, with royal jewels aplenty. Good for the whole family, and under 5s get in free. Avoid the queues by booking ahead.
- **The V&A Museum Of Childhood** (Cambridge Heath Road, E2 9PA, 020 8983 5200) This lesser known gem of the Victoria & Albert Museum houses the national childhood collection, which basically means it's full of toys, games, dolls, dollhouses, nursery antiques and children's costumes. There's no shortage of activities and events going on here to keep your kids occupied, and it's free.

Classes

A recent resurgence in the amount of out of school programmes being implemented in the capital means that there's more for your kids to do than ever before.

- **Art Club** (Orleans House Gallery, Riverside, TW1 3DJ, 020 8831 6000) A rare opportunity for 5-10 year olds to work with practicing artists and explore new techniques and materials. Every Wednesday and Thursday from 3.45-5pm.
- **Barnsbury One O'Clock Club** (Barnard Park, Hemingford Road, N1 0JU, 020 7278 9494) Fun and games for the under 5s.
- **Brixton Recreation Centre** (27 Brixton Station Road, SW9 8QQ, 020 7926 9779) Recently refurbished, this centre includes The Energy Zone (ages 5-15) for ball games and The Fitness Zone (ages 8-15) with SHOKK fitness equipment specifically designed for the younger body builder/steroid abuser.
- **Camden Square Play Centre** (Camden Square, NW1 9RE, 020 7485 6827) After school (and school holiday) centre with fun activities for children aged 4-12.
- **Camden Swiss Cottage Swimming Club** (Swiss Cottage Leisure Centre, Winchester Road, NW3 3NR, 020 7974 5440) Swimming lessons for children aged 4 and upward.
- **Chang's Hapkido Academy** (Topnotch Health Club, 3 Tudor Street, EC4Y 0AH, 07951 535876) Martial arts school with classes for ages 12 and upward.

- **The Circus Space** (Coronet Street, N1 6HD, 020 7613 4141) Prepare your children for a life in the circus with The Circus Space's variety of classes and workshops for all ages.
- **Crazee Kids** (Jackson Lane Community Centre, Archway Road, N6 5AA, Tuesdays), (Union Church & Community Centre, Weston Park, N8 9TA, Saturdays) 020 8444 5333, Weekly term-time dance, drama and music classes. Summer workshops.
- **Harringay Club** (Hornsey YMCA, 50 Tottenham Lane, N8 7EE, 020 8348 2124) A range of things to do for those aged up to 15, including a pre-school programme, gymnastics, ballet, street dance and kickboxing.
- **The Kids' Cookery School (**107 Gunnersbury Len W3 8HQ, 020 8992 8882) Get your kids cooking at this fine venue which offers classes and workshops for those aged 3 and upwards.
- **Kite Art Studios** (Priory Mews, 2B Bassein Park Road, W12 9RY, 020 8576 6278) Courses and workshops on painting, pottery and jewellery making amongst other fun activities for kids of all ages. Mother and toddler sessions too.
- **London Irish Centre (**50-52 Camden Square, NW1 9XB, 020 7916 7222) Irish dancing classes for beginners upwards, every Monday at 6pm, courtesy of the Barrett Semple-Morris School.
- **The Little Angel Theatre (**14 Dagmar Passage, Cross Street, N1 2DN, 020 7226 1787) Children's theatre offering after-school courses in puppet making, the art of puppetry performance and a Saturday Puppet Club.
- **The Little Gym (**Compass House, Riverside West, Smugglers Way, SW18 1DB, 020 8874 6567) Gymnastics and skills development within a relaxed environment for children aged up to 12.
- **Music House For Children (**Bush Hall, 310 Uxbridge Road, W12 7LJ, 020 8932 2652) Whether it's instrumental or singing lessons, this wonderful place can provide individual and group tuition and even caters for 1 year olds!
- **Painted Earth** (Arch 65, The Catacombs, Stables Market, NW1 8AH, 020 7424 8983) Ceramic arts classes supervised by staff. Children can make their own mugs and plates.
- **Pirate Castle** (Oval Road, NW1 7EA, 020 7267 6605) Kids can canoe or Kayak around Camden's only castle at this outdoor adventure club, which moonlights as a school and youth services centre.
- **Richmond Junior Chess Club (**ETNA Community Centre, 13 Rosslyn Road, TW1 2AR, 07720 716336) Chess classes with a mixture of instruction and play for those up to the age of 18.
- **Sobell Leisure Centre** (Hornsey Road, N7 7NY, 020 7609 2166) No need to book, just turn up for coached sessions in basketball, badminton, football and ice hockey amongst other sports. Children aged 7 and under must be accompanied by an adult.
- **Tricycle Theatre** (269 Kilburn High Road, NW6 7JR, 020 7328 1000) Not just a theatre/ cinema/gallery, the Tricycle also runs term-time workshops in drama, storytelling and music.
- **Triyoga** (6 Erskine Road, NW3 3AJ, 020 7483 3344) Let the kids get their Zen on at after school yoga classes for ages 5 and over.
- **Westway Stables** (20 Stable Way, Latimer Road, W11 6QX, 020 8964 2140) Horse riding lessons for the over 5s in the heart of Notting Hill.

Babysitting/Nanny/Services

- **Nannies Unlimited** 11 Chelveton Road, SW15 1RN, 020 8788 9640
- **Nanny Search** 1st Floor, 1 Shepherds Hill, N6 5QJ, 020 8348 4111
- **Sleeptight Nannies** 20 Nursery Road, N14 5QB, 020 8292 2618
- **Top Notch Nannies** 49 Harrington Gardens, SW7 4JU, 020 7259 2626

Where to Go for More Info

www.dayoutwiththekids.co.uk

Shopping Essentials

- **Baby Dior** 6 Harriet Street, SW1X 9JW, 020 7823 2039 – Encourage label envy as soon as possible.
- **Baby Munchkins** 186 Hoxton Street, N1 5LH, 020 7684 5994 – Baby wear.
- **Balloonland** 12 Hale Lane, NW7 3NX, 020 8906 3302 – Balloons and party supplies.
- **Benjamin Pollock's Toyshop** 44 The Piazza, Covent Garden WC2E 8RF, 020 7379 7866 – Toys.
- **Biff** 43 Dulwich Village, SE21 7BN, 020 8299 0911 – Designer and street brands.

- **Boomerang** 69 Blythe Road, W14 0HP, 020 7610 5232 – Clothes and necessities for tots.
- **Bonpoint** Chic clothes.
  17 Victoria Grove, W8 5RW – 020 7584 5131
  197 Westbourne Grove, W11 2SE – 020 7792 2515
  256 Brompton Road, SW3 2AS – 020 3263 5057
  35B Sloane Street, SW1X 9LP – 020 7235 1441
  38 Old Bond Street, W1S 4QW – 020 7495 1680
- **Burberry** 21-23 New Bond Street, W1S 2RE, 020 7839 5222 – Clothes.
- **Caramel** 291 Brompton Road, SW3 2DY, 020 7589 7001 – Cool clothes.
- **Catamini** – Babies and children's clothes. 33C King's Road, SW3 4LX – 020 7824 8897, 52 South Molton Street, W1Y 1HF – 020 7629 8099
- **Cheeky Monkeys** – Mainly wooden toys. 202 Kensington Park Road, W11 1NR – 020 7792 9022, 94 Kings Road, SW6 4UL – 020 7731 3037
- **Children's Book Centre** 237 Kensington High Street, W8 6SA, 020 7937 7497 – Books.
- **D2 Leisure** 201-203 Roman Road, E2 0QY, 020 8980 4966 – Bicycle shop.
- **Daisy & Tom** 181 King's Road, SW3 5EB, 020 7352 5000 – Clothes, toys and a carousel.
- **Davenports Magic Shop** 7 Adelaide Street, WC2N 4HZ, 020 7836 0408 – Magic shop.
- **Early Learning Centre** 36 King's Road, SW3 4UD, 020 7581 5764 – Educational toyshop.
- **Disney Store** – Disney merchandise.
  Unit 10, The Piazza, WC2E 8HD – 020 7836 5037
  22A & 26 The Broadway Shopping Centre, W6 9YD – 020 8748 8886
  360-366 Oxford Street, W1N 9HA – 020 7491 9136
- **Eric Snook's Toyshop** 32 Covent Garden Market, WC1 8RE, 020 7379 7681 – Toys and teddies.
- **The Farmyard** 63 Barnes High Street, SW13 9LF, 020 8878 7338 – Toys for younger children and babies.
- **GapKids/Baby Gap**
  35 Hampstead High Street, NW3 1QE – 020 7794 9182
  146-148 Regent Street, W1B 5SH – 020 7287 5095
  Brent Cross Shopping Centre, NW4 3FB – 020 8203 9696
  122 King's Road, SW3 4TR – 020 7823 7272
  4 Queens Road, SW19 8YE- 020 8947 9074
  101-111 Kensington High Street, W8 5SA – 020 7368 2900
  260-262 Chiswick High Road, W4 1PD – 020 8995 3255
  47-49 St John's Wood High Street, NW8 7NJ – 020 7586 6123
  151 Queensway, W2 4YL – 020 7221 8039
  330-340 Cabot Place East, E14 4QT – 020 7513 0241
  121-123 Long Acre, WC2E 9PA – 020 7836 0646
- **Green Rabbit** 20 Briston Grove, N8 9EX, 020 8348 3770 – Contemporary kids' wear.
- **Hamley's** 188-196 Regent Street, W1B 5BT, 020 7153 9000 – Toys galore, tourists galore.
- **Happy Returns** 36 Rosslyn Hill, NW3 1NH, 020 7435 2431 – Toys again!
- **Honeyjam** 267 Portobello Road, W11 1LR, 020 7243 0449 – Retro and vintage toys and rocking horses.
- **Igloo Kids** Wide range of kids' clothes. 300 Upper Street, N1 2TU – 020 7354 7300, 80 St John's Wood, NW8 7SH – 020 7483 2332
- **International Magic** 89 Clerkenwell Road, EC1R 5BX, 020 7405 7324 – Magic shop.
- **Joujou & Lucy** 32 Clifton Road, W9 1ST, 020 7289 0866 – Children's boutique.
- **Kent & Carey** 154 Wandsworth Bridge Road, SW6 2UH, 020 7736 5554 – Classic children's clothes.
- **Little Stinkies** 15 Victoria Grove, W8 5RW, 020 7052 0077 – Dolls' houses, toys and puppet theatres.
- **MIMMO** 602 Fulham Road, SW6 5PA, 020 7731 4706 – Designer duds.

- **Mothercare** – The leading chain for baby stuff in the UK; will sell you everything but the baby.

  Brent Cross Shopping Centre, NW4 3FD – 020 8202 5377

  416 Brixton Road, SW9 7AY – 020 7733 1494

  Unit 7, The Waterglade Centre, 1-8 The Broadway, W5 2ND – 0208 579 6181

  Ravenside Retail Park, Angel Road, N18 3HA – 020 8807 5518

  146 High Street, SE9 1BJ – 020 8859 7957

  4 Palace Gardens, EN2 6SN – 020 8367 1188

  316 North End Road, SW6 1NG – 020 7381 6387

  Kings Mall Shopping Centre, W6 0PZ – 020 8600 2860

  448 Holloway Road, N7 6QA – 020 7607 0915

  112 High Street, TW3 1NA – 020 8577 1767

  Unit 1A, Richmond Retail Park, Mortlake Road, Kew – 020 8878 3758

  41 Riverdale High Street, SE13 7EP – 020 8852 2167

  526-528 Oxford Street, W1C 1LW – 0845 365 0515

  Unit 2, Aylesham Centre, Rye Lane, SE15 5EW – 020 7358 0093

  33-34 The Mall, E15 1XD – 020 8534 5714

  BHS Surrey Quays Shopping Centre, Redriff Road, SE16 7LL – 020 7237 2025

  Unit 59, Southside Shopping Centre, SW18 4TF – 020 8877 4180

  Unit Lsu4, Centre Court, SW19 8YA – 020 8944 5296

  38-40 High Road, N22 6BX – 020 8888 6920

  62 Powis Street, SE18 1LQ – 020 8854 3540

- **Never Never Land** 3 Mildhurst Parade, Fortis Green, N10 3EJ, 020 883 3997 – Toys and dolls.

- **Olive Loves Alfie** 84 Stoke Newington Church Street, N16 0AP, 020 7241 4212 – Children's lifestyle boutique.

- **Patrick's Toys & Models** 107 Lillie Road, SW6 7SX, 020 7385 9864 – Outdoor games and equipment.

- **Patrizia Wigan** 19 Walton Street, SW3 2HX, 020 7823 7080 – Clothing boutique.

- **Petit Bateau** 62 South Molton Street, W1K 5SR, 020 7491 4498 – Luxurious baby wear.

- **Petite Ange** 6 Harriet Street, SW1X 9JW, 020 7235 7737 – Exclusive clothing.

- **Please Mum** 85 Knightsbridge, SW1X 7RB, 020 7486 1380 – Expensive clothing.

- **Pom D'Api** 3 Blenheim Crescent, W11 2EE, 020 7243 0535 – Classy shoes.

- **QT Toys** 90 Northcote Road, SW11 6QN, 020 7223 8637 – Toys, games and gifts.

- **Rachel Riley** 14 Pont Street, SW1X 9EN, 020 7935 7007 – Clothes.

- **Showroom** 64 Titchfield Street, W1W 7QH, 020 7636 2501 – Funky children's clothes.

- **Soup Dragon** 27 Topsfield Parade, Tottenham Lane, N8 8PT, 020 8348 0224 – Toys and clothes.

- **The Shoe Station** 3 Station Approach, Kew Gardens, TW9 3QB, 020 8940 9905 – Shoes and footwear.

- **Their Nibs** 214 Kensington Park Road, W11 1NR, 020 7221 4263 – Designer clothes and bedding.

- **Tots** 39 Turnham Green Terrace, W4 1RG, 020 8995 0520 – Clothes boutique.

- **Toys R Us** - Toys, toys, toys.

  Tilling Road (opposite Brent Cross Shopping Centre), NW2 1LW – 020 8209 0019

  Great Cambridge Road, EN1 3RN – 020 8364 6600

  Hayes Road, UB2 5LN – 020 8561 4681

  760 Old Kent Road, SE15 1NJ – 020 7732 7322

- **Traditional Toys** Chelsea Green, 53 Godfrey Street, SW3 3SX, 020 7352 1718 – Timeless toys.

- **The Little White Company** 261 Pavillion Road, SW1X 0BP, 020 7881 0783 – Clothing, bed linen and furniture.

For many, the Internet is *the* key to the city. Before the dawning of the Internet, we Dickensian scamps had to scurry around in the filth foraging for information in 'books' and by talking to actual 'people'. Now that the future is here, Londoners can navigate their city's streets, explore its dark history, organise a debauched weekend in Chiswick or, as is more likely, peer over the shoulder of men in raincoats in Internet Cafes.

Internet Cafes are everywhere. In fact you probably live in one. They can range from the dimly lit 'Money Transfer' shacks that have an air of illegality, to chains that dominated the market before home internet use skyrocketed in the late 90s. To be fair, internet use in these places is usually criminally cheap: as low as 50p per hour in the non-tourist areas. For a large list of London internet cafes check out: www.allinlondon.co.uk/directory/1166.php.

London was one crowned WiFi capital of the world, owing to its astronomical rate of increase in WiFi networks in 2007. Today, it is difficult to move in your local cafe without catching the edge of a laptop. An alternative to those of you who have joined the growing legion of smartphone users and don't want the commitment of a long-term contract try **Gifgaff** (www.giffgaff.com). For £10 you can get 250 minutes, unlimited texts and unlimited data for a month with no additional cost incurred. They offer a best in business rate for the Internet addicts among you.

Useful and/or Fun London Links

www.fedbybirds.com
www.royalparks.org.uk
www.tfl.gov.uk
www.londonist.com
www.londonfreelist.com
www.davehill.typepad.com
www.shadyoldlady.com
www.derelictlondon.com
www.walk-london.blogspot.com
www.hiddenlondon.com
www.londonbloggers.iamcal.com
www.london-underground.blogspot.com
www.fancyapint.com
www.dailycandy.com/london
www.gumtree.com
www.timeout.com
www.brickads.blogspot.com
www. wildinlondon.blogspot.com
www. westlondonblogger.blogspot.com
www. dalstonoxfamshop.blogspot.com
www.viewlondon.co.uk
www.lecool.com/cities/london
www.deadcafesociety.org.uk
www.londonreviewofbreakfasts.blogspot.com
www.beerintheevening.com
www.london-se1.co.uk
www.talkonthetube.com
www.london.thewayweseeit.org
londoncabby.blogspot.com

The doom-sayers have less cause to complain about the decline of Gayhood in London recently, what with **Heaven** (London's self-proclaimed most famous gay club) hanging on and new nights popping up everywhere. Yes, popular indie discos **Popstarz** and **Rebel Rebel** have relocated but **Girl's Action** at Ghetto promises great things and we are so in love with 'polysexual' club **Dalston Supermarket** at the moment. Of course every time one door (read: gay club) closes another one opens, and let's face it, the latter will probably open later and sell you even cheaper Red Bull and vodka.

One of the most exciting developments in the past few years has been the advent of what has been dubbed London's new 'Gay Village'—the cluster of clubs, saunas and after-hours hangover incubators that have sprung up in Vauxhall. Now it's possible, though still just as inadvisable, to party from Thursday through to Tuesday without stopping to reapply deodorant, or think about the consequences of what you're doing—hooray. The small outcrop of gay and 'polysexual' nights in the East End, is still thriving, and offers another refreshing alternative to Soho for those in search of an aggressive fashion consciousness and a less cruisy atmosphere. This said, if you can handle bright lights, pop music, tight t-shirts and a lot of hair gel, you'll still have massive amounts of fun around Soho and Old Compton Street, the traditional central London gay epicentre. This area is always buzzing, day and night, and is a great place to sit back and do some people watching as well as to go out and, y'know, go crazy.

For girls there is still room for improvement, with options fewer and less centralised, but **The Minories'** new Girls' night is a blast and the continuing women-only nights at **Village** and **Element** are cause for celebration. Many mixed and polysexual nights (such as Motherfucker at **Barden's Boudoir**) also draw large female crowds, and though dedicated lesbian bars and clubs are few and far between, there is enough going on in the city to make any day of the week a possible night out.

Websites

www.dirtydirtydancing.com - Super-airbrushed photos from many of the trendier Soho and east London nights.
http://scene-out.com - Comprehensive mainstream scene guide.
www.gingerbeer.co.uk - Lesbian guide to London.
www.girlguidelondon.co.uk - Does what it says on the tin.
www.gmfa.org.uk - Gay men's health charity.
www.patroc.com/london/clubs.html-Great source for upcoming gay events.
www.pinkdate.com - Speed dating events for gay men and women in central London.

Publications

The following are all free listings/scene magazines that can be found in most gay shops and venues (anywhere on Old Compton Street should have some copies lying around):

Boyz Magazine - Weekly scene news and listings, out Thursdays. www.boyz.co.uk

G3 Magazine - Lesbian scene, monthly. www.g3mag.co.uk

Out in the City Mag - Monthly London lifestyle magazine for gay men. www.outmag.co.uk

Qx Magazine - Gay men's mag. www.qxmagazine.com

Shops

Gay's the Word, 66 Marchmont Street, WC1N 1AB, 020 7278 7654, http://freespace.virgin.net/gays.theword/, The only dedicated Gay and Lesbian Bookshop in London, recently threatened by rising rent. Visit whilst it's still there!

Prowler, 5–7 Brewer Street, W1F 0RF, 020 7734 4031, The ultimate gay men's shop, stocking everything from (skimpy) clothes to sex toys plus mountains of lube, pornography, and the other usual suspects.

Sh! Women's Erotic Emporium, 57 Hoxton Square N1 6PD, 020 7697 9072, http://www.sh-womenstore.com/, London's only female-orientated sex shop, run by women, for women.

Sexual Health

A comprehensive list of London clinics that offer same day HIV testing and PEP treatments for gay/bisexual men is available at www.gmfa.org.uk/londonservices/clinics. CLASH, below, is particularly recommended.

CLASH (Central London Action on Street Health), 11 Warwick Street, W1B 5NA, 020 7734 1794, Friday night clinic for gay men, with incredibly friendly staff who will offer comfort and advice. Same day (often instant) HIV testing, PEP treatment. Fridays, 5 - 8.30pm, call for an appointment.

Support Organizations

Again, a more comprehensive list can be found at the GMFA website: www.gmfa.org.uk/londonservices/support-groups/index

Stonewall, Tower Building, York Road, SE1 7NX, www.stonewall.org.uk, Gay rights charity and lobbying group.

PACE Youthwork Service, 34 Hartham Road, N7 9LJ, 020 7700 1323, www.outzone.org, Support organization for gay and lesbian youths under 25. Organizes regular social events and offers one to one consultations with advisors: phone or visit the website to get involved.

London Friend, 86 Caledonian Road, N1 9DN, 020 7833 1674, www.londonfriend.org.uk, Voluntary organization which runs several helplines, group workshops and social events, as well as offering advice on reporting hate crime.

London Lesbian and Gay Switchboard, 0300 330 0630, www.llgs.org.uk, Counselling and information service.

Kairos in Soho, Unit 10, 10-11 Archer Street, W1D 7AZ, 020 7437 6063, www.kairosinsoho.org.uk, Gay and lesbian charity which organises a variety of recreational events to promote the health, well being and development of the LGBT community.

Naz Project London, Palingswick House, 241 King Street, W6 9LP, 020 8741 1879 www.naz.org.uk, Charity that organizes support and sexual health services for black and ethnic minority communities in London. Various services, including free one-on-one counselling and support groups are available, phone or check website for details.

GALOP, PO Box 32810, N1 3ZD, 020 7704 6767, www.galop.org.uk, Charity specialising in advice about reporting hate crime.

Annual Events

Pride London, www.pridelondon.org, Large pride festival, takes place every July.

GFEST – www.gaywisefestival.org.uk, London's premier cross-arts festival, GFEST features a variety of established and new LBG&T artists. The festival promotes the queer arts scene while keeping LBGT human rights the underlying focus of proceedings.

London Lesbian and Gay Film Festival, www.bfi.org.uk/llgff, Film festival at the BFI on South Bank, March–April.

London LGBT History Month, www.lgbthistorymonth.co.uk, Nationwide awareness month, with various talks and events staged in London, every February.

Gay/Mixed Venues

Soho:

The Admiral Duncan, 54 Old Compton Street, W1D 4UB, 020 7437 5300

Barcode Soho, 3-4 Archer Street W1D 7AT, 020 7734 3342

Comptons, 53–57 Old Compton Street, W1D 6HN, 020 7479 7961, Crammed gay pub.

Duke of Wellington, 77 Wardour Street, W1D 6QA

G-A-Y Bar, 30 Old Compton Street, W1D 5JX, 020 7494 2756, Poptastic bunker. Video walls and cheap drinks.

G-A-Y Late, 5 Goslett Yard, WC2H 0ER, 020 7734 9858, Cheap drinks and pop videos wipe out brain functions 'til 3am.

Ghetto, Falconberg Court, W1D 3AB, 020 7287 3726, Loud electro at this busy gay club. Thursday is ladies night.

Halfway to Heaven, 7 Duncannon Street, WC2N 4JF, 020 7321 2791.

Heaven, Under the Arches, Villiers Street, WC2N 6NG, 020 7930 2020, Legendary gay club. An institution.

Ku Bar, 30 Lisle Street, WC2H 7BA, 020 7437 4303, Newly relocated bar for the young and clueless.

Profile, 56–57 Frith Street, W1D 3JG, 020 7734 8300

Soho Revue Bar, 11 Walkers Court, Brewer Street, W1F 0ED, Cabaret acts followed by dancing 'til late.

The Village, 81 Wardour Street, W1D 6QD, 020 7434 2124, Tacky, flirtatious bar spread across two floors.

North:

Cosmo Lounge, 43 Essex Road, N1 2SF, 020 7688 0051, Subdued bar, normally full of regulars.

Central Station, 37 Wharfdale Road, N1 9SD, 020 7278 3294. Pub/club with ominously blacked out windows.

The Green, 74 Upper Street N1 0NY, 0871 971 4097, Innocuous gay bar/restaurant frequented by many unsuspecting straight couples.

King Edward VI Pub, 25 Bromfield Street, N1 0PZ

The Black Cap, 171 Camden High Street, NW1 7JY, 020 7428 2721, Slightly crummy gay pub.

East:

Bistrotheque, 23–27 Wadeson Street, E2 9DR, Jonny Woo's restaurant, great food and drag acts.

The Black Horse, 168 Mile End Road, E1 4LJ, 020 7790 1684

Joiners Arms, 116–118, Hackney Road, E2 7Q, Late opening free-for-all with a wonderfully mixed crowd. ('til 2/3am most nights)

South:

The Two Brewers, 114 Clapham High Street, SW4 7UJ, 020 7498 4971

Depot, 66 Albert Embankment, SE11 7TP, Sister club of Area, with a more cruisy vibe.

Fire, South Lambeth Road, SW8 1RT, 020 7434 1113, The quintessential Vauxhall club. Open pretty much forever, bulging muscles everywhere.

The Fort, 131 Grange Road, Bermondsey, SE1 3AL - Themed cruising/fetish/sex bar.

Kazbar Clapham, 50 Clapham High Street, SW4 7UL, 020 7622 0070

Little Apple Bar, 98 Kennington Lane, SE11 4XD Mixed/lesbian bar.

Royal Vauxhall Tavern, 372 Kennington Lane, SE11 5HY, 020 7820 1222

South Central, 349 Kennington Lane, SE11 5QY, 020 7793 0903

Substation South, 9 Brighton Terrace, SW9 8DJ, 020 7737 2095

XXL, 51–53 Southwark Street, SE1 1TE, www.fatsandsmalls.com, Busy bear club.

West:

Bromptons, 294 Old Brompton Road, SW5 9JF, 020 77370 1344

The Coleherne, 261 Old Brompton Road, SW5 9JA020 7244 5951

Recommended Nights

Club Motherfucker, second Saturdays @ Barden's Boudoir, 38 Stoke Newington Road, Dalston, N16 7XJ, Polysexual band night. Sweaty, noisy, very much about the music.

Circus, Fridays @ Soho Revue Bar, 11 Walkers Court, Brewer Street, W1F 0ED, Drag Queen Jodie Harsh's long running night attracts its fair share of celebrities from both on and off the scene. Get there early or be prepared to queue.

DTPM, www.myspace.com/dtpm, Legendary event, no longer with a fixed location. See site for details of upcoming parties.

For3ign, Saturdays @ Bar Music Hall, 134 Curtain Road, EC2A 3AR, 020 7613 5951, Outlandish costumes and, of course, thumping electro.

Horsemeat Disco, Sundays @ South Central, Italo and 70s Disco bring all sorts to this fantastic night, originally a bear love club.

Icon, Sundays @ Essence, 562a Mile End Road, E3 4PH, 0208 980 6427, mob 07843 440 443 (weekly), New night in the East End. Yet to prove itself.

Matinee, monthly (check site) @ Fabric, 77a Charterhouse Street, EC1M 3HN, 020 7335 8898, www.matineelondon.com, Irregular gay night at this enormous club in Farringdon.

Popstarz, Fridays @ Sin, 144 Charing Cross Road, WC2H 0LB, 020 7240 1900, Gay indie institution, recently relocated.

Trailer Trash, Fridays @ On the Rocks, 25 Kingsland Road, E2 8AA, 020 7688 0339, The dirtiest electro and the drunkest you've ever been. Crammed with sweating fashionistas.

Wet Yourself, Sundays @ Aquarium, 256–264 Old Street, EC1V 9DD, 020 7251 6136, This used to be the place to be after Boombox. It's lost only a little of its charm since (mixed polysexual crowd).

Lesbian Venues

Blush Bar, 8 Cazenove Road, Stoke Newington N16, 020 7923 9202, www.blushbar.co.uk

First Out Café Bar, Soho - 52 St Giles High St, WC2H 8LH, 020 7240 8042, Cafe with nightly events. All girls on Friday.

Oak Bar, 79 Green Lanes, N16, www.oakbar.co.uk, 020 7354 2791,

The Star At Night, 22 Great Chapel Street, Soho, W1 8FR, 020 7434 3749, Mixed cocktail bar with a predominantly female crowd.

Recommended Nights

100% Babe, Bank Holiday Sundays @ The Roxy, 3 Rathbone Place, W1P 1DA, 020 7636 1598, Irregular party for fans of funky house, R&B, old skool and electropop.

Blue Light, last Saturdays @ Bar Med, Triton Court, 14 Finsbury Square, EC2, 020 7588 3056

Club Wotever, first Saturday of the month @ The Masters Club, 12 Denman Street, Piccadilly, W1D 7HH, 020 7734 4243, Draggy night with a large 'King' quota.

Code, irregular night @ the Enclave, 25–27 Brewer Street, W1F 0RR, www.club-code.net - check website for details.

Girls on Girls, Wednesdays @ Village, 81 Wardour Street, W1D 6QD, 020 7434 2124

Lounge, second Thursdays @ Vertigo, 1 Leicester Square, WC2H 7NA, 020 7734 0900, Relaxed cocktail night at this swish Leicester Square club.

Miss Shapes, Thursdays @ Ghetto, Falconberg Court, W1D 3AB, 020 7287 3726, Popular girls-only indie night.

Pink, Wednesdays @ Element, 4-5 Greek Street, W1D 4DD, 020 7434 3323.

Play, irregular night @ Bar Rumba, 35 Shaftesbury Ave, W1D 7EP, 020 7287 2715, www.myspace.com/_clubplay

Rumours, last Saturday of the month @ 64–73 Minories, EC3, 07949 477 804

Smack, irregular night @ various venues, check website, www.myspace.com/smackclub

Wish, first Saturdays @ Gramophone, 60–62 Commercial Street, E1 6LT, Style conscious night for young techno-heads and indie girls.

Women's Anarchist Nuisance Cafe, Penultimate wednesdays @ the RampART Creative Centre and Social Space, Rampart St, Aldgate, E1 2LA, Social group and cooperative vegan women's cafe.

Stickier Options

Club Fukk, second Fridays @ Central Station, 37 Wharfdale Road, N1 9SD, 020 7278 3294, www.centralstation.co.uk or www.woteverworld.com/id12.html, Predominantly Lesbian fetish/play club. One of many sex/cruising nights at the venue – check site for details.

Chariots, www.gaysauna.co.uk, Popular chain of gay saunas, with branches at the following locations: *Shoreditch*: 1 Fairchild Street, EC2A 3NS, *Waterloo*: 101 Lower Marsh, SE1 7AB, 020 7401 8484, *Limehouse*: 574 Commercial Road, E14 7JD, 020 7791 2808, *Streatham*: 292 [rear of] Streatham High Road, SW16 6HG, 020 8696 0929, *Farringdon*: 57 Cowcross Street, EC1M 6BX, 020 7251 5553, *Vauxhall*: 63-64 Albert Embankment, SE1, 020 7247 5333

The Fort,131 Grange Road, Bermondsey, SE1 3AL , Themed cruising/fetish/sex bar.

Hard On, monthly @ Hidden, 100 Tinworth Street, SE11 5EQ, www.hardonclub.co.uk, Rubber and fetish sex club for gay and bisexual men and women.

Nudity, first Fridays @ Hidden, 100 Tinworth Street, SE11 5EQ, Nude men's dance/play club.

London Timeline

A timeline of significant events in London's history.

50: The Romans found Londinium, building the first London Bridge.

61: Queen Boudicca burns Londinium down.

100: Londinium becomes the capital of Roman Britain.

200: The Romans build the London Wall.

410: Roman occupation ends and Londinium is largely abandoned for many years.

604: King Aethelbert of Kent completes the first St Paul's Cathedral.

700: The Saxons build Lundenwic a mile to the west of old Londinium.

851: The Vikings burn Lundenwic down (starting to see a pattern, here?)

878: Alfred The Great defeats the Vikings and establishes a new settlement within the Roman Walls.

1013: The Viking King Canute besieges London.

1066: William The Conqueror becomes the first king to be crowned at Westminster Abbey.

1088: William The Conqueror builds the Tower Of London.

1097: William Rufus builds Westminster Hall—later part of the Houses Of Parliament.

1176: The wooden London Bridge is replaced by a stone structure.

1343: 'The Canterbury Tales' author Geoffrey Chaucer is born in London.

1348: The Black Death wipes out between a third and half of London's population in 18 months.

1381: Peasants revolt, storming the Tower Of London.

1599: William Shakespeare's theatre company The Chamberlain's Men build the Globe Theatre.

1605: Guy Fawkes' Gunpowder Plot fails to blow up the Palace Of Westminster.

1635: Hyde Park opens to the public.

1649: King Charles I is beheaded at Whitehall.

1665: The Great Plague kills a fifth of London's population (starting to see another pattern, here?)

1666: The Fire of London destroys 60% of the city, including St Paul's Cathedral, but wipes out the plague. This really must have been a great year.

1708: The new St Paul's Cathedral is completed by Sir Christopher Wren.

1732: Downing Street becomes the home of the Prime Minister.

1750: Westminster Bridge is built.

1814: Lord's Cricket Ground is opened.

1829: Robert Peel establishes the Metropolitan Police force, policemen known as 'Bobbies' or 'Peelers'.

1831: London becomes the world's biggest city.

1834: The Houses Of Parliament are built.

1843: Nelson's Column is completed in Trafalgar Square.

1851: Six million people gawp at newfangled technology and design at The Great Exhibition.

1858: The Great Stink inspires the 19th century's biggest civil engineering project—London's sewerage system.

London Timeline

1863: The first London Underground line is built.

1876: The Albert Memorial to Queen Victoria's husband Prince Albert is completed.

1877: The first Wimbledon Championship takes place. A Brit wins, but only Brit's are playing.

1884: An imaginary line through Greenwich Royal Observatory is internationally accepted as the Prime Meridian. Except by the French.

1887: Arthur Conan Doyle publishes the first Sherlock Holmes story 'A Study In Scarlet.'

1888: Jack The Ripper's first victim, Mary Ann Nichols, is murdered.

1908: London hosts the Olympics for the first time.

1915: German Zeppelin airships launch first air raids on London, ultimately killing over 700 people.

1923: Wembley Stadium is built in 300 days, costing £750,000.

1940: The Blitz begins—German bombs kill over 30,000 Londoners by the end of WW2 and destroy large areas of the city.

1946: Heathrow Airport opens for commercial flights.

1948: The second London Olympics is held.

1951: The Royal Festival Hall is built as part of the Festival Of Britain.

1952: The Great Smog, caused by a combination of fog and coal smoke, kills 4000 people in five days.

1956: The Clean Air Act puts an end to London's smog problems.

1965: The Notting Hill Carnival is established by West London's Caribbean community

1966: England win the FIFA World Cup at Wembley stadium, better still, against Germany.

1969: The Beatles play their last ever gig on the roof of the Apple building.

1976: The Sex Pistols play at the first 'International Punk Festival' at the 100 Club on Oxford Street.

1981: The first London Marathon.

1983: Six people are killed when the IRA bombs Harrods.

1991: London's tallest building, One Canada Square (better known as Canary Wharf), is completed.

2000: Ken Livingstone becomes London's first directly-elected Mayor.

2005: 52 people are killed by four suicide bombers on Underground trains and a bus.

2007: The rebuilt Wembley Stadium is completed after four years, costing £778 million.

2008: Boris Johnson defeats Red Ken in the London Mayoral Election with a promise to re-instate the Routemaster.

2011: Royal Wedding mania.

2012: London's third Olympics held; Danny Boyle adapts NHS as West End spectacular.

2012: Queen Elizabeth II celebrates her Diamond Jubilee with a rainy-day boat show.

2013: Prince George of Cambridge born.

ondon is an egotist—it just *loves* to talk about self. As you might expect, there's a vast array f print and online publications, not to mention adio stations, designed to let the city do exactly hat. Single-handedly forcing the environmental novement back twenty years are freebie dailies he **Metro** and the more fiscally orientated **City .M.** Free weeklies to look out for include **Stylist** n Wednesday's for girls, **ShortList** on Thursday's r boys and **Sport** on Friday's for, well, sports nthusiast. The Aussies are pushing **TNT** at tube tations on Monday, but it lacks the wider appeal. newer addition to the freesheet line-up is he substantial **Evening Standard**, which went ee in January 2009, and is the preferred news-oundup du jour of suburbanites and city types like, if only for the sudoku and quick crossword uzzles. Online, **www.thisislocallondon.co.uk** ondenses forty local newspapers into 'one online oice'. On the wireless, **Capital Radio** broadcasts n irksome parade of popular hits and frenetic Js, whilst **Heart** and **Magic** corner the market on p-trembling power ballads, mid-paced chart rock nd wacky quizzes. All of the British Broadcasting Corporation's national radio stations—including he snazzy, young(ish) **Radio 1** and ovaltine-rinkers' choice **Radio 2**—are based in London, s is (surprisingly) **BBC London**, a decent option or weekend sports coverage. Cooler, urban types re more likely to be tuning into **Kiss FM** (dance, ip hop), **Smooth FM** (jazz, soul) or **Choice** dancehall, roots), while alternative rockers tune heir dials anguishedly to **XFM**, and the talkative ndulge in unreserved subjectivity over at **LBC.** Of ourse, the undisputed king of alternative London roadcasting is Resonance FM, a 'community un' station. Expect everything from 'Calling All ensioners' to live psycho-geographic wanders round city's warped dark streets. Un-licensed nd illegal pirate radio stations offer a slightly un-inged ear into the fringes of London's musical ociety. Twiddle your dials around the extreme nds of the FM spectrum for pirate stalwarts **Rude M** and **Kool FM**. On the telly-box, the latest news s spoon-fed to you on ITV's **London Tonight** how and delivered in short slots at the end of the BC and ITV national news programs. For those ctually risking going outside, **Time Out** remains he socialite's sacred text.

Print

The Evening Standard Northcliffe House, 2 Derry Street, W8 5TT, 020 7938 6000, Newly reinstated as a freesheet, it continues to be London's favourite journey home read.

Metro Northcliffe House, 2 Derry Street, W8 5TT, 020 7651 5200, Free underground daily from same stable.

City AM New London Bridge House, 25 London Bridge St, SE1 9SG, 020 7015 1200, Free morning business bulletin for city-goers.

Sport Third Floor, Courtyard Building, 11 Curtain Road, EC2A 3LT, 0207 375 3175 Free sports overview every Friday.

TimeOut London 251-255 Tottenham Court Road, Universal House, W1T 7AB, 0207 813 3000, Listings & reviews across the city. Pretty damned comprehensive.

Literary Review 44 Lexington Street, W1 0LW, 020 7437 9392, Fortnightly publication for the bookish.

London Gazette PO Box 7923, SE1 5ZH, 020 7394 4517, Capital's oldest paper—official journals record of the government.

The London Magazine 32 Addison Grove, W4 1ER, 020 8400 5882, Bi-monthly Arts reviews.

TNT London 14-15 Childs Place, Earls Court, SW5 9RX, 020 7373 3377, Info and opinion for the antipodean set.

Loot 31 John Street, WC1N 2AT, 0871 222 5000, Classifieds: flats, bought/sold and lonely hearts.

The Voice GV Media Group Ltd, Northern & Shell Tower, 6th Floor, 4 Selsdon Way, E14 9GL, 020 7510 0340, African-British national.

Polish Express 603 Cumberland House, 80 Scrubs Lane, NW10 6RF, 020 8964 4488 , News and info for the Polish community.

Live Listings Magazine Keith Villa (House), 102 Mallinson Rd, SW11 1BN, 020 7207 2734 Guide to what's on in multicultural London.

ShortList 6 Emerald Street, London, WC1N 3QA, 020 7242 5873, A Thursday freebie for metrosexuals.

Sport 18 Hatfields, London SE1 8DJ, 020 7959 7800, A free Friday magazine dedicated to, you guessed it, sports.

Stylist 6 Emerald Street, London, WC1N 3QA, 020 7242 5873, London's first free women's glossy. Handed out on Wednesdays.

Public Radio

FM

89.1 BBC Radio Two: Middle-aged music and chat.
91.3 BBC Radio Three: Classical.
93.5 BBC Radio Four: Current affairs, comfort listening.
94.9 BBC London: Chat, sport.
95.8 Capital FM: Chart, capers.
96.9 Choice FM: Hip Hop, R&B.
97.3 LBC: Phone in, chat.
98.8 BBC Radio 1: Pop, rock, more pop.
100.0 Kiss FM: Dance, urban.
100.9 Classic FM: Classical.
102.2 Smooth FM: Jazz, soul.
102.6 Essex FM: Audible in East London.
103.3 London Greek Radio: Um, Greek.
103.5 BBC Essex: Audible out East.
104.4 Resonance FM: Always bizzare, always brilliant.
104.9 Xfm: Alternative, rock.
105.4 Magic: Pop, slush.
105.8 Virgin Radio: Pop, rock.
106.2 Heart: Chart, pop.
106.6 Time: West London only.
107.3 Time: South East London only.

AM

252 Atlantic: Rock.
558 Spectrum International: Multi-ethnic.
648 BBC World Service: Global.
720 BBC Radio Four: Spoken word.
909 BBC Radio Five Live: Sport, phone in.
963 Liberty Radio: 70s, 80s pop.
1035 Ritz: Country.
1089 talkSPORT: Sports phone in.
1152 LBC News: News, weather.
1215 Virgin Radio: Pop, rock.
1305 Premier Radio: Christian.
1458 Sunrise: Asian.
1548 Capital Gold: Rock 'gold', sport.
1584 London Turkish Radio: Turkish community.

Essential London Books

The Diary of Samuel Pepys (1825): Samuel Pepys: eyewitness accounts of the Restoration, Great Plague and Fire of London from noted sixteenth century scribbler.

Oliver Twist; Hard Times; Great Expectations (1837, 1854, 1860): Charles Dickens: any Dickens novel paints Victorian London at its most exacting.

The Strange Case of Dr. Jekyll and Mr. Hyde (1886): Robert Louis Stevenson: the book that enthralled a city unnerved by Jack the Ripper.

The Adventures of Sherlock Holmes; The Hound of the Baskervilles (1892): Arthur Conan Doyle: classic whodunits featuring Holmes and Watson.

The Inimitable Jeeves (1923): P.G. Wodehouse: prewar upper class tomfoolery in London Town.

Mrs Dalloway (1925): Virginia Woolf If you know London you can follow Clarissa Dalloway every step of the way – in real time.

Londinium: London in the Roman Empire, John Morris (1982): London's rise from a Roman outpost into a debauched medieval mecca.

V For Vendetta (1982-1989): Alan Moore, The world's greatest comic writer blows up London in a fit of Anarchist fantasies.

London Fields (1989): Martin Amis: post-modern jaunt through London at the end of the millennium.

London – The Biography, and ***Illustrated London*** (2000): Peter Ackroyd: definitive, eight hundred page mother lode of remarkable city history, and lavish pictorial version.

London's Disused Underground Stations (2001): JE Connor documenting forgotten, ghostly tube stations beneath the pavements.

London Orbital and Hackney That Rose Red Empire (2002): Iain Sinclair: London's premier scribe continues to fill our brains with joy despite being ripped off by devotee Peter Ackroyd.

The Clerkenwell Tales (2003): Peter Ackroyd: corking murder mystery set in the time of Chaucer.

Brick Lane (2003): Monica Ali: award winning coming-of-age tale centred on Brick Lane's Muslim community.

Art Deco London (2003): Colin Michael Hines: Wistful but enjoyable stroll around London's Art Deco heritage.

Intimate Adventures of a London Call Girl (2005): Belle de Jour: steamy, real-life shenanigans ahoy.

From Here to Here (2005): Simmons, Taylor, Lynham, Rich: 31 top notch short stories about Circle Line destinations, includes Simon Armitage.

Secret London: Exploring the Hidden City, with Original Walks and Unusual Places to Visit (2006): Andrew Duncan: an explorer's dream.

The London Bombings: An Independent Inquiry (2006): Nafeez Mosaddeq Ahmed: balanced, subtle overview of 2005 Underground bombings.

Around London with Kids – 68 Great Things to See and Do (3rd edition; 2006): Eugene Fodor: should keep the little rascals from breaking into cars.

I Never Knew That About London (2007): Christopher Winn: Well, did you?

The London Encyclopaedia (2008): Ben Weinreb and Christopher Hibbert: London's history and culture documented in minutest detail

Derelict London (2008): Paul Talling: The urban explorers bible!

Essential London Songs

Lambeth Walk, Noel Gay/Douglas Furber (1937): All together! *Doing the Lambeth Walk! Oi!*

A Nightingale Sang in Berkeley Square, Judy Campbell (1940): Wartime cheer made famous by Vera Lynn.

London Pride, Sir Noel Coward (1941): Written during the Blitz, this sensational ballad gave comfort to Londoners being bombed nightly.

Maybe It's Because I'm a Londoner, Hubert Gregg (1944): Pearly Queen favourite crammed with WWII spirit.

A Foggy Day (In London Town), Ella Fitzgerald (1956): Definitive recording of Gershwin classic.

Waterloo Sunset, The Kinks (1967): Timeless paean to the nation's capital.

Consider Yourself, Lionel Bart (1968): Oliver Twist hoodwinked into a life of crime by the Artful Dodger, the rascal.

Primrose Hill, John and Beverly Martyn (1970). Folk rock's second couple never had to deal with Katie Frost and Kate Moss when they were watching the sun set, did they?

Streets Of London, Ralph McTell (1974). Cool folk dude destroys credibility forever with international monster hit.

Baker Street, Gerry Rafferty (1978): Feel that sax line, air that guitar.

London Calling, The Clash (1979): Joe Strummer paints an apocalyptic vision of a city in post-punk transition.

Electric Avenue, Eddy Grant (1983): Roots-rock champion name checks 80s Brixton scene.

London, The Smiths (1983): Morrissey lugubriously debates a trip south. Miserable shite.

West End Girls, Pet Shop Boys (1986): East London working class meets West London affluence in electro-pop classic.

Pump Up London, Mr. Lee (1988). Squelchy Chicago House dude makes London sound amazing whilst name checking every British town he can think of: Leeds! Manchester! Scatland!

Parklife, Blur (1994): Home counties-boys get cockney makeover while eyeing London's jogging scene.

Sunny Goodge Street, Donovan (2002). Folk crooner sings of a hippy London goneby.

The London Underground Song, Amateur Transplants (2005): Sweary, infectiously catchy and a comical ballad to the tube, rings painfully true.

Sheila, Jamie T (2006): Mr. T delivers an excellent poetic diatribe on what being young and hopeless in London is like.

Hometown Glory, Adele (2007): This song will make you fall in love with the city all over again.

Essential London Films

The 39 Steps (1935): Hitchcock adaptation of John Buchan novel.

Pygmalion (1938): Leslie Howard as Henry Higgins and Wendy Hiller as Eliza Doolittle prove Shaw's classic comedy does very well without music.

Great Expectations (1946): Rare Richard Attenborough acting outing in classic Dickens adaptation.

The Ladykillers (1955): Superb black comedy from the Ealing canon, with pre-Obi Wan Alec Guinness.

One Hundred and One Dalmations (1961): Innocent pelt-seeker tortured by 101 belligerent pups. For shame.

Mary Poppins (1964): Notable for Dick Van Dyke's confounding, lanky turn as cockney chimney sweep.

A Hard Day's Night (1964): Classic, swinging 60s' comedy from the Fab Four.

Alfie (1966): Caine in much-lauded role as audience-addressing lothario.

Carry On Doctor (1967): Critically-panned, guilty-pleasure raunchfest from Pinewood Studios.

The London Nobody Knows (1967): The greatest film about London ever. Period.

Oliver! (1968): Sprightly musical adaptation of Dickens classic.

A Clockwork Orange (1971) Kubrick's dystopian masterpiece was set in Thamesmead, which is still, "Feeling a bit shagged and fagged and fashed."

The Elephant Man (1980): John Merrick 'accepted' by London's polite Victorian-era society in David Lynch masterpiece.

An American Werewolf in London (1981): US student attacked on moors; gets haunted; romps with Jenny Agutter; becomes werewolf; slaughters innocents; is shot in alley; credits roll.

My Beautiful Launderette (1985): Hanif Kureishi's controversial depiction of cross-culture, same-gender love in the Thatcher-era.

Muppet Christmas Carol (1992): That Michael Caine, he sure can act. But he sure can't sing.

London (1994): Patrick Kellier's abstract ramble through 'the most unsociable and reactionary of cities.'

Lock, Stock and Two Smoking Barrels (1998): East End crime capers from Madonna's (not from the East End) husband.

Notting Hill (1999): Hugh Grant as mumbling, bumbling, lovesick fop.

Bridget Jones's Diary (2001): Rene Zellweger goes Sloane in adaptation of Helen Fielding novel.

28 Days Later (2002): Us Londoners finally erupt in pandemic rage at how slow tourists are on the tube.

Love Actually (2003): Expansive Richard Curtis romcom with Grant in slightly-less mumbly, slightly-more bumbly form.

Shaun of the Dead (2003): Fighting off zombies at the local pub. Hilarious.

The Kings Speech (2010): A stuttering King finds his voice and wins a few Academy Awards for his efforts.

There can't be anything worse than the inconvenience of trying to find a convenience when nature takes an unexpected hold of your nether regions; you may choose to follow the lead of many a Saturday evening reveller and use a public doorway, but is it really worth the £80 fine that will be levied if caught in the act (and let's face it, it's hard to conceal the evidence)?

Unfortunately, London has seen a recent decline in the provision of public toilet facilities, as local councils seem to have decided that they are under no obligation to provide such a service; you'll also be hard pushed to find a toilet attendant manning a lavatory these days, and the dubious goings-on in some loos may not be quite what you had in mind, unless your name has a "Michael" in it. Most surviving public toilets seem also to emit their own particular aroma of…well, you don't really have to use your imagination. But don't get down in the dumps!

The most obvious place to go to when in need is McDonald's. Despite what some may say about their food, their outlets are the place to go when caught short and not wishing to pay to pee. Usually maintained and cleaned throughout opening hours, they can also be used inconspicuously and without purchasing anything; and let's face it, you can't move without the glow of those golden arches following you across London. It's also a safe bet to use Starbucks, Caffe Nero and Costa Coffee bars, although they often have a policy of access to toilets by key only, which can be a bit of a bummer (groan).

It may seem like a good idea to visit pubs or bars solely for their toilets, but you might find yourself being hauled out by an irked landlord mid-act. Furthermore, don't expect luxury; pub toilets are usually fairly scummy and often not furnished with toilet paper. It's also unlikely to find a men's cubicle that will have a working lock in it; do you really wish to have an unwanted visitor whilst on the throne? Exceptions are the Wetherspoon's chain, which prides itself on having toilets cleaned on the hour, and the nicest of gastro pubs, which can offer commodious and clean facilities (at least during the day). Otherwise, if desperate, at least go for a pub or bar that's busy.

Also bear in mind that if you find yourself in need in the City of Westminster, you can use a toilet text service from your mobile phone! Known as SatLav, texting the word 'Toilet' to 80097 will result in a message being sent to your phone informing you of the nearest public convenience. It may prove to be the most relieving 25p you'll ever spend in London…

A good and extensive list of London public toilets can be found at www.lastrounds.co.uk/public_toilets.html.

If none of the afore-mentioned places are available, there are other options:

Other street public toilets—yes, those bizarre futuristic looking structures on some of London's central streets are toilets. Known as sanisettes or "superloos", there is a charge to use them and once in, you've got 15 minutes before the door automatically opens (don't get extended stage-fright). They're self-cleaning, which usually means that they're in a right state, and are also quite popular with junkies and prostitutes, so best saved for when extremely desperate.

There are also a few pop up toilettes which, although intended for the right use, unfortunately stink like hell and fortunately return back there during the day. These are only suitable for (drunk) men and rise to the challenge of channelling away an evening's excesses from 7pm to 6am. Located at notorious 'wet spots' in the West End, they are linked to the main sewerage system; taking the piss, indeed…

Stations—including almost all large railway stations and a few central London tube stations. There will usually be a cost for these facilities though (around 30p).

Department Stores—All the large ones, including John Lewis, Selfridges, Debenhams and Harrods. Smaller shops rarely have toilets for public use.

Supermarkets—many larger branches of Sainsbury's and Marks & Spencer.

Museums—the majority of London's large museums and galleries are free to enter (erm, and have toilets).

Libraries—most libraries will have an area of salvation for the needy.

Universities and Colleges—and you get to pass yourself off as a student or lecturer (in need of the loo).

Hospitals—you can also drop in on that relative that you always meant to visit, or maybe leave a stool sample; just try not to leave with a superbug.

Parks—not on the grass, please.

Hotels—larger hotels shouldn't pose a problem.

London has some of the finest hospitals in the world, attracting top-notch specialists who carry-out state-of-the-art procedures—the trick is, getting in to see one of them. An appointment at a specific hospital, or with a specialist, requires a referral from your GP and plenty of patience. In an emergency go to your nearest A&E—bring a book and some earplugs. On the weekends after eleven, waiting times for non-urgent problems can be measured in aeons, but rest assured, if something is seriously wrong you'll be seen very quickly—lucky ol' you. For non serious injuries or illnesses, find your nearest Minor Injuries Unit or Walk-in Centre on www.nhs.uk. You'll spend less time hanging around and free up A&E for critical cases and over-cidered teens needing stomach pumps. The ever-friendly 24 hr NHS Direct 0845 4647 is also always available for advice.

If you have the money, numerous private sector hospitals and clinics are available to cure what ails you, or to pander to your hypochondriacal needs. You won't necessarily get better treatment, but there'll be less waiting, more pampering and more grapes by your bedside. For information, start at www.privatehealth.co.uk.

A & E	*Address*	*Phone*	*Map*
Charing Cross Hospital	Fulham Palace Rd & St Dunstan's Rd	020 3311 1234	41
Chelsea and Westminster Hospital	369 Fulham Rd	020 8746 8000	43
Homerton University Hospital	Homerton Row	020 8510 5555	90
King's College Hospital	Denmark Hill & Champion Park	020 3299 9000	128
Moorfields Eye Hospital	162 City Rd	020 7253 3411	84
Royal Free Hospital	Pond St & Fleet Rd	020 7794 0500	57
Royal London Hospital	Whitechapel Rd & Vallance Rd	020 7377 7000	96
St Mary's Hospital	Praed St & Winsland St	020 3312 6666	31
St Thomas' Hospital	Westminster Bridge Rd & Lambeth Palace Rd	020 7188 7188	131
University College Hospital	235 Euston Rd	0845 155 5000	4
Western Eye Hospital	173 Marylebone Rd	020 7886 6666	2
Whittington Hospital	Magdala Ave	020 7272 3070	59

Other Hospitals	*Address*	*Phone*	*Map*
Bupa Cromwell Hospital	162 Cromwell Rd	020 7460 2000	35
Capio Nightingale Hospital	11 Lisson Grove	020 7535 7700	76
Charing Cross Hospital	Fulham Palace Rd & St Dunstan's Rd	020 3311 1234	41
Chelsea and Westminster Hospital	369 Fulham Rd	020 8746 8000	43
City Medical	17 St Helen's Pl	0845 123 5380	17
Dove Clinic	19 Wimpole St	020 7580 8886	2
Eastman Dental Hospital	256 Gray's Inn Rd	020 7915 1000	5
Elizabeth Garrett Anderson Hospital	Huntley St	0845 155 5000	4
Fitzroy Square Hospital	14 Fitzroy Sq	020 7388 4954	3
Gordon Hospital	Bloomburg St & Vauxhall Bridge Rd	020 8746 8733	21
Great Ormond St Children's Hospital	34 Great Ormond St	020 7405 9200	5
Guy's Hospital	Great Maze Pond & St Thomas St	020 7188 7188	106
Heart Hospital	16 Westmoreland St	020 7573 8888	2
Highgate Private Hospital	17 View Rd	020 8341 4182	51
Homerton University Hospital	Homerton Row	020 8510 5555	90

Other Hospitals	*Address*	*Phone*	*Map*
Hospital For Tropical Diseases	Martimer Market & Capper St	0845 155 5000	4
Hospital of St John and St Elizabeth	60 Grove End Rd	020 7806 4000	68
King Edward VII Hospital For Officers	5 Beaumont St	020 7486 4411	2
King's College Hospital	Denmark Hill & Champion Park	020 3299 9000	128
Lambeth Hospital	108 Landor Rd	020 3228 6000	144
Lister Hospital	Chelsea Bridge Rd	020 7730 7733	20
London Bridge Hospital	27 Tooley St	020 7407 3100	106
London Chest Hospital	Bonner Rd & Approach Rd	020 7377 7000	93
London Independent Hospital	1 Beaumont Sq	020 7780 2400	97
London Welbeck Hospital	25 Welbeck St	020 7224 2242	2
Marylebone Consulting Rooms	10 Bulstrode Pl	020 8872 3838	2
Maudsley Hospital	Denmark Hill & Champion Park	020 3228 6000	104
Mile End Hospital	Bancroft Rd & Alderney Rd	020 7377 7000	93
Moorfields Eye Hospital	162 City Rd	020 7253 3411	84
National Hospital for Neorology and Neurosciences	Queen Sq & Great Ormond St	0845 155 5000	5
Portland Hospital For women and Children	209 Great Portland St	020 7580 4400	3
Princess Grace Hospital	42 Nottingham Pl	020 7486 1234	2
The Rosenheim Building	25 Grafton Way	0845 155 5000	4
Royal Brompton Hospital	Sydney St & Cale St	020 7352 8121	45
Royal Free Hospital	Pond St & Fleet Rd	020 7794 0500	57
Royal London Homeopathic Hospital	60 Great Ormond St	020 7391 8888	5
Royal London Hospital	Whitechapel Rd & Vallance Rd	020 7377 7000	96
Royal Marsden Hospital	Fulham Rd & Sydney Close	020 7352 8171	45
Royal National Orthopaedic Hospital	51 Bolsover St	020 8954 2300	3
Royal National Throat, Nose and Ear Hospital	330 Gray's Inn Rd	020 7915 1300	5
St Bartholomew's	West Smithfield & Hosier Ln	020 7377 7000	15
St George's at St John's Therapy Center	162 St John's Hill	020 8812 5385	139
St Mary's Hospital	Praed St & Winsland St	020 3312 6666	31
St Pancras Hospital	4 St Pancras Way	020 7530 3500	78
St Thomas' Hospital	Westminster Bridge Rd & Lambeth Palace Rd	020 7188 7188	131
University College Hospital	235 Euston Rd	0845 155 5000	4
Wellington Hospital	8 Wellington Pl	020 7586 5959	76
Western Eye Hospital	173 Marylebone Rd	020 3312 6666	2
Whittington Hospital	Magdala Ave & Dartmouth Park Hill	020 7272 3070	59

Overview

Librarians love nothing more than a warm cardigan and a complex cataloguing system, nevertheless, they've done themselves proud with London's libraries. London boasts an enormous, if somewhat eccentric and confusing, network of over 360 libraries. In 2009 the Chief Librarians initiative passed and 4,000 libraries in England, Wales and Northern Ireland can now be easily accessed and used for all library services including checking out books, as long as you have an existing library card and proof of address. This excludes the elite British institutions (see below) and all books must be returned to a library in the same area.

London's libraries vary enormously in subject, range and facilities, with some accessible for free, some for a fee, some with an appointment and some only if you are very very nice and give the curator a chocolate digestive. But the treat of such a large network, apart from the world-class breadth, depth and quality of collections, is that many of the libraries have a unique personality to make them a treasured part of London. For example, £10 will get you a day's membership to the **London Library (Map 23)**, an atmospheric labyrinth where you can browse alongside ghosts of past members including Dickens, Tennyson and Darwin, and feel several IQ points higher than before you went in. In Tower Hamlets, libraries are now **"Ideas Stores" (Map 92, 101, 96)**, because Tower Hamlets is, like, cool. In addition to the books, magazines, music and internet facilities which are available at most public libraries, these superb spaces also offer activities such as free PopLaw legal advice clinics, homework clubs and jazz classes. The borough has built four of these wonders; find them in Bow, Whitechapel, Canary Wharf and on East India Dock Road. London linguists are spoiled with the excellent **French Institute (Map 36)**, **Instituto Cervantes (Map 19)** and the **Goethe Institut (Map 37)**, while more cunning linguists may prefer the eye-opening gynaecological collection among the 2.5 million medical-related works in the **Wellcome Library (Map 4)**. Poets should meander their way to the **Saison Poetry Library (Map 104)**, ensconced within the South Bank Centre, for a little inspiration. Artists will enjoy the **National Art Library (Map 36)**, which nestles within the V&A Museum. You can use many of London's academic and specialist libraries through the Inspire London scheme, which grants one-day reference access to collections throughout London; ask your local library to refer you.

However, the Daddy of them all is the **British Library (Map 78)**. This behemoth receives a copy of every publication printed in the UK and Ireland, and requires 625km of shelving space to accommodate its 150million items. But it's just such a tease. You cannot borrow books, and to even access the collections you need to obtain a Reader Pass, via an introductory discussion to establish why you need it and whether you're likely to doodle on the books. This requires two forms of ID, no compromise: refer to www.bl.uk for the latest guidelines. Once you have your pass you can access the Reading Rooms, albeit with your personal belongings in a clear plastic bag (or stored in a locker). But if you just fancy seeing the Magna Carta, Shakespeare in Quarto or some Beatles manuscripts, you can access the book-free visitor areas without appointment and still gain an impressive look at one of the world's greatest information resources.

General Information

Important phone numbers:
All emergencies: 999
Non-emergencies: 101
Anti-terrorism hotline: 0800 789 321
Crime Stoppers: 0800 555 111
Neighbourhood Watch: 020 79934709
Missing Persons: 0500 700 700
Complaints: 08453 002 002
Websites:
www.met.police.uk
www.cityoflondon.police.uk (Separate police force specifically covering the Square Mile).
www.btp.police.uk (Separate police force specifically covering public transport).

Statistics* (Greater London)

	2008/09	2009/10	2010/2011
Murder	146	113	124
Rapes	2,177	2,839	3279
GBH	11,212	10,525	8374
Burglary (res)	59,176	60,909	60803

* all sourced from the MPS Crime Website http://content.met.police.uk

Police Stations

	Address	*Phone*	*Map*
Albany Street Police Station	60 Albany St	030 0123 1212	77
Battersea Police Station	112 Battersea Bridge	030 0123 1212	132
Belgravia Police Station	202 Buckingham Palace Rd	030 0123 1212	20
Bethnal Green Police Station	Cambridge Heath Rd & Roman Rd	030 0123 1212	92
Bow Road Police Station	111 Bow Rd	030 0123 1212	94
Brick Lane Police Station	25 Brick Ln	030 0123 1212	91
Brixton Police Station	367 Brixton Rd	030 0123 1212	144
Camberwell Police Station	22 Camberwell Church St	030 0123 1212	122
Cavendish Road Police Station	47 Cavendish Parade	030 0123 1212	149
Charing Cross Police Station	Agar St & Strand	030 0123 1212	24
Chelsea Police Station	2 Lucan Pl	030 0123 1212	46
Chiswick Police Station	209 Chiswick High Rd	030 0123 1212	38
Clapham Police Station	51 Union Grove	030 0123 1212	51
Deptford Police Station	114 Amersham Vale	020 8297 1212	126
East Dulwich Police Station	173 Lordship Ln	030 0123 1212	129
Fulham Police Station	Fulham Rd & Heckfield Pl	030 0123 1212	42
Greenwich Police Station	31 Royal Hill	030 0123 1212	120
Hackney Police Station	2 Lower Clapton Rd	030 0123 1212	87
Hammersmith Police Station	226 Shepards Bush Rd	030 0123 1212	33
Hampstead Police Station	26 Rosslyn Hill	030 0123 1212	56
Harrow Road Police Station	325 Harrow Rd	030 0123 1212	26
Holborn Police Station	10 Lamb's Conduit St	030 0123 1212	5
Holloway Police Station	284 Hornsey Rd	030 0123 1212	61
Hornsey Police Station	98 Tottenham Ln	030 0123 1212	54
Isle of Dogs Police Station	165 Manchester Rd	030 0123 1212	103
Islington Police Station	2 Tolpuddle St	030 0123 1212	80
Kennington Police Station	49 Kennington Rd	030 0123 1212	104
Kensington Police Station	72 Earl's Court Rd	030 0123 1212	35
Kentish Town Police	12 Holmes Rd	030 0123 1212	72
Lavender Hill Police Station	176 Lavender Hill	030 0123 1212	140
Limehouse Police Station	29 West India Dock Rd	030 0123 1212	100
Marylebone Police Station	1 Seymour St	030 0123 1212	1
Notting Hill Police Station	100 Ladbroke Grove	030 0123 1212	28
Paddington Green Police Station	2 Harrow Rd	030 0123 1212	31
Peckham Police Station	177 Peckham High St	030 0123 1212	123
Rotherhithe Police Station	99 Lower Rd	020 7378 1212	110
Shoreditch Police Station	4 Shepherdess Walk	030 0123 1212	83
Southwark Police Station	323 Borough High St	030 0123 1212	106
St John's Wood Police Station	20 Newcourt St	030 0123 1212	69
Stoke Newington Police Station	33 Stoke Newington High St	030 0123 1212	64
Tooting Police Station	251 Mitcham Rd	030 0123 1212	152
Walworth Police Station	12 Manor Pl	030 0123 1212	113
Wandsworth Police Station	146 Wandsworth High St	030 0123 1212	138
West End Central Police Station	27 Savile Row	030 0123 1212	10

N8
N15
N6
N4
N19
N16
E5
NW3
NW5
N7
N5
E8
E9
NW6
N1
NW8
NW1
E2
E3
W9
WC1
EC1
W10
EC2
E1
W1
WC2
EC4
EC3
W11
W2
W12
E14
SE1
W8
SE16
SW7
SW1
W14
SW5
SE11
SE17
W4
SW3
SE8
SW10
SE10
SW13
SW8
SE14
SE5
SW6
SE15
SW9
SW11
SW4
SE24
SE22
SW15
SW18
SW2
SW12
SW17

Overview

London hotels can be sources of hopelessly romantic creativity. In 1899 Claude Monet painted the Houses of Parliament from his balcony at the Savoy hotel. About 100 years later, Fay Weldon moved in with her typewriter as writer in residence. If you've got visitors in town, fancy giving Claude a run for his money, or just can't face going back to your dump of a flat, you'll need the services of a hotel. When choosing your hotel, think carefully about what kind of London you're looking to experience and whom the room is for. We've identified a few of the usual suspects for whom you may find yourself booking a hotel room, and heartily offer you our best suggestions for each. Just don't expect to emerge from any of them clutching a masterpiece penned overnight.

Only the Best, Daah-ling

So you need to find a hotel for a VIP client who will accept nothing but the best. Where to start? Since you don't have to cover the bill yourself, here is where you can really dig into London hospitality at its most deluxe. Start by trying to book **The Ritz (Map 9)**, with its amazing views of Green Park, Rococo detailing and killer high tea. **Brown's (Map 9)** is a stunning five-star and was the first hotel in London to have a lift. There is also the **Dorchester (Map 9)**, and its neighbour the **Hilton Park Lane (Map 9)**, where you may see a celebrity stumbling back to their quarters at four in the morning, if you're very, very lucky. **The Landmark (Map 76)** is a wonderfully Victorian retreat in the centre of ritzy Marylebone and has a rather fine atrium. But the granddaddy of luxury London must be the **Savoy (Map 24)**. This elegant old-timer stunk of old money until its temporary closure in 2007 for a £100 million spruce-up. It was built on the location of the Savoy Palace, which burned down during the Peasants' Revolt in 1381. We say let them eat cake (and tea).

A Dirty Weekend

This can be any weekend where a Londoner decides booze-goggled sex and/or quick-to-bed access after a night of clubbing is worthy of dishing out the dosh on an über-chic central hotel. It's one (giant) step up from splurging on a taxi and is the realm of the London boutique hotel where location is everything. **Hazlitt's (Map 12)** is right in the middle of Soho yet still wonderfully intimate. **Andaz Hotel (Map 8) (formerly Great Eastern Hotel)** is in the heart of the City, with funky Shoreditch on its doorstep, whilst the 'modern English' style of the **Charlotte Street Hotel (Map 3)** is painfully hip and sophisticated.

The Tea-and-Crumpet Tourist

Then there's the hotel for your sweetly naïve cousin that sees London through rose-tinted Ray Bans: full of scones, Mary Poppins and the chimes of Big Ben. You wouldn't want to burst her cute little bubble, would you? Not to worry, there are plenty of hotels to satisfy the Harrods tourist. **San Domenico House London (Map 46)** is a Chelsea boutique hotel that is about as warm and cuddly as a cup of sugary tea. **The Rookery (Map 15)**, built amongst a row of once derelict Georgian townhouses in Clerkenwell, is cluttered with museum-worthy furniture, open fires and ye oldey worldey frippery. Or, if she can't bear to be too far away from Buckingham Palace, there's the nearby **Windermere (Map 20)**.

Parents in Town?

If your parents have spent their nest egg on bailing you out of your London-induced debt, they will probably want to get the most out of London for the least money possible. But if the hotel you pick for their stay is anything short of perfect, you'll never hear the end of it. If they have loyalty cards with any of the bigger hotel chains, now is a good time to use them. **The London Bridge Hotel (Map 22)** is an independent four-star that usually has good deals and is conveniently close to Borough Market and London Bridge station. Gower Street has a wealth of small family-run hotels at reasonable prices, including the **Cavendish (Map 23)**, within stumbling distance of the British Museum. There's also the nearby **Crescent Hotel (Map 4)**, next to Russell Square. If you miss home cooking, get your 'rents a serviced apartment with a kitchenette. Marlin Apartments and Think London have a few different properties, often ripe for the celeb sighting as pop stars are known to hitch up their wagons there during drawn-out tours.

In Lieu of a Couch to Crash On

Then you get your university friend still in strong denial of the real world, who refuses to get a real job. The amount of times this sponger has crashed on your sofa has been enough to send your might-be-the-one girl/boyfriend packing. Instead of blaming him/her for your future life of loneliness, banish them from the flat and call in the services of one of London's cheapies. They do exist, you just have to look hard. The **Hoxton Hotel (Map 84)**, an urban cheap boutique founded by the owner of Pret a Manger, is famous for its £1 hotel room sales. Cheap but cheerful chain Premier Inn (multiple locations) boasts rooms from £29 a night. Sometimes short-term rental companies, like **Airbnb** (www.airbnb.com), offer shared facility flats at very cheap prices. This is perfect if a guest is wishing to stay for a week or more. Airbnb has over 9,000 listings in London, which start as low as £10 a night. This can be a necessary and friendly alternative to endless weeks of friends imposing on your hospitality.

Where to Stick Your Best Friend From School

(And Her Husband, Two Perfect Kids and a Dog)

Unfortunately, for some people visiting London, a dodgy guesthouse isn't going to cut it. You want to show them how your city can be just as perfect as their countryside home and how not jealous you are of them! Of course, they don't see the point in paying tons either. This is where the few and far between bed and breakfasts come out of the woodwork. Most of these are small, so book in advance. London's best is the warm and welcoming **Bay Tree House and Annex B&B (Out of coverage)**. Great for families or singletons alike, it's in New Southgate (about 25 minutes by tube from central London) but can be a relaxing retreat. **Barclay House (Map 43)** is a hidden gem in Fulham Broadway (make sure you write down the address as it's not signposted and can blend in). **Aster House (Map 45)** is a bit pricier but close enough to posh High Street Kensington to give a glimpse of how the other half live.

With all these hotels, compare prices online, ask for their best rate and/or call for last minute deals, you may be surprised at the reductions available. Good offers mean you can pay less than you'd think for the best, and London does really have the best.

As you might expect from a site constantly inhabited since the Roman invasion of Britain, and probably before, London has managed to assemble a vast array of good, bad and ugly landmarks. The city is, in fact, stuffed with them, and the following is a slightly subjective rumination on a small proportion of some of the most noteworthy.

Historical

London gracefully bears a massive weight of history, and many of its landmarks reflect this. One of the oldest is the remains of the **Temple of Mithras (Map 16)** on Walbrook, built by the Romans when London was Londinium. Parts of the **London Wall (Map 18)**, also originally built by the Romans, still exist, the best fragments are around Tower Hill station. In Medieval times London became a bustling place; celebrate one of its most beautiful churches by visiting the oddly named **St Giles' Cripplegate (Map 7)**, which is ensconced within the brutal **Barbican Centre (Map 7)**, a landmark itself. By the 1600s, London was bustling so hard it got the plague and then some idiot burnt the entire city down in 1666. Celebrate three days of the Great Fire by climbing to the top of the 202 feet high **Monument (Map 18)**, before visiting post-fire architect Christopher Wren's masterpiece, **St Paul's Cathedral (Map 16)**. Into the 18th century, things became a little more sophisticated and some of London's prettiest domestic architecture bloomed. Stroll down Bloomsbury's **Doughty Street (Map 5)**, stopping at Charles Dickens' House, for perfectly proportioned Georgian elegance. The Victorians had a huge impact on London, with whole tracts of the city bearing the stamp of the starched times of chimney sweeps and empire bashing. For the lighter side of Victorian London, poke about the museums quarter from the **Victoria & Albert Museum (Map 37)** up to the **Albert Memorial (Map 36)**. For the darker, dodge the elderly at the **St Pancras Hospital (Map 78)**, an ex-workhouse.

Tourist Bait

London has a host of over-exposed landmarks that are honey to the swarms of tourist worker-bees but over-rated in the eyes of many Londoners. We don't necessarily share this view, but if you want to venture beyond the crowds at **Big Ben (Map 22)**, try some of the following. The aforementioned **St Paul's Cathedral (Map 16)** is an absolute wonder, although try the smaller **Southwark Cathedral (Map 106)** for a more intimate option. **The British Museum (Map 4)** is a beauty made fairer by its recent courtyard renovation; peruse the library to see where Marx pondered upon 'Das Kapital'. **The Burlington Arcade (Map 10)** is how shopping should be. The crypt under **St Mary-le-Bow Church (Map 16)** is 11th century weirdness complete with its own vegetarian restaurant. The Thames is long enough to provide you with your own spot of riverside tranquillity. If you're scared of bridges, burrow under the river at the **Greenwich Foot Tunnel (Map 120)**, or chug across it on the free Woolwich Ferry. For a weekend mooch, try the **Grand Regent's Canal (Map 71)**.

Modern Landmarks

The 20th century blessed the city with some opinion splitting contributions. **The Hayward Gallery (Map 104)** and **National Theatre (Map 104)** are both concrete frighteners which we are learning to love. Despite originally housing a power station, **Tate Modern (Map 105)** has been more graciously received. Meanwhile, further down the river, long abandoned **Battersea Power Station (Map 133)** will be undergoing major developments in 2013 and will be replaced by some form of flashy money-without-substance monstrosity. The **BT Tower (Map 3)** is like a 1960s lighthouse for central London drunks. **The Lloyds Building (Map 18)** and **Tower 42 (Map 18)** are both absorbing odes to the banker and glare menacingly at new rival **One Canada Square (or Canary Wharf Tower) (Map 100)**. A more recent contribution to the city is the **Canary Wharf Underground Station (Map 100)**. Until at least 2014 the 150-year squabble over what to put in **Trafalgar Square's (Map 24)** fourth and only empty plinth rages on. Expect modern, classic and performance art in this space for the time being, at least, until they add a statue of Britain's future supreme commander Rupert Murdoch strangling Lady Justice in 2014.

Lowbrow

In these clean times of starchitects, steel and glass, a few minutes spent gawping at **Elephant and Castle (Map 105)** shopping centre is enough to remind anyone how awry a landmark can go. Even a quick squizz at the nearby **Faraday Memorial (Map 105)** may not lift your gloom, largely as it now forms the body of a clogged roundabout. However, London can do lowbrow with the best of them, starting with the **Westway Flyover (Map 31)**: a noisy, dusty shard of concrete to remind you that the car is still king. The disused **Kingsway Tram Tunnel (Map 4)** is a forgotten piece of prime underground real estate and **Centre Point (Map 4)** and **Millbank Tower (Map 21)** are good examples of dodgy skyscrapers that no-one needed. **Battersea Park Gasometers (Map 133)** are imposing monsters, whereas **Lots Road Power Station (Map 50)** is fast becoming London's trendiest disused power station. If you must jump upon band wagons, keep your eyes peeled around east London for art left on walls by Banksy. Mobile lowbrow starts with a trip on a Routemaster, despite the buses being withdrawn in 2005, two heritage routes are still running. Lowbrow (along with logic, aesthetic quality and planning) finishes with **Euston Station (Map 78)**, which is, simply, disgusting.

Map 1 • Marylebone (West)

Marble Arch	Oxford St & Park Ln	Randomly plonked gateway to nowhere.
Speakers' Corner	Cumberland Gate & Park Ln	It's easy—stand on the corner and listen to the 'speeches.'

Map 2 • Marylebone (East)

Hertford House	Manchester Sq & Hinde St	Terribly twee home of the Wallace Collection.
Jimi Hendrix Memorial Blue Plaque	23 Brook St	Jimi lived here. Some bloke called Handel lived next door.

Map 3 • Fitzrovia

BT Tower	60 Cleveland St	A 574 foot tall official government secret until 1993.
Charlotte Street	Charlotte St	Restaurant strip for the advertising in-crowd.
Middlesex Hospital	Mortimer St & Cleveland St	Closed-down and spooky-looking.
Pollock's Toy Museum	1 Scala St	Brimming with delightful, traditional toys and Dickensian atmosphere.
Sinner Winner Man	216 Oxford St	Are you a sinner? Or a winner? London's top preacher's patch.
Tottenham Court Road	Tottenham Ct Rd	Buy your electronics 'ere, innit?

Map 4 • Bloomsbury (West)

The British Museum	Great Russell St & Museum St	Newly-covered Great Court is architectural manna.
Centre Point	101 New Oxford St	Ugly skyscraper looking kinda out of place.
Kingsway Tram Tunnel	Theobalds Rd & Southampton Row	Spooky remnant of London's defunct Tram network.
SOAS	Thornhaugh St	University focused on Africa, Asia and the Middle East.
Senate House	Malet St & Torrington Sq	Ominous art deco building; Orwell's Ministry of Truth.
Student Central	Malet St	University of London's giant students' union.
Tavistock Square	Tavistock Sq	Has a statue of Gandhi looking as cool as ever.
University College London	Gower St	London's "Global University," upholding progressive ideals since 1826.

Map 5 • Bloomsbury (East)

The Dickens House Museum	48 Doughty St	Unassuming from the outside, mecca for Dickens' fans on the inside.
Doughty Street	Doughty St & Guilford St	Exquisite Georgian street in heart of literary land.
Gray's Inn Field	Theobald's Rd	Holborn Hideaway.

Map 7 • Barbican / City Road (South)

Barbican Centre	Silk St & Whitecross St	An architectural eyesore. Bloody good events though.
Bunhill Fields	38 City Rd	120 thousand dead people, including William Blake. All buried, luckily.
Church of Saint Bartholomew the Great	6 Kinghorn St	Stroll in for your daily dose of frankincense and choir song.
LSO St Luke's	161 Old St	Home to the London Symphony Orchestra. Peaceful gardens for relaxation.
St. Giles-without-Cripplegate	Fore St & Wood St	Medieval church which defied the Blitz. Catch an organ recital.

Map 8 • Liverpool Street / Broadgate

Fulcrum at Broadgate	Broadgate	Richard Serra's overwhelming steel megalith.

Map 9 • Mayfair / Green Park

50 Berkeley Square	50 Berkeley Sq	The most haunted house in all of London town!
Apsley House	149 Piccadilly	"Number One, London"—former hip address of Duke of Wellington.
Buckingham Palace	The Mall	Unofficial HQ for Fathers For Justice.
Down Street Station	Down St & Piccadily	Bricked-up Underground station. The Turtles didn't live here.
Hard Rock Cafe	150 Old Park Ln	Original location; check out free Vault memorabilia collection downstairs.

Map 10 • Piccadilly / Soho (West)

Burlington Arcade	Burlington Arcade & Piccadilly	Welcoming shoppers since 1819.
Carnaby Street	Carnaby St	Will anything innovative ever come from here again?
Kingly Court	Kingly St & Foubert's Pl	Flash the cash to cut a dash.
Statue of Eros	Piccadilly Circus	God of Love, smothered in pigeon crap: a cautionary tale.

Map 11 • Soho (Central)

Huge Tree In Pub (Waxy O'Connor's)	14 Rupert St	No, you're not drunk, it really is a tree.
John Snow Water Pump	Broadwick St	Source of 1854 Cholera outbreak identified by Snow.
Berwick Street Market	Berwick St & Rupert St	Arrive early for traditional Cockney trader songs / off-duty hookers.

Map 12 • Soho (East)

Denmark Street	Denmark St & Charing Cross Rd	Guitar land. 'Enter Sandman' forbidden in most stores.
FA Headquarters	25 Soho Sq	Home of English football's top brass.
Old Compton Street	Old Compton St	Dubious gay hub.
The Phoenix Garden	21 Stacey St	A beautiful green mini-oasis in the middle of the city.
Soho Square	Soho Sq	Great atmosphere on hot summer days.

Map 13 • Covent Garden

Oasis Lido	32 Endell St	A lido in central London! In a 50s housing estate!
Seven Dials	Upper St Martin's Ln & Earlham St	Slum area in the past. Now great for shopping!

Map 14 • Holborn / Temple

Aldwych tube station	Strand & Surrey St	Creepy abandoned tube station. With a photo booth... of doom?
BBC Bush House	Aldwych & Kingsway	London calling the world, since 1940.
Hatton Garden	Hatton Garden	Historic jewelry and diamond district
Inner Temple Garden	Inner Temple	So peaceful even the lawyers look relaxed.
Lincoln's Inn Fields	High Holborn & Chancery Ln	Largest public square in London.
The Old Curiosity Shop	13 Portsmouth St	The oldest shop in London is truly Dickensesque.
Royal Courts of Justice	Strand & Bell Yard	Witness justice meted out to all, even the McCartneys.
Sir John Soane's Museum	13 Lincoln's Inn Fields	Spooky museum dedicated to the great 18th century architect.
Site of Sweeny Todd's Barber Shop	186 Fleet St	Swing by for a demon haircut and lovely pie.
Somerset House	Strand	18th century palace, beautiful fountains; has various modern functions.

Map 15 • Blackfriars / Farringdon

Daily Express Building	121 Fleet St	Art Deco sleeper.
Millennium Bridge	Millennium Bridge	Footbridge famous for wobbling alarmingly when it was opened.
Postman's Park	King Edward St & Little Britain	Tile memorial for 'average' people who did really cool things.

Map 16 • Square Mile (West)

The Guildhall	Gresham St & Basinghall St	Big, posh, old... Like Prince Phillip but less entertaining.
St Mary le Bow Church	Cheapside & Bow Ln	A historic place for City tycoons to save their souls.
St. Paul's Cathedral	St. Paul's Church Yard & Cannon St	Magnificence since 604AD.
Temple of Mithras	Queen Victoria St & Queen St	3rd century Roman temple foundations. Discovered 1954 and moved here.

Map 17 • Square Mile (East)

Bank of England	Threadneedle St	The 'Old Lady' still churns out the pounds.
London Stone	111 Cannon St	Possibly used by Romans to measure all distances in Britannia.
Threadneedle Street	Threadneedle St & Prince's St	London's original Grope Cunt Lane. Seriously, it's a true story.

Map 18 • Tower Hill / Aldgate

The Gherkin	30 St Mary Axe	Phwoar.
Leadenhall Market	Leadenhall Market	Designed by Horace Jones (Billingsgate and Smithfield Markets)
The Lloyds Building	1 Lime St	Dystopia's nicer side.
London Wall	Cooper's Row & Trinity Sq	Ruins, should be re-built to keep Northerners out.
The Monument	Monument St & Fish St Hill	Climb 311 coronary-inducing steps for unique, unsung London views.
Pudding Lane	Pudding Ln	Starting point for Great Fire of 1666. No smoking.
Royal Raven Lodgings	Wakefield Tower	Want to upgrade your pokey flat? Become a raven.

Soup Kitchen for the Jewish Poor	Brune St & Tenter Ground	The kitchen's gone; the stunning ornate façade is still there.
Thames Clipper	Tower Pier	
Tower 42 (Natwest Tower)	25 Old Broad St	One of London's skyscrapers. Great view (and restaurant) at top.
Tower of London	The Tower of London	Kings and Queens. Surprisingly insightful, annoyingly expensive.

Map 20 • Victoria / Pimlico (West)

Little Ben	Victoria St & Vauxhall Bridge Rd	Big Ben's runty kid brother.
Westminster Cathedral	42 Francis St	Yep, impressive.

Map 21 • Pimlico (East)

Millbank Tower	21 Millbank	Ugly sore thumb. And Labour Party HQ!

Map 22 • Westminster

Big Ben	House of Commons	The world's most famous clock and pretty damn cool.
Bolan Rock Shrine	Queen's Ride, Putney	Memorial shrine where 70s rock star Marc Bolan died.
Field of Remembrance	Victoria St & Dean's Yard	Sea of crosses and poppies to honour veterans.
New Scotland Yard Sign	8 Broadway	It spins!! Just like on the telly!!
Smith Square	Smith Sq	Square with great concert venue--watch out for MPs.
UK Parliament	Victoria St & Abingdon St	Parliament buildings where you can watch government debates.
Westminster Tube Station	Bridge St & Victoria Embankment	A daunting, soulless, engineering playground. Good and bad both extinct here...

Map 23 • St. James's

Economist Plaza	25 St James's St	Rotating sculpture installations from bratty young artists.
Giro the Nazi Dog	9 Carlton House Terrace	London's sole Nazi memorial. You'd think there'd be more…
Leicester Square	Leicester Sq	Tragic, tacky, always inexplicably heaving. Avoid.
TKTS	Leicester Square & St Martin's St	Cheapo tickets to sometimes worth-seeing shows.

Map 24 • Trafalgar Square / The Strand

10 Downing Street	10 Downing St	The Prime Minister's house.
The Actors' Church	29 Bedford St	Somewhat hidden and unique church long-associated with thesps.
The Banqueting House	Whitehall & Horse Guards Ave	Unsullied Renaissance cum-shot. Still does private parties.
Cleopatra's Needle	Embankment	Ancient-Egyptian Empire esoterica, with additional Luftwaffe-era 'distressed' styling.
Eleanor Cross	Charing Cross Station, The Strand	A mourning King's tribute to his expired Queen.
Jane Austen Residence	10 Henrietta St	The first Bridget Jones' bachelorette crashed here for a time.
Right-hand Drive Street	Savoy Ct	Britain's only right-hand-drive street. Like being on holiday! (Ish)
Sewer Lamp	Carting Lane & Strand	Lit by the power of your bowels.
St Martin-in-the-Fields	St Martin's Pl & Duncannon St	Was indeed surrounded by fields once. Just TRY to imagine!
Top Secret Tunnels	6 Craig's Ct	Government's WWII tunnels, 100ft below London. But shhh: top secret.
Trafalgar Square	Trafalgar Sq	Hardly an oasis but space to sit, look and think.

Map 25 • Kensal Town

Trellick Tower	5 Golborne Rd	Grade II listed 1960s council estate inspiring love/hate reactions.

Map 29 • Notting Hill Gate

Portobello Road Market	223 Portobello Rd	Antiques, clothes, food and more. A London institution.

Map 31 • Paddington

Paddington Bear Statue	Paddington Station	The statue's pleasant. But they're milking it with the crap shop.
Tony Blair's house	Connaught Square & Seymour St	Promise not to do anything naughty now.
Westway Flyover		Coolest car route into London

Map 33 • Shepherd's Bush

BBC Television Centre	Wood Ln & Ring Rd	Treasure it before the BBC moves out in 2013.

Map 34 • West Kensington / Olympia

Kyoto Garden (Holland Park)	100 Holland Park Ave	Traditional Japanese Garden in Holland Park offering peace and tranquility.

Map 35 • Kensington

Kensington Palace Gardens	Kensington Palace Gardens	Billionaire's Row. Stunning street to amble down and gawp at the mansions.

Map 36 • South Kensington / Gloucester Rd

Albert Memorial	Kensington Gardens	The shiniest balding head in town.
Royal Albert Hall	Kensington Gore	One stunner of a music hall, inside and out.

Map 37 • Knightsbridge

Holy Trinity Brompton	Brompton Rd & Knightsbridge	Historic HTB is home to the Alpha course. Even Guy Ritchie's been!
Victoria & Albert Museum	Cromwell Rd & Thurloe Pl	Victorian treasure trove, building a beauty itself.

Map 42 • Baron's Court

Empress State Buidling	Lillie Rd & North End Rd	Awesome Art Deco building now a scary cult center.

Map 43 • West Brompton / Fulham Broadway / Earl's Court

Stamford Bridge	Fulham Road & Moore Park Rd	That's not sweat you smell but money at Chelsea FC's HQ.

Map 46 • Sloane Square

Saatchi Gallery	Duke of York HQ, King's Rd	See rich dude's great art collection, for free.

Map 48 • Fulham

Putney Bridge Tube Pill Box	Putney Bridge Station	"We will fight them on the platforms!"

Map 50 • Sand's End

Lots Road Power Station	27 Lots Rd	Pint-sized power station, now disused.

Map 51 • Highgate

Highgate Cemetery	1 Swain's Ln	Eerily gothic home to Karl Marx and The Highgate Vampire.
Karl Marx's grave	Highgate Cemetry	Exactly what it says on the tin.

Map 52 • Archway (North)

Parkland Walk Nature Reserve	Parkland Walk	Hedgehogs and graffiti to be spotted along this abandoned railway.
Suicide Bridge	Hornsey Ln & Archway Rd	Former London entry point, now very much an exit point.

Map 53 • Crouch End

Abandoned Warehouse	Parkland Walk & Crouch End Hill	Dereliction galore along one of the best walks in London.

Map 55 • Harringay

Railway Fields Nature Reserve	381 Green Lanes	Calm oasis at former railway depot near Green Lanes station.

Map 56 • Hampstead Village

Hampstead Observatory	Lower Terrace & Hampstead Grove	The highest point in London, and open to the public!

Map 57 • Hampstead Heath

John Keats House	38 Heath Hurst Rd	Here lived a writer whose name was writ with water.
Lawn Road Flats	Lawn Rd & Garnett Rd	c.1934 modern living. Learn to love concrete.

Map 60 • Archway

Banksy's Hitchhiking Charles Manson	Tally Ho Corner (off Highgate Hill)	Early stencil by internationally renowned graff artist.
Dick Whittington's Cat	89 Highgate Hill	Small stone statue of obscure Mayor's cat.

Map 62 • Finsbury Park

North London Central Mosque (Finsbury Park)	7 St Thomas's Rd	New name, ethos for once controversial, now myth-dispelling, mosque.

Map 63 • Manor House

The Castle Climbing Centre	Green Lanes & Lordship Park	Fake castle, real climbers.

Map 64 • Stoke Newington

Newington Green Church	39 Newington Green	'ERECTED 1708, ENLARGED 1860'...well, it made us laugh.

Map 67 • Belsize Park

Freud Statue	Fitzjohn's Ave, opposite Maresfiend Gardens Junction	Statue by Oscar Nemon near the psychoanalyst's Hampstead home.
St Stephen's	Rosslyn Hill	Gothic awesomeness. Currently being restored to its former glory.

Map 68 • Kilburn High Road / Abbey Road

Abbey Road Zebra Crossing	3 Abbey Rd	Go on. Take THAT photo. You know you want to.

Map 70 • Primrose Hill

3 Chalcot Square	3 Chalcot Sq	Home of poet Sylvia Plath, 1960-61.

Map 71 • Camden Town / Chalk Farm / Kentish Town (West)

Camden Market	Camden Lock Pl	Shop, hang, drink, listen, pose, watch, chill, rock, laugh.
Grand Regents Canal	Grand Regents Canal	London's best bike lane. Or canoe to Birmingham.
The Roundhouse	Chalk Farm Rd & Crogsland Rd	Prominent round building and historic performance venue.

Map 74 • Holloway Road / Arsenal

Gillespie Park	191 Drayton Park	Weird and wonderful nature park along the train tracks.

Map 75 • Highbury

St Paul's Shrubbery	St Paul's Rd & Northampton Park	All Monty Python jokes welcome, in fact, positively encouraged.

Map 76 • Edgeware Road / Marylebone (North)

Sherlock Holmes' House	221 Baker St	It's elementary my dear Watson!

Map 77 • Mornington Crescent / Regent's Park

Euston Tower	286 Euston Rd	Quite an impressive erection.
Greater London House	180 Hampstead Rd	Crazy Art Deco building.

Map 78 • Euston

The British Library	96 Euston Rd	Prestigious research library with unmatched collection.
Camden High Street	Camden High St & Delancey St	'Alternative' tourist mecca.
Cheney Road	Cheney Rd & Weller's Ct	"Chaplin, "Alfie" and many more were filmed on these cobbles.
Euston Station	Eversholt St & Doric Way	So ugly it's oogly.
Platform 9¾	King's Cross Station	This Harry Potter thing has gone way too f'ing far.
St Pancras Station	St Pancras Way	Listed Gothic frontage, massive modern Eurostar hangar behind.
St Pancras	Pancras Rd & Euston Rd	Ex-Victorian workhouse turned superbug den.

Map 80 • Angel / Upper St

Angel Station Roof	Angel	You can get on the roof here, you epic teens.
The Bull	100 Upper St	Hands up: who loves beer?

Map 81 • Canonbury

Gladiators Paving Slab	10 Canonbury St	Logo of fighty telly show built into pavement. Me neither.

Map 82 • De Beauvoir Town / Kingsland

Suleymaniye Mosque	212 Kingsland Rd	Striking minaret silhouetted against Shoreditch Church spire and Broadgate Tower.

Map 84 • Hoxton

Hoxton Square	Hoxton Sq	Great in summer. Buy some cans and join the hipsters.
Village Underground	54 Holywell Ln	How did they get the trains up there?
White Cube	48 Hoxton Sq	Jay Jopling's homage to modern art

Map 85 • Stoke Newington (East)

Abney Park Cemetery	Stoke Newington High St & Rectory Rd	Egyptian revival-style, spooky nature reserve.

Map 86 • Dalston / Kingsland

Centreprise	136 Kingsland High St	Multi-cultural art centre, cafe, bookshop and venue.
Holy Trinity, The Clowns Church	Beechwood Rd & Kirkland Walk	Every Feb, clowns mourn Grimaldi. In full costume.

Map 87 • Hackney Downs / Lower Clapton

London Orphan Asylum	Lower Clapton Rd & Linscott Rd	Grandiose remains of historic site now beloved of enviornmental artists.
The Strand Building	29 Urswick Rd	Beautiful Art Deco building, NOT the subject of Roxy Music song.
Sutton House	2 Homerton High St	Music and arts in the oldest house in East London.

Map 88 • Haggerston / Queensbridge Rd

Geffrye Museum	136 Kingsland Rd	English interior design from 1600 to today.
St Mary's Secret Garden	50 Pearson St	A bit calm amongst the bees and the butterflies.

Map 89 • London Fields / Hackney Central

London Fields Lido	London Fields Westside	Open-air swimming for hardy Hackney folk.

Map 91 • Shoreditch / Brick Lane / Spitalfields

Brick Lane Mosque	59 Brick Ln	The area's changes reflect on the building – once a synagogue, now a mosque.
Christ Church Spitalfields	2 Fournier St	Star architect Nicholas Hawksmoor's pretty masterpiece.
Dennis Severs' House	18 Folgate St	Candle-lit cellar, parlour, smoking room - step 300 years back in time.
Spitalfields Market	105 Commercial St	No bargains but certainly one-of-a-kind fashions.
Sweet Toof Graffiti Alley	Pedley St & Brick Ln	Signature sweeties and skulls – just off Brick Lane.
Ten Bells	84 Commercial St	Where Jack the Ripper got his victims.
Truman's Brewery	91 Brick Lane	Beautiful old building now a hip weekend market. That's progress...

Map 92 • Bethnal Green

Bethnal Green Tube Station	Bethnal Green Tube Station	Scene of the worst civilian loss of the Second World War.
London Buddhist Centre	51 Roman Rd	Get your freak om.

Map 93 • Globe Town / Mile End (North)

Art Pavillion	221 Grove Rd	Arts center seemingly designed by the Teletubbies.
Mile End Climbing Wall	Haverfield Rd & Grove Rd	Classic climbing centre - one of London's big three.

Map 95 • De Beauvoir Town / Kingsland

The Sun HQ	1 Virginia Street	It's probably not legal to stake out Page 3 girls.

Map 96 • Whitechapel (East) / Shadwell (West) / Wapping

Battle of Cable Street Mural, St George's Hall	236 Cable St	Celebrating an almighty multi-faith bashing of a 1930s fascist march.
Blind Beggar Pub	337 Whitechapel Rd	A killing here finally led to Ronnie Kray doing porridge.

Map 98 • Mile End (South) / Limehouse

Ragged School Museum	46 Copperfield Rd	Barnado's school 'for the deserving poor' turned East End museum.

Map 100 • Poplar (West) / Canary Wharf (West)

Canary Wharf Tower	1 Canada Sq	You can smell the money yards away. Look, don't touch.
Canary Wharf Tube Station	Canary Wharf	Norman Foster's Jewel in the Jubilee Line Extension.

Map 102 • Millwall

The Docklands Sailing & Watersport Centre	235 Westferry Rd	Award-winning sailing centre.

Map 104 • South Bank / Waterloo / Lambeth North

County Hall	Westminster Bridge Rd & Belvedere Rd	One of London's most historical and vast buildings.
The Hayward Gallery	Southbank Centre	Revered and reviled bruiser.
The London Eye	Westminster Bridge Rd	Two words: Tourist. Trap. Nice view though.
Low Tide at South Bank	South Bank	Go for a walk on the exposed riverbed.
National Theatre	Waterloo Rd & Upper Ground	South Bank centre-piece, looked like it was from 2050 in 1960.
The Pier at OXO Tower	Barge House St & Upper Ground	Screw OXO! Have a picnic on the pier instead.
South Bank Book Market	Under Waterloo Bridge	Little-known outdoor market; heaps of vintage and second-hand reads.
Waterloo Bridge	Waterloo Bridge	When tired with London, come here and watch the sunset.

Map 105 • Southwark / Bankside (West)

Buskers' Archway	Southbank	Excellent acoustics make the decorated tunnel a coveted buskers' spot.
Elephant & Castle	Elephant & Castle	Everything that was wrong with 60s town planning. Concrete hell.
Michael Faraday Memorial	Elephant & Castle	He gave us electromagnetism, we gave him a roundabout.
The Ring	72 Blackfriars Rd	London's first boxing ring was here; now a characterful pub.
Shakespeare's Globe	21 New Globe Walk	The Bard's famous playhouse reconstructed.
Tate Modern	Bankside	Herzog and de Meuron dazzler.

Map 106 • Bankside (East) / Borough / Newington

Borough Market	8 Southwark St	London's best food market. Enjoy the free samples.
Cross Bones Graveyard	Redcross Way & Union St	Medieval resting place for London's ladies of the night.
Female Gladiator	159 Great Dover St	1st centruy AD grave of London's very own Xena.
The Golden Hinde	Clink St & Stoney St	Amazing replica of Francis Drake's Tudor war ship.
The London Tombs	2 Tooley St	Lesser known Tower experience—beware the plague pits.
Mint Street Park	Southwark Bridge Rd & Marshalsea Rd	Open space on the site of the old Evelina Children's Hospital.
Old Operating Theatre Museum	9 St Thomas St	Macabre ancient operating theatre, with gallery for eager spectators.
The Shard	32 London Bridge St	72-storey Renzo Piano glass pyramid along the river.
Southwark Cathedral	Cathedral St & Montague Close	Worth the diversion to see Chaucer and Shakespeare's stomping grounds.
St George the Martyr	Borough High St & Tabard St	Look for the homage to Dickens.
Winchester Palace	Clink St & Storey St	Random 13th century ruins with remarkable rose window.

Map 107 • Shad Thames

City Hall	Queen's Walk, More London	Dubbed 'The Testicle' by Mayor Ken Livingston. Nice.
Design Museum	Shad Thames	Fairly unsatisfying shows - drool-worthy bookshop.
Fashion and Textile Museum	83 Bermondsey St	DAH-ling, it's just fabulous!
Floating Gardens	31 Mill St	Gardens. Mad tramps. On Boats. What else do you want?
HMS Belfast	Morgan's Lane & Tooley St	Floating WW2 killing machine, much beloved of children.
Stompie	Mandela Way & Page's Walk	Sounds like a baby elephant. But it's a Soviet tank.
Tower Bridge	Tower Bridge Road	Messing about on the water.

Map 110 • Rotherhithe (West) / Canada Water

Brunel Museum	Railway Ave & Rotherhithe St	Where engineering geeks can seek refuge from being picked on.

Map 111 • Rotherhithe (East) Surrey Quays

Surrey Docks Farm	Rotherhithe St & Salter Rd	Show the kids what their bacon used to look like.

Map 113 • Walworth

East Street Market	Walworth Rd & East St	Gloriously useless stuff.
Heygate Estate	Deacon Way & Heygate St	A testament to urban planning gone horribly wrong.

Map 114 • Old Kent Road (West) / Burgess Park

The Animatronic Fireman	Old Kent Rd	Be afraid. Be very afraid.
Peckham Library	122 Peckham Hill St	Groundbreaking modern architecture or huge, carelessly dropped Tetris block?

Map 116 • South Bermondsey

Millwall FC Stadium	Zampa Road & Bolina Rd	A football mecca for somebody?

Map 120 • Greenwich

Cutty Sark Gardens	King William Walk & Romney Rd	Where the Archbishop of Canterbury was murdered in 1012.
Greenwich Foot Tunnel	Greenwich Church St & Thames St	Walk/crawl/skip/limp under the Thames.

Map 126 • New Cross

Ben Pimlott Building	University of London, New Cross	A building of cheerful, dreary, warped, modern fascist fun.

Map 131 • Vauxhall / Albert Embankment

Lambeth Palace	Lambeth Palace Rd & Lambeth Rd	Where the Archbishop of Canterbury lives; no, not in Canterbury, stupid.
Secret Intelligence Service HQ (MI6)	85 Vauxhall Cross	Real life James Bonds in a not-so-secret location.
Vauxhall City Farm	165 Tyers St	So that's where an egg comes from.

Map 133 • Battersea (East)

Battersea Dogs' Home	4 Battersea Park Rd	Re-house a pooch. Now does cats too.
Battersea Park Gasometers	Queenstown Rd & Prince of Wales Dr	Rusting monsters.
Battersea Power Station	188 Kirtling St	The world's most beautiful power station, surely.

Map 140 • Clapham Junction / Northcote Rd

Northcote Road	Northcote Rd	Middle-class marketing-types mecca.

Map 143 • Clapham High Street

Clapham Common Air-Raid Shelter	Clapham High St	The depths of government paranoia.

Map 144 • Stockwell / Brixton (West)

Brixton Market	Electric Ave & Electric Ln	Caribbean flavours, smells and sounds.
Electric Avenue	Electric Ave & Brixton Rd	First shopping area in Britain lit by electricity, in 1880.

Map 145 • Stockwell / Brixton (East)

Stockwell Bowls	Stockwell Rd & Stockwell Park Walk	70's concrete skatepark, take quads and get beaten-up.

Map 152 • Tooting Broadway

Gala Bingo Hall	50 Mitcham Rd	Bingo hall with Grade One listed interior.

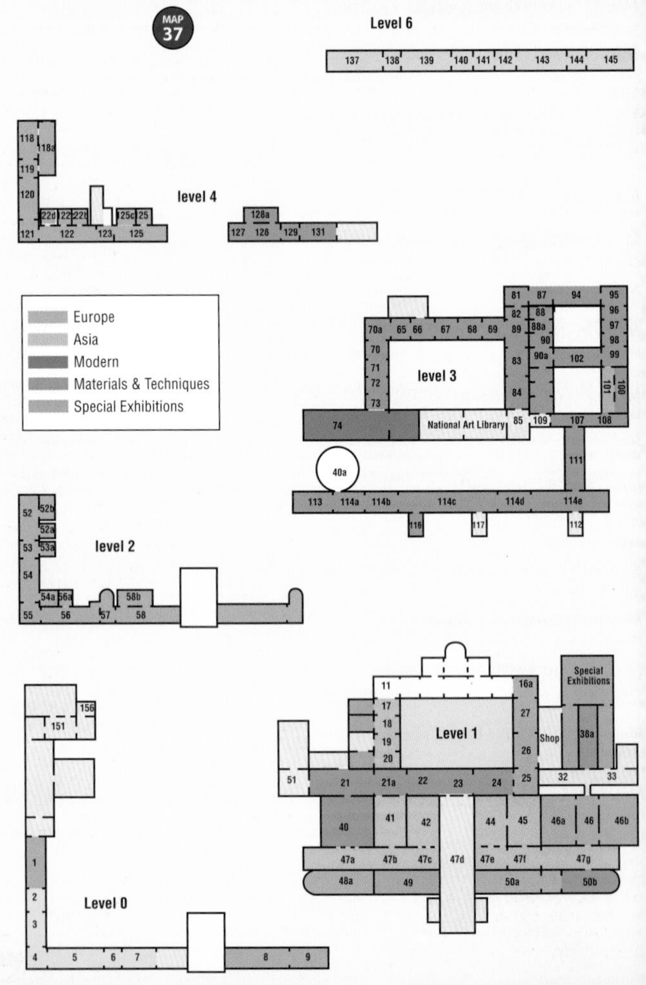
MAP 37
Level 6
137
138
139
140
141
142
143
144
145
level 4
118
118a
119
120
122d
122c
122b
125c
125
121
122
123
125
128a
127
128
129
131
Europe
Asia
Modern
Materials & Techniques
Special Exhibitions
level 3
70a
65
66
67
68
69
89
81
87
94
95
82
88
96
88a
97
90
98
90a
102
99
70
71
72
73
83
84
100
101
74
National Art Library
85
109
107
108
111
40a
113
114a
114b
114c
114d
114e
116
117
112
level 2
52
52b
52a
53
53a
54
54a
56a
58b
55
56
57
58
Level 0
156
151
1
2
3
4
5
6
7
8
9
Level 1
11
16a
17
18
19
20
27
26
Special Exhibitions
Shop
38a
51
21
21a
22
23
24
25
32
33
40
41
42
44
45
46a
46
46b
47a
47b
47c
47d
47e
47f
47g
48a
49
50a
50b

General Information

NFT Map: 37
Address: Cromwell Road
London SW7 2RL
Phone: 020 7942 2000
Website: www.vam.ac.uk
Hours: 10am – 5.45pm daily. Select areas open until 10pm every Friday. National Art Library open 10am – 5.30pm daily and 6.30 on Fridays. Check website for areas/ activities that require booking. Closed 24th, 25th and 26th of December.

Admission: Free to the permanent collection. There is a charge for temporary exhibitions. Tickets have an allotted time slot and although they can be purchased on the day, it is recommended you book ahead of time by phone or online, especially with the more popular exhibitions.

Overview

The Victoria and Albert Museum, or the V&A, calls itself the world's greatest museum of art and design and nowhere has there ever been such an eclectic collection of objects inducing so many 'oooohs', 'aaaaahs' and 'holy shits!'. With a permanent collection of over 4.5 million objects, pretty much all on display in the 145 galleries, you can go everyday for a lifetime and be blown over by something you hadn't noticed before. For the tourist and non-tourist alike, the V&A is a wonderful maze of cultural ramblings. You'll get lost, overwhelmed and flustered, but we promise you won't get bored.

The V&A is a cabinet of curiosities of gargantuan proportions, boasting 5000 years of art and design, in every medium imaginable (from wax dioramas to a little black dress made of bras), spread over seven levels and organised by five themes—Asia, Europe, Materials & Techniques, Modern and Exhibitions. The trouble is where to start. You'll no doubt spend the first 10 minutes mesmerised by the glass Chihuly chandelier over the information booth, but what you do afterwards depends on how much time you have. Got hours? Avoid structure and just wander. Got an hour? Take a look at the map, see what strikes your fancy and head straight there. Just don't forget to hit up the gift shop afterwards—it's killer.

The Greatest Hits

There's no real method to the V&A's madness. Despite their best efforts to categorise everything, Vivienne Westwood gowns are just a stumble away from 1000 year-old Buddhas. But this is a great thing. The best advice is really to ditch the guidebook and go with your instincts. To make sure you take in the best stuff, start in the basement (having arrived through the Tunnel Entrance from the tube station), where you'll find the 17th century **Cabinet of Curiosities**—predecessors to the modern museum—which will get you in the right mind set. Weaving past bits and pieces of **Versailles**, you emerge onto the ground floor (Level 1) which covers fashion, Asia and both Medieval and Renaissance Europe. Highlights of which include the **cast courts**, which boast a life-size replica of **Trajan's Column** in plaster, then onto ancient **samurai swords** and spectacular **kimonos** in Asia, the **Ardabil Carpet**—the largest and most amazing Islamic carpets in existence dating from 1539 (lit up on the hour and half-hour), an extensive costume room covering everything from **18th century crinolines** to **Juicy Couture** worthy of Paris Hilton, and lastly, **Raphael's cartoons**—massive sketches for a 1515 commission of tapestries that now hang in the Vatican. Before heading on, stop for a tea in the **Morris, Gamble & Poynter Rooms** café for teacakes in 1860s arts and crafts surroundings. Level 2 consists of the tucked away **British Galleries**, including the **Great Bed of Ware** as well as the endearing **Lord and Lady Clapham** dolls bedecked in miniature turn-of-the-18th century outfits. Up again on Level 3, you'll find the Materials & Techniques rooms, with its vast collections of **silver, ironwork and musical instruments**, as well as some dynamite paintings. Don't miss **Rossetti's The Daydream** and then **Ron Arad's Chair** in the modern rooms. This floor also houses the **National Art Library**—an art history student's research dream (you have to get a reading pass to study here though). Level 4 has a wonderfully tactile display of **glasswork**, as well as **architecture** and more **British Galleries from 1760-1900**. If you've made it this far, you deserve a knighthood.

MAP
4

Ancient Greece & Rome
Middle East
Asia
Egypt
Enlightenment
North & Central America
Africa
Exhibitions and changing displays
Europe
Lift
Stairs

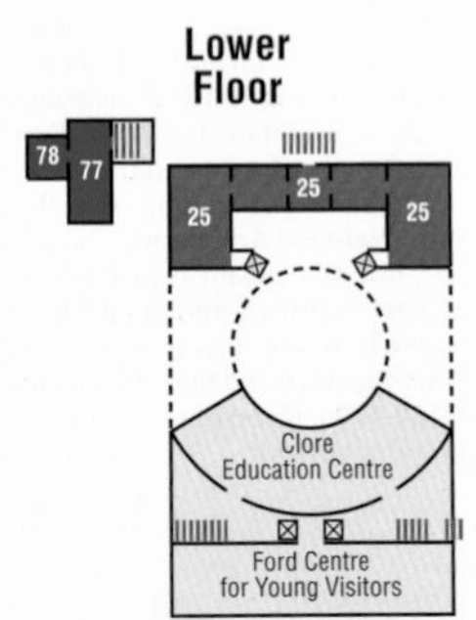
Lower Floor
78
77
25
25
25
Clore Education Centre
Ford Centre for Young Visitors

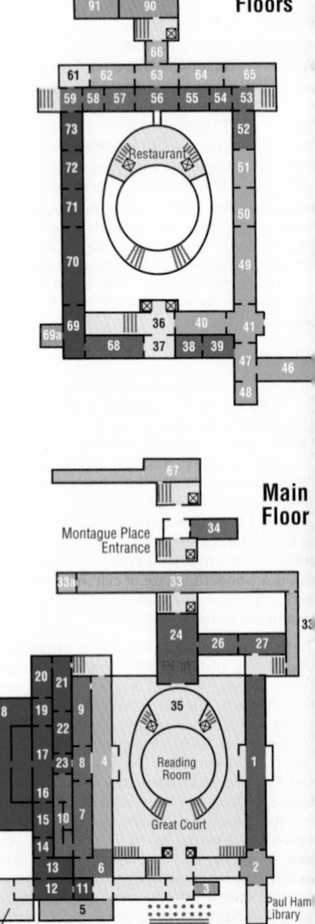
Upper Floors
94
93
92
91
90
66
61
62
63
64
65
59
58
57
56
55
54
53
73
72
71
70
69
69a
52
51
50
49
Restaurant
36
37
38
39
40
41
68
47
46
48
Main Floor
67
Montague Place Entrance
34
33a
33
24
26
27
35
Reading Room
Great Court
18
19
20
21
9
22
17
23
8
4
1
16
15
10
7
14
13
6
2
12
11
3
5
Restaurant
Main Entrance Great Russell Street
Paul Ham
Library

General Information

NFT Map: 4

Address: Great Russell Street, WC1B 3DG

Phone: 020 7323 8299 (information) or 020 7323 8181 (exhibition tickets)

Website: www.britishmuseum.org

Hours: The galleries open daily 10am – 5.30pm and until 8.30pm on Fridays. The Great Court is open 9am – 6pm and 8.30pm on Fridays. Check website for planned maintenance causing gallery closures. Closed 1st of January and 24th, 25th and 26th of December.

Admission: Free, with a charge for some special exhibitions.

Overview

Unless you're Indiana Jones, combining archaeological expertise with the swashbuckling energy to defeat obnoxious school groups, then do not attempt to cover the British Museum in a day. With 13 million items covering two million years of human history in almost 100 permanent and temporary galleries, you are better off treating yourself to different sections when the mood takes you—a perk of having one of the world's largest museums on your doorstep and open for free.

At 250 years, it is also the oldest museum in the world, but forget preconceptions of dusty urns and endless Roman coins—they're there if that's your bag, but this is a very modern organisation. The permanent displays include some of the world's most fascinating treasures, while the temporary exhibitions bring London a chance to break and pose artefacts which have seen some of the greatest moments of history, such as the recent display of drawings by Michelangelo, Raphael, Leonardo, and some other Renaissance scribblers who didn't make Ninja Turtle status.

However, while preserving artefacts to inspire its visitors, the Museum can also be seen as a testament to the great British pastime of looting. Some of the shining lights of its collection were acquired under the shadiest of circumstances, and the countries which were plundered so that snotty kids could chortle at the genitalia of their sculptures are increasingly vocal about getting the items back. For example the Elgin Marbles, rechristened with their pleasantly playful English name after the earl who helped himself to them, are huge slabs hacked from the 2500 year old Athenian Parthenon (albeit Elgin's entire nose later rotted off due to syphilis: a gratifying example of one-upmanship by nature). The legality of this move is hotly debated, but apart from the damage to the Parthenon, the Marbles undeniably suffered when they were cut into smaller pieces for transport to Britain, and when rowdy schoolboys bopped the leg off a centaur in 1961. The Museum holds firm that returning debated items would empty the museums of the world, but it has extended the occasional olive branch to ease the controversy; compensation was paid for the display of drawings stolen by Nazis, and they returned the Tasmanian Ashes (aboriginal human remains) to Australia after a 20-year battle.

The Greatest Hits

The **Great Court** is not just a Greatest Hit of the Museum, but of London as a whole. Being "the world's largest covered public square" may sound too niche an accolade to be impressive, but it really is stunning. The 150 year old **Reading Room** at its centre is a delight, both for the excellent library and for the wall-mounted list of major historical figures who have sought inspiration within its round walls. Whatever your ethics on plunder, some of the most morally-dubious exhibits are among the absolute must-sees: the **Elgin Marbles** in Room 18 are remarkable, while the **Rosetta Stone** in Room 4 gives you the irresistible buzz of seeing something so legendary up close, or as close at the backpacked hordes will allow, in your own town. A whole **Moai Statue** from Easter Island is in Room 24, the **Lewis Chessmen** set is in Room 42, and the **Mausoleum of Halikarnassos** exhibition displays some of the last remaining fragments of one of the Seven Wonders of the World. However, it is the stories of heartache, adventure, mystery and passion behind the items which bring them to life. Asking the steward of Rooms 62-3 how the **mummies** came to be in the museum, or seeing the pages from **The Book of the Dead** which recorded lives of the deceased, is a fascinating way to gain insight to people around the world and throughout time. And if that's a bit too deep, just head to one of the four **shops** for a mummy-shaped pencil case or replica Rosetta Stone.

General Information

NFT Map:	36
Address:	Cromwell Road, SW7 5BD
Phone:	020 7942 5000
Website:	www.nhm.ac.uk
Hours:	Daily 10 am–17.50 pm (Last admission 17.30) "After Hours" events run on the last Friday of each month during Nov–Apr. 24–26 Dec: closed.
Admission:	Free access to most of the Museum. Fee charged for some special exhibitions (free to Members).

Overview

Visiting the Natural History Museum is like reading National Geographic, if it was edited by JK Rowling. As imagination-tingling to adults as it is to kids, you can mull over serious questions about genetic modification and the environmental cost of modern life, while walking inside a termite mound or knocking on a petrified tree.

With more than 70 million specimens in their collection, you simply won't see it all at once, or for most of us—ever. But with free entry, regularly refreshed exhibits and unforgettable special exhibitions, it's worth dropping in when you have the opportunity. Grab a free map at the entrance to work

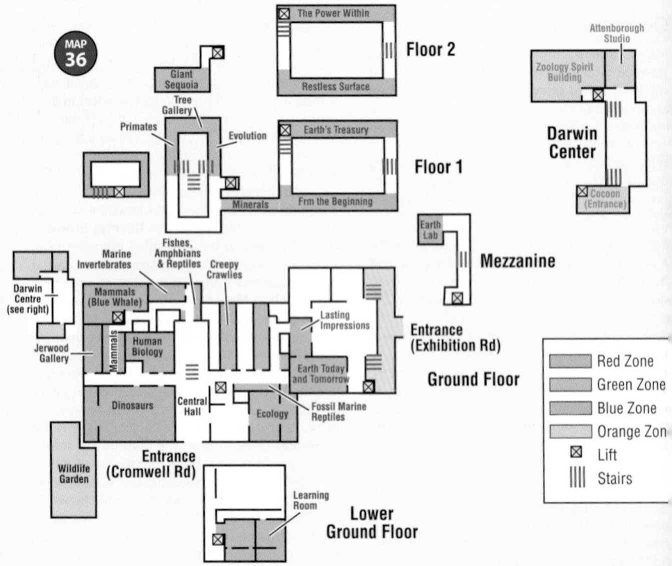

ut your route, which is colour-coded for a lightly) easier life: Red Zone for the planet nd forces of nature; Green for ecology nd the environment; Blue for dinosaurs, ıammals and biology; and Orange for the /ildlife Garden and behind-the-scenes eeks.

/eekends are inevitably heaving with yperactive button-pressing families, oellbound tourists and Londoners trying to ebuild the brain cells they killed off with the ight before's drinking; weekdays are amok vith school groups. But don't let this put ou off. If there's a queue outside the main ntrance on Cromwell Road, and you don't ıncy killing time by spotting all the different reatures carved around the entrance arch, op 'round the side to Exhibition Road ntrance and you'll fast-track yourself in. ou can go early or late for fewer crowds, or tick with the permanent exhibitions, which re superb but not as sexy as the world-lass special exhibitions which draw in the nasses. Or, if all else fails, just shove the kids ut the way: they're smaller than you and the uttons are *so much fun* to press.

The Greatest Hits

ınyone who didn't see the **Dinosaur xhibition** as a child really missed out: run ıere and rectify the situation immediately you haven't been, or revisit and enjoy ne modernised exhibits if you have. 'he **Mammals Exhibition** will get you vondering exactly *how* someone stuffs giraffe, and gives you a chance to get lose to the gaping jaws of a hippo. For a lifferent perspective on this room, go up o the balcony around it: watching people tare agog at the brilliantly-displayed **blue vhale** is as entertaining as the exhibits hemselves. For proof that even history eeks can make the earth move for you, visit the **Power Within** exhibition which recreates an earthquake (though don't expect a Universal Studios experience. The will is there, bless, but the budget just isn't…). Watch blushing parents introduce their kids to the birds and the bees in the **Human Biology** section, where an 8-times-life sized model of a **foetus** will put you off pregnancy forever. The **Wildlife Garden** is an oasis of serenity open from April–October, or you can impress a date (or not, depending on your coordination) by **ice-skating** next to the stunning Victorian building from November–January.

The Museum's Special Exhibitions are superb—check the website for current information. The annual **Veolia Wildlife Photographer of the Year**, October–April, is utterly inspirational, while a varying daily programme of events includes **lectures, behind the scenes tours** of the botany department, and **fossil workshops** for kids. Due to the success of the children's version, the museum is now running Dino Snores sleepovers for adults, which includes a three course meal, life drawing classes and an all night monster movie marathon. So if you fancy yourself as Ben Stiller in Night at The Museum start saving, as the stay will cost you a whopping £175.

Like the creatures it displays (except for the Dodo—you'll find one in the Green Zone), the museum keeps evolving. Aptly, the latest major development is the Darwin Centre, where you can stoke your nightmares by checking out the giant tarantulas, experience life in a cocoon (like life in a London flat, but more spacious), and watch scientists at work. You might not think that watching scientists analysing and cataloguing bits of plant would be much of a spectator sport, but an hour in the centre will whiz by and leave you bursting with new knowledge to irritate your mates with.

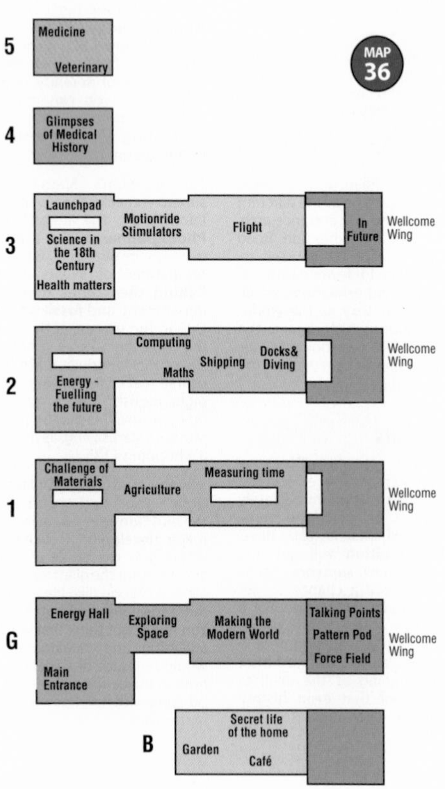
MAP
36
5
Medicine
Veterinary
4
Glimpses of Medical History
3
Launchpad
Science in the 18th Century
Health matters
Motionride Stimulators
Flight
In Future
Wellcome Wing
2
Energy - Fuelling the future
Computing
Maths
Shipping
Docks& Diving
Wellcome Wing
1
Challenge of Materials
Agriculture
Measuring time
Wellcome Wing
G
Energy Hall
Main Entrance
Exploring Space
Making the Modern World
Talking Points
Pattern Pod
Force Field
Wellcome Wing
B
Garden
Secret life of the home
Café

General Information

NFT Map: 36
Address: Exhibition Road, South Kensington, London SW7 2DD.
Phone: 0870 870 4868
Website: www.sciencemuseum.org.uk
Hours: Open 10 am–6 pm every day except 24 to 26 December. check website for special school holiday and summer opening hours.
Admission: Free, but charges apply to IMAX 3D Cinema, simulators & a few special exhibitions.

Overview

Museum and Science. Two words known to strike fear into the heart of many a child. And many a grown-up, come to that. But the Science Museum is one of the most visited museums in London. How so? Perhaps it's the heady mix of mildly erotic pistons and shafts; 60s room-sized computers and Bakelite ashtrays; special effects simulators and the mighty IMAX theatre? Or maybe it is the multitude of buttons; red and blue and green actual buttons, as well as Minority Report-style touch screens? We know they're aimed at kids, but we like. Oh and levers, did we mention levers?

The museum has its origins in the popular Great Exhibition of 1851. Prince Albert (no laughing in the back please) suggested the extra cash made by the Exhibition be used to found a number of educational establishments. Following a number of building moves and expansions the Science Museum as we know and love it opened in 1885.

The Greatest Hits

The museum's 300,000 gidgets, gadgets and gizmos attract 2.5 million visitors a minute or something, but venture above the third floor, to the **medical floors**, and you will have the place almost to yourself. The most popular area is the main drag along the ground floor which includes **Exploring Space** hung with real life space probes and other relics that look like they've come from the Doctor Who costume and props department, and **Making of the Modern World** featuring **Stephenson's Rocket**, to titillate your dormant trainspotter.

The third floor's **Launchpad** area has as many interactive displays as an 8-year-old could ever want. Parents hope their little darlings are actually learning something as they race from exhibit to exhibit whirling wheels, spinning liquids in plastic tubes and grimacing through head-sized lenses till tiredness or RSI sets in. For younger kids the tactile **Pattern Pod** on the ground floor makes up for its lack of buttons by its immensely pleasing shape.

The museum has its own Imax to impress the grown-ups and to make whimpering children cower as 3D Rexes loom into their faces. Don't even think about going in with a hangover. A huge silver hoop joins the **Energy exhibition** on the second to the ground floor. Answer a question on a nearby monitor, (don't worry they are easy) and watch your initials and age whiz around the inside of the ring. But what's that BUZZ? Like a huge electric fly killer? It's the inspired **'don't touch' display**—irresistible for the naughtiest in the class, one small electric shock later, the rest of the lemmings race over for a turn. Hilarious.

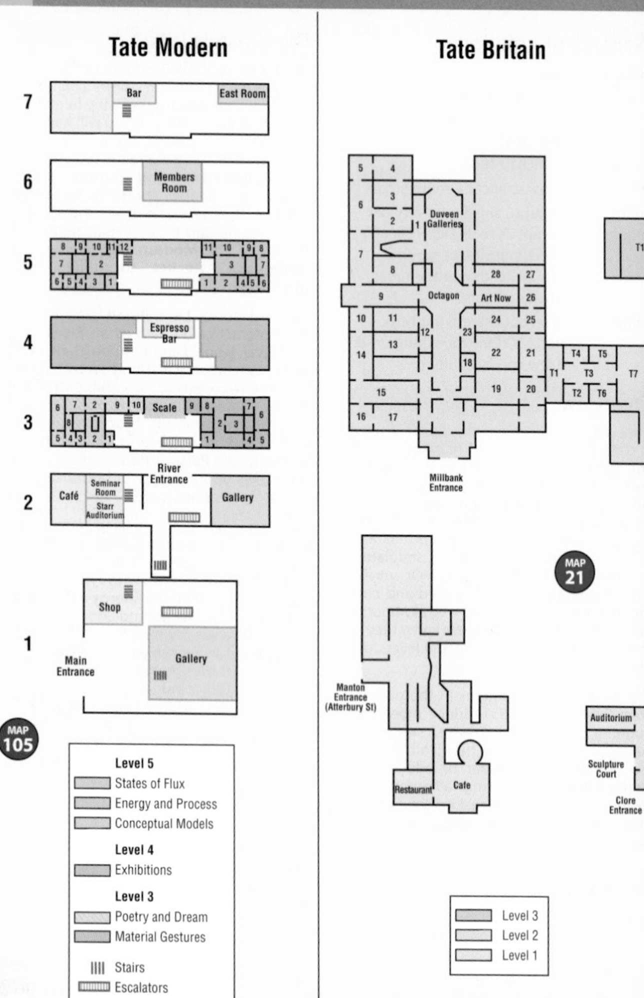

Tate Modern
7
Bar
East Room
6
Members Room
5
4
Espresso Bar
3
Scale
2
Café
Seminar Room
Starr Auditorium
River Entrance
Gallery
1
Shop
Gallery
Main Entrance
MAP 105
Level 5
States of Flux
Energy and Process
Conceptual Models
Level 4
Exhibitions
Level 3
Poetry and Dream
Material Gestures
Stairs
Escalators
Tate Britain
Duveen Galleries
Octagon
Art Now
T10
Millbank Entrance
MAP 21
Manton Entrance (Atterbury St)
Auditorium
Sculpture Court
Clore Entrance
Restaurant
Cafe
Level 3
Level 2
Level 1

General Information

Tate Britain:

NFT Map:	21
Address:	London SW1P 4RG
Phone:	020 7887 8888
Website:	www.tate.org.uk/britain
Hours:	Open 10am – 6pm Saturday to Thursday, and until 10pm on Fridays. Last admission to special exhibitions is 45 minutes before closing time.

Tate Modern:

NFT Map:	105
Address:	London SE1 9TG
Phone:	020 7887 8888
Website:	www.tate.org.uk/modern
Hours:	Open 10am—6pm daily. Last admission to special exhibitions is 45 minutes before closing time.

Overview

In a city renowned for its galleries and museums, London's Tate galleries shine from the banks of the Thames. The first Tate was founded in 1897 as the National Gallery of British Art, but was renamed soon afterwards after its main patron Henry Tate—he of Tate and Lyle and the sugar cube. Originally on the site of the former Millbank Prison (where Tate Britain remains), the gallery gradually expanded and divided its collection over the four sites, two in London, one in Liverpool and the last in St Ives. In London, Tate Britain houses British art dating from 1500 to the present day, while Tate Modern was created to house—yes you've guessed it—more modern work from 1900 to the present day, and is reportedly the most visited modern art gallery in the world.

The two Tates carry the same trendy Tate logo and the shops contain much of the same avant-garde merchandise with a great range of children's stuff available in both. But while the more traditional Tate Britain more closely resembles the National Gallery in architectural and artistic flavour, Tate Modern has a very hip feel and draws a slightly broader audience, in part due to its location on the increasingly buzzy South Bank.

Both museums have popular restaurants and cafes, but to encourage those without a membership to sign up, each offers an exclusive members' room. These provide the best views, nicest toilets, designated staff and ever so slightly self-important customers, and are always a safe bet to impress a date.

Tate Modern

Based in the former Bankside Power Station, Tate Modern has proved to be an extremely popular attraction for tourists and Londoners alike since its opening in 2000. It houses the national collection of modern art, so expect plenty of inspirational and challenging works alongside exhibits that look like your cat sicked them up. The temporary art installations of the five-storey tall Turbine Hall provide much of the draw to the gallery. This huge space displays specially commissioned works from October to April of each year—a programme which was intended to run for only five years, but was extended due to its popularity. Quirky exhibitions fill the vast Turbine Hall, like Olafur Eliasson's 'Weather Project' which encouraged visitors to lie back on the floor in their thousands, gazing at the shadows cast by the synthetic sun. Ai Wei Wei's Sunflower Seeds, in 2010/11, was probably his most ambitious and attention-grabbing work before going MIA—ironically and probably due to the unwanted exposure it brought to the Chinese government. That and the fact punters had to be forbidden from walking on the seeds due to the fine dust the porcelain they were made from produced which could have been inhaled and damage the lungs. Again, ironically. As always, we await with baited breath who will fill the Turbine Hall and with what. If it all seems like you could have created better art yourself, then try one of the gallery's excellent workshops or courses and give it a go.

Tate Britain

The Tate Britain boasts the most comprehensive collection of British art in the world, and is home to the annual and unmissable Turner Prize show. Stone steps lead up to the portico and once inside, the Duveen Galleries' ethereal sculptures lie straight ahead, giving the first taste of a breathtaking collection of artwork. Tate Britain's collection is divided chronologically and dedicates space exclusively to notable artists, such as Turner, Blake and Constable. The gallery also includes significant works by William Hogarth, Stanley Spencer and Francis Bacon. Look out for the themed guides to suit your mood, such as "The I've Just Split Up", "The I'm In A Hurry" and "The I Haven't Been Here For Ages" collections: a highly endearing way ease you through the 500 years of exhibits.

General Information

NFT Map: 24
Address: Trafalgar Square
London WC2N 5DN
Phone: 020 7747 2885
Website: www.nationalgallery.org.uk
Hours: 10 am–6 pm daily,
Fridays until 9 pm.

Admission: Free to the permanent collection and temporary exhibitions in the Sunley Room, Room 1 and The Space on Level 2. There is a charge for temporary exhibitions held on Level 2 in the Sainsbury Wing. Tickets have an allotted time slot and although they can be purchased on the day, it is recommended you book them ahead of time online, especially with the more popular exhibitions.

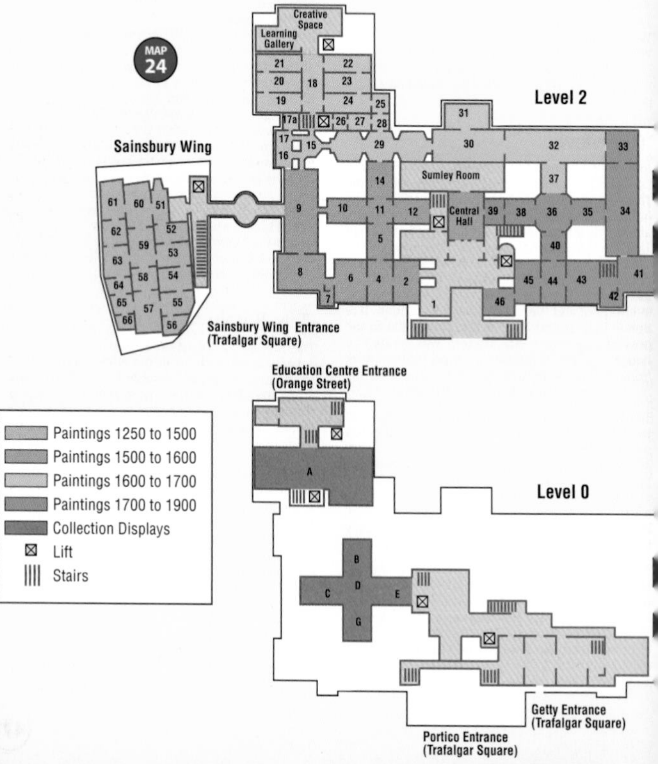

Overview

The National Gallery is home to one of the best and largest collections of Western European painting in the world, coming in at around 2100 paintings on display at any one time. An emphasis on *Western* and *painting* is needed. If you're looking for Roman antiquities or Persian miniatures, head for the British Musuem or the V&A—this is not where you're going to get it. Furthermore, if you're into anything post-Impressionist, make an about face for the Tate Britain. This is a celebration of the arts of Europe in all their old-school occidental glory. Taking the surprisingly manageable tour around the galleries (most of which are on one floor) will leave you wowed by how many works of art you will recognise. This is a collection that has been branded deep into your subconscious—with its oh-yeah-that-one Turners, Hogarths, Rembrandts and Leonardos. Bring a date and even the most culturally challenged will be able to impress.

The collection came into being in 1824 when the House of Commons paid £57,000 for 38 paintings belonging to a banker, using his Pall Mall home as the exhibition space. Compared to the Louvre, calling a few paintings in some guy's house the National Gallery was a little too embarrassing for the British public. So the great and the good demanded the Government pull their finger out and get to work on a purpose-built gallery worthy of a national art collection. In 1832, architect William Wilkins was given the job, constructing the recognisable porticoed façade in an up-and-coming area known as Trafalgar Square, called by one trustee 'the very gangway of London'. The most recent addition to the gallery is the Sainsbury Wing, designed in 1991 by leading contemporary architects Robert Venturi and Scott Brown after much controversy. Prince Charles, notoriously fussy when it comes to architecture, dismissed one suggested design as "a monstrous carbuncle on the face of a much-loved and elegant friend".

The National Gallery can be tackled in one exhausting afternoon, if you put your mind to it. Take advantage of the fancy benches, as many of the more epic paintings are best viewed from a distance. Be sure to get lost in the many smaller galleries, which house some dynamite, lesser-known, works. If you're feeling hungry, the National Dining Rooms is a critically acclaimed (read: expensive) restaurant, serving up the best in British fare. If you're feeling like a little culinary nationalism, the more casual National Café serves a very good cream tea.

The Greatest Hits

Starting with the Sainsbury Wing, the collection snakes around, covering European painting in chronological order from 1250 to 1900. There are a lot of paintings and it can get slightly overwhelming, so if you're pressed for time and want to make sure you've 'done' the National Gallery, try one of their 60 minute taster tours or pick up their guide to the 30 must-see paintings. Don't miss the **Arnolfini Portrait** (signed with 'Van Eyck was here' above the mirror—hilarious), **Botticelli's Venus and Mars**, **The Wilton Diptych**, and **Uccello's The Battle of San Romano**. Moving onto the 1500-1600 range, you'll recognise **Leonardo's cartoon of The Virgin and Child with St Anne and St John the Baptist**, **'The Ambassadors'** by Hans Holbein the younger (the one where you have to crouch to see the skull), the still-hilarious portrait of **A Grotesque Old Woman** by Quinten Massys (a 1664 example of the classic conundrum—a 64 year-old trying desperately to look 16) and **Titian's Bacchus and Ariadne**. Moving on, the collection houses a rather large collection of Dutch masters, including **Rembrandt, Rubens and van Dyck**. If you're sick of 2-D, a rather cool contraption is **Samuel von Hoogstraten's peepshow**. Peer through the peep hole in this painted box for an eye-popping view of the interior of a Dutch house. Very cool. A trip to the museum is never complete without viewing a **Gainsborough, Turner and Hogarth**, all of which are housed in the 1700-1900 galleries. Do not miss Hogarth's **Marriage a la Mode** a comical rendition of an 18th century arranged marriage—in a series of six paintings. Last but not least, onto the juxtaposition of three epic 19th century history paintings depicting corporal punishment with chilling realism—**Manet's Execution of Maximillian, Delaroche's Lady Jane Gray and Puvis de Chavanne's Beheading of St John the Baptist.** What a way to end it all, quite literally.

General Information

Address:	Peninsula Square, London, SE10 0DX
Website:	www.theO2.co.uk
General Information:	020 8463 2000
Tickets:	0871 984 0002

Overview

Exactly how the Millennium Dome transformed itself from national embarrassment and vortex for millions of taxpayers' money to the slick new home of groovy events is a bit of a mystery. Or maybe it's blindingly obvious—suits are better than politicians at this kind of thing. Anyway, on the outside it looks the same—the oversized lovechild of a jellyfish and hedgehog. Inside, gone are the attractions and concepts of 1999, aimed at celebrating all things British, so visionary that visitors stayed away in droves. Instead, the contents of an above-average high street have been stuffed inside—generic bistro food and wine bars, a multi-screen cinema. Whoope-doo you might think. But hold on—people come for the music. No really, they do.

Enter the O2 Arena or its little sis, the IndigO2 (see what they did there?) and be very impressed. The Arena has been engineered to provide sight lines that older venues can only dream of. The air conditioning—usually a rarity at London gigs, actually works. The acoustics have to be heard to be believed. It might not be a destination venue for mosh-loving purists and those who like the sweat and beer to fly, but if you like your music with a bit of comfort and luxury, you know, like toilets that work and don't stink of piss (548 of them!) then the 02 is well worth a look. Wheelchair users are catered for with fully accessible facilities. London seems to have its first venue that feels like some real thought has gone into its creation. If the organisers get their act together and diversify the bands appearing, including more that veer away from mainstream bands then it could become unstoppable.

How to Get There—Driving

Driving to the O2 isn't as daft as it might sound considering its location—previously un-chartered industrial wastelands of south east London. 2,000 parking spaces can be reserved in advance. With decent road links, traveling after rush hour should be bearable. The A102 linking north and south London runs through the Blackwall Tunnel, right next to the venue.

How to Get There—Mass Transit

In theory, the O2 has excellent transport links no matter how you travel. In practice, there's a good chance that your gig coincides with engineers digging up the precise bit of track you need to travel on. Check www.tfl.gov.uk before you travel. But when everything is working, then the Jubilee line at nearby North Greenwich connects directly with Waterloo and London Bridge. The Docklands Light Railway is one stop away and several bus routes drop off right outside. But the best way to arrive has to be by boat— the high speed Thames Clipper runs every 20-30 minutes. from several piers including Greenwich, Embankment and Waterloo. It's not only relaxing, but you get to see London at its best on the trip.

How to Get Tickets

Ticketmaster. Naturally. Try Gumtree and Craigslist for swaps, unwanted tickets and scum-of-the-earth touts.

Life in London can sometimes seem like one continuous, eventful film, but if you like your plots to take place on screen then the city has a lot to offer. Going to catch a flick in London can often unravel like some kind of Indiana Jones-esque adventure—the Holy Grail being a reasonably-priced ticket in a clean, comfortable theatre, that can only be sought after battling hundreds of tourists and fellow Londoners all with the same thought. Every year 164 million people visit London's cinemas; now that's a fair few ticket stubs.Thankfully, by leaving The Twilight Zone (a.k.a. the tourist trap of the West End) there are plenty of cinematic treasures to be plundered. Whatever genre of film takes your fancy, whatever time of night and whether you want a velour seat and popcorn or a leather chair and glass of champagne, you are sure to find it in the nation's capital.

For those who are desperate to catch Spielberg's latest offering, and are crazy enough to stick it out in the West End, chain cinemas abound. You'll find **Odeon (Maps 1, 4, 23, 30, 35, 61, 66, 71, 111 & 136)**, **Vue (Maps 12, 33, 43, 66 & 80)** and **Cineworld (Maps 11, 23, 40, 43, 45, 100 & 138)** theatres all over London. If you're brave, or just fancy seeing a star or two at one of the regular premiers, **Odeon Leicester Square (Map 23)** (made up of two separate theatres) could be for you. Another monster on the square is the historic **Empire (Map 11)**, seating an impressive 1,300 patrons is a landmark in itself, although she is a slightly faded leading lady these days. Beware though. While the price of a cinema ticket in the big smoke is normally enough to make you choke on your Butterkist, wandering into any of the theatres in Leicester Square may force you to re-mortgage with prices as high as £22.50 a ticket at peak times. **Apollo West End Multiplex (Map 23)** on Lower Regent Street was formerly the home of Paramount Pictures in the UK but now houses five small, luxurious theatres showing the latest flicks on general release.

It's not hard to find cinemas offering art house and independent films in London. Finding a good one, however, can be more of a challenge. **The Barbican (Map 7)** is always a good bet, and you can take in an exhibition before your film to really beef up your grey matter. We highly recommend the **Curzon Soho (Map 11)** offering not only a wide range of cinematic gems but also a plush bar to loosen you up for that three hour Kurasawa number. Remember if the queue is snaking along the pavement, tickets can be bought at the bar downstairs too. Check out the cinema's cousin in **Mayfair (Map 9)** as well as the slightly shabby **Renoir (Map 5)** in Brunswick Square. **Cineworld Chelsea (Map 45)** on the lustrous King's Road is one of London's premier art houses with two-seaters available for the perfect smooching experience. **The Gate (Map 29)** in Notting Hill was created from a restaurant in 1911 and now offers independent releases in a luxurious setting. **BFI Southbank (Map 104)** specializes in film through the ages as well as hosting frequent events. Who would have thought old Charlie would help us save our pennies? **The Prince Charles Cinema (Map 11)** off Leicester Square sits in a perfect location and offers revivals, cult and foreign language films for as low as £1.50. Now that's a bloody bargain. For those with a penchant for 'le cine' courtesy of our French neighbours visit **Cine Lumiere (Map 36)** in South Kensington. Uber-cool Clapham has an equally trendy art house cinema, the **Clapham Picturehouse (Map 143),** Dalston's Art Deco gem the **Rio Cinema (Map 86)** is worth a look, while Bloomsbury offers up **The Horse Hospital (Map 4)**—the name's almost as avant-garde as the films they show. Just leave Dobbin behind.

There are some wonderful cinematic experiences to be had too. **BFI IMAX (Map 104)** is housed in a curious circular building, south of Waterloo Bridge, with the biggest screen in the UK—the size of five double-decker buses. Then there are those three magic words—**The Electric Cinema (Map 29)** on Portobello Road. Grab a Pinot Grigio, rest your derriere on a soft leather seat and munch away at home-made ice cream all the way from sunny Hampshire while catching the latest Polish release. We now have the first British cinema to be opened in the 21st century: **Shortwave (Map 107)**, popped up in 2009 in the stylish Bermondsey Square, and among its 50 seats are some which were shrewdly rehoused from the Electric Cinema. And treat your mates to another round and a packet of crisps, because there are increasing numbers of mini-cinemas in pubs and bars such as **The Garrison (Map 107)** and **The Roxy (Map 106)**.

Cinemas	*Address*	*Phone*	*Map*
Aldwych Film	1 Aldwych	020 7300 1000	14
Apollo Cinema Piccadily Circus	19 Lower Regent St	0871 2233 444	23
Barbican Centre Cinema	Silk St & Whitecross St	020 7638 4141	7
BFI London IMAX	1 Charlie Chaplin Walk	0870 787 2525	104
BFI Southbank	Belverdere Rd & Waterloo Rd	020 7928 3232	104
Cine Lumiere	17 Queensberry Pl	020 7073 1350	36
Cineworld Chelsea	279 King's Rd	0871 200 2000	45
Cineworld Fulham Road	142 Fulham Rd	0871 200 2000	43
Cineworld Hammersmith	207 King St	0871 200 2000	40
Cineworld Haymarket	63 Haymarket	0871 200 2000	23
Cineworld Shaftesbury Avenue	13 Coventry St	0871 200 2000	11
Cineworld Wandsworth	Wandsworth High St & Ram St	0871 220 8000	138
Cineworld West India Quay	11 Hertsmere Rd	0871 200 2000	100
Clapham Picturehouse	76 Venn St	020 7498 2242	143
Curzon Chelsea	206 King's Rd	020 7351 3742	45
Curzon Mayfair	38 Curzon St	020 7495 0501	9
Curzon Renoir	1 Brunswick Sq	033 0500 1331	5
Curzon Soho	99 Shaftesbury Ave	020 7292 1686	11
The Electric Cinema	191 Portobello Rd	020 7908 9696	29
Empire Leicester Square	5 Leicester Sq	020 7437 9011	11
Everyman Baker Street	96 Baker St	020 3145 0565	1
Everyman Belsize Park	203 Haverstock Hill	020 3145 0520	67
Everyman Hampstead	5 Hollybush Vale	0870 066 4777	56
Everyman Screen on the Green	83 Islington Green	020 3145 0525	80
The Exhibit	12 Balham Station Rd	020 8772 6556	148
Frontline Club	13 Norfolk Pl	020 7479 8950	31
Gate Picturehouse	87 Notting Hill Gate	020 7727 4043	29
Genesis Mile End	93 Mile End Rd	020 7780 2000	97
Greenwich Picturehouse	180 Greenwich High Rd	087 0755 0065	120
Hackney Picturehouse	270 Mare St	0871 90 25 734	89
ICA Cinema	The Mall & Horse Guards Rd	020 7930 3647	23
Lux	18 Shacklewell Ln	020 7503 3980	86
Notting Hill Coronet	103 Notting Hill Gate	020 7727 6705	29
Odeon Camden Town	14 Parkway	020 7482 4576	71
Odeon Holloway	419 Holloway Rd	0871 22 44 007	61
Odeon Kensington	Kensington High St & Edwards Sq	0871 22 44 007	35
Odeon Leicester Square	24 Leicester Sq	0871 22 44 007	23
Odeon Marble Arch	10 Edgware Rd	0871 22 44 007	1
Odeon Panton Street	11 Panton St	0871 22 44 007	23
Odeon Putney	26 Putney High St	0871 22 44 007	136
Odeon Surrey Quays	Redriff Rd & Surrey Quays Rd	0871 22 44 007	111
Odeon Swiss Cottage	96 Finchley Rd	0871 22 44 007	66
Odeon Tottenham Court	30 Tottenham Ct Rd	0871 22 44 007	4
Odeon West End Cinema	40 Leicester Sq	0871 22 44 007	23
Odeon Whiteleys	Queensway & Porchester Gardens	0871 22 44 007	30
Peckham Multiplex	95 Rye Ln	0870 0420 299	123
Phoenix Cinema	52 High Rd	020 8444 6789	na
Prince Charles Cinema	7 Leicester Pl	020 7494 3654	11
Renoir Cinema	1 Brunswick Sq	0870 0420 299	5
Rich Mix Centre	34 Bethnal Green Rd	020 7613 7490	91
Rio Cinema	107 Kingsland High St	020 7241 9410	82
Ritzy Picturehouse	Coldharbour Ln & Brixton Oval	020 7733 2229	150
Riverside Studios	Crisp Rd & Queen Caroline St	020 8237 1111	41
Shortwave	10 Bermondsey Square	0207 357 6845	107
Vue Finchley Road	Finchley Rd & Blackburn Rd	08712 240 240	66
Vue Fulham	Fulham Rd & Cedarne Rd	08712 240240	43
Vue Islington	36 Parkfield St	08712 240240	80
Vue Piccadily Circus	19 Regent St	087 1224 0240	23
Vue Shepherds Bush	Shepherds Bush Green & Rockley Rd	08712 240 240	33
Vue West End Cinema	3 Cranbourn St	08712 240 240	12

It seems that every pub, bench and bridge in London has a tale to tell of past literary greats mulling over their troubles, weeping over lovers lost or launching themselves into the Thames. Ours is a city saturated in literary history and literature-lovers, with an abundance of bookshops and diversity of readers. While so many other retailers are homogenising, our independent bookshops—with their knowledgeable staffs and their often narrow focus—remain as eclectic and enthusiastic as ever. As well as a great selection of specialist independent stores, London is also home to dozens of second-hand bookshops, book markets, a literature festival, a major international book trade fair, and Europe's largest bookshop.

General

The **Foyles** flagship store on Charing Cross Road **(Map 12)** is a London institution, with a history as eccentric as its stock. Along with mainstream books and best-sellers, it offers a good range of second hand and out-of-print books, as well as a specialist Antiquarian department and a chilled jazz café. Venerable **Hatchard's (Map 10)** has been hawking books for over 200 years, making it London's oldest bookstore. The **London Review Bookshop (Map 4)** offers a huge range of constantly updated books with an intellectual bent and intellectual staff. **Metropolitan Books (Map 6)** is small but perfectly stocked, and Phil the owner makes time for any customer seeking advice or a friendly chat. Kids can find a bookshop wonderland in **Tales on Moon Lane (Map 128)** while parents can find the books they grew up with at **Ripping Yarns (Map 51).** The excellence of the independent stores has meant the chains have had to up their game—and loath though we are to say it, some, such as academic specialists **Blackwells (Maps 4, 12 & 74)** has gotten it very right indeed. In particular, **Waterstone's** in Piccadilly **(Map 23)** attracts all sorts of excitable superlatives, being the largest bookshop in Europe, running a range of literary activities to complement their stock, and even hosting a bar with some of the finest views of London.

Second Hand

Sadly, the world-renowned status Charing Cross Road used to command as the Mecca of second-hand bookstores is fading, and those who go looking for the genteel expertise immortalised in Helene Hanff's bestseller *84 Charing Cross Road* will find a "Med Kitchen" (shudder) at number 84. Many shops still cling to their ideals however, such as **Any Amount of Books (Map 12)** selling titles from as little £1 and offering a leather-binding service so your books can furnish your room as well as your mind. Good places to start if you are scouting for quality second-hand bookshops are: the tardis-like **The Bookshop (Map 129)** staffed by bookworms who have read *everything* (or so it seems) and can always help you find a gem; **John Sandoe (Map 46)** for true bookshop charm (rickety staircases, passionate staff, enchanting atmosphere); and the **Trinity Hospice (Map 136)** and **Oxfam Bookshops (Maps 38, 51, 86)**—not only an astonishingly cheap and broad collection of works, but all for charidee.

Specialist

Finding a bookshop devoted to your passion is like finding a club of old friends, and London caters for all tastes. Bored of cheese toasties? **Books for Cooks (Map 29)** smells as good as the recipes look, as they're tested in their kitchen first, while in-store cooking workshops teach new skills to avid customers. Sci-Fi nerds will be in their element at **Forbidden Planet (Map 179)**. **Gekoski (Map 4)** stocks a good range of modern first editions, or for older and rarer first editions try **Henry Sotheran (Map 10)**: a unique, but pricey, treat for any enthusiast. Head to **Atlantis (Map 4)** for all your occult needs (though no doubt the Spirits had already tipped you off on that one). Arty types are extensively catered for: **The Photographers' Gallery (Map 3)**, a treat in itself, has a substantial shop stocking photography titles, artists' monographs and unusual cameras; the **ICA Bookshop (Map 23)** is a great destination for art and film fans, and you can take in an exhibition while you're there; **Travis & Emery (Map 24)** stocks a vast range of music books and scores; comic geeks can get their fix at **Gosh! (Map 4)**. And for those with a passion for passion, pop along to the book section of **Coco de Mer (Map 13)**. Head to **Artwords (Map 84)** for books on—nope, I'll see if you can guess. Or to **Chappell (Map 11)** to supplement your Abba Hits keyboard book with some of their 50,000 music titles. **Motor Books (Map 24)**, surprisingly London's only shop dedicated to motoring, rail, aviation and military books, is the ideal repository for your menfolk when you need some peace.

Travel

Feeling lethargic? Head to one of the city's superb travel bookshops to have your energy restored. **Stanford's (Map 13)** has been inspiring London for 150 years, with its enormous collection of travel books and maps. A bookshop for travellers who like to read, **Daunt Books (Maps 2, 28, 57 & 67)** arranges all its books by geographical location, so even its fiction, cookbooks and history are shelved by country. Or to learn any of over 150 languages, head to **Grant & Cutler (Map 10),** the UK's largest foreign-language specialist.

Politics

Bookmarks (Map 4) stocks left-leaning works on a huge range of issues and takes a lively role in political activism, giving it a real and infectious sense of purpose. Also hugely right-on, both representing and driving several lefty social movements, is **Housmans (Map 78)**. Or for a more balanced approach with political works across the parties and even the odd Minister browsing for ideas, try **Westminster Bookshop (Map 22).**

Talks and Events

Publishing is a cut-throat business, and many writers have to sell their soul to get noticed. For them, it means an endless round of book signings and talks; for us, it means a fabulous chance to hobnob with our favourite authors. Most bookshops host occasional signings, but for regular events from the most celebrated authors, the big boys predictably have all the clout. **Foyles (Maps 12, 33, 78, 104)** and **Waterstone's (see p.489)** attract huge names: recent guests have included JK Rowling, Louis de Bernières, Salman Rushdie and AS Byatt. **Stanford's (Map 13)** offers opportunities to hear well-known travel editors, writers and photographers for an inspirational and sometimes career-changing evening. For intellectually stimulating debates and literary discussions, check out the **London Review Bookshop (Map 4)** and **Bookmarks (Map 4)**. Some events are free, some as much as a theatre ticket, but all should be booked in advance to ensure a place.

Bookshops	*Address*	*Phone*	*Map*
Any Amount of Books	56 Charing Cross Rd	020 7836 3697	12
Artwords	65 Rivington St	020 7729 2000	84
Atlantis	49 Museum St	020 7405 2120	4
Bargain Bookshop	153 Stoke Newington High Street	020 7249 8983	85
Bertram Rota	31 Long Acre	020 7836 0723	13
Blackwell Business + Law Bookshop	243 High Holborn	020 7831 9501	14
Blackwell Medical Bookshop	St Thomas Street	020 7403 5259	106
Blackwells	183 Euston Road	020 7611 2160	4
Blackwells	100 Charing Cross Rd	020 7292 5100	12
Bookmarks	1 Bloomsbury St	020 7637 1848	4
Books for Cooks	4 Blenheim Crescent	020 7221 1992	29
The Bookshop	1 Calton Ave	020 8693 2808	129
Chappell of Bond St	152 Wardour St	020 7432 4400	11
Coco de Mer	23 Monmouth St	020 7836 8882	13
Daunt Books	83 Marylebone High St	020 7224 2295	2
Daunt Books	193 Haverstock Hill	020 7794 4006	67
Daunt Books	51 S End Rd	020 7794 8206	57
Daunt Books	112 Holland Park Ave	020 7727 7022	28
Donlon Books	77 Broadway Market	020 7684 5698	89
The Dover Bookshop	18 Earlham St	020 7836 2111	12

Bookshops	*Address*	*Phone*	*Map*
Forbidden Planet	179 Shaftesbury Ave	020 7420 3666	12
Foyles	113 Charing Cross Rd	020 7437 5660	12
Foyles	Upper Ground	020 7440 3212	104
Foyles	Pancras Road	020 3206 2650	78
Foyles	Westfield	020 3206 2656	33
Gay's the Word	66 Marchmont St	020 7278 7654	5
Gosh! Comics	39 Great Russell St	020 7636 1011	4
Hatchard's	187 Piccadilly	020 7439 9921	10
Henry Sotheran	2 Sackville St	020 7439 6151	10
Housmans Bookshop	5 Caledonian Rd	020 7837 4473	78
ICA Bookshop	The Mall	020 7766 1452	23
John Sandoe	10 Blacklands Terrace	020 7589 9473	46
Librairie La Page	7 Harrington Rd	020 7589 5991	7
The Lion and Unicorn Bookshop	19 King Street	020 8940 0483	n/a
London Review Bookshop	14 Bury Pl	020 7269 9030	4
Magma	8 Earlham St	020 7240 8498	12
Motor Books	13 Cecil Court	020 7836 5376	24
Oxfam	80 Highgate High St	020 8340 3888	51
Owl Books	209 Kentish Town Rd	020 7485 7793	72
Pages of Hackney	70 Lower Clapton Rd	020 8525 1452	87
The Photographers' Gallery	16 Ramillies St	020 7831 1772	10
Quinto	72 Charing Cross Rd	020 7379 7669	12
R. A. Gekoski	15 Bloomsbury Square	020 7706 2735	4
Ripping Yarns	355 Archway Rd	020 8341 6111	51
Southbank Book Market	Under Waterloo Bridge	0871 663 2501	104
Stanford's	Long Acre	020 7836 1321	13
Stoke Newington Bookshop	159 Stoke Newington High Street	020 7249 2808	85
Tales on Moon Lane	25 Half Moon Ln	020 7274 5759	128
Travis & Emery	17 Cecil Ct	020 7240 2129	24
Trinity Hospice Bookshop	208 Upper Richmond Rd	020 8780 0737	136
Village Books	1 Calton Ave	020 8693 2808	129
Waterstone's	421 Oxford St	020 7495 8507	2
Waterstone's	82 Gower St	020 7636 1577	4
Waterstone's	Spencer Street	020 7608 0706	6
Waterstone's	9 Garrick St	020 7836 6757	13
Waterstone's	176 Fleet St	020 7353 5939	14
Waterstone's	Ludgate Circus	020 7236 5858	15
Waterstone's	54 London Wall	020 7628 9708	17
Waterstone's	1 Whittington Ave	020 7220 7882	18
Waterstone's	206 Piccadilly	020 7851 2400	23
Waterstone's	Trafalgar Square	020 7839 4411	24
Waterstone's	151 King's Rd	020 7351 2023	45
Waterstone's	255 Finchley Road	020 7433 3299	66
Waterstone's	128 Camden High Street	020 7284 4948	78
Waterstone's	45 Bank Street	020 7719 0688	100
Waterstone's Economists' Bookshop	Clare Market	020 7405 5531	14
Westminster Bookshop	8 Artillery Row	020 7802 0018	22
WHSmith	124 High Holborn	020 7242 0535	14
WHSmith	Fenchurch Street Station	020 7480 7295	18
WHSmith	Surrey Quays Shopping Centre	020 7237 5235	111
WHSmith	Elephant and Castle Shopping Centre	020 7703 8525	112

Yep you've heard the news. Theatre in the capital is all commercial. Predictable. Repetitive. Uncontroversial. If you believe the whingers, it's all boring stuff. Don't, because it's not. Yes, the West End, that heartland of commercial theatre around Shaftesbury Avenue, is filled with tourist-grabbing, crowd-pleasing musicals. Yes, there are more star-dominated, tried-and-tested plays than ever. Yes, the Mousetrap is still taking up the space at St Martin's after 58 years of we-bloody-well-know-whodunit.

But all that's only half the story. To find the other half, look beyond the glittering billboard signs to find the daring, small West End theatres, such as the **Donmar Warehouse (Map 13)**, bringing the innovative and unusual to Theatreland. There are the Off-West End theatres that proudly fly the flag for new writers, unafraid of being political, controversial and in-yer-face: **The Royal Court (Map 19)**, **The Soho (Map 11)**, **The Bush (Map 33)**. There are the unconventional, anarchic ensemble companies, such as PunchDrunk, shaking up things all the way from the fringe to the West End, while innovative short-play evenings are popping up at pubs across the city (see below).

But let's not forget the cracking double-whammy of the **National Theatre (Map 104)** and **The Old Vic (Map 104)**, two artistic powerhouses currently going from strength to strength. At the National, the unstoppable Nicholas Hytner brings original works to this Southbank concrete colossus (coupled with a £10-tickets offer), while down the road, Hollywood-star-turned-theatre-connoisseur Kevin Spacey is returning the Old Vic into its former glory. The refurbished **Young Vic (Map 104)**, meanwhile, is one of the best places to see fresh, new theatre (and get drunk afterwards). And, whatever you do, you're never far from a good Shakespeare production.

Keeping It Real in the West End

The Donmar Warehouse (Map 13), the West End's smallest theatre, has gained a reputation for being one of Theatreland's most innovative, yet still crowd-pleasing houses. It's quite common for good new plays that have successfully kicked off at a fringe or Off-West End venue to transfer to the West End, such as Tom Stoppard's guitars-meet-politics cracker Rock'n'Roll. **Dean Street's Soho Theatre (Map 11)** hunts out some of the most original, fearless or hilarious theatre around, while the **Comedy Theatre (Map 23)** may play it a little more safe but packs its shows with jaw-dropping casts. The West End is also a great place to catch up on those classics you always wanted to see but never got round to: from Beckett to Shakespeare.

Off-West End & The Fringe—The Best

The underground-led, breakneck guerrilla heyday might be over, but theatre outside the West End is in rude health. Head to rough-around-the-edges Dalston, where the **Arcola Theatre (Map 86)** continues to thrive in its scruffy ex-factory home, thanks to eclectic programming, an early-fringe-days feel and heaps of creative energy. The tiny **Bush Theatre (Map 33)** has long been a fierce champion of new work, and after being rescued by a star-studded tantrum in the face of funding cuts in 2008 it will doubtless continue to discover exciting new talent. So will **The Royal Court (Map 19)** on Sloane Square, which is one of London's finest. For new, innovative work, also keep your eyes on the **Battersea Arts Centre (Map 140)**, to watch what others will pay £50 to see next year (such as its premiere of Jerry Springer The Opera while other theatres nervously wrung their hands).

Theatre can't change society? Try telling that to the conviction-led crew of Kilburn's **The Tricycle (Map 65)**—easily London's most radical and most dedicated, political theatre. Islington's **Almeida (Map 80)** is far more conventional, but pretty—and that's got to count for something. If you're up for a laugh, check **The Hackney Empire (Map 87)**, a turn-of-the-century music hall, hosting some of London's best variety shows. **The Old Red Lion (Map 80)**, home inside an Islington pub, stubbornly clings to its unconventional, ale-fuelled fringe attitude while **Battersea's Theatre 503 (Map 132)** is as provocative as ever. Be surprised.

If the thought of being in a theatre at all is too bourgeois for you, then you're still well catered for. London thesps it up wherever it can so you're never too far from a performance and its sometimes unwitting audience. Recent outings have included an opera about domesticity and flatpack furniture in the Wembley Ikea, and a thriller performed in an office while the audience watch with binoculars and audiophones from the terrace opposite.

Tickets

If you know what you're after, check the theatre's website—they will either have their own system, a link to a ticket selling site, or provide a phone number. If not, check www.officiallondontheatre.co.uk, which lists shows by name, theatre and genre. The site also displays shows that are just opening, or just closing, and links straight to the appropriate ticketing website, once you have made your mind up. There's a handy map of all West End venues, too.

Fancy a bargain? The iconic TKTS ticket booth on Leicester Square sells on-the-day tickets for most big shows, half-price. The queue can be mind-boggling, so go early. There's a £2.50 booking fee, but it's included in the price shown. Many theatres also have their own discount schemes. If you don't mind standing, you can get Royal Court tickets for as little as 50p. Yes, that's 50p. Just show up between 6 pm and 6.30 pm on the day of the performance. The National has £5 standing tickets for all shows, but the view ain't always great.

Exciting & New

Enter the ensemble. They are multi-skilled, imaginative and are shaking the cosy, venue-obsessed Theatreland with a vengeance. Ensemble companies like PunchDrunk and Kneehigh are touring their way through London's venues in vigorously anarchic fashion. The result is increasingly physical, increasingly unconventional—and increasingly exciting theatre, which you'd be mad to miss.

PunchDrunk (punchdrunk.com) have gained a reputation for site-specific productions, inviting the audience to walk around and follow actors and themes as they please. Their 2006 treatment of Goethe's Faust at the National Theatre was widely hailed as one of the best things to have happened to British theatre in years. Kneehigh (www.kneehigh.co.uk) enjoy setting their nightmarish productions in outside mystical locations, but aren't afraid of West End constraints either. The award-winning Cheek by Jowl (www.cheekbyjowl.com), which have been producing Shakespeare and European classics since 1982, keep discovering hot talent—and ways to innovate.

If that's not grassroots enough, visit one of the themed short-play evenings that are popping up across town. Bringing together writers, actors and directors for twenty-minutes-or-so mini-shows, they have become a popular theatre alternative. Take your pick: Established organisers Nabokov (www.nabokov-online.com) have found a West End home at the **Trafalgar Studios (Map 24)** and relative newcomers DryWrite have made Whitechapel's **The George Tavern (Map 97)** their own. The message is spreading. What you thought was a boozer, really is a stage. The possibilities are endless.

Contemporary Dance

From small company shows to big stage spectacles, contemporary dance is having one hell of a ride. **Sadler's Wells (Map 6)** (www.sadlerswells.com), the grand old lady of dance venues, is still doing a fine job bringing some of the world's best dance to London. Check their Sadler's Wells Sampled programme, showcasing dazzling future talent for as little as £10. **The Barbican (Map 7)** (www.barbican.org.uk) has established itself as a reliable source of powerful dance performances, while the **Royal Festival Hall (Map 104)** attracts increasingly bold and interesting works to its refurbished riverside location. For London's most innovative dance performances, check **The Place (Map 4)**, a stylish venue that combines performance, training and dance education (www.theplace.org.uk).

Theatres	*Address*	*Phone*	*Type*	*Map*
Adelphi Theatre	The Strand	020 3725 7060	West End	24
The Albany	Douglas Way	020 8692 4446	Performing Arts	119
Aldwych Theatre	49 Aldwych	0870 4000 805	West End	14
Almeida Theatre	Almeida St	020 7359 4404	Fringe	80
Ambassadors Theatre	West St	084 4811 2334	West End	12
Apollo Theatre	Shaftesbury Ave	084 4579 1971	West End	11
Apollo Victoria Theatre	17 Wilton Rd	020 7834 6318	West End	20
Arcola Theatre	27 Arcola St	020 7503 1646	Fringe	86
ArtHouse	159 Tottenham Ln	020 8245 3099	Performing Arts	54
Arts Theatre	6 Great Newport St	084 5017 5584	West End	12
Barbican Centre	Silk St & Whitecross St	020 7638 4141	Performing Arts	7
Barons Court Theatre	28 Comeragh Rd	020 8932 4747	Fringe	42
Battersea Arts Centre	Lavender Hill & Theatre St	020 7223 2223	Fringe	140
Bloomsbury Theatre	15 Gordon St	020 7388 8822	Fringe	4
Brixton Academy	211 Stockwell Rd	020 7771 3000	Performing Arts	145
Bush Theatre	2 Shepherd's Bush Rd	020 8743 3584	Fringe	33
Cadogan Hall	5 Sloane Terrace	020 7730 4500	Performing Arts	19
Cambridge Theatre	Earlham St	084 4412 4652	West End	13
Chats Palace Arts Centre	42 Brooksby's Walk	020 8533 0227	Performing Arts	90
Comedy Theatre	Panton St	087 1297 5454	West End	23
Criterion Theatre	218 Piccadilly	087 0060 2313	West End	10
The Dogstar	389 Coldharbour Ln	020 7733 7515	Fringe	150
Dominion Theatre	268 Tottenham Court Rd	020 7413 3546	West End	4
Donmar Warehouse Theatre	41 Earlham St	020 7438 9200	West End	13
The Drill Hall	16 Chenies St	020 7307 5060	Fringe	4
Duchess Theatre	Catherine St	084 5434 9290	West End	14
Duke of York's Theatre	St Martin's Ln	087 0060 6623	West End	24
Etcetera	265 Camden High St	020 7482 4857	Fringe	71
Fortune Theatre	Russell St	020 7369 1737	West End	13
Garrick Theatre	Charing Cross Rd	020 7520 5690	West End	24
Gate Theatre	11 Pembridge Rd	020 7229 0706	Fringe	29
The George Tavern	373 Commercial Rd	020 7790 7335	Fringe	97
Gielgud Theatre	Shaftesbury Ave	084 4482 5130	West End	11
Greenwich Theatre	Crooms Hill & Nevada St	020 8858 7755	Fringe	120
Hackney Empire	291 Mare St	020 8985 2424	Fringe	89
Hampstead Theatre	Eton Ave	020 7722 9301	Fringe	66
Hammersmith Apollo Theatre	Queen Caroline St	020 8563 3800	West End	41
The Hen & Chickens Theatre Bar	109 St Paul's Rd	020 7354 8246		109
Her Majesty's Theatre	Haymarket	0844 412 2707	West End	23
Indigo2	Millenium Way	020 8463 2000	Performing Arts	na
Jermyn Street Theatre	16 Jermyn St	020 7287 2875	Fringe	23
King's Head Theatre & Pub	115 Upper St	020 7226 1916	Fringe	80
Koko	1 Camden High St	087 0432 5527	Performing Arts	71
Leicester Square Theatre	5 Leicester Pl	020 7534 1740	West End	11
Little Angel Theatre	14 Dagmar Passage	020 7226 1787	Performing Arts	80
London Palladium	Argyll St	020 7494 5020	West End	10
Lyceum Theatre	21 Wellington St	020 7432 4220	West End	14
Lyric Theatre	29 Shaftesbury Ave	020 7494 5045	West End	11
National Theatre	South Bank	020 7452 3400	West End	104

Theatres	*Address*	*Phone*	*Type*	*Map*
New London Theatre	Drury Ln	0870 890 0141	West End	13
Noël Coward Theatre	St Martin's Ln	084 4482 5140	West End	24
Novello Theatre	Aldwych	084 4482 5170	West End	14
Old Red Lion	418 St John St	020 7837 7816	Fringe	6
The Old Vic Theatre	103 The Cut	084 4871 7628	West End	104
Palace Theatre	Shaftesbury Ave	020 7870 6876	West End	12
Park Theatre	Clifton Terrace	087 0890 0142	Fringe	62
Phoenix Theatre	Charing Cross Rd	087 0060 6629	West End	12
Piccadilly Theatre	16 Denman St	020 7478 8800	West End	10
The Place	17 Duke's Rd	020 7121 1000	Performing Arts	4
Playhouse Theatre	Northumberland Ave	084 4871 7631	West End	24
Prince Edward Theatre	28 Old Compton St	084 4482 5151	West End	12
Prince of Wales Theatre	Coventry St	084 4482 5115	West End	11
Queen Elizabeth Hall	South Bank Centre	020 7960 4200	Performing Arts	104
Queen's Theatre	Shaftesbury Ave	084 4482 5160	West End	11
Riverside Studios	Crisp Rd & Queen Caroline St	020 8237 1111	Fringe	41
Ronnie Scott's	47 Frith St	020 7439 0747	Performing Arts	12
The Roundhouse	Chalk Farm Rd & Crogsland Rd	020 7424 9991	Performing Arts	71
Royal Albert Hall	Kensington Gore	020 7589 8212	Performing Arts	36
Royal Court Theatre	Sloane Sq	020 7565 5000	West End	19
Royal Festival Hall	Belvedere Rd	084 4875 0073	Performing Arts	104
Royal Opera House	Bow St	020 7304 4000	Performing Arts	13
Sadler's Wells	Rosebery Ave	084 4412 4300	Performing Arts	6
Savoy Theatre	The Strand	0870 164 8787	West End	24
Scala	275 Pentonville Rd	020 7833 2022	Performing Arts	78
Shaftesbury Theatre	210 Shaftesbury Ave	020 7379 5399	West End	13
Shakespeare's Globe	21 New Globe Walk	020 7902 1400	West End	105
Shepherd's Bush Empire	56 Shepherd's Bush Green	084 4477 2000	Performing Arts	33
Soho Theatre	21 Dean St	020 7478 0100	Fringe	11
Southwark Playhouse	77 Newington Causeway	020 7407 0234	Fringe	106
The Space	269 Westferry Rd	020 7515 7799	Fringe, Performing Arts	na
St John's	Smith Square	020 7222 1061	Performing Arts	22
St Martin's Theatre	West St	020 7836 1443	West End	12
Sutton House	2 Homerton High St	020 8986 2264	Performing Arts	87
Theatre 503	503 Battersea Park Rd	020 7978 7040	Fringe	132
Theatre Royal Drury Lane	Catherine St	087 0890 6002	West End	13
Theatre Royal Haymarket	Haymarket	020 7930 8890	West End	23
Toynbee Studios	28 Commercial St	020 7650 2350	Fringe	91
Trafalgar Studios	14 Whitehall	087 0060 6632	West End	24
The Tricycle Theatre	259 Kilburn High Rd	020 7372 6611	Fringe	65
Vaudeville Theatre	404 Strand	087 0890 0511	West End	24
Victoria Palace Theatre	Victoria St	084 4248 5000	West End	20
Wembley Stadium	Wembley Hill Rd	0800 169 2007	Performing Arts	na
Wigmore Hall	36 Wigmore St	020 7935 2141	Performing Arts	2
Wilton's Music Hall	Graces Alley & Ensign St	020 7702 2789	Fringe	95
Wyndham's Theatre	32 Charing Cross Rd	084 4482 5120	West End	12
The Young Vic Theatre	66 The Cut	020 7922 2922	West End	104

There are many great things about London's vibrant art world. The best? It's free. Granted, if you want to see some of the big show-stopping exhibitions that pass through the **Tates (Maps 21 & 105)**, **British Museum (Map 4)**, **National Gallery (Map 23)** and **Royal Academy (Map 2)** you'll have to pay quite a hefty sum, but overall, you can experience visual arts throughout the capital without coughing up much dough. This might be a contributing factor to London's sprawling art scene, as it is so easy to duck in and out of the capital's 300+ museums and galleries on a lunch break.

Of course, there are concentrations of art in locations around Piccadilly and Bond Street (check out Cork Street for its galleries, such as **Messum (Map 10)** and the **Adam Gallery (Map 10)**, running parallel with Savile Row), the East End (funkier affair and an artistic hipster breeding ground—check out Vyner Street in Bethnal Green), South Kensington/ Chelsea (a major culture scene as a result of the Great Exhibition of 1851) and various institutions dotted along the Thames (as seen from the Tate to Tate boat service). If your feeling really adventurous/ bored pretend you're really in the know and head to the New Cross, Peckham and Camberwell areas of South London where artists and galleries are pushing new boundaries in creativity/ pretentiousness. Great art is all over the this city, so get out your Oyster Card, and get ready to cover a lot of ground.

Starting with London's modern art, the **Tate Modern (Map 105)**, with its massive smoke stack, has become a major London landmark. This is despite it only existing as a separate entity from the **Tate Britain (Map 21)** since 2000. Check out its spacious Turbine Hall, with often spectacular installations.

It's not surprising that the Tate Modern is often the London tourist's first stop these days, as the city has become well-known for contemporary art. Due in part to the too-cool-for-school London art scene of the 1990s, which saw the establishment of Turner Prizers Tracy Emin, Rachel Whiteread and Damien Hirst, and made a major mark under Saatchi's guiding light. This light has faded somewhat, as the movement's personalities have slowly sold out a little (Emin designing for Longchamp is a case and point). But certain London galleries remain as monuments to this explosion of counter-culture, and, in addition to the **Saatchi Gallery (Map 46)**, these include the **Serpentine Gallery (Map 30)**, **Haunch of Venison (Map 10)**, and **Victoria Miro (Map 31)**. Other inspiring alternatives include the **Riflemaker (Map 10)**, **South London Gallery (Map 122)**, **Camden Arts Centre (Map 66)**, the **White Cube** at Mason's Yard **(Map 23)**, Hoxton Square **(Map 84)**, and Bermondsey **(Map 107)**.

London is a city with a lot on offer, and if you're looking for something a bit more traditional, start with the **National Gallery (Map 24)** in Trafalgar Square, moving onto the **National Portrait Gallery (Map 24)** next door, which presents you with a who's who of British culture past and present. Stroll up Charing Cross Road to the awesome **British Museum (Map 4)** with its jaw-dropping two acre roof over the Great Court (yet another example of Norman Foster's obsession with glass and geometry). Be sure to take in the Parthenon Marbles, aka Elgin Marbles, before the Greek government makes any attempt to get them back. Then over to the not-nearly-praised-enough **Wallace Collection (Map 2)** behind Selfridge's for some tea and Watteau action. A traditional art-lover's tour of London is not over without a trip to the **Royal Academy (Map 2)** with its epic exhibitions and finally to the **Tate Britain (Map 21)**, where the Pre-Raphaelites reign supreme.

Feeling a little non-conformist? London has a brilliant array of cultural institutions that offer more than just marble and canvas. From ceramics to dolls houses, kimonos to plaster casts of just about every great sculpture in the world—the V&A has it all (not to mention an awesome gift shop). Other alternatives to the mainstream include **The Photographers' Gallery (Map 13)** by Leicester Square, which not only squeezes in the best photographic exhibitions in town, but also boasts the best bookshop on the subject. Odd in its own way is the **Museum of London (Map 7)**, which walks you through the history of the city from prehistoric times to the present day. Recent London museum gems also include the newly renovated **London Transport Museum (Map 24)**, **Fashion and Textile Museum (Map 107)**, **Museum of Brands**, **Packaging and Advertising (Map 29)** and the **Design Museum (Map 107)**, with cars and video games in case you're stuck entertaining your nephew. Or check out one of London's hidden glories, from the The Vault at The Hard Rock Café (Map 9) by Hyde Park, or the mind blowing **Hunterian Museum (Map 14)** for fans of fetuses in jars and other macabre wonders (although be warned, do not go suffering from a weak stomach). The Horniman (*snigger*) Museum is a legacy of Victorian curiosity, starring an overstuffed walrus whose taxidermist didn't realise that walruses are supposed to have wrinkles.

The **Geffreye Museum (Map 88)** is a good one to check out when you're in Shoreditch and tired of being hip. Just up Kingsland Road from **Flowers (Map 91)** (a good British contemporary art gallery), this museum of domestic interiors runs through the history of Britain one living room at a time. Somewhat forgotten are the weird and wonderful **Sir John Soane's Museum (Map 14)**, **Leighton House (Map 35)** and **Dennis Severs' House (Map 91)**—but we'll let you discover these gems for yourself.

So forget Pret a Manger—feed your soul in one of London's many museums and galleries. They certainly have more to offer than one of those crappy no bread sandwiches, anyway.

Museums & Galleries	*Address*	*Phone*	*Map*
2 Willow Road	2 Willow Road	020 7435 6166	56
19 Princelet Street—Museum of Immigration and Diversity	19 Princelet St	020 7247 5352	91
7 Hammersmith Terrace	7 Hammersmith Terrace	0208 741 4104	39
Adam Gallery	24 Cork St	020 7439 6633	10
Apsley House	149 Piccadilly	020 7499 5676	9
Arsenal Museum and Stadium Tour	Drayton Park	020 7704 4504	74
Bank of England Museum	Threadneedle Street	020 7601 5545	17
The Banqueting House	Whitehall & Horse Guards Ave	020 3166 6000	24
Benjamin Franklin House	36 Craven St	020 7839 2006	24
The Bramah Museum of Tea and Coffee	40 Southwark Street	020 7403 5650	106
Britain At War Experience	66 Tooley Street	020 7403 3171	107
The British Library	96 Euston Rd	084 3208 1144	78
The British Museum	Great Russell St & Museum St	020 7323 8299	4
Brunel Museum	Railway Ave & Rotherhithe St	020 7231 3840	110
Brunswick House	30 Wandsworth Rd	020 7394 2100	134
Camden Arts Centre	Arkwright Rd	020 7472 5500	66
Cartoon Museum	35 Little Russell St	020 7580 8155	4
Chelsea FC Museum and Stadium Tour	Stamford Bridge	087 1984 1955	43
Chelsea Physic Garden	66 Royal Hospital Rd	020 7352 5646	45
Churchill Museum and Cabinet War Rooms	King Charles Street	020 7930 6961	24
Clink Prison Museum	1 Clink St	020 7403 0900	106
Clockmakers' Museum	Aldermanbury	020 7332 1868	16
Cuming Museum	151 Walworth Rd	020 7525 2332	113
Dennis Severs' House	18 Folgate St	020 7247 4013	91
Design Museum	Shad Thames	020 7403 6933	107
The Dickens House Museum	48 Doughty St	020 7405 2127	5
Dr Johnson's House	17 Gough Square	020 7353 3745	15
Fan Museum	12 Croom's Hill	020 8305 1441	120
Fashion and Textile Museum	83 Bermondsey St	020 7407 8664	107
Florence Nightingale Museum	2 Lambeth Palace Rd	020 7620 0374	131
Flowers	82 Kingsland Rd	020 7920 7777	91
Foundling Museum	40 Brunswick Square	020 7841 3600	5
Geffrye Museum	136 Kingsland Rd	020 7739 9893	88
Grant Museum of Zoology	Malet Place	020 7679 2647	4
Guards Museum	Birdcage Walk	020 7414 3428	22
Hampstead Museum	New End Square	020 7431 0144	56
Handel House Museum	25 Brook St	020 7495 1685	2
Haunch of Venison	6 Burlington Gardens	020 7495 5050	10
Hayward Gallery	Belvedere Rd	0871 663 2501	104
Horniman Museum & Gardens	100 London Rd	020 8699 1872	n/a
Hunterian Museum	35 Lincoln's Inn Fields	020 7869 6560	14
Imperial War Museum	Lambeth Road	020 7416 5000	104
Jewish Museum	129 Albert St	020 7284 7384	71
King's Place Gallery	90 York Way	020 7520 1485	79
Kirkaldy Testing Museum	99 Southwark St	013 2233 2195	105
The Library and Museum of Freemasonry	60 Great Queen St	020 7395 9251	13
Linley Sambourne House	18 Stafford Terrace	020 7602 3316	35
London Canal Museum	12 New Wharf Rd	020 7713 0836	79
London Dungeon	29 Tooley St	020 7403 7221	106
London Fire Brigade Museum	94 Southwark Bridge Rd	020 8555 1200	106

Museums & Galleries	*Address*	*Phone*	*Map*
London Sewing Machine Museum	293 Balham High Rd	020 8767 4724	151
London Transport Museum	Covent Garden Piazza	020 7379 6344	24
Marylebone Cricket Club Museum	St John's Wood Rd	020 7616 8656	76
Messum	8 Cork St	020 7437 5545	10
Museum in Docklands	Hertsmere Road	020 7001 9844	100
Museum of Brands, Packaging and Advertising	2 Colville Mews	020 7908 0880	29
Museum Of Childhood	Cambridge Heath Road	020 8983 5200	92
Museum of Fulham Palace	Bishops Avenue	020 7736 3233	48
Museum of Garden History	Lambeth Palace Road	020 7401 8865	131
Museum of London	150 London Wall	020 7001 9844	7
Museum of Methodism & Wesley's Chapel	49 City Rd	020 7253 2262	7
Museum of the Order of St John	26 St John's Ln	020 7324 4005	15
Museum of the Royal Pharmaceutical Society	1 Lambeth High St	020 7572 2210	131
National Army Museum	Royal Hospital Road	020 7881 2455	46
National Gallery	Trafalgar Square	020 7747 2885	24
National Maritime Museum	Park Row	020 8312 6565	n/a
National Portrait Gallery	St Martin's Place	020 7306 0055	24
Natural History Museum	Cromwell Rd	020 7942 5460	36
The Old Operating Theatre, Museum & Herb Garret Venue	9 St Thomas St	020 7188 2679	106
Petrie Museum of Egyptian Archaeology	Gower St	020 7679 2884	4
Pollock's Toy Museum	1 Scala St	020 7636 3452	3
Ragged School Museum	46 Copperfield Rd	020 8980 6405	98
Riflemaker Gallery	74 Beak St	020 7439 0000	10
Rootstein Hopkins Parade Ground	16 John Islip St	020 7514 8514	21
Rotherhithe Picture Research Library	82 Marychurch St	020 7237 2010	109
Royal Academy of Music Museum	Marylebone Rd	020 7873 7373	2
Saatchi Gallery	King's Road	020 7823 2332	46
Science Museum	Exhibition Rd	087 0870 4868	36
Serpentine Gallery	Kensington Gardens	020 7402 6075	30
Sherlock Holmes Museum	221 Baker St	020 7224 3688	76
Sikorski Museum	20 Princes Gate	020 7589 9249	37
Sir John Soane's Museum	13 Lincoln's Inn Fields	020 7440 4263	14
Smythson Stationery Museum	40 New Bond St	020 7629 8558	10
South London Gallery	65 Peckham Rd	020 7703 6120	122
Spencer House	27 St James's Pl	020 7499 8620	23
St Bartholomew's Hospital Museum	West Smithfield	020 7601 8152	15
Tate Britain	Millbank	020 7887 8888	21
Tate Modern	Bankside	020 7887 8888	105
Tower Bridge Exhibition	Tower Bridge	020 7403 3761	107
Victoria & Albert Museum	Cromwell Rd & Thurloe Pl	020 7942 2000	37
Victoria Miro Gallery	16 S Wharf Rd	020 7336 8109	31
Wallace Collection	Manchester Square	020 7563 9500	2
Wellcome Collection	183 Euston Rd	020 7611 2222	4
Westminster Abbey	Parliament Square	020 7222 5152	22
White Cube	26 Mason's Yard	020 7930 5373	23
White Cube	48 Hoxton Square	020 7930 5373	84
White Cube	144 Bermondsey St	020 7930 5373	107

Overview

Stumbling out teary-eyed into the light, pallid skin wrecked by long hours in darkness and surrounded by strangers, it's hard to believe that this time last year we were counting out our coppers and begging our friends to buy us another drink. Okay, so we're not completely in the red and London's cash registers may not be overflowing with moolah as they once were but we've managed to open new bars, forget about old ones, sing ourselves raw in amateur karaoke sessions, break a few bones dancing in scary clubs we shouldn't be in—you know, the usual. What is scary though is how fast the night-time landscape is changing around us. These days walking around Soho is like picking your way through a war zone; with The Astoria and its surrounding area now bulldozed, it sometimes feels the heart of London's soul has been ripped out by greedy developers. Maybe it has, but we're not dwelling on all those bad vibes: we're too busy digging amateur folk in Stokey, or quaffing luxurious cocktails in the depths of Old Street, or down the front at some dingy gig hellhole in the depths of Brixton having the time of our sorry little lives. As you may have gathered by now, London's options are as endlessly varied as her tastes. And being children of the post-modern age (or is that post-post-modern age?) we've given up caring about tribalism and consistency and have dived head-first into everything at once. Economy, what economy?

Local Pubs for Local People

North to South, East to West, whether in Zone 1 or Zone 6 the London 'local' encapsulates the city itself. That calm beating heart of the old geezer talking of times gone by in Limehouse or the adrenaline-fuelled racing heart of the City's next 'big thing' in Farringdon—all echoing around a city that tells its stories, shares its woes and gets itself together over a pint of 'Pride' in the local boozer. The cavernous bowels of Dickens' favourite local **Ye Olde Cheshire Cheese (Map 15)** now provide tourist-free shelter for City folk. Borough's **George Inn (Map 106)**, with a dazzling selection of ales, is as ancient as they get. **The Lamb (Map 14)** is where to go after your office job if you want to pretend you're a writer, while the Grade-II-listed **Princess Louise (Map 4)** is sparkling with old man-ness but in the heart of London. In Hampstead, it's got to be the pretty, and pretty hidden, **Holly Bush (Map 56)**. And while it's been gentrified since it was run by the Kray's mum, **The Carpenter's Arms (Map 91)**, is still a great, tiny little foreign beer-heaven. Modern rot has yet to set in at Highgate's old-school **The Winchester (Map 52)** and you can eyeball woodworm in the brilliant **The Compton Arms (Map 80)**. The old-timers in Rotherhithe's dream-of-your-dad **The Mayflower (Map 109)**, and Brixton's **The Effra (Map 150)** will have never heard of the 'Inter-web', never mind Facebook. Way out west, **The Dove (Map 40)** draws the local collective with its cosy fire, relaxed chatter and river spectacular.

Keep-It-Real Ale

The Carling brigade can take a hike, this town takes Price (sic) in its real brews. **The Wenlock Arms (Map 83)** proves we can do down-to-earth ale-enthusiast and **The Jerusalem Tavern (Map 3)** shows we can do fake ye olde times with amazing beer selection as well as any Lancashire local. Borough's **Market Porter (Map 106)** has a great selection, and is full of market traders counting their cash. Lovers of the Belgian stuff (and trendy Hackney-ites) will feel at home in **The Dove (Map 89)** and those after an even greater selection of European ales without the pretentiousness should head to **Quinns (Map 71)** in Camden. Too fancy? For great ale selections, there's **The Royal Oak (Map 106)** also in Borough, where the taps come courtesy of the Harveys brewery. Pitfield, Freedom and St Peter's, meanwhile, supply Islington's **Duke of Cambridge (Map 83)** with organic beer, if you like that kind of stuff. In Parson's Green **The White Horse (Map 49)** is a Victorian gem and the **Roebuck (Map 38)** provides Chiswick with an ever changing selection of local and national brews.

Good Mixers

While our ale keeps us down to earth, it's the lure of the cocktail that causes us to show off. Shaken or stirred, it doesn't matter. It's all about looking good with a long glass of the colourful sugary stuff dressed to the nines, glace cherry 'n all. For aesthetic hedonism we love **Loungelover (Map 91)** and **Lounge Bohemia (Map 8)**. Martinis? You'll find us at the **Charlotte Street Hotel (Map 3)**. At **5th View (Map 9)** there's vistas of Big Ben with your Kir Royal and the secretive speak-easy mood of **Milk & Honey (Map 10)** comes with eight handy house rules, including "no star fucking." See also the plush Art Deco heaven that is **Claridge's Bar (Map 2)**, while **Montgomery Place (Map 29)** serves Notting Hill a bit of old world cool. If you find yourself on Clapham High Street then you could do a lot worse than heading to **The Loft (Map 143)**—a modern, lush escape. One can feel studious while nursing a punch bowl at **The Cinnamon Club (Map 22)**, nestled perfectly inside the old serenity of the Old Westminster Library. On the contrary, vivacious **Buena Vista (Map 143)** brings a bit of Havana to the streets of Clapham and is the perfect spot for a mojito.

Weirdos

Let's face it, sometimes the booze just isn't enough to keep you entertained. Destroying your internal organs with the stuff is just sometimes a little boring, right? **Jamboree at Cable Street Studios (Map 97)** is an artist-run warehouse space that does hipster rave-offs. **The Windmill (Map 150)** of Brixton is a handmade weirdo magnet and **The Battersea Barge (Map 134)** is a friendly old pub—on a very thin barge. **The Coronet (Map 74)** in Holloway has a desolate, nostalgic charm as does perhaps the weirdest pub of them all, the **Palm Tree (Map 93)**, a celebration of British antiquity with crooners of a certain age most nights.

Smoker-Friendly

If the merciless prohibition regime of 2007 hasn't resulted in reluctant surrender, don't despair: from provisionally erected patios to all-year beer gardens to secret backdoors, London's ban-bashing creativity knows no boundaries. Great fag spots include the terrace at **Proud (Map 71)**, overlooking Camden's roofs, the barbeque-and-beer-can courtyard of **93 Feet East (Map 91)** and the tree-shaded garden of the **Edinboro Castle (Map 77)**. Hang out in front of Highgate favourite **The Flask (Map 51)** or combine a late-night pint with a rollie in the backyard of the **The Dolphin (Map 89)**. For clubbing, consider **Egg (Map 79)**, where you're allowed to smoke in the massive garden. **The Owl & Pussycat (Map 91)** is not just a surprisingly pleasant pub in Shoreditch, it's also got a surprisingly nice garden, where smoking is not just allowed, dear friends, but encouraged.

We're Raving, We're Raving

While the fierce bass from the basement at **Plastic People (Map 84)** reverberates around Shoreditch, over at superclub **Fabric (Map 15)** the cool kids of the capital are bringing down the house with ... er, a bit of House music. For the groovier seeking a smaller joint try **Guanabara (Map 13)**. The ever-so-eclectic **Notting Hill Arts Club (Map 29)** continues to come up with exhilarating and inventive nights, as does Brick Lane's 93 **Feet East (Map 91)** and **333 (Map 84)**. **Cargo (Map 84)** is for those who like a deep seated couch with their DJ while **Madame Jojo's (Map 11)**. As long as lip fuzz is still trendy there's always the **Moustache Bar (Map 86)** and for quirky, artsy fartsery head to **Passing Clouds (Map 88)**, both in Dalston, natch. For serious rockabilly, find **Ye Olde Axe (Map 91)** gentlemen's club on Hackney Road, where the rock 'n' roll starts as soon as the last naked girl has disappeared behind the big-mirrored wall.

Great Bars

George Orwell's ideal pub was all about "draught stout, open fires, cheap meals, motherly barmaids and no radio." These days we'd maybe add music straight from a blog, handmade decor and a dangerous vibe. For some if not all of these try up-beat **Jaguar Shoes (Map 91)**. **Freud (Map 13)** or the **French House (Map 11)** in the West End are also solid contenders for boho schlock. But there's so much more: crawl from **Barrio North's (Map 80)** caravan to the country-house of **Lost Society (Map 142)**, from the **Island Queen (Map 83)** to the Moijto-fuelled **Mau Mau (Map 29)**. We like standing next to (would-be) artists at the **ICA Bar (Map 23)** and actor types on the terrace of **The Cut Bar (Map 104)**. Or in front of a movie screen, at **Roxy Bar and Screen (Map 106)**. Later on, you'll find us nibbling cheese in Dalston's **Jazz Bar (Map 82)**, dancing to trashy music at **Da Vinci's (Map 104)**.

Best of the Rest

Want to feel exclusive? Members-only clubs are not only becoming ever more popular, but also ever more accessible. So there. Escape Shoreditch's terrifying hordes to the rooftop swimming pool of **Shoreditch House (Map 91)** or the boredom of Shepherd's Bush to the underground ex-toilets that have become

Ginglik (Map 33). Of course, most of those in the know will drag you to the various warehouse raves that fire up every weekend. People like **Real Gold** (http://wearerealgold.com) are a good place to start if you fancy some of this awfulness. Remember it's not who you know but, oh wait, it is who you know.

To create your own entertainment and/or embarrass yourself, **Lucky Voice (Maps 10, 80)** is one of many joints offering private karaoke booths for you and some people who will most probably cease to be your friends after they hear you massacre 'Time After Time.' Shoreditch's exposed brick joint **The Book Club (Map 8)** has a bit of 'Social Athletics' on the bill—ping pong, old chap? If relying on that notoriously joke-cracking ex-friend of a friend for your evening's amusement sounds a bit risky, consider these alternatives: The standard-setting **Comedy Store (Map 11)** (book in advance) and **Covent Garden Comedy Club (Map 24)**, or, at the pub end of things, **The Bedford (Map 148)** and the **Camden Head (Map 78)**. If you think that YOU should in fact provide the evening's amusement, well, the **Poetry Café (Map 13)** gives you the stage. Or stay at home and talk to yourself; it's cheaper.

Music, Sweet Music

London's veins are pumped by its mellifluous melodies, the driving sound of grime, the sneers of angry young men and the coos of sweet maidens. Whether you're dub-stepping in the dark or jamming along at folk night there'll be something to hear at any given time of the week.

Strummin' Mental

This city's music scene is in a constant state of flux with bands, venues and styles falling in and out of cool lists quicker than a Ramones song. What never changes though is that there always is a scene and with that scene comes the venue. The good news is that there are so many great places to do this in. Yes we've got our share of corporate megaliths (that means you **O2**) but for every church of Carling there are two or three brilliant dives like the punky **Grosvenor (Map 145)** or the ever-mobbed **Stag's Head (Map 84)**.

For the sweatily inclined there are infinite choices. Bethnal Green's **Star of Bethnal Green (Map 92)** (formerly the Pleasure Unit), Highgate's **Buffalo Bar (Map 80)** and Angel's **Lexington (Map 79)** are as pant-wettingly indie as they come but if you like harder or weirder stuff the **Camden Underworld (Map 71)** does all the metals while **Cafe Oto (Map 86)** handles experimental and improv. **The MacBeth (Map 84)** is very popular yet somehow suffers from a fun bypass but **Monto Water Rats (Map 5)** is an unshakeable legend. The refurbished **Old Blue Last (Map 84)** or Vice Magazine party HQ has surfed to the crest of the trend wave fueled by young kids attempting to be sexually harassed by older men like in their favourite adverts for American Apparel. Mid-sized venues for mid-fame bands? The **Scala (Map 78)** is a brilliant converted cinema. The now legal **Barden's Boudoir (Map 86)** has come a long way since it was a dingy dive run by gangsters and of course the **ICA (Map 23)** is the 'art-space' par excellence for all artistes who insist on that 'e' at the end of 'artist.' The **Amersham Arms (Map 126)** is a good place to watch some twonks you've been told to like by Dazed. The city's electronic music scene generally piggy-backs the guitars, but check out **Cable (Map 107)** and **Lightbox (Map 134)**.

As for the classics, the **Shepherd's Bush Empire (Map 33)** and the breathtakingly beautiful **Bush Hall (Map 32)** remain west London's finest, while Camden stalwart **Koko (Map 71)** keeps rocking in the free world. The north London show is being stolen by **Roundhouse (Map 71)**, though, boasting a healthy "I am Legend"-attitude and some bloody horrible Anthony Gormley statues waiting to jump from the top. **Brixton Academy (Map 145)** might be slightly overrated, but its sky-like ceiling remains awesome. If you have to do stadium-size, do stadium-size in style and get your seat in the **Royal Albert Hall (Map 36)**, which is increasingly luring good non-classical acts. The refurbishment of the **Royal Festival Hall (Map 104)**, meanwhile, has kick-started more pop-oriented programming on the South Bank.

A World of Jazz and Blues

Camden's intimate **Jazz Café (Map 71)** seems to have no intention of stopping its relentless stream of first-rate jazz performances, getting in more soul, funk and pop at the same time, while **Ronnie Scott's Jazz Club (Map 12)**, London's undisputed grandaddy of jazz original continues to offer up an eclectic programme of past and present. For some of the freshest jazz, alongside great contemporary folk and world music, head to Dalston, where the plush **Vortex (Map 82)** is a-buzz with free-spirited legends. On the other side of town, Fulham's small but perfectly formed **606 Club (Map 50)** sets the tone with crammed, small tables within slobbering distance from the saxes. Catch excellent blues and singer/songwriter stuff every night of the week at **Ain't Nothing But The Blues Bar (Map 10)**, or Denmark Street's **12 Bar Club (Map 12)**. Latin jazz breezes through the air at Archway's **Caipirinha Jazz Bar (Map 52)**. For world music, the **Barbican Centre (Map 7)** leads the pack, but is easily beaten in atmosphere stakes by the **Union Chapel (Map 80)**, an Islington church doubling as one of London's most beautiful venues and in scummy stakes by **Dingwalls (Map 71)** who continue to expand their programming. The home of folk is the brilliant **Cecil Sharp House (Map 70)**. If classical music floats your boat, look beyond the obvious venues and settle amid the great acoustics of Chelsea's **Cadogan Hall (Map 19)**, the historical brilliance of Hackney's **Sutton House (Map 87)** or the magnificent **Wigmore Hall (Map 2)**, in Mayfair.

Map 1 • Marylebone (West)

Duke of York	45 Harrowby St	020 7262 9129	The ideal local.

Map 2 • Marylebone (East)

Claridge's Bar	55 Brook St	020 7629 8860	Posh and plush and Art Deco. More champagne!
Gunmakers	33 Ayrbrook St	020 7487 4937	Nice boozer on quiet street.
Inn 1888	21 Devonshire St	020 7486 7420	Quiet pint perfection.
The Phoenix	37 Cavendish Sq	020 7493 8003	A quirky gem amidst an ocean of crappy chain bars.
Purl	50-54 Blandford St	020 7935 0835	Victorian themed experimental cocktail bar.

Map 3 • Fitzrovia

100 Club	100 Oxford St	020 7636 0933	Ancient club that's seen off Nazi bombs and Sex Pistols.
The Albany	240 Great Portland St	020 7387 0221	Swanky, but nice. And the music's good.
Bourne & Hollingsworth	28 Rathbone Pl	020 7636 8228	Fine Fitzrovian basement boutique.
Bradley's Spanish Bar	42 Hanway St	020 7636 0359	60's rock joint with awesome jukebox and disgusting toilets.
Bricklayers Arms	31 Gresse St	020 7636 5593	Advertising types fake no-nonsense boozing.
Charlotte Street Hotel	15 Charlotte St	020 7806 2000	Dirty gossip over dirty martinis.
The Cock	27 Great Portland St	087 2107 7077	Cheap, cheerful and central.
The Fitzroy Tavern	16 Charlotte St	020 7580 3714	Sam Smith's, anyone?
Hakkasan	8 Hanway Pl	020 7927 7000	Sleek, blue-lit boutique. For saketinis and rose petal martinis.
The Jerusalem Tavern	55 Britton St	020 7490 4281	A tiny old wooden gem of a pub. And organic ale.
Market Place	11 Market Pl	020 7079 2020	Warm buzz. Hot crowd. Cool prices.
The Northumberland Arms	43 Goodge St	020 7580 7975	Cosy, old-style bar with a local feel.
The Remedy	124 Cleveland St	020 3489 3800	Deep dive into wine, with food pairings, too.
Rising Sun	46 Tottenham Ct Rd	020 7636 6530	Bordering studentland and Fitzrovia; pretty name, less pretty pub.
The Roxy	3 Rathbone Pl	020 7255 1098	Hip subterranean hangout. More chicks than dicks.
Shochu Lounge	37 Charlotte St	020 7580 6464	Japanese-styled cocktails underneath Roka restaurant.
The Social	5 Little Portland St	020 7636 4992	Fab music, nonchalant surroundings and plenty of trendsters.
Yorkshire Grey	46 Langham St	020 7636 4788	Upstairs is perfect when Oxford Street's pissing you off.

Map 4 • Bloomsbury (West)

All Star Lanes	Bloomsbury Pl	020 7025 2676	You'll be bowled over. Oh yes you will.
Bloomsbury Bowling Lanes	Bedford Way	020 7183 1979	As cool as bowling gets.
Marquis Cornwallis	31 Marchmont St	020 7278 8355	Chilled couches.
The Old Crown Public House	33 New Oxford St	020 7836 9121	After-work bar that takes itself very seriously.
The Plough	27 Museum St	020 7636 7964	Fancy a bite? London Vampyre Society meetings held here monthly.
The Princess Louise	208 High Holborn	020 7405 8816	Victorian gin palace now serving cheap but good lager.
ULU	Malet St	020 7664 2000	Student union, student prices, student bands.

Map 5 • Bloomsbury (East)

)6 St Chad's Place	6 St Chad's Pl	020 7278 3355	Stylish wine bar with plastic chairs? SOOO avant-garde, dahhhling!
The Blue Lion	133 Grays Inn Rd	020 7405 4422	Pool table!
Calthorpe Arms	252 Gray's Inn Rd	020 7278 4732	Impressive old man pub.
The Clerk & Well	156 Clerkenwell Rd	020 7837 8548	You and a hundred cycle couriers.
Monto	328 Grays Inn Rd	020 3589 5983	No rats here, only the best up-and-coming bands.
The Perseverance	63 Lamb's Conduit St	020 7405 8278	Bustling, young and semi-trendy.
Pimp Shuei	59 Mount Pleasant		Kung fu-themed bar.
Smithy's	15 Leeke St	020 7278 5949	Our lunchtime to late-night-wind-down friend.

Map 6 • Clerkenwell

1920	19 Great Sutton St	020 7253 1920	Classic American pool hall with occasional DJ events.
Bandstand Busking	Northampton Square		Free acoustic gigs in summer. Dreamy.
The Betsey Trotwood	56 Farringdon Rd	020 7253 4285	Thoroughly likable Shepherd Neame pub renowned for live music.
Café Kick	43 Exmouth Market	020 7837 8077	Creaky, Latin American table football cafe.
The Dovetail	9 Jerusalem Passage	020 7490 7321	Small, but perfectly formed Clerkenwell sister to Broadway Market's The Dove.
The Harlequin	27 Arlington Way	079 7565 2669	Livingroom boozer.
Old Red Lion	418 St. John St	020 7833 3053	Theatre pub legend.
The Slaughtered Lamb	34 Great Sutton St	020 7253 1516	Dimly-lit pub that's still packing in the Clerkenwell crowd.
The Three Kings	7 Clerkenwell Close	020 7253 0483	Quirky pub that dies on weekends.
The Wilmington Arms	69 Rosebery Ave	020 7837 1384	Staff have 'arsehole' tattooed on their foreheads.

Map 7 • Barbican / City Road (South)

Nightjar	129 City Rd	020 7253 4101	Like Fat Sam's Grand Slam.
The Two Brewers	121 Whitecross St	020 7819 9539	Traditional English pub with a young hip crowd.

Map 8 • Liverpool Street / Broadgate

The Book Club	100 Leonard St	020 7684 8618	All day food and drink venue with outdoor space and basement club.
Callooh Callay	65 Rivington St	020 7739 4781	Not-so-secret cocktail bar in The City; enter through a wardrobe.
Casita	5 Ravey St	020 7729 7230	Generous cocktails and entertaining bar staff.
Lounge Bohemia	1 Great Eastern St	077 2070 7000	Vintage martinis make up for neo-avant-garde pretenses.
Red Lion	1 Eldon St0	20 7247 5381	Drinkers near Moorgate can't be choosers. So there.
Worship Street Whistling Shop	63 Worship St	020 7247 0015	Wet your whistle.
XOYO	32 Cowper St	020 7354 9993	Concrete music bunker with quality acts and a buzzing vibe.

Map 9 • Mayfair / Green Park

707 Wine Bar	181 Piccadilly	020 7734 8040	Empty Fortnum & Mason's wine cellar.
Funky Buddha	15 Berkeley St	020 7495 2596	Overpriced, overrated, tacky Z-list haunt. Apart from that, it's great!
Mahiki	1 Dover St	020 7493 9529	Crushingly tropical cocktail bar. Pineapples a-go-go.
Shepherd's Tavern	50 Hertford St	020 7499 3017	For drinking within Shepherd's Market.
Whisky Mist	35 Hertford St	020 7208 4067	High-end hotel bar with a huge selection of whiskies.

Map 10 • Piccadilly / Soho (West)

h View	203 Piccadilly	020 7851 2433	Spill Bloody Marys over books in full view of Big Ben.
.n't Nothing But...	20 Kingly St	020 7287 0514	Bracingly raw music in a tiny frontroom.
he Blind Pig	58 Poland St	020 7993 3251	Challenging cocktails above Social Eating House.
ourthouse Bar	19 Great Marlborough St	020 7297 5555	Drink where Oscar Wilde was in the clink.
he John Snow	39 Broadwick St	020 7437 1344	Yet another cheap, old school boozer from Samuel Smith Brewery.
ucky Voice	52 Poland St	020 7439 3660	Why is this London's best karaoke bar? The dress up box.
he Red Lion	14 Kingly St	020 7734 4985	Amazingly cheap for such a central spot.
rawberry Moons	15 Heddon St	020 7437 7300	Dig the cheese, with your new squeeze.
he Windmill	6 Mill St	020 7491 8050	Fab beers on tap but you come here for the pies.

Map 11 • Soho (Central)

ue Posts	22 Berwick St	020 7437 5008	Unreformed, scuzzy boozer.
he Blue Posts	28 Rupert St	020 7437 1415	Hey, a decent pub in Soho.
he Comedy Store	1 Oxendon St	084 4847 1728	It ain't world famous for no reason, chuckles.

De Hems	11 Macclesfield St	020 7437 2494	Dutch bar with brain-cell-annihilatingly strong beer. Hic!
Experimental Cocktail Club	13 Gerrard St	020 7434 3559	The modern-day speakeasy: reservation by email only.
Freedom	66 Wardour St	020 7734 0071	Neon green cocktail kitsch.
The French House	49 Dean St	020 7437 2799	Boho Soho hang-out for eccentrics.
The Lyric	37 Great Windmill St	020 7434 0604	Charming Victorian pub with many draughts.
Old Tom & English	187 Wardour St	020 7287 7347	Sleek cocktails in mid-century modern atmosphere.
The Shadow Lounge	5 Brewer St	020 7317 9270	Gay chi chi lounge.
Village	81 Wardour St	020 7478 0530	Tacky, flirtatious Soho gay bar.

Map 12 • Soho (East)

68 and Boston	5 Greek St	020 7287 3713	68's wine is on ground floor; Boston's cocktails live above.
Ape & Bird	142 Shaftesbury Ave	020 7836 3119	Italian-focused beverages from folks behind Polpo.
Bar Termini	7 Old Compton St	07860 945018	Italian coffee and cocktails; efficiently scheduled.
The Borderline	Orange Yard	020 7734 5547	Cool basement club, bizarrely got up in Tex-Mex decor.
Cafe Boheme	13 Old Compton St	020 7734 0623	Beautiful bar to prop up and people watch.
Comptons	53 Old Compton St	020 3238 0163	Crammed gay pub.
The Crobar	17 Manette St	020 7439 0831	Heavy metal and cheap bourbon. Be a man for once.
G-A-Y Bar	30 Old Compton St	020 7494 2756	Poptastic gay bunker.
G-A-Y Late	5 Goslett Yard	020 7734 9858	Cheap drinks and pop videos wipe out brain functions 'til 3am.
Garlic & Shots	14 Frith St	020 7734 9505	Drunken vampires beware.
Green Carnation	5 Greek St	020 8616 8087	Sexy, Oskar Wilde-inspired lounge that Oskar would have approved of.
Jazz After Dark	9 Greek St	020 7734 0545	Tunes and cheap drinks, until LATE.
Karaoke Box	18 Frith St	020 7494 3878	A bit gritty but one of London's cheaper karaoke bars.
Ku	30 Lisle St	020 7437 4303	Newly relocated gay bar for the young and clueless.
LAB Bar	12 Old Compton St	020 7437 7820	London Academy of Bartending—they know how to make martinis.
The Montagu Pyke	105 Charing Cross Rd	020 7287 6039	Cheap beer—in the West End.
Ronnie Scott's	47 Frith St	020 7439 0747	Original, and still the best.
The Royal George	133 Charing Cross Rd	020 7734 8837	Busy, but the crowd's nice. Board games and food.
The Three Greyhounds	25 Greek St	020 7494 0953	Recall glory days of Soho hunting grounds with real ale.
The Toucan	19 Carlisle St	020 7437 4123	Small and snug central bolthole for Guinness.

Map 13 • Covent Garden

Compagnie Des Vins Surnaturels	8-10 Neal's Yard	020 7734 7737	Encyclopedic wine bar with French-Italian focus.
The Cross Keys	31 Endell St	020 7836 5185	Tiny old-school boozer.
Freud	198 Shaftesbury Ave	020 7240 9933	Intimate basement bar that used to be Alex of Blur's living room. Literally.
Guanabara	Parker St	020 7242 8600	Brasil. But in Holborn.
Lamb and Flag	33 Rose St	020 7497 9504	Cobbled lane leads to a crowded but gloriously timeless inn.
Poetry Cafe	22 Betterton St	020 7420 9888	Eat, drink, write, listen or, yes, PERFORM!

Map 14 • Holborn / Temple

Bar Polski	11 Little Turnstile	020 7831 9679	With 50 types of vodka, even beetroot soup tastes good.
Bounce	121 Holborn	020 3657 6525	Anyone for (table) tennis?
Cittie of Yorke	22 High Holborn	020 7242 7670	Soe olde it's name has extra e's. A marvellouse pube.
The Craft Beer Co.	82 Leather Ln		Beer drinkers heaven, albeit with a scramble to get served
The Enterprise	38 Red Lion St	020 7404 8461	More Captain Cook than Captain Kirk.
The Lamb	94 Lamb's Conduit St	020 7405 0713	Legendary little place with Victorian touches.
The Seven Stars	53 Carey St	020 7242 8521	Tiny, slightly dusty bar frequented by barristers.
Volupte	9 Norwich St	020 7831 1622	They call it burlesque, we call it strippers with tassles.

Map 15 • Blackfriars / Farringdon

The Cocktail Trading Co.	50-52 Long Ln	020 7427 6097	Mixologically compelling drinks; fun attitude.
Fabric	77 Charterhouse St	020 7336 8898	Debauched club mecca for gurners of all persuasions.
Fox and Anchor	115 Charterhouse St	020 7250 1300	Amazing interior and the tankards make up for the wankers.
The Hat and Tun	3 Hatton Wall	020 7242 4747	Home of the original politically incorrect 100 shooter list.
Ye Olde Cheshire Cheese	145 Fleet St	020 7353 6170	Get tanked up where Dickens used to. Historic.
Ye Olde Mitre	1 Ely Pl	020 7405 4751	Elizabeth I used to dance here, don't you know?!

Map 16 • Square Mile (West)

The Hatchet	28 Garlick Hill	020 7236 0720	Lost in the City? Escape here.
Planet of the Grapes	74 Queen Victoria St	020 7248 1892	The clue is in the name.
The Samuel Pepys	Stew Ln	020 7489 1871	Find it and be rewarded with Thames views.
Ye Olde Watling	29 Watling St	020 7248 8935	Squeeze in.

Map 17 • Square Mile (East)

The Counting House	50 Cornhill	020 7283 7123	A truly magnificent (former) bank. That sells beer now.
Royal Exchange Grand Café and Restaurant Sauterelle	Royal Exchange	020 7618 2480	The courtyard of the Royal Exchange. Fancy, eh?

Map 18 • Tower Hill / Aldgate

Dion	52 Leadenhall St	020 7702 9111	Veuve Clicquot La Grande Dame Rose, anyone?
Kenza	10 Devonshire Sq	020 7929 5533	Belly-dancers, cocktails & couscous.
Mary Janes	124 Minories	020 7481 8195	Inconspicuous perspex floor catches out the knickerless.
The Minories	64 Minories	020 7702 1658	Cavernous boozer by day, thumping disco by night.
Revolution	140 Leadenhall St	020 7621 9955	Vodka-drenched, vault-like DJ bar that couldn't care less about the revolution.

Map 19 • Belgravia

The Blue Bar	Wilton Pl	020 7235 6000	It's blue. Mindboggingly so.
The Nag's Head	53 Kinnerton St	020 7235 1135	No mobiles allowed. Says it all.
The Plumber's Arms	14 Lower Belgrave St	020 7730 4067	Tradesman's pub from days of yore. Ask about Lord Lucan.
The Wilton Arms	71 Kinnerton St	020 7235 4854	A Shepherd Neame pub? In Belgravia?

Map 20 • Victoria / Pimlico (West)

The Cask & Glass	39 Palace St	020 7834 7630	Teeny tiny, English country garden-esque drinking hole. Flower-festoned frontage, real ale.
The Warwick	25 Warwick Way	020 7834 4987	Gastropub with fine selection of booze.
Windsor Castle	23 Francis St	020 7834 7260	Easier to like than to find.

Map 21 • Pimlico (East)

Morpeth Arms	58 Millbank	020 7834 6442	Where Millibank prisoners used to escape to.

Map 22 • Westminster

The Albert	52 Victoria St	020 7222 5577	Distinguished, well-preserved period pub. Tourist haunt but rightly so.
The Cinnamon Club	30 Great Smith St	020 7222 2555	Cocktail classiness inside the Old Westminster Library. Try finding it.
The Speaker	46 Great Peter St	020 7222 1749	Good after-worker with guest ales.
St. Stephen's Tavern	10 Bridge St	020 7925 2286	Tiny pub with character, despite being on tourist trail.
Two Chairmen	39 Dartmouth St	020 7222 8694	Public servants galore! Decent pub for this area though.

Map 23 • St. James's

Aura	48 St James's St	020 7499 9999	If you ain't on the list, you ain't coming in. Seriously.
Dukes Hotel	35 St James's St	020 7491 4840	Channel 007 and have a martini at Ian Fleming's haunt.
Institute of Contemporary Arts	The Mall	020 7930 3647	Cutting edge arts complex/bar, weirdly stuck on the upper-crust Mall.

Map 24 • Trafalgar Square / The Strand

Asia de Cuba	45 St Martin's Lane	020 7300 5588	For rum-drinking with the jet set.
BYOC	28 Bedfordbury	020 7240 7810	Underneath Juice Bar. Bring Your Own Cocktails to this intimate den.
The Chandos	29 St Martin's Ln	020 7836 1401	All Trafalgar Square pubs tourist traps? Think again.
The Coal Hole	91 Strand	020 7379 9883	Genuine old style.
Covent Garden Comedy Club	The Arches	079 6007 1340	Good acts play to a friendly crowd drinking awful beer.
Gordon's Wine Bar	47 Villiers St	020 7930 1408	Candle-lit vaults. Romantic perfection.
The Harp	47 Chandos Pl	020 7836 0291	Covent Garden's secret spot for sausage and a good brew.
Heaven	The Arches	020 7930 2020	Epicentre of London's late night gay scene.
Maple Leaf	41 Maiden Ln	020 7240 2843	Just don't ask which State they're from.
Punch & Judy	The Covent Garden Piazza	020 7379 0923	Naff, naff, naff. 'Nuff said?
Retro Bar	2 George Ct	020 7839 8760	Chilled gay bar, hiding from Charing Cross in a small alley.
Roadhouse	The Covent Garden Piazza	020 7240 6001	"You're the one that I want, ooh-ooh-ooh"
The Sherlock Holmes	10 Northumberland St	020 7930 2644	Unintentionally sinister, must-see Holmes waxwork upstairs. Expect bad dreams.
The Ship and Shovell	1 Craven Passage	020 7839 1311	A pub made of two pubs, both obsessed with Sherlock Holmes.
Terroirs	5 William IV St	020 7036 0660	Non-pretentious wine bar with good eats too.
Zoo Bar & Club	13 Bear St	020 7839 4188	Wake up with someone new.

Map 26 • Maida Hill

The Union Tavern	45 Woodfield Rd	020 7286 1886	A pub that bakes its own bread! Oh, and it's canal side...

Map 27 • Maida Vale

The Bridge House	13 Westbourne Terrace Rd	020 7266 4326	Canal views and comedy. Lovely.
The Warwick Castle	6 Warwick Pl	020 7266 0921	Down-to-earth drinking in Maida Vale. Indeed.
The Waterway	54 Formosa St	020 7266 3557	Try not to fall into the canal.

Map 28 • Ladbroke Grove / Notting Hill (West)

Julie's Restaurant & Champagne Bar	135 Portland Rd	020 7229 8331	Pleasantly posh wine bar full of pleasantly posh ladies.

Map 29 • Notting Hill Gate

Mau Mau	265 Portobello Rd	020 7229 8528	Ace mojitos and Thursdays open-mic. Wear your dancing shoes.
Notting Hill Arts Club	21 Notting Hill Gate	020 7460 4459	Indie cave with bands, lurid projections and teenagers.
Sun in Splendour	7 Portobello Rd	020 7792 0914	Notting Hill denizens' choice.
Trailer Happiness	177 Portobello Rd	020 7313 4644	Step back in time.
Uxbridge Arms	13 Uxbridge St	020 7727 7326	Warm little place full of eccentric old toffs.
Windsor Castle	114 Campden Hill Rd	020 7243 8797	A wood-panelled piece of pub history.

Map 30 • Bayswater

All Star Lanes	6 Porchester Gardens	020 7313 8363	Glitzy bowling madness.
The Cow	89 Westbourne Park Rd	020 7221 0021	Lovely pub. Let down by braying trustafarians.

Map 31 • Paddington

Royal Exchange	26 Sale Pl	020 7723 3781	Salt beef sarnies and hot and cold Guinness.
The Victoria	10 Strathearn Pl	020 7724 1191	British pub straight from a Richard Curtis film. Simply perfect.

Map 32 • Shepherd's Bush (West)

Bush Hall	310 Uxbridge Rd	020 8222 6955	The red carpet, the ornate walls...the sheer beauty!
The Queen Adelaide	412 Uxbridge Rd	020 8746 2573	Chic gastropub serving the West Bush.
White Horse	31 Uxbridge Rd	020 8723 4531	Did you call my pint a slag? Outside, now!

Map 33 • Shepherd's Bush

Albertine	1 Wood Lane	020 8743 9593	Drink wine with the Beep set.
The Defector's Weld	170 Uxbridge Rd	020 8749 0008	Tarted up boozer.
O2 Shepherd's Bush Empire	Shepherd's Bush Green	020 8354 3300	Still among London venueland's finest.

Map 34 • West Kensington / Olympia

The Cumberland Arms	29 North End Rd	020 7371 6806	Where long hard days become good again.
Famous 3 Kings (F3K) Bar	171 North End Rd	020 7603 6071	Brilliant atmosphere for big matches especially rugby. Poo tables too.
Society Bar	380 Kensington High St	020 7603 3333	Dying for a drink in Kensington? Well there.

Map 35 • Kensington

The Builders Arms	1 Kensington Ct Pl	020 7937 6213	Boozy haven from High Street Kensington's shopping madness.
The Devonshire Arms	37 Marloes Rd	020 7937 0710	Warm and cosy for a roast on a rainy Sunday.

Map 36 • South Kensington / Gloucester Rd

Boujis	43 Thurloe St	020 7584 2000	If you want to see the two princes drunk. And only then.
The Queen's Arms	30 Queen's Gate Mews	020 7823 9293	South Ken's secret drinking spot. Close to the Royal Albert Hall.

Map 38 • Chiswick

Carvosso's	210 Chiswick High Rd	020 8995 9121	For a glass of wine before dinner.
George IV	185 Chiswick High Rd	020 8994 4624	Fullers pies, real ale and a comedy club on the High Road? Sweet.
Packhorse & Talbot	145 Chiswick High Rd	020 8994 0360	A Chiswick institution. Proper British pub...with live jazz?! Truly.
The Roebuck	122 Chiswick High Rd	020 8995 4392	Best pub in West London. Unpretentious charm, killer Sunday roast.

Map 39 • Stamford Brook

The Raven	375 Goldhawk Rd	020 8748 6977	A bit grubby on the outside but £4 handmade pies are pa of the appeal.

Map 40 • Goldhawk Rd / Ravenscourt Park

The Dove	19 Upper Mall	020 8748 9474	So perfect for dates that Charles II brought Nell Gwynne here.

Map 41 • Hammersmith

Brook Green	170 Shepherd's Bush Rd	020 7603 2516	Lost between Hammersmith and Shepherd's Bush? Fear not.
The Distillers	64 Fulham Palace Rd	020 8748 2834	Chandelier clad pub-bar with ace live music and comedy in The Regal Room.
Hammersmith Apollo	45 Queen Caroline St	020 8563 3800	Still West London's best music venue.
The Hampshire Hog	227 King St	020 8748 3391	Relaxing spot for a Pinot Noir after a hard day.
Lyric Hammersmith	King St	020 8741 6850	Hammersmith's hottest home of hentertainment.

Map 42 • Baron's Court

Colton Arms	187 Greyhound Rd	020 7385 6956	If you're not already a regular, you'll wish you were.
The Curtains Up	28 Comeragh Rd	020 7386 7543	Pub which keeps actors in the basement.
The Fulham Mitre	81 Dawes Rd	020 7386 8877	Young, trendy Fulhamites like it. We don't.
The Queen's Arms	171 Greyhound Rd	020 7823 9293	Relaxed and comfy local boozer with tip top Sunday roasts.

Map 43 • West Brompton / Fulham Broadway / Earls Court

The Blackbird	209 Earl's Court Rd	020 7835 1855	Proper London local amidst the chaos of Earl's Court Road.
Chairs & Coffee	512 Fulham Rd	020 7018 1913	Friday is aperitivo night.
The King's Head	17 Hogarth Rd	020 7373 5239	Tucked away with British style tapas. Who knew!
Onboard Karaoke	8 Kenway Rd	020 7244 6850	Truly authentic Japanese karaoke at truly authentic London prices.
Prince Of Teck	161 Earl's Court Rd	020 7373 4291	Locals and tourists receive a friendly welcome in this pub.

Map 44 • Chelsea

Brinkley's	47 Hollywood Rd	020 7351 1683	Enter the cougar's lair.
The Drayton Arms	153 Old Brompton Rd	020 7835 2301	Low-lit Victorian pub with mismatched chairs and a great beer selection.
The Duke of Clarence	148 Old Brompton Rd	020 7373 1285	All leather seats and wooden floors. Cool spot for a drink after work.

Map 45 • Chelsea (East)

The Anglesea Arms	15 Selwood Terrace	020 7373 7960	4th Best Pub in the UK, says The Morning Advertiser Industry.
Chelsea Potter	119 Kings Rd	020 7352 9479	Chelsea old school.
The Pig's Ear	35 Old Church St	020 7352 2908	Relaxed, tasteful, friendly.

Map 47 • Fulham (West)

The Crabtree	Rainville Rd	020 7385 3929	The Thames view from the garden is reason alone to visit.

Map 49 • Parson's Green

Amuse Bouche	51 Parsons Green Ln	020 7371 8517	Fizzy fun.
Duke on the Green	235 New King's Rd	020 7736 2777	If only all pub food was this good (but half the price).
The White Horse	1 Parsons Green	020 7736 2115	Victorian pub and a beer drinker's heaven. Book a table.

Map 50 • Sand's End

606 Club	90 Lots Rd	020 7352 5953	Great jazz venue. If you like ten minute sax solos.

Map 51 • Highgate

The Angel Inn	37 Highgate High St	020 8341 5913	Lively local with board games and unusual beers.
The Boogaloo	312 Archway Rd	020 8340 2928	Not as cool as it thinks it is.
The Flask	77 Highgate West Hill	020 8348 7346	Great beers, great food, great place. Really, it is.
Prince of Wales	53 Highgate High St	020 8340 0445	Friendly local for posh Highgaters and their even posher dogs.
The Victoria	28 North Hill	020 8340 6091	Try to catch the Sunday sing-along sessions.
The Woodman	414 Archway Rd	020 8340 3016	Reformed fight club with gastropub intentions.
The Wrestlers	98 N Rd	020 8340 4297	Branded "best pub in Highgate" by residents.

Map 52 • Archway (North)

Caipirinha Bar	177 Archway Rd	020 8340 2321	Cosiness! Cocktails! Latin jazz! Sherpa required to find it!
The Winchester Pub Hotel	206 Archway Rd	020 8374 1690	Wonky-floored palace of boozy delight.

Map 53 • Crouch End

The Harringay Arms	153 Crouch Hill	020 8292 3624	No music, plenty of beer.
King's Head	2 Tottenham Ln	020 8340 1028	Plenty of funny business.
The Queens	26 Broadway Parade	020 8340 2031	God save the Queens.
The Shaftesbury	534 Hornsey Rd	020 7272 7950	Family-friendly local with hearty food menu.
Stapleton Tavern	2 Crouch Hill	020 7272 5395	Super laid-back local.

Map 54 • Hornsey

The Hope & Anchor	128 Tottenham Ln	020 8340 3051	Proper local.

Map 55 • Harringay

The Beaconsfield	359 Green Lanes	020 8800 2153	Friendly local. The footy's always on!
Brouhaha	501 Green Lanes	020 8348 8563	Friendly, laid back atmosphere and varied clientele.
Jam In A Jar	599 Green Lanes	079 5176 9981	Reliably good local watering hole.
The Salisbury	1 Green Lanes	020 7836 5863	A local's secret...no longer! Exceptional.

Map 56 • Hampstead Village

Duke of Hamilton	23 New End	020 7794 0258	Lovely local, nicely tucked away.
The Flask	14 Flask Walk	020 7435 4580	Hampstead alleyway classic that's been refitted. But nicely so.
The Freemasons Arms	32 Downshire Hill	020 7433 6811	Lovely beer garden.
The Holly Bush	22 Holly Mount	020 7435 2892	It's hidden. It's a gem. Really.
The Horseshoe	28 Heath St	020 7431 7206	Birthplace of Camden Town Brewery.

Map 57 • Hampstead Heath

The Garden Gate	14 S End Rd	020 7435 4938	Nice pub with garden for those sunny days. (yeah right)
Roebuck	15 Pond St	020 7435 7354	Somewhere between cosy pub and stylish bar. And good at it.
The White Horse	154 Fleet Rd	020 7485 2112	Yet another pub on the thai food bandwagon.

Map 58 • Parliament Hill / Dartmouth Park

The Bull and Last	168 Highgate Rd	020 7267 3641	Good place for a post-Heath pint.
The Southampton Arms	139 Highgate Rd	079 5878 0073	Best pub in the area. A real ale lover's dream.

Map 59 • Tufnell Park

Aces And Eights Saloon Bar	156 Fortress Rd	020 7485 4033	Rock n roll n pizza.
Boston Arms	178 Junction Rd	020 7272 8153	Ferociously scruffy but friendly Irish pub, with rock pit attached.
The Hideaway	114 Junction Rd	020 7561 0779	Beer, pizza, dancing. What else do you need?
The Lord Palmerston	33 Dartmouth Park Hill	020 7485 1578	Gone a bit plastic, but still worth it.
The Star	47 Chester Rd	020 7272 2863	It's a star.

Map 60 • Archway

Mother Red Cap	665 Holloway Rd	020 7263 7082	Begorra! Bejesus! Be better off going to another boozer!

Map 61 • Holloway (North)

The Quays	471 Holloway Rd	020 7272 3634	Into bad U2 cover bands? Then you'll love it here.
The Swimmer	13 Eburne Rd	020 7281 4632	No running, diving in the shallow end, or heavy petting.

Map 62 • Finsbury Park

Faltering Fullback	19 Perth Rd	020 7272 5834	Tardis-like local. Avoid match nights unless you're a Gooner.
The Old Dairy	1 Crouch Hill	020 7263 3337	Great food, great drink, great place.
The Silver Bullet	5 Station Pl	020 7619 3639	Mix-and-match music, edgy vibe, and very cheap drinks.
WB Yeats	20 Fonthill Rd	020 8617 3400	Good selection of craft beers.
The World's End	21 Stroud Green Rd	020 7281 8679	Football and live music, sometimes at the same time.

Map 63 • Manor House

The Brownswood	271 Green Lanes	020 8802 0494	Enter, before Manor House drives you mad.
The Happy Man	89 Woodberry Grove	020 8800 0074	Great sunny day spot, looks naff but never disappoints.

Map 64 • Stoke Newington

Auld Shillelagh	105 Stoke Newington Church St	020 7249 5951	The best Guinness in London; you won't leave standing up.
The Londesborough	36 Barbauld Rd	020 7254 5865	Stokey trendies on leather sofas.
The Rose and Crown	199 Stoke Newington Church St	020 7923 3337	Sunday roasts to die for and step-back-in-time décor.

Ruby's	76 Stoke Newington Rd		Underneath the cinema sign.
Ryan's Bar	181 Stoke Newington Church St	020 7275 7807	Boho cafe and venue with a noise limiter! Pussies.
The Shakespeare	57 Allen Rd	020 7254 4190	The Bard would be proud.
White Hart	69 Stoke Newington High St	020 7254 6626	Huge pub, huge beer garden—really it's huge.

Map 65 • West Hampstead

The Black Lion	274 Kilburn High Rd	020 7624 1424	Popular local since the 6th century.
Czech and Slovak Bar	74 West End Ln	020 7372 1193	Go Czech.
The Good Ship	289 Kilburn High Rd	079 4900 8253	Where Kilburn takes music seriously.

Map 66 • Finchley Road / Swiss Cottage

Ye Olde Swiss Cottage	98 Finchley Rd	020 7722 3487	What can we say.

Map 67 • Belsize Park

The Washington	50 England's Ln	020 7722 8842	Monday night is pub quiz night.

Map 68 • Kilburn High Road / Abbey Road

Love & Liquor	34 Kilburn High Rd	020 7625 7500	Niteclub evoking "Brooklyn, USA"; cocktails, bottle service.

Map 69 • St. John's Wood

The Star	38 St. John's Wood Terrace	020 7722 1051	Drink face-to-face with a huge Highland Terrier.

Map 70 • Primrose Hill

The Albert	11 Princess Rd	020 7722 1886	A local. Cosy and relaxed.
Cecil Sharp House	2 Regent's Park Rd	020 7485 2206	Sword dancing and Olde Stuffe.
The Lansdowne	90 Gloucester Ave	020 7483 0409	Home of the beautiful people.
The Princess of Wales	22 Chalcot Rd	020 7722 0354	Traditional pub with occasional jazz performances.
Sir Richard Steele	97 Haverstock Hill	020 7483 1261	Friendly local with quirky decor.

Map 71 • Camden Town / Chalk Farm / Kentish Town (West)

Bar Vinyl	6 Inverness St	020 7485 9318	DJ Bar. And good coffee.
Brewdog	113 Bayham St	020 7284 4626	Original London branch of the Fraserburgh craft beer renegades.
Camden Town Brewery Bar	55 Wilkin Street Mews	020 7485 1671	Where better for a pint of Camden Ink.
The Constitution	42 St Pancras Way	020 7387 4805	Proper boozer away from the madness of Camden Taaahn.
Dingwalls	Middle Yard	020 7428 5929	Camden Lock's guitar-smashing heartland.
The Dublin Castle	94 Parkway	020 7485 1773	Famous, small, LOUD.
Electric Ballroom	184 Camden High St	020 7485 9006	Scruffy but essential rock haunt, perennially threatened by developers.
The Enterprise	2 Haverstock Hill	020 7485 2659	Literary Irish pub with tiny indie venue upstairs.
Fiddler's Elbow	1 Malden Rd	020 7485 3269	Live music venue pub sans pretention.
The Good Mixer	30 Inverness St	020 7916 7929	Ah, remember those halcyon days of Britpop?
The Grafton	20 Prince of Wales Rd	020 7482 4466	Hosts regular DJs from renowned Dirty Water Club.
The Hawley Arms	2 Castlehaven Rd	020 7428 5979	The Hawley will rise from the ashes. Camden needs it.
The Jazz Cafe	5 Parkway020 7485 6834	A relentless stream of excellent gigs.	
KOKO	1 Camden High St	087 0432 5527	From Charlie Chaplin to Lenny Kravitz, playing Koko still kicks ass.
The Lock Tavern	35 Chalk Farm Rd	020 7482 7163	Great gigs, Sunday roasts and (unpainfully) hip clientele.
Oxford Arms	265 Camden High St	020 7267 4945	Theatre pub where you may stumble upon Amy Winehouse, stumbling.
Proud Camden	Stables Market	020 7482 3867	Oh-so-casual, trendy little bar. Fairy lights and arty types.
Quinn's	65 Kentish Town Rd	020 7267 8240	More German beer than you can pronounce.
The Underworld	174 Camden High St	020 7482 1932	Throbbing pit of angry rock and even angrier metal.

Map 72 • Kentish Town

The Abbey Tavern	124 Kentish Town Rd	020 7267 9449	Fairy-lit, casual beer garden with talented DJs on Saturdays.
The Assembly House	292 Kentish Town Rd	020 7485 2031	Massive pub with friendly atmosphere.
Club Fandango @ The Bull & Gate	389 Kentish Town Rd	020 7704 0187	A gigging institution.
The Forum	9 Highgate Rd	020 7428 4099	Good venue for medium-sized bands.
Ladies and Gentlemen	2 Highgate Rd		Once a disused Victorian lav, now a gin palace.
The Lion and Unicorn	42 Gaisford St	020 7267 2304	Old school pub, with upstairs theatre space.
The Pineapple	51 Leverton St	020 7284 4631	Backstreet Victorian with good beers and Thai grub.
Rio's	239 Kentish Town Rd	020 7485 0607	Bored of your wife? Swap her here.

Map 73 • Holloway

The George Shillibeer	Carpenter's Mews	020 3218 0083	For relaxed drinking on comfy couches.
The Lord Stanley	51 Camden Park Rd	020 7428 9488	Dark wood, Edwardian interior, fireplace and secret walled garden.
Shillibeer's Bar and Grill	1 Carpenter's Mews	020 3218 0083	Warehouse-style venue good for large groups.
The Unicorn	227 Camden Rd	020 7485 3073	Venue for the brilliant club Garageland.

Map 74 • Holloway Road / Arsenal

The Coronet	338 Holloway Rd	020 7609 5014	The smell of old men's piss is abound, but it's cheap!
The Garage	20 Highbury Corner	020 7619 6720	Bad sound and a guaranteed black hole in your evening.
Hen and Chickens	109 St. Paul's Rd	020 7704 2001	All the best pubs have theatres. Fact.
The Horatia	98 Holloway Rd	020 7682 4857	Forward thinking live music gem, packs a sexy crowd.

Map 75 • Highbury

The Alwyne Castle	83 St. Pauls Rd	020 7359 7351	Alright for a pint
Snooty Fox	75 Grosvenor Ave	020 7354 9532	Strangely empty—shame for such a great pub.

Map 76 • Edgware Road / Marylebone (North)

twotwentytwo	222 Marylebone Rd	020 7631 8000	Grand is the word.
The Volunteer	245 Baker St	020 7486 4091	Grand old Victorian taphouse great for a lively post-work pint.

Map 77 • Mornington Crescent / Regent's Park

The Crown & Anchor	137 Drummond St	020 7383 2681	A pub makeover masterpiece.
The Edinboro Castle	57 Mornington Terrace	020 7255 9651	Huge outdoors bit, great BBQ on summer weekends.
Euston Tap	190 Euston Rd	020 3137 8837	Post journey boozer with an award winning variety of beer.
Queen's Head & Artichoke	30 Albany St	020 7916 6206	The pinchos are addictive. We have warned, friends.

Map 78 • Euston

The Camden Head	100 Camden High St	020 7485 4019	Pre-gig/post gig boozer.
The Doric Arch	1 Eversholt St	020 7383 3359	Impressive range of all things ale.
Lincoln Lounge	52 York Way	020 7837 9339	Arty, quirky and cool. Does King's Cross proud.
The Purple Turtle	65 Crowndale Rd	020 7383 4976	Rock club that looks like a wacky goth spaceship.
Scala	275 Pentonville Rd	020 7833 2022	Historic venue with plush edges. If these walls could talk...
Searcys St Pancras Grand Brasserie	Pancras Rd	020 7870 9900	Miss your train!

Map 79 • King's Cross

The Big Chill House	257 Pentonville Rd	020 7427 2540	Allow staff 28 working days to process your drinks order.
Canal 125	125 Caledonian Rd	020 7837 1924	Upmarket local bar that draws a swanky crowd.
Central Station	37 Wharfdale Rd	020 7278 3294	Ominous looking cabaret bar-cum-cruise emporium. Check site first.
Drink, Shop & Do	9 Caledonian Rd	020 7278 4335	Perfect cocktails, art to buy, and lovely atmosphere.
EGG	200 York Way	020 7871 7111	Big club, big garden, big night out.
The Hemingford Arms	158 Hemingford Rd	020 7607 3303	Full of local aleheads.
The Lexington	96 Pentonville Rd	020 7837 5371	Come and support your boyfriend's shit band.
Simmons	32 Caledonian Rd	020 7278 5851	The bar Alice goes when Wonderland's closed.
Tarmon	270 Caledonian Rd	020 7607 3242	Character. Lots of character.

Map 80 • Angel / Upper St

'Round Midnight Jazz and Blues Bar	13 Liverpool Rd	020 7837 8758	Great music and a good atmosphere.
69 Colebrooke Row	69 Colebrooke Row	075 4052 8593	The kind of bar Hemingway would drink in.
The Angel	3 Islington High St	020 7837 2218	Students. The elderly. The unemployed.
The Angelic	57 Liverpool Rd	020 7278 8433	A sophisticated local.
Camden Head	2 Camden Walk	020 7359 0851	Comedians debut new gags upstairs. Cheap—and mostly cheerful.
The Castle	54 Pentonville Rd	020 7713 1858	Needs breaking in.
The Compton Arms	4 Compton Ave	020 7359 6883	Islington's only real pub—or so they say.
The Crown	116 Cloudesley Rd	020 7837 7107	Jovial spot for a quiet pint and Sunday roasts.
Dead Dolls House	181 Upper St	020 7288 1470	Sign up online and bring a bottle of the hard stuff.
The Drapers Arms	44 Barnsbury St	020 7619 0348	Celeb backlash against new CCTV. Big Brother really is watching.
Hope And Anchor	207 Upper St	020 7354 1312	Scuzzy pub with even scuzzier bands in the basement.
King's Head Theatre Pub	115 Upper St	020 7478 0160	Proper, good-time boozer.
Lucky Voice	173 Upper St	020 7354 6280	Singing in private? Like a bathroom with beer.
O2 Academy	16 Parkfield St	020 7288 4400	Grubby live music. Slap on some skinny jeans first.
Public House	54 Islington Park St	020 7359 6070	This boutique pub offers an escape from hedonistic Upper Street.
The Regent Pub	201 Liverpool Rd	020 7700 2725	Good news: it's finally starting to fray.
Union Chapel	Compton Terrace	020 7226 1686	God's favourite music venue. Hell, everyone's.

Map 81 • Canonbury

The Lord Clyde	342 Essex Rd	020 7288 9850	Like boozing in Land of Leather.
Marquess Tavern	32 Canonbury St	020 7359 4615	Scruffy locals live on, despite gastro revolution.
Myddleton Arms	52 Canonbury Rd	020 7226 4595	Don't those people have, y'know, jobs?

Map 82 • De Beauvoir Town / Kingsland

Dalston Boys Club	68 Boleyn Rd		Keep your eyes peeled for gigs at this place.
Dalston Jazz Bar	4 Bradbury St	020 7254 9728	Kitschy cool and not suffocatingly trendy, but no jazz, figure?
The Duke of Wellington	119 Ball's Pond Rd	020 7275 7640	Nice little boozer, as they say.
The Hunter S	194 Southgate Rd	020 7249 7191	As Hunter says, "Buy the ticket, take the ride."
The Northgate	113 Southgate Rd	020 7359 7392	Reliable local despite being—gasp!—a gastro.
Rosemary Branch Theatre	2 Shepperton Rd	020 7704 2730	Theatre pub with great selection of ales and hearty fare.
The Vortex	11 Gillett Sq	020 7254 4097	Dalston's only real jazz bar.

Map 83 • Angel (East) / City Rd (North)

Barrio North	45 Essex Rd	020 7749 3940	Groovy little bar with friendly international vibe. And a caravan!
The Duke of Cambridge	30 St. Peter's St	020 7359 3066	Feel self-righteous in the world's first organic pub.
The Earl of Essex	25 Danbury St	020 7424 5828	For drinking in the day. In the dark.
Island Queen	87 Noel Rd	020 7354 8741	Where NFT planned the London guide. Sweet.
The Mucky Pup	39 Queen's Head St	020 7226 2572	The dog's bollocks.
The Narrow Boat	119 St Peters St	020 7400 6003	Cheerful canal-side pub for lazy pints and people watching.
The Old Queen's Head	44 Essex Rd	020 7354 9993	Trendier than the name suggests.
The Wenlock Arms	26 Wenlock Rd	020 7608 3406	Threadbare, battered old boozer with a magnificent range of real ales.

Map 84 • Hoxton

333 Mother	333 Old St	020 7739 5949	Mama told you not to come, but you need it.
Cargo	83 Rivington St	020 7739 3440	Cavernous hole with bad sound but good gigs.
Charlie Wright's	45 Pitfield St	020 7490 8345	Does anyone turn up here sober?
Club Aquarium	256 Old St	020 7251 6136	After-hours swimming pool scuzzfest.
Happiness Forgets	9 Hoxton Sq	020 7613 0325	No door policy just no wallies.
Howl at the Moon	178 Hoxton St	020 7739 9221	Chuffing good little pub serving burgers.
Hoxton Square Bar and Kitchen	2 Hoxton Sq	020 7613 0709	Snotty bands and doormen. Wear something uber.
The Macbeth	70 Hoxton St	020 7749 0600	Hot new bands love it. And so do we.
The Old Blue Last	38 Great Eastern St	020 7739 7033	Until the bass drum WILL bring down that pub ceiling.
PortSide Parlour	14 Rivington St	020 3662 6381	Friendly rum bar.
Red Lion	41 Hoxton St	020 7729 7920	Stay forever if you bag the chaise lounge...
The Stag's Head	55 Orsman Rd	020 7739 5186	Run down boozer currently being used for hip gigs.
Strongroom	120 Curtain Rd	020 7426 5103	Shoreditch's last stronghold of unpretentiousness?
Troy Bar	10 Hoxton St	079 5829 8607	A semi-hidden gem with soul and funk music most nights.
Zigfrid	11 Hoxton Sq	020 7613 1988	Cross between a club and an antique store.

Map 85 • Stoke Newington (East)

Blush	8 Cazenove Rd	020 7923 9202	Pink pint-parlour with poker and personable patrons (oh please!)
The Jolly Butchers	204 Stoke Newington High St	020 7249 9471	Revamped but unpretentious pub with great beer selection.
Royal Sovereign	64 Northwold Rd	020 8806 2449	Drink with the locals.

Map 86 • Dalston / Kingsland

The Alibi	91 Kingsland High St	020 7249 2733	The kids like it.
Bar 23	23 Stoke Newington Rd	020 7241 2060	A slice of weirdness with wacked out DJing and drinking.
Bardens Boudoir	36 Stoke Newington Rd	020 7923 9223	Anything can happen in this basement. The beating heart of Dalston's music shenanigans.
Cafe Oto	18 Ashwin St	020 7923 1231	Mysterious new venue importing music from the hinterlands of psychedelia.
Dalston Superstore	117 Kingsland High St	020 7254 2273	Uber hip polysexual squelch-a-thon.
Efes Pool Club & Bar	17 Stoke Newington Rd	020 7249 6040	Down some pints at this great spot to play pool.
The Haggerston	438 Kingsland Rd	020 7923 3206	Artist-run flea pit. Chaotic crowd surfing most nights.
Moustache Bar	58 Stoke Newington Rd	075 0715 2047	Follow the moustache (sticker) trail to this trendy/grimy subterranean bar.
The Nest	36 Stoke Newington Rd	020 7354 9993	Electronic dance club in basement.
Passion Social Club	251 Amhurst Rd	020 7254 3667	Tiny basement venue that hosts massive all-nighters.
The Prince George	40 Parkholme Rd	087 1934 1384	Buzzing local favourite. Renowned Monday quiz night, great jukebox.
Ridley Road Market Bar	49 Ridley Rd		A contender for best little bar in Dalston.
The Shacklewell Arms	71 Shacklewell Ln	020 7249 0810	Relive your punk youth.
VFD	66 Stoke Newington Rd	020 7249 2733	The latest place to Vogue.

Map 87 • Hackney Downs / Lower Clapton

Biddle Brothers	88 Lower Clapton Rd	020 8985 7052	Almost trendy oasis for the trendy in an eccentric neighbourhood.
The Crooked Billet	84 Upper Clapton Rd	020 3058 1166	Proof that Clapton can still be f***ing terrifying.
The Pembury Tavern	90 Amhurst Rd	020 8986 8597	Large selection of microbrews.
Star by Hackney Downs	35 Queenstown Rd	020 7458 4481	Fun, circus themed pub.

Map 88 • Haggerston / Queensbridge Rd

Passing Clouds	1 Richmond Rd	020 7241 4889	Back alley arts collective and live venue.

Map 89 • London Fields / Hackney Central

Baxter's Court	282 Mare St	020 8525 9010	A chain pub, okay, okay. But check the ladies' toilets!
The Dolphin	165 Mare St	020 8985 3727	Pathos sodden karaoke occasionally ruined by post-opening art people.
The Dove	24 Broadway Market	020 7275 7617	Belgian beer paradise.
Draughts	337 Acton Mews	020 7254 1572	A library of 500 board games to choose from.
The Old Ship	2 Sylvester Path	084 4264 1444	Nicely refurbed ex-dive.
Pub on the Park	19 Martello St	020 7923 3398	Tap for London Fields.

Map 90 • Homerton / Victoria Park North

Chats Palace	42 Brooksby's Walk	020 8533 0227	Fantastic community arts venue—Hackney classic.
The Kenton	38 Kenton Rd	020 8533 5041	Local favourite.
The Lauriston	162 Victoria Park Rd	020 8985 5404	As vamped up as its would-be-village surroundings.
Royal Inn on the Park	111 Lauriston Rd	020 8985 3321	Victoria Park's prime boozer.

Map 91 • Shoreditch / Brick Lane / Spitalfields

93 Feet East	150 Brick Ln	020 7247 3293	Enthusiastic, trendy club (to impress out-of-towners).
The Archers	42 Osborn St	020 7247 3826	Nice ole pub that's resisted Shoreditchification. Perfect for pre-curry pints.
Bar Kick	127 Shoreditch High St	020 7739 8700	Lemon-yellow table football gaff.
Bar Music Hall	134-136 Curtain Rd	020 7729 7216	Nice wallpaper, free music. Who's complaining?
The Big Chill Bar	Dray Walk	020 7392 9180	Still among Brick Lane's better drinking spots.
The Birdcage	80 Columbia Rd	020 7739 0250	Karaoke! Til 3am!
Browns	1 Hackney Rd	020 7739 3970	Now really. What would your mother say?
Café 1001	91 Brick Ln	020 7247 6166	Like a house party. But one where cans cost £3.
The Carpenters Arms	73 Cheshire St	020 7739 6342	No longer run by the Kray twins' mother, still felonious fun.
Catch	22 Kingsland Rd	020 7729 6097	Reliable active dancefloor, reliable silly hats, reliable good fun.
The Cocktail Trading Co.	68 Bethnal Green Rd	020 7427 6097	Mixologically compelling drinks; fun attitude.
The Commercial Tavern	142 Commercial St	020 7247 1888	Quirky Shoreditch traditional.
The Culpeper	40 Commercial St	020 7247 5371	Used to be The Princess Alice. Beautiful interior.
Golden Heart	110 Commercial St	020 7247 2158	Has it all: fires, pints and a lazy resident dog.
Jaguar Shoes	32 Kingsland Rd	020 7729 5830	Happy hipsters behind wide windows.
Loungelover	1 Whitby St	020 7012 1234	Kitsch-colonial glitter-ball of a cocktail bar.
The Love Shake	5 Kingsland Rd	07850 383178	Chic media-café-cum-bar with mid Atlantic vibe.
The Old Shoreditch Station	1 Kingsland Rd	020 7729 5188	Used to be cool. When it was a train station.
The Owl & Pussycat	34 Redchurch St	020 3487 0088	Crooked little place, tucked in the folds of Shoreditch's blubber.
Prague	6 Kingsland Rd	020 7739 9110	The closest you'll ever get to a romantic bar in Shoreditch.
The Pride of Spitalfields	3 Heneage St	020 7247 8933	The only East End boozer left on Brick Lane.
The Redchurch	107 Redchurch St	020 7739 3440	Late, loud DJ box.
The Royal Oak	73 Columbia Rd	020 7729 2220	Gentrifying, gentrifying...gentrified.
Sager + Wilde	193 Hackney Rd	020 8127 7330	Get yer wine on.
Shoreditch House	Ebor St	020 7739 5040	Last one in the rooftop pool buys the drinks!
The Ten Bells	84 Commercial St	075 3049 2986	Jack The Ripper's local. An oddly nice place for an evening drink.
Vibe Bar	91 Brick Ln	020 7247 3479	Bar in a brewery. Feel the vibe?
The Water Poet	9 Folgate St	020 7426 0495	Mismatched chairs, over-stuffed sofas, philosophy and beer.
Ye Olde Axe	69 Hackney Rd	020 7729 5137	Rockabilly-only weekends. That's right: rockabilly-only. Occasional gentleman's club.

Map 92 • Bethnal Green

Bethnal Green Working Men's Club	44 Pollard Row	020 7739 7170	Saucy amateur burlesque that still confuses the resident Working Men.
The Florist Arms	255 Globe Rd	020 8981 1100	The Camel's naughty little sister.

Satan's Whiskers	343 Cambridge Heath Rd	020 7739 8362	Devilishly good cocktails.
Sebright Arms	31 Coate St	020 7729 0937	Meantime lager and Lucky Chip burgers.
The Star Of Bethnal Green	359 Bethnal Green Rd	020 7458 4480	Formerly the Pleasure Unit. Still Bethnal Green's live music best.

Map 93 • Globe Town / Mile End (North)

The Approach	47 Approach Rd	020 8983 3878	Great if you can tolerate the ironic haircuts crew.
Morgan Arms	43 Morgan St	020 8980 6389	Grab a pint with some gourmet food.
Palm Tree	Haverfield Rd	020 8980 2918	Brass walls and retired crooners! Amazingly old-fashioned boozer.
The Victoria	110 Grove Rd	020 8980 6609	Coolified old man's boozer turned hipster joint.

Map 94 • Bow

Coborn Arms	8 Coborn Rd	020 8980 3793	Nice ales, nice beer garden.
Lord Morpeth	402 Old Ford Rd	020 3022 5888	Bow boozing's best.
The Lord Tredegar	50 Lichfield Rd	020 8983 0130	Trusty local boozer.
Young Prince	448 Roman Rd	020 8980 1292	If on Roman Road...

Map 95 • Whitechapel (West) / St Katharine's Dock

The Dickens Inn	St Katharine's Way	020 7488 2208	Proof that an awesome location can conquer all.
Rhythm Factory	16 Whitechapel Rd	020 7375 3774	The Libertines' old haunt, with all the grimy 'chic' that implies.
Simmons	61 Mint St	020 7702 9481	Reliable good time place.

Map 96 • Whitechapel (East) / Shadwell (West) / Wapping

Captain Kidd	108 Wapping High St	020 7480 5759	Pub with nice Thames-side beer garden.
Indo	133 Whitechapel Rd	020 7247 4926	Very narrow and everything but narrow-minded.
Town of Ramsgate	62 Wapping High St	020 7481 8000	Get nautical.
Victualler	69 Garnet St	020 7481 9694	Natural, organic and biodynamic wines in shop setting.

Map 97 • Stepney / Shadwell (East)

Cable Street Studios	566 Cable St	020 7790 1309	'Artists.' 'Warehouse studios.' 'Parties.' It'll never work.
The George Tavern	373 Commercial Rd	020 7790 7335	Old men, hipsters and blue-collar poets in imperfect harmony.
The Prospect of Whitby	57 Wapping Wall	020 7481 1095	Ye olde pub(e) on ye Thames(e).
Troxy	490 Commercial Rd	020 7790 9000	Glorious art deco palace.

Map 98 • Mile End (South) / Limehouse

The Grapes	76 Narrow St	020 7987 4396	True to its roots East End boozer—natural survivor.

Map 100 • Poplar (West) / Canary Wharf (West)

Davy's	31 Canary Wharf	020 7363 6633	Traditional-style with fine ales, wine and food.
Via Fossa	18 Hertsmere Rd	020 7515 8549	Three floors of bankers...

Map 101 • Poplar (East) / Canary Wharf (East)

The Greenwich Pensioner	28 Bazely St	020 7987 4414	No pensioners and not in Greenwich.

Map 102 • Millwall

Hubbub	269 Westferry Rd	020 7515 5577	Oasis in Docklands desert.

Map 103 • Cubitt Town / Mudchute

The Ferry House	26 Ferry St	020 7537 9587	Beer-drenched docks time capsule.
The Lord Nelson	1 Manchester Rd	020 7987 1970	Can I have a half, Nelson?

Map 104 • South Bank / Waterloo / Lambeth North

The Anchor & Hope	36 The Cut	020 7928 9898	For that intellectual pre-theatre/dinner chat.
Benugo Bar & Kitchen	Belvedere Rd	020 7401 9000	Long tables, sofas, soft lighting. Sup cocktails, feel cultured.
Concrete	Southbank Centre	020 7921 0758	Restaurant/bar features Russian beer, food, absinthe.
Cubana	48 Lower Marsh	020 7928 8778	Still riding the mojito trend. But good at them.
The Cut Bar	66 The Cut	020 7928 4400	Enjoy the outdoor terrace with trendy media types and thesps.
The Pit Bar	The Cut	020 7928 2975	Guzzle champagne with Kevin Spacey and friends.
Royal Festival Hall	Belvedere Rd	020 7960 4200	Increasingly exciting programming amid nicely refurbished surroundings.
Skylon	Belvedere Rd	020 7654 7800	Impress someone with the view, then split the bill.

Map 105 • Southwark / Bankside (West)

Albert Arms	1 Gladstone St	020 7401 2362	Where yuppies meet students meet blow-ins meet locals.
The Libertine	125 Great Suffolk St	020 7378 7877	Pizza and beer, what more do you want?
Lord Nelson	243 Union St	020 7207 2701	Like a student union.
Ministry of Sound	103 Gaunt St	087 0060 0010	The sound really IS amazing.
The Prince of Wales	51 St George's Rd	020 7582 9696	Cheap local with downright scary karaoke.

Map 106 • Bankside (East) / Borough / Newington

The Anchor	34 Park St	020 7407 1577	Did Samuel Johnson have to battle this many tourists?
Belushi's	161 Borough High St	020 7939 9710	Drunk Antipodeans. Karaoke. General carnage.
The Blue-Eyed Maid	173 Borough High St	020 7378 8259	It's never too late for a last drink in Borough.
Brew Wharf	Stoney St	020 7378 6601	Beer lovers' heaven.
The George Inn	77 Borough High St	020 7407 2056	Grab a home brew in the dazzlingly ancient George Inn.
The Globe	8 Bedale St	020 7407 0043	Bridget Jones' home? Do we care?
The Market Porter	9 Stoney St	020 7407 2495	Market traders and suits neck real ale. Smell the testosterone.
The Rake	14 Winchester Walk	020 7407 0557	Tiny place with a hundred different beers. Honestly, a hundred.
The Roebuck	50 Great Dover St	020 7357 7324	Cool but calm drinkerie for a pre-night-out drink.
The Rose	123 Snowfields	020 7378 6660	Backstreet boozer full of human oddities.
Roxy	128 Borough High St	020 7407 4057	Mingle with baby yuppies at the Roxy Bar & Screen.
The Royal Oak	44 Tabard St	020 7357 7173	Possibly the friendliest landlords in London.
Southwark Tavern	22 Southwark St	020 7403 0257	Traditional ambience and ordinary fare in ye olde Southwark Tavern.
Wine Wharf	Stoney St	020 7940 8335	If you're as crazy about wine as they are.

Map 107 • Shad Thames

Cable	33 Bermondsey St	020 7403 7730	Get messed up in a dark tunnel. Again.
The Hide	39 Bermondsey St	020 7403 6655	Slightly odd vibe, but cracking drinks.
Hilton London Tower Bridge	5 More London Pl	020 3002 4300	Super-chilled, low lit relaxation zone for the wealthy.
Village East	171 Bermondsey St	020 7357 6082	Wine buffs and cocktail lovers will lap it up.
The Woolpack	98 Bermondsey St	020 7357 9269	Filling lunches, comfy sofas, great garden. Job done.

Map 109 • Southwark Park

The Ancient Foresters	282 Southwark Park Rd	020 7394 1633	Surprise charmer in an otherwise grimy area.
The Angel	101 Bermondsey Wall E	020 7394 3214	Sam Smith pub with great views across the river
The Mayflower	117 Rotherhithe St	020 7237 4088	Used to be The Shippe from whenst the Mayflower departed

Map 110 • Rotherhithe (West) / Canada Water

The Albion	20 Albion St	020 7237 0182	Only if three generations of your family drank here first.
Old Salt Quay	163 Rotherhithe St	020 7394 7108	Pub-by-numbers, but the riverside patio of dreams.
The Ship	39 St Marychurch St	020 7237 4103	Sunny day? Settle in with a beer and a sarnie.

Map 111 • Rotherhithe (East) Surrey Quays

The Blacksmith's Arms	257 Rotherhithe St	020 7064 4355	Good enough for the Queen Mum: good enough for us.
The Moby Dick	6 Russell Pl	020 7231 6719	Once here, it's hard to leave. Because it's really far from the tube.
The Ship & Whale	2 Gulliver St	020 7237 7072	So good we even come for breakfast.
Whelan's	11 Rotherhithe Old Rd	020 7237 9425	Looks rough around the edges, but you could do worse.
Wibbley Wobbley	Rope St	020 7232 2320	Great dinky boat-bar, for short people.

Map 112 • Kennington / Elephant and Castle

Brasserie Toulouse Lautrec	140 Newingtion Butts	020 7582 6800	Eclectic music venue in the Belle Epoque tradition.
Corsica Studios	5 Elephant Rd	020 7703 4760	Sweaty music venue with 'home-made' vibe.
The Dog House	293 Kennington Rd	020 7820 9310	Like your scruffy, unpretentious younger brother. Made for chill-axing.
The Doghouse	293 Kennington Rd	020 7820 9310	Solid local drinking hole.
The Old Red Lion	42 Kennington Park Rd	020 7735 4312	Best pub in the area.
Prince of Wales	Cleaver Sq	020 7735 9916	Stuart's favourite pub in Kennington.
South London Pacific	340 Kennington Rd	020 7820 9189	Step off Kennington Road into the heart of Honolulu.

Map 113 • Walworth

Banana's Bar	374 Walworth Rd	020 7703 3295	New party bar for excitable funsters.
The Beehive	60 Carter St	020 7703 4992	The local bit of nice.
Red Lion	407 Walworth Rd	020 7703 7075	They'll look at you funny, but you'll be welcome enough.

Map 118 • Deptford (Central)

Lord Palmerston	81 Childers St	020 8692 1575	Fewer brawls than your average Deptford pub.

ap 119 • Deptford (East)

e Bird's Nest	32 Deptford Church St	020 8692 1928	Hilarious 'locals vs. trendies' vibe. Go for monthly Flesh Dunce!
e Bunker Club	46 Deptford Broadway	020 8691 0000	The name tells all.
e Dog & Bell	116 Prince St	020 8692 5664	Now why can't ALL pubs in Deptford be like this?

ap 120 • Greenwich

e Greenwich Union	56 Royal Hill	020 8692 6258	Beers galore.
e O2	O2 Arena	020 8463 2000	The grandaddy of mainstream live music.
e Old Brewery	Pepys Building	020 3327 1280	Get the excellent range of Meantime beers direct from the source.
The Creek	302 Creek Rd	020 8858 4581	Comedy club (plus comedy dancing at the disco)

ap 121 • Camberwell (West)

e Joiners Arms	35 Denmark Hill	020 7701 1957	Friendly local with occasional Irish dancing.
e Sun of Camberwell	61-63 Coldharbour Ln	020 7737 5861	Same owners and decor as nearby Tiger. Great beer garden.

ap 122 • Camberwell (East)

e Flying Dutchman	156 Wells Wy		Old man's boozer given an outrageously camp revamp.
and Union	26 Camberwell Grove	020 3247 1001	By far the best of the Grand Union chain.
ermit's Cave	28 Camberwell Church St	020 7703 3188	Log fire and Deuchars on the pump.
ormbird	25 Camberwell Church St	020 7708 4460	Insane selection of beers makes the bland décor bearable.

ap 123 • Peckham

r Story	213 Blenheim Grove	020 7635 6643	Peckham's first and finest cocktail bar. Best when sunny.
navan's Peckham Pool Club	188 Rye Ln	075 6348 2439	Where art students meet alcoholics in late, late night harmony.
e CLF Art Cafe	133 Rye Ln	020 7732 5275	Ex-cricket bat factory hosting galleries, studios and anything goes raves.
e Four Quarters	187 Rye Lane	020 3754 7622	Arcade games bar: Hadouken!
ank's Cafe	95 Rye Ln	075 2860 0924	Cheap Campari cocktails in a multi-story car park. Pure class.
he Montpelier	43 Chomert Rd	020 7635 9483	Cosy pub with free regular and eclectic film nights.
eckham Palais	1 Rye Ln		Sprawling old club recently given new hipster lease on life.

ap 126 • New Cross

mersham Arms	388 New Cross Rd	020 8469 1499	Art school hipdom in grimy New Cross's coolest venue.
arquis of Granby	322 New Cross Rd	020 8692 3140	Lovely old corner pub with mix of students and oldtimers.
ew Cross Inn	323 New Cross Rd	020 8355 4976	Someone's gotta keep "the scene" going.

ap 127 • Coldharbour Lane / Herne Hill (West)

he Commercial	212 Railton Rd	020 7733 8783	Roaring fire and mulled wine in winter. Fits like a glove.
he Florence	133 Dulwich Rd	020 7326 4987	Microbrewery on premises.
he Prince Regent	69 Dulwich Rd	020 7274 1567	Life drawing on Wednesdays to titillate posh diners.

29 • East Dulwich

ast Dulwich Tavern	1 Lordship Ln	020 8693 1316	Jeremy Clarkson was once thrown out for nefarious activities.

ap 130 • Peckham Rye

he Gowlett	62 Gowlett Rd	020 7635 7048	Shabby local serving pizzas famous across the area.
he Rye	31 Peckham Rye	020 7639 5397	For lazy lunches on summer Sundays.

ap 131 • Vauxhall / Albert Embankment

agle London	349 Kennington Ln	020 7793 0903	Fur on tap throughout the week. Sundays recommended.
he Royal Vauxhall Tavern	372 Kennington Ln	020 7820 1222	Fun gay pub with trashy cabaret.
eitgeist at the Jolly Gardeners	49 Black Prince Rd	020 7840 0426	German gastropub with uber-extensive collection of beer and sausages.

ap 132 • Battersea (West)

arrio	14 Battersea Sq	020 7801 9548	What balmy Sunday evenings were made for.
he Draft House	74 Battersea Bridge Rd	020 7228 6482	A great pub well worth the trek.
e QuecumBar	42 Battersea High St	020 7787 2227	Gypsy jazz, honkytonk and frogs legs in bygone Parisian chic.
he Prince Albert	85 Albert Bridge Rd	020 7228 0923	Enjoy a regal roast with a view of the park.
he Woodman	60 Battersea High St	020 7228 2968	A nice Fire. Pint of Badger. Luverleee.

Map 133 • Battersea (East)

The Mason's Arms	169 Battersea Park Rd	020 7622 2007	Perfect local boozer with quality Sunday roasts.

Map 134 • South Lambeth

Bar Estrela	113 S Lambeth Rd	020 7793 1051	Portugal transplanted to South London. Beer, tapas and football.
The Battersea Barge	Nine Elms Ln	020 7498 0004	Bouncy, buoyant, thrilled to see you—the Labrador puppy of venues.
The Cavendish Arms	128 Hartington Rd	020 7498 7464	Shabby, unpretentious pub with comedy nights and a cool streak.
Fire	38 Parry St	020 7820 0550	Legendary gay terrordrome with LED ceiling.
Lightbox	6 S Lambeth Pl	020 3242 0040	15,000 LED lights. Enough to give us all seizures.
The Priory Arms	83 Lansdowne Way	020 7622 1884	Renowned for their excellent selection of proper, geeky rea ales.
The Vauxhall Griffin	8 Wyvil Rd	020 7622 0222	Theme nights to knock your socks off

Map 135 • Oval

The Brown Derby	336 Kennington Park Rd	020 7735 5122	A ray of rock n' roll sunshine in South East's dubstep wastelands.
The Fentiman Arms	64 Fentiman Rd	020 7793 9796	The staff believe that smiles kill kittens.

Map 136 • Putney

The Boathouse	Brewhouse Ln	020 8789 0476	Riverside pub with loadsa outdoor space.
Duke's Head	8 Lower Richmond Rd	020 8788 2552	Typical gastro pub upstairs. Dark DJ bar downstairs.
The Jolly Gardeners	61 Lacy Rd	020 8789 2539	Like all good pubs. And sock monkey classes on Wednesdays.
Star & Garter	4 Lower Richmond Rd	020 8788 0345	Upscale Saturday night hotspot on the Thames.

Map 138 • Wandsworth (Central)

The Cat's Back	88 Point Pleasant	020 8874 7277	Atmospheric and busy with loadsa obscure decoration.
GJ's	89 Garratt Ln	020 8874 2271	Party with snow bunnies.

Map 139 • Wandsworth (East)

Powder Keg Diplomacy	147 St Johns Hill	020 7450 6457	Like stepping into a colonial Victorian plantation.
The Waterfront	Juniper Dr	020 7228 4297	No Marlon Brandos here. Not much of a view either.

Map 140 • Clapham Junction / Northcote Rd

B@1 Cocktail Bar	85 Battersea Rise	020 7978 6595	Be at one with a cocktail menu the size of a book.
Humble Grape	2 Battersea Rise	020 3620 2202	Unpretentious wine bar—hurray!

Map 141 • Battersea (South)

The Lost Angel	339 Battersea Park Rd	020 7622 2112	Put this in your pipe and smoke it, Shoreditch.

Map 142 • Clapham Old Town

Prince of Wales	38 Old Town	020 7622 3530	Eccentric, friendly. Run by a magpie.
Rose & Crown	2 The Polygon	020 7923 3337	For the CAMRA purists.
The Sun	47 Old Town	020 7622 4980	Nice pub. Ruined by surfeit of twats.

Map 143 • Clapham High Street

The Alexandra	14 Clapham Common South Side	020 7627 5102	Join an up-for-it crowd as multinational as the sport here.
Bread and Roses	68 Clapham Manor St	020 7498 1779	Surprisingly pleasant socialist boozer. Without Clapham tossers.
Buena Vista Cafe	19 Landor Rd	020 7326 0280	Sunday at this Cuban hangout features dirty mojitos and tunes.
The Clapham North	409 Clapham Rd	020 7274 2472	A bit 'Clapham', but pretty likable really.
The Coach and Horses	173 Clapham Park Road	020 7622 3815	Honest little boozer.
The Falcon	33 Bedford Rd	020 7274 2428	"I told Daddy, I've nowhere to even PARK a GTi!"
Infernos	146 Clapham High St	020 7720 7633	Oh God no.
Inn Clapham	15 The Pavement	020 7652 2948	Charmingly tatty and full of French people
The Loft	67 Clapham High St	020 7627 0792	A welcome oasis from Clapham High Street.
The Railway Tavern	18 Clapham High St	020 7622 4077	Half-trendy, half-local, three-quarters cool.
Two Brewers	114 Clapham High St	020 7819 9539	Club nights, gay cabaret, lots of fu-un!

Map 144 • Stockwell / Brixton (West)

he Duke of Edinburgh	204 Ferndale Rd	020 7326 0301	Warm, traditional pub with massive beer garden.
arquis of Lorne	49 Dalyell Rd	020 7771 9408	A dying breed.
lan B	418 Brixton Rd	020 7733 0926	Has made a name for itself, but pretty lame really.
he Prince of Wales	469 Brixton Rd	020 7095 1978	Behind dealers chanting skunk lies a nothin' special pub.
he Queen's Head	144 Stockwell Rd	020 7737 3519	Bastion of true Brixton.
even at Brixton	7 Market Row	0207 998 3309	Cheap cocktails taken seriously with board games to boot.
he Swan	2 Stockwell Rd	020 7978 9778	Don't worry about spitting on the floor.

Map 145 • Stockwell / Brixton (East)

ixton Academy	211 Stockwell Rd	020 7771 3000	Overrated, but still a tad awesome.
mm	261 Brixton Rd	020 7274 5537	The real deal a little way out.

Map 146 • Earlsfield

ar 366	366 Garratt Ln	020 8944 9591	Chilled, lounge-type bar.
alfway House	521 Garratt Ln	020 8946 2788	Slinky, chardonnay-swilling pub with terrific terrace.
Gothique	Windmill Rd & John Archer Wy	020 8870 6567	The answer to: "Open a bar! What could go wrong?"

Map 147 • Balham (West)

he Hope	1 Bellevue Rd	020 8672 8717	Consider nearby Wandsworth Common an extension of the beer garden.
he Nightingale	97 Nightingale Ln	020 8673 1637	Untrendified local. Long may it stay so.

Map 148 • Balham (East)

he Avalon	16 Balham Hill	020 8675 8613	Beer garden for lazy Sunday lunches and, er, Japanese whisky.
alham Bowls Club	7 Ramsden Rd	020 8673 4700	A pub. In a bowling club circa 1950. Genius.
he Bedford	77 Bedford Hill	020 8682 8940	Music and comedy pub with great bands but crappy beer.
he Exhibit	12 Balham Station Rd	020 8772 6556	Bar with indie cinema attached
agen & Hyde	157 Balham High Rd	020 8772 0016	Popular boozer.

Map 150 • Brixton

he Dogstar	389 Coldharbour Ln	020 7733 7515	The burritos are great, but leave before the tunes get cheesy.
he Effra	38 Kellett Rd	020 7274 4180	A slice of the real Brixton.
ffra Social	89 Effra Rd	020 7737 6800	Retro pub in former Brixton Conservative Club.
ectric Brixton	Town Hall Parade	020 7274 2290	DJs and live music venue in former Fridge space.
rand Union	123 Acre Ln	020 7274 8794	Come for the tiki shacks and burgers.
remio de Brixton	St. Matthew's Rd	020 7924 0660	Spanish tapas bar in church crypt.
ootananny	95 Effra Rd	020 7737 7273	Great gigs—many for free
rince Albert	418 Coldharbour Ln	020 7274 3771	It's charming, trust us. In a not too obvious kindaway.
tay	447 Coldharbour Ln	084 4474 6080	Cocktails to suit the snobbiest of drinks connoisseurs
pstairs at the Ritzy	Brixton Oval	020 7326 2627	Where Brixton sparkles. Cinema, bar, café and free live music.
he Windmill	22 Blenheim Gardens	020 8671 0700	Rough-edged weirdo magnet. Unique and brilliant.

Map 151 • Tooting Bec

he Bec Bar	26 Tooting Bec Rd	020 8672 2979	Pleasant enough. Go for sport.
he King's Head	84 Upper Tooting Rd	020 8767 6708	Former gin palace brings yesteryear flair to the wasteland.

Map 152 • Tooting Broadway

he Little Bar	145 Mitcham Rd	020 8672 7317	It's a bar and it's little
he Ramble Inn	223 Mitcham Rd	020 8767 4040	Irish/locals bullcrap-free boozer.
he Secret Bar	Totterdown St	07508 369 722	Convivial Portuguese bar.
ooting Tram and Social	46 Mitcham Rd	020 8767 0278	Cavernous, funky and cool without trying.
nwined	21 Tooting High St	020 3286 4631	Pop up turned permanent providing excellent wines.

British food and British chefs had a pretty bad reputation until fairly recently; greasy piles of stodge topped off with gravy was the general consensus for what to expect in a London restaurant. A couple of years back France's premier chef Alain Ducasse upped the ante for the London dining scene by declaring it the 'restaurant capital of the world.' While there are still numerous naff cafes around they're far outnumbered by brilliant bistros, bountiful brunch places, bodacious BBQs and boatloads of other badass eateries.

As one of the most multicultural cities in the world, London is packed with cuisine from around the world, with some areas dedicated to a signature cuisine. We've got Jewish, Indian, Peruvian, Mexican, Vietnamese, Moroccan, hell even Mongolian. Visitors don't even have to look at a Yorkshire pudding, roast beef, a full English, or fish & chips if there're not so inclined but anyone would be a fool to miss out on some of the better English places.

Foodie trends come and go in this dusty old town so if you really want be down with the urban gourmands you'll need to know what's hot right now. It would be terribly embarrassing to be caught nibbling on sushi when munching on king ribs is the in thing. Then there's the staple and stable cool places that manage to keep the hungry masses happy no matter what's cool.

What you spend on food is as flexible as British weather too; street food provides some of London's most famed snacks while places like Hix's **Tramshed** dishes out minimalist done well, and old English favourites like **The Ritz** stick to the traditional-type menu its customers expect. For everyone else in between there's everything else in between. London even does Vegetarian, apparently.

Eating for Britain

In a country whose national dish is reportedly a Chicken Tikka Masala, pin-pointing what British cuisine actually is doesn't come easy. Taking a traditional approach we've got those archetypal dishes like the Sunday Roast, Full English, Fish & Chips, and Jellied Eels; if visitors believed every stereotypical image of the British it would stand to reason that these dishes make up our standard diet, along with bucket loads of builder's tea, of course.

Delve a little deeper though and you'll find a revolutionised British menu brought about by the demand of a newly sophisticated palate. We still do the soggy seaside favourite but you're just as likely to find grilled mackerel with potato salad on a chip-shop menu as you are a battered saveloy which is what you'll see at **Poppie's** in Spitalfields (Map 91). We still do Sunday lunch but you're more likely to be served the rarest of beef, a whole Poisson, or tenderloin pork than a leathery piece of gravied meat. Breakfast is a class of its own and though we're still to see a food revolution hit the East End pie shops, some things are best left as they are like the centuries-old **F.Cooke (Map 89)** on Broadway Market.

We're partial to a fusion, too; it's not unusual to see British tapas on a pub menu – expect things like mini toad-in-the-hole, bite sized beef wellington and pork belly squares served with apple sauce. We're seeing things like whole Indian menus that are made entirely of British ingredients to keep the eco-warriors happy, and we're munching on American-style pulled pork that is smoked over English craft ales.

Our adopted second cuisine award goes to the Indian sub-continent whose spicy dishes us Brits consider to be synonymous with a night out on the tiles or a night in front of the telly. Samosas as a snack, bhajis on the way home from work, and a five course special of a Sunday eve; it's all good.

Hold the Pesticides

You'd think that with all the smog the city creates and the pollution that's pumped around this place that Londoners would have come to accept the pesticides and chemicals often found in food, you would, of course, be wrong. London loves a good farmer's market and all organic café, and a good serving of local produce and meat. Weekly farmer's markets like those in **Islington (Map 80)**, London Fields and **Borough (Map 106)** are credited with starting the trend for street food in London, a few years back. The vendors would cook each other's produce to sell to hungry shoppers which in turn created a demand for top end, tasty, chemical-free food.

Any café worth its salt uses free-range eggs, bacon from British pigs, lamb (from Wales not New Zealand), apples from Somerset orchards and oysters from Whitstable. There's certainly no crime in sticking to produce form British soils, serving misshapen tomatoes, and purple carrots, just be aware that more than a handful of 'organic' places like to charge over the odds for the pleasure of non-tainted meals.

Breakfast & Lunch—Brunch

Any good Londoner values their weekend days off like a dog loves his bone. The working week leaves time for no more than coffee and a croissant at breakfast time which is why we revel so much in a weekend brunch date. Be it with a lover, a group of rowdy friends, or visiting family members, we've developed the act of brunching into an art form in its own right.

You'll still see the off greasy spoon around, serving lukewarm baked beans, fatty bacon, and pebbly scrambled eggs but chances are that the dove grey (or Victorian green) painted shop two doors down will be packed to the proverbial rafters with a convivial young crowd of foodies and hipsters. There's a lot to be said for the Full English; it's a world-famous classic, and done well, it's the breakfast of kings. We've even branched out into providing grease-free breakfasts for the more delicate morning palate.

Nothing beats the Veggie Breakfast at the **Counter Café (Near Map 94)** in Hackney Wick, and **Pavilion Café (Map 93)** in Victoria Park is a close contender for feeding the east's foodies – kippers with potato cakes and poached eggs is a fantastic Irish classic. **Caravan (Map 6)** has enjoyed its time at the top for a City brunch and it looks set to stay in the number one spot for some time; the chefs here are renowned for mixing up exotic flavour and creating elixical hangover cures. For American treats **The Breakfast Club (Map 80)** is a firm favourite and with three locations there's a seat for everyone. **Dukes Brew and Que (Map 82)** is a sneaky American brekkie place vying for the winner's ribbon and Scandinavian-influenced **Cooper and Wolf (Near Map 87)** has some wholesome northern European options on offer for the more health conscious.

Street Is Sweet

Eating on the street might mean using a plastic fork and sitting on a kerb but it certainly doesn't mean dissecting your way through a soggy sarnie or pulling half-eaten burgers out of the bin. It does mean queuing for a while to eat at the best places, trying to decide which of the tempting street stalls to eat from, and possibly dripping mustard down your best top.

You can literally find everything on the streets of London; from cockroaches to sleeping people, dog shit and hypodermics. Quite delightfully you can also find the much more attractive options of food from all over the world – we've got Peruvian, Polish, Vietnamese, Mexican, French, and pretty much everything else you can think of.

The humble burger has enjoyed huge acclaim over the past year with stalls like **Lucky Chip** reinventing the British BBQ classic to resemble something much more palatable. **Bahn Mi** is a travelling Vietnamese baguette specialist that keeps chiming in reward for serving the best pork rolls in town, and the East.St collective have a permanent spot at Kings Cross where they present the baying public with things like **The Wild Game Co (Map 11)**, and **Engine** with its haute-gourmet Hot Dogs. Even city centre workers have taken the bait for their bait though there is a heavy lean towards superfood salads and sushi in the city, the current bento leader is also perfectly positioned for visitors; right outside of Liverpool Street Station, **Wasabi** has a stall where you can pick up a salad, a couple of bits of sushi, and a delicious miso soup for less than a fiver.

Camden Market food used to be famous for all the wrong reasons; overcooked noodles, oily fried chicken, watery curry and cardboard pizzas, there's still plenty of that around but a newer set of stalls also caters to more refined tastes. What's on offer can be interchangeable but there are a few stalwarts that are worth a go. There's a French stall that does mushrooms and sauté potatoes in a Roquefort sauce and there's no exceptions made just because the chefs are serving from a stall instead of inside a restaurant; these things are literally sit-down-white-table-cloth standard.

The absolute upside to street food stalls, which we've cleverly held back 'til last, is the ability to enjoy top-notch, amazing food for a fraction of the price that a restaurant would charge for the same dish. We're talking £5-6 a go for a main meal that might be paella, Moroccan tagine, Goan curry, or an Argentinian steak. A little cake for afters should knock you back a couple of quid and will round off your stand-up meal quite nicely —**Violet's (Map 89)** lemon drizzle cake makes the proverbial icing on your day.

Doffing Hats to a Trend

The London food scene can be a fickle thing. One day it's Gin and Venison that's the reigning king of the food world and the next it's knocked off its perch by a BBQ rib and a craft beer. See, once the masses have caught onto a top secret food trend, the gourmands move on to new pastures where The Guardian is yet to report, and a license is yet to be passed.

We've lately seen some foodie revolutions, the death of others, and the birthing of a few. While the burger has surely enjoyed its time, one of the new kids on the block, Peruvian, is sticking around for a while, and crawling across the city like a drunk crab – the **Last Days of Pisco** pops up in venues across the city which can be a bit pesky if you turn up the day after it has moved on but their ceviche is possibly one of London's best new additions. Out in the West, the aptly named **Ceviche (Map 12)** does more of the fish-cooked-with-citrus thing and complements each dish with lashing of Peruvian firewater, Pisco which comes on its own, in dessert, and as a range of cocktails.

Onto another trend which is set to stay; the French have hors d'oeuvres the Spanish have tapas, the Swedish have smorgasbord and now the British have small plates, and we love them. Russell Norman's **Polpo (Map 10)** restaurants will remain as popular as ever to serve up shareable small plates in a New York diner-style setting. Expect to see things like Anchovy & Chickpea Crostini, Spicy Pork & Fennel Meatballs, and Rabbit & Chicory Salad, all made in perfect proportions whether you're planning to take a couple for yourself or share a load with friends.

Yauatcha (Map 10) is Soho's answer to the small plate influx where head chef Tong Chee Whee is renowned for combining complicated flavours and adding delicate notes to create things like Venison Puffs. **Brawn (Map 91)** on Columbia Road is in a class of its own when it comes to creating meaty feasts; the restaurant shamelessly rejoices in all things pig and waives any requests for a veggie option. The menu is dependent on season and on what the chefs feel like cooking; you might find salted ox tongue, pork scratching, or pickled wild boar here and it will all be delicious and meaty.

Pop-Up, Pop-Down

Providing a location for these pop up restaurants and supper clubs can be a challenge, mainly because the very nature of them means that most don't stay in the same place for too long, instead choosing to change venues every 3-6 months, allowing each little part of insular London to enjoy the experience.

Some of the more business-inclined places choose to pop in the same place, say, once a month, which makes it easier to pinpoint them but harder to actually get a table. Other that started as a travelling-circus version of a restaurant have settled into grown-up, permanent accommodation, or at least rented a kitchen to become semi-perm tenants. The **Seagrass (Map 80)** in Islington is one of the second type – started as a pop-up and matured to a mainstay; they take over a pie & mash shop three nights a week to serve up a menu heavy on game and fish, you're also invited to bring your own booze.

Disappearing Dining Club follows a similar vein. Having started as a pop-up group offering tea dances and three course dinners, it recently moved out of its student digs into a parently home on Brick Lane where they're operating under the name of **Back in Five Minutes (Map 91)**. It's hidden behind a clothes shop, limited to thirty guests, and operates from Wednesday to Saturday.

Pay for What You Eat

It seems only sensible and fair that you should only pay for what you eat, right? Think about how much of your evening dining bill is often down to the sheer amount of booze you've put away though. Now imagine that you don't have to pay for that portion of the bill.

London has its fair share of bring your own bottle restaurants and the best part is that they're not all of one vein i.e Oriental, dingy, or in one place; even high-end Mayfair has BYOB bottle restaurants. There does seem to be a higher than normal number of BYOB eateries in the east but that's just because hipsters are skint, preferring to spend their cash on purple leggings and (il) legal highs.

By day **Hurwendeki (Map 92**) is a standard little coffee shop, tucked in a railway arch with a unique terrace, by night it is a Korean restaurant with perfect ambiance a brilliant, affordable menu and a BYOB policy. **Little Georgia (Map 92)** is a darling of a place; pretty pale green with a warm, inviting basement, and hearty portions of Georgian food is what to expect here. Kingsland Road is scattered with Vietnamese places where u can BYOB and while they're all fairly good **Mien Tay (Map 91)** is always packed out.

Key: £ : Under £10 / ££ : £10–£20 / £££ : £20–£30 / ££££ : £30–£40 / £££££: £40+
** : Does not accept credit cards./ † : Accepts only American Express / ††: Accepts only Visa and Mastercard*
Time listed refers to kitchen closing time on weekend nights

Map 1 • Marylebone (West)

Abu Ali	136 George St	020 7724 6338	£		Good cheap 'n chearful Lebanese joint among many similar in the area!
Beirut Express	112 Edgware Rd	020 7724 2700	££	2 am	Chaotic, rude and the best Lebanese in town.
Daisy Green	20 Seymour Street	020 7723 3301	££		Aussie style easy eating.
Locanda Locatelli	8 Seymour St	020 7935 9088	££££	11.30 pm	Outstanding Italian food.
Maroush VI Express	68 Edgware Rd	020 7224 9339	££	12 am	Wax philosophical while smoking a hookah out front.
Twist	42 Crawford St	020 7723 3377	£££		Italian-focused small plates.

Map 2 • Marylebone (East)

Casa Becci	32 Paddington Street	020 7935 7031		11 pm	Cosy Lady and the Tramp-style Italian eaterie
Chiltern Firehouse	1 Chiltern St	020 7073 7676	£££	12 am	Delicious food and celeb-spotting.
Comptoir Libanais	65 Wigmore St	020 7935 1110	£	8 pm	Uncompromisingly cheap and cheerful mezes.
Diwan	31 Thayer St	020 7935 2445	££	11 pm	Lebanese gorge spot.
Fischer's	50 Marylebone High St	020 7466 5501	£££		Pitch-perfect Viennese cafe.
Galvin Bistrot de Luxe	66 Baker St	020 7935 4007	£££	11 pm	Veloutés, ballatines, tartares and escargots. Delicieux? Mais oui.
The Golden Hind	73 Marylebone Ln	020 7486 3644	££	10 pm	Fish and chips from the top-drawer. Can do BYOB
Goodman Mayfair	24-26 Maddox St	020 7499 3776	£££££		London steak institution.
Hush Brasserie	8 Lancashire Ct	020 7659 1500	££££	11 pm	European food al fresco. Go on a lunch hour holiday.
Meat Liquor	74 Welbeck St	020 7224 4239	£	12 am	Best burgers and chilli cheese fries in town.
MEATliquor	74 Welbeck St	020 7224 4239	£		No reservations, queues round the block but it's worth it.
No. 5 Cavendish Square	5 Cavendish Sq	020 7079 5000	£££	11 pm	A No. 5 desperately trying to be as opulent as Chanel's.
Patisserie Valerie	105 Marylebone High St	020 7935 6240	£	9 pm	Boho coffee and pastry.
Patty & Bun	54 James St	020 7487 3188	£		Exactly what a burger should be. Be prepared to wait.
Pollen Street Social	8 Pollen St	020 7290 7600	£££££		The mighty Jason Atherton's flagship restaurant.
The Providores and Tapa Room	109 Marylebone High St	020 7935 6175	££	11 pm	Sip Rioja and gorge on tapas for the cognoscenti.
Royal China	24-26 Baker St	020 7487 4688	£££		Cantonese culinary powerhouse flagship; dim sum mandatory.
Royal China Club	40-42 Baker St	020 7486 3898	££££		More upscale iteration of Cantonese culinary powerhouse; dim sum mandatory.
Trishna	15 Blandford St	020 7935 5624	££££		Starred Indian cuisine highlighting the subcontinent's coastal regions.
Zoilo	9 Duke St	020 7486 9699	££££		Haute Argentine transcending beef-industrial complex.

Map 3 • Fitzrovia

Archipelago	53 Cleveland St	020 7383 3346	£££££	10.30 pm	London's best, alright only, chocolate-covered scorpions and crocodile steaks.
Ask	48 Grafton Way	020 7388 8108	£	11.30 pm	...for pizza.
Bao	31 Windmill St		££		Scrumptious meat-filled buns.
Barnyard	18 Charlotte St	020 7580 3842	££		Muscular New British cuisine.

Key: £ : Under £10 / ££ : £10–£20 / £££ : £20–£30 / ££££ : £30–£40 / £££££: £40+
** : Does not accept credit cards./ † : Accepts only American Express / ††: Accepts only Visa and Mastercard*
Time listed refers to kitchen closing time on weekend nights

Barrica	62 Goodge St	020 7436 9448	£££		Tapas and sherry-forward bar.
Berners Tavern	10 Berners St	020 7908 7979	£££	10:30 pm	One for special occasions.
Beyond Bread	2 Charlotte Pl	020 7636 7055	££		Breads and pastries made from alternative grains.
Bonnie Gull	21 Foley St	020 7436 0921	££	10 pm	Best fish and chips.
Boopshi's	31 Windmill St	020 3205 0072	££	10 pm	Schnitzel and every kind of Spritz.
Brazilian Gourmet	70 Cleveland St	020 7018 0879	£	6 pm	Authentic and friendly.
Crazy Bear	26 Whitfield St	020 7631 0088	££££	10.30 pm	Thai deluxe. Where the media world feeds its clients.
Gitane	60 Great Titchfield St	020 7631 5269	£	6 pm	Parisian meets Persian
Govinda's	10 Soho St	020 7440 5229	£*	8 pm	Cheap Krishna food. You know the deal.
Hakkasan	8 Hanway Pl	020 7927 7000	£££££	12 am	Soho's sexiest subterranean Chinese. China-chic dining for the beautiful people.
Honey & Co	25 Warren St	020 7388 6175	£	10:30 pm	Husband and wife run.
Iberica	195 Great Portland St	020 7636 8650	££	4 pm	Jamon Jamon
Italiano Coffee Co.	46 Goodge St	020 7580 9688	£	11 pm	Zen it is not—but who cares at £3.50 a pizza?
Kin Cafe	22 Foley St	020 7998 4720	£	5:30 pm	Father and son team cooking fresh and healthy.
Koba	11 Rathbone St	020 7580 8825	£		A Korean delight! Set lunch is a bargain.
Latium	21 Berners St	020 7323 9123	£££	10.30 pm	Romantic (and pricey) first date place.
Market Place	11 Market Pl	020 7079 2020	£	1 am	Warm buzz all day/night. Hot clientele/tepid Prices.
Navarro's	67 Charlotte St	020 7637 7713	£££	10 pm	Delicioso! Smells like Seville, tastes like Seville.
Nyonya	11 Warren St	020 7387 0300	£	7pm	Peranakan Chinese food!
Picture	110 Great Portland St	020 7637 7892	£	10:30 pm	Bistro fayre for sharing. Date night?
Portland	113 Great Portland St	020 7436 3261	££	11 pm	For when you want to impress the parents.
Ragam	57 Cleveland St	020 7636 9098	££	10.45 pm	Can't dis these dosas (potato crepes) at very decent prices.
The Riding House Cafe	43 Great Titchfield St	020 7927 0840	££		Ignore the stuffed squirrels and focus on the buttermilk pancakes.
Roka	37 Charlotte St	020 7580 6464	£££	11 pm	Dazzling Izakaya concept Japanese.
Salt Yard	54 Goodge St	020 7637 0657	£££	11 pm	Intimate and sexy. Take a date. Get laid. Possibly.
Sardo	45 Grafton Way	020 7387 2521	££	10 pm	Hit after hit. Try the crab pasta.
Stef's	3 Berners St	020 3073 1041	££	11 pm	You can't knock the gnocchi.
Thai Metro	38 Charlotte St	020 7436 4201	££	11 pm	Thai food, cooked well, served well, job done.
Villandry	170 Great Portland St	020 7631 3131	££		Hot, tasty, homemade feel and very ready-to-eat.
Yalla Yalla	12 Winsley St	020 7637 4748	£	11:30 pm	Shawarma-rama.

Map 4 • Bloomsbury (West)

Alara	58 Marchmont St	020 7837 1172	£££	7 pm	Hardcore veggie/vegan mecca, surprisingly good.
Bi Won	24 Coptic St	020 7580 2660	£	10 pm	Manhandling staff but great food.
Hummus Bros	37 Southampton Row	020 7404 7079	£		Second branch of independent chain serving hummus and meze.
Savoir Faire	42 New Oxford St	020 7436 0707	££	10.30 pm	Sweet little rustic restaurant, a stroll from Soho.

Map 5 • Bloomsbury (East)

Banh Mi Bay	4-6 Theobalds Rd	020 7831 4079	£		One of the originator's of London's bahn mi craze.
Ciao Bella	86 Lamb's Conduit St	020 7242 4119	££	11 pm	Authentic, rustic feel Italian complete with piano.
Cigala	54 Lamb's Conduit St	020 7405 1717	££	10.45 pm	Great service and gorgeous salty Spanish bread.
The Food Bazaar	59 Grays Inn Rd	020 7242 6578	£*	9 pm	Casual and friendly with great hot food selection.
Fryer's Delight	19 Theobald's Rd	020 7405 4114	£*	10 pm	No frills chippie; big portions of chunky, salty, greasy tastiness.

Itadaki Zen	139 King's Cross Rd	020 7278 3573	£	10 pm	Get your zen on.
The Lady Ottoline	11 Northington St	020 7831 0008	£££		Great gastropub from owner's of Shoreditch's Princess.
Mary Ward Centre	42 Queen Sq	020 7269 6000	£*	5 pm	Hippy educational centre with a great organic cafe.
Paolina Snack Bar	181 King's Cross Rd	020 7278 8176	£*	10 pm	Grotty exterior disguises this diamond of cheerful authentic Thai.
The Perseverance	63 Lamb's Conduit St	020 7405 8278	££	10.30 pm	Good quality gastropub food.
You Me Sushi	180 Gray's Inn Rd	020 7278 8699	£££		Burgeoning sushi empire; good for takeout.

Map 6 • Clerkenwell

Caravan	11 Exmouth Market	020 7833 8115	£		Exceptional coffee and food.
Dans Le Noir	30 Clerkenwell Green	020 7253 1100	££££	9 pm	Blind waiters serve in pitch darkness: don't wear white.
The Eagle	159 Farringdon Rd	020 7837 1353	££	10.30 pm	London's first gastro pub—just look what they started.
Little Bay	171 Farringdon Rd	020 7278 1234	££	12 am	Posh-people food at pikey-people prices.
The Modern Pantry	47 St Johns Sq	020 7553 9210	££		From breakfast through brunch to lunch and dinner with a modern twist.
Morito	32 Exmouth Market	020 7278 7007	£££		Moro's tapas-mezze sister restaurant.
Moro	34 Exmouth Market	020 7833 8336	££££	11 pm	DO believe the hype.
Pham Sushi	159 Whitecross St	020 7251 6336	£££		Central independent sushi for great healthy lunch.
The Sandwich Man	23 Easton St	020 7833 9001	£*	2.30 pm	Office delivery returns. Gourmet—and just 65p. Best lunch in London.
Sushi Tetsu	12 Jerusalem Passage	020 7278 0421	££££		Tiny, unpretentious, and world class.

Map 7 • Barbican / City Road (South)

Bavarian Beerhouse	190 City Rd	084 4330 2005	££	11 pm	Unlace your lederhausen for some serious schnitzel madness.
Carnevale	135 Whitecross St	020 7250 3452	££	11 pm	Veggie on the cheap.
De Santis	11 Old St	020 7689 5626	££	9.30 pm	Like being in Milan; owner Enzo takes care of you
Nusa Kitchen	9 Old St	020 7253 3135	£*	5 pm	People queuing? For ages? For soup? Now I've seen everything.

Map 8 • Liverpool Street / Broadgate

Duck & Waffle	110 Bishopgate	020 3640 7310	£££		Remarkably good value for such an 'elevated' dining experience.
Eyre Brothers	70 Leonard St	020 7613 5346	££	10.45 pm	Great place run by the Eyre brothers—Jane no relation.
Gaucho Broadgate	5 Finsbury Ave	020 7256 6877	££££	11 pm	Divine, ohmigod, melt-in-your-mouth steak. Oops, drooling!
Hoxton Grill	81 Great Eastern St	020 7739 9111	£££		Very sexy. Very nice. Very expensive.
The Princess of Shoreditch	76 Paul St	020 7729 9270	££		Gastropub and drinking hole for city workers and slackers.

Map 9 • Mayfair / Green Park

Alain Ducasse at The Dorchester	Park Ln	020 7629 8866	££££	10 pm	Better known for its extortionate prices than michelin-starred food
Burger & Lobster	29 Clarges St	020 7409 1699	££		Burger or lobster or both? Greedy!
Citrus	112 Piccadilly	020 7499 6321	££££		High-end Italian at the Sheraton Park Lane.
Corrigan's	28 Upper Grosvenor St	020 7499 9943	£££££		When in Rome/ Mayfair...
El Pirata of Mayfair	5 Down St	020 7491 3810	£££	11.30 pm	Don't be put off by stuffy location—this is f'ing good tapas.
The English Tea Room at Brown's	Albemarle St	020 7518 4155	££££	11 pm	Ah, so that's what a £48 cup of tea tastes like.
Galvin at Windows	22 Park Ln	020 7208 4021	£££££	11 pm	Art Deco French overlooking Buckingham Palace. We're not worthy!
Gymkhana	42 Albemarle St	020 3011 5900	££££		Posh four-star Indian with slightly disarming colonial flourishes.

Key: £ : Under £10 / ££ : £10–£20 / £££ : £20–£30 / ££££ : £30–£40 / £££££: £40+
** : Does not accept credit cards./ † : Accepts only American Express / ††: Accepts only Visa and Mastercard*
Time listed refers to kitchen closing time on weekend nights

Kitty Fisher's	10 Shepherd Market	020 3302 1661	£££		Mediterranean-British in cozy digs.
L'Autre	5 Shepherd St	020 7499 4680	££££	11 pm	Polish meets Mexican. Surprisingly well.
Momo	25 Heddon St	020 7434 4040	££		Tea, cous-cous, shisha, and tagines; perfectly Moroccan.
Nobu	19 Old Park Ln	020 7447 4747	£££££	12 am	Rob a bank on the way as it's bloody expensive!
The Ritz	150 Piccadilly	020 7493 8181	£££££	10 pm	High tea amidst ornaments and swank—resist temptation to swipe towels.
Theo Randall	1 Hamilton Pl	020 7318 8747	£££££	11 pm	Sincere and stylish cuisine unfortunately hidden behind a hotel faÃ§ade.

Map 10 • Piccadilly / Soho (West)

Bao	53 Lexington St		££		Scrumptious meat-filled buns.
Bob Bob Ricard	1 Upper James St	020 3145 1000	£££	11.30 pm	Proper posh British diner serving Cornish crab cake and...Ribena.
Bodean's BBQ	10 Poland St	020 7287 7575			Resistance is futile. Soho Special—great way to end a night.
Brasserie Zedel	20 Sherwood St	020 7734 4888	£		Service so-so, atmosphere tres Parisian. Great value.
Cecconi's	5 Burlington Gardens	020 7434 1500	££££	11.15 pm	All day menu for the spoilt. Delicious breakfasts.
Cha Cha Moon	15 Ganton St	020 7297 9800	££	11 pm	Like Wagamamas but for Chinese.
Dehesa	25 Ganton St	020 7494 4170	£££	11 pm	Faux-rustic protein-rich tapas, sweetie.
Detox Kitchen	10 Kingly Street	0207 498 6417	££	6:30pm	Clean eating made simple.
Dishoom	22 Kingly St	020 7420 9322	££		All-day Parsi cafe straight outta Bombay.
Kulu Kulu	76 Brewer St	020 7734 7316	£	10 pm	Great, fresh, fast sushi for people on the go. Sit down is 45 minutes only.
Le Pain Quotidien	18 Great Marlborough St	020 7486 6154	£	10 pm	Feel like a right old tartine.
Mildred's	45 Lexington St	020 7494 1634	££	11pm	Even non-vegetarians are fans.
Nordic Bakery	14 Golden Sq	020 3230 1077	£	7 pm	Authentic sticky cinnamon buns, Karelian pies and smoked Moomin.
The Photographers' Gallery	16 Ramillies St	020 7087 9300	£*	5.30 pm	Artsy coffee spot with photos on view.
Ping Pong	45 Great Marlborough St	020 7851 6969	££	11 pm	Don't leave without trying a char sui bun!
Pitt Cue Co.	1 Newburgh St	020 7287 5578	£££		Best Southern BBQ this side of Austin, Texas.
Polpo	41 Beak St	020 7734 4479	£		Venetian-style bacaro.
San Carlo Cicchetti	215 Picadilly	020 7494 9435	£££		Seasonal Italian; fresh ingredients; all-day menu.
Sartoria	20 Saville Row	020 7534 7000	£££££	11 pm	The pick of the Conran restaurants.
Sketch	9 Conduit St	020 7659 4500	£££	1 am	Colossally trendy kitsch palace.
Social Eating House	58 Poland St	020 7993 3251	££££		Fun, creative cuisine with studiously low-key vibe.
Taro	61 Brewer St	020 7734 5826	£££	10.30 pm	Where London's Japanese locals eat sushi.
Ten Ten Tei	56 Brewer St	020 7287 1738	£££££	10 pm	The Japanese restaurant Japanese people love.
Tibits	12 Heddon St	020 7758 4110	££	12 am	Buffet: sans meat, sold by weight. Genius!
Wagamama	10 Lexington St	020 7292 0990	£	11 pm	Reliable, speedy noodle chain.
Wild Honey	12 St George St	020 7758 9160	£££	10.30 pm	This Michelin star's got skillz (and a damn good tête de veau).
Yauatcha	15 Broadwick St	020 7494 8888	£££££	11.45 pm	Traditional Chinese tea-house meets star-spangled media haunt.
Yoshino	3 Piccadilly Pl	020 7287 6622	££	10 pm	Back alley bentos so good you'll pretend they were your discovery.

Map 11 • Soho (Central)

Ba Shan	24 Romilly St	020 7287 3266	££		User-friendly Szechuan from Barshu folks.
Balans	60 Old Compton St	020 7439 2183	££	3 am	Share a 4am breakfast with the likes of Amy Winehouse.
Bar Bruno	101 Wardour St	020 7734 3750	£*	10 pm	Hidden Italian cafe gem. Authentically loud and friendly.
Blanchette	9 D'Arblay Street	020 7439 8100	££		Three French brothers bring modern bistro to Soho.
Bocca di Lupo	12 Archer St	020 7734 2223	£££	12 am	Italian for 'break a leg'; authentic fare gets your bocca watering.

Bone Daddies	31 Peter Street	020 7287 8581	£	11:30pm	Tonkotsu ramen, slurp.
Busaba Eathai	110 Wardour St	020 7255 8686	£££		Never mind the shared benches, the food's too yummy.
Cafe Espana	63 Old Compton St	020 7494 1271	££	11 pm	Highly recommended. 10% off for eating with castanets (possibly).
Copita	27 D'Arblay St	020 7287 7797	£££		Continually changing tapas menu and full bar.
Ember Yard	60 Berwick St	020 7439 8057	£££		Tapas-y charcoal-grilled meats and charcuterie via Spain & Italy.
Foxcroft & Ginger	3 Berwick Street		£	10 pm	Casual cafe eating all day.
The Full English	83 Wardour St		£		Proper British comfort food at unbelievably reasonable prices.
Gelupo	7 Archer St	020 7287 5555	£		Grab a granita, close your eyes and you're in Sicily.
Grace	42 Great Windmill St	020 7851 0800	££££	10.30 pm	Wannabe a WAG? Get in 'ere!
Honest Burgers	4 Meard St	020 3609 9524	£		Why keeping it simple works. A+ reasonably priced burgers.
Hummus Bros	88 Wardour St	020 7734 1311	££	11 pm	Where hummus is the main dish.
Imli	167 Wardour St	020 7287 4243	£	11 pm	Tapas + curry. Fusion gone insane but somehow works.
Jazz Club	10 Dean St	084 5602 7017	£	11 pm	Surprisingly, jazz takes the mediocre chain up a notch.
Jerk City	189 Wardour St	020 7287 2878	£	10 pm	Jamaican fast food. In doubt? Go for ackee and saltfish.
Kirazu	47 Rupert St	020 7494 2248	£££		Artfully crafted Japanese tapas.
Leong's Legends	4 Macclesfield St	020 7287 0288	££	11 pm	A Taiwanese Chinatown legend.
Maoz	43 Old Compton St	020 7851 1586	£*	1 am	Falafeltastic!
Morada Brindisa Asador	18-20 Rupert St	020 7478 8758	££££		Wood-fired pig via Spain.
The Palomar	34 Rupert St	020 7439 8777	££££		Open-kitchen gastroexperimentation.
Paul	49 Old Compton St	020 7287 6261	£	10 pm	French cafe/bakery chain. Amazing baguettes!
Pizzeria Malletti	26 Noel St	020 7439 4096	£*	3 pm	Amazing! Use your mobile and you won't get served.
Princi	135 Wardour St	020 7478 8888	£		Italian deserts you didn't know existed. Tempting new pizzeria area.
Randall & Aubin	16 Brewer St	020 7287 4447	£££	11 pm	Over-indulgently carnal seafood delights which only call for champagne.
Soho Joe	22 Dean St	075 3413 4398			Darn good pizza with the locals that won't break the bank.
Spuntino	61 Rupert St		£££	12 am	Hidden nameless bar serving up tasty bites.
St Moritz	161 Wardour St	020 7734 3324	££££	11.30 pm	Swiss cheese heaven.
Thai Square	27 St. Annes Ct	020 7287 2000	££	11 pm	Thai with a good range. In set meals—go for starter NOT dessert.
Tokyo Diner	2 Leicester St	020 7287 8777	£		One of London's best for katsu curry. No tipping!
Wong Kei	41 Wardour St	020 7437 8408	££	10 pm	AKA Wonky's: institutionally rude service, cheap fast Chinese.
Yoshino Delicatessen	59 Shaftesbury Ave	020 7287 6622	£	10 pm	Cheap as chips but with sushi.

Map 12 • Soho (East)

10 Greek Street	10 Greek St	020 7734 4677	£££		Farm—and sea-to-table; courier font and slate.
Abeno Too	17 Great Newport St	020 7379 1160	££	11 pm	Addictive Okonomiyaki (pancakes) flipped and fried on the table.
Arbutus	63 Frith St	020 7734 4545	£££	11 pm	Chocolate soup! Worth it for that alone.
Assa	53 St Giles High St	020 7240 8256	££	12 am	Cheerful eager-to-please Korean cafe
Baiwei	8 Little Newport St	020 7494 3605	££		Highly recommended Szechuan; encyclopedic menu.
Baozi Inn	26 Newport Court	020 7287 6877	£		No frills, quality Szechuan.
Bar Italia	22 Frith St	020 7437 4520	££	4.30 am	Soho institution; perfect for people watching at any hour.
Barrafina	54 Frith St	020 7813 8016	£££	11 pm	Seriously, the best (and hippest) place for tapas.
Barshu	28 Frith St	020 7287 8822	£££		Hot 'n' heavy Szechuan in well-appointed digs.
Bi Bim Bap	11 Greek St	020 7287 3434			Cheap and healthy Korean rice bowls.
Bo Drake	6 Greek St	020 7439 9989	£££		Asian meets American barbecue.

Key: £ : Under £10 / ££ : £10–£20 / £££ : £20–£30 / ££££ : £30–£40 / £££££: £40+
** : Does not accept credit cards./ † : Accepts only American Express / ††: Accepts only Visa and Mastercard*
Time listed refers to kitchen closing time on weekend nights

Boheme Kitchen and Bar	19 Old Compton St	020 7734 5656	£££	11.45 pm	You want frites with that? Deliciously snobby comfort food.
Ceviche	17 Frith St	020 7292 2040			Brining Peruvian to the perverted.
Corean Chilli	51 Charing Cross Rd	020 7734 6737	££	12 am	Karaoke and stir-fries with the Korean cool kids.
Ed's Easy Diner	12 Moor St	020 7434 4439	££	11 pm	It's like, you know? Soooo, like, American? You know?
The Friendly Inn	47 Gerrard St	020 7437 4170	£	1 am	Where Londoners go for Chinese in Soho.
Gaby's Deli	30 Charing Cross Rd	020 7836 4233	££	10 pm	High on tradition, low on frills. Authentically spartan.
Garlic & Shots	14 Frith St	020 7734 9505	££££	1 am	Garlic, garlic and more garlic. No-go zone for vampires.
Gay Hussar	2 Greek St	020 7437 0973	££	10.45 pm	Everything from strudel to cherry soup at this old-school Hungarian.
Haozhan	8 Gerrard St	020 7434 3838	£££	11 pm	Can't pick? This is the one.
Imperial China	25 Lisle St	020 7734 3388	££		Solid dim sum option.
The Ivy	1 West St	020 7836 4751	£££		Dining experience that will prove memorable.
Koya	49 Frith St	020 7434 4463	£		Blink and you'd miss London's worst-kept udon secret.
La Bodega Negra	16 Moor St	020 7758 4100	££		Shh, it's a secret! Mexican food underneath a Soho sex shop.
La Porchetta Pollo Bar	20 Old Compton St	020 7494 9368	£££	12 am	Cheap and cheerful Italian. In the West End? Well, exactly.
Le Beaujolais	25 Litchfield St	020 7836 2955	££	10 pm	Get insulted by a Frenchman here in London—Mai oui!
New World	1 Gerrard Pl	020 7434 2508	£	11.45 pm	Crispy duck, Dim Sum, custard dumplings... bring it on!
Pizza Express	20 Greek St	020 7734 7430	£		Pizza. Really fast.
Sartori	15 Great Newport St	020 7836 6308	££		Hit and miss service but all is forgiven with metre long pizzas.
Smoking Goat	7 Denmark St		£££		Stylish, adventurous full-service Thai restaurant.
Soho's Secret Tea Room	29 Greek St	020 7437 5920	£		Secret tea! Hoorah!
The Stockpot	18 Old Compton St	020 7287 1066	££*	12 am	Fantastically cheap stodge.
Taro	10 Old Compton St	020 7439 2275	££	10.30 pm	Like Taro Brewer Street. But gayer, obviously.
Yang Guang Supermarket	28-29 Newport Ct	020 8494 9222	£		Pork buns and coconut jam waffles from vendors outside.

Map 13 • Covent Garden

Battersea Pie	28 The Market	020 7240 9566	£	6 pm	Who ate all the pies?
Belgo Centraal	50 Earlham St	020 7813 2233	£££	11 pm	Thoroughly enjoyable moules et frites. And beer... mmm... beer.
Café Mode	57 Endell St	020 7240 8085	££	11.30 pm	Pizza, pasta, salad. No fuss.
Flesh & Buns	41 Earlham St	020 7632 9500	£££		Fun izakaya and bun spot from folks behind Bone Daddies.
Great Queen Street	32 Great Queen St	020 7242 0622	£££	11 pm	Affordable and might be London's best gastropub.
Jar Kitchen	176 Drury Ln	020 7405 4255	£££		Farm-to-table modern British.
Kulu Kulu Sushi	51 Shelton St	020 7240 5687	££	10 pm	Tiny conveyor belt sushi joint. Bang on the money.
Lima Floral	14 Garrick St	020 7240 5778	££££		Elegant Peruvian, the way it's meant to be.
Mon Plaisir	21 Monmouth St	020 7836 7243	£££	11.15 pm	Not up to typical Paris standards, but still tres bon!
Punjab	80 Neal St	020 7836 9787	£££	11:30 pm	Relive the days of the Raj in this old-school curry house.
Rock & Sole Plaice	47 Endell St	020 7836 3785	£££	11 pm	London's oldest chippie. Est. 1871. On-street, fairy-lit picnic benches. Huge portions.
Rossopomodoro	50 Monmouth St	020 7240 9095	£	12 am	Chain Italian with very tasty pies. Cutlery prohibited!
Sarastro	126 Drury Ln	020 7836 0101	££	11.30 pm	Hilarious over-the-top decor; includes fornicating cherubs.
Souk Medina	1 Shorts Gardens	020 7240 1796	££	11 pm	Atmospheric Morrocan joint. Free refills on mouthwatering £20 set menu.
Wild Food Cafe	14 Neal's Yard		££	10pm	Delicious, vibrant and healthy.

Map 14 • Holborn / Temple

Asadal	227 High Holborn	020 7430 9006	£££	10.30 pm	Go on—venture down those stairs—it's worth it.
Casanova's Treats	13 Lamb's Conduit Passage	020 7405 5505	£	4 pm	Come get seduced by this tasty Casanova.
Indigo	1 Aldwych	020 7300 0400	£££	11 pm	Sunday brunch and a movie—all in the same place!
The MEATmarket	Jubilee Market Hall, Tavistock St	020 7240 4852	££		Try the hard shakes.

Map 15 • Blackfriars / Farringdon

Beppe's Sandwich Bar	23 W Smithfield	020 7236 7822	££	3 pm	As classically Italian as oversized sunglasses. Only much, much better.
Bleeding Heart	Bleeding Heart Yard	020 7242 2056	£££	10.30 pm	Historic, hard to find, eccentric beauty.
Foxlow	69-73 St John St	020 7014 8070	£££		Neighborhood-friendly meat-forward comfort cuisine.
Gaucho Smithfield	93 Charterhouse St	020 7490 1676	££	11 pm	Where cows would choose to be eaten.
Hix Oyster & Chop House	36 Cowcross St	020 7017 1930	££		Never tried beef and oyster pie?
Kurz + Lang	1 St. John St	020 7993 2923	£	11.30 pm	Ze German Bratwurst sausage at its zizzling best.
Le Cafe du Marche	22 Charterhouse Sq	020 7608 1609	£££	11 pm	Wonderful French cuisine in delightful venue. Tucked away in Charterhouse Square.
Pho	86 St. John St	020 7253 7624	£	10.30 pm	Steaming bowlfuls for hungry Clerkenwell workers. Specialises in street food.
Poncho 8	11 Queens Head Passage	020 7248 6744	£		St. Paul's branch of the Mexican restaurant.
Portal	88 St John St	020 7253 6950	££££	10.15 pm	Astoundingly good Portuguese. Swanky but not stuffy.
Shosharu	64 Turnmill St	020 3805 2304	££££		Exquisite multi-level Anglo-Japanese cuisine.
Smiths of Smithfield	67 Charterhouse St	020 7251 7950	£££	10.45 pm	Overflowing with yuppies and trendy types; pricey but tasty.
St John	26 Saint John St	020 7251 0848	££	11 pm	Nose to tail eating.
St. John	26 St John St	020 7251 0848	£££	11 pm	This place is ALL about the offal.
Tinseltown	44 St. John St	020 7689 2424	£	24 hrs	Funky diner serving great late-night milkshakes.
Vivat Bacchus	47 Farringdon St	020 7353 2648	£££	9.30 pm	Three wine cellars and a cheeseroom. A ROOM of cheese.

Map 16 • Square Mile (West)

Barbecoa	20 New Change Passage	020 3005 8555	££££		Steak-y Jamie Oliver fire-cooked joint.
Planet of the Grapes	74 Queen Victoria St	020 7248 1892	££	12 am	Finally, a reason to go to the Square Mile.
Pull'd	61 Cannon St	020 3752 0326	£	9 pm	Pulled pork/beef/chicken.
Sweetings	39 Queen Victoria St	020 7248 3062	£££	4 pm	Old fashioned institution for nostalgia trips. Lunch only.

Map 17 • Square Mile (East)

Gaucho City	1 Bell Inn Yard	020 7626 5180	££££	11 pm	The best steakhouse in the city. Located in former gold vaults.
The Mercer	34 Threadneedle St	020 7628 0001	££	9.30 pm	Proper British grub in a light contemporary atmosphere.
Nusa Kitchen	2 Adams Ct	020 7628 1149	£	4 pm	Fresh soup made daily.
Simpson's Tavern	38 Ball Court Alley	020 7626 9985	££		Perfectly cooked classics in a pub full of history.
Wasabi	52 Old Broad St	020 7374 8337	£*	10 pm	Delicious sushi and bento for those in a rush.

Map 18 • Tower Hill / Aldgate

Jeff's Cafe	14 Brune St	020 7375 2230	£*	10 pm	Cheap as chips (which they serve here, incidentally).
La Pietra	54 Commercial St	020 7247 0988	£		Hey mambo, mambo Italiano.
Poncho 8	5 Steward St	020 7247 2008	£		Spitalfields branch of the Mexican restaurant.

Key: £ : Under £10 / ££ : £10–£20 / £££ : £20–£30 / ££££ : £30–£40 / £££££: £40+
** : Does not accept credit cards./ † : Accepts only American Express / ††: Accepts only Visa and Mastercard*
Time listed refers to kitchen closing time on weekend nights

Map 19 • Belgravia

Amaya	Motcomb St	020 7823 1166	££££	11.30 pm	Where the trendies go for their curry fix.
Boisdale	15 Eccleston St	020 7730 6922	£££££	11 pm	Posh Scottish nosh. No deep-fried Mars Bars, sadly.
Noura	12 William St	020 7235 5900	££	11 pm	Frequently orgiastic Lebanese pig-outs, habibi.
One-O-One	101 Knightsbridge	020 7290 7101	££££	10 pm	One man's fish is another man's pleasure.
The Pantechnicon	10 Motcomb St	020 7730 6074	£££££		One to impress the parents.
Yo! Sushi	109 Knightsbridge	020 7841 0775	££	10 pm	A London institution—we dream in sashimi on conveyor belts.

Map 20 • Victoria / Pimlico (West)

Grumbles	35 Churton St	020 7834 0149	££	11 pm	Unfashionably unfussy Brit/French home-cooking. Gorgeous pies, no grumbles.
Pimlico Fresh	86 Wilton Rd	020 7932 0030	££		Best bet for a quality bite before your show.

Map 21 • Pimlico (East)

Regency Cafe	17 Regency St	020 7821 6596	£*	7 pm	Proper British fry-ups and atmosphere in this 1940's cafe.
The Vincent Rooms	76 Vincent Sq	020 7802 8391	£££	7 pm	Brilliant food served by awkward catering students.

Map 23 • St. James's

Laduree	71 Burlington Arcade	020 7491 9155	£££	10 pm	Grande Dame of Parisian tearooms and purveyor of cult macaroons.
The Stockpot	38 Panton St	020 7839 5142	££*	10.45 pm	Treacle pud & custard. Bish bash bosh.
The Wolseley	160 Piccadilly	020 7499 6996	££	12 am	Step back in time for an elegant afternoon tea.

Map 24 • Trafalgar Square / The Strand

Cafe in the Crypt	6 St Martin's Pl	020 7766 1158	££	10 pm	Spooky sandwiches and fruit crumble.
Gourmet Burger Kitchen	13 Maiden Ln	020 7240 9617	££	11 pm	Go for the Kiwiburger. Don't question the ingredients. Trust us.
Herman Ze German	19 Villiers St	020 7839 5264	£		Great currywurst for the brave, fab hot dogs for the rest!
India Club	143 The Strand	020 7836 4880	£	11 pm	Quirky run-down BYOB eaterie; more character than Brick Lane equivalents.
J Sheekey	28 St. Martin's Ct	020 7240 2565	££££	11 pm	Old-fashioned seafood haven that the celebs still love.
Portrait Restaurant	St Martin's Pl	020 7312 2490	£££	10.30 pm	Exceptional view over London; dinner Thursday and Friday only.
R.S. Hispaniola	Victoria Embankment	020 7839 3011	£££	10 pm	Feel the bloat, on a boat.
Rules	35 Maiden Ln	020 7836 5314	£££££	10.30 pm	London's oldest restaurant with old-fashioned comfort food to match.
Scott's Sandwich Bar	10 New Row	020 7240 0340	££	4 pm	Gets very busy at lunch mainly for the salt beef.
Thai Pot	1 Bedfordbury	020 7379 4580	££	11 pm	Busy but fast with fresh and generous helpings. Delicious Massaman curry.
Wahaca	66 Chandos Pl	020 7240 1883	£££	11 pm	Tasty Mexican market food/tapas. Always busy.

Map 25 • Kensal Town

Boom Burger	272 Portobello Rd	020 8960 3533	££	11 pm	Jamaican burgers, jerk chicken and red snapper. Irie.
Lowry and Baker	339 Portobello Rd	020 8960 8534	££		Top notch eggs benedict.
Snaps + Rye	93 Golborne Road	020 8964 3004	££	6 pm	London's only Danish restaurant.
Thai Rice	303 Portobello Rd	020 8968 2001	££	10.30 pm	Jaw-dropping food in sterile, bland enviornment.

Map 26 • Maida Hill

Mosob	339 Harrow Rd	020 7266 2012	£	11:30pm	Fresh, spicy home-cooked food.

Map 29 • Notting Hill Gate

Beach Blanket Babylon	45 Ledbury Rd	020 7229 2907	££££	12 am	Maze of baroque nooks and crannies where celebs nibble discreetly.
Cafe Diana	5 Wellington Terrace	020 7792 9606	£	10.30 pm	Creepy, kitsch shrine to Princess Diana with so-so food.
Crazy Homies	125 Westbourne Park Rd	020 7727 6771	££	10.15 pm	Avoid first date awkwardness over quality Mexican at this lively get-up.
The Elgin	96 Ladbroke Grove	020 7229 5663	££		Gussied up pub classics.
Geales	2 Farmer St	020 7727 7528	£££	10.30 pm	Feels ever-so-slightly like a front to appease visiting Americans.
Lucky 7	127 Westbourne Park Rd	020 7727 6771	£££	10.30 pm	Atmospheric diner for wistful yuppies.
Manzara	24 Pembridge Rd	020 7727 3062	£	10 pm	Burek Obama for president! Arf.
Nama	110 Talbot Rd	020 7313 4638	££	10 pm	Raw food nirvana.
Osteria Basilico	29 Kensington Park Rd	020 7727 9957	£££	11.30 pm	Quaint, buzzing and full of Italian rustic charm. A local hot spot.
The Rum Kitchen	6-8 All Saints Rd	020 7920 6479	££		Fun beach shack themed Jamaican joint.
The Shed	122 Palace Gardens Terr	020 7229 4024	£££		Best of British seasonal.
Taqueria	139 Westbourne Grove	020 7229 4734	££	11 pm	Wash down these fresh mini-tacos with a good tequila.

Map 30 • Bayswater

Al Waha	75 Westbourne Grove	020 7229 0806	££		Highly regarded Lebanese.
The Cow	89 Westbourne Park Rd	020 7221 0021	£££	9.45 pm	Top end bar food. Smart restaurant upstairs.
Royal China	13 Queensway	020 7221 2535	£££	11.15 pm	Keep the Cantonese dim sum comin'!
Tiroler Hut	27 Westbourne Grove	020 7727 3981	££££	1 am	Dementedly kitsch Austrian madhouse with lederhosen-clad waiters.

Map 31 • Paddington

Bonne Bouche	129 Praed St	020 7724 5784	£	4.30 pm	Deli counter is popular with local workers for sandwiches.
Casa Malevo	23 Connaught St	020 7402 1988	££££		Warm, welcoming Argentine steakhouse.
Mandalay	444 Edgware Rd	020 7258 3696	£	10.30 pm	Cheap treats await, despite the God awful situation.
Ranoush Juice Bar	43 Edgware Rd	020 7723 5929	£		Stalwart late night Lebanese cafe.

Map 32 • Shepherd's Bush (West)

Abu Zaad	29 Uxbridge Rd	020 8749 5107	£	11 pm	A colourful Syrian welcome. Posh Kebabs.
Esarn Kheaw	314 Uxbridge Road	020 8743 8930	£	11.30 pm	Outstanding Thai. Transport your taste buds to Bangkok.
Vine Leaves Taverna	71 Uxbridge Rd	020 8749 0325	£	1 am	Friendly staff, traditional grub, huge portions.

Map 33 • Shepherd's Bush

Busaba Eathai	Westfield Shopping Centre	020 3249 1919	££		Westies can now chow down on great Mussaman closer to home.
Jasmine	16 Goldhawk Rd	020 8743 7920	££	11 pm	Awesome Thai.
Kerbisher & Malt	164 Shepherd's Bush Rd	020 3556 0228	£		Making fish and chips contemporary, ketchup 'n all.
Mr Falafel	Units T4-T5, New Shepherd's Bush Market	077 9890 6668	£		Contender for best falafel in the city.
Patio Restaurant	5 Goldhawk Rd	020 8743 5194	££		Highly regarded home-style Polish.
Piansu	39 Bulwer St	020 8740 4546	£		Steam rising, Nihao at the door. China right here in SheBu.
Popeseye	108 Blythe Rd	020 7610 4578	££££	10.30 pm	London's ONLY member of the Aberdeen Angus Society.

Map 34 • West Kensington / Olympia

Belvedere	Abbotsbury Rd	020 7602 1238	£££	11 pm	Sublime setting—the same cannot always be said for the service.

Key: £ : Under £10 / ££ : £10–£20 / £££ : £20–£30 / ££££ : £30–£40 / £££££: £40+
**: Does not accept credit cards./ † : Accepts only American Express / ††: Accepts only Visa and Mastercard*
Time listed refers to kitchen closing time on weekend nights

Map 35 • Kensington

Bone Daddies	63-97 Kensington High St	020 7368 4575	££		Rock 'n' roll ramen.
Byron	222 Kensington High St	020 7361 1717	££	10 pm	London's best burger? Locals in the know say so.
Cable Bar and Cafe	8 Brixton Rd	020 8617 9629	£		Charming 50s style hangout. Cocktails at night.
Clarke's	124 Kensington Church St	020 7221 9225	££	10 pm	Elegant, English fine dining. Perfect brunch spot if feeling refined.
Maggie Jones's	6 Old Court Pl	020 7937 6462	£££	10.30 pm	A British culinary time warp, but we like it anyway.
The Roof Gardens & Babylon Restaurant	99 Kensington High St	020 7368 3993	££££	1 am	Truly spectacular roof gardens and devine restaurant 100 foot above HS Ken.
Yashin	1 Argyll Rd	020 7938 1536	£££		Sushi that's Japanese fresh, venue that's London cool.

Map 36 • South Kensington / Gloucester Rd

Caffe Forum	146 Gloucester Rd	020 7259 2322	£*	11 pm	Strange proverbs about cows on the wall and £3.75 pizza. Student digs.
Cremerie Creperie	2 Exhibition Rd	020 7589 8947	£*	11 pm	The best sweet and savoury crepes in London.
Da Mario	15 Gloucester Rd	020 7584 9078	£££	11.30 pm	Apparently Princess Di's local Italian Pizzeria. Affordable and A+ pizza.
Jakobs	20 Gloucester Rd	020 7581 9292	££	10 pm	Brave the slow service for delicious veggie dishes and fresh juices.
Little Japan	32 Thurloe St	020 7591 0207	£*	11.30 pm	Wowzers: bento for a fiver? Suspicious and delicious.
Oddono's	14 Bute St	020 7052 0732	£	11 pm	Gelato fix for homesick Italians and ice-cream freaks alike.
Zack's Deli	115 Gloucester Rd	020 7373 2221	£		More cafe than deli but has tasty home-cooked food.

Map 37 • Knightsbridge

Bar Boulud	66 Knightsbridge	020 7201 3899	££		Best burger in town.
Daquise	20 Thurloe Square	020 7589 6117	£££		Haute Polish cuisine.
Ognisko	55 Prince's Gate	020 7589 0101	£££		Schmancy Polish.
Zuma	5 Raphael St	020 7584 1010	£££	12 am	If your gal likes sushi, ideal for a romantic night out.

Map 38 • Chiswick

Boys Authentic Thai	95 Chiswick High Rd	020 8995 7991	££	10.30 pm	The staff are as funky and fresh as the food.
Chris' Fish Bar	19 Turnham Green Terrace	020 8995 2367	£*	12 am	It's all British-ness wrapped in warm, greasy paper.
Foubert's	2 Turnham Green Terrace	020 8994 5202	£	11 pm	Little Italian owned cafe. Excellent ice gream and gelato.
Franco Manca	144 Chiswick High Rd	020 8747 4822	££	10 pm	London's best pizza with longer opening hours.
High Road Brasserie	162 Chiswick High Rd	020 8742 7474	££	11 pm	As good as it looks. The continent comes to the High Road.
Kalamari	4 Chiswick High Rd	020 8994 4727	££	12 am	For those with a feta fetish.
La Trompette	5 Devonshire Rd	020 8747 1836	£££	10.30 pm	Unpretentious French restaurant with excellent service and set menus.
Le Pain Quotidien	214 Chiswick High Rd	020 3657 6933	£		Lacks the charm of its W11 cousin but delivers fine pastries.
Maison Blanc	26 Turnham Green Terrace	020 8995 7220	£		Windows full of divine cupcakes; wait until you get inside.
Union Jacks	217 Chiswick High Rd	020 3640 7086	££		Mr Oliver's fused British and Italian. Flats and Perry! Genius.
Zizzi	235 Chiswick High Rd	020 8747 9400	££	11.30 pm	Skip the mains—cut straight to the heavenly Apple Crumble.

Map 39 • Stamford Brook

Azou	375 King St	020 8563 7266	££	11 pm	Chilled, candle lit place in amongst a heap of other places. Great tagines.
The Carpenter's Arms	89 Black Lion Ln	020 8741 8386	£££	11 pm	As gastropub as it gets.
Lola & Simon	278 King St	020 8563 0300	££		Cosy and welcoming Kiwi-Argentine eatery serving a great brunch.
Saigon Saigon	313 King St	020 8748 6887	££		Inside and outside are charming, the pho and welcome authentic.
Tosa	332 King St	020 8748 0002	£	10 pm	Low-key authentic yakitori (fried skewered meat) joint. Easy on the wallet.
Upsy Daisy Bakery	387 King St	020 0011 3387	£		Like your Mum's front room but with nicer cakes. Friendly staff.

Map 40 • Goldhawk Rd / Ravenscourt Park

Mahdi	215 King St	020 8563 7007	££	12 am	Truly authentic, unpretentious Iranian place—menu in Arabic 'n all. Tasty!
Sagar	157 King St	020 8741 8563	££	11 pm	Yummy South Indian veggie food at a great price.
Zippy Diner	42 Goldhawk Rd	020 8740 5473	£		Local greasy spoon diner from the old school. Hearty breakfasts.

Map 41 • Hammersmith

The Gate	51 Queen Caroline St	020 8748 6932	££££	10 pm	Light and airy by day, cosy at night. Lovely food.

Map 42 • Baron's Court

Best Mangal	104 North End Rd	020 7610 1050	££	1 am	Proper good kebabs with heeeeaps of nosh. Can sit in too—a rarity.
The Malt House	17 Vanston Pl	020 7084 6888	££		Vogue Livingesque interiors with the poshest pork scratchings money can buy.

Map 43 • West Brompton / Fulham Broadway / Earls Court

Bodean's BBQ	4 Broadway Chambers	020 7610 0440	£££	11 pm	Stuff yourself on BBQ pulled-pork sandwiches. Yee haw!
Cafe Brazil	511 Fulham Rd	020 7385 2244	£	10:30pm	Brazilian pizza and other delights.
Chutney Mary	535 King's Rd	020 7351 3113	££££	11.30 pm	Get coddled over a curry (at a price).
The Harwood Arms	Walham Grove	020 7386 1847	£££		Michelin-starred cheese and Guinness on toast and a pint!
Megan's Deli & Restaurant	571 King's Rd	020 7348 7139	£		Boiled eggs in the calm and beautiful courtyard. Ah, bliss...
Pizza@Home	350 Old Brompton Rd	020 7244 8080	£*	10 pm	Maybe London's most authentic Italian pizza. Fast and cheap as chips!!
Vingt-Quatre	325 Fulham Rd	020 7376 7224	£	24 hrs	24 hour booze! Incidentally, the food is very good.

Map 44 • Chelsea

Bluebird Chelsea	350 King's Rd	020 7559 1000	£££	10.30 pm	So it seems you can get a bacon butty and look cool on the Kings Road.
Eight Over Eight	392 King's Rd	020 7349 9934	££££	11 pm	Exotic and dripping with celebs.
Haché	329 Fulham Rd	020 7823 3515	£		Top notch gourmet burgers—check out the £1 lunch voucher!

Map 45 • Chelsea (East)

Big Easy	332-334 King's Rd	020 7352 4071	££		Tuesdays are all you can eat shrimp, Louisiana style.
The Chelsea Kitchen	451 Fulham Rd	020 3055 0088	£	11 pm	New place, same affordable stodge. A Winner.
Four o Nine	409 Clapham Rd	020 7737 0722	££££	10.30 pm	Inviting and intimate, it's nice.
Made In Italy	249 King's Rd	020 7352 1880	££	11 pm	"Food Mama used to Make." Unless you're not Italian, obviously.
My Old Dutch Pancake House	221 King's Rd	020 7376 5650	£	11.30 pm	Sweet or savory pancakey goodness in the heart of Chelsea.
The Pig's Ear	35 Old Church St	020 7352 2908	££	10 pm	Quirky, restored boozer. Deep fried pigs ear anyone? Seriously.

Key: £ : Under £10 / ££ : £10–£20 / £££ : £20–£30 / ££££ : £30–£40 / £££££: £40+
** : Does not accept credit cards./ † : Accepts only American Express / ††: Accepts only Visa and Mastercard*
Time listed refers to kitchen closing time on weekend nights

Map 46 • Sloane Square

The Admiral Codrington	17 Mossop St	020 7581 0005	£££	10.30 pm	Go for simplicity here. Even the chips they get exactly right.
Bibendum Restaurant & Oyster Bar	81 Fulham Rd	020 7581 5817	£££££	11 pm	French institution with a cool (literally) oyster bar.
Foxtrot Oscar	79 Royal Hospital Rd	020 7352 4448	££	10 pm	Tango Alpha Sierra Tango Yankee.
The Good Life Eatery	59 Sloane Ave	020 7052 9388	££		Seriously good, yah.
Restaurant Gordon Ramsay	68 Royal Hospital Rd	020 7352 4441	£££££	11 pm	Mmmmmm...debt...

Map 47 • Fulham (West)

The River Café	Rainville Rd	020 7386 4200	£££	11 pm	Fine dining by the Thames for champagne socialists.

Map 48 • Fulham

The Drawing Room Cafe	Bishop's Ave	020 7610 7160	£	5 pm	A historical and elegant spot for a cup of Earl Grey and a scone.
Fisher's Fish & Chips	19 Fulham High St	020 7371 5555	£	10 pm	Quality chips AND quality punning. It's why Britain's Great.
Royal China	805 Fulham Rd	020 7731 0081	£££		Cantonese culinary powerhouse; dim sum mandatory.

Map 49 • Parson's Green

Little H	267 New Kings Rd	020 3417 8228	£		Cali-style eating in Parson's Green.
Tendido Cuatro	108 New King's Rd	020 7371 5147	£££	12 am	Perfecto! Mouth watering iberico jamon, buzzing and friendly Spanish staff.

Map 50 • Sand's End

Blue Elephant	The Boulevard	020 7751 3111	££££	11:30 pm	A classy new location but still damn fine Thai food.
The Sands End	135 Stephendale Rd	020 7731 7823	£££	10 pm	Hearty, rustic Irish fare. Nowt much else around but makes the grade.

Map 51 • Highgate

The Bull	13 N Hill Ave	020 8341 0510	£££	12 am	Chic eatery with perfectly positioned front terrace.
Cafe Rouge	6 S Grove	020 8342 9797	££	11 pm	Decent French restaurant and cafe chain.
Papa Del's	347 Archway Rd	020 8347 9797	££	11 pm	Nice place. Good cookies. £3 pizzas after 9pm!
The Red Lion & Sun	25 North Rd	020 8340 1780	££££	10 pm	Excellent Sunday roasts.

Map 52 • Archway (North)

Bengal Berties	172 Archway Rd	020 8348 1648	££	11 pm	Spit and sawdust venue with excellent nosh.
Fish Fish	179 Archway Rd	020 8348 3121	££	11 pm	Outstanding fresh fish joint flies beneath radar.

Map 53 • Crouch End

Hot Pepper Jelly	11 Broadway Parade	020 8340 4318	££*	5 pm	Pepperphobes probably shouldn't come to this culinary wonder.
Jai Krishna	161 Stroud Green Rd		£	11pm	Super delicious vegetarian Indian food.
Wow Simply Japanese	18 Crouch End Hill	020 8340 4539			Naff name, good food.

Map 54 • Hornsey

Ridge Cafe	97 Tottenham Ln	077 3305 0375	£		Good place for quick lunch or just a caffeine boast.

Map 55 • Harringay

Antepliler	46 Grand Parade, Green Lanes	020 8802 5588	££		Turkish pide pizzas and grilled meat. Lots of it.
Autograf Grill	499 Green Lanes	020 8347 7788	££		Colorless gut-busting cuisine. And delicious.
Blend	587 Green Lanes	020 8341 2939	£		Cafe and seasonal dishes.
Bun & Bar	553 Green Lanes	020 8348 5111	££		Burgers & live music.
Cafe Moka	5 Wightman Rd	020 8340 8664			Oasis in area somewhat of a culinary desert.
Devran	485 Green Lanes	020 8340 2288	£	2 am	Complementary baklava (if you have any room left!)
Fogo Vivo	Harringay Green Lanes Station	078 7707 4062	£		Hearty Brazilian home cooking and great caipirinhas.
Gokyuzu	26-27 Grand Parade, Green Lanes	020 8211 8406	££		Wear stretchy trousers.
Hala	29 Grand Parade	020 8802 4883	£	2am	Delicious Turkish breakfast.

Map 56 • Hampstead Village

Carluccio's	32 Rosslyn Hill	020 7794 2184	£££	11 pm	Deli by day, diner by night.
Jin Kichi	73 Heath St	020 7794 6158			Great range of reasonably priced Japanese favourites.
La Creperie De Hampstead	77 Hampstead High St	020 7445 6767	£*	11 pm	No crap crepes at this sublime French street stall.
Louis Patisserie	32 Heath St	020 7435 9908	£	6 pm	Tea and gorgeous cakes beloved of elderly Eastern European gentlemen.
Tinseltown	104 Heath St	020 7435 2396	£	3 am	Welcome to milkshake heaven!

Map 57 • Hampstead Heath

Mimo La Buffala	45 South End Rd	020 7435 7814	£££		Charming neighborhood Italian.
Paradise	49 S End Rd	020 7794 6314	£££		Excellent Indian with a modern twist.
Polly's	55 S End Rd	020 7431 7947	£	5 pm	Sometimes you just fancy a sarnie and a cuppa.

Map 58 • Parliament Hill / Dartmouth Park

Al Parco	2 Highgate West Hill	020 8340 5900	£	10 pm	Probably the best pizza in London.
Bistro Laz	1 Highgate West Hill	020 8342 8355	£	11 pm	Lovely meze. Or order in pizza if next door's full.
Carob Tree	15 Highgate Rd	020 7267 9880	£££	11 pm	Swanky Greek place with nice terrace in summer.
Lalibela	137 Fortress Rd	020 7284 0600	££		Steaming pots of Ethiopian stew mopped up with injera.

Map 59 • Tufnell Park

Nuraghe Trattoria	12 Dartmouth Park Hill	020 7263 4560	££		Stylish urban Italian joint with a quirky atmosphere.
Rustique Cafe	142 Fortess Rd	020 7692 5590	££	8 pm	Damn those tasty tasty cookies for being so small.
The Spice	161 Fortess Rd	020 7482 2700	££	11.30 pm	Top-notch curries

Map 60 • Archway

500 Restaurant	782 Holloway Rd	020 7272 3406	££		Excellent homemade gnocchi.
Il Mio Mosaic	24 Junction Rd	020 7272 3509	££	10.30 pm	Head for the back garden sun-trap in Summer.
Junction Café	61 Junction Rd	020 7263 2036	£*	10 pm	Greasy. Spoon.
Nid Ting	533 Holloway Rd	020 7263 0506	£££	11.15 pm	Bigger, meatier portions than most Thai restaurants.
St John's Tavern	91 Junction Rd	020 7272 1587	££££	11 pm	Gastro pub oasis stranded among the pound-shops of Archway.

Map 61 • Holloway (North)

El Molino	379 Holloway Rd	020 7700 4312	£	11 pm	One of those, and those, and that..oh and that!
The Landseer	37 Landseer Rd	020 7263 4658	££	9.30 pm	Gastropub extraordinaire.
North Nineteen	194 Sussex Way	020 7281 2786	££		A bright spark in an area of surrounding darkness.

Key: £ : Under £10 / ££ : £10–£20 / £££ : £20–£30 / ££££ : £30–£40 / £££££: £40+
** : Does not accept credit cards./ † : Accepts only American Express / ††: Accepts only Visa and Mastercard*
Time listed refers to kitchen closing time on weekend nights

Map 62 • Finsbury Park

Dudley's Pancake House	119 Stroud Green Rd	020 8447 3966	££		Damn good pancakes.
Exeter Street Bakery	Morris Pl	020 7272 8266	££	9:30 pm	Italian-inspired cafe.
Fassika	152 Seven Sisters Rd	020 7272 7572	££	12 am	Intimate with lovely food. Distinctly flirty waitresses though...
Girasole	150 Seven Sisters Rd	07870607959	£		Parmigiana like mama used to make.
Hana Sushi	150 Seven Sisters Rd	020 8964 3333	££	11pm	Authentic sushi.
Le Rif	172 Seven Sisters Rd	020 7263 1891	£*	10 pm	Essential for all your banter and microwaved Tagine needs.
Lulu's Caribbean Cuisine	84 Stroud Green Rd	020 7263 9690	£	11 pm	Caribbean food done just right. Irie.
N4 Street Burger & Burrito	8 Clifton Terrace	020 7502 7741	£	11 pm	Gourmet junk food comes to N4.
Osteria Tufo	67 Fonthill Rd	020 7272 2911		11 pm	Delicious authentic Italian.
Petek	96 Stroud Green Rd	020 7619 3933	£	10.45 pm	Classy but cheap Turkish.
Pizzeria Pappagone	131 Stroud Green Rd	020 7263 2114	££		Has NFT's very own Italian seal of approval.
Season	53 Stroud Green Rd	02072635500	££	10:30 pm	Delicious seasonal food.

Map 63 • Manor House

Fink's Salt & Sweet	70 Mountgrove Rd	020 7684 7189	££	11 pm	Restaurant/deli/wine/coffee/everything you could want.
Il Bacio	178 Blackstock Rd	020 7226 3339	££	11 pm	Friendly, reliable and huge portions.
New River Cafe	271 Stoke Newington Church St	020 7923 9842	£	11 pm	Steamy windows and top hangover cure fry-ups.

Map 64 • Stoke Newington

Anglo-Asian Tandoori	60 Stoke Newington Church St	020 7254 3633	££	11.30 pm	Classic curry house right down to the free sherry.
The Blue Legume	101 Stoke Newington Church St	020 7923 1303	£	11 pm	Dreamy eggs benedict, served under a giant aubergine.
El Olivo	24 Stoke Newington Church St	020 7254 7897			Welcome Spanish addition to areas Turkish foodie landscape.
Homa	71-73 Stoke Newington Church St	020 7254 2072	£££		Upmarket Italian catering to Stokeys buggy parade.
Rasa N16	55 Stoke Newington Church St	020 7249 0344	££	11.30 pm	Vegetarian-style Indian cooking at its mouth-watering best.
Yum Yum	187 Stoke Newington High St Mussaman.	020 7254 6751	£££	11 pm	Tasty tasty, Thai Thai. Go for the Kang

Map 65 • West Hampstead

Barraco Cafe	10 Kingsgate Place	020 7604 4664	£	11 pm	Boteca bar frequented by Brazilians.
Small & Beautiful	351 Kilburn High Rd	020 7328 2637	£		Small and beautiful indeed, as is the bill.

Map 66 • Finchley Road / Swiss Cottage

Bradleys	25 Winchester Rd	020 7722 3457	£££	11 pm	Your friendly face in the neighbourhood that loves wine.
Camden Arts Centre	Arkwright Rd	020 7472 5500	£	6 pm	Excellent food in buzzing artistic setting.
Loft Coffee Company	4 Canfield Gardens				Simple, tiny cafe, with brilliant coffee.
Singapore Garden	83 Fairfax Rd	020 7328 5314	££	11 pm	Surprising flavours make a welcome alternative on a night out.

Map 67 • Belsize Park

Artigiano	12 Belsize Terrace	020 7794 4288	£££	11 pm	Fancy some fancy pasta?
Paradiso	36 England's Ln	020 7586 9001	££	11.30 pm	For those on a carbs, cheese and cream diet.
Retsina	48 Belsize Ln	020 7431 5855	£££	11 pm	Lively Greek—grilled meat galore!
Violette Cafe	2 England's Ln	020 7586 4326	££	6.30 pm	Cakey goodness.

Map 68 • Kilburn High Road / Abbey Road

Little Bay	228 Belsize Rd	020 7372 4699	££*	11 pm	Crazy cheap. Crazy cute!
Tamada	122 Boundary Rd	020 7372 2882	£££		Proper Georgian winter food.

Map 70 • Primrose Hill

The Hill	94 Haverstock Hill	020 7267 0033	£££	11 pm	The Hill is an ideal place to meet friends before heading off to a show.
J Restaurant	148 Regent's Park Rd	020 7586 9100	££	11 pm	Excellent food, especially brunch. Tempestuous service.
The Legal Cafe	81 Haverstock Hill	020 7586 7412	£	6 pm	Great coffee, good food and wifi: a pleasant working environment.
Lemonia	89 Regent's Park Rd	020 7586 7454	£££	11.30 pm	Fancy a real Greek meal?
Manna	4 Erskine Rd	020 7722 8028	££	11.30 pm	Aesthetically gorgeous veggie restaurant, serving scrumptious food.
Melrose and Morgan	42 Gloucester Ave	020 7722 0011	£	8 pm	Scrumptious food and coffee. Good for solo snacks.
Odette's	130 Regent's Park Rd	020 7586 8569	£££	1 am	Delectably dainty restaurant, high-class service.
Primrose Bakery	69 Gloucester Ave	020 7483 4222	£	6 pm	A delectably dinky bakery. These cakes can't be missed.
Tandis	73 Haverstock Hill	020 7586 8079	££		Iranian food with a touch of elegance.

Map 71 • Camden Town / Chalk Farm / Kentish Town (West)

Andy's Taverna	81 Bayham St	020 7485 9718	££	11 pm	Big Greek restaurant with a garden.
Anima e Cuore	129 Kentish Town Rd	020 7267 2410	££		BYOB affordable fan-favorite Italian.
Arancini Factory Cafe	115 Kentish Town Rd	020 3583 2242	£	5 pm	Aussie guys making risotto balls.
Bar Gansa	2 Inverness St	020 7267 8909	££	12 am	More buzzing and pleasurable than a Rampant Rabbit.
Bento Cafe	9 Parkway	020 7482 3990	££	11 pm	Exquisite Japanese food at very reasonable prices.
Cafe Chula	89 Camden Lock Pl	020 7284 1890	££		Mexican, for brunch?! Si, si si! A+ Huevos Rancheros.
Cottons	55 Chalk Farm Rd	020 7485 8388	££	10 pm	No hustle and bustle, just chill Jamaican style.
Falla and Mocaer	82 Parkway	020 7428 7586	£		Great cakes and snacks.
Haché	24 Inverness St	020 7485 9100	££	10.30 pm	Burger heaven for both vegetarians and carnivores.
Kim's Vietnamese Food Hut	Stables Market		£*	11 pm	Once you pass the Spanish Inqusition, some excellent slop.
Marathon Kebab House	87 Chalk Farm Rd	020 7485 3814	£*	4 am	Legendary late-night venue serving kebabs, chips and beer.
Marine Ices	8 Haverstock Hill	020 7482 9003	£	11 pm	Fantastic ice cream restaurant with '70s decor and autographed photos.
Muang Thai	71 Chalk Farm Rd	020 7916 0653	£	11 pm	Quiet vibe, tinkly music, reliably decent food.
My Village	37 Chalk Farm Rd	020 7485 4996	£	9 pm	Cute ethnic organic shop serving food, tea and coffee.
Q Grill	29-33 Chalk Farm Rd	020 7267 2678	£££		Fun, festive New World-themed barbecue.
Thanh Binh	14 Chalk Farm Rd	020 7267 9820	£	10 pm	Excellent Vietnamese with very friendly and chatty staff.
Woody Grill	1 Camden Rd	020 7485 7774	£*	12 am	Late night post-alcohol food without salmonella poisoning.
Yumchaa	91 Camden Lock Pl	020 7209 9641	£*	6 pm	The carrot cake...oh mama!
Zorya Imperial Vodka Room	48 Chalk Farm Rd	020 7485 8484	££	12 am	Vodka, vodka and more vodka. Oh ...and gorgeous food too.

Map 72 • Kentish Town

Bengal Lancer	253 Kentish Town Rd	020 7485 6688	£££		The best (and priciest) indian in the area.
Cafe Renoir	244 Kentish Town Rd	020 7485 7186	£		Nice and bright with simple food and decent coffee.
Dirty Burger	79 Highgate Rd	020 3310 2010	£	12 am	Burgers that are dirty.
ta	225 Kentish Town Rd	020 7267 5622	£	10 pm	Awesome pizza for those on a budget.
Mario's Cafe	6 Kelly St	020 7284 2066	£*	10 pm	Saint Etienne's local greasy spoon.
The Oxford	256 Kentish Town Rd	020 7485 3521	££	9.45 pm	Smug comfort eating.
ane Vino	323 Kentish Town Rd	020 7267 3879	££	10.30 pm	Staff can be Italian. Food can be fantastic.
Phoenicia	186 Kentish Town Rd	020 7267 1267	£	10 pm	Coffee 'n baclava, falafel, meze. All a steal.

Key: £ : Under £10 / ££ : £10–£20 / £££ : £20–£30 / ££££ : £30–£40 / £££££: £40+
** : Does not accept credit cards./ † : Accepts only American Express / ††: Accepts only Visa and Mastercard*
Time listed refers to kitchen closing time on weekend nights

Map 74 • Holloway Road / Arsenal

El Rincon Quiteno	235 Holloway Rd	020 7700 3670	££		A ray of South American sunshine on bleak Holloway Road.
Kokeb	45 Roman Way	020 7609 9832	£	10 pm	Getenesh will look after you.
Wolkite Kifto	82 Hornsey Road	020 7700 3055	£	11 pm	Good veggie options as well as kitfo.

Map 75 • Highbury

Firezza	276 St. Paul's Rd	020 7359 7400	£		Up market-esque stone baked pizza joint.
Highbury Arts Club	73 Highbury Park	07826 899499	££	11 pm	Cosy space with live events.
Prawn on the Lawn	220 Saint Paul's Rd	020 3302 8668	£££	12 am	As fresh as it gets.
Primeur	116 Petherton Rd	020 7226 5271	£££		Fun, fresh European menu with French focus.
San Daniele Del Friuli	72 Highbury Park	020 7226 1609	£££	12 am	Like mama used to make—well someone had to say it.
Trullo	300-302 St Paul's Rd	020 7226 2733	£££		Well-done rustic seasonal Italian.
Ustun Lahmacun	107 Green Lanes	020 7704 0360	£*	10 pm	Very nice lamachun.

Map 76 • Edgware Road / Marylebone (North)

The Sea Shell Lisson Grove	49 Lisson Grove	020 7224 9000	££	10.30 pm	Pescatarians will love this place—sorry, carnivores!

Map 77 • Mornington Crescent / Regent's Park

Chutneys	124 Drummond St	020 7388 0604	££	11.30 pm	Flavoursome, no-frills, fill-yer-boots affair. Bargainous buffet colossal.
Diwana Bhel Poori House	121 Drummond St	020 7387 5556	££	11 pm	South-Indian veggie with tasty dosai and puris.
Mestizo	103 Hampstead Rd	020 7387 4064	£££	11 pm	Great. The margarita is made by the devil himself.
York & Albany	127 Parkway	020 7388 3344	£££	11 pm	Gordo on a budget.

Map 78 • Euston

Asakusa	265 Eversholt St	020 7388 8533	£££	11.30 pm	Authentic Japanese.
Banger Bros.	Euston Station	020 7387 6958	£	7.30 pm	Sing it: It's a small world (of sausages) after all!
The Booking Office	St Pancras Renaissance London Hotel, Euston Rd	020 7841 3566	££		Where the lucky few have pre Eurostar cocktails and snacks.
Camino Cruz del Rey	3 Varnisher's Yard	020 7841 7330	£££	12 am	Sophisticated Spanish restaurant in Kings Cross. Seems wrong, somehow.
Caravan	1 Granary Building	020 7101 7661	££	11:30 pm	Industrial space serving food and awesome coffee.
Chop Chop Noodle Bar	1 Euston Rd	020 7833 1773	£	11 pm	Great for a quick and cheap meal. Massive portions.
El Parador	245 Eversholt St	020 7387 2789	££	11 pm	Great tapas. A little ray of sunshine in your mouth.
Grain Store	1-3 Stable St	020 7324 4466	££		United Nations of food; good vegan and vegetarian options.
Great Nepalese	48 Eversholt St	020 7388 6737	££	11 pm	Really the only option in the area.
Kerb	Kings Blvd		£		Ever changing market showcasing best in London street food.
Kitchin N1	8 Caledonia St	020 7713 8777	££	11 pm	Round-the-world all-you-can-eat. Vile and great.
Rodon Live	Pratt St	020 7267 8088	£££	11 pm	Friendly rotund owner masks just above average food.
The Somers Town Coffee House	60 Chalton St	020 7387 7377	££	10 pm	Bistro food in grade II listed pub. Excellent se menu.

Map 79 • King's Cross

Addis	42 Caledonian Rd	020 7278 0679	££	11 pm	Lovely food with convivial sloth-like service.
Cafe Oz	53 Caledonian Rd	020 7278 9650	£*	10 pm	Unusually well-kempt greasy spoon.
Euro Café	299 Caledonian Rd	020 7607 5362	£	10 pm	Loveable caff with some unusual specials.
Marathon	196 Caledonian Rd	020 7837 4499	££	12 am	Raw meat, ritualistic coffee and crazed dancing.
New Didar	347 Caledonian Rd	020 7700 3496	£	12 am	Friendly staff willing to strike deals. Haggling gets you everywhere.

Map 80 • Angel / Upper St

Afghan Kitchen	35 Islington Green	020 7359 8019	£££*	10.45 pm	Only a few tables; Islington's smallest—and biggest—Afghan place.
Alpino	97 Chapel Market	020 7837 8330	£	4 pm	This, guv'nor, is a proper tea'n'two slices caff. Alright?
The Breakfast Club	31 Camden Passage	020 7226 5454	££	9.30 pm	Not just breakfast, not a club. But just so gooood.
Candid Café & Courtyard	3 Torrens St	020 7278 9368	£	10 pm	Laid-back, arty cafe for dreamy types. Candle-lit. Perfect for lingering.
Dead Dolls House	181 Upper St	020 7288 1470	££	11 pm	Hand illustrated walls using marker pen.
Desperados	67 Upper St	020 7226 5055	££	11.30 pm	Garish. More like the Mexico of MTV than the real world.
The Elk in the Woods	39 Camden Passage	020 7226 3535	££	10.30 pm	Laid-back, hunting-themed eatery.
Fig and Olive	151 Upper St	020 7354 2605	££	11 pm	Incredibly busy at weekends which can affect service and quality.
Fredericks	Camden Passage	020 7359 2888	££	11 pm	Swanky Euro-flash bistro.
Gem	265 Upper St	020 7359 0405	£££	4 am	A good vibe is precious.
Indian Veg Bhelpoori House	93 Chapel Market	020 7833 1167	£	10 pm	Honest all-you-can-eat Indian. Veggie propaganda on walls.
Isarn	119 Upper St	020 7424 5153	££	11 pm	Pretty, flower-adorned food, green curry cooked to perfection. Candle-lit courtyard.
Le Mercury	140 Upper St	020 7354 4088	££	1 am	This place will seduce you AND your mother.
Masala Zone	80 Upper St	020 7359 3399	££	11 pm	Cheap, good thalis served on metal trays.
Mem & Laz	8 Theberton St	020 7704 9089	££	11 pm	Mediterranean chaos by candlelight.
Oldroyd	344 Upper St	020 8617 9010	£££		Ever-changing pan-European menus using seasonal ingredients.
Ottolenghi	287 Upper St	020 7288 1454	££	10 pm	Staff you'll want to take home to meet your mum.
Pera	170 Upper St	020 7704 6888	££		It's all about the Turkish brunch in this friendly joint!
Pizzeria Oregano	19 St. Alban's Pl	020 7288 1123	££	11 pm	Great pizza and lentil soup. Delicious odd couple.
Rodizio Rico	77 Upper St	020 7354 1076	£££	11 pm	Meat. And lots of it.
The Seagrass	74 Chapel Market	079 0201 5200	££		Authentic 19th century décor, cockney culture, pie and mash perfection.
Tortilla	13 Islington High St	020 7833 3103	££	10 pm	Damn good burritos!
Zaffrani	47 Cross St	020 7226 5522	££	11 pm	Thinking man's curry.

Map 81 • Canonbury

Raab's Bakery	136 Essex Rd	020 7226 2830	£	6 pm	Use your loaf sunshine.

Map 82 • De Beauvoir Town / Kingsland

De La Panza	105 Southgate Rd	020 7226 0334	£££	12 am	Bodegon-style eating.
Duke's Brew & Que	33 Downham Rd	020 3006 0795	£		Whatchoo want to eat? Ribs.
Mother Earth	101 Newington Green Rd	020 7359 7353	£	8 pm	Wholesome cafe food.
Peppers and Spice	40 Balls Pond Rd	020 7275 9818	£*	10.30 pm	The real deal: jerk, oxtail, festival, plantain, ackee. Everyting irie.
Pond	3 Gillett St	020 3772 6727	££	11pm	Hawaiian, anyone?
Vietnamese Canteen Huong Viet	12 Englefield Rd	020 7249 0877	££	11 pm	A crumbling old bath house? Look again.

Key: £ : Under £10 / ££ : £10–£20 / £££ : £20–£30 / ££££ : £30–£40 / £££££: £40+
** : Does not accept credit cards./ † : Accepts only American Express / ††: Accepts only Visa and Mastercard*
Time listed refers to kitchen closing time on weekend nights

Map 83 • Angel (East) / City Rd (North)

The Shepherdess	221 City Rd	020 7253 2463	£	5 pm	Cafe offering no-frills traditional English fare.
William IV	7 Shepherdess Walk	020 3119 3012	££	12 am	Lovely gastropub, off the beaten track and with delicious food.

Map 84 • Hoxton

The Barrel Boulangerie	110 Hoxton St	020 7683 0353	£	10 pm	Local favourite spot for pizza.
Big Apple Hot Dogs	239 Old St	079 8938 7441	£		Offers a gourmet British twist on a classic American treat.
The Clove Club	380 Old St	020 7729 6496	££££		Nu British tasting menus in grand setting.
The Diner	128 Curtain Rd	020 7729 4452	£££	10.30 pm	Door-stopper burgers that should come with health warnings.
Jamie Oliver's Fifteen	15 Westland Pl	020 3375 1515	£££££	10 pm	Lots of Jamie Oliver. Lots of great, expensive food.
The Jones Family Project	78 Great Eastern St	020 7739 1740	££		Excellent steak and fish dishes.
Meat Mission	15 Hoxton Market	020 7739 8212	£	12 am	Sister restaurant to Meat Liquor.
MEATmission	14-15 Hoxton Market	020 7739 8212	££		Make sure to try the Peckham dip.
Rivington Grill	28 Rivington St	020 7729 7053	££	11 pm	Emin on the walls, meat in the buns.
Tramshed	32 Rivington St	020 7749 0478	££		A.K.A The Cow and Chicken.

Map 85 • Stoke Newington (East)

19 Numara Bos Cirrik	34 Stoke Newington Rd	020 7249 0400	££	10 pm	Meat, meat, meat—oh and onion, pomegranate and turnip salad.
Addie's Thai Cafe	3 Northwold Rd	020 7249 2618	££		Deceptively pokey, unimaginatively named, yet brilliant.
The Bagel House	2 Stoke Newington High St	020 7249 3908	£*	10 pm	Bagels to rival Brick Lane and without the queues.
Cafe Z Bar	58 Stoke Newington High St	020 7275 7523	£*	11 pm	Popular grease-shop/hangover center for Stokey Lefties.
Tatreez Cafe	188 Stoke Newington High St	020 8616 5434	££		Charming Palestinian restaurant; beer and wine available.
Testi	38 Stoke Newington High St	020 7249 7151	£££	12 am	It's the dog's bollocks.
The Three Crowns	175 Stoke Newington High St	020 7241 5511	££		Impressive Victorian pub that's undergone gastropubification.

Map 86 • Dalston / Kingsland

A Little Of What You Fancy	464 Kingsland Rd	020 7275 0060	££		A bit like being in a friend's kitchen/dining room.
Arancini Brothers	592 Kingsland Rd	020 3583 7303	£	10 pm	This is how you do fast food (and coffee).
The Best Turkish Kebab	125 Stoke Newington Rd	020 7254 7642	£*	12 am	Feed your soul. Always buzzing.
Dalston Eastern Curve Garden	13 Dalston Lane		£	11pm	Check website for days when food is served.
Evin	115 Kingsland High St	020 7254 5634	££	11 pm	Fantastic Turkish place without the grease factor. Speciality is gozleme.
Mangal 1	10 Arcola St	020 7275 8981	£*	12 am	May the grill's smoke guide you, meat-loving friends.
Mangal 2	4 Stoke Newington Rd	020 7254 7888	££	12 am	Gilbert & George aren't the only ones loving this one.
The Russet	Amhurst Terrace	020 3095 9731	£		Hanging out with the creatives.
Shanghai	41 Kingsland High St	020 7254 2878	££	10.30 pm	Tasty, good-value Chinese hiding behind the facade of a dingy old Kaff.
Somine	131 Kingsland High St	020 7254 7384	£*	24-hrs	Reanimating red lentil soup, Turkish style. Around the clock.
Stone Cave	111 Kingsland High St	020 7241 4911	££	12 am	Cave look and cave feel. Up-scale(ish) Turkish And great.
The Tea Rooms	155 Stoke Newington Rd	020 7923 1870	£	10 pm	Stokey in a tea-cup. Pleasant...
Voodoo Ray's	117 Kingsland High St	020 7254 2273	£		All American late night pizza from folk behind Dalston Superstore.

Map 87 • Hackney Downs / Lower Clapton

Mess Café	38 Amhurst Rd	020 8985 3194	£*	5 pm	All manner of breakfast all the time.

Map 88 • Haggerston / Queensbridge Rd

Beagle	397 Geffrye St	020 7613 2967	£££		Tasteful Modern British cuisine plus cocktails and all-day coffee.
Berber & Q	Arch 338, Acton Mews		£££		BBQ meets mezze under railroad arches.
Chicks n Sours	390 Kingsland Rd		££	10:30pm	Fried chicken and cocktails. Of course.
Fabrique Bakery	385 Geffrye St	020 7033 0268	£		Great Nordic bakery and cafe.
Faulkners	424 Kingsland Rd	020 7254 6152	£	10 pm	Legendary and traditional with traditional opening times.
Hackney City Farm	1 Goldsmith's Row	020 7729 6381	££	4.30 pm	Animals! In Hackney! And some overpriced fry-up.
Song Que	134 Kingsland Rd	020 7613 3222	££	11 pm	Still Little Vietnam's queen. An authentic, no-nonsense affair.
Uludag	398 Kingsland Rd	020 7241 1923	£		Great falafels and a bit of a nutter hub to boot.
Viet Hoa Cafe	70 Kingsland Rd	020 7729 8293	£	11.30 pm	Bland looking cafe hides gorgeous delicacies.

Map 89 • London Fields / Hackney Central

Buen Ayre	50 Broadway Market	020 7275 9900	££££	10.30 pm	Vegetarians take note—run for the hills.
Cafe Bohemia	2 Bohemia Pl	020 8986 4325	£	11 pm	Feeling Bohemian? Quirky cafe with live blues/jazz/world Saturday nights.
The Cat and Mutton	76 Broadway Market	020 7254 5599	££	10 pm	Gastropub without the gastropub nastiness.
The Corner Deli	121 Mare St	020 8986 0031	£	9 pm	Nice spot for brunch away from the bustle of Broadway Market.
Hai Ha	206 Mare St	020 8985 5388	££*	11 pm	Brilliant BYO Vietnamese cafe.
Ombra	1 Vyner St	020 8981 5150	£		Neighbourhood Italian, good honest food.
Pidgin	52 Wilton Wy	020 7254 8311	£££		Ever-changing seasonal set menus, charming digs.
The Spurstowe Arms	68 Greenwood Rd	020 7249 2500	££	11 pm	Suntrap beer garden, good wine selection and gamey menu. Marvellous.

Map 90 • Homerton / Victoria Park North

Eat 17	64-66 Brooksby's Walk	020 8986 6242	££		Convenience store, burger bar, restaurant, florist, bakery, off licence, etc.
The Empress	130 Lauriston Rd	020 8533 5123	£££	10 pm	Spiffy menu from brekkie through to dinner in Hackney Village.
Fish House	126 Lauriston Rd	020 8533 3327	££	9.45 pm	Not as cheap as chips but still very good.
Machete	91 Lauriston Rd	020 8533 3100	££	11:30 pm	Great cocktails too.
Well Street Kitchen	203 Well St	020 8533 6275	£	5 pm	Good honest caff food.

Map 91 • Shoreditch / Brick Lane / Spitalfields

Andina	1 Redchurch St	020 7920 6499	££		Fun Peruvian beyond the usual.
Back in 5 Minutes	222 Brick Ln	075 0775 4318			Pop in a pop up for shopping and a 3 course.
Beigel Shop	155 Brick Ln	020 7729 0826	£*	24 hrs	For 3am cravings; salted beef bagel from the Beigel Shop.
Boundary	2 Boundary St	020 7729 1051	£££	10.30 pm	Warehouse conversion, great view, some major boxes being ticked here.
Brawn	49 Columbia Rd	020 7729 5692			No pig left unturned.
Cafe Bangla	128 Brick Ln	020 7247 8981	££	12 am	Popular Bangladeshi adorned with psychedelic and surreal fantasy art.
Chez Elles	45 Brick Ln	020 7247 9699	£££		Out-Frenches most actual French bistros, and does it deliciously.
Clipper Bangladeshi Cusine		104 Brick Ln020 7377 0022			££ 12 am For less spice-oriented connoisseurs, Bengali Clipper's exceptional lamb korma.
The Culpeper	40 Commercial St	020 7247 5371	££	2 am	Seasonal and local food.
Dishoom	7 Boundary St	020 7420 9324	££		All-day Parsi cafe straight outta Bombay.
The Drunken Monkey	222 Shoreditch High St	020 7392 9606	££	12 am	Debauched, dimly-lit dim-sum drinking hole. Chinese lanterns and lethal mojitos.
Ethiopian Food Stall	Brick Ln		£*		One of many great food stalls, get Brazilian desert after!
Frizzante	1 Goldsmith's Row	020 7739 2266	££		All the Italians go to Agriturismo night (Thurs) just sayin'.
Gourmet San	261 Bethnal Green Rd	020 7729 8388	£*	11 pm	Whole crabs and minimal English.

Key: £ : Under £10 / ££ : £10–£20 / £££ : £20–£30 / ££££ : £30–£40 / £££££: £40+
** : Does not accept credit cards./ † : Accepts only American Express / ††: Accepts only Visa and Mastercard*
Time listed refers to kitchen closing time on weekend nights

Hanoi Cafe	98 Kingsland Rd	020 7729 5610	££	11 pm	Cosy Viet joint, where the whole family's around.
Hawksmoor	157 Commercial St	020 7426 4850	£££	10.30 pm	France and America forget their differences for some serious steakage.
Les Trois Garcons	1 Club Row	020 7613 1924	££££	11 pm	Kitch décor/slick service/fantastic grub.
Lyle's	56 Shoreditch High St	020 3011 5911	££££		Modern British.
Marksman Public House	254 Hackney Rd	020 7739 7393	£££		Cut-above pub grub.
Mien Tay	122 Kingsland Rd	020 7729 3074			Kingsland's supreme Vietnamese.
Mr Buckley's	277 Hackney Rd	020 3664 0033			Uber hip without falling into usual cliches.
Noodle King	185 Bethnal Green Rd	020 7613 3131	£*	11.30 pm	Half the normal price; double the normal portions. Come hungry.
Poppies	6 Hanbury St	020 7247 0892	£		The Great British dish served '50's style.
The Premises	209 Hackney Rd	020 7729 7593	££	11 pm	Bistro swarming with musicians thanks to next door's recording studio.
Rosa's	12 Hanbury St	020 7247 1093	££	11 pm	Quirky, warm little Thai place.
St. John Bread and Wine	94 Commercial St	020 7251 0848	£££	11 pm	Minimalist and meaty. Anyone for deep-fried pig's head?
Taberna do Mercado	107 Commercial St	020 7375 0649	£££		Stylish, tasty Portuguese.
Tay Do	65 Kingsland Rd	020 7729 7223	£	11 pm	Squish 'em in, feed 'em quick variety of cheap & filling Vietnamese cuisine.
Troy Cafe	124 Kingsland Rd	020 7033 9514	£	7 pm	Delicious lunchtime buffet.

Map 92 • Bethnal Green

Bistrotheque	23 Wadeson St	020 8983 7900	££	11 pm	Brunch, burlesque and pianist playing Smells Like Teen Spirit. Fabulous.
E. Pellicci	332 Bethnal Green Rd	020 7739 4873	£	4.30 pm	Challenge your hangover to survive their fry-ups.
The Gallery Cafe	21 Old Ford Rd	020 8980 2092	£	9 pm	Veggie/vegan haven.
Little Georgia	87 Goldsmiths Row	020 7739 8154	££	10 pm	Hearty fayre from the former Soviet State. No drinks licence.
Mission	250 Paradise Row	020 7613 0478	£££	12 am	Californian high-end drinking and eating.

Map 93 • Globe Town / Mile End (North)

Greedy Cow Burgers & Steaks	2 Grove Rd	020 8983 3304	$$		Burger and exotic meat taste explosion.
Morgan Arms	43 Morgan St	020 8980 6389	£££	12 am	Which joker invented the term "gastropub"? This is one of them.

Map 94 • Bow

Chicchi	516 Roman Rd	020 8141 4190	£*	7 pm	The Italians reclaim Roman Road
G. Kelly Noted Eel & Pie Shop	526 Roman Rd	020 8980 3165	£	7 pm	Servin' 'ot 'ome-made pies, jellied eels 'n mash since 1937.
Pavilion Victoria Park	Old Ford Rd	020 8980 0030			Kippery breakfast with a view

Map 95 • Whitechapel (West) / St Katharine's Dock

Cafe Spice Namaste	16 Prescot St	020 7488 9242	££	10.30 pm	Open-minded Indian that strays far from run of the mill.
The Empress	141 Leman St	020 7265 0745	£	11.45 pm	Forget Brick Lane. This is where it's at.

Map 96 • Whitechapel (East) / Shadwell (West) / Wapping

Lahore Kebab House	2-10 Umberston St	020 7488 2551	$		Pakistani grub gives new insight to 'eyes bigger than stomach'.
Needoo Grill	87 New Rd	020 7247 0648	££		For when Tayyabs queue is just too long.
Tayyabs	83 Fieldgate St	020 7247 6400	£	12 am	Lipsmacking seekh kebabs alone are worth the queues.

Map 97 • Stepney / Shadwell (East)

Dirty Burger	27 Mile End Rd	020 3727 6165	£	11 pm	East London outpost of this gourmet fast food fave.
Foxcroft & Ginger	69 Mile End Rd		£	10 pm	Sister to popular Soho cafe.

Map 98 • Mile End (South) / Limehouse

The Narrow	44 Narrow St	020 7592 7950	£££	11 pm	Gordon Ramsay's nod to gastropubs—cracking views.
The Orange Room	63 Burdett Rd	020 8980 7336	£££	11.30 pm	Tasty, fresh Lebanese food in a wasteland of stodgy takeaways.

Map 100 • Poplar (West) / Canary Wharf (West)

Browns	Hertsmere Rd	020 7987 9777	£££	11 pm	Always reliable.
Nicolas	1 Canada Sq	020 7512 9092	££	10.30 pm	Micro French restaurant and vintners in one.
Plateau	Canada Pl	020 7715 7100	££££	10.30 pm	Striking views and truffle gnocchi.
Royal China	30 Westferry Circus	020 7719 0888	£££		Cantonese culinary powerhouse; dim sum mandatory.

Map 101 • Poplar (East) / Canary Wharf (East)

The Gun	27 Coldharbour	020 7515 5222	£££	11 pm	Enjoyed by 18th century dockers and city workers alike.
Jamie's Italian	2 Churchill Pl	020 3002 5252	£££	11 pm	Bang-on Jamie O on the cheap.

Map 103 • Cubitt Town / Mudchute

Mudchute Kitchen	Pier St	020 3069 9290	££	5 pm	Food companion to the farm bit. Chi chi children.

Map 104 • South Bank / Waterloo / Lambeth North

The Anchor & Hope	36 The Cut	020 7928 9898	££££	10.30 pm	A British gastro-pub obsession, long waits though.
Canteen	Belvedere Rd	084 5686 1122	££	10.30 pm	A menu that sums up the best of British food with aplomb.
Concrete	Southbank Centre	020 7921 0758	£	1 am	Restaurant/bar features Russian beer, food, absinthe.
The Cut Bar	66 The Cut	020 7928 4400	£££	11 pm	Brilliant chips. A cut above the rest.
Giraffe	Riverside	020 7928 2004	££	10.45 pm	Good crowd pleaser. Though too much world music and balloons.
Marie's Cafe	90 Lower Marsh	020 7928 1050	£	10.30 pm	Greasy spoon by day, a no-frills, super-yum BYO thai by night.
OXO Tower Wharf	Barge House St	020 7803 3888	££££	11 pm	You might have to rob a bank, but the view's amazing.
RSJ	33 Coin St	020 7928 4554	££	11 pm	Forget about those crappy South Bank chains. Go here.
Skylon	Belvedere Rd	020 7654 7800	££££	10.45 pm	Expensive but staffs' uniforms and view make up for it.
Studio 6	56 Upper Ground	020 7928 6243	££	11 pm	Service with a reluctant grunt doesn't stop the crowds.
'as	33 The Cut	020 7928 2111	££	11.30 pm	Blink and you'll miss it. Buzzing Turkish cafe—best hummous in London.

Map 105 • Southwark / Bankside (West)

altic	74 Blackfriars Rd	020 7928 1111	££££	10:30 pm	Try Polish Hunters stew: made with real Polish Hunters. Probably.
l Vergel	132 Webber St	020 7401 2308	£*	10 pm	It's Latin breakfast: Oh. My. God. Soooooo good.
estaurant at Tate Modern	Bankside	020 7887 8888	££	6 pm	Stunning views, crap food, clueless staff.
he Table	83 Southwark St	020 7401 2760	£*	10.30 pm	Go and find out why we're all obsessed.
erry's Cafe	158 Great Suffolk St	020 7407 9358	£	2 pm	Mom & Pop British fare including mushy peas.

Key: £ : Under £10 / ££ : £10–£20 / £££ : £20–£30 / ££££ : £30–£40 / £££££: £40+
** : Does not accept credit cards./ † : Accepts only American Express / ††: Accepts only Visa and Mastercard*
Time listed refers to kitchen closing time on weekend nights

Map 106 • Bankside (East) / Borough / Newington

Name	Address	Phone	Price	Time	Comment
Arabica Bar & Kitchen	3 Rochester Walk	020 3011 5151	££		Fresh, fun, game-upping Middle Eastern cuisine.
The Boot and Flogger	10 Redcross Way	020 7407 1184	££	8 pm	Splendidly gentleman's club-esque—all savile row suits and chesterfield sofas.
Brew Wharf	Stoney St	020 7378 6601	££	11 pm	Unusual comfort food and tasty home brews.
Champor-Champor	62 Weston St	020 7403 4600	£££	10.15pm	Jaw-droppingly inspired high-end Malaysian cuisine. Totally impressive.
Elliot's Cafe	12 Stoney St	020 7403 7436	£££		Rumoured by some to serve London's best burgers.
Feng Sushi	13 Stoney St	020 7407 8744	££	10 pm	The best sushi in London and available to takeaway. Dangerous!
Fish!	Cathedral St	020 7407 3803	££	10.30 pm	Great fish. Simple. Let it have its exclamation mark.
Hing Loong	159 Borough High St	020 7378 8100	£	11 am	Stupidly cheap. Very cheerful. The duck rocks.
Nando's	225 Clink St	020 7357 8662	££	11 pm	Peri-peri madness underneath the arches.
Roast	Stoney St	084 5034 7300	££	9.30 pm	Meat, glorious meat. High-end food. Fab location.
Silka	6 Southwark St	020 7378 6161	£££	11.30 pm	Curry house that won't damage your arse in the morning.
Tapas Brindisa	18 Southwark St	020 7357 8880	££	11 pm	If you can bear the crowds; lovely market-bordering eaterie.
Tas	72 Borough High St	020 7403 7200	££	11 pm	Reduce your carbon footprint: come here and feel 1000 miles away.
Wright Bros Oyster & Porter House	11 Stoney St	020 7403 9554	£££	10.30 pm	Tastebuds say no, but libido says YES.

Map 107 • Shad Thames

Name	Address	Phone	Price	Time	Comment
Butlers Wharf Chop House	36 Shad Thames	020 7403 3403	£££	11 pm	What better place for British best than under Tower Bridge?
Casse-Croute	109 Bermondsey St	020 7407 2140	£££		Fun French bistro with chalkboard menu.
Jose	104 Bermondsey St	020 7403 4902	£££		Sister sherry bar and restuarant to nearby Pizarro. More casual.
Le Pont de la Tour	36 Shad Thames	020 7403 8403	£££££	11 pm	Blair & Clinton's rendezvous. Posh but gosh!
M. Manze Pie and Mash	87 Tower Bridge Rd	020 7407 2985	£	2.30 pm	As English as it gets. Try it once.
Magdalen	152 Tooley St	020 7403 1342	££££	10.30 pm	Forever fascinating Franco-Spanish cuisine.
Pizarro	194 Bermondsey St	020 7378 9455	£££		A slice of Spain south of the river, top Menu del Dia.
Pizarro Tapas	104 Bermondsey St	020 7256 5333	££	10:15 pm	The real deal for tapas.
Village East	171 Bermondsey St	020 7357 6082	£££	11 pm	Superior food. Slick surroundings.

Map 108 • Bermondsey

Name	Address	Phone	Price	Time	Comment
Poppy Hana	168 Jamaica Rd	020 7237 9416	£	11 pm	Cute as a button Japanese. Don't be put off by the food sculptures.
Tentazioni	2 Mill St	020 7237 1100	££	10.45 pm	Stunningly sophisticated for a neighbourhood eaterie.

Map 109 • Southwark Park

Name	Address	Phone	Price	Time	Comment
The Mayflower	117 Rotherhithe St	020 7237 4088	£££		The pub Sunday Lunch was invented for.

Map 110 • Rotherhithe (West) / Canada Water

Name	Address	Phone	Price	Time	Comment
Café Silka	30 Albion St	020 7237 2122	££		Wishes it were somewhere else, but nicely done.
Simplicity	1 Tunnel Rd	020 7232 5174	££	10:30 pm	Boldly goes where no restaurant has gone before: Rotherhithe.

Map 111 • Rotherhithe (East) Surrey Quays

Cafe East	100 Redriff Rd	020 7252 1212	££		Best Vietnamese pho this side of the Kingsland Road.

Map 112 • Kennington / Elephant and Castle

Brasserie Tolouse Lautrec	140 Newington Bts	020 7582 6800	££££		French cuisine as excellent as the owners are eccentric.
Brasserie Toulouse Lautrec	140 Newingtion Butts	020 7582 6800	££	12 am	French brasserie and bar.
Chatkhara	84 Walworth Rd	020 7701 8899	£		Possibly the best value lunch deal in the city.
Dragon Castle	100 Walworth Rd	020 7277 3388	££	11 pm	Odd locale for such a curious pocket of culinary authenticity.
La Bodeguita	Elephant & Castle Shopping Centre	020 7701 9166	££		Colombian home cooking and salsa parties. Whats not to like?
The Lobster Pot	3 Kennington Ln	020 7582 5556	£££	10.30 pm	Dine to a soundtrack of seagull caws. We don't kid.
Mamuska	233 Elephant & Castle Shopping Centre	020 3602 1898	£		Hearty polish grub to stave off winter blues.

Map 113 • Walworth

Aobaba and Longdan Express	128-132 Walworth Rd	020 7701 2566			Canteen serving proper bahn mi, with adjoining oriental supermarket.
Bagel King	280 Walworth Rd	020 7277 4060	£		Refuge in the night.
La Luna	380 Walworth Rd	020 7277 1991	££	11 pm	Ignore exterior. It's the garlic bread inside that counts.

Map 114 • Old Kent Road (West) / Burgess Park

Shu Castle	194-202 Old Kent Rd	020 7703 9797	£££		£££

Map 115 • Old Kent Road (East)

Roma Café	21 Peckham Park Rd	020 7639 7730	£	10 pm	Escape Peckham and enjoy a good fry-up here.

Map 119 • Deptford (East)

The Big Red Pizza Bus	30 Deptford Church St	020 3490 8346	£	11 pm	It's a bus. Where you can get pizza!
Chaconia	26 Deptford High St	020 8692 8815	£		Lip-tingling rotis made by the Trinidadian version of your Granny.
Panda Panda	8 Deptford Broadway	020 8616 6922	£		Bahn mi and other Vietnamese treats.
The Waiting Room	142 Deptford High St	079 6803 6562	£	7 pm	Veggie and vegan heaven

Map 120 • Greenwich

Craft London	1 Greenwich Place	020 8465 5910	£££	10:30 pm	Stevie Parle and Tom Dixon collaboration celebrating British fayre.
Goddards at Greenwich	22 King William Walk	020 8305 9612	£	6 pm	Pie n' mash n' eels. Only at the weekend.
Greenwich Tavern	1 King William Walk	020 8858 8791	£££	10 pm	Kobe steak burgers. Nuff said.
The Hill	89 Royal Hill	020 8691 3626	£££	10 pm	Bistro food. Local favourite.
The Langos Company	5 Greenwich Market	075 2586 1964	£		Deep fried flatbread like no other.
Piano Restaurant	131 Greenwich High Rd	020 8853 3020	£££££	2 am	Fish swim in the chandeliers. Get the idea?
Rivington	178 Greenwich High Rd	020 8293 9270	£££	11 pm	Good for brekkie or dinner before a Picturehouse movie

Map 121 • Camberwell (West)

Kazakh Kyrgyz	158 Camberwell Rd	020 7871 9963	££	1 am	Unsuspectingly tantalising Central Asian cuisine—belly dancer included
New Dewaniam	225 Camberwell New Rd	020 7703 9318	£	12 am	Mouth-watering Indian takeaway for a tenner.
Rock Steady Eddie's	2 Coldharbour Ln		£		Where Elvis would eat if he was born in King's College.
Zeret Kitchen	216 Camberwell Rd	020 7701 8587	£	11 pm	Order the special to try a bit of everything.

Map 122 • Camberwell (East)

Angels & Gypsies	33 Camberwell Church St	020 7703 5984	££		Like some kind of Dali-Almodovar fantasy.
Caravaggio	47 Camberwell Church St	020 7207 1612	£	11 pm	Cheap Italian with impressive fare. Stands out from the rest.
Crooked Well	16 Grove Ln	020 7252 7798	££££		A damn fine taste of the genteel side of Camberwell.
Falafel	27 Camberwell Church St	020 7277 2573	£		Better bet for an evening snack than stale friend chicken.
FM Mangal	54 Camberwell Church St	020 7701 6677	££		Book a taxi because the monstrous portions seriously hinder mobility.
Silk Road	49 Camberwell Church St	020 7703 4832	££		As far away from chicken chow mein as Chinese gets.
Wuli Wuli	15 Camberwell Church St	020 7708 5024	££		Go for the regional Sichuan dishes.

Map 123 • Peckham

Agrobeso African Cuisine	139 Peckham High St	020 7501 8792	£		For anyone mad enough to try honeycomb tripe.
The Begging Bowl	168 Bellenden Rd	020 7635 2627	£££		Great food, outstanding cocktails.
Ganapati	38 Holly Grove	020 7277 2928	£	10:30 pm	Influenced by street food of South India.
M. Manze Pie and Mash	105 Peckham High St	020 7277 6181	£		One of the only remaining original pie and mash shops.
Miss Tapas	45 Choumert Rd	07838 821 836	£		Andalucian fare.
Obalende Suya Express	43 Peckham High St	020 7703 7033	£		Nigeria's answer to a kebab shop.
Peckham Refreshment Rooms	12 Blenheim Grove	020 7639 1106	£	12 am	Mediterranean influenced eats in New York style surrounds.

Map 124 • Peckham East (Queen's Road)

805	805 Old Kent Rd	020 7639 0808	£££	12 am	West African oasis. In Peckham.
Tops Carribean Takeaway	173 Queens Rd	020 7732 7557	£		Eat incredible fried dumplings under a massive Obama mural.

Map 125 • New Cross Gate

Hong Kong City	43 New Cross Rd	020 7252 9888	££		Tastes like it's in a much better part of town.
Smokey Jerky	158 New Cross Rd	020 7639 6204	£		Some of the best, messiest jerk in South London.

Map 126 • New Cross

Birdie Num Nums	11 Lewisham Way	020 8692 7223	£	7 pm	Smashing cafe with occasional evening events.
The London Peculiar	399 New Cross Rd	020 8692 6149	£		Quaint little cafe.

Map 127 • Coldharbour Lane / Herne Hill (West)

Beanery	Coldharbour Ln	077 3431 9081	£		Good strong coffee to perk you up before your train.
Café Prov	2 Half Moon Ln	020 7978 9228	£££	10 pm	Local art (for sale) decorates this relaxed restaurant/bar/ cafe.
Ichiban Sushi	58 Atlantic Rd	020 7738 7006	£	11 pm	The bee's knees.
Naughty Piglets	28 Brixton Water Ln	020 7274 7796	££		Nouveau bohemian French cafe-inflected menu.
New Fujiyama	5 Vining St	020 7737 6583	£	10.30 pm	This place blows Wagamama's out of the water.

Map 128 • Denmark Hill / Herne Hill (East)

Lombok	17 Half Moon Ln	020 7733 7131	£££	10.30 pm	From Stir-fries to curries, a no-fuss pan-Asian standby.
Number 22	22 Half Moon Ln	020 7095 9922	££££	10.30 pm	Gorge yourself on Spanish wine, sherry and loads of brilliant tapas.

Map 129 • East Dulwich

Anderson & co	139 Bellenden Rd	020 7469 7078	££	10:30 pm	Fresh and delicious.
The Palmerston	91 Lordship Ln	020 8693 9662	££££	10 pm	Gastropub that's a lot more gastro than pub.

Map 130 • Peckham Rye

Artusi	161 Bellenden Rd	020 3302 8200	££	10 pm	Italian-inspired seasonal menu.
Pedler	58 Peckham Rye	020 3030 5015	£	11pm	Vibrant neighbourhood eaterie.
Thai Corner Cafe	44 North Cross Rd	020 8299 4041	££*	11 pm	Tiny, laidback neighbourhood cafe.

Map 132 • Battersea (West)

Ransome's Dock	35 Parkgate Rd	020 7223 1611	£££	11 pm	Friendly, stylish, likes wine and children.

Map 134 • South Lambeth

A Toca	343 Wandsworth Rd	020 7627 2919	£££		Football on numerous screens, as if you were in Lisbon!
Bar Estrela	113 S Lambeth Rd	020 7793 1051	£	11 pm	Like mama used to make. Probably.
Brunswick House	30 Wandsworth Rd	020 7394 2100	££	12 am	Opulent setting.
Canton Arms	177 S Lambeth Rd	020 7582 8710	£££	10 pm	Recently acquired by Anchor & Hope folks. Bring on the yuppies.
Hot Stuff on Wheels	19 Wilcox Rd	020 7720 1480	£	10 pm	Hard to find. Slightly dinghy. Mental Staff. Amazing food.
O Moinho	355 Wandsworth Rd	020 7498 6333	£££		Well-done traditional Portuguese.
Tia Maria	126 South Lambeth Rd	020 7622 3602	£	1 am	Known for its tapioca wraps.

Map 135 • Oval

Adulis	44 Brixton Rd	020 7587 0055	£	11 pm	C'mon, it's yummmy and cheap. And we can't cook Eritrean.
Bonnington Café	11 Vauxhall Grove	Check Website	£*	10.30 pm	Wonderful vegetarian meals in a communified (ex-squat) environment.
Oval Kebab	32 Clapham Rd	020 7820 8846	£*	10 pm	Fancy a doner kebab? Go nowhere else.

Map 136 • Putney

Enoteca Turi	28 Putney High St	020 8785 4449	£££		Aperol Spritz followed by some homemade ravioli?
Ma Goa	242 Upper Richmond Rd	020 8780 1767	££	11 pm	Amazing regional Goan cuisine.
Talad Thai	320 Upper Richmond Rd	020 8789 8084	££	10.30 pm	Thai-ny, family-run restaurant with Thai supermarket, cooking classes and Thai regulars.

Map 137 • Wandsworth (West)

Miraj	123 Putney Bridge Rd	020 8875 0799	£	10 pm	Curry in a hurry? Cheap, tasty take away joint.

Map 138 • Wandsworth (Central)

Brady's	Smugglers Way	020 8877 9599	££	11 pm	Up-market fish and chip cafe and take-away.
Kathmandu Valley	5 West Hill	020 8871 0240	££	11.45 pm	Nepalese is the new black (read: curry).

Map 139 • Wandsworth (East)

The Fish Club	189 St. John's Hill	020 7978 7115	££	10 pm	The thinking man's chippie.
Gazette	79 Chatfield Rd	020 7223 0999	£££		Unpretentious French brasserie fare that is tres sophistique.

Map 140 • Clapham Junction / Northcote Rd

Gail's Bread	64 Northcote Rd	020 7924 6330			Clapham branch of North London artisanal chain.
Jack's At The Junction	252 Lavender Hill	020 7228 9111	£		There's only one rule here—be a very hungry Jack.
Mien Tay	180 Lavender Hill	020 7350 0721			Kingsland Road stalwart brough to Lavender Hill.
Parisienne	225 Lavender Hill	020 7924 5523	£	5 pm	Massive sarnies and baked potatoes.
Pizza Metro	64 Battersea Rise	020 7228 3812	£££		Pizza by the metre!

Map 141 • Battersea (South)

The Lavender	171 Lavender Hill	020 7978 5242	££	11 pm	Rustic European eclectic—stellar cassoulets.

Map 142 • Clapham Old Town

Nardullis Ice Cream	29 The Pavement	020 7627 1515	£		Real Italian gelato to smear over your chops.
Trinity	4 The Polygon	020 7622 1199	£££	10.30 pm	How to do local dining really quite fantastically well.

Map 143 • Clapham High Street

Brickwood	16 Clapham Common South Side	020 7819 9614	£	6.30 pm	Top brunch.
The Dairy	15 The Pavement	020 7622 4165	£££		Charming seasonal British cuisine.
Gastro	67 Venn St	020 7627 0222	££	12 am	Low-lit gallic bistro extraordinaire
The Pepper Tree	19 Clapham Common South Side	020 7622 1758	£*	11 pm	Speedy Thai with soul.
Roti Joupa	12 Clapham High St	020 7627 8637	£	11 pm	Pick up some real Trinidadian food and enjoy it on the common.
San Marco Pizzeria	126 Clapham High St	020 7622 0452	££~	11.30 pm	Arguably the best pizza outside Italy—take that New York!
Tsunami	5 Voltaire Rd	020 7978 1610	££££	10.30 pm	The new Nobu. Unbelievable. Unfortunate name.

Map 144 • Stockwell / Brixton (West)

Agile Rabbit	24-25 Coldharbour Ln	020 7738 7646	££*		Tough contender with Franco Manca. Plus live music.
Bellantoni's	81 Granville Arcade	078 7294 5675	££		Artisan homemade pasta for date night at Brixton Village.
Breads Etcetera	88 Brixton Village Market	077 1764 2812	££		DIY toast comes to Brixton.
Brixton Cornercopia	65 Coldharbour Ln	079 1954 2233	££		Ultra-local fare with a changeable menu to match.
Casa Morita	9 Market Row	020 8127 5170	£££		Try-hard and pricey taqueria. Decent tacos; less decent guacamole.
Falafel Van	Station Rd		£		Tasty falafel from a man with a nice Muhammad Ali portrait.
Honest Burgers	12 Brixton Village	020 7733 7963	££		Best British burgers in Brixton. Not gonna lie.
Jeff the Chef	Station Rd				Proper oil drunk jerk and fresh coconuts.
Mama Lan	18 Brixton Village Market		£		Slap-up corner joint selling nom noodle soups and dumplings.
SW9 Bar	11 Dorrell Pl	020 7738 3116	£	9 pm	Great hangover curing breakfasts (and hangover causing booze).

Map 146 • Earlsfield

Amaranth	346 Garratt Ln	020 8874 9036	££*	10 pm	Rarefied, bustling restaurant with tacked-on takeout element.

Map 147 • Balham (West)

Chez Bruce	2 Bellevue Rd	020 8672 0114	££££	10.30 pm	Worth its fancy-pants (read Michelin) star.

Map 148 • Balham (East)

Brickwood	11 Hildreth Street		£	6 pm	Top brunch.
The Exhibit	12 Balham Station Rd	020 8772 6556	£££	2 am	Cool event space: friendly, laid back vibe.
Hagen & Hyde	157 Balham High Rd	020 8772 0016	££	2 am	Modern British pub food.
Harrison's	15 Bedford Hill	020 8675 6900	££	10.30 pm	Great food if you can tolerate the 'look at me!' crowd.

Map 149 • Clapham Park

Bistro Union	40 Abbeville Rd	020 7042 6400	£££		All-day bistro featuring well-crafted modern fare.

Map 150 • Brixton

Asmara	386 Coldharbour Ln	020 7737 4144	££	11.15 pm	Disconcerting but delicious curry with pancakes to mop it up.
Boqueria	192 Acre Ln	020 7733 4408	£££		Insanely good croquetas de jamon. Excellent value too.
Curry Ono	14 Market Row	020 7326 1399	£££		Katsu curry that makes Wagamama's taste like a crying shame.
Duck Egg Cafe	424 Coldharbour Ln	020 7274 8972	££		Unassuming brunch. Go duck eggs, ginger beer and hash browns.
Elephant	55 Granville Arcade	075 9038 9684	£	10 pm	Hip, understated and authentic Pakistani street food. Go thali.
Franco Manca	4 Market Row	020 7738 3021	££	10 pm	London's best pizza? Eclectic concoctions of sour dough goodness comes west.
KaoSarn	Coldharbour Ln	020 7095 8922	££		The beating heart of Brixton Village. Half-chicken or bust.
Khan's of Brixton	24 Brixton Water Ln	020 7326 4460	££	11 pm	Great curry, and BYO to boot. Have it!
Lounge	56 Atlantic Rd	020 7733 5229	£	10 pm	A local favourite for breakfast, recovery and hanging on weekends.
Negril	132 Brixton Hill	020 8674 8798	£	10 pm	Tasty Carribean with veg options (which are joy).
Opus Café	89 Acre Ln	020 7737 1414	£	6 pm	Cakes and coffee. Niceness.
The Phoenix	441 Coldharbour Ln				Old school institution. Good bubble and squeak.
Refill	500 Brixton Rd	020 7274 5559	£		24 hour with suprisingly good patties and jerk sandwiches.
Yum-D	14 Market Row	020 7274 8824	£		Thai deli that makes tasty beef salads to order.

Map 151 • Tooting Bec

Al Mirage	215 Upper Tooting Rd	020 8772 4422	£	10.30 pm	Better than Mirch Masala? We think so.
Masaledar Kitchen	121 Upper Tooting Rd	020 8767 7676	££	11 pm	Last word in top-notch Indian cuisine
Mirch Masala	213 Upper Tooting Rd	020 8672 7500	£	12 am	Cheap, no frills, award-winning curries. Sublime.
Spice Village	32 Upper Tooting Rd	020 8672 0710	£	11 pm	Go for grilled.

Map 152 • Tooting Broadway

Dosa n Chutny	68 Tooting High St	020 8767 9200	£		Breakfast, South Indian style. Amazing.
Jaffna House	90 Tooting High St	020 8672 7786	££	12 am	Mediocre curry fare beneath flourescent bulbs.
Radha Krishna Bhavan	86 Tooting High St	020 8682 0969	££	11.30 pm	Busy, buzzing, bhavan of South Indian curry.
Rick's Restaurant	122 Mitcham Rd	020 8767 5219	£££	11 pm	Tooting's best kept culinary secret.

So are we still in the Recession? Who knows? Who cares? We're getting used to this boom and bust cycle but we've cut up all our credit cards. When it comes to retail, people will always spend whether money or no (that's how we got in this fine mess remember Stanley?), it's just that with little of the stuff about, people are more discerning about what they spend their hard earned cash/State Benefits on. And of course if we didn't spend we would never collectively crawl out of this endless dirge of gloom. As the well-observed slogan on the reusable eco-shopping bag from Modern Toss (available at **Magma, Maps 5, 12)** says, "Buy More Shit Or We're All Fucked". Indeed. But if the economic crisis is teaching us anything it's to be more picky about what we purchase and for retailers not just to deliver the goods but also all the extras that we, as polite English people, so foolishly see as just "extras". Primarily what we mean is, that intangible thing that contributes to a satisfying shopping experience and brings a customer back to the same store again and again: excellent service—helpfulness, genuine smiles and interest in the product and the customer. Beautiful packaging, loyalty cards, discounts, samples, invites to in-store events all help, too. In an adverse way, consumers have never had more power than now to demand what they want or—as important—don't want. So just make sure you buy more cool shit as opposed to any old shit.

The British High Street is certainly changing and support for independent shops is growing. A leaning towards handmade items and crafts which support local designers and artisans—Columbia Road and Cheshire Street are hotspots for this kind of thing. Yes there are a lot of these shops cropping up that purely sell "beautiful things" like **Of Cabbages And Kings (Map 64)** and (if it's a beauty of a decaying kind you're looking for) **Viktor Wynd's Shop of Horrors (Map 87)** to name just a couple (and we like them). But when it comes to fashion we also like to know that a little bit of love has been sprinkled into the making of an item. Special mention here must go to Amy Anderson of **Comfort Station (Map 91)** who produces the most thoughtful and whimsical pieces of jewellery and **Vivien of Holloway (Map 74)** who has built a real niche following but whose fabulous 1950s tailoring would make any gal feel like a doll. Both have gorgeous, well-fitted, unique shop spaces, too. For blokes, **Folk (Map 5)** are renowned for their limited collections, particularly shoes which are hand-stitched (hence the price tag).

Part of this trend is Pop-Up Shops which are installed for a few months at a time sometimes displaying the work of a single designer/company or else a co-operative of independent designers. Not only is this a thrifty way of setting up shop in these uncertain times, it also provides a showcase for new young things so always worth a look. These tend to appear around Carnaby Street and Spitalfields, especially in the summer.

The Big Boys

When it comes to department stores, **Selfridges (Map 2)** is without a doubt the daddy of them all—arguably, (and the emphasis is on that word depending on your budget) you can just get everything you need from here but if you're strapped, at least go and marvel at the window displays. **Harvey Nics (Map 37)** and **Harrods (Map 37)** are very much for ladies who lunch, and the Knightsbridge set use them like corner shops—that's not to say they don't have their uses. For a more personal touch, **Fenwick (Map 2)** and **Liberty (Map 10)** are wonderful British institutions which take you far from the madding crowd. If all these close-quarters encounters get up your nose head to **Whiteleys (Map 30)** or the Behemoth that is **Westfield Shopping Centre (Map 33)**.

Haute Et High Street

For flexing that plastic, Bond Street has always been the place to spend but Bruton Street, which branches off the main drag, is setting quite a precedent with **Matthew Williamson (Map 9)**, **Stella McCartney (Map 9)** and **Diane Von Furstenburg (Map 9)** all in residence. Always one to mix things up and throw us off track, **Marc Jacobs' (Map 9)** London store is to be found on Mount Street—check out the Marc for Marc Jacobs range for affordable designer garb—by which we mean £3 and upwards. Yes, really. If you want to feel like Alice down the rabbit hole, make a trip to **Dover Street Market (Map 9)**, owned by Rei Kawakubo of Comme Des Garçons—a real experience even if you're not buying. Throwing down the gauntlet when it comes to experiential retail is **LN-CC (Map**

86). For those of us in the real world, **Topshop (Map 3)** is the grand kahuna of high street shopping—seventh heaven on three floors for fashionistas. For super-slick, sharp ready-to-wear you can't beat Spanish stores, **Zara (Map 2)** and **Mango (Map 3)** which both do high street with an edge and turnover is pretty quick to ensure their stock remains covetable. New contenders for higher end high-street include **Cos (Map 10)** and **Hoss Intropia (Map 10)**, and let's not forget our Stateside cousins who have sent ripples of excitement through the fash pack by opening flagship stores of **Anthropologie**, **Banana Republic**, and **Abercrombie & Fitch (Map 10)** all in the big smoke. There are also little shopping oases to be found in the capital. St Christopher's Place is hidden behind the hustle and bustle of Oxford Street and houses cool European brands like **Marimekko (Map 2)** alongside more familiar fare. Kingly Court (behind Carnaby Street—itself a great shopping spot for trend-led labels) has independent boutiques. The area around Seven Dials in Covent Garden which includes Neal's Yard is eclectic with high-end boutiques like **Orla Kiely (Map 13)** on Monmouth and skatewear at **Slam City Skates (Map 13)** and **Superdry (Map 13)** on Earlham. Edgy fashion abounds out East: head to **Good Hood (Map 84)** to start your shopping crawl.

Back to the Future

'Vintage' seems to be the term for anything over five years old nowadays but London's vintage (and secondhand) scene is thriving. Some of the best-known, best-loved shops include **Rellik (Map 25)** in Portobello, **Annie's (Map 80)** in Islington (a favourite of La Moss), and **Beyond Retro (Map 91)** and **Absolute Vintage (Map 91)** in Shoreditch (famous hunting ground for stylists). If you want to hear what the young, stylish and clueless get up to head to **Rokit (Maps 13, 71)** and eavesdrop on the staff's mindnumbing conversations. For genuine thrift, the turnover of goods in our charity shops is mind-boggling. **Oxfam Dalston (Map 86)** is renowned for being a good rummage: it's hit and miss but then that's the nature of the thrifting beast. Most hardy shoppers will happily tread the city twice over for good charity shop finds but if you want some certainty of finding designer threads you can't beat the **British Red Cross (Map 45)** where you will discover the likes of Ralph Lauren, Armani and pairs of Manolos amongst the usual flotsam and jetsam. The **Octavia Foundation Charity Shop (Map 35)** is also a reliable source of local celebrities' cast-offs from like, yesterday. For all you true vintage fashion fiends who want to mingle with like-minded souls and find genuine vintage togs (i.e. pre-1980s) the **Frock Me! Vintage Fashion Fair (Map 45)** and **Anita's Vintage Fashion Fair (Map 135)** are unequalled for choice and variety. Wake up and smell the mould.

Keep on Running, Cycling, Skating Etc.

Lillywhite's (Map 10) is the obvious place to go for cheap sportswear—it has earned a bit of a bargain basement tag where once it was prestigious (the Lillywhites were instrumental in the game of cricket during the 19th century) but it doesn't stop the shoppers pouring in, and tourists buying their favourite London football team shirts. A good indie chain is **Runners Need (Map 20)**. If it's sweatshop-made kit you're after head to **Niketown (Map 2)**, which is as scary as the name suggests. Though we're no Amsterdam, the economic shitstorm has inspired many Londoners to don skintight clothes and take to two wheels. If you're after a battered old charmer of a bike, **Recycling (Map 112)** does a fab job at selling secondhand wheels. If you've had your designer bike nicked, head down to Brick Lane at the weekend and buy it off some dodgy geezer. **Slam City Skates (Map 13)** is the only dedicated place for Southbank skaters to get their duds.

Home Sweet Home

John Lewis (Map 2) is a British standard (read: very sensible) and has been the store of choice for middle-class couples' wedding lists for decades. With fantastic staff (who all get a share of the profits) and well-made stuff, their maxim is "never knowingly undersold." **Twentytwentyone (Map 80)** is a designer's wet dream selling originals as well as new items. So impressive is their collection that they often lend out furniture to film companies who want the authentic look of an era on set. **SCP**

(Maps 30, 84) is perfect for unnecessary-yet-tasteful knick-knacks. The wonderfully named **Timorous Beasties (Map 6)** make wickedly amusing wallpapers—their most famous being a toile de jouy design for modern days (spot the alcopop-drinking chavs and the Gherkin in the background). **Labour and Wait (Map 91)** does the retro home stuff better than most. If you want personable, "Where can I find one of these?" type of service try **Russell's Hardware & DIY (Map 151)** in Tooting or **KTS The Corner (Map 86)** in Dalston.

Electricity for You and Me

Apple have done a very good job at monopolising our lives and getting everyone to 'Think Different,' so why you'd need to go anywhere other than the **Apple Store (Map 10)** we're not sure. However, traditionally, Tottenham Court Road is the hideout for the anally retentive hi-fi nut and the nerdoid pirate radio enthusiast a-like. The area positively thrums with electricity. In all cases it's best to shop around, play prices against each other and barter until you get the lowest price—often cash payment will get you well below the RRP. **Computer Exchange (Map 3)** is the one-stop shop for gaming, DVDs, computing and phones, which—as the name suggests—will part-exchange and knock money off for cash transactions. For audiovisual, **Richer Sounds (Map 106)** is a trusted chain, and if we're talking electronics in the purist sense, **Maplin (Map 3)** is geek central. Whether you'll get anyone who knows what they're talking about is another matter. Photography enthusiasts should check out the **London Camera Exchange (Map 24)** for old-school SLRs and digital cameras and **Red Dot Cameras for Leicas (Map 7)**.

Food for Thought

We like our food in London and the more diverse the better. Whether it's chowing down on burgers from Lucky Chip and Vietnamese baguettes from Banh Mi 11 down **Broadway Market (Map 89)** or fresh scallops and some raclette down Borough Market (Map 106) before moseying on down to **Maltby Street Market (Map 107)** for gelato, we're not afraid to say, "Please Sir, I want some more" (mainly because we're paying for it). **Whitecross Street (Map 7)** also has an impressive selection of foodie stalls. We have New York (and in particular, the Magnolia Bakery) to thank for the invasion of cupcake stores but the original and best is the **Hummingbird Bakery (Maps 29, 45)** which makes Red Velvet cupcakes that taste like little pieces of baked orgasm. Just try and restrain yourself from licking the last morsels of frosting from the paper. Nostalgia for old style sweetie shops can be bought at **Mrs. Kibble's Olde Sweet Shop (Map 10)** whether your fetish is for cola cubes, sherbet flying saucers or Wham bars. Numerous Italian delis can be found around the city selling cured meats, buffalo mozzarella, biscotti and everything else that Mama used to make—**I Camisa & Son (Map 11)** is small but crammed full of delicacies, while **Spiazzo (Map 53)** is bigger and sparklier. Organic freaks can bypass the rather average Whole Foods chain and head to local independent places like **The Grocery (Map 91)** or **Mother Earth (Map 75)**. For the cheapest and best coffee-to-go in Soho try the **Algerian Coffee Stores (Map 11)**. Looking for Unicum? Look no further than **Gerry's Spirits Shop (Map 11)** where you can find obscure liquors like Zubrowka Bison Grass Vodka and good quality Cachaça.

Art and Craft Supplies

Crafty types and closet Van Goghs can pick up supplies at **Cass Art's (Map 80)** three-storey flagship store in Islington. There's everything here for aspiring Manga cartoonists and weekend watercolourists alike, and lots of fun bits and pieces for school holiday/rainy day projects in the basement. Much of the high quality stock can be found at cut-price throughout the year—stock up on Moleskine note and sketchbooks which are frequently marked down. **The London Graphic Centre (Map 13)** has more design-led stock as well as fine art material attracting architects and graphic designers. Known for its greeting cards and stationery, **Paperchase (Map 3)** on Tottenham Court Road also has—true to its name—an astonishing array of handmade papers on its top floor—from flocked designs to fibrous papers made with dried flowers. You've got to love **Blade Rubber (Map 4)** just for its name, and for keeping sketches, photos, and memories intact. **Wyvern Bindery (Map 6)** is one of few of its kind to offer book-making services.

Axes, Saxes, Drums, Strums…

Traditionally, Tin Pan Alley (real name: Denmark Street) has always been the hub of musical creativity in the city. Back in the day when rents were affordable, a community grew up around this little side street which went on to see Jimi Hendrix and The Beatles record in the basements, and a young Elton John sitting on the rooftops penning "Your Song". Nowadays you may spot Jack White trying out a Digitech Whammy or Jonny Greenwood looking for some new toy to replace his Marshall Shred Master. If we had to choose a couple, we'd bug **Macari's (Map 12)** for cheapness and **Wunjos (Map 12)** for friendliness. There are plenty of independent music stores to be found in London's boroughs, and often they are specialists, happy to have a natter about what exactly it is that you're looking for and what the weather's like. Try **Top Wind (Map 104)** for all your flute needs, Duke of Uke (Map 91) for banjo and ukulele-lovers, though the staff are a little arsey, and **Phil Parker (Map 1)** for all you jazz cats needing a hand with your brass. For the medieval troubadour in your life, **Hobgoblin (Map 3)** has its own luthier who makes lutes. Try **Ray Man (Map 71)** in Camden for unusual ethnic instruments and drone boxes. For the largest collection of sheet music in Europe, **Chappell of Bond Street (Map 11)** (now on Wardour Street but they've kept the name) is your destination. One thing though, will you instrument shop assistants please stop jamming while you're talking to us?

Music Nonstop

The slow, painful death of the CD can be seen in almost every indie music store in London, and it coincides with the financial doom and gloom that has befallen Virgin Records, Zavvi and Sanctuary (thankfully we still have one branch of **Fopp (Map 12)** left). Bizarrely, the death march of the traditional record shop has become a moonwalk: more and more boutique record shops are springing up selling new and used wax. The Berwick Street vinyl epicenter may have been drained of late, but other parts of London have become haunts for us of haunched posture and good taste. **Sister Ray (Map 11)** is forever teetering on the edge, but **Reckless Records (Map 11)** seems here to stay. If you find yourself on the Essex Road, have a gander at **Flashback (Maps 53, 83)** and **Haggle Vinyl (Map 83)**: you're sure to find something to please and appeal in the former and appall in the latter. The **Music & Video Exchange (Map 29)** in Notting Hill was way ahead of its time and has been the swapshop of choice for years, it's still the king as far as we're concerned. When south of the river, do as Camberwellians do and drop in at **Rat Records (Map 121)**. To guarantee a withering look from a record shop lifer go and discuss the use of naivety in Legowelt's output at **Phonica (Map 10)** in Soho. Many a muso's all-round fave, **Sounds of the Universe (Map 11)** is owned by the **Soul Jazz** label.

Antiques and Bric-A-Brac, Flea Markets and Stalls

There may have been a time, dear reader, when markets sold fleas. And brics and bracs. Perhaps we used to know what these elusive words meant. Frankly, we numbskulls at NFT don't care about etymology unless it's secondhand and collectable. First stop on many shoppers' lists—both serious collectors and weekend browsers—are **Alfie's Antique Market (Map 76)** and **Gray's Antique Market (Map 2)**. Here you'll find art, antiques, jewellery, vintage clothing and rare books all housed under one roof.

Once the centre of the Britpop phenomenon in the '90s and a thriving mini-metropolis for vintage and antique stalls, Camden is now rather anaesthetised, but packs of German and French kids on school trips still rifle through the emo and goth gear that overfloweth. There is some gold to be found in shops like **Episode (Map 71)** and **Rokit (Map 71)**, and **Aldo Liquidation (Map 71)** is good for a bargain (or practising your rugby tackle). Certainly the place still has atmosphere.

Well-known to scavengers, **Camden Passage (Map 80)** in Angel rather confusingly, is a welcome retreat from the mallrat-filled N1 centre across the road in Islington. The Mall and also Pierrepoint Arcade (tucked away behind the passage) offer a cornucopia of clothing, jewelry, military paraphernalia, homewares, prints, and a host of other bits and bobs. On

Saturdays, market stalls set up in the street and surprises like original Givenchy earrings from 1978 (4 quid!) can be salvaged from amongst the knick-knacks. This is another brilliant little vintage bazaar continually threatened by chains and redevelopment. Go protest by buying any old crap.

Brick Lane (Map 91) also opens up on Sunday and in the summer there is a real carnival feel with fruit and veg, plumbing and DIY bits and pieces, electricals, toiletries, furniture (dentist's chair anyone?), clothes, DVDs lining the lane and spilling into Sclater Street. Watch your bags and all the silly haircuts. Brick Lane also has the added advantage of having many a watering hole and curry house where you can stop and people-watch if it all makes you want to go all 'Falling Down' on their asses. If that's not your thing, (Up)Market is held in the **Truman Brewery (Map 91)** every Sunday and showcases new designers as well as housing some vinyl, vintage and gourmet street food. **Spitalfields Market (Map 91)** has been tarted up to be a sanitized precinct of chain stores but there are still some unusual boutiques and independent shops.

The triumvirate of hipster markets consists of **Columbia Road Market (Map 91)**, **Broadway Market (Map 89)**, and Chatsworth Road Market (just north of Map 90). Also in the East is **Roman Road Market (Map 94)**. It's proper gorblimey, lor' love a duck cockerney territory but you may find yourself soaking up the atmosphere more than finding anything of real interest. If Lady Luck is stroking your inner thigh you get some great bargains Sarf of the river at **Deptford Market (Map 119)**.

Though certainly not as bountiful in treasure as the car boot sales of other parts of the country, London does have some. The best in Zone 2 is definitely the **Battersea Car Boot Sale (Map 141)**, a sprawling mess that kicks off around midday is a godsend to all us alcoholics and narcoleptics.

Map 1 • Marylebone (West)

Maroush Deli	45 Edgware Rd	020 7723 3666	Lebanese food emporium—fresh coffee, ice-creams and best houmous in town.
Phil Parker	106 Crawford St	020 7486 8206	Brass-o-rama.
Primark	499 Oxford St	020 7495 0420	Enter the scrum.
Spymaster	3 Portman Sq	020 7486 3885	Stab-proof vests, in house P.I., you know, the usual.
Totally Swedish	32 Crawford St	020 7224 9300	Salt liquorice and Plopp bars for scandiphiles.

Map 2 • Marylebone (East)

Browns	24 S Molton St	020 7514 0016	Sleep with someone rich, then bring them here.
Content Beauty & Wellbeing	14 Bulstrode St	020 3075 1006	Exceptional selection of organic beauty products.
Daunt Books	83 Marylebone High St	020 7224 2295	Almost intimidatingly beautiful book shop.
Divertimenti	33 Marylebone High St	020 7486 8020	Go and pretend you need a £500 coffee machine.
Fenwick	63 New Bond St	020 7629 9161	A welcome escape from Oxford Street for those in the know.
French Sole	61 Marylebone Ln	020 7486 0021	Spendy but these pumps can withstand London's terrible pavements.
Gray's Antique Market	58 Davies St	020 7629 7034	A world of bygone beauty a skip away from Bond Street.
John Lewis	300 Oxford St	020 7629 7711	Where John Betjeman would have gone if the world exploded.
Monocle	2 George St	020 7486 8770	Super stylish travel gear from the folks behind the magazine.
Niketown	236 Oxford St	020 7612 0800	Like a real town! Owned by Nike! But without sweatshops.
Paul Smith	38 Marylebone High St	020 7935 5384	Kitsch and dolls from the fashion designer. Don't ask why.
Postcard Teas	9 Dering St	020 7629 3654	Taste tea. Send tea. Love tea. Right here.
Selfridges & Co.	400 Oxford St	080 0123 400	A Mecca for the shopping elite who want everything.
Skandium	86 Marylebone High St	020 7935 2077	Ikea for grown-ups.
VV Rouleaux	102 Marylebone Ln	020 7224 5179	Trimmings and ribbons like you've never seen.
The Widescreen Centre	47 Dorset St	020 7935 2580	Telescopes, binoculars, projectors, screens, film cameras & virtual reality.
Zara	242 Oxford St	020 7318 2700	Spiffy suits and cute casualwear from the Balearic brand.

Map 3 • Fitzrovia

The Aquatic Design Centre	107 Great Portland St	020 7580 6764	You will want an aquarium after visiting this place.
Ben's House	64 Grafton Way	020 7388 0850	Impeccable curation of delectable treats.
Computer Exchange	32 Rathbone Pl	084 5345 1664	Good selection of secondhand DVDs, games and gadgets.
Harmony	103 Oxford St	020 7734 5969	Also known as Butt Plugs R Us.
Hobgoblin Music	24 Rathbone Pl	020 7323 9040	Folky paradise; impressive/amusing collection of alternative instruments.
Mango	225 Oxford St	020 7534 3505	Let's go Mango!

Maplin	218 Tottenham Court Rd	084 3227 7353	A whole world of technical geeketry to immerse yourself in.
Paperchase	213 Tottenham Court Rd	020 7467 6200	More than meets the eye to this high street card shop.
Scandinavian Kitchen	61 Great Titchfield St	020 7580 7161	Smorgasbord!
Stargreen Box Office	21 Argyll St	020 7734 8932	Try here for tickets to sold-out gigs.
Topshop	216 Oxford St	020 7636 7700	Kate Moss still loves it. We do too.
Topshop	36 Great Castle St	084 4848 7487	Clothing for the New Generation.
Trimmings	14 Great Titchfield Street		Treasure trove for craftsy folk.
Urban Outfitters	200 Oxford St	020 7907 0800	Heaps of streetwear and crazy things for your house.

Map 4 • Bloomsbury (West)

Aperture	44 Museum St	020 7242 8681	Specialists in new and vintage cameras.
Blade Rubber Stamps	12 Bury Pl	020 7831 4123	Scrapbooking materials plus traditional and made-to-order rubber stamps.
Gosh!	1 Berwick St	020 7636 1011	A Japanese school boy's wet dream. Comics galore!
James Smith & Sons	53 New Oxford St	020 7836 4731	Umbrella shop—because you might just need one.
London Review Bookshop	14 Bury Pl	020 7269 9030	Big books, big name personal appearances—and cake!
York Cameras	18 Bury Pl	020 7242 7182	New and secondhand, specializing in Canon.

Map 5 • Bloomsbury (East)

Antoni & Alison	43 Rosebery Ave	020 7833 2141	Home of "bonkers" fashion duo.
Bibas Hair and Beauty	72 Marchmont St	020 7837 9555	Lovely, friendly hair salon, excellent prices, 15% student discount.
The Brunswick	Hunter St	020 7833 6066	Brutalist shopping centre pushing the utopian/dystopian envelope.
The Flash Centre	68 Brunswick Centre	020 7837 5649	Studio lighting specialists.
Folk	49 Lamb's Conduit St	020 7404 6458	Great clothes, even better shoes.
Gay's the Word	66 Marchmont St	020 7278 7654	Britain's only dedicated Gay & Lesbian book store.
International Magic	89 Clerkenwell Rd	020 7405 7324	When you need some tricks up your sleeve.
JOY	22 Brunswick Centre	020 7833 3307	Funky Urban Outfitters type stuff, but cheaper.
Magma	117 Clerkenwell Rd	020 7242 9503	Funky book & novelty shop.

Map 6 • Clerkenwell

EC One	41 Exmouth Market	020 7713 6185	Gorgeous sparkly fings.
The Family Business Tattoo Shop	58 Exmouth Market	020 7278 9526	Tatts for all the family.
London Tattoo	332 Goswell Rd	020 7833 5996	Was on the telly. Caused quite a buzz.
M & R Meats	399 St. John St	020 7837 1781	So meat-savvy they'll even know the best cut on you.
Metro Imaging	32 Great Sutton St	020 7865 0000	Photo processing.
Timorous Beasties	46 Amwell St	020 7833 5010	Outlandish prints for the daringly tasteless home.
The Wyvern Bindery	56 Clerkenwell Rd	020 7490 7899	Book binding for theses, portfolios and presentations. Repairs and restoration.

Map 7 • Barbican / City Road (South)

Red Dot Cameras	68 Old St	020 7490 8444	Like yer Leica.
Whitecross Market	Whitecross St		Street food central.

Map 9 • Mayfair / Green Park

Diane Von Furstenberg	25 Bruton St	020 7499 0886	Forget the LBD, every girl needs a DVF.
Dover Street Market	17 Dover St	020 7518 0680	Serious designer wear for people with serious money.
Marc Jacobs	24 Mount St	020 7399 1690	Never out of fashion.
Matthew Williamson	28 Bruton St	020 7629 6200	The boy who knows how to dress real girls.
Stella McCartney	30 Bruton St	020 7518 3100	Stella's star keeps rising despite initial doubts in Fahionland.

Map 10 • Piccadilly / Soho (West)

Abercrombie & Fitch	7 Burlington Gardens	084 4412 5750	Like GAP but more expensive.
American Apparel	3 Carnaby St	020 7734 4477	25% off all sexual harrassment lawsuits.
Anthropologie	158 Regent St	020 7529 9800	Go check out the innovative window dressing if nothing else.
Apple Store	235 Regent St	020 7153 9000	Get your hardware here so you can buy NFT apps.
Banana Republic	224 Regent St	020 7758 3550	Your Stateside buddies don't need to ship over your clothes anymore
Beyond Retro	58 Great Marlborough St	020 7434 1406	Biggest, original, live-bands-on-Saturday vintage.
Burlington Arcade	Piccadilly	020 7493 1764	Welcoming shoppers since 1819.
COS	222 Regent St	020 7478 0400	COS you can. See what I did there?
The European Bookshop	5 Warwick St	020 7734 5259	For when you get sick of English.
Fortnum & Mason	181 Piccadilly	020 7734 8040	The world's poshest marmalades.
Freggo	27 Swallow St	020 7287 9506	Argentinean ice cream for insomniacs. About freakin' time.
Hamley's	188 Regent St	087 1704 1977	World's biggest toy store. Terrifying just before Christmas.
Hatchards Bookshop	187 Piccadilly	020 7439 9921	Still musty, floors still creak, despite being owned by The Man.
Hoss Intropia	211 Regent St	020 7287 3569	High-end high street.
Lazy Oaf	2 Ganton St	020 7287 2060	Rockin good little design shop with the emphasis on illustration.

Liberty	214 Regent St	020 7734 1234	Splendid wood-panelled department store. Beautiful and obscure scents and perfumes.
Lillywhites	24 Regent St	084 4332 5602	Good if you know exactly what you're looking for.
Muji	41 Carnaby St	020 7287 7323	Japanese chain hits London—simple, minimalist goods but great quality.
Phonica	51 Poland St	020 7025 6070	Cutting edge vinyl/CD shop; alas, no Michael Bolton in stock.
Richard James	29 Savile Row	020 7434 0605	Bespoke contemporary Savile Row tailoring.
Rigby & Peller	22 Conduit St	020 7491 2200	Furnishers of the Queen's basement.

Map 11 • Soho (Central)

Algerian Coffee Store	52 Old Compton St	020 7437 2480	Pick up some Blue Mountain beans and a 95p cappu-to-go.
Calumet Photographic	175 Wardour St	020 7434 1848	Cameras and accessories.
Chappell of Bond Street	152 Wardour St	020 7432 4400	Which is actually on Wardour Street.
Gerry's	74 Old Compton St	020 7734 2053	A veritable alcoholic's Utopia.
I. Camisa & Son	61 Old Compton St	020 7437 7610	The best Italian deli outside of Italy.
Reckless Records	30 Berwick St	020 7437 4271	Sickly phoenix risen from the ashes of Reckless Records.
Sister Ray	34 Berwick St	020 7734 3297	Alternative vinyl, CDs and DVDs.
Sounds of the Universe	7 Broadwick St	020 7734 3430	Blow your friends' minds with obscure African vinyl.

Map 12 • Soho (East)

Angels Fancy Dress	119 Shaftesbury Ave	020 7836 5678	Chock full of fancy dress outfits.
Fopp	1 Earlham St	020 7845 9770	May Fopp never, ever die again. Long live the music bargain!
Forbidden Planet	179 Shaftesbury Ave	020 7420 3666	Cult/film/TV memorabilia shop that will leave Star Wars fans salivating.
Foyles	113 Charing Cross Rd	020 7437 5660	Convivial shop/cafe. Essential for Americana and, uh, jazz!
Kokon to Zai	57 Greek St	020 3601 1414	Mad fashion laboratory providing competition for The Pineal Eye.
Macari's	92 Charing Cross Rd	020 7836 2856	Family run instrument shop with historic roots.
Magma	16 Earlham St	020 7240 7571	Super-cool housewares and knick-knacks from the Magma gods.
Porselli Dancewear	9 West St	020 7836 2862	Before American Apparel...when only dancers wore dancewear.
Quinto Bookshop	72 Charing Cross Rd	020 7379 7669	Pretend you're a character in Black Books.
Rockers	5 Denmark St	020 7240 2610	Quiffs, picks, riffs and licks. Sick.
Wunjo Guitars	20 Denmark St	020 7379 0737	Mind-bendingly friendly Scot selling lovely vintage gear...

Map 13 • Covent Garden

Artbox	29 Earlham St	020 7240 0097	Hello Kitty overload.
The Astrology Shop	78 Neal St	016 2482 7000	For people who believe that shit—and people who don't.
Beadworks	21 Tower St	020 7240 0931	Great resource for amateur beaders and professional designers
Ben's Cookies	13 The Piazza	020 7240 6123	Cookie chain good. Chips in dough yum.
Blackout II	51 Endell St	020 7240 5006	Vintage heaven.
Cath Kidston	28 Shelton St	020 7240 8324	Kitsch at its most chic, and vice-versa.
Coco de Mer	23 Monmouth St	020 7836 8882	High-class, kinky fun.
Cybercandy	3 Garrick St	084 5838 0958	For when a plain old Mars bar just won't cut it.
David and Goliath	4 The Market	020 7240 3640	Droll, funky t-shirts and other fun stuff.
Libidex at Liberation	49 Shelton St	020 7836 5894	Caters for all your kinks. Yes, even that one.
London Graphic Centre	16 Shelton St	020 7759 4500	One stop shop for graphics geeks.
Neal's Yard Dairy	17 Shorts Gardens	020 7240 5700	Follow your nose to very fine cheeses.
Nigel Hall	18 Floral St	0207 836 8223	Where to get business casualed well.
Octopus	54 Neal St	020 7836 2911	Makes the everyday so much more fun.
Orla Kiely	31 Monmouth St	020 7240 4022	Trademark cutesy prints from the Irish designer.
Pop Boutique	6 Monmouth St	020 7497 5262	Retrotastic!
Rokit	42 Shelton St	020 7836 6547	Vast array of vintage clothing.
Slam City Skates	16 Neal's Yard	020 7240 0928	Rambunctious skate shop.
Stanfords	12 Long Acre	020 7836 1321	Treasure trove of maps, travel books and accessories.
Superdry	24 Earlham St	020 7240 9437	Super funky pseudo-Japanese urbanwear. Friendly staff.
Tabio	66 Neal St	020 7836 3713	Only the Japanese could create such an array of socks.
Urban Outfitters	42 Earlham St	020 7759 6390	Heaps of streetwear and crazy things for your house.

Map 14 • Holborn / Temple

Konditor & Cook	46 Grays Inn Rd	084 4854 9365	Unusual location to find K&C's famous Magic Cakes.
Topshop	60 The Strand	020 7839 4144	Clothing for the New Generation.

Map 16 • Square Mile (West)

Church's	90 Cheapside	020 7606 1587	An English shoe institution.

Map 17 • Square Mile (East)

Lulu Guinness	23 Royal Exchange	020 7626 5391	Eccentric yet stylish bags and purses.
Paul A. Young Fine Chocolates	20 Royal Exchange	020 7929 7007	"Everytime you go away..." you take a piece of chocolate.
Pretty Ballerinas	30 Royal Exchange	020 7929 6994	Find rich banker, take to fabulous shoe shop.

Map 18 • Tower Hill / Aldgate

Montezuma's	51 Brushfield St	020 7539 9208	Chocolate you'd leave your boyfriend for.
Petticoat Lane Market	Middlesex St		No petticoats here love, but look for the FCUK stall.
Precious	16 Artillery Passage	020 7377 6668	One of few independent boutiques left standing.

Map 19 • Belgravia

Daylesford Organic Farmshop and Cafe	44 Pimlico Rd	020 7881 8060	Fresh as you can get ingredients from their Gloucestershire farm.
Mungo & Maud	79 Elizabeth St	020 7467 0823	Real dogs don't wear clothes! Chihuahuas do though...and pugs.

Map 20 • Victoria / Pimlico (West)

Capital Carboot Sale	Lupus St	084 5094 3871	We love a rummage through other people's rubbish.
Grays of Westminster	40 Churton St	020 7828 4925	Charming period shop specializing in Nikon.
La Bella Sicilia	23 Warwick Way	020 7630 5914	Old-skool deli with cheery old owners and pasta aplenty.
Rippon Cheese Stores	26 Upper Tachbrook St	020 7931 0628	A world of cheese.
Runners Need	24 Palace St	020 7630 5056	Place for all you joggers "who go round and round."
Topshop	18 Victoria St	020 7828 6139	Clothing for the New Generation.

Map 21 • Pimlico (East)

Black Rose	112 Belgrave Rd	020 8279 2014	Gothic. Very, very gothic.

Map 22 • Westminster

Haelen Centre	41 Broadway	020 8340 4258	All your hippy, wholemeal, organic needs under one roof.

Map 23 • St. James's

Richard Caplan	60 Pall Mall	020 7807 9990	New and used equipment, specializing in Leica.

Map 24 • Trafalgar Square / The Strand

Austin Kaye	425 The Strand	020 7240 1888	Vintage watches. Don't expect e-bay prices.
London Camera Exchange	98 Strand	020 7379 0200	My lens is longer than yours.
Stanley Gibbons	399 Strand	020 7836 8444	World's leading stamp dealer attracts collectors, investors and the curious.

Map 25 • Kensal Town

Honest Jon's	278 Portobello Rd	020 8969 9822	Obscure and rare Jazz, Funk, Reggae and Hip-Hop.
Trellik	8 Golborne Rd	020 8962 0089	Opposite the Trellik Tower—geddit? Specialises in Queen Viv (Westwood).
What Katie Did	281 Portobello Rd	084 5430 8743	Fabulous 1940s-inspired boudoir boutique for rib-crushing corsets, stockings and pointy bras.

Map 28 • Ladbroke Grove / Notting Hill (West)

Cowshed	119 Portland Rd	020 7078 1944	Express mani-pedis for women who have places to go etc.
The Cross	141 Portland Rd	020 7727 6760	The original London boutique, still going.
Gelato Mio	138 Holland Park Ave		Get ice-cream, head to park.
Jeroboams	96 Holland Park Ave	020 7727 9359	London's largest independent wine merchant.
Virginia	98 Portland Rd	020 7727 9908	If money is no object, what you want is here.

Map 29 • Notting Hill Gate

Bodas	36 Ledbury Rd	020 7727 5063	Everyday underwear that gives M&S a run for its money.
Clarke's	124 Kensington Church St	020 7221 9225	All-butter brioche and honey loaves for Harvey Nicks, Selfridges—and you.
Diane Von Furstenberg	83 Ledbury Rd	020 7221 1120	High end wear for those who can afford it.
The Grocer on Elgin	6 Elgin Crescent	020 7221 3844	Restaurant standard ready-meals for lazy people.
The Hummingbird Bakery	133 Portobello Rd	020 7851 1795	Takeaway cupcakes reminiscent of New York's Magnolia Bakery.
Melt Chocolates	59 Ledbury Rd	020 7727 5030	Posh chocs made before your bulging eyes.
Mr Christian's Delicatessen	11 Elgin Crescent	020 7229 0501	Great little deli with non-Portobello Rd prices.
Music & Video Exchange	38 Notting Hill Gate	020 7243 8573	Invented second hand record shops. Best in London.

Negozio Classica	283 Westbourne Grove	020 7034 0005	Half bar, half store selling high-end Italian kitchen goods.
Portobello Road Market	Portobello Rd	020 7727 7684	The Notting Hill institution.
R. Garcia and Sons	246 Portobello Rd	020 7221 6119	Overwhelming selection of Spanish groceries.
Retro Man	34 Pembridge Rd	020 7792 1715	Vintage fixes for modern men. And men only.
Retro Woman	32 Pembridge Rd	020 7598 2233	Exclusive vintage ware that's worth it.
Rough Trade West	130 Talbot Rd	020 7229 8541	More character and better records than the soulless East Branch.

Map 30 • Bayswater

Al Saqi Bookshop	26 Westbourne Grove	020 7229 8543	Specialist book shop for anything and everything Middle Eastern.
Planet Organic	42 Westbourne Grove	020 7727 2227	Organic heaven.
Porchester Gate Spa	Queensway & Porchester Rd £25!	020 7792 3980	Proper old school art deco Turkish baths and spa for less than
SCP	87 Westbourne Grove	020 7229 3612	Design-led homeware.
Whiteleys Shopping Centre	Queensway	020 7229 8844	Slightly more soulful than Smithfields.

Map 32 • Shepherd's Bush (West)

Damas Gate	81 Uxbridge Rd	020 8743 5116	Incredible range of Middle Eastern food.
Nut Case	352 Uxbridge Rd	020 8743 0336	About time nuts got some respect.

Map 33 • Shepherd's Bush

Westfield Centre	Ariel Way	020 3371 2300	Very likable shopping center. Really.

Map 34 • West Kensington / Olympia

Homebase	195 Warwick Rd	084 5640 7062	So much stuff that you never knew you needed.

Map 35 • Kensington

Ben's Cookies	12 Kensington High St	020 7376 0559	Chunky cookies in wonderous flavours. Hidden in High Street Ken station.
Octavia Foundation Charity Shop	57 Kensington Church St	020 7937 5274	There's gold in them thar (clothes) hills.
Trailfinders	194 Kensington High St	020 7938 3939	Personable one-stop shop for travel bookings, advice and services.
Urban Outfitters	36 Kensington High St	020 7761 1001	Heaps of streetwear and crazy things for your house.
Whole Foods Market	63 Kensington High St	020 7368 4500	Overwhelming selection of organic exotica.

Map 36 • South Kensington / Gloucester Rd

Maitre Choux	15 Harrington Rd	020 3583 4561	Pimp your choux!
Partridges	17 Gloucester Rd	020 7581 0535	Family run mega-deli to the queen.
Snog	32 Thurloe Pl	020 7584 4926	Crazy frozen yoghurt joint with an interior mad enough to be in Tokyo.

Map 37 • Knightsbridge

Burberry	2 Brompton Rd	020 7980 8426	Flagship store of the classic British brand.
Divertimenti	227 Brompton Rd	020 7581 8065	Go and pretend you need a £500 coffee machine.
Harrods	87 Brompton Rd	020 7730 1234	Arch conspiracy theorist Mr Al-Fayed's still classy department store.
Harvey Nichols	109 Knightsbridge	020 7201 8081	Not sure who really shops here.
Rigby & Peller	2 Hans Rd	020 7225 4760	Sexy lingerie fit for a queen...for THE Queen?
Skandium	247 Brompton Rd	020 7584 2066	For lottery winners who can't shake their love of Ikea.
Space NK Apothecary	307 Brompton Rd	020 7589 8250	Skincare heaven.

Map 38 • Chiswick

As Nature Intended	201 Chiswick High Rd	020 8742 8838	Main store from organic food company. Pricey but worth the trek.
Chiswick Health & Wellness Spa	300 Chiswick High Rd	020 8995 2293	A calming oasis hidden on the High Road. Fantastic products.
Gail's Bread	282 Chiswick High Rd	020 8995 2266	Enough artisan pastries to tempt you for seconds. Busy weekends.
Mortimer & Bennett	33 Turnham Green Terrace	020 8995 4145	Gourmet deli that is guaranteed to get you excited about pickled asparagus.
Outsider Tart	83 Chiswick High Rd	020 7096 1609	Two American dudes start a US baked goods revolution—cupcakes!
Oxfam Books	90 Turnham Green Terrace	020 8995 6059	Fantastic fiction selection—the rich read too!
Wheelers Flowers	Turnham Green Terrace	020 8747 9505	Last chance station for forgotten occasions next to Turnham Green tube.

Map 39 • Stamford Brook

Thai Smile	287 King St	020 8846 9960	Heaven for those who love Asian cooking. For the rest it's just intriguing.

Map 40 • Goldhawk Rd / Ravenscourt Park

Bushwacker Wholefoods	132 King St	020 8748 2061	Small and friendly organic and health food shop. Booja Booja ice-cream!
Patisserie Sainte-Anne	204 King St	020 8563 2046	Heavenly Parisian cakes, breads, and pastries.

Map 41 • Hammersmith

Bakehaus	71 King St	020 3490 3231	Traditional German baking through and through, Bratwurst roll an' all.

Map 43 • West Brompton / Fulham Broadway / Earl's Court

Vagabond Wines	18-22 Vanston Pl	020 7381 1717	Try before you buy wine.

Map 44 • Chelsea

The Furniture Cave	533 Kings Rd	077 6771 3314	Swanky. Huge. Quintessentially Kings Road.
Richer Sounds	258 Fulham Rd	033 3900 0027	Chain selling all things electronic, technologic, and so forth.
The Shop At Bluebird	350 King's Rd	020 7351 3873	Spend a fortune here and become an "edgy" individual.
Worlds End	430 King's Rd	020 7352 6551	Ever changin outlet of Dame Viv.

Map 45 • Chelsea (East)

Ad Hoc	153 King's Rd	020 7376 8829	Gold sequin knickers—what more do you want?
British Red Cross	69 Old Church St	020 7376 7300	Known locally as La Croix Rouge Boutique.
Frock Me! Vintage Fashion Fair	Kings Rd	020 7254 4054	Held every couple of months, "pre-war" tearoom refreshes shopping casualties.
The Hummingbird Bakery	47 Old Brompton Rd	020 7851 1795	Notting Hill's big brother with seating to devour Red Velvets and lattes.
Nomad Books	781 Fulham Rd	020 7736 4000	Glorious little place with added coffee shop.
Sweaty Betty	125 King's Rd	020 7349 7597	Clothes for you to stretch in, Gretchen.

Map 46 • Sloane Square

Partridges	2 Duke of York Sq	020 7730 0651	Family run mega-deli to the queen.
Rigby & Peller	13 Kings Rd	020 7824 1844	Sexy lingerie fit for a queen...the queen?
Space NK Apothecary	307 King's Rd	020 7351 7209	The Superdrug for the Sloane Square ladies who lunch.

Map 48 • Fulham

Hurlingham Books	91 Fulham High St	020 7736 4363	More stacked than Arnie was in the 70s.

Map 51 • Highgate

The Corner Shop	88 Highgate High St	020 8340 1118	Locals' favourite fending off the advance of Tesco's.
Highgate Butchers	76 Highgate High St	020 8340 9817	Reassuringly expensive meat. Them cows must have lived like kings.
Hops N' Pops	389 Archway Rd	020 8348 0624	Great selection for all budgets.
Mind	329 Archway Rd	020 8341 1188	Great selection for skint book worms.
Oxfam	80 Highgate High St	020 8340 3888	Musty bookstore with some cracking titles.
Wild Guitars	393 Archway Rd	020 8340 7766	Get your retro gear in this brilliant guitar shop.

Map 52 • Archway (North)

The Green Room	192 Archway Rd	079 6144 1722	Amazing selection of weird things you probably don't need.
Pax Guns	166 Archway Rd	020 8340 3039	Errm..."best" gun shop in the area?

Map 53 • Crouch End

Flashback	144 Crouch Hill	020 8342 9633	2nd hand vinyl and DVD goldmine.
Italian Farmers	186 Stroud Green Rd	020 3719 6525	Gorgeous produce direct from Italian farmers.
Organic Food	196 Stroud Green Rd	020 7281 1115	Well-stocked local shop.
Riley Ice Cream Cafe	32 The Broadway	020 8347 7825	Particularly creamy and good ice cream.
Soup Dragon	27 Topsfield Parade	020 8809 6123	Paradise for yummy mummies and their tots.
Walter Purkis And Sons	17 The Broadway	020 8340 6281	Proof that fish don't need their tasty batter skins.

Map 54 • Hornsey

Micycle N4	8 Ferme Park Rd	020 8347 9180	Friendly bike repairs and cafe.

Map 55 • Harringay

Beans and Barley	595 Green Lanes		Organic emporium.
Harringay Local Stores	581 Green Lanes	020 8347 6070	Hipsters do their grocery shopping.
Yasar Halim	495 Green Lanes	020 8340 8090	Amazing Turkish grocery store.

Map 56 • Hampstead Village

Happy Returns	36 Rosslyn Hill	020 7435 2431	Boring posh toys...and some cool stuff for normal kids.
Keith Fawkes	1 Flask Walk	020 7435 0614	Books, books, books. A glorious mess of a shop.
Mystical Fairies	12 Flask Walk	020 7431 1888	It's a fairy shop. Really.

Map 57 • Hampstead Heath

Daunt Books	51 S End Rd	020 7794 8206	A right daunty little shop.
Giocobazzi's Delicatessen	150 Fleet Rd	020 7267 7222	The taste of posh Italy.

Map 58 • Parliament Hill / Dartmouth Park

Baba	11 Swain's Ln	020 8442 9111	Quirky kitchenware and gifts.
Corks	9 Swain's Ln	020 8340 4781	Superb selection of interesting wines and beers.
Forks	7 Swain's Ln	020 8340 1695	Friendly, well-stocked deli. Fresh crepes in summer!

Map 59 • Tufnell Park

The Hornsey Trust Charity Shop	124 Fortess Rd	020 7267 2338	Eccentric staff? Check. Affluent, moth-eaten cast offs? Check.
North London Adoption Centre	135 Junction Rd	020 7272 6048	Need a cat? Of course you do! Miaow!

Map 60 • Archway

Second Chance	7 St John's Way	020 7281 5449	Heaps of rubbish and the occasional incredible find.
Super Persia	621 Holloway Rd	020 7272 2665	Very proud little shop specializing in Iranian sweets.

Map 61 • Holloway (North)

Holloway Car Boot	Opposite Odeon Cinema	019 9271 7198	Scavenge with North London's finest.
Michael's Fruiterers	56 Seven Sisters Rd	020 7700 1334	Fruit n veg fest. Nowhere's fresher.

Map 62 • Finsbury Park

The Deli at 80	80 Stroud Green Rd	020 7272 6622	Epicurean delights.
The Happening Bagel Bakery	284 Seven Sisters Rd	020 8809 1519	Another Haringey gem, with some delicious pastries too!
Hettie Holland	19 Charter Court	020 7272 2002	Gorgeous gifts and homewares.

Map 63 • Manor House

Bennet & Brown	84 Mountgrove Rd	020 7704 9200	Secondhand furniture and interesting things.
Sargent & Co.	74 Mountgrove Rd	020 7359 7642	Passionate about bike building and bespoke.
Simply Organique	316 Green Lanes	020 8800 4668	Local organic store.
Sylvanian Families	68 Mountgrove Rd	020 7226 1329	It is indeed a shop that solely sells Sylvanian Families.

Map 64 • Stoke Newington

The Ark	161 Stoke Newington Rd	020 7275 9311	Cute little interiors and gift shop.
Beaucatcher Salon	44 Stoke Newington Church St	020 7923 2522	Hairdressers and community hub.
Belle Epoque Patisserie	37 Newington Green	020 7249 2222	Fancy schmancy, delicious pastries.
Bridgewood & Neitzert	146 Stoke Newington Church St	020 7249 9398	Renowned string section repair, exchange and sales.
Church Street Bookshop	142 Stoke Newington Church St	020 7241 5411	Great shack with out-of-print books and shite records.
Metal Crumble	13 Stoke Newington Church St	020 7249 0487	Affordable, flippin' gorgeous, jewellery made on site.
Of Cabbages & Kings	127 Stoke Newington High St	020 7998 3282	Another of those crafty little shops that keep popping up.
Pelicans & Parrots	81 Stoke Newington Rd	020 7249 9177	Boutique hipster fashion joint which mixes oddness with elegance.
Ribbons and Taylor	157 Stoke Newington Church St	020 7254 4735	Long-standing vintage clothes shop—Stokey original.
Rosa Lingerie	3 Church Walk	020 7254 3467	The oldest knickers in Stokey.

Route 73 Kids	92 Stoke Newington Church St	020 7923 7873	Bus inspired toy shop.
S'Graffiti	172 Stoke Newington Church St	020 7254 7961	You've been framed.
Sacred Art Tattoos	148 Albion Rd	020 7254 2223	(Needles + Ink + Skin) x Pain = Art.
The Spence Bakery & Cafe	161 Stoke Newington Church St	020 7249 4927	Bread elevated to an art form.
Stoke Newington Farmers' Market	Stoke Newington High St	020 7502 7588	Overpriced, organic, natural, hea... Zzzzzzzz

Map 65 • West Hampstead

Party Party	206 Kilburn High Rd	020 7624 4295	Party Party Stuff Stuff!

Map 67 • Belsize Park

Belsize Village Delicatessen	39 Belsize Ln	020 7794 4258	For a truly international picnic basket.
Lotus and Frog	32 England's Ln	020 7586 3931	Quirky gifts for young and old.

Map 70 • Primrose Hill

Nicolas	67 Regent's Park Rd	020 7722 8576	A wide range of wines, including some cheap ones.
Press	3 Erskine Rd	020 7449 0081	Impressive array of brands for a boutique. Good sales.
Primrose Hill Books	134 Regent's Park Rd	020 7586 2022	Fabulously curated selection of new books.
Primrose Hill Pets	132 Regent's Park Rd	020 7483 2023	Everything your handbad mutt could need.
Primrose Newsagent	91 Regent's Park Rd	020 7722 0402	Newsagent, stationers, post office, drycleaners and internet cafe.
Richard Dare	93 Regent's Park Rd	020 7722 9428	Quite lovely kitchen/cooking products.
Shepherd Foods	59 Regent's Park Rd	020 7586 4592	Highly priced but quaint local deli.
Shikasuki	67 Gloucester Ave	020 7722 4442	Affordable vintage and modern design.
Sweet Pea	77 Gloucester Ave	020 7449 9292	Unusual handmade jewelry.
Tann Rokka	123 Regent's Park Rd	020 7722 3999	Wildly expensive "lifestyle store" in old Primrose Hill train station.

Map 71 • Camden Town / Chalk Farm / Kentish Town (West)

AcuMedic	105 Camden High St	020 7388 6704	Chinese medicine centre offering acupuncture AKA polite masochism.
Aldo Outlet	231 Camden High St	020 7284 1982	If you find shoes that fit they're free. Not really.
Cyberdog	Stables Market	020 7482 2842	Enormous sci-fi set displaying PVC, neon, and leather clubbing gear.
Escapade	45 Chalk Farm Rd	020 7485 7384	Dress up as Wonder Woman! Also caters for females.
Eye Contacts	10 Chalk Farm Rd	020 7482 1701	Opticians that sells uber-trendy spectacles.
Graham and Green	164 Regent's Park Rd	020 7586 2960	Wonderfully dinky yet scarily pricey shop.
Proud Camden	Stables Market	020 7482 3867	Stock up on contemporary photography.
Ray Man Music	54 Chalk Farm Rd	020 7692 6261	Wonderful shop full of exotic instruments. Bavarian noseflute, anyone?
Rokit	225 Camden High St	020 7267 3046	Secondhand, sorry, vintage clothing store to the stars.
Three Amigos Skateboard Shop	118 Camden Rd	020 7284 4515	Skater owned, skater run. Best in London.
TRAID	154 Camden High St	020 7485 5253	Characterful recycled clothes. Touch of wank, but still we like.
Village Games	65 Camden Lock Pl	020 7485 0653	Huge selection of boardgames.
Whole Foods Market	49 Parkway	020 7428 7575	Organic and wholefood oasis with eat-in possibilities.

Map 72 • Kentish Town

Phoenicia	186 Kentish Town Rd	020 7267 1267	Olives, just-roasted nuts, baclava, ice-cream bar. Meze heaven. Ditch Sainsburys.
Ruby Violet	118 Fortress Rd	020 7609 0444	Housemade ice cream with bold, inventive flavours.

Map 73 • Holloway

Bumblebee Natural Foods	33 Brecknock Rd	020 7284 1314	Hot veggie lunches, lush cakes. Organic fruitopia over the road.

Map 74 • Holloway Road / Arsenal

Vivien of Holloway	294 Holloway Rd	020 7609 8754	Want to dress like Joan from Mad Men?

Map 75 • Highbury

Cabbies Delight Autospares Car Parts	9 Green Lanes	020 7226 1692	21,000 car parts and 21 years experience.
Highbury Vintners	71 Highbury Park	020 7226 1347	Discount when you buy 6 or 12 bottles.
La Fromagerie	30 Highbury Park	020 7359 7440	Blow your inheritance on some Abbaye De Trois Vaux.
Mother Earth	282 St. Paul's Rd	020 7354 9897	Unfortunate New Age name, decent little shop.
Prawn on the Lawn	220 Saint Paul's Rd	020 3302 8668	Ethically and sustainably sourced fish.

Map 76 • Edgware Road / Marylebone (North)

Alfie's Antiques Market	25 Church St	020 7723 6066	Kitsch oddball sanctuary for vintage treats.
Archive Bookstore	83 Bell St	020 7402 8212	Old and unusual books.
London Beatles Store	231 Baker St	020 7935 4464	All you need is love, and no taste.
Lord's Cricket Store	Lisson Grove	020 7616 8570	They won't even ask why you want a cricket bat.

Map 77 • Mornington Crescent / Regent's Park

Calumet Photographic	93 Drummond St	020 7380 1144	Cameras and accessories.

Map 78 • Euston

All Ages Records	27 Pratt St	020 7267 0303	Truly independent punk & hardcore record shop. F*** the system!
Housman's Bookshop	5 Caledonian Rd	020 7837 4473	Bookshop for progressive peaceniks and radical revolutionaries.
Peyton & Byrne	Pancras Rd	020 7278 6707	Cupcake perfection.
Transformation	52 Eversholt St	020 7388 0627	The world's largest shop for transvestites and transexuals. Seriously.

Map 79 • King's Cross

Cosmo Cornelio	182 Caledonian Rd	020 7278 3947	Old-skool, moustache trimming Italian barbers.

Map 80 • Angel / Upper St

After Noah	121 Upper St	020 7359 4281	Stuff your Nintendo Wiis—these are proper toys, retro-style.
Annie's Vintage Costume and Textiles	12 Camden Passage	020 7359 0796	Proper vintage—1900s to 1940s.
Camden Passage	Camden Passage		Thingamebobs, whatsits and doodahs aplenty.
Cass Art	66 Colebrooke Row	020 7354 2999	Large, neat-as-a-pin, extremely pleasing art supply shop.
Gill Wing Cook Shop	190 Upper St	020 7226 5392	Splendid array of kitchen gadgetry to keep foodies amused.
Little Paris	262 Upper St	020 7704 9970	A Francophile's paradise.
Micycle N1	47 Barnsbury St	020 7684 0671	Friendly and knowledgeable. With cafe!
Monte's Italian Deli	23 Canonbury Ln	020 7354 4335	Tasty, but look elsewhere if you need a hearty meal.
Paul A. Young Fine Chocolates	33 Camden Passage	020 7424 5750	"Everytime you go away..." you take a piece of chocolate.
twentytwentyone	274 Upper St	020 7288 1996	Bauhaus to Boontje and beyond.

Map 81 • Canonbury

Get Stuffed	105 Essex Rd	020 7226 1364	Polar bear for the living room, anyone? Taxidermy emporium.
HG Lockey & Sons	8 Halton Cross St	020 7226 7044	For all your, er, coal and smokeless fuel needs.
James Elliott Butchers	96 Essex Rd	020 7226 3658	So much choice they'd probably stock human if they could.
Planet Organic	64 Essex Rd	020 7288 9460	Organic heaven.
Sew Fantastic	107 Essex Rd	020 7226 2725	If you'd thought it up, you'd have opened it too.
Steve Hatt	88 Essex Rd	020 7226 3963	A fishmonger's so good, people queue to get in.

Map 82 • De Beauvoir Town / Kingsland

2&4	4 Southgate Rd	020 7254 5202	Independent shop selling furniture but coffee too.
Mother Earth	101 Newington Green Rd	020 7359 7353	Organic, vegan and raw produce.
North One Garden Centre	25 Englefield Rd	020 7923 3553	Dinky little garden centre catering for dinky little London gardens.

Map 83 • Angel (East) / City Rd (North)

Flashback	50 Essex Rd	020 7354 9356	Don't come in whistling Barbie Girl.

Map 84 • Hoxton

Good Hood	41 Coronet St	020 7729 3600	Like American Apparel before it got shit.
Hoxton Street Monster Supplies	159 Hoxton St	020 7729 4159	World's only grocer for monsters, don't forget your fang floss.
SCP	135 Curtain Rd	020 7739 1869	Design-led homeware.
Sh!	57 Hoxton Sq	020 7613 5458	Dildo-tastic! Guys must come (ahem) accompanied by a galpal.
Tord Boontje Shop	23 Charlotte Rd	020 7717 5398	Whimsical, magical things.

Map 85 • Stoke Newington (East)

Bargain Bookshop	153 Stoke Newington High St	020 7249 8983	Books! Bargains! AH!
Hamdy's	167 Stoke Newington High St	020 7254 0681	Porn-free newsagents run by stubborn maverick.
Rouge	158 Stoke Newington High St	020 7275 0887	Cool Chinese housewares. Via Belgium of course.
Stoke Newington Bookshop	159 Stoke Newington High St	020 7249 2808	Long-standing local stellar indie bookshop.

Map 86 • Dalston / Kingsland

Centre Supermarket	588 Kingsland Rd	020 7241 4472	Beers from all corners of the globe.
Dalston Mill Fabrics	69 Ridley Rd	020 7249 4129	Veritable treasure trove for budding Vivienne Westwoods and John Gallianos.
Healthy Stuff	168 Dalston Ln	020 7812 9604	Fresh health foods and organic goods in Hackney.
LN-CC	18 Shacklewell Ln	020 7275 7265	Appointment only darling.
Oxfam	514 Kingsland Rd	020 7254 5318	Flagship charity shop. Go find treasures!
Party Party	9 Ridley Rd	020 7254 5168	Fancy dress and party supplies plus an outstanding cake decorating department.
Ridley Road Market	Ridley Rd	084 4657 4634	Giant (live!) snails, Nigerian DVDs, fresh fish, 'taters, "Pound a bowl!"
St Vincent's	484 Kingsland Rd	020 7249 3511	Christian charity shop. Jesus galore.
Turkish Food Centre	89 Ridley Rd	020 7254 6754	Olives and feta galore, bakery onsite, plus other fresh groceries.

Map 87 • Hackney Downs / Lower Clapton

Kate Sheridan	112 Lower Clapton Rd	020 8985 7500	Covetable prints.
Palm 2	152 Lower Clapton Rd	020 8533 1787	Legendarily friendly corner shop beloved of bloggers.
The Pet Shop	40 Amhurst Rd	020 3330 2520	Brilliant local pet shop.
Salvation Army Clapton	122 Lower Clapton Rd	020 8985 3902	Come all ye unfaithful...
Umit & Son	35 Lower Clapton Rd	020 8985 1766	Crazed film buff selling vintage porn, super 8 and crisps?!
Viktor Wynd's Little Shop of Horrors	11 Mare St	020 7998 3617	Macabre and marvellous shop and gallery.
X Marks The Bokship	44 Copperfield Rd		Interesting bookshop specialising in independent publishers and small presses.

Map 88 • Haggerston / Queensbridge Rd

KTS The Corner	415 Kingsland Rd	020 7249 3199	Helpful DIY store if you can't do it yourself.

Map 89 • London Fields / Hackney Central

Broadway Market	Broadway Market		Yummy mummies and Guardian-reading couples peruse.
Burberry Factory Shop	29 Chatham Pl	020 8985 3344	Ever wondered how Burberry became associated with chavs?
Candle Factory	184 Mare St	020 8986 6356	Well-made, well-priced candles.
E5 Bakehouse	395 Mentmore Terrace	020 8525 2890	Sour dough to make you happy.
L'eau a la Bouche	35 Broadway Market	020 7923 0600	Cute French delicatessen shop.

Map 90 • Homerton / Victoria Park North

Eat 17	64-66 Brooksby's Walk	020 8986 6242	A bit like a farmers' market but you don't have to wait for the weekend.
The Ginger Pig	99 Lauriston Rd	020 8986 6911	Brilliant butcher bequeathing beef to the Borough.
Perlie Rides	137 Well St	020 8525 5694	Need a Dick Van Dyke? (Bike)
Sublime	225 Victoria Park Rd	020 8986 7243	Boudoir-like boutique selling select and independent labels.
Work Shop	77 Lauriston Rd	020 8986 9585	Beautiful handmade pottery for home and kitchen by Caroline Bousfield Gregory.

Map 91 • Shoreditch / Brick Lane / Spitalfields

A Child of The Jago	10 Great Eastern St	020 7377 8694	Slapdash assortment of otherworldy vintage.
A Portuguese Love Affair	142 Columbia Rd	020 7613 1482	Wonderfully curated collection of beautifully packaged items from Portugal.
Absolute Vintage	15 Hanbury St	020 7247 3883	If Imelda Marcos ran a misanthropic clothes shop.
Bangla City	86 Brick Ln	020 7456 1000	Breaks the rule saying you should avoid smelly supermarkets.
Bernstock Speirs	234 Brick Ln	020 7739 7385	Look no further if you're searching for a signature titfer.
Blackman's Shoes	42 Cheshire St	078 5088 3505	Chaotic hole-in-the-wall selling £5 plimsolls.
Caravan	5 Ravenscroft St	020 7033 3532	Quirky interiors shop with items new and old on offer.
Comfort Station	22 Cheshire St	020 7033 9099	Quirky and comforting collection of handmade jewellery.
Duke of Uke	88 Cheshire St	020 3583 9728	For all your many ukelele and banjo needs.
Dum Dum Donutterie	2-4 Bethnal Green Rd	020 7426 0436	Baked not fried, with a patissier's craftsmanship.
Fairy Goth Mother	72 Commercial St	020 7377 0370	Not entirely "Goth"—a Dita Von Teese of a shop.
The Grocery	54 Kingsland Rd	020 7729 6855	Selling the good life to lower Kingsland Road.
Junky Styling	91 Brick Ln	020 7247 1883	Bespoke tailoring from old rags. But posher.
Labour And Wait	85 Redchurch St	020 7729 6253	Brilliant wee shop selling old and old-looking goods.
The Laden Showroom	103 Brick Ln	020 7247 2431	Eclectic bazaar of small labels scavenged by stylists and starlets.
Lily Vanilli	6 Ezra St		Cult bakery.
Luna and Curious	24 Calvert Ave	020 3222 0034	Curiouser and curiouser..lovely local artists' and designers' co-operative.
Mast Brothers	19 Redchurch St	020 7739 1236	Bearded brothers from Brooklyn set up in Shoreditch.
Peloton & Co	4 Market St	020 7183 5530	Get off your face on coffee before buying some cycling gear.
Present	140 Shoreditch High St	020 7033 0500	Fashionable designer menswear shop with a coffee bar.
Rough Trade East	91 Brick Ln	020 7392 7788	East London outpost of the absurdly cool Rough Trade Records.
Ryantown	126 Columbia Rd	020 7613 1510	Home of the ever popular paper cutter Rob Ryan.
Sunday (Up)Market	Brick Ln	020 7770 6028	Great Sunday market with lots of food and cool clothes.
Taj Stores	112 Brick Ln	020 7377 0061	Weird and wonderful Eastern food.
Tatty Devine	236 Brick Ln	020 7739 9191	Bonkers jewellery loved by celebs, fashionistas and hipsters.
Taylor Taylor	12 Cheshire St	020 7033 0330	Salon for the indulgent customer.
Taylor Taylor	137 Commercial St	020 7377 2737	French boudoir-style hairdressers with free cocktail bar. Feel like a princess.
Treacle	110 Columbia Rd	020 7729 0538	Dreamy cupcakes. Don't ask for coffee—this is a TEAshop!

Map 92 • Bethnal Green

AP Fitzpatrick Fine Art Materials	142 Cambridge Heath Rd	020 7790 0884	Art supplies and expert advice.

Map 94 • Bow

Roman Road Market	Roman Rd	020 7364 1717	Big, colourful, cheap as chips—bargain tat hawked by lively east-end traders.
Sew Amazing	80 St Stephens Rd	020 8980 8898	Long established sewing machine shop. Repairs and recycling service provided.
South Molton Drug Store	583 Roman Rd	020 8981 5040	Branded cosmetics and toiletries at knock-down prices.

Map 95 • Whitechapel (West) / St Katharine's Dock

Freedom Press	84 Whitechapel High St	020 7247 9249	Long running bastion of radical thinking.

Map 97 • Stepney / Shadwell (East)

East End Thrift Store	1 Assembly Passage	020 7423 9700	Come on Thursday nights for the in-store parties.
John Lester Wigs	32 Globe Rd	020 7790 2278	Need a syrup?

Map 101 • Poplar (East) / Canary Wharf (East)

Billingsgate Fish Market	Trafalgar Way	020 7987 1118	Slice of real London in the shadow of Canary Wharf.

Map 104 • South Bank / Waterloo / Lambeth North

Calder Bookshop & Theatre	51 The Cut	020 7620 2900	Enduringly fashionable hub for the unfashionably literate.
Greensmiths	27 Lower Marsh	020 7921 2970	Old skool greengrocer's and fine foods.
I Knit London	106 Lower Marsh	020 7261 1338	The UK's only knitting shop with a licensed bar. Wool is cool.
Konditor & Cook	22 Cornwall Rd	084 4854 9361	Yummy scrummy choccies and cake.
The Oasis	84 Lower Marsh	020 7401 7074	Friendly independent salon for massages, waxing, facials and pedicures.
Radio Days	87 Lower Marsh	020 7928 0800	Cave of vintage wonders.
ScooterCaffe	132 Lower Marsh	020 7620 1421	Scooter shop has superb coffee. Word spreads. Becomes café too.
Southbank Centre Book Market	Belvedere Rd	087 1663 2501	Fun little scribe's market in brilliant surroundings.
Top Wind	2 Lower Marsh	020 7401 8787	Serious flute worship.
What The Butler Wore	131 Lower Marsh	020 7261 1968	60s, 70s vintage boutique—retro-glam party garments plus resident moggy, Binky.

Map 105 • Southwark / Bankside (West)

Elephant & Castle Shopping Centre	Elephant & Castle	020 7703 5678	An anti-Portobello Road Market...slightly dodgy but dirt-cheap.
Silverprint	120 London Rd	020 7620 0169	Photographic retailer specialising in analogue and alternative photography.

Map 106 • Bankside (East) / Borough / Newington

Borough Market	8 Southwark St	020 7407 1002	Go on an empty stomach and feast on samples.
Brindisa Shop	Borough Market	020 7407 1036	Chorizo, salchichon, Serrano ham—famed importers Brindisa have it all.
Paul Smith	13 Park St	020 7403 1678	Kitsch and dolls from the fashion designer. Don't ask why.
Richer Sounds	2 London Bridge Walk	033 3900 0021	The original store of this small chain offering low prices.
Vinopolis	1 Bank End	020 7940 8300	Wine tasting and buying megastore. Spitting optional.

Map 107 • Shad Thames

Design Museum Shop	28 Shad Thames	020 7940 8775	Stuff you wish you'd thought of.
Fine Foods	218 Long Ln	020 7403 7513	Little, local Italian deli to coo over.
Maltby Street Market	Maltby St		Snapping at the ankles of Borough Market.

Map 108 • Bermondsey

The Kernel Brewery	11 Dockley Road Industrial Estate	020 7231 4516	Open on Saturdays for brewskis.

Map 111 • Rotherhithe (East) Surrey Quays

Decathlon	Surrey Quays Rd	020 7394 2000	The Daddy of sports & outdoors shops.

Map 112 • Kennington / Elephant and Castle

Pricebusters	311 Elephant & Castle	020 7703 8244	Impressively cheap, friendly staff and an amusing collection of bric-a-brac.
Recycling	110 Elephant Rd	020 7703 7001	They sell'em bikes, they fix'em bikes. Secondhand.

Map 113 • Walworth

Threadneedleman	187 Walworth Rd	020 7701 9181	Outfitter to Suggs, David Haye and countless other suave gentlemen.
Walworth Surplus Stores	211 Walworth Rd	020 7703 4759	Decades worth of dust and grumpiness to boot.

Map 119 • Deptford (East)

Deptford Market	Deptford High St		Cheap, busy, eclectic: Proof that there IS life in Deptford.

Map 120 • Greenwich

The Beehive	320-322 Creek Rd	020 8858 1964	Greenwich's quirky vinyl-vintage cohabitation.
Bullfrogs	22 Greenwich Church St	020 8305 2404	Strange name, decent shop. Independent boutique.
The Cheeseboard	26 Royal Hill	020 8305 0401	Buy your cheese then head to Theatre of Wine.
The Junkshop	9 Greenwich South St	020 8305 1666	Voodoo masks, Guiness mugs and everything in between.
Meet Bernard	23 Nelson Rd	020 8858 4047	Dapper gents outfitters.
Mr Humbug	Greenwich Market	020 7871 4944	Infinitissimal old-fashioned sweets to relive your childhood sugar buzzes.
Music & Video Exchange	23 Greenwich Church St	020 8858 8898	Greenwich branch of the second hand empire.

Map 121 • Camberwell (West)

Butterfly Walk	Denmark Hill		The usual attractions.
Men's Traditional Shoes	171 Camberwell Rd	020 7703 4179	Visit Fred "The Shoe" Harris for classic mod footwear.
Pesh Flowers	31 Denmark Hill	020 7703 9124	Freshest daisies for miles around.
Rat Records	348 Camberwell New Rd	077 9542 4575	Ramshackle and friendly. There's bargains if you've got superhuman patience.

Map 122 • Camberwell (East)

Architectural Rescue	1-3 Southampton Way	020 7277 0081	Dig through the architectural salvage of South London's past.
Cowling and Wilcox	8-12 Orpheus St	020 7703 1342	Suppliers to the local art school hordes.

Map 123 • Peckham

Persepolis	30 Peckham High St	020 7639 8007	Can a deli change your life? Yes. Yes, it can.
Primark	51 Rye Lane	020 7639 9655	More of a chance of scoring that 'it' item at this branch.

Map 127 • Coldharbour Lane / Herne Hill (West)

Blackbird Bakery	208 Railton Rd	020 7095 8800	London needs more lovely independent bakeries (like this).

Map 128 • Denmark Hill / Herne Hill (East)

Tales on Moon Lane	25 Half Moon Ln	020 7274 5759	Cute children's bookshop (as if there were any other kind!).

Map 130 • Peckham Rye

Flock and Herd	155 Bellenden Rd	020 7635 7733	Posho butchers for Peckhams new residents. Good sausages.

Map 133 • Battersea (East)

London Recumbents	Battersea Park	020 7498 6543	Much more fun in theory than in practice.

Map 134 • South Lambeth

Fetish Freak	76 Bolton Crescent	020 7091 0031	Witness the wall of dildos.
LASSCO	30 Wandsworth Rd	020 7394 2100	Homebase for the unique, antique, or eccentric.
New Covent Garden Market	New Covent Garden Market	020 7720 2211	Known as London's Larder. Nowhere near Covent Garden
The Nine Elms Sunday Market	New Covent Garden		Challenge yourself to think of something this place doesn't sell.

Map 139 • Wandsworth (East)

Cake Boy	2 Kingfisher House	020 7978 5555	Cookery school and cake emporium extraordinaire.

Map 140 • Clapham Junction / Northcote Rd

The Hive Honey Shop	93 Northcote Rd	020 7924 6233	Every kind of honey you could want.
Huttons	29 Northcote Rd	020 7223 5523	Eclectic mix of unusual clothes, furniture and gifts.
Party Superstores	268 Lavender Hill	020 7924 3210	The queues on Halloween will scare you to death.
Space NK Apothecary	46 Northcote Rd	020 7228 7563	Skincare heaven.
Sweaty Betty	136 Northcote Rd	020 7978 5444	Look like a total Betty, like, even when you're sweaty.
TK Maxx	St John's Rd & Barnard Rd	020 7228 8072	The best bargains in town.
TRAID	28 St John's Rd	020 7924 3065	Characterful recycled clothes. Touch of wank, but still we like.
Whole Foods Market	305 Lavender Hill	020 7585 1488	Overwhelming selection of organic exotica.

Map 141 • Battersea (South)

Battersea Boot	401 Battersea Park Rd	079 4138 3588	Yeah! A huge, tumultous boot sale that starts mid afternoon!
Comet Miniatures	44 Lavender Hill	020 7228 3702	Get your Airfix fix. Model shop and sci-fi.
Get A Grip Bicycle Workshop	19 Lavender Hill	020 7223 4888	These people know their stuff.

Map 142 • Clapham Old Town

M. Moen & Sons	24 The Pavement	020 7622 1624	Butcher for the bourgeoisie, incredibly good, massively expensive.
Puppet Planet	787 Wandsworth Rd	020 7627 0111	Not great if you're pupaphobic but otherwise rather charming.

Map 143 • Clapham High Street

Apex Cycles	40 Clapham High St	020 7622 1334	Bikes fixed, bikes sold.
Esca	160 Clapham High St	020 7622 2288	Your Clapham Common picnic starts here.
Today's Living Health Store	92 Clapham High St	020 7622 1772	Health foods, herbal remedies and other jiggery pokery.

Map 144 • Stockwell / Brixton (West)

A & C Co. Continental Grocers	3 Atlantic Rd	020 7733 3766	Portuguese-owned institution, famous for pestos, chorizo and mamma's tortilla.
Brixi	7 Second Ave	079 1916 2428	A look inside an eccentric's closet.
Funchal Bakery	141-143 Stockwell Rd	020 7733 3134	Portuguese grocery with good coffee and better pastel de nata.
Lisa Stickley London	74 Landor Rd	020 7737 8067	Dotty 1940s-inspired handbags to tea-towels. Cath Kidston but better.
The Old Post Office Bakery	76 Landor Rd	020 7326 4408	Disused P.O turned artisan baker's. Local loaf? The Brixton Rye.

Map 147 • Balham (West)

Bon Vivant	59 Nightingale Ln	020 8675 6314	Great local deli.

Map 148 • Balham (East)

Moxon's Fishmongers	Westbury Parade	020 8675 2468	Fresh fish for foodies with deep pockets. Knowledgeable staff.

Map 149 • Clapham Park

MacFarlane's	48 Abbeville Rd	020 8673 5373	Gourmet goodness galore.

Map 150 • Brixton

Bookmongers	439 Coldharbour Ln	020 7738 4225	Truly great local bookshop with friendly staff and dog.
Lab G	6 Granville Arcade	078 0392 2616	End your Brixton night right here with salted caramel gelato.
Ms. Cupcake	408 Coldharbour Ln	020 7733 9438	A lactose-intolerant 1950s housewife's wet dream (in 120 flavours).
Supertone Records	110 Acre Ln	020 7737 7761	Legendary reggae shop.
Tasty Rich Bakery	Brixton Village Market		Spicy lamb patties like you've never had before.
TRAID	2 Acre Ln	020 7326 4330	Characterful recycled clothes. Touch of wank, but still we like.

Map 151 • Tooting Bec

Crazy Horse Bike Workshop	275 Balham High Rd	020 8767 5614	Bikes and bike repairs.
Russell's Trade & DIY	46 Upper Tooting Rd	020 8672 1576	DIY treasure chest. Friendly, helpful owners.
Wandsworth Oasis HIV/AIDS Charity Shop	40 Trinity Rd	020 8767 7555	Thrift store treasure trove.

Map 152 • Tooting Broadway

Tooting Market	21 Tooting High St	020 8672 4760	Quaint indoor labyrinth worth nosing about.

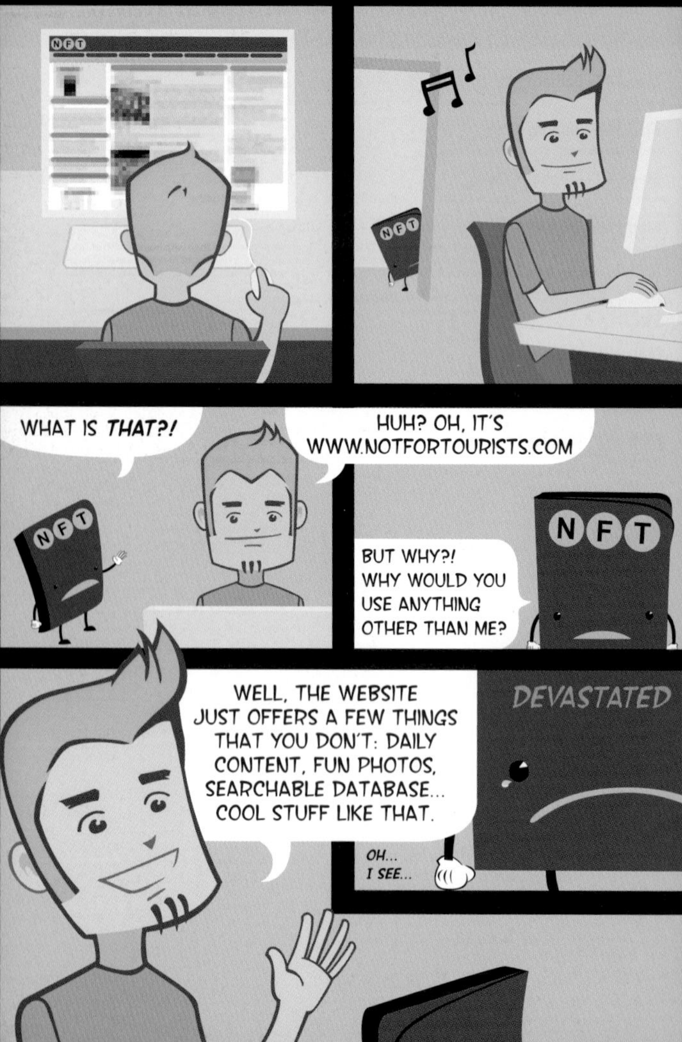

NFT
NFT
WHAT IS THAT?!
HUH? OH, IT'S WWW.NOTFORTOURISTS.COM
NFT
NFT
BUT WHY?! WHY WOULD YOU USE ANYTHING OTHER THAN ME?
WELL, THE WEBSITE JUST OFFERS A FEW THINGS THAT YOU DON'T: DAILY CONTENT, FUN PHOTOS, SEARCHABLE DATABASE... COOL STUFF LIKE THAT.
DEVASTATED
OH... I SEE...

BUT I FIT IN YOUR POCKET. YOU CAN TAKE ME ANYWHERE.
SWOOP!
NFT
OH!
TUCK
TUCK
OH PLEASE. THE WEBSITE COULD NEVER REPLACE YOU. I NEED YOU BOTH TO GET THE MOST OUT OF MY CITY!

A

Street Index

Street Index

B

Street Index

Street Index

Street Index

Street Index

Street Index

Street Index

Street Index

F

Street Index

Street Index

H

Street Index

Street Index

I

Street Index

L

Street Index

M

Street Index

Street Index

N

O

P

Street Index

Street Index

Q

R

Street Index

Street Index

S

Street Index

Street Index

Street Index

T

Street Index

W

Street Index

Y

Z

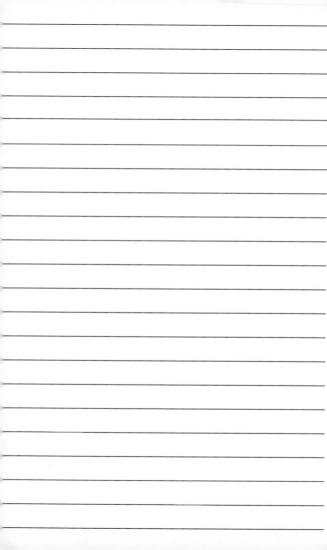